The Daily

THE
GOOD
GARDENS
GUIDE 2006

EDITED BY PETER KING
& KATHERINE LAMBERT

FRANCES LINCOLN

This paperback edition published 2006

Peter King has asserted his right to be identified as the author
of this work under the Copyright, Designs and Patents Act 1988

Botanical Editor: Ruth Stungo
Administrator: Anita Owen
Disk Editor: Peter Champness
Maps: Neil Hyslop
Index: Angie Hipkin

Frances Lincoln Ltd,
4 Torriano Mews, Torriano Avenue, London NW5 2RZ

A CIP catalogue record is
available from the British Library

ISBN 0 7112 25672

10 9 8 7 6 5 4 3 2 1

Typeset by SMI India
Printed in Great Britain

The Daily Telegraph

THE GOOD GARDENS GUIDE 2006

Contents

THE GARDENS

Acknowledgements

This is the seventeenth annual edition of the *Guide*. All of the gardens described are open to the public, and there is an emphasis on those open frequently or by appointment over several months of the year. Certain gardens only open once or twice are included on merit. Our thanks to everyone who has helped with the preparation of the *Guide* – to owners, custodians, professional gardening staff, and many others. In particular, we thank our inspectors and those who advised them. Some of those who have given advice do not wish to be listed and, although anonymous, they have been every bit as valuable. We are also obliged to staff of The National Trust, The National Trust for Scotland and English Heritage for their co–operation.

The following include inspectors (plus some past inspectors) and advisors: Barbara Abbs, Miranda Allhusen, Jane Allsopp, Gillian Archer, Diana Atkins, Rosie Atkins, Diane and Peter Baistow, David Baldwin, Jenny Baldwin, Susan Barnes, Mr and Mrs Basten, Kenneth and Gillian Beckett, June Beveridge, Lavender Borden, Kathryn Bradley–Hole, Hilary Bristow, Cecil Brown, Jennifer Brown, Christina Campbell, Adam Caplin, Shirley Cargill, Dr Joan Carmichael, Brian and Gillian Cassidy, Lady Cave, Liz Challen, Anne Chamberlain, Sir Jeremy and Lady Chance, Annabelle Chisholm, Timothy Clark, Sarah Coles, Anne Collins, E. Anne Colville, David Conway, Guy Cooper, Beatrice Cowan, Simon Cramp, Janet Cropley, Jo, Penelope, Rosie and Trixie Currie, Wendy Dare, Margreet Diepeveen–Bruins Slot, Marilyn Dodd, Rosemary Dodgson, Daphne Dormer, Lady Edmonstone, Matthew Fattorini, Sir Charles and Lady Fraser, Daphne Fisher, Kate Garton, Leslie Geddes–Brown, Lucy Gent, Alison Gregory, Gwynne Griffiths, Fenja Gunn, Elizabeth Hamilton, Stuart Harding, Anne Harrison, Sunniva Harte, Charles Hawes, Tara Heinemann, Jane Henson, Steve Hipkin, Judith Hitchings, Hilary Hodgson, Christopher Holliday, Mariana Hollis, Caroline Holmes, Jacky Hone, Sophie Hughes, Pam Hummer, Jill Husselby, David Jacques, Judith Jenkins, Valerie Jinks, Vanessa Johnston, Rosemarie Johnstone, Belinda Jupp, Mary Keen, Jo Kenaghan, Margaret Knight, Jean Laughton, Virginia Lawlor, Andrew Lawson, Dr Elizabeth Lazenby, Anne E. Liverman, Malcolm Lyell, Charles Lyte, Rhian de Mattos, Pat McCrostie, Anna McKane, Christopher McLaren, Deirdre McSharry, Bettine Muir, Dr Charles Nelson, Hugh Palmer, Lucinda Parry, Victoria Petrie–Hay, David Pettifer, Lady Pigot, Stephen Player, Jocelyn Poole, Heather Prescott, Lorna Ramsay, Terence Reeves–Smith, Finola Reid, Anne Richards, Tim Rock, Christopher Rogers, Sue Roscoe Watts, Dorothy Rose, Jane Russell, Alison Rutherford, Sarah Rutherford, Peter de Sausmarez, Kathy Sayer, George and Jane Scott, Barbara Segall, Marjorie Sime, Gillian Sladen, Dr Gordon Smith, Michael Smith, Lady Smith–Ryland, Elaine Snazell, Margaret Soole, Camilla Swift, Marlene Storah, Vera Taggart, Sally Tamplin, Gordon Taylor, Caroline Todhunter, Michael Tooley, Annetta Troth, Marie–Françoise Valery, Jackie Ward, Ian Warden, Anne Wareham, Jenifer Wates, Myra Wheeldon, Susan Whittington, Cynthia Wickham, Nigel Wilkins, John Wilks, Martin Wood. The editors also express their appreciation of the dedicated assistance of Peter Champness, Angie Hipkin, Pam Rainbow and Ruth Stungo, and especially of the *Guide's* invaluable administrator, Anita Owen.

Foreign Exchanges and Ideas

Va et viens

Despite the wars of religion, which had for so long held Europe in thrall, a steady flow of English travellers sailed from south coast ports as pilgrims to France, Italy, Spain and the Holy Land. By the fourteenth and fifteenth centuries, their number had increased year on year; in 1434 alone, King Henry VI licensed no fewer than 2433 to visit the shrine of St James of Compostella. Not all had a religious motivation. Erasmus, who arrived in Cambridge in 1498 after teaching pupils – including Lord Mountjoy – in Paris, condemned pilgrimage as a feckless form of travel, undertaken largely by the rich and the dissipated. For himself, Erasmus had no hesitation in declaring it 'very necessary' to visit Italy, 'to achieve for his poor learning some authority from the celebrity of the place.'

Journeys between England and Europe began in earnest in the sixteenth century, as relative political stability gradually opened up opportunities. Henry VIII led by example in sponsoring the education and travel of talented young men, and Elizabeth I followed suit by maintaining 'young men of promising hopes in Foreign countries for the more complete polishing of their Parts and Studies'. Courtiers such as Sir John Harington, the Earl of Essex, the Earl of Hertford, Sir Christopher Hatton and Sir Philip Sidney left England so that they might return 'acceptable servants' to their sovereign. Philip Sidney was abroad for three years, while Thomas Coryate announced that his travels would occupy him for ten. They might well have done, had he not died on the way.

Religious and intellectual betterment may been at the forefront, but historical and horticultural curiosity was not far behind. The first chronicler to record the parks and gardens of England was John Leland (1506–52). Having been in quick succession chaplain and librarian to Henry VIII, he was rewarded in 1533 with a post as the king's antiquarian. Between 1540 and 1546 he travelled the length and breadth of the country collecting a mass of historical evidence, and 'notid yn so doing a hole world of things memorable', including 'fair made' walks, gardens and orchards'. Four years later he went insane, and his proposed book, *History and Antiquities* never saw the light of day.

The first topographical guide for visitors to England, William Camden's *Britannia*, written in Latin, appeared in 1586 and went into three editions. The *va et viens* had begun. It gathered pace following the marriage in 1625 of Charles I to Henrietta Maria, the King of France's sister, which left England at peace with France and Spain. By 1600 Italianate gardening had also begun to make an impression, after the return of Inigo Jones from an Italian journey with his patron Lord Arundel and the subsequent remodelling of Arundel House. The two French brothers Salomon and Isaac de Caus were also in England after studying hydraulics in Pratolino. While Salomon was set to work for James I's consort, Anne of Denmark, at St James's Palace and Wimbledon, Isaac found employment with the Countess of Bedford at Moor Park and at Wilton with the Earl of Pembroke.

The dissemination of botanical and horticultural knowledge had been hastened by the invention of printing in the fifteenth century. To begin with, printed books were imported from France and Italy, but herbals and books on gardening soon began to be produced in England. Jacques le Moyne, who escaped religious persecution in

France some time after 1580, became tutor to the Sidney household; his illustrated book *Le Clef des Champs*, published in 1586, was dedicated to Lady Mary Sidney. In 1597 John Gerard, Lord Burghley's gardener at Theobalds in Hertfordshire and Cecil House in the Strand, dedicated his *Herball* to his master. Gerard lived in Holborn, one of London's many villages, and his garden contained 'strangers' – plants introduced to western Europe via Constantinople.

The 1st Earl of Salisbury was among the first of a number of rich seventeenth – century landowners to plant tulips in his parterres at Hatfield. John Tradescant the Elder, the Earl's gardener, who travelled extensively in Europe and the Mediterranean region, sent him a bill at the start of the New Year 1611 for 'Routes, flowers, Seeds, trees and plants by him bought for my Lo: in Holland. From Haarlem 800 tulip bulbs at ten shillings the hundred.' The cost of the tulips alone was the equivalent of a gardener's half-yearly wage. Tradescant may also have brought back tulips from Russia, for he was in Archangel in 1618 knowing full well that 'thear groweth in the land both tulips and narsisus'.

The first Englishman to document the gardens of both England and Europe was John Evelyn (1620–1706). His voluminous diaries record select visits to English gardens. More surprising is his roll call of gardens visited in Europe: Blois, the Pitti Palace in Florence, Fontainebleau, gardens in Geneva and The Hague, Leyden's famed collection of 'simples', Pierre Morin's garden in Paris, the Tuileries, the Pisa Physic Garden, the Palazzo d'Este at Tivoli. Visiting the gardens of the Luxembourg in Paris, he was amazed by Boyceau's great embroidered parterre, 'so rarely designed and accurately kept cut that the *embroiderie* makes a wonderful effect'. The impressive grotto there was a 'very rare extravagance of elaborate shell work in the shape of satyrs and other wild fancies', and the artificial cascade 'rolled down a very steepe declivity, and over the marble steps and basins with an astonishing noyse and fury terminating in a grotto'.

When Evelyn returned to England to make his own garden at Deptford, he modelled it on Morin's. Sayes Court was famed for its glass beehives, its walled garden filled with rare flowers, and its vast holly hedge – Evelyn's pride and joy, destroyed by his impossible tenant Peter the Great. One entry makes for sad reading: 'June 9, 1698 I went to Deptford to view how miserably the Tsar of Muscovy had left my house after 3 months making it his court having gotten Sir Cr: Wren to his Majesties Surveyor and Mr London his Gardener to go down and make an estimat of the repairs.' Thereafter Evelyn was regularly consulted on the French style of gardening: in 1664 for the Earl of Clarendon at Cornbury Park, in 1671 for the Earl of Arlington at Euston Hall and in 1680 for the Earl of Essex at Cassiobury.

For Evelyn's contemporary, Henry Compton (1632–1713), the magnet was not garden–visiting but plant–collecting. The sixth son of the staunchly royalist Earl of Northampton started his career as a soldier, but by 1666 his thoughts had turned to the church, and in no time he was ordained and installed as Master of St Cross in Winchester – a position he held for eight years. It was at St Cross that he learnt to garden. Alongside him throughout was Alexander Marshal, his Steward, best known for his 'curius booke of flowers in miniature' – now in the Royal Library at Windsor Castle, and published for the first time in 1985 as a florilegium – who imparted his extensive botanical knowledge to his master.

In 1675 Compton was made Bishop of London, and as such automatically became head of the Church in the American colonies, known as the Plantations. Although he never actually visited America, he was responsible for appointing its chaplains, and was accordingly in a unique position to ensure that those with a particular interest in botany were selected. New species of trees and shrubs, together with seeds, were earmarked for Fulham Palace, but other interested collectors such as Jacob Bobart of the Physic Garden at Oxford and members of the Temple Coffee House Botany Club also benefited. Compton's passion, knowledge and collection grew. On Compton's death, Stephen Switzer described him as 'one of the first that encouraged the Importation, Raising, and Increase of Exotics, in which he was the most Curious Man of that Time.'

The interaction between garden–makers was by no means confined to countries on the Grand Tour. In 1772 Catherine the Great of Russia wrote to the French philosopher Voltaire: 'I love English gardens to the point of folly: serpentine lines, gentle slopes, marshes turned into lakes, islands of dry ground, and I deeply despise straight lines. I hate fountains which torture water to take a course contrary to nature; in a word, my plantomania is dominated by anglomania.' Voltaire had spent the years 1726–9 in exile in England. He later told a visitor to Ferney, his house in Switzerland, that he had made his garden in the English taste. 'There says he is the Thames – and there is Richmond Hills. No French gewgaws. – All is Nature.'

Catherine's anglomania extended to her choice of head gardener. Charles Cameron (1743 – 1812) travelled to Russia in 1779 to work as her decorator, architect and landscape designer. Employed first at Tsarskoye Selo, he went on to design the Palladian palace and its landscape setting at Pavlovsk. In all, his landscape work amounted to many thousands of hectares of the land encompassing both these royal palaces. After Catherine's death in 1796, he was dismissed, only to be re-employed five years later as architect-in-chief to the Admiralty. He also restored the Khan's palace and estate at Bakhtchisarai in the Crimea.

Thomas Blaikie (1758–1838) another Scot, who worked mainly in France, introduced gardeners from England and Scotland to his French employers and made frequent visits to England to collect plants for his clients. He was a powerful advocate of the English style of gardening and did not conceal his contempt for France's hybrid – the *jardin anglais–chinois*. His first post was with the Comte de Lauragais, who soon introduced him to Bélanger, one of France's foremost architects. Almost immediately Blaikie found employment with the Comte d'Artois (the future Charles X) for whom, together with Bélanger, he laid out the famous gardens of the Bagatelle. His next projects were equally important – the Parc Monceaux and Le Raincy for the Duc de Chartes (later Duc d'Orléans). Despite a constant flow of work, Blaikie managed extensive excursions to French gardens round Paris and described them in *The Diary of a Scotch Gardener*, not published until nearly 100 years after his death.

The English style also found an echo in Germany. The dashing but impecunious Prince Hermann von Pûckler-Muskau, visiting England in 1826 in an unsuccessful quest for a rich English wife, introduced the English style into his estate in Silesia after studying the work of Nash in Regent's Park and St James's Park. In the process – like Charles Hamilton at Painshill – he allowed his passion for gardening to devour his family fortune.

The exchange of horticultural ideas across nations is as powerful today as it has ever been. Travel now is swifter, modern gardening more universal. Tom Stuart-Smith has worked in Paris, Alain Cousseran and Alain Provost in London, Rupert Golby at Ninfa, Arabella Lennox-Boyd in Italy and in France. Piet Oudolf has found commissions in Sweden, New York and England. Gardening has become truly international.

'American Roots' and The World Map of Plants

By the eighteenth century, the opening up of Asia, Africa, North America and the Caribbean had led to an influx of exotic animals and plants into Britain. The Dukes of Chandos and Richmond, Viscount Weymouth and the Earl of Northampton were just four of the aristocratic enthusiasts who establish private menageries in their parks. Many of these patrons collected rarities both zoological and horticultural. Princess Augusta imported kangaroos, Algiers cows, Chinese and Tartary pheasants and 'small exotic birds and gold fish' to enliven the grounds at Kew, which were described by the London-based horticultural agent Peter Collinson as 'the Paradise of our World, where all the plants are found, that money or interest can procure'.

At Painshill in Surrey, the princess's contemporary Charles Hamilton (1704-86), very much the youngest son of the 6th Earl of Abercorn, was also in close contact with Collinson and subscribed to his opinion that 'England must be turned up side down & America transplanted Heither'. He signed up for some of the five-guinea boxes of seeds and plants shipped over from the east coast of North America by Collinson's plant-collector colleague, the Philadelphia Quaker farmer John Bartram.

Hamilton was, however, more than just a horticultural magpie. Intellectually he was a mould-breaker, one of those responsible for moving landscape tastes away from the rigid formality of the Baroque age to a more fluid, fanciful and floriferous interpretation of a pastoral ideal. Like Henry Hoare at Stourhead, he was a masterly sculptor of the landscape, turning Painshill into a ravishing piece of theatre with majestic spaces, choreographed vistas and carefully placed temples and follies. Horace Walpole, never wanton with his compliments, said of the result: 'He has really made a fine place out of a most cursed hill.' Hamilton's American acquisitions were destined to be the garden's rich trimmings.

The eighteenth-century walled garden at Painshill is currently the scene of a long-running exhibition, 'American Roots', which celebrates the fruitful collaboration between Hamilton and his suppliers. Narrow slip-beds nurturing plants earmarked for permanent homes in the park, a decorative conical bed representing a nosegay of rare and familiar flowers, a plant theatre with a black-painted interior – these are the main elements in an authentic reconstruction which purveys the excitement, high seriousness and attention to detail that would have attended the receipt, planting and propagation of Hamilton's new treasures. Containers for shipment, raised beds, barrels especially designed for seedling plants, miniature sunshades and even a bird scarer in the shape of a winged potato have all been faithfully reproduced to a high standard of workmanship.

By no means all the plants are native to North America – most of the bulbs, annuals and succulents come from other parts of the globe – but all are in period and the New World takes pride of place, not only in the exhibition space but also within the rolling acres of the park. As visitors walk out from the walled garden into the fir walk, the theatrical amphitheatre encircled by tiers of mounded shrubs, the young arboretum shading more conical beds of flowers, they become steeped in Hamilton's vision of transforming the English landscape with the aid of rare exotica. Horticultural institutions both sides of the Atlantic have supplied plants and expertise to the exhibition. Fittingly, Professor Mark Laird, author of the seminal

The Flowering of the Landscape Garden and the man responsible for much of the background research and design for the restoration at Painshill, is British by birth, teaches at Harvard, and lives in Toronto.

Contemporary with Painshill's, the walled garden at fourteenth-century Lullingstone Castle in Kent is in the shape of a distorted square, sloping gently and dipping in places. It seems an unlikely setting for a unique and grandiose horticultural venture.

The great botanist and explorer Joseph Banks wrote towards the end of his life to the 28-year-old William Hooker: 'Let me hear from you how you feel inclined to prefer Ease & indulgence to Hardship and activity I was about 23 when I began my Peregrinations you are somewhat older but you may be assured that if I had Listend to a multitude of voices that were Raisd up to dissuade me from my Enterprise I should... probably have attained to no higher Rank in Life than that of a countrey Justice of the Peace.' Hooker went on to become Director of Kew and to father the intrepid Joseph, who was to spend six weeks in 'durance... somewhat of the vilest' while on an expedition to Tibet and Sikkim in 1849.

Tom Hart Dyke's resolve to lay out a world map using plants indigenous to every country and continent was conceived in similar circumstances. He was 24 at the time. 'It all started on 16 June 2000 with an AK-47 aimed at my temple and a machete caressing the side of my neck in the depths of the Colombian jungle. An orchid-hunting trip to the Darien Gap had gone seriously wrong, and I had been taken hostage. As yet another threat of my gruesome execution was issued by my captors, I decided to draw up a garden design plan for Lullingstone in my diary. This horticultural occupation got me through that day, and all the others through my nine-month kidnap ordeal, and it stayed with me after my release.'

Five years on, his dream – 'the World in One Acre', no less – is becoming reality. Poetic licence has been taken with sizing the land masses. Africa is just 7.5 metres across and 18.5 metres long, while the tiny Canaries weigh in at 2 x 6 metres, Japan at 2 x 7 metres, and the UK at 3 x 5.5 metres. Within Australia, Tasmania (a favourite spot for Tom after a four-month seed-collecting expedition in 1999) takes up fully half of mainland Australia. The Arctic and Antarctic regions are not represented at all, and the oceans have been distorted to allow wheelchair access along these arterial pathways. It smacks of the early 'here be dragons' maps in three dimensions, with the added advantage of being able to stroll around landscape features like Mount Everest or Ayer's Rock and to smell and examine at close range the 10,000 different plants – colourful, exotic, humble or assertive – that will eventually find a home there.

The coastlines of this world are edged with rocks from a selection of British quarries, with the UK islands represented by fiery red granite, the seas by superbly reflective Cornish grit. The original alkaline soil has been retained, but over 100 tonnes of acid soil has been brought in to keep rhododendrons and suchlike from Japan and mainland Asia in good health. British plants include fennel and sea kale, common spotted orchids, cornflowers, betony, vervain, red and white campion, *Campanula glomerata*, *Daphne mezereum*, rowan, bird cherry and Scots pine.

Tom Hart Dyke's moment of wild surmise in the Darien Gap has turned into one of those strange British gambles (£150,000's worth) which stands a remarkably good chance of succeeding. If he achieves his primary ambition of highlighting and quantifying the debt we owe to the intrepid plant hunters of the past and to present-day breeders and nurserymen – given that nearly 80 per cent of the plants commonly grown in our gardens are not native to Britain – this 'self-taught plant nut' will be well satisfied. He may not however, get round to becoming a country Justice of the Peace.

A dialogue with Piet Oudolf
by Isabelle Van Groeningen

Nowadays it is no more difficult – and often quicker – to travel from Britain to any major European city than it is to make the journey from London to Glasgow. As travel becomes faster and cheaper, and technology makes international communications forever easier, there are no longer any barriers to designing and planting gardens across borders. Or are there? What about climate, plant availability, language difficulties? What about differences in national tastes, customs and traditions?

The success of the Dutch plantsman and designer Piet Oudolf is taking him further and further afield. Besides a string of projects throughout Europe, including the UK, he is now increasingly being asked to undertake schemes in the USA. Professionally, I have quite a lot in common with Piet. Belgian by birth and upbringing, as part of Land Art Ltd working with the German-born garden architect Gabriella Pape I have been designing and planting gardens and public spaces in the UK and Germany, but also elsewhere in Europe and as far afield as South America and the Far East.

Due to the number and scale of the projects we run in Germany, and the fact we speak the language and understand the system, we usually keep control ourselves; elsewhere we tend to work with local companies. Likewise, when he is working abroad, especially in the States, Piet usually collaborates with larger companies that help him run the project. This can create a problem of approach: 'I can never get used to these large offices which in a first phase work very schematically, developing the overall concept, when I am already fully into the small details in my mind.'

Whether working at home or abroad, Piet and I find that when we are planting private gardens it is not always necessary to get outside contractors involved: we can liaise directly with the client and the head gardener and leave the execution of the design to them. We like to procure the plants ourselves to ensure quality and authenticity, and once the planting areas are prepared we come to site to lay out the plants. This is important, as inevitably small adjustments need to be made, and it is often difficult for others to interpret elaborate planting plans.

The differences in climate within northern Europe alone can throw up surprises, both positive and negative. By comparison with the Netherlands and Germany, Britain has the kindest climate: no great extremes of temperature (neither excessively hot nor cold), and regular rainfall but no continuous periods of wet weather. As a maritime nation the weather changes quickly in the UK, so that you may have rain in the morning and sunshine in the afternoon, while a little breeze dries off any residual dampness. Wet is a bigger killer than cold, affecting many of the evergreen small shrubs, particularly those with silver or felty foliage. 'Planting is easier in the UK, everything is possible there,' reckons Piet. I have noticed that about one-third of the plants I use regularly in UK schemes would not be hardy for most of Germany. Even common ivy has been known to suffer frost damage in Berlin, where winter and summer temperatures can vary by 60°C.

Plant availability is another issue. With hundreds of small specialist nurseries, Piet's view is that 'in the UK everything is available, but not in any quantity, whereas in the Netherlands we can get the quantity, but not the variety'. Added to that are differences in opinion on nomenclature. It is difficult enough to ensure that all plants carry the correct name in one country (something which in Britain has improved since the publication of *The Plant Finder*), but across borders there are still some differences. *Persicaria polymorpha* is sold as *Polygonum alpinum* in Germany, and *Achillea* 'Moonshine' is a different plant from that offered by UK nurseries.

And then there are the clients. Gabriella and I have noted a distinct difference between our German and English clients: the Germans rarely know the name of the plants we have used in their gardens, but will know the price, whereas the British will never talk about the money spent, but will know the name of every plant. Piet has found this too: 'In the UK there is an enormous appreciation for my work, the clients have great knowledge and I enjoy the dialogue I have with them. I do regret, however, not having enough time to go back and revisit the gardens regularly.' His recent projects in the States have been public spaces – different again. 'You do not have the cosy conversations you have with private clients, nor the flexibility. Instead you have to operate within set budgets and a specific brief, but this does allow you to work with strong conceptual ideas. I also like confronting the public and capturing people's imagination. There will be visitors who have never seen anything like it, or have never paid plants much attention, but they will walk out of the space saying "I want this in my garden," and that is very rewarding.'

All the travelling we do is far from glamorous, and very time-consuming, but when you ask Piet why he accepts these commissions in other countries, his reply comes instantly. 'Pure ambition drives me, but also the appreciation for my work abroad.' More unexpected, but ever so important, is his third reason: 'I get 100% more success because of the way my schemes are maintained by dedicated professionals. Even the public spaces I have designed in the USA are immaculately kept, and the long-term maintenance is budgeted for from the start. Each project has a highly trained, motivated person in charge who sees to its daily needs.' He is quite right – the most stunning schemes are a waste of time if appropriate maintenance by skilled gardeners is not budgeted for.

I would like to add another reason to his list: the sheer challenge of tackling a different and possibly unfamiliar climate that will influence the range of plants you can use. This can of course work both ways. When I am planting in Berlin, I find that although I have to watch the hardiness of some plants, species such as North American prairie plants actually love the continental climate and are perfectly geared up for cold, snow-laden winters and hot dry summers, thriving much better than they do in the UK. Each garden is a challenge. Being able to push the boundaries outwards makes it even more fun.

Three case studies:
Le Bois des Moutiers

Varengeville-sur Mer is one of many small villages lining the coast between Dieppe and St Valéry. It stands high on the cliffs, and off the road leading to the twelfth-century church is a big-boned, irregular house framed by an equally strong-minded garden, with a vast woodland garden behind stretching down to the sea. The story of Le Bois des Moutiers is a classic case of client-designer partnership: the collaboration between an Anglophile banker, Guillaume Mallet, and an up-and-coming English architect, Edwin Lutyens. The two met during the run-up to the 1900 *Exposition Universelle*, for which Lutyens had been commissioned to build an English house, and he set to work almost straight away.

Lutyens's design for the garden is the perfect foil for the Arts-and-Crafts house. He laid out a succession of distinctive enclosures ornamented by beautifully crafted and intricately detailed paths, paving, walls, a pergola and a summerhouse. Mallet, a connoisseur and lover of the new, filled his house with Mackintosh furniture, ceramics and works of art by Burne-Jones, while Lutyens collaborated with Gertrude Jekyll to fill his garden rooms with the plants that she had made popular in England. Thus the white garden to the east of the house has box-edged beds filled with such things as 'Iceberg' roses and 'White Triumphator' tulips, the generous twin border on the south facade are planted rhythmically with shrubs, roses, hostas, irises, lilies and other English herbaceous favourites, while the sturdy brick and wooden pergola is hung with roses, clematis and vines.

Lutyens enjoyed working with the vocal and excitable French builders and craftsmen. In a letter to his wife Emily he described the scene: 'Such a day of it yesterday. Seven French builders, the different trades. Oh such a talking – such tremendous demonstrations and the excitement at times beyond all description.' And he loved the place itself: 'Oh Emy it is so lovely here, so quiet and delicious, gloriously fine, yet quite cool and pleasant and the smells are all so good.' His association with the Mallet family was long and close – he went on to build two other houses for them in France. There was, however, a twist in the tale, for after a visit to Varengeville in 1910 Emily embraced Mme Mallet's theosophist beliefs, and the universal brotherhood, vegetarianism and sexual abstinence involved were to make life increasingly uncomfortable and lonely for poor Ned.

Woolton House

The landscaping and planting of the gardens at Woolton House is another remarkable example of Anglo-French collaboration, but with the nationality of client and designer reversed. Rosamund Brown, married to an American architect with an international practice and homes in London, Paris and Hong Kong, commissioned one of France's foremost landscape plantsmen to reinvent the gardens surrounding their country house on the Berkshire-Hampshire border. The combination of the owners' architectural expertise and artistic panache and Pascal Cribier's landscaping skill and use of colour has resulted in the creation of one of the most intriguing modern gardens in the UK.

Cribier had worked previously with Louis Benech on a widely acclaimed scheme to renovate the gardens of the Tuileries in Paris. Together they gave a contemporary gloss to André Le Nôtre's formal layout of water, lawn and parterre, in the same way that Tom Stuart-Smith and Piet Oudolf are achieving at Trentham Gardens in Staffordshire (see below). For the garden at Woolton House, set within traditional English parkland, he used a different canvas and painted with still more vibrant colours.

Mondrian provided the inspiration for the four-acre walled kitchen garden. Vegetables are regimented into waves, stripes and hatchings of grey, blue, yellow and green; another part of the garden blazes with species tulips, hot red geums and dahlias grown between slender lines of turf. Inside, the walls conceal a red Chinese picking garden and, as its companion, a succulent hosta walk. From the house the view is of a pool garden massed with roses – apricots, reds and yellows – with an extensive ornamental pool in the centre. Everywhere sculpture is to be found, modern and sited with an unerring eye.

Trentham Gardens

At Chelsea 2005 a gold medal was awarded to Tom Stuart-Smith for his atmospheric show garden. It was in fact, unusually, an impressionistic interpretation of the grandiose restoration and revival of an actual garden – Trentham in Staffordshire. In 1833 the 2nd Duke of Sutherland commissioned Charles Barry to turn the 1707 house into a magnificent Italian *palazzo*. Barry also created broad flower-filled terraces separated by steps. On the upper level an intricate square of beds intersected by narrow paths was filled with the bedding plants and colour-themed arrangements for which head gardener George Fleming was to become celebrated. The 10-acre rectangular lower garden leading down to 'Capability' Brown's lake was even more intricately patterned and ornamented with an array of statues and temples.

Three different designers have been employed at Trentham to reinvent Barry's grandiose concept. Dominic Cole and Land Use Consultants were made responsible for restoring the upper flower garden to its colourful Victorian formality, while the vast lower parterre garden was handed over to Tom Stuart-Smith and Piet Oudolf. The work on the lower terrace has been likened by Tom to making a sandwich, with Piet responsible for the 'bread' – twin herbaceous borders flanking his own substantial 'filling'. Challenging the underlying Victorian rigidity, Tom has filled the beds with a spider's web mesh of over 70,000 Mediterranean and meadow-like perennials, using the combinations and colours for which he in his turn has become famous. Where George Fleming had planted a rivulet of blue and white forget-me-nots to meander through the pleasure grounds, he has planted a ribbon of grasses to represent the River Trent which flows through the property and which for Tom has become a metaphor of Trentham's decline and resurgence .

Professor Mark Laird, who has done so much to reinvent Painshill, believes that Piet Oudolf, following in the pioneering footsteps of the likes of Charles Hamilton and Gertrude Jekyll, 'gains painterly strength by drawing on and departing from three centuries of experimenting with planting'. His work at Scampston Hall was earlier proof of his 'sublime flair'. The Anglo-Dutch partnership at Trentham was an inspired piece of commissioning.

Notes on Great Gardeners

Sir Charles Barry (1795–1860) A highly successful architect (Houses of Parliament etc), he popularised the formal Italian style of gardening in the mid-nineteenth century, creating impressive designs incorporating terraces, flights of steps, balustrading, urns, fountains and loggis. His most notable gardens were at Trentham, Dunrobin, Cliveden, Shrubland Hall and Harewood.

Christopher Bradley-Hole (b. 1955) He worked first on a range of architectural projects before moving over to landscapes and gardens. He can claim to be among the first of British minimalists to practise the art of garden design. Winner of many Chelsea gold medals, he works chiefly for private clients.

Charles Bridgeman (d. 1738) Famous for the way in which he exploited the outstanding features of the sites for which he designed gardens, he provided the link between the rigid formality of much seventeenth-century garden design and the apparent freedom of the landscape movement pioneered by William Kent and ʻCapabilityʼ Brown. While retaining features such as geometric parterres close to the house and straight allées, he also incorporated wilderness and meadow areas linked by meandering paths, and by his use of the ha-ha wall he made vistas of the surrounding landscape part of his designs. Apart from work for royal patrons in gardens such as Richmond and Kensington Gardens, he carried out important works at Blenheim, Claremont, Rousham, Cliveden and Stowe.

John Brookes (b. 1933) Designer of over 700 gardens here and abroad, he is in Jane Brownʼs estimation ʻthe most talented Modernist who has worked in Britain since the warʼ. His Mondrianesque garden for Penguin Books in Harmondsworth is his most elegant modern garden, Denmans his best-known.

Lancelot ʻCapabilityʼ Brown (1716–83) Having worked as head gardener and clerk of works at Stowe early in his career, Brown became familiar with the work of Bridgeman and Vanbrugh and helped to execute the designs of William Kent and James Gibbs. However, he was more radical than any of them, discarding formality when creating natural-looking landscapes with large stretches of water and impressive clumps of native trees, and confining flowering plants and vegetables to walled gardens well away from the house. Examples of his work in the *Guide* are: Audley End, Berrington, Blenheim, Bowood, Burghley, Cadland House, Chatsworth, Claremont, Harewood, Highclere, Holkham, Leeds Castle, Longleat, Petworth, Sheffield Park, Sledmere, Syon, Temple Newsam, Trentham, Warwick Castle, Weston House, Wimpole Hall and Wrest Park.

Brenda Colvin (1897–1981) A highly influential landscape architect who worked at both ends of the scale – large projects such as land reclamation schemes and new towns, small gardens for private clients. She helped to found the Landscape Institute, serving as its President from 1951 to 1953, and her *Land and Landscape* became a prime reference book for the profession.

Dame Sylvia Crowe (1901–98) She was responsible for many large-scale projects for a crop of new towns and became an acknowledged expert on the sympathetic integration of development schemes, such as the construction of power stations, with the surrounding landscape. She was President of the Landscape

Institute from 1957 to 1959. Examples of her work may be seen at Blenheim, Cottesbrooke and Lexham Hall.

Margery Fish (1888–1969) An informed plantswoman and influential lecturer and author, a partisan of William Robinson's naturalistic approach to gardening. This she developed in her own garden at East Lambrook, which became a haven for endangered garden plants. Her style of mixing semi-formal features with traditional planting has been influential.

Henk Gerritsen (b. 1948) One of a famous group of Dutch garden designers, he has been involved in turning the 40-acre garden at Waltham Place into a wholly organic garden.

Isabelle Van Groeningen (b. 1965) She arrived in the UK in 1983 from Belgium to train at Wisley and Kew, and in 1992 formed the Land Art practice with the German landscape architect Gabriella Pape. Together they have tackled an range of projects both in Europe and elsewhere — historic gardens, new private gardens, public parks and commercial sites. Examples of their work in the *Guide* are at Eltham Palace, Cliveden, Ryton Organic Garden and The London Wetland Centre.

Charles Hamilton (1704–86) Under the influence of William Kent between 1738 and 1773, when he was obliged to sell the estate at Painshill Park in Surrey to pay his debts, Hamilton created one of Britain's most picturesque landscape gardens. As well as being a talented designer, he was an exemplary plantsman, incorporating many exotics in his schemes. He also designed a cascade and grotto at Bowood in Wiltshire and advised on work at Holland Park in London and Stourhead.

Ian Hamilton Finlay (b. 1925) A calligrapher and sculptor of the highest order, he is best known for his home in Lanarkshire, Little Sparta, which has been described by Sir Roy Strong as 'the most original contemporary garden in the country'. This is modernism at its most elegant and refined, and a showcase for a lifetime of his own work.

Gertrude Jekyll (1843–1932) Both by her writing and her planting (much of it accomplished in partnership with the architect Sir Edwin Lutyens), she has probably had as much influence on the appearance of British gardens as any other designer. Her great strength was in carefully considered and subtle use of plant colour. Finding inspiration in the informality of cottage gardens, she created large interwoven swathes of plants rather than confining them to precise `spotty' patterns. One of the best examples of her work with Lutyens is Hestercombe; others are Barrington Court, Castle Drogo, Folly Farm, Goddards, Hatchlands, Knebworth, Upton Grey Manor House, Munstead Wood, Tylney Hall, Vann and Yalding.

Sir Geoffrey Jellicoe (1900–96) Shortly after becoming an architect, he made an extensive study of Italian gardens with J.C. Shepherd, which led in 1925 to their classic book, *Italian Gardens of the Renaissance*. The publication of *Gardens and Design* in 1927 helped to bring him interesting commissions, such as the design of a large formal garden at Ditchley Park in Oxfordshire, giving scope for the strongly architectural quality of his work. After World War II he was given much public work, including the Cathedral Close in Exeter, the Kennedy Memorial at Runnymede and a large theme park at Galveston in Texas. Among his work for private clients, the gardens at Sutton Place and Shute House are notable. His work may also be seen at Cliveden, Cottesbrooke, Mottisfont and Sandringham.

Charles Jencks (b. 1939) An American academic long resident in the UK, he is best known for his re-landscaping of the garden at Portrack in the Scottish Borders with his wife Maggie Keswick. The principal landscape elements, monumental earthworks, echo the Land Art movement of the 1960s. Since his wife's death he has created the Garden of Cosmic Speculation (a scientific theme park) at Portrack, and the new Landform Ueda for the Scottish Gallery of Modern Art in Edinburgh.

Lawrence Johnston (1871–1948) One of the most outstandingly stylish twentieth-century gardeners, he was an American who spent much of his youth in Paris and built two great gardens in Europe which influenced the design of a great many others, including Sissinghurst. In 1905 he began to make the garden at Hidcote, where he pioneered the creation of a series of sheltered and interconnected garden rooms, each of which surprised by its different content and treatment.

William Kent (1685–1748) The former apprentice coach painter from Hull twice made the Grand Tour of Italy with his most influential patron, Lord Burlington. Heavily influenced by the paintings of Claude and Salvator Rosa, he later tried to introduce the type of romantic landscape encountered in their canvases into his gardens, freeing them from much of the formality which had dominated previous British gardening. His work at Rousham, Holkham, Chiswick House, Claremont and Stowe had a great influence on 'Capability' Brown, Charles Hamilton and Henry Hoare of Stourhead.

Arabella Lennox-Boyd (b. 1938) Italian by birth and upbringing, she has designed some 300 gardens — in Europe, Barbados, Canada, the United States and Mexico. She is renowned for the clarity and elegance of her designs and planting, and is a Chelsea gold medallist five times over.

Christopher Lloyd (b. 1921) The doyen of garden-makers and one of the most stimulating of garden writers. He is the son of Nathaniel Lloyd, the architectural writer, who commissioned Edwin Lutyens to extend his house at Great Dixter and to design the garden. Christopher Lloyd has brought to it his great skill as a plantsman and an almost iconoclastic approach to Lutyens' planting.

Sir Edwin Lutyens (1869–1944) A fine architect who between 1893 and 1912 created approximately 70 gardens in partnership with Gertrude Jekyll. Her subtle planting always softened and complemented the strong architectural nature of his garden designs, and they in their turn splendidly integrated the house with the garden and its site. A fine example is at Hestercombe; others are at Abbotswood, Ammerdown, Castle Drogo, Folly Farm, Goddards, Heywood, Knebworth, Misarden, Munstead Wood and Parc Floral des Moutiers.

Thomas H. Mawson (1861–1933) A Lancastrian who trained in London and set up a landscape practice in Windermere in 1885, his reputation quickly grew and he was chosen by many of the rich northern industrialists to landscape the gardens of their Lakeland holiday homes. Examples of his work may be seen at Brockhole, Dyffryn, Graythwaite, The Hill Garden, Holker, Little Onn, Rivington Terraced Garden, Tirley Garth and Wightwick.

Hal Moggridge (b. 1936) He trained as an architect before working for Geoffrey Jellicoe. He started his own practice in 1967 after advising the GLC on suitable sites for new towns, then two years later joined Brenda Colvin in practice as Colvin and Moggridge. As a firm they have designed industrial landscapes, public gardens and private parks, landscaped the National Botanic Garden of Wales and planted William Morris's diminutive garden at Kelmscott.

William E. Nesfield (1793–1881) Working often in partnership with the architect Salvin, his style was eclectic, usually reflecting that of the houses they surrounded; he was responsible for the reintroduction of the parterre (a good example is at Holkham) as a garden feature. He worked also at Alton, Blickling, Cliveden, Dorfold Hall, Holkham, Kew, Rode Hall, Shugborough, Somerleyton and Trentham.

Piet Oudolf (b. 1944) One of the best-known proponents of naturalistic planting with perennials and grasses, he is a nurseryman as well as a garden designer, and won 'Best in Show' at Chelsea 2000. He has made a number of gardens in Britain – at Wisley, Bury Court, Pensthorpe and Scampston. His latest *grand projet* is in collaboration with Tom Stuart-Smith at Trentham.

Russell Page (1906–85) Trained as a painter, he quickly became absorbed by garden design, working for several years in association with Jellicoe. After the war he secured many commissions in Europe and America, including the garden at the Frick in New York and the Battersea Festival Gardens in London. He encapsulated many of his ideas about garden design in *The Education of a Gardener*, first published in 1962. Examples of his work are at Longleat and Port Lympne.

Sir Joseph Paxton (1803–65) Gardener at Chatsworth for 32 years from 1826, where he made the great fountain and the pioneering conservatory. One of the early designers of public parks, including those at Birkenhead and Halifax, he was also influential as a writer and a founder of *The Gardener's Chronicle*. Other examples of his work are at Birkenhead, Capesthorne, Somerleyton and Tatton.

Dan Pearson (b. 1964) He began his professional career in 1987, and has completed a wide range of private and public sector commissions. He was responsible for re-landscaping the grounds of Althorp and for the landscape design surrounding the Millennium Dome. He is also well known as an author, a columnist and a TV presenter.

Harold Peto (1854–1933) A talented architect working for the partnership which later employed the young Lutyens, who undoubtedly influenced his style. A lover of Italianate formal gardens, one of his best-known works was his own garden at Iford Manor, but the canal garden at Buscot Park and the Casita garden at Ilnacullin are also notable achievements. Other examples are at Easton Lodge, Greathed Manor, Heale House, Wayford Manor and West Dean.

Humphry Repton (1752–1818) The most influential eighteenth-century landscaper after the death of Lancelot Brown, he was a great protagonist of Brown's ideas but tended to favour denser planting, and his parkland buildings were rustic rather than classical. He restored formality to gardens with terracing, flights of steps and balustrading. He produced over 400 of his famous 'before and after' Red Books and worked tireleslly on such fine estates as Holkham, Sheffield Park, Woburn and

Sheringham. Other examples in the *Guide* are at Ashridge, Attingham, Corsham, Hatchlands, Kenwood, Longleat, Rode Hall and Ston Easton.

William Robinson (1838–1935) An Irishman who settled in England and became one of the most prolific writers and influential designers of his epoch. By his teaching and example he liberated gardeners from the prim rigidity which had begun to dominate garden design in the mid-nineteenth century, advocating a free and natural attitude towards the creation of herbaceous and mixed beds. His planting philosophy which early inspired Gertrude Jekyll. He founded a weekly journal, *The Garden* and wrote the best-selling *The English Flower Garden*. Examples of his work are at Gravetye Manor, High Beeches, Killerton, Leckhampton College (Cambridge) and Shrubland Park.

Lanning Roper (1912–83) A Harvard graduate from New Jersey who adopted Britain as his home and became one of the most popular landscapers in the 30 years after World War II. His best schemes, such as that at Glenveagh Castle, involved a subtle handling of plants combined with interesting formal features. One of his most controversial designs is the ornamental canal in the RHS garden at Wisley. Other examples of his work are at Anglesey Abbey, Broughton Castle, Fairfield House, Lower Hall and Orford Old Rectory.

Vita Sackville-West (1892–1962) With her husband, Harold Nicolson, she made the famous garden at Sissinghurst Castle, begun in 1932. The couple were friendly with and influenced by Lawrence Johnston. Another example of her work may be seen at Alderley Grange. Although she was the propagandist of the pair, some think that her husband's conception of structure made a great contribution to twentieth-century garden design.

Tom Stuart-Smith (b. 1960) A superb plantsman and a perennial Chelsea gold medallist. He aims to create 'informal and wild' gardens, and indeed his gardens are becoming increasingly naturalistic. Although most of his work is for private clients, he has created a garden at Wisley, another at Windsor Castle, and is currently a key player in the vast restoration project at Trentham.

Sir John Vanbrugh (1644–1726) A considerable dramatist and spectacular architect of palaces like Blenheim in Oxfordshire and Castle Howard in Yorkshire. Although he did not generally design landscapes, he ensured that his houses were magnificently sited and often created buildings for their gardens, such as the bridge at Blenheim and for landscapes made by other designers such as Stowe and Claremont.

Rosemary Verey (1918–2001) A renowned plantswoman who created a famous garden at Barnsley House, and designed others for private clients. Other examples of her work are at Holdenby House and The Old Rectory in Sudborough. She was also an inspiring lecturer and one of England's foremost gardening writers, author of 17 books.

Kim Wilkie (b. 1955) A landscape architect, urban designer and an environmental planner, expert at introducing modern designs into historic landscapes. Responsible for the Thames Landscape Strategy, he threaded together the eighteenth-century waterside villas and landscape and made the administrative authorities along the Thames look anew at their heritage. He has helped to revive the cult of earth sculpting with his grass terraces at Great Fosters and Heveningham Hall. His new garden at the V&A in London is restrained, practical and elegant.

Glossary of Garden Terms

Arbour Any sheltered covered area open to one side which usually contains a seat. Often surrounded by masonry, hedging or trelliswork covered with climbing plants.

Allée **or alley** A path either cut through a thick shrubbery or woodland or closely flanked by a hedge or wall.

Auricula theatre A shelter rising in tiers housing a collection of auriculas – an early-nineteenth-century collectors' craze.

Bath house A rectangular sunken pool for cold-water bathing, with seating approached by steps.

Bosquet **or bosket** A block of closely planted trees with *allées* between.

Canal An ornamental water basin made in the form of an elongated rectangle. It can either be excavated into the ground or confined above ground within masonry walls.

Clair-voie or *clair-voyée* A gap in a wall or hedge which extends the view by allowing a glimpse of the surrounding countryside; also an openwork gate, fence or grille at the end of an *allée*.

Cottage orné A deliberately picturesque rustic dwelling designed to ornament a park.

Crinkle-crankle wall A serpentine wall sheltering fruit trees within its walls.

Exedra An area of turf within a semi-circular hedge which is commonly used to display ornaments or to locate a semi-circular seat; or the seat itself.

Eye-catcher A building such as a tower, temple, obelisk, etc., or sometimes merely a bench, large urn or outstanding long-lived plant designed to beckon the eye towards a particularly rewarding view.

Finial An ornament such as an urn or a pointed sculptural form used to cap features like gateposts, the tops of spires, the top corners of buildings, etc.

Folly A decorative building with no serious function except perhaps to lure attention along a vista or to improve the composition of the garden 'picture'.

Gazebo Dog latin for 'I will gaze', used to describe a building usually sited on a high terrace from which the surrounding countryside can be enjoyed.

Grotto/Nymphaeum An artificial garden feature made to simulate an underground cavern and usually dimly lit from a single small natural light source such as the cave mouth or an oval occulus pierced through the roof or wall. But when formally shaped and lined with statuary and a sophisticated encrustation of shellwork, a grotto can become a nymphaeum.

Ha-ha A deep ditch separating the garden from the landscape beyond. It allows the unscreened view to be enjoyed from the house but is profiled in such a way that livestock cannot enter the garden.

Hermitage A rustic building popularised in the eighteenth century, supposedly as a hermit's retreat.

Knot garden Geometric patterns of low-growing hedge plants such as box or shrubby germander which are made to appear as though they intertwine like knotted cord. The areas between the hedges are filled with plants or decorative gravel.

Moon door or gate A circular opening in a door or wall.

Mount An artificial hill usually surmounted by an arbour from which landscapes both inside and beyond the garden can be enjoyed from a different perspective.

Obelisk A tall, thin vertical column diminishing in width as it rises, and frequently tapered to a pyramid. Large-scale examples have been built to commemorate great events or notable people and often to act as eye-catchers in great landscape schemes. Smaller *treillage* versions have been used to beckon for attention in smaller gardens or to act as vertical frames for climbing plants.

Pagoda A feature in a few great landscape gardens based on Buddhist multi-storey towers of spiritual significance. In Britain they were first introduced during the eighteenth-century craze for things Chinese.

Palladian bridge A bridge with a classical superstructure, usually open-sided with columns supporting a roof.

Parterre An intricately patterned formal garden which usually includes other features such as statuary, water basins and fountains; much larger than a knot garden.

Patte d'oie Literally 'goose foot'; a series of usually three formal paths or grand avenues leacing fan-wise from a single point through densely planted trees.

Pergola A framework of columns supporting beams, usually clad with climbing plants such as roses, clematis or wisteria.

Pleaching Training the branches of a line of trees horizontally by pruning and attaching them to wires, so that the remainder can be intertwined as they grow to form a screen of foliage.

Quincunx A pattern (sometimes a repeat-pattern) of four trees at the corners of a square and one at the centre.

Red Book Bound books of proposals including 'flap' overlays, drawn by Humphry Repton for his clients.

Rotunda Strictly, circle of classical columns on a raised circular plinth supporting a domed roof. Instead of a solid dome it may be topped with an open ironwork dome. Sometimes loosely called a kiosk.

Rustic work Garden features, such as garden houses, fences or seats, made from unbarked tree branches, and frequently embellished with such decoration as patterns made from sectioned pine cones.

Souterrain An underground chamber, usually in a grotto.

Stumpery Roots and stumps arranged upside down and covered with trailing plants.

Stilt hedge Clipped trees, such as limes, which have all their branches removed for several feet above the ground to reveal a line of bare trunks like stilts.

Théâtre de verdure Similar to but usually more spacious than an exedra, a turf 'stage' with a backcloth of trimmed hedge and sometimes other hedges disposed like the wings of a theatre.

Treillage Architectural features such as arbours, obelisks or ambitious screens made out of trellis.

Trompe-l'oeil A feature designed to deceive the eye, such s a path which narrows as it recedes from a viewpoint to exaggerate the perspective and make the garden seem larger.

Wilderness Bosquet, grove or wood traversed by paths.

Two-Starred Gardens in the *Guide*

Buckinghamshire
Ascott; Cliveden, The Manor House, Bledlow;
Stowe Landscape Garden; Waddesdon Manor;
West Wycombe Park

Cambridgeshire
Anglesey Abbey; Christ's College; University
Botanic Garden

Cheshire
Ness Botanic Gardens; Tatton Park

Cornwall
Caerhays Castle Garden; Chyverton; Heligan;
Trebah; Tresco Abbey; Trewithen

Cumbria & Isle of Man
Holker Hall; Levens Hall

Derbyshire
Chatsworth

Devon
Castle Drogo; Knightshayes; Marwood Hill;
RHS Rosemoor

Dorset
Abbotsbury Sub-Tropical Garden; Cranborne
Manor; Forde Abbey; Mapperton

Essex
Beth Chatto Garden

Gloucestershire
Hidcote; Kiftsgate; National Arboretum
Westonbirt; Sezincote

Hampshire & Isle of Wight
Exbury Gardens; Longstock Park; Mottisfont
Abbey; The Sir Harold Hill ier Gardens; West
Green House

Hertfordshire
Benington Lordship; Hatfield House

Kent
Goodnestone Park; Hever Castle; Sissinghurst
Castle

Lancashire
Gresgarth Hall

London
Chiswick House; Hampton Court Palace; Royal
Botanic Gardens Kew

Norfolk
East Ruston Old Vicarage; Houghton Hall

Northamptonshire
Coton Manor; Cottesbrooke Hall

Northumberland
Belsay Hall

Oxfordshire
Blenheim Palace; Oxford Botanic Garden;
Rousham; Westwell

Shropshire
Hodnet Hall; Wollerton Old Hall

Somerset
Cothay Manor; Greencombe; Hadspen Garden

Staffordshire
Biddulph Grange

Suffolk
Helmingham Hall; Somerleyton Hall

Surrey
Painshill; RHS Garden Wisley; Savill Garden; Valley
Gardens

East Sussex
Great Dixter; Sheffield Park

West Sussex
Leonardslee; Nymans; Wakehurst Place

Wiltshire
Iford Manor; Stourhead

North & East Yorkshire
Castle Howard; Newby Hall; Studley Royal &
Fountains Abbey

Northern Ireland
Annesley Gardens; Mount Stewart; Rowallane

Republic of Ireland
Dillon Garden; Mount Congreve; Mount Usher

Scotland
Arduaine; Benmore Botanic Garden; Castle
Kennedy; Crarae Garden; Crathes Castle; Culzean
Castle; Drummond Castle; House of Pitmuies;
Inverewe Garden; Little Sparta; Logan Botanic
Garden; Manderston; Mount Stuart; Royal Botanic
Garden Edinburgh

Wales
Bodnant; Powis Castle

France
Château de Brécy; Château de Canon; Parc Floral
des Moutiers; Le Vasterival

Belgium
Annevoie

Netherlands
Paleis Het Loo

How to Use the *Guide*

The *Guide* is **arranged by counties.** Within each of these the gardens are listed alphabetically by the normal name of the garden/house. The index at the end of the book can also be used to find a garden whose name only is known to the reader.

Readers who do not have a specific garden in mind may like to take the following **procedure to discover gardens** in their particular area which are available for viewing:

1. Choose the county or neighbouring counties which will be your target area.
2. Search out (in these counties) the gardens which are open all year round, i.e. those marked with ○.
3. Having listed these gardens, pay particular attention to ★ ★ and then ★ gardens on the list.

Alternatively, readers can concentrate on the starred gardens, checking which of these are open on the days available to the visitor.

Symbols: These are intended to convey some useful information at a glance. [NEW] entries new for 2006 edition; ○ open all year; ☾ open most of year; ◑ open for main season; ◖ open on a certain number of days and/or by appointment; ☕ teas/light refreshments; ✕ meals; ▉ picnics permitted; WC toilet facilities; WC toilet facilities, inc. disabled; ♿ garden partly wheelchair-accessible; ꜛ dogs permitted on lead; ✿ plants for sale; ▥ shop; ♟ events held; ꝋ children-friendly; B&B bed and breakfast.

This list is repeated in various places throughout the book and further explanation of symbols is given under **Detailed Use of the *Guide*** (below).

Detailed Use of the *Guide*
(information listed in order used in entry)

Garden name The name of the garden, or the building with which it is associated.

Stars To help give the reader the opinion which inspectors and editors have formed about the status of certain gardens, over 100 properties have been marked with ★ ★ indicate that in our opinion these are amongst the finest gardens in the world in terms of design and content. Many are of historic importance, but some are of recent origin. Readers will appreciate that direct comparisons cannot be made between a vast estate like Chatsworth with its staff of professional gardeners and a tiny plantsman's garden behind a terraced house, although both may be excellent of their kind. Those gardens which are of high quality, though not perhaps as outstanding as the ★ ★ ones, are given a single ★ . The latter will be worth travelling a considerable distance to see, and sometimes the general ambience of the property as a whole will make the visit especially rewarding. The bulk of the gardens in the *Guide* are not given a mark of distinction, but all have considerable merit and will be well worth visiting when in the region. Some of them will have distinctive features of design or plant content, noted in the description, which will justify making a special journey. To give readers an idea of scale, we estimate that some 5000 properties in the UK are open to the public on announced dates in the year, plus public parks and green spaces. We list well over 1200, of which over 100 have ★★ status, that is about ten per cent of the total listed by us, but two and a half per cent of the total open. On the maps at the end of the *Guide*, those gardens given ★★ status are distinguished from the others by being boxed in bold.

Address This is the address supplied by the owner or some other reputable source. In the index, gardens with street numbers are listed under the initial letter of the street name.

Telephone numbers Except where owners have specifically requested them to be excluded, telephone numbers to which enquiries may be directed are given for each property. To maintain the support and co-operation of private owners, it is suggested that the telephone be used with discretion. Where group visits are proposed, owners should be advised in advance and arrangements preferably confirmed in writing. Telephone code numbers are given in brackets. Visitors calling the Republic of Ireland from Britain should phone 00353 followed by the code (Dublin is 1) followed by the subscriber's 6-figure number. Northern Ireland and the Channel Islands follow the mainland system. France has 9-figure numbers prefixed by 0033, Belgium by 0032 and Netherlands by 0031.

Website Many gardens in the *Guide* now have their own websites, and we include these in a separate list on pages 591–7.

Owners' names given are those available at the time of going to press. In the case of The National Trust, some properties may be the homes of tenants of the Trust. Some other gardens are owned or managed by other trusts.

Location, travel and parking This information has been supplied by inspectors and is intended to be the best available to those travelling by car. No specific details are given where to park because it is assumed that most owners make some convenient arrangement for visitors' cars. However, if special circumstances apply (i.e. if parking is a long walk away) this is usually mentioned under **Other Information**. The unreliability of train and bus services makes it unrewarding to include many details, particularly as very many garden visits are made on Sundays. However, a number of properties can be reached by public transport.

Opening dates and times (see also symbols as opening indicators, below). Dates and times given of access to house (if open) and to garden are usually the best available at the moment of going to press, but some may have been changed subsequently. Some owners unavoidably cannot give their opening information before we go to press. The details given are the most helpful we can present. Many gardens open under the National Gardens Scheme, so check the Yellow Book; and if in doubt telephone in advance of a visit. The dates and times given for all entries are inclusive – that is, an entry such as May to Sept means that the garden is open from 1st May to 30th Sept inclusive, and 2 – 5pm also means that visits will be effective during that period, although some gardens may close to visitors beforehand, and it is wise to arrive half an hour before closing time. Many owners open their gardens to visitors by appointment, and will often arrange to give a personally conducted tour.

Gardens in Britain which are open by courtesy of the owners for one of many charities are included where the gardens are of special interest even if, as on some occasions, they are open in this way on only one day in the year. Some owners will, however, also open by appointment on other days. However, such gardens may also open at other specific times, such as for local charities or church restoration funds, and it is not generally possible to give dates for all these locally publicised openings. Readers should note that other nearby gardens, not listed in this guide for one reason or another, may well be open at similar times to those of listed gardens.

Entrance fees As far as is known, these are correct at time of going to press, but changes may be made without notice. Where there are variations, these will be upwards, but the amount of increase is usually small. Family tickets may be available with children charged at a lower rate. Numbers of children included in the family ticket may vary. Charges for parties are often at special rates. National Trust charges are explained in their literature with special concessions for members. Accompanied children are normally admitted by the Trust at half price and this is why no specific charge for children is usually listed for Trust properties. Figures for the Republic of Ireland are given in Euros. The Royal Horticultural Society, in addition to its own properties, has a 'free access' scheme to a wide range of other British gardens. RHS members will find details in the Society's annual *Handbook*; otherwise consult the website (www.rhs.org.uk).

Other information This section gives helpful information notified to us which we pass on to the reader. It includes: extra attractions in or near the garden (eg a musem or nursery); facilities outside the garden but nearby (eg toilet facilities); facilities which are limited either by availability (eg teas on charity open days only), or by location (eg picnics in park only); warnings (eg no coaches), and helpful hints (eg possible for wheelchairs but some gravel paths).

Disclaimer

The information given is believed to be correct at the time of going to press but changes do occur, properties are sold or ownership varied. There may also be closures of over-visited properties, or limitations imposed on opening times. Prices of entry may be changed without notice.

It has not been possible for *Guide* inspectors to visit every garden which was open to the public at some time in the year, and certain gardens in the *Guide* may not have been visited for over twelve months. In general, inspections have been made on an anonymous basis to ensure objectivity.

Symbols

NEW New garden this year.

○, ◑, ◐, ◕ **Opening times** These symbols indicate gardens are open as follows: ○ throughout the year; ◑ most of the year; ◐ more or less throughout the season from Easter to October for several days (i.e. more than two or three) each week; and ◕ on a certain number of days and/or by appointment.

■, ✕, 🍴, **Refreshments:** a guide only. Where ■ is given, this means that the owners have arranged to serve a simple tea or light refreshments on the property, or near at hand, at reasonable prices during opening hours. ✕ indicates that meals are served. ⛱ means that picnics are permitted, although probably in certain areas only.

WC, <u>WC</u> Toilet facilities WC indicates that access to a toilet or toilets is provided, while <u>WC</u> means that the toilet facilities are also suitable for disabled visitors. Where neither symbol is given, no specific toilets are available and enquiries will have to be directed to staff or owners.

♿ **Wheelchair suitability** Inspectors have told us where they believe a garden is partly or wholly negotiable by someone in a wheelchair. This symbol refers to the garden only and if a house or other building is also open, it may or may not be suitable for wheelchairs.

🐾 **Dogs** They are allowed in the property on leads (very often in restricted areas only).

🌿 **Plants for sale** Often these are grown on the property, but some owners now buy in plants from a commercial source for re-sale.

🛍 **Shop** refers to a sales outlet on the premises, such as National Trust shops, those selling souvenirs, etc.

🎭 **Events** These may be held during, or as well as, normal garden opening times. Those wishing to participate in (or to avoid) events should check before travelling.

👶 **Children-friendly** Some owners pay particular attention to expanding the attractions for the whole family, while other gardens are by their design and content intriguing to children.

B&B **Bed and Breakfast** An increasing number of owners offer accommodation – a fine way for visitors to become acquainted with a garden.

No symbol means either that a certain facility is not available at a garden or that we have not been notified of it. However, it is worth checking under **Other Information** for details of partial availability.

BEDFORDSHIRE

Kings Arms Path Garden

Ampthill, Bedford MK45. Tel: (01525) 755648/403945

Ampthill Town Council • Opposite Market Square, Ampthill, down Kings Arms Yard via public footpath • Open 29th Jan, 26th Feb, 2 – 4pm; 26th March, 16th April, 28th May, 18th June, 30th July, 27th Aug, 24th Sept, 2.30 – 5pm; 29th Oct, 2 – 4pm, and for parties by appt • Entrance: £1 (£2 on 16th April), children free ● ● & ℘

This unusual and most atmospheric garden was created in his retirement by William Nourish between 1970 and 1986. Long and narrow, it has its own microclimate, kept moist by a pond at the top and water gullies under the little valley floor. A path runs beside the gullies, designed with viewing points. A magnificent swamp cypress stands on an island with *Lysichiton americanum*, a huge wisteria clambers up into a 23-metre Scots pine, and the fine contrasting trees include a *Fagus sylvatica* 'Purpurea Tricolor', an American buckeye chestnut and a collection of handsome variegated hollies. Azaleas and rhododendrons give colour in May, with irises and lilies to follow. The ground cover and underplanting are good too, with many varieties of snowdrops, narcissi, hellebores, primulas and epimediums, and collections of geraniums, hemerocallis, magnolias and many others.

The Manor House ★

Church Road, Stevington, Bedford MK43 7QB. Tel: (01234) 822064

Kathy Brown • 5m NW of Bedford off A428, through Bromham. In Stevington, turn right at crossroads; garden is on left after 0.25m • Open 28th May, 25th June and 30th July, 2 – 6pm; 21st June, 6 – 9pm, and for parties by appt • Entrance: £3.50, children £1 ● ● WC & ℘ ⚜

A garden of exuberant imagination, atmospheric and brimful of ideas, with a strong emphasis on garden art. Each of the twenty distinct areas is completely different in atmosphere. The summer garden planted around the old fish pond is colourful and strongly Mediterranean, with a variety of succulents and imposing echiums followed by a fine display of aeoniums, agaves and dasylirions. Beautifully understated by contrast is the avenue of *Betula utilis* var. *jacquemontii* 'Grey Ghost' underplanted with acanthus. It leads to a flowery meadow through beds of grasses (dressed with pebbles or slate) which prolong the attraction into autumn and winter. The French garden is an essay in formal design; the yew hedges that back the box parterres commemorate Fouquet's famous 1661 trial with 12 'jurors' clipped into shape. Moving swiftly forward in time, the visitor comes to a 'Rothko room' glowing with purple beech, berberis and prunus, and an airy 'Hepworth room' of grasses mingling with herbaceous plants. Major collections of clematis and roses are dotted around the garden.

Seal Point ★

7 Wendover Way, Luton LU2 7LS. Tel: (01582) 611567

Mrs Danae Johnston • In NE of Luton. Turn N off Stockingstone Road into Felstead Way and take second turning on left • Open for individuals and parties by appt • Entrance: £2.50 ◕ 🖰 🖫 WC ⚲

This small, sloping town garden with a Japanese theme goes from good to better, with interesting plants and gorgeous colour schemes. A hardy standard fuchsia is now over three metres high, and 20 or more different grasses are integrated into the borders. There is something unusual at every turn: a wildlife copse, a tiny bonsai garden, three pools (one with a waterfall), yin and yang beds, amusing topiary, original ornaments, and much more. The garden is run organically and with log piles, ladybird lodges, bumble bee nests and nectar plants the accent everywhere is on nurturing wildlife.

Stockwood Park

Stockwood Craft Museum, Farley Hill, Luton LU1 4BH. Tel: (01582) 738714

Borough of Luton • Leave M1 at junction 10 for Luton. Take Farley Hill (Chapel Street) turn off A505 Dunstable road out of Luton. Signposted from A1081 • Open April to Oct, daily except Mon (but open Bank Holiday Mons), 10am – 5pm; Nov to March, Sat and Sun, 10am – 4pm • Entrance: free • Other information: Craft museum in stable block ◔ 🖰 WC ♿ 🚻 ☕ ⚲

A series of period gardens – medieval, seventeenth-century knot, cottage and Victorian – has been assembled within the walled gardens of the old house. In the park is a landscape garden with sculpture by Ian Hamilton Finlay, whose work gives a convincing continuity to the landscape tradition by its location alongside the original ha-ha. Another of his sculptures is a curved inscribed wall, and his modern fragments of 'antique' buildings, partly buried, suggest the eighteenth-century ideal of a harmonious blend of parkland, planting, architecture and sculpture.

The Swiss Garden [Historic Garden Grade II*]

Old Warden Park, Biggleswade SG18 9ER. Tel: (01767) 627666

Bedfordshire County Council • 6m SE of Bedford. Take A1 to Biggleswade and follow signposts from roundabout. Also signposted on A600 Shefford – Bedford road. Entrance via Shuttleworth Collection • Open all year, daily, 10am – 5pm (closes 4pm Nov to March). Guided tours available • Entrance: £4, concessions £3, children free. Special rates for parties • Other information: Restaurant adjacent to garden in grounds of Shuttleworth Collection. Disabled parking. Two wheelchairs available for loan ◔ 🖰 ✕ WC ♿ ⚲ 🚻 ☕

The 10-acre landscape garden was laid out in the 1820s by Lord Ongley for his Swiss mistress, complete with a rustic thatched cottage of unpeeled bark and a series of canals crossed by ornate hump-back iron bridges made by the blacksmith uncle of Emma Hamilton (Admiral Nelson's mistress was once a nurserymaid at a local house). The Swiss cottage is the main focus for a series of contrived vistas, but there are plenty of other elements of interest in this unusual and atmospheric garden: a grotto and fernery, a thatched tree shelter, an Indian pavilion, two ponds and many fine shrubs and conifers, plus some remarkable trees.

Toddington Manor ★

Toddington LU5 6HJ. Tel: (01525) 872576

Sir Neville and Lady Bowman-Shaw • 8m NW of Luton, 1m NW of Toddington, 1m W of M1 junction 12. Signposted from village • Open probably 29th May, 11am – 5pm, and for parties by appt • Entrance: charge • Other information: Rare breeds of goats and pigs. Vintage tractor collection ● & ⬥ 🐾

The garden is maintained to the highest standards but the shrubs and plants are allowed to grow and flower and seed in abundance. Each area is themed individually. The pleached lime walk – a most successful *allée* – is paved and surrounded by large herbaceous borders displaying an exuberance of hostas with many variations of leaf, blue delphiniums, white astilbes and hellebores, euphorbias and angelicas. Inside the walled garden are borders with dramatic sweeps of delphiniums, peonies, clematis and grasses, backed by shrubs. In the rose garden the air is scented by yellow and white floribunda roses and philadelphus, with wonderful eremurus growing through; under the roses violas have spread in sheets. A stream flows through and feeds the ponds and the fountain. There is a good herb garden and greenhouse, and beyond the walls a wildflower meadow, orchards and 20 acres of woodland contribute to a fine display of natural beauty.

Tofte Manor

Souldrop Road, Sharnbrook MK44 1HH. Tel: (01234) 781425

Mr and Mrs C. Castleman • Off A6 between Bedford and Rushden. Exit at roundabout signed to Sharnbrook, and through village towards Souldrop. At Y-junction take right fork; house is 400 yards ahead on left, through large black wrought-iron gates • Open May to July and Sept, Tues and Wed, 9am – 5pm, and at other times for individuals and parties by appt • Entrance: £3.50, children free ● WC

In 1995 the present owners moved into the 1613 manor house and began work on a site that was flat and neglected although well furnished with magnificent cedars and other mature trees. This they landscaped, creating a large sunken garden, borders, a rose arbour and water feature. Wonderful spring bulbs, hot and cool colour-themed herbaceous borders, wild areas and a parterre garden with statues give the whole place great atmosphere and charm. There are contemporary sculptural touches too: a copper ball, lit at night by candles, hangs from the branches of a giant cedar as an unusual seat, and in the sunken garden an illuminated ball running with water glows after dark. A copy of the labyrinth at Chartres Cathederal, incorporating crystals and sacred geometry, can be walked by visitors in search of a still moment.

Woburn Abbey [Historic Park Grade I]

Woburn MK17 9WA. Tel: (01525) 290666

The Duke of Bedford and Trustees of Bedford Estates • 11m NW of Luton between A5 and M1 (follow signs from junction 13) • Open Easter to Oct, daily, 11am – 4pm

(telephone or consult website at back of Guide for exact details) • *Entrance: House and garden £9.50, OAPs £8.50, children (5–15) £5, plus additional £4 per car (2005 prices)* ☾ 🍽 ✕ 🏠 <u>WC</u> ♿ ♨ ☕

Early in the seventeenth century, Woburn was established as the principal seat of the 4th Earl of Bedford, who extended the abbey buildings and commissioned Isaac de Caus to build a grotto in the new north wing. At the Restoration, a series of enclosed gardens had been laid out to the west of the house and woodland planted with rides cut through. By 1714, the park had been extended and George London's Bason Pond created as an integral part of his grand Baroque west approach, and by 1738 Charles Bridgeman had largely removed all the formal gardens around the house. In 1780 Holland designed a greenhouse (later a sculpture gallery) and the Chinese dairy overlooking a small lake with a covered walk. At the same time informal gardens were created and enclosed to the east and south. The 6th Duke then employed Humphry Repton to draw up a landscape scheme for the park as a whole, and by 1805 the result was Repton's finest Red Book. His proposals were a triumph, and he was able to claim that 'The improvements I have had the honour to suggest have nowhere been so fully realised as at Woburn Abbey.' These comprised the creation of a group of linked yet separate areas of garden: an American and a Chinese garden, a rosery, a menagerie and an aviary. He also reshaped the lakes westwards from the abbey and rerouted the southern approach drive. In the 1930s the gardens were again developed by Percy Cane, and the 42 acres of gardens today are those made in the twentieth century. The park is still a deer park, largely pasture, and surrounds the gardens and pleasure grounds of the past. The private gardens, which are rarely open to the public, contain a large hornbeam maze, formal gardens, good herbaceous borders, and a most successful rose garden by Anita Pereire.

Wrest Park [Historic Park Grade I]

Silsoe, Bedford MK45 4HS. Tel: (01525) 860152

English Heritage • *10m S of Bedford, 0.75m E of Silsoe off A6* • *Open April to Sept, Sat, Sun and Bank Holiday Mons, 10am – 6pm; Oct, Sat and Sun only, 10am – 5pm (last admission 1 hour before closing). Advisable to check times before travelling* • *Entrance: £4.30, OAPs £3.20, children (5–15) £2.20, family £10.80 (2005 prices)* ◑ 🍽 🏠 WC ♿ ⬦ ♨ ☕

One of the few places in England where it is possible to see a Baroque formal garden of the early-eighteenth century. The Long Water – a canal – dominates the 'Great Garden', made for the 1st Duke of Kent. It provides the main axis of the grounds, and cuts through thick blocks of woodland. At its head stands the Banqueting House, a beautiful Thomas Archer pavilion with strong echoes of a similar pavilion designed by Daniel Marot, only recently discovered. 'Capability' Brown worked here later, creating a naturalistic river to surround the grounds at their perimeter. The woods on either side of the Long Water are intersected by avenues and dotted with 'incidents of delight' and giant urns set in grassy glades by Thomas Acres. The later Bath House was built as a romantic classical ruin. Water catches the eye in every direction. The nineteenth-century house (not open) was built in the French style, fronted by terraces and parterres. The large orangery was designed by Cléphane.

BERKSHIRE

Some gardens have postal addresses in one county and are physically situated in another. If in doubt, a check in the index will direct the reader to the page on which the garden appears.

Two-starred gardens are marked on the map with a black square.

Chieveley Manor

Chieveley, Newbury RG20 8UT. Tel: (01635) 248208

Mr and Mrs C.J. Spence • 4m N of Newbury, 0.5m from M4 junction 13 via A34. In Manor Lane by church • Open 25th June, 2 – 5pm • Entrance: £3, children free ● 🍽 WC ♿ 🌳

This well-presented garden provides a pleasing setting for the old brick manor house. Generous lawns, with some fine trees, merge into the immaculate paddocks of the adjacent stud farm. Brick steps edged with roses lead up from the lawn to the gravelled drive and the house, where borders of mixed planting soften the walls. The grassed walled garden at the back of the house has attractive trees, including a variegated maple and a tulip tree. Herbaceous borders with bold groups of perennials flank the entrance from a sunken stone terrace: here the colour scheme has been carefully conceived with deep colours counterbalanced by pinks and white. A variety of clematis in the walled garden and elsewhere catches the eye. Four beds surrounding a circular stone sink are filled with purple sage interspersed with *Geranium sanguineum* 'Album', which together create the rich but muted colour effect of an old carpet. A swimming pool garden with a Mediterranean atmosphere leads off the main walled enclosure.

Englefield House ★ [Historic Garden Grade II]

Englefield, Theale, Reading RG7 5EN. Tel: (0118) 930 2221

Sir William and Lady Benyon • 5m W of Reading. Entrance on A340, near Theale • Open all year, Mon; plus April to Nov, Tues – Thurs; all 10am – 6pm • Entrance: £3, children free ◑ 🍽 ♿ 🌳 ☕

There has been a garden here since the seventeenth century, and today its seven acres have achieved a rare and successful balance between the formal and informal. Stone-balustraded terracing close to the house provides an appropriately grand setting for the historic building and a place to view the surrounding deer park descending to the lake. On the terraces box-edged and less formal borders set against stone walls are planted with climbers, shrubs, perennials and annuals giving interest and colour through the seasons. An informal touch is added by swathes of meadow grass, where cowslips, tulips, anemones and camassias have established themselves under trees within an area of formal lawn. The ground rises steeply behind the terraces into tree-covered slopes underplanted with thickets of colourful shrubs – the glory of this garden. A stream edged with candelabra primulas, ferns and bog plants winds below a slope covered with azaleas and maples; a flint- and rock-faced grotto, its interior lined with a mosaic of fir cones, stands at the top of the stream.

There are well-placed seats in pleasant intimate corners, and a place has been found for the carved wooden bear rising among bluebells and a most imaginative children's garden.

Folly Farm [Historic Garden Grade II*]

Sulhamstead, Reading RG7 4DF. Tel: (Contact: Janet Findon) (01635) 841541

7m SW of Reading, 2m W of M4 junction 12. Turn onto A4 and left at road signed to Sulhamstead at Spring Inn 1m after Theale roundabout; entrance 0.75m on right • Open all year for parties of 10 – 25 by appt • Entrance £6, incl. coffee and biscuits ● ● WC

The gardens surrounding the timber-framed farmhouse, with its distinctive extensions added in 1906 and 1912, remain in essence an outstanding example of the Lutyens-Jekyll partnership. House and garden were designed to blend together in a series of walled courts connected by brick-arched doorways and herringbone brick paths. The tank cloister and canal (now planted with pastel-coloured water lilies) and the octagonal pool in the rose garden show Lutyens' skill with water. Although the planting of the gardens is no longer maintained according to Jekyll's plans, nothing has been done to obscure or detract from the quality of Lutyens' garden architecture. Contemporary plantings of grasses have supplanted the iris border, and a mixture of disease-resistant modern roses has replaced the original scheme in the dramatic circular sunken rose garden, with its intriguing changes of level and tall yew hedges. Organic vegetables are now grown in the once-neglected kitchen garden and the original greenhouses provide a home for a remarkable collection of tropical rainforest plants.

Frogmore Gardens [Historic Garden Grade I]

Windsor SL4 2JG.

H.M. The Queen • At Windsor Castle. Entrance via signed car park on B3021 between Datchet and Old Windsor. Pedestrian access only from Long Walk • House open as garden in Aug • Garden usually open several days in late May and Aug – telephone (020) 7766 7305 for information • Entrance: house, gardens and mausoleum £5.50, OAPs £4.50, children £3.50 (2005 prices) ●

The 35 acres of landscaped gardens are set within the home park of Windsor Castle. The estate has been under royal ownership and Crown tenancy since the sixteenth century, and in 1792 it was purchased for Queen Charlotte, who lavished large sums of money on the gardens, introducing rare plants and developing the landscape in Picturesque style. From the nineteenth century come James Wyatt's delightful wisteria-festooned Gothick ruin overlooking the lake, the Duchess of Kent's mausoleum, and other commemorative and architectural features, including Queen Victoria's tea house, an exquisite white marble Indian kiosk, and the royal couple's imposing mausoleum. The feeling of harmony and tranquillity which prompted them to choose this site for their final resting place still prevails – the lake and meandering canal, and the fine mature trees casting their shadows over immaculate swathes of lawn contribute to the sense of Victorian peace and plenty.

The Living Rainforest

Hampstead Norreys, Nr Newbury RG18 0TN. Tel: (01635) 202444

The Living Rainforest • 7m NE of Newbury. Follow signs from M4 junction 13 • Open all year, daily except 25th and 26th Dec, 10am – 5.15pm (last admission 4.30pm) • Entrance: £5.30, concessions £4.60, children (5 – 14) £3.50, children (3 – 4) £1.95 (2005 prices) ○ 🍴 🏪 <u>WC</u> ♿ ⌖ 🏛 ⚲ ⚲

A remarkable 1860-square-metre glasshouse with a fine collection of exotic plants, splendidly grown, which educates visitors in the beauty and diversity of the rainforest. The plants are displayed in an imaginative way, with paths at various levels allowing them to be enjoyed from above. There are two distinct environments – an area known as Lowland which mimics conditions of lowland rainforest, and one called Amazonica which emphasises life in the forest canopy. In each is a representative collection of the animals to be found there, chosen to illustrate the symbiotic relationship between animals and plants in their natural environment.

Mariners ★

Mariners Lane, Bradfield RG7 6HU. Tel: (0118) 974 5226

Anthony and Fenja Anderson • 10m W of Reading. From M4 junction 12 take A4 W for 1m; at roundabout take A340 signed to Pangbourne, then turn left after 400 yds signed to Bradfield. After 1m turn left signed to Southend Bradfield; after 1m opposite signpost to Tutts Clump turn right into Mariners Lane; house is on left at bottom of hill • Open 18th June, 2 – 6pm, for charity, and by appt 19th – 28th June • Entrance: £3, children under 16 free • Other information: Plants for sale on charity day only. Wheelchair access limited due to slopes. No dogs please ● ♿ ⌖

The present owners have consulted the genius of their sloping 1.5-acre site with intelligence and imagination. This is especially true of the bank above the broad terrace, where two borders have been contoured so that the colour and texture of imaginatively chosen flowers and foliage may be enjoyed at close quarters; one is planted in a predominantly wine and red colour theme, the other in soft blues, creams and yellows. The main herbaceous border and the bank border opposite, which incorporates a bog garden, is the backbone of the garden. Lawns planted with unusual trees link the various areas and lead the eye upwards to the highest level, where there is an orchard, a sundial garden, a border of grasses and a hexagonal arbour supporting vines and clematis. Beyond is a one-acre wildflower meadow with a charming 'borrowed' tower terminating the view. The most atmospheric part of the garden is the sunken rose garden, a fabulous sight in June and gloriously scented by many old varieties of shrub roses underplanted with herbaceous perennials; an arbour and moon gate are festooned with clematis and rambling roses. From there a path leads down under trees to a streamside walk.

Meadow House

Ashford Hill, Thatcham RG19 8BN. Tel: (0118) 981 6005

Antony and Harriet Jones • 8m SE of Newbury. From B3051 take turning at SW end of village to Wolverton Common. After 350 metres turn right down track to house

• Open by appt; parties of up to 40 welcome • Entrance: £3, children free • Other information: Park cars in meadow and coaches at top of lane. Plants for sale in nursery ● ⬥ ℘

The house is secluded among fields and the two-acre garden blends harmoniously with the surrounding countryside. From the entrance a five-bar gate opens into a drive fringed with *Alchemilla mollis* which curves its way along a border of towering old shrub roses and a small lake sheltered on one side by shrubs and trees and edged with candelabra primulas. The house sits prettily among lawns, herbaceous borders and a stone terrace with a generous scattering of attractively planted pots. The steep bank to one side, planted with sun-lovers, has a Mediterranean feel, while the surrounding borders are a delightful blend of shrubs, roses and perennials in a subtle and delicately balanced range of colours – Mrs Jones is a fastidious and di cerning plantswoman, and it is her planting schemes that give this garden its distinction. The small nursery, enclosed by a trellis covered with wisteria, clematis, roses and honeysuckle, sells plants propagated by Mr Jones, many of which can be seen in the garden.

The Old Rectory

Burghfield, Reading RG30 3TH.
Tel: 07791 0692170 or (0118) 983 3141 (Neil Collins)

Mr A.R. Merton • 5m SW of Reading. Turn S off A4 to Burghfield village and right after Hatch Gate Inn • Open 6th Aug, 2 – 5pm, and by appt all year • Entrance: £3, children free • Other information: Rare plant sale in June (telephone for details) ● ⬛ WC ⬥ ℘ ⬤

The planting of this now gracefully mature garden was conceived in 1950 by an exceptional plantswoman, the late Esther Merton, and its structure, including the fine yew hedges, was planned by her husband Ralph. An atmosphere of harmony is created by a simple, uncluttered layout with a generous sweep of lawn dominated by a cedar of Lebanon and an elegant gazebo. Yew hedges screen the swimming pool garden with its pretty pavilion. Climbers festoon mellow brick walls. The planting remains much as it was in Mrs Merton's day: a choice and subtly coloured palette of old roses, irises, tender shrubs, hellebores and spring bulbs. One of the most understated but ingeniously planted areas is the shade garden close to the house where the planting scheme is sustained by a variety of greens. The pots on the terrace – her particular speciality – are crammed still with an exotic mixture of plants. The double herbaceous borders flanking a grass path between yew hedges produce their best show in late summer and early autumn. The view from the house through these borders to the large pool which terminates the vista is dominated by the impressive classical stone figure which looms out of the water.

The Old Rectory, Farnborough

(see Oxfordshire)

Potash

Mariners Lane, Southend Bradfield, Reading RG7 6HU. Tel: (0118) 974 4264

Mr and Mrs J.W.C. Mooney • 10m W of Reading. From M4 junction 12 take A4 W for 1m. At roundabout take A340 signed to Pangbourne, then turn left signed to

Bradfield. After 1m turn left signed to Southend Bradfield; 1m further, opposite
Southend Bradfield sign turn right, and garden is 370 metres on left by beech hedge
• Open all year by appt to parties and individuals • Entrance: £3, children free
● wc ⅏ ⏏

The garden is continually being enriched with fresh plants and new areas of interest, such as the Mediterranean planting on the banks above the recessed tennis
court. Mr Mooney was a forester by profession, and so the character of the place is
dominated by mature and handsome trees, many of them unusual. The site sweeps
down from lawns and shrubberies to a winding stream crossed by a wooden
Japanese bridge. A large pond has a richly planted bog area, and the rising ground
beyond is edged with a dense cordon of specimen shrubs blending into carefully
planned young woodland. At the start of the year a spectacular show of snowdrops
fringes the banks of the pool and stream, followed by crocuses and daffodils in their
thousands. Early-flowering shrubs and trees provide points of interest throughout
the garden, with roses and a herbaceous border for summer colour and autumn
leaves to complete the cycle.

Scotlands ★

Cockpole Green, Wargrave, Reading RG10 8QP. Tel: (01628) 822648

The Payne family • 4m E of Henley-on-Thames, off A4 at Knowl Hill, halfway
between Warren Row and Cockpole Green • Open for various charities, and by appt
• Entrance: £3, children free • Other information: Picnics permitted on Cockpole
Green ● 🍴 ⅏

The five-acre garden, created since 1980, uses slopes and undulations of its landscape to great effect. In the dip of a valley a large lake scooped out of a wet and
boggy area now reflects the surrounding trees and waterside plants, with a Repton-
style summer house overlooking the quiet scene. Water is also a feature of the
meticulously tended woodland garden beyond the summer house and lake. Here are
rivulets, channels, still pools and a waterfall, all surrounded by specimen trees, well-
chosen shrubs and a rich variety of waterside plants. The ground rises steeply from
the lake to the small formal gardens clustering round the chalk-and-flint house. The
original low-walled kitchen garden, which now has a handsome architectural brick
tool shed in one corner, is planted with roses mixed with cottage-garden plants,
herbs and cardoons. Its criss-crossing pathways are punctuated by clipped box and
pots. Herbaceous borders edge the path leading to the oval swimming pool
enclosed by yew hedging west of the house, and on to a spacious shady area of trees
and grass overlooked by an arbour surrounded by shrub roses.

Waltham Place ★

White Waltham, Maidenhead SL6 3JH. Tel: (01628) 825517

Mr and Mrs N.F. Oppenheimer • 3.5m S of Maidenhead. From M4 junction 8/9
take A404M and follow signs to White Waltham. Turn left to Windsor and Paley
Street. Parking signposted at top of hill • Open May to Sept, Wed, 10am – 4pm, and
Fri by appt for guided tours only • Entrance: £3.50, children £1 (2005 prices) • Other
information: Organic meals available for groups by prior arrangement ● 🍽 wc ⅏
⏏ 🌿 ♿

The ornamental gardens lie within a walled enclosure of mellow brick, the oldest dating from the seventeenth century; substantial brick-pillared pergolas support an abundance of roses and climbers and provide shady walks. In striking contrast to this traditional formality are the naturalistic plantings created by the Dutch designer Henk Gerritsen. He has filled one small enclosed garden mainly with plants to attract butterflies, another with herbs and native species. The Square Garden combines lawns and generous sweeps of gravel, dotted with a variety of grasses, in a freely drawn design separated by newly scalped box hedges. A large area of rich herbaceous planting holds some surprises, such as that familiar invader, ground elder, introduced deliberately for its striking leaves and subtle flowers. Beyond the *potager*, knot garden and Japanese garden are long, densely packed herbaceous borders, where newly planted beech alcoves shelter tall weedbeds including our native bindweed. The original formal yew hedges have been transformed into billowing shapes, as if by a creative giant with hedge cutters. Within these 40 acres are other gardens, and a lake, and a maze cut through long grass — all part of the 170-acre estate, which also includes an organic farm.

White Knights

The Ridges, Finchampstead, Wokingham RG40 3SY. Tel: (0118) 973 3274

Mrs Heather Bradly • 9m SE of Reading between A327 and A321, midway along Finchampstead Ridges on B3348. Turn in through white gateposts on right between Crowthorne station and war memorial • Open 7th May, 13th Aug, and by appt • Entrance: £3 • Other information: Refreshments available. Guide dogs only ● 🖵 &
♨ ♿

This is more a series of gardens than one cohesively designed site, reflecting the owner's interest in producing her own interpretation of various styles of garden and then planting them appropriately. The area immediately behind the house is planted in Mediterranean style with sun-loving and drought-resistant plants which contrast with the adjacent green garden of low-growing and dwarf conifers. A winding path leads between borders, trees and rhododendrons to a tennis court edged with a variety of small gardens, including a grass garden, a cactus bank and a Japanese garden with its tea house and series of waterlily pools fringed by waterside plants. The vegetable garden bears witness to the owner's skill at growing plants. A path skirting one side of the house leads to a courtyard garden where all the artefacts and decoration have been chosen to enhance its Chinese character — a small pool even features a puffing dragon. Plenty of ideas here, although many may feel that the fairy grotto is a bridge too far.

HOW TO FIND THE GARDENS
Directions to each garden are included in the entry. This information has been supplied by the owners and garden inspectors. It is aimed to be the best available to those travelling by car, and has been compiled to be used in conjunction with a road atlas. Some gardens may be reached by train or bus, but the unreliability of these makes it unrewarding to include details, particularly as many garden visits are made on Sundays.

BIRMINGHAM AREA

Ashover

25 Burnett Road, Streetly B74 3EL. Tel: (0121) 353 0547

Mr and Mrs Martin Harvey • 8m N of Birmingham. Take A452 towards Streetly, then B4138 alongside Sutton Park. Turn left at shops into Burnett Road • Open for NGS 21st May and 6th Aug, 1.30 – 5.30pm, and by appt • Entrance: £2.50, children 50p • Other information: Teas and plants on NGS open days only ● ● WC

This is a garden for all who love colour – a third of an acre cleverly planted for year-round interest, from bulbs and azaleas in the spring through roses, clematis, lilies and herbaceous plants, both traditional and unusual, in summer and autumn, with a 'hot' border featuring large in July and August. Colour-themed beds and an attractive water feature catch the eye and close planting constantly challenges the interest of the discerning visitor. Surprises round every turn make the garden appear larger than it actually is, and a luxuriant atmosphere is generated by the sheer variety, quality and quantity of plants amassed here.

The Birmingham Botanical Gardens and Glasshouses ★ [Historic Garden Grade II*]

Westbourne Road, Edgbaston B15 3TR. Tel: (0121) 454 1860

2m SW of city centre. Approach from Hagley Road or Calthorpe Road, following tourist signs • Open all year, daily, 9am – 7pm, or dusk if earlier (opens 10am on Sun) • Entrance: £5.90 (£6.20 on summer Suns and Bank Holiday Mons), OAPs, disabled, students and children £3.50, family £16 (£17 on summer Suns and Bank Holiday Mons). Parties of 10 or more £4.80 per person, concessions £3 (2005 prices) • Other information: Manual and electric wheelchairs available free of charge ○ ● ✕ ● WC ₺ ℗ ⛪ ❢ ✆

This 15-acre ornamental garden will appeal both to the keen plantsperson and to the everyday gardener. In addition to the unusual plants in the tropical and Mediterranean houses, there is a sub-tropical house and an arid house, a small display of carnivorous plants, aviaries with parrots and macaws, peacocks and a waterfowl enclosure. Less rarefied gardeners will enjoy the beautiful old trees, the border devoted to E.H. Wilson plants, the raised alpine bed and the sunken rose garden beside the Lawn Aviary. The rock garden contains a wide variety of alpine plants, primulas, astilbes and azaleas. There are also herbaceous borders, a quaint cottage-style garden, a herb garden and model historic and organic gardens, plus a trials area and a sculpture trail, where many of the exhibits are for sale. An attractive courtyard houses a National Collection of bonsai, and a Japanese garden is intended to create a mood of harmony, reflection and relaxation. The alpine yard has examples of the many ways to grow plants in a variety of raised beds and containers. An imaginative children's discovery garden, a playground and adventure trail make this a pleasant place for a family outing. Bands play on summer Sundays and Bank Holidays, and there are events throughout the year to suit all ages.

Castle Bromwich Hall Gardens ★ [Historic Garden Grade II*]

Chester Road, Castle Bromwich B36 9BT. Tel: (0121) 749 4100

Castle Bromwich Hall Gardens Trust • 4m E of city centre, 1m from junction 5 of M6 northbound; southbound leave M6 at junction 6 and follow A38 and A452. Signposted • Open April to Sept, Wed – Fri, 1.30 – 4pm, Sat, Sun and Bank Holiday Mons, 1 – 5.30pm. Guided tours daily • Entrance: £3.50, OAPs £2.50, children £1.50 ❶ 💻 🏠 WC ♿ ⇎ ✿ ❦

The hall (not open), was built at the end of the sixteenth century and sold to Sir John Bridgeman in 1657. His wife, with expert help from John Evelyn, Captain William Winde, George London and Henry Wise, created a garden famous in its time. It fell into decay, but now has a series of formal connecting gardens – 10 acres in all contained within a west-facing slope – which have gradually been restored by a dedicated team of volunteers to give them the appearance and content of a garden of 1680–1740. They contain a large collection of rare period plants and a nineteenth-century holly maze. An elegant greenhouse and summerhouse stand at each end of a broad holly walk. In the formal parterre, re-created to a 1728 design and bordered by culinary and medicinal herbs, several heritage vegetables are grown, such as skirrets, scorzonera, orache, cardoons and salsify. Fruit trees have been planted in orchards and along paths.

City Centre Gardens

Cambridge Street B1 2NP.

Birmingham City Council • Off Cambridge Street, to rear of theatre and Symphony Hall on Broad Street • Open all year, daily, during daylight hours • Entrance: free ○ 🏠 ♿ ⇎

Half an acre of rough ground remaining after building demolition and subsequently used as a car park has been converted into a garden for all seasons. The layout is formal, the planting skilful and exuberant, with a great variety of bulbs, shrubs, perennials, roses and annuals, many of them less usual and all blending harmoniously. Climbers cover the walls and fences.

University Botanic Garden ★

Winterbourne, 58 Edgbaston Park Road, Edgbaston B15 2RT. Tel: (0121) 414 4944

University of Birmingham • 2m SW of city centre, off A38 Bristol road. On university campus • Open all year, Mon – Fri (but closed Bank Holiday Mons and some university holidays), 11am – 4pm • Entrance: £2 (2005 price) • Other information: Events at weekends ● 🏠 WC ♿

The six acres of garden belonging to a Grade-II-listed Arts and Crafts house owe much to the landscape style developed by Edwin Lutyens and Gertrude Jekyll. Its wide range of plants and different features make it of interest to the ordinary gardener as well as the botanist. Geographical beds show typical trees and shrubs from Europe, Australasia, the Americas, China and Japan. The pergola is swathed in clematis and roses and there are extensive herbaceous borders backed by brick walls covered with climbers. A miniature arboretum contains interesting specimens, including acers, conifers and a *Ginkgo biloba*, together with hedges of yew and copper beech. In the Commemorative Garden is a black mulberry planted to mark the centenary of Birmingham's status as a city. The range of plants continues with the sandstone rock garden, troughs, rhododendrons, heathers and alpines. Unusual features include a nut walk containing several varieties of *Corylus avellana* trained over an iron framework, and a crinkle-crankle wall. A special feature is the walled garden laid out with beds showing the history of the European rose. There are also water gardens, rock and scree gardens, a meadow, a bog garden and a Japanese tea house.

Wightwick Manor [Historic Garden Grade II]

Wightwick Bank, Wolverhampton WV6 8EE. Tel: (01902) 761400

The National Trust • 3m W of Wolverhampton off A454. Turn by Mermaid Inn up Wightwick Bank • House open Thurs and Sat, 12.30 – 5pm (last entry 4.30pm). Timed tickets • Garden open March to Dec, Wed, Thurs and Sat, plus Bank Holiday Suns and Mons, 11am – 6pm, and other weekdays by appt. Pre-booked parties accepted Wed and Thurs; family days in Aug • Entrance: £3.40, children free (house and garden £6.50) • Other information: Possible for wheelchairs but sloping site. Braille guide available ☕ 🍽 🎁 <u>WC</u> ♿ ⚓ 🌳 🏛 ♨

This 17-acre garden, designed by Alfred Parsons and Thomas Mawson for Theodore Mander, the paint and varnish manufacturer, surrounds an 1887 neo-Tudor house strongly influenced in its design by William Morris and his Movement. Large trees form a delightful framework, the main feature of which is the magnificent octagonal arbour in the centre of the rose garden, hung with climbing roses and clematis. Through an old orchard is a less formal area with pools surrounded by shrubs and rhododendrons. There are herbaceous borders, two rows of barrel-shaped yews and beds containing plants from gardens of famous men. The peach house and the rose garden have been restored, and the Mathematical Bridge, giving access to the Bridge Garden filled with spring bulbs, is now reconstructed.

FEEDBACK

Readers are invited to advise the *Guide* of any gardens which in their opinion should be listed in future editions, and where possible arrangements will be made to review such suggestions. Readers who would like to add information about gardens listed are warmly invited to write to the *Guide* with their comments, which may be used in future editions without attribution. Please send letters to the publishers, Frances Lincoln Ltd, 4 Torriano Mews, Torriano Avenue, London NW5 2RZ. All letters are acknowledged by the editors.

BRISTOL AREA

Algars Manor

Iron Acton, Bristol BS37 9TB. Tel: (01454) 228372

Dr and Mrs John Naish • 9m N of Bristol between M5 and A432. Turn S from Acton bypass (B4059) and pass village green; garden is 180 metres beyond level crossing • Open by appt (for NGS) • Entrance: £3 ◑ 🍴 **WC** ⅋

The seventeenth-century manor house stands on the edge of a rocky bank bordering the River Frome. The dendrologically minded visitor can learn a great deal about magnolias and camellias interplanted with a wide range of rare and specimen trees after an enlightening tour of the woodland garden with the owners, who like to share its fifty-year history under their devoted care. The natural surroundings of quarry, river and mill stream contribute to the garden's very special atmosphere.

Ashton Court Estate [Historic Park Grade II*]

Long Ashton BS41 9JN. Tel: (0117) 963 9174

Bristol City Council • SW of city off A369 • Open all year, daily, 8am – dusk • Entrance: free ◯ 🍴 🍴 **WC** ⅋ ⤴ 🏛 ♿

The Ashton estate is an astonishing survival to find on the edge of a major city. It has two deer parks, and its 850 acres include many ancient oaks. The house itself is fifteenth-century with a handsome seventeenth-century wing. The park was first landscaped in the 1600s; two hundred years later, with advice from Humphry Repton, it was redesigned. The year 2004 saw the start of major restoration with help from the Heritage Lottery Fund.

Blaise Castle House Museum ★ [Historic Garden Grade II*]

Henbury BS10 7QS. Tel: (0117) 903 9818 (Museum);
(0117) 950 3732 (Estate Office)

4m N of city, W of Henbury, N of B4057 • Museum open all year, Sat – Wed, 10am – 5pm • Entrance: free pedestrian access to green • Other information: Visitors requested not to picnic or invade privacy of cottage owners ◯ **WC** ⅋ ⤴ ♿ ♿

Blaise Hamlet is a picturesque village owned by The National Trust in the form of a green surrounded by nine cottages with private gardens, designed by John Nash with George and John Repton in 1809 for the pensioners of John Harford's estate. The village pump and sundial of 1812 remain. Jasmines, ivies and honeysuckles were planted around the cottages to reflect their picturesque names ('Jessamine', 'Rose Briar'), with ornamental shrubs added to the woodland setting. A spectacular drive can be taken from Henbury Hill to the entrance lodge of Blaise Castle House – another charming *cottage orné* is half-way. The driveway into the gorge and up to the house passes a Robber's Cave and Lovers' Leap. Near the house are the ornamental dairy and elegant orangery, both by Nash.

Bristol Zoo Gardens
Clifton BS8 3HA. Tel: (0117) 974 7399

Bristol Zoo Gardens • Signposted from M5 junctions 17 and 18 and from city centre
• Open all year, daily except 25th Dec, 9am – 5.30pm (closes 4.30pm in winter)
• Entrance: £9.70, concessions £8.50, children (3 – 14) £6.20, family £28.50.
Special rates for parties of 10 or more ○ 🅿 ✕ 🍴 <u>WC</u> ♿ 🏛 ♀ ⚲

Set up in 1835 as a garden as well as a zoo, the gardens will satisfy those with a Victorian taste in colour. Displays range from formal to informal, and botanically inter-esting plants are highlighted. The vibrantly colourful terrace bedding is complemented by herbaceous borders, a lake, rose and rock gardens, indoor displays and numerous interesting trees and shrubs. All is well contrived and maintained with evident love and care. Two National Collections, of hedychiums and caryopteris, are held here.

Emmaus House
Retreat and Conference Centre, Clifton Hill, Clifton BS8 4PD.
Tel: (0117) 907 9950

Sisters of La Retraite • From city centre take A4018 W to Clifton, then A4176 past Bristol Zoo, and turn left into Clifton Down Road. Follow through to Regent Street; house is at bottom of drive on right • Open by appt (for NGS) • Entrance: £2.50, children free ● 🅿 ✕ <u>WC</u> ♿ ⚘ ♀ B&B

Covering one and a half acres, the gardens lie hidden from the road behind two impos-ing eighteenth-century merchants' houses. Walking down from the front entrance and around the side of the property, the visitor enters a succession of separate gardens set on different levels, all carefully linked and with extensive views towards the har-bour and beyond. They have been considerably altered in recent years, but the Victorian kitchen garden is substantially intact, supplying fruit and vegetables to the house. The old greenhouse is still in use, containing apricots and a 150-year-old Black Hamburg vine. A formal herb garden framed by clipped box pyramids surrounds an ornamental fishpond. This leads down to a Zen Garden, where large stones and run-ning water are imaginatively used to represent the Zen concepts of life and rebirth. At a lower level, the visitor enters the Secret Garden containing many old apple trees and underplanted with spring bulbs. Then, continuing round the beech lawn, the courtyard garden is enclosed by high walls with macleayas, robinias and vigorous euphorbias; an old pump delivers the soothing noise of running water. A newly discovered eighteenth-century coach house in the woodland garden is an ideal place to sit and enjoy views of the gardens and to the countryside of South Bristol beyond.

Goldney Hall [Historic Garden Grade II*]
Lower Clifton Hill, Clifton BS8 1BH. Tel: (0117) 903 4873/4880

University of Bristol • In city centre at top of Constitution Hill, Clifton • Open 30th April, 2 – 6pm, and three other days for charity – telephone for details • Entrance: £3, concessions £1.50, children under 12 free, guided tours £2 ● 🅿 WC <u>WC</u> ♿ ♀

The eighteenth-century garden is a thrilling discovery in the middle of the city. Perched on a hillside, it is full of surprises, not least the small formal canal with an orangery at its head. From the largely nineteenth-century house the visitor is led through the shadows of an *allée* of yews to a dark grotto entrance, the facade of which is a striking example of early but sophisticated Gothick. The grotto itself is astonishingly elaborate: water really gushes through it and the walls are liberally encrusted with shells and minerals. Passing through the grotto and out by narrow labyrinthine passages, suddenly there is a terrace, a broad airy grass walk with magnificent views over the old docks. At the far end of the terrace is a Gothick gazebo, and towering above the other end a castellated tower. Although a new student hall has been allowed to encroach upon this historic setting, it is alleviated by Michael Balston's stylish planting and landscaping, which includes a circular pool and a brick amphitheatre as a crossing point for paths. Goldney also has follies, a parterre and a herb garden packed into its nine acres.

The Red Lodge

Park Row BS1 5LJ. Tel: (0117) 921 1360

Bristol City Council • In city centre • House open • Garden open April to Oct, Sat – Wed, 10am – 4.30pm • Entrance: free ◐

This is a good reconstruction of the early-seventeenth-century garden of a merchant's town house, with old varieties of roses, shrubs and other plants, trelliswork re-created from a seventeenth-century design, and a knot garden based on a plasterwork pattern in the house. A list of plant names is available for a small charge. The early-Georgian *Queen Square* in the city has also undergone major restoration with Lottery funding. Six miles south of Bristol on the A37 is *Blackmore and Langdon's Nursery*, open daily, a pleasure at any time, but particularly when the roses and delphiniums are blooming (Tel: (01275) 525455).

9 Sion Hill

Clifton, Bristol BS8 4BA. Tel: (0117) 973 2761

Mr and Mrs R.C. Begg • In city, 100 metres from Clifton Suspension Bridge • Open by appt • Entrance: £2 (2005 price) ◐ ✿

This is not a typical town garden – on the contrary, twenty-five years of profuse planting have produced an overall impression of peace and plenty on a scale which belies the garden's true size. Entering through a working conservatory, a small grassed area is dominated by a vigorous black mulberry tree (planted by the owners and for once not in King James's time) and surrounded by densely planted borders. This leads to a central path, the axis of which is established by the 'temple', an ivy-clad terracotta architectural finial from which paths radiate to various points. Looking back from the house, the garden is terminated by a seven-metre-high wall which acts as a backdrop. The timber pergola, unusual in spanning the entire width of the garden, is smothered in roses and clematis. The play of light and shade ensures a constantly changing effect. A town garden full of interesting ideas – the subtle placing of pots of various kinds is particularly successful.

University Botanic Garden

The Holmes, Stoke Park Road, Stoke Bishop, Bristol. Tel: (0117) 331 4912

University of Bristol • From city centre, take A4108 north to end of Whiteladies Rd, turn left at roundabout into Stoke Rd, then 2nd right into Stoke Park Rd. Garden is opposite Churchill Hall of Residence • Open from March 2006 – telephone for details, or consult www.bris.ac.uk/Depts/BotanicGardens • Entrance: charge ○ **WC**

The new four-acre botanic garden designed by Land Use Consultants (of Eden Project fame) is a happy marriage of education and contemporary design. The relaxed and fluid layout is focused on a lake surrounded by groups of local flora and threatened native plants. A sunken dell is connected by paths that meander through formal and informal plantings charting the seminal stages of the evolution of plants on our planet, from primitive liverworts and tree ferns through to a spectacular flowering of magnolias. The fine collection of Mediterranean plants built up at the botanic garden's former home has been relocated here, and the Chinese medicinal herb collection flourishes now in the shadow of a splendid mature ginkgo.

OPENING DATES AND TIMES
Times of access given are the best available at the moment of going to press, but some may have been changed subsequently. In the entries, the times given are inclusive — that is, an entry such as May to Sept means that the garden is open from 1st May to 30th Sept inclusive, and 2 — 5 pm means that entry will be effective during that period. Please note that many owners will open their gardens to visitors by appointment, and they will often arrange to give a personally conducted tour on these occasions. Unavoidably some owners cannot give their opening details before we go to press, and in such cases we attempt to give the best guidance we can. If in doubt, it is wise to telephone before making a long journey.

GUIDANCE ON SYMBOLS
Wheelchair users: the symbol ♿, denoting suitability for wheelchairs, refers to the garden only — if there is a house open, it may or may not be suitable. Additionally, some areas of the garden may not be accessible by wheelchair, or may require assistance.
Dogs: ⊕ indicates that there is somewhere on the premises where dogs may be walked, preferably on a lead. The garden itself is often taboo — parkland, or even the car park, are frequently indicated for the purpose.
Picnics: ⏛ means that picnics are allowed, but usually in certain restricted areas only. It does not give visitors the all-clear to feast where they please!
Children-friendly: the bat-and-ball symbol ⚇ suggests that there are activities specifically designed for children, such as an adventure playground or a discovery trail, or that the garden itself is likely to appeal to them.

BUCKINGHAMSHIRE

Two-starred gardens are marked on the map with a black square.

Ascott ★★ [Historic Garden Grade II*]

Wing, Leighton Buzzard, Bedfordshire LU7 0PS. Tel: (01296) 688242

The National Trust • 7m NE of Aylesbury, 0.5m E of Wing, S of A418 • House and gardens open March to Aug – telephone for details. Parties must pre-book • Entrance: £4, children £2 (house and garden £6.50, children £3.25) (2005 prices) • Other information: Parking 220 metres from house ❍ WC ᕫ

Thirty acres of Victorian gardening at its best, laid out with the aid of Veitch and overlaid with more recent designs and planting. It is notable for its collection of mature trees set in rolling lawns. Fascinating topiary includes an evergreen sundial with a yew gnomon and the inscription 'Light and shade by turn but love always' in golden yew. Wide lawns slope away to magnificent views across the Vale of Aylesbury, glimpsed between towering cedars. Formal gardens include the Madeira Walk with sheltered flower borders, and the bedded-out Dutch garden. The Long Walk leading to the lily pond has been imaginatively reconstructed by Arabella Lennox-Boyd as a serpentine walk with beech hedging, and a wild garden planted in Coronation Grove. Two stately fountains were sculpted by Thomas Waldo Story in the nineteenth century. Spring gardens feature massed carpets of bulbs.

Blossoms

Cobblers Hill, Great Missenden HP16 9PW. Tel: (01494) 863140

Dr and Mrs Frank Hytten • 8m NE of High Wycombe. From Great Missenden follow Rignall Road towards Butlers Cross. After 1m turn right into Kings Lane and up to top of Cobblers Hill. At T-junction turn right at yellow stone marker in hedgerow, and after 50 metres right again • Open by appt (for NGS) • Entrance: £2 ● ● WC ᕫ ᕫ

The five-acre garden has a good variety of trees: an acre of beech woodland under-planted with bluebells and other spring-flowering bulbs, an old apple orchard, collections of eucalyptus, acers and salix, plus other fine specimen trees. Interesting features include rock and cutting gardens, a small lake with an island, and sculpture by the owner and friends; two water gardens and a paved well garden with sundial are linked by woodland paths.

Chenies Manor House ★

Chenies, Rickmansworth, Hertfordshire WD3 6ER. Tel: (01494) 762888

Mrs MacLeod Matthews • 3m E of Amersham off A404. If approaching via M25, exit at junction 18 • House open (extra charge) • Garden open April to Oct, Wed, Thurs and Bank Holiday Mons, 2 – 5pm • Entrance: £3.50, children £1.50 ❍ ● ● WC ᕫ ᕫ ᕫ ᕫ ᕫ

The fine linked gardens, highly decorative and maintained to the highest standards, are in perfect keeping with the fifteenth- and sixteenth-century brick manor house. Planted for a long season of colour and using many old-fashioned roses and cottage plants, there is always something to enjoy here: formal topiary in the white garden, collections of medicinal and poisonous plants in a physic garden, a parterre, an historic turf maze, an intricate yew maze over two metres high, and a highly productive kitchen garden. On her visits here, Queen Elizabeth I had a favourite tree and the 'Royal Oak' survives.

Cliveden ★★ [Historic Garden Grade I]

Taplow, Maidenhead, Berkshire SL6 0JA. Tel: (01628) 605069

The National Trust • 6m NW of Slough, 2m N of Taplow off A4094 • House open April to Oct, Thurs and Sun, 3 – 6pm • Woodlands open all year, daily except 22nd Dec to 2nd Jan, 11am – 6pm (closes 4pm Nov to 16th March). Estate and gardens open 15th March to Oct, daily, 11am – 6pm; Nov to 22nd Dec, daily, 11am – 4pm. Closed Jan and Feb • Entrance: £7, family £17.50 (house £1 extra, entry by timed ticket) • Other information: Refreshments in Conservatory Restaurant, 16th March to Oct, daily. Dogs allowed in specified woodlands only ○ ● ✕ ● WC & ⬦ ⬧ ♀ ♀

The setting of the house is one of the most beautiful in Britain. The flamboyant Duke of Buckingham found it and William Winde exploited it, taking the raw material – 'a cliffy ground as hanging over the *Tamise* and sum Busshis groinge on it' and creating, by excavation and earth-moving, a platform for the house and a terrace for access. John Evelyn's verdict was that 'the house stands somewhat like *Frascati* on the platform . . . a circular view of the uttmost verge of the Horison, which with the serpenting of the *Thames* is admirably surprising . . . The *Cloisters*, Descents, Gardens, & avenue through the wood august and stately.' The present house (now an hotel), designed by Sir Charles Barry, incorporates a terrace with a balustrade brought by the 1st Viscount Astor from the Villa Borghese in Rome in the 1890s. There is an attractive water garden, a secret garden and herbaceous borders, formal gardens below the house, the Long Garden, and fountains, temples and statuary galore. Among famous designers who have worked on the grounds are Bridgeman (walks and amphitheatre), Leoni (Octagon Temple) and John Fleming (parterre). From the ilex grove a shaded path leads through a gate to the Secret Garden, planted originally by the 3rd Lord Astor in the 1950s to the designs of Geoffrey Jellicoe. Once a rose garden, it has been planted anew by Isabelle Van Groeningen with a mixture of perennials and grasses to give year-round interest.

Gracefield

Main Road, Lacey Green, Princes Risborough HP27 0QU. Tel: (01844) 345560

Mr and Mrs B.C. Wicks • 5m N of High Wycombe off A4010. In Bradenham turn right by Red Lion towards Walters Ash, then left at T-junction to Lacey Green. House is beyond church facing Kiln Lane • Open May to Aug for parties by written appt • Entrance: £2.50, children free • Other information: Park at village hall ● &

A steeply terraced water garden is a fine feature in this varied one-and-a-half-acre garden, which includes plants for the flower arranger, new designs for paved terraces and trough gardens, and collections of clematis and shrub roses. Among the specimen trees *Malus* 'Marshal Oyama' gives fantastic crab apple jelly. The owners are self-confessed plantaholics and have thoughtfully labelled many specimens in their unusual collection.

Hughenden Manor [Historic Garden Grade II]

High Wycombe HP14 4LA. Tel: (01494) 755573

The National Trust • 1.5m N of High Wycombe on A4128 • House open as garden, but 1 – 5pm • Park and woodland open all year. Garden open March to Oct, Wed – Sun and Bank Holiday Mons; all 11am – 5pm. Parties not admitted on Sat, Sun or Bank Holiday Mons, and must pre-book at other times • Entrance: £1.90, children 95p (house and garden £5, children £2.50, family £12.50. Party rates on application) (2005 prices) ◑ ● ✕ 🐛 WC ➻ ⬥ 🌿 ⛪ 🍴 ⚲

A High-Victorian garden created by Mrs Disraeli in the 1860s and recently restored; particularly pleasing is the human scale of house and gardens. The five acres include lawns, a terraced garden with a Mediterranean planting scheme, formal brightly coloured annual bedding on the lower level (Mrs Disraeli's guests commented at the time on the blinding colour schemes she chose), woodland walks, and an orchard with old varieties of apples and pears. Additional Victorian flower beds are usually at their best in July. The three walled gardens are undergoing full restoration over the next few years, and Black Hamburgh grapes are growing again inside the refurbished vine house.

The Manor House ★★

Bledlow, Princes Risborough HP27 9PB.

Lord and Lady Carrington • 8m NW of High Wycombe, 0.5m E of B4009 in middle of Bledlow • Manor House Garden open 7th May, 18th June, 2 – 6pm, and May to Sept for groups by written appt. Lyde Garden open all year, daily • Entrance: Manor House Garden £4.50, children free. Lyde Garden free • Manor House Garden: ● ● WC ➻ 🌿 *Lyde Garden:* ○ WC ➻

With the help of landscape architect Robert Adams, Lord and Lady Carrington have created an elegant English garden of an exceptionally high standard. The productive and colourful walled vegetable garden has York-stone paths and a central gazebo. Formal areas are enclosed by tall yew and beech hedges; in the centre of one is a water feature by William Pye. Mixed flower and shrub borders feature many roses and herbaceous plants around immaculately manicured lawns. Another garden approached through a yew and brick parterre was planned around existing mature trees on a contoured and upward-sloping site with open views. It is now thoroughly established, with its trees and lawns fulfilling the original landscaping design, and incorporates several modern sculptures including a second water feature by William Pye and two works by Peter Randall Page. The *Lyde Garden*, across the lane, is a magnificent wild water garden of great beauty and tranquillity. A note of caution: children need watching here.

Nether Winchendon House

Nether Winchendon, Aylesbury HP18 0DY. Tel: (01844) 290101

Mr and Mrs R. Spencer Bernard • 7m SW of Aylesbury, 5m NE of Thame. Near church in Nether Winchendon • Open 2 days for NGS, and at other times by appt • Entrance: £2, children under 15 free (2005 prices) ☕ 🍴 WC ⚙ ☙

The gardens surround a romantic brick and stone Tudor manor which is approached by an unusual line of dawn redwoods planted in 1973, continuing a centuries-old tree planting tradition by the Spencer Bernard family. Small orchards on either side of the house combine with fine specimen trees, including mature acers, catalpas, cedars, paulownias, liquidambars and, dominating the lawns at the back of the house, an eighteenth-century variegated sycamore and a late-1950s' oriental plane of almost equal height. There are also well-kept lawns, shrub and flower borders, and walled gardens, including a productive kitchen garden.

Stowe Landscape Gardens ★★ [Historic Garden Grade I]

Buckingham MK18 5EH. Tel: (01280) 822850

The National Trust • 3m NW of Buckingham via Stowe Avenue off A422 Buckingham – Brackley road • House (Stowe School) may be open in holidays, telephone (01280) 818166 to check before visiting • Garden open 2nd March – 30th Oct, Wed – Sun 10am – 5.30pm (last admission 4pm); 5th Nov to 26th Feb, Sat and Sun, 10am – 4pm (last admission 3pm). Closed 24th and 25th Dec • Entrance: £5.80, children £2.90, family £14.50, discount for parties of 15 or more. All parties must pre-book • Other information: Refreshments for parties must be pre-booked through Group Bookings Co-ordinator. Self-drive powered 2-seater batricars available, must be pre-booked (telephone (01280) 818825) ☕ 🍴 ✕ 🛍 WC ♿ 🏛 🌿 ⚘

This is garden restoration on an heroic scale. Stowe has had enormous influence on garden design from the mid-seventeenth century onwards under a succession of distinguished designers, including the owner, Viscount Cobham: Vanbrugh, Bridgeman, Kent, 'Capability' Brown, and then the new owner Lord Temple, who thinned out Brown's plantings after 1750. What remains today is a *locus classicus* of eighteenth-century landscaping, with a nineteenth-century overlay diversifying the landscape into distinct 'scenes', each with its own character. The aim over the last twenty years has been to reinstate them. The concept of the restoration was brilliantly planned, using the Trust's considerable management and computer resources to reinstate lost plantings and remove recent irrelevant additions. There are two ways of visiting. One is just to wander through the gardens enjoying the wonderful views, the water, the splendid trees and autumn colour and the historic buildings – Stowe has more than twice as many listed garden buildings as any in England – and its statuary. The other approach is to step back in time and try to understand what was meant by the political and philosophical programme that fashioned the landscape movement. In the past decade land has been bought back – 320 acres including the home farm and deer park, which included the Wolfe obelisk, the Gothic umbrello and a superb set of 1790s' farm buildings. The Chinese house has been returned from Ireland as a memorial to Gervase Jackson-Stops, six of the seven Saxon deities have reappeared, and the Corinthian Arch has been restored. What is staggering is that the Trust has to date restored 70 per cent of the listed buildings at Stowe and Cobham is back on his column. Heroic indeed.

Turn End ★

Townside, Haddenham, Aylesbury HP17 8BG. Tel: (01844) 291383/291817

Mr and Mrs P. Aldington • 7m SW of Aylesbury. From A418 turn to Haddenham. From Thame Road turn at Rising Sun pub into Townside; garden is 250 metres on left • Open by appt for parties of 10 or more • Entrance: charge • Other information: No parking at garden ● WC & ⌂

Peter Aldington's RIBA-award-winning development of three linked houses (now listed) is surrounded by a series of garden rooms which have evolved since the 1960s. A sequence of spaces, each of individual character, provides focal points at every turn. There is a fishpond courtyard, a shady court, a formal box court, an alpine garden, hot and dry raised beds and climbing roses, all contrasting with lawns, borders and glades. A wide range of plants is displayed to good effect against a framework of mature trees, and spring and early summer are the best seasons to visit.

Waddesdon Manor ★★ [Historic Garden Grade I]

Waddesdon, Aylesbury HP18 0JH. Tel: (01296) 653211; advance house bookings with charge, garden tours and events (01296) 653226

The National Trust • 6m NW of Aylesbury, 11m SE of Bicester on A41. Entrance in Waddesdon village • House (inc. wine cellars) open 29th March to 29th Oct, 15th Nov to 23rd Dec, Wed – Sun and Bank Holiday Mons, plus 18th and 19th Dec; all 11am – 4pm (opens 12 noon Wed to Fri, Nov to Dec; timed-ticket system in operation; recommended last admission 2.30pm) • Grounds (inc. gardens, aviary, restaurant and shops) open 7th Jan to 26th March, Sat and Sun; 10am – 5pm; then 29th March to 23rd Dec, Wed – Sun and Bank Holiday Mons, plus 18th and 19th Dec; all 10am – 5pm • Entrance: £5, children £2.50 (house and grounds £12, children £8.50) • Other information: Parking for disabled. Guide dogs only. Many special events – brochure on request ◐ ☕ ✕ 🍽 WC & ♨ 🏛 ♟ ♿ B&B

Baron Ferdinand de Rothschild's grandiloquent château (built 1874–89) is set in 165 acres of appropriately grand grounds with fountains, vistas, terraces and walks laid out by Elie Lainé, his landscape designer with an extensive collection of Italian, French and Dutch statuary. The extensive parterre and fountains to the south require over 100,000 plants in the main summer display alone; the theme changes every year. According to a Victorian head gardener here, one yardstick of wealth was by the size of their bedding-out plant list: 10,000 for a squire, 20,000 for a baronet, 30,000 for an earl and 50,000 for a duke. Waddesdon is truly regal. Parterres used to require a large staff but Lord Rothschild has called on experts who use their computer skills to assemble the design. To the west of the parterre, an ornate, semi-circular aviary of eighteenth-century French Rococo style, erected in 1889, provides a distinguished home for many exotic birds. It also acts as an *exedra*, focusing on the pleasure grounds and the expansive views of the landscape beyond. The area in front of it has been restored to its original bedding-plant scheme. The gardens undergo changes almost annually, with old features being restored and new ones added. Wildflower Valley has daffodils in spring, and in summer wild flowers, including cowslips, ox-eye daisies and a range of orchids, which are encouraged to seed. Close by, over 20,000 camassias, colchicums, lilies-of-the valley and wild garlic have been naturalised in grassland and in the woodland garden.

West Wycombe Park ★★ [Historic Garden Grade I]

West Wycombe HP14 3AJ. Tel: (01494) 513569

The National Trust • 2m W of High Wycombe, at W end of West Wycombe, S of A40 Oxford road • House open as garden but June to Aug (weekday entry by guided tour) • Grounds open 2nd April to Aug, Sun – Thurs, 2 – 6pm (last admission 5.15pm) • Entrance: £3, children £1.50 (house and grounds £5.70, children £2.80, family £14.50) ◗ wc ⴵ

The park was largely created by the second Sir Francis Dashwood and was influenced by his experiences on the Grand Tour, which included visits to Asia Minor and Russia. The first phase involved the creation of the lake with meandering walks, completed by 1739. Numerous classical temples and statues were added subsequently, as well as the delightful little flint and wooden bridges which span the streams. Later still, in the 1770s, the park was enlarged; Nicholas Revett was employed to design yet more temples and follies, including a particularly fine music temple on one of the three islands. Thomas Cook, a pupil of 'Capability' Brown, was entrusted with the planting of trees and alterations to the landscape. There are splendid vistas, especially towards the lake which is in the shape of a swan.

Wotton House [Historic Garden Grade II*]

Wotton Underwood, Aylesbury HP18 0SB.

Mrs April Gladstone • 8m W of Aylesbury off A41 • Open 12th April to 13th Sept, Wed, 2 – 5pm, and for parties of no more than 25 by appt in writing • Entrance: £5, concessions £3, children free ◖ ⴵ ⬳

This remarkable landscape garden (250 acres) with over a dozen follies and other attractions shares a history with Stowe (see entry). Derelict after World War II, it has been painstakingly restored. Much, however, remains to be done. George London's early-eighteenth-century design is still evident, with the remains of his two double avenues east and west of the house. The third avenue, to the south-west, was the work of 'Capability' Brown. South of the house is London's walled garden with a terrace, an orangery below it, a double staircase with a shell niche between its wings, and a pavilion, formerly the coach house. The unchanged wider view remains splendid, and was shaped by Brown between 1750 and 1767. His main work was to remodel the contours and create a large lake, connecting it to a smaller, existing lake by a serpentine canal. Note the bridges and the two Tuscan pavilions overlooking the water. The island grotto, the strikingly handsome Turkey Building and the rotunda are contemporary, but not Brown's handiwork.

CAMBRIDGESHIRE

Two-starred gardens are marked on the map with a black square.
A few gardens with Peterborough postcodes are to be found in the Northamptonshire section.

Abbots Ripton Hall ★ [Historic Garden Grade II]

Abbots Ripton, Huntingdon PE28 2PQ. Tel: (01487) 773555

Lord and Lady De Ramsey • 2m N of Huntingdon, approached from B1090 • Open 21st May, 28th June, 9th July and 23rd July, 6th Aug for charities, 2 – 5pm, and for individuals and parties by appt • Entrance: £3 on charity days; £8 (including plant guide) for parties of 12 or more ◐ 🍵 <u>WC</u> & ✿

A superb garden in which many of the great twentieth-century gardeners have had a hand. In the 1950s Humphrey Waterfield designed the Rose Circle – a ring of historic roses with a circular lawn at its centre – and planted the Grey Border with alpines and sun-loving perennials. His dedicated work ended abruptly in 1971 when he was killed in England, absentmindedly driving on the right-hand side on his return from France. At the foot of a memorial urn is the inscription: 'Remember Humphrey Waterfield who made this garden anew'. Between 1960 and 1970 Lanning Roper also advised on planting and design. The follies – the work of Peter Foster, Surveyor of the Fabric at Westminster Abbey – range from two large Gothic screens in the spectacular herbaceous borders stretching from the eighteenth-century house, which are backed by columns of yew and philadelphus, to the Chinese pagoda at the end of the lake. Jim Russell advised on trees and added a plantation along the earth bank to protect the garden from the noise of traffic, and Peter Coates and Tony Venison also worked here. The present Lady De Ramsey is a keen gardener, and with Peter Beales has replanted the Rose Circle and many of the borders. With her husband she has started a collection of rare oaks from acorns collected all over the world.

Anglesey Abbey Gardens and Lode Mill ★★ [Historic Garden Grade II*]

Lode, Cambridge CB5 9EJ. Tel: (01223) 810080

The National Trust • 6m NE of Cambridge off A14, on B1102 • House open 22nd March to 29th Oct, Wed – Sun and Bank Holiday Mons, 1 – 5pm • Garden open 22nd March to 29th Oct, Wed – Sun and Bank Holiday Mons, and 3rd July to 3rd Sept, daily, 10.30am – 5.30pm (last admission 4.30pm). Winter garden open 2nd Nov to 20th March, Wed – Sun, 10.30am – 4pm. Closed 23rd to 29th Dec • Entrance: £4.50, winter £4 (house, garden and Lode Mill: £8). Charge made for tours with Head Gardener • Other information: Five single and one double electric buggies available. Lode Mill machinery working first and third Sat of month ◐ 🍵 ✗ <u>WC</u> & ✿ 🏛 🍴 ♿

The Abbey's setting is one of England's finest twentieth-century gardens for high maintenance, superb plantsmanship and statuary of exceptional quality. It was the visionary creation of one man, the 1st Lord Fairhaven, started in the 1930s. Avenues of mature trees lead to intimate gardens enclosed by meticulous hedges; smooth lawns give way to meadows awash with wild flowers; visitors will unexpectedly come upon dramatic vistas lined by superb trees, or glimpse the peaceful Bottisham Lode and Lode Mill. A semi-circular garden with a deep encircling herbaceous border is a highlight for the summer; the bold, imaginative planting of perennials is splendid, plumes of seakale and spires of delphinium mingling with mysterious sages. The rose garden (previously kept for Lord Fairhaven's private use) is now open on specific weekends throughout the summer season. In another garden, 4500 hyacinths bloom in spring while dark-foliaged dwarf dahlias take their place in late summer. Narcissus gazes at his reflection surrounded by scented white- and yellow-blossomed shrubs. A curved border of randomly planted late-summer dahlias may not be to everyone's taste, but what garden is ever entirely perfect? This place is almost so. It is vast, too – 100 acres. The mile-long Winter Walk, underplanted with thousands of early small bulbs, features a serpentine walk and woodland path which has areas for hedgehogs to overwinter (hedgehog hotels!). A grove of giant redwoods marks the start of the walk, a forest of white-stemmed birches underplanted with the black-stemmed *Cornus alba* 'Kesselringii' its conclusion.

Cambridge College Gardens

Most colleges are helpful about access to their gardens, although the Master's or Fellows' Gardens are often strictly private or rarely open. Specific viewing times are difficult to rely on because some colleges prefer not to have visitors in term time or on days when a function is taking place. The best course is to ask at the porter's lodge or to telephone in advance. However, some college gardens will always be open to the visitor, by arrangement with porters. Several now charge for entry.

Amongst college gardens of particular interest are the following: *Christ's* (see entry). *Clare* (see entry). *Downing College*: Spacious neo-classical domus (founded 1800), covering 16 acres, with lawns and many fine trees, including a cedar of Lebanon in the East Lodge Garden [Open most days by application to the porter's lodge]. *Emmanuel* [Historic Garden Grade II*]: large gardens with herb garden designed by John Codrington. Also memorable for its fine trees, including a Caucasian wing nut, swamp cypress, dawn redwood and the splendid plane tree, cloaked to the ground, in the Fellows' Garden. Informal shrubberies and herbaceous borders skirt the lawns, and there is a pond with a restrained piece of modern sculpture nearby [Open daily, 9am – 5pm; College Gardens and Fellows' Garden open one day in summer]. *Jesus*: a must for those interested in sculpture; there are a number of interesting pieces throughout the grounds including the Flanagan Venetian horse in First Court and 'The Head' in the cloisters. An award-winning nature trail follows the bank of Jesus Ditch. Elsewhere the St Radegund's garden has planting derived from the sixth-century garden in Poitiers, France [Open daily, but closed during Easter term – May to mid-June]. *King's* [Historic Garden Grade II*]: one of the greatest British architectural experiences, set off by fine lawns [College and Chapel open daily until 6.30pm, but grounds closed mid-April to mid-June, 9.30am – 4.30pm, and closed over Christmas period. Entrance: £4, children and concessions £3 &]. Fellows' Garden with magnificent old specimen trees [Open one day in summer for NGS, 2 – 6pm]. *Leckhampton* (part of *Corpus Christi*) at 37 Grange Road: laid out by William Robinson, originally seven acres with two acres added [Open one day for charity ♥ WC]. *Magdalene*: Fellows' Garden [Open daily, 1 – 6pm. Closed May and June &]. *Pembroke*: extensive and varied garden, including orchard and winter bed, with notable range of unusual plants, most of which benefit from shelter provided by various walls, and a good selection of herbaceous perennials. Recent landscaping projects by Marina and Robert Adams [Open daily during daylight hours. Closed May and June &]. *Peterhouse*: varied, smallish gardens and interesting octagonal court with hot and cool sides. Extensive naturalised daffodils in spring [Open Mon – Fri, 1 – 5pm. Closed mid-May to early June &]. *Robinson*: Warden and Fellows' Garden, Grange Road [Open daily, 10am – 6pm]. This modern college was built around the edge of a 10-acre site so as to preserve the character of the Edwardian gardens in the centre. The older individual gardens now interconnect and merge around a wide lawn and small lake. Memorable old trees are preserved and the original flower borders have been renewed. Wild areas benefit local wildlife. *St John's* [Historic Garden Grade II*]: huge park-like garden with eight acres of grass, fine trees and good display of bulbs in spring. Wilderness (nearly three acres) introduced by 'Capability' Brown has spring bulbs including, from June to July, the spectacular Turk's cap lily. In the Master's Lodge Garden are quantities of *Arabis turrita*, probably the only specimens in the country. Rose garden [Open Mon – Fri, 10am – 5pm, Sat and Sun, 9.30am – 5pm]. *Trinity* [Historic Garden Grade II]: a garden and grounds of 45 acres with good trees [Grounds open daily although restricted access with charge for entry, March to Sept; opening times from porter's lodge. Fellows' Garden open one day, 2 – 6pm]. Nearby is *Little St Mary's Church*: wild and natural garden developed since 1925 [Open all year].

Childerley Hall [Historic Garden Grade II*]

Dry Drayton, Cambridge CB3 8BB. Tel: (01954) 210271

Mr and Mrs John Jenkins • 6m W of Cambridge on A428 opposite Caldecote turn • Open mid-May to mid-July by appt • Entrance: £2.50 ● WC

The hall lies between the sites of the two vanished villages of Great and Little Childerley, and the drive leading to the house, chapel and four-acre garden is nearly a mile and a half through flat open country, making it seem particularly still and remote. To one side is an ornamental Tudor moat and a yew hedge crowned by topiary birds. The south front of the house is on a raised terrace. From here the main garden, sunken and surrounded by raised grass walks, can be viewed; the corners of these walks were originally Tudor mounts. The backbone of the garden is a collection of over 350 different shrub and species roses flourishing in mixed borders – secret corners accessed by paths winding through trees and shrubs.

Chippenham Park ★

Ely CB7 5PT. Tel: (01638) 720221

Mr and Mrs Eustace Crawley • 5m NE of Newmarket, 1m off A11 • Open 2nd April, 18th June, 22nd Oct, 11am – 5pm, and at other times for parties of 20 or more by appt. Guided tours (£7.50) by arrangement NEW ● ●● ⬛ WC & ⬥ ✿

William Emes filled the gap between Brown and Repton, landscaping over 100 parks and bringing flowers back to the garden. The perimeter drive and tadpole-shaped lake and island are typical of his style. As a designer he was sensitive, retaining many of the original features; at Chippenham the old formal water garden was allowed to remain, also the trees planted by Admiral Russell in the seventeenth century to echo the formation of the ships drawn up at the battle of La Hogue. The present owners have created a 15-acre garden within the park, embellishing Emes's work with distinction. The great canal has been strengthened by the introduction of a glowing copper beech, and in Adrian's Walk (named after a still-serving gardener of 53 years) the colourful plantings are reflected in the waters of the lake. The long south border grows peonies and alliums to perfection, while the Victorian box walk preserves an air of mystery at the entrance to the woodland garden. The old vegetable garden, divided into four, includes a mound and a quince garden, a Spanish garden with olive trees and a green theatre, and a memorial garden to Admiral Russell planted around the magnificent statue of a begging hare. With over 750 rose bushes and a wide selection of acers and rarer trees, this garden never gives the feeling of being too large or too busy to comprehend. The daffodils are in period with the 1886 house, and the spires of eremurus in season reflect the grandeur of its gables. One of the county's most original gardens.

Christs College ★★ [Historic Garden Grade II]

St Andrew's Street, Cambridge CB2 3BU. Tel: (01223) 334900

In city centre • Open mid-June to Sept, Mon – Fri, 9.30am – 12 noon; Oct to April, Mon – Fri, 9.30am – 12 noon and 2 – 4pm. Closed Bank Holidays, Easter Week, exam period (May and early June) and 23rd Dec to 2nd Jan • Entrance: free • Other information: parties over 8 people must book in advance ❍ ♿ ♞

First impressions are telling, and the court beyond the porter's lodge is a sight that proclaims excellence. The summer display of fuchsias and petunias in window boxes and tubs is refined and peaceful, and tubs of hydrangeas welcome visitors into the immaculate gardens beyond. The well-planned herbaceous borders with considerable panache are augmented by bedded-out plants. On a mound in the far corner the venerable mulberry, contemporary with Milton, sheds its fruit onto the exemplary lawn. There are many other lovely trees, including *Catalpa bignonioides* in bloom in midsummer, and the cypress grown from seed from the tree on Shelley's grave in Rome. Darwin's garden with its canal intrigues the visitor by the use of false perspective.

Clare College Fellows' Gardens [Historic Garden Grade II]

Trinity Lane, Cambridge CB2 1TL. Tel: (01223) 333200

In city centre. Entry from Queens Road and Trinity Lane • Open April to Sept, daily inc. Bank Holidays, 10am – 4.30pm. Closed on graduation, May Ball and special events days • Entrance: College and garden £2 ◗ ♿

Reached by crossing the oldest bridge over the Cam from the college itself, or from Queens Road by walking along the avenue laid out in 1690, there are two gardens between the college buildings and the bridge. To the north the private Master's Garden and to the south the Scholars' Garden, where the planting relies on silver, blue, purple and white. Professor E.N. Willmer designed the present, well-regarded planting scheme for the Fellows' Garden; the fine trees are mainly the legacy of his predecessors. At the garden's heart, concealed by hedges, is a formal pool; adjoining this and enclosed by shrubs is a new sub-tropical planting of bananas, canna lilies and plants for foliage effect. The double herbaceous borders have a yellow and blue theme, while along the northern boundary is a ribbon of silver with a mass of white flowers, including some that show up well against walls and hedges. Summer bedding is used to insert oranges and reds in island beds by the river. Elizabeth Banks

Associates has prepared a master plan for development over the next ten years, which will be implemented from 2006.

Crossing House Garden ★

78 Meldreth Road, Shepreth, Royston, Hertfordshire SG8 6PS.
Tel: (01763) 261071

Mr and Mrs Douglas Fuller • 8m SW of Cambridge, 0.5m W of A10 • Open all year, daily, dawn – dusk • Entrance: free ○ WC ♿

Highly recommended, a delightful, eccentric place which proves that plantsmanship is alive and well in Cambridgeshire. A small garden, started by the present owners over thirty years ago, it is crammed full of plants and is an eye-opener about what can be achieved in a small space. There are little pools, excellent dwarf box edging, an arbour in clipped yew, rockeries and a lawn, and two tiny glasshouses full of orchids and alpines. In all there are estimated to be about 5000 different plants here, so a visit at any time of year will be rewarding. Docwra's Manor (see below) is about 250 metres away.

Docwra's Manor

2 Meldreth Road, Shepreth, Royston, Hertfordshire SG8 6PS.
Tel: (01763) 261473/261557/260235

Mrs John Raven • 8m SW of Cambridge, 0.5m W of A10. Opposite war memorial • Open all year, Wed and Fri, 10am – 4pm, first Suns of Mar to Oct, 2 – 5pm, and at other times by appt. Parties welcome • Entrance: £3, accompanied children under 16 free. Extra charge for guided and out-of-hours parties • Other information: Park in village hall car park ◔ WC ♿

'Simply a garden as reasonably varied as could be' – that was John and Faith Raven's original intention when they bought the manor house with two and a half acres of land in 1954, and this they achieved. Divided into unexpected compartments by buildings, walls and hedges, it contains many choice plants. The effect is wild in parts; other areas are more formal, with hosts of roses, spurges, clematis, eryngiums and philadelphus. Few gardens arouse so many mixed emotions in visitors – some consider that its romantic atmosphere of *temps perdu* makes it one of the greatest of East Anglian gardens, others find the casual emergence of chance seedlings an irritation. It is best viewed perhaps as the creation of cultured minds – John Raven was a classicist and an eminent field botanist, and his book, *A Botanist's Garden* (1971; reissued) describes the plants he and his wife grew together here. The Crossing House Garden (see above) is within easy walking distance.

Elgood's Brewery

North Brink, Wisbech PE13 1LN. Tel: (01945) 583160

Elgood's Brewery • In Wisbech, at W end of North Brink • Brewery open as garden for tours, Tues – Thurs, 2pm (£6 inc. tasting) • Garden open 2nd May to 28th Sept, Tues – Thurs, 11.30am – 4.30pm • Entrance: £2.50, OAPs and children £2 • Other information: Guide dogs only ◑ WC ♿

Wisbech is an elegant market town and among its delights are several splendid Georgian terraces. North Brink, along the River Nene, is arguably the most spectacular. Peckover House (see entry) is near the eastern end of the Brink, while the brewery dominates the western end. Behind it is a large enclosed garden, now restored, with some superlative trees. The *Ginkgo biloba* near the public entrance catches the eye first. A few paces away stands a tulip tree (*Liriodendron tulipifera*) the like of which you will rarely see; in June every shoot bears a flower, a cup of orange and jade. Other dignitaries are a mulberry, a variegated sycamore, a weeping willow, a tree of heaven (*Ailanthus altissima*) and an oak. The deep pool is home to a colony of great crested newts. Paths have been reinstated, and colourful herbaceous borders, a rockery, a herb garden and a thuja and laurel maze planted. The rose garden is now a sensory garden, with aromatic plants and grasses set in gravel and water emerging from stainless steel shapes. Onto this new planting the trees look down with grace and dignity.

Elton Hall [Historic Garden Grade II*]

Peterborough PE8 6SH. Tel: (01832) 280468 (during office hours)

Sir William and Lady Proby • 8m W of Peterborough in Elton, just off A605 • Hall open as garden • Garden open 28th and 29th May; June, Wed; July and Aug, Wed, Thurs, Sun and Bank Holiday Mon; all 2 – 5pm. Hall and garden open for tours by appt April to Sept • Entrance: £4 (hall and garden £6, accompanied children under 16 free) ● ● ✕ wc & ℗ ▥

Steps cloaked in aubrieta and lavender, guarded by two sphinxes, ascend to the low castellated house, parts of which date from 1475. Beside the steps is a knot parterre in box, elegantly wrought, and in front a smooth lawn rises to meet the surrounding pasture. A sunken pool, enveloped in a billow of whites and blues with some purple, is the first feature visitors see as they enter the main garden through an archway. Take the gravel path that encircles the lawn, which has an ornamental well-head offset in the middle, and wander past the immaculately clipped low yew hedges, tumps of golden yew and the short ha-ha to the restored rose garden, full of old-fashioned roses and herbaceous favourites – summer scents and colours. The distant sound of water will eventually beckon you on, across a hornbeam-lined avenue punctuated with pyramids of box, into an informal silvery shrubbery and under a fine *Paulownia tomentosa*, to discover a new Gothick orangery set in an ornamental garden.

Florence House

Back Road, Fridaybridge, Wisbech PE14 0HU. Tel: (01945) 860268

Mr and Mrs A. Stevenson • 3.5m S of Wisbech on B1101. In Fridaybridge turn right at Chequers pub • Open for NGS 19th March, 28th May, 10th Sept, 12 noon – 4pm; 19th April, 21st June, 19th July, 16th Aug, 10am – 4pm, and by appt • Entrance: £2.50, children 50p • Other information: Unusual plants for sale. Teas on Suns only ● wc & ℗

Although 25 years have gone into its making, this is essentially a garden in the contemporary style, filled with an array of choice plants. One-and-a-half acres of lawns, borders, trees and shrubs benefit from some of the most fertile soil in the country. The paddock borders, planted in 2000, are big-boned and colour-themed, starting with grasses and boldly architectural and exotic plants – cannas, phormiums, heleniums, phlomis, euphorbias and eryngiums. The mood changes as the colours shade into greens and creams, then finishes with a flourish of mauves, reds and blues. Mrs Stevenson likes to experiment with colours and combinations, and the borders change from year to year. Beyond, the woodland area is underplanted with ferns, hellebores and bulbs.

Hardwicke House

High Ditch Road, Fen Ditton, Cambridge CB5 8TF. Tel: (01223) 292246

John Drake • 3.5m E of Cambridge off A14, 0.5m from centre of Fen Ditton. From A1303 Newmarket road turn N by borough cemetery • Open one day in late May for NGS, and by appt • Entrance: £3, children free ◐ ↧ ✍ 🎇 ⚲

A garden of originality and inventiveness now settling into a rich maturity, best seen in the company of its owner, who can name the host of unusual species and elaborate on his ideas for its further improvement. Towering hedges of beech and closely clipped *leylandii* enclose compartments, some with splendid sculptures in a grassy setting, and emphasise its long axis, in part lined by birch trees alternating with yellow-blossomed *Rosa* 'Cantabrigiensis'. In late spring and early summer the place is awash with columbines and cranesbills and filled with the fragrance of old roses; in autumn there are colchicums in abundance, while hellebores and daffodils provide spring colour. There are orchids appearing in the lawn, and a National Collection of aquilegias is held here.

Island Hall

Post Street, Godmanchester PE29 2BA. Tel: (01480) 459676

Mr Christopher and Lady Linda Vane Percy • 2m S of Huntingdon, in centre of Godmanchester • Open 28th May, 12 noon – 5pm, for NGS, and for parties by appt, May to July and Sept • Entrance: £2 ◐ ⬤ 🍴 WC ↧

The garden is in two parts, separated by a mill-race yet linked by a Chinese-style wooden bridge erected in 1988. The Island was the pleasure garden in Victorian times – today it has tall trees, mainly horse-chestnuts, underneath which cow-parsley and other wild flowers are being encouraged. There are lovely views across the River Ouse to Portholme Meadow. Returning via the bridge, another vista embraces two fine cedars of Lebanon, one standing in front of the eighteenth-century house. On the terrace is a formal parterre with clipped variegated box hedges, box spirals and yew pyramids; the Mill Garden has a sundial ensconced in another parterre spilling over with white shrubby cinquefoil, white Scotch roses and columbines.

21 Lode Road ★

Lode, Cambridge CB5 9ER. Tel: (01223) 811873

Richard Ayres • 6m NE of Cambridge. From A14 take B1102 to Lode • Open for charity 17th, 18th, 24th, 25th June, 11am – 5pm, and by appt • Entrance: £2 • Other information: Parking facilities at village hall. Possible for wheelchairs but narrow paths ◐ ⬤ ⬬

The owner is the well-known retired head gardener from Anglesey Abbey, and his years there are reflected in his accomplished use of foliage – golden, feathery, silvery, opulent – in his own garden. All the plants are placed to their best advantage, the colours blending delightfully without too much emphasis on any particular individual. Twenty years ago this was a vegetable patch; it now contains over 150 cultivars of snowdrop and a wide selection of shrubs and herbaceous plants. The satisfying design of small island beds was completed and cut out in a single day. Although the climbing rose 'Erinnerung an Brod' dominates the entrance, the garden is not over-rosed. There is a modern stone water feature and a row of tubs showing how delightful hostas can be if they are well grown and kept free of slugs.

Madingley Hall

Madingley, Cambridge CB3 8AQ. Tel: (01954) 280272

University of Cambridge • 3m W of Cambridge in village of Madingley. Accessible from M11, A14 and A428 • Open one day for charity, and in 2006 for our readers, by special permission from the Warden, on 27th May, 8th July and 9th September for parties of 10-20 (1 party on each day only – telephone to book) • Entrance: charge • Other information: Refreshments available if booked in advance NEW ● WC

The hall was built in 1543 by Sir John Hynde and remained in the family until 1871, and the gardens embrace three main periods of activity. The Kip engraving of c.1705 reveals elaborate formal Dutch gardens laid out around the house; these were swept away by 'Capability' Brown after 1756 when he refashioned the landscape as parkland, built a new coach road and created an S-shaped pond. When Colonel Walter Harding bought the estate in 1905, he introduced terraces and symmetry on the north side; his son contributed yew hedges and topiary and a rose garden. In 1948 the estate passed to the University, and since the mid-1980s the eight acres surrounding the house have been restored and developed by the Warden and Richard Gant and his team with sense and sensitivity. The atmosphere is not that of an institutional garden but of an English country house – an achievement so rare it deserves comment. The delightful ornamental walled gardens to the south of the stable courtyard include a rose pergola and a nut walk to give height and shade and have been planted with a wide range of hardy plants, alpines and medicinal herbs, while the Alberni Border in the formal garden has been planted for year-long colour and interest. The hall (not open) is listed Grade I by English Heritage, and the twelfth-century parish church beside the entrance bridge is well worth a visit.

The Manor

Hemingford Grey, Huntingdon PE28 9BN. Tel: (01480) 463134

Diana Boston • 4m SE of Huntingdon off A14. Access off river tow path • House open by appt; tours daily in May, 11am and 2pm – booking advisable • Garden open all year, daily, 11am – 5pm (closes dusk in winter) • Entrance: £2, children free (house £5, OAPs £4, children £1.50) • Other information: Park in High Street ○ WC & ⏃ ✿ ⚏ ⚒

A storybook garden for children of any age – but there is much more than a garden here, for the wonderful moated Norman manor (c. 1130) is perhaps the oldest continuously inhabited house in England. It was the home of Lucy Boston from 1939 and the setting for her *Green Knowe* children's books. She designed the garden, intermixing old-fashioned roses with herbaceous perennials, creating parallel herbaceous borders, a formal rose garden and topiary in the form of chess pieces. Trees in the lawns are underplanted with autumn crocuses. At the Norman front are ancient yews and a superb copper beech that has layered itself. Parts of the garden are left wild deliberately. From mid-May through to the end of June a profusion of irises and old roses make this an especially magical time to visit.

Netherhall Manor

Tanner's Lane, Soham, Ely CB7 5AB. Tel: (01353) 720269

Timothy Clark • 6m SE of Ely on A142; pass church and war memorial and take second road on left. From Newmarket turn right in Soham at second road after cemetery • Open 2nd April, 7th May, 6th and 13th Aug, 2 – 5pm, and for parties of 10 or more by appt • Entrance: £1 ● ▇

An elegant garden, touched with antiquity, and full of old-fashioned plants. In spring it blazes with Victorian hyacinths, crown imperials and old primroses, followed by a display of florists' tulips and florists' ranunculus. There are Elizabethan daisies, the rare double-flowered white Turk's cap lily originated here, and the very rare rose 'Jules Margottin', mentioned in Mary's Meadow, also flowers here. Entering through a courtyard with box-edged beds and a handsome fountain, visitors first glimpse the formal aconite garden (later filled with old fuchsias); behind is the organic vegetable garden. To the right runs a colonnade of lichen-encrusted columns linked by a balustrade on which pots of seasonal flowers are displayed; summer is represented by gold and silver tricolour pelargoniums, yellow and golden-brown calceolarias, heliotropes and double lobelias. Notable too are the old apples, specimen trees, vast clumps of violets and hepatica and, most remarkably, the double-flowered ornamental blackberry (*Rubus ulmifolius* 'Bellidiflorus') trained against the gable wall. 3m SW of Soham is the *Wicken Fen National Nature Reserve*, one of the wild treasures of Cambridgeshire, and the simple effective garden of *Fen Cottage* (National Trust) is open April to October on Sundays and Bank Holiday Mondays, 2 – 5pm.

Peckover House [Historic Garden Grade II]

North Brink, Wisbech PE13 1JR. Tel: (01945) 583463

The National Trust • In centre of Wisbech on N bank of River Nene • House open as garden, but 1 – 4pm • Garden open 25th March to 30th April, 2nd Oct to 5th Nov, Sat, Sun, Good Friday and Bank Holiday Mon; 2nd May to 30th July, 2nd Sept to 1st Oct Tues, Wed, Sat, Sun and Bank Holiday Mon; 31st July to 1st Sept, Mon – Wed, Sat and Sun; all 12 – 5pm • Entrance: £2.50 (house and garden £4) (2005 prices) • Other information: electric wheelchair available by prior application ◔ ▇ ✗ <u>WC</u> ♿ ⚘ ♨ ☕ ⚲

The red-brick town house was built in 1722, whereas the elongated, two-acre garden has a distinctly late-Victorian ambience. Stepping from the house onto the croquet lawn, the visitor is surrounded by greenery, mature trees and evergreen shrubs. In summer, bedding plants add colour and the scent of a host of roses is an invitation to bear westwards, passing a (reconstruction) formal pool, into compartments variously planted with flowering shrubs, perennials and those perfumed roses. Topiary peacocks overlook a second pool and summerhouse; beyond are two wide borders designed by Graham Stewart Thomas in the 1960s. Lilies, peonies, hydrangeas and 'Mrs Sinkins' pinks provide a succession of blooms in the walled garden, at the end of which is the orangery, full to bursting with flowering pot plants and three mature, fruiting orange trees. Abutting one another at a corner of the orchard lawn are two borders backed by espalier pears, one planted in shades of red, the other in pastel colours. Cut flowers are grown for the tea room and house and everything is neat and orderly, bearing out the claim that this garden is 'the product of prudent tidiness, a period piece'. A new pathway (constructed over the Victorian carriage way) leads visitors past a scented shrubbery to the seventeenth-century threshing barn, used now as the tearoom. Elgood's Brewery (see entry) is close by.

South Farm

Shingay, Royston, Hertfordshire SG8 0HR. Tel: (01223) 207581

Mr P. Paxman • 11m SW of Cambridge, 6m NW of Royston off A1198, via Wendy • Open 28th May for charity, one day in June for NGS, and by appt May to July. Gardening clubs especially welcome • Entrance: £2.50 ● ● ● WC ● ●

The main flower garden is enclosed and protected by a tall cypress hedge, pierced frequently by gates that allow you to glimpse the long fields of wheat. The hedge even has a *trompe-l'oeil* cut into it – not a bad use for the loathsome *leylandii*. A lily pond in one corner is awash with sedges and monkey flowers and around it an informal garden with such beauties as *Rosa chinensis* 'Mutabilis'. Familiar flowers abound: Jacob's-ladders, daylilies, plume poppies, loosestrife. On the other side of the farmhouse is a pool terrace and an exotic conservatory, and a 1000-metre-square vegetable garden enclosed by espalier fruit trees and totally netted. Each rotation plot is subdivided by gravel paths, parterre-style, into some 15 beds holding over 150 varieties of vegetables and fruit. Beyond is a small wildflower meadow, and more wheat. A happy, not-too-tidy garden – the lucky ducks and their companion rare breeds have some well-trained humans to keep it for them. Nearby is a private nature reserve with a three-acre lake, which is open to the public. *Brook Cottage* (Mr and Mrs Charvil), four minutes' walk away, is a much smaller garden with a crystal-clear stream – a real cottage garden with vegetables and poultry as well as honey suckles and horsetails.

Thorpe Hall [Historic Garden Grade II*]

Longthorpe, Peterborough PE3 6LW. Tel: (01733) 330060

Sue Ryder Care • In Longthorpe, on W edge of Peterborough between A47 and A605 • Ground floor of house open for some events • Garden open all year, Mon – Fri, except Good Friday, Bank Holiday Mons, 25th and 26th Dec and 1st Jan, 10am – 5pm (closed on event days) • Entrance: by donation ○ WC ● ●

A wooden door lets the visitor out of the courtyard into the L-shaped garden comprising a series of parterres and borders. Two elegant Georgian pavilions, far apart, are linked by a long vista which is interrupted as it pierces a third pavilion. A boldly planted herbaceous border and a restrained, lavender-hedged rose garden around an oval pond occupy parts of a longer axis. On the shorter axis is an architectural Victorian parterre laid out with a strange mixture of perennials, including ornamental grasses, clipped bay laurel, box and yew, and bedded-out plants. The south court is planted with

Cromwellian plants, the east border with 1850s' plants, while the west end has rose gardens typical of the 1920s and '30s. What has been achieved so far is pleasing and worthwhile, providing a diverting small garden with echoes of former grandeur, especially in its Grade-II-listed pavilions, ancient yews and spreading cedar trees.

University Botanic Garden ★★ [Historic Garden Grade II]

Cambridge CB2 1JF. Tel: (01223) 336265

University of Cambridge • In S of city, on E side of A1309 (Trumpington Road). Entrance off Bateman Street • Open all year except 25th Dec to 1st Jan inclusive, 10am – 5pm (closes 6pm in summer and 4pm in winter) • Entrance: March to Oct, Mon – Fri, and weekends and Bank Holidays all year £3; Nov to Feb, Mon – Fri, free. Other information: Café open Feb to Nov; shop open March to Oct ○ 🍽 🥪 WC ♿ 🏛 🚻 ♺

This diverse and impressive garden covers 40 acres, and admirably fulfils its three purposes – research, education and amenity. A visit at any time is worthwhile, even during the coldest months when the winter garden, especially on a sunny day, is dramatic. The various dogwoods with red, black, green and yellow-ochre stems contrast with *Rubus biflorus*, while the pale pink trunk of the birch *Betula albo-sinensis* var. *septentrionalis* is stunning. The garden has the best collection of trees in the east of England, with limes, chestnuts, willows and conifers featuring prominently. Exotic trees include pawpaw (*Asimina triloba*), and good specimens of madrona (*Arbutus andrachne*), black walnut (*Juglans nigra*) and dawn redwood (*Metasequoia glypostroboides*). The historic systematic beds display the hardy representatives of 90 families of flowering plants, and there are both limestone and sandstone rock gardens. The glasshouse range is always fascinating, and in winter the tropical section can be a welcome retreat. It contains a green-flowered jade vine (*Strongylodon macrobotrys*), cycads, tropical economic plants and much more. In the alpine house, plants are changed regularly as they come into flower. The Dry Garden investigates how design and plant selection can eliminate the need for watering in a typical city garden. Local habitats are displayed nearby. Recently a major fenland display has been opened which illuminates the wildlife and human activity associated with this precious and unique area. The Genetic Garden shows how the huge variety of flowering plants results from genetic variation due to mutation and how humans have exploited this in the development of crops. The figure of 'Healthy Herbie' and a display about compost and compost-making highlight current concerns about chemicals, drugs, recycling and sustainable living.

Wimpole Hall [Historic Garden Grade I]

Arrington, Royston SG8 0BW. Tel: (01223) 206000

The National Trust • 7m SW of Cambridge, signed off A603 at New Wimpole • House open as garden, but 1 – 5pm (closes 4pm Nov) • Garden open 1st to 16th March, Sat – Wed, 11am – 4pm; 19th March to 31st July, Sat to Wed, 10.30am – 5pm; Aug, daily except Fri, 10.30am – 5pm; 3rd Sept to 30th Oct, Sat – Wed, 10.30am – 5pm; 31st Oct to 21st Dec, Sat – Wed, 11am – 4pm; 27th Dec to 4th Jan 2007, daily, 11am – 4pm. Pre-booked guided tours for parties with head gardener. Park walks open all year • Entrance: £2.70 (hall and garden £6.90, children £3.40) • Other information: Pre-booked guided tours for parties with head

gardener. Pre-booked self-drive vehicles available for disabled visitors ☾ 💬 ✕ ♿ <u>WC</u>
 🚻 ⬗ ♨ ⚕ 🅿️ ♒

Historically this is the most important garden in Cambridgeshire: the vast landscape park has features by Bridgeman (1720s), 'Capability' Brown (1760s) and the little-known but widely admired William Emes (1790s). The Trust has lavished money on this property and it shows. The rebuilt greenhouses in the walled garden are matched in quality by the planting surrounding them, and restoration continues. The parterre on the north front is decorated with some modern sculpture which may astonish the viewer. Vast avenues lead to the cardinal points of the compass, past lakes, bridges and a splendid 1770 folly – soothing the eye from the shock of the parterre. Fine trees embellish the walk to the folly which takes an hour to reach (a leaflet is available for an alternative tour). The home farm contains a remarkable collection of rare breeds of cattle and sheep.

Wytchwood

Owl End, Great Stukeley, Huntingdon PE28 4AQ. Tel: (01480) 454835

Mr David Cox • 2m N of Huntingdon off B1043. In Great Stukeley, turn at village hall into Owl End • Open 25th July, 1.30 – 5.30pm, and at other times by appt in writing • Entrance: £2, children 50p • Other information: Parking at village hall ☾ 💬 ♿ ⬗

Cascades of petunias in a wooden wheelbarrow and hanging baskets are a vibrant prelude to the garden proper. An island bed is planted with grasses and perennials, and perennials and grasses feature too beside a small pool and a blue spruce framing the patio. A few steps further on and the garden becomes different again, and wilder. At the back of the house a dry garden is planted in gravel, and set among one and a half acres of mown grass with large uncut islands full of wild grasses and native plants, especially attractive to amphibians, butterflies and dragonflies. The restraint of the meadow islands, filled with lady's bedstraw and poppies, set with rowans, maples and birches, is inspired. A spinney has been planted with native trees, ferns, hostas, foxgloves and spring bulbs.

THE HERITAGE BULB CLUB

This is both a commercial venture and a conservation-minded horticultural service, based at Tullynally (see entry in Ireland). The club has over 500 members, who receive a year's worth of bulbs, chosen so that a different variety is in flower each month. The choice is between the Heritage Collection and the Plantsman Collection. The stories surrounding the discovery of these bulbs or the uses put to them are written up, as are growing requirements, with the help of renowned bulb expert Martyn Rix. Membership fees range from £45 to £110 p.a., and a sample box is also available for £25. The club aims to kindle interest and spread knowledge, with visits to gardens here and abroad, expeditions to see wild species in flower (Turkey in 2006) and the opportunity to buy normally unobtainable bulbs and exchange seeds. A wholesale list of bulbs for naturalising and a heritage vegetable seed list are also available. Enquiries to Heritage, Tullynally Castle, Castlepollard, Co. Westmeath, Ireland. Tel: 0845 300 4257 (UK), 044 62744 (Ireland); info@heritagebulbs.com; www.heritagebulbs.com.

CHESHIRE

We have included some gardens with Cheshire postal addresses in the Manchester Area for convenience. So before planning a day out in Cheshire it is worthwhile consulting pages 271–275.

Two-starred gardens are marked on the map with a black square.

Adlington Hall [Historic Garden Grade II*]

Adlington, Macclesfield SK10 4LF. Tel: (01625) 820875

Mrs C.J.C. Legh • 5m N of Macclesfield off A523. Signed in Adlington • House and garden open June to Aug, Wed, 2 – 5pm, and for parties all year, Mon – Fri, by appt • Entrance: hall and garden £6, children £3, parties of 20 or more £5.50 per person ● ● WC & ❦

The attractive woodland park was mostly landscaped in the eighteenth century in the style of 'Capability' Brown. To the Georgian south front of the house a gravelled carriage-sweep encircles an oval lawn with a sundial at its centre, then leads through a pair of iron gates to a lime avenue dating from 1688; a path bears eastwards to a small brick building embellished with shells in the mid-nineteenth century. The wilderness to the west of the house offers pleasant walks, especially along the small river bank. In the centre, close to a Chinese bridge, is a temple to Diana and several other follies. Formal gardens re-created in front of the early Elizabethan north front of the house include a maze and rose garden and a herbaceous border. East of the house across a cobbled area is a water garden with ponds, rills, fountains and a water cascade, and a new penstemon garden.

Arley Hall and Gardens ★ [Historic Garden Grade II*]

Arley, Great Budworth, Northwich CW9 6NA. Tel: (01565) 777353/777284

The Viscount Ashbrook • 5m W of Knutsford off A50, 7m SE of Warrington off A559. Signed from M6 junctions 19 and 20 and M56 junctions 9 and 10 • Hall open • Garden open 16th April to Sept, Tues – Sun and Bank Holiday Mons; Oct, Sat and Sun; all 11am – 5pm • Entrance: £4.50, OAPs £3.90, children £2 (hall extra) (2005 prices) • Other information: Spring plant fair 2nd April, 10am – 4pm, garden festival 24th and 25th June, 10am – 5pm ● ● ✕ ● WC & ⬥ ♪ ♨ ❦ ✎

The gardens consist of many distinct areas, each with its own character and charm, but it is for its superb herbaceous border that Arley is most famed. Dating from before 1846, it is one of the earliest of its kind in England. A watercolour by George Elgood of 1889 shows it looking much as it does today, with a broad grass walk and clipped yew buttresses. At one end a classical pavilion provides a focal point framed by chess-piece topiary, and a little to one side is a fine wrought-iron gate. The large range of perennials includes some varieties used here a century ago. Designed to give colour from June to September, the season begins with soft yellows, blues and silvers before the spires of delphiniums and aconitums make their impact along with the softer forms of gypsophila and achillea; towards the end of the year the hotter colours of sedum, helianthus and crocosmia come to the fore. There is plenty of interest elsewhere too: the walled garden has perennials and shrubs grown in attractive combinations, and in the walled kitchen garden is a vinery containing a good collection of tender plants and a fine border with shrub roses, irises and peonies. Some areas, such as the flag garden and herb garden, are intimate in scale, while others have wide open vistas. Topiary, mellow brickwork and stone ornaments contribute to the structure and character throughout. Away from the more formal areas an extensive woodland garden has been created by the present Viscount Ashbrook, where 300 varieties of rhododendron grow amongst a collection of rare trees and shurbs in a delightfully tranquil setting. Attached to the gardens is a nursery selling some unusual plants, especially perennials.

Bluebell Cottage Gardens (Lodge Lane Nursery)

Lodge Lane, Dutton, Nr Warrington WA4 4HP. Tel: (01928) 713718

Jack and Anne Stewart • 4m SE of Runcorn, 6m NW of Northwich, S of M56 and A533. Signposted • Gardens, meadow and woodland open May to Aug, Fri, Sat, Sun and Bank Holiday Mons, 10am – 5pm, and for parties by appt • Nursery open mid-March to mid-Sept, Wed – Sun and Bank Holiday Mons, 10am – 5pm • Entrance: £3, children free ◑ 💻 WC ⅄ 🌿 🍴 🚻

Set around an old cottage, the gardens include six acres of woodland and wildflower meadow and a large well-run nursery. Clustered around the cottage are several small gardens divided by hedges and trellises covered in climbers. Each is devoted to a different theme, and there is also a patio with a large collection of pelargoniums and other tender perennials grown in pots. In a larger open area sloping up to the canal a scree bed runs down to a pool; cut into the lawn is a series of large herbaceous borders giving an impressive display from May through August. In a garden with little natural shade, a corner next to the canal bridge has been developed as a woodland haven.

Bridgemere Garden World ★

Bridgemere, Nantwich CW5 7QB. Tel: (01270) 521100

On A51 7m SE of Nantwich. Signed from M6 junctions 15 and 16 • Open all year, daily except 25th and 26th Dec, 9am – 7pm (closes 6pm in winter) • Entrance: free ○ 💻 ✕ WC ⅄ 🌿 🚻 🍴 🅿

The 25-acre garden centre has some 5000 different plants for sale including several rare and unusual varieties. There are also six acres of display gardens, some modern in feel and others more traditional. They change with the seasons and are constantly being altered. One is Mediterranean in feel with an area of terracotta, a fine stout pergola and many plants with striking foliage, another has mock ruins overlooking a moat and an area devoted to damp lovers. A rockery and a pool (filled with water lilies and surrounded by varieties of iris and astilbe) are backed by a collection of pines; close by is a bed of euphorbias that reminds one just how many fine varieties of this plant there are. The displays of tulips are particularly impressive, and a good selection of azaleas and rhododendrons grows around the mound, which gives a fine view across the whole garden. Statuary, trellises, grottoes and garden ornaments are used to good effect throughout.

Capesthorne Hall and Gardens ★

Macclesfield SK11 9JY. Tel: (01625) 861221

Mr W.A. Bromley Davenport • 7m S of Wilmslow, 1m S of Monks Heath on A34 • House open as gardens but 1.30 – 3.30pm only • Gardens open April to Oct, Wed, Sun and Bank Holidays, 12 noon – 5pm • Entrance: gardens, hall and chapel £6, OAPs £5, children (5–18) £3 • Other information: Lunches, teas and suppers by arrangement ❶ 🍽 🌸 WC ♿ 👓 ♿

Set within a large estate, the gardens have something of a quiet majesty about them and include fine architectural features. The surrounding parkland was laid out in the seventeenth and eighteenth centuries with three lakes forming the southern perimeter. Vernon Russell-Smith designed the formal lakeside garden in the 1960s to replace the large kitchen gardens. It is mainly laid to lawn, but also has herbaceous borders containing a good variety of plants and a wonderful set of Rococo Milanese gates. There is a serene view from here across the lake with its attractive brick bridge and memorial garden alongside. The mellow brickwork of the eighteenth-century chapel sets off the glossy foliage of the *Magnolia grandiflora*, camellias and cherry in the small garden which surrounds it. On the north side the old rock garden has been replanted with ferns and tree ferns, and there are many new artefacts. Azaleas and rhododendrons lead to the 'Millennium Dome' in the arboretum, which includes two enormous sweet chestnuts, some giant redwoods and a more recently planted selection of maples. The surrounding park and woodland offer excellent walks.

Cholmondeley Castle Gardens ★ [Historic Garden Grade II]

Malpas SY14 8AH. Tel: (01829) 720383

The Marquess of Cholmondeley • 7m W of Nantwich, 6m N of Whitchurch on A49 • Open April to Sept, Wed, Thurs, Sun and Bank Holiday Mons, 11.30am – 5pm, and on other days by prior appt for parties of 20 or more • Entrance: £4, children £1.50 (2005 prices) ❶ 🍽 🌸 WC ♿ 👓 🐾 ♿ ♿ ☕

Of the great formal garden laid out by George London in 1690 no trace remains. His canal and fruit garden are gone, as is his vast kitchen garden (138 x 246 metres with some 40 compartments), which was almost on the scale of Louis XIV's *potager* at Versailles. Instead, set in idyllic parkland and blessed with a most extensive range of mainly acid-loving trees and shrubs, the present gardens are designed to take advantage of spectacular views. The nineteenth-century castle perches majestically on a hill overlooking the estate, which includes two lakes and a superbly sited cricket pitch. The lawns which slope up to the castle are covered with bulbs in spring. The gardens to the west have some of the most interesting plants. In the glade, sheltered by large trees, are varieties of magnolia and cornus, an *Abutilon vitifolium*, a *Davidia involucrata*, species rhododendrons and a large liquidambar. On a lower level are primulas, narcissi and cyclamens. The rose garden, containing a mixture of old and new varieties, is one of the few formal areas: a pleasant layout of beds divided by stone-flagged paths, with a fine *Magnolia sieboldii* standing at the entrance. The most impressive area of all is the temple garden, where the landscaping and architecture give a classical feel – a Claude painting contrived by a horticulturist. Around a pool with its two grassed islands are some attractive combinations of shrubs and trees, good use being made of purple, gold and blue foliage. Tower Hill is a wilder area, where mature woodland of beech, oak and sweet chestnut is underplanted with camellias, more magnolias, azaleas, cornus and rhododendrons. Another water garden, known as the Duckery, has recently been restored and planted with rhododendrons, shrubs and trees; a collection of ferns surrounds the two Victorian waterfalls.

Dorfold Hall [Historic Garden Grade II]

Chester Road, Acton, Nantwich CW5 8LD. Tel: (01270) 625245

Mr R. Roundell • 1m W of Nantwich, S of A534 • Hall open • Garden open April to Oct, Tues and Bank Holiday Mons, 2 – 5pm • Entrance: House and garden £5, children £3 ◑ ঌ

A woodland garden of spring-flowering shrubs and bulbs is the chief horticultural attraction here. The formal gardens around the house, once laid out in ornate Elizabethan style, are now fairly austere, confined to large areas of lawn edged by narrow herbaceous borders. A statue of Shakespeare stands to one side of the house and a fine Jacobean gate to the other. A new garden against the old walled garden, enclosed by a yew hedge and a wrought-iron gate, shows promise, with borders of peonies, hostas, tulips and shrub roses backed by wall climbers. The woodland garden itself, set within a dell, has clipped grass paths running among areas of long grass planted with spring bulbs and clumps of azaleas giving off a heady scent. The valley then slopes steeply down towards a small stream fringed by primulas and arums, beneath a dense canopy of oak and sycamore. The landscaping has been well designed, with gravel paths winding among large boulders and revealing views across the garden.

Dunge Valley Hidden Gardens

Windgather Rocks, Kettleshulme, Whaley Bridge, High Peak SK23 7RF. Tel: (01663) 733787

David and Elizabeth Ketley • 6m NE of Macclesfield, 12m SE of Stockport in Kettleshulme. Signed from B5470 Macclesfield – Whaley Bridge road • Open March to Aug, Thurs – Sun and Bank Holiday Mons; plus Tues and Wed in May; all 10.30am – 5pm • Entrance: £3 weekdays, £3.50 weekends, children £1, season ticket £6 • Other information: Mini-buses up to 16 seats only. Telephone for appt at other times to buy plants at Hardy Plant Nursery ◑ ▬ ✕ WC ✿

A superbly sited garden nestling in a small valley high in the Pennines; the location is so remote that often only the song of the lark or the cry of the curlew can be heard. Walks wind across and around the rocky valley, disclosing wonderful views over the garden and into the rugged landscape beyond. It is a superb natural setting for many rhododendrons, camellias, acers and magnolias, with shrub and species roses providing interest later in the season. When the garden was begun in 1983, pine, larch and hemlock were planted as shelter belts and now, even at an altitude of 300 metres, some surprisingly tender specimens – embothriums, *Eremurus robustus* and *Desfontainia spinosa* – survive. Rodgersias, rheums, primulas and other moisture-lovers cluster around the stream that runs through the valley, and close to the stone farmhouse are cultivated pockets of choice plants, including collections of meconopsis and peonies. The expanding nursery stocks such things as American magnolias, plus sorbus and meconopsis grown from seed collected by the owners in Nepal and Arunachal Pradesh. The garden has expanded to seven acres with over 600 new shrubs added.

Eaton Hall ★ [Historic Garden Grade II*]

Eccleston, Chester CH4 9ET. Tel: (01244) 684400

The Duke of Westminster • 4m S of Chester off A483 Chester – Wrexham road • Open 16th April, 29th May, 28th Aug, 1.30 – 5.30pm • Entrance: £3, children £1 ● ● WC & ⬦

The gardens and parkland surrounding the modern hall are vast. There are several fine features, including well-kept herbaceous beds and many stone statues and urns. A long, narrow greenhouse contains camellias, and a deep bed backing against the walled garden is planted for dramatic effect with hot-coloured perennials, cotinus and dark-flowering dahlias. There is also a large lake and a small Gothic-style cottage with stone and brick paths set within its own small herb garden. Close to the house is the imposing Italian garden surrounded by a high yew hedge; a large dragon fountain stands at the centre of a pool, and there are beds of annuals and more statues. Arabella Lennox-Boyd has been working on the garden since 1990.

Gawsworth Hall [Historic Garden Grade II*]

Macclesfield SK11 9RN. Tel: (01260) 223456

Mr and Mrs T. Richards • 3m S of Macclesfield off A536. Signposted • Hall open • Garden open Easter to mid-June, Sun – Wed and Bank Holiday Mons (advisable to telephone in advance); then mid-June to Aug, daily; Sept to early Oct, Sun – Wed; all 2 – 5pm • Entrance: hall, park and garden £5, children under 16 £2.50, parties of 20 or more £4 per person (2005 prices) • Other information: Open-air theatre in garden mid-June to mid-Aug ● ● WC & ●

The hall is approached by a drive leading between two lakes to the north end, where there is a large yew tree and lawns sloping down to one of the rhododendron-fringed lakes. A formal garden on the west side has beds of modern roses edged with bright annuals and many stone ornaments, including a sundial and a circular pool with a fountain; stone steps lead to a sunken lawn and mixed beds. To the south is another lawned garden surrounded by a high yew hedge and herbaceous borders. A grassed area containing mature trees lies to the west of these formal areas, from where there is a view of the groundwork for a Williamite garden begun but not completed by the Earl of Macclesfield, who died in 1694.

Hare Hill Gardens
Hare Hill, Over Alderley, Macclesfield SK10 4QB. Tel: (01625) 584412

The National Trust • 5m NW of Macclesfield, N of B5087 between Alderley Edge and Prestbury at Greyhound Road • Open 5th April to 7th May, Wed; then 31st May to Oct, Wed, Thurs, Sat, Sun and Bank Holiday Mons, all 10am – 5pm. Special opening for rhododendrons and azaleas 8th to 28th May, daily, 10am – 5pm. Parties by written appt • Entrance: £2.70, children £1.25. £1.50 per car refundable on entry to garden • Other information: Picnics at lakeside only ❶ WC &

Hybrid and species rhododendrons, some of enormous size, are the main attraction here. Other acid-lovers – azaleas, magnolias, acers and tree-like pieris – thrive in the damp, lush setting and sheltering canopy of beech and oak. A pool at the heart of the wood gives a break in the trees, and the colours of the rhododendrons are reflected in its waters; rustic timber bridges cross to a central island. There is also a walled garden, once used for growing vegetables but now rather sparsely planted, laid mainly to lawn with beds of roses and some good climbers. Along the drive to the south, majestic conifers and pines tower above rhododendrons and azaleas. Although at its peak in spring and early summer, the rolling countryside surrounding the garden and the views of the Pennines to the east make it a good centre for walks at any time of the year.

Henbury Hall ★
Macclesfield SK11 9PJ.

Mr S.Z. de Ferranti • 2m W of Macclesfield on A537 • Open one day for NGS • Entrance: £5, children £1 ❶ 🐛 WC ⚗

The hall, modelled on the Villa Rotunda, sits confidently on a gentle eminence at the heart of parkland. The remarkable 12-acre *giardino segreto* is skilfully hidden from the park by a backcloth of trees. The main garden to the north-east, centred around a lake with a high jet, has steep banks planted with rhododendrons, azaleas and small trees such as acers, laburnums and birches, which give it something of the aura of Stourhead; around the margins are beds of hostas, candelabra primulas, gunneras, irises and royal ferns. The garden buildings here include a Chinese bridge, a small Chinese summerhouse and a Gothick folly. Beyond is a walled garden with a double herbaceous border and a tennis court discreetly hidden, as is the swimming pool sited within a conservatory. At the entrance to the house is a small sunken garden with a round pool and a fountain and quadripartite lawns edged with miniature box. Three fine statues by Simon Verity are placed around the garden.

73 Hill Top Avenue
Cheadle Hulme SK8 7HZ. Tel: (0161) 486 0055

Mr and Mrs Martin Land • 2m S of Cheadle. From A34 follow B5094 to Cheadle Hulme. Take 2nd left turn into Gillbent Road, go to end and turn right at roundabout into Church Road, then 2nd left into Hill Top Avenue • Open two days for NGS, and by appt • Entrance: £2.50, children free ❶ 🐛 WC ⚗

Perennials are the mainstay of this small suburban garden, and the variety is huge. A lawn snakes through the length of the garden. To one side is a border in full sun, its soil lightened over the years, which contains delphiniums, campanulas, penstemons, hemerocallis, achilleas and other sun-lovers. Shade-lovers, including ferns, are grown in the opposite border in heavier soil. Providing colour later in the year are phlox in variety, dahlias, asters and crocosmias. A selection of small shrubs has been chosen for foliage colour: *Cercis canadensis* 'Forest Pansy', berberis, golden elm (*Ulmus minor* 'Dampieri Aurea'), *Salix exigua* and silver elaeagnus. A small pool has a selection of moisture-lovers, and there are shrub roses and clematis. Don't get the impression, however, that this is just an impressive plant collection, for the planting has been planned for its aesthetic effect and the result is a most attractive garden.

Jodrell Bank Arboretum

Macclesfield SK11 9DL. Tel: (01477) 571339

Manchester University • 11m W of Macclesfield, on A535 between Holmes Chapel and Chelford, 5m NE of M6 junction 18. Signposted • Open mid-March to Oct, daily, 10.30am – 5.30pm; Nov to mid-March, Tues – Fri, 10.30am – 3pm, Sat and Sun, 11am – 4pm. Closed several days over Christmas and New Year – telephone to check • Entrance: free (charge for 3D-theatre and parking) ☯ 🍽 🍴 WC 🚻 ♿ 🎫 🍴 ⚲

The arboretum, begun in 1972 largely at the instigation of Professor Sir Bernard Lovell, is set in a flat landscape with all views to the west dominated by the massive radiotelescope. The large collection of trees, wonderful in their autumn colours, covers 35 acres and includes National Collections of malus and sorbus. There is also a collection of hornbeams and shrubs such as berberis, fine specimens of *Ulmus minor* (syn. *U. elegantissima*) 'Jacqueline Hillier' and the cut-leaved form of the common walnut (*Juglans regia* 'Laciniata'). Broad grass walkways lead among the trees, and small natural ponds are dotted around the garden; there are also beds of shrub roses and azaleas. A new apple orchard is based on varieties that originated in Cheshire.

Little Moreton Hall

Congleton CW12 4SD. Tel: (01260) 272018

The National Trust • 4m SE of Congleton on E side of A34 between Congleton and Newcastle-under-Lyme • Open 25th March to 5th Nov, Wed – Sun and Bank Holiday Mons, 11.30am – 5pm; 11th Nov to 17th Dec, Sat and Sun, 11.30am – 4pm • Entrance: £5.50, children £2.80, family £13, party rates £4.70 per person (hall and gardens) • Other information: Wheelchair for loan. Guide dogs and hearing dogs only ◑ 🍽 ✕ 🍴 WC 🚻 ♿ 🍴 ⚲

The extraordinary timber-framed house, built between 1440 and 1580, is undoubtedly the magnet for visitors, but its quiet, contemplative gardens play their part in establishing the aura of the place. Designed to frame the building in suitable style, they are actually a modern creation. The most outstanding feature, the knot garden, was laid out by Graham Stuart Thomas using a simple geometric seventeenth-century pattern of gravel, lawn and box edging; enclosed by a high yew hedge. There is also a yew tunnel and four beds of period herbs and vegetables, and a small orchard set within a lawn. The perimeter of the garden is defined by a moat, its clear waters filled with golden orfe and overhung by trees, including a fine old willow. A gravel walk follows the moat, giving views back across the garden to the unforgettable hall.

The Manor House ★

Chelford, Macclesfield SK11 9AH. Tel: (01625) 861038

Lynne Murphy • 6m E of Macclesfield on A537 at roundabout in Chelford • Open 7th May, 9th July, 3rd Sept, 2 – 5.30 pm, and for parties of 12 or more by appt • Entrance: £3.50, children free • Other information: NEW ● ● WC ♨

A garden of 12 acres with some fine planting and well-designed areas, and many large and interesting sculptures. In the intimate-feeling walled garden pebble and stone paths radiate out from a large central urn; the planting is exotic, with tree ferns, palms, cannas, cleomes and dahlias and a Victorian conservatory stuffed with more tender species. Beyond the walls, the mood is more expansive, taking in large lawns and a lake with an impressively high water geyser. There are many good herbaceous borders, and a prairie garden is developing nicely with drifts of grasses, salvias, sedums, monardas and achilleas. A stream winds through the lower garden. A gate leads into the courtyard garden of *Honeysuckle Cottage*. It is filled with small shrubs, perennials and annuals, many of them in pots; water features add movement and variety. Taken together, an imaginative and thoroughly modern ensemble that works well on very different scales.

Mellors Gardens [Historic Garden Grade II]

Hough Hole House, Sugar Lane, Rainow, Macclesfield SK10 5UW. Tel: (01625) 573251

Mr and Mrs A. Rigby • From Macclesfield take B5470 Whaley Bridge road. In Rainow turn off to N opposite church into Round Meadow, then turn first left into Sugar Lane and follow road down to garden • Open 29th May and 28th Aug, 2 – 5pm, and for parties of 10 or more by appt • Entrance: £1.50, children free ● ● WC

Where can you pass through the Valley of the Shadow of Death, climb Jacob's Ladder, see the Mouth of Hell and visit the Celestial City, all within the space of ten minutes? Here, at the heart of a valley in a rugged but attractive part of the Peak District, during the second half of the nineteenth century, James Mellor, much influenced by Swedenborg, designed a unique allegorical garden which attempts to re-create the journey of Christian in Bunyan's *Pilgrim's Progress*. There are many small stone houses and other ornaments to represent features of the journey. Most areas are grassed, with stone paths running throughout; at one end a large pond is overlooked by an octagonal summerhouse. Excellent guide book.

The Mount

Andertons Lane, Whirley, Henbury, Macclesfield SK11 9PB.

Mr and Mrs Nicholas Payne • 2m W of Macclesfield off A537. Turn into Pepper Street opposite Blacksmith's Arms, and left into Church Lane which becomes Andertons Lane. Garden is 200 metres further on. Signposted • Open one day for

NGS, and by written appt at other times for parties of 10 or more • Entrance: £4, children 50p • Other information: Plants for sale on NGS day only ● ● ● WC �),

The two-acre garden, originally planted in the 1920s but enlarged, improved and replanted by the present owners, is a fine setting for the Regency house. Each distinct area has its own individual style. The terrace garden has an Italian feel, with a swimming pool, many architectural features and brightly planted terracotta pots. The shade garden is more informal, with rhododendrons, azaleas and camellias underplanted with hostas and other shade-lovers. A lawned area has two herbaceous borders; opposite is another small border planted entirely with astilbes, and a conservatory containing a climbing pelargonium. In one corner of the garden an area of grass has been cut to different heights, forming patterns and paths leading to an obelisk looking across the Cheshire plain towards Wales.

Ness Botanic Gardens ★★ [Historic Garden Grade II]

Neston Road, Ness, Wirral CH64 4AY. Tel: (0151) 353 0123

University of Liverpool • 10m NW of Chester, 2m off A540 between Ness and Burton • Open daily except 25th Dec: March to Oct, 9.30am – 5pm, Nov to Feb, 9.30am – 4pm • Entrance: charge • Other information: Guide dogs only ○ ● ✕ ● WC ☒ ℗ ⊞ ☕ ♀

Arthur Kilpin Bulley, a Liverpool cotton broker, began gardening on this site in 1898, using seeds from plants collected for him by George Forrest, the noted plant hunter. The gardens extend to over 60 acres, and those who have experience of the north-west winds blowing off the Irish Sea will marvel at the variety and exotic nature of the plant life. The secret is in trees planted as shelter belts. The aim has been to provide interest from spring onwards, through the herbaceous garden of summer, to the heather and sorbus collections of autumn. There are in addition areas of specialist interest, such as the Pinewood and adjacent areas, home to the best collection of rhododendrons and azaleas in the north-west of England. A new sedum-roofed visitor centre opened in 2005.

Norton Priory Museum and Gardens ★

Tudor Road, Manor Park, Runcorn WA7 1SX. Tel: (01928) 569895

The Norton Priory Museum Trust • 2m E of Runcorn. From M56 junction 11 turn for Warrington and follow signs to Norton Priory. From all other directions follow signs to Runcorn, then Norton Priory • Open all year, daily, 12 noon – 5pm (closes 6pm Sat, Sun and Bank Holiday Mons; 4pm Nov to March). Walled garden open April to Oct, daily, 1.30 – 4.30pm • Entrance: £4.50, concessions £3.25, family £12 (2005 prices) • Other information: Museum open. Teas and snacks in museum ○ ● ✕ ● WC ☒ ⟐ ℗ ⊞ ☕ ♀

The woodland garden, covering 30 acres and containing many fine mature trees, surrounds the remains of the twelfth-century Augustinian priory. The stream glade is the most attractive area, planted with azaleas and candelabra primulas; a water-lily tank has a statue of Coventina (goddess of wells and streams) at its centre. There are many modern sculptures dotted around both parts of the garden. At some distance to the north is the clearly signposted walled garden, built in the mid-eighteenth century and now redesigned on more ornamental lines with a rose walk running down the centre and two broad borders containing a variety of shrub roses. It also contains an orchard of pears, plums, greengages and quinces (a National Collection of *Cydonia oblonga*, tree quince, is held here), a vegetable garden and a distinctive herb garden. Along the south-facing wall a series of brick arches, covered with vines and honeysuckles and sheltering two large figs, is fronted by beds of perennials, strongly planted with kniphofias, euphorbias, salvias and geums. Indeed the walled garden is a good illustration of the twin strengths of the garden as a whole – a bold, coherent design and a great variety of plants.

Peover Hall [Historic Garden Grade II]

Over Peover, Knutsford WA16 9HW.

Mr R. Brooks • 4m S of Knutsford off A50 at Whipping Stocks Inn, down Stocks Lane, signposted • Hall open April to Oct, Mon only (but closed Bank Holiday Mons), 2 – 5pm • Gardens open April to Oct, Mon and Thurs, 2 – 5pm • Entrance: £3, children £2 (hall, stables and garden £4.50, children £3) ◑ WC

Peover Hall (pronounced Peever) and its 15-acre gardens are surrounded by a large expanse of flat parkland laid out in the early eighteenth century. The gardens themselves are mainly Edwardian and include some historic and unusual features. On the north side of the Elizabethan house a broad grass walk extends from the forecourt through an avenue of pleached limes to a yew-hedged enclosure where a summerhouse overlooks a small circular lawn. Around the house is a series of formal gardens with distinctive and ornate topiary combining perfectly with the old brick walls and stone paths. A lily-pool garden has a summerhouse with a stone-tiled roof and Doric columns. To the west of the gardens is a wooded area underplanted with rhododendrons, azaleas and other shade-lovers; the grassy dell with its banks of flowering shrubs looks particularly attractive in late spring and early summer. Be sure to see the fine Caroline stables and church when visiting.

Queen's Park, Crewe [Historic Park Grade II]

Victoria Avenue, Wistaston Road, Crewe CW2 7SE. Tel: (01270) 537882

Crewe and Nantwich Borough Council • 2m W of town centre, S of A530 • Open all year, daily, 9am – sunset • Entrance: free • Other information: Parking off Queen's Park Drive ○ 🍴 ♿ WC ♿ 🐕 🌷 ⚲

Although the 45-acre park, first opened in 1887, has continued over the last few years to suffer from vandalism and neglect, it is still impossible not to be impressed by its fine Victorian landscaping and many fine mature trees – conifers, pines and some ancient oaks. Financed originally by the London and North Western Railway, the company's own designers, F.W. Webb and Edward Kemp, dammed the small valley and fashioned the shapely curves of the lake that give the oval-shaped park its distinctive character. The clock tower and the two lodges at the main entrance, looking along a birch avenue to the central boating lake and cafe, are typically Victorian in character. To the west the wooded valley with its small artificial stream is now very overgrown, many paths have been badly cracked by tree roots and most other areas of ornamental planting are virtually abandoned. A restoration scheme is, however, a possibility.

The Quinta ★

Swettenham, Congleton CW12 2LD.

Sir Bernard Lovell, Cheshire Wildlife Trust and Tatton Garden Society • 5m NW of Congleton, E of A535 Holmes Chapel – Alderley Edge road, near Twemlow Green. Follow signs for Swettenham Village; arboretum is next to Swettenham Arms • Open all year, daily except 25th Dec, 9am – dusk, twice for NGS and for parties by appt • Entrance: £2.50 • Other information: Teas on NGS Sun openings only ● & ⬢

Sir Bernard Lovell began planting this garden in 1948 to satisfy his love of trees. It now contains a large variety of trees and shrubs. There are National Collections of pine and ash, good collections of birch, five of the six varieties of wingnut and an Oriental plane directly descended from the Hippocratic tree on the island of Cos. Most areas are informally planted and interspersed with grassed glades; several avenues pass up and down the garden, including one of red-twigged limes planted in 1958 to commemorate Sir Bernard's Reith lectures, and one of *Populus nigra* to celebrate his knighthood; to mark his 90th birthday collections of camellias, rhododendrons, primulas and malus were assembled. To the west of the garden a walk taking in some marvellous views across the Dane Valley (SSSI) leads to the 39 steps that descend into the wooded valley of a small brook (one mile from the car park and back).

Reaseheath College

Reaseheath, Nantwich CW5 6DF. Tel (01270) 625131

Reaseheath College • 1.5m N of Nantwich on A51 • Open for College Open Day 14th May, 11am – 5pm, and for NGS, 1 – 5pm • Entrance: by donation. Guided tours available. Prices on application ● ⬤ ⬢ WC & ⅋ ⬛

From the old brick hall a large lawn sweeps southwards to a lake, flanked on one side by a heather garden and on the other by a rockery. The lake is spanned by a wooden bridge and stocked with a variety of water lilies and marginals. On the south side is a woodland garden with many fine trees, including a large cut-leaf beech, underplanted by primulas, hostas, azaleas and other shade-loving plants. To the west of the lake another lawned area has island beds with a variety of small trees, shrubs and perennials. Other areas of interest include a garden with water features, a herb garden, a model fruit garden, a gravel garden, a range of glasshouses and a nursery.

Rode Hall [Historic Garden Grade II]

Church Lane, Scholar Green ST7 3QP. Tel: (01270) 882961

Sir Richard and Lady Baker Wilbraham • 5m SW of Congleton between A34 and A50 • House open as garden from April, but Wed and Bank Holidays only, and for parties by appt at other times • Garden open 4th to 26th Feb (for snowdrops), daily except Mon, 12 noon – 4pm; April to Sept, Tues – Thurs and Bank Holiday Mons,

2 – 5pm; and for parties by appt at other times • Entrance: £3, OAPs £2.50 (house and garden £5, OAPs £4. Special parties at other times £8, including tea) ◑ ☕ WC ♿ ⬦ ✍

A long drive leads through parkland to an attractive red-brick house with fine stable buildings. The gardens lie to the north and east, with many areas remaining as planned by Repton in 1790. The rose garden and formal areas were designed by Nesfield in 1860; these are mainly lawn, with gravel paths and clipped yews, and good views from here of the surrounding countryside and Repton's lake. In a dell to the west is a woodland garden with hellebores and flowering shrubs, rhododendrons, azaleas and some fine climbing roses. Old stone steps ascend the opposite side of the dell to a grotto and early-nineteenth-century terraced rock garden. A small stream is dammed at the open end of the dell with the resulting pond surrounded by marginals; a path leads from here to the lake. Snowdrops, daffodils and bluebells light up the early months, while the two-acre Georgian walled kitchen garden is at its best from June to August. The ice-house in the park is also worth a visit.

Stapeley Water Gardens

London Road, Stapeley, Nantwich CW5 7LH. Tel: (01270) 623868

Mr R.G.A. Davies • 1m SE of Nantwich on A51. Signed from M6 junction 16 • Open all year, daily except 16th April and 25th Dec. Opening and closing times vary from 9am – 10am and 4pm – 8pm • Entrance: Display gardens free. The Palms Tropical Oasis £4.45, OAPs £3.95, children £2.60. Season tickets available • Other information: Wheelchairs available ○ ☕ ✕ 🍴 WC ♿ ✍ 🏛 ♿ ☕

Two acres of garden shopping under cover form the world's largest water-garden centre. Within it a few areas are attractive gardens in their own right. At the back are many pools containing a National Collection of water lilies; the land around is landscaped with lawns and shrub borders. Another area has small demonstration gardens. Across the car park is The Palms Tropical Oasis. This huge greenhouse has none of the architectural merit of a Victorian palm house, but the main hall is impressive, with a long rectangular pool flanked by huge palm trees, the Jungle Floor (a variety of exotic plants and animals), and other exhibits. Those with an interest in water gardens might comment that this is a bleak description – think of the giant *Victoria amazonica* water lily from Brazil, the rare breeding sting-rays, the *Nymphaea gigantea* from Australia. There's also an angling centre for the non-horticultural.

Tatton Park ★★ [Historic Garden Grade II*]

Knutsford WA16 6QN. Tel: (01625) 534400

Cheshire County Council/The National Trust • 3m N of Knutsford, signed from M6 and M56 • House open 25th March to 1st Oct, daily, 12 noon – 4pm • Gardens open 25th March to 1st Oct, daily except Mon, 10am – 7pm (last admission 6pm); 3rd Oct to 23rd March 2007, daily except Mon, 11am – 4pm (last admission 3pm). Closed 25th Dec • Entrance: gardens £3, children £2, family £8, park £4 per car (2005 prices) • Other information: RHS Flower Show here probably 26th to 30th July (telephone to check) ○ ☕ ✕ 🍴 WC ♿ ✍ 🏛 ♿ ☕

Tatton Park was, throughout four centuries, the home of the Egertons, an immensely rich family who could indulge their every whim on their vast estate. The 50 acres of gardens here are among the finest in England and contain some unique features created by the best designers in the country. Repton made a 'Red Book' for Tatton in 1791 and much of his work is still visible in the wonderful rolling parkland that surrounds the gardens. When Lewis Wyatt completed his work on the house in 1815 he was asked to design the kidney-shaped flower garden and the elegant orangery. From 1859 Paxton was at work, and his fernery was built to take the collection of plants made by Lord Egerton's brother; it now houses New Zealand tree ferns. Also by Paxton is the Italian garden, the grandest and most formal part of the gardens: an arrangement of terraces spaciously laid out with an ornate design of clipped hedges and beds. They are overlooked by the south-facing portico of the house and fine views stretch out across the parkland from here. The Japanese garden constructed in 1910 by Japanese workmen and recently restored has a wholly different feel. Set in a small valley, the contrasting textures of mounds of moss, delicate acer leaves, large stones and a gently flowing stream give this garden its particular charm, while large conifers provide a backdrop and lend it intimacy. Tatton has much more besides: pools and lakes, huge numbers of rhododendrons and azaleas, a rose garden that has something of the feel of Lutyens about it, a maze and an arboretum with especially fine pines. With the help of Heritage Lottery Funding, a huge project is underway to restore the walled gardens to their former working glory, with areas of fruit and vegetables and large greenhouses, including a pinery for forcing pineapples. One problem – these marvellous gardens attract huge numbers of visitors at peak times.

Tulip Tree Cottage

85 Warmingham Road, Coppenhall, Crewe CW1 4PS. Tel: (01270) 582030

Mr and Mrs A. Mann • 3m N of Crewe off A530 between Warmingham and Leighton Hospital near White Lion Inn • Open mid-Feb to Sept by appt for parties of up to 40 • Entrance: £2, children free (2005 price) ◕ ⬤ 🐌 WC ⓵ ☙

Two-thirds of an acre with a small woodland, a large herbaceous border and a good display of hellebores and snowdrops. Many and various alpines are to be found here. In the first section of the garden, paths run among lushly planted beds lightly shaded by trees; there are perennials and small shrubs as well as a collection of lilies, and a small pond in the centre is planted with marginals such as golden sedge. Beyond this area is a lighter, more open section containing gravel screes, a rock garden and a peat bed. Diascias, violas and geraniums abound. There are also two greenhouses, one with a good collection of cacti and succulents.

Walton Hall Gardens

Walton Lea Road, Higher Walton, Warrington WA4 6SN. Tel: (01925) 601617

Warrington Borough Council • 2m SW of Warrington on S side of A56 in Walton • Open all year, daily, 8am – dusk • Entrance: free • Other information: Pay-and-display car park. Heritage centre, children's zoo and play area, pitch and putt, crazy golf, bowls ○ ⬤ 🐌 WC ⓵ ◁▷ 🏛 ♟ ☙

The gardens are dominated by the dark brick Victorian mansion with its distinctive clock tower. To one side of the building a large pool containing carp is backed by an impressive rockery well planted with azaleas, rhododendrons, birches and other small shrubs and trees. Water cascades down the rocks to a pool furnished with water lilies and marginals, including a clump of gunneras. Behind the hall is a series of formal gardens separated by yew hedges and low stone walls and containing beds of bright tulips and annuals. Beyond some large beech trees, modern roses are set out in formal beds. The walk back down the west side of the garden passes through light woodland with a collection of camellias and some fine acers and magnolias.

85 Warmingham Road
(see TULIP TREE COTTAGE)

Weeping Ash

**Glazebury, Warrington Road, Warrington, Cheshire WA3 5NT.
Tel: (01942) 266303 (Bents Garden Centre)**

John Bent • 14m W of Manchester. Turn S off A580 at Greyhound Hotel roundabout onto A574 to Culcheth. Garden is 0.25m further on left • Open Feb to Nov, 3rd Sun in each month, 11am – 5pm • Entrance: £2, children free • Other information: Parking, teas, toilet facilities, plants for sale and shop at adjacent garden centre ● ▆
✕ wc �& ♨ ⊞ ♟

This garden has been created by a retired nurseryman, so it is only to be expected that a great variety of plants is found here: an extensive collection of small trees, particularly sorbus, shrubs, roses, and a large range of perennials, including over 50 hellebores and many bulbs. One large bed is devoted to lilies. But it is his ideas on design that bring so much to the garden. The herbaceous border is 90 metres long. Broad grass paths snake around the mixed beds, small offshoot paths give interesting glimpses back into the main areas, and there are views over the whole garden from a ruined Doric temple on a mound. Many structures have been created as hosts to climbing plants, the best being a rustic gazebo built entirely from scrapwood, which is now covered by a passion flower and a golden hop.

The Well House

Tilston, Malpas SY14 7DP. Tel: (01829) 250332

Mrs S.H. French-Greenslade • 3m NW of Malpas, 12m SW of Chester off A41. Turn right after Broxton roundabout, then continue on Malpas road through Tilston. Garden is at antique shop • Open one day for NGS, 2 – 5.30pm, and March to July by appt • Entrance: £2, children 25p • Other information: Plants sometimes for sale. Teas by arrangement ● wc ⇱ ⊞ ♟ ℺

A one-acre garden set around a small natural stream, well worth visiting both for the range of plants grown and the natural landscaping of the site; the land rises steeply from the stream, giving views back over the garden. Close to the house is a geometric layout of beds containing perennials such as campanulas and alstroemerias, backed by a rose-covered pergola and with a sundial at the centre. There is also an area devoted to rock plants and a patio on which a large number of plants are grown in containers – an inspiration for those with small gardens. Another area has plants chosen for foliage colour, including yellow gleditsia, purple berberis and silver pyrus. Moisture-lovers, including many ferns, line the stream that divides the garden, and a bridge leads across to a small hexagonal summerhouse. In the upper garden is a new triple waterfall feature. There is also a wildflower meadow and a natural bog area massed with kingcups and ragged robin.

PARKS AND GARDENS DATA PARTNERSHIP
A major new national database is being set up under the aegis of the Association of Gardens Trusts, the Welsh Historic Gardens Trust and the University of York, funded by a £1-million grant from the Heritage Lottery Fund. This ambitious three-year project, which will complement English Heritage's *Register* of fewer than 1600 properties, aims ultimately to make available to the general public detailed information on some 30,000 historic parks, gardens and landscapes throughout Britain. The initial database will be established in 2006 and some 6000 records provided by 2008.

GARDEN AND FLOWER SHOWS 2006
- 11th to 14th May: Spring Gardening Show, Malvern
  (Three Counties Showground, Malvern, Worcestershire)
  Ticket hotline: (01684) 584924; www.threecounties.co.uk
- 23rd to 27th May: Chelsea Flower Show
  (Royal Hospital, Chelsea, London SW3)
- 6th to 8th June: Wisley Show
  (RHS Garden, Wisley, Woking, Surrey)
- Mid-June: BBC *Gardeners' World* Live
  (National Exhibition Centre, Birmingham)
  Ticket hotline: (0870) 902 0555; www.necgroup.co.uk
- 16th to 18th June: Three Counties Show, Malvern
  Ticket hotline: (01684) 584924
- 4th to 9th July: Hampton Court Flower Show
  (Hampton Court Palace, East Molesey, Surrey)
- 26th to 30th July (probable dates): RHS Flower Show, Tatton Park
  (Tatton Park, near Knutsford, Cheshire)
- 22nd to 24th Aug: Wisley Show
- 23rd and 24th Sept: Autumn Garden & Country Show, Malvern
  Ticket hotline: (01684) 584924

Unless otherwise given, for details of all these shows telephone the Royal Horticultural Society on (020) 7834 4333 or consult www.rhs.org.uk.

CORNWALL

Two-starred gardens are marked on the map with a black square.

Antony ★ [Historic Garden Grade II*]

Torpoint PL11 2QA. Tel: (01752) 812364

The National Trust/Trustees of Carew Pole Garden Trust • 2m W of Torpoint on A374, 16m SE of Liskeard. From Plymouth use Torpoint car ferry • House open as formal gardens • Formal gardens open April to Oct, Tues – Thurs and Bank Holiday Mons; also June to Aug, Sun; all 1.30 – 5.30pm (last admission 4.45pm). Woodland gardens open March to Oct, Tues – Thurs, Sat, Sun and Bank Holiday Mons, 11am – 5.30pm • Entrance: £4 (house and formal gardens £4.60, children £2.20, pre-booked parties £3.80 per person, family £11.50) (2005 prices) • Other information: Separate car parks for formal and woodland gardens ◑ 🍽 ✕ 🧺 <u>WC</u> ♿ ⛩ ♗

Antony is a little off the beaten track, but it is well worth the effort to visit one of the country's finest early-eighteenth-century houses in its magnificent natural setting. The house and adjacent formal gardens now belong to the National Trust, while the woodland gardens, which lie between the parkland and the River Lynher and are also open, belong to the family trust. The formal gardens, with a terrace round the house, wide lawns, extensive vistas, yew hedges and old walls, are of the highest quality. A water feature by William Pye on the west lawn mirrors the yew topiary nearby. Eighteenth-century statues, modern sculpture and topiary are features of the yew walk and of the formal compartments of the summer garden; the latter includes a pleached lime hedge, mixed shrub and herbaceous borders with roses, and a knot garden. The woodland gardens, also known as the wilderness – the central section – include Jupiter Hill and a late-Georgian bath house and are planted with superb camellias, magnolias and rhododendrons, with scented rhododendrons outstanding in May. A standing stone of Cornish granite has been erected on top of Jupiter Hill in memory of the present owner's parents, who created the woodland gardens. In the neighbouring woodland walk is a ruined fifteenth-century dovecote and Richard Carew's sixteenth-century Fishful Pond, and there are fine walks along the river banks. Two National Collections are held here: hemerocallis (610 cultivars) and *Camellia japonica* (300 cultivars).

Barbara Hepworth Museum and Sculpture Garden [Historic Garden Grade II]

Barnoon Hill, St Ives TR26 1AD. Tel: (01736) 796226

Administered by The Tate Gallery • In centre of St Ives. Signposted • Open March to Oct, daily, 10am – 5.30pm; Nov to Feb, Tues – Sun, 10am – 4.30pm • Entrance: museum and sculpture garden £4.50, concessions £2.25, OAPs and children free ○ WC ♿

The wonderful collection of Hepworth's own sculptures combines superbly with the architectural planting of her garden as a permanent testimonial to her importance. The house and half-acre sloping garden are kept as they were in her lifetime. The strong vertical and other architectural statements and the soft underplanting occlude views outside and provide a soft contrasting background for the sculptures. Trees shade the upper part of the garden and give transient light effects in the sun. They include *Cordyline australis*, bamboos and a metasequoia on the back wall, and below them *Magnolia grandiflora*, a ginkgo, and a row of *Prunus* 'Amanogawa' providing cover for a small but important pond and separating the upper garden from the small open lawn which forms the lower part. Below are herbaceous beds and a silver-grey path. The garden is within walking distance of the Tate St Ives; the small but attractive *Trewyn Garden*, well planted and with an immaculate lawn, adjoins [open all year, daily].

Boconnoc [Historic Garden Grade II*]

The Estate Office, Boconnoc, Lostwithiel PL22 0RG. Tel: (01208) 872546

Mr and Mrs J.D.G. Fortescue • Between Lostwithiel and Liskeard, S of A390. Well signed on open days between Lostwithiel and Middle Taphouse • Open 7th, 14th, 21st and 28th May, 2 – 5pm, and for parties of 10 or more by appt • Entrance: £5, children free • Other information: Guided tours of house, garden, church and estate, with refreshments, by prior arrangement. Holiday accommodation available ● ➤ WC & ⬧ ⌇ ♀ B&B

The superb parkland was first laid out by Thomas Pitt, Lord Camelford (grandfather of Pitt the Elder), in the eighteenth century. With its sweeping views and enormous hardwoods, it is a fine example of the Picturesque landscape and makes a wonderful backdrop for the garden. This too is of great quality, with trees and shrubs vast even by Cornish standards. Along the drive rhododendrons, azaleas and camellias thrive on a carpet of bluebells; on the lawns around the house are camellias and large clumps of *luteum* and 'Cornish Red' rhododendrons. A Golden Jubilee walk around the lake has been planted with daffodils. The magnificent woodland garden, covering some 20 acres, contains fine flowering shrubs and many large and unusual trees. Using the original 1840 list, the circular pinetum is being replanted into sections based on the points of the compass: the Americas, Europe and Asia, with 'play' areas for Chile and New Zealand.

Bonython Estate Gardens ★

Cury Cross Lanes, Helston TR12 7BA. Tel: (01326) 240234

Mr and Mrs R. Nathan • 5m S of Helston on A3083. Turn left at Cury Cross Lanes (Wheel Inn), and take entrance on right signposted 'Bonython Estate' • Open April to Sept, Tues – Fri, 10am – 4.30pm • Entrance: £5, children £1.50, parties of 10 or more £5 per person (incl. guided tour) ● ➤ WC & ⌇

A major new and exciting garden still being developed. The owners started in 1999 with an old walled garden, a few ornamental trees and shrubs, background trees and essential shelter belts (now extended by another 15,000 trees!). A complex water feature, planted with grasses, herbs and bamboos, was completed in the new courtyard garden of the Georgian house during 2004. The lawn is surrounded by rhododendrons and azaleas. The walled garden is amazingly mature only four years after planting: the upper part contains herbaceous and shrub borders themed with colours that change throughout the year; the lower is a newly designed parterre planted with flowers and ornamental vegetables. The areas below the walled garden are more sheltered, and an orchard with wild flowers beneath the trees slopes down to Lake Joy against a background of specimen trees and shrubs. The sunny bank which dams it has a bold display of South African and Mediterranean plants with camassias congregated beside the water course. Below this Lake Sue is surrounded by masses of ornamental grasses, and hot red colours stand out in late summer. From here a stream leads through the woodland dell, full of wild flowers, new rhododendrons and young Arctic ferns, to the Quarry Lake with vertical cliffs beyond.

Bosahan

Manaccan, Helston TR12 6JL. Tel: (01326) 231351

Mr and Mrs R.J. Graham-Vivian • 10m SE of Helston, 1m NE of Manaccan • Open by appt for parties of 6 or more • Entrance: £4 per person • Other information: Coach companies must confirm in advance ● WC ⬧ ℘ ℀

The 100-year-old garden, with fine views from the top, runs from the house down to an attractive stream and pond in the valley. Its four acres contain mature conifers and rhododendrons as well as camellias, magnolias, tree ferns and other specimens; there are also palm trees and more recent plantings near the house. Beyond the main garden a mature wooded valley, where tree ferns and pittosporums grow, shadows the stream down to the Helford River. The adventurous can follow its bank to the left and return up the old fern glen, where ancient rhododendrons grow alongside tree ferns.

Bosvigo ★

Bosvigo Lane, Truro TR1 3NH. Tel: (01872) 275774

Michael and Wendy Perry • 0.75m W of Truro. From A390, turn into Dobbs Lane adjacent to Sainsbury supermarket roundabout. Entrance is 500 metres down lane on left, just after sharp left bend • Open March to Sept, Thurs, Fri, 11am – 6pm • Entrance: £3.50, children free • Other information: Rare and unusual plants for sale in nursery ◑ WC ♿ ℘

An immaculately maintained garden of great artistry and imagination. The two acres surrounding the Georgian house consist of several delightful enclosed and walled areas. The hot garden displays red, yellow and orange flowers, the Vean Garden white and yellow, and the walled garden many rare plants. Flowers and foliage are grouped with boldness or subtlety to enchanting effect. Though not a typical Cornish garden (rhododendrons and camellias do not play a major part), there is a wonderful spring section with a woodland walk containing many treasures such as hellebores, epimediums and erythroniums The garden as a whole, however, is at its best in summer when the mainly herbaceous plants start their display.

Burncoose Gardens

Gwennap, Redruth TR16 6BJ. Tel: (01209) 860316

Burncoose Nurseries • On A393 Redruth – Falmouth road between Lanner and Ponsanooth. Signposted • Open daily except 25th Dec, 8.30am – 5pm (opens 11am Suns) • Entrance: £2, children free ○ 🍽 🍴 wc & ⬦ ⌨ ⛪ ☕

This woodland garden, belonging to the Williams family of Caerhays Castle (see entry), was laid out originally at the turn of the twentieth century; it is now allied to the Burncoose Nurseries. It contains many fine camellias, magnolias, rhododendrons, acers and other spring-flowering shrubs and ornamental trees. The woodland extends to more than 30 acres and is accessible by a network of paths; the main planted areas lie either side of the main drive and beside the pond.

Caerhays Castle Garden ★★ [Historic Garden Grade II*]

Caerhays, Gorran, St Austell PL26 6LY. Tel: (01872) 501310

Mr F.J. Williams • 10m S of St Austell, on coast by Porthluney Cove between Dodman Point and Nare Head • House open 13th March to May, Mon – Fri, 12.15 – 4pm • Garden open 13th Feb to May, daily, 10am – 5.30pm • Entrance: £5.50, children under 16 £2.50 (under 5 free) (house and garden £9.50, children under 16 £3.50. Party rates for 15 or more • Other information: Car park by beach; short walk to garden entrance ● 🍽 ✕ wc & ⬦ ⌨ ⛪

Caerhays, unsurpassed as a spring garden and one of the greatest of all Cornish and British gardens, fully deserves its international reputation. Principally a woodland garden, it stretches up and around the extensive hillside above the romantic early-nineteenth castle. It can claim its collection of camellias and rhododendrons to be amongst the finest and its magnolias to be unrivalled. All of these, as well as many other fine shrubs and trees, are not only huge themselves but bear flowers of a remarkable size and depth of colour. The extensive replanting in the higher garden after the storm of 1990 has matured with great effect, while the felling of a stand of mature beech trees for safety reasons has revealed wonderful new views looking down on many of the most spectacular magnolias. A large number of plants are raised from material brought back by famous plant hunters or sent recently from China, and it was at Caerhays that the famous 'Williamsii' camellias were originally propagated.

Carwinion

Mawnan Smith, Falmouth TR11 5JA. Tel: (01326) 250258

Mr and Mrs H.A.E. Rogers • 5m SW of Falmouth. From Mawnan Smith take left road by Red Lion. 500 metres up hill on right is white gate marked 'Carwinion' • Open all year, daily, 10am – 5.30pm • Entrance: £3, children free (2005 prices) ○ 🍽 🍴 wc & ⬦ ⌨ ☕ B&B

The garden is notable for its bamboos – the Bamboo Society's reference collection is held here. They are planted intensively in the walled section and, accompanied by camellias, rhododendrons and other shrubs, in other parts of the garden. Among these is a fine *Michelia doltsopa* and a good *Drimys winteri*. The lawn below the house is adorned with shrubs and bamboos, and a series of small valleys with an attractive high-level path converges to form ponds and a bog of gunnera. This leads past the open lawns of the new quarry garden through woodland sheltering tree ferns and hellebores, and on down to the Helford river. Much impressive clearing and replanting has taken place in the fourteen acres here since 1998.

Chyverton ★★ [Historic Garden Grade II]

Zelah, Truro TR4 9HD. Tel: (01872) 540324

Mr N. Holman • 8m NE of Redruth, 1m W of Zelah on A30. At end of bypass, turn N at Marazanvose; entrance is 0.5m on right • Open March to May by appt only by personally conducted tour • Entrance: £6, parties of 20 or more £5 per person ● 🌿 *WC* ♿

Chyverton is one of the greatest of Cornish and of woodland gardens. It covers perhaps 140 acres, depending on the distinction between garden and woods, and is maintained virtually single-handedly by the owner without the use of chemical sprays. It has benefited from seventy years of unbroken planting, hence the outstanding collection of magnolias in particular, but also of rhododendrons, camellias, ferns and many other plants of the greatest interest. All these thrive in an unspoilt setting which is certainly not over-manicured, aptly described by the owner as a 'magic jungle', and a photographer's paradise; such are the growing conditions that collectors and great botanical institutions send their rare plants and collections here. The garden surrounds the 1730s' house, which has a contemporary copper beech and stretches under mature trees along the bottom of the adjacent valley. It is being divided into 29 separate 'rooms', some of them given added interest by a new collection of statues.

Cotehele ★ [Historic Garden Grade II*]

St Dominick, Saltash PL12 6TA. Tel: (01579) 351346

The National Trust • 12m NE of Liskeard, 8m SW of Tavistock. Turn S off A390 at St Anne's Chapel • House open 18th March to Oct, daily except Fri (but open Good Friday), 11am – 5pm • Garden open all year daily, 10.30am – dusk • Mill open daily except Fri (but open Good Friday); July, Aug, daily; all 1pm – 5.30pm; Oct, daily except Fri, 1 – 4.30pm • Entrance: garden and mill £4.40 (house, garden and mill £7.40, pre-booked parties £6.40 per person) • Other information: Holiday cottages available ○ 🍴 ✕ 🛍 WC ♿ ♿ 🚼 ⛲ 🏵 ⚘

There are two separate parts to this 19-acre garden. The upper gardens around the beautiful sixteenth-century house are largely formal, with courts, herbaceous borders, walls, yew hedges, fine lawns, a pool and a formally planted terrace falling away from the east front of the house. There is a daffodil meadow, a grove of acers and an orchard. This area is probably at its peak in the late spring and early summer. The woodland valley garden lies in the view below the formal terrace. Here beneath large conifers and hardwoods are many colourful flowers, shrubs and ornamental trees; rhododendrons and azaleas are especially striking in spring. The valley tumbles down towards the River Tamar, and from a hilltop behind the house a tower offers fine views.

Creed House

Creed, Grampound TR2 4SL. Tel: (01872) 530372

Mr and Mrs W.R. Croggon • Mid-way between St Austell and Truro. Take A390 to Grampound, then road in main street signed to Creed. After 1m, opposite Creed church, turn left; entrance to house and garden is on left • Open all year, daily, 10am – 5.30pm, and 4th June for NGS, 2 – 5.30pm • Entrance: £3, children free • Other information: Teas, toilet facilities and plant sales on charity open days only ○ ♿ B&B

The seven-acre garden, which has been devotedly restored and developed by its present owners, surrounds a fine Georgian rectory and has views of the country-side through mature trees. The beautiful trees and shrubs include camellias, magnolias and rhododendrons. A most enjoyable concealed walk leads through the shrubs surrounding the lawn. Below the lawn the pond is a focus, while herbaceous borders in the walled garden behind the house and elsewhere give particular summer interest. For maximum enjoyment, use the garden guide to be found beside the front door and view the historical photographic montage in the stable-block garage.

Eden Project

Bodelva, St Austell PL24 2SG. Tel: (01726) 811911

1.5m off A391 NE of St Austell, or by Luxulyan Road, St Blazey Gate on A390 E of St Austell, or from A30 (all signposted). Open all year, daily: April to Oct 10am – 6pm (last admission 4.30pm); Nov to March 10am – 4.30pm (last admission 3pm). Closed 24th and 25th December • Entrance: £12, OAPs £9, students £6, children (5–16) £5, under 5 free, family £30 (2005 prices) • Other information: Students must have ID ○ ✕ WC ♿

This mammoth project was created in 2001 from a vast disused china clay pit which contains two huge, transparent geodesic lean-to conservatories – biomes – and a landscaped outdoor area. The larger, humid tropics biome houses a large waterfall and flowing river planted with species from Amazonia, West Africa, Malaysia and Oceania. The plants apparently are fully mature and some of them look as if they will, literally, soon go through the roof. The smaller, but still huge, warm-temperate biome is now clad with plants that have come of age. The outdoor area is spectacularly landscaped, though the bright colours at some times of year may not appeal to all tastes; it now features an ice-rink, in use from November to February. Eden is a resounding success, hardly a project any more, and not a garden but a spectacular educational theme park of botany and ecology. It hammers home how vital it is to protect the world's ecology and it does it in such a way as to catch the imagination of the young. A new education building opened for schools and the general public in autumn 2005. Eden has developed into a tremendously powerful tourist magnet far beyond initial forecasts – 1.8 million people pass through every year, nearly double the figure originally projected. They have already made this the third most-visited tourist attraction in Britain and a real earner for the Cornish economy.

Fox Rosehill Gardens

Melville Road, Falmouth TR11 4DB. Tel: (01872) 224400

Carrick District Council • From A39 follow signs to beaches and hotels • Open all year, daily, 8am – dusk • Entrance: free • Other information: Plant sale in early June ○ 🐌 �& ⬗ 🌷

Established by the Fox family, owners of the Falmouth Packet Line, with specimens brought back by ships' captains, this is a truly remarkable small park of two acres. It is famous for its many exotic trees and shrubs, including an *Embothrium coccineum* (Chilean firebush) and a *Syagrus romanzoffiana* (queen palm). There are also collections of myrtus and bamboo, all set amongst paths and two lawns. A delight for the ordinary visitor and of great interest to the plantsman.

Glendurgan Garden ★ [Historic Garden Grade II]

Mawnan Smith, Falmouth TR11 5JZ. Tel: (01326) 250906

The National Trust • 4m SW of Falmouth, 0.5m SW of Mawnan Smith on road to Helford Passage • Open 11th Feb to 28th Oct, Tues – Sat and Bank Holiday Mons, 10.30am – 5.30pm (last admission 4.30pm). Closed 14th April • Entrance: £5, children £2.50, family £12.50, booked parties £4.25 ◑ � ✕ 🐌 <u>wc</u> �& 🌿 🏛 🌷 ℀

Set, like Trebah (see entry), in a ravine with a fine view of the Helford River, and adjacent and similar in size to it, Glendurgan is predominantly a springtime and sub-tropical garden. It contains many fine mature trees and shrubs, including rhododendrons, camellias, a vast 150-year-old liriodendron and a large michelia. An attractive pond graces the lower valley, together with tree ferns, gunneras, hydrangeas and bamboos. There is also an 1833 maze of cherry laurel, and a Giant Stride for children. Its upkeep is immaculate.

Godolphin House [Historic Garden Grade II*]

Godolphin Cross, Helston TR13 9RE. Tel: (01736) 763194

Mr and Mrs L.M.P. Schofield • 6m NW of Helston between B3302 and B3280. From Helston take A394 Penzance road. Turn right before Jet garage onto Camborne road, and sharp left at sign to Godolphin Cross. Go through village; entrance is on left • Open April to Sept – telephone for details – and for parties by appt • Entrance: £2, children free (house and garden £6, concessions £5, children (5-15) £1.50, under 5 free) ◑ � ✕ 🐌 <u>wc</u> �& 🌿 🏛 🌷 ℀

The Side Garden at Godolphin is a fascinating survival. Not all of it is a garden in the usual sense at present. One third is 700 years old and still gardened; the remainder, discernible under grass, awaits revival. In 1300 it consisted of nine compartments (3 x 3: a concept derived from the Holy Trinity) covering 4.5 acres with the original castle at its heart. In the late fifteenth century the garden was remodelled when the house beside which it now lies replaced the castle; interestingly, the nine-compartment concept was retained, as it was when the garden was remodelled again a century later. Extensive surveys have been carried out and repair of the surrounding wall-walks has begun (the one on the east side will be accessible in 2006). The aim now is to line two pools and resurface the wall-walks, and in the long run to discover and make use of the most interesting and best of the structures and ideas from the historic garden to realise a garden for the present day.

Headland

Battery Lane, Polruan–by–Fowey PL23 1PW. Tel: (01726) 870243

Jean Hill • 8m E of St Austell off A3082. Take passenger ferry from Fowey and 7-minute walk up hill, or take car ferry from Fowey to Bodinnick and follow signs for Polruan (3m). Ignore first car park, turn left for second car park overlooking harbour, then turn left (on foot) down St Saviour's Hill • Open for charity 4th May to 7th Sept, Thurs only, 2 – 6pm • Entrance: £2.50, children £1 • Other information: Beach for swimming ● 🅿 WC

This unique garden, set on a steep cliff face with fine sea views, has been developed with great determination and ingenuity by the present owner. The narrow interlocking paths and archways reveal hidden areas and intimate seats on many different levels which maximise the feeling of space. Despite the salt spray and gales, a fine collection of temperate, alpine, antipodean and sub-tropical plants with a sheltered aspect gives a colourful display, especially in summer. A path lined with trees and a steep flight of steps lead to a small sandy beach. This is a garden of tremendous character, but definitely not for the disabled, and small children should be supervised.

Heligan ★★ [Historic Garden Grade II]

Pentewan, St Austell PL26 6EN. Tel (01726) 845100

The Lost Gardens of Heligan • 5.5m S of St Austell off A390. Take B3273 signed to Mevagissey past Pentewan • Open all year, daily except 24th, 25th Dec, 10am – 6pm (closes 5pm in winter) (last admission 4.30pm in summer, 3.30pm in winter). Guided tours by arrangement • Entrance: £7.50, OAPs £7, children (5–16) £4, family £20 ○ 🅿 ✕ 🍴 WC ♿ ⚘ 🏛 🍼 ✿

Started in the late eighteenth century but neglected since 1914, the renaissance of this large garden is, rightly, a well-known story. The restored productive gardens to the north of the house, a superb demonstration of horticultural archaeology (the pineapple pits are particularly fascinating), are surrounded by Victorian pleasure grounds laid out as a series of secluded enclosures with fountains and a sundial. Massive, mainly red rhododendrons enclose the large lawn; some were collected by Sir Joseph Hooker and show signs of their age. The Jungle, some ten minutes walk away, is a wild, beautiful valley where rhododendrons, bamboos, tree ferns and Chusan palms flourish. Further on, magical woodland walks can be taken in the Lost Valley. The Steward's House has a well-planted young garden with magnolias, and beyond that a pioneering wildlife conservation project is being developed. Like the Eden Project, Heligan is a busy tourist target; plan your visit carefully, especially at holiday times.

Ince Castle

Saltash PL12 4QZ. Tel: (01752) 842672

The Viscount and Viscountess Boyd of Merton • 3m SW of Saltash off A38 at Stoketon Cross. Turn at sign for Trematon and then for Elmgate • Open 12th March,

9th April, 14th May, 16th July, all 2 – 5pm, and for parties by appt • Entrance: £3, children under 14 free • Other information: Due to very narrow lanes, no large coaches. Picnics in car park only ● ● WC & ◁

Five acres of formal and informal gardens are knit together here by strong design and the personalities of its two generations of creators. The formal areas and lawns, enhanced by statues and planted with summer flowers, are set round the castle, with dramatic views over the Lynher River and a background of mature trees. Daffodils and other bulbs create colour early in the year, while the woodland areas, with paths and an elliptical open space, contain camellias, rhododendrons, azaleas and other fine shrubs. The summerhouse is decorated internally with shells collected during the 1960s. The castle itself is romantic and stands at the end of a very long lane.

Ken Caro

Bicton, Liskeard PL14 5RF. Tel: (01579) 362446

Mr and Mrs K.R. Willcock • 5m NE of Liskeard. Turn off A390 at St Ive and follow brown tourist-signs • Open 26th Feb to Sept, daily except Sat, 10am – 6pm • Entrance: £3.50, children £1 ● ● WC & ℗

These four acres, expanded gradually since 1970, are planted in two sections. One consists of a series of small enclosed areas interconnected by well-kept paths and filled with shrubs, conifers, rhododendrons and herbaceous plants, all labelled. Some rare shrub specimens include *Eucryphia* x *nymansensis* and *Lomatia ferruginea*. The second part, by contrast, is open to pleasing views of the surrounding landscape. Beds with a fine collection of hemerocallis are well kept, and there is a large fish pond; a further large lily pond is flanked by island beds. A good visit for plantsmen and gardeners alike.

Ladock House

Ladock, Nr Truro TR2 4PL. Tel: (01726) 882274

Mr G.J. and Lady Mary Holborow • 7m E of Truro on B3275. Entrance by church • Open 30th April and 14th May, 2 – 5pm, and for parties by appt • Entrance: £2.50, children free ● WC & ◁ ℗

The Georgian rectory is set in six and a half acres of garden and woodland, all reclaimed and planted during the past thirty years. Spacious lawns are embellished with shrubs and flower beds, and a spring garden has clearings in wooded areas planted with rhododendrons, azaleas and camellias. On the other side of a park-like field is a woodland walk with wild flowers and another shrub garden.

Lamorran House ★

Upper Castle Road, St Mawes TR2 5BZ. Tel: (01326) 270800

Mr and Mrs R. Dudley-Cooke • Above St Mawes turn right at garage. Signposted at castle. Continue for 0.5m, and house is on left set behind line of pine trees • Open April to Sept, Wed and Fri, 10.30am – 5pm, and at other times by appt • Entrance: £5.50, children free • Other information: Coaches by prior appt only ◑ WC &

This four-acre garden on a south-facing slope above the sea enjoys a most favoured microclimate that supports wonderful collections of plants from the southern hemisphere, sub-tropical plants flourishing in the lower sections of the garden, temperate plants higher up. The latter include rhododendrons, evergreen azaleas and camellias. The garden has a fine collection of palms (over 30 varieties) and tree ferns, including varieties of cyathea. Paths in an intricate pattern zigzag down the steep hillside between enclosed compartments, some designed in Japanese or Italian style, and all with fine views over the sea to St Anthony's Head. There are many imaginative neo-classical statues and columns, and streams and pools permeate the whole slope. The planting is so dense and comprehensive that the paths, though there is often little space between them, are well screened from each other and so appear to magnify the total area. The immaculate upkeep of the garden enhances the overall effect. Nearby, in the grounds of *St Mawes Castle*, is another sub-tropical garden, with good views.

Lanhydrock ★ [Historic Garden Grade II*]

Bodmin PL30 5AD. Tel: (01208) 265950

The National Trust • 2.5m SE of Bodmin off A38 and A30, or off B3268 • House open 18th March to Oct, Tues – Sun and Bank Holiday Mons, 11am – 5.30pm (closes 5pm Oct) • Garden open all year, daily, 10am – 6pm (closes 5pm in Oct) • Entrance: garden and grounds £4.70, children £2.35 (house, garden and grounds £8.40, children £4.20, family £20.95, pre-booked parties of 15 or more £7.40 per adult, £3.70 per child) • Other information: Parking 550 metres from garden but disabled may park adjacent to garden ○ 🍵 ✕ 🛍 <u>WC</u> ♿ ℗ ⛲ 🍺 ⚘

Although the collection of trees was started as early as 1634, the bones of this superb 30-acre garden, in a dramatic woodland and parkland setting, were put in place in 1857 by the first Baron Robartes. The architect of his choice was George Gilbert Scott, who had been brought in to restore and extend the seventeenth-century house, and to redesign the garden. The formal gardens remain largely as he conceived them. Behind the original seventeenth-century gatehouse is a formal lawn with 29 topiary yews in the shape of truncated cones and with rose beds in between, and, beside the house, a Victorian parterre flanked by six similar yews has spring and summer bedding plants. The herbaceous circle is planted for both spring and autumn. A shady stream fringed by water-loving plants runs off the hill behind the house. The Higher Garden, planted with large groups of 'Cornish Red' and other rhododendrons, many camellias, azaleas, magnolias and *Viburnum plicatum*, has a new border planted with perennials. The hillside woods have fine walks beneath mature trees underplanted with large-leaved rhododendrons and bluebells, although for some visitors the heavily gravelled paths introduce a somewhat artificial note.

Marsh Villa Gardens

Marsh Villa, St Andrew's Road, Par PL24 2LU. Tel: (01726) 815920

Mrs Judith Stephens • 5m E of St Austell. Leave A390 at St Blazey traffic lights, then take first left; garden is 700 metres on left • Open April to Oct, Sun – Wed, 10am – 6pm • Entrance: £3, children free ◑ 🍵 🛍 WC ♿ ⊲⊳ ℗

This magical garden has been created since 1986 from a poorly drained meadow. Although it is worth visiting at any time, the herbaceous plantings ensure that it is at its best in summer. A hornbeam avenue forms the main axis of the garden, with sinuous paths of gravel and grass leading off to areas of varying character and interest. The formal herbaceous garden is enclosed by an escallonia hedge; there are many mixed borders and underplanted woodland areas, and a large natural pond over-looked by a capacious summerhouse. Beyond the main garden of three acres lie fourteen more of wild garden and marshland, where native irises, willows and alders thrive.

Morrab Subtropical Garden [Historic Garden Grade II]

Penzance. Tel: (01736) 336621 (Open Spaces Manager)

Penwith District Council • In centre of Penzance. Entrances in St Mary's Terrace, Morrab Road and Coulson's Place • Open all year, daily, dawn – dusk • Entrance: free ○ 🐝 👍 🖾 🍷 ☕

This garden, though only of three acres and in the centre of Penzance, is genuinely sub-tropical and successfully creates its own atmosphere. It is beautifully maintained and planted with, *inter alia*, tree ferns, cabbage palms, myrtles, drimys, camellias and magnolias. It contains a fine bandstand, two ponds and a fountain.

Mount Edgcumbe House and Country Park ★ [Historic Garden Grade I]

Cremyll, Torpoint PL10 1HZ. Tel: (01752) 822236

Cornwall County Council and Plymouth City Council • Access from Plymouth by Cremyll ferry (pedestrian) to park entrance or Torpoint ferry (vehicle) via A374 and B3247. Access from Cornwall via A38 to Trerulefoot roundabout then A374 and B3247 • House open as Earl's Garden • Park and formal gardens open all year, daily, 8am – dusk. Earl's Garden open 2nd April to 28th Sept, Sun – Thurs, 11am – 4.30pm • Entrance: Park and formal gardens free. Earl's Garden and house £4.50, concessions £3.50, children £2.25, family £10, season ticket £7.50, groups £3.50 per person • Other information: Coaches must pre-book ○ 🍽 ✕ 🐝 WC 👍 🖾 🐾 🏛 🍷

The gardens and Grade-I landscaped park created by the Edgcumbe family in the eighteenth century were praised by William Kent and Humphry Repton. There are three main areas of interest. Surrounding the house is the Victorian Earl's Garden, with a fine formal east lawn containing flower beds, statues and urns, and with superb views down the wide hardwood avenue to the formal gardens below. In the landscaped woodland above and beside the house a National Collection of camellias (1000 cultivars), currently semi-mature, is developing attractively. The entrance to the formal gardens, best reached from below, has a fine view of the house. With a background of holm oaks and other mature trees, they include a formal Italian garden with orange trees, less formal English and French gardens, and two commemorating the Edgcumbe family's connection with America and New Zealand. In the centre of these is the 2002 Jubilee Garden. Rhododendrons and azaleas make late spring an attractive time to visit, and a rose garden gives summer interest.

The Old Mill Herbary

Helland Bridge, Bodmin PL30 4QR. Tel: (01208) 841206

Brenda and Robert Whurr • 1m N of Bodmin between A30 and B3266 • Open April to Sept, daily except Wed, 2 – 5pm • Entrance: £4, Children £2.75 • Other information: Coaches strictly by arrangement ○ 🐌 **WC** 🐦 ℘

The five-acre garden on the banks of the gently flowing River Camel, with its fourteenth-century bridge, has intriguing and original features, and something of interest and colour at every season. In April and May wild daffodils, wood anemones and bluebells abound. An open meadow between the river and an old mill-race is planted with individual and interesting specimen trees, while three sizeable islands support mature woodland trees, some 400 years old. The semi-wild garden on the slope above the mill-leat consists of horizontal paths and borders with many rare herbs and other plants. Here and around the buildings, the statuary, based on an unabashed Mediterranean fertility theme, is another unusual feature. A camomile lawn gives off an impressive scent.

Pencarrow ★ [Historic Garden Grade II*]

Washaway, Bodmin PL30 3AG. Tel: (01208) 841369

The Molesworth-St Aubyn family • 4m NW of Bodmin. Signed from A389 Bodmin – Wadebridge road and from B3266 at Washaway • House open 2nd April to 26th Oct, Sun – Thurs, 11am – 4pm • Garden open March to Oct, daily, 9am – 5.30pm • Entrance: £4, children £1 (house and garden £7.50, children £3.50, parties of 20 – 30 £6.50 per person, parties of 31 and over £5.50 per person) • Other information: Craft gallery ◐ 🍴 ✕ 🐌 <u>WC</u> ♿ 🐦 ℘ 🏛 ♿ ✎

The magnificent Palladian mansion lies at the end of an impressive one-mile drive, planted with flowering shrubs, conifers and hardwoods. The setting is superb, with formal gardens on two sides, a rock garden above, and wide and beautiful lawns in front of mature trees; these include an open beech grove. The trees are underplanted with shrubs, including azaleas and huge mounds of 'Cornish Red' and other rhododendrons. There is a fine view over the formal garden with its circular lawn from the main facade of the house. The park and woodland, which extends to 50 acres, contain many rhododendrons and camellias, and a woodland walk leads to a lake covered with water lilies. A new memorial garden is planted to fill the gap between spring and later in the year.

Penjerrick [Historic Garden Grade II]

Budock, Falmouth TR11 5ED. Tel: (01872) 870105

Mrs R. Morin • 3m SW of Falmouth between Budock and Mawnan Smith. Entrance opposite Penmorvah Manor Hotel • Open March to Sept, Wed, Fri and Sun, 1.30 – 4.30pm • Entrance: £2.50, children £1 • Other information: Parking for one coach only, at gate. Plants for sale on charity days only ◐ 🐦

This is a magical 10-acre garden, wild and romantic, and overgrown in parts; most years it is probably at its best from mid- to late-April. The principal horticultural interest is in the area above the road. Although famous as the home of the rhododendron hybrids 'Penjerrick' and 'Barclayi', the Loderi cultivars are also outstanding, as are *R. falconeri, R. augustinii,* and several of the fragrant species. There are also large camellias and tree magnolias, and a giant *Podocarpus salignus.* Below the road recent clearing has opened up a walk beside the ponds with some venerable rhododendrons of considerable interest and beauty, as well as tree ferns, bamboos and gunneras, and a fine view up the verdant stream. The atmosphere here is jungle-like, the going sometimes damp underfoot.

Pine Lodge Garden and Nursery ★

Holmbush, St Austell PL25 3RQ. Tel: (01726) 73500

Mr and Mrs R. Clemo • Just E of St Austell off A390 between Holmbush and turning for Tregrehan. Signposted • Open all year, except 24th to 26th Dec, daily, 10am – 6pm. Guided tours for parties of 20 or more by appt all year • Entrance: £5.50, children £3.50 ◑ 💻 ✕ 🌿 wc & ♨ 🏛 ♟

Assembled in this immaculately maintained 30-acre garden is a wide-ranging collection of over 6000 different plants, all of them labelled. In the formal gardens, many less familiar shrubs from around the world complement the magnolias, camellias, rhododendrons and azaleas surrounding the perfect lawns, adding to the year-round interest from spring bulbs to herbaceous perennials and autumn stalwarts. There are statues, too, and several ponds, including separate ones for koi carp, newts and frogs. Beyond is a tightly planted arboretum with tidily mown grass, flanked on one side by a four-acre pinetum with its collection of 80 different conifers and on the other by parkland leading down to the lake, where an island is home to black swans and many waterfowl. A Japanese garden has recently been added and a bell tower sited in a wildflower meadow. A National Collection of grevilleas is held here, and plants for sale in the extensive nursery include some raised from seed collected on annual plant-hunting expeditions.

Polgwynne

Feock, Truro TR3 6SG. Tel: (01872) 862612

Mrs P. Davey • 5m S of Truro. Take A39, then B3289 to first crossroads. Continue past garage on right following signs to Feock. At T-junction turn left down steep hill; garden is at bottom on right • Open 30th April, 28th May, 25th June, 2 – 5pm, and by appt all year • Entrance: £3 for charity, children free • Other information: Refreshments and plants for sale on open days only ◐ wc & ⬦

Though comparatively small, this garden is superb in every respect: the layout, the rare and interesting plants growing in benign conditions, and the immaculate but not over-tidy upkeep, the whole pervaded by the personalities of the owner and her late husband, who created it over the last forty years. The principal garden, four acres in extent, slopes sharply down towards the sea and is protected by an 2.5-metre wall. Within is a croquet lawn and less formal lawns featuring a stream and ponds, all surrounded by shady walks and borders. The upper part of the protective wall and some of the plants, including what may be the oldest female ginkgo in the country and a superb wisteria, predate the present ownership. Beside the walled garden is a similar area consisting of a formal garden and, below, a Victorian stepped wall and kitchen garden, surrounded by a grass bank with primroses.

St Martin's Manor

St Martin-by-Looe, Looe PL13 1NX. Tel: 01503 262825

Dr Kenneth Olson • 1m NW of Looe off B3253 Plymouth road. Go down small lane almost opposite Looe Garden Centre to St Martin's Church; garden is adjacent • Open by appt only • Entrance: £2.50, children (over 6) £1 (2005 prices) ● WC ⬧

The garden is that rarity, a plantsman's delight that is also beautifully designed and planted, reflecting the creativity of its owner. Its four acres are on a hillside and surround a Georgian rectory. Much of the lower garden, including the pond, is visually enclosed, while the upper part has views of the countryside. The borders are closely planted with rare shrubs and perennials, and ferns and many tender plants are concentrated round the pound. Attractive all through the year, the garden is at its peak from mid-June to August.

St Michael's Mount ★ [Historic Garden Grade II]

Marazion, Penzance TR17 0EF. Tel: (01736) 710507

The National Trust • 0.5m from shore at Marazion, 0.5m S of A394. Access by ferry or across causeway • Castle open April to Oct, Mon – Fri, 10.30am – 5.30pm (last admission 4.45pm), and most weekends from June to Sept for charity, when NT members are asked to pay for admission. From Nov to March essential to telephone for opening arrangements in advance • Garden open April and May, plus weekends as above • Entrance: April and May gardens only £2.50, castle £4.80, family £13, pre-booked parties of 20 or more £4.40 per person) (2005 prices) • Other information: Parking in Marazion ◑ 🍴 ✕ WC 🅿 ♿

It is the private eighteenth-century walled garden belonging to the St Aubyn family that is important here. Rising in terraces from just above sea level at the south-eastern corner of the castle to the foot of its southern wall, such is the microclimate that, despite constant exposure to salt spray and gales, many tender and exotic subtropical plans thrive. Escallonia hedges provide some shelter, and much of the planting is amongst granite boulders. The private garden, laid out on several terraces near the top, is approached along an informal avenue of kniphofia across rough grass. Both here and above are groups of striking plants: *Agave americanum*, aeoniums, succulents, *Euphorbia mellifera* and yuccas. The view down from the higher terraces and the castle walls is outstanding, but the climb is steep and rough; sensible shoes are advised.

Trebah ★★ [Historic Garden Grade II]

Mawnan Smith, Falmouth TR11 5JZ. Tel: (01326) 250448

Trebah Garden Trust • 4m SW of Falmouth. Signed from A39/A394 junction at Treliever Cross roundabout, 500 metres W of Glendurgan Garden • Open all year, daily, 10.30am – 5pm (or dusk if earlier) • Entrance: £5.50, OAPs £5, disabled and children (5–15) £3, RHS and NT members free Nov to Feb • Possible for wheelchairs but paths steep in places • Other information: Powered wheelchairs available ○ 💺 ✕ 🏵 <u>wc</u> ♿ ⬆ 🌳 🎁 ⚲

The most remarkable feature of Trebah – apart from its fascinating history of fame and fortune, decline and fall, and rejuvenation – is the spectacular view over the massive clumps of rhododendrons, tree ferns and bamboos and into the ravine, which runs between tall trees down to the Helford River. The garden is about 25 acres in all and contains many beautiful mature trees and shrubs. April is the winning month by a short head, but there is colour and interest at every season. An extensive collection of sub-tropical Mediterranean plants, a stream and some carp ponds occupy the upper reaches, while in the lower parts is a lake, a vast plantation of gunnera, and acres of blue and white hydrangeas giving summer colour. Superbly maintained throughout, but in no way over-manicured.

Tregrehan ★ [Historic Garden Grade II*]
Par PL24 2SJ. Tel: (01726) 814389

The Carlyon Estate/Mr T. Hudson • 2m E of St Austell, on A390 Lostwithiel – St Austell road. Entrance opposite Britannia Inn 1m W of St Blazey • Open mid-March to mid-June, Wed – Sun and Bank Holiday Mons, 10.30am – 5pm (closed 16th April); mid-June to Aug, Wed, 2 – 5pm • Entrance: £4, children free. Guided tours for groups by prior arrangement; holiday cottages available ◐ 💺 🏵 <u>wc</u> ♿ 🌳

A wonderful spring garden, much restored since 1989 by the new owner. Its 20 acres are mainly planted woodlands, but there is a nineteenth-century walled garden which contains a magnificent, newly restored Victorian glasshouse range, an arch of *Acer palmatum* and interesting spring- and summer-flowering climbers. A formal yew walk, dark in itself, effectively frames the upper gardens. The woodland dell is furnished with huge and interesting conifers and native hardwoods. The near, steep side features very fine rhododendrons and camellias, whilst in the newly cleared areas beside the stream at the bottom and on the opposite bank – beautifully light on a sunny day – are young and rare shrubs and trees from the southern hemisphere. A bluebell walk is magical in spring. The views into the dell are magnificent, ranking with the best in any Cornish garden.

Trelissick ★ [Historic Garden Grade II*]
Feock, Truro TR3 6QL. Tel: (01872) 862090

The National Trust • 4m S of Truro on B3289 above west end of King Harry Ferry (boat services from Falmouth, Truro and St Mawes, April to Sept) • Open 11th Feb to Oct, daily, 10.30am – 5.30pm (or dusk if earlier); telephone for winter opening times • Entrance: £5.50, children £2.75, family £13.75, one adult family £8.75, pre-booked parties £4.60 per person. Parking charge £3 (refundable) • Other information: Wheelchairs and batricar available. Theatrical events during season plus autumn and winter events programme ◐ 💺 ✕ 🏵 <u>wc</u> ♿ 🌳 🍴

Trelissick ranks among the most beautiful of Cornish spring gardens, and also has many summer-flowering shrubs. It covers 27 acres, set in the middle of 500 acres of park and farm land, and offers panoramic views down Carrick Roads to the open sea. It is young compared to many similar gardens, and the plantings and layout date only from 1937. It has fine open lawns, particularly in the area known as the Carcaddon, and is known both for its collection of camellias, magnolias and rhodo-dendrons in the spring, and for its large collection of hydrangeas and other tender and exotic plants. The woodland walks, surrounded by shrubs, have attractive views across the water below.

Trengwainton Garden ★ [Historic Garden Grade II*]

Madron, Penzance TR20 8RZ.Tel: (01736) 363148

The National Trust • 2m NW of Penzance on B3312, 0.5m N of A3071 • Open 13th Feb to 30th Oct, Sun – Thurs (but open Good Friday), 10am – 5.30pm (closes 5pm Feb, March and Oct) • Entrance: £4.50, children £2.20, family £11, single-adult family £6.70, pre-booked parties £3.80 per person (2005 prices) ➊ 💭 ✕ 🍱 <u>WC</u> ⟐ ⟪⟫ ⌗ 🏛 💡 ⚲

The garden enjoys a particularly benign climate, and the drive, broad and sweeping uphill, is unsurpassed for its grandeur and planting. Near the entrance an old walled garden is divided into five primary bays containing huge and impressive magnolias as well as tender and exotic shrubs and plants of the greatest interest. Beyond this on the right a shrub garden with many camellias under mature hardwoods leads to open lawns studded with ornamental trees and divided by shrub beds. On the left of the drive, beyond a narrow lawn, is a small stream fringed colourfully with astilbes, primulas, arisaemas, lilies and lysichitums. Visitors may be disappointed to find that the upper reaches of the garden are private property; however, there is fine compensation as the garden spreads out to the left across the stream with magnificent rhododendrons and azaleas surrounding the ponds and lawn.

Tresco Abbey ★★ [Historic Garden Grade I]

Tresco, Isles of Scilly TR24 0PU.
Tel: (01720) 424105 (Garden Curator: Mike Nelhams)

Mr R.A. Dorrien-Smith • On island of Tresco. Travel by helicopter from Penzance heliport to Tresco heliport (reservations (01736) 363871 and (01720) 422970) or from St Mary's by launch • Open all year, daily, 10am – 4pm • Entrance: £8.50, children free, weekly tickets (7 days) £15 • Other information: Possible for wheelchairs but some paths very steep. Wheelchairs available at gate. New garden visitor centre ○ 💭 ✕ 🍱 WC ⟐ ⟪⟫ ⌗ 🏛 💡 ⚲

Tresco, located in the Scilly Isles 28 miles off Land's End and in the full Gulf Stream, is a unique sub-tropical garden of the very highest quality. Within a formal framework of paths, steps, the ruined walls of the old abbey and high hedges is a lush profusion of flourishing exotic plants that soften the outlines and provide striking colour and contrasting shapes and textures. Set on a south-sloping hillside with horizontal walks, the gardens are visually quite self-contained. From the top terrace views slant downwards to the sea, revealing the wonderful plantings below, especially those in the more open areas such as the pond, where four Mediterranean cypresses form strong verticals. Myrtles notably various met-rosideros, are set amongst the background trees. Aeoniums, cacti, puyas, proteas and huge agaves (some with leaves 46 cms wide) stand out, and callistemons, banksias, agapanthus, *Geranium maderenese* play a major part. Just five gardeners plus some student help maintain the 17 acres. The gardens are probably at their peak from March to the autumn, and at their most colourful from late April to the end of June.

Trevarno Estate and Gardens and The National Museum of Gardening ★

Trevarno Manor, Helston TR13 0RU. Tel: (01326) 574274

Mr M. Sagin and Mr N. Helsby • 3m NW of Helston off A394 or B3302 • Open all year, daily except 25th, 26th Dec, 10.30am – 5pm • Entrance: £5.15, concessions £4.45, children (5 – 14) £1.95 (garden and museum of gardening), under 5 free ○ 🍴 🏠 <u>WC</u> ♿ 🌱 🐶 🏛 🍽 ⚲

Great and continuing restoration has taken place on the estate and in the gardens, which combine formal and less formal elements. The lawn, with a splendid avenue of Japanese cherries to one side, leads to the formal Italian garden; from here a woodland walk descends to the lake, which sports a Victorian boathouse and a cascade at its top end and a fine rhododendron rockery beyond. Above this is the pinetum underplanted with shrubs, and the Georgian walled gardens and glasshouses. With rhododendrons, Japanese cherries, camellias and bluebells in the woodlands, it is probably at its best in the spring. The National Museum of Gardening is located near the entrance, and there are interesting craft workshops nearby.

Trewidden ★

Chyandour, Penzance TR18 3LW. Tel: (01736) 363021

Bolitho Estates • 2m W of Penzance on A30 • Open 15th Feb to 1st Oct, Wed – Sun and Bank Holiday Mons, 10.30am – 4.30pm • Entrance: £4, under 16 free 🍴 🍴 🏠 <u>WC</u> ♿ 🌱 🐶

Until 2002 this wonderful sub-tropical spring garden, created by the Bolitho family in the nineteenth century, was only rarely open to the public; now, after recent restoration after storm damage and pruning of over-mature camellias, it is essential visiting for serious gardeners. It covers 12 acres, including the separate South Garden, and consists mostly of informal woodland paths, some leading to an attractive pond with a Japanese lantern and a whale-tail sculpture. Although chiefly renowned for its camellias, of which there are over 300 varieties from India, China and other parts of the Far East, equally fine are the early-flowering magnolias, which shine forth above the other shrubs throughout. These include huge specimens of *M.* x *veitchii* 'Peter Veitch' and *M. hypoleuca (obovata)*, as well as outstanding examples of *M.* 'Trewidden Belle', *M. sargentiana* and varieties of *M. campbellii*. There is also a magnificent stand of tree ferns set in the remains of an early open-cast tin mine. The south-facing walled garden is under restoration, with an emphasis on summer-flowering plants and artefacts from the tin industry.

Trewithen ★★ [Historic Garden Grade II*]

Grampound Road, Truro TR2 4DD. Tel: (01726) 883647

Mr and Mrs A.M.J. Galsworthy • On A390 between Truro and St Austell • House open April to July, Mon and Tues, 2 – 4pm • Gardens open Feb to Sept, Mon – Sat, 10am – 4.30pm (also Suns in Feb and May) • Entrance: £4.75, parties of 20 or more £4.25 per person (house and garden £8) ◑ ⬛ 🍴 <u>WC</u> ও ⬥ ৺ 🏛 ৎ

Trewithen is one of the greatest of all gardens. It covers 30 acres, mainly of woodland, and is known internationally for its great collections, often formed from the wild, of magnolias, camellias and rhododendrons, as well as of many other rare trees and shrubs. The most striking feature is the long lawn in front of the 1730s' house, flanked by sinuous borders of mature rhododendrons, magnolias, acers and other shrubs and ornamental trees, and backed by mature hardwoods. The enormous size of many of the rhododendrons and magnolias is particularly exciting. To the west the shrub beds and paths are sheltered by beech and other woodland trees. To the south-west is the main camellia collection, with the specimens noticeable for their huge flowers, and many other wonderful shrubs. Three viewing platforms have been erected to give a new perspective of the camellias from canopy level. A deep sunken garden contains tree ferns as well as acers and camellias, and a newly commissioned *camera obscura* has been sited in one of the glades. The walled garden (not always open) is contemporary with the house and is laid out as a herb and rose garden with herbaceous borders; it has a fish pond, an old summerhouse and a wisteria-clad pergola. Many hybrid rhododendrons and camellias originated at Trewithen, some of them named by George Johnstone, the garden's creator, after members of his family. The inspiration for Tom Leaper's magnolia fountain derived from the great specimens to be found here.

Trewoofe House

Lamorna, Penzance TR19 6PA. Tel: (01736) 810269

Mr and Mrs H.M. Pigott • 6m SW of Penzance. Take B3315 from Penzance via Newlyn towards Lamorna. At top of hill take sharp right turn signed to Trewoofe • Open May, Wed; June, Wed and Sun; July, Sun; all 2 – 5pm. Also open by appt May to Sept. Coaches and groups must pre-book • Entrance: £2.50, children under 16 free ◐ WC ও ৺

This two-acre garden, situated at the head of the Lamorna valley, is planted informally with shrub and herbaceous beds that give colour all year round. There are several interesting mature trees. An ancient mill leat runs through it, enabling a bog garden to be developed with a wide range of moisture-loving plants, including many iris species and varieties. The garden is on two levels, linked by two bridges over the leat and using local granite. There is a small fruit garden with cordon- and espalier-trained trees, and a conservatory with semi-tender climbers.

CUMBRIA & ISLE OF MAN

Two-starred gardens are marked on the map with a black square.

Acorn Bank Garden and Watermill

Temple Sowerby, Penrith CA10 1SP. Tel: (01768) 361893

The National Trust • 6m E of Penrith off A66 N of Temple Sowerby • Woodland walk open 4th to 19th March, Sat and Sun, 11am – 4pm, for snowdrops. Garden, Woodland walk and watermill open 25th March to 29th Oct, Wed – Sun and Bank Holiday Mons, 10am – 5pm • Entrance: £3, children £1.50, family £7.50, pre-booked parties £2.50 per person ● ● ✕ ● WC & ♥ ♫ ♣ ♥

The 'acorn bank' is the ancient oakwood sloping down to the Crowdundle Beck behind the house. In spring it is a carpet of daffodils and narcissi in many varieties planted profusely in the 1930s, and there are some 60,000 Lent lilies. The walled gardens are then also a mass of blossom from the old varieties of apple, medlar, pear and quince, carpeted with wild tulips, anemones and narcissi. The orchard trees include later-blossoming apple varieties. Along the three sheltering walls are herbaceous and shrub borders, backed by good clematis and other climbers. A bed of species roses flanks the steps to a picturesque sunken garden, with a pond and alpine terraces. Through a gateway lies a splendid walled herb garden – a well-tended collection of some 250 medicinal and culinary herbs, now being redesigned and replanted. For those interested in alpines, it is worth taking the A686 over the spectacular Hartside fell to *Hartside Nursery Garden* about 14 miles away near Alston. [Open mid-March to Oct, Mon – Fri, 9.30am – 4.30pm (12.30 – 4pm weekends and Bank Holiday Mondays) and otherwise by appointment – telephone (01434) 381372.]

Ballalheannagh ★

Glen Roy, Lonan, Isle of Man IM4 7QB. Tel: (01624) 861875

Mrs Maureen Dadd • On E of island in Glen Roy, 2m inland from Laxey • Open April to Sept, daily except Wed, 10am – 4.30pm, and at other times by appt • Entrance: £2.50, children free ○ ♫

Take a steep-sided valley, a ladder, some seedlings of exotic rhododendrons and forget all about digging holes to accommodate the roots. Just stick them into crevices among the mosses and ferns and wait a few years, never giving up. Outcome – paradise for plant-lovers. You expect to find a garden like Ballalheannagh in Cornwall or Kerry – but this is the middle of the Isle of Man. No visitor with an interest in gardening who is marooned on the island need fear boredom, for this is a botanical garden, not in name, but surely in content. Steep winding paths cling to the valley sides, and crystal water cascades below, carrying the bells of pieris to the Irish Sea. The lower portion contains lofty rhododendrons, while the upper parts of the valley have newer plantings that will certainly delight in years to come. Here are eucalyptus, drimys, epacris, epigaeas, megacarpaeas and betulas, and a host of others too, and the native mosses and ferns are a wonderful sight. The garden has been extended to more than 20 acres, with four miles of gravel walks and new oriental features, plus a millennium window.

Brantwood

Coniston LA21 8AD. Tel: (01539) 441396

Brantwood Trust • On E side of Coniston Water off B5285, signposted. Coniston Launch provides hourly service to Brantwood and other points around lake. Steam yacht 'Gondola' sails regularly from Coniston Pier • House open as garden • Garden open 13th March to 12th Nov, daily, 11am – 6pm; winter season Wed – Sun, 11am – 4.30pm, but closed 25th and 26th Dec • Entrance: £3.75 (house and garden £5.50, students £4, children under 16 £1) ○ ➋ ✕ ▧ <u>WC</u> ⬦ ℘ ⛪ ▮ ⚭

A superb site with wonderful views, atmosphere and history. The rocky hillside behind the house is threaded with a wandering network of paths created by John Ruskin to delight the eye and please the mind. A succession of eight small, individual gardens threads the landscape, exploring the many themes that fascinated the artist and visionary social reformer, and this 'living laboratory' of ideas is being revived by Sally Beamish and her small team. Ruskin's own Professor's Garden, the woodland pond and harbour walk are maturing beautifully. An extensive collection of British native ferns surrounds an ice-house and several waterfalls. There is a British herb garden, and the allegorical Zig-zaggy depicting the levels of Purgatory found in Dante's *Divine Comedy* is now complete. The High Walk, actually a Victorian viewing platform, encourages contemplation of the magnificent Lakeland scenery beyond the garden. The high points of the year here are spring and autumn.

Brockhole ★ [Historic Garden Grade II]

Lake District Visitor Centre, Windermere LA23 1LJ. Tel: (01539) 446601

Lake District National Park Authority • 1.5m N of Windermere on A591 • Grounds and gardens open all year, daily, 10am – dusk • Entrance: parking fee only; minibuses and coaches free if pre-booked • Other information: Centre open with slide theatre and exhibition. Cruises from jetty ○ ➋ ✕ ▧ <u>WC</u> & ⬦ ℘ ⛪ ▮ ⚭

A garden blessed with the Lakeland combination of western aspect and water to the hills beyond, in this case notably the Langdale Pikes. To frame this view Thomas Mawson worked closely (*c.*1900) with his architect colleague Dan Gibson. The ornamental terraces drop through old-fashioned rose beds, herbaceous borders and shrubbery to a wildflower meadow flanked by mature woodland. The original kitchen and herb garden has been restored; other special features are herbaceous plants, tender shrubs and rarities and the constantly changing colour from spring rhododendrons and azaleas through to late Chilean hollies, maples and eucryphias. In Troutbeck, between Windermere and Ambleside, is *High Cross Lodge*, a small fell-side garden planted with rhododendrons, foliage and tender plants. [Open several times for NGS and by appointment – write to Mr and Mrs Sydney Orchant, High Cross Lodge, Bridge Lane, Troutbeck LA23 1AA.]

Copt Howe

Chapel Stile, Great Langdale, Ambleside LA22 9JR.
Tel: (01539) 437685 (Infoline)

*Professor R.N. Haszeldine • 3m W of Ambleside on B5343 • Open 29th, 31st March;
7th, 14th to 17th, 21st, 28th to 30th April; 1st, 5th, 10th, 17th, 24th, 26th to 29th
May; 2nd, 7th, 9th, 14th, 16th, 17th, 21st, 28th and 29th June; 3rd, 5th, 12th and
14th July; all 12 noon – 5pm; plus many days mid-April to Sept (telephone for recorded
weekly information). Private visits and parties by appt • Entrance: £3, children free*
❶ 🍴 WC ♿ ⬥ ♨ ♘

This plantsman's fellside woodland two-acre garden, with magnificent views of the
Langdale Pikes and interesting geological features, has an exceptionally wide range
of rare acid-loving plants from many mountainous countries, including expedition
plants from the Himalayas, China, Tibet, Japan, Bhutan, Tasmania, New Zealand and
North and South America. The extensive collections includes acers, camellias, azaleas, quercus, fagus, large and dwarf conifers, pieris, kalmias, tilias, bamboos, cercis and
cercidiphyllums; among herbaceous plants are many bulbous species with orchids
and species lilies, *Tropaeolum tuberosum, T. tricolor* and *T. speciosum*. The varied plantings extend to alpine troughs, streams and woodland with mountain primulas,
species tulips, anemones, orchids, nomocharis, trilliums, hepaticas, hellebores,
cardiocrinums, *Myosotidium hortensia* and many species of meconopsis, including
M. punicea. Dramatic spring, early summer and autumn colours.

Dalemain Historic House and Gardens ★ [Historic Garden Grade II*]

Dalemain Estate Office, Penrith CA11 0HB. Tel: (01768) 486450

*Mr and Mrs R.B. Hasell-McCosh • On A592 3m W of Penrith on Ullswater road
• House open as garden but 11am – 4pm • Garden open 26th March to 29th Oct,
Sun – Thurs, 10.30am – 5pm; Nov to March, Mon – Thurs, 10am – 2pm
• Entrance: £3.50, children free (house and garden £5.50, children (6–16) £3.50,
family £14.50 (2005 prices). Special prices for pre-booked parties) • Other information: Wheelchair and electric scooter available by prior arrangement. Dogs outside
garden only, on lead* ❶ 🍽 ✕ 🍴 WC ♿ ♨ 🏛 ♘

Dalemain has evolved in the most natural way from a twelfth-century pele tower
with its kitchen garden and herbs. The Tudor-walled knot garden remains, as do the
Stuart terrace (1680s) and the walled orchard where apple trees like 'Nonsuch' and
'Keswick Codling', planted in 1728, still bear fruit. The gardens were re-established
by the late Mrs Sylvia McCosh during the 1960s and '70s with shrubs, a collection
of over 100 old-fashioned roses, and other rarities, together with richly planted
herbaceous borders along the terraces and around the orchard; maintained and
developed by her daughter-in-law, Mrs Jane Hasell-McCosh, they continue to
improve. The wild garden on the lower ground features an outstanding display of
Himalayan blue poppies in early summer and a walk past the Tudor gazebo into
woods overlooking the Dacre Beck. Some thoughtful planting in the woodland
augurs well for the future. A plantsman's garden with an artist's appreciation of form,
texture and colour.

Graythwaite Hall ★

Ulverston, Graythwaite LA12 8BA. Tel: (01539) 531248

Graythwaite Estate • 4m N of Newby Bridge on W side of Lake Windermere • Open April to June, daily, 10am – 6pm • Entrance: £2, children free ◑ **WC** ♿ ⬧

Essentially a spring garden landscaped by the late Victorian Thomas Mawson in partnership with Dan Gibson in a beautiful parkland and woodland setting. Azaleas and rhododendrons yield to cultivars of late spring-flowering shrubs, and there is a formal terraced rose garden. The finely wrought sundials and gate by Gibson, the Dutch garden and the stream and pond all add charm to this serene garden. For topiary admirers, Mawson employed interesting effects to contrast with his more billowy plantings: notable are the battlemented yew hedge and some yew globes with golden yew in the top half and green in the bottom. While in Hawkshead, those interested by sculpture in nature should visit the *Grizedale Sculpture Trail*, organised by the Forestry Commission (Tel: (01229) 860373). The first piece was placed there in 1977 and there are now about 90 sculptures.

Halecat

Witherslack, Grange–over–Sands LA11 6RU.
Tel: (01539) 552536 (Contact: Mrs K. Willard)

Mrs M. Stanley • 14m SW of Kendal, off A590. Signposted • Garden open all year, daily, 9am – 4.30pm (opens 12.30pm Sun) • Entrance: free • Other information: Plants, especially hydrangeas, for sale in adjoining nursery ○ 🐌 **WC** ♿ ⬧ ⬧ ⬧ ⬧

These two acres are the front garden of the mid-nineteenth-century house which stands at the head of a small valley with distant views of Arnside Knott and the Forest of Bowland. Mrs Stanley created this pleasing, personal garden as a series of terraces and squares, and the limestone quarried from the borders has been used to build the retaining walls and the perimeter wall separating the garden from the surrounding woodland. An azalea bed has been made on the bottom terrace by removing rock and filling the beds with peat from a nearby bog. The mixed borders are well maintained and filled with many shrubs, clematis, herbaceous plants, and shrub and climbing roses. There is also a wildflower meadow and a damson orchard. Look out for unusual wooden animals, especially the bear. The gazebo with stained glass quarries was designed by the architect Francis Johnson.

High Cleabarrow

Windermere LA23 3ND. Tel: (01539) 442808

Mr and Mrs R.T. Brown • 3m SE of Windermere off B5284 (opposite Windermere Golf Course) • Open for NGS and for parties by appt, April to Oct • Entrance: £3, children under 12 free • Other information: Teas by prior arrangement ◑ 🅿 **WC** ♿ ⬧

A two-acre plantswoman's garden of restful charm and year-long interest, created by the owners since 1990 and continually expanding and evolving. Set over 200 metres above sea level in a shallow bowl sloping gently to a pond with waterside planting, a wealth of shrubs and hardy perennials, many of them unusual and rare,

are to be found in island beds and in a wide border running the length of the garden. Large collections of hellebores, hardy geraniums, roses, clematis, hostas, hydrangeas, rhododendrons and azaleas give interest at all times. A knot garden filled with old-fashioned roses underplanted with violas, geraniums and campanulas is a fragrant summer secret concealed behind a beech hedge. At the rim the garden is sheltered by woodland, but also includes a large rocky outcrop 24 metres high. Bracken and brambles have been cleared, pathways struck, a glade of azaleas planted, terracing furnished with dwarf rhododendrons and more azaleas, a raised bed planted with alpines and a cobble bed created for succulents and grasses. For the owners the challenges go on and on, but visitors can relax in the summerhouse, from which fine views of the surrounding countryside open up.

Holehird ★

Patterdale Road, Windermere LA23 1NP. Tel: (01539) 446008

Lakeland Horticultural Society • 1m N of Windermere on A592 Patterdale road • Open all year, daily, sunrise – sunset. Garden tours available April to Oct, 11am – 5pm • Entrance: by donation (minimum £2 appreciated) • Other information: Annual plant sale 7th May in local school ○ WC ᗊ

Managed by a charity dedicated to promoting and developing the science, practice and art of horticulture with special reference to the conditions in Lakeland, this garden is maintained to an exceptionally high standard, largely by its members, who are all volunteers. It lies on a splendid hillside site alongside the house with a natural water course and rock banks looking over Windermere to the Langdale Pikes. The Society has 10 acres of attractive gardens and trial areas. Much of the earlier planting has been preserved, including many fine specimen trees, together with acid-loving plants that do well in the free-draining soil. Highlights are the summer-autumn heathers, winter and spring-flowering shrubs, alpines and National Collections of astilbes, hydrangeas and polystichum ferns. The walled garden, now accessible for wheelchairs, has fine herbaceous borders, herbs and climbers. The site has expanded to encompass the lower Victorian terrace of the estate and includes original Victorian features, such as the restored greenhouses. The views of the fells from the garden are breathtaking.

Holker Hall ★★ [Historic Garden Grade II]

Cark-in-Cartmel, Grange-over-Sands LA11 7PL. Tel: (01539) 558328

Lord and Lady Cavendish • 4.5m W of Grange-over-Sands, 4m S of Haverthwaite on B5278 • House open as garden, but 11am – 4pm • Garden open 26th March to 29th Oct, daily except Sat, 10.30am – 5pm (last admission 4.30pm) • Entrance: wide variety of entrance prices depending on visitor requirements – telephone or contact website at back of Guide for details • Other information: Holker Garden Festival 2nd to 4th June ◑ ⏻ ✕ ▓ WC ᗊ ⏏ ℘ ⛪ ⛾ ✑

Set in 125 acres of parkland, the award-winning 25 acres of woodland walks and formal gardens at Holker (pronounced Hooker) have been constantly developed by the family ever since Lord George Cavendish established his 'contrived natural landscape' over 200 years ago. The woods now contain many rare and beautiful specimens, most of them tagged and chronicled in the excellent guide to the garden walks. A National Collection of styracaceae is maintained here. Other features are the impressive cascade, evocative of the Villa d'Este, and a beautifully contrived transformation of the croquet lawn into summer gardens. This combination of formal beds and inventive planting makes a wonderful Italianate-cum-English garden that typifies the spirit of the place. There is also a sunken garden, which was formerly the rose garden and contains many sub-tropical plants. Notable too are the Elliptical Garden, the rhododendron and azalea walk and the new labyrinth in the wildflower meadow. Designed in part to link the formal gardens with the parkland and wider landscape, it is based on a Hindu temple motif allied to a contemporary version of a Cumbrian stone circle.

Holme Cragg

Blea Cragg Bridge, Witherslack, Grange-over-Sands LA11 6RZ.
Tel: (01539) 552366

Mr J. Watson • 14m SW of Kendal, 3m N of Grange-over-Sands, off A590. From A590, follow signs to Witherslack. Past telephone kiosk in Witherslack, turn first left, first left again and follow signs to Newton (past Halecat) for 1.25m over small bridge to third gate on left • Open all year, daily • Entrance: by donation • Other information: Coaches must pre-book ○ ♿

This is an amateur's and a plantsman's garden which has made magnificent use of natural features of the site. Every rocky outcrop is clothed in alpines, sedums, sempervivums and saxifrages. Azaleas and rhododendrons are an important feature, as are the irises and candelabra primulas around the pond. The shaded areas are filled with the blue of the Himalayan meconopsis, a grass bank is covered with double and single Welsh poppies in colours ranging from deep orange to pale yellow, and there is an interesting natural wildflower area. Rhododendrons are followed by shrub roses; later the foliage of acers starts to flame.

Hutton-in-the-Forest [Historic Garden Grade II]

Penrith CA11 9TH. Tel: (01768) 484449

Lord and Lady Inglewood • 6m NW of Penrith on B5305 (M6 junction 41) • House open 12th April to 1st Oct, Wed, Thurs, Sun and Bank Holiday Mons, 12.30 – 4pm • Garden open March to Oct, daily except Sat, 11am – 5pm. Private parties by arrangement from April • Entrance: £3.50, children £1 (house and garden £5.50, children (7–16) £3.50, family ticket £15) • Other information: Electric scooter available for disabled (donation requested). Light lunches and teas when house open, other meals on request ● 🍴 🛍 wc ♿ ♿ 🏬 🎁 ✿

This garden, a compelling setting for the appealing house, which ranges across the centuries from a thirteenth-century pele tower to Salvin's handsome alterations, is itself a mixture of features from the seventeenth to the twentieth centuries. It has great visual appeal, with a magnificent view from the seventeenth-century terraces embellished with Victorian topiary. The beautiful walled garden, dating from the 1730s, is divided into compartments and has excellent herbaceous borders, trained fruit trees and roses. The backdrop of the house, the surrounding yew hedges and compartments and well-filled herbaceous borders combine to make a dramatic composition. Some of the mature woodland trees were planted in the early eighteenth century. Other features include a seventeenth-century dovecot and an eighteenth-century lake.

Levens Hall ★★ [Historic Garden Grade I]

Kendal LA8 0PD. Tel: (01539) 560321

Mr C.H. Bagot • 5m S of Kendal on A6 (M6 junction 36) • House open as garden, but 12 noon – 5pm • Garden open April to mid-Oct, Sun – Thurs, 10am – 5pm • Entrance: £5.90, children £2.70, family £17 (house and garden £8, children £3.80, family £22). Party rates available (2005 prices) ◑ ♉ ✕ 🍴 **WC** ♿ ⚘ 🛍 ♧

James II's gardener, Guillaume Beaumont, designed this famous topiary garden in 1694; it is one of very few to retain its original trees and design. The impeccably clipped yews and box hedges are set off by colourful spring and summer bedding and borders, and the primroses may be the start of a permanent collection. To celebrate the tercentenary of the garden in 1994 a new area, the Fountain Garden, was created with lime avenues meeting at the pool. Indeed there is much to see in addition to the topiary. Massive walls of beech hedge open to vistas over parkland, and one avenue leads to the earliest English ha-ha. There is a picturesque herb garden behind the house. The record of only 10 head gardeners in 300 years, and the affectionate care by the Bagot family, account for the rare harmony of this exceptional garden, which clearly still has a stylish hand at the helm. Further developments include the installation of two pairs of clematis gates, a green-oak ticket booth disguised as a garden pavilion, and a pair of gates with hearts as handles – celebrating the old legend that a gambler acquired the property in the seventeenth century by turning over the ace of hearts.

Muncaster Castle [Historic Garden Grade II*]

Ravenglass CA18 1RQ. Tel: (01229) 717614

Mr and Mrs Gordon-Duff-Pennington • 15m S of Whitehaven on A595 • Castle open 19th Feb to 5th Nov, daily except Sat, 12 noon – 5pm, or dusk if earlier • Gardens, owl centre and meadow vole maze open Feb to Dec, daily, 10.30am – 6pm (or dusk if earlier) • Entrance: £6.50, children (5-16) £4.50 (under 5 free), family £20, parties of 12 or more £6, children £3.50 per person. Inclusive price for all attractions £9, children £6, family £25, parties of 12 or more £7.50, children £4.50 per person • Other information: Wheelchairs available for pre-booking ○ ♉ ✕ 🍴 **WC** ♿ ⬦ 🛍 B&B

The castle is set against the splendid backdrop of Scafell and the hills, with a remarkable panoramic view from the terrace, described by Ruskin as the 'Gateway to Paradise'. The acid soil and the Gulf Stream warmth provide ideal conditions for one of the most extensive collections of species rhododendrons in Europe, substantially from plant-hunting expeditions to Nepal in the 1920s (Kingdon Ward, Ludlow and Sherriff). There are fine azaleas, camellias, magnolias, hydrangeas and maples, plus many unusual trees. The Sino-Himalayan Walk, one part of a network of over six miles of paths, gives a real taste of the Orient.

Rydal Mount Gardens [Historic Garden Grade II]

Ambleside LA22 9LU. Tel: (01539) 433002

Rydal Mount Trust • 1m N of Ambleside on A591 • House open • Gardens open March to Oct, daily, 9.30am – 5pm; Nov to Feb, daily except Tues, 10am – 4pm • Entrance: £2 (house and garden £4.50, OAPs £3.75, students £3.50, children (5–15) £1.50, parties of 10 or more pre-booked £3.50 per person, non-booked £3.75 per person. Reciprocal discounts with Dove Cottage and Wordsworth's House) • Other information: Limited parking with awkward entry/exit ○ 🕭 WC ☞ ♿ ⚲

The carefully maintained grounds of Wordsworth's house still follow the lines of his own plan, and it is easy to imagine the poet wandering along the upper terrace walk ('the sloping terrace') and down through winding, shaded paths to the lawns, or across a terrace to the ancient mound with its distant glimpse of Windermere. Apart from its poetic association the garden is also a visual delight, with good herbaceous borders, shrubs and unusual trees (e.g. the fern-leaf beech). Dora's Terrace is named after the poet's daughter, and a bank of daffodils dances in nearby Dora's Field. Wordsworth's other house at Cockermouth has a pleasant town garden, but it is only worth it if the house, too, is to be visited.

Sizergh Castle ★ [Historic Garden Grade II]

Kendal LA8 8AE. Tel: (01539) 560951

The National Trust • 3.5m S of Kendal on A590 (M6 junction 36) • Castle and garden open 2nd April to 29th Oct, 12 noon – 5pm (castle open 1pm) • Entrance: £4, children £2 (castle and garden £6.20, children £3.10, family £15.50, parties of 15 or more £5.20 per person) • Other information: Manual wheelchair and powered buggies available. Guided walks available ➊ 🍴 🕭 WC ♿ ☞ ⚲ ♀

An exceptionally varied garden with colour from early spring daffodils to summer borders and climbers, culminating in glorious autumn tints – the Japanese maples all fiery red is a memorable sight. To the east of the castle's fourteenth-century tower is a remarkable rock garden, built in 1926 by a local Ambleside firm, T.R. Hayes & Sons, in the form of a bowl of rough limestone terraces within a dell fed by the pond above. The 16-acre garden around the tower includes the restored Dutch garden with its avenue of spring-flowering 'Shirotae' cherries. There are also wildflower banks with native limestone flora, including species orchids, and an orchard. What stays in the memory is the rolling parkland and beyond, the looming Howgill hills.

Stagshaw

Ambleside LA22 0HE. Tel: (01539) 446027

The National Trust • 0.5m S of Ambleside on A591 • Open April to June, daily, 10am – 6.30pm, July to Oct by appt (s.a.e. to NT Property Office, St Catherine's, Patterdale Road, Windermere LA23 1NH) • Entrance: £2, children free • Other information: Limited parking ☾

Set on a west-facing hillside of oak trees with spendid views looking out over the head of Lake Windemere is a little gem of a garden, beautifully planted and maintained. Azaleas and rhododendrons have been carefully blended among camellias, magnolias and other fine shrubs with unusual underplanting, and another area is massed with pink erythroniums. Rather difficult of access, with the volume of traffic on A591 making the exit especially dangerous, but worth the effort.

Yewbarrow House

Hampsfell Road, Grange-over-Sands LA11 6BE. Tel: (01539) 532469

Jonathan Denby • 15m SW of Kendal off A590. Take B5277 to Grange-over-Sands, continue up main street past railway station to mini roundabout and turn right. At crossroads turn right, then left up Hampsfell Road. Road narrows and goes into woodland; pass cottage on left, take left fork at footpath signed to Yewbarrow Wood, then left again up narrow unmade road to entrance gates • Open 4th June, 2nd July, 6th Aug, 3rd Sept, 11am – 4pm, and by appt • Entrance: £3 • Other information: Parking very limited. Unsuitable for coaches ● 🏞 WC ⊲⊳ ℘ ℺*

This interesting two-acre fellside garden with a breathtaking view over Morecambe Bay has been redesigned by the owner with help from Christopher Holliday. It is on the site of a Victorian garden which had mostly, except for the kitchen garden, reverted to woodland; the mild west-coast climate, shelter from the prevailing wind by boundary trees, well-drained soil and an almost frost-free micro-climate enable exotica from all over the world to flower and survive. There are several individual gardens, divided by attractive limestone walls: Mediterranean and gravel gardens, ferns in woodland, a Japanese garden with a swimming pool disguised as a hot spring pool and a tea house, flower terraces and a rhododendron area. There are olive trees bearing flowers and some ripe fruit, phormiums, palms, yuccas, *Magnolia grandiflora*, *Paulownia tomentosa*, cannas and much more. The owner's aim is to have something in flower throughout the year alongside ever-green plants providing colour and structure. This is surely a Lakeland garden with a difference.

SYMBOLS

[NEW] entries new for 2006; ○ open all year; ◔ open most of year; ◑ open during main season; ◕ open rarely and/or by appt; ☕ teas/light refreshments; ✕ meals; 🏞 picnics permitted; WC toilet facilities; <u>WC</u> toilet facilities, inc. disabled; ♿ partly wheelchair-accessible; ⊲⊳ dogs on lead; ℘ plants for sale; 🏬 shop; ♛ events held; ℺ children-friendly; B&B bed and breakfast available.

DERBYSHIRE

Two-starred gardens are marked on the map with a black square.

Calke Abbey [Historic Garden Grade II*]

Ticknall DE73 7LE. Tel: (01332) 863822 (office)

The National Trust • 10m S of Derby, off A514 at Ticknall • House and church open 18th March to 29th Oct (closed 14th Aug), Sat – Wed and Bank Holiday Mons, 12.30 – 5pm • Park open all year, daily except 24th Dec. Garden open as house, 11am – 5pm, plus Thurs and Fri, 29th June to 1st Sept • Entrance: £4.20, children £2.10 (house and garden £6.80, children £3.40). £3.50 vehicle charge for entry to park • Other information: Dogs and picnics in park only. Restaurant closed Thurs and Fri ◑ ● ✕ <u>WC</u> ✿ ⚙ ☕

Previously owned by the Harpur Crewe family, Calke has a long history punctuated by neglect; the Trust has slowly and sensitively brought the garden back from the brink of decay. The vinery in the physic garden has been restored, as have the tomato house, frames, pits, backsheds and the only early-nineteenth-century auricula theatre left in England; in summer pelargoniums replace the auriculas on its shelves. The gardeners are growing flowers, fruit and old varieties of vegetables in the two walled compartments formerly kept for flowers and herbs. The third compartment is the kitchen garden, overlooked by an orangery and housing a head gardener's office of 1777. An orchard of old local apple varieties is of particular interest.

Chatsworth ★★ [Historic Garden Grade I]

Bakewell DE45 1PP. Tel: (01246) 582204

The Duke and Duchess of Devonshire and the Chatsworth House Trust • 4m E of Bakewell, 10m W of Chesterfield on B6012, off A619 and A6 • House open • Garden open mid-March to mid-Dec, daily, 11am – 6pm • Entrance: £5.75, OAPs and students £4.25, children £2.50, family £14 (house and garden £9.50, OAPs and students £7.50, children £3.50, family £22.50) (2005 prices). Parking charge for cars only £1.50 ◑ ● ✕ 🍽 <u>WC</u> ✿ ♿ ⚘ ⚙

The 105 acres of garden at Chatsworth have developed over 400 years and many areas still reflect the fashions of each century. The seventeenth-century gardens of London and Wise remain only as the cascade, the canal pond to the south and the copper 'willow tree' with water pouring from its branches. During the eighteenth century 'Capability' Brown destroyed much of the formal gardens to create a land-scaped woodland park. Notable is the vista he created from the Salisbury Lawn to the horizon, which remains unchanged, as does the lawn itself since no liming or fertilisers are used, allowing many varieties of wild flowers, grasses, moss and sedges to thrive. Paxton's work still gives pleasure, including some rare conifers and the magnificent 84-metre water jet from the Emperor Fountain. Although his Great Conservatory was a casualty of the 1914–18 war and metre-wide stone walls in the old conservatory garden are all that remain to give an idea of its size, as part of the celebration of the bicentenary of Paxton's birth in 1803, damaged areas of his giant rockeries were rebuilt. From the twentieth century come the orange borders and blue and white borders, the terrace, display greenhouse, rose garden and old conservatory garden, which has lupin, dahlia and Michaelmas daisy beds, and a yew maze planted in 1963. In the arboretum and pinetum the suffocating rhododendrons, laurels and sycamores have been removed and many new trees planted. The double rows of pleached red-twigged limes added in 1952 and the 1953 serpentine beech hedge are both now rewarding features. The epitome of a cottage garden has two new neighbours: a flight of yew stairs leading to a 'bedroom' where the four-poster is of ivy and the dressing-table of privet, and a sensory garden. The kitchen garden has been resited and redesigned – it has been called 'indelibly British'. The first major piece of garden statuary to be placed in the garden for 150 years, 'War Horse' by Dame Elisabeth Frink, is sited at the south end of the canal, and her 'Walking Madonna' is a new and important presence.

Dam Farm House ★

Yeldersley Lane, Ednaston, Ashbourne DE6 3BA. Tel: (01335) 360291

Mrs Jean Player • 8m NW of Derby, 5m SE of Ashbourne on A52. Opposite Ednaston village turn, gate is 500 metres on right • Open by appt. Groups and coach parties welcome • Entrance: £3, children free ● WC & ⚘

This wonderful garden, created from a field, owes its existence to the inspiration of the owner, whose knowledgeable eye for good plants of all kinds – trees, perennials, shrubs and roses – is evident throughout. It is this planting that gives the garden, including the vegetable garden, its special character. Garden rooms span outwards from the house, most enclosed by high beech and yew hedges and an evergreen tapestry hedge dividing the arboretum from the main garden. The scree is filled with choice alpines. Climbers are used abundantly for clothing walls, pergolas, even spilling down over high retaining walls. The farmyard has several stone troughs, now used for plants. One of the best gardens in Derbyshire, maturing after 26 years of collecting and intermittent planting.

Derby Arboretum [Historic Garden Grade II*]

Arboretum Square, Derby DE23 8FN. Tel: (01332) 292612

Derby City Council • Between Reginald Street and Arboretum Square with entrances on either side of Royal Crown Derby Factory • Open all year, daily • Entrance: free ○ 🏠 WC & ⚘

The first specifically designed urban arboretum in Britain, this was commissioned in 1839 from John Claudius Loudon, whose original plans involved the planting of 1000 trees. A useful leaflet now lists 40 varieties, many from around the world, all individually numbered, and also describes other parks in Derby, including the well-known *Markeaton Park*. While in the city, try to visit the refurbished market place, where there is a splendid water sculpture by William Pye, of free-falling water over a bronze cascade – it will give you the sensation of walking behind a waterfall.

Dove Cottage
Clifton, Ashbourne DE6 2JQ. Tel: (01335) 343545

Mr and Mrs S.G. Liverman • 1.5m SW of Ashbourne off A515. In Clifton turn right at crossroads then first left down lane (signed 'Mayfield Yarns'). House is 200 metres on left by River Dove • Open by appt for parties of 10 or more, and certain Suns April to July for charity, 1 – 5pm • Entrance: Parties £3.50 per person for guided tour (£2.50 on charity open days), children free • Other information: Teas on charity days only ● WC ⁂ ♟

It is only to be expected that this richly stocked cottage garden is above the average, for it has had the benefit of being developed and nurtured by an owner who is a qualified horticulturist. April brings a spectacular daffodil display, and there are several hardy plant collections, including alliums, campanulas, euphorbias, geraniums and variegated plants; hardy perennials are being nurtured in a dry woodland area. A pleasant walk leads between a flower bed and the River Dove, where kingfishers may sometimes be spotted.

Elvaston Castle Country Park ★ [Historic Garden Grade II*]
Borrowash Road, Elvaston DE72 3EP. Tel: (01332) 571342

Derbyshire County Council • 2m SE of Derby on B5010 between Borrowash (A6005) and Thulston (A6). Signed from A6 and A52 • Open all year, daily, 9am – 5pm • Entrance: free, but parking charge ● ● ✕ 🖢 WC ⅄ ⬦ ⚒ ♟

The gardens were designed by William Barron in the early nineteenth century for the 4th Earl of Harrington and include Italian, parterre and Old English gardens, all enclosed within 11 miles of hedges. It is probable that these were the first 'garden rooms', which influenced others when, twenty years after their establishment, they were opened to the public. Discover the extensive topiary, tree-lined avenues and large ornamental lake, search out the golden gates, boat house and Moorish temple, and wonder at the distinctive cedars of Lebanon. Barron transplanted mature trees as high as 13 metres from as early as 1831, using his unique transplanting machines, one of which is housed at the Royal Botanic Gardens, Kew. For those who find a park out of scale with their own smaller gardens, a tiny 'romantic' garden nearby, *White Gate* at Arleston Meadows, is recommended. The owner, Mrs Judy Beba-Thompson, welcomes private visits and small parties by prior appointment (Tel: (01332) 763653).

Fanshawe Gate Hall
Holmesfield S18 7WA. Tel: (0114) 289 0391

Mr and Mrs John Ramsden • 6m NW of Chesterfield, 6m SW of Sheffield, 1m E of Holmesfield. Follow B6054 and turn first right after Penny Acres School • Open 25th June, 2nd, 16th and 23rd July, 11am – 5pm, for NGS, and for parties (min. 10 persons) by appt June and July • Entrance: £2 ● ● WC ⅄ ⬦ ⁂

Topiary, mixed borders, a variegated border, an Elizabethan garden and a sixteenth-century dovecot are features of this two-acre garden. The upper walled garden displays herbaceous plants, shrubs, ferns, water features and roses, while the lower courtyard has a knot garden and a herb border. The owners, who moved here in 1959, have sought to use plants appropriate to the setting of the 700-year-old hall. The orchard has been redesigned and replanted with old varieties of English fruit trees, and a wildlife pond created. A *potager* is planned for the vegetable garden.

Fir Croft

Froggatt Road, Calver, Hope Valley S32 3ZD.

Dr S.B. Furness • 4m N of Bakewell, between Power filling station and A625/B6001 junction • Open 23rd April, 7th, 21st May, 4th June, 2 – 5pm • Entrance: by donation • Other information: Plants for sale at adjoining nursery ● &

The owner is a botanist and botanical photographer who has put his expertise into an extensive alpine garden. Started from scratch in 1985 and considerably extended in 2002, it has been planted with many new varieties and now contains one of the largest and most eclectic collections of alpines in the UK. A 'must' for those interested in alpine and scree gardens. There is also a substantial collection of dwarf conifers.

Gamesley Fold Cottage

10 Gamesley Fold, Glossop SK13 9JJ. Tel: (014578) 67856

Mrs G. Carr • 2m SW of Glossop off A626 – Marple road near Charlesworth. Turn down lane opposite St Margaret's School • Open for NGS, and May to Aug, Thurs – Sat, 2 – 5pm, and for parties by appt. Coach parties welcome • Entrance: £2, children free • Other information: Wildflower nursery open all year, but telephone to check opening times ● ● WC & ☙

Although all gardeners will find much of interest here, those who like native or 'wild' flowers will be particularly impressed. The loosely planted beds are crammed with primulas, violets, campions and poppies, many of them self-seeded. Mixed in is a good variety of perennials, notably campanulas, euphorbias, geraniums, verbascums, meconopsis and others that go well with their wild neighbours. There is also a vegetable garden, an orchard and woodland. Wildlife abounds within the garden, especially butterflies lured here by the flowers, trees and shrubs; looking outward are extensive views of the surrounding countryside and hills.

Haddon Hall ★ [Historic Garden Grade I]

Bakewell DE45 1LA. Tel: (01629) 812855

Lord Edward Manners • 2m SE of Bakewell, 6.5m N of Matlock on A6 • House open • Garden open: telephone for dates and times • Entrance: hall and gardens £7.25, OAPs £6.25, children £3.75, family £19. Parking charge for cars £1, coaches free ◑ ● ✕ WC ⬛

The hall, perched high on a rocky outcrop, looks down to the River Wye over mature woodland. In origin a medieval house, it has gradually grown over the centuries into every semblance of a castle. Rex Whistler painted a delightful water-colour conversation piece of the 9th Duke with his young son and heir on the hillside above the hall – lords of all they surveyed. The gardens retain a seventeenth-century atmosphere. The south garden is terraced with views of the river below, flowing in a series of loops across the valley landscape. It is above all a haven for roses – an immense collection built up by the 9th Duchess, set against the massive house walls and buttresses – and in June and July they create a spectacular floral display.

Hardwick Hall ★ [Historic Garden Grade I]

Doe Lea, Chesterfield S44 5QJ. Tel: (01246) 850430

The National Trust • 9.5m SE of Chesterfield, 6.5m NW of Mansfield. Approach from M1 junction 29 take A6175 • House open April to Oct, Wed, Thurs, Sat, Sun, Bank Holiday Mons and Good Friday, 12 noon – 4.30pm • Garden open April to Oct, Wed – Sun, 11am – 5.30pm. Country park open all year, daily, 8am – 6pm • Entrance: £4.20, children £2.10, family £10.50 (house and garden £7.60, children £3.80, family £19) • Other information: Refreshments on days hall is open ◑ ⬤ ✕ <u>WC</u> ♿ ⌂ ⚑ ⚲

This famous Elizabethan mansion was built by Bess of Hardwick and designed by Robert Smythson in the late sixteenth century. Mature yew hedges and stone walls provide necessary protection in an otherwise exposed escarpment site. The borders of the south court have shrubs and herbaceous planting to give structure and extend the flowering period, while the west court's herbaceous borders are planted in strong, hot colours graduating to soft hues, with the peak flowering season in late summer and autumn. The newly redesigned herb garden is outstanding. In the south-east quarter is an orchard, with varieties of apples, pears, plums, gages and damsons, and the north-east orchard has been progressively replanted with old varieties such as crab apples, with the grass left long for naturalised daffodils and wild flowers. At Hall View Cottage in Hardstoft, 3 miles away, is *The Herb Garden*, which has physic, scented pot-pourri and lavender gardens and a parterre to visit, and there is a wide range of herbs to buy. [Open mid-March to mid-Sept, Wed – Sun, 10am – 5pm.]

Kedleston Hall ★ [Historic Garden Grade I]

Kedleston, Derby DE22 5JH. Tel: (01332) 842191

The National Trust • 4.5m NW of Derby on Derby – Hulland road between A6 and A52. Signposted • Hall open 11th March to 29th Oct, Sat – Wed, 12 noon – 4.30pm • Park open 11th March to 29th Oct, daily, 10am – 6pm; 2nd Nov to 10th March, daily, 10am – 4pm. Garden open 25th March to 30th Oct, daily, 10am – 6pm • Entrance: park £2.70 per vehicle; park and garden £3.10, children £1.55, family £7.70 (hall, park and garden £6.90, children £3.30, family £17) • Other information: Coaches must pre-book by writing to Property Manager. Electric stairclimber and batricar sometimes available ◑ ⬤ ✕ <u>WC</u> ♿ ⚘ ⌂ ⚑

The extensive gardens do not compete with this neo-classical Robert Adam palace – the ancient home of the Curzon family – but are of mature parkland where the eye is always drawn to the house. The rhododendrons when in flower are worth seeing in their own right, otherwise visit the gardens as a pleasurable way to view not only Adam's magnificent south front but also the hexagonal-domed summerhouse, the orangery, the Venetian-windowed fishing house, the bridge across the lake, the aviary and slaughterhouse (now a loggia) and the main gateway. The formal gardens have a sunken rose garden. The Sulphur Bath House, one of the earliest eighteenth-century landscape park features, where a small spa used to operate, has been restored but is not accessible to the public.

Lea Gardens

Long Lane, Lea, Matlock DE4 5GH. Tel: (01629) 534380

Mr and Mrs Tye • 5m SE of Matlock E off A6 • Open 20th March to 30th June, daily, 10am – 5pm, and at other times by appt • Entrance: £3.50, children 50p (season ticket £6) • Other information: Coaches by appt ◑ 🍽 wc ♿ ⏏ ⌖ 🜨 ♀ ✿

This garden has a comprehensive collection of rhododendrons, azaleas, alpines and conifers, all brought together in a beautiful woodland setting. John Marsden Smedley started his rhododendron garden in 1935, inspired by his visits to Bodnant and Exbury, and the collection now comprises some 550 varieties of rhododendrons and azaleas in a much-increased area.

Melbourne Hall Gardens ★ [Historic Garden Grade I]

Melbourne DE73 8EN. Tel: (01332) 862502

Lord Ralph Kerr • 8m S of Derby between A514 and A453, off B587 in Melbourne • House open Aug, daily except 7th, 14th and 21st, 2 – 5pm (last admission 4.15pm) • Garden open April to Sept, Wed, Sat, Sun and Bank Holiday Mons, 1.30 – 5.30pm • Entrance: £3, OAPs and children £2 (house and gardens £5.50, OAPs £4.50, children £3.50) ◑ 🍽 ✕ wc ♿ ⌖ 🜨

There has been little alteration to Thomas Coke's formal plan, so this is a visual record of a complete late seventeenth-/early eighteenth-century design laid out by London and Wise in the style of Le Nôtre. It is in immaculate condition with some unusual magnolias flowering in early April. Avenues culminate in exquisite statuary and fountains, including a lead urn of The Four Seasons by van Nost, whose other lead statuary stands in niches of yew. A series of terraces runs down to a lake, the Great Basin, and a grotto has an inscription by George Lamb. Unique in English gardens is the Birdcage iron arbour of 1706, which can be seen from the house along a long walk hedged with yews. Also in Melbourne, on the site of the fourteenth-century castle, is *Castle Farm*, a garden of interesting plants, open for private visits and groups by appointment; telephone Mr and Mrs John Blunt on (01332) 864421.

Pavilion Gardens

St John's Road, Buxton SK17 6XN. Tel: (01298) 23114

High Peak Borough Council • Near town centre • Open all year, daily, from 10am • Entrance: free • Other information: Refreshments in complex ○ 🍽 ✕ 🍴 wc ♿ ⏏ 🜨 ♀

Twenty-three acres of landscaped park, woodland and ornamental lakes, this updated pleasure garden of 1871 has the distinction of having been laid out by Edward Milner, Paxton's chief assistant at Crystal Palace. The gardens are well maintained and the 1875 octagon (now used for events) is a graceful backdrop. The conservatory is well stocked but many find the colour schemes of the bedding plants harsh; there are, however, band concerts to soothe shattered nerves. In the nearby Crescent, examples of the arcane art of well-dressing may be seen during summer. A Heritage grant has aided a refurbishment programme costing £4m over five years.

Renishaw Hall [Historic Garden Grade II*]

Renishaw, Sheffield S21 3WB. Tel: (01246) 432310

Sir Reresby and Lady Sitwell • 6m SE of Sheffield, 5m NE of Chesterfield on A6135. From M1 at junction 30, take A616 towards Sheffield for 3m through Renishaw • Open 13th April to Sept, Thurs – Sun and Bank Holiday Mons, 10.30am – 4.30pm • Entrance: £3.60, OAPs £2.80 (2005 prices) • Other information: Sitwell museum, costume museum, art gallery, performing arts gallery ◑ 🍽 ✕ 🥾 <u>WC</u> ♿ 🕊 🌿 🏛 🍷 ☕

For nearly twenty years Renishaw had 'the most northerly vineyard in western Europe'. Also astonishing to see at this northerly latitude and on top of a hill are enormous specimens of rare and slightly tender shrubs. Sir George Sitwell spent much of his life in Italy and this is the style he re-created at Renishaw a century ago. Within a framework of vistas, walks and topiary, plants riot in ordered confusion in the sheltered gardens to the south of the house. Statues, terraces and the sound of splashing water enhance the Italianate atmosphere, and the present incumbents have added a stupendous water jet to increase the effect. They have also increased the number of different gardens (10 in all), divided and protected by yew hedges and columns, enlarged the borders, introduced innovative planting, and linked the garden to the wood with new planting and paths. At the end of the lime avenue on the top lawn stands Sir Hamo Thornycroft's statue of the Angel of Fame, regilded by Lady Sitwell. Beyond the brick wall is a greenhouse that contains the National Collection of yuccas, and below that winds a spinney that badgers now share with a statue walk. A nature trail leads to an avenue of camellias on to a bluebell wood – an azure carpet in early May – and on still to the classic temple, Gothick lodge, old sawmill, cave and lakes.

NCCPG

The National Council for the Conservation of Plants and Gardens publishes a *National Plant Collections Directory*. Those interested in seeing some of the rarer species and garden varieties of particular families of plants will find this an invaluable publication. The latest edition, which offers information on about 600 collections comprising more than 50,000 plants and contains articles by holders of the collections, is available from NCCPG, The Stable Courtyard, RHS Garden, Wisley, Woking GU23 6QP (Tel: (01483) 221465; Fax: (01483) 212404; Website: www.nccpg.com. The new edition will be published in February or March 2006.

DEVON

Two-starred gardens are marked on the map with a black square.

Andrew's Corner

Belstone, Okehampton EX20 1RD. Tel: (01837) 840332

Mr and Mrs R.J. Hill • 3m E of Okehampton off A30, signed to Belstone then Skaigh • Open 16th and 30th April, 14th and 28th May, 4th and 18th June, 2.30 – 5.30pm; 28th and 29th July, 7 – 10pm, and by appt at other times • Entrance: £2, children free (evening openings £3.50 incl. wine and refreshments) • Other information: Teas on open days only ● ◗ ⬤ ⑂ ✿ ◔

High above sea level on north Dartmoor, facing the Taw valley and the high moor, in only one and a half acres (amazing that it is not larger) grows a wide variety of plants of all sorts not normally seen at such an altitude. The sense of space is achieved by the division of the garden into different levels by rhododendrons and trees, each area having its own microclimate, and all with glimpses through to other areas and to the wider landscape. Colour in spring comes from bulbs and meconopsis, in summer from herbaceous plants and lilies, in autumn from maples (many grown from seed) and gentians. There are drystone walls (a speciality of the area), a paved area and ponds with water plants; in stone and paving cracks lewisias and other alpines flourish.

Arlington Court [Historic Garden Grade II*]

Arlington, Barnstaple EX31 4LP. Tel: (01271) 850296

The National Trust • 8m NE of Barnstaple on A39 • House and carriage collection open as garden • Garden open 26th March to 29th Oct, daily except Sat, 10.30am – 5pm • Entrance: garden and carriage collection £5, children £2.50 (house, carriage collection and garden £7, children £3.50, family £15.80, parties of 15 or more £6 per person, children £2.40) ◐ ◗ ✕ ▥ <u>WC</u> ⑂ ⬠ ✿ ⚘ ◔

The Georgian house is set in a largely informal garden extending to 30 acres. The combination of a mild, damp climate and acid soil provides a perfect home for a wide range of plants, particularly rhododendrons, with many species of tree-like proportions; hydrangeas also thrive here. In spring, drifts of bulbs carpet the grass, followed by wild flowers. The wilderness pond is surrounded by rhododendrons, contrasting with the formal and symmetrical terraced Victorian garden with its annual bedding. There is also a double herbaceous border, a rockery and a conservatory. The one-acre walled kitchen garden is being restored, and the Victorian lean-to greenhouse has been rebuilt to the original design. A few miles N of Barnstaple on the A39, in Pixie Lane, Umberleigh, *Glebe Cottage Plants* (the nursery owned by Chelsea gold-medal winner Carol Klein) stocks a mouth-watering range of rare and newly introduced perennials. [Tel: (01769) 540554.]

Bickham House

Kenn, Exeter EX6 7XL. Tel: (01392) 832671

Mr and Mrs John Tremlett • 6m S of Exeter on A38 before junction with A380. Leave dual carriageway at Kennford Services and follow signs to Kenn, then take first right and follow lane for 0.75m to end of no-through road • Open 2nd, 4th, 5th April, 14th, 16th, 17th May, 11th, 13th, 14th June, 9th, 11th, 12th July, 13th, 15th, 16th Aug, all 2 – 5pm, and by appt at other times • Entrance: £3, children free ● ▆ ▆ WC & ✿

Six acres of garden in a peaceful wooded valley, overlooking a small lake. The house has been in the family since it was built in 1682, but the garden has been extensively remodelled over the last few years, and new features are being added all the time. There are lawns and fine trees, spring-flowering shrubs and many naturalised bulbs, and a box-hedged parterre around a lily pond; banks around the main lawn are left uncut to encourage butterflies. In the mixed borders great attention is paid to colour co-ordination. The one-acre walled garden, divided into rose beds, a formal herb garden and a highly productive flower and vegetable section, is full of colour and interest throughout the year; an avenue of palm trees leads to a summerhouse. Colourful too is the small water garden, and the spinney full of cowslips and naturalised aquilegias. There is also a conservatory, opening onto an enclosed cobbled area with raised beds and a wall fountain.

Bicton College

East Budleigh, Budleigh Salterton EX9 7BY. Tel: (01395) 562427

2m N of Budleigh Salterton on A376 • Open all year: April to Sept, daily; Nov to March, Mon – Fri, (closed 25th Dec to 1st Jan); all 10am – 4.30pm • Entrance: £2, children free (2005 price) • Other information: Parking beyond student car park, short walk to garden ○ ▆ WC & ✿ ♟

The gardens of this Georgian house, set in parkland with a lake, form the horticultural department of Bicton College, and as such contain a large number of plants laid out for both study and general interest – truly a plantsman's paradise. As well as fine herbaceous borders there is an arboretum worth visiting at any time of the year and an old walled garden, all approached by an avenue of araucarias (monkey puzzle trees). Amongst the plants which provide both information and effect are National Collections of agapanthus and pittosporums. Ten miles to the north is *Escot Place*, Ottery St Mary, where the latest project of the designer Ivan Hicks is evolving in 220 acres of traditional woodland garden. Telephone (01404) 822188 for more information, or visit the website at www.escot-devon.co.uk.

Bicton Park Botanical Gardens ★ [Historic Garden Grade I]

East Budleigh, Budleigh Salterton EX9 7BJ. Tel: (01395) 568465

Bicton Park • 2m N of Budleigh Salterton on B3178 • Open daily except 25th and 26th Dec, 10am – 6pm (closes 5pm in winter) • Entrance: £5.75, children (3–15) £4.50, concessions £4.50, family £18.95 (2005 prices) ○ ▆ ✕ ▆ WC & ♿ ✿ ♛ ♟ ♞

There is much to see in the 60 acres. The formal and informal gardens date from c.1735, largely landscaped in the style of Le Nôtre. There is a stream garden with a 150-year-old mulberry, azaleas, camellias and flowering cherries, herbaceous borders against magnolia-clad walls, an American garden established in the 1830s, and a hermitage garden with a lake and water garden. The pinetum, first planted in 1839 and extended in 1910 to take the collection of the famous botanist and explorer 'Chinese' Wilson, has some rare conifers, including the tallest Grecian fir ever recorded (41 metres). Perhaps Bicton's greatest glory is the palm house, built between 1825 and 1830, one of the oldest in the country; inside, endangered species such as bottle, loulu, triangle, cotton and kentia palms, and outside a Chinese tea plant. There are also arid and temperate houses, and a tropical house for bananas, bromeliads, figs and bougainvilleas. The Countryside Museum, one of the largest in the West Country, houses a collection of farm machinery, gardening tools and craft exhibits, reflecting changes in rural life since the 1700s. There is a new display of cacti and other succulents in a naturalistic desert-like landscape in the arid house, and one of Britain's earliest Victorian ferneries has been re-established by the planting of a large collection of ferns, including dicksonias, among the rocks around the shell house. Nearby, Sidmouth's *Connaught Gardens* [Historic Garden Grade II], originally designed in the 1930s, combine breathtaking views across its beautiful and mercifully still unspoilt bay, stunningly colourful traditional bedding displays and a large and varied collection of unusual and tender shrubs and plants; also herbaceous borders with new varieties introduced on a regular basis, all immaculately kept – very different from the expected seaside public garden. Meandering paths lead from sheltered walled areas to the clifftop walk, with seats everywhere.

Blackpool Gardens

Blackpool Sands, Blackpool, Dartmouth TQ6 0RG. Tel: (01803) 770606

Sir Geoffrey Newman, Bt • 3m S of Dartmouth on A379. Parking by beachside café. Entrance through Blackpool Sands car park • Open April to Sept, daily (subject to weather), 10am – 4pm, and to private and school parties by appt • Entrance: £2.50 (tickets available at Blackpool Sands ticket office), children free • Other information: Refreshments and toilets available at Blackpool Sands ◑ 🍽 ✕ <u>WC</u> ♿

An engrossing secret garden, entered through a small green-painted door overhung by a cascade of *Fuchsia magellanica* and set into a wall of beautifully laid Devon stone. Facing south and rising steeply, it overlooks the perfect crescent of Blackpool Sands. This chunk of Devon's Heritage Coast has been in the same family since the late eighteenth century, but the landscaping of the three-acre woodland garden was begun by Robert Lydston Newman, Deputy Governor of the Bank of England, in 1896. He carved out four wide parallel paths the length of the garden, joining them by further paths and steps so that they climb upwards in a gentle zig-zag. The hillside between is filled with a wide variety of sub-tropical, temperate and antipodean trees and shrubs, some of great age, others introduced more recently, and all testimony to the fact that succeeding generations of Newmans have been keen collectors and plantsmen. An 1848 Monterey pine and an 1896 avenue of cork oaks with venerably pitted bark survive from the earliest period. The award of a European grant in 2000 enabled the present owner to regenerate the landscaping and rejuvenate the plantings. A new water garden is planned, centred on an existing pond garden above the terraces, so that water may in time cascade back down towards the stunning views, far below, of beach, craggy headlands and a shoreline fading away to distant Start Point. Then it's time to make your way back through the secret door, enjoy a swim, hire a kayak, and return to the real holiday world.

Buckland Abbey

Yelverton PL20 6EY. Tel: (01822) 853607

The National Trust and Plymouth City Council • 6m S of Tavistock, 11m N of Plymouth. Turn off A386 0.25m S of Yelverton • House open as garden • Garden open 25th March to 29th Oct, daily except Thurs,10.30am – 5.30pm; 18th Feb to 25th March, 30th Oct to 17th Dec, Sat and Sun, 12.30 – 5pm. Closed 21st Dec to 20th Feb • Entrance: £3.70, children £1.80 (abbey and grounds £7, children £3.50, family £17.50) • Other information: Possible for wheelchairs but steep site. Motorised buggy usually available ○ ● ✕ ● WC & ℘ ⬚ ℀

The garden is largely a twentieth-century creation. There is a box hedge parterre between the 30-metre-long medieval barn and the abbey, its pockets filled with over 50 different herbs, reputedly inspired by Vita Sackville-West. *Magnolia delavayi* and *M. grandiflora* grow against the abbey walls. A line of ailing yews on the north border of the lawn has been replaced by an Elizabethan garden, and a thyme area has been created. Delightful estate walks and glorious views of Devon and Cornwall.

Burrow Farm Gardens ★

Dalwood, Axminster EX13 7ET. Tel: (01404) 831285

Mr and Mrs John Benger • 4m W of Axminster off A35 Honiton road. After 3.5m turn N near Shute garage onto Stockland road. Garden is 0.5m on right • Open April to Sept, daily, 10am – 7pm • Entrance: £3.50, children 50p, parties (discount rate) by appt ○ ● ● WC & ⬚ ℘

These lovely 10-acre gardens, created from pasture land, are the inspiration of Mary Benger and her family. Foliage effect has been admirably achieved with a colourful array of azaleas and rhododendrons. A former Roman clay pit is graded from top to bottom through mature trees and shrubs to an extensive bog garden with a marvellous show of candelabra primulas and native wild flowers during the early part of the season. In summer the pergola walk, with its old-fashioned roses and herbaceous borders, is a picture, and a courtyard garden and a terraced garden feature late-flowering herbaceous plants. The rill garden has ponds, a classical summerhouse and a ha-ha laid out in a formal design, luxuriantly and informally planted. The setting and sense of grandeur are more typical of gardens of greater repute. Magnificent views. A new azalea glade was added in 2004 to look down past the thatched summerhouse towards the lake, rich in wildlife and surrounded by a subtle blend of cultivated and wild flowers.

Castle Drogo ★★ [Historic Garden Grade II*]

Drewsteignton EX6 6PB. Tel: (01647) 433306

The National Trust • Between Okehampton and Exeter, 5m S of A30 or 4m NW of Moretonhampstead on A382; follow signs from Sandy Park • Castle open as garden until 4th Nov, but closed Tues • Garden open 4th, 5th, 11th, 12th March, 10.30am – 4.30pm; 18th March to 5th Nov, daily, 10.30am – 5.30pm (closes 4.30pm 30th Oct to 5th Nov); 6th Nov to 17th Dec, Fri – Sun, 11am – 4pm • Entrance: £3.50 (£1.10 Nov to Feb), children £2 (house and garden £6.30, children £3.10, family £15.50) (2005 prices). Reduced rate for parties by appt • Other information: Coaches by appt only. Disabled parking. Access for wheelchairs by arrangement at reception. Croquet equipment for hire ❶ ☕ ✕ 🍴 wc ♿ ♨ 🏛 ♟ ❀

The last castle to be built in England (begun 1910) was designed by Sir Edwin Lutyens. The plans for the planting of the garden were by George Dillistone of Tunbridge Wells. Evergreen oaks survey the magnificent views over the Teign Gorge, and a valley planted with rhododendrons, magnolias, camellias, cornus and maples. Nearer the house are formal terraces and borders with walls of granite, sharp-edged yew hedges with rose beds and arbours of *Parrotia persica*. The paths and parrotia arbours echo Lutyens' circle and square theme. Herbaceous borders are full of old varieties of crocosmia, lychnis, campanula, iris and kniphofia. Under the granite walls perennials – euphorbias, hellebores, alchemillas and rodgersias – mingle with spring bulbs. Steps lead to a second terrace with yuccas and wisterias and a fragrant garden; then on up to shrub borders of enkianthus, azaleas, magnolias and lilies; and finally comes a splendid circular lawn surrounded by a tall yew hedge at the top, a huge green circle and a perfect stage set for croquet. Near Chagford, off A30 via Whiddon Down, are *Stone Lane Gardens*, Kenneth and June Ashbourner's informally landscaped five-acre arboretum. An annual sculpture exhibition is held from May to September. [Open by appt – ring (01647) 231311, or consult website on www.mythicgarden.com.]

Castle Hill ★ [Historic Garden Grade I]

Filleigh, Barnstaple EX32 0RQ. Tel: (01598) 760336 Ext.4

The Earl and Countess of Arran • 7m SE of Barnstaple, 19m NW of Tiverton off A361. Leave A361 at roundabout after South Molton, heading for Filleigh. Take second right, then after 2.5m turn right into drive at yellow lodge • Open 2nd April to Aug, daily except Sat, 11am – 5pm • Entrance: £4. Other information: Teas on Suns and Bank Holiday Mons ☕ 🍴 wc ♿ ♟ ❀

The eighteenth-century landscape garden and park, leading away from the magnificent Palladian house, were created by the 1st Lord Fortescue in 1730 with temples, follies, ponds and across the valley a triumphal arch. At the top of the hill above the house is a castle (complete with cannons) from which Dartmoor, Exmoor and Lundy Island are visible on a clear day. The woodland garden shelters magnolias, camellias, rhododendrons, azaleas, a two-acre daffodil wood, thousands of bulbs, and there are also some renowned trees in the Easter Close. As if this were not enough, the millennium garden designed by Xa Tollemache has herbaceous borders planted with lilies, agapanthus, phlox and penstemon edged with box and lavender in gentle curves lining gravel paths. There is an avenue of formal clipped *Quercus ilex* underplanted with *Viburnum tinus* and a spectacular water sculpture by Giles Rayner.

Cleave House

Sticklepath, Okehampton EX20 2NL. Tel: (01837) 840481

*Ann and Roger Bowden • 3.5m E of Okehampton on old A30 towards Exeter.
House is in Sticklepath on left just past small right turn for Skaigh • Open for NGS,
and by appt at other times – parties and individuals welcome • Entrance: £2
(2005 price)* ● WC & ✍

For the Bowdens, hostas are not just a business, they are an abiding passion. Their
one-acre garden, tucked away at the heart of a small Devon village, boasts some
delightful mixed planting – both trees and shrubs – but hostas are the dominant feature. A few varieties, notably the brightly coloured, have been imported from the
United States. This Mecca for the hosta enthusiast includes demonstration beds
resplendent with over 1000 different varieties, displaying fascinating variations in
both colour and size. The collection has been designated an NCCPG reference (of
modern hybrids).

Clovelly Court

Clovelly, Nr Bideford EX39 5SZ. Tel: (01237) 431200

*The Hon. John Rous • 8m W of Bideford off A39, on B3237. In village next to All
Saints Church • Open March to Oct, daily, 10am – 4pm • Entrance: £1.50,
children free* [NEW] ◐ 🥬 WC & ✍ 🍴 ⚲

New life has been breathed into the gardens here, especially within the classic
Victorian kitchen garden surrounded by ancient stone walls. The five greenhouses
lining the south-facing wall have been lovingly restored; despite no extra heating,
they now house vines, nectarines, peaches, lemons, apricots and melons. Tomatoes,
cucumbers, chillies and aubergines grow in another greenhouse in the centre of the
garden. Perfectly tended espaliers and fan-trained apple, pear, plum, cherry and fig
trees line the walls, and in midsummer the herbaceous borders add a riot of colour
to the lower half of the garden. Organically grown vegetables, fruit, cut flowers and
pot plants are for sale in the potting shed. An ornate wrought-iron gate opens to
reveal a formal garden with terraced lawns and a magnificent view of Lundy Island,
and the Long Walk through woodland recently planted with bulbs and rhododendrons leads to the village of Clovelly with its steep cobbled street tumbling down
to the sea. Hartland Abbey (see entry) is just along the coast.

Coleton Fishacre Garden ★ [Historic Garden Grade II*]

Brownstone Road, Kingswear, Dartmouth TQ6 0EQ. Tel: (01803) 752466

*The National Trust • 3m E of Dartmouth, 3m S of Brixham off B3205. 2.5m
from Kingswear, take Lower Ferry Road and turn off at toll house • House open
as garden from 29th March, 11am – 4.30pm • Garden open 4th to 26th March,
Sat and Sun, 11am – 5pm; 29th March to 29th Oct, Wed – Sun and Bank Holiday
Mons, 10.30am – 5.30pm • Entrance: £4.10, children £2, pre-booked parties of 15
or more £3.50 per person (house and garden £5.25, children, £2.60, family £13,
pre-booked parties £4.50) (2005 prices) • Other information: Holiday cottages
available* ◐ 🍽 ✕ WC & ✍ 🏛 ⚲

Oswald Milne, a pupil of Edwin Lutyens, designed the house and the architectural features of this garden for Rupert and Lady D'Oyly Carte; the house was completed and the garden begun in 1926. The exceptionally mild setting is a Devon combe, sloping steeply to the cliff tops and the sea, and sheltered by belts of Monterey pines and holm oaks. The streams and ponds make a humid atmosphere for moisture-loving and sub-tropical plants. There is a collection of unusual trees like dawn redwood, swamp cypress and Chilean myrtle, and dominating all a tall tulip tree and tree of heaven (*Ailanthus altissima*) the same age as the house. The Paddock Woodland Walk runs from the Gazebo Walk near the house through woodland to a main viewing area. Formal walls and terraces create a framework round the house for a large number of sun-loving tender plants. There are various water features, notably a stone-edged rill and a circular pool in the herbaceous-bordered walled garden.

Dartington Hall ★ [Historic Garden Grade II*]

Dartington, Totnes TQ9 6EL. Tel: (01803) 862367

Dartington Hall Trust • 2m NW of Totnes, E of A384. In Dartington, turn left past church (from London and north) or right before church (from west • Open all year, daily, dawn – dusk. Parties by appt only • Entrance: by donation £2, guided tours by arrangement £5 • Other information: Coaches by appt ○ ⬤ ✕ WC & ♿ B&B

In 1925, Leonard and Dorothy Elmhirst purchased the ancient and dying estate in order to launch their great experiment in rural regeneration. The hall is one of the most beautiful medieval manor houses in Devon. Standing at the crest of its sheltering coombe and commanding a triangular green tiltyard, the garden is an astonishing piece of theatre. Eleven Irish yews in apostolic procession (Judas Iscariot debarred) face a wall of tall and narrow turfed terraces, crowned by a line of chestnut trees and a majestic Henry Moore *Reclining Figure* in Hornton stone. Low, clipped yew screens loosely close the triangle, and Percy Cane's grand stone staircase leads to the upper level. Cane also planted a glade and an azalea dell, while the American Beatrix Farrand transformed the courtyard and opened up the woodland walkways. There are three walks, each using yew and holly as background plantings for collections of camellias, magnolias and rhododendrons. More recently, Preben Jacobsen redesigned the sunny herbaceous border in quiet shades of cream, blue and purple, Philip Booth laid out a Japanese garden and Georgie Wolton rationalised the forecourt entrance. Over the seasons, the spotlight of colour sweeps around the garden, but the overall effect is strongly architectural, with the tiltyard and terraces at its heart. Arguably the best view of these is from the top of the new wheelchair-accessible path, signalled by Peter Randal-Page's *Jacob's Pillow*.

Docton Mill Gardens ★

Lymebridge, Hartland EX39 6EA. Tel: (01237) 441369

Mr and Mrs J. Borrett • 14m W of Bideford, 12m N of Bude off A39. From north Devon travel via Hartland to Stoke or from north Cornwall to West Country Inn, then turn left signed to Elmscott towards Lymebridge in Spekes Valley • Open March to Oct, daily, 10am – 6pm • Entrance: £4, OAPs £3.75, children under 16 free • Other information: Coaches by appt ◑ ⬤ ✕ 🍽 WC ♿ ♿ ♿ ♿ B&B

The garden and the water mill of Saxon origin were rescued from dereliction in 1980. The mill was restored, the ponds, leats and smaller streams were cleared, a bog garden was created and a vast number of trees planted. The start of the new Millennium saw another burst of activity with the planting of a woodland garden and the transformation of the old donkey paddock into a magnolia garden with large herbaceous borders. The intention is to blend the garden into the natural landscape of valley and water. In spring there are displays of narcissi, primulas, camellias, rhododendrons and azaleas, with bluebells carpeting the woods; in summer the garden abounds in roses, including a bank of 'Felicia' and 'Pax', and the adjacent herbaceous border is in full flower.

The Garden House ★

Buckland Monachorum, Yelverton PL20 7LQ. Tel: (01822) 854769

The Fortescue Garden Trust • 10m N of Plymouth, 2m W of Yelverton off A386 • Open March to Oct, daily, 10.30am – 5pm • Entrance: £5, OAPs £4.50, children £1 ◑ ◻ ✕ 🐾 <u>WC</u> ⚘ ℺

A garden in the 'new naturalism' style, providing colour and interest from spring through summer and into autumn. Largely north-facing and nearly 150 metres above sea level, it has to contend with up to 150 centimetres of rain *per annum*. Its origins are deep in the past, but in gardening terms its story began when Mr and Mrs Lionel Fortescue arrived in 1945 to breathe life into the derelict walled garden which surrounded the ruins of a medieval vicarage and included a thatched barn and a tower. Through years of painstaking toil, it has become one of the finest of its type in the country. In 1978 Keith and Ros Wiley came here and continued the work, transforming eight acres of pasture and paddock by the planting of more than 3000 trees and shrubs, more than 1000 herbaceous plants and thousands of spring bulbs. A wisteria wood is now maturing, and the latest departures under Matt Bishop are a quarry garden with ponds and waterfalls and associated bog planting, and an area filled with South African perennials and annuals.

Gidleigh Park ★

Chagford TQ13 8HH. Tel: (01647) 432367

Andrew and Christina Brownsword • Off A382 11m SE of Okehampton. In Chagford Square turn right into Mill Street by Lloyds TSB. After 150 metres fork right (virtually straight across junction), and go to end of road – about 2m • Open all year, Mon – Fri (but closed Bank Holiday Mons) • Entrance: £6 (inc. coffee or tea with biscuits) • Other information: Lunches and teas served in hotel ○ ◻ ✕ <u>WC</u> ♿

Gidleigh Park, the acclaimed hotel and restaurant, is set in 45 acres of magnificent and secluded grounds on the north bank of the River Teign, within Dartmoor National Park. The woodland garden and parkland were created between 1850 and 1930. Since 1980 the owners have undertaken an extensive programme of restoration. Among the many interesting features is a delightful water garden, rebuilt and planted in 1986 and extended significantly into the woodland in 1997. Visitors can take this in on their way round the Boundary Walk – a 45-minute stroll through natural mixed woodland, underplanted with azaleas and rhododendrons. The Teign is

never far away, tumbling over granite boulders, past spring displays of rhododendrons. The mock-Tudor house gives way to a terrace resplendent with summer
colour, while a parterre and a herb garden add a touch of formality. There is an interesting avenue of young pleached limes adjacent to the front lawn, and mention must
be made of the croquet lawns, the very upmarket golf 'putting garden' and the pavilion – the final decadent flourishes.

Greenway

**Greenway Road, Galmpton, Churston Ferrers, Brixham TQ5 0ES.
Tel: (01803) 842382**

*The National Trust • 4m W of Brixham. From A3022 Paignton – Brixham road, take
road to Galmpton, then towards Greenway quay and ferry. Vehicles now strictly regulat-
ed, and no parking allowed in lanes outside property. Parking spaces for mini-coaches
must be pre-booked. If possible, visitors should park at Dartmouth park-and-ride, then
take river cruise to Greenway (telephone ferry service on (01803) 844010). Allow 4
hours • Open 1st March to 7th Oct, Wed – Sat, 10.30am – 4.30pm • Entrance:
£4.80, children £2.40* ● ● ✕ ● WC ⬩ ⌖ ⛪

The 30-acre ancient Devon garden is set high on the curving bank of the tree-lined
Dart river which has beautiful woodland walks. The Trust's researches indicate that
Repton may have worked here. There are so many indigenous trees over 150 years
old, that in high summer the river is completely hidden from the house, and even
from Dittisham on the opposite bank the house is barely visible. This natural paradise is gorgeous at every season, starting with camellias, rhododendrons, magnolias,
davidias and michelias underplanted with narcissus, cyclamen, primroses and bluebells, followed by paulownias, embothriums and *Cornus capitata* with their understorey of campions, foxgloves and ferns. The camellia and fernery gardens and the
vinery have been restored, the border in the top garden redeveloped. The house
(Agatha Christie's holiday home for many years) and the area immediately around it
are not open.

Hartland Abbey

Bideford EX39 6DT. Tel: (01237) 441264/441234

*Sir Hugh and Lady Stucley • 15m SW of Bideford off A39 Bideford – Bude road.
Follow signs to Hartland; drive through village, take road to Hartland Quay.
Signposted • House open April to 1st Oct, Wed, Thurs, Sun, Good Friday and
Bank Holiday Mons, plus Tues, July and Aug; all 2 – 5.30pm • Garden and
grounds open April to 1st Oct, daily except Sat, 2 – 5.30pm, and by appt at
other times • Entrance: gardens and grounds £4.50, children 50p (house, gardens
and grounds £7, OAPs £6.50, children £1.50) • Other information: Shop open as
house* ◑ ● ● WC ⬩ ⌖ ⛪ ♦ ⚲

Once an Augustinian monastery, the abbey is set across a narrow sheltered valley.
Due to Atlantic gales, gardens were not created around the house – although a row
of 100-year-old bay trees survives – but were planted either side of the valley with
azaleas, rhododendrons, camellias, hydrangeas, gunneras and many other shrubs and

trees. Some paths in the bog garden were designed by Gertrude Jekyll, who used to be a guest at the abbey, and the Victorian fernery, also thought to be by her, has been replanted. The walk to the Atlantic, a mile away, is carpeted in spring with bluebells, primroses and violets; a newly-restored nineteenth-century gazebo faces out to sea. A series of eighteenth-century walled gardens, set in a south-facing, gently sloping valley five minutes' walk away, is filled with vegetables, herbaceous plants, roses, climbers and tender perennials – *Echium pininana* thrives here.

Heddon Hall

Parracombe EX31 4QL. Tel: (01598) 763541

Juliet and Fred de Falbe • 10m NE of Barnstaple off A39. 360 metres up hill from village centre, entrance to drive is on right • Open Feb, Sun, 1 – 5pm (for hellebores and snowdrops); then May to July, Wed and Sun, 2 – 5.30pm, and for partes by appt all year • Entrance: £3.50, children free [NEW] 🅿 🐕 **WC** ♿ ⬀ 🌿 🍴

Nestling in a valley with views of Exmoor, the five-acre Georgian rectory garden was renovated in the mid-1980s by Joan Keatley, a keen plantswoman, and is full of horticultural delights. Through the cobbled courtyard lies a walled garden with an elaborate formal design of box hedges and step-over fruit trees designed by Penelope Hobhouse; the imaginative combination of flowers, fruit, herbs and vegetables between the intricate hedges is the work of Carol Klein. Next door, in the secret garden, cordoned and pleached limes line colour-themed beds planted with unusual herbaceous plants brought back from various plant-hunting trips. On the steeply sloped Himalayan bank bulbs and shade loving plants, including many unusual epimediums, flower beneath an abundance of rhododendrons, azaleas, camellias and acers. The young River Heddon flows first through the water garden and then into three ancient stew ponds separated by cascades. Snowdrops and hellebores start the gardening year, followed by magnolias, rhododendrons, new English and shrub roses, going out in a blaze of foliage colour from the large collection of specimen acers in the arboretum.

Higher Knowle

Lustleigh, Newton Abbot TQ13 9SP. Tel: (01647) 277275

Mr and Mrs D.R.A. Quicke • 13m NW of Torquay, 8m NW of Newton Abbot, 3m NW of Bovey Tracey on A382 towards Moretonhampstead. After 2.5m, turn left at Kelly Cross for Lustleigh; after 0.25m left then right at Brookfield along Knowle Road; after 0.25m steep drive on left • Open 19th March to 29th May, Sun and Bank Holiday Mons, 11am – 6pm, for NGS, and by appt between these dates • Entrance: £2.50, children free ◖ **WC** ⬀

The three-acre woodland garden surrounds a stone house built in 1914 with many Lutyens-style features by his pupil Fred Harrild as architect. Situated on a steep hillside with spectacular views to Dartmoor, the sheltered garden usually avoids late frosts and is home to tender plants. The old oak wood is carpeted with primroses and bluebells in spring, with mature Asiatic magnolias providing a fine display in late March, followed by camellias, new hybrid magnolias, many rhododendrons and azaleas, and tall embothriums. Giant Dartmoor granite boulders add natural sculpture to the woodland walks, which include a water garden.

Hill House Nursery and Garden ★

Landscove, Ashburton, Newton Abbot TQ13 7LY. Tel: (01803) 762273

Mr and Mrs Raymond Hubbard and Mr Matthew Hubbard • 3m S of Ashburton. From Plymouth-bound A38, take second exit signed to Ashburton, then left signed to Landscove, or from A384 Totnes – Buckfastleigh road follow signs to Landscove. Signposted • Open all year, daily, 11am – 5pm. Closed 19th Dec to 5th Jan. Booking required for parties • Entrance: free • Other information: Tea room open March to Sept only ○ ☕ wc ⅋ ✿

Hill House, once a Victorian vicarage next to its church – both by John Loughborough Pearson – is known to enthusiasts for the garden created by Edward Hyams and filled by him with rare, exotic and tender plants. Since the 1980s it has been restored by the present owners, plantsmen Raymond and Matthew Hubbard, both as a private garden and a family-run nursery; so too has the eighteenth-century Grecian temple installed by Hyams. By the pond is a pretty conservatory also designed by him and containing a grape vine, passion flowers and a lemon tree. An integral feature of the garden is the commercial nursery, which offers both everyday plants and tender, exotic and rare species.

Killerton ★ [Historic Garden Grade II*]

Broadclyst, Exeter EX5 3LE. Tel: (01392) 881345

The National Trust • 7m NE of Exeter on W side of B3181 • House and costume museum open 1st March to Oct, daily except Tues, 11am – 5.30pm • Park and garden open all year, daily, 10.30am – dusk • Entrance: £6.50 (2005 price) • Other information: Tea room limited opening in winter. Motorised buggies with drivers available for disabled. Dogs in park only ○ ☕ ✕ 🍴 wc ⬠ ✿ 🏛 ℗ ✎

This large hillside garden surrounded by woods, park and farmland extends to over 6000 acres. It was created by John Veitch in the late eighteenth century and later involved the famous Victorian gardening writer William Robinson. The actual garden area of 18 acres is a haven of delight. It will provide pleasure and interest to all but particularly to the tree and shrub enthusiast. Many of the plants for sale were propagated here. Besides the avenue of beeches, there are Wellingtonias (the first plantings in England), Lawson cypresses, oaks, maples and many other fine broad-leaved trees. Trees and shrubs introduced by Veitch are now reaching an imposing size. Terraced beds and extensive herbaceous borders provide summer colour. Killerton has a rhododendron collection with 95 different species, many brought back from China and Japan. There is also an early-nineteenth-century summerhouse, the Bear's Hut, an ice-house and rock garden. The handsome chapel has its own three-acre grounds containing many other fine trees, notably an enormous tulip tree.

Knightshayes ★★ [Historic Garden Grade II*]

Bolham, Tiverton EX16 7RQ. Tel: (01884) 254665 (Property Manager); (01884) 253264 (Garden Office)

The National Trust • 16m N of Exeter, 2m N of Tiverton. Turn off A396 at Bolham • House open 23rd March to 31st Oct, daily except Fri (but open Good Friday),

*11am – 4.30pm (closes 4pm in Oct) • Gardens open 4th to 20th March, Sat – Mon,
11am – 4pm; 25th Mar to 31st Oct, daily, 11am – 4.30pm (closes 4pm in Oct)
Entrance: £5.40, children £2.70, (house and gardens £6.90, children £3.40 • Other
information: Dogs on lead in park and Impey Walk only* ◐ 💻 ✕ 🏠 **WC** ♿ 🌿 🏛
🔦 ♿

The garden and landscaping was originally planned by Edward Kemp in the late
1870s when the house was being completed. It remained essentially unchanged until
Sir John and Lady Amory began replanting in the 1950s. The terraces are planted
with shrub roses, tree peonies and herbaceous plants in soft colours and silvers.
Yew encloses a paved garden in shades of pink, purple and grey with two standard
wisterias. Battlemented hedges frame the pool garden with a backdrop of *Acer
pseudoplatanus* 'Brilliantissimum', and topiary hounds endlessly chase a fox on a
lower terrace. The Garden in the Wood shelters magnolias, rhododendrons, cornus,
hydrangeas and other rare and tender plants, some grown in raised peat blocks.
Drifts of pink erythroniums, white foxgloves and cyclamen appear in their seasons.
The Victorian walled kitchen garden has recently been restored and opened; constructed in tiers with a central ornamental pool, it provides organic vegetables, fruit
and cut flowers.

Lee Ford

Budleigh Salterton EX9 7AJ. Tel: (01395) 445894

*Mr and Mrs N. Lindsay-Fynn • 3.5m E of Exmouth on B3178 Budleigh Salterton –
Knowle road • Open for charity for parties of 20 or more by appt • Entrance: £4,
children £2, (£5 with guided tour with head gardener, children £3) • Other information: Refreshments by special arrangement* ◐ **WC** ♿ 🌿

Inspired by the Savill Gardens (see entry in Surrey), the present owner's father
developed this woodland garden in the 1950s. Although at its peak in spring, with
acres of daffodils followed by rhododendrons, azaleas and magnolias, there is now
plenty to see later in the year. Following much recent landscaping, the formal garden
round the house merges into the woodland rising above it, with curving beds full of
new planting that includes collections of hydrangeas and fuchsias, together with
many grasses and a bog garden. In the woodland, with its fine tall trees and distant
views of the sea, the mown glades are surrounded by masses of azaleas, *R. ponticum*
and other species rhododendrons, some rare; the large collection of camellias
includes white varieties which are often in flower on Christmas Day. The nineteenth-
century walled garden is still run as a traditional vegetable garden, with flowers for
cutting and greenhouses. There is also a conservatory, an Adam pavilion and a little
herb garden.

Lukesland

Harford, Ivybridge PL21 0JF. Tel: (01752) 893390

*Mrs R. Howell • 1.5m N of Ivybridge off A38, on Harford road • Open 19th March
to 11th June, Wed, Sun and Bank Holiday Mons; all 2 – 6pm • Entrance: £3.50,
children free • Other information: Teas during main season only. Coaches by appt* ◐
💻 **WC** ♿ 🌿 ♿

More a botanical park than a garden – entering the grounds you could be forgiven for believing you were in the foothills of the Himalayas. Lying on the hem of Dartmoor, Lukesland is Victorian in both origin and taste. The house was built in 1862 in the Victorian Gothic style by W.E. Matthews. The delightfully secluded valley of Addicombe Brook is the setting here for 15 acres of flowering shrubs, trees and carpets of wild flowers – a gem of its kind. Although recent planting has ensured a greater variety of all-year interest, it is in spring that the profusion of rhododendrons, camellias and azaleas show the garden at its resplendent best. The magnificent *Magnolia campbellii*, over 19 metres tall and nearly one metre in diameter, is registered as a champion tree, and the pocket-handkerchief tree planted in 1936 is thought to be one of the largest in the country. The brook, which tumbles and gurgles its way over ponds and waterfalls, is criss-crossed by a series of delightful bridges which enable the visitor to wander at leisure amid scenes of great tranquillity. James McAndrew undertook the first major landscaping of the garden in the 1880s. The late owner and his family have carried out further planting, including a fine pinetum, and the construction of more ponds and bridges, all in the spirit of the original, and this is continuing.

Marwood Hill ★★

Marwood, Barnstaple EX31 4EB. Tel: (01271) 342528

Dr J. Snowdon • 4m NW of Barnstaple off A361. Signposted • Open all year, daily except 25th Dec, dawn – dusk • Entrance: £3, accompanied children under 12 free (2005 prices) • Other information: Teas on Sun and Bank Holidays and for parties by arrangement ○ 💻 WC ♿ 🌿

With its wonderful collection of plants and its delightful setting, this 20-acre garden is of special interest to the connoisseur but could not fail to give pleasure to any visitor. Five thousand different varieties of plants cover collections of willows, ferns, magnolias, eucryphias, rhododendrons and hebes, plus a fine collection of camellias in a glasshouse. There is also a large planting of eucalyptus and betulas. Other features include a pergola draped with 12 varieties of wisteria, raised alpine scree beds, three small lakes with an extensive bog garden and National Collections of astilbes, clematis, *Iris ensata* and tulbaghias. As always, the garden continues to evolve; new prairie-style plantings of herbaceous perennials, grasses and wild flowers are being developed in a further few acres.

Overbecks Museum and Garden ★ [Historic Garden Grade II*]

Sharpitor, Salcombe TQ8 8LW. Tel: (01548) 842893

The National Trust • 1.5m S of Salcombe, SW of South Sands • Museum open late March to Oct – telephone for details • Garden open all year, daily, 10am – 6pm • Entrance: £5 (museum and garden £5.50) • Other information: No coaches ○ 💻 ✕ 🍴 WC 🌿 ♿ 🍼 ♿

Palms stand in this exotic garden high above the Salcombe estuary, giving a strongly Mediterranean atmosphere. The mild maritime climate enables it to be filled with exotics such as myrtles, daturas, agaves and the rare example of a large camphor tree, *Cinnamomum camphora*. The Himalayan *Magnolia campbellii*, over 100 years old and 12 metres high and wide, is a sight to see in February and March. The steep terraces were built in 1901 and lead down through fuchsia trees, huge fruiting banana palms and myrtles to a wonderful *Cornus kousa*. In the centre of the garden are four beds packed with herbaceous perennials, many of them rare and tender; they are spectacular from July through to September. The parterre of classical design is enlivened in season by orange and lemon trees. The range of unusual and exotic plants is being extended and some of the more hidden areas at the perimeters of the garden made more accessible.

Paignton Zoo Environmental Park

Totnes Road, Paignton TQ4 7EU. Tel: (01803) 697500

The Whitley Wildlife Conservation Trust • 1m W of centre of Paignton on Totnes Road • Open all year, daily except 25th Dec, from 10am (closing times vary according to season) • Entrance: £10, OAPs £8.25, children £6.70 (2005 prices) ○ ➐ ✕ 🐾 WC ♿ ♨ ♋

Those with mixed views on zoos may be won over by Paignton; it is in the forefront of animal and plant conservation and one of the zoos worldwide involved in the breeding of endangered species. As well as the healthy and happy animals there are the plants. Over 80 acres in size, this was the first zoo in the country to combine animals and a botanic garden, laid out 80 years ago and added to over the years. There are five habitat areas: wetland, desert, savannah, forest and tropical forest. Plant selection is governed by many factors including toxicity and suitability for particular animals. Garden areas are themed geographically and botanically: hardy Chinese plants surround the baboon rock, while medicinal plants are used around the veterinary centre. One of the large glasshouses contains a desert exhibit with plants from arid areas. A tropical display area, complete with birds and reptiles, gives visitors the experience of this very different environment, and a garden of tender plants from around the world has been established outside the restaurant.

RHS Garden Rosemoor ★★

Great Torrington EX38 8PH. Tel: (01805) 624067

The Royal Horticultural Society • 7m SE of Bideford, 1m SE of Great Torrington on A3124 • Open all year, daily except 25th Dec, 10am – 6pm (closes 5pm Oct to March) • Entrance: £5.50, children £1.50 ○ ➐ ✕ 🐾 WC ♿ ♨ ♋ 🍴 ♋

Lady Anne Berry created the original garden here and her eight acres contain over 3500 plants from all over the world, many of them collected by her. Rosemoor was the Society's first regional garden, second in importance only to Wisley, with which it has a certain stylistic affinity. The 40 acres include a new formal garden with 2000 roses in 200 varieties, colour-themed gardens, a herb garden, a *potager*, cottage, foliage and winter gardens, an alpine terrace, three model gardens and extensive herbaceous borders. The new garden designed by Tom Stuart-Smith displays a range of plants grown mainly for their leaves, particularly grasses. The eighteenth-century gazebo from the grounds of Palmer House in Great Torrington has been reconstructed in the south arboretum, giving fine views across the garden and the valley. Elsewhere are stream and bog gardens and a large walled fruit and vegetable garden. National Collections of ilex (over 100 kinds) and cornus are planted throughout.

Lectures, talks, garden walks and demonstrations are held all year; there are also many events (telephone for full programme) and free guide books for children.

Saltram House [Historic Garden Grade II*]

Plympton, Plymouth PL7 1UH. Tel: (01752) 333500

The National Trust • 3m E of Plymouth. From A379 turn N to Billacombe and after 1m turn left to Saltram • House open 25th March to Sept, daily except Fri (but open Good Friday), 12 noon – 4.30pm; 1st to 29th Oct, daily except Fri, 11.30am – 3.30pm • Park open all year, daily, dawn – dusk. Garden and gallery open all year, daily except Fri, (but open Good Friday), 11am – 4pm. Closed 23rd to 31st Dec, and 1st Jan 2007 • Entrance: £3.50, children £1.80 (house and garden £7, children £3.50) ◑ 🍽 ✕ <u>WC</u> & ✆ 🏠 🎔 ⚲

The original garden dates from the 1740s, with Victorian and twentieth-century overlays. There are three eighteenth-century buildings – a castle or folly, an orangery (home to orange and lemon trees during the winter months) and a classical garden house named Fanny's Bower after Fanny Burney, who came here in 1789 in the entourage of George III. A long lime avenue is underplanted with narcissi in spring and *Cyclamen hederifolium* in autumn, and a central glade has specimen trees like the stone pine and Himalayan spruce. Set against rolling lawns are several walks with magnolias, camellias, rhododendrons and Japanese maples which, with other trees, make for dramatic autumn colour; new plantings in the serpentine walk provide scent and extra winter interest. A tree walk guide is available. The restored Graham Stuart Thomas border provides colour through the summer months, as do a wide variety of hydrangeas. Many areas of long grass abound with wild flowers throughout the spring and early summer.

Tapeley Park ★ [Historic Garden Grade II*]

Instow EX39 4NT. Tel: (01271) 342558

Mr Hector. Christie • 2m N of Bideford S off A39 Barnstaple – Bideford road • House open for pre-booked parties (additional £2.50 per person) • Gardens open 20th March to Oct, daily except Sat, 10am – 5pm • Entrance: £4, OAPs £3.50, children £2.50. Special rates for parties of 5 or more ◑ 🍽 🛍 <u>WC</u> & ⬙ ✆ 🏠 🎔 ⚲

The mellow red-brick William and Mary house bestrides the narrow estuary of the River Torridge. It was the nobility of its elevated setting that inspired a much later hand – the architect John Belcher – to create a triple cascade of Italian terraces at the beginning of the twentieth century. These have now been restored to startling effect by Mary Keen, with planting of longitudinal bands of colour emphasising their length and formality. The way from the house to the lake winds down a beautiful woodland walk; the water is backed by magnificent *Thuja plicata*, said to be the oldest in the country. Within the gardens is a set of small buildings, which include a circular shell-lined grotto, a brick ice-house, a Georgian dairy, a handsome neo-Grecian lodge and a fine 1855 obelisk. The eighteenth-century walled kitchen garden is very much a working area, and there is a new organic garden producing fruit, vegetables, nuts and herbs. The wild garden houses farm animals and an adventure playground. For plantsmen there are fine specimens including exotics (*Abelia floribunda*, sophoras

and accas from Brazil), and for those interested in landscape design there is ornamental water, yew hedges, an ilex tunnel, giant beeches and oaks. A garden for all
tastes and all seasons, and a house owned by a family with a fascinating history – the
Christies of Glyndebourne in Sussex. Mary Keen was also responsible for the new
gardens around the rebuilt opera house at *Glyndebourne* itself, where Christopher
Lloyd and head gardener Chris Hughes are also reinvigorating the existing planting
schemes.

Tudor Rose Tea Rooms and Garden

36 New Street, The Barbican, Plymouth PL1 2NA. Tel: (01752) 255502

*Plymouth Corporation • In old town centre • Open all year, Tues – Sun, 10am – 5pm.
During summer season also open Mons, 10am – 5pm, and Thurs – Sat, 10am –
7.30pm • Entrance: free* ○ ⬛ ✕ WC ⬦

An integral part of an area of Plymouth that is being refurbished, this is an interesting reconstruction of the type of Tudor garden that would have existed behind the
houses in this ancient street. As far as possible only plants which grew in Elizabethan
England have been established. Elsewhere in Plymouth the Corporation commemorates great Victorian seaside gardening with colourful carpet bedding, hanging baskets and tubs.

University of Exeter ★

Streatham Estate, Prince of Wales Road, Exeter EX4 4PX. Tel: (01392) 263059

*University of Exeter • On N outskirts of Exeter on A396, turn E onto B3183.
Signposted • Garden open all year, daily • Entrance: free • Other information:
Coaches by appt only* ○ ♿ ⬦

High above Exeter with views over the city, the 300-acre university campus contains
an impressive collection of unusual trees and shrubs from the temperate regions
of the world – all credit to the authorities for the sensitivity with which they
have woven the modern buildings into this mature arboretum. In the 1860s, an East
India merchant who had inherited a fortune made by blockade-running in the
Napoleonic wars employed the Exeter firm of Veitch to lay out the original 15-acre
garden. Veitch's plant collectors, among them E.H. Wilson and the Lobb brothers,
brought back numerous species from around the globe; many, such as the wingnut
tree (*Pterocarya stenoptera*) and one of the first Wellingtonias to be planted in this
country, are still flourishing. The sheltered site is perfect for tender plants, including
hardy bananas, podocarpus and callistemons, and for a large range of magnolias,
rhododendrons and camellias growing in woodland. A stream has been dammed
to create three ponds, and this contrasts with the formal bedded area and the
scented garden on the site of the original orangery. The garden holds a National
Collection of azaras. A sculpture walk includes works by Barbara Hepworth and
Henry Moore.

DORSET

Two-starred gardens are marked on the map with a black square.

Abbotsbury Sub-Tropical Gardens ★★ [Historic Garden Grade I]

Abbotsbury, Weymouth DT3 4LA. Tel: (01305) 871387

Ilchester Estates • 9m NW of Weymouth, 9m SW of Dorchester off B3157 • Open March to Oct, daily, 10am – 6pm; Nov to Feb, daily except Christmas and New Year period (telephone to check), 10am – dusk • Entrance: £6.80, OAPs £6, children £4
○ ● ✕ ● wc ᠔ ⟳ ℘ ⛪ ❢ ⚲

The walled garden was established by the 1st Countess of Ilchester in 1765, as a kitchen garden for the nearby castle, which burned down in 1913. It forms the nucleus of these famous gardens, which contain a rich selection of plants from the Mediterranean – proximity to the sea and shelter from the north create the microclimate that has turned the area into a botanical treasure trove. A Mediterranean bank grows exotics from Australia, South Africa and Mexico, including proteas, banksias, agaves and olive trees. In 1899 a catalogue of 5000 plants was produced; today there must be many more within the 20-acre site, which has been extensively restored and replanted over the last two decades. Rare trees abound: a fine and ancient wingnut, 100-year-old Chusan palms over 20 metres tall, and the beautiful *Cornus* 'Bentham's Cornel', bright with sulphur yellow bracts in July. Bamboo groves, bog gardens, bananas from Ethiopia, masses of hydrangeas, azaleas, hostas and much else besides are all to be seen on the well-marked woodland walk, where peacocks, golden pheasants and other exotic birds may be spotted among the trees. A lush waterside planting of primulas, hostas, rogersias and other moisture-lovers is maturing well. A new magnolia walk, 250 metres long, leads out of the garden up to a high point giving spectacular views of the World Heritage Jurassic coast. The nearby swannery at the eastern end of the village should not be missed.

Arnmore House

57 Lansdowne Road, Bournemouth BH1 1RN. Tel: (01202) 551440

Mr and Mrs David Hellewell • On B3064 just S of hospital • Open all year, by appt • Entrance: £3, children free ● ᠔

A garden of considerable personality, created by a composer who also has a strong feeling for Chinese art. His planting is tactile and shape, colour and texture all matter – hence the unusual specimen trees, the topiary against walls and the patterned paving. The formal parterre is a striking composition of diagonals, with *Buxus sempervirens* accompanied by clipped balls of *B.s.* 'Aureovariegata'. Trees and shrubs chosen for year-round colour are all around, some in pots and many pruned and trained to give exactly the desired effect. Ease of maintenance has also been a priority as Mrs Hellewell is disabled.

Athelhampton House Gardens ★ [Historic Garden Grade I]

Athelhampton, Puddletown, Dorchester DT2 7LG. Tel: (01305) 848363

Patrick Cooke • 5m NE of Dorchester, 1m E of Puddletown off A35 at Northbrook junction • House and gardens open March to Oct, Sun – Thurs; Dec to Feb, Sun; all 10.30am – 5pm (or dusk if earlier) • Entrance: house and garden £7.95, OAPs £7, children free, parties of 12 or more £5.50 per person) • Other information: Picnics in riverside area only. Self-catering accommodation available ☽ 🍽 ✕ 🛍 WC ♿ ⚘ 🚻 ☕

The four gardens and two pavilions of the Tudor manor house were designed for Alfred Cart de La Fontaine in 1891 by F. Inigo Thomas. The late Robert Cooke extended the garden with great sensitivity during the 1960s and '70s. Courts and walls follow the original plan with beautiful stone and brickwork arches. Visitors will take away with them an abiding memory of some of the most stylish architectural topiary in England, and of the River Piddle, girdling the garden in its own right and busily harnessed within it to service pools, fountains and a long canal studded with water lilies. Major features are a fifteenth-century circular dovecot on the lawn facing the west wing of the house, and the pleached lime circular grove behind the Pyramid Garden. Here, twelve massive yews are fashioned to echo the obelisks on the raised terrace walk, which has a matching pair of charming pavilions standing at each end. The toll house to the south has been restored, and a new raised boardwalk extends over 200 metres along the River Piddle. The planting, including tulips, rambling roses, clematis and jasmine, is big-boned, low-key and sophisticated. A remarkable, unforgettably atmospheric interpretation of the late-medieval ideal.

Chettle House

Chettle, Blandford Forum DT11 8DB. Tel: (01258) 830858

Mr and Mrs Peter Bourke • 6m NE of Blandford on A354, turn left to Chettle • House and garden open. Telephone for opening times. • Entrance: £3.50, children free (2005 price) ☽ 🍽 WC ♿ ☕ ⚬

The tranquil site is approached through mature trees where a number of different horse chestnut species may be seen. There is an elegant church in the grounds. Beyond the wide lawns framing the impressive Queen Anne house (designed by the Baroque architect Thomas Archer, of rounded style and inverted scrolls fame), vistas appropriate to that period are preserved, with a paddock on the south slope. Lavish herbaceous borders contain many chalk-loving plants, including no fewer than 20 varieties of honeysuckle and some fine clematis.

Chideock Manor

Chideock, Bridport DT6 6LF. Tel: (01297) 489890

Mr and Mrs Howard Coates • 2m W of Bridport on A35. In centre of village turn right by church; entrance to house on right along narrow lane • Open for NGS, and weekends by appt • Entrance: £3.50 [NEW] ☽ 🍽 WC ♿

The attractive driveway leads through downland and woodland and over a stream to the imposing Regency mansion (not open), home from 1803 to 1996 to the Weld family; the adjoining chapel was added in 1879. They left a legacy of magnificent mature trees, an imposing yew walk, a walled kitchen garden and several fine statues, but the garden seen today is largely the creation of the present owners. The layout is formal in parts, and the Welds' statues take their place in the new scheme, relocated as focal points in the Lady Garden, the lime walk and other distinctive areas. From the knot garden with its whorls of santolina, paths lead to the old yew walk and on to woodland, where masses of *Zantedeschia aethiopica* grace the extensive bog garden in summer. More developments are promised; meanwhile, visitors can sit in the stone belvedere and admire the fine views of the surrounding landscape.

City Farmhouse

Sydling St Nicholas, Dorchester DT2 9NX. Tel: (01300) 341593

Nigel and Angela Shaw • Open 28th and 29th May, 3rd and 4th June, 2 – 6pm • Entrance: £3 in May (includes 15 other village gardens), £1.50 in June ◐ 🐌 ♿ 🐾

Set in one of Dorset's most unspoilt villages in the Sydling Valley, the farm was at one time owned by Winchester City, hence the name of the thatched Dorset longhouse, which dates from the early seventeenth century. Now separated from the actual farm, the attractive old building divides the half-acre garden into two parts. Behind, a spacious lawn is partly bordered by cottage-garden flower beds and a stream where trout rise to be fed, and here the planting is in traditional cottage-garden style, colourful, informal and intermingled. There are 70 different roses in the garden, mainly trusty David Austin varieties – the house walls alone carry four, with three wisterias as companions, while on the eastern side an immaculate grass tennis court is a true feature, surrounded by a striking hedge of alternate box and yew trees, now some 4 metres tall and carefully topiaried and trimmed. The setting exudes the peaceful, unchanging spirit of this beautiful village – well worth exploring, especially the church bordering the gardens of the manor house, which is famous for its massive and ancient yew hedge.

Cranborne Manor Garden ★★ [Historic Garden Grade II*]

Cranborne, Wimborne Minster BH21 5PP. Tel: (01725) 517248

The Marquess and Marchioness of Salisbury • 10m N of Wimborne on B3078. Entrance via garden centre • Open March to Sept, Wed only, 9am – 5pm, and some weekends for charity – telephone to check dates • Entrance: £4, OAPs £3.50 (2005 prices) • Other information: Garden centre open all year ◐ 🍵 WC ♿ 🐾 🏛

Tradescant established the basic framework in the early seventeenth century, but little is left of the original plan. Neglected for a long period, the garden has been revived in the last three generations and now includes several smaller areas surrounded by tall clipped yew hedges, a walled white garden at its best in midsummer, wide lawns (again yew-lined) and extensive woodland and wild areas. The high-walled entrance courtyard to the south is approached through an arch between the two Jacobean gatehouses. Here the plant selection along the lengthy borders is delightfully imaginative, providing the perfect introduction to what has been called 'the most magical house in Dorset' (not least for the garden which surrounds it). The excellent nursery garden specialises in traditional rose varieties, but also carries a wide selection of other plants, particularly clematis and herbaceous

perennials; the tearoom is excellent too. Another garden with an interesting historical pedigree, but an entirely different experience, is to be found at nearby *Ashley Park
Farm*, Damerham. Created by a dedicated conservationist, there are unusual trees and
shrubs in attractive woodland walks, ponds and a wildflower meadow, a farm and wild
fowl and rare sheep. [Open for NGS and by appt. Tel: (01725) 518200.]

Dean's Court

Wimborne Minster BH21 1EE. Tel: (01202) 886116

*Sir Michael and Lady Hanham • In centre of Wimborne off B3073 • Open for NGS
16th, 17th and 30th April, 1st, 28th and 29th May, 18th June, 27th and 28th Aug,
10th Sept, Suns 2 – 6pm, Mons 10am – 6pm • Entrance: £3, OAPs £2, children £1*
● ● WC & ●

Originally the deanery to the minster, the mainly eighteenth-century house has
sixteenth-century origins; it is set in 19 acres of parkland with a number of interesting trees, including a vast Mexican swamp cypress and a 30-metre tulip tree. Others
that survived the 1990 storm include two mulberries, medlars, a ginkgo and a false
nutmeg. There are few formal beds, but there are over 100 varieties of herbs in the
courtyard, and a 1.25-acre kitchen garden, built by Frenchmen taken prisoner
during the Napoleonic wars and surrounded on two sides by a serpentine wall, one
of the longest in the country. The landscaped rose garden is enclosed to keep out
the deer, and the monastic stewpond, fed by the River Allen and recently restored,
is still stocked with carp as it was in the days of the Saxon monastery once sited in
this peaceful haven.

Domineys Yard

Buckland Newton DT2 7BS. Tel: (01300) 345295

*Mr and Mrs William Gueterbock • 11m N of Dorchester, 2m E of A352. From B3143
take no-through road between church and Gaggle of Geese inn; entrance 90 metres on
left • Open 2nd April, 14th May, 25th June, 13th Aug, 22nd Oct, all 2 – 6pm. Also
by appt • Entrance: £3, children free* NEW ● ●

When the present owners bought the sixteenth-century thatched house, it was
surrounded by open fields. Over the years their plantings have prospered in the
greensand, and their 2.5-acre garden now has a rich seasonal display of bulbs, herbaceous plants, shrubs and trees. The adaptable soil allows for both lime- and acid-
loving plants, many cultivated from seed and some for sale. There is also a thriving
vegetable and fruit garden and another with a formal layout, and visitors may park
and picnic in the 4.5-acre arboretum with its charming rural backdrop.

Edmondsham House

Edmondsham, Cranborne, Wimborne Minster BH21 5RE. Tel: (01725) 517207

*Mrs J. Smith • 9m N of Wimbourne, 1m S of Cranborne. From A354 turn at
Sixpenny Handley crossroads signed to Ringwood and Cranborne • House open April
and Oct, Wed and Bank Holiday Mons, 2 – 5pm • Garden open April to Oct, Wed
and Sun, 2 – 5pm, and by appt • Entrance: £2, children 50p, season ticket £10*

(house and garden £4, children £1, under 5 free) • *Other information: Refreshments April and Oct, Wed only* ◑ 🍴 <u>WC</u> ♿ 🌣

The visitor should allow time for a tour of the interesting family house and dairy before venturing out into the large walled kitchen garden with its large herbaceous border planted to ensure interest from spring through to the end of October. No chemical fertilisers or pesticides are used here. Admire the beds of Russian comfrey, rhubarb, Jerusalem artichokes and asparagus, the herb gardens and the fruit cage before taking the path to the lean-to peach house. The Pit House is a sunken greenhouse, restored in 1990. The arch of the walled garden leads to the paddock and on to the drive and the dell. The pond has an island of *Sasa palmata* and a dawn redwood (*Metasequoia glyptostroboides*). An unusual circular grass hollow is said to have been a cockpit, one of only a very few 'naturalised' areas of the sort in the country. The massed spring bulbs together with the many spring-flowering shrubs make this the best season, but the peaceful, mellow atmosphere pervades the garden throughout the year. Allow time to visit the church to look for the clumps of mistletoe, the cucumber tree (*Magnolia acuminata*) and the foxglove tree (*Paulownia tomentosa*).

Forde Abbey ★★ [Historic Garden Grade II*]

Chard, Somerset TA20 4LU. Tel: (01460) 221290

Mr M. Roper • 8m NW of Beaminster, 7m W of Crewkerne, 4m SE of Chard off A30 • House open April to Oct, Tues – Fri, Sun and Bank Holiday Mons, 12 noon – 4pm • Garden open all year, daily, 10am – 4.30pm • Entrance: £5.50, OAPs £5, children under 15 free (house and garden £7.50, OAPs £7, children under 15 free) (2005 prices) • Other information: Parties of 20 or more telephone 01460 220231 for bookings ○ 💬 ✕ 🍴 <u>WC</u> ♿ ⬳ 🌣 🏛

This unique and fascinating former Cistercian abbey, inhabited as a private house since 1649, is set in a varied and pleasing garden. A canal at the end of the long set of buildings which comprises the stately abbey, and a large lake some distance away, are major features of the extensive garden. Old walls and colourful borders, sloping lawns, lush ponds and cascades, graceful statuary and enormous mature trees combine to create an atmosphere of timeless elegance. A new 160-foot fountain celebrates the Roper family's 100 years at Forde Abbey. There is something here for every gardener to appreciate: the bog garden displays a large collection of primulas and other Asiatic plants; the shrubbery contains a variety of magnolias, rhododendrons and other delightful specimens. The rock garden was revolutionised by the late Jack Drake, and a fine arboretum has been built up since 1947; at the back of the abbey is an extensive kitchen garden and a nursery selling rare and unusual plants which look in fine health. In nearby Bettiscombe, Penelope Hobhouse's renowned garden at *The Coach House* is open for parties by appointment (telephone (01308) 868560) and in conjunction with other village gardens on 2nd July.

Frankham Farm

Ryme Intrinseca, Sherborne DT9 6JT. Tel: (01935) 872304

Mr and Mrs R.G. Earle • 6m SW of Sherborne off A37 Yeovil – Dorchester road. 3m S of Yeovil turn left; garden is 0.25m on left • Open for NGS, and for parties and individuals by appt • Entrance: £2.50, children free ◑ 💬 ✕ <u>WC</u> ♿ 🌣

In spring and early summer, visitors to this charming garden can be assured of plenty of colour. Developed since the 1960s, the flat site of over two acres includes extensive plantings of roses and clematis. Well-stocked herbaceous borders frame a fine view of adjacent fields, with grass walks meandering through woodland and a wild garden planted with spring bulbs and shrubs making a pleasing contrast. A striking group of *Cornus kousa* with white foxgloves under eucalyptus leads from the neat and productive kitchen garden into a small plantation of unusual trees, including the Chilean firebush (*Embothrium coccineum*) and *Aesculus pavia*, alongside rhododendrons, azaleas and camellias. Many of the plants and trees have been grown from seed by the owners. Farm buildings form an attractive backdrop.

Horn Park

Beaminster DT8 3HB. Tel: (01308) 862212

Mr and Mrs David Ashcroft • 1.5m N of Beaminster on A3066 on left before tunnel • Open two days in June for NGS, and April to Oct, Tues – Thurs, by appt • Entrance: £3.50 • Other information: Teas by prior arrangement ◐ 🏠 WC ♿ 🐕

Although the impressive house designed by Lawrence Dale, a pupil of Lutyens, dates from 1910, the garden is based partly on features discovered as the work progressed. A drive through parkland leads to the wide gravel sweep before the entrance porch, with terraced lawns to the front of the house and a panoramic view towards Beaminster and the distant coast. Other features include rock areas, herbaceous and rose borders, unusual plants and shrubs, a water garden beneath a steep azalea bank, ponds, a woodland garden and walks among wild flowers, including orchids and bluebells in spring. The natural wildflower meadow, with over 160 different flowers and grasses, is listed as a site of nature conservation interest. Just south of Beaminster on the A3066, the dramatic topiary and flower gardens of *Parnham House* will host the Dorset Gardens Trust Open Day on 6th July, 10am – 5pm. Well-known lecturers and many specialist plant stalls – telephone Serena Hichens on (01308) 488232 for details.

Ivy Cottage ★

Aller Lane, Lower Ansty, Dorchester DT2 7PX. Tel: (01258) 880053

Anne and Alan Stevens • 12m NE of Dorchester, 10m W of Blandford in centre of triangle between A352, A354 and A3030. Take turning near Fox Inn, Ansty • Open May to Sept, Thurs, 10am – 5pm, and for parties by appt at other times • Entrance: £3, children free ◐ 🏠 WC

Mrs Stevens trained and worked as a professional gardener before coming to her cottage in 1964. Although chalk underlies the surrounding land, this one-and-three-quarter-acre informal cottage garden is actually on greensand; it has springs and a stream that keep it well watered and is therefore an ideal home for plants such as primulas, irises, gunneras, and in particular trollius and moisture-loving lobelias. Other delights are a thriving and ordered kitchen garden (which hardly ever needs a hose), large herbaceous borders giving colour all year round, drifts of bulbs and other spring plants surrounding specimen trees and shrubs, and three most interesting raised beds for alpines. The new roof garden on the garage can be seen from a high path nearby. Wildlife is actively encouraged.

Kingston Lacy ★ [Historic Garden Grade II]

Wimborne Minster BH21 4EA. Tel: (01202) 883402

The National Trust • 1.5m NW of Wimborne on B3082 • House open 18th March to 29th Oct, Wed – Sun, 11am – 5pm (last admission 4pm) • Park and garden open 18th March to 29th Oct, daily, 10.30am – 5.30pm; 3rd Nov to 17th Dec, Fri – Sun, 10.30am – 4pm; Feb and March, Sat and Sun, 10.30am – 4pm. Additional opening for snowdrops – telephone for details • Entrance: garden and park: £4.50, children £2.25, family £11 (house, garden and park £9, children £4.50, family £22, parties of 15 or more £6.80 per person, children £3.40) • Other information: Volunteer-driven buggy on house open days ☺ 💷 ✕ 🥘 <u>WC</u> ⬥ ⬥ 🏛 ⚑ ⚲

This 32-acre formal garden, with nine acres of lawn, also has a wonderful lime avenue planted in 1668, which leads to the Nursery Wood containing a fine collection of rhododendrons and azaleas. The terrace displays urns, vases and lions in bronze and marble, and there are interesting marble wellheads or tubs for bay trees; also an Egyptian obelisk and a sarcophagus. The parterre was laid out in 1899 for Henrietta Bankes in memory of her husband and is still planted in the seasonal bedding schemes designed for her. The Victorian fernery, planted with 25 different types of fern and a National Collection of *Anemone nemorosa*, leads to the once-fine cedar walk, where one of the trees was planted by the Duke of Wellington in 1827 and others by visiting royalty. Snowdrops, daffodils and bluebells abound, and in summer the spectacular display of roses includes 'Bonica', 'Cardinal Hume', 'Nozomi' and 'Amber Queen'. The restored Japanese gardens lie in 7.5 acres of the southern shelter belt. Originally laid out by Henrietta Bankes c.1910, they are the largest of their kind in England and include a formal tea garden complete with a stone 'stream', a tea house and a waiting arbour. The garden holds a National Collection of convallarias. There is a circular woodland walk, including a children's playground. In spring, many areas are covered in snowdrops, daffodils and bluebells.

Kingston Maurward Gardens ★ [Historic Garden Grade II*]

Dorchester DT2 8PY. Tel: (01305) 215003

Kingston Maurward Gardens • E of Dorchester off A35. Turn off at roundabout at end of bypass • Open all year, daily, 10am – 5.30pm. Closed 21st Dec to 4th Jan. Guided tours by appt • Entrance: £5, children £3, under 3 free. Family season tickets available to gardens and farm animal park ☺ 💷 🥘 <u>WC</u> ♿ ⬥ 🏛 ⚑ ⚲

Three distinct periods coexist harmoniously here. In 1720 the handsome house was built, dignified by a contemporary landscape park with 35 acres of fine trees, water and woodland. Then, between 1918 and 1920, the formal gardens to the west of the mansion were laid out by the Hanbury family, who also owned the celebrated La Mortola in Italy. Within splendid stone terraces, balustrading, steps and yew hedges, they made a series of intimate enclosures, including water features, topiary, a yew maze, and other requisites of a grand Edwardian garden. Positioned on a steep hillside overlooking the 8-acre lake, the views are outstanding. The most recent phase in the gardens' history has been their determined restoration since 1990 by the present incumbents, the staff and students of Kingston Maurward College. Their utilitarian training facilities might occupy the perimeter, but the formal gardens are resplendent once more. National Collections of penstemons and salvias are held here, together with a large collection of herbaceous perennials; in spring drifts of bulbs occupy the sweeping lawns and the margins of the lake. Of particular interest is the statuary on long loan from the Palace of Westminster and the restored Grecian temple at the lake's edge. There is also a Japanese-style garden with Chusan palms, bamboos and maples, a tree trail with 65 different species to discover, and an animal park for children. *Hardy's Cottage*, now a National Trust property with a small colourful garden, is nearby.

Knoll Gardens and Nursery ★

Hampreston, Wimborne Minster BH21 7ND. Tel: (01202) 873931

Mr Neil Lucas • Between Wimborne and Ferndown, off Ham Lane (B3073). Leave A31 at Canford Bottom roundabout. Signed after 1.5m • Open all year, Wed – Sun and Bank Holiday Mons, 10am – 5pm (or dusk if earlier). Closed 19th Dec to 1st Jan • Entrance: £4.25, concessions £3.75, children (5–15) £2.75, family £10.50. Reductions for parties of 20 or more ☼ 🍽 <u>WC</u> ♿ ♨ ♀

Twenty-five years ago this was a private botanic garden, but it is now laid out in an informal English setting with mature specimen trees and shrubs creating a relaxed and intimate atmosphere. Although only a little over four acres, the many different areas, winding pathways and constantly changing views give an impression of a much larger area. The owners continue to develop the garden. A naturalistic border commemorating the owners' tenth anniversay at the gardens was planted in 2004 with over 800 grasses and hardy perennials. The summer garden has a collection of exotic-looking tender perennials, the water garden several waterfalls, while the Dragon Garden boasts a nationally acclaimed collection of modern perennials and grasses, displayed to their best effect. There are areas planted for dry shade and for moisture and a newly extended gravel garden for drought-tolerant plants. National Collections of deciduous ceanothus, phygelius and pennisetums are held here. Christopher Bradley-Hole's new amphitheatre garden at *Portland Castle* is 12 miles away.

Langebride House

Long Bredy, Dorchester DT2 9HU. Tel: (01308) 482257

Mrs D. Greener • 8m W of Dorchester off A35 Dorchester – Bridport road. Turn S to Long Bredy • Open several days for NGS, and by appt at other times • Entrance: £3 ☼ WC ♿

This garden has so many desirable features it is impossible to avoid making a list: a 200-year-old copper beech rising from wide, lush lawns, underplanted with carpets of spring bulbs; a thriving enclosed vegetable garden of manageable size, backing onto a sloping grass area with colourful mixed borders along the tile-topped walls; a rising slope to the mixed wild woodland behind, where favourite trees have been planted in groups to allow for culling as they enlarge; a formal yew-lined lawn with pond, fountain and old stone features, from which steps descend through sloping shrubberies towards the front of the house. A miniature area of greensand allows a patch of acid-loving plants to provide contrast. A long line of pleached limes runs parallel with the bi-colour beech hedge along the road. There is also a sloping orchard, a tennis court with a tall rockery behind, planted with alpines, which acts as a viewing point and sun-trap, beds and borders, trellises for climbing plants and low stone walls for those that prefer to hang. All around, thousands of bulbs hide in waiting for the spring explosion which, in the owner's opinion, is the best season to visit.

Loscombe House

Bridport DT6 3TL. Tel: (01308) 488361

Derek Andrewes • 3m N of Bridport, 2m SE of Beaminster, 1m E of A3066. In Melplash take Loscombe turn opposite Half Moon Inn and after 0.5m turn right (signed to Loscombe). Continue 1m to bottom of lane • Open April to Sept, Sat – Tues, 11am – 6pm • Entrance: free (donations to Macmillan Cancer Relief welcome)
❶ 🛍 ♿

A woodland garden, in a secluded valley, this is Dorset at its most rural. Set in a four-acre site, the garden designed by the late Mrs Andrewes has a background of hills which drop down close to the boundary. Hillside tree-planting undertaken in 1970 has now developed into woodland, improved from 1984 when the valley bog was drained. An attractive flowing stream is a focus, with grass paths winding among well-maintained and decorative shrubs and perennials, including roses, berberis and spiraeas, sustained by the microclimate within this sheltered site. A delightful, peaceful scene, far indeed from the madding crowd.

The Manor House

Sandford Orcas, Sherborne DT9 4SB. Tel: (01963) 220206

Sir Mervyn Medlycott, Bt • 2.5m N of Sherborne, off B3148, house is next to village church • House open • Garden open 17th April, 10am – 6pm, then May and July to Sept, Sun and Mon, 2 – 5pm, and by appt for parties at other times • Entrance: house and garden £4, children £2. Reduced rates for pre-booked parties of 10 or more
❶ WC ⬦

Looked at purely as a garden, this is not exceptional. It is the medieval house, ancient and redolent of its long history, which permeates the scene and dominates the garden. Two giant clam shells brought from Tahiti ornament the terrace. An old, flagged path slopes up between bordered lawns towards an open field. The stone walls at either side are attractive, and where they stop the eye travels on into the countryside beyond. At the end of the lower lawn along the south side of the house, a viewpoint back towards the south front allows the attractive planting below the herb garden to show at its best. Roses and other climbing plants clinging to the honey-grey walls harmonise well with this gracious setting.

Mapperton ★★ [Historic Garden Grade II*]

Beaminster DT8 3NR. Tel: (01308) 862645

The Earl and Countess of Sandwich • 5m NE of Bridport, 2m SE of Beaminster between A356 and A3066 • House open 26th June to 4th Aug, Mon – Fri, plus 29th

May, 28th Aug, all 2 – 4pm, and by appt • Garden open March to Oct, daily except Sat, 11am – 5pm. House and garden tours available by prior appt (£2 extra) • Entrance: £4, children (5–18) £2.50, under 5 free ◐ ⚑ ✕ <u>WC</u> ♿ ⚲ ⛪ ☕

Dorset's combes are famously intriguing, and Mapperton offers one of the county's most atmospheric gardens set into a unique stepped valley. This is garden-as-opera-set, beginning on the first of three levels with the courtyard garden at the front of the charming sixteenth- and seventeenth-century manor house which introduces a cast of old roses and clematis. To the east, beyond the seventeenth-century house and below the main lawn, the drama quickens as the land falls to the Fountain Court with its sculptured topiary and Italianate features. Pools of water, carved stone steps, a pergola and foaming Mediterranean borders, including *Artemisia* 'Powis Castle'. *Phlomis italica* and species salvias face the classical orangery built by the current owner's father in 1968. A golden hamstone wall shows off a living wallpaper of pink *Erigeron karvinskianus* and a tree poppy, *Romneya coulteri*. The Baroque-inspired fountain, beautifully restored, is surrounded by box and yew to evoke the original 1920s' design (probably by Pike, a local architect) for the then owner, Mrs Labouchère. Below are deep fishponds reflecting 'walls' of yew and the tower house above. These yew walls repay attention, for their niches display evocative statuary. Down on the third level – the floor of the valley – is a small arboretum of species trees and shrubs, which opens into the 'wild' countryside beyond with cattle looming. There is flower and leaf interest throughout the visiting season from the first magnificent pink flowers of *Magnolia campbellii* to the fruits and berries appearing among the tints in the valley garden. Mapperton is a draw for garden lovers and for photographers and watercolourists in particular, because of the play of light across the planes of this extraordinary north-south valley.

Melbury House ★ [Historic Park and Garden Grade II*]

Melbury Sampford, Dorchester DT2 0LF. Tel: (01935) 83699 (Garden Office)

Mr James and The Hon. Mrs Townshend • 13m NW of Dorchester on A37 Yeovil – Dorchester road. Signposted • Telephone for opening dates and times • Other information: Guided walks by appointment. ◐ ⚑ WC ⚲

The outstanding eighteenth-century historic house (not open) is approached by a long drive through open parkland. Visitors are directed to the west side and enter through the large walled garden, a good part still maintained as a productive kitchen garden. A walk through the western part of the arboretum ends at the bottom of the south lawn with fine views of the house and across the lake to the deer park. The main part of the arboretum with its massed spring bulbs lies to the east in the Valley Garden, overlooked by the ancient family church (open). There are over 130 different trees, many of them rare and of impressive size. Herbaceous borders along the south of the house lead to a colourful walled flower garden. Recent seasons have seen much replanting so this garden will be a source of continuous interest.

Melplash Court

Melplash, Bridport DT6 3UH

Mrs T. Lewis • 5m N of Bridport on A3066 • Open for NGS, and by written appt only • Entrance: £3 ◐ ⚑ WC ♿ ⟿ ⚲

The elegant sixteenth-century house, set among the Dorset hills with the sea over the horizon, is approached through an avenue of mature chestnut and lime trees. The owners respected plans for the garden as laid out by a previous owner, Lady Diana Tiarks, but have extensively restored and extended the area so that new planting is a feature without disturbing the general concept. On the whole, muted colours are preferred and expressed in a wonderful variety of foliage, particularly on the banks of the stream garden. Each section, including the outstanding Japanese garden, is a surprise as the visitor progresses via walled areas into carefully planned bedding that dramatises the sloping contours. A walled kitchen garden features knots where again leaf shape, in the form of rhubarb, leek, cabbage, angelica, creates attractive patterns. Herbaceous borders have recently been planted on the croquet lawn stretching out from the house. Maintenance is first-class.

Minterne ★ [Historic Garden Grade II]

Minterne Magna, Dorchester DT2 7AU. Tel: (01300) 341370

The Hon Mr and Mrs Henry Digby • 9m N of Dorchester, 2m N of Cerne Abbas on A352 • Open March to Oct, daily, 10am – 6pm • Entrance: £4, accompanied children free ◑ WC ⬦

Minterne is a grand house in a magnificent setting. There are many rare trees, and one and a half miles of walks with palm trees, cedars, beeches, etc giving spectacular spring and autumn colour. At the lower end of the valley the stream with its lakes and waterfalls is surrounded by splendid tall trees, among which the paths wind back towards the house. The lakes contain many water lilies, and ducks have been introduced to deal with the duckweed. The garden has an interesting collection of Himalayan rhododendrons and azaleas, spring bulbs, cherries and maples. A restful and attractive atmosphere – the informative and personally written labels will encourage visitors to linger.

Moreton Gardens

Moreton DT2 8RF. Tel: (01929) 405084

Richard and Liz Frampton-Hobbs • 7m E of Dorchester off B3390 • Open all year, daily, 10am – 5pm, and by appt for evening parties • Entrance: £3, accompanied children under 16 free (2005 prices) • Other information: Moreton Tea Rooms open daily, 10am – 5pm, catering for parties and coaches by appt (Tel: (01929) 463647) ○ 🛍 WC ♿ ⚲ 🏛 🍴 ⚘

These tranquil three acres, re-created within the gardens of a now-detached house, have matured well since opening to the public in 1997. Some original trees remain and a delightful stream flows through the grounds. There is evidence of Gertrude Jekyll's influence in the design of paved roundels, pergolas and long views, softened now by a profusion of roses, herbaceous borders and a woodland area abounding in hostas, azaleas and lilies. The planting is varied, with something for all seasons, especially along the waterside. The church received a stray bomb during the Second World War and has replacement windows engraved by Lawrence Whistler; Lawrence of Arabia is buried in the churchyard.

The Old Rectory

Litton Cheney, Dorchester DT2 9AH. Tel: (01308) 482383

Mr and Mrs Hugh Lindsay • 9m W of Dorchester, 1m S of A35 • Open possibly during Feb for snowdrops (see local press), for NGS 16th April, and one Sun in May and one Tues in June, all 2 – 6pm. Open at other times by appt • Entrance: £2.50, children free ● ● WC ⑂ ⬦ ⚘

The house rests comfortably below the church and is approached by a gravel drive which circles a small lawn; a thatched summerhouse stands to one side like a massive beehive. The small walled garden has outhouses and a large barn on two sides and borders around three, prolifically stocked with well-chosen and favourite plants in specific colour bands, including many roses. A steep path leads down into the four acres of natural woodland, a surprisingly extensive area of mature trees with many springs, streams and ponds – never a water shortage here, even in the driest of summers. This area was reclaimed by the current owners, who are adding new young trees and shrubs as well as successfully encouraging many spring-flowering plant colonies, mostly native. Climbing back above the house, the visitor arrives at the belvedere giving views over trees to farmland on the other side of the valley. Spring and autumn are the best times to see this garden, from which Reynolds Stone, the wood-engraver, drew inspiration. In the same village, *Tithe Barn House* in Chalk Pit Lane has a charming small garden with a wealth of plants and pots, a reflecting pool and sweeping valley views. [Open one day in June for NGS, and for parties of 10 or more by appointment – telephone Mr and Mrs Antony Longland on (01308) 482219.]

The Old Rectory

Pulham, Dorchester DT2 7EA. Tel (01258) 817595

Mr and Mrs N. Elliott • 13m N of Dorchester, 8m SE of Sherborne on B3143. Turn E at Pulham crossroads and continue to church • Open for NGS, and for parties by appt • Entrance: £3.00, children free ● WC ⑂ ⚘

A well-maintained three-acre garden with superb views, developed around a fine eighteenth-century house. Plants, sometimes rare and often for sale, are attractively placed within box parterres sheltered by yew hedging and mature trees. Beyond the three acres of formal gardens lie a further four-and-a-half acres of recently planted woodland and shrubbery, with pleasant walks along mown paths. There are also two ponds, one with a waterfall, and a small arboretum. There are fine views to Bulbarrow, Nettlecombe Tout and the Dorset Heights.

The Old Rectory

Tarrant Gunville, Nr Blandford Forum, DT11 8JN. Tel: (01258) 830309

Mr and Mrs John Stoller • 7m NE of Blandford, off A354 at Tarrant Hinton • Open for small groups by prior arrangement only. Please write or telephone • Entrance: by donation to designated charity ●

The entrance to the handsome eighteenth-century house is dominated by a towering evergreen oak, indication of the climatic advantages of this tucked-away village. The owners, originally gardeners in Minnesota, where they faced extremes of seasonal temperature, have resurrected the one-acre garden from near-dereliction, inheriting high brick walls and a backdrop of tall trees. Within the garden their use of contrasting greens is original, varying textures and tones against good stonework; the whole effect gives a sense of theatre. Sculptured yew and box planting breaks up the grass area, and attractive divisions are made by alternating juniper and laurel. Where borders do occur, their curving edges trimmed to perfection, planting is colourful, immaculate and interesting. Roses and clematis grace the walls. An altogether serene and sophisticated place.

The Priest's House Museum

23–27 High Street, Wimborne Minster BH21 1HR. Tel: (01202) 882533

The Priest's House Museum • In centre of Wimborne • Museum open • Garden open April to Oct, Mon – Sat, 10am – 4.30pm. Advisable to check before travelling • Entrance: £3, OAPs £2, children £1 (museum and garden) • Other information: Refreshments in summer only ◑ 🖵 WC & ♿ 🍴 ✎

In the heart of this small town lies a walled garden, hidden from the busy shopping thoroughfare by the frontage of the museum. Both are well worth a visit. The 100-metre-long garden is laid out with some formal beds but mostly lawn, herbaceous and herb borders. In late spring the wisteria on the back of the house is particularly appealing. Sit on one of the seats dotted around and enjoy the peaceful atmosphere of this well-cared-for garden staffed by volunteers who are only too pleased to answer questions about the plants.

Sherborne Castle ★ [Historic Park Grade II*]

Sherborne DT9 5NR. Tel: (01935) 813182 (Estate Office); (01935) 812072 (Castle)

The Wingfield Digby family • Signed from Sherborne • Castle and garden open April to Oct, Tues – Thurs, Sat, Sun and Bank Holiday Mons, 11am – 4.30pm (castle opens Sat 2.30pm) • Entrance: £3.50, children free (castle and grounds £7.50, OAPs £7, children free, parties of 15 or more £6.50 per person) (2005 prices) • Other information: Private viewings for parties of 15 or more by arrangement ◑ 🖵 ✗ 🛍 WC & ✍ ♿ 🍴

As they are seen today, the castle grounds are based on landscaping undertaken in the late eighteenth century by 'Capability' Brown for the 6th Lord Digby, when the lake was created out of the then-flowing River Yeo, and the famous hanging gardens enjoyed by Sir Walter Raleigh and his wife Bess a century earlier were lost forever. Sweeping acres of deer park surround the impressive castle, and masonry salvaged from the crumbling ruin of the old castle, destroyed during the Civil War in 1645, gave rise to fine stable blocks, courtyards and nearby Castleton Church. The gardens on the north side of the lake have been extended to the east of the ruins to take in the late-eighteenth-century Dry Grounds Walk, an eight-acre avenue with many fine specimen trees and a serpentine trail of original pathways. A charming walled flower garden has been designed within one of the courtyards near the orangery, but the main attraction lies surely in the site's unique history, the colourful scene of water against graceful sloping lawns, and the ancient ruin visible across the lake. A visit to the delightful and comprehensive *Castle Gardens Plant Centre*, established in the original walled kitchen garden of the castle and accessible from the main road, is worth a detour.

Shute House ★

Donhead St Mary, Shaftesbury SP7 9DG. Tel: (01935) 814389

Mr and Mrs John Lewis • 5m NE of Shaftesbury, off A30. Near Donhead St Mary church • Open all year, Mon – Fri, by appt only, for parties of 20 to 40 • Entrance: £3.50 • Other information: Teas by arrangement ● 💷 ✕ <u>WC</u> & ℘

The handsome early-eighteenth-century house (originally a fifteenth-century pilgrims' inn) standing at the edge of the estate close to the road is surrounded by a garden of many springs and ponds – the source of a river. The marvellous site faces south, overlooking a slope to farmland. Behind, mysterious shrubberies have a magical hold on the visitor, who is led by paths through groves of camellias and rhododendrons into knot gardens and borders and by placid pools and canals. The late Sir Geoffrey Jellicoe designed the musical cascade that tumbles down the slope over projecting copper Vs set in concrete – a 1972 flashback to his earlier involvement in the Modern Movement. This famous feature has been revived and replanted, while other structural features are being created by the present owners, who are respecting Jellicoe's overall design 'while introducing their own sense of fun'.

Snape Cottage

Chaffeymoor, Bourton SP8 5BZ Tel: (01747) 840330

Ian and Angela Whinfield • 5m NW of Gillingham off A303, at W end of Bourton • Open Feb to Sept, last 2 Suns each month, plus May to Aug, Thurs; all 10.30am – 5pm • Entrance: £2.50 NEW ● 💷 WC ℘ 💠

This small garden hidden away at the end of a wooded lane has attracted a band of enthusiasts. It is planted with a profusion of old-fashioned and uncommon perennials – snowdrops and hellebores, old border auriculas and daffodils, tall-bearded, Siberian and Pacific Coast irises, with phlox and asters to round off the visiting season. All are well-labelled, and many of them are for sale. New borders, designed in a naturalistic cottage-garden style, reach their peak in June and July, but the main theme, which will strike a chord with many gardeners today, is wildlife conservation and especially the encouragement of pond-loving insects and fauna.

Springhead

Fontmell Magna, Shaftesbury SP7 0NU. Tel: (01747) 811853/811206

The Springhead Trust • 5m S of Shaftesbury, 6m N of Blandford Forum on A350 • Open by appt • Entrance: £3, children free • Other information: Difficult for wheelchairs (many levels). Children must be supervised. Plant sales and teas on official open days only ● 💷 & ⬦ ℘ ℃

Although the *raison d'être* of Springhead is the promotion of ecology, education and the arts, its magical garden is also developing fast under the direction of the daughter of the original owners, Rolf and Marabel Gardiner, who created here in the 1930s a centre for rural regeneration and planted over a million trees. Day and residential courses are held in the house, which is based on several cottages on the site of an old mill and overlooks a sweeping view of the lake. At the far end emerge the springs of absolutely clear water which give the place its name and its spirit – it is indeed a haven of peace and privacy, nestling in a small green valley below the Cranborne Chase. The upper garden surrounds the lake, informal planting (including a fine copper beech framing wild flowers and magnolias in the spring) giving way to a more formal area along the banks. A grant from the Dorset Gardens Trust has enabled a bridge to be built over the stream to give views over the clear water. Wildlife abounds. A walk leads up to the chalk down glorious with wild flowers and orchids in summer and spectacular views all year.

Stanbridge Mill ★

Gussage All Saints BH21 5EP. Tel: (01258) 841067

James Fairfax • 7m N of Wimborne on B3078 Cranborne road • Open 14th June, 10.30am – 6pm, for NGS, and for parties by written appt • Entrance: £4, children 50p ● ● wc & ✍

Designed in its initial stages by Arabella Lennox-Boyd with sensitive later additions by the present owner and head gardener, the 50-acre site greets the summer visitor with clouds of white ox-eye daisies either side of the drive. This wild theme is paramount throughout. Extensive water meadows, now tamed, harvest an abundance of wild flowers; grass drives meander alongside streams towards an elegant thatched summerhouse – an ideal point from which to view this pleasing profusion. The house itself, once a water mill, is surrounded by more formal areas, although the millstream remains a key part of the design. A particular feature is the Mound Garden, from where tiers of hedges – ranging from diminutive box through yew and beech to pleached lime – lead up to a higher level with a magnificent swimming pool and a pavilion. All is rectangular, with clever planting edged by neat box. A striking white-flowered *allée* lies beneath a series of iron archways; a prairie planting is now adjacent to the ensuing wisteria walk with herbaceous borders stretching for some 60 metres. A new feature is a processional grass maze with willow sculpture up-river from the ha-ha. Everything is well maintained and shown off to perfection by paving and steps created in patterns by up-ended tiles, flints and bricks.

Stapehill Abbey, Crafts and Gardens

276 Wimborne Road West, Stapehill, Nr Wimborne BH21 2EB.
Tel: (01202) 861686

Mr and Mrs J. Pickard (Directors) • On old A31 Wimborne – Ferndown road, 0.5m E of Canford Bottom roundabout • Abbey open • Garden open April to Sept, daily, 10am – 5pm; Oct to March, daily except Mon and Tues (but closed 22nd Dec to 1st Feb), 10am – 4pm • Entrance: £7.50, OAPs and students £7, children (4–16) £4.50, family £18.50 • Other information: Guide dogs only. Craft shops ○ ● ✕ ▦ wc & ✍ ♠ ♀ ♙

Formerly home for 200 years to Cistercian nuns, this lovely old abbey has now been restored and the grounds transformed into award-winning gardens, including a Victorian cottage garden, a wisteria walk, a tropical house, a lake, a woodland walk and picnic area, a large rock garden with waterfall and pools, and a Japanese garden. Craft shops in the abbey offer demonstrations of traditional crafts on most days. The restaurant is in the former refectory, off a lovely walled terrace so that one can eat out of doors in summer. The Country World museum has a good collection of tractors etc., and overlooks the farmyard. Nearby, between Wimborne and Ferndown, is *Trehane Camellia Nursery*, with a vast range of camellias, magnolias and other acid-lovers. [Open all year, Mon – Fri, 9am – 4.30pm; spring weekends, 10am – 4pm.]

Sticky Wicket ★

Buckland Newton, Dorchester DT2 7BY. Tel: (01300) 345476

Pam Lewis • 11m from Dorchester and Sherborne, 2m E of A352, or take B3143 from Sturminster Newton. At T-junction midway between church and school • Open June to Sept, Thurs and Fri, 10.30am – 8pm, plus Sat and Sun for parties by appt; also open 18th June and 20th Aug, 2–8pm, for NGS • Entrance: £3.50, children £1.50
● ● WC ㅊ ❦ ❦

The three-acre gardens and meadows are divided into four areas; each has an individual focus of wildlife interest with varied planting styles and harmonious colouring to complement and enhance the environment. Information boards guide visitors through gardens which are specially designed with features and planting to attract frogs, birds, bees and butterflies. Wildflower meadows are a particular attraction. This is very much the garden of conservation-minded plant lovers and is not suitable for most children; if the progress of recent years is maintained it is destined to become outstanding.

Weston House

Buckhorn Weston, Gillingham SP8 5HG. Tel: (01963) 371005

Mr and Mrs E.A.W. Bullock • 4m W of Gillingham, 4m SE of Wincanton. From A30 turn N to Kington Magna, continue towards Buckhorn Weston and after railway bridge take left towards Wincanton. House is second on left • Open May to July by appt for charity • Entrance: £2.50, children free • Other information: Teas by arrangement ● ● WC ㅊ ❦

Although centred around an exceptional collection of old-fashioned and English roses – currently 92 varieties, all clearly labelled – this is not merely a rose garden. Near the house stone walls are enveloped in 'Paul Lédé', 'Aloha', 'White Cockade' roses and many clematis, and to one side is a small, fragrant garden enclosed by mellow stone walls, with a great variety of roses and other climbers and skilfully chosen companion plants. Elsewhere, hot colours, a herb collection and a large *Buddleia alternifolia* attract the butterflies. The transition to the main garden is marked by splendid borders of *Nepeta* 'Six Hills Giant' flanked by 'Polar Star' standards, with an arch smothered in ramblers at the house end. Borders fan out at the sides of the extensive lawn, which reaches outwards to the meadows and trees of the Blackmore Vale. Part of an adjoining natural hayfield has been added to the garden and seeded with additional wild flowers; it is edged with a grass 'step' cut slightly higher than the mown paths and the main lawn. Around the perimeter there is more to explore: a plantation of old-fashioned roses, an area of perennials and grasses leading down to woodland and a wildlife pond – a delightful shady contrast much enjoyed by children.

DURHAM

Some gardens have postal addresses in one county and are physically situated in another. If in doubt, check the index.

Auckland Castle Deer Park [Historic Park Grade II*]

Auckland Castle, Bishop Auckland DL14 7NR.
Tel: (01325) 462966 (Smiths–Gore Chartered Surveyors)

The Church Comissioners for England (leased to Wear Valley District Council)
• Leave A1(M) at junction 60 signed to Bishop Auckland. Follow A689 W through Rushyford past Windlestone Hall and Coundon into Bishop Auckland • Castle state rooms and St Peter's Chapel open 17th April to Sept, Sun and Mon, plus Weds in Aug; all 2 – 5pm • Park open all year, daily, 7.30am – dusk • Entrance: Deer park free (state rooms, chapel and gardens within inner wall £4, OAPs £3, children under 12 free, family £10) • Other information: Symbols relate to castle only – no facilities in park ○ WC ⑁ ⚑

A remarkable survival of an eighteenth-century deer house enclosed within part of the original park in the well-wooded valleys of Coundon Burn and Gaunless River, a tributary of the River Wear. Visitors enter through the Gothick gateway crowned by a turreted clock and weather vane and walk past the entrance to the castle, glimpsed through a *clairvoyée*. Suddenly, through Bishop Barrington's screen of 1796, designed by James Wyatt, they see the twelfth-century banqueting hall converted into a chapel by Bishop Cosin in the late seventeenth century. The inner and outer parks extend to 160 acres, with the remainder of the 800-acre deer park leased to local farmers and the golf club. Within them, the river traces a meandering course among precipitous bluffs and craggy outcrops. It has been canalised in places with a weir dating from the eighteenth century. There are avenues of Austrian pine and sweet chestnut and circular stands of trees, groves of ancient alders and clumps of holly trees amongst which dog roses climb. The gnarled and ancient hawthorns are also a feature. A scheduled ancient monument under the guardianship of English Heritage exists within the park: the deer house, designed in 1757 for Bishop Trevor by Thomas Wright, the Wizard of Durham.

Bedburn Hall Gardens

Hamsterley, Bishop Auckland DL13 3NN. Tel: (01388) 4888231

Mr I. Bonas • 9m NW of Bishop Auckland, W of A68 at Witton-le-Wear. 3m SE of Wolsingham off B6293 • Open one day in summer for NGS, 2 – 6pm, and by appt at other times • Entrance: £3, children 50p • Other information: Teas and plants for sale on NGS open day only ● ⑀ WC ⑁ ⚑

A medium-sized terraced garden, largely developed by the present owner, beautifully situated by Hamsterley Forest. It is dominated by a lake with associated rhododendrons and bamboos. A 17-metre lavender bed and a fruit cage of similar size are recent additions. A well-established conservatory contains passion flowers and other exotics. Lilies and fuchsias are a speciality. Azaleas and rhododendrons, roses, lilies, fuchsias and autumn-tinted leaves give a long season of colour and interest.

The Bowes Museum Garden [Historic Garden Grade II]

Barnard Castle DL12 8NP. Tel: (01833) 690606

The Bowes Museum Charitable Trust • In Barnard Castle • Garden and park open all year, daily (except 25th and 26th Dec and 1st Jan), 11am – 5pm • Entrance: free (museum £7, OAPs £6, children under 16 free) ○ 🍴 ✕ 🏬 WC ♿ 🐕 🏛 ♥ ✇

In front of the museum to the south, beneath a stone balustrade, a traditional herbaceous border announces a formal parterre, laid out in 1982 to complement the style of the building designed in 1869 by Jules Pellechet for John Bowes. The raised beds of the parterre are edged with box, which if laid out would stretch for over one and a half miles. There are 20 acres of grounds, planted with 56 different tree species. A double avenue starts behind the east lodge and follows the park perimeter; the trees mark a carriageway which once led from the main gate to the first site of the Bowes chapel. The low terrace wall and enclosed garden and tennis courts are on the site of this chapel, now a picnic area, and the yews survive from this scheme. (The chapel itself was moved to a new site near the main gates.) The trees continue as a windbreak round the whole of the northern edge of the grounds, with exotics such as Wellingtonias and a monkey puzzle planted in front of the native species. The mound behind the car park has been designed as a retreat, with shrubs and statues (removed from the Houses of Parliament during restoration work in the 1970s), and there is also a tree trail.

Crook Hall and Gardens

Sidegate, Durham City DH1 5SZ. Tel: (0191) 384 8028

Mr and Mrs K. Bell • In centre of Durham, near Millburn Gate shopping centre and car park. Follow road next to river bank • House and gardens open 14th to 17th April; 29th May to 2nd June; 23rd April to Sept, Suns and Bank Holiday Mons; Aug, daily except Fri; all 1 – 5pm • Entrance: £4, concessions £3.50, family £12 ◑ 🍴 🏬 WC 🐾 🏛 ♥ ✇

The medieval manor house is surrounded by romantic themed gardens. These include secret walled gardens, a Shakespeare garden with Elizabethan plants, and the Cathedral Garden with magnificent views of the cathedral and castle. There is also a moat pool, a wildflower meadow and a maze. An attractive, peaceful place and a must for visitors to Durham.

East Durham and Houghall Community College

Houghall, Durham DH1 3SG. Tel: (0191) 386 1351

1m SE of Durham city S of A177 Durham – Stockton-on-Tees road. Or leave A1(M) at A177 signed to Peterlee and continue towards Durham • Open all year, daily, 1 – 4pm • Entrance: free ○ 🍴 WC ♿ 🐾

These campus grounds have been developed since the 1970s as the county's main horticultural educational and training facility. They comprise some 24 acres of sports fields and ornamental features, including National Collections of sorbus and meconopsis and one of the largest collections of hardy plants in north-east England. There is a water garden, woodland garden, alpine house, display greenhouses, rock garden, raised beds, troughs, narcissi naturalised under trees, heather garden and arboretum. Since this is a working college the visitor may see empty beds and much work in progress.

Eggleston Hall Gardens

Eggleston, Barnard Castle DL12 0AG. Tel/Answerphone: (01833) 650115

Gordon Long and Malcolm Hockham • *5m NW of Barnard Castle on B6278*
• *House not open but available for private functions – telephone (01833) 650553*
• *Garden open daily except 25th Dec, 10am – 5pm* • *Entrance: £1, guided tours for parties £1 per person* • *Other information: Catering and guides for parties by arrangement* ○ ◗ ✕ <u>WC</u> & ⌖ ⌖ ⌖ ⚲

The early-nineteenth-century house and its lodge were designed by Ignatius Bonomi, and the four acres of walled gardens include many plants of note – *Syringa emodi*, veratrums, epimediums, fritillaries, meconopsis and a host of rare perennials. The signature plant here is *Celmisia spectabilis* 'Eggleston Silver' from New Zealand. The winding paths within the main garden hold much excitement, rounding corners to reveal colourful vistas that change with the seasons. The old churchyard, with gravestones dating from the seventeenth century, has been lovingly restored and there are interesting plantings among the re-erected gravestones and within the sheltered, roofless area inside the church walls. Three Victorian greenhouses are still in working order and everyday use.

Raby Castle Gardens [Historic Garden Grade II*]

Staindrop, Darlington DL2 3AH. Tel: (01833) 660202

The Rt Hon. The Lord Barnard • *1m N of Staindrop on A688 Barnard Castle – Bishop Auckland road* • *House open as garden, 1 – 5pm* • *Garden open May and Sept, Wed and Sun; June to Aug, daily except Sat; plus Bank Holidays (incl. Easter), Sat – Wed; all 11am – 5.30pm* • *Entrance: £4, OAPs/students £3.50, children £2.50, family £12.50, season ticket (house extra charge). Other information: Annual Orchid Show 29th April to 1st May* ◑ ◗ ✕ ⌖ <u>WC</u> & ⌖ ⌖ ⚱ ⚲

One of the country's most impressive medieval castles, once the seat of the Nevills and home to Lord Barnard's family for 380 years, is set in a 200-acre deer park and has an interesting walled garden. This formal garden, dating from the mid-eighteenth century, was designed by Thomas Wright (the Wizard of Durham) for the 2nd Earl of Darlington and has a wide array of trees, shrubs and herbaceous plants; the borders in late June are colourful and impressive. Thomas White advised on the landscaping along with Joseph Spence. The garden walls built from locally hand-made bricks have flues which used to enable sub-tropical fruits to be grown on the south terrace. The famous white Ischia fig tree, brought to Raby in 1786, still survives. Rose garden, shrub borders, original yew hedges, lakes and ornamental pond – all exceptionally well maintained.

University Botanic Garden
Hollingside Lane, Durham DH1 3TN. Tel: (0191) 334 5524

Durham University • 1m from city centre, E of A1050. Accessible from A1(M). From S leave A177 and drive NW through Bowburn and Shincliffe to Durham. From N leave at A690 and drive SW to Durham. Garden off Hollingside Lane • Open all year. Glasshouses open all year, daily, 10am – 5pm. Visitor centre open March to Oct, daily, 10am – 5pm; Nov to Feb, daily except Christmas week and bad weather, 10am – 4pm • Entrance: £1.75, concessions £1, children 50p (2005 prices) • Other information: Wheelchair and map of wheelchair route available ○ ● ● WC ♿ ☂ ♨ ☕

Established in 1970 as a centre for botanical study, this is now one of the few botanical gardens in the north of England. Of special interest are woodland walks with exotic trees from the Americas and the Himalayas. There is little in the way of herbaceous borders because throughout the garden trees and herbaceous plants are grown together as they would be found in the wild. There are, however, individual features devoted to heathers and conifers and to woodland plants, plus a North American arboretum, a Himalayan valley, a gazebo garden overshadowed by a huge monkey puzzle tree, and an alpine/scree garden. The greenhouses shelter tropical and Mediterranean plants and cacti, while the Prince Bishop's Garden contains sculptures originally designed for the 1990 Gateshead Garden Festival. While this has potential to be a very interesting botanical garden, some improvement in maintenance in specific areas will be required. Eighteen acres in all.

Westholme Hall
Winston, Darlington DL2 3QL. Tel: (01325) 730442

Mr and Mrs J.H. McBain • 5m E of Barnard Castle on B6274 between Staindrop and Winston • Telephone for opening dates and times • Entrance: £2.50, children 50p • Other information: Teas available on open days ● ● ● WC ♿ ☂ ♨ ☕

The Jacobean house and the garden (which was laid out in 1890) are reached by a short drive of limes with mature hollies on the north side. To the south is parkland. Immediately inside the garden enclosure (about five acres), there are lawns: on the right an old tree supports a 'Félicité et Perpétue' rose and a 'Comtesse de Bouchaud' clematis. From the front door in the south elevation an axial line leads to a stone-flagged bridge over a stream, the Westholme Beck, to the River Tees. A stone retaining wall parallel to and south of the house forms the backing for a grass walk running east-west; then a grass slope descends to a wide croquet lawn with bold plantings of rhododendrons and thence to grass walks with cherries and specimen trees. Cross the stream that bisects the garden and there is a paddock and more walks through maturing woodland; one vista through what will one day become an avenue of beeches is closed by a massive stone plinth. Elsewhere the long grass terrace walk is terminated by a wall and an urn, and stone parapets salvaged from the Streatlam Park demolition sale of the 1930s now adorn the garden. There is a delightful shrub rose garden to the west of the house, partly sunken and overlooked by a summerhouse, with a good collection of Albas, Bourbons, etc. A woodland walk which has become a wildlife corridor leads up the old Pennine Railway, making a 20-minute round trip from the garden to a large pond, home to many birds.

ESSEX

Two-starred gardens are marked on the map with a black square.

Amberden Hall ★

Widdington, Saffron Walden CB11 3ST. Tel: (01799) 540402

Mr and Mrs D. Lloyd • 6m S of Saffron Walden, E of B1383 near Newport. Follow signs to Mole Hall Wildlife Park. Hall is 0.5m past park on right • Open by appt only • Entrance: £3, children free ◕ **WC**

Lovely old walls covered in a variety of climbers, some of them rare, enclose this medium-sized garden set at one side of a fine house. The colour-themed borders are cleverly designed so that not all of the garden is visible at once. A *leylandii* hedge has been clipped and the sides corrugated. There is a good vegetable garden with raised beds to make it easier to cope with the heavy clay soil. The garden has been extended beyond the walls with an ivy *allée* – this has two viburnum hedges with poles rising out of them supporting different ivies. More recent additions are a secret garden inside a dismantled barn and a woodland walk.

Audley End [Historic Garden Grade I]

Saffron Walden CB11 4JF. Tel: (01799) 522399

English Heritage • 1m W of Saffron Walden on B1383 • House open as grounds but different opening and closing times • Garden open April to Sept, daily except Tues, 10am – 6pm; Oct, daily except Tues and Wed, 10am – 5pm. Last admission 1 hour before closing • Entrance: £4.50, OAPs £3.40, children under 16 £2.30, family £11.30 (house and grounds £8.50, OAPs £6.40, children under 16 £4.30, family £21.30) (2005 prices) • Other information: Snowdrop walks in spring (Sat and Sun only) – telephone for details. Picnics in park only ◑ 🍽 🐌 **WC** ♿ 🏵 🐾 🏛 🔦

The house has long been a fascinating relic of an extraordinary Jacobean pile. Now visitors can enjoy an early version of the parterre garden, restored to the plans developed by the 3rd Lord Braybrooke and his wife *c.* 1830, advised by William Sawrey Gilpin. The design was inspired by classic seventeenth-century French parterres but with sheltering shrubberies to relate to the contemporary (1830) interiors. English Heritage has introduced the whole repertory of the flower garden of the period – irises, martagon lilies, roses, peonies and astrantias, violas, hypericums along with spring and summer bedding – all planted in some 170 beds. The herbaceous borders leading into the parterre have recently been planted out with a wide variety of perennials. The restoration has taken ten years and has been completed without interfering with the surrounding 'Capability' Brown landscape. His park buildings included a circular temple, a bridge, Lady Portsmouth's Column by Robert Adam, and a cascade constructed in the same year on the site of an ancient mill dam. There are fine planes, oaks and tulip trees, and a pond garden, laid out in 1868, containing many scented old roses and sub-tropical bedding, with a Pulhamite rock garden at one end. Everything is immaculately maintained. The walled kitchen garden, which includes a 52-metre-long vine house, a full set of service buildings, a gardeners' bothy and an orchard house, has been developed into a working organic kitchen garden laid out in the Victorian style, including fruit trees on the walls and a splendid variety of Victorian vegetables, which are also for sale in season.

The Beth Chatto Gardens ★★

Elmstead Market, Colchester CO7 7DB. Tel: (01206) 822007

Mrs Beth Chatto • 3m E of Colchester, 0.25m E of Elmstead Market on A133 • Open March to Oct, Mon – Sat, 9am – 5pm; Nov to Feb, Mon – Fri, 9am – 4pm, and for parties by appt • Entrance: £4, accompanied children under 14 free • Other information: Parties by appt ○ 🍽 🚭 WC ᕫ ℗ ℺

Beth Chatto designed these gardens in the 1960s from a neglected hollow which was either boggy and soggy or exceedingly dry. She, more than anyone else, has influenced gardeners by her choice of plants for any situation, and her ability to show them off to perfection. Her planting is a lesson to every gardener on how to use both leaf and flower to best advantage. The large gravel garden which she planted to replace the old car park is maturing well as a home for beautiful plants which can thrive in very dry conditions. In the last few years some of the earliest borders have been renewed, and part of the Mediterranean garden has been given over to scree beds – a setting for the smaller plants in the form of five irregular islands. The other major change has taken time to evolve: the creation of five large ponds, each slightly lower than the other, at the heart of the garden. On the perimeter of the garden, a patch of woodland garden nurtures shade-loving plants. The beautifully designed and photographed handbook (£3) includes a fully descriptive catalogue. Adjoining is the excellent *Unusual Plants* nursery. All compulsory visiting.

Bridge End Gardens [Historic Garden Grade II*]

Bridge Street, Saffron Walden.

In town centre; entrance in Bridge Street and Castle Street • Gardens and hedge maze open Mon – Fri (telephone Tourist Information Office on (01799) 510444 for details of opening times) • Entrance: free ○ 🚭 WC ᕫ 🚹 ℺

The early Victorian gardens were started by Atkinson Francis Gibson. The yew hedge maze, planted in 1840 in the Italian Renaissance style, has 610 metres of pathways, originally embellished with statues and columns and richly ornamented iron gates. After some fifty years of vandalism and neglect, restoration began in 1984, when the maze was replanted with 1000 yews; these have now reached maturity. The award of a lottery grant has enabled further restoration, but the kitchen garden with its tantalising traces of heated tomato and peach houses, cold frames and beehives remains to be tackled. Upkeep and maintenance remain problematic, and an appeal has been launched for volunteer workers. Other features include a rose garden, a Dutch garden with elaborate topiary, and a viewing platform looking over lawns to Saffron Walden church. On the common nearby is the ancient *Turf Maze of Saffron Walden* [Historic Garden Grade II], a circular labyrinth of medieval Christian design, 29 metres in diameter with only four outer bastions. It is probably the largest of its kind in the world and one of only eight in England.

Cracknells ★

Great Yeldham CO9 4PT. Tel: (01787) 237370

Mr and Mrs T. Chamberlain • 10m N of Braintree, on A1017 between Halstead and Haverhill • Open by appt • Entrance: by donation to collecting box ◐

Mr Chamberlain started contouring this large plot even before he started building his house. The landscape rolls away down to the lake, also excavated at the start. This is not a garden in the accepted sense but 'a garden picture painted with trees', to use his own words. He has gathered together an impressive collection from all over the country. Here is the rare cut-leaf beech, *Fagus sylvatica* var. *heterophylla*, and its purple- and pink-leaved forms, 'Rohanii' and 'Purpurea Tricolor', as well as the variegated tulip tree, *Liriodendron tulipifera* 'Aureomarginatum'. There are also collections of birches, acers, sorbus and oaks. If you are a lover of trees, make your pilgrimage.

Easton Lodge, The Gardens [Historic Garden Grade II]

Easton Lodge, Little Easton, Great Dunmow CM6 2BB. Tel: (01371) 876979

Mr and Mrs B. Creasey • 11m W of Braintree, 1m N of Great Dunmow on B184. Signposted • Open 14th April to Oct, Fri – Sun and Bank Holiday Mons (snowdrop season open daily, Feb and March – telephone for details), 12 noon – 6pm, and at other times by appt • Entrance: £3.80, OAPs £3.50, children under 12 £1.50. Discount for parties (2005 prices) ◑ ☕ 🍽 <u>WC</u> ⅄ ⬥ ℘ 🐕 ℀

The old west wing survives of Easton Lodge where 'Darling Daisy' Countess of Warwick, mistress of Edward VII, spent vast sums on making a wonderful garden and grounds and entertaining her royal lover. Harold Peto designed the garden for her in 1902. In 1950 the house was demolished and the garden abandoned, but in 1996 the pavilion was restored with a grant from Essex County Council, and latterly a vast amount of work has been done. The glade, originally a Japanese garden dug by hand by 69 Salvation Army inebriates, has been cleared to reveal Peto's design of a gently sloping mown valley planted with mature trees and bulbs ending in a viewing platform overlooking a large lake. The ornamental pond with its stone balustrading has been revitalised by water lilies and massed penstemons and agapanthus, the fine vistas framed by yew hedges beckon once more. In the cobbled courtyard stone pots contain pine trees, and the raised terrace is massed with pink roses and charming bantams and peacocks. This is, alas, a requiem for a beautiful garden. Although maintenance continues, restoration has ceased as Stansted Airport is coming alarmingly close – an extension would bring a flight path directly overhead.

7A Ellesmere Gardens

Redbridge, Ilford IG4 5DA. Tel: (020) 8550 5464

Cecilia Gonzalez • Travelling E, off A12 Eastern Avenue between Redbridge roundabout (M11 interchange) and Gants Hill roundabout • Open by appt (garden only takes two at a time) • Entrance: £2.50 ◐

The charming split-level courtyard garden, only six metres square, is a treasure trove of unusual plants such as *Podranea ricasoliana, Cassia corymbosa, Grevillea rosmarinifolia,*

Impomoea indica and *Solanum rantonnetii*, all thriving in the south-west-facing plot encased in greenery. The upper level is filled with imaginatively planted containers, the lower with dense tropical planting. Between May and mid-August it has a cottagey feel, with favourites old and newer – clematis, gauras, campanulas, *Verbena bonariensis*, *Knautia macedonica, Hesperis matronalis* – then from August onwards the tropical plants come into their own.

Feeringbury Manor

Coggeshall Road, Feering, Colchester CO5 9RB. Tel: (01376) 561946

Mr and Mrs Giles Coode-Adams • 6m E of Braintree between Coggeshall and Feering • Open April to July and Sept, Thurs and Fri, 8am – 4pm, and by appt • Entrance: £2.50 ❶ 🏠 WC ♿ ◈

This 10-acre garden is distinguished by structured designs and good detailed planting. An excellent variety of plants is grown, from moisture-lovers beside the ponds and streams to semi-tender specimens in sheltered areas. The owners specialise in clematis and sweet peas, and the fine selection helps to prolong the season. Visitors are drawn by a succession of imaginative colourful planting schemes from one vista to the next. A garden of atmosphere and tranquil charm. Notable, too, are the sculptured gates and benches by Ben Coode-Adams, including a galvanized-steel rose arbour 65 metres long with a vigorous abstract design of trees and bowling hoops.

Folly Faunts House

Goldhanger, Maldon CM9 8AP. Tel: (01621) 788213

Mr and Mrs J.C. Jenkinson • 12m E of Chelmsford, 2m E of Maldon on B1026 • Open for charity several days in summer, 2 – 5pm, and at other times for parties of 6 or more by appt • Entrance: £2.50 • Other information: Teas and plants for sale on charity open days only ◑ 🏠 WC ♿ ◈ ⚲

The twenty acres of woodland, parkland and garden surrounding the eighteenth-century house, old barn and farm buildings have been created by the present owners since 1962, with 5000 trees and a small arboretum planted, ironically, in 1987, the year of the Great Storm. Five of these acres are gardens, well-structured and furnished with a catholic array of plants (some 1000 in all). Only the fittest survive, for this is alternately drought and rain-sodden country, with Dutch elm disease and pockets of heavy clay putting in an appearance too. The owners' philosophy of combining variety and a long season of interest is exemplified by the trees they have chosen for the six double avenues to be found in the park and leading up to the house – all have two or three different species peaking variously in spring, summer and autumn. Near the house different areas are grouped around a series of formal and informal water features, notably a steep-banked round pond planted with *Salix elaeagnos* subsp. *angustifolia, Cornus nuttallii*, gleditsias, gunneras, rheums and flax. A formal paved sunken garden is contained within railway sleepers and planted with unusual shrubs, and the top garden is divided by hedges into compartments where attractive colour combinations persist for many months. A triumph of persistence over adversity.

The Gibberd Garden [Historic Garden Grade II]

Marsh Lane, Gilden Way, Harlow CM17 0NA. Tel: (01279) 442112

Gibberd Garden Trust • E of Harlow between A414 and B183. From M11 junction 7 take A414 to Harlow, follow signs to Old Harlow onto B183 (Gilden Way) and continue for 1m. Marsh Lane is on left • Open for snowdrops 6th and 13th Feb, 11am – 4pm; then April to Sept, Wed, Sat, Sun and Bank Holiday Mons, 2 – 6pm; also Autumn Festival 23rd Oct, 11.30am – 4pm • Entrance: £4, concessions £2.50, children free ● ● ● WC & ⊕ ⊕ ⊕ ⊕

This is the extremely individual creation of the architect and art collector Sir Frederick Gibberd and an outstanding example of twentieth-century garden design. Hugh Johnson has stated that it 'must certainly be one of the most important [gardens] in the history of the twentieth century'. The nine-acre sloping site comprises a series of rooms designed to display his remarkable collection of modern sculpture and architectural artefacts. The structure is not restrictive; tranquillity as well as drama is provided by glades, groves and *allées*, as they open up vistas or focus on sculpture. A waterfall and quiet pools have been incorporated into a small brook which borders the east of the property and towards which run lushly planted channels of water. At one end of the brook stands a moated castle. There are also natural ponds, a tree house and a gazebo. The garden is now in the enthusiastic hands of the Gibberd Garden Trust, which is aiming to realise his wish that it be kept open to the public in perpetuity.

Glen Chantry ★

Wickham Bishops, Witham CM8 3LG. Tel: (01621) 891342

Wol and Sue Staines • 9m NE of Chelmsford off A12, 2m SE of Witham. Turn left off B1018 towards Wickham Bishops. Pass golf course, cross River Blackwater bridge and turn left up Ishams Chase by Blue Mills • Open 7th April to 2nd Sept, Fri and Sat, 10am – 4pm • Entrance: £3.50, children 50p • Other information: D.I.Y. teas ● ● ● WC & ⊕

The present owners started laying out their garden on an awkwardly sloping 3.5-acre site in 1976, and it is now at the peak of its maturity, magnificent and impeccably maintained. The design is both elegant and rather informal, with lawns swooping around beds massed with the rare and the unusual. Plants with different requirements thrive in a variety of carefully cultivated habitats, and the enviably wide range that results is maintained throughout the year. Spring sees an abundance of bulbs, woodland plants and early alpines, and in early summer the beds are beautifully planted with many euphorbias, plants with variegated foliage, grasses lightened by groups of *Allium sieboldii* and *A. christophii*, some very pretty irises, and much more. And so on, to autumn colour, seed heads and berries, and the brave flowers of winter. Two pools patterned with water lilies are densely fringed with moisture-lovers, and a large tufa rockery has areas of shingle planted with alpines and scree-loving plants. The adjoining nursery sells a wide variety of excellent plants – some are old favourites, others uncommon or more of a challenge to grow.

Hill House

Chappel, Colchester CO6 2DX. Tel: (01787) 222428

Mr and Mrs R. Mason • 8m W of Colchester on A1124 between Colchester and Earls Colne • Open by appt • Entrance: by donation to charity ◗

The large garden was designed by the owners on formal lines, using yew hedging and walls to create vistas, and with a lime avenue sited to lead the eye out into the country. A mixed planting of tough native trees like sorbus and hawthorn has been established as a windbreak. A small courtyard with a raised pool, reminiscent of a London plot, is planted with green-leaved plants and white flowers only. Another feature is a pond with two black swans. The bones of the garden are in place including urns, statues and seats, and all the colour and secondary planting has now been introduced. Further land has been acquired giving a fine view over the Colne Valley and Chappel Viaduct, and hedges and trees are being established here.

Ingatestone Hall

Ingatestone CM4 9NR. Tel: (01277) 353010

Lord Petre • 7m SW of Chelmsford on A12. From Ingatestone main street, take Station Lane at SW end. Signposted • House open • Garden open 15th April to 16th July, 2nd Sept to 1st Oct, Sat, Sun and Bank Holiday Mons; 19th July to 3rd Sept, Wed – Sun and Bank Holiday Mon; all 1 – 6pm • Entrance: £4, OAPs and students £3.50, children £2 ◑ ● WC ♿ ✿ ♨ ⌀

There have been buildings here since 950 AD, and the hall (well worth a visit) was built in the 1540s. A large stewpond, contemporary with the house, provided fish and fresh-water mussels; it is now bordered by huge gunneras and shady walks. The walled garden has magnificent standard roses and a lily pond. There is a nut walk and a grass walk, but the lime walk is haunted by Bishop Benjamin Petre's dog, which saved his life when he was set upon in 1740. His ghost still patrols. The extensive, immaculate lawns have specimen trees: mulberries, *Magnolia grandiflora* and weeping beeches.

Langthorns Plantery

High Cross Lane West, Little Canfield, Dunmow CM6 1TD. Tel: (01371) 872611

Mr and Mrs David Cannon and Edward Cannon • 3m W of Great Dunmow, 5m E of M11 junction 8, on A120 • Plantery open daily, 10am – 5pm • Garden open by appt (telephone or ask at Plantery) • Entrance: free ◗ ♨

The owners, avid collectors of unusual plants propagated in the nursery, which stocks one of the widest ranges of good-quality plants in the country, including trees, shrubs, conservatory plants, alpines and herbaceous perennials. There are also clematis and honeysuckles, and many unusual forms of tricyrtis, geraniums and salvias. The garden has now been revamped and is open to the public on a limited basis.

The Magnolias

18 St John's Avenue, Brentwood CM14 5DF. Tel: (01277) 220019

Mr and Mrs R.A. Hammond • From A1023 turn S to A128. After 300 metres turn right at traffic lights, over railway bridge. St John's Avenue is third on right • Open 19th and 26th March, 2nd, 16th, 23rd and 30th April, 14th and 21st May, 18th June, 16th July, 13th Aug, 17th Sept, 22nd Oct, all 10am – 5pm, and for parties by appt • Entrance: £1.50, children 50p ● ✿

The garden may be a bit of a jungle, but it is a plantsman's delight, with 70 different magnolias, camellias, hostas, bamboos and epimediums. The front garden (7.5 x 6 metres) has impressive trees and shrubs – *Carpenteria californica* with white-flowered *Solanum jasminoides* growing through it, *Cercis canadensis* 'Forest Pansy', *Sophora microphylla* and *Cytisus battandieri*. A dark path leads to a long narrow garden with seven ponds, and mature trees and plantings, including trilliums, *Embothrium coccineum* (Chilean firebush), a *Magnolia campbellii* which did its first reasonable flowering twenty-five years after planting, in time for the owners' silver wedding anniversary, and several flowering cornus including 'Norman Hadden'.

Olivers

Olivers Lane, Colchester CO2 0HJ. Tel: (01206) 330575

Mr and Mrs David Edwards • 3m SW of Colchester off B1022 Maldon road. Follow signs to Colchester Zoo. From zoo continue 0.75m towards Colchester and at round-about turn right. After 0.25m turn right again into Olivers Lane. From Colchester pass Shrub End church and Leather Bottle pub then turn left at second roundabout • Open 30th April and 1st May, and by appt • Entrance: £3, children free ● 🍴 ♿ WC ♿ ✿ ☕

A wonderfully atmospheric garden surrounded by woodland originally planted in the seventeenth century with rides cut through; many fine old trees survive. The Georgian-fronted house is sited on a hill with a fine view of the gardens and woodland. In spring the generous York-stone terrace and in front of the house blossom into a spectacular display of tapestry bedding, with tulips, white myosotis and wallflowers planted closely together. Wicker fighting-cock baskets used as frost protectors make an amusing feature early in the year. Yew hedges divide the well-planted borders below the terrace into small sections, each with a different colour theme; *Ceanothus repens* is a wonderful sight in full bloom. A 'willow pattern' bridge crosses the first of a succession of pools dropping down to an ancient fish pond; *Taxodium distichum*, metasequoia, ginkgo and tree ferns flourish by the waterside. Beyond, an orchard and a collection of quinces and medlars merge into a natural meadow – cut only to encourage wild flowers and grasses – which spreads out to the trees bordering the river. There is also a delightful woodland walk, where mature native trees shelter rhododendrons, azaleas and shrub roses in the rides.

Perrymans

Dedham Road, Boxted, Colchester CO4 5SL. Tel: (01206) 272297

Mr and Mrs R. Human • 4m NE of Colchester station to Boxted on Dedham road • Open by appt • Entrance: £2.50 ● ● 🏠 WC ♿ ⬥ ⚲

An interesting seven-acre garden developed since 1970 from a cottage garden which had some magnificent elm trees and a patch of ground grazed by goats. Ponds were dug on the site of the old Boxted sewage works and are now established lakes. In 1973 Beth Chatto came to advise and the garden began to take its present shape. New trees have been planted alongside existing ones and a three-acre woodland was created in 1996. Spring colour comes from bulbs, followed by cherry blossom rhododendrons, azaleas and camellias, with wisteria, tulips and irises for added appeal. In June the rose garden overlooking one of the lakes, itself bordered by roses, comes into its own, with a huge 'Paul's Himalayan Musk' threatening to engulf the host tree. There is also a most productive and attractive vegetable garden, and in 2002 a contemporary garden was added.

RHS Garden Hyde Hall

Rettendon, Chelmsford CM3 8ET. Tel: (01245) 400256

The Royal Horticultural Society • 7m SE of Chelmsford, signed from A130 • Open all year, daily except 25th Dec, 10am – 6pm (last admission 5pm), (closes dusk Oct to March) • Entrance: £4.50, children (5–16) £1. Parties of 10 or more £3.50 per person • Other information: Guide dogs only ● ● ✕ 🏠 WC ♿ ⚲ 🏛 ⚑ ⚲

The 28-acre hilltop garden is perched above the East Anglian wheatfields in a truly Tuscanesque manner. Notable are the beds of species roses with white peonies and naturalised *Eremurus robustus* growing through them. There is much else to see: a colour-themed herbaceous border; two informal ponds; a spring garden of massed hellebores and many bulbs; a formal enclosed rose garden with pillars behind a broad planting of alliums and half-hardy salvias. This is on a double crossfall which poses a severe problem – but although it is against all classical garden design principles, it still produces a stunning display. A National Collection of viburnums is here. Three thousand young trees have been planted, the upper and lower ponds are being opened up and replanted, and the terrace (entered through a massive oak pergola adorned with clematis and wisteria) is being enlarged. Much new planting and several wildflower areas have been established in the Malus Field, and work is continuing on the winding, shallow riverbed, display and shrub beds and a shrub rose garden. The new dry garden is on fertile alkaline clay with huge glacial boulders from Scotland, and grows things like the self-seeding *Eremurus robustus*, *Erigeron karvinskianus*, a thousand bulbs and much more.

R. and R. Saggers ★

Waterloo House, High Street, Newport, Saffron Walden CB11 3PG. Tel: (01799) 540858

R. and R. Saggers • 6m S of Saffron Walden on B1383 through Newport • Open all year, daily except Mon (but open Bank Holiday Mons), 10am – 5pm (closed Suns,

Jan to March and Aug) • Entrance: free • Other information: Wedding list and full floristry service available, inc. hire of plants and trees for functions ○ 🐞 **WC** ♿ ◁▷ 🌿 🏛

This small, immaculately kept nursery has a charming town garden running down to a stream between flint walls. An amusing clipped box character in a hat carries a vase under his arm overflowing with running water. Old-fashioned roses and many rare and unusual trees and plans are propagated and grown *in situ*, and there is a new trend towards Mediterranean species such as the hardy *Poncirus trifoliata*, with its white flowers and plentiful crop of oranges, olive trees, bananas and others that require some winter protection. Also on sale is a good range of statues, urns, Whichford pots and armillary sundials.

Saling Hall ★ [Historic Garden Grade II]

Great Saling, Braintree CM7 5DT.

Mr and Mrs Hugh Johnson • 6m NW of Braintree, halfway between Braintree and Dunmow on B1256; turn N at Blake End • Open for NGS May to July, Wed, 2 – 5pm, and for parties by written appt, Mon – Fri • Entrance: £3, children free ◐ **WC** ♿

Hugh Johnson's wonderful garden is clearly the work of a tree lover – a rare example of a picturesque landscape created by a very wide-ranging dendrological collection. When the huge elms of Saling died, he turned the 12 acres of chalky boulder clay into an arboretum of genera that thrive on alkaline clay or gravel. A marvellous collection of pines, quercus, sorbus, aesculus, acers, prunus, tilias, fraxinus, fagus, salix and betulas leads the eye to a classical Temple of Pisces. There are many rarities like *Carpinus fangiana*, *Tilia oliveri*, *Toona sinensis*, *Staphylea colchica*, weeping Chinese juniper, incense cedars from Oregon seed, and unusual pines. Japanese maples have also been a striking success. In the south-west facing walled garden apple trees are trimmed into parasol shapes to provide shade on parallel lawns between beds and borders planted informally and generously with roses, shrubs and perennials. The whole garden is planned as a succession of vistas given definition and mood by the choice of trees. There is also a vegetable garden, a Japanese garden, a water garden, a secret garden and a strange menhir in its private yew-hedged 'chapel'. The old moat with its cascade boasts some substantial carp.

Stone Pine ★

Hyde Lane, Danbury, Chelmsford CM3 4LJ. Tel: (01245) 223232

Mr and Mrs David Barker • 4m E of Chelmsford from Runsell Green, 1m S of A414 leaving Danbury towards Maldon • Open by appt • Entrance: by donation to collecting box ◐ 🐞 **WC**

This small garden, owned by a former Chairman of the Hardy Plant Society, is filled with choice and unusual varieties. The area of grass is minimal and paths wind around borders crammed with trees, acers being particularly popular, and shrubs. Surprising plants appear around each corner, like the rarely seen *Paris quadrifolia*, several sorts of disporum with their delicate hanging bells, and enjoying this shady woodland garden trillium and epimediums. A National Collection of epimediums includes most of the recently discovered species.

Tye Farm

Colchester Road, Elmstead Market, Colchester CO7 7AX. Tel: (01206) 822400

Mrs A. Gooch • 2m E of Colchester on A133, 0.5m W of Elmstead Market • Open for parties by appt • Entrance: £2.50 ● 🌡 WC ☀️ ⬇ ⚘

This one-acre garden is cleverly planted with hedges to make compartments to break the prevailing wind. The shrubs and perennials complement one another, and tulips and irises are followed by a fine display of old and modern roses, and good autumn colour. The small walled garden has a yellow theme. There is a formally planted, box-edged area in front of the conservatory, which contains many unusual plants.

Warwick House

(see EASTON LODGE, THE GARDENS)

ASSOCIATION OF GARDENS TRUSTS
Founded in 1993 in response to growing unease among conservationists and owners of historic gardens about their future security, 36 individual county garden trusts shelter under its umbrella. They are charitable bodies with no legal powers, able to influence planning and other governmental decisions only through vigilance and lobbying. For further details, contact: The Association of Gardens Trusts, 75 Cowcross Street, London EC1M 6EL (Tel: (020) 7251 2610, Tues and Thurs only; www.gardenstrusts.org.uk).

GARDENING WEBSITES
Many gardens now have their own websites, and we list these at the back of the *Guide*. Others useful for garden visitors are:
  Dept of Environment (Ireland): www.heritageireland.ie
  English Heritage: www.english-heritage.org.uk
  Historic Houses Association: www.hha.org.uk
  Historic Royal Palaces: www.hrp.org.uk
  Historic Scotland: www.historic-scotland.gov.uk
  Landmark Trust: www.landmarkrust.org.uk
  National Gardens Scheme: www.ngs.org.uk
  National Trust: www.nationaltrust.org.uk
  National Trust for Scotland: www.nts.org.uk
  Royal Horticultural Society: www.rhs.org.uk
  Welsh Historic Monuments: www.cadw.wales.gov.uk

GLOUCESTERSHIRE

Some gardens have postal addresses in one county and are physically situated in another. If in doubt, a check in the index will direct the reader to the page on which the garden appears.

Two-starred gardens are marked on the map with a black square.

Abbotswood ★ [Historic Garden Grade II*]

Stow-on-the-Wold GL54 1EN. Tel: (01451) 830173

Dikler Farming Co • 1m W of Stow on B4077 • Open 9th April, 7th May, 4th June, 2nd July, 6th Aug, 10th Sept, 1.30 – 6pm • Entrance: £3, children free • Other information: Coaches must drop passengers at top gate and park in Stow ● ● WC ♿

In this most beautiful of Cotswold settings the 20-acre garden retains its Edwardian charm, merging gently into the landscape with descending streams, surrounding woodland and pastoral views. The elegant formal gardens around the house were originally designed by Lutyens with a spectacular fountain, a terraced lawn, a sunken garden, a lily pond and a rose garden, all planted in harmonious Jekyll style. The box-edged blue garden, with its deep blue forget-me-nots and later *Salvia farinacea*, is particularly attractive. Herbaceous borders are full of interest and colour, and there are extensive heather beds, flowering shrubs, specimen trees and, artfully framed by dense foliage, luscious rhododendrons in shades of pink (no shrieking oranges here). In spring fritillaries yield to spotted orchids in the wild garden beside the stream that meanders down into the wooded ravine, its slopes massed with bulbs, and into the Dikler river, widened to form a lake in the field beside the drive. The prolific and immaculate walled garden, usually open later in the season, is well worth the short walk.

Alderley Grange [Historic Garden Grade II]

Alderley GL12 7QT. Tel: (01453) 842161

Mr Guy and The Hon. Mrs Acloque • 6m N of Chipping Sodbury, 2m S of Wotton-under-Edge. Turn NW off A46 Bath – Stroud road at Dunkirk • Open during June by appt • Entrance: £3.50, children free ● WC ♿

A garden of character and charm in a tranquil walled setting, renowned for its collection of aromatic plants and scented flowers. Designed by the late Alvilde Lees-Milne, it is believed to be the last garden in which Vita Sackville-West had a hand. The fine house and a mulberry tree date from the seventeenth century; a pleached and arched lime walk leads to a series of enclosed gardens. There is a notable hexagonal herb garden with many delightful perspectives of clipped, trained or potted shrubs and trees, and abundant plantings of old roses, tender and unusual plants.

Barnsley House ★

Barnsley, Nr Cirencester GL7 5EE. Tel: (01285) 740421

Rupert Pendered and Tim Haigh • 4m NE of Cirencester on B4425 • Open for NGS, and for small parties throughout the year, strictly by prior appt • Entrance: £5 (2005 price) • *Other information: Coaches on open days only by prior appt. Refreshments available at Village Pub opposite house* ● WC ♿

This was a highly influential garden in its day, comprising many garden styles from the past, carefully blended by Rosemary and David Verey after 1951. The 1697 Cotswold stone house (now a country-house hotel and restaurant) is set in the middle of the four-acre garden, surrounded on three sides by a 1770 stone wall. Borders create vistas and divide the garden into areas of distinct and individual character, and great attention is paid to colour and texture. The laburnum, allium and wisteria walk and the *potager* with its numerous small beds were renowned in their day; the latter has been enlarged into the adjacent field to meet the demands made upon it by the hotel kitchen. Although it is impossible for Rosemary's unique planting style to be perpetuated indefinitely, Barnsley will remain both her creation and her memorial.

Batsford Arboretum ★ [Historic Garden Grade I]

Batsford Park, Moreton-in-Marsh GL56 9QB. Tel: (01386) 701441

The Batsford Foundation • 1.5m NW of Moreton-in-Marsh on A44 to Evesham. Opposite entrance to Sezincote (see entry) • Arboretum open Feb to mid-Nov, daily; mid-Nov to mid-Feb, Sat, Sun and 26th Dec, 1st Jan; all 10am – 5pm • Entrance: £5, OAPs £4, children £1 ● ⬛ ✕ 🖳 WC ♿ ⬥ ℘ ⏃ ♟ ⚲

Over 1500 different species and varieties of trees, shrubs and bamboos in 55 acres plus an unusual collection of exotic shrubs and bronze statues from the Far East. There are also fine collections of magnolias, a National Collection of Japanese cherries, aconites, snowdrops and daffodils for spring and excellent autumn colour. A 'swampery' combines elements of a bog and a stumpery. Good views of the house (not open).

Bourton House ★

Bourton-on-the-Hill, Moreton-in-Marsh GL56 9AE. Tel: (01386) 700754

Mr and Mrs R. Paice • 2m W of Moreton-in-Marsh on A44 • Open 31st May to Aug, Wed – Fri; Sept to Oct, Thurs and Fri; also 28th and 29th May, 27th and 28th Aug; all 10am – 5pm • Entrance: £5, children free • Other information: Parking across road ● ⬛ 🖳 WC ♿ ℘ ⏃

The handsome eighteenth-century Baroque Cotswold house with fine views is enhanced by its medium-sized garden which is an inspiring alternative to traditional country-house acres. The diminutive geometrical *potager* is a particular delight. Well-kept lawns, quiet fountains, a knot garden and Cotswold stone walls are set off by a number of herbaceous borders which make skilful use of current fashions in garden design. The colours and choice of plants are bold and sophisticated, mixing spiky, semi-tropical, traditional and unusual species in a versatile display. Each year there are new interests – a raised pond in the top garden, a topiary walk, and long terraces on the main lawn planted with low-growing shrubs, perennials and roses. The plantation in the field opposite is a pleasure to roam, and a gallery of local arts, crafts and design has opened in the tithe barn. The cocoon-like shade-house is a flourishing environment for novel shade-loving plants. Many of the plants may be unfamiliar to visitors; labels would be welcome.

Cerney House Gardens

North Cerney, Cirencester GL7 7BX. Tel: (01285) 831300/831205

Sir Michael and Lady Angus • 3.5m N of Cirencester off A435 Cheltenham road. Turn left opposite Bathurst Arms, follow road up hill past church, signed to Bagendon, and turn in through gates on right • Open April to July, Tues, Wed, Fri and Sun, 10am – 5pm, and for parties by appt at other times • Entrance: £3, children £1 • Other information: Lunches and high teas by arrangement. Picnics in car park only ◑ ◖ ◉ <u>WC</u> ♿ ⚘ ♨ ✿

Around the house remodelled by Decimus Burton in 1791, goats, sheep and horses graze and wild flowers flourish in their meadow. The garden laid out in a sheltered hollow surrounded by woodland is a dream. The 3.5-acre walled garden – filled with vegetables, riotous herbaceous borders, old-fashioned roses and clematis – is overlooked by delightful stripy Berkshire pigs scampering beneath the apple trees in the orchard above. As you enjoy the view down the gazebo walk you may, if you are lucky, see the resident peacock in full display framed by roses at the far end. In May thousands of tulips displayed in informal groups among the herbaceous plants and formally in beds and pots. The woodland walk is carpeted with snowdrops and bluebells, with abundant spring bulbs all around. The rockery, geranium and thyme bank and pink border beside the swimming pool are well established, the herb garden richly stocked. A genera garden leads down to a pond and a tree trail. The happy and unrestrained plants include a National Collection of tradescantias. Informative labelling is a bonus, including those in the new beds to the side of the house telling the stories of plant-hunters and famous nurserymen. The locality is rich in history, with Chedworth Roman Villa a few miles away (note the attractive Roman snails meandering along the paths). The beautiful twelfth-century church nearby is well worth a visit.

The Chipping Croft

26 The Chipping, Tetbury GL8 8EY. Tel: (01666) 503178

Dr and Mrs P. Taylor • In town centre proceed between The Snooty Fox and 'Ultima One' shop past parking in Chipping Square. Garden is at bottom of hill on left behind wall with tall trees, entrance in driveway to courtyard • Open by appt • Entrance: £3.50 • Other information: Teas by arrangement ◉ ♿

This is a most unusual town garden because of its size and secret character. Entering through a courtyard leading to a terrace, sunken patio and large lawn bordered by mature trees and a wooded walk, it extends to about two acres and is on three levels. At one time, the mostly late-seventeenth century house was used as a school, and since 1985 Dr Taylor has transformed a playground area into a courtyard with a small rectangular raised pool and a conservatory. He has replanted extensively, constructed a summerhouse/potting shed and added new steps connecting the various levels. Three formal terrace gardens contain a variety of perennials and cottage-garden flowers as well as unusual plants, fruit trees, vegetables and herbs, with the kitchen garden proper laid out as a *potager* on a higher level. Beneath the terraces is a wide walk with roses and perennials in borders either side and arches covered with roses, honeysuckle, wisteria and clematis leading back to the house. The garden has colour and interest from mid-April through to September, and the huge 'Kiftsgate' rose towering above a mass of colourful border plants is a wonderful sight in mid-June.

Colesbourne Park ★

Near Cheltenham GL53 9NP. Tel: (01242) 870264

Henry and Carolyn Elwes • 6m S of Cheltenham on A435 • Open 4th to 26th Feb, Sat and Sun, for snowdrops; then 26th March, 15th to 17th April, 1st May (plant sale); all 1 – 4.30pm • Entrance: £5, children free ● ● WC & ⊕ ⊯

One of the joys of late-winter and early spring in the Cotswolds is a visit to the famous snowdrop collection at Colesbourne Park, and the season has now been extended with a three-year restoration project to celebrate the great days of that celebrated Victorian plantsman and collector, Henry John Elwes. Then the garden was world-famous for its trees as well as its bulbs, and now early-flowering scented shrubs and many thousands of small-flowered daffodils have been planted to sparkle in meadow and lakeside, and a superb collection of hellebores is flourishing among other bulbs in woodland. But the glory of the garden is still the snowdrops – great swathes and drifts spreading in variety through the woods and beside the lake, and some 200 rare and beautiful cultivars displayed in raised beds near the house, where newly planted formal beds open onto wide lawns with vistas and gentle prospects across the surrounding parkland.

Cotswold Farm

Duntisbourne Abbots, Cirencester GL7 7JS. Tel: (01285) 821857

Iona Birchall • 5m NW of Cirencester off A417. From Cirencester turn left signed to Duntisbourne Abbots, then at once right, right again after 270 metres, under the new dual carriageway, and house drive is opposite. From Gloucester 1m past Highwayman Inn, turn left signed 'Duntisbourne Abbots/Services', turn right at once, and the drive is 270 metres on left • Open 5th and 6th Feb for snowdrops, 12 noon to 4pm; 23rd April, 20th Aug, 2 – 6pm; and by appt at other times (good notice appreciated) • Entrance: £3 ● ● WC & ⊯

A mature garden planted in grand style and sustained with sensitive artistry surrounding a fine old house in a superb Cotswold setting. The terrace was designed by Norman Jewson in 1938. The formal walled gardens have a pool and are planted with shrub, bush and climbing roses, alpines, lavender and a collection of scented flowers. There are also established plantings of shrubs, herbaceous perennials and many small treasures overlooking an unspoilt wooded valley. A charmed garden redolent of another age in a remote and lovely situation.

Daylesford House ★ [Historic Garden Grade II*]

Daylesford, Moreton-in-Marsh GL56 0YH. Tel: (01608) 659888

Sir Anthony and Lady Bamford • As we go to press, we learn that the garden will not be open during 2006

Warren Hastings, the first Governor-General of Bengal, bought the estate in 1785 and the house was designed by Samuel Pepys Cockerell in the Anglo-Indian style.

Hastings employed John Davenport to lay out the bones of the garden, including the splendid Gothick orangery, walled garden and magnificent lakes. The present owners have re-created the original combination of semi-natural parkland, naturalised wild-flower meadows and woodland, and more formal areas. Every aspect is a delight. The orangery has a sensational display of blue *Salvia guaranitica* across the length of the large south-facing wall, as well as a collection of citrus and vine arches and exotics in huge clay pots. Behind the orangery is the secret garden, with a pavilion and a pool presided over by a seventeenth-century Neptune, *Rosa banksiae alba* tumbling down the balustrades and stunning blue and white planting schemes continuing into the spring border outside. Beyond the scented walk and stumpery is the two-acre walled garden. This was laid out by Mary Keen (who also designed the rose trellis terrace and the parterre in front of the house), with subsequent work by Rupert Golby. It contains peach and orchid houses and a series of yew-hedged areas leading to a raised rose garden and cutting border. There are also espaliered fruit trees and a large *potager* producing unusual organic vegetables. The top lake cascades into the dell and stream, a shady area with the accent on texture and foliage, behind which the wood is carpeted in spring with bluebells and colonies of wood anemones, myosotis and spotted orchids.

Dyrham Park [Historic Garden Grade II*]

Chippenham SN14 8ER. Tel: (0117) 937 2501

The National Trust • 4m S of Chipping Sodbury, 8m N of Bath, 12m E of Bristol on A46. Take M4 junction 18 in direction of Bath • House (including Victorian domestic areas) open as garden but 12 noon – 4.45pm (last admission 4pm) • Garden open 24th March to 29th Oct, Fri – Tues, 11am – 5pm • Park open all year except 25th Dec, daily, 11am – 4.45pm or dusk if earlier • Entrance: park only (when house closed) £2.25, children £1.10; park and garden £3.40, children £1.70, family £7.75 (house, garden and park £8.80, children £4.35, family £21.75) (2005 prices) • Other information: Possible for wheelchairs on terrace but park steep in places. All cars in car park at East Lodge, bus link to house and garden. Dogs in dog walking area only, on lead • Garden: ◑ ▣ ✕ 🍴 WC ♿ ⛲ ♥ ☕ *Park:* ○ 🍴 ☕

Only a tiny fragment of the extensive London and Wise Baroque garden shown in the view by Kip in 1710 survives. The terraces were all smoothed out in the late eighteenth century to form an 'English' landscape with fine mature beech, Spanish chestnut, Lucombe oak, red oak and black walnut. Avenues of elms survived until the mid-1970s; they have since been replanted with limes. The cascade in the garden on the west side is still working and one can make out the form of the original garden and enjoy the terrace and Talman's orangery, all 30 metres now splendidly transformed and wonderfully scented. The views towards Bristol and the elegance of the 'natural' landscape, with the house and church tucked into the hillside, make this an outstanding example of English landscape gardening. In all, 263 acres of ancient parkland.

Eastleach House ★

Eastleach Martin, Cirencester GL7 3NW.

Mrs David Richards • 6m SW of Burford off A361 Lechlade road or off A40 via Westwell and Eastleach Turville. House opposite church gates, up steep drive • Open

June, July, Fri, 2 – 5pm. Guided tours by owner for parties of 10 or more at other times. Requests only in writing please • Entrance £5, accompanied children free • Other information: Limited parking and no access for coaches. Lunches and teas available in village at Victoria Inn ● ✿

A beautiful and relatively unknown garden, twenty years in the making. The owner interweaves plants and combines colours and textures with skill and sensitivity, handles changes of level with panache, and creates interlocking spaces and outdoor rooms to form a coherent flow. The house, which is turn-of-the-twentieth-century, sits on the top of a hill and faces the four points of the compass. It has become the reference point, the fulcrum of the design. The rear facade looks out across lawn to the countryside through a pair of wrought-iron gates decorated with clematis. Beyond, a newly planted lime avenue leads to a yew roundel encircling the statue of a stag. Only one secret is hidden from the house – the sunken wildlife pond beyond the walled garden. Roses wind through clematis and around fastigiate Irish yews; a meandering path through the miniature arboretum brings the visitor to the edge of the croquet lawn. Ascend the broad steps and opposite is an arbour and a tapestry border of shrubs. Stand finally at the west end of the house, look down onto the rill and have your eye caught by the perfectly shaped balls of *Sorbus aria* 'Lutescens' beyond the borders of perennials embracing the entire colour spectrum. A garden of sheer delight. Sorry, don't miss the herb garden.

The Ernest Wilson Memorial Garden

Leasbourne, High Street, Chipping Campden. Tel: (01386) 840884 (Dick Smith)

N of A44 between Evesham and Stow-on-the-Wold and S of Stratford-upon-Avon off A46 E of Broadway • Open all year, daily except 25th Dec, 9am – dusk • Entrance: free, but contributions welcome (donation box) ○ ♿

A garden opened in 1984 in memory of Ernest 'Chinese' Wilson, who was born in Chipping Campden in 1876. The famous collector is estimated to have introduced 1200 species of trees and shrubs during his career, and there are several of his introductions here, including *Acer griseum*, a handkerchief tree (*Davidia involucrata*) planted in the early 1980s, and the plant for which he wished to be remembered, *Lilium regale*. It is a peaceful oasis, with seats and shade, backed by the beautiful church tower. Other gardens in Chipping Campden are open on certain days, and the charity Action Research arranges for some 20 gardens to open on the third weekend in June, 2 – 6pm.

Ewen Manor

Ewen, Cirencester GL7 6BX. Tel: (01285) 770206

Lady Gibbs • 4m S of Cirencester off A429. Turn at signpost for Ewen, and garden is 1m further on • Open 25th, 26th, 30th and 31st May; 1st to 29th June, Tues – Thurs; all 11am – 3.30pm, and probably two days for charity • Entrance: £2.50 • Other information: Teas on charity days only ● 🧺 ♿ ✿

In the late 1940s this was a run-down manor garden which had in part been used as a Dig-for-Victory patch. The Georgian house had been moved here from across the Thames 200 years earlier. Backed by magnificent trees, it now contains a series of gardens with architectural features, and everywhere the planting is profuse. There are views across the pattern-mown lawn to the circular summerhouse with its conical Cotswold stone-tiled roof, and to the 200-year-old cedars of Lebanon in the woodland area all around. The main herbaceous border is backed by a high yew hedge, behind which is a large rectangular lily pool surrounded by masses of helianthemums, overlooked by the garden room (once the stables) with its plant-filled terrace and pots. Daffodils and spring bulbs abound. One of the most charming of traditional manor house gardens.

Frampton Court [Historic Park Grade I]

Frampton-on-Severn GL2 7EU. Tel: (01452) 740268

Mr and Mrs Rollo Clifford • SW of Gloucester, 2m from M5 junction 13, signposted. On left-hand side of village green through gates in long wall • House open all year for parties of 10 or more by appt (by guided tours, £5) • Garden open all year by appt • Entrance: £3 • Other information: Refreshments by arrangement ● ● WC & ℘ B&B

Home of the remarkable Clifford family of female artists, who created the *Frampton Flora* (1830-1860), the elegant 1730s' house stands on land owned by the family since the twelfth century. It was possibly designed by John Strahan in the style of Vanbrugh; the interior has exquisite woodwork and furnishings. The park overlooks a lake and the five-acre garden, with fine trees and a formal water garden of Dutch design. The Strawberry Hill Gothick orangery of 1750 (not always open but available for holiday letting), where the ladies are believed to have executed their work, stands reflected in the still water, planted with lilies and flanked by a mixed border. The walled garden at the orangery is now home to *Pan Global Plants*, a rare plants nursery. [Open all year, Wed – Sun and Bank Holiday Mons (closed first Sun in Sept), 11am – 5pm; 1st Nov to 31st Jan by appt only – telephone (01452) 741641]. Visitors to the garden at Frampton Court may also be able to see that of *Frampton Manor*, also occupied by Cliffords, where a boldly planted walled garden with many old roses is set off splendidly by a fine fifteenth-century timbered house. [Open 27th April to 21st July, Thurs and Fri, 2.30 – 5pm].

Grange Farm

Evenlode, Nr Moreton-in-Marsh GL56 0NT. Tel: (01608) 650607

Lady Aird • 3m N of Stow-on-the-Wold, E of A429 Fosseway. 1.5m from Broadwell • Open for NGS, 11am – 6pm, and May to July by appt • Entrance: £2.50, children free • Other information: Teas and plants for sale on June open day ● ● WC & ⬦ ℘

This charming traditional English country garden at the edge of the village blends gently into the surrounding Evenlode valley, overlooking waterside meadows with a cleverly hedge-framed vista. Lawn, herbaceous borders, wild areas and sunken garden complement one another, full of interest and subtle planting schemes. The water garden in May is sensational: deep pink tulips, narcisssi and cow parsley beneath the apple blossom is reminiscent of a Beatrice Parsons painting. June sees the flowering of masses of roses. A yew circle surrounds an old russet apple tree – perfect for hide-and-seek. The productive vegetable garden is immaculate, mown paths meander through the wild areas, and there are many places to sit and appreciate the peaceful atmosphere.

Hidcote Manor Garden ★★ [Historic Garden Grade I]
Hidcote Bartrim, Chipping Campden GL55 6LR. Tel: (01386) 438333

The National Trust • 3m NE of Chipping Campden. Signposted • Open 23rd March to Oct, Sat –Wed, plus Good Friday, 10.30am – 6pm (closes 5pm Oct); Parties by written appt only. On fine weekends and Bank Holidays garden less crowded after 3pm • Entrance: £7, children £3.50, family £17.10 • Other information: Coaches by prior arrangement only ◗ ▆ ✕ <u>WC</u> & ♨ ⚙ ♟

One of the most famous gardens in Britain, impeccably kept throughout its 10 acres, particularly the miles of sculptured hedges. It is famous especially for its highly disciplined formal outdoor rooms, many of them filled with wonderfully dramatic plantings. It was created in the early years of the twentieth century by Lawrence Johnston, an American with a strong sense of design and great planting skills. He made many new introductions and rediscovered many forgotten plants, some of which he collected himself; several varieties now bear the Hidcote name. The Trust has, since its acquisition in 1948, done its best to retain the spirit of the original, but its researches and some new evidence suggests that his planting legacy has been eroded over the years. The plan now is to make a gradual return to Johnston's own stated vision of 'a wild garden in a formal setting'. His plant house may be re-created and other features reinstated. As always, a garden to watch.

Hodges Barn ★
Shipton Moyne, Tetbury GL8 8PR. Tel: (01666) 880202

Mrs Charles Hornby • 3m S of Tetbury, 3m NW of Malmesbury, just outside Shipton Moyne on Malmesbury side • Open 26th and 27th April, 21st and 22nd May, 3rd, 4th and 7th July, 2 – 6pm, and at other times by appt; parties welcome • Entrance: £5, children free ◖ ⛟ WC & ⬠

In 1499 this was built as a dovecot or columbarium to a large house nearby which burnt down in 1556; it was converted to a home in 1938 and bought by the Hon. Mrs Arthur Strutt, the late Mr Hornby's grandmother, in 1946. She set about creating the basic structure of the garden with good stone walls and topiary, and had planted most of the trees before her death in 1973. It is an extensive eight-acre garden, with plenty of interest for everyone – above all those who like roses (there are well over 100 different varieties). The spring garden, the water garden, the little wild woodland, the large cleared wood, the topiary and the splendid lawns are all enjoyable. The plantings reflect a preoccupation with colour, scent and variety, uninhibited by a desire to prevent one flower or shrub from growing into another. Note the planting in gravel along some of the many beds, and the tapestry hedges. This is a garden which breathes knowledge and enthusiasm.

Hullasey House
Tarlton, Cirencester GL7 6PA. Tel: (01285) 770132

Mr and Mrs Jonathan Taylor • 5m SW of Cirencester off A433. In Tarlton, follow lane marked 'Church'; drive is on right • Open 10th to 12th June, 2 – 5pm for NGS, and May and June by appt • Entrance: £2.50, children free ◖

A medium-sized traditional Cotswold garden which has succeeded in overcoming the problem of a windy situation. Commanding spectacular views, the front of the house is a formal area with a sweeping lawn and octagonal box-edged beds in purple, mauve, white and silver. The luxuriant herb garden is contained within a walled parterre, with fruit trees, yet more roses and a miniature camomile lawn. There is a splendid walled garden with an exuberant mixture of herbaceous plants and roses of every description, rambling around and beside the walls and over arches, intertwined with honeysuckle. Beyond is the spring garden, planted with wild daffodils and naturalised tulips, and a garden filled with wild roses.

Hunts Court

North Nibley, Dursley GL11 6DZ. Tel: (01453) 547440

Mr and Mrs T.K. Marshall • 1.5m SW of Dursley, 2m NW of Wotton-under-Edge near North Nibley. Turn E off B4060 in Nibley at Black Horse Inn and fork left after 0.25m • Open all year except Aug, Tues – Sat and Bank Holiday Mons, 9am – 12.30pm, 1.45pm – 5pm, and some Suns for NGS, 2 – 6pm. Closed 14th April and 25th Dec to 2nd Jan • Entrance: £3, children free • Other information: Teas on Suns only ☺ 🐝 wc ♿ ✿

A must for those with a love of old roses. June sees in excess of 400 varieties – species, climbing and shrub – filling the borders, cascading over rails, pergolas and trees and spilling out over the informal grass paths which weave a passage through rare shrubs and herbaceous perennials. Summer is inevitably dominated by roses, but this is not to deny interest in other seasons, from spring-flowering shrubs to trees with good autumn colour. A more formal sundial garden with beds intersected by gravel paths provides a home for hardy geraniums, penstemons and diascias. In another area mown paths draw the eye towards the Cotswold escarpment which commands the eastern landscape. In the adjoining nursery many of the plants growing in the garden are for sale, and the owner is on hand with advice. An arboretum has been added with acers and other more unusual trees and shrubs.

Kiftsgate Court ★★ [Historic Garden Grade II*]

Chipping Campden GL55 6LW. Tel: (01386) 438777

Mr and Mrs J.G. Chambers • 3m NE of Chipping Campden and near Mickleton, very close to Hidcote, which is signposted • Open April, Aug and Sept, Sun, Mon, Wed, 2 – 6pm; May, June, July, daily 12 noon – 6pm (Note: opening times not identical to Hidcote's) • Entrance: £5.50, children £1.50 • Other information: Coaches by appt only ➊ 🍵 🐝 wc ✿

The house was built in the late nineteenth century on a magnificent site surrounded by three steep banks, and the garden was largely created by the present owner's grandmother after World War I. Her work was carried on by her daughter, Diany Binny, who made a few alterations but followed the same colour schemes in the borders, and by her grand-daughter Anne Chambers, who continues to perfect her vision. In spring, the white sunken garden is covered with bulbs, and there is a fine show of daffodils along the drive. June and July are the peak months for colour and scent, but the magnificent old and species roses are the glory of this garden, home of *Rosa filipes* 'Kiftsgate'. Notable too are perennial geraniums, a mighty wisteria and many species of hydrangea, some very large. In autumn, Japanese maples glow in the bluebell wood. Unusual plants are sometimes amongst those available for sale. Most visitors had thought of Kiftsgate as trapped in a charming time warp, when, lo and behold, the owners add a serenely simple flower-free water garden – flower-free, that is, apart from Simon Allison's inspired foliage sculpture reflected in the black water of the pool. Note: young children and the elderly should take care on the steep, uneven and sometimes slippery paths.

Lydney Park Gardens

Lydney GL15 6BU. Tel: (01594) 842844

The Viscount Bledisloe • 20m SW of Gloucester. N of A48 between Lydney and Aylburton • Open late March to early June, Wed, Sun and Bank Holiday Mons, 11am – 6pm. Parties and guided tours by appt • Entrance: £4 (£3 on Weds), accompanied children 50p (2005 prices) • Other information: Picnics in deer park; Iron Age fort, Roman temple site and New Zealand museum ● ☕ 🍽 WC ♿ ⌦ ℘ ⚜ ♟

The park dates from the seventeenth century, and although it has been in the hands of one family since 1723, a new house was built in 1875 and the old one demolished. An area near the house has an interesting collection of magnolias, and a picturesque sight is the bank of daffodils and cherries, splendid in season. From 1955 a woodland garden was developed in the wooded valley behind and below the house, with the aim of achieving bold colour at different times between March and June. Near the entrance to the main part of the gardens is a small pool surrounded by azaleas and a collection of acers. From here the route passes through carefully planted groups of rhododendrons and past a folly, brought from Venice, which overlooks a valley and bog garden. Criss-crossing the hillside are rare and fine rhododendrons and azaleas, including an area planted with unnamed seedlings. Enormous effort has gone into the plant design, colour combination and general landscaping. Nearby is the Roman camp and museum containing the famous bronze Lydney dog, while the park has a fine collection of trees and herds of fallow deer.

Mill Dene

Blockley, Moreton-in-Marsh GL56 9HU. Tel: (01386) 700457

Mr and Mrs B.S. Dare • 3m W of Moreton-in-Marsh on A44. Follow brown tourist-signs from Bourton-on-the-Hill • Open April to Oct, Tues – Fri and Bank Holiday Mons (except Easter), 10am – 5pm, and for individuals and parties by appt • Entrance: £4.50, children £1. Special rates for parties ◑ ☕ WC ♿ ℘ ♟ B&B

A 2.5-acre garden, built around the mill pond and stream and climbing in steep terraces, each with its own character and colour scheme, to a *potager* and fruit garden with a summerhouse and little fountain at the top and a new rose walk and cricket lawn on the way. Scented plants are a priority, and there are splendid views of the Cotswold hills and surrounding picturesque village. Quirky surprises include a grotto and *trompe-l'œil* effects. Rupert Golby helped design the North Shade garden, which has garden sheds with planted roofs and a disguised telegraph pole and is decorated with glass fossil sculptures. Up to a dozen other gardens in this popular hillside village are open on one day in June for the NGS and are well worth a

visit. Nearby is *Peartrees*, a small cottage garden full of treasures, open by appointment (telephone (01386) 700464).

Misarden Park Gardens ★ [Historic Garden Grade II*]

Miserden, Stroud GL6 7JA. Tel: (01285) 821303

*Major M.T.N.H. Wills • 6m NW of Cirencester, 3m off A417. Signposted • Open
April to Sept, Tues – Thurs, 10am – 5pm, and for parties by appt • Entrance: £4
(inc. printed guide), children free. Reduction for parties of 20 or more. Guided tour
extra • Other information: Adjacent nursery open daily except Mon ◑ 🏠 WC ♿ ☕*

This lovely, timeless English garden, which commands spectacular views over the
Golden Valley, has most of the features to be expected of a garden started in the
seventeenth century. There are extensive yew hedges, a York-stone terrace, a Lutyens
loggia overhung with wisteria, and a good specimen of *Magnolia* x *soulangeana*. The
south lawn sports splendid grass steps. West of the seventeenth-century manor
house (not open) the ground ascends to the nursery in a series of grassed terraces.
Two good herbaceous borders lead to a parterre of tulips, alliums, hebes, lavender
and roses, and a rill and summerhouse were added to mark the Millennium. There
are many fine specimen trees, and the spring show of blossom and bulbs is notable.

Moor Wood

Woodmancote, Cirencester GL7 7EB. Tel: (01285) 831397

*Mr and Mrs Henry Robinson • 3.5m N of Cirencester off A435. At North Cerney
turn uphill to Woodmancote. In Woodmancote go through white gates on left beside
lodge. Parking at end of drive • Open for NGS 28th June and 2nd July, 2 – 6pm,
and by appt • Entrance: £3, children free • Other information: Teas on open days
only ◑ 💻*

With its attractive valley setting, this is the perfect home for a National Collection
of rambler roses – 140 in all, crawling over every wall surrounding the gardens of
this Cotswold family house and its cottages and stables. Since 1984 the owners have
been gradually building up the collection and restoring the gardens, a continuing
process. There are two acres of cottage gardens, a formal lawn and borders, an
orchard and a terraced garden. The wildflower planting in the old walled garden is
being revitalised, contributing to the garden's delightfully natural atmosphere in
keeping with the surrounding farmland.

The National Arboretum, Westonbirt ★★ [Historic Arboretum Grade I]

Westonbirt, Tetbury GL8 8QS. Tel: (01666) 880220

*The Forestry Commission • 3m SW of Tetbury on A433, 5m NE of A46 junction
• Open all year, daily, 10am – 8pm (or dusk if earlier) • Entrance: Charges vary
seasonally – maximum for individuals £7.50, OAPs £6.50, children £1, family £15
(reduced rates for disabled, educational, and parties) (2005 prices) ○ 💻 ✕ 🏠 WC ♿
↩ ☕ 🏛 ♨ ⚲*

This is perhaps the finest arboretum in Britain – 600 acres in all. Started in 1829 by
Robert Stayner Holford, it was expanded and improved by successive generations

of the same family until it was taken over by the Forestry Commission in 1956. Numerous grass rides divide the trees into glades used for special plantings. Westonbirt is noted for its vast range of stunning mature specimen trees. Across the valley from the original arboretum is Silkwood, with collections of native, Asian and American species that in spring are carpeted with primroses, wood anemones and bluebells. There are in excess of 17,000 numbered trees, including an exceptional National Collection of Japanese maples, extended in 2006 by the newly planted Rotary Glade. Colour is best in May (rhododendrons, magnolias, etc.) and October (Japanese maples, Parrotias, cercidiphyllums, etc.). From early December until Christmas the Enchanted Wood is illuminated at weekends with a wonderful festive display, and many champion trees are floodlit. In 2006 the arboretum will celebrate fifty years of Forestry Commission ownership with a plethora of events and guided walks.

Newark Park [Historic Garden Grade II]

Ozleworth, Wotton-under-Edge GL12 7PZ. Tel: (01453) 842644

The National Trust (contact: Michael Claydon) • 1.5m E of Wotton-under-Edge, 1.75m S of A4135 and B4058. Follow signs for Ozleworth • Open April and May, Wed, Thurs and Bank Holiday Mons, plus 14th – 16th April; June to Oct, Wed, Thurs, Sat, Sun and Bank Holiday Mons; all 11am – 5pm • Entrance: House and garden £5, children £2.50 🕐 🏠 **WC** ♿ ☂ 🍽 **B&B**

The former deer park, set within 700 acres, leads to the Tudor hunting lodge, and beyond to a landscape of hills and wild woodland brought vividly to life by the drama of a vertical drop on the southern side. The sixteenth-century house, greatly enlarged and Gothicised by James Wyatt in the 1790s, has now been rehabilitated with great taste; much of the credit for this goes to Robert Parsons, who was tenant here from 1970 to 2000 and whose work is continued with the Trust's support by Michael Claydon. The house is set amongst woodland walks which end at the foot of the escarpment (the planting here is yet to be restored) with a carp pond partially enclosed by a crinkle-crankle wall, a summerhouse and an arbour. Wild flowers abound in their season. No lover of classic English landscape should miss a visit to Newark with its majestic panoramic views to the distant Mendip Hills.

The Old Barn

Upper Dowdeswell, Cheltenham GL54 4LT. Tel: (01242) 820858

Dawn and Jamie Adams • 5m E of Cheltenham off A40. Turn right after reservoir to Dowdeswell, then right at crossroads at top of hill past church and after 180 metres right again into Upper Dowdeswell. Park outside manor on left and walk short distance to garden • Open 3rd and 4th June, and by appt • Entrance: £3, children free ● ✿

Dawn Adams, a garden designer, has cleverly combined style and naturalism in this beautifully kept three-quarter-acre hillside garden, which perfectly complements its fine Cotswold setting and splendid views. Developed from a field over the past twenty years and following gently sloping contours, individual areas are bounded by immaculate beech and yew hedges and stone walls. Planted for year-round appeal with many unusual species, there are traditional colour-themed borders, a rose-and-clematis-covered pergola, a croquet lawn, a fruit garden and a white garden – something of interest in and around every corner. Snowdrops and bluebells, auriculas and hellebores flower in profusion in their seasons. A one-acre woodland walk on the other side of the road overlooks the Severn Vale and Malvern Hills.

The Old Rectory ★

Duntisbourne Rouse, Daglingworth, Cirencester GL7 7AP

Charles and Mary Keen • 3m NW of Cirencester off A417. From Daglingworth take narrow valley road for the Duntisbournes. After 0.5m house is on right next to church • Open by written appointment only for parties of 10 or more • Entrance: charge ☻

Since 1983 the garden writer and designer Mary Keen has created an intimate and inspiring 1.5-acre garden full of colour, variety and interest at every season. House and garden nestle among softly wooded Cotswold hills beside a tiny, unspoilt Saxon church. The garden has been designed with its exceptional setting in mind, its views drawing the eye towards the surrounding countryside. Visitors should start their tour by taking themselves up to the former schoolroom and browsing through the latest collection of cuttings and comments about the garden, giving themselves time to take in the peaceful atmosphere. It is divided into many different areas of changing levels and moods, separated by yew or box hedges. The initial calm expanse of lawn at the front of the house gives way to sunken areas of exuberant colour, an auricula house, a winter garden and a dark reflective pool. A partially hidden pathway lined with snowdrops leads to a shrub dell carpeted by wood anemones and more snowdrops. Behind the house, steps lead up through seasonally changing borders past the recently restored schoolhouse, to a greenhouse filled with special treasures, a gooseberry garden, a wildflower orchard with a hazel walk and mown pathways, and on into the vegetable garden and borders facing the churchyard.

The Old Rectory

Quenington, Nr. Fairford, Cirencester GL7 5BN. Tel: (01285) 750358

Mr and Mrs D. Abel Smith • 2m N of Fairford, 9m E of Cirencester on A417 • Open 9th April, 23rd April (rare plant sale), 25th June for NGS, and by appt • Entrance: £3 on charity days only • Other information: Biennial show of contemporary sculpture usually July. Refreshments on open days ☻ WC ♿ ⟁ ❦

The owners have taken full advantage both of the River Coln meandering through their garden and the more formal mill race (constructed by the Knights Hospitallers) to display their growing collection of sculpture. Personally chosen works are to be found in the formal garden behind the house, and more can be discovered when walking among the trees towards the river and its bridge – a natural setting for the collection of permanent works in many materials (note the growing interest in glass). Some 200 works are displayed during the biennial show. Today sculpture 'parks' are far from rare, but few enjoy the benefit of the fine riverside setting here which has the feeling of an amphitheatre. Four other pretty gardens are open in Quenington on the NGS day in June.

Owlpen Manor [Historic Garden Grade II]

Uley, Dursley GL11 5BZ. Tel: (01453) 860261

Mr and Mrs N. Mander • 6m SW of Stroud, 3m E of Dursley off B4066, 1m E of Uley. Signposted • House open • Garden open May to Sept, Tues, Thurs and Sun, 2 – 5pm • Entrance: £2.80 (house and garden £4.80, children £2) ◑ 💷 ✕ WC ঙ B&B

Situated in a remote, beautiful and vertiginous Cotswold valley, this is an unusually complete survival of a small formal manorial garden of the seventeenth century. Laid out on seven hanging terraces with topiary yews, box parterres, old roses, and steps leading steeply down to the stream, the garden plays a major role in creating a romantic setting for the house and its church. Today, however, the topiary has lost some of its crispness, the infilling of the parterres its freshness, the espaliered trees their rhythm. An unsympathetic modern viewing platform gazes out across the stream to a slightly dispirited garden – but it is a magical place nonetheless.

Ozleworth Park ★

Ozleworth, Wotton–under–Edge GL12 7QA. Tel: (01453) 845591

Michael Stone • 5m S of Dursley off A4135 Tetbury – Dursley road. At junction with B4058, turn S on single-track lane signed to Ozleworth, and follow signs for 2m until reaching gates with eagles on gate posts • Open one day for NGS, and one day for charity ◑ 💷 WC ঙ

The garden surrounding the handsome house is quite simply magnificent: in the generosity of its spaces, the scale and sophistication of its plantings and the artistry of its design, carried out by Antony Young, Jane Fearnley-Whittingstall, Charles Hornby and the head gardener Colin Durber. Behind the house three venerable cedars stand on a huge lawn sweeping to a quarter-mile-long ha-ha. The stable courtyard to the east is substantial too, and the octagonal-towered Norman church is drawn into the assembly of outbuildings. There is space here only to hint at a few of the multiple enclosures laid out within yew hedges or beautiful old walls: a stepped rill with slabs of stone and square ponds, rising up a steep hillside to a wild area at the top; an espaliered pear pergola underplanted with alliums and agapanthus reached by a green yew corridor; an 1806 bath house encircled by a walkway; wide and deep borders planted with a subtle, exuberant range of shrubs and perennials; a rose garden that really is given over to roses; a little stream crossed by a wooden bridge and thickly planted with moisture-lovers. One of the most successful spaces is the water garden, tucked away at the perimeter, where two long rectangular pools studded with water lilies and separated by a bronze girl with a bow are flanked by a plump lavender hedge and a low yew hedge. Plus greenhouses, and a cutting garden, and a vast vegetable garden. Ten acres in all, this is a twenty-first-century garden of truly Edwardian opulence and panache.

Painswick Rococo Garden ★ [Historic Garden Grade II*]

Painswick GL6 6TH. Tel: (01452) 813204

Painswick Rococo Gardens Trust • 0.5m from Painswick on B4073. Signposted • Open 10th Jan to Oct, daily, 11am – 5pm • Entrance: £5, OAPs £4, children £2.50 • Other information: Coaches by appt ◑ 💷 WC ◈ ৶ ⛪ 🍴

A great deal of time, money and effort is going into the continuing restoration (almost complete redevelopment) of this rare Rococo survival. Much of the work is now completed, with new plantings becoming established. At present, the best features are the eighteenth-century garden buildings, the views into beautiful surrounding countryside, and the marvellous snowdrop wood spanning a stream that flows from a pond at the lower end. This must be one of the best displays of naturalised snowdrops in England. There are some splendid beech woods and older specimen trees. Wild flowers are allowed complete freedom. Rococo gardening was an eighteenth-century combination of formal geometric features with winding woodland paths, revealing sudden incidents and vistas – in essence, a softening of the formal French style, apparent from about 1715 onwards in all forms of art. The basis for Painswick's present restoration is a painting of 1748 by Thomas Robins (1716–78) for Benjamin Hyett, who created the garden in the grounds of the house built by his father in 1735. To celebrate the 250 years of its existence, Painswick's owners have planted a yew hedge maze, designed by Angela Newing, in adjoining farmland; something to look forward to as it matures. In total it is a large estate and visitors (who should be fit for some steep inclines) must allow three-quarters of an hour even for a brisk walk round its many beauties.

Rockcliffe ★

Lower Swell, Stow–on–the–Wold GL54 2JW.

Mr and Mrs Simon Keswick • 3m W of Stow-on-the-Wold on B4068 • Open June and July, Wed, 2 – 5pm • Entrance: £3.50, children under 15 free ◗ **WC**

The house was built in the late nineteenth century for the dowagers of Eyford Park, the estate that marches with it, and looks due west towards a glorious stretch of unspoilt country enclosed by a curving shelter belt of mature park trees. Two elegant pavilions added by Nicky Johnson to the house pull the whole composition together and create a generous forecourt. Here the garden starts. On the stone slabs is a series of geometric box patterns, intertwined and tubular, including a centrepiece in the form of a box-edged spoked wheel with a stone wellhead in the centre; the paving froths lime-green with *Alchemilla mollis*. From the forecourt the view is of beech obelisks stalking up the broad grass ride towards the new ha-ha and beyond to open countryside. Between the terrace and the tree-lined boundary to the north is a shady enclosure where a stone-edged pool is overhung by six elegant *Cornus controversa* 'Variegata'. This lower-level garden leads to another where two simple canals of reflective water are framed by York-stone paving. In this placid green space are parallel lines of pleached hornbeams; a deep herbaceous border in pastel shades is relegated to a supporting role. Then come three flower-filled *boîtes* – two yew-edged rooms, richly planted in shades of white and purple-blue, and a scented swimming-pool garden with four huge standard bay trees and a pool-house covered with *Rosa* 'Zéphirine Drouhin'. The walled kitchen garden is productive and pretty, but on the other side of the kitchen garden is the *pièce de résistance*: topiary yew birds perch in pairs on the slope leading through the orchard to a recently completed octagonal stone dovecote.

Rodmarton Manor ★ [Historic Garden Grade II*]

Rodmarton, Cirencester GL7 6PF. Tel: (01285) 841253

Mr and Mrs Simon Biddulph • 6m SW of Cirencester, 4m NE of Tetbury off A433, halfway between Cirencester and Tetbury • House open as garden, and for pre-booked guided group visits at other times • Garden open for snowdrops 12th, 16th and 19th Feb, 1.30pm to dusk; then May to Sept, Wed, Sat and Bank Holiday Mons, 2 – 5pm • Entrance: £4, accompanied children 5-15 £1 (house and garden £7, children £3.50) • Other information: Coaches use holly (west) drive ❶ 💷 🏠 WC ♿

The manor and its garden, designed by Ernest Barnsley for the Biddulphs from 1909, is an excellent example of the English Arts and Crafts Movement at its best. The drive lies between impeccably clipped tapestry hedges, and the garden, which retains virtually all its original features, comprises a series of outdoor rooms, each with its own character, bordered by the fine hedges of yew, beech, holly and box for which it is famous. In front of the house is the terrace and topiary garden, the recently replanted trough garden, the sunken garden and white borders leading to the cherry orchard, which has a wide variety of snowdrops in early spring as well as shrubs and roses. There is a good rockery, a wild garden with a hornbeam avenue, and many attractive vistas. The large working kitchen garden features both culinary and ornamental plants, old apple arches, a collection of old-fashioned and scented roses, and a row of sinks. Several areas have been replanted since 1991 when the present owners moved into the manor, including parts of the leisure garden and the four large herbaceous borders, which are now quite magnificent. The shrubbery has also been renovated. Beautifully kept, this garden is full of romance and excitement.

Sezincote ★★ [Historic Garden Grade I]

Moreton-in-Marsh GL56 9AW.

Mr and Mrs E. Peake • 1.5m W of Moreton-in-Marsh on A44 just before Bourton-on-the-Hill • House open May to July, Sept, Thurs, Fri, 2.30 – 6pm (no children in house) • Garden open Jan to Nov, Thurs, Fri and Bank Holiday Mons, 2 – 6pm (or dusk if earlier), and one day for NGS • Entrance: £4, children £1.50, children under 5 free (house and garden £6) • Other information: Teas on NGS open day only ❍ 🏠 WC ♿

The entrance to Sezincote is up a long dark avenue of holm oaks that opens into the most English of parks, with a distinct Reptonian feeling – fine trees and distant views of Cotswold hills. Turning the last corner is the surprise, for there is that fascinating rarity, an English country house built in the Moghul architectural style by Samuel Pepys Cockerell. The form of the garden has not changed since Repton's time, but the more recent planting was carried out by Lady Kleinwort with help from Graham Stuart Thomas, and on her return from India in 1968 she laid out the Paradise Garden in the south garden with canals and Irish yews. Behind this is the curved orangery, home to many tender climbing plants. The house is sheltered by great copper beeches, cedars, yews and limes, which provide a fine backdrop for the exotic shrubs. Streams and pools are lined with great clumps of bog-loving plants, and the stream is crossed by an Indian bridge, adorned with Brahmin bulls. Planted for year-round interest, the garden is particularly strong on autumn colours. Graham Stuart Thomas's instructive guidebook is highly recommended.

Snowshill Manor ★ [Historic Garden Grade II]

Broadway WR12 7JU. Tel: (01386) 852410

The National Trust • 3m S of Broadway off A44 • House open as garden but 12 noon – 5pm • Garden open 25th March to 28th Oct, Wed – Sun and Bank Holiday Mons, 11am – 5.30pm • Entrance: gardens £4, children £2, family £10 (house and gardens £7.80, children £3.65, family £18.50) • Other information: Coaches and school parties by written appt only. No entry from Snowshill village. Car park 500 metres from manor with entry via footpath; motorised buggy available ◑ 😐 ✕ ● WC ♿ 🐾 🏬 🍽 ☕

From a design by the Arts and Crafts architect M.H. Baillie-Scott, Charles Wade transformed a 'wilderness of chaos' on a Cotswold hillside into an interconnecting series of outdoor rooms from the 1920s onwards. Wade was a believer in the Arts and Crafts rustic ideal and the garden, like the house, expresses his eccentricities. Seats and woodwork are painted 'Wade blue', a powdery dark blue with touches of turquoise which goes well with the Cotswold stone walls. The simple cottage style conceals careful planting in shades of blue, mauve and purple. Organic gardening is employed here.

Special Plants Nursery (Hill Farm Barn Garden)

Greenways Lane, Cold Ashton, Chippenham SN14 8LA. Tel: (01225) 891686

Derry Watkins • 7m N of Bath just S of junction A46 and A420. Turn into Greenways Lane (signed to nursery) • Open July and Aug, Wed, 11am – 5pm; also four Thurs, June to Sept for NGS, and for parties by appt • Entrance: £2.50 • Other information: Lectures and courses in autumn and winter; telephone for details ● 😐 🏬 WC 🐾

Set high on the Cotswold Way is the small garden of Derry Watkins, owner of the adjacent Special Plants Nursery. Entirely created over the last eight years, the structure and imaginative modern design are the work of her architect husband, Peter Clegg, while she has employed her discerning eye for colour and knowledge of a vast range of unusual perennials to produce a dramatic and brilliant display rising to a climax in late summer. The steepness of the south-facing site, mercifully sheltered by mature willows, ash and horse chestnut, enables many borderline tender plants and shrubs to flourish and grow to immense size in deep gravel terraces and richly planted borders. Bold shapes in gravel, water and grass echo the outlines of the magnificent surrounding scenery, and there are superb colour-associations, such as the deep crimson/almost black border and the shades of apricot edging the new gravel garden. The garden is still developing – the productive vegetable garden and a peaceful woodland walk are new features. The nursery itself is outstanding, selling a wide range of beautifully grown and well displayed perennials, both hardy and tender, and many new introductions.

Stancombe Park ★ [Historic Garden Grade I]

Stancombe, Dursley GL11 6AU. Tel: (01453) 542815

Mrs Gerda Barlow • Between Wotton-under-Edge and Dursley on B4060 • Open for parties by appt • Entrance: £3 ◑ 💬 WC

People still rush to view the most curious park and garden south of Biddulph Grange (see entry in Staffordshire), built in 1811. Set on the Cotswold escarpment, it has all the ingredients of a Gothick best-seller. A narrow path drops into a dark glen, roots from enormous oaks, copper beeches and chestnuts trip your feet, ferns brush your face, walls drip water, and ammonites and fossils loom in the gloom. Rocks erupt with moss, Egyptian tombs trap the unwary, tunnels turn into grottoes. Even plants live in wire cages. But it is not a place of gloom; indeed the secret garden can be light and friendly when it is not raining. A millennium folly with a peace motif, placed at the head of a small pond, has reused the facade of a ruined chapel found in the woods; a bog garden has been planted behind. The upper garden around the house has a new pattern border, created by the owner and the designer Nada Jennett.

Stanway House [Historic Garden Grade I]

Winchcombe, Cheltenham GL54 5PQ. Tel: (01386) 584469

Lord Neidpath • 1m E of B4632 Cheltenham – Broadway road, 4m NE of Winchcombe • House open as garden but closed Sat • Garden open June, Tues and Thurs; July and Aug, Tues, Thurs and Sat; all 2 – 5pm. Tours for parties at other times by appt • Entrance: £4, children £1 (house and garden £6, OAPs £4.50, children £1.50 ◑ 💬 WC ⬧

Stanway is a honey-coloured Cotswold village with a Jacobean great house which has changed hands just once since AD 715. The garden rises in a series of dramatic terraced lawns and a rare, picturesque grasswork to the pyramid, which in the eighteenth century stood at the head of a 190-metre-long cascade descending to a formal canal on a terrace above the house. This was probably designed by Charles Bridgeman, and exceeded in length and height (36 metres) its famous rival at Chatsworth (see entry in Derbyshire). Inside the house is a fascinating painting recording the cascade as it looked in the eighteenth century. The canal, the upper pond behind the pyramid, a short section of the cascade, and the upper fall below the pyramid were restored in 1998, and a 100-metre-high single-jet fountain (the tallest garden fountain in the world) added in the middle of the canal. The medieval pond in the Lower Garden, recently restored, has enhanced the beauty of the fourteenth-century tithe barn. It is hoped soon to restore the pyramid itself, a banqueting house from which guests could watch the sluices being opened and the water falling down towards the house. A high walk along the hillside above the cascade reveals the splendid park trees.

Stone House

Wyck Rissington GL54 2PN. Tel: (01451) 810337

Mr and Mrs Andrew Lukas • 1.5m S of Stow-on-the-Wold off A429 just NE of Bourton-on-the-Water. Last house in village, past church on opposite side of road

• *Open April to Oct for individuals and parties by appt* • *Entrance: £4* • *Other information: Teas by prior arrangement. Plant fairs 29th May and 19th Sept* ● ● WC &

This plantsman's garden is the perfect antidote to all those daffodil-lined Cotswold lanes, as it avoids horticultural clichés all year round. Note, for example, the bold use of euphorbias. Its two acres are filled with unusual bulbs, shrubs and herbaceous perennials, including an abundance of aquilegias and hostas. There is a crab-apple walk, rose borders and a herb garden, and fritillaries are naturalising in the meadow walk. A spring-fed stream flowing into the River Dikler bubbles throughout; the area of sloping, box-edged lawns leading down from a terrace via rounded Lutyensesque brick steps to the water's edge is especially charming. The overall design makes full and sensitive use of the sloping site and the views out across a ha-ha to unspoilt countryside; major elements such as a swimming pool and tennis court are cunningly concealed. The annual plant fairs are prized for their wide range of good and unusual plants, with some of the stands manned by professional nurserymen. The attractive village has an unusual church with a fine tower, where Gustav Holst was organist for a period at the princely annual stipend of £4.

Sudeley Castle and Gardens ★ [Historic Garden Grade II*]

Winchcombe, Cheltenham GL54 5JD. Tel: (01242) 602308

Henry and Mollie Dent-Brocklehurst • 8m NE of Cheltenham off B4632 at Winchcombe • Castle and gardens open main season – telephone or check website at back of Guide for details. Private guided tours in and out of season by arrangement • Entrance: castle and gardens £7.70, concessions £6.70, children £4.70, family £22.80; party rates and season tickets available (2005 prices) ● ● × ● WC & ● ● ● ● ●

There has been a house on this magnificent site, with views of the surrounding Cotswold hills at every turn, for over 1000 years; today the emphasis is on tourism. The extensive grounds contain ten integrated but individual gardens, notably the Queen's Garden with its outstanding collection of old-fashioned roses, surrounded by immaculately clipped double yew hedges. These were laid out in the nineteenth century by an ancestor of the present owners on the site of the original Tudor parterre. In recent years Jane Fearnley-Whittingstall guided the restoration of this area, as well as designing the knot garden and a newly planted buddleia walk featuring 23 different varieties. The gardens surrounding the ruins of the banqueting hall and the tithe barn with its carp pond are exceptionally lovely, with old climbing roses and (should you be lucky enough to avoid the coachloads) a romantic atmosphere. There is a white garden, a secret garden replanted by Charles Chesshire, and a tree peony garden. The Victorian kitchen garden is managed in collaboration with the Henry Doubleday Research Association to produce seed for propagation.

Througham Court ★

Througham GL6 7HG. Email: cafacer@netcom.co.uk

Dr Christine Facer • 8m W of Cirencester. From Birdlip, follow the B4070 until left turn signed to The Camp; after The Camp take first left signed to Througham. Take second left turn down hill; house immediately on right • Open May to Sept by appt • Entrance: £5, children free; parties of up to 15 welcome (with lecture tour: fee negotiable) [NEW] ●

The intriguing house – a Jacobean, eighteenth-century and Arts-and-Crafts hybrid, listed Grade II* – lies at the heart of the garden, and the garden acts as a viewing platform for the landscape beyond. It is a fascinating amalgam of the traditional (garden compartments, topiary, courtyards and terraces) and the contemporary (a wild grass meadow, a magical black bamboo maze, a mound planted with late perennials). Science has been a deep inspiration on both the design and the details: reminders of the cosmos are expressed in stone, statuary and in a host of allusive names such as the Garden of Cosmic Evolution, Fibonacci Jumps, Entry Into Chaos Gate, Molecule Seat. It comes as no surprise that the owner, a scientist turned landscape designer, has worked closely with Charles Jencks. There are witty and light-hearted touches too: a rippling photinia hedge as background to a series of sculptured slate shards cascading down a slope; steps covered with a surprising red astroturf 'carpet', shimmering banners by Shona Watts. High-quality is the workmanship of the complex stainless-steel gates, perfectly formed and engraved Ancaster stone balls and slate starburst linked to a black reflective pool and a rill, and the planting shows the same fine eye for colour and a talent for blending and juxtaposing plants in subtle or startling groups. A remarkable contemporary garden, still in the making.

Trull House

Trull, Tetbury GL8 8SQ. Tel: (01285) 841255

Caroline and Simon Mitchell • 3m E of Tetbury, 7m SW of Cirencester off A433. Signposted • Open 30th April to 3rd Sept, Wed, Sun and Bank Holiday Mons, 11am – 5pm, plus June, Tues and Fri, 6 – 8.30pm, and by appt at other times; coaches welcome • Entrance: £3, children free [NEW] ● ● WC & ℗ ⏏ ℺

In a beautiful Cotswold setting, the eight acres of garden surrounding the 1841 house (not open) were laid out at the beginning of the twentieth century. They are in the best English tradition, with expansive lawns, mature trees, shrubs and wild areas; large walled gardens contain a series of lush herbaceous borders overflowing with popular country-house favourites in shades of pink, blue and purple. A sunken lily pond and a rockery evoke its Edwardian past. The evening openings especially, when the light heightens the peaceful atmosphere and intensifies the colour schemes and picks out the magnificent delphinium spires, are a perfect restorative after a tiring summer day.

Upton Wold

Northwick Estate, Moreton–in–Marsh GL56 9TR. Tel: (01386) 700667

Mr and Mrs I.R.S. Bond • 5m NW of Moreton-in-Marsh on A44. Pass Batsford, Sezincote and Bourton House, continue up Bourton hill, pass Troopers Lodge Garage at A424 junction, and drive is 1m further on right • Open two days for NGS, 2 – 6pm, and by appt May to July, 10am – 6pm • Entrance: NGS openings £4, children free; May to July openings £6 ● ● & ℗

The newest and best-concealed of the four fine gardens lying along this stretch of the A44 is the garden set around a small seventeenth-century manor house hidden in a wold. The owners arrived here in the 1970s and have created, from scratch, what is now one of the most distinguished of typical Cotswold gardens. The view from the south-east facade of the house (not open) stretches out across a lawn and ha-ha to the valley. To the left is a long border, which leads to the pond and wild garden (fritillaries bursting through in season), to the right a more formal space with a canal and fountains. The walk on the opposite side of the central lawn is bordered by a tunnel of yew. Beyond this the ground slopes up through the Hidden Garden and hedged croquet lawn to a long level area containing an ornamental fruit garden, a fine vegetable garden and greenhouses. Imaginative planting is evident everywhere (note the owners' passion for standards), with particular care taken to provide pleasing views from the house windows, such as the bank of old roses below the dovecot. A small arboretum on the south side of the garden holds a National Collection of walnuts.

The Urn Cottage

19 Station Road, Charfield, Wotton–under–Edge GL12 8SY. Tel: (01453) 843156

Mr A.C. and Dr L.A. Rosser • 3m E of M5 junction 14. In Charfield turn off main road at Railway Tavern; garden is 370 metres on left, a short walk from parking area • Open by appt only • Entrance: £3, children £1 (2005 prices) ◕ ● WC & ♨

This splendidly varied garden around an old stone cottage has been entirely created by the owners since 1982. The trees they planted for shelter have now matured and frame beautiful views of the Cotswolds from its edge-of-village setting. Dr Rosser is a horticultural design consultant and lecturer, and her expertise is evident in the skilful design and planting of this attractive 0.75-acre garden. Her preference for well-behaved plants results in a wide and remarkably healthy selection, all maintained to a high standard. Long-season interest is achieved throughout the garden, from the stylish schemes around the house to planting beside a shady stream and even on a patch of volcanic rock. A small vegetable garden is cleverly terraced with wooden railway sleepers, and interesting sculptures are imaginatively displayed.

Westbury Court Garden [Historic Garden Grade II*]

Westbury-on–Severn GL14 1PD. Tel: (01452) 760461

The National Trust • 9m SW of Gloucester on A48, close to church • Open 8th March to 30th June, Wed – Sun and Bank Holiday Mons; July to 29th Aug, daily; 30th Aug to 29th Oct, Wed – Sun; all 10am – 5pm. Individuals at other times by appt and parties of 15 or more by written appt • Entrance: £4, children £2 • Other information: Braille plan available ◑ ● WC & ♥

The future of this remarkable Dutch water garden – restored by the Trust in the 1960s – is still in jeopardy following an outbreak of phytophthora in 2002. Substantial sections of the formal yew hedging flanking the Tall Pavilion have died and therefore disfigure one fundamental component of the ensemble of *allée*, canal, *clairvoyée* and vista, and the Trust has been advised that the garden could be flooded with increasing frequency in the decades to come. Nevertheless, the replanting of the hedges is said to be under positive review. The other elements of this rare seventeenth-century survival remain in good shape and retain their interest for garden historians. Parallel to the long canal and its unhappy yews is a T-shaped canal with Neptune bestriding a dolphin in the centre of the arm. There is an elaborate seventeenth-century seat in the 'bowling green', a central area which has been returned, as in the Kip engraving, to growing period vegetables, fruit and herbs. To the north-east is a charming gazebo, one side of which overlooks a small walled enclosure where species of plants to be found growing in England prior to 1900 grow now in box-edged beds. A small sliver of the original rabbit warren shown in the 1708 Kip engraving, where conies were bred for their meat and fur, has been re-created round the back of the walled garden. Beyond is the parterre: beds of simple shape containing box topiary; this in turn is surrounded by the quincunx, a formal arrangement of small trees and clipped evergreens.

Westonbirt Arboretum

(see THE NATIONAL ARBORETUM, WESTONBIRT)

Westonbirt School Gardens [Historic Garden Grade I]

Tetbury GL8 8QG. Tel: (01666) 880333

Westonbirt School • 3m SW of Tetbury on A433 opposite Westonbirt Arboretum • Open two days for NGS, 2 – 4.30pm, at certain times during school holidays (telephone for details or see website at back of book), and at other times by appt • Entrance: £3.50, children £2 (2005 prices) ● & ⚘ ☕

The house was built by the eminent Victorian plant collector Robert Stayner Holford, who had already started to plant trees when he inherited the estate and spectacular 40-acre gardens from his father in 1839. After his death in 1892 his son George, who became one of the most successful amateur gardeners of his time, continued the development of both arboretum and garden; he was particularly keen on orchids and exotics. The garden is designed to have leisurely walks and a few surprises. Sweeping lawns and terraces lead down to the fountain pool, with views across the ha-ha, which hides the road, to farmland beyond. The other axis leads from the church to the sunken garden, with its pond and statue of Mercury. An Italian garden with exuberant ogee-roofed pavilions and a pergola walk complete the formal eastern side of the house, while the other side is more informal, with irregular groups of trees and shrubs (many rare and exotic), a lake, a grotto and a rockery. Many trees are over 100 years old, and some are the largest of their kind in the country.

HAMPSHIRE &
THE ISLE OF WIGHT

Gardens on the Isle of Wight will be found at the end of the Hampshire section.
Two-starred gardens are marked on the map with a black square.

Abbey Cottage

Rectory Lane, Itchen Abbas, Winchester SO21 1BN. Tel: (01962) 779575

*Col. Patrick Daniell • 2m W of New Alresford on B3047, 1m E of Itchen Abbas
• Open 5th and 6th April, 2 – 5pm; 30th April and 1st May, 12 noon – 5pm;
14th and 15th June, 8th and 10th Aug, 10.30am – 5pm; 27th and 28th Aug,
12 noon – 5pm • Entrance: £2.50. Other information: teas on Suns and Mons only*
● WC ⅙

A series of vistas linked by steps, slopes and hedge corridors leads the visitor into this
one-and-half-acre organic garden with varied levels and enclosures. The framework
of yew and other hedging makes a satisfying foil to shrubs and perennials, while an
oval window cut through the hedge of one garden gives glimpses into the next, of a
pond and an immaculate box bench with box cushions. Walls are covered with
unusual species clematis and the perennial climber *Malvastrum lateritium*; among
many striking plants are *Magnolia* x *loebneri* 'Merrill', flowering against the yew hedge
in spring, *Cornus alternifolia* 'Argentea' and ancient, well-groomed apple trees.
One meadow is planted with spring bulbs and young specimen trees, another with
late-summer wild flowers, and at the highest point in the garden there is a new
plantation containing native trees.

Amport House [Historic Garden Grade II]

Amport House Chaplaincy Centre, Amport, Andover SP11 8BG.

*4m W of Andover, S of A303 • Open by appt only in writing to the Principal
• Entrance: £5* ● B&B

This little known Lutyens and Jekyll garden surrounds a yellow brick Jacobean-style
house built in 1857 for the Marquis of Winchester. Jekyll's contribution has faded but
Lutyens' is very evident in the raised rock garden, the broad steps and wide terraces
inlaid with millstone shapes, and the water parterre said to be the prototype of his
water garden in New Delhi. It has a wide oval pond and is surrounded by rills
holding water lilies, all overlooking spreading chalk countryside and grazing deer.
Mature trees along the drive include limes, copper beeches, cedars of Lebanon and
Wellingtonias. A knot garden established in Victorian times bears the marquis's
motto 'Aymez Loyauté', which also adorns the house. Beyond are nicely maintained
cordon lime walks, each with three swagged laterals; some of these march in parallel
lines and some are solo. Reminiscent of cloisters, they seem entirely fitting for a
chaplaincy, as does the notice by a pond: 'Please do not walk on the water.'

Apple Court

Hordle Lane, Hordle, Lymington SO41 0HU. Tel: (01590) 642130

Charles and Angela Meads • 200 metres N of A337 between Lymington and New Milton along Hordle Lane opposite Royal Oak • Open March to Oct, Fri – Sun and Bank Holiday Mons, 10am – 5pm • Entrance: £2.50 • Other information: Plants for sale in adjoining nursery ☕ 🍽 **wc** &

The garden, created by the previous owners, Diana Grenfell and Roger Grounds, is a showcase for a National Collection of hostas and the only American Hemerocallis Society display garden in Europe. The daylily garden, with a frothy rectangle of ornamental grasses at its centre, is at its peak in July and August, when the flowers are mixed with agapanthus, crocosmias, kniphofias and phormiums. The white garden has a different drama – a square of yew hedging contains an oval border of white flowers and silvery-leaved grasses viewed through an inner oval of pleached hornbeams which frames them like a series of lit pictures. The effect is architectural, like entering a square with a circular colonnade. Three rectangular ponds are connected by cascading rills, and a Japanese garden with a Koi pond was added in 2004. There is also a fern path and herbaceous borders lined with rose-covered rope swags.

Bramdean House ★ [Historic Garden Grade II]

Bramdean, Alresford SO24 0JU. Tel: (01962) 771214

Mr and Mrs H. Wakefield • 9m E of Winchester, 5m SE of New Alresford on A272 in middle of Bramdean • Open 19th Feb, 19th March, 16th April, 11th June, 9th July, 13th Aug, 10th Sept, 2 – 5pm, for NGS, and by appt at other times • Entrance: NGS days £3.50, other days £4.50, children free ☕ 🍽 **wc** & 🐾

The mellow brick eighteenth-century house is well protected from the main road by a huge undulating yew and box hedge. The six-and-a-half-acre garden on chalk slopes away from the house and is divided into three parts. One contains the famous mirror-image herbaceous borders, while surrounding beds have a large array of usual and unusual plants, shrubs and small trees. Fine wrought-iron gates lead through into the walled working kitchen garden, cultivated entirely by hand, containing fruit and vegetables grown for the house, old-fashioned sweet peas, perpetual carnations, a peony walk and a trial area for plants. Ornamental flower beds along a central path lead through a second wrought-iron gate into the orchard area, featuring fruit trees underplanted with massed daffodils and terminated by a blue-doored apple house and belfry. To the east are interesting shrubs and trees and castellations of yew. In spring there are carpets of aconites, snowdrops, crocuses and other early bulbs, and a large collection of tender and hardy nerines adds autumn colour.

Brandy Mount House

Brandy Mount, Alresford SO24 9EG. Tel: (01962) 732189

Mr and Mrs M. Baron • In town centre. Take first right in East Street before Sun Lane • Open early Feb for snowdrops (telephone or see website for dates), 11am – 4pm;

and for NGS 5th March, 2 – 5pm • Entrance: £2, children free (2005 prices) • Other information: No vehicular access. Parking in station car park and Broad Street. Teas available except in Feb. Children must be supervised ● ● ● ● ●

This informal one-acre garden of trees, shrubs, beds and grass is very much for the plantsman, with unusual species and varieties to be discovered at every turn. Michael Baron is on hand to guide visitors through his National Collections of at least 220 named snowdrops in winter and spring, and over 130 varieties of daphne, and will discuss the problems of growing plants on dry chalk. There are woodland plants by the pond, and hellebores, ferns, trilliums, pulmonarias, epimediums, erythroniums. The alpine house has a good display of dwarf narcissi and alpine primulas, where they are a delight on cold spring days. The *potager* is packed with vegetables.

48 Broad Street

New Alresford, Alresford SO24 9AN. Tel: (01962) 732441

Mr and Mrs David Ashdown • In town centre • Open by appt • Entrance: £4 ●

This town garden turns a long and narrow plot into a journey of light and dark through varied passages and rooms. Near the house are pots, paving, *Trachelospermum jasminoides* and the silver-leaved *Elaeagnus angustifolia* grown as a standard with *Clematis viticella* 'Etoile Violette' weaving through it. Next comes the lawn, sculpture and box-edged beds of lilies, perennials and roses, followed by miniature woodland and a geometric garden in shades of lavender with slate chippings, and the transition to Hampshire countryside is completed by a nut walk leading to a view of fields and a glimpse of Alresford pond. Everywhere there is the sound of water bubbling from low fountains. Visit in spring for the hellebores and bulbs, and in June when the herbaceous borders are in full fig.

Bury Court

Bentley, Farnham, Surrey GU10 5LZ. Tel: (01420) 520351

John Coke • 6m NE of Alton, 5m SW of Farnham, 1.5m N of Bentley on road signed to Crondall • Open for parties by appt • Entrance: £2 ● **WC** ●

The walled garden is the work of the Dutch designer Piet Oudolf and displays both his naturalism and his characteristic use of grasses. Surrounded by walls of brick and stone, curved oast houses and other buildings with a glimpse of the countryside beyond, the asymmetrical beds are dominated by robust perennials and varied grasses, planted so as to evoke an idealised or dreamlike natural landscape. With lawns, cambered sett paths, a set-piece of planks emerging from water, sculptural clipped box, and a fine gravel bed with blue-flowered and grey-leaved plants, it is a good example of Oudolf's work. A new garden has been made with help from the minimalist designer Christopher Bradley-Hole, using raised beds edged with rusted steel and planted with drifts of grasses and wild-looking but non-weedy perennials.

Cadland Gardens ★ [Historic Garden Grade II*]

Fawley, Southampton SO45 1AA.

Mr and Mrs Maldwin Drummond • 16m SE of Southampton off A326/B3053
• Open May to July, Sept and Oct, by written appt for parties of 20 or more
• Entrance: £4 • Other information: Teas by arrangement. House also open by
arrangement ● **WC** &

The landscape garden of eight acres, laid out for the banker Robert Drummond in 1775, is 'Capability' Brown's smallest surviving pleasure ground. It has been restored to the original plan, using plants available before 1780. A path with tiered shrubs underplanted with wild flowers winds from the modern house (encapsulating the original thatched *cottage orné* designed by Brown and Henry Holland), along the Solent shore and back through a lime walk and a Georgian flower border. Broad vistas alternate with carefully orchestrated views of the sea. There is a kitchen garden with fruit houses and a gravel garden. A second walled garden has a red border, a cool grey border and rare plants – *Astelia chathamica, Pileostegia viburnoides*, tender acacias and leptospermums.

Conholt Park ★

Chute, Nr Andover SP11 9HA. Tel: (07803) 021208

Professor Caroline Tisdall • 5m NW of Andover off A342. Turn N at Weyhill church
and continue 5m through Clanville and Tangley Bottom. Turn left for Conholt; house
is 0.5m on right just off Chute causeway • Open 11th and 25th June, 2 – 5pm, and
for private visits by appt • Entrance: £3, children free ● ● ● **WC** ⬧ ⬧ ⬧

Surrounding the Regency house is an imaginative 10-acre garden created over the past few years. Spacious lawns, towering cedars and fine views are grace-notes providing a dignified setting for a variety of individual spaces, including rose, secret, winter and Shakespeare gardens, an Edwardian Ladies' Walk and a laurel millennium maze, in the shape of a foot and possibly the longest in the country. The walled kitchen garden has good glasshouses, a sunken pool and tunnels of runner beans, herbs and flowers. Future plans include a meadow rose garden with the roses allowed free growth through an existing meadow – something which has been done in France but rarely over here.

Exbury Gardens ★★ [Historic Garden Grade II*]

Exbury, Southampton SO45 1AZ. Tel: (023) 8089 1203

Mr E.L. de Rothschild • 15m S of Southampton. From M27 west junction 2 take
A326 then B3054. 2.5m SE of Beaulieu, after 1m turn right for Exbury.
Signposted • Open 25th Feb to 5th Nov, daily, 10am – 5.30pm (or dusk if earlier)
• Entrance: high-season £7, OAPs £6.50 (£6 on Tues, Wed and Thurs),
children (3–15) £1.50, family £17. Seasonal discounts (2005 prices) ● ● ✕ ●
WC & ⬧ ⬧ ⬧ ● ⬧

Established between the wars by Lionel de Rothschild, these gardens of rhododendrons and azaleas are the most outstanding of their kind in the south. Winding paths meander over 200 acres and proceed under a light canopy of trees, mostly oak and pine, over a bridge and beside ponds to the Beaulieu River. Many rhododendrons and azaleas, such as *R. yakushimanum* and *R.* (Hawk Group) 'Crest', were introduced here and are to be found growing beside purple Japanese maples and candelabra primulas. At times the colour associations seem brash – harsh orange beside blush, metallic magenta beside pale blue – but a glade of towering white blooms, pink in bud, more than makes up for this. In March early rhododendrons, camellias and the daffodil meadow flower; in April the rock garden, miniature mountain scenery with screes and valleys, is at its peak with alpine rhododendrons flowering among 'Skyrocket' junipers. May is the high season. In summer the herbaceous and grass garden is a mass of colour and variety, while the recently planted exotic garden is full of unusual plants. For autumn interest there is a superb collection of deciduous trees, shrubs, notably acers, which exhibit fiery hues next to the ponds. The Summer Lane Garden, planted in a contemporary design inspired by Piet Oudolf, combines huge swathes of herbaceous plants, grasses, bulbs and wild flowers, and includes an apple and pear orchard. A steam railway has opened up the south-east corner of the gardens, offering visitors a 20-minute journey in comfort.

Farleigh House ★

Farleigh Wallop, Basingstoke RG25 2HT. Tel: (01256) 842684

The Earl and Countess of Portsmouth • 3m SE of Basingstoke off B3046. Leave M3 at junction 7 and follow signs from Dummer • Open for parties by appt • Entrance: £5 ● ● &

An exemplary modern garden in the classic tradition, designed by Georgia Langton, immaculately maintained and complementing the knapped-flint house. The large kitchen garden has a herbaceous border running with blue clematis *C. durandii*, and culminates in a conservatory (with a pond), scented by various brugmansis, rare passion flowers and other choice plants. The quadripartite fountain garden, of roses, nepeta and alchemilla, is followed by an area of species roses with silver metallic seagulls wheeling overhead. A simple maze leads, via two topiary peacocks pecking at strawberries, to a rectangular waterlily garden; beyond, at the end of the Scots pine walk new wrought-iron gates open onto a 1.5-acre lake. Note the details: a huge smooth granite apple in woodland lit by a shaft of light … another pair of wrought-iron gates decorated with tools, flowers and abstract geometrical patterns … hedges dipping to give glimpses of gardens beyond … the little barrel seat above the ice-house. Good shrubs and trees, including a fine *Cornus controversa* 'Variegata'.

Furzey Gardens

Minstead, Lyndhurst SO43 7GL. Tel: (023) 8081 2464

Mrs M.M. Cole (Administrator) • 8m SW of Southampton, 1m S of A31, 2m W of Cadnam and end of M27, 3.5m NW of Lyndhurst • Open daily except 25th and 26th Dec, 10am – 5pm (earlier in winter) • Entrance: summer: £3.50, OAPs £2.80, children £1.50, families £9; winter: £1.50, OAPs £1, children 50p, family £3. Reductions for parties by arrangement • Other information: Galleries and cottage open March to Oct, daily; Nov to Dec, Sat and Sun only. No toilet facilities when galleries closed ○ ● ● WC & ✿ ● ●

The informal 10-acre garden was established in 1922. At the entrance are several thatched buildings, including a restored forest cottage and a craft and art gallery, and nearby is Furzey House, the largest thatched cottage in the forest. Fine views look down to a Chilean fire bush, *Embothrium coccineum*, and over the woodland beyond. Narrow paths, winding past acid-loving plants from Chile and Japan, lead to tree houses for children, a bog garden with a raised walk through lysichitons and ferns, and a waterlily pond surrounded by *Iris sibirica*. Low banks of rhododendrons, azaleas, cistus and hydrangeas slope down from Furzey House. Blue and red meconopsis flower in June and July, followed in August by six varieties of eucryphia. There are many different kinds of birch, a fine *Cornus kousa* and various acers.

The Garden Gallery

Broughton, Nr Stockbridge SO20 8AZ. Tel:(01794) 301144

Mr and Mrs G. Bebb • 12m W of Winchester • Telephone for exhibition opening times or see website at back of Guide; also open by appt • Entrance: £2 ● &

Rachel Bebb's one-acre cottage garden, designed as a series of stylishly informal enclosures with varied plantings, displays a range of modern sculpture for sale. Some are set among flowers beside the small formal pond, others on gravel, in an orchard, or showing up against a background of shrubs. Abstract forms, pots, benches, tables, sundials and figures in stone, bronze, resin, ceramic, clay, wood, steel and copper – all are harmoniously sited, encouraging visitors to relate them to their own gardens.

Gilbert White's Garden

Selborne GU34 3JH. Tel: (01420) 511275

Oates Memorial Trust • 4.5m S of Alton, 8m N of Petersfield on B3006 • Open April to 24th Dec, 11am – 5pm • Entrance: £5, OAPs and students £4.50, children £3. Special rates for parties • Other information: Public car park behind Selborne Arms. Unusual plant fair 17th and 18th June, other non-horticultural events later (telephone to check dates) ● ● WC & ● ● ●

Here the naturalist Gilbert White wrote his classic *The Natural History of Selborne* (published 1788), and the garden is exceptionally well documented. The sundial and ha-ha beyond the lawn, with its splendid views of the beech-clad hanging wood, were there in his day. A copy of the amusing wooden cut-out of the Hesperian Hercules which he set up in the park in 1758 is the work of sculptor David Swinton. The quincunx, a square pattern of five cypresses on a mound, was also originally conceived by White. Borders and beds near the house contain many plants from his time, including hollyhocks ('hollyoaks'), sweet Williams, pinks, species foxgloves, santolinas, martagon lilies and old roses, Gallicas, Damasks, etc. Later additions include a laburnum tunnel, a herb garden, a fine tulip tree planted in 1910 and some yew topiary. The garden is being restored to its eighteenth-century form with historic varieties of fruit (including White's favourite melons), vegetables, herbaceous plants, annuals and wild flowers. Look out for the revolving wine barrel.

Heathlands ★

47 Locks Road, Locks Heath, Southampton SO31 6NS. Tel: (01489) 573598

Dr John Burwell • 5m W of Fareham. Leave M27 at junction 9. Locks Road runs due S from A27 at Park Gate • Open 5th March, 2nd April, 7th May, 27th Aug, 2 – 5.30pm • Entrance: £2.50, children free ● ● ● WC & ⬦ ⬦ ⬦

The garden is approached along a roadside planted with a row of paulownias raised from seed by the owner. The sylvan setting is reinforced by the *Styrax japonicus*, sweet chestnut, camellias, embothriums and crinodendrons surrounding the lawn and by the woodland beyond. There are 1000 different plants here, with flowering interest maintained from bulbs and an acacia in March and earlier to hydrangeas and scented eucryphias in August. Notable are a gigantic flowering phormium, yuccas, a tree fern, *Abutilon megapotamicum* and many clematis. A splendid holly drum, over ten feet high, becomes sculpture among the natural planting, and a yew hedge leading to the kitchen garden sports a topiary peacock, its tail in low relief against the hedge and its head and crown outlined above. Fine rhododendron hedges line a walk focused on an obelisk and delineate secret areas with ponds and ferns; they are cut through at intervals to give glimpses of the woodland beyond.

Highclere Castle and Gardens [Historic Garden Grade I]

Highclere, Newbury, Berkshire RG20 9RN. Tel: (01635) 253204 (infoline)

The Earl and Countess of Carnarvon • 4.5m S of Newbury, W of A34 • House open as garden • Garden open June to Aug, Mon – Fri, 11am – 4pm, plus some weekends (telephone for exact dates) • Entrance: Grounds and gardens free (house £7.50, concessions £6, children £4, family £18. Special rates for parties of 20 or more (2005 prices) ● ● × ● WC & ● ●

At first glance it seems that the Houses of Parliament have flown and settled in a parkland setting of lawns and cedars. Not surprising, since Highclere Castle (1840) was designed by the same architect, Sir Charles Barry, who remodelled a Georgian mansion to create a fine Victorian home for the 3rd Earl of Carnarvon. Three follies, a rotunda beside the lake, a roofless temple called Jackdaw's Castle, and Heaven's Gate on Sidown Hill opposite the castle are remnants of the garden before 'Capability' Brown remodelled the grounds in 1774 to give a gloriously simple vista of valley and hills. Tucked out of sight is the walled garden and the flower garden, designed by the late James Russell.

Hillier Gardens

(see THE SIR HAROLD HILLIER GARDENS AND ARBORETUM)

Hinton Ampner ★

Hinton Ampner, Bramdean, Alresford SO24 0LA. Tel: (01962) 771305

The National Trust • 8m E of Winchester, 1m W of Bramdean on A272 • House open 19th March to 11th Oct, Sun, Tues and Wed, 1.30 – 5pm, plus Sat in Aug • Garden open 18th March to 11th Oct, Sat – Wed, 11am – 5pm. Parties of 15 or

more by appt • Entrance: £5.50, children (5–16) £2.75. Extra charge for house
• Other information: Coaches must use entrance through village ◑ ⚑ <u>WC</u> ⚐ ⚘

The garden was created by Ralph Dutton, later Lord Sherborne, who inherited the estate in 1935. The terraces below the Georgian style house command fine views over downland. Their cross-axes, revealing glimpses of urns, statues or an obelisk, are almost Italianate in feel, but this is a classic English garden of lawns and avenues, deep borders and secret places. The yew and box hedging and topiary are dense and crisp, the giant yew mushrooms surreal in feel. Among the wide range of unusual plants are *Syringa* x *laciniata*, *Abelia triflora* and *A. floribunda* with raspberry tubes, *Amorpha fruticosa* and *Gymnocladus dioica* (the Kentucky coffee tree). The plants are unlabelled but the gardeners happy to identify. As befits a large formal house, the climbers, punctuated by pillars of yew and holly, are trained to reach high and grow wallpaper-tight with never an overlapping stem. The old walled kitchen garden is now laid out as a formal orchard. A new rose garden has been planted, and interest extends to September and beyond with salvias and autumn crocuses, and the late-flowering *Heptacodium miconioides*.

Houghton Lodge [Historic Garden Grade II*]

Stockbridge SO20 6LQ. Tel: (01264) 810912/810502

Mr and Mrs Martin Busk • 1.5m S of Stockbridge. Signposted • Open March to Sept, daily, except Wed, 2 – 5pm (opens 10am Sat, Sun and Bank Holiday Mons). Telephone for winter opening times • Entrance: £5, children free ◑ ⚑ <u>WC</u> ⚐ ⚐ ⚘ ⚑

Superbly sited on an eminence, overlooking an open and gently curving stretch of the River Test with its swans and water meadows, the early eighteenth-century *cottage orné* (some cottage!) and its garden is the centrepiece of a miniature 30-acre estate. The lodge stands at the corner of a stable yard with 'stabling for fourteen and four carriages'. Beyond is the one-acre organic kitchen garden. Divided in two by a central path, it is contained by chalk cob walls. Fine mature specimen trees, all of them proper parkland stock – planes, oaks and horse chestnuts – stand proudly on the ridge beyond the lawns. The garden abounds in topiary, including a peacock garden with a patterned box parterre, and in spring is a mass of snowdrops and daffodils. Dr David Jacques advised on the restoration. There is also a modern hydroponicum in which plants are cultivated without soil, and a new orchid collection. In addition to the 12 acres of garden proper a further 18 acres have been opened up to give meadow walks through the peaceful and unspoilt surroundings of the River Test.

53 Ladywood ★

Eastleigh SO50 4RW. Tel: (02380) 615389

Mr and Mrs D. Ward • Leave A33/M3 at junction 12 on A335 signed to Eastleigh, turn right at roundabout into Woodside Avenue, second right into Bosville, 5th right into Ladywood • Open for NGS on three Suns, 11am – 5.30pm, and by appt April to Sept, Tues, 2 – 5.30pm • Entrance: £2.50, children £1 • Other information: Parking in Bosville only ◗ ⚘

This suburban garden, 14 metres square, containing 1800 different labelled plants, is subdivided into several more miniscule areas: a water garden with water hawthorn (*Aponogeton distachyos*) and water lilies, a scree garden, a shade garden with hostas and variegated plants and a tiny oval lawn. Among the healthy plants are alpines, erodiums, hardy geraniums galore, the white *Clematis* 'Henryi', *C. viticella* climbing through shrubs and trelliswork, roses, grasses, the miniature *Philadelphus* 'Manteau d'Hermine', and a good collection of *Phlox paniculata*. All are sensitively arranged with good colour associations and contrasts – for example, the black viola 'Molly Sanderson' and black grasses *Ophiopogon planiscapus* emerging from pale shingle. In April many small bulbs are interplanted with unusual woodland plants, and in June and July roscoeas and dactylorhizas put on a fine display. A new summerhouse is hung with the owner's botanical drawings.

Lake House

Northington, Alresford SO24 9TG.

Lord Ashburton • 3m NW of Alresford off B3046. Follow English Heritage signs for Northington and The Grange, and turn sharp left before entrance to Grange • Open probably two days for NGS • Entrance: £3, children free ● 🍴 🛈 WC ♿ ⌘ 🐾

The tall and handsome walls of the old kitchen gardens of the ruined Grange make a pleasing contrast with the low modern house nearby. The walled garden has herbaceous borders and box-edged plots filled with old roses and perennials, as well as a vegetable and cutting area with espalier apples, a rose and wisteria pergola and an avenue of Irish yews leading to a moon gate. There are large areas of naturalised daffodils and a snakes'-head fritillary meadow. The house – surrounded by a conservatory, a terrace, a formal pond and pots – looks across lawns to the lake with a scenic walk which includes views of the neo-classical shell of the old house, a nineteenth-century cascade, ancient cedars, a castle folly and an arched flint bridge. *The Grange* itself, designed by William Wilkins and formerly home of the Ashburton family, is now in the guardianship of English Heritage [Historic Park Grade II*] and may be visited at any time.

The Little Cottage

Southampton Road, Lymington SO41 9GZ. Tel: (01590) 679395

Peter and Lyn Prior • On northern outskirts of Lymington on A337 opposite Tollhouse Inn • Open 13th June, 4th July, 1st Aug, 5th Sept, 10am – 1pm, 2 – 5pm, and by appt between those dates • Entrance: £2 ◐

Drama is the essence of this splendidly over-the-top town garden divided into four rooms with a connecting corridor. Every path and vista is focused on an ornamental seat, door, arbour or urn, and exploring it is like walking through a series of stage sets. First comes the blue and yellow garden, where the path is lined with gold and green standard *Euonymus japonicus* 'Aureus' surrounded by flowers like morning glory and *Commelina tuberosa*; their blueness is echoed in vases, seats, balls and ceramic cats. The shady blue and white corridor leads to the courtyard garden with white flowers and ornamental doves. There are two side gates, one opening to a soft pastel garden, the other to a geometric black and white Gothick garden with glittering white chippings and black paving, black pots, seats and ceramic balls which Lyn Prior hopes will 'frighten the good-taste brigade'. Heaven and hell lie side by side. Among the black plants are chocolate cosmos and chocolate mint, the millet 'Purple Majesty', a ruffled black basil, *Persicaria microcephala* 'Red Dragon' and *Sambucus* 'Black Lace' contrasting with artemesias and other grey-leaved plants. In the New Forest area with its sandy acid soil it is refreshing to find a garden without a single rhododendron, and one that flourishes in late summer.

Longstock Park Water Garden ★★

Longstock, Stockbridge SO20 6EH. Tel: (01264) 810904

John Lewis Partnership (Leckford Estate Ltd) • 5m S of Andover, 2m N of Stockbridge. From A30 turn N on A3057. Signposted • Open April to Sept, first and third Sun of each month, 2 – 5pm, and by appt for parties • Entrance: £4, children £1 • Other information: Refreshments and plants for sale at nursery ● ▣ WC & 🌿 ⛪

The seven acres of these superb water gardens, created by John Spedan Lewis in 1948, are fed from the River Test and surrounded by acid-loving trees and shrubs. They form an archipelago connected by narrow bridges and causeways. Gunneras and swamp cypresses, surrounded by stilts, royal ferns and *Aralia elata* are just some of the plants reflected in the clear waters moving with gold carp, and a walk along the paths gives a succession of views followed by more intimate spaces. Aquatics include 48 different water lilies. Do not miss a visit to *Longstock Park Nursery* nearby (also open daily), set in a walled garden with climbing plants, and the fine herbaceous border reached through a gate in its wall. This runs parallel to a pergola planted with roses and an exquisite and extensive collection of *viticella* clematis. A National Collection of buddleias, with over 100 varieties, may be seen by request.

The Manor House ★ [Historic Garden Grade II*]

Upton Grey, Basingstoke RG25 2RD. Tel: (01256) 862827

Mr and Mrs J. Wallinger • 6m SE of Basingstoke in Upton Grey, on hill immediately above church • Open April to Oct, Mon – Fri (but closed Bank Holiday Mons), by appt only • Entrance: £5 (includes refreshments) ● WC & 🌿

The garden has been meticulously restored since 1985 by Mrs Wallinger to the original 1908 Gertrude Jekyll planting plans, copies of which are on display, and the tender care invested makes it more than a unique museum piece. Here are formal beds with lilies, peonies and roses edged with lamb's ears, drystone walls clothed with plants, terraces, pergola and yew hedging, as well as Jekyll's only surviving restored wild garden with a pond, daffodils and rambling roses. A living example of many Jekyll theories, it is worth noting her use of colour, with hot reds moving through yellows to distant greys and blues, the proportions of the steps, and the relation of the garden to the house (designed in grand vernacular style with hung tiles, etc by Ernest Newton for Charles Holme, founder and owner of *The Studio* magazine). This is claimed to be the most authentic Jekyll garden reconstruction, supported by a useful booklet and plant list.

Marycourt

43 High Street, Odiham, Hook RG29 1LF. Tel: (01256) 702100

Mrs A. Conville • 7m E of Basingstoke, 7m W of Aldershot off A287 1.5m from M3 junction 5 • Open 25th June and 2nd July, 2 – 6pm, 5th July, 9am – 6pm, and by appt • Entrance: £2.50, children free ● ❧ <u>WC</u> ও ⬧

The large, long town garden is approached from the drive in the High Street. Splendid mixed borders (alpines, clematis, honeysuckles, roses, shrubs, bulbs, phormiums, perennials) along the walls open out to a riot of primary colours (ligularias, heleniums, bergamot, achilleas) beside the swimming pool. The detail and the variety of plants in the alkaline soil of this garden is remarkable; note particularly the half-hardy plants. A collection of ivies and climbing roses help distract the eye from the grass tennis court. Blue and white beds are planted with agapanthus, white roses and delphiniums and edged with lavender. Hostas grown with Solomon's seal and *Lilium regale* in a tunnel of overhanging apple trees are most effective.

Mottisfont Abbey Garden ★★ [Historic Garden Grade II]

Mottisfont, Romsey SO51 0LP. Tel: (01794) 340757

The National Trust • 15m NW of Southampton, 4.25m NW of Romsey, 0.5m W of A3057 • Open 4th to 26th Feb, 2nd to 10th Dec, Sat and Sun, 11am – 4pm; 25th Feb to 31st May, 2nd Sept to 26th Oct, Sat – Wed (and Good Friday), 11am – 5pm; 3rd to 30th June, daily, 11am – 8.30pm; 1st July to 3rd Sept, daily except Fri, 11am – 5pm • Entrance: £7, children £3.50, family £17.50. Party rates on application (2005 prices) • Other information: Coaches must pre-book. Four-seater golf buggy available. No smoking in walled garden during rose season ◑ ☛ ✕ ❧ <u>WC</u> ও ♨ ⊞ ☕ ⚭

This famous collection of historic roses, based on the design and selection by Graham Stuart Thomas, was established in 1972 in the original walled kitchen garden, quartered with paths and box hedging – a formal design given additional interest by herbaceous borders, a central pond and a fountain. Here are the Albas, Damasks and Gallicas of the Middle Ages, cabbage and moss roses, and the earliest Chinas, Bourbons, hybrid perpetuals, French nineteenth-century Gallicas and Albas as well as Rugosas, and ramblers up walls, arches and stands – in all, a National Collection of 300 old-fashioned roses (also a few species and New English roses), now being renovated. The best time to visit is on midsummer evenings, when there are fewer visitors and the scent is at its strongest. Sweeping lawns around the house, cedars, the largest London plane tree in the country, a magically deep and bubbling pool, and a spring running down to the River Test provide a tranquil contrast to the heady and scented delights of the roses. The simple but effective design of grass terraces, yew octagon and pollarded lime walk is the work of the late Sir Geoffrey Jellicoe, while Norah Lindsay contributed the small lavender- and box-edged parterre infilled with spring bulbs and summer annuals.

Redenham Park ★

Redenham, Nr Andover SP11 9AQ. Tel: (01264) 772511

Lady Clark • 4m NW of Andover on A342 • Open for parties by appt • Entrance: £5.50 • Other information: Teas by arrangement ● ⓑ WC ♨

The perfect setting for a Jane Austen novel, this classic five-acre garden embraces its early-nineteenth-century ashlar-faced house. Views of parkland with sheep and cedars are followed by an enclosed paved rose garden with a circular pond (home to zantedeschias and white irises) and a fountain, then by herbaceous borders leading to a pleached lime walk and a moon gate. There are also fine borders, sculptural clipped yews, a tapestry hedge of copper- and green-leaved beech bordering a croquet lawn, and a low pear and apple espalier in a walled garden, where walls and paths drip in June with scented roses. The walled kitchen garden is immaculate, and there is a mass of exotic fowls.

Rotherfield Park [Historic Garden Grade II*]

East Tisted, Alton GU34 3QE. Tel: (01420) 588207

Sir James and Lady Scott • 4m S of Alton on A32 • Open for NGS, and for parties by appt in May and Sept • Entrance: £2.50, children free ● ⓟ ⓑ WC ☒

The Grade-I-listed house was built between 1815 and 1822 by the Scott family, with later additions in a medley of medieval and Tudor styles – note the laundry house chimney like Rapunzel's tower – and is an integral part of the Picturesque landscape, looking to the church which was rebuilt as a *point de vue* complete with little tower. The quadripartite walled garden is approached via splendid yew hedges supported by golden yew buttresses, and entered through magnificent wrought-iron gates. These open to herbaceous borders terminated by a Victorian summerhouse with enamelled tiles. There is a fruit section with espalier apples and pears along the walls, standard gooseberries and other fruits, a vegetable plot and flower and shrub sections. In May the 60-acre pleasure ground is a haze of bluebells. Elsewhere, an orchard and maze, an ice-house and a ha-ha, and many fine trees and shrubs.

Sandhill Farm House

Rogate, Petersfield GU31 5HU. Tel: (01730) 818373

Mrs Rosemary Alexander • 4m E of Petersfield off A272. From crossroads in Rogate, take road signed to Nyewood and Harting. Follow road for 1m over small bridge; house is on right over cattle grid • Open 2nd April, 11th June, 2 – 5pm, and by appt • Entrance: £3, children free WC ◑ ♨

There are two gardens here, lying either side of the house, and each is different in mood. The first – informal, shady and enclosed – is approached by an opening cut through a beech hedge underplanted with *Hedera helix* 'Maple Leaf'. Beyond is a woodland garden contoured by peat bricks, with gravel paths winding around trees and shrubs such as ginkgo, *Ilex aquifolium* 'Hascombensis', a fatshedera, the white-stemmed and golden-leaved *Rubus cockburnianus* 'Goldenvale' and two birches whose silky grey and pink barks are scrubbed every Easter Sunday. Beside the house are the rarely seen pineapple guava *Acca sellowiana* and *Lyonothamnus floribundus* with its little white flowers appearing in early summer. The other garden is laid out in patterns with a *potager* and a tiny gazebo, herbaceous borders and a lawn overlooking the surrounding countryside. One border is planted in shades of red, yellow and orange; the other, complemented by a variegated Italian buckthorn, has mauves, delicate blues, greys and pinks. Vistas are everywhere carefully controlled.

The Sir Harold Hillier Gardens ★★ [Historic Garden and Arboretum Grade II]

Jermyns Lane, Ampfield, Romsey SO51 0QA. Tel: (01794) 368787

Hampshire County Council • 3m NE of Romsey, 9m SW of Winchester, 0.75m W of A3090 along Jermyns Lane. Signed from A3090 and A3057 • Open all year, daily, except 25th and 26th Dec, 10.30am – 6pm (or dusk if earlier) • Entrance: £6, concessions £5.50, children under 16 free, parties of 10 or more £5 per person (2005 prices) • Other information: Plants for sale and shop in adjacent nursery ○ 💻 ✕ WC ⚹ ⛪ ⚐ ✑

Administered by Hampshire County Council since 1977, this collection of hardy trees and shrubs, the largest in the world, was begun in 1953 by the late Sir Harold Hillier, using his house and garden as a starting point. It extends to 180 acres and includes approximately 12,000 different species and cultivars, with many rarities. Eleven National Collections are held here, more than any other garden, including quercus and hamamelis. Weekly lists of plants of current-season interest are produced, and lead the visitor to herbaceous, scree, heather and bog gardens. With a total of about 42,000 plants it is impossible at any time of year not to be impressed or learn something about what, where and how to plant. Notable among the trees are *Eucalyptus nitens* and *E. niphophila*, *Magnolia cylindrica*, *Zanthoxylum* spp. (the prickly ash or toothache tree) as well as acers and sorbus. Among the shrubs is a wide range of rhododendrons, azaleas, camellias and hydrangeas. The winter garden specialises in plants at their best from November to March, and includes gold- and black-stemmed bamboos and the white-stemmed *Rubus thibetanus*. Much more than an arboretum, this attractively laid-out garden can be enjoyed at many levels. The visitor education pavilion is approached by a curved walk of *Metasequoia glyptostroboides*, and the visitor now approaches the arboretum with a view of rare trees merging with the Hampshire countryside beyond. Nearby at *Broadlands* there is a 'Capability' Brown landscape [Historic Park Grade II*]. It is also worth the detour into Winchester to view *Queen Eleanor's Garden*, the re-creation of a small medieval plot designed by Dr Sylvia Landsberg behind the Great Hall of Winchester Castle.

Spinners ★

School Lane, Boldre, Lymington SO41 5QE. Tel: (01590) 673347

Mr P.G.G. Chappell • 1.5m N of Lymington. Follow county signs on A337 between Brockenhurst and Lymington • Open April to 12th Sept, Tues – Sat, 10am – 5pm, and at other times by appt; mid-Sept to March nursery and part of the garden open on same days – telephone for details • Entrance: £2.50 • Other information: Plants for sale in nursery ◗ 🌿 WC ⚐

This informal woodland garden on the acid soil of the New Forest, created by the Chappells and praised by plantsmen, is remarkable for its plant associations and the owner's careful choice of scale. Nothing is over-large or dwarfs the smaller pleasures. In spring the sun shines through the canopy of trees, lighting camellias and dwarf rhododendrons, exochordas, magnolias, *Cornus kousa* and the brilliant coral leaves of *Acer palmatum* 'Shishio Improved'. Many of the rarer magnolias and tree cornus have been planted recently, and the numbers of species and lace-cap hydrangeas, particularly the new Teller selections, increased to extend the flowering season. Admire at ground level the carpets of cyclamen, *Erythronium revolutum* like pale pink stars, and the white and strange maroon trilliums. Beside the spring near the house the yellow-greens of ferns and variegated iris synchronise with white and yellow skunk cabbage. Ferns, primulas and hostas thrive in the bog garden, and good autumn colouring comes from *Nyssa sinensis* and other trees.

Staunton Country Park [Historic Park Grade II*]

Middle Park Way, Havant PO9 5HB. Tel: (023) 9245 3405

Hampshire County Council and eight other public bodies • 2m N of Havant on B2149. Signposted • Open all year, daily, 10am – 5pm (closes 4pm in winter) • Entrance: £4.60, OAPs £4, children £3.50 ○ 🅿 ✕ 🛍 <u>WC</u> ♿ 🐕 🌳 🏛 🍴 ⚲

The park was formerly the Leigh estate, belonging to the nineteenth-century horticulturist and adventurer Sir George Staunton. The walled garden has a crinkle-crankle wall to the south, and within it lies a major restoration of Victorian green-houses. Here are the passion flowers, pepper vines and exotics grown by him, including the giant *Victoria amazonica* lily in its original circular pool. The great house has gone and the park is split by a main road, but fine specimen trees remain, as well as the Gothick library and follies such as the shell house and the beacon, also the terrace and the lakes, the Chinese bridge, and the remains of the lake fort where Staunton used to fire guns and fly the imperial yellow flag of China. Don't miss the ornamental Regency farm, stocked, as in the 1800s, with peacocks, deer, pigs, sheep, goats and horses. A yew maze has hand-crafted arbours and gates and reflects the spirit of the formal gardens and rose displays that existed in his time. A sensory garden was planted in autumn 2003.

Tylney Hall Hotel ★ [Historic Garden Grade II*]

Rotherwick, Hook RG27 9AZ. Tel: (01256) 764881

Access from M3 junction 5 (take A287 via Newnham) or from M4 junction 11 (take B3349 via Rotherwick) • Open for NGS, and for non-residents eating at hotel • Entrance: £2, children free • Other information: Refreshments and plants for sale on open days ● 🅿 ✕ <u>WC</u> ♿ 🌳 🍴 B&B

An Edwardian period piece. The elaborate brick house with gardens stretching to 66 acres was built in 1900 by Seldon Wornum for Sir Lionel Phillips, a South African diamond merchant. Wornum and Robert Weir Schultz designed the gardens, with an Italian terrace and fountain overlooking the boathouse lake, a Dutch garden, a fine avenue with Wellingtonias and splendid vistas framed by trees to the north and south. Designs were obtained from Gertrude Jekyll for the wild water garden, where two rivulets fell from one lake to another. When the house became a school in 1946, hard tennis courts were built on the Italian terrace, the lakes became choked and balustrades and statuary were lost. It is now a hotel, and the gardens have been restored and replanted by estate manager Paul Tattersdill and five gardeners. A fountain plays again on the Italian terrace, the boathouse lake is cleared and its bridge rebuilt, the water gardens are restored with rivulets, lakes and bogside planting, the kitchen garden has regained its rose pergola, the orchards stock 20 varieties of apple, and the vistas with their mature trees now look better than in the photographs of earlier days. Fine specimen trees.

West Green House Garden ★★

West Green, Hartley Wintney, Hook RG27 8JB. Tel: (01252) 844611

Miss Marylyn Abbott • 10m NE of Basingstoke, 1m W of Hartley Wintney, 1m N of A30 • Open 14th April to Aug, Thurs – Sun and Bank Holiday Mons; Sept, Sat and Sun; all 11am – 4.30pm. • Entrance: £5 • Other information: Many events – telephone for details ◑ 💶 ✕ WC & ♨ 🏛 ♣

Nestling in a wooded corner of Hampshire is this ravishingly attractive 1720s' manor house, where busts of gods, emperors and dukes look down from the walls onto two major gardens. The inner gardens, enclosed by eighteenth-century walls, are all devoted to parterres. One is filled with water lilies, another is of classical design with box topiary, and a third enacts the whimsy of *Alice in Wonderland* with the story's characters in ivy and box topiary surrounded by roses of red and white. The main walled garden is planted in subtle hues of mauve, plum and blue, contained in beds that have been faithfully restored to their original outlines. Flamboyant groups of tulips echo the walled garden's imaginative colour schemes. A decorative *potager* is centred around berry-filled fruit cages where herbs, flowers and unusual vegetables are designed into colourful patterns. All this is surrounded by a second garden, a remarkable neo-classical park studded with follies, birdcages and monuments designed by Quinlan Terry. The entrance to the park is through a tunnel of hornbeams, pleached to direct the eye to two Chinese pagodas, where a 'dragon garden' reveals two monsters devised by Nick Muscamp, surrounded by black-red peonies. Water is everywhere. There is a tree-fringed lake, especially attractive in spring with its drifts of fritillaries and other bulbs, and a grand water garden, the Nymphaeum, spills down rills and steps from a devil's mouth into serene ponds. Between the two is a new paradise garden – a geometric parterre of moated trees and grass rectangles which seem to float above the water. Lines of water play. A green theatre, a picturesque orangery and long *allées* of green all add to a fine and dramatic restoration undertaken by the well-known Australian gardener Marylyn Abbott.

West Silchester Hall

Silchester RG7 2LX Tel: (0118) 970 0278

Mrs Jenny Jowett • 7m N of Basingstoke, 7m S of Reading, off A340. Signed from centre of village • Open 28th and 29th May, 2nd and 30th July, 2 – 6pm, and for parties by appt • Entrance: £3, children free NEW ● 💶 & ◁▷ ♨

The house is in fact the west wing of Silchester Hall, a Victorian mansion built of London stocks. At first sight its 1.5-acre garden seems a romantic English creation that has grown of its own accord, reaching down to great conifers and a hidden pond, with never a straight line in sight. Curving borders display a mass of shrubs, clematis, roses and herbaceous plants. It is very much a plantsman's garden, and inspection reveals a mass of unusual plants flourishing in the acid soil, such as a cut-leaved alder, a grey-leaved *Parahebe perfoliata*, *Omphalodes linifolia*, *Lilium* x *dalhansonii* (deep red and ochre), *Kniphofia thomsonii* var. *snowdenii*, *Rhododendron* 'Jalisco Eclipse', *Rubus spectabilis*, *Cynoglossum nervosum* and many more, not forgetting the half-hardies, including a large collection of salvias. There are nice colour pairings, such as a cream iris with a cream green-edged hosta. The seasonal colour of the borders is extended by nipping the tops out of plants such as phlox. The hellebores become ground cover in high summer, roses follow rhododendrons, and are in turn followed by *viticella* clematis on hoops. The owner has been awarded three RHS Gold Medals for her botanical paintings; her studio lies within the garden and is open to visitors.

White Windows ★

Longparish, Andover SP11 6PB. Tel: (01264) 720222

Mrs Jane Sterndale-Bennett • 5m E of Andover. Turn off A303 to Longparish on B3048 • Open four days for NGS, 2 – 6pm, and by appt April to Sept, Wed, 2 – 6pm • Entrance: £2.50 ● WC ও ⌖

Over the years the trees and shrubs have matured and are now thinned, the lower branches cut to raise the canopy and allow glimpses into adjoining areas. Three mini-gardens curve in sequence from the house, each with a couple of sentinel plants such as pruned balls of *Prunus laurocerasus* 'Otto Luyken' ushering the visitor through. They are crammed with a wealth of shrubs and hardy perennials, with interest maintained by contrasting leaf shapes, textures, colours, and an abundance of flowers. Each garden has its own mood, with an unobtrusive red border, a blue border and a yellow border that looks translucent on a grey day. In shady areas good use is made of ferns, woodruff, *Thalictrum delavayi* 'Album' and geraniums such as *G.* 'Sue Crug' and *G. phaeum* 'Margaret Wilson'. In late summer icicles hang from the itea, and the white mounds of *Hydrangea arborescens* 'Annabelle' and *H. quercifolia* with pink-tinged leaves, as well as grasses and late alpines like roscoea are at their best, while the scrambling *Geranium* 'Rozanne' carries bowls of blue flowers with white centres all summer. This immaculate garden of the former chairman of the Hardy Plant Society is a year-round inspiration to anybody gardening in a limited space.

ISLE OF WIGHT

Barton Manor

Whippingham, East Cowes PO32 6LB. Tel: (01983) 528989

Robert Stigwood • From East Cowes take A3021, 500 metres beyond Osborne House on left • Open for four themed charity days, 10am – 5pm • Entrance: £3, children £1 • Other information: Coaches welcome. Guide dogs only ● ☕ ⚐ WC ও ♿

Prince Albert's original design included fine trees and the cork grove; the grand terraces were added by Edward VII. In 1968 Hillier's laid out an intriguing water garden on the far side of the lake, home to carp and waterfowl, on what was originally Queen Victoria's skating rink. There is also a secret garden planted with azaleas and roses and impressive herbaceous borders. The present owner (a keen conservationist) has spared no effort in restoring and maintaining the estate. National Collections of kniphofias and watsonias are here. The most recent addition is a rose hedge maze which is the largest such attraction on the island – it is now tall enough to get lost in. Another former royal residence, Osborne (see entry), is nearby.

Morton Manor

Brading, Sandown PO36 0EP. Tel: (01983) 406168

J.A. Trzebski • 3m from Ryde on A3055. Turn right at Brading traffic lights, signposted 100 metres up hill • Manor open (guided tours) • Garden open 16th April to Oct, daily except Sat, 10am – 4.30pm • Entrance: £3.75, children (6-16) £2 (house and garden £4.75, OAPs £4.25, children (6–16) £2) • Other information: Vineyard and winery ❶ 🍽 ✕ 🛍 <u>WC</u> ♿ ⟳ 🌳 ❀

The history of Morton goes back to the thirteenth century. The Elizabethan sunken garden has old-fashioned roses and is shaded by a magnificent *Magnolia grandiflora*. The terraces are nineteenth-century with extensive herbaceous borders and a huge London plane. Masses of spring bulbs are followed by rhododendrons and traditional herbaceous displays. Among the wide range of fine trees is an Indian bean (*Catalpa bignonioides*) and a *Cornus kousa*; particularly lovely in early June is *Robinia hispida*. There are also 100 different varieties of Japanese maple, and several varieties of acer imported from New Zealand are now on sale. Another feature is a pagoda covered with the vine variety 'Baco'. Little remains of the old walled garden, but in the corner behind the herbs are the restored bee boles (an old telephone box has a beehive inside so that visitors can view in safety). Also a turf maze made for children and a vineyard.

North Court ★

Shorwell, Newport PO30 3JG. Tel: (01983) 740415

Mr and Mrs J. Harrison • 4m S of Newport on B3323. Entrance on right after rustic bridge, opposite thatched cottage • Open one Sun in May, 2 – 5.30pm, for NGS, and by appt • Entrance: £4 ❶ 🍽 WC B&B

Fifteen acres of wooded grounds surround a Jacobean manor house, with varied gardens consisting of seventeenth-century landscaped terraces leading down to the stream and water gardens, herbaceous borders, woodland walks, a sunken rose garden and a walled kitchen garden. Terraces with a south-easterly aspect have been made into a maritime garden with far-reaching views of the sea. The garden specialises in more tender plants – abutilons, salvias, diascias and argyranthemums all thrive here, especially in the new Mediterranean garden. The 'secret walled garden' at the top has been cleared and planted in sub-tropical style. The cottage garden of *Little Northcourt* (open at the same time as North Court), is full of hidden delights, especially in May and June. Swinburne, the poet, stayed and wrote at the big house. 3m W on B3399, the National Trust's *Mottistone Manor* has a herb garden and good views of the Channel.

Nunwell House [Historic Garden Grade II]

Coach Lane, Brading PO36 0JQ. Tel: (01983) 407240

Col. and Mrs J.A. Aylmer • 3m S of Ryde, signed off A3055 in Brading into Coach Lane • House open, tours 1.30pm, 2.30pm, 3.30pm • Garden open 28th and 29th May, 3rd July to 6th Sept, Mon – Wed, 1 – 5pm, and for parties by appt • Entrance: £2.50 (house and garden £4, OAPs and students £3.50, accompanied children under 10 £1) ◑ 🐌 WC ♿

The house stands in six acres of gardens with wonderful views across the park to Spithead. The rose garden (a bowling green in the seventeenth century) is set at the top of a slope in front of the walled garden, which is now replanted with a double herbaceous border. The Long Walk leads down past the side of the house to the front garden. Among the varied shrubs and plants in the borders are several pretty *Lavatera* 'Barnsley', a notable acanthus, an enormous *Elaeagnus* x *ebbingei* and a *Cotoneaster* x *watereri* 'Cornubia'. There is also a 45-metre run of *Rosa* 'Frensham' and a *Cornus kousa*, and on the front of the house are three large myrtles. A steep flight of steps bordered by lavender leads up to the woods. To the rear of the house is an arboretum laid out by Vernon Russell-Smith in 1963.

Osborne House [Historic Garden Grade II*]

East Cowes PO32 6JY. Tel: (01983) 200022

English Heritage • 1m SE of East Cowes off A3021 • House open as grounds, 10am – 5pm • Grounds open April to Oct, daily, 10am – 6pm (closes 4pm Oct). Telephone for winter opening times • Entrance: £5.30, OAPs £4, children £2.70 (house and grounds £8.95, OAPs £6.70, children £4.50, family £22.40) ◑ 💷 ✕ 🐌 WC ♿ 🅿 ♿ ☕

Built by Queen Victoria in 1845–51 as a family retreat, the gardens, designed jointly by the royal couple in the formal Italianate style, are now being restored and replanted to the original designs. Old cultivars have been used for the Victorian-style bedding on the terraces, and the borders have been replanted with plants of the period. The park and gardens are notable for their magnificent trees. The Swiss Cottage Garden, in what were the royal children's gardens, has nine plots, each with 14 beds, planted with old varieties of soft fruit, flowers and vegetables. The Swiss Cottage museum is here, plus curiosities such as a mock fort and Queen Victoria's bathing machine. There is also a wildflower meadow and an orchard. The one-acre walled garden has been restored sympathetically by Rupert Golby using historic plants within a modern design. The plantings here exploit fully the island climate, enhanced by the protective walls of the garden. The usual wall-trained fruit of vines, figs, pears, plums and cherries are complemented by an olive, an orange and a lemon tree. Drifts of multiple plantings span the length and width of the garden, ensuring a continuous display of striking colour throughout the summer, and broad rows of herbaceous plants are offset by extensive plots of annually sown flowers, herbs and vegetables. The glasshouses commissioned by Prince Albert have been restored and house collections of plants from South Africa and plants introduced to Britain during the Victorian period. The entwined V & A motifs to be seen in the furnishings of the house are also used here on ironwork arches, garden benches and terracotta pots.

Pitt House

Love Lane, Bembridge PO35 5NF.

L.J. Martin • Near village centre and Maritime Museum • Open June to Aug, Thurs, 2 – 5pm • Entrance: by donation ● &

Four acres with lovely views of the Solent through the trees. On a lower level from the house is a delightfully shady dell with a waterfall, ponds and water plants. In the main part of the garden are pergolas hung with roses and honeysuckle, and a Victorian greenhouse with two magnificent yellow daturas.

Ventnor Botanic Garden ★ [Historic Garden Grade II]

Undercliff Drive, Ventnor PO38 1UL. Tel: (01983) 855397

Isle of Wight Council • 1m SW of Ventnor. Signed from A3055 • Garden open all year, daily, dawn – dusk. 'Green' House and visitor centre open March to Oct, daily; Nov to Feb, Sat and Sun; all 10am – 4pm • Entrance: Garden free; charge for 'Green' House and car parking. Guided tours for parties by appt, £3 per person • Other information: New visitor centre with exhibition area, gift shop and restaurant ○ 🍽 ✕ 🍴 <u>WC</u> & 🍴 🌿 🏛 🎈 ℺

Twenty-two acres, sheltered from the south by *Quercus ilex* and escallonias, and from the north by an escarpment growing cistus, echiums and olearias, were originally planted by Sir Harold Hillier to house the tender trees and shrubs in his collection. Almost destroyed by the gales of 1987 and 1990, the collections have been restored, and *Acer sikkimense, Citrus ichangensis* from China, the flowering tree *Lyonothamnus floribundus* subsp. *asplenifolius* from California, *Cestrum elegans* from Mexico, banana plants from Japan, and olive trees from the Mediterranean are but a few of the exotics to flourish in the unique microclimate of the Undercliff. A National Collection of pseudopanax is held here, including *P. ferox* and *P. crassifolius*. The New Zealand garden holds the largest collection of native plants grown in this country, and in July the South African garden includes a beautiful array of agapanthus. On the sunny slopes an amazing colony of four-metre-tall *Echium pininana* has naturalised. In the Palm Garden stately foliage plants like yuccas, cordylines, phormiums and beschornerias are underplanted with watsonias, cannas and kniphofias. The only drawback to this attractive municipal garden is that the labelling of plants leaves much to be desired. The 'Green' House has been re-landscaped with a series of water features, and the adjoining plant sales area has a range of unusual varieties on offer, mostly raised from seed and surplus to the garden's requirements. In nearby Godshill, *Deacon's Nursery* [open Oct to March, Sat only] has a large variety of fruit trees and bushes together with hops and nut trees, and their catalogue contains over 200 varieties of apples. A few miles inland is the ruined shell of the eighteenth-century *Appuldurcombe House*, now owned by English Heritage, which stands in grounds landscaped by 'Capability' Brown. [Open April to Oct, daily, 10am – 5pm.]

HEREFORDSHIRE

Abbey Dore Gardens ★

Abbey Dore, Hereford HR2 0AD. Tel: (01981) 240419

*Mrs C.L. Ward • 11m SW of Hereford off A465 • Open April to Oct, Tues, Thurs,
Sat, Sun and Bank Holiday Mons, 11am – 5.30pm, and by appt • Entrance: £3.50,
children 50p* ◐ ⬤ ✕ <u>WC</u> ♿ ⚘

Only first-rate plants are allowed to grow here: flower, colour or shape – everything
is in some way exemplary. The six acres, two of them left wild, incorporate a large
part of the original Abbey Dore Court garden (laid out in 1858 but developing its
present character and plantings since the late 1970s). A new area, designed around
a delicate gazebo, is quickly becoming established. The purple, gold and silver
borders, created at the suggestion of Graham Stuart Thomas, are eye-catching and
retain year-round interest. They lead to a wild riverside walk, and across the River
Dore a meadow is planted with rare trees and shrubs, intersected by mown paths.
A walled Victorian garden with wide borders punctuated by white foxgloves and
cimicifugas has been developed with a sure eye for colour and form. The fruit trees
have now all gone and a wide path dissects the old orchard area. There is a wire seat
at the end looking down to an original water feature, and in the west-facing corner
a slate table raised by terracing catches the evening sun. Extravagant plantings, laid
out with flair and imagination, delight the eye on every side. Hellebores, peonies and
astrantias are specialities.

The Arrow Cottage Garden

Ledgemoor, Weobley HR4 8RN. Tel: (01544) 318468

*Mr and Mrs D. Martin • 10m NW of Hereford between A4110 and A480, 1.5m E of
Weobley • Open April to Sept, Wed and Sat, 11am – 5pm • Entrance: £3.75 • Other
information: Refreshments on Sat only* ◐ ⬤ WC ⚘

The clever layout of this garden, created by the designer Lance Hattatt, makes it
seem much larger than its two-acre site. A series of well-defined areas, each named
(Zion, for instance, is planted with ten *Malus* 'Ten Commandments') offers the
visitor a cornucopia of contrasting shapes, colours and moods. A long, peaceful rill
of water, punctuated by pots of agapanthus, terminates in a simple and elegant
fountain. Elsewhere, old shrub roses flower in informal profusion.

Berrington Hall [Historic Garden Grade II*]

Leominster HR6 0DW. Tel: (01568) 615721

*The National Trust • 4m N of Leominster, W of A49 • House open as garden, but
1 – 5pm • Garden open 25th March to 29th Oct, Sat – Wed (but open Good Fri),
12 noon – 5pm (closes 4.30pm Oct and Nov). Park walk open July to 17th Dec, 12
noon – 5pm. Parties of 15 or more by written appt • Entrance: £3.50 (house and*

grounds £5, children £2.50, family £12.50) • Other information: Two wheelchairs and one batricar available for pre-booking ◑ 💬 🖥 <u>WC</u> ♿ ♨ ♨ ♀

Spherical golden yews line the path to the formal eighteenth-century house designed by Henry Holland. The grounds, landscaped by 'Capability' Brown, are an excellent example of naturalistic parkland, containing many specimen trees. The walled garden houses a small orchard of pre-1900 apple varieties and handsome mixed borders which include lupins and red-hot pokers. A children's play area nearby sports a living willow tunnel.

Bryan's Ground ★

Letchmoor Lane, Stapleton, Nr Presteigne LD8 2LP. Tel: (01544) 260001

David Wheeler and Simon Dorrell • The garden will be closed during 2006 but will reopen in 2007

Home of *Hortus*, the widely acclaimed quarterly magazine, this eight-and-half-acre garden is a feast of horticultural delights. The entrance sets the tone: the orchard plats flanking the main drive are thickly planted with squares of blue *Iris sibirica*, stunning against the ochre-yellow walls of the Edwardian house. Colour, both strong and subtle, is used everywhere to great effect. The Sulking House (hung with tattered velvet, adorned with dried teasels) looks out onto a double border where dark red, mauve and purple predominate, backed by copper beeches. At every turn, strong architectural lines of clipped yew or box hedging are softened by exuberant clumps of aquilegia, cranesbill, astrantia. The square pool in one quarter of the walled kitchen garden is as peaceful as a chapel, enclosed by its hornbeam cloister; water materialises also as a 19-metre canal in the Dutch Garden, and a 'cold bath' with a water spout in the old kitchen garden. Other delights include a crinkle-crankle beech hedge, a three-storey timber-framed dovecot, a restored Edwardian greenhouse and a large collection of hellebores in a wild woodland area. The arboretum has been extended to the river bank, and there is a new vegetable garden.

Croft Castle [Historic Garden Grade II*]

Leominster HR6 9PW. Tel: (01568) 780246

The National Trust • 5m NW of Leominster off B4362 • Garden open 4th to 26th March, Sat and Sun; April to Sept, Wed – Sun and Bank Holiday Mons; all 12 noon – 5pm; Oct to 26th Nov, Sat and Sun, 11am – 4pm. Parties of 15 or more by written appt. Parkland open all year • Entrance: £3.10. Car parking charge £2 per car (refundable on entry), £10 per coach (2005 prices) • Other information: Picnics in car park only. Braille guides available. Dogs in parkland only, on leads ◑ 💬 <u>WC</u> ♿ ♨ ♨ ♀ ♐

The Welsh Marches castle dates from the fourteenth century and commands a spectacular landscape of open countryside. The walled garden has a collection of interesting and unusual plants, while the park is notable for its fine avenue of Spanish chestnuts, possibly 350 years old, and for its venerable pollarded oaks. There are charming walks in the Fishpool valley.

Eastnor Castle [Historic Park Grade II*]

Eastnor, Ledbury HR8 1RL. Tel: (01531) 633160

Eastnor Estate • 8m SW of Great Malvern, 2m E of Ledbury on A438 • Castle open selected days • Garden open 16th April to 1st Oct, Sun and Bank Holiday Mons; July, Aug, daily except Sat; all 11am – 5pm • Entrance: £5, OAPs £4, children £3 (house and garden £7, OAPs £6, children £4, family £18) • Other information: Refreshments on castle open days ◑ 💭 🐚 WC ♿ ⬥ ♨ ♀ ✆

The arboretum here contains some of the earliest plant-hunter collections of exotic trees in the country, especially of conifers. Roughly contemporary with Westonbirt, the main collection was established between 1840 and 1860, with seed being brought from around the world throughout the nineteenth century. A tree trail leads to the most important and interesting specimens, and to far-flung areas of the extensive grounds. A lakeside walk gives fine views back to the fairytale Gothick castle designed by Robert Smirke. Restoration is ongoing: new groves of cercidiphyllums and acers, for example, will add to the variety of colour and texture for all seasons. Near to the castle, the terraces have not been restored to their nineteenth-century character; instead, a long border is planted for mid- to late-summer colour, while the upper terrace has an iris border, together with lavenders, santolinas and other sun-loving shrubs. A cottage-style garden is being planted near the maturing yew maze.

Hampton Court Gardens ★

Nr. Hope under Dinmore, Leominster HR6 0PN. Tel: (01568) 797777

Hampton Court Gardens (Herefordshire) Ltd • 5m S of Leominster, on A417 near junction with A49 between Leominster and Hereford • Property is on market – telephone for details of opening times and charges 🐚 💭 ✕ 🐚 WC ♿ ⬥ ♨ ♀ ✆

This fine garden has only been in creation since 1996, and its future is sadly now in doubt. Surrounding a fifteenth-century Grade-I-listed building, the grounds have been designed on a suitably grand scale by Simon Dorrell. A *potager*-style kitchen garden is now established, producing organic fruit and vegetables. The water garden is a large, geometrically laid-out walled enclosure, with a pair of octagonal pavilions surrounded by canals and ornamental water steps; the borders, lushly planted with lilies, lavenders, macleayas and cardoons, create an effective contrast to their crisp formality. It is worth puzzling your way through the intricate yew maze to reach the tower, from where a bird's eye view of the walled garden – like a medieval pleasaunce with the crenellated house beyond – is especially beguiling. From the tower a subterranean tunnel leads to a thatched hermitage beside a cascade and sunken pool. A nineteenth-century wisteria arch is magically sweet-smelling in flower, and leads to the calm tranquillity of a Dutch-inspired water garden. Wide lawns surround the house; the ha-ha allows a view of cattle grazing under magnificent trees in the park beyond. Visit while you still can.

Hergest Croft Gardens ★ [Historic Garden Grade II*]

Kington HR5 3EG. Tel: (01544) 230160

W.L. Banks • 14m W of Leominster, 0.5m W of Kington off A44 • Open March, Sat and Sun; April to Oct, daily, all 12.30 – 5.30pm; May and June, daily, 12 noon – 6pm • Entrance: £5, children under 16 free, season ticket £17, pre-booked parties of 20 or more £4 per person ❶ 🍴 🏠 WC ♿ 🐕 🌳 ♨ ❦

A large, varied garden, created over a period of 100 years by three generations of the Banks family. Over 50 acres, the design was much influenced by the writings of William Robinson, and is laid out in four sections: the plantings around the house itself, the kitchen garden, an azalea garden and Park Wood. The lawns and borders surrounding the Edwardian house are filled with a large collection of herbaceous plants and shrubs, backed by some outstanding specimen trees, including a huge sycamore planted c. 1800. The croquet lawn is like a restful, empty room amid all this fascinating variety, featuring only clipped yew hedges and large urns filled with lilies. The kitchen garden is traditional, with an avenue of ancient apple trees and double borders of spring flowers, with many coloured tulips and forget-me-nots under the blossoming trees – an ordinary enough combination, but somehow particularly pretty here. The double herbaceous borders blaze with colour in summer. The exotically coloured azalea garden is outstanding, shaded by many of the magnificent birches and maples that form part of National Collections. A grove of maples, designed by Elizabeth Banks and planted since 1985, includes many new or re-introduced species from China and elsewhere. The outer reaches of Park Wood are retained as natural beech and oak woodland, carpeted with anemones and bluebells in spring, but at its heart lies a secret valley of giant rhododendrons, a positively Himalayan scene.

How Caple Court

How Caple, Hereford HR1 4SX. Tel: (01989) 740626

Mr and Mrs Roger Lee • 10m S of Hereford on B4224. Turn right at crossroads in How Caple • Open 13th March to 15th Oct, daily, 10am – 5pm, and for parties by appt • Entrance: £2.50, children free ❶ 🍴 🏠 WC 🐕 ❦

This important Arts and Crafts garden deserves to be better known. It first appeared in the *Guide* in 1991. Laid out by the great-grandfather of the present owner, it is intensely romantic and full of surprises. Immediately below the seventeenth-century manor house, formal stone-flagged terraces descend the hillside via broad stone steps, past a rose garden, a summerhouse and clipped Irish yews, with a magnificent view westward across the Wye valley. Below, intriguingly almost lost in the woodland, is a stunning Italianate water garden with a great rill at its heart, set with Irish yews and bounded by a pavilion and pergola. Nearby, Tuscan columns adorn the viewing terrace for a long-gone tennis court, redolent of that lost 'golden afternoon'. Woodland, lawn, shrubbery and rockery complete the picture. Although not a plantsman's garden, and gently decaying and unkempt in parts, its particularly special atmosphere makes it worth visiting at any time of year.

Kingstone Cottages

Weston under Penyard, Nr Ross-on-Wye HR9 7PH. Tel: (01989) 565267

*Michael and Sophie Hughes • 2m E of Ross-on-Wye off A40. Turn left at Weston
Cross public house signed to Bromsash, then left signed to Rudhall. Garden is 0.75m
down this lane, on left • Open 1st May to 7th July, daily except Sat, 10am – 5pm,
and by appt • Entrance: £2, children free • Other information: Refreshments by
arrangement for pre-booked parties* ● & ♨*

The garden has only been in existence since 1976, but thanks to the owners' skilful
use of reclaimed brick and stone it has the mellow atmosphere of a much older one.
The planting is subtle and varied, well balanced between flowering plants and foliage.
A pond, full of bulrushes and water lilies, is overhung by a cleverly constructed
summerhouse, creating a magically secret spot. Other plantings frame fine views out
to the Black Mountains. A grotto, a honeysuckle and clematis tunnel and a small
formal water garden are other attractions, with a 'scrap-iron garden' adding a more
surreal note. A special feature is a National Collection of old dianthus, with 140
varieties on show, and many of these and other unusual plants are for sale.

The Lance Hattatt Design Garden

(see ARROW COTTAGE)

The Long Barn

Eastnor, Ledbury HR8 1EL. Tel: (01531) 632718

*Roger and Fay Oates • 8m SW of Great Malvern, 2m E of Ledbury on A438
Tewkesbury road. House approximately 0.5m from junction with Ledbury – Malvern
road • Open late-May to mid-Sept, Wed – Fri, 10am – 5pm, and at other times by
appt • Entrance: donation to NGS* ◑ WC ♿

In 1995 the owners were faced with a quarter-acre blank canvas at the edge of an
orchard in the Malvern Hills, its boundaries fixed by stone pigsties, a tall hedge, a
brick barn, and a green lane. Now the garden sits contentedly in the landscape,
anchored by a strong and simple structure of enclosures bounded by walls, hedges
and trellises festooned with honeysuckles and roses. The enjoyment comes from the
way Roger Oates (a textile designer) has woven together a profusion of herbaceous
plants, herbs and vegetables within square plots, divided by grass and gravel paths,
with giant perennials towering overhead and mingling happily. The whole profusion
is carefully colour-themed, with white and silver, dark reds and purples
predominating. An enclosed area given over to grasses creates a calm and neutral
backdrop. He consults no rulebook, relying on instinct, experiment and the plants'
own wayward inclinations; the effect is loosely disciplined, at times rather shaggy, and
absolutely delightful.

Lower Hope

Ullingswick HR1 3JF. Tel: (01432) 820557

*Mr and Mrs Clive Richards • 7m NE of Hereford. At roundabout on A465 near
Burley Gate take A417 towards Leominster. After 2m turn right, signed to Pencombe*

and Lower Hope; garden is 0.5m on left. Signposted • Open for NGS 2nd April, 21st May, 9th July, 6th Aug, 1st Oct, 2 – 5pm • Entrance: £3, children £1 • Other information: Guide dogs only ● ● WC & ✿

The eight-acre garden is dazzlingly colourful and immaculately maintained. Bog gardens boast impressive gunneras and swathes of candelabra primulas, and the swimming-pool garden, with its palm trees and air of quiet seclusion, feels positively Mediterranean. A laburnum walk is magnificent in early summer. The many large island beds are sheets of bright flowers and coloured foliage, and interesting sculptures are artfully placed within the grounds. Bananas, palms, melons, orchids and other exotic plants flourish in a fine glasshouse fronted by an enclosed garden filled with English roses and lavenders and a herb and vegetable garden. A tree fern stumpery has been added. Clive Richards has a Paxtonian passion for damming, diverting and pumping water with virtuoso inventiveness and skill, into streams, fountains and ponds. A lime tree walk leads to a lake surrounded by wild flowers and marginal bog plantings and home to water birds, dragonflies and other wildlife. Prize-winning pedigree Hereford cattle and Suffolk sheep graze in the surrounding farmland.

Lower Hopton Farm

Stoke Lacy, Bromyard HR7 4HX. Tel: (01885) 490294

Mr and Mrs Giles Cross • 10m NE of Hereford off A465 Bromyard – Hereford road • Open for individuals and parties of 20 or more only, by personal introduction, to be confirmed in writing • Entrance: By donation – guideline individuals £10 per person, parties of 45-50 £6 per person ● ● WC

This five-acre garden, created from a field since 1992, is a testament to the skill and vision of Mrs Cross (the garden designer Veronica Adams), who tends it single-handedly. Rare plants abound. There are over a hundred named cultivars of snowdrops, unusual coloured roses – grey, green, buff – and splendid, towering cardiocrinums. The moated island holds rare shrubs and ferns and unusual varieties of peony, hellebore and magnolia among many other treasures. The prize in this collection is the ethereal, mauve-white giant bell-flower (*Ostrowskia magnifica*), flowering happily in a sunny border. These wonderful rarities are seamlessly woven into an imaginative design, with subtle colour schemes and light, humorous touches: two clipped yew giraffes are growing well, and a topiary fox peers out from a border. An elegant gazebo gives a view upstream to a series of small waterfalls, with climbing roses cascading from overhanging trees, and 'Paul's Himalayan Musk' towering overall. A new area, planted with white Judas trees, arching white wisteria and 'Debutante' roses, leads to a small fountain. A tunnel of airy robinias heralds a garden of old shrub roses, and a lacquer-red Chinese bridge adds an exotic note, leading to an area of pink and lime-green plants – a refreshing colour combination. The cleverly created 'ruin' provides a sheltered spot for tender perennials. Overall a triumph of creativity and much hard work.

Monnington Court

Monnington–on-Wye HR4 7NL. Tel: (01981) 500264

John and Angela Bulmer • 9m W of Hereford, off A438. Turn left opposite Portway pub, follow lane to end • Open 27th to 29th May, 10am – 5pm, and by appt

• *Entrance: £5* • *Other information: Special Morgan Horse displays 3.30pm each open day* ● �'' ✕ ▣ <u>WC</u> ♿ ⟠ ♨ ♥ ✎

The 20 acres around this medieval house are full of surprises and delights: black swans swim on the large, man-made lake, peacocks show off their fine plumage and all around are many interesting sculptures, both abstract and figurative, including most recently a bronze of the late Queen Mother by Mrs Bulmer – she is the well-known sculptor Angela Conner. Monnington Walk, a mile-long avenue of pine and yew trees, leads to the house, and the land is bounded by a rack alongside the River Wye. This is also the Foundation Farm of the Morgan Horse in Britain, a beautiful, old-fashioned-looking breed shipped to the United States in the 1700s and now returned to Europe.

Stockton Bury Gardens

Kimbolton, Leominster HR6 0HB. Tel: (01568) 613432

Mr G. Fenn and Mr R. Treasure • *1m NE of Leominster. From A49, turn right onto A4112 Kimbolton road. Garden is 300 metres on right. Signposted* • *Open April to mid-Oct, Wed – Sun and Bank Holiday Mons, 12 noon – 5pm* • *Entrance: £4* • *Other information: Unsuitable for children* ◑ �'' ✕ <u>WC</u> ♿ ✿

A true plantsman's garden, thoughtfully laid out and beautifully cared for, containing a wealth of unusual clematis, shrubs, climbers and herbaceous plants. The four-acre site is divided into different areas by brick and stone walls and yew hedges. The Dingle, created from an old quarry, is the most recently cultivated and beginning to look well established, with clumps of marginal plants fringing the water's edge. Many cultivars are grown, especially of peonies, pulmonarias, viburnums and lilacs; rare and beautiful plants greet the visitor round every corner. The enchanting little double wood anemone, (*Anemone nemorosa* 'Vestal') makes a delightful underplanting. Many of the more unusual plants are for sale, all of them of good size, well labelled and reasonably priced – typical of the owners' meticulous attention to detail.

The Weir Garden

Swainshill, Hereford HR4 8BS. Tel: (01981) 590509 (Infoline)/(01684) 855372

The National Trust • *5m W of Hereford on A438* • *Open 21st, 22nd, 28th and 29th Jan; 1st to 26th Feb, Wed – Sun; all 11am – 4pm; 27th Feb to 1st May, daily; 3rd May to 30th Sept, Wed – Sun; 1st to 29th Oct, Sat and Sun; all 11am – 5pm* • *Entrance: £3.80, children £1.90, family £9* • *Other information: Coaches by appt* ◑ ▣

The woodland garden which runs along the northern banks of the River Wye is at its best in spring when daffodils, bluebells, chionodoxas, camassias and naturalised tulips carpet the ground. The rockery (made with stone from Cheddar Gorge) contains a selection of colourful Japanese maples, conifers and ferns. A newly created willow arbour frames a seat giving a delightful view over the river to the weeping willows on the opposite bank, peaceful meadows beyond, and the Black Mountains in the distance. A collection of tightly clipped yew balls sits rather oddly in this otherwise 'wild' garden – have the aliens landed?

Westonbury Mill Water Gardens
Pembridge HR6 9HZ. Tel: (01544) 388650

Richard Pim • Off A44 between Leominster and Kington. From Pembridge take Kington road for 1.5m; garden is signed on left • Open 13th April to Sept, Thurs to Mon, 11am – 5pm • Entrance: £3.50, children £1 • Other information: teas available, plants for sale; dogs allowed NEW 🍴 🛒 WC ♿ ⚐ ✿ ♺

This is a beautiful and highly individual water garden with a broad collection of damp and water-loving plants laid out around a maze of leats, channels, streams and in a bog criss-crossed with narrow paths. Views to the hills and across the old meadows surrounding the garden are emphasised by the planting, and an adjacent 1.5-acre meadow with streamside walks to the weir is being developed as a wildflower area. The garden has been landscaped and planted by the owner, a retired hydrogeologist with a flair for quirky constructions. These include an African-style open hut, a willow tunnel and a stone tower with gargoyles spouting intermittent chutes of water – reminiscent of watery Renaissance jokes in Italian villas. The water is raised by a belt of buckets driven by a water wheel. A fern grotto has a domed roof made of wine bottles which glow in the sun like cathedral windows. Massed plantings include *Iris pseudacorus* var. *bastardii*, *I. laevigata* 'Snowdrift', *I.* x *robusta* 'Gerald Darby', *I. sibirica* 'Perry's Blue', *Primula wilsonii*, *Ligularia* x *hessei*, *Rodgersia podophylla* and *Gunnera manicata*.

Whitfield House [Historic Garden Grade II]
Wormbridge HR2 9BA. Tel: (01981) 570202

Mr and Mrs Edward Clive • 8m SW of Hereford on A465 Abergavenny road • Open by appt only • Entrance: £2.50, children free ● WC ♿ ⚐

A splendid 15-acre garden surrounds the house, plus extensive woodland walks. The estate boasts some magnificent trees, including a stand of giant redwood planted in the mid-nineteenth century and reputed to be the largest in Europe. The gardens adjacent to the house have been redesigned by Arabella Lennox-Boyd, and are currently under construction; cubes of yew and pleached limes will add a crisp formality. A string of lakes leads away from the facade, where golden orfe fry turn the water in the Fountain Pool positively gold in early summer. Castle Pool has a folly island devised by the late owner, a rare creation in the twentieth century. A fernery, punctuated with martagon lilies, flourishes in the shade of a large copper beech, and there are some fine magnolias. An extensive walled garden is reached through the camellia house, with a classical portico; a vinery and a ginkgo tree with the greatest girth in the country are amongst the delights therein. The epitome of the English country house garden, on a grand scale, Whitfield is a tribute to the knowledge of the late owner, George Clive (a dendrologist of renown), the enthusiasm of the present owners and the energy of their gardener.

HERTFORDSHIRE

Two-starred gardens are marked on the map with a black square.

The Abbot's House

10 High Street, Abbots Langley WD5 0AR. Tel: (01923) 264946

Peter and Sue Tomson • 5m N of Watford, in Abbots Langley. Approach via M25 junction 19 (from W) and 21A (from E) or M1 junction 6 • Open 30th April, 11th June, 30th Aug, 2 – 5pm. Parties welcome by appt • Entrance: £3, children free • Other information: Plants for sale in nursery ◐ ☕ WC ♿ ✿

This plantsman's garden is full of delights: *Crinodendron hookerianum, Itea ilicifolia, Hoheria sexstylosa* 'Stardust' and *Halesia carolina*, and many outstanding shrub and tree specimens, some of which must be tender. The sunken garden has plants thriving between the brickwork. There is also a Mediterranean semi-formal garden, a shrub border with contrasting foliage, borders of differing colour schemes, an annual and wildflower meadow and a conservatory.

Ashridge Management College [Historic Garden Grade II*]

Berkhamsted HP4 1NS. Tel: (01442) 843491

Ashridge (Bonar Law Memorial) Trust • 3.5m N of Berkhamsted (A41), 1m S of Little Gaddesden off A4146 • Open 14th April to Sept, Sat, Sun and Bank Holiday Mons, 2 – 6pm • Entrance: £3, OAPs and children £1.50 ◐ ♿ ◁▷

A total of 190 acres, comprising 90 acres of garden with the rest woodland. The nineteenth-century design was influenced by Humphry Repton; following his death the gardens were laid out by Sir Jeffry Wyatville, retaining many of Repton's suggested small gardens. An orangery with an Italian garden and fountain leads round to the south terrace, which is dominated by venerable clipped yews and spring and summer bedding. The main lawn in front of the terrace links many small gardens and has within it a group of ancient yews and a large oak. The circular rosary is sited virtually where Repton intended. The Monk's Garden and Holy Well comprises box laid out to represent an armorial garden. The conservatory dates from 1864 and was used as a fernery. The grotto is constructed of Hertfordshire pudding-stone, and the *souterrain* leading from it of flints hung on an iron framework. Crossing the main lawn brings visitors to a sunken garden formerly used as a skating pond. Beyond a disused moat is an avenue of Wellingtonias planted in 1858 and underplanted with rhododendrons, leading to the arboretum with many specimen trees and a Bible garden featuring a circle of incense cedars.

The Beale Arboretum

West Lodge Park Hotel, Cockfosters Road, Hadley Wood EN4 0PY.
Tel: (020) 8216 3900

Beales Hotels • Leave M25 at junction 24 and take road S towards Cockfosters (A111). West Lodge Park is 1m further on left • Open all year, daily, 2 – 5pm, and

for parties of 10 or more by appt all year • Entrance: £2.50, children free (2005 price)
• Other information: Possible for wheelchairs but undulating gravel paths ● ● ✕
& ✈ ♞ B&B

The late Edward Beale bought West Lodge Park Hotel in 1945 with the intention of enriching its fine eighteenth-century park with many more trees. Today, there are 10 acres of arboretum, and these, together with the three acres of more formal garden, the lake, the many azaleas and rhododendrons, and the impressive four-star hotel, make a visit to this little-known gem memorable. The strawberry tree said to have been there when John Evelyn visited in 1675 has become one of the largest in England.

Benington Lordship ★★ [Historic Garden Grade II]

Benington, Stevenage SG2 7BS. Tel: (01438) 869668

Mr and Mrs R. R. A. Bott • 5m E of Stevenage • Open for snowdrops 28th Jan to 17th Feb, 12 noon – 4pm; 30th April, 1st, 28th and 29th May, 2 – 5pm (opens 12 noon Mons); then 24th June to 2nd July, 2 – 5pm. Also open by appt all year • Entrance: £3.80, children free. Other information: Refreshments on open days only ● ⊛ WC & ℗

Surrounding the manor house, Norman gatehouse and Victorian folly is a romantic hill-top garden with fine views over the lake and open countryside. The massive and well-filled herbaceous double borders are designed with a glorious feeling for texture and colour, backed by the kitchen garden wall and a sloping bank planted with an informal mixture of foliage and flowering plants. The old rock garden has been bulldozed and grassed over, and its original three pools now sit serenely among newly planted ornamental trees. There are formal areas too: the Shylock Garden with a statue of Shakespeare's villain at its heart; and a lavender-edged rose garden set in a square in the centre of the old bowling green. There is also a shrub rose border, and the kitchen garden has ornamental borders as well as functional rows of vegetables. The display of snowdrops in the moat and the surrounding grounds is outstanding, followed by drifts of scillas.

Bromley Hall

Standon, Ware SG11 1NY. Tel: (01279) 842422

Julian and Edwina Robarts • 6m W of Bishop's Stortford near A120 and A10 on Standon – Much Hadham road • Open 4th June for NGS, and for parties by appt • Entrance: £3.50, children free ● ● WC & ℗

The four-acre garden, distinguished by its architectural qualities and its plantsmanship, has reached a wonderful maturity. The site is windy and exposed, and all possible use has been made of walls and hedges, including one of copper beech. The wide border flanking the drive flowers in early summer with a pleasing mixture of syringa, foxgloves, poppies and the lovely *Allium christophii*, and another startles with its bold mixture of red brooms, pink cistus and other hot-coloured flowers. A new sculptural addition is an obelisk with a striking gilded pattern of intertwining leaves and lizards. The kitchen garden contains an array of mouth-watering produce, helped into immaculate growth by curly ornamental steel pea-sticks and terracotta rhubarb forcers. Vistas reveal glimpses of mown paths, rough grass, mature trees, and the countryside stretching out in the distance.

Great Munden House

Dane End, Ware SG11 1HU. Tel: (01920) 438244

Mr and Mrs D. Wentworth-Stanley • 7m N of Ware off A10. Turn off W of Puckeridge bypass • Open April to June for small parties by appt only, with refreshments • Entrance: £4 ◐ WC

The charming three-and-a-half-acre garden, beautifully planned, immaculately kept and containing a great variety of plants, is situated down the side of a valley with a backdrop of wheatfields and trees. Beech hedges surrounding lawns act as necessary windbreaks against the wind funnelling down the valley. The mixed borders are imaginatively planted with shrubs, shrub roses, phlox and excellent foliage plants. Spring colour and interest come from bulbs and blossom, and the main border in May is blue, mauve and pink with early irises, pale and dark alliums, aquilegias and perennial geraniums. A paved pond area is surrounded by silver plants and roses, with a *Juniperus virginiana* 'Skyrocket' in each corner. Many climbing roses ramble through old apple trees, and there is an additional damp area with shade-loving plants. Primulas and hostas surround a small statue, and the herb garden is protected by a clipped *Lonicera nitida* hedge.

Hanbury Manor Hotel

Ware SG12 0SD. Tel: (01920) 487722

Hanbury Manor Hotel • 2m N of Ware off A10 • Open all year • Entrance: free (charge on charity days) • Other information: Refreshments, toilet facilities and shop in hotel ○ ♿

Edmund Hanbury inherited the property in 1884 and replaced the old house with a Jacobean-style mansion. The Hanbury family were gifted horticulturists and the original gardens, now part of the hotel complex, were widely acclaimed for their species trees and orchid houses. Today, a colourful pre-Victorian walled garden with a listed moon gate has extensive herbaceous borders, a herb garden and fruit houses. The original pinetum with its centuries-old sequoias still stands, and major restoration work has seen the revival of the period rose gardens and bulb-planted orchard. A more recent secret garden in a woodland setting is well worth a visit. On the outskirts of Ware, on A1170, is *Van Hage's Nursery*, superbly run with top-class plants and a wide range of garden furniture and accessories. [Open daily except Easter Sun, Christmas Day and Boxing Day, Mon – Sat, 10am – 6pm, Sun, 10.30am – 4.30pm.]

Hatfield House ★★ [Historic Garden Grade I]

Hatfield AL9 5NQ. Tel: (01707) 287010

The 7th Marquess of Salisbury • 2m from A1(M) junction 4 off A414 and A1000, opposite Hatfield railway station • House open Wed – Sun and Bank Holiday Mons, 12 noon – 4pm (guided tours Thurs only) • Park, West Garden, restaurant and shop open 15th April to Sept, daily, 11am – 5.30pm. East Garden open Thurs only

• *Entrance: Park and West Garden £4.50, children £3.50. Park only £2, children £1 (house, park and West Garden £8, children £4; Thurs, park and gardens £7, house tour £5 extra)* • *Other information: Dogs in park only* ❶ 🍵 ✕ 🏪 <u>WC</u> ♿ 🏛 🌡 ♻

Laid out originally in the early seventeenth century by Robert Cecil and planted by John Tradescant the Elder, the garden underwent various changes in the following centuries, particularly in the Victorian era, but during the past three decades it has enjoyed a splendid transformation at the hands of the Dowager Marchioness of Salisbury. She began the work of restoration with an imaginative and bold stroke – a new garden as the setting for the Old Palace. The plantings are her particular skill – see the pleached *Quercus ilex* imported especially for the garden, and the wild garden around the New Pond (formed in 1607), landscaped and planted since the devastation by two hurricanes. There are many splendours here: an inner courtyard on the south front, varied knot gardens and a charming herb garden in the scented garden, all planted following her own designs, and sited, like those in Tudor times, to be viewed from above; they are filled with plants used from the fifteenth to seventeenth centuries. In the Wilderness, up to 20,000 bulbs are planted each year.

Hopleys ★

Much Hadham SG10 6BU. Tel: (01279) 842509

Aubrey Barker • *5m W of Bishop's Stortford off A120. In Much Hadham 50 metres N of Bull pub* • *Open March to Oct, Mon, Wed – Sat, 9am – 5pm, Sun, 2 – 5pm, on special days for charities, and by appt* • *Entrance: free (donations welcome)* • *Other information: Self-service refreshments* ◷ 🍵 WC ♿ 🌿 🏛 🌡

A remarkable four-acre garden and nursery with a most interesting structure and layout. The pool and bog garden are now well established, and developments continue: a new gravel garden is in the making and a hornbeam avenue has been planted. There are some lovely mature trees, including mulberries and several different chestnuts, fine shrubs and much more. The extensive nursery sells many rarities. Much Hadham has two other properties of interest to gardeners. In Bourne Lane is the headquarters of *Andrew Crace* (Tel: (01279) 842685), who designs and sells a wide range of fine garden furniture and bronze and stone ornaments. *Dane Tree House* is the home of the *Henry Moore Foundation* and his collection, studios and workshops stand in parkland, with larger works placed in the surrounding fields. [Open April to Sept, Tues – Thurs, mornings only by appointment, or 2.30pm for tour. Tel: (01279) 843333.]

Jenningsbury

Hertford SG13 7NS. Tel: (01992) 583978

Mr and Mrs Barry Fox • *3m SE of Hertford between A414 and A10. Take B1197 to Hertford Heath and Haileybury College; garden is 0.5m on right* • *Open for NGS, and by appt* • *Entrance: £3* • *Further information: Teas on open day* ◐ 🌿

The seventeenth-century farmhouse stands in eight acres of ground encompassed by two-thirds of a thousand-year-old moat haunted by the Mayor of Hertford who drowned in it, and includes two acres of wonderfully atmospheric flower meadow. Cut-grass paths wander through a profusion of camassias, tradescantias, ox-eye daisies, orchids and much else. The path leads past a large pond, a bog garden with *Geum rivale*, primulas, handsome grasses and a fernery. Round the pond, stocked with water lilies and teeming with wildlife is a mixed planting of wild and cultivated species; a wide border, hiding the farm buildings, contains purple-leaved hazel, yew, golden comfrey and huge, massed *rugosa* roses. By contrast, the garden round the house is immaculate: white and purple wisteria and roses on the pergola. Then out into the field by the car park where Daisy Roots' exciting nursery has many rare plants.

Knebworth House ★ [Historic Garden Grade II*]

Knebworth, Nr Stevenage SG3 6PY. Tel: (01438) 812661

The Hon. Henry Lytton Cobbold • Signposted from A1(M) junction 7 • House open as garden, 12 noon – 5pm • Garden open 1st to 17th April, 27th May to 4th June, 1st July to 3rd Sept, daily, 11am – 5.30pm. Also open 25th and 26th March; 22nd April to 1st May, 6th to 21st May, 10th to 25th June, 9th to 24th Sept, Sat, Sun and Bank Holiday Mon; all 11am – 5.30pm • Entrance: £9.00, OAPs and children £8.50 • Other information: Guided tours available. Dogs in park only, on lead
❶ ➲ ✕ 🍴 wc ⅊ 🅿 ⌂ ♿ ♛

The ancient home of the Lytton family has seen many alterations. The gardens evolved from a simple Tudor green and orchard to Sir Edward Bulwer Lytton's elaborate Jacobean-style design of the 1880s. In 1909 Edwin Lutyens, who married into the family, remodelled and simplified them. His scheme included pollarded lime walks, rose gardens and pools. Beyond a tall yew hedge lie his Green Garden, Gold Garden and Brick Garden (with a blue and silver theme), and a pergola-covered with clematis and roses. To one side is a pets' cemetery, to the other a crab-apple walk. The Victorian maze was replanted in 1995, and the herb garden, designed by Gertrude Jekyll in 1907, was laid out in 1982. The redeveloped walled garden has a collection of culinary herbs and vegetables. The Wilderness is a carpet of daffodils in spring followed by blue alkanet, foxgloves and other wild flowers; life-size dinosaurs are to be found grazing in three of its seven acres. In all there are 25 acres of garden to explore – a good day out for the whole family.

Pelham House

Brent Pelham, Buntingford SG9 0HH. Tel: (01279) 777473

David and Celia Haselgrove • 7m NW of Bishop's Stortford, E of Brent Pelham on B1038 Buntingford – Newport Road • Open 26th March, 9th April and 7th May, 1 – 5pm, and by appt at other times • Entrance: £4 ❶ ➲ wc ⅊ ♿ 🅿

The garden was created from a cold and windswept field by the present owners. Beds were raised, tons of topsoil and mulch carted in, sheltering hedges of yew, beech and thuja planted. David Haselgrove is an excellent plantsman and grows rare and exotic varieties from seed, some of them collected by him from the wild – *Cornus capitata* is now a substantial tree, and exciting peonies come in many colours. Among the interesting trees is a cut-leaved oak, *Cornus* 'Eddie's White Wonder', and a good collection of birches. It is a lovely place to wander in spring among unusual hellebores, erythroniums, trilliums and many bulbs. A shingle garden holds a collection of daphnes, gentians and alpines, and there are fine statues by Antony Turner and Dominic Welsh. Beside the church in the same village, and open on the same NGS days, is *Church Cottage*, an interesting and imaginative 0.75-acre cottage garden with delightful hidden corners, a winding pond and a bog garden.

St Paul's Walden Bury ★ [Historic Garden Grade I]

Whitwell, Hitchin SG4 8BP. Tel: (01438) 871218

Sir Simon Bowes Lyon and family • 5m S of Hitchin, 0.5m N of Whitwell on B651 • Open 23rd April, 14th May, 4th June, 2 – 7pm, and for parties at other times by appt • Entrance: £3.50, children 50p, private visits £6 per person ● 🍴 🐾 WC & 🐾

The formal landscape garden was laid out in 1730 and is one of the few to survive; the Bowes Lyon family have lived at St Paul's Walden for more than 250 years. It covers an area of 60 acres. The long mown rides or *allées* are lined with clipped beech hedges and fan out from the eighteenth-century house – the heart of the layout – through *bosquets* to temples, statues, ponds and a medieval church. In one of the *bosquets* is a green theatre. The lake, with its temple and wonderful vistas, is worth walking to see, but in the formal areas near the house the previously impeccable standards of maintenance have been allowed to lapse.

Vineyard Manor

Much Hadham SG10 6BS Tel: (01279) 843761

Mr and Mrs H. Tee • 5m W of Bishop's Stortford off A120 • Open May to Aug by appt • Entrance: £3 • Other information: Teas by arrangement ● 🐾 &

A garden of vivid imagination created by the present owners since 1995, and at its peak in high summer. Visitors enter up a slope planted with ferns, exciting hostas and other shade-loving plants under mature trees, past an amusing man's head with two clutching hands by Mark Hall. Behind the house a terrace with a wide border let into the hillside is planted in shades of gold, silver and bronze with good colour contrasts. This leads to a swimming pool surrounded by, and lined with, grey Chinese slate – a most ingenious solution. An old dew pond restored by Anthony Paul has been taken into the garden and planted in generous blocks of colour, with a mass of dark sedums, vast drifts of ligularias, *Gunnera manicata* and drifts of tall grasses in variety.

FEEDBACK
Readers are invited to advise the *Guide* of any gardens which in their opinion should be listed in future editions, and where possible arrangements will be made to review such suggestions. Readers who would like to add information about gardens listed are warmly invited to write to the *Guide* with their comments, which may be used in future editions without attribution. Please send letters to the publishers, Frances Lincoln Ltd, 4 Torriano Mews, Torriano Avenue, London NW5 2RZ. All letters are acknowledged by the editors.

KENT

We have included some gardens with Kent postal addresses in the London section for convenience. So before planning a day out in Kent it is worthwhile consulting pages 234–70.

Two-starred gardens are marked on the map with a black square.

Abbotsmerry Barn

Salmans Lane, Penshurst TN11 8DJ. Tel: (01892) 870900

Mr and Mrs K. Wallis • 5m SW of Tonbridge off B2176 towards Leigh. Turn left 180 metres N of Penshurst; house is 1m down lane • Open for NGS and for parties by appt • Entrance: £3, children free ● ● WC ⬡

The south-facing seven-acre garden with distant views towards Penshurst is an object lesson in how to exploit a challenging sloping site. The handsome converted Kentish barn, sheltered by mature trees and a stilted lime hedge, stands at the highest point. A sunny circular terrace, surrounding a large well, is filled with sun-loving plants, and impressive herbaceous borders in shades of purple and silver curve along the hillside towards bold groups of fragrant shrub roses. The latest area, planted with native trees, joins the existing woodland, with its shady dells and paths mown through swaying grasses, and the wildflower meadow sweeping into the valley. Further exploration reveals a dramatic quarry with huge gnarled cherries, roses and foxgloves emerging from fissures in the sandstone, set around a tranquil oriental pool and a lush bog garden.

Bedgebury National Pinetum and Forest Gardens ★ [Historic Arboretum Grade II*]

Goudhurst, Cranbrook TN17 2SL. Tel: (01580) 211781

Forestry Commission • 10m SE of Tunbridge Wells off A21, on B2079 Goudhurst – Flimwell road • Arboretum open all year, daily, 10am – 5pm (closes 4pm in winter) • Entrance: £3.50, OAPs £3, children £1.50, family £9 (2005 prices) ○ ● ● WC ⬡ ⬡ ⬡ ⬡ ⬡

The modern pinetum was founded in 1924, but some of the larger specimen trees dating from 1850 are still flourishing. The conifer collection has been listed as the best in the world by the International Dendrological Research Institute. In addition it has many deciduous trees, including rare oaks and maples, and a wide range of rhododendrons flowers from January to August. The pinetum holds five National Collections: of Lawson and Leyland cypresses, junipers, yews and red cedars. A few miles away, south of Lamberhurst, lies *Bewl Water*, a splendid man-made stretch of water surrounded by woods and meadows. Water sports galore, and a 12.5-mile route around the reservoir for walkers and wildlife enthusiasts. [Open all year, daily, except one Sat in July and 25th Dec, 9am – sunset.]

Belmont ★ [Historic Garden Grade II]

Belmont Park, Throwley, Faversham ME13 0HH. Tel: (01795) 890202

*Harris (Belmont) Charity • 4m SW of Faversham, 1.5m W of A251 Faversham –
Ashford road. From A2 or M2 junction 6, take A251 S towards Ashford. Signed at
Badlesmere • House open as garden, but Sat, Sun and Bank Holiday Mons • Garden
open April to Sept, daily except Fri, 10am – 6pm • Entrance: £2.75, children £1
(house, clock museum and gardens £5.25, concessions £4.75, children £2.50)
• Other information: Teashop open from 3pm Sat, Sun and Bank Holiday Mon only*
● ● ● wc & ⬧ ⌖ ⛪ ♟

The eighteenth-century house by Samuel Wyatt was built at a time when beautiful
country-house architecture was required to blend in with equally beautiful and
well-planned surroundings, exemplified here by 40 acres of formal and informal
gardens merging into 150 acres of parkland to give marvellous vistas of aged and
noble trees. There is also a yew walk and a pinetum. The walled garden includes
borders, a pool and a rockery; note also the shell grotto and folly. The two-acre
kitchen garden has been imaginatively restored and replanted by Arabella
Lennox-Boyd, and the surrounding area transformed with grasses, wild flowers and
nut trees; it contains a formal garden based on a Hindu design, thus perpetuating the
Harris family's long connection with India.

Broadview Gardens

Hadlow, Tonbridge TN11 0AL. Tel: (01732) 850551

*Hadlow College • 8m SW of Maidstone, 3m NE of Tonbridge, on A26 • Open all
year, daily, 10am – 5pm (closes 4pm Suns) • Entrance: £2* ● ● ✕ wc & ⌖ ⛪ ♟

The gardens in the grounds of Hadlow College – 10 acres and growing – offer an
inspiring range of old and new designs in a series of well-planted areas. The
sub-tropical garden with four different varieties of musa, canna lilies, stooled
paulownia and golden catalpa, leads to a double100-metre-long herbaceous border.
The cottage garden has dwarf trained fruit trees, herbs and flowers, and in the
Sensory Garden a water rill at waist height falls over cobbles and raised beds. The
symbolism of the Paradise gardens is achieved by planting one with scented herbs
and subtly varied foliage, the other with hot colours in both flowers and foliage.
A half-acre Japanese garden has all the requisite oriental elements and appropriate
planting. There is also a low-maintenance gravel garden, an Italian garden and a
one-acre lake edged with bog plants. National Collections of hellebores and
Japanese anemones are held here, and many snowdrops, tulips and irises flower in
season.

Chart's Edge

Westerham TN16 1PL. Tel: (01732) 504556

*Mr and Mrs Bigwood • S of M25 and A25, 0.5m S of Westerham on B2026 towards
Chartwell • Open mid-April to mid-Sept, Wed and Fri, 2 – 4.30pm; for NGS, 14th
May, 11th June, 16th July, 2 – 5pm; and for parties of 5 or more by appt*

• *Entrance: £3.50, children free* • *Further information: Refreshments on NGS days only* ◐ 💬 WC ♿ ⬦ 🌿

The sweeping lawns are the start of a voyage of discovery through vast dells of magnificent azaleas and rhododendrons, their colours mercifully subtle and harmonious, and on into intimate and exotic areas designed and planted to make the most of the varying levels and vistas. The Dell Garden, filled with acers, tree ferns and hostas, leads to a flint-lined Victorian grotto adjoining a brick-lined room with a sunken bath. On the wide terraces cut into the valley side, water flows down through a series of gravel gardens; nearer the house colour comes from roses, a large and well-planted rockery and a bank of *Rhododendron yakushimanum*.

Chartwell [Historic Garden Grade II*]

Mapleton Road, Westerham TN16 1PS. Tel: (01732) 866368 (Infoline)

The National Trust • *S of M25 between junctions 5 and 6, 2m S of Westerham off B2026* • *House open* • *Garden open 25th March to 29th Oct, Wed – Sun and Bank Holiday Mons; plus Tues in July and Aug: all 11am – 5pm (last admission 4.15pm)* • *Entrance: £5, children £2.50, family £12.50 (house and garden £10, children £5, family £25)* ◑ 💬 ✕ WC ♿ ⬦ 🏛 🍽 ☕

Within this garden on a hill, with vast views over the Weald of Kent, the first feature to greet the visitor is the water garden with fish ponds and the swimming pool constructed by Sir Winston Churchill. Well-established trees along a path lead the way to a walled rose garden, its perimeter planted with herbaceous plants such as hostas, peonies and penstemons. A cloud of shrub roses perfumes the terrace, and ceanothus, white potentillas and dark red double *rugosa* roses invite the visitor on towards the house, one wing of which is covered by a huge *Hydrangea petiolaris*; against the south wall stands a large *Magnolia grandiflora*. A vine-covered pergola leads to a gazebo and viewpoint. There is also a series of smaller terraces, one planted with silver-foliage plants, and a Golden Rose walk bordered by clipped beech hedges. Maintenance and labelling are excellent.

Copton Ash Garden

105 Ashford Road, Faversham ME13 8XW. Tel: (01795) 535919

Drs Tim and Gillian Ingram • *1m S of Faversham. Just N of M2 junction 6 on A251 Faversham – Ashford road* • *Garden and nursery open March to Oct, Tues – Sun, 2 – 6pm, but check before travelling. Gardening parties welcome by appt* • *Entrance: £2 (but free for nursery visitors), accompanied children free* ◐ ♿ 🌿

Despite its position close to the M2, there is a pleasant atmosphere in this plantsman's garden created since 1978 on the site of an old cherry orchard. About one and a half acres in extent, it accommodates over 3000 species in herbaceous borders and island beds. A collection of over 100 different snowdrops and early bulbs, along with hellebores and other woodland plants, make visits early in the year particularly rewarding. Alpines are grown in raised beds and there is also a collection of fruit. Some significant new plantings have been and are being made, including many novel and rarely seen species from wild-collected seed, and experiments are underway to examine the hardiness of species from Australia, New

Zealand and South America. A specialist nursery has been developed with an emphasis on plants for dry situations. The nearby *Brogdale Horticultural Trust* holds a National Collection of fruit – over 4000 varieties. Seek them out in Brogdale Road, Faversham – open Easter to Dec, 9.30am – 5pm.

Cottage Farm

Cacketts Lane, Cudham TN14 7QG. Tel: (01959) 532506

Phil and Karen Baxter • 5m NW of Sevenoaks, 4m SW of Orpington, signed to Cudham from Green Street Green roundabout on A21. 3m into village, turn left past garage to second row of cottages on right. Entrance through working farm to parking • Open June, Sun, 1.30 – 5.30pm, and for parties by appt • Entrance: £3 NEW ● 🍵 ♿ ⬦ ⌓ ♒ B&B

Tucked well away in the byways of the North Downs, farmer Phil Baxter has created a delightful series of intimate garden spaces around a row of eighteenth-century brick and flint cottages. Visitors enter through an immaculate kitchen garden laid out in sturdy raised beds. Rustic pergolas clothed in richly scented roses provide shade, seclusion and secret sitting places, old-fashioned sweet peas scramble up tripods, clematis and honeysuckles festoon old apple trees, and the cottage-garden planting spilling over narrow paths is masterly. A sheltered terrace blooms with exotics such as daturas, strelitzias, palms, cordylines and cannas. Self-sufficiency is obviously part of the philosophy: tropical plants and fruits flourish in heated glasshouses, and there is also a well-stocked fruit-cage and a greenhouse with tomatoes and peppers. Fuchsia displays, a vine-covered dome, a wildlife pond and a stumpery planted with ferns add further interest to a most individual garden.

Doddington Place Gardens [Historic Garden Grade II]

Doddington, Sittingbourne ME9 0BB. Tel: (01795) 886101

Richard and Amicia Oldfield • 6m S of Sittingbourne. From A20 turn N at Lenham, from A2 turn S at Teynham. Signposted • Open 16th April to June, Suns and Bank Holiday Mons, plus 6th, 26th Aug, 17th Sept, all 2 – 6pm (opens 11am Bank Holiday Mons), and at other times for parties by appt • Entrance: £4, children (over 5) £1, groups £3.50 per person ● 🍵 🧺 WC ♿ ⬦ ♀

The theatrical quality of the gardens where, appropriately, open-air opera is performed each year, is significantly heightened by newer features. The scale is intrinsically grand – smooth lawns are punctuated by towering specimen trees and enclosed by extraordinary yew hedges pruned into amorphous, cloud-like shapes, and a Wellingtonia avenue planted in the mid-nineteenth century is contemporary with the house. A young *allée* of upright *Sorbus aucuparia* 'Beissneri' accentuates the geometry of the Pond Walk, and a mirror-glass obelisk is the striking focus of the flower-filled grasses of the Spring Walk. A new brick-and-flint Gothick folly marks the transition between the formality of the Folly Walk and the wildness of the three-acre woodland garden beyond, where camellias, rhododendrons, acers and bulbs are spectacular in May and June. The formal rose and sunken gardens have imaginative modern planting schemes, and a pool has been added to the Edwardian rock garden, which is the subject of a major restoration project.

Edenbridge House

Main Road, Edenbridge TN8 6SJ. Tel: (01732) 862122

*Mrs M.T. Lloyd • 1.5m N of Edenbridge on B2026 • Open April to Sept, Tues and
Thurs, 2 – 5pm, plus some Suns and Weds for NGS. Also open for parties by appt
• Entrance: £3 • Other information: Refreshments on charity open days only* ◑ WC
♿ ⌖ ▱

This five-acre garden, originally made in the 1930s, is set on a south-facing slope. The
part-sixteenth-century house is surrounded on three sides by a wide terrace on
which a large variety of tender plants flourishes in pots. A walled courtyard to one
side of the house contains a parterre filled with displays of annuals. Roses, *Itea
ilicifolia, Clerodendrum bungei*, wisteria, jasmine and a *Magnolia grandiflora* drape the
walls. Garden rooms are linked to the house by a lawn containing a fountain pool
guarded by elegant drum-shaped golden yews. A small stream, crossed by two
wisteria-clad bridges, meanders down to a small lower pool; the banks of the stream
are edged with rocks and planted with moisture-loving plants. There is a large
kitchen garden, a soft-fruit cage and an apple and cherry orchard. Part of the kitchen
garden has been turned into an arboretum and planted with a selection of trees and
shrubs to give a wide range of colour. A 21-metre-long peach house now contains
plumbago, passiflora and a large *Cobaea scandens* f. *alba*. A gravel garden, which is hot
and sheltered with the added benefit of a boggy area, has hostas, bamboos, various
grasses, ferns, spiky agaves and palms. This is a plantsman's garden, with year-round
interest provided by displays of early spring bulbs, colourful summer herbaceous
borders and the foliage colours of autumn.

Emmetts Garden ★ [Historic Garden Grade II]

Ide Hill, Sevenoaks TN14 6AY. Tel: (01732) 868381

*The National Trust • 1.5m S of A25 and M25 junction 5, 1.5m N of Ide Hill off
B2042 Edenbridge – Sundridge road • Open 25th March to 31st May, Tues – Sun
and Bank Holiday Mons; 1st June to 2nd July, Wed – Sun; 5th July to 29th Oct,
Wed, Sat and Sun; all 11am – 5pm (last admission 4.15pm) • Entrance: £5,
children £1, family £11 • Other information: Buggy available from car park to
entrance* ◑ ➊ ▦ WC ♿ ⌖ ▥ ♆ ⚘

The garden gives a superb view over the Weald of Kent and provides an impressive
setting for this plantsman's collection of trees and shrubs. It is particularly fine
in spring, with its bluebell woods and flowering shrubs. Noted especially for
its rhododendrons and azaleas, it follows the late-nineteenth-century style of
combining exotics with conifers to provide a 'wild' garden; the plants are all listed
in the guidebook. A rose garden, a rock garden and a collection of acers planted
for autumn colour extend the interest throughout the year. The enforced
clearance of some trees and shrubs after the gales of 1987 has enabled new
planting to keep the traditions of the garden and also to expand it – the rock
garden in particular is becoming established. A splendid site and a fascinating
garden.

Godinton House [Historic Garden Grade I]

Godinton Lane, Ashford TN23 3BP. Tel: (01233) 620773

The Godinton House Preservation Trust • Off M20 junction 9, 1.5m NW of Ashford in Godinton Lane at Potter's Corner (opposite Hare and Hounds pub) • House open 7th April to 8th Oct, Fri – Sun • Garden open 25th March to 29th Oct, Thurs – Mon, 2 – 5.30pm • Entrance: £3, children free (house and garden £6, children free) • Other information: Coaches by appt only. Garden tours available by prior arrangement. Refreshments available when house is open and for pre-booked parties
◑ 🏠 WC ☕ ✈ 🌿 🍴 ♿

The gardens surrounding the house have evolved over centuries, and in 1902 were redesigned by architect Reginald Blomfield, an exponent of the revival of the formal gardens of the seventeenth century. As restored, it is now in essence an elegant formal garden with a modern sensibility. Its stylish simplicity is evident in the entrance courtyard, where four *Acer pseudoplatanus* 'Brilliantissimum' glow against the great yew boundary hedge, cut to echo the Flemish gables of the house. Beyond, elegant terraces defined by topiary link different areas, such as the box-hedged Pan Garden and huge formal herbaceous borders leading to the lily pond, originally an Edwardian swimming pool. A redesigned rose garden burgeons with boldly underplanted fragrant shrub roses; another is filled with bulbs and wild flowers bordering an informal pond; while the intimate Italian Garden, approached via a classical colonnade, has been replanted with Mediterranean plants. The major work-in-progress is the walled kitchen garden, where gravel paths lined with espalier fruit have been restored and a Victorian glasshouse replaced. Borders maintained by the Delphinium Society line the walls, and new beds are being planted with decorative mix of cutting flowers and produce.

Goodnestone Park ★★ [Historic Garden Grade II*]

Goodnestone, Nr Wingham, Canterbury CT3 1PL. Tel: (01304) 840107

Lady FitzWalter • 5m E of Canterbury. Take A2 signed to Dover, turn left at junction B2046 for Wingham/Aylesham, then E after 1m • House open by appt for pre-booked parties • Garden open 12th Feb to 19th March, Sun, 12 noon – 5pm; then 20th March to 29th Sept, Wed – Sun, 11am – 5pm (opens 12 noon Sat and Sun). Pre-booked parties daily • Entrance: £4, OAPs £3.50, children (under 12) 50p, family £6.50 (guided tours £5.50 per person) • Other information: Teas available April to Sept only. Gardening lectures spring and summer – telephone for details ◑ 🍽 🏠 WC ☕ 🍴 ♿

Goodnestone (pronounced Gunston) Park is a 14-acre garden in a rural setting. Built in 1700 by Brook Bridges, the Palladian-style house was rebuilt and enlarged by his great-grandson, Sir Brook Bridges, 3rd Baronet, whose daughter Elizabeth married Jane Austen's brother Edward. In her letters Jane makes frequent reference to Goodnestone and her Bridges cousins. There are pleasant vistas within the garden and good views out to open countryside. The garden ranges in time from the walled area behind the house, which dates from the sixteenth and seventeenth centuries, to mid-eighteenth-century parkland with fine trees and cedars. The tour leads along a broad terrace in front of the house, planted with a parterre for the Millennium, to a lime avenue. Next comes a new venture – a gravel garden designed by Graham Gough, inspired in part by Beth Chatto. The small woodland, laid out in the 1920s, gives pleasant walks among rhododendrons, camellias, magnolias, hydrangeas and many cornus; beyond is a golden arboretum designed by Tom Wright and planted in 2001. A cedar walk leads, between spring borders on the left and a red and grey border on the right, to a walled garden overlooked by the church tower. Old roses mingle with mixed underplanting, and walls bear clematis, jasmine and climbing roses.

Great Comp ★

Comp Lane, Platt, Borough Green, Sevenoaks TN15 8QS. Tel: (01732) 886154

Great Comp Charitable Trust • From M20 junction 2, take A20 towards Maidstone. At Wrotham Heath take B2016. Signposted • Open April to Oct, daily, 11am – 5.30pm • Entrance: £4, children £1, annual ticket £12, OAPs £8 ◑ 🍽 ✕ <u>WC</u> ♿ ⚘ ♨ ♟

A half-day may be required to do justice to this imaginatively planned seven-acre garden, which offers all-year interest. Although the setting for an early-seventeenth-century house, it was only created after 1957 out of the neglected earlier garden, rough woodland and paddock. Long grass walks intersect the beds and borders, providing ever-changing views to tempt visitors to stray from their intended route. Focal points and interest are given by statuary, a temple and ruins built from the tons of ironstone dug up over the years. There are woodland areas, herbaceous borders, a heather garden, a rose garden, formal lawns and an Italianate garden designed to set off a collection of Mediterranean plants. Hellebores, especially *H. orientalis*, are a feature, and the introduction of salvias, dahlias, kniphofias and crocosmias has given the garden a new exoticism. The *Taxus baccata* at the front of the house was planted in 1840. Other specimen trees include a young dawn redwood (*Metasequoia glyptostroboides*) and a Californian redwood (*Sequoia sempervirens* 'Cantab'). A music festival is held here each year, with recitals in the former stables.

Groombridge Place ★ [Historic Garden Grade I*]

Groombridge, Tunbridge Wells TN3 9QG. Tel: (01892) 861444

4m SW of Tunbridge Wells. Take A264 towards East Grinstead, then after 2m B2110 to Groombridge • Open April to 5th Nov, daily, 10am – 5.30pm • Entrance: £8.70, OAPs £7.20, children £7.20, family £29.50 • Other information: Canal boat rides, birds of prey ◑ 🍽 ✕ 🍴 <u>WC</u> ♿ ⚘ ♨ ♟ ⚲

Half hidden in a broad wooded valley, the handsome moated manor house (not open) was built in 1662 by Philip Packer, Clerk of the Privy Seal to Charles II. Centuries have gone into the making of the gardens within the ancient walls of the original 1230 moated castle, but recently the seventeenth-century formal gardens have been imaginatively restored. From a magnificent border on the highest terrace, a gravelled path leads between a striking double procession of 24 drum-shaped yews. On either side are garden rooms of differing character: the Oriental Garden inspired by the colours of an oriental rug, the Drunken Garden of misshapen junipers, the former kitchen garden now the White Rose Garden. A narrow canal feeds a tranquil lake, originally the village millpond, and there are newer features such as the Giant Chessboard, the Golden Key Maze and a new knot garden. An exciting aerial walkway leads to the Enchanted Forest, created by land artist Ivan Hicks and designer Myles Challis, where extraordinary sculptures and mysterious pools provide imaginative challenges for children and adults.

115 Hadlow Road

Tonbridge TN9 1QE. Tel: (01732) 353738

Mr and Mrs Richard Esdale • 1m N of Tonbridge. From High Street take A26 signed to Maidstone. House is 1m on left in service road • Open 16th to 30th July, 27th Aug, 2 – 6pm, and by appt • Entrance: £2 ● ⬤

A third-of-an-acre terraced suburban garden with many interesting specimen trees such as *Catalpa bignonioides* 'Aurea', *Acer negundo* 'Flamingo', *A. japonicum* 'Aureum', golden elm and *Sorbus cashmiriana*. A herbaceous border and an array of clematis, hardy fuchsias, ferns, grasses (*Stipa gigantea*), hostas, alpines, roses, shrubs and summer bedding provide additional colour, and a small pool with a fountain contains water-loving plants. There is also a small, well-stocked fruit and vegetable garden.

Hever Castle and Gardens ★★ [Historic Garden Grade I]

Hever, Edenbridge TN8 7NG. Tel: (01732) 865224

Broadlands Properties Ltd • 3m SE of Edenbridge off B2026, between Sevenoaks and East Grinstead • Castle open as garden, but from 12 noon • Gardens open March to Nov, daily, 11am – 6pm (close 4pm March and Nov). Pre-booked guided tours available for both castle and gardens for parties • Entrance: £7.30, OAPs £6.30, children (5–14) £4.80, family £19.40; castle and gardens £9.20, OAPs £7.70, children (5–14) £5, family £23.40. Rates for parties of 15 or more available (2005 prices) ● ⬤ ✕ 🪑 <u>WC</u> ♿ 🐕 🌳 🏛 🍴 ✿

The gardens were laid out between 1904 and 1908 to William Waldorf Astor's designs. One thousand men were employed, 800 of whom dug out the 35-acre lake; steam engines shifted rock and soil to create apparently natural new features, and teams of horses moved mature trees from Ashdown Forest. Today the gardens have reached their maturity and are teeming with colour and interest throughout the year. Among the many superb features is an outstanding four-acre Italian garden, the setting for a large collection of classical statuary; opposite is a magnificent pergola, supporting camellias, wisteria, crab apple, Virginia creeper and roses. It fuses into the hillside beyond, which has shaded grottoes of cool damp-loving species such as hostas, astilbes and polygonums. Less formal areas include the rhododendron walk, Anne Boleyn's orchard and her walk, which extends along the full length of the grounds and is particularly attractive in autumn. A Tudor herb garden has been added, and the Sunday Walk nearby runs beside a stream past newly created borders in mature woodland. The 110-metre herbaceous border has been re-created and the water maze on Sixteen-Acre Island, planted with a range of aquatic plants, offers peaceful walks down to the millennium fountain.

Hole Park

Rolvenden, Cranbrook TN17 4JA. Tel: (01580) 241344/241386

Mr and Mrs Edward Barham • 4m W of Tenterden, on B2086 between Rolvenden and Benenden • Open 2nd April to 2nd July, Wed, Thurs, Sun and Bank Holiday Mons; then 5th July to 26th Oct, Wed and Thurs; plus 8th, 15th and 22nd Oct; all 2 – 6pm. Open by appt at other times • Entrance: £4, children (under 12) 50p • Other information: Refreshments and plants for sale on Suns and Bank Holiday Mons ● ● ● WC & ♨ ♀

Majestic chestnut trees line the drive through beautiful parkland to the superb early eighteenth-century house surrounded by 14 acres of tranquil and immaculate gardens. A series of formal garden spaces enclosed by yew hedges planted by the owner's grandfather contrasts with smooth lawns offset with towering specimen trees, topiary, classical statuary, and a theatrical wisteria-clad pergola. Around the house, elegant garden rooms are sheltered by old walls, where climbers and herbaceous plants are used to great effect, including a pool garden with sun-loving plants and shrubs. Further delights lie in the extensive woodland valley, where bulbs and ornamental trees lead through magnificent azaleas and rhododendrons to a stream and secret shady pool with lush marginal planting and fine autumn colour. The views towards Rolvenden postmill and the villages and landscape of the Weald of Kent make a visit a rewarding and pleasurable experience.

Ightham Mote

Mote Road, Ivy Hatch, Sevenoaks TN15 0NT. Tel: (01732) 810378

The National Trust • 6m E of Sevenoaks off A25, 2.5m S of Ightham off A227 • House open • Garden open 12th March to 29th Oct, daily except Tues and Sat, 10am – 5.30pm • Entrance: £8.50, children £4, family £21 • Other information: Disabled parking ● ● ✕ ● WC & ● ♀ ╰

Situated in a wooded cleft of the Kentish Weald, this medieval and Tudor manor house lies in the valley of Dinas Dene, where a stream has been dammed to form small lakes and the moat which surrounds the house. The design of the gardens has evolved over several centuries – the present lawn replaces the medieval stewpond, which was used for breeding fish for the table; further domestic needs were satisfied with vegetables and herbs for culinary and medicinal purposes, and flowers for decorating and scenting the house. During the nineteenth century the garden emerged as an excellent example of the ideal Old English garden, and the Trust is gradually restoring this with extensive replanting. Six acres of woodland walks with fine rhododendrons are re-established and the long border has returned to its former glory.

Ladham House ★

Goudhurst TN17 1DB.

8m E of Tunbridge Wells, NE of Goudhurst off A262 • Open two days for NGS, 2 – 5.30pm, and by written appt for individuals and parties • Entrance: £3.50, children 50p, £4.50 for private visits (2005 prices) • *Other information: Teas must be pre-booked* ● WC ⅃ ⬧

The house, Georgian with additional French features, is surrounded by 37 acres of garden and parkland. It is interesting to see the bog garden replacing a leaking pond, and the arboretum replacing the old kitchen garden. The mixed shrub borders are attractive; notable are the magnolias – two *M.* x *wieseneri* over 10 metres tall and a deep-red-flowering 'Betty Jessel', a seedling from Darjeeling. Among other rarer trees and shrubs are *Cornus kousa*, embothriums, American oaks, *Aesculus parviflora*, *Carpenteria californica* and *Azara serrata*. The arboretum is maturing and has some unusual and interesting trees. Developments continue: the Fountain Garden has been completely reconstructed, the rock garden restored with a waterfall incorporated, a 200-metre-long Kentish ragstone ha-ha built to the north of the house, and a woodland walk down the side of the park opened up. A new garden close to the swimming pool uses tropical and hot-coloured plants.

Laurenden Forstal

Laurenden Forstal, Blind Lane, Challock TN25 4AU. Tel: (01233) 740310

Mrs M. Cottrell • *6m N of Ashford near junction of A251 and A252, with access from both* • *Open 25th June and 20th August, 2 – 6pm, and by appt* • *Entrance: £2.50, children free* • *Other information: Parking village hall car park behind house. Disabled parking at house* ● ⬤ ⬧

The two-acre gardens surrounding the handsome fourteenth-century timber-framed house, said to be the birthplace of William Caxton, are the domain of Amanda Cottrell. During the last few years, she has revitalised the traditional framework. Near the house are sunny terraces and a charming courtyard planted mainly with white flowers. Tall buttressed yew hedges enclosing velvety lawns contrast with burgeoning herbaceous planting, including a recent 'hot' border, and a romantic rose-swagged pergola leads to the Victorian lady's walk through a flower-spangled meadow. A natural wildlife pond, recreated from a sunken garden, is fringed by candelabra primulas, ligularias and loosestrife; vegetables flourish in tiny raised beds. A charming touch is the living willow tunnel which overlooks the pond, supporting rampant honeysuckle and sheltering a fragrant thyme seat. A woodland glade is delightful in spring, and decorative chickens, ponies and a resident donkey add to the welcoming atmosphere.

Leeds Castle ★ [Historic Garden Grade II*]

Maidstone ME17 1PL. Tel: (01622) 765400

Leeds Castle Foundation • *7m E of Maidstone on B2163 near M20 junction 8* • *Castle opens 11am (10.15am in winter)* • *Park and garden open all year, daily except 24th June, 1st July, 4th Nov, 25th Dec, 10am – 7pm (last admission 5pm) (closes 5pm Nov to March, last admission 3.30pm)* • *Entrance: castle, park and gardens £13, OAPs and students £11, children (4 – 14) £9, family £39 (2005 prices)* ○ ⬤ ✕ ▥ WC ⅃ ⬧ ⏣ ♟ ⚲

Visit the castle and grounds for its romantic, wooded setting, covering some 500 acres; the woodland garden, with its old and new plantings of shrubs, is especially beautiful at daffodil time. The Culpeper Garden, in a secluded area beyond the castle, provides the main interest for the keen gardener. This is not a herb garden as often thought, though a small area does include some herbs, but is named after a seventeenth-century owner, distantly related to the herbalist. Started in 1980 by Russell Page on a slope overlooking the River Len, and surrounded by high brick walls of stabling and old cottages, it consists of a simple pattern of paths lined with box contains areas of old roses, riotously underplanted with herbaceous perennials. National Collections of monardas are situated in one corner. The terraced Italian-style Lady Baillie Garden overlooking the Great Water has stunning sub-tropical plants. Don't miss the spectacular 1987 grotto beneath the maze. The garden is complemented by some rare and attractive birds in the duckery and aviary, which are well placed amid numerous shrubs and small trees.

Longacre

Perry Wood, Selling, Faversham ME13 9SE. Tel: (01227) 752254

Dr and Mrs G. Thomas • 5m SE of Faversham. From A2 (M2) take A251 S signed to Selling. Pass White Lion on left, second right, then left, continue for 0.25m. From A252 at Chilham, take road to Selling at Badgers Hill Fruit Farm, turn left at second crossroads, first right, next left, then right • Open 16th, 17th and 30th April, 1st, 14th, 28th and 29th May, 27th and 28th Aug, and by appt at other times • Entrance: £2.50, accompanied children free • Other information: Teas and plants for sale on NGS open days only ◑ ● WC & ℗

This is a jewel of a small garden in a tranquil country setting next to Perry Woods into which the borders of the garden melt. Created entirely by the present owners, it is at its best in spring and early summer, but offers all-year interest of colour and form, replicating in miniature woodland, damp and dry areas. There are mixed borders, a small pond with running water and a large gravel garden. Trellis around the area supports sun-loving climbers, and vegetables in raised beds are cropping well, and a new conservatory displays a wide range of tender plants.

Lullingstone Castle

Eynsford DA4 0JA. Tel: (01322) 862114

The Hart Dyke family • On A225 midway between Dartford and Sevenoaks. In Eynsford, turn at church and cross bridge, then turn left and pass Roman villa. Park at castle gatehouse • Open April to Oct, Fri and Sat, 12 noon – 5pm, Sun and Bank Holiday Mon, 2 – 6pm (closed Good Friday), and to parties of 15 or more by appt, Wed – Sun • Entrance: £5.50, OAPs £5, children (5-15) £2.50, family £12.50 [NEW] ◑ ● WC & ♿

The World Garden of Plants being created here is the vision of Tom Hart Dyke, a young plant hunter who became newsworthy in 2000, when he was kidnapped by armed guerrillas whilst on an orchid-hunting expedition in the Colombian jungle. During his nine months of captivity, he dreamed of making a garden of plants collected from all parts of the world, and this is now taking shape in the two-acre walled garden of the castle where his family have lived since the fifteenth century. With unstoppable energy, he has laid out a huge map of the world using boulders to delineate the shapes of the continents and countries, with the beds contoured to emulate the topography. Planting began in 2005 and on completion these areas will hold over 10,000 different species planted to show their relative habitats. It is a bold concept, and visitors will see the collection developing over time. Education is high on the agenda with the aim of showing how many familiar plants have come from far-flung and often inhospitable places, and of telling the extraordinary stories of Victorian and Edwardian plant hunters. The garden is set in 120 acres of peaceful Kentish countryside, with the handsome manor and castle gatehouse overlooking a beautiful 15-acre lake.

Marle Place Gardens and Gallery ★
Brenchley, Tonbridge TN12 7HS. Tel: (01892) 722304

Mr and Mrs G. Williams • 5m E of Tunbridge Wells, 1m SW of Horsmonden, W of B2162. Signposted • Open April to 1st Oct, Fri – Mon, 10am – 5.30pm, and by appt at other times • Entrance: £4.50, OAPs and children (4–12 years) £4, wheelchair users free • Other information: Art exhibitions in gallery throughout season ❶ 💷 🍴 WC & 🌿 🍴 ⚲

The 10-acre garden surround a seventeenth-century house hidden away in the byways. Close to the house a small shady fern garden and a border of several varieties of cistus are set off by an old wall furnished with interesting climbers. A double herbaceous border leads to an area of alliums and ornamental grasses. Near the house too is an old ornamental pool garden with a wildflower bank and aromatic plants, a croquet lawn and several interesting specimen trees. The use of tapestry hedges as a background to many of the borders illustrates the artistic flair of the owner (her studio is open to garden visitors). Other features include a Victorian gazebo, an Edwardian rockery and two small lakes approached by a woodland walk. A red Chinese bridge leads over a boggy area backed by bamboos, and a mosaic terrace has been laid within a blue-and-yellow border. There are areas of wild flowers both within the garden and in the 10-acre wood of native trees. Several large iron skeletal sculptures of horses and other work by varied artists, plus carved wooden furniture made by the owners' daughter, add to the eclectic charm. Along the woodland walk visitors come upon a two-acre 'gallery wood', where they are invited to participate in creating artworks made from the natural objects surrounding them. A recently planted five-acre arboretum is carpeted with buttercups and scented clover. Within the yew-hedged kitchen garden are a new box parterre and a raised-bed rose garden.

Mount Ephraim [Historic Garden Grade II]
Hernhill, Faversham ME13 9TX. Tel: (01227) 751496

Mrs Mary Dawes and Mr and Mrs E.S. Dawes • 6m W of Canterbury, 3m E of Faversham off A299. At Duke of Kent pub turn to Hernhill; garden is through village on left, signposted • Open 1st April to Sept, Wed, Thurs, Sat, Sun and Bank Holiday Mons, all 1 – 5pm (Bank Holiday weekends 11am – 5pm) • Entrance: £3.50, children £1, parties £3 per person • Other information: Craft shop Sun afternoon only ❶ 💷 🍴 WC & 🌿 🍴 ⚲

The fine 10-acre gardens surrounding the house mirror two centuries of changing horticultural fashions. From its eminent position, with far-flung views over fruit orchards to the Thames estuary, the house overlooks sweeping lawns, huge borders and magnificent specimen trees, including a sweet chestnut planted to commemorate the Battle of Waterloo. The steeply sloping site retains the original formal plan in the rose terrace, with flights of steps hedged in venerable yew, leading to the tranquil lake and a water garden. The restored Japanese-influenced rock gardens are a turn-of-the-century feature. In 1950 the indefatigable Mary Dawes and her husband began the restoration work, which continues today with the creation of an elegant millennium garden filled with fragrant new and old-fashioned roses. Nigel Lee Evans was responsible for its layout of the new rose garden, Sarah Morgan for its planting; she also carried out the design of the Ivan-Hicks-inspired grass maze on the side of the old vineyard. A long herbaceous border, skilfully planted and sheltered by old stable walls, lines the topiary garden with its idiosyncratic collection of birds, animals and First World War memorabilia in clipped yew. The arboretum was planted in 1995.

Nettlestead Place ★

Nettlestead, Maidstone ME18 5HA. Tel: (01622) 812205

Mr and Mrs R.C. Tucker • 6m SW of Maidstone off B2015. Next to church • Open for NGS 4th June and 10th Sept, 2 – 5.30pm, and at other times by appt • Entrance: £4 ● ● ● WC & ◁

An avenue of Irish yews leads down from the early-fourteenth-century gatehouse to the thirteenth-century manor house set in seven acres on the banks of a tranquil stretch of the River Medway. A long gravel garden planted with rock plants and dwarf bulbs lies along the eastern side of the house, which is clothed with akebia, sophora, fremontodendron and *Rosa* 'Frances Lester'. A large sunken pond bounded by a ragstone wall provides a sheltered environment for tender plants, and a natural spring flowing down the hill in the glen garden is edged with hostas, primulas, dwarf pines, astilbes and other damp- and shade-lovers. Beyond this a woodland garden sheltered by a steep bank leads through to a collection of bamboos. The astounding plantsman's collection continues throughout the garden – shrubs, hybrid tea and floribunda roses in the large rose garden, specialised trees and shrubs in a series of island beds, a comprehensive range of plants in the herbaceous garden, and a small, recently planted China rose garden. An arboretum containing over 30 different acers delights in spring with its interesting bark variations and in autumn with its vibrant foliage colours.

Old Buckhurst

Markbeech, Nr Edenbridge TN8 5PH. Tel: (01342) 850825

Jane and John Gladstone • 4m SE of Edenbridge via B2026. At Queen's Arms turn E to Markbeech; after 1.5m garden is first on right after leaving village • Open May to July, Wed; plus 6th and 27th May, 3rd and 24th June, 1st and 29th July; and for NGS; all 11am – 5.30pm • Entrance: £3, children free ● ● WC & ◈

The fifteenth-century farmhouse, draped in wisteria, roses, a fig and summer jasmine, sits on top of a wide, flat ridge. It is surrounded by an acre of garden containing an exuberance of cottage-garden plants, old-fashioned roses and clematis. The planting becomes wilder towards the perimeter, the better to blend into the countryside, but in the heart of the garden native species give way to more sophisticated effects. A courtyard enclosed by low walls has a silver pear tree and a series of box globes for structure and winter interest. A short pergola leads to the kitchen garden; a small pond surrounded by damp-loving plants and a gravel garden provide contrasts. The wide variety of plants propagated from the garden for sale in the little nursery is an added bonus. The owners' daughter, Claire Gladstone, is a garden designer who keeps a watching brief on this charming place.

Old Place Farm

High Halden, Ashford TN26 3JG. Tel: (01233) 850202

Mr and Mrs J. Eker • 10m SW of Ashford. From A28, opposite Chequers pub in High Halden, take Woodchurch road and follow for 0.5m • Open by appt only • Entrance: £3.50, guided tour £5 per person • Further information: Teas by arrangement ● ▣ WC ఉ

A four-acre garden surrounding a period house and farm buildings, created since 1968, mainly by Anthony du Gard Pasley. The lake of two-thirds of an acre provides a near focus from the house, and an elegant gazebo is an idyllic setting for contemplation. The borders behind have an apricot, gold and cream colour theme offset by blues, purples, silvers and greys. An avenue of *Crataegus prunifolia*, underplanted with white-flowering bulbs from February to May, leads to a fine sheep statue. There is a nut plat, a philadelphus walk and, to provide summer shelter from the sun, two large *Catalpa bignonioides*. A parterre herb garden is linked to a circular brick feature with a sundial by an avenue of *Malus* 'Golden Hornet'. A pergola draped with the rose 'New Dawn', white wisteria and purple vines divides the cutting garden from a small *potager*. Two new bridges over the stream connect the garden to the wood and fields beyond.

Owl House Gardens

Lamberhurst TN3 8LY. Tel: (01892) 891290

Estate of the late Maureen, Marchioness of Dufferin and Ava • 6m SE of Tunbridge Wells, S of Lamberhurst off A21. Signposted • Open all year, daily except 25th Dec and 1st Jan, 11am – 6pm • Entrance: £4, children £1 (2005 prices) • Other information: Coaches by appt. Tea room closed Sept to April ○ ▣ ▣ WC ఉ ⟨⟩ ℘

In 1952 Lady Dufferin fell in love with a cottage which had the crookedest chimney in Kent and was the county's oldest building. In 1522 its tenants paid a yearly rental of one white cockerel to the monks at Bayham Abbey, and during the sixteenth century it was a hiding place for wool smugglers who, at the approach of the law, hooted their warning, hence its name. Within its 16.5 acres a beautiful year-round garden was created over the years by Lady Dufferin. Swathes of daffodils and bluebells start the season, followed by camellias, azaleas and rhododendrons. Summer interest is ensured by large numbers of old roses – *R. longicuspis*, 'Bobbie James' and 'Rambling Rector' – climbing into the many fine trees; philadelphus and clematis also abound. Statues of owls are dotted about the garden, with seats placed to overlook viewpoints. There is a wisteria temple, a grove of *Parrotia persica*, and four walks: of iris, apple blossom, laburnum and blue hydrangeas. Three water gardens provide a peaceful setting for contemplation.

Penshurst Place and Gardens ★ [Historic Garden Grade I]

Penshurst, Tonbridge TN11 8DG. Tel: (01892) 870307

Lord De L'Isle • 5m SW of Tonbridge on B2176, 7m N of Tunbridge Wells off A26 • House open as garden, but 12 noon – 4pm • Gardens open weekends from 4th March, then daily from 25th March to 29th Oct, 10.30am – 6pm. Tours available for parties of 20 or more • Entrance: £6, children £4.50, family £18 (house and gardens £7.50, OAPs and students £7, children £5, family £21). Parties of 20 or more £7 per person • Other information: Garden history exhibition. Guide dogs only ◑ 💺 🏦 WC ♿ ♨ ⚑ ☕

The 600-year-old gardens, contemporary with the house, reflect their creation under the Tudor owner, Sir Henry Sidney, and their restoration by the present owner, his father and his grandfather. An example is the 640-metre double line of oaks, their planting completed in 1995 as part of a 15-year programme to re-create the historic parkland structure. The many separate enclosures, surrounded by trim and tall yew hedges, offer a wide variety of interesting planting, with continuous displays from spring to early autumn. Just inside the entrance is a garden for the blind, with raised beds of aromatic plants, a small wooden gazebo and the constant music of water splashing on pebbles. The Italian garden with its oval fountain and century-old ginkgo dominates the south front of the magnificent house. Herbaceous borders are teeming with colour. Note also the borders designed by Lanning Roper in the late 1960s and the blue and yellow border. Contrast is made by the nut trees and over a dozen different crab apples underplanted with daffodils, myosotis, tulips, bluebells, Lenten lilies, and a magnificent bed of peonies bordering the orchard. Even in late summer the rose garden is colourful with 'Anisley Dickson' and 'Anna Olivier', and their perfumes mingle with those of mature lavender bushes. A lake and woodland trail have been developed so that the style of design so much enjoyed here by Gertrude Jekyll and Beatrix Farrand is fully recaptured. Two medieval fish ponds have been reclaimed and stocked with fish. There is an imaginative play area for children.

The Pines Garden

Beach Road, St Margaret's Bay CT15 6DZ. Tel: (01304) 851737

St Margaret's Bay Trust • 3m NE of Dover off A258, through St Margaret's at Cliffe, just before beach • Open all year, daily, 10am – 5pm • Entrance: £3, concessions £2.50, children 50p, wheelchair users £1 (2005 prices) • Other information: Teas and gift shop in St Margaret's Museum opposite (open at peak seasons, Wed – Sun, 2 – 5pm) ○ 🏦 WC ♿ ◁

It is hard to believe that this well-stocked and organically maintained garden was scrubland until 1970. Fred Cleary, founder of the St Margaret's Bay Trust, transformed the original six-acre site, known as the Barrack Field, once the home and training ground for soldiers in the Napoleonic Wars. Now the garden has a good variety of trees, gently undulating lawns, flowering shrubs, bulbs and herbaceous plants. The lake with its cascade of waterfalls provides further interest; adjoining it is a new grass labyrinth. A bronze statue of Churchill by Oscar Nemon looks across the garden to the famous white cliffs of Dover, and at the other end is a seventeenth-century facade from a London Cheapside property, and a newly built roundhouse shelter for picnics if the weather is breezy. For the Millennium a large new bed near the entrance to the garden was filled with perennial plants introduced into Kent over the past few hundred years. A new water feature has been built at the entrance, with a lily pool and two terraced gardens leading up to the visitor centre.

Port Lympne [Historic Garden Grade II*]

Lympne, Hythe CT21 4PD. Tel: (01303) 264647

The Aspinall family • 3m W of Hythe, 18m S of Canterbury on B2067 • House open • Garden open all year, daily, 10am – 6pm (last admission 4.30pm, 3pm in winter) • Entrance: £12.95, OAPs and children £9.95 (house, garden and wild animal park) ○ 💷 ✕ 🍴 WC ♿ 🅿 ⛪ 🍽 ♺

This is one of those gardens which is hugely enjoyed by some people and leaves others cold. It stands in a 600-acre wild animal park with views across the Channel. The interior of the Lutyens-style house is noted for the murals by Rex Whistler and Spencer Roberts. After a period of distinction in the 1920s and '30s it fell into decay until it was rescued in the 1970s by the late John Aspinall, who wanted the surrounding land for his private wild animal park. He reconstructed the 15-acre garden to something like its original design with advice from experts, including the late Russell Page. Visitors enter down a great stone stairway of 125 steps, flanked by clipped yews, to the paved west court and lily pool. Beyond is the lime tree walk and a series of terraces planted with standard fig trees and vines. Everywhere there is fine stone paving and walls with appropriately placed urns, statues from Stowe, etc. Bedding and bedding-out are used extensively. Although the late Arthur Hellyer admitted that 'for years it has been fashionable to denigrate Port Lympne', he admired it; he also waxed lyrical about the beautiful wrought-ironwork by Bainbridge Reynolds.

Riverhill House Gardens [Historic Garden Grade II]

Sevenoaks TN15 0RR. Tel: (01732) 458802/452557

The Rogers family (correspondence to Mrs John Rogers) • 2m S of Sevenoaks on A225 • House open to bona fide booked parties only. No children inside house • Garden open 2nd April to 18th June, Sun and Bank Holiday Mons, 11am – 5pm • Entrance: £3, children 50p (house and garden for parties of 20 or more £4.50 per person) • Other information: Coaches by appt 🌙 💷 🍴 WC 🅿 ⛪

This was originally one of the great smaller country-house gardens, housing a plantsman's collection of trees and species shrubs as introduced by John Rogers, a keen horticulturist, in the mid-1800s. Massive rhododendrons, many of them species, are topped by a cedar of Lebanon planted in 1815, and azaleas and outstanding underplanting of bulbs make a fine show in spring and early summer. Other features include a woodland garden with bluebells, a rose walk, an orchard with a Wellingtonia planted in 1860, magnolias and much more.

Rock Farm ★
Gibbs Hill, Nettlestead, Maidstone ME18 5HT. Tel: (01622) 812244

Mrs P.A. Corfe • 6m SW of Maidstone. From A26 turn S onto B2015, then turn right 1m S of Wateringbury • Open 10th, 13th, 17th, 20th May; 7th, 10th, 14th, 17th, 21st, 24th, 28th June; 1st, 5th, 8th July; all 11am – 5pm; and for private visits by appt • Entrance: £4 ◑ **WC** B&B

The Kentish farmhouse, set on an east-facing slope, is surrounded by a two-acre plantswoman's garden. The entrance is along a colourful iris border, and the best season is May to July when the large herbaceous border is at its peak. The soil is alkaline and there are excellent specimens of ceanothus, a huge *Solanum crispum*, a *Fremontodendron californicum* and a *Magnolia grandiflora*. Of special interest is the *Chionanthus virginicus* or fringe tree. Natural springs supply water for two ponds bordered by cupressus of various foliage colour and for a small stream whose banks are planted with primulas and other moisture-lovers. A *Catalpa bignonioides* 'Aurea' is cut annually to give huge golden leaves, and a *Sequoia sempervirens* is also pruned drastically, resulting in rarely seen new foliage of this coniferous forest tree.

Rogers Rough
Chicks Lane, Kilndown, Cranbrook TN17 2RP. Tel: (01892) 890554

Mr and Mrs Richard Bird • 10m SE of Tonbridge off A21. 2m S of Lamberhurst turn left to Kilndown, and in village take 1st right into Chicks Lane; garden is on right • Open 28th May and 1th June, 11am – 5.30pm, and by appt for individuals and parties • Entrance: £3, children 50p NEW ◑ 🖳 WC ♿ ⌨

A gem of a garden – one and a half acres created by a plantsman who is also a garden writer. The setting is idyllic, with views out to farmland and Bedgebury Pinetum, where the neutral pH of the soil allows a wide variety of plants to be grown. Hedges of beech and yew enclose individual rooms filled with cottage-garden plants, and the small, well-planted pond is fringed with interesting moisture-lovers. The scent within the rose garden is almost overwhelming. The meandering paths encourage the visitor to seek out surprises round every corner – *Azara lanceolata*, a white-berried sorbus, magnolias, mature shrubs with decorative foliage and a *Drimys winteri*.

Scotney Castle Garden and Estate ★ [Historic Garden Grade I]
Lamberhurst, Tunbridge Wells TN3 8JN. Tel: (01892) 891081

The National Trust • 8m SE of Tunbridge Wells, 1m S of Lamberhurst on E side of A21 • Old Castle open as garden • Garden open late March to Oct – telephone for details • Entrance: £4.80, children £2.40, family £12. Pre-booked parties (weekdays only) £4.20 per person • Other information: Possible for wheelchairs but hilly approach. Dogs in park only ◑ 🏮 <u>WC</u> ♿ ⌨ 🏧 🍴 ⌕

This is an unusual garden designed in the Picturesque style by the Hussey family, following the tradition established by William Kent and using the services of the artist and landscape gardener William Gilpin, who also advised on the site of the new house, completed in 1843. The landscape garden includes smaller garden layouts in the overall area. A formal garden overlooks a quarry garden and the grounds of the Old Castle enclose a herbaceous border backed by roses and clematis; there is also a herb garden. The lakeside planting adds an air of informality. Evergreens and deciduous trees provide the mature planting, linking shrubs and plants to give something in flower at every season. Daffodils, magnolias, rhododendrons and azaleas are the most spectacular; also notable are the kalmias, hydrangeas and wisterias. In a good autumn, the colours are amazing. The planting is intentionally occasional and haphazard, 'Picturesque' in the true sense, but visit this garden for its setting on a slope that gives fine views of open countryside, and for the romantic eighteenth- to nineteenth-century theme uniting it.

Sissinghurst Castle Garden ★★ [Historic Garden Grade I]

Sissinghurst, Cranbrook TN17 2AB. Tel: (01580) 710700 (Infoline)

The National Trust • 13m S of Maidstone, 2m NE of Cranbrook, 1m E of Sissinghurst on A262 • Open 18th March to 29th Oct, Mon, Tues, Fri, 11am – 6.30pm, Sat, Sun and Bank Holiday Mons, 10am – 6.30pm (last admission 5.30pm or dusk if earlier). Parties of 11 or more by appt. Garden much quieter after 3.30pm • Entrance: £7.50, children £3.50, family £18.50 • Other information: Coaches by appt. Wheelchairs restricted to two chairs at one time because of narrow, uneven paths; pushchairs not admitted ● ⬤ ✕ 🍴 WC ♿ ♨ 🏠 ♀ ♋ B&B

'Profusion, even extravagance and exuberance within the confines of the utmost linear severity', was Vita Sackville-West's description of her design when creating Sissinghurst with her husband Harold Nicolson. It is a romantic garden within a formal framework, with seasonal features throughout the year. Certain colour schemes have been followed, as in the purple border, the orange and yellow cottage garden, and the white garden, which is probably the most beautiful garden at Sissinghurst, itself one of the outstanding gardens in the world. The Nicolsons added little to, but saved much of, the Elizabethan mansion. The site was first occupied in the twelfth century, when a moated manor was built where the orchard now stands. The long library and Elizabethan tower are open and the latter is well worth climbing in order to see the perspective of the whole garden and surrounding area. All is kept in immaculate condition, well labelled, with changing vistas at every turn of the winding paths or more formal walks. The rose garden contains many old-fashioned roses as well as flowering shrubs such as *Ceanothus impressus* and *Hydrangea villosa*, which together with iris, clematis and pansies fill the area. There is a thyme lawn leading to the herb garden filled with fragrance and charm. It is a truly magnificent example of Englishness and has had immense influence on garden design because of its structure of separate outdoor rooms within the garden. *Knole*, home to the Sackville family since 1603, will also be of interest to Vita's admirers, since she was born and brought up there. The house and its park (listed Grade I by English Heritage) were in her bones: 'It has the tone of England. It melts into the green of the garden turf, into the tawnier green of the park beyond, into the blue of the pale English sky.' (Park open daily, Lord Sackville's garden on the first Wednesday of each month, May to September.)

Southover

Grove Lane, Hunton, Maidstone ME15 0SE. Tel: (01622) 820876

Mr and Mrs David Way • 6m S of Maidstone between A229 and B2010. From Yalding take Vicarage Road to Hunton. Almost opposite school turn left into Grove Lane; house is about 180 metres on right. From Coxheath turn down Hunton Hill to Hunton; Grove Lane is immediately past school • Open for NGS, and by appt; parties welcome • Entrance: £3, accompanied children free • Other information: Wheelchair users must be accompanied ● ⅃

The typical fifteenth-century timber-framed Kentish house lies in the centre of a gently south-sloping site and is surrounded by a garden full of plants and diversity. Work started in 1980. The foundations of a much larger house were uncovered and planted with hedges to enclose a true garden room. Two ponds, filled in over the centuries, have been redeveloped – one re-excavated, the other planted as a damp garden. Higher up, a bank flows with ground-cover plants. Beyond is a woodland walk and wildflower meadow. The upper spring garden is complemented by an autumn border, with three new beds of winter- and spring-flowering bulbs, including many snowdrop cultivars. Nearer the house are two 'secret' garden rooms. The one adjoining the house has a large central paved area surrounded by borders containing a wide range of perennials blended with biennials and annuals, at its best in May and June. The other has recently been replanted in a formal design with cool greens and soft yellows. A third enclosure has been developed as a *potager*. Impressive herbaceous borders to the south of the house contain many unusual plants, especially penstemons. Other features are a sunken walk in green and white, a fern bank and a brown garden featuring sedges and grasses.

Squerryes Court [Historic Garden Grade II]

Westerham TN16 1SJ. Tel: (01959) 562345/563118

Mr and Mrs John Warde • 0.5m W of Westerham on A25, near M25 junctions 5 and 6 • House open as garden, but 1 – 5pm • Garden open April to Sept, Wed, Thurs, Sun and Bank Holiday Mons, 12 noon – 5.30pm. Parties of 20 or more by appt • Entrance: £3.60, OAPs £3.30, children under 14 £2, family £7; (house and garden £5.50, OAPs £5, children £3, family £13) (2005 prices). Reduced rates for pre-booked parties ◑ ▆ ▆ wc ⅃ ✑ ⚏

The 20 acres of gardens, laid out around 1700 in the formal Anglo-Dutch style, were landscaped again in the eighteenth century. The view over the large lake leads to a gazebo, built around 1740, from where a former member of the family used to watch his racehorses in training; nearby is a fine old dovecot. The main feature is the restored formal area to the rear of the house; a 1719 print has been used as an outline on which to base the changes. These reflect the mellow brickwork of the handsome house; beds, edged with box, contain lavender, purple sage and santolina, and two long Edwardian borders have been planted with roses and herbaceous perennials. All are framed by well-kept yew hedges. There are several other mixed borders and a Victorian rockery with fine examples of topiary. The woodland garden, currently being restored, contains rhododendron and azalea shrubberies and a broad variety of spring bulbs. Many fine magnolias around the house and a cenotaph in memory of General Wolfe (a family friend) complete a most attractive garden.

Stoneacre

Otham, Maidstone ME15 8RS. Tel: (01622) 862871

The National Trust • 3m SE of Maidstone, 1m S of A20 from Bearsted, at N end of Otham • House open • Garden open mid-March to mid-Oct, Wed, Sat and Bank Holiday Mons, 2 – 6pm (last admission 5pm), and at other times by appt • Entrance: house and garden £2.60, children £1.30 • Other information: Disabled parking at gate. Picnics in car park ◑ & ⚘

The Kentish hall house was restored and embellished in the 1920s by Aymer Vallance, Oxford aesthete, writer and friend of William Morris. Rosemarry Alexander of The English Gardening School was the Trust's tenant until she moved to Sandhill Farm House (see entry in Hampshire). Within the framework of yew hedges and ragstone walls, the current tenants have considerably reworked the charming garden of borders and lawns along more sculptural and textured lines. The lawns and hedges have been reshaped to reflect the surrounding landscape. The gardens at the front of the house contain borders with unusual colour schemes, including one with many interesting black and dark plants. At the rear of the house is a wild garden – particularly beautiful when the cow parsley is in bloom – with an apple orchard and three ponds.

Walmer Castle [Historic Garden Grade II]

Kingsdown Road, Walmer, Deal CT14 7LJ. Tel: (01304) 364288

English Heritage • On coast 2m S of Walmer on A258, off M20 at junction 13 or from M2 to Deal • Castle open • Garden open March to Sept, daily, 10am – 6pm (closes 4pm March); Oct, Wed – Sun, 10am – 4pm; Closed Nov to Feb and when Lord Warden in residence. Telephone in advance of visit to check, particularly in Oct and winter months • Entrance: castle and garden £5.95, concessions £4.50, children (5–16) £3, family £14.90 (2005 prices) • Other information: Pre-booked guided garden tours for parties £40. Electric wheelchair available. Guide dogs only ◐ ● ✕ 🍴 wc & ⚘ ⊞ ℗ ℺

English Heritage is restoring the gardens of this, the official residence of the Warden of the Cinque Ports, to their former status in the early twentieth century. The castle overlooks the sea and the 10-acre gardens are surrounded by shelter belts and meadows. The formal core of the garden consists of three areas. The first is a double herbaceous border backed by large crinkle-crankle yew hedges ending in terraces with a croquet lawn. Then comes a traditional kitchen garden with a cut-flower area producing decoration for the castle, and a vegetable area with espaliered apple and pear trees, cold frames and glasshouses. Finally the late Queen Mother's Garden, situated in the old walled garden, was redesigned by Penelope Hobhouse to commemorate her late Majesty's 95th birthday. It includes a 30-metre-long formal pond, yew pyramids, box topiary and a mount topped by yew hedges clipped in the shape of a castle. A dry moat is planted with roses and shrubs. An informal woodland walk encircles a wildflower meadow, and there are picnic tables and deck chairs on the oval lawn from which to relax and enjoy it all. The restored glasshouse displays a range of conservatory plants, providing an added attraction in winter and early spring.

Waystrode Manor ★

Spode Lane, Cowden, Edenbridge TN8 7HW. Tel: (01342) 850695

Mrs Jill Wright • 8m W of Tunbridge Wells, 4.5m S of Edenbridge, off B2026 Edenbridge – Hartfield road • Open some Weds and Suns from May to July for NGS • Entrance: £3, children £1 ◐ ☕ WC ♿ ✿ 🛍

This eight-acre garden on Wealden clay has been developed over the last thirty years and surrounds a beautiful half-timbered sixteenth-century house. An avenue of red-candled horse chestnut trees leads to the house, which is flanked on one side by an old barn supporting wisteria, clematis, actinidia and schizophragma. A stone-flagged area at the rear has herbs growing out of it and, as a central feature, an old mill grinding-wheel planted with low-growing plants. From the house the eye is led via the serpent fountain garden to a small yew-enclosed white garden. A large and decorative wooden building contains tender and tropical plants. There are several pergolas, clad with wisteria, laburnum and roses. Two small pools connected by a waterfall are crossed by a charming arched bridge. Borders of irises, old roses and geraniums are dotted around, and the whole is complemented by some excellent and unusual specimen trees, such as *Ulmus minor* 'Dampieri Aurea', *Abies koreana*, *Betula utilis* var. *jacquemontii*, *Cedrus deodara* 'Pendula' and a collection of unusual oaks.

Weeks Farm

Bedlam Lane, Egerton Forstal, Ashford TN27 9DA. Tel: (01233) 756252

Robin and Monica De Garston • 2.5m E of Headcorn. From Headcorn, take Smarden road, then third turning on left. House is 1.5m on right • Open for NGS, and by appt (please telephone evenings) • Entrance: £2 (2005 price) ◐ WC ♿ 💡

The two-acre garden is informally laid out round a typical Kent farmhouse. The prime asset here is a glorious annual display of naturalised spring bulbs, started thirty years ago by the previous owner on a badly drained site, and topped up annually with more bulbs – hyacinths, daffodils and tulips. A new pond, linked to an older one, is generously stocked with fish. The overall effect is much more than a cottage garden, with subtle oriental elements such as bamboos repeated throughout, and for good measure there are two deep mixed borders lining the sweeping drive.

Yalding Organic Gardens

Benover Road, Yalding, Maidstone ME18 6EX. Tel: (01622) 814650

HDRA – the organic organisation • 6m SW of Maidstone, 0.5m S of Yalding on B2162 • Open April to Oct, Wed – Sun and Bank Holiday Mons; Nov to Dec, Sat and Sun; all 10am – 5pm • Entrance: £4, concessions £3.50, children £1, parties of 14 or more £3 (£1 extra for garden tour) ◑ ☕ ✕ WC ♿ ✿ 🛍 💡 🔍

The pergola of hop poles at the heart of Yalding links the gardens closely to the surrounding oasts and hop gardens of Kent. They offer a tour through gardening history, beginning with the natural woodland that once dotted our hills and valleys. Visitors pass through a thirteenth-century apothecary's garden, an Elizabethan Paradise Garden and Tudor knot, an early-nineteenth-century cottager's plot, a Victorian artisan's garden with an original nineteenth-century glasshouse, sweeping Edwardian borders and a utilitarian 1950s' allotment before being shown an organic vision of the future. A children's garden ands a new garden aimed at encouraging beginners of all ages to grow their own organic food complete the tour. Impressive, well-kept and an experience for the whole family.

POSTCODE PLANTS DATABASE

It is often difficult to find out which plants are local to an area. The Postcode Plants Database locates the names of flowers, trees, butterflies and birds for each of Britain's 26 million home addresses. The website is www.nhm.ac.uk/science/projects/fff; simply by typing in the first four characters of their postcode, householders, schools, garden centres and councils can obtain tailor-made lists of local plants which are both hospitable and garden-worthy. Also included are the names of butterflies and birds most likely to visit gardens in each area. The lists come from innovative software, developed by Royal Mail and *FLORA-for-FAUNA* in conjunction with the Natural History Museum, which searches through hundreds of distribution maps of fauna and flora in the British Isles.

GARDENING WEBSITES

Many gardens now have their own websites, and we list these at the back of the *Guide*. Others useful for garden visitors are:

Dept of Environment (Ireland): www.heritageireland.ie
English Heritage: www.english-heritage.org.uk
Historic Houses Association: www.hha.org.uk
Historic Royal Palaces: www.hrp.org.uk
Historic Scotland: www.historic-scotland.gov.uk
Landmark Trust: www.landmarkrust.org.uk
National Gardens Scheme: www.ngs.org.uk
National Trust: www.nationaltrust.org.uk
National Trust for Scotland: www.nts.org.uk
Royal Horticultural Society: www.rhs.org.uk
Welsh Historic Monuments: www.cadw.wales.gov.uk

SYMBOLS

NEW entries new for 2006; ○ open all year; ◔ open most of year; ◑ open during main season; ◕ open rarely and/or by appt; ☕ teas/light refreshments; ✕ meals; 🧺 picnics permitted; WC toilet facilities; WC toilet facilities, inc. disabled; ♿ partly wheelchair-accessible; 🐕 dogs on lead; ✿ plants for sale; 🛍 shop; 🎈 events held; ⚲ children-friendly; B&B bed and breakfast available.

LANCASHIRE

Two-starred gardens are marked on the map with a black square.

Ashton Memorial [Historic Garden Grade II]

Williamson Park, Quernmore Road, Lancaster LA1 1UX. Tel: (01524) 33318

E of Lancaster town centre. Signposted • Open all year, daily except 25th, 26th Dec and 1st Jan, 10am – 5pm (closes 4pm Oct to March) • Entrance: park and ground floor of memorial with exhibition free; memorial viewing gallery 50p; butterfly house, mini-beast house, conservation garden and free-flying bird enclosure £3.50, OAPs £3, children £2 ○ 💀 WC ᓬ 💠 ⛫ 🍴 ♿

Ashton Memorial, designed in 1906 by John Belcher in Baroque Revival style and described by Pevsner as 'the grandest monument in England', stands at the highest point of Williamson Park looking down on the town of Lancaster. There are many views of the surrounding country from various points in the superbly landscaped park. Broad paths run through the grounds, much of which is woodland with an underplanting of rhododendrons and other shrubs. A small lake is spanned by a stone bridge, and nearby a large stairway leads to the huge domed monument. Not far away is the butterfly house (also by Belcher) and pavilion. A three-year restoration programme for the park and woodland is due to be completed in 2007.

Clearbeck House

Higher Tatham, Lancaster LA2 8PJ. Tel: (01524) 261029

Peter and Bronwen Osborne • 10m E of Lancaster. From M6 junction 34 take A683 towards Kirkby Lonsdale, turn right on B6480 and follow signposts from Wray village • Open 28th May, 25th June, 2nd July, 11am – 5pm, and for parties by appt • Entrance: £2.50, children free ● 💀 WC ᓬ 💠 🌿 ♿

An individual creation that works on many levels. On the bigger plan Rousham (see entry in Oxfordshire) has been of influence, with vistas presenting views across stretches of water and swathes of grass to the impressive moorland beyond, punctuated by sculptures, ornaments and follies. In some areas space is more enclosed, and here the influence is Sissinghurst (see entry in Kent). An allegorical theme inspires some parts – the Garden of Life and Death with its unique pyramid, a maze and a folly named Rapunzel's Tower all have a story behind them. A most successful recent addition is a temple sitting at the base of a group of noble poplar trees and overlooking a pool. Behind is a mount where some visual trickery is intended – indeed a sense of fun pervades the garden. The sculpture is varied and often thought-provoking, but whether classical or modern it is placed to play an integral role in the structure of the garden. There is strong planting too, with beds of mixed perennials surrounding the stone cottage, marsh lovers fringing the pools and streams, and a large collection of shrub roses with many scented varieties. Water is present throughout, and the largest pool attracts a lot of wildlife – 67 bird species noted in a single year. Perhaps the greatest achievement here is the way the garden sits so perfectly within the landscape.

Gawthorpe Hall [Historic Garden Grade II]

Padiham, Burnley BB12 8UA. Tel: (01282) 771004

Lancashire County Council (on lease from National Trust) • 2.5m NW of Burnley, N of A671 just E of Padiham town centre • Hall open April to Oct, daily except Mon and Fri (but open Good Friday and Bank Holiday Mons), 1 – 5pm • Gardens open all year, daily, 10am – 6pm • Entrance: free (hall £3, concessions £1.50, children free) • Other information: Refreshments only when hall open ○ 🍺 🍴 WC ♿ ✧ 🏛 ♿

This garden, though botanically not particularly special, sets off the Elizabethan hall. To the front is a formal layout of lawns and gravel paths, and to the rear a parterre by Sir Charles Barry in the form of a sunburst overlooks the River Calder. The woodlands that surround the formal garden are planted with rhododendrons and azaleas and traversed by many walks, with views back to the house and across the valley.

Gresgarth Hall ★★

Caton LA2 9NB. Tel: (01524) 771838

Sir Mark and Lady Lennox-Boyd • 4m NE of Lancaster. From M6 junction 34 take A683 towards Kirkby Lonsdale, then turn right in Caton village, signed to Quernmore • Open 9th April, 14th May, 11th June, 9th July, 13th Aug, 10th Sept, 11am – 5pm • Entrance: £5 ● 🍺 WC ♿ ✿

You expect something special from the garden of such a renowned designer as Arabella Lennox-Boyd, and you will not be disappointed. Over this large area she has experimented with different styles of gardening and produced some superb results – all the more surprising since the weather in this part of northern Lancashire can be harsh. At the front of the house are formal areas – herbaceous borders, protected by yew hedges and to the south a pool and bog garden with a large selection of ferns and other moisture-lovers. An arboretum contains a large sequoiadendron, acers, lilacs and many other fine specimens, while the walled garden has a happy mix of vegetables, fruit and flowering plants. To the east an attractive terrace and belvedere overlook a rocky beck that rushes through this part of the garden. A Chinese bridge leads to a woodland garden where azaleas, cornus, magnolias and many unusual plants flourish in the light shade. Sculpture, classical and modern, is used creatively throughout. There are woodland walks, a huge variety of plants and so much else that this description can only serve as the briefest of introductions to a fine garden. Evolution continues: several hundred trees and shrubs and a new herbaceous border were planted in 2004.

Hawthornes Nursery Garden

Marsh Road, Hesketh Bank, nr Preston PR4 6XT. Tel: (01772) 812379

Mr and Mrs Richard Hodson • 10m SW of Preston. Take A59 towards Liverpool, turn right at traffic lights signed to Tarleton, then on to Hesketh Bank • Open several days for NGS, and by appt • Entrance: £2, children free • Other information: Telephone for nursery opening times NEW ● 🍺 WC ♿ ✧ ✿ ♿

There is a welcome trend among nurserymen to open their own private gardens to visitors, enabling them to see many of the specimens for sale in their full mature splendour. Here, laid out informally as beds and sweeping grass paths, a tremendous number and variety of plants that thrive in a rich silt marshland with a high pH grow within the one-acre garden. There are over 150 shrub roses, including many species and old-fashioned varieties – damasks, hybrid musks, centifolias and a few Bourbons. Old and new varieties of *rugosa* hybrids feature too. Clematis are Mr Hodson's other love. He has managed to assemble 200 of them, including many *viticella* hybrids and some rare herbaceous varieties; many begin flowering as the roses come to an end. Perennials are abundant too, with pulmonarias, campanulas, geraniums, hemerocallis and aconitums extending the flowering season. Close to the entrance is a large wildlife pond.

Hoghton Tower [Historic Garden Grade II]

Hoghton, Preston PR5 0SH. Tel: (01254) 852986

Hoghton Tower Preservation Trust • 5m SE of Preston, mid-way between Preston and Blackburn, on old A675 • House open for guided tours (£5, OAPs and students £4, children £4, family £16) • Garden open July to Sept, Mon – Thurs, 11am – 4pm, Sun, 1 – 5pm; also Bank Holiday Suns and Mons (except Christmas and New Year). Private tours by arrangement • Entrance: £2 ◐ 💺 ✕ <u>WC</u> ও ⬸

The Tower, a sixteenth-century fortified manor house built of local stone, occupies a hilltop position with good views to all sides and outwards to the surrounding countryside. The house and outbuildings are constructed around two courtyards which, although not qualifying as gardens, are fine spaces. Surrounding the house are three walled gardens. The first, the Wilderness, contains a large lawn and herbaceous borders. The second, the rose garden, has a rectangular lawn flanked on two sides by clipped yews; in the centre is a raised square pond with an elaborate stone fountain. The third is mainly lawn with access to the tops of two crenellated towers. Around the walled gardens runs the Long Walk, which passes under large beech trees and holly trees (especially weeping hollies) and is planted with shrubs, mainly rhododendrons and azaleas. There is a tradition that Shakespeare lived here during a formative period, and James I knighted a piece of beef 'Sirloin' on 17th August 1617.

Leighton Hall

Carnforth LA5 9ST. Tel: (01524) 734474

Mr R.G. Reynolds • 8m N of Lancaster, 1m W of Yealand Conyers, signed from M6 junction 35 • House open as garden • Gardens open May to Sept, Tues – Fri, Bank Holiday Suns and Mons, 2 – 5pm (opens Aug, Tues – Fri, Suns and Bank Holiday Mon, 12.30 – 5pm). Open in winter for parties only by appt • Entrance: house and garden £5.50, OAPs £5, children £4, parties of 25 or more £4.50 per person, schools £3 per child (2004 prices) • Other information: Dogs in park only, on lead ◐ 💺 🏵 <u>WC</u> ও 🌿 ⛪ 🍴 ☕

Very striking when first seen from the entrance gates, the white stone facade (c. 1822) shines out in its parkland setting with the hills of the Lake District visible beyond. The most interesting area of the gardens, which lie to the west of the house, is the walled garden with its unusual labyrinth in the form of a gravel path running under an old cherry orchard. Opposite is a vegetable garden made in a geometric design with grass paths. There are also herbaceous borders and an aromatic herb garden containing a wide variety of perennials, with climbing roses on the wall behind. High summer is a good time to visit.

Mill Barn ★

Goose Foot Close, Samlesbury Bottoms, Preston PR5 0SS. Tel: (01254) 853300

Dr C.J. Mortimer • 6m E of Preston on A677 Blackburn road, turn S into Nabs Head Lane, then Goose Foot Lane • Open 17th and 18th June, 11am – 5pm, and mid-June to mid-July by appt • Entrance: £2, children free • Other information: 'Art and Garden' exhibition 17th and 18th June. Refreshments and plants for sale on open days ● WC ♿ ⟐ ☕ ♿ B&B

On the site of an old mill by the River Darwen, this garden has been designed to make the most of its superb setting. A path leads along a high stone embankment overlooking the fast-flowing river. It passes through a series of features: a unique temple to alchemy created from an old sluice gate, a rose-clad pergola, a picturesque ruin constructed to hide a septic tank. Near here a fine 'Paul's Himalayan Musk' rose climbs high up into a tree. Finally there is a rectangular pool set into the wall containing a good variety of water plants and marginals, with a stretch of lawn and an heptagonal summerhouse beyond. A long herbaceous border runs back to the house, containing plants chosen for their contrasting foliage and architectural effects. A bridge crosses the river giving access to a belvedere looking back over the garden. The quarry is becoming a secret garden in a modern style.

The Old Zoo Garden ★

Brockhall Village BB6 8DX. Tel: (01254) 244330

Gerald and Linda Hitman • 5m N of Blackburn, turn N off A59, W of junction with A666. Take minor road signed Old Langho and Brockhall Village • Open 30th June, 2nd July, 2 – 6pm. Also open all year for guided tours of parties of 20 or more staying or eating at Avenue Hotel nearby • Entrance: £4, children £1.50 NEW ● ⬤ ✕ WC ♿ ⟐ ♨ ☕ ♿ B&B

Although these sensational gardens are thoroughly modern in concept and design, there is an underlying feeling of the medieval pleasure grounds about them. The asymmetric and slightly austere house designed by Homa and Sima Farjardi sits perfectly within the 15-acre gardens and surrounding landscape. The use of water is spectacular. At the front a clear pool and canal are surrounded by a dramatic planting of phormiums, bamboos, rhus and pines, and from these a stream passes through a series of rocky pools under the house to emerge at a large area of decking that converts to a swimming pool. A long rill projects outwards across the terrace towards a stunning panorama of the Ribble Valley. To the north, looking for all the world like a medieval mount inverted, is an excavated spiral with a cascade flowing to a pool at its base. Below the terrace a unique step maze and an elongated hedge maze set out to puzzle the visitor. Magnificent sculptures appear throughout the garden, together with some notable green oak shelters designed by Derek Goffin. A small wooded valley is well planted with drifts of primulas, gunneras, hostas, hemerocallis and ligularias and backed by golden elder. There are more fine sculptures here and a bridge that incorporates a large curved tree trunk. A hot tub has a lid that has to be seen to be believed, and a *boules* rink is set within a glade of alders. Further up is a croquet lawn surrounded by banks of thickly planted *Rosa alba* 'Meidiland', with gravel paths and rough-hewn stone steps winding up through swathes of hostas and grasses, tubs of cloud trees also add a distinctive note. At the bottom of the valley is a wildlife lake surrounded by lush green foliage with a plantation of Lancashire apple trees on one bank. A garden of many delights.

Pendle Heritage Centre

Park Hill, Barrowford, Nelson BB9 6JQ. Tel: (01282) 661701

The Heritage Trust for the North West • N of Nelson, near M65 junctions 13 and 14. In Barrowford at A682/B6247 junction • Open all year, daily except 25th Dec, 10am – 5pm. Parties welcome by appt • Entrance: Walled garden, barn and woodland £1.20, concessions 80p. Museum £1, concessions 80p (2005 prices) ○ 🍽 ✕ <u>WC</u> ♿ ℗ 🏛 ♨ ❧

In the centre of Barrowford among a group of fine old stone buildings (eight Grade-II-listed) is a walled garden dating from the 1780s. This has been restored and replanted under the guidance of the NCCPG, using only plants that were available in the eighteenth century. There are culinary and medicinal herbs and plants that were used in the production of dyes, as well as traditional varieties of fruit and vegetables. All plants are organically grown in beds divided by gravel paths and edged in clipped box. A woodland walk takes the visitor up a steep wooded bank planted with native wild flowers to a viewing point that looks back over the garden and surrounding countryside to a cruck-frame barn saved and re-erected on the site.

The Ridges

Limbrick, Chorley PR6 9EB. Tel: (01257) 279981

Mr and Mrs J.M. Barlow • From M61 junction 8 follow signs for Chorley on A6, then for Cowling and Rivington • Open June and July, Wed and Bank Holiday Suns and Mons, 11am – 5pm (closed Easter); and by appt at other times • Entrance: £2.50, children free ● 🍽 WC ♿ ✑ ℗ B&B

In the first area of the garden, shaded by fruit trees, a herbaceous border reaches its full flowering in mid- to late summer. The eighteenth-century house has French windows leading onto a small lawn. This is part of the old walled garden, where two arches over seating have been thoughtfully planted with jasmines, fragrant climbing roses and herbs. Highly scented David Austin rambling roses trail through apple trees and trellises. A natural-looking stream fringed by wild flowers and moisture-lovers ends in a little pool, and an Italianate water feature is set into the old orchard wall, with a dovecot standing on a circle of paving nearby. A path leads beneath a laburnum arch and between two large thujas into another garden where a mock-ornamental pool and urn are at the centre of a large rectangular lawn surrounded by woodland, with beds of perennials, shrubs and trees.

Rivington Terraced Gardens

(see Manchester)

Rufford Old Hall

Rufford, Ormskirk L40 1SG. Tel: (01704) 821254

The National Trust • 7m NE of Ormskirk, N of Rufford, E of A59 • House open as garden but 1pm – 5pm. Garden open 25th March to 29th Oct, Sat – Wed, 11am – 5.30pm. Telephone for winter opening times • Entrance: £2.80, children £1.30 (house and garden £4.90, children £2.50, family £12) ◑ 💻 ✕ 🍴 <u>WC</u> ♿ 🚾 ☕

The gardens complement the exceptional sixteenth-century timber-framed house, having been laid out by the Trust in the style of the Victorian/Edwardian period. On the south are lawns and gravel paths designed in a formal manner. The many island beds are formal in layout, too, but the shrubs, small trees and herbaceous plants they contain are planted in a more relaxed way. In the centre, a path leads from two large topiary squirrels to a beech avenue that extends beyond the garden towards Rufford. There are many mature trees and rhododendrons in this area dating back to the 1820s. To the east of the house by the stables is an attractive cobbled space with climbing plants on the surrounding walls. Look out for the cottage garden to the north side of the house, in which grow many old-fashioned plants enclosed by a rustic wooden fence.

Towneley Park [Historic Park Grade II]

Todmorden Road, Burnley BB11 3RQ. Tel: (01282) 424213

Burnley Borough Council • 1.5m SE of Burnley on A671 • House open all year, Mon – Thurs, Sat and Sun, 12 noon – 5pm. Closed Christmas week • Park open all year, daily during daylight hours • Entrance: free • Other information: Shop in hall ◯ 🍴 <u>WC</u> ♿ 🕮 ☕

The hall dates from 1500, but its exterior is largely the work of 1816 to 1820. The frontage looks out over a pond and beyond a ha-ha to open parkland laid out in the late eighteenth century. There are some formal beds to the east of the house planted with bright annuals. Herbaceous plants and shrubs have been chosen for the area around the hall, and the Small Lime Walk has been opened up by removing old rhododendrons, replacing them with a better selection of choice shrubs and ground cover. Further to the east, as well as to the south and west, are extensive woodlands containing many large rhododendrons, and long walks. There is also a museum of local history.

Woodside

Princes Park, Shevington, Wigan, Manchester WN6 8HY. Tel: (01257) 255255

Barbara and Bill Seddon • 3m NW of Wigan. From M6 junction 26 or 27 follow signs for Shevington • Open by appt • Entrance: £2, children 50p ◕

This is a suburban garden of two thirds of an acre on an attractively undulating site, surrounded by mature trees. Broad grass paths designed to accentuate the landscaping lead round beds of mainly acid-loving plants – azaleas, rhododendrons, camellias, magnolias, acers and conifers. Of particular note are collections of hostas, peonies and hellebores. An attractive water feature stands at the centre of the garden – a large stone trough with water bubbling up through stones guarded by a pair of ornamental geese. The well-established herbaceous border is delightful from mid-June until September, and in August dozens of hydrangeas and three mature *Eucryphia x nymansensis* are in flower. There is also a stone-banked dell excavated at one end of the garden and a waterfall. Everything is exceptionally well kept, and there is a surprising amount to see and an enviable number of plants. Recent additions are a well-planted gravel bed with driftwood features and a greenhouse imaginatively screened by a clematis-covered trellis.

Worden Park [Historic Garden Grade II]

Leyland PR25 2DJ. Tel: (01772) 422316

Borough of South Ribble • 4m S of Preston. Take B5253 S from Leyland. Signposted • Open all year, daily, 8am – dusk • Entrance: free • Other information: Refreshments at craft centre ○ 🏠 WC & ⊕ ⚑ ⚲

The gardens are set around part of an old house and a stable block that now contains craft and theatre workshops (the rest of the house was burnt down in the 1940s). The maze is unusual, being made of hornbeam hedges in a circular pattern. A little distance away is a large conservatory with a rockery to one side and a herbaceous border to the other, facing a formal sunken lawned area enclosed by a low balustrade and some fine ironwork gates. Large areas of open parkland surround the gardens, which contain a children's adventure play area, mini golf, a model railway, an ice-house and an arboretum. Areas in the parkland are being developed to attract wildlife.

RESEARCHING GARDEN HISTORY

The Register of Parks and Gardens of Special Historic Interest is the official record of the nation's historic landscapes produced by English Heritage. It has been substantially revised and upgraded, parks and gardens added, and threatened landscapes 'spot-registered'. At the beginning of August 2005, the total number of entries was 1588. Each site is documented in a description of its historical evolution, accompanied by specially drawn paper maps delineating the historical boundaries of the park or garden and chronicling its development.

The *Register* is available for public consultation at English Heritage's National Monuments Record Centre in Swindon (open Tues – Fri, 9.30am – 5pm). Copies of individual entries or complete county registers can also be purchased and sent by post. For more information contact NMR Enquiry & Research Services (Tel: (01793) 414600; Fax (01793) 414606; Email: nmrinfo@english-heritage.org.uk). Additionally, each local planning authority will have a copy of the relevant descriptions and maps within their jurisdictions. Be sure to telephone in advance of a visit.

LEICESTERSHIRE

For gardens in Rutland, see pages 333–335.

Beeby Manor ★

Beeby LE7 3BL. Tel: (01162) 595238

Mr and Mrs Philip Bland • 5m E of Leicester. Turn off A47 in Thurnby and follow signs through Scraptoft • Open by appt • Entrance: £2 ◐ 🏠 WC ♿

This atmospheric garden runs uphill from the house to a series of 'rooms' which feel lived-in and welcoming. The terrace near the house is laden with planters. In late April the purple tulips in tubs are sensational, with *Rosa banksiae* going mad on the wall behind. Different species of narcissus also abound. To the west of the front lawn a doorway beckons the visitor into a great hall of old clipped yew hedges, left quite plain with a formal lily pond in the centre. The exit on the other side leads to an impressive modern sculpture in a bay of its own with a swimming-pool garden on one side and a wild garden on the other; beyond is an infant arboretum. A long and wide herbaceous border returns to the house, where an old, poodle-clipped Portuguese laurel looks positively Japanese. A lot of variety here.

Belvoir Castle [Historic Garden Grade II]

Belvoir, Grantham, Lincolnshire NG32 1PD. Tel: (01476) 871002

The Duke of Rutland • 10m NE of Melton Mowbray off A607 by Belvoir. Signposted • Castle open • Garden open April to Sept, Tues – Thurs, Sat, Sun and Bank Holiday Mons; Oct, Sun; all 11am – 5pm (last admission 4pm). Spring garden open all year for pre-booked parties • Entrance: £5 (castle, rose and spring gardens £10, OAPs £9, children £5, family £26) (2005 prices). Telephone for details of spring garden charges for groups ◐ 💺 ✕ 🏠 WC ♿ 🎔 ⚑

The castle, straddling an isolated hill at the edge of the Vale of Belvoir, is the fourth to occupy this dramatic natural belvedere. The first was eleventh-century Norman, rebuilt after the Wars of the Roses, the third a mid-seventeenth-century house by John Webb with a remarkable sloping formal garden. All were swept away at the beginning of the nineteenth century, and James Wyatt's mock Gothic castle for the 5th Duke stands in their stead. On her return from the Grand Tour in 1819 the Duchess redesigned the garden in the Renaissance manner. By the mid-nineteenth century terraced gardens had been created, divided into smaller enclosures by the discreet use of topiary and hedging. During the 1870s spring bedding was introduced; now various areas are devoted to roses and peonies, and elsewhere snowdrops and daylilies are naturalised. In the early twentieth century the rose garden was laid out and yew hedges were planted around two sides of the garden. To the north-east runs a curving terrace path, probably the broadwalk depicted in Badeslade's view of 1731; some of the Caius Cibber statues which lined it are now in the Statue Garden. The present Duchess is moving the restoration and upkeep of these historic gardens forward with great care and taste. Her private woodland garden, known as the Spring Garden, was laid out in 1810; it is set in a natural amphitheatre and contains statuary and a recently restored hexagonal root house dating from 1841.

Goadby Hall

Goadby Marwood, Melton Mowbray LE14 4LN. Tel: (01664) 464202

Mr and The Hon. Mrs Westropp • 4m NE of Melton Mowbray between A606 and A607 • Open by appt only • Entrance: £3 • Other information: Teas by arrangement 🥢 WC ♿ 🔄 ♀ B&B

The approach to this exciting and romantic garden is at the head of a string of five ornamental lakes extending to over a mile. These have been dredged and restored to the beauty the Duke of Buckingham must have imagined when he created them in the eighteenth century. Surrounding the handsome manor house remodelled in the 1760s is a variety of separate gardens planted often in creams and greens and variegated plants to offset the dominance of the ironstone buildings and walls with many varieties of daffodils and tulips for spring colour. A children's garden leads to the croquet lawn, then past the church to the secret rose and west walled gardens. There is also a *potager* and a recently restored stable garden, and a small orchard. All have been brought back to life over the past three years with the love, imagination and hard work of the knowledgeable owner.

Long Close ★

Main Street, Woodhouse Eaves, Loughborough LE12 8RZ.
Tel: (01509) 890616 (business hours)

Mr J.T. Oakland and Miss P. Johnson • 5m S of Loughborough between A6 and M1 junctions 22 and 23 • Open March to July, Sept to Oct, Tues – Sat and Bank Holiday Mons, 9.30am – 1pm, 2 – 5.30pm, and two Suns for NGS. Parties by appt • Entrance: £3, children 50p • Other information: Tickets for daily visits to be purchased from Pene Crafts gift shop opposite the garden. Park in adjacent public car park. Teas on NGS open days, and for parties by arrangement only ◑ 🥢 WC ♿ 🔄 🌿 🍽 🍴

When Mr and Mrs George Johnson bought Long Close in 1949, they began to restore the five-acre garden, based on the framework and potential left by their predecessor, Colonel Gerald Heygate. Taking advantage of the lime-free loam, they nurtured a large collection of rhododendrons, azaleas and magnolias, which are now in magnificent maturity, adding many camellias and other shrubs and trees. Formal terraces lead to more informal gardens, with winding paths between specimen trees and finally to a natural dappled pool. In spring there are drifts of snowdrops, daffodils and bluebells and in summer prolifically planted herbaceous borders. The present owners have extended the plantings, created a *potager* and penstemon collection in the old walled kitchen garden, and laid out a new cottage garden. A courtyard plays its sheltered part with magnificent wall-covering plants. This is sometimes described as a Cornish garden in Leicestershire owing to the many quite tender trees and plants rarely to be found elsewhere so far north. Truly a plantsman's garden. For contrast, take a stroll along the ancient pasture wildflower meadow walk, freckled with orchids in June.

Orchards ★

Hall Lane, Walton, Lutterworth LE17 5RP. Tel: (01455) 556958

Mr and Mrs Graham Cousins • 4m E of M1 junction 20. In Lutterworth turn right at police station and follow signs to Kimcote and Walton. From Leicester take A5199 to Shearsby, then turn right signed to Bruntingthorpe and follow signs for Walton • Open 21st, 28th, 29th May, 18th June, 2 – 5pm, and by appt 21st May to 18th June • Entrance: £2.50, children free 🅿️ 🧺 WC ♿ ℗

An unusual garden of 1.25 acres, very much the creation of Mr Cousins. Vistas have been created throughout, and at one point the garden peers out over the surrounding countryside to remind one that there is a world outside this enchanting enclosure. There are a number of distinct areas, bounded by hornbeam hedges or upright shrubs such as hazel and viburnum, some cool and green, others bright with flowers chosen to emphasise the passage of the seasons. Trees, shrubs and climbers are shaped to underline their natural form and this gives the garden a sculptural quality. Though not primarily a plantsman's garden, there are many interesting and unusual plants here. Other features include an old orchard, an impressive wisteria draped over a large pergola, a circular reflective pool and a number of carvings and slate paving patterns by the owner's brother, Patrick Cousins.

Pine House

Gaddesby, Leicester LE7 4XE. Tel: (01664) 840213

Mr and Mrs Timothy Milward • 9m SW of Melton Mowbray off A607. At Rearsby turn E to Gaddesby • Open for private visits by appt • Entrance: £3, children free NEW ℗

The facade of the house is completely clothed in clipped pyracantha and the terrace looks out across a grass tennis court to open countryside. On either side are mature trees including a Wellingtonia, yews, oaks pines and a fine copper beech, with a woodland walk and water garden to be discovered amongst them. Behind the herbaceous border a hidden winding path leads to a rockery on one side with interesting plants everywhere. Behind the house is a small yellow and green topiary garden and a wisteria walk unusually planted for summer interest with gourds which hang down attractively to resemble Chinese lanterns. The tunnel goes to a Victorian vinery and a pot garden growing a wide variety of plants. A large gravel garden is a recent venture.

Stoke Albany House

Stoke Albany, Market Harborough LE16 8PT. Tel: (01858) 535227

Mr and Mrs Alfred Vinton • 4m E of Market Harborough. Turn S off A427 onto B669. Garden is 0.5m on left • Open 2nd April (Daffodil Sunday), then 7th, 14th, 21st, 28th June, 5th and 12th July, all 2 – 4.30pm • Entrance: £3, children free • Other information: Teas on Daffodil Sun only ℗ ♿ ℗

A country-house garden set in four acres with picturesque landscape sweeping beyond. There are fine trees and wide herbaceous borders, striped lawns, good displays of bulbs in spring and roses in June. The walled garden contains a *potager* with topiary, a grey garden, an avenue of *Nepeta* 'Six Hills Giant' arched with 'Mme Alfred Carrière' roses and clematis, a garden centred around a water feature, and a beautifully maintained greenhouse. There is also a Mediterranean garden, a rose-filled parterre and an autumn garden – tradition brought up to date in a perfect English setting.

Thorpe Lubbenham Hall

Lubenham, nr Market Harborough LE16 9TR. Tel: (01858) 433960

Sir Bruce and Lady McPhail • 3m W of Market Harborough on A4304 • Open by appt for individuals and groups • Entrance: £2.50, children free NEW ●

The red-brick Edwardian mansion stands handsomely in its spacious park. Dotted with fine trees ranging from oaks to Wellingtonias, the land rises on the southern side from the main façade of the house. The park was planted by the Philips family in the early twentieth century, while the 13 acres of garden are being restored and renewed by the present owners. The sunny front garden is sheltered by shrubberies. Here a terrace bears a fine array of daturas and other tender plants in pots; a sunken central area has a circular pool with a fine fountain edged with 'Iceberg' roses and lavender. Impressive herbaceous borders stretch along a walk near the house, and the enormous swimming pool, concealed behind clematis, a grape vine and wisteria, is surrounded by fragrant and colourful plantings of irises, hydrangeas, roses, dahlias and other perennial favourites. Most interesting of all, a short distance from the entrance driveway the moated site of a ruined house is being developed as a conservation garden, enticing birds, butterflies and wildlife with an array of nectar-bearing flowers, berries, seedheads and plenty of nesting boxes.

Ulverscroft Close

Ashby Road, Gilmorton LE17 5LY. Tel: (01455) 553226

Mr and Mrs Michael Maddock • 10m S of Leicester • Open by appt • Entrance £2.50 ● 💭 🏵 WC 🦽 🐾

Entered off the village street, the half-acre garden has great atmosphere and gives the immediate impression of being in loving hands. A fine conservatory containing, among other interesting plants, a *Lapageria rosea* stands on the upper level; from here a brick path leads to a short avenue of mop-head robinias adjoining a small box parterre. On the lower level is a pond and bog garden. A pergola of green oak supports roses and some of the 100 or so varieties of clematis to be found in the garden (July or August is the time to catch these at their best). Through an archway cut through the beech hedge may be glimpsed the vegetable garden, charmingly laid out in formal style and bordered by fruit trees and bushes.

Wartnaby Gardens ★

Wartnaby, Melton Mowbray LE14 3HY. Tel: (01664) 822549

Lady King • 4m NW of Melton Mowbray. From A606 turn W in Ab Kettleby for Wartnaby • Open April to July, Tues, 9.30am – 12.30pm, and by appt • Entrance:

£2.50, children free • Other information: Spring plant fair 26th Feb, 11am – 3pm, and 30th April, 11am – 4pm; summer plant fair and picture exhibition 18th June, 11am – 4pm ● ● ✕ wc ⓺ ⬀ ⁹

The garden has delightful little gardens within it, including a white garden, a rose garden, a border of shrubs and roses, good herbaceous borders, climbers and old-fashioned roses. Three large pools with primulas, astilbes, ferns, gunneras and several varieties of willow extend to further pools and woodland walks. There is an arboretum with a good collection of trees and shrubs. A long drive leads to the house, with an avenue of lime trees underplanted with beech hedging in a crenellated pattern. To round it all off is a well-furnished kitchen garden and orchard with arches and a collection of climbing roses and clematis.

GARDENING FOR THE DISABLED
- The Gardening for the Disabled Trust (Charity No. 255066) collects donations to assist people with improvements to their gardens, or to supply equipment which will enable them to continue to garden. Information from Mrs Angela Parish, Frittenden House, Nr Cranbrook TN17 2DG (Fax: (01580) 852120; Email: aparish@hotmail.com.
- Thrive is a national charity promoting the use of gardens and horticulture as a therapy for restricted or disabled gardeners (Tel: (0118) 988 5688; Email: info@thrive.org.uk; Website:www.thrive.org.uk or www.carryongardening.org.uk
- For information on the Disabled and Older Gardeners' Association (including workshops etc.), write to Growing Point, Holme Lacy College, Hereford or telephone Sue Eaton on (01432) 268876.
- Demonstration gardens to assist the disabled are on view at a number of properties open to the public and are also featured in the *Guide*. They include two in Battersea Park (for an appointment with the Horticultural Therapy Unit telephone (020) 7720 2212), Capel Manor and Broadview Garden.

GUIDANCE ON SYMBOLS
Wheelchair users: the symbol ⓺, denoting suitability for wheelchairs, refers to the garden only — if there is a house open, it may or may not be suitable. Additionally, some areas of the garden may not be accessible by wheelchair, or may require assistance.
Dogs: ⬀ indicates that there is somewhere on the premises where dogs may be walked, preferably on a lead. The garden itself is often taboo — parkland, or even the car park, are frequently indicated for the purpose.
Children-friendly: the bat-and-ball symbol ♘ suggests that there are activities specifically designed for children, such as an adventure playground or a discovery trail, or that the garden itself is likely to appeal to them.
Picnics: ● means that picnics are allowed, but usually in certain restricted areas only. It does not give visitors the all-clear to feast where they please!

LINCOLNSHIRE

Aubourn Hall ★

Aubourn, Lincoln LN5 9DZ. Tel: (01522) 788270

Lady Nevile • 7m SW of Lincoln between A46 and A607 • Open for charity some Suns, 2 – 5pm, and for parties by appt (telephone (0781) 6202 353) • Entrance: £3
◑ wc &

First impressions of the 10 acres of gardens surrounding the fine red-brick hall (c. 1600) are of spacious simplicity. Undulating lawns and borders sweep through rose arches or along grassy swathes to further lawns and gardens beyond. The enviably deep and diverse borders are carefully planted to give maximum effects of colour, shape and texture. There are also secluded areas in which to linger: the formal rose garden with its central tiered copper planter, the Golden Triangle edged with yew and planted with ornamental crab apple trees and spring bulbs, the ponds, the woodland dell and walks, and the swimming pool surrounded by a rose- and clematis-covered pergola. The grass maze is a new attraction. The nearby church, one of the smallest in Lincolnshire, is also open to visitors.

Ayscoughfee Hall [Historic Garden Grade II]

Churchgate, Spalding PE11 2RA. Tel: (01775) 761161

South Holland District Council • In centre of Spalding • Museum closed for refurbishment until Easter 2006 • Gardens open all year, daily except 25th Dec and 1st Jan, 8am – dusk • Entrance: free • Other information: Refreshments in main season ○ ⬤ ✕ 🦃 wc & 🍴

The gardens of the late-medieval wool merchant's house are in a beautiful setting next to the River Welland. Entirely enclosed by mellow old walls, they are worth visiting for the bizarrely shaped clipped yew walks, the old rectangular fish pond with fountains, and the interesting late-medieval red-brick hall, now housing the Museum of South Holland Life. In addition there are good bedding displays, particularly in the 1995 Garden of Peace, an ice-house, a garden for the visually impaired, lawns, a pergola and wall shrubs, including a fruiting vine.

Belton House ★ [Historic Garden Grade I]

Belton, Grantham NG32 2LS. Tel: (01476) 566116

The National Trust • 3m N of Grantham off A607 • House open 12.30 – 5pm • Gardens open 5th, 12th, 19th Feb for snowdrops; then 25th March to 29th Oct, Wed – Sun and Bank Holiday Mons, 11am – 5.30pm. Free access to park on foot from Lion Lodge gates all year (closed for special events), but this does not give admittance to house, garden or adventure playground • Entrance: gardens and grounds £6, children £3.50, family £15.50 ◑ ⬤ ✕ wc & ♿ 🍴 ✂

The park and gardens are, like the house, composed with perfect harmony and proportion. There are good views from first-floor windows of the formal gardens and of the East Avenue rising imperiously to the distant Bellmount Tower. The extensive woodland has two lakes, a small canal and noble cedars, and a maze re-created from the 1890 original. The radiating avenues are an impressive reminder of the late seventeenth- and early eighteenth-century predilection for introducing drama into the landscape. However, it is the formal area to the north of the house that makes a visit memorable. The 1870s' Dutch garden is a satisfying composition with pillars of green yew and cushions of golden yew, pale gravel, formal beds cleverly planted and edged with lavender, and generously filled urns. The earlier sunken Italian garden is more reliant on Wyatville's architectural features: a large central pond with a fountain, a lion-headed exedra and, the high point, the restored and replanted orangery. Behind the orangery a little church is glimpsed; it is filled with memorials to generations of Custs, who built the house, and Brownlows, who created the gardens.

Burghley House [Historic Park and Garden Grade II*]

Stamford PE9 3JY. Tel: (01780) 752451

Burghley House Preservation Trust. Custodian: Lady Victoria Leatham (née Cecil)
• 0.5m E of Stamford on Barnack road, close to A1. Signposted • House open April
to Oct, daily except Fri, 11am – 5pm • Entrance: £8.20, concessions £7.20, children
£3.70, family £21.00 • Sculpture garden and parkland open daily, 10am – 5pm
(closes 4pm in winter); South Garden open April • Entrance: £3, children £1
(free admission Nov to May) • Other information: Limited access for wheelchairs.
Dogs in park only, on lead ◑ 🍽 ✕ 🥾 <u>WC</u> ♿ 🍵 ⚲

The main attraction at Burghley is the Elizabethan house with its immense collection of art treasures, built by William Cecil, created Lord Burghley by his Queen. The parkland, landscaped by 'Capability' Brown, is delightful and extensive, even though in the process he swept away the George London Baroque garden of 1700 which had 'canals, rising flights of terraces, ornamental fish-pools, a maze, a vineyard and other conceits'. In addition to creating a large serpentine lake, Brown built a new stable block and an orangery. The finest surviving small building is his restored lakeside 'temple', which can be seen while the South Garden is open for its display of spring flowers in April. Twelve acres of garden have been reclaimed from woodland and extensively planted with specimen trees and shrubs. This area has an annually changing display of contemporary sculpture alongside a number of permanent sculptures, one of the most dramatic being a group emerging Excalibur-like from the surface of the lake.

21 Chapel Street

Hacconby, Bourne PE10 0UL. Tel: (01778) 570314

Mr and Mrs C. Curtis • 3m N of Bourne off A15, turn E at crossroads to Hacconby
• Open 18th and 19th Feb, 11am – 4pm (snowdrop and hellebore weekend), 2nd
March, 2 – 5pm, 17th April and 1st Oct, 11am – 5pm, and by appt • Entrance:
£1.50, children (under 16) free ◐ 🍽 🥾 <u>WC</u> ⚲

The gay and cottagey impression of this village garden has been achieved by minimising lawn area and replacing it with planting space. The circuitous path passes rockeries and scree beds, small trees and shrub roses, rustic arches, troughs and a pond, all exuberantly planted and underplanted to ensure year-round colour, from snowdrops in February to red, yellow and gold herbaceous plants in late summer and asters extending the season into October. There are hundreds of varieties of bulbs, alpines and herbaceous plants here to satisfy both the casual gardener and the seeker of the rare.

Croft House

Pitmoor Lane, Ulceby, Brigg DN39 6SW. Tel: (01469) 588330

Mr and Mrs P. Sandberg • 9m NW of Grimsby, 7m SE of Barton-upon-Humber on A1077 • Open for NGS, and by appt • Entrance: £2, children under 12 free • Other information: Refreshments by arrangement and plants for sale on open days ● ● ● ●

Although set within a formal design of high walls, clipped *Lonicera nitida* hedges, a pergola walk and gravel paths, this two-acre garden could not seem less formal. The eclectic planting of old favourites among sought-after varieties gives a refreshingly cottage air, intensified by flowers allowed to seed freely in the gravel. In fact the owners have a rare affection for garden 'thugs', using them to advantage throughout the garden. There is a tiny, paved secret garden with an unusual thyme table, and many other features and areas of interest, including mixed, herbaceous and woodland borders, a meadow, a gravel bed, a loggia and a Victorian vinery.

Doddington Hall [Historic Garden Grade II*]

Doddington, Lincoln LN6 4RU. Tel: (01522) 694308

Mr and Mrs J. Birch • 5m W of Lincoln on B1190 • House open as garden but 1 – 5pm (closed 19th Feb) • Garden open 19th Feb, then May to Sept, Wed, Sun and Bank Holiday Mons, all 12 noon – 5pm. Parties welcome at other times by appt • Entrance: £3.80, children £1.80 (house and garden £5.50, children £2.65, family £14.80), special rates for disabled in wheelchairs and parties of 20 or more. Other information: Please telephone about wheelchair access ● ● WC ● ● ●

The large gardens of large houses (Elizabethan in this case) do not often impart an air of intimacy, but here grandeur and formality sit happily alongside the casual, comfortable style of the present owner. Formality is represented by a gravel, box and lawn courtyard, complete with topiary unicorns from the family crest, as well as beds of flag irises and a yew *allée* giving views along an extensive avenue of limes. The wild gardens beyond offer a choice of meandering walks through ancient trees, past a stream edged with flourishing *Lysichiton americanus*. From the Temple of the Winds, designed by the present owner, the natural landscape opens up. Snowdrops are followed by equally naturalistic plantings of narcissi and erythroniums, and then by rhododendrons. In May and June there is a tapestry of colour in the walled garden where box-edged parterres are filled with flag irises and herbaceous borders are massed with towering echiums, syringas, peonies, alliums and phlox. A turf maze designed by the owner's father is popular with children and adults alike.

Easton Walled Gardens

Easton, Grantham NG33 5AP. Tel: (01476) 530063

Sir Fred and Lady Cholmeley • 7m S of Grantham, 1m E of A1 off B6403 N of Colsterworth roundabout. Follow signposts to village • Open 11th to 19th Feb for snowdrops, then April to Sept, Wed, Fri, Sun and Bank Holiday Mons, plus 8th June for NGS; all 11am – 4pm • Entrance: £3.50, children free • Other information: Range of garden events, including RHS snowdrop previews, sweet pea and cut flower days, and Gardener's Fair 17th April, 10am – 4pm [NEW] ⚇ ✕ ᴡᴄ ♿ ♫ ⅏ ♀ ⚭

The 12 acres of garden date back to at least 1592. 'Improved' by the Victorians, photographs from *Country Life* in 1903 show an impressive array of glasshouses, lawns with statues, fountains and bedding schemes, ha-has, great terraces, fine trees and tremendous views. The manor house, however, was pulled down in 1951 and the garden lay untouched for fifty years. In 2002 Lady Cholmeley, aided by a dedicated team of helpers and volunteers, began to uncover the skeleton of the Victorian gardens in a massive undertaking to reclaim, restore and develop them. Already avenues have been cleared, glasshouses and stonework restored and planting schemes devised. Hand-in-hand with the ancient yew tunnel are new features such as the Pickery, in which a changing display of flowers for cutting is grown. New, too, are areas dedicated to herbaceous plantings, wild flowers and woodland plants, and collections of narcissi and syringas are expanding. A garden to revisit year by year as the restoration unfolds.

Goltho House

Lincoln Road, Goltho LN8 5NF. Tel: (01673) 857768

Mr and Mrs S. Hollingworth • 10m E of Lincoln on A158, 1m on left before reaching Wragby • Open 19th April to Sept, Wed, 10am – 4pm, and by appt • Entrance: £3 • Other information: Teas on open days and by arrangement ● ♫

This 4.5-acre garden was only started in 1998, but already looks established and holds out much promise for the future. A long grass walk flanked by abundantly planted mixed borders forms a focal point; paths and walkways span out to other features – a nut walk, planted mostly for spring interest, an experimental prairie border, a small woodland area (still in its infancy, but maturing) and a stunning wildflower meadow. Nearer the house and its range of interesting old farm buildings lies a large pond area, still undergoing development, a peony and iris garden and a delightful rose garden. In contrast to the large-scale effect of the garden as a whole, the *potager*, with its brick and stone paths and geometric planting, offers an intimate experience of a wide variety of herbs and vegetables. The garden is laid out with a strong feeling for colour, form and texture in flowers and foliage, and reflects the owners' interest in a wide range of plants, many of them rare. A winter walk has been planted up, and a dry garden is in the offing.

Grimsthorpe Castle [Historic Garden Grade I]

Grimsthorpe, Nr Bourne PE10 0LY. Tel: (01778) 591205

Grimsthorpe and Drummond Castle Trust Ltd • 4m NW of Bourne on A151 Colsterworth – Bourne road • House open as garden but from 1pm, last admission

4.30pm • Park and garden open April to July, Sept, Thurs, Sun; Aug, Sun – Thurs; all 12 noon – 6pm • Entrance: £3, OAPs £2.50, children £2 (house, park and garden £7, OAPs £6, children £3.50) ◑ 💺 ✕ 🍽 <u>WC</u> ♿ 🐕 ♿ 🎋 🌡 ⚲

The impressive house, part-medieval, part-Tudor and part-eighteenth-century, with a dramatic forecourt and north front by Vanbrugh, is surrounded on three sides by good pleasure gardens in which 'Capability' Brown had a hand. The Victorian knot garden to the east of the house has beds of lavender, roses and catmint edged by clipped box. To the south are two yew-hedged gardens with topiary, a yew broad walk and a retreat. Leading to the west terrace is a double yew walk with classic herbaceous borders, and beyond is a shrub rose border. The yew hedging throughout the garden is superbly maintained and differs in design from one area to another. Beyond the pleasure gardens is an arboretum, a wild garden, an unusual geometrically designed kitchen garden with clipped box and bean pergola, and extensive parkland. Views of the old oak and chestnut avenues and of the parkland with its lake and Vanbrugh summerhouse are provided by cleverly positioned vistas and terraces.

Gunby Hall ★ [Historic Park and Garden Grade II]

Gunby, Spilsby PE23 5SS. Tel: (01909) 486411

The National Trust • 7m NW of Skegness, 2.5m NW of Burgh-le-Marsh on S of A158 • Hall and garden open as house, but Wed only, 2 – 6pm • Garden open 29th March to Sept, Wed and Thurs, 2 – 6pm, and Tues, Fri by written appt to Mr and Mrs J.D. Wrisdale. Coaches and parties pre-book in writing • Entrance: £3, children £1.50, family £7.50 (hall and garden £4.20, children £2.10, family £10.50) • Other information: Possible for wheelchairs but some gravel paths; no wheelchair access to hall ◑ 🍽 <u>WC</u> ♿ 🐕 ✍ 🌡

The charming William and Mary house, its walls smothered in fine plants, sits in parkland with avenues of lime and horse chestnut. The shrub borders, wild garden, lawns with old cedars and restrained formal front garden of catmint and lavender beds backed by clipped yew provide a startling contrast to the main attraction of Gunby – its walled gardens. The dazzling pergola garden with its apple-tree walkway has a maze of paths leading to beds of old roses, a herb garden and brimming herbaceous and annual borders. The second walled area houses an impressive kitchen garden reached after passing more borders of perfectly arranged herbaceous plants and hybrid musk roses. Backing onto its wall is another wonderfully classic herbaceous border and, beyond that an early-nineteenth-century long fish pond, a focal point for walks on either side. April brings a dazzling display of bulbs and wildflowers, in June the roses steal the show, and in July the herbaceous borders are at their splendid best. This is a gorgeous garden. It is fitting that it was the subject of Tennyson's *Haunt of Ancient Peace*.

Hall Farm and Nursery ★

Harpswell, Gainsborough DN21 5UU. Tel: (01427) 668412

Mr and Mrs M. Tatam • 7m E of Gainsborough on A631 • Open all year, Mon – Fri, 8am – 5.30pm (closes 8.30pm, Thurs), plus some Sat and Sun for NGS (please telephone for dates). Also open by appt • Entrance: donation to charity • Other information: Coaches by appt. Teas on charity open day only ○ **WC** ⟨symbols⟩

This garden combines the formal and the informal in a most imaginative way. The owners' delight in plants, satisfied by their adjoining nursery, is evident everywhere; there are hundreds of varieties of unusual herbaceous plants, roses and shrubs. A rose pergola leads from a decorative paved terrace to the main area behind the farmhouse. Subdivided into six separate areas, each with at least two entry points, the whole becomes an intriguing maze of garden rooms linked by border-edged paths and pergolas; they include a walled top terrace, a formal double border walk, a sunken garden with seasonal planting, an orchard with a giant chessboard and a set of chessmen and a newly restored wildlife pond and walkway. Here the borders have been planted with moisture-lovers, grasses and bamboos, providing a peaceful contrast to the other, floriferous areas.

Harrington Hall ★ [Historic Garden Grade II]

Harrington, Spilsby PE23 4NH. Tel: (01790) 754570 (Gardener)

Mr and Mrs D.W.J. Price • 5m E of Horncastle, 2m N of A158 • Open 4th, 25th June, 16th July, 6th Aug, 2 – 5pm, and by appt • Entrance: £2, children free ● ▪ **WC** ⟨symbol⟩

Given an idyllic setting in the wolds, the mellow red-brick walls of the Tudor and seventeenth-century hall and gardens provide the perfect backdrop for a variety of superb wall shrubs, climbers and deep herbaceous and mixed borders. No visitor would guess that the hall itself was practically destroyed by fire during the tenure of the present owners. Referred to in Tennyson's *Maud*, it is hard to imagine that these romantic gardens, walks and famous terraces have ever changed, although they were in fact replanted during the 1950s after a spell of wartime vegetable cultivation. Ironically, the one-acre kitchen garden immediately east of the house is a much more recent restoration. Formal in design and subdivided by a variety of hedges and paths, it is a happy combination of the functional and the purely decorative, with trained fruit trees, borders and a raised sitting area with a pond. Two new hedge-enclosed areas and their surrounding slopes are still in the early stages of development, but the inclusion of ornamental native trees screen a swimming-pool pavilion and link the formal pleasure gardens to the parkland beyond.

25 High Street

Rippingale, Bourne PE10 0SR. Tel: (01778) 440693

Mr Beddington • 6m N of Bourne off A15 • Open by appt • Entrance: £1.50, children free • Other information: Refreshments and plants for sale on open days only ● ✕ &

What at first seems a small informal garden of lawn, borders and island beds in fact provides half an acre of many delightful surprises. There are shady paths and secret corners, a bog garden, ponds and paved areas, and through a small gate an inspirational vegetable garden complete with a fruit cage and rhubarb pots. The assiduous care of the owner ensures a display of unusual herbaceous plants, shrubs and bulbs throughout the year. With its almost exclusively pastel palette, gentle curves and emphasis on wildlife habitats, the garden invites the visitor to linger and absorb its tranquillity.

Holmdale House

55 High Street, Martin, Lincoln LN4 3QY. Tel: (01526) 378838

Ian Warden and Stewart MacKenzie • 15m SE of Lincoln, 4m SW of Woodhall Spa on B1191 • Open all year, Tues – Sun and Bank Holiday Mons, 10am – 5pm • Entrance: free 🅿 WC ♨ ♿

Cleverly arranged around the Victorian farmhouse and spacious courtyard (used as the owners' plant nursery), three intimate gardens have evolved here, each with a different aspect and conditions. In the first a natural pond is edged by a gravel path and walled border. This leads to a grass walk flanked by deep rambling borders. The third area is a bordered lawn divided by a well-planted central bed. Existing trees and shrubs have been underplanted and supplemented, resulting in an eclectic mix of colour and texture. Although there are flowers here, this garden, with its hosta bed, grasses and choice variegated plants, will appeal particularly to foliage lovers. Combining unusual plants, imaginative planting and quirkily placed seats and containers, a traditional acre plot has been transformed into a garden with a highly individual feel.

Kexby House

Kexby Lane, Kexby, Gainsborough DN21 5NE. Tel: (01427) 788338

Herbert and Jenny Whitton • 12m NW of Lincoln, 6m E of Gainsborough on B1241, on outskirts of Kexby village • Open for NGS 30th April, 4th and 25th June, 6th July and 3rd Sept (seed collecting day – free), and at other times by appt. Parties welcome (45 max) • Entrance: £3.00, children free 🅿 🛍 WC ♿ ♨ ♨ 🍴

The four-acre garden, begun at least as far back as 1881 when the impressive Victorian country house was built, is a visual feast. Stunningly impressive herbaceous borders betray the owners' passion for sumptuous colour combinations – sometimes subtle, sometimes vividly arresting, always striking. Swathes of geraniums, irises, lupins, aquilegias, paeonies, poppies, nepetas, euphorbias and a multitude of other well-grown plants spill over from the wide herbaceous vistas, enhancing the garden's defined Victorian structure. Cottage-garden stalwarts jostle with less well-known hardy plants, the whole herbaceous effect supported by judicious planting of shrubs, hundreds of roses and some fabulously ancient trees. It is obvious that an artist's eye has guided the design and planting, as one perspective after another invites the visitor on. There is no feeling of an endless series of disconnected rooms, however, for the division of the garden into more intimate spaces, each with its own character and interest, creates a natural movement and sense of progression throughout. To list the features – wildlife pond, bog garden, mixed and colour-coordinated borders, scree – doesn't begin to capture the spirit of a garden with a long history, tempered by the personal and modern approach of its present owners.

The Lawn

**Sir Joseph Banks Conservatory, Union Road, Lincoln LN1 3BL.
Tel: (01522) 560306.**

Lincoln City Council • Off Burton Road beside Lincoln Castle • Open all year, daily: summer, 10am – 5pm (closes 4.30pm Fri); winter 10am – 4.30pm (closes 4pm Fri and Sun) • Entrance: free, but parking charge ○ 🍵 🅿 <u>WC</u> ♿ ⛪ ⚲

When Lincoln City Council bought this disused Georgian mental hospital in 1985 they aimed to establish a botanic collection to represent Lincoln's partnership with cities and countries around the world. Central to this is the Sir Joseph Banks Conservatory. Here, an excellent use of water and arrangements of plants in areas corresponding with parts of the world visited by Banks on his three-year voyage with Captain Cook have made this small area both exotic and interesting. The nearby walled *John Dawber Garden* continues this international theme, with mini-gardens representing England, Germany, China and Australia.

Lincoln Contemporary Heritage Garden

Medieval Bishops' Palace, Minster Yard, Lincoln LN2 1PU. Tel: (01522) 527468

English Heritage • On S side of Lincoln Cathedral • Open April to Oct, daily, 10am – 5pm (closes 6pm in July and Aug); Nov to March, daily except Tues and Wed, 10am – 4pm. Closed 24th to 26th Dec, 1st Jan • Entrance: £3.60, OAPs £2.70, children £1.80, family £9 (2005 prices) ○ 🅿 ⚲ ⛪ ♿

Mark Anthony Walker's heritage garden is a landscaper's answer to the New York loft conversion. In this case an antique terrace, first recorded as a garden site in 1320, has been given a pure, uncluttered design which must surely convert the anti-modernist. Deceptively simple, it makes clever allusion to the garden's history, linking it perfectly to the surrounding ruins and nearby cathedral. Brick paths create a lattice pattern across a lawn, and fastigiate hornbeams have been planted within steel discs at the intersections. Like the ribs and bosses of the cathedral's vaulted ceilings which inspired the design, the lattice succeeds in resolving the problem of asymmetry created by the irregular quadrilateral site. Clipped lavender – a splendid sight in flower in summers – and the red 'Guinée' rose give localised colour. The garden may be enjoyed from two seats set in yew niches, but the best views are from the East Hall terrace, where the full impact of what is in effect a contemporary knot garden can be appreciated. The entry charge includes access to the palace ruins and the flourishing vineyard on a lower terrace.

Manor Farm

Keisby, Lenton, Bourne PE10 0RZ. Tel: (01476) 585607

Mr and Mrs C.A. Richardson • 9m NW of Bourne, N of A151 between Lenton and Hawthorpe • Open by appt only • Entrance: £1.50 ●

Artistically planned and planted in harmonious colours, this pretty, informal garden is a delight. The tiny paths to the pergola, the stream and the one formal area of herbaceous beds and clipped yews meander through the garden, allowing close inspection of the many choice plants, including perennials, shrub roses, ramblers and clematis.

A walk along the stream bank leads to a new half-acre garden made in a former farmyard. In complete contrast to the cottagey style of the original, this open, south-facing area of lawns, gravel and beds is hot and continental in feeling. Here the emphasis is on outdoor living, with sitting areas and a gazebo from which to enjoy the variety of grasses and sun-loving plants. There is also a large collection of hellebores and snowdrops, plus other rarities for the plantsperson.

Marigold Cottage

Hotchin Road, Sutton-on-Sea LN12 2JA.
Tel: (01507) 442151.

Betty and Stephanie Lee • 16m N of Skegness off A52 • Open 14th May, 11th June, 2nd and 30th July, 13th Aug, 3rd Sept, 11am – 4pm, and at other times by appt • Entrance: £2 & ⬤ ℗

When the clear, white North Sea light falls on this half-acre garden, clearly defining edges and shadows, it truly sparkles. Essentially it is a cottage garden, with brimming mixed borders, plant-laden pergolas, arches and trellises, secret paths and tiny lawns. However, artefacts and ideas gathered over two decades of living in Asia, plus the skill and enthusiasm of a mother-and-daughter duo, have combined to create a garden of great originality. There is a Japanese *tori* entrance and corner, two new raised beds in the courtyard (ideal for disabled gardeners) and a newly established moon gate leading to the plant sales area. Original ideas include a Chinese corner with a viewing window and bamboos, a dry water feature made of slate, and a small domed water fountain with two huge pots as water features. Rare and tender plants flourish in the practically frost-free climate but old favourites grow alongside them – there is no plant snobbery here.

Normanby Hall ★

Normanby Hall Country Park, Normanby, Scunthorpe DN15 9HU.
Tel: (01724) 720588

North Lincolnshire Council • 4m N of Scunthorpe on B1430 • House and farm museum open April to Oct, daily, 1 – 5pm • Park open all year, daily, 9am – dusk (closes 9pm in summer). Victorian walled garden open daily except 25th and 26th Dec and 1st Jan, 10.30am – 5pm (4pm in winter) • Entrance: hall, gardens and farm museum £4.20, concessions £3.80, family £15. Season tickets available (2005 prices) ○ ➾ ✕ ▤ wc & ⬤ ℗ ♿ ⬤ ♒

The Regency house designed by Sir Robert Smirke is set in 300 acres of parkland boasting some fine mature trees, including a grand old holm oak looking like a surreal climbing frame and good avenues of copper beech and Wellingtonia. There are also stream walks, a bog garden, a Christmas garden, a newly planted woodland garden and an accessible deer park (open March 2006). A Victorian woodland garden has been planted with Japanese maples, camellias and azaleas, and acid-loving woodland perennials like the Himalayan blue poppy. Great improvements have been made to restore the pleasure gardens to their former beauty. The formal area south of the hall includes a 'boar's head' parterre and a sunken garden with a rectangular pond surrounded by herbaceous borders. Further away are two gardens enclosed by tall old walls and holly and conifer hedges. The first has good wall shrubs and climbers and double herbaceous borders planted Gertrude-Jekyll-fashion, moving from hot to cool colours along its length. The second is a lavish reconstruction of the original Victorian kitchen garden, complete with a potting shed, bothy, a vinery with a bed of subtropical plants, a fern house and a display house. Fruit trees are trained against the walls and over arches; those in the south-facing peach cases are under glass. There are decorative borders and four box-edged plots filled with organically grown fruit and vegetables varieties true to the period.

The Old Rectory

Church Lane, East Keal, Spilsby PE23 4AT. Tel: (01790) 752477

Mrs R.F. Ward • 12m W of Skegness, 2m SW of Spilsby on A16 • Open for NGS probably 23rd April, 28th May and 27th Aug, 2 – 5pm, and for individuals and parties by appt • Entrance: £2, children free • Other information: Refreshments by arrangement ● ● WC ℘

Nestled on a hillside in the Wolds, this gorgeous three-quarter-acre garden boasts possibly the best views of all those listed in Lincolnshire. It has been planted by the friendly owners to complement the many old walls, paved areas and rejuvenated yew hedges. There are paths everywhere – grass, brick, stone and granite-sett – all meandering from one delight to another, and seats sited for peaceful contemplation or to enjoy vistas. Lawn is kept to a minimum and masses of flowers tumble over rockeries, ponds, borders and retaining walls. Great efforts are made to introduce changes in planting, style and mood, which results in a wide variety of plants for the enthusiast to appreciate. There is also an extensive vegetable garden, an orchard, a rhododendron walk and a swimming pool area converted into an enclosed pool garden with a bog surround, and a new dry garden is planned.

The Old Rectory

Somerby, Nr Brigg DN38 6EX. Tel: (01652) 628268

Denise and Derrick Targett • 4m E of Brigg off A1084 • Open May to Sept, daily, 10am – 5pm, and for parties of up to 50 people by appt • Entrance: £2.50 NEW ● WC ℘ ℘

Although little remains of the original nineteenth-century garden there is still a feeling of Victorian opulence in the two acres here, due to a preference for shrubs and herbaceous plants with form and stature. Specimens are permitted space to develop to their full potential in the wonderfully generous borders (up to 10 metres deep in places) that edge the sweeping lawns. No froth or clutter, no island beds or secret walks, but anything that may have been forfeited in mystery has been gained in unobstructed views and plant beauty, epitomised by the exotic hot border with excellent rheums and *Lobelia tupa*. There is also a well-planted pergola, raised display beds and a formal fish pond. Hostas are a particular passion, displayed in a hosta walk, a large collection of unusual American hybrids (including a National Collection of 'Mildred Seaver' hybrids), and the adjoining specialist nursery. It is worth visiting the Norman church sheltering on the wooded hillside opposite the house, and Normanby Hall (see entry) is only 14 miles away.

4 Ringwood Close

Birchwood, Lincoln LN6 OLN. Tel: (01522) 683960

Margaret and John Brown • 2m SW of Lincoln. From A46 Lincoln by-pass take Skellingthorpe Road, signed to Birchwood. Turn right at traffic lights, then first right and first right again • Open 25th June, 11am – 5pm, and by appt • Entrance: £2
● ● WC ♨

For many, gardening on the edge of a wood could be dispiriting, but here the owners have used their sylvan backdrop to enhance the colour and composition of their young plantings. From a paved driveway with planters and conifers, the small back garden sweeps away into the distance, encompassing very different growing conditions. All the boundaries are covered in climbers, and the damp shaded courtyard allows hostas, ferns and acers to flourish, while the dry wide borders flanking the meandering lawn paths contain an exciting mix of desirable herbaceous plants, roses, shrubs and grasses. The recently planted Blue Garden, a final project for a design course, provides a perfect spot in which to sit and contemplate the different areas.

GARDEN AND FLOWER SHOWS 2006
- 11th to 14th May: Spring Gardening Show, Malvern
  (Three Counties Showground, Malvern, Worcestershire)
  Ticket hotline: (01684) 584924; www.threecounties.co.uk
- 19th to 21st May: Journée des Plantes de Courson (Château de Courson, Bruyères-le-Châtel, France)
  Tel: (0033) 1 64 58 90 12; www.coursondom.com
- 23rd to 27th May: Chelsea Flower Show
  (Royal Hospital, Chelsea, London SW3)
- 6th to 8th June: Wisley Show
  (RHS Garden, Wisley, Woking, Surrey)
- 15th to 19th June: BBC *Gardeners' World* Live
  (National Exhibition Centre, Birmingham)
  Ticket hotline: (0870) 902 0555; www.necgroup.co.uk
- 16th to 18th June: Three Counties Show, Malvern
  Ticket hotline: (01684) 584924
- 4th to 9th July: Hampton Court Flower Show
  (Hampton Court Palace, East Molesey, Surrey)
- 19th to 23rd July: RHS Flower Show, Tatton Park
  (Tatton Park, near Knutsford, Cheshire)
- 22nd to 24th Aug: Wisley Show
- 23rd and 24th Sept: Autumn Garden & Country Show, Malvern
  Ticket hotline: (01684) 584924
- 13th to 15th Oct: Journée des Plantes de Courson

Unless otherwise given, for details of all these shows telephone the Royal Horticultural Society on (020) 7834 4333 or consult www.rhs.org.uk.

LIVERPOOL & WIRRAL

Birkenhead Park ★ [Historic Park Grade I]

Birkenhead, Wirral CH41 4HY. Tel: (0151) 637 6218
or (0151) 652 5197 (Park Manager)

*Metropolitan Borough of Wirral • 1m from centre of Birkenhead, S of A553 • Open
all year, daily, during daylight hours • Entrance: free* ○ 🐾 **WC** ♿ ⟁ 🔦 ✆

Historically Birkenhead Park is a milestone in garden history. Opened in 1847, it was
the world's first urban park to be built at public expense. Designed by Joseph Paxton,
it was also highly influential in the creation of New York's Central Park. Paxton's mas-
ter-stroke at Birkenhead was to separate 'through' from peripheral traffic; he also
banked up the edges of the lakes to keep them hidden, and made them sinuous in
shape to provide walkers with a constantly changing view. No subsequent public park
has succeeded in fashioning such a subtle yet masterly landscape. The banks on the
eastern side of the lake are planted with trees and shrubs; a Swiss-style bridge links
two islands, and a fine stone boathouse has recently been restored. The western lake
has weeping willows and rhododendrons planted around its edge. The park is currently undergoing a £11 million restoration, funded by the Heritage Lottery Fund, the
European regional Development Fund and the Metropolitan Borough of Wirral. Most
of the landscaping work will be completed before the end of 2006.

Croxteth Hall [Historic Garden Grade II]

Croxteth Hall Lane, Liverpool L12 0HB. Tel: (0151) 228 5311

*Liverpool City Council, Leisure Services • Turn N off A5058 Liverpool ring road
into Muirhead Avenue on NE side of city. Signposted • House and Victorian farm also
open • Garden open 14th April to 24th Sept, daily, 10.30am – 5pm (winter times on
request) • Entrance: grounds free; walled garden £1.50, OAPs and children 80p (all
facilities £4.50, OAPs and children £2.30, family £11) • Other information: Dogs in
outer park only. Shop in house* ◑ 💺 ✕ **WC** ♿ ⟁ 🌿 🏪 🔦 ✆

The hall, formerly the ancestral home of the Barons Sefton, stands in 500 acres of
its original parkland, with large areas of woodland and many rhododendrons. For
gardeners the centre of interest is the large walled garden to the north of the
house. Interpreted as a working Victorian kitchen garden and divided up by gravel
paths, this contains a great variety of fruit, vegetables and decorative plants,
organically cultivated; espalier fruits are grown against the walls and trained on wire
fences, and the south-facing wall has a broad herbaceous border containing a good
variety of perennials and ornamental grasses. Several greenhouses and a mushroom
house are also open, and there is a small herb garden.

Liverpool Botanic Gardens ★

Calderstones Park, Liverpool L18 3JD. Tel: (0151) 225 4877

*Liverpool City Council, Environmental Services • 4m SE of city centre, S of A562
• Park open all year, daily. Old English garden and Japanese garden open all year,*

daily except 25th Dec, 8am – 5pm (closes 4pm Oct to March) • Entrance: free ○ 💺
🏠 WC ♿ ☕ 🌳 🍽 ♨

Essentially this is a large, well-landscaped park with mature trees, a lake and a rhododendron walk. At its heart, close to the house, a series of gardens is set around the old walled garden. To the front a long herbaceous border, 6 metres deep, has a range of strong-growing perennials; beyond, the flower garden features large clumps of grasses and daylilies and beds of annuals. Overlooking it is a greenhouse containing a sample of National Collections of codiaeums, dracaenas and aechmeas, many fine orchids in season, an impressive collection of cacti, and much else besides. To the rear of the greenhouse the Old English flower garden has beds of perennials, bulbs and shrubs set within a formal layout of paths, with a circular lily pool and pergolas bearing clematis, vines, golden hops and honeysuckle at its centre. In the Japanese garden a chain of rocky streams and pools is fringed by acers, pines and clumps of bamboo. On the outer edges of the park is a recently restored rock garden, a large lake, a bog garden and a rose garden. Children will enjoy the 'text garden' maze and the £100,000 millennium playground. Altogether one of the best 'free' gardens in the country.

Reynolds Park Walled Garden

Church Road, Woolton, Liverpool L24 0TR. Tel: (0151) 724 2371

Liverpool City Council (controlled by Environmental Services, Calderstones Park) • 4.5m SE of Liverpool city centre. Turn left off A562 up Beaconsfield Road to end and right into Church Road; park is on left • Open all year, daily except 25th Dec, 10am – 6pm (closes 4pm winter) • Entrance: free ○

The diamond-shaped walled garden, set within an attractive part of Liverpool on a surprisingly high hill, has traditional formal beds of dahlias and seasonal bedding; cordylines are used for their structural shape within the scheme. Along the south-facing walls it is a different story: broad herbaceous borders containing a great range of perennials – phlox, acanthus, achilleas, lilies, echinops, heleniums and hostas – backed by wisteria, clematis and roses. There are also collections of azaleas and conifers. In the park outside, an unusual clipped yew garden was laid out in the 1920s in Art Deco style. East of the city centre in Knowsley, within the 35-acre Victorian Court Hey Park, *The National Wildflower Centre* has demonstration areas of different plantings, including a garden of medicinal plants and herbs, plus a sculpture garden, workshops and activities for children. [Open April to Sept, Wed – Sun and Bank Holiday Mons, Oct to March Wed only, 11am – 4pm.]

Sefton Park [Historic Park Grade II*]

Liverpool. Tel: (0151) 225 4868; (0151) 726 9304 (Palm House enquiries)

Liverpool City Council • 3m SE of Liverpool city centre, N of A561 • Open all year, daily • Entrance: free • Other information: Palm house used for functions, so not always open ○ 💺 🏠 WC ♿ ☕ 🍽

One of the country's most impressive Victorian parks, endowed by the Sefton family, conceived on a vast scale, and close in size to Hyde Park. It was planned as one of a series of parks ringing Liverpool to serve as an amenity for the growing population of the city. The competition for its design was won by Edouard André and Lewis Hornblower. Its layout of huge ellipses and circles owes much to Parisian gardens – André had worked with Haussmann in his grand bid to transform the French capital. For this English park he devised many views towards the interior, cleverly using planting to enhance perspective, with large-leaved trees around the perimeter and finer-leaved varieties in the centre. Hornblower, who had worked under Paxton at Birkenhead, was responsible for the many fine lodges, gates and kiosks dotted around the park. The most magnificent building of all is not, however, his. The palm house was built in 1896 thanks to the generosity of a local millionaire; octagonal in plan, it is 39 metres across with a vast glass dome built in three tiers, and contains tropical and exotic plants from Africa, Asia and Australasia. Each continent has an excellent guidebook. Its recent restoration is greatly to be welcomed, although it is unfortunate that much of the floor has been concreted over to enable a wide range of public and private events to be held. Subject to Stage 2 Heritage Lottery Fund approval, a major programme is planned to restore and improve the landscape, features and facilities of the park itself.

Speke Hall

The Walk, Liverpool L24 1XD. Tel: (0845) 585702 (Infoline) or (0151) 427 7231

The National Trust • 8m SE of city centre, S of A561. Signposted • House open – telephone for details • Garden open all year, daily, 11am – 5.30pm (closes 4.30pm in winter). Closed 24th to 26th and 31st Dec, 1st Jan • Entrance: £3.50, children £1.80, family £10 • Other information: Picnics at Home Farm only. Accessible path around Stocktons Wood for wheelchair users ○ ☕ 🧺 WC ⅗ 🏬 ⚑ ⚑

The remarkable gardens at Speke are neither as old nor as impressive as the Elizabethan hall. They are extraordinary, however, for although they are situated in one of the most heavily industrialised areas of south Liverpool and close to the airport, they seem to be set in the heart of the countryside. In front of the house is a large lawn with shrub borders to the sides containing mainly rhododendrons and hollies. On the side opposite the house a ha-ha allows views to the fields and woodland. A stone bridge leads over a drained moat to the ornate stone entrance of the hall. The moat continues to the west where there is a herbaceous border with a variety of perennials; a large holm oak stands opposite. To the south are new Victorian borders, and a formal rose garden contains fragrant varieties of old-fashioned roses. In the centre of the house is a large cobbled courtyard in which grow two enormous yews. The Trust is continuing to develop many areas of the gardens: a mid-Victorian-style stream garden has been planted with rhododendrons, azaleas, camellias, ferns and other plants, and new beds have been created on the south lawn.

LONDON AREA

At the end of this section we include some of London's most attractive open spaces: City parks and gardens, squares and other retreats. The famous parks justify an entry of their own, but we have listed others of merit with a brief description under 'London's Open Spaces'.

Two-starred gardens are marked on the map with a black square.

33 Balmuir Gardens

Putney, London SW15. Tel: (020) 8788 0931

Mrs Gay Wilson • Nearest station Putney mainline (5 mins). Buses 14, 74, 377, along Upper Richmond Road • Open by appt only • Entrance: £3 (2005 price) ☽

Pleasure in Putney: a small garden with romantic mixed planting for sun and shade. A paved path patterned with slate and pebble mosaics meanders between a small lawn and under trees to a dipping pool and wall pond. The garden designer owner intersperses the densely planted borders of shrubs, ferns and hostas with a soft colour palette of perennial plantings, and the many climbers – roses, clematis and the like – are discreetly nipped and tucked to give an abundant backdrop to this delightful garden.

Barbican Conservatory

The Barbican Centre, Silk Street, London EC2Y 8DS. Tel: (020) 7638 4141/8891

City of London • In Barbican Centre, on 3rd floor • Open all year, Sun and Bank Holiday Mons only, 10am – 5.30pm. Telephone to confirm opening times as conservatory is sometimes used for conferences • Entrance: free ☽ WC &

The lift to the third floor of the Barbican propels you from the streets of the City to a lush jungle of temperate and semi-tropical plants. Planted in the autumn of 1980–81 using 1600 cubic metres of soil, the imaginative conservatory was opened in 1984 and is arguably the best single piece of architecture of the whole of the Barbican. Twin *Dicksonia antarctica* grace the main entrance, while a vast banyan tree (*Ficus bengalensis*) in the eastern section threatens to burst through the roof. Many familiar houseplants like *Ficus benjamina* have reached gigantic proportions, and a colossal Swiss cheese plant (*Monstera deliciosa*) produces edible fruits after flowering. The arid house on the second level, added in 1986, contains epiphyllums and cacti. There are finches in the aviary and the ponds are alive with fish. Another interesting contemporary garden is at the *Broadgate Arena* at the far end of Liverpool Street Station concourse.

Battersea Park [Historic Park Grade II*]

Battersea, London SW11 4NJ. Tel: (020) 8871 7530/8800

Wandsworth Borough Council • On S side of River Thames, from Chelsea Bridge to Albert Bridge • Open all year, daily, 7am – dusk • Entrance: free, but parking charge ○ ☽ ✕ 🖼 WC & 🏛 ♀ ♒

There is something for everyone in this 200-acre Victorian park. Much of the nineteenth-century landscape and the 1951 Festival of Britain pleasure gardens, designed by Russell Page, have been restored, with thousands of specimen trees and shrubs and acres of ornamental planting. The grand Riverside Promenade alongside the Thames now includes the Buddhist peace pagoda. More than 60 jets of water play in the Vista Fountains. The Subtropical Garden, the first of its kind open to the public in this country, has now been restored to its original combination of lush sub-tropical plants and vibrant bedding. Other popular attractions include the Pulhamite cascade on the 13-acre lake, where boats can be hired, the Pump House Gallery showing contemporary art, the otter and owl wildlife centre, the lakeside café and important sculptures by Henry Moore and Barbara Hepworth.

80 Bromfelde Road

London SW4 6PR. Tel: (020) 7720 4080

Susan Collier • N of Clapham High Street off Gauden Road. Nearest underground station Clapham North; buses 77, 77A, 88, 155, 255, 322, 345, 355 • Open for NGS, and for parties of 4 or more by appt end-May, June, Aug and Sept • Entrance: £2 [NEW] ●

A garden of secrecy and surprise, created by an artist for whom gardening and textile design are mutually inspiring. The conservatory, with its pretty frame of blue and red stained glass, looks across paving studded with pots of pelargoniums, hostas and lilies to a winding gravel path almost submerged under a wash of vibrant, scented or textural perennials. The garden appears to end with a flourish of bamboos. Not so. Beyond are three other chambers packed with flowers and foliage. One has a contemplative bench, the next a mosaic table and an industrial-looking fountain backed by decorative clapboarding (the owner is an accomplished reclaimer). Step up to the final surprise: an enclosed lawn where a little Buddha on a wall faces a studio room across an expanse of lawn backed by mature trees.

Buckingham Palace [Historic Garden Grade II*]

Westminster, London SW1A 1AA. Tel: (020) 7766 7300

Crown Estate Commissioners • On N end of Buckingham Palace Road, on N side beyond Royal Mews and Royal Gallery. Entrance through courtyard to S of palace • Open Aug and Sept (but opening and closing dates may vary), daily, 9.30am – 4.30pm by timed ticket • Entrance combined with admission to State Rooms: £13.50, over 60s £11.50, children under 17 £7, children under 5 free, family £34, group rate (min. 15 persons) £12 per person (2005 prices) • Other information: Advance tickets available via website or by telephone on (020) 7766 7300. Ticket office in Green Park Aug and Sept. Coaches must contact visitor officer (Tel: (020) 7766 7321) well in advance ● WC ♿

Visitors to the Palace end their tour of the State Rooms along a 450-metre guided route on the south side of the garden, and halfway along the three-acre lake are then directed out into Grosvenor Place. Although they may not roam freely they will be able to marvel at a 39-acre walled garden in central London – part parade ground, part ecological and dendrological oasis and part wildlife habitat. The magnificent trees were planted by William Aiton – head of Kew in the nineteenth century – and latterly by the Royal Family in acts of commemoration. The romantic and naturalistic lake is host to more than 30 types of bird. The visitors' view of Nash's handsome garden front of the palace is a privilege in itself.

15A Buckland Crescent ★

London NW3 5DH.

Lady Barbirolli • As we go to press, we learn that the garden will be closed to visitors in 2006, but is due to reopen for the NGS and by appt in 2007

The strong sense of space and line that musicians often possess is expressed in this dignified third-of-an-acre town garden, in which the ground plan combines flowing unfussy lines and ingenious geometry. Planting is everywhere discriminating, ranging from a functional but decorative vegetable patch to some unusual plants such as citrus and other interesting shrubs, including a small bamboo 'grove'. A generous terrace is enhanced by boldly planted urns.

5 Burbage Road

Herne Hill, London SE24 9HJ. Tel: (020) 7274 5610

Crawford and Rosemary Lindsay • Close to Half Moon Lane. Nearest station: Herne Hill • Open for NGS (telephone for information), and by appt • Entrance: £2.50
● ℘

An attractive garden in a tranquil and sheltered setting, with well-kept lawns, a quietly splashing fountain and herb beds. There is year-round interest and a continual introduction of unusual plants; borders are filled with choice arrangements of herbaceous perennials and shrubs, and good use is made of a variety of pots holding climbers, ferns and tender plants.

Bushy Park [Historic Park Grade I]

Hampton, Surrey. Tel: (020) 8979 1586

Royal Parks • N of A308 Hampton Court road, between Kingston Bridge and Hampton Court Bridge. Access from Hampton Court or Twickenham. Entrance to Waterhouse Plantation via gate on Hampton Court road • Open all year, daily, 9am – dusk • Entrance: free ○ ☕ WC ♿

Once a royal hunting ground, the park adjoins Hampton Court (see entry) to the north. The vast avenue of four rows of limes and one of chestnuts planted by Henry Wise for William III created a grand approach to the palace. It was punctuated by a formal basin to which Queen Anne removed the Arethusa fountain (long called the Diana fountain) from the Old Privy Garden. In the *Waterhouse Plantation* paths wind round mass shrub plantings and open onto small lakes and the Longford River with many bridges.

7 The Butts

Brentford TW8 8BJ. Tel: (020) 8232 8597

Mrs Susan Sharkey • Off Manor Road and Half Acre (A3002), a short walk from Brentford High Street. Buses 235 and 267. Nearest mainline station Brentford • Open for NGS, and by appt • Entrance: £2 ● &

A garden designer's garden (27 x 14 metres) cleverly planted with an abundance of foliage plants. It is separated into three sections. Next to the house a terrace has raised beds, distinguished by a strong use of colour. Then, leading from a plant-festooned pergola to a well-kept lawn framed by cloud-pruned box-edged beds, the garden opens up and gives a feeling of space, before revealing the final secret area with an original water feature and unusual planting for year-round interest.

Camley Street Natural Park

12 Camley Street, London NW1 0PW. Tel: (020) 7833 2311

London Borough of Camden; managed by London Wildlife Trust • Off Goods Way, near King's Cross railway station • Open all year, daily except Fri and Christmas period, 9am – 5pm (opens 11am Sat and Sun; winter, 10am – 4pm or dusk if earlier) • Entrance: free, but donations welcome ○ 🅱 <u>WC</u> & 🍴 ℺

An innovative project created in the early 1980s and now a designated local nature reserve, this is an example of a successful and thriving urban wildlife park and garden created against all the odds. Just over two acres between the Regent's Canal and the railway have been landscaped with a large pond and include a visitors' centre with an environmental education classroom. This tranquil space has a fine sighting record of birds and other wildlife. Views of the canal and passing narrow boats are offset somewhat romantically by relics of Victorian industry. The park will remain open throughout the Channel Tunnel rail link works in the area.

Cannizaro Park [Historic Park Grade II*]

West Side Common, Wimbledon, London SW19 4UE. Tel: (020) 8946 7349

London Borough of Merton • West Side Common, Wimbledon • Open all year, daily, 8am – sunset (opens 9am Sat, Sun and Bank Holidays) • Entrance: free • Other information: Teas on summer Suns only. Sculpture exhibition in June, open-air theatre season July and Aug. Top garden possible for wheelchairs ○ 🍱 🅱 WC & ⇦ 🍴

Formerly the grounds of Cannizaro House, the park is entered through imposing gates up a formal drive, lined with beautifully kept seasonal bedding. The trees are the principal attraction here: cork oaks, mulberries and sassafras, enormous and beautiful beeches and mature red Japanese maples are among the many attractions. At the southern wooded end of the park, in Lady Jane's Wood, the main feature is the magnificent and vibrantly colourful azalea dell. In the midst of the trees a secluded picnic area, set with tables, contains – somewhat unexpectedly – a bust of the Emperor Haile Selassie of Ethiopia, who sought refuge in Wimbledon. There is also a small aviary, a pretty walled rose garden, an azalea and a rhododendron collection. The old garden, a formal garden and a pool are found down a steep slope directly in front of the house, with a wild garden in the same location.

Capel Manor College

Bullsmoor Lane, Enfield EN1 4RQ. Tel: (020) 8366 4442

Capel Manor Charitable Corporation • From M25 junction with A10, via Turkey Street/Bullsmoor Lane (signposted), or walk from railway station • Open March to Oct, daily; Nov to Feb, Mon – Fri; all 10am – 6pm (last admission 4.30pm). Closed 25th Dec to 1st Jan • Entrance: £5, OAPs £4, children £2, family £12. Special rates for winter and show weekends • Other information: Plants for sale at special events
○ 🍽 🏠 <u>WC</u> ♿ 🐕 🌳 🏛 ☕

These busy and popular gardens of this well-known horticultural college have been developed to support the needs of the students attending its horticultural, garden design, floristry and arboricultural courses. Feature gardens created by ex-students in the grounds include Kim Wilde's ultra-modern 'jungle gym' garden. They are also educational and interesting for visitors, featuring a variety of plants and combination plantings, and hard landscaping materials and water features. The largest of the five main areas is the historic landscape around the eighteenth-century house, and this includes a walled garden, a wilderness, a magnolia border and seventeenth-century gardens. The area of modern gardens (which includes the National Gardening Centre) offer an all-year version of the ephemeral gardens at the Chelsea Flower Show. The extensive experimental and trials gardens are run by *Gardening Which?* and provide much of the editorial and photographs featured in their publications. There is also a lakescape garden and an area of theme gardens covering everything from topiary to flower arranging. Suitable for a family outing, enhanced by a maze and an animal area which includes Kune Kune pigs and Clydesdale horses.

Chelsea Physic Garden ★ [Historic Garden Grade I]

66 Royal Hospital Road, Chelsea, London SW3 4HS. Tel: (020) 7352 5646

Chelsea Physic Garden Company • Entrance in Swan Walk, off Chelsea Embankment and, for wheelchair users only, in Royal Hospital Road • Open 5th and 12th Feb, 11am – 3pm; April to Oct, Wed, 12 noon – 5pm, Sun, 2 – 6pm; also during Chelsea Flower Show and Chelsea Festival Week, 12 noon – 5pm • Entrance: £6.50, students, children and unemployed £4 🍴 🍽 <u>WC</u> ♿ 🌳 🏛 ☕

The garden was established in 1673 as the first botanical grounds and training establishment, to widen herbal knowledge increasingly used by the apothecaries of the time. The crimson-flowered apothecary's rose, *R. gallica* var. *officinalis*, can be found in the Medical Quadrant, and some of the trees introduced by these early botanists still stand, including a fruiting pomegranate reputed to the one painted by Elizabeth Blackwell for the two-volume record of the plants growing in the Physic Garden, published in a bid to buy her husband out of a debtors' prison in the eighteenth century. A statue of Sir Hans Sloane, who gave the land in perpetuity to the Society of Apothecaries in 1722, dominates the central core of the garden, which is devoted to systematically ordered beds of plants. Another plot makes reference to plants introduced by previous botanists and curators. One of the earliest rock gardens in Europe was created from basaltic lava brought back by Sir Joseph Banks from Iceland in 1772. In one glasshouse is the rare *Musschia aurea* with starry cream flowers pollinated in the wild by lizards living on the volcanic slopes of Madeira; another houses an exceptional collection of species pelargoniums. This historic garden reveals something new and fascinating on every visit.

Chiswick House ★★ [Historic Park and Garden Grade I]

Burlington Lane, Chiswick, London W4 2RP. Tel: (020) 8995 0508

London Borough of Hounslow and English Heritage • 5m W of central London; entrance on A4 • House open April to Oct, Wed – Sun, 10am – 5pm (closes 2pm Sat). Private tours by arrangement Nov to March; telephone for details • Gardens open all year, daily, 8am – dusk • Entrance: garden free (house £4, concessions £3, children £2) • Other information: Dogs outside Italian garden only ○ 💷 🍴 wc ♿ 🍵 🏛

The handsome eighteenth-century gardens, stretching over many acres, with a lake, statues, monuments, bridges and magnificent trees, were created from 1726 and extended by William Kent to complement the Palladian villa built by Lord Burlington in 1729. They are full of splendid vistas, avenues and changes of contour. Drawings of the time show the degree of perfection the English landscape had reached even in the early eighteenth century. The large canal-shaped lake has at its southern end a cascade designed by Kent in 1738 to mimic an underground river flowing from a rocky hill. He failed to make the cascade work but English Heritage – using information from archaeological excavation and from the archives at Chatsworth – has succeeded. After Kent's day, the Victorian garden with parterres was created and is now filled with vividly coloured bedding plants in front of a handsome conservatory. In co-operation with the London Borough of Hounslow, English Heritage plan to complete the restoration of the Victorian gardens; a first bid is in for a major lottery grant. West of the lake, the oriental plane walk has been restored with holly hedges, re-creating the walk in the manner of the mid-nineteenth century. William Kent's carriage drive and the raised walk that flanked the drive have also been re-created. Although this is not yet open to the public, visitors can walk the length of the *allée* leading from the Burlington Gate to the classical bridge. There is an outstanding camellia collection with early-nineteenth-century specimens; a new outdoor camellia garden is envisaged to the south of the Italian garden. Further work is expected to take place in Burlington's Orange Tree Amphitheatre and in the northern and western wildernesses. From about Easter there are two return trips a day by boat from Westminster (telephone (020) 7930 4721) – but note these are lengthy.

College Garden and Little Cloister

Westminster Abbey, London SW1P 3PA. Tel: (020) 7222 5152

Dean and Chapter of Westminster • Entrance via Broad Sanctuary (west end of Abbey) then Dean's Yard, Great Cloister and Fountain Court (signposted) • Open April to Sept, Tues to Thurs, 10am – 6pm (closes 4pm Oct to March) • Entrance: free

but donations welcome • Other information: Band concerts (free) July and Aug, Wed,
12.30 – 2pm as advertised ○ ⬤ ⬤ ⬤ ⬤

The eleventh-century College Garden (a little over one acre) has been under cultivation for more than 900 years, and therefore qualifies as one of the oldest in England. It was originally the source for herbs used in the monastic infirmary of the Benedictine Abbey, and this theme is continued by the growing of herbs in the knot garden. Landscaping by John Brookes encourages visitors to move towards the south and east, from where some of the best architecture of the abbey may be viewed. In the south-west corner is a shaded area with a crucifixion group in bronze. Some interesting small gardens with topiary and intensive planting adjoin the buildings to the north of the area. The Little Cloister Garden is a miniature study in green and white, with a fountain and fish pond in the centre. There are fine trees throughout, and for flowers the best time to visit is February to May.

156 Dalling Road

Hammersmith, London W6 0EU. Tel: (020) 8741 2994

Kim Whatmore • Off King Street, Hammersmith. Buses 27, 190, 266; underground
station Hammersmith (10 mins) or Ravenscourt Park (5 mins) • Open by appt
• Entrance: £1.50 ⬤ ⬤

Key plants – large tree ferns, camellias and box – are repeated throughout the small and tranquil garden to give cohesion. Trellis covered with *Clematis* 'Nelly Moser' and purple wisteria make secret partitions; York-stone paving liberally interspersed with pebbles and planting leads to an arbour painted pale green. This is a garden where every inch of space is made to count.

Dolly's Garden

43 Layhams Road, West Wickham, Kent BR4 9HD. Tel: (020) 8462 4196

Mrs Dolly and Miss Mary Robertson • Off A232 and A2022. Semi-detached house
opposite Wickham Court Farm • Open all year by appt only • Entrance: by donation
to collecting box. Other information: Teas by arrangement ⬤ WC ⬤ ⬤

The waist-high 'allotment' garden, open to visitors since 1980, was designed for the late Dolly Robertson, a permanent wheelchair user. Organic since 1941, excellent fruit and vegetables continue to be raised by her daughter, who has set up the Dolly Robertson Trust for Disabled Gardeners in her memory (visitors' donations welcomed). Perennials, combined with shrubs and climbers, are surrounded by native trees, holly, bay and bamboo, with a purpose-built greenhouse tucked among the raspberry canes. It remains a happy and fiercely fruitful place, brimming with ideas for disabled and organic gardeners, where the emphasis is on year-round self-sufficiency.

Down House [Historic Garden Grade II]

Luxted Road, Downe, Kent BR6 7JT. Tel: (01689) 859119

English Heritage • 2m NE of Biggin Hill off A21 • Open 5th Feb to 23rd Dec, Wed –
Sun and Bank Holiday Mons, 10am – 6pm (closes 4pm in winter) • Entrance: £6.60,
OAPs £5, children £2.30 (house and garden) ○ ⬤ WC ⬤ ⬤ ⬤ ⬤

Charles Darwin and his family lived in the house for forty years from 1842, and his daughter wrote: 'Many gardens are more beautiful and varied but few could have greater charm or repose.' The great scientist used the garden, woodland and meadows as his open-air laboratory while he formulated the theories which culminated in his ground-breaking work, *On the Origin of Species*, and for visitors one of the most famous features of the garden is his 'Sand-walk' or 'thinking path'. The garden is being restored using plants described by Darwin in his notes and letters, including the greenhouse where he studied plant growth and pollination and which now houses orchids, carnivorous and climbing plants. The flower borders lead to the small kitchen garden, which provided material for his experiments as well as fruit, vegetables and flowers for the household; it was replanted in 2005. The flower garden outside the drawing room, now restored to its appearance during the late 1870s, was used by the family as an extra room. Outside, on the lawn, is a 'wormstone' laid out by Darwin's son Horace in an experiment to measure soil displacement.

66A East Dulwich Road

East Dulwich, London SE22 9AT. Tel: (020) 8693 3458

Kevin Wilson • Behind Goose Green, opposite Dulwich swimming baths. Buses 37, 175, 176; underground station East Dulwich (20 mins) • Open by appt; parties of 10 or more welcome • Entrance: £2.50 ● &

The 30-metre-long garden is distinguished by lush planting, ponds, a willow tree and climbing plants used to great advantage. The owner is an artist and a garden designer, and his unique method of festooning may-poles with climbers, head-height seating areas and plant-filled antique hip baths defy all the rules. Large plantings of slug-free hostas and hanging baskets of ferns line the gravel path leading to a decking area, and pots of soleirolias march up wooden steps. Before reaching the large workroom, a pole with a mirrored top reflects the abundant planting. A viewing platform made from decking, with a double swing underneath, a seating area and a plunge pool near the summerhouse/studio entice you to the end of this unusual garden. Kevin Wilson has now annexed a third of his neighbour's garden. Part is given over to vegetables, but lo and behold another verandah, sundeck and summerhouse have sprung up alongside the original. This is the shelter Robinson Crusoe would have built for himself given the skill and the tools to do a proper job.

The Elms

13 Wolverton Avenue, Kingston upon Thames, Surrey KT2 7QF. Tel: (020) 8546 7624 or (07885) 045685

Professor and Mrs R. Rawlings • 1m E of Kingston on A308, 100 metres from Norbiton station. Entrance opposite flats in Manorgate Road • Open 11th and 12th March, 8th and 9th April, 13th and 14th May, 2.30 – 4.30pm, and for parties of 10 or more by appt • Entrance: £1.50 • Other information: Parking restricted on Sats ● ● ♨

This is a true collector's garden with some rare and unusual plants, featuring rhododendrons, magnolias, camellias, conifers and a wide range of evergreen and deciduous shrubs. In a very small area (just 16.5 x 7.5 metres) are small trees, herbaceous ground cover, and a two-level pool with a geyser and well-planted margins; room is even found for plums, pears and soft fruit. The roof garden (open to private visitors only) is an object lesson in the possibilities of such high-level spaces.

Eltham Palace Gardens [Historic Garden Grade II*]

Court Road, Eltham, London SE9 9QE. Tel: (020) 8294 2548

English Heritage • Near Eltham High Street, 0.5m from Eltham railway station (then Bus 161) or 0.75m from Mottingham railway station (then Bus 126 or 131) • Palace open as garden • Garden open all year, except Jan, 10am – 5pm (closes 4pm Nov to March). Closed 24th Dec to 1st Feb • Entrance: £4.60, OAPs £3.50, children £2.30 (house and garden £7.30, OAPs £5.50, children £3.70, family £18.30)

● ● ● ● WC & ● ●

The original moated manor house had royal connections stretching back from Henry VIII to Edward II. By 1933, when Stephen and Virginia Courtauld bought the site and built their Art Deco House with its splendid interiors adjoining, only the Great Hall remained. The garden that exists now is largely their creation. The wisteria pergola is supported by eighteenth-century Ionic columns salvaged by Courtauld money. The sunken rose garden has been replanted with the early hybrid tea and hybrid musk roses popular at the period. The Westmorland stone rock garden, housing now shrubs and alpine plants, originally featured a series of pools and cascades descending to the moat – these will be restored, funds permitting. Banks have been laid to mown grass or mass-planted with clipped laurel. Contemporary planting in the 120-yard-long South Moat border and White Wood by designer Isabelle Van Groeningen is likewise in the spirit of the 1930s: within a series of enclosures created by unusual evergreen shrubs and trees spring- and summer-flowering shrubs are underplanted with a variety of bulbs and perennials – *Salvia coccinea*, for example, and delphiniums grouped in single colours. The smooth reflective surface of the moat is a magnet for visitors, but a walk up to the wildlife lawn for wide views of London brings home the timeless allure of this remarkable historic enclave.

Fenton House

Hampstead Grove, London NW3 6RT. Tel: (020) 7435 3471

The National Trust • In centre of Hampstead in Hampstead Grove behind Heath Street • House open • Garden open 4th to 26th March, Sat and Sun, 2 – 5pm; 29th March to 29th Oct, Sat, Sun and Bank Holiday Mons, 11am – 5pm, Wed – Fri, 2 – 5pm. Parties at other times by appt • Entrance: £2, children £1 (house and garden £4.90, children £2.45 family £12) • Other information: Toilet facilities if house visited ● WC & ● ●

The entrance to the handsome seventeenth-century house – described by *Country Life* as 'London's most enchanting country house' – and the garden is through the grand iron gate into an avenue of robinias or by a side gate near the yew bower, from which the south garden is visible. The one-and-a-half acre walled garden is formal, with gravel walks and herbaceous borders planted to give summer-long interest, edged by neatly clipped box. Standard hollies are a feature, and the walls are particularly well planted; note the collection of *Clematis viticella* varieties. The ground drops on several levels to a sunken rose garden and a late-summer/autumn border surrounded by tall yew hedges dividing the formal lawn area from the rose garden. Steps then lead down to an ancient orchard delightful in spring with narcissi, fritillaries and bluebells. At one end is the reinstated glasshouse with a herb border alongside (note the two olive trees in pots), at the other the vegetable garden and cutting borders. In collaboration with the HDRA, the garden was chosen to be part of a pilot project aimed at providing the Trust with an organic gardening blueprint for the future.

Fulham Palace [Historic Garden Grade II*]

Bishop's Avenue, London SW6 6EA. Tel: (020) 7736 3233

London Borough of Hammersmith and Fulham • Off Fulham Palace Road down Bishop's Avenue • Museum open all year, Thurs – Sun, 2 – 4pm • Garden open all year, daily except 25th Dec, 1st Jan, 8am – dusk. Tours of Palace and garden 2nd and 4th Sun of each month, 2pm; other tours by appt • Entrance: free (museum tours 3 per person) • Other information: Plants for sale in nearby nursery. Annual plant sale end April/early May, 11am – 4pm. Garden walks once a season ○ 🐌 ♿ ♨ ♀ ☕

A place of faded grandeur, steeped in history. The palace, surrounded on three sides in its prime by a moat, was once the home of the Bishops of London; in the seventeenth century, Bishop Compton established here a vast collection of shrubs and trees sent back from America by his missionaries. The back of the palace, with its long, shuttered Georgian windows outlined by clipped pyracantha, looks over a sweeping lawn with a tall copper beech, an enormous Atlas cedar and other venerable trees. The holm oak, estimated to be over 500 years old, has been nominated a Great Tree of London. The old walled garden, with a gem of a small Tudor gateway to find, contains a sprawling specimen of a rare small-flowered fremontodendron and a long (if decayed) vinery along a curving wall. An elliptical box-edged herb garden dating from 1828 is enclosed by a pergola supporting a magnificent 100-year-old wisteria. The wilderness garden, long frequented only by green and spotted woodpeckers and other wildlife, is due to re-open after restoration late in 2006.

Geffrye Museum Gardens

136 Kingsland Road, London E2 8EA.
Tel: (020) 7739 9893/(020) 7739 8543 (Infoline)

Geffrye Museum Trust • 200 metres N of Shoreditch Church. Take underground to Liverpool St. (Bishopsgate exit) then buses 149 or 242. Front garden open all year, daily except 1st Jan, 14th April, 24th to 26th Dec; herb garden and period garden rooms open April to Oct, daily except Mon (but open Bank Holiday Mons); all 10am – 5pm (opens 12 noon Suns and Bank Holiday Mons) • Entrance: free • Other information: Guide dogs only ○ 💻 ✕ 🐌 <u>WC</u> ♿ ♨ ♀ ☕

The enjoyable museum and gardens are on the site of eighteenth-century almshouses formerly belonging to the Ironmongers' Company; the entrance to the walled herb garden is tucked away by the side of the museum. This mature garden has 170 different herbs, including sweet woodruff (*Galium odoratum*), sweet cicely (*Myrrhis odorata*) and buckler-leaf sorrel (*Rumex scutatus*). Flower beds contain informal, labelled groupings of herbs showing those for aromatic, culinary, cosmetic, dye, household and medicinal uses, and a special bed is designed to attract bees.

Secluded arbours with roses and climbing plants surround a delightful fountain. Period gardens lead from the herb garden and are arranged chronologically to reflect the museum's main displays of period rooms. These include a seventeenth-century garden of raised beds for herbs and vegetables, a Georgian garden with box edging, York-stone paths and clipped yew; a Victorian garden with seasonal, massed bedding; and an Edwardian garden with a pergola, a circular pool and informal planting of cottage-garden favourites.

70 Gloucester Crescent

London NW1 7EG. Tel: (020) 7485 6906

Lucy Gent and Malcolm Turner • Near junction of Gloucester Crescent and Oval Road 350 yards SW of Camden Town underground • Open by appt; visitors most welcome • Entrance: £2 ●

Mrs Charles Dickens once lived in this end-of-crescent house, and the garden, with its idiosyncratic shape, is strong on character. The three areas – a square at the front, a triangle at the side and a wedge at the back – show how a difficult town site may successfully be exploited. The owner, a garden designer and author, has created a place of strong geometry and infinite interest throughout the seasons, with August the high point for colour. The contrast with the bustle of nearby Camden Lock is quite something.

4 The Grove ★

Highgate Village, London N6 6JU.

Mr Cob Stenham • In Highgate Village, near Hampstead Lane • Open 4th June, 2 – 5pm, and May and June by appt only • Entrance: £2, OAPs/children £1 ● ♨

The seventeenth-century house sits behind a dignified front courtyard, beautifully paved with brick and surrounded by lush plantings of evergreens such as skimmias and ivy grown along the railings, with spring-flowering magnolias in the borders. A side passage brings the visitor through to an outstanding vista: the terrace, with a formal pool surrounded by dramatic planting, is the foreground to an immaculate lawn with well-planted mixed borders. Beyond this is an extensive backdrop to the wooded slopes of Hampstead Heath. An arbour of silver pears overlooks this stunning view, and a ceanothus arch leads down, through a tunnel of *Vitis coignetiae*, to the lower garden. This comprises an orchard with an old mulberry tree and some good statuary. One yew hedge conceals the well-ordered compost/bonfire area, and another balances this to enclose a secret garden dominated by a *Cladrastis kentukea*. *Rosa* 'Cooperi' flourishes on the south wall of the house, and the whole garden, which is beautifully designed and maintained, has exceptional charm. No. 7. The Grove (see below) is open on the same day in June.

7 The Grove ★

Highgate Village, London N6 6JU. Tel: (020) 8340 7205

Thomas G. Lyttelton • In Highgate Village, off Hampstead Lane • Open 26th March and 4th June, 2 – 5.30pm • Entrance: £3.50, OAPs and children £1.50 • Other information: Teas available on open days ● 🖳 ♿ ♞

A half-acre London walled town garden behind a handsome Victorian house of *c.*1830, splendidly designed by the owner for low maintenance, but with a variety of good planting schemes and ideas. Tunnels, arbours and screens abound, providing inspiration for busy garden-owners who would still like to have an interest outside the house. A series of nineteenth-century brick-built arches across the width of the garden separates it into two compartments. The area near the house is formal with a lawn, the area beyond the screen much less so, with fine compartments and features. Secret paths and unexpected views make this a magical place for children. Much use is made of evergreens and there are some exquisite shrubs, including a row of camellias down one wall and a massive *Hydrangea petiolaris*. There are many species and varieties of a particular genus – five varieties of box and even more of ivies, for example. The owner describes it as a green and yellow garden, with glimpses of white and red here and there. The canal feature was restructured and enhanced into a water garden in autumn 1996. No. 4. The Grove (see above) is also open on the charity day in June.

Hall Place [Historic Garden Grade II*]

Bourne Road, Bexley, Kent DA5 1PQ. Tel: (01322) 526574

Bexley Heritage Trust • Just N of A2 near A2/A223 junction • House open April to Oct, daily, 10am – 5pm, (opens 11am Sun); Nov to March, Tues – Sat, 10am – 4.15pm • Garden open all year, daily, 9am – dusk. Model allotment, parts of nursery and glasshouses open all year except 25th Dec, Mon – Fri, 9am – 5pm (closes 4pm in winter) • Entrance: free ○ 🍽 🏠 WC ♿ 🌐 🏛 🍵 ♺

Surrounding a splendid Tudor mansion, this is arguably the most interesting and best-kept public garden in south-east London. Although there is a strong emphasis on municipal annual bedding plants (geraniums, lobelias and marigolds) to provide summer colour, they are used with restraint and good taste, as are the roses in the large classical rose garden and the herbaceous plants in two splendid borders separated by a turf *allée* and backed by a characterful old brick wall on one side and a tightly clipped yew hedge on the other. Features include a raised walk overlooking one of Britain's finest topiary gardens, several rich shrubberies, a large and beautifully designed patterned herb garden, a wildlife friendly garden, a rock garden, meandering stretches of the River Cray, a heather garden and acres of lawn studded with evergreen and deciduous trees to provide vistas. The working nursery has a wide range of tropical floral displays, including model gardens and an orchard, carpet bedding and an environmental garden with pond-dipping, a wildflower meadow and a time garden reflecting the origins of the house.

Ham House ★ [Historic Garden Grade II*]

Ham Street, Richmond, Surrey TW10 7RS. Tel: (020) 8940 1950

The National Trust • On S bank of Thames, W of A307 at Petersham • House open 25th March to 29th Oct, Sat – Wed, 1 – 5pm • Garden open all year, Sat – Wed, 11am – 6pm (or dusk if earlier). Closed 25th, 26th Dec, 1st Jan • Entrance: £4, children £2, family £9. House and garden £8, children £4, family £19 • Other information: Parking 400 metres by river, disabled on terrace. Orangery café open as house at winter weekends ○ 🍽 🏠 WC ♿ 🌐 🏛 🍵 ♺

The approach to the impressive house is along an avenue running through meadows bordering the River Thames, giving no hint of the architectural framework of the seventeenth-century gardens beyond. Clipped balls of santolina and lavender set amongst parterres of box and hedged with yew lead to the raised south terrace, where historic pots and planting are backed by healthy pomegranate trees. Beyond lie the grass plats. The Trust is in the process of returning the gardens to their appearance c. 1670–80. The restoration of the wilderness as it lies on the main axis of the house re-creates one of the highlights of the original garden. Replicas of seventeenth-century lead statues mark its entrance, and hornbeam hedges provide a setting for spring bulbs and summer wild flowers. The walled kitchen garden, planted with period herbs, fruit and vegetables, is the perfect adjunct to the earliest surviving orangery in the country. Then cross the river by ferry to Marble Hill (see entry), or visit the *Palm Centre* at Ham Central Nursery. [Open Mon – Fri, 10am – 6pm. Tel: (020) 8255 6191.]

116 Hamilton Terrace

St Johns Wood, London NW8. Tel: (020) 7625 6909

Mr and Mrs I.B. Kathuria • Nearest underground station Maida Vale (5 mins), St John's Wood (10 mins). Buses 16, 98 from Marble Arch to Cricklewood. Parking in Hamilton Terrace • Open for NGS, and by appt • Entrance: £2 ● ● WC

Spot the house duck on the small front-garden pool in this prize-winning garden. The considerable visual appeal of the neighbouring church and surrounding trees gives a peaceful quality to the large and interesting back garden. Prize hostas flourish at different levels and the walls are covered with a variety of clematis, roses and other climbers. The garden reflects the owners' interest in a wide range of plants. Exuberance is balanced by restraint in many effective planting combinations, as the changes are rung in open areas, damp and shady sites, and containers, all beautifully maintained.

Hampton Court Palace ★★ [Historic Park and Garden Grade I]

East Molesey, Surrey KT8 9AU. Tel: (0870) 950 4499

Historic Royal Palaces Trust • On A308 at junction of A309 on N side of Hampton Court Bridge over Thames • Palace open • Gardens and park open all year, daily except 25th Dec • Entrance: Rose, Wilderness and Tiltyard Gardens free; Maze £3.50, children £2.50; Great Fountain Garden, Twentieth-Century Garden, Privy Garden, Sunken Garden and Great Vine £4, Concessions £3, children £2.50, family £12 (free to palace ticket-holders). Afternoon garden history tours, weekends only from May to Sept for garden or palace ticket-holders (limited places); special pre-booked morning tours by arrangement. Admission fees may change at short notice • Other information: Exhibition on history of Hampton Court gardens behind garden shop on East Front ○ ● ✕ ● WC & ⬧ ⬛

The gardens, which provide the setting for the palace, are an exciting and eclectic mixture of styles and tastes, with many different areas of character and interest. They are traditionally famous for the Great Vine, planted in 1768 – probably the oldest in the world and still producing hundreds of 'Black Hamburg' grapes each year (for sale to the public when harvested in late August) – and the maze, the oldest hedge-planted maze in Britain. The Pond Gardens offer a magnificent display of bedding plants, and there is a 1924 knot garden with interlocking bands of dwarf box, thyme, lavender and cotton lavender infilled with bedding plants. On a truly grand scale, the Great Fountain Garden, an immense semi-circle of grass and flower beds with a central fountain, is probably the most impressive element, but the Wilderness Garden in spring, with its mass of daffodils and spring-flowering trees, has the most charm. The laburnum walk – a tunnel of trained trees with butter-coloured rivulets of flowers in May – off the Wilderness Garden is another great attraction. The former kitchen garden now houses a rose garden. The restored Privy Garden of William III is a spectacular and unique example of the Baroque, with parterres, cutwork, clipped yews and spring and summer displays of seventeenth-century plants; it now forms a magnificent setting for Sir Christopher Wren's south front of the palace and the elaborate gilded ironwork railings by Jean Tijou. An area of the gardens sometimes missed by visitors is the secluded Twentieth-Century Garden, an area developed originally for the training of apprentices, but now also open to all. It is located just over the canal next to the Fountain Garden (signposted). Too much to see in one day – plan at least two trips; one in spring and one in summer to walk in only part of the 66 acres of gardens and the informal deer park ten times that size. A double row of 544 lime trees has been planted to flank the Longwater in Home Park, bringing Charles II's Long Walk Avenue back to its 1661 glory. By-the-by, try making the journey by boat from Westminster pier down to Hampton Court – the most charming approach to the garden – although be aware that it can take four hours. The park is also the venue for the annual RHS Hampton Court Palace International Flower Show in July. Bushy Park (see entry) lies across Hampton Court Road.

The Hill Garden [Historic Garden Grade II*]

Inverforth Close, North End Way, London NW3 7EX. Tel: (020) 8455 5183

Corporation of London • From Hampstead pass Jack Straw's Castle on left hand side on road to Golders Green. Inverforth Close is off North End Way (A502) • Open all year, daily, 9am – dusk • Entrance: free ○ 💬 ✗ WC ♿

Overgrown in parts, the chief charm here lies in the secluded setting. The pergola, now restored, was built between 1906 and 1925 to a design by Thomas H. Mawson to screen Lord Leverhulme's house, The Hill (now known as Inverforth House), from its kitchen gardens and to shield it from people walking on the Heath. It is one of the best examples of its type, with all its columns and timber features intact. The pergola walk and the former kitchen garden have both been replanted. Other features include a large formal lily pond, herbaceous borders, undulating lawns and many shrubs and trees. There are wonderful views across the Heath.

Holland Park [Historic Park Grade II]

Kensington, London W8/W11. Tel: (020) 7471 9813

Royal Borough of Kensington and Chelsea • Between Kensington High Street and Holland Park Avenue, with several entrances • Parking (pay and display) from Abbotsbury Road entrance • Open all year, daily, 7.30am – dusk • Entrance: free
○ 💬 ✗ 🍴 WC ♿ 🎭 💡 ♺

Most of the famous Holland House was destroyed by bombs in World War II, but the formal gardens, created in 1812 by Lord Holland, have been maintained. The 53-acre park contains some rare trees such as Pyrenean oak, Chinese sweet gum, Himalayan birch, violet willow and the snowdrop tree, which flowers in May. The rose walk has now been replanted with a variety of azaleas, and a small iris garden surounds a fountain. Peacocks strut the lawns and drape the walls with their tail feathers, and in the woodland section birds and squirrels find sanctuary from London's noise and traffic. There are excellent children's play areas. In 1991 the charming and beautifully maintained one-acre Kyoto Garden was opened as a permanent souvenir of the Japanese Festival. This is one of the most pleasant small London parks, although paths and grass can look worn and tired after the busy summer period, and not everyone will admire the bedding plants. Don't miss William Pye's fountain in the garden behind the orangery.

The Holme

Inner Circle, Regent's Park, London NW1 4NT.

Crown Estate Commissioners • In Regent's Park, just W of Inner Circle • Open several days for NGS • Entrance: £2.50, children £1 (2005 prices) • Other information: Parking in Outer Circle. Refreshments and toilet facilities in café opposite ● &

The garden was designed to enhance the setting of one of the best-positioned houses (by Decimus Burton) in central London, overlooking Heron Island in Regent's Park Lake; wisely, waterfowl are excluded. A gravel path leads down through a shrubbery towards sweeping lawns and herbaceous beds at the back of the house. A spectacular rock garden with stream, pond and waterfall is not to be missed, nor is the formal garden with its pool, fountain and arbours. Find time to sit at some of the many vantage points to admire the mature trees, good planting schemes and views.

239A Hook Road

Chessington, Kingston–upon–Thames, Surrey KT9 1EQ. Tel: (020) 8397 3761

Derek and Dawn St Romaine • On Hook road (A243) close to Hook underpass and A3. Opposite recreation ground • Open for NGS, and by appt • Entrance: £2 • Other information: Parking in recreation ground opposite ● & B&B

Created since 1985, this garden of many visual delights reflects the artistic skill of the garden-photographer owner and his wife. An attractive patio leads out onto a gravel garden and dining area planted with grasses and drought-tolerant plants. Around the circular lawn are standard hollies and box balls act as edging to the wide and effective borders. A circular pond and an L-shaped rose tunnel lead into the *potager*, where thriving vegetables are given designer willow supports and fruit trees are underplanted with patterns of herbs, vegetables and low hedges. Look out for the picturesque garden shed with its cobwebby windows, which puts in an appearance in many garden photographs.

Horniman Museum and Gardens [Historic Public Park Grade II]
100 London Road, Forest Hill, London SE23 3PQ. Tel: (020) 8699 1872

Horniman Museum • On South Circular at 100 London Road, SE23 • Open all year, daily except 25th Dec, 7.15am – sunset (opens 8am Sun and Bank Holiday Mons) • Entrance: free ○ 💬 ✕ 🖼 wc ♿ ⚐ ⚜ ♀ ♀

The museum and gardens were Frederick Horniman's gift to the people of London in 1901 'for their recreation, instruction and enjoyment'. The high standard of maintenance, impressive planting under the creative eye of the head gardener and stunning views across London make them a place of year-round interest. The 16.5 acres include herbaceous borders distinguished by subtle shades and innovative plant combinations, a delightful rose and sunken garden planted in strong colours with interesting annuals, and an imaginative mix of tropical and traditional bedding schemes. An historic bandstand stands at the centre of the gardens, and the Grade-II-listed Victorian conservatory has been restored and resited. There is also an animal enclosure and a 5-acre nature trail along a stretch of disused railway line. An enjoyable visit for the whole family.

1A Hungerford Road
London N7 9LA. Tel: (020) 7607 0072

David Matzdorf • Short walk from Caledonian Road tube station. Buses 29, 253 to Hillmarton Road stop in Camden Road, 17, 91, 259 to last stop in Hillmarton Road, 10 to York Way and 274 to junction of Market Road and Caledonian Road • Open one day in August for NGS, 1 – 6pm, and by appt • Entrance: £1.50, children 50p ● wc

The small walled garden in front of the eco-house co-designed by the owner and architect Jon Broome is planted as an exotic sub-tropical space with acacias, palms, brugmansias in plunge pots, bananas, cannas and ginger lilies – in essence a conservatory without a roof. The 'green roof' of the house (accessible at visitors' own risk) is fashioned with a densely packed array of alpines, sedums, grasses and aromatic herbs. An unusual house and garden, and a good example of creativity in a small space.

Hyde Park [Historic Park Grade I]
Rangers Lodge, London W2 2UH. Tel: (020) 7298 2100

Royal Parks • Open all year, daily, 5am – midnight • Entrance: free • ○ 💬 ✕ 🖼 wc ♿ ⚜ ♀ ♀

One of the great Royal Parks that now provide Central London with highly valued open space, Hyde Park has something for everyone – and this is perhaps its weakness as well as its strength. For those with an interest in plants it is best explored on foot, although a ride up from Hyde Park Corner to Marble Arch, preferably on the top of a bus, is perhaps the best way to appreciate the bold and colourful seasonal plantings in Park Lane. You can make up your mind at the same time what you think of the curious Queen Elizabeth gates erected in 1993. The south side of the park near Hyde Park Corner has most to offer gardeners, particularly the newish and very English rose garden, which is maturing well. Summer brings a profusion of roses in beds and on arches, with pinks and creamy yellows predominating, and tall foxgloves and eremurus adding an unexpected note. A short walk away the Dell has waterfowl enjoying the waterfall and the iris-lined stream. On the opposite side of the path is a quiet grove of silver birch under planted with epimediums, cotoneasters and junipers, where a sombre holocaust memorial stone is set in gravel. It is tempting to nibble away at Hyde Park round the edges, enjoying the pockets of rich planting to be found around its entrances. You get a much better feel for the place, however, by walking from edge to edge, or better still making an entire circuit. It takes a surprisingly short time. That way you cannot fail to appreciate the glory of its trees, and its stately avenues with cool shade. Step away from the main paths and you will find patches of longer grass, dells of golden buttercups, distant views of the Albert Memorial above the trees of nearby Kensington Gardens. There are many curiosities to discover. The Reformers' Tree south-west of Speakers' Corner turns out to be a fine memorial mosaic rather than an actual tree, commemorating one burned down in the Reform League riots of 1866. Nearby is the gaunt shaft of a large oak struck by lightning in 1999. You may, if you pass the right way, find the bird sanctuary memorial to the naturalist W.H. Hudson, with its Epstein sculpture, or the perched dolmen-like boulder given by Norwegian seamen in gratitude for friendship and hospitality during World War II. The Diana Princess of Wales memorial fountain, whose agitated waters rather too closely mirror her troubled life, is the best-known and most recent of the monuments that mark the history of the place. Good maps at strategic points are a source of as much information as the average visitor could need.

Isabella Plantation ★

Richmond Park, Richmond, Surrey TW10 5HS. Tel: (020) 8948 3209

*Royal Parks • Richmond Park, Broomfield Hill • Open all year, daily, dawn – dusk • Entrance: free • Other information: Parking in Broomfield Hill car park, Pembroke Lodge, Roehampton Gate, disabled at north entrance by way of Ham Gate. Refreshments at Pembroke Lodge. Motorised wheelchair available weekdays. Telephone to book by 12 noon previous day ○ **WC** & ⇪*

Hidden away behind a wrought-iron gate within the sweeping tracts of Richmond Park is a remarkably rich wooded plantation of 40 acres. Fine native trees – oaks, beeches and birches – shelter spring-flowering bulbs, colourful magnolias, camellias, rhododendrons and azaleas (a National Collection of Kurume azaleas is held here), coloured autumn leaves, and scented winter-flowering shrubs. Ponds, streams and a bog garden are planted with irises, daylilies and candelabra primulas. The garden is a notable bird sanctuary – nuthatches, tree-creepers, kingfishers, woodpeckers and owls have all been spotted, and herons fish regularly in the ponds. It is worth driving around the park perimeter to appreciate the majesty of the trees and the fine views over London, marred only by a battalion of tower blocks.

Kensington Gardens [Historic Park and Garden Grade I]

London W2 2UH. Tel: (020) 7298 2100

Royal Parks • Entrances off Bayswater Road, Kensington Gore and West Carriage Drive, Hyde Park • Palace state apartments open all year, daily, 10am – 5pm (closes

6pm Sun, 4pm Nov to Feb). Orangery open daily; for information telephone (020)
7937 9561 • Gardens open all year, daily, from 6am (closing time displayed at gate)
• Entrance: free (state apartments £10, OAPs/students £7.50, children £6.50, family
£30) ○ 🍽 🍴 <u>WC</u> ⌖ ⬦ 🔦 ⚲

The 274 acres of finest park adjoining Hyde Park have their own pleasures, including sculpture by G.F. Watts. Children and older enthusiasts will relish on the north side of the park at the western corner a whole new imaginative Peter Pan world – a playground in memory of Diana, Princess of Wales, which features a pirate ship, wigwams, a tree house and a splendidly realistic crocodile among its many attractions (telephone (0207) 298 2141 for details). Also commemorating the late princess is a seven-mile-long memorial walk, charted by 90 plaques set in the ground, which crosses Kensington Gardens and Hyde, Green and St James's Parks. The Albert Memorial is a glittering treat, and the elegant Baroque orangery by Hawksmoor and Vanbrugh, with decoration by Grinling Gibbons, is well worth a visit. So, too, is the sunken water garden surrounded by beds of bright seasonal flowers, which can be viewed from 'windows' in a lime walk. From the Broad Walk east to the Albert Memorial, semi-circular flower beds are kept planted against a background of flowering shrubs. *The Serpentine Gallery*, host to some of London's most exciting and talked-about modern exhibitions, is situated at the convergence of two of Bridgeman's avenues. It is distinguished by a crescent of slate benches and a stone circle by Ian Hamilton Finlay inscribed with the Latin names of all the trees in the park, and other outdoor sculpture is also sometimes on display.

Kenwood [Historic Park Grade II*]

Hampstead Lane, London NW3 7JR. Tel: (020) 8348 1286

English Heritage • On N side of Hampstead Heath, on Highgate-Hampstead road
• House open April to Oct, daily, 11am – 5pm (closes 4pm Nov to March) • Park
open all year, daily, 8am – 8.30pm (closes 4.30pm in winter) • Entrance: free
• Other information: Parking at West Lodge car park, Hampstead Lane (charge)
○ 🍽 ✕ 🍴 <u>WC</u> ⌖ ⬦ 🌳 🏛 🔦 ⚲

The picturesque landscape, which is currently being restored, was laid out by Humphry Repton at the end of the eighteenth century. Today the Kenwood estate covers 112 acres, and walks follow Repton's original plan. Vistas, sweeping lawns from the terrace of Kenwood House and views over Hampstead Heath (and London) predominate, and the magnificent mature trees include oak and beech. Large-scale shrubberies are dominated by rhododendrons. The pasture ground slopes down towards two large lakes, and woods to the south of the lakes fringe the heath side of the pasture ground, with several gates onto the heath itself. It is a good place to walk at any season, but particularly when the trees are turning in autumn, to recall that the lime walk was a favourite of that great gardener of the eighteenth century, Alexander Pope. Look out for the ivy arch which opens out on to the lakes (one of Repton's famous 'surprises') and the sham bridge on the Thousand Pound Pond, which has been faithfully rebuilt with its single upside-down baluster. There is also some worthwhile modern sculpture, including a Henry Moore and a 1953 Barbara Hepworth. On the western side are haymeadows which change colour from May to July; natural regeneration of the ancient woodlands (SSSI) is being encouraged.

Kew Gardens
(see ROYAL BOTANIC GARDENS)

38 Killieser Avenue
Streatham Hill, London SW2 4NT. Tel: (020) 8671 4196

Mrs Winkle Haworth • Off Streatham Hill, near Streatham Hill station. From Sternhold Avenue take second turning right • Open for NGS and by appt for parties of 5 or more • Entrance: £3 ◐ ▦ B&B

This much-visited South London garden is lovingly tended and full of carefully chosen plants and shrubs evoking a romantic atmosphere. Lush and skilful planting divides the garden into two distinct areas where perennials and annuals with a restrained colour palate blend harmoniously – box topiary, old-fashioned roses, clematis and violas. An obelisk, a rose arch and a water cascade give architectural interest, while box cones beside a delightful rose-clad Gothick arbour introduce visitors to a second level, with a parterre filled with white roses and a wall fountain providing an element of formality.

London Wetland Centre
Queen Elizabeth's Walk, Barnes, London SW13 9WT. Tel: (020) 8409 4400

The Wildfowl and Wetlands Trust • From M4 junction 1 take A4 to Hammersmith, then follow signs to Barnes (A306), crossing Hammersmith Bridge. Travel 0.75m along Castelnau to traffic lights; at Red Lion pub turn left into Queen Elizabeth's Walk. Nearest underground station Hammersmith. Buses from Hammersmith Bus Depot, 33, 72, 209 (alight at Red Lion pub) and 283, the dedicated 'Duck Bus', direct to Centre • Open all year, daily, except 25th Dec, 9.30am – 6pm (closes 5pm in winter) (last admission 1 hour before closing) • Entrance: £6.75, OAPs £5.50, children £4, family £17.50 (2005 prices) ○ ▦ ✕ ▦ WC ໓ ☺ ♨ ☻ ⚲

Within 105 acres of the wetlands in an area close to the visitors' centre, three high-profile young garden designers have focused on the theme of sustainability and created gardens to motivate and encourage conservation gardening. The first, designed by Land Arts, has a loosely laid spiralling path of slate curving from the outer edge of the garden to finish in a tight central oval resembling a butterfly's proboscis. Block planting of perennials rich in pollen and scent has been chosen to give interest for the partially sighted and to attract insects. By contrast, Arne Maynard's garden consists of structured formal planting with turf-topped walls formed from split oak logs, radiating across the site in undulating curves; the planting is meadow-like. The third garden is a tongue-in-cheek Bouncing Bomb/Barnes Wallis/Barnes Wetlands by Cleve West and Johnny Woodford. It is surrounded by cobalt-blue spikes, with a seat resembling sharp teeth. The eye is led to the central pond with the 'bouncing bomb' skimming the surface; reed beds surround the pond and planting is simplified to increase the sculptural impact. Find time to include the Wildfowl and Wetland Trust areas, and look out for the hides with their roofs of succulents.

London Zoo

Regent's Park, London NW1 4RY. Tel: (020) 7722 3333

London Zoo • In Regent's Park to N of Outer Circle. Take Bus 274 from Camden/ Baker Street to Prince Albert Road and walk across bridge to main gate; tube to Camden Town/Baker Street; waterbus from Camden Lock or Little Venice • Open all year, daily except 25th Dec, 10am – 5.30pm (closes 4pm in winter) • Entrance: £14, OAPs and students £12, children under 15 £10.75, under 3 free, family £45 • Other information: Car park at zoo or metered parking in Outer Circle. Wheelchairs available from information kiosk at main gate ○ 💷 ✕ 🍴 WC ♿ ❢ ⚲

Listen to the dramatic cries of the macaws in the distance as you enter the main gate and observe the mixed carex planted in front of their enclosure. All the enclosures are designed to provide the conditions the animals need. The keepers choose the most appropriate materials, all grown on site for each species: sand or earth for burrowing animals, hard surfaces for hoofed animals, branches and perches for arboreal species. Note the tree of heaven (1870) with the listed penguin pool built around it, and the old black mulberry (wrongly labelled 'white' a century ago). Find time to walk over the timber bridge below the 'stream' of blue slate in the Water-wise Garden. As part of the 'Bugs' exhibition, housed within the millennium conservation centre, a native wildlife garden has been created. This includes habitats such as meadows, woodland and hedgerow, along with ideas for a domestic garden including a rockery and a herb garden, and reveals ways that birds, butterflies and animals can be attracted to a city garden.

4 Macaulay Road

Clapham, London SW4 0QX. Tel: (020) 7627 1137

Mrs Diana Ross • Off Clapham Common Northside • Open by appt only • Entrance: £5 per person (10 people min.) inclusive of guided tour ● ♿

A walled garden (24 x 15 metres) set out on strong, clear lines with formality heightened by trees, box hedges, topiary and lots of pots. A circular lawn is surrounded by dense mixed planting, arches and a pergola, and the patterned shell of a grotto is softened by ferns. The garden has been designed to look as good in winter as in summer, and to foster wildlife, especially birds and frogs. No pesticides allowed here.

Marble Hill [Historic Park Grade II*]

Richmond Road, Twickenham TW1 2NL. Tel: (020) 8892 5115

English Heritage • S of Richmond Bridge off Richmond Road. Additional access by river launch • House open April to Oct, Sat, Sun and Bank Holiday Mons, 10am – 5pm (closes 2pm Sat); Nov to March, by appt only • Park open all year, daily, 7.30am – dusk • Entrance: £3.70, concessions £2.80, children £1.90 ○ 💷 🍴 WC ♿ ⬧ 🏛 ❢

The gardens, originally laid out in the 1740s for the Countess of Suffolk, are still being restored by English Heritage and awaiting the implementation of a landscape management plan as part of the Thames Landscape Strategy – a conservation plan for the whole of this historic area. Alexander Pope, a neighbour of the Countess, took an interest in the layout, and excavations have revealed one of the two grottoes known to have been constructed. There is an ice-house and a young Sweet Walk. The gardens (if they can be called that, as now they are largely sports pitches and a venue for summer music concerts) lay claim to one of the largest and oldest black walnuts in the country and also some of the tallest bay willows (*Salix pentandra*) and Italian alders (*Alnus cordata*). Then take the ferry to Ham House (see entry) over the river. You can also visit *Strawberry Hill* (eponymous station nearby) where Horace Walpole's 'little Gothick castle' and Grade-II* garden can be seen from Easter to Oct on Sunday afternoons for parties by appointment. Telephone (020) 8892 0051.

Mile End Park

Mile End Road, London E3. Tel: (020) 7364 5000

London Borough of Tower Hamlets • Access from Burdett Road (A1205), St Paul's Way, Mile End Road (A1), Grove Road (A1205). Nearest underground station: Mile End • Open all year, daily • Entrance: free ○ 🏧 ♿ � 🍴 ♋

Not great gardening, but is a must for residents and for anyone following the development of new city parks. Created by linking small parcels of open space, it was designed to provide a range of activities for local people. Clever landscaping helps disguise its narrowness and block out much of the sound of busy main roads; at times birdsong wins over traffic noise. A long ribbon of green stretching from the edge of Victoria Park south almost to Limehouse basin, hugged on its eastern side by Regent's Canal, it is now developing its own special character. Its best-known feature, the green – actually yellow – bridge with its silver birch and pine trees spanning the Mile End Road, has had its problems, and does not prepare you for the impressively lush growth elsewhere. Now that it has had time to settle, there is a feeling that nature and man are beginning to modify – and in places even perhaps to improve on – the designs of the planners. New footpaths are etched where they are needed. Survival of the fittest (there isn't much money for maintenance in this part of London) brings pleasant surprises – rich purple geraniums sprawling through rough grass, thickets of escallonia alive with bumblebees. While the older buildings in the park look distinctly tatty, nature flourishes.

Museum of Garden History

Lambeth Palace Road, London SE1 7LB. Tel: (020) 7401 8865

In Lambeth Palace Road, parallel to River Thames on S bank, hard by Lambeth Bridge • Open all year, daily, 10.30am – 5pm (closed Christmas period – telephone for details) • Entrance: Voluntary admission charge £3, concessions £2.50 • Other information: Historic collection of garden tools and artefacts. Courses, exhibitions, lectures, plant fairs and concerts ○ 🍽 ✕ <u>WC</u> ♿ ♨ 🏛 🍴

The garden in the churchyard was created in 1981. It commemorates the two John Tradescants (father and son), gardeners to Charles I and II, who are buried in a fine tomb in the replica seventeenth-century garden, which contains plants grown at that time. Lady Salisbury's knot garden design incorporates some of the Tradescants' own introductions. Well-labelled herbs abound amongst pretty perennials, making a delightful backcloth for the table tombs, whilst the walls are clothed in Virginia creeper, ivy, roses and clematis. In 2006, thanks to a £40,000 lottery grant, a multi-media display will be integrated around one of the Museum's oddities – a total immersion font dating back to its days as an Anglican church. The installation aims to tell the story of the local area and some of its more famous associates: the Tradescants, Elias Ashmole, Captain Bligh, William Blake and the late-eighteenth-century botanical artist James Sowerby.

Museum of London Nursery Garden

London Wall, London EC2Y 5HN. Tel: (020) 7600 3699

Museum of London • Take underground to St Paul's or Barbican, then follow signs • Open 14th April to Oct, daily, 10am – 5.30pm (opens Sun 12 noon) • Entrance: free • Other information: Possible for wheelchairs but shallow steps make assistance necessary ❶ 🍽 ✕ <u>WC</u> ♿ 🚻 ⚲

Garden designers Colson and Stone totally revamped the internal courtyard in 1990 to coincide with the exhibition of London's gardens, and have transformed an almost lifeless area into a living history of plantsmanship in the City from medieval times to the present day. Legendary names like Henry Russell, who sold striped roses in Westminster, and James Veitch, who sold exotica like the monkey-puzzle tree from his nursery in Chelsea, are represented. This tiny roof garden is flanked on four sides by high buildings, yet the designers have still managed to incorporate a tumbling rill and a rock garden.

Myddelton House Gardens ★ [Historic Garden Grade II]

Bulls Cross, Enfield EN2 9HG. Tel: (01992) 702200

Lee Valley Regional Park Authority • S of M25 on A10 (junction 25), turn first right into Bullsmoor Lane, left into Bulls Cross; house is on right at junction with Turkey Street • Open all year, Mon – Fri, 10am – 4.30pm (closes 3pm Oct to March); plus Suns and Bank Holiday Mons, 16th April to Oct, 12 noon – 4pm; and for NGS. Closed Christmas week and Bank Holidays • Entrance: £2.40, concessions £1.80 • Other information: Teas on NGS Suns and charity days only ○ <u>WC</u> ♿ 🅿 ⚲

A magnificent, diverse plant collection set in four acres was built up by the famous E.A. Bowles and is now restored. Splendid spring bulbs, followed by an award-winning iris collection, then by autumn crocus, cyclamen and autumn-remontant iris, make this garden a joy all year round. Sternbergia and nerines are just a few of the autumn bulbs, and there is a fine *Crinum moorei* near the old conservatory. This is by no means a municipal garden, and the impressive plant collection is displayed attractively in a well-designed area surrounding the Regency house. The garden is still unified by Bowles's plants and vision and it is worth reading details of his plan, which included a Lunatic Asylum planted with botanical misfits. Other attractions include the carp lake, a magnificent wisteria and part of the old London Bridge.

17A Navarino Road

Hackney, London E8 1AD. Tel: (020) 7923 2696 (Alex Ratcliffe)

John Tordoff • Off London Fields, near Hackney Central station. Buses 30, 38 • Open by appt for parties of 10 or more • Entrance: £2.50 ☕ ⚲

An imaginative explosion of design occupies just 25 x 8 metres, yet this garden visit must not be hurried, starting with the Italianate courtyard with its fountain guarded by white pottery doves – the doves, archways, Mount Fuji, tea house and mirrored alcove are recycled or made by the owner. Clipped yews lead to a new perspective – a Japanese garden. Do not miss the seating area on the right which shares the pool with neighbours. Miniature conifers and well-placed rocks bring the eye down to the small scale of the design, and the whole is kept together by the rich green carpet of *Soleirolia soleirolii* (baby's tears). The clear stream is a haven for many birds. Memorable.

Noel–Baker Peace Garden

Elthorne Park, Hazelville Road, London N19.

London Borough of Islington • Entrances to Elthorne Park in Beaumont Road and Sunnyside Road • Open all year, daily, 8am – dusk (opens 9am Sat, 10am Sun) • Entrance: free • Other information: Toilet facilities in adjacent playground ○ &
⟁

This is a small, well-designed formal garden within a London park, created in 1984 in memory of Philip Noel-Baker, winner of the Nobel Peace Prize in 1959. It is an interesting example of late-twentieth-century garden design and planting, centering on a water feature and a striking bronze figure (with a horizontal bronze reflection). Much use is made of brick and York-stone paving, and raised beds together with lawns; the overall effect is softened and enlivened by the excellent planting, with many unusual species (e.g. *Acca sellowiana, Clerodendrum bungei, C. trichotomum*). The emphasis is on green, grey and white, lifted here and there by splashes of colour and linked by the strong lines of the asymmetrical design. There are several secluded sitting areas. The garden receives extensive use and support from the local community, and although the results of limited maintenance are sometimes apparent, the overall impression is of well-loved amenity. Also in Hazelville Road is another neighbourhood amenity: *Sunnyside Community Gardens*, with flower borders, a wildflower patch and a pond, while *Elthorne Park* itself has a good children's playground and a fitness trail.

Pembridge Cottage

10 Strawberry Hill Road, Twickenham TW1 4PT. Tel: (020) 8287 8993

Ian and Lydia Sidaway • 1m from Twickenham town centre, approached from Cross Deep or Waldegrave Road. Strawberry Hill station; buses 33, 110, 267, 281, 290, 490, R68, R70 • Open 18th and 25th June, 2 – 6pm, and by appt • Entrance: £2 ●

A carefully maintained artist's garden which is an excellent example of a green garden without the ubiquitous lawn. Interesting at all seasons, the long and narrow plot is designed with recessed areas framed by structural shrubs – bay, elaeagnus, fig, olive, viburnums, box and photinia. Gravel paths are outlined by groups of large river stones. Bamboos, strong ferns and grasses have stylishly planted terracotta pots placed among them. The journey ends at the artist's studio. Ask to see the imaginative scrapbook showing the garden's progress over the past six years.

Priory Gardens [Historic Garden Grade II]

Orpington, Kent. Tel: (020) 8464 3333 ext. 4471

London Borough of Bromley • Off Orpington High Street • Open all year, daily, 7.30am – dusk (opens 9.30am Sat, Sun and Bank Holiday Mons) • Entrance: free • Other information: Separate area for dogs ○ 🐾 WC <u>WC</u> ⅅ ⟐ ⚲ ⚬

Adjacent to an attractive medieval priory building (now Bromley Museum), this is one of the most tastefully gardened public spaces in outer London, documentation of which dates from 1634. Pre-1939 the gardens were extended in the formal Arts and Crafts style. It has an excellent example of patterned annual bedding, a recently replanted herbaceous garden, a rich rose garden, fine mature trees and shrubs and a refurbished lake.

Regent's Park ★ [Historic Park and Garden Grade I]

Inner Circle, Regent's Park, London NW1. Tel: (020) 7298 2000

Royal Parks • Off Marylebone Road. Many other entrances to park • Open all year, daily, dawn – dusk • Entrance: free • Other information: Dogs in park only ○ ● ✕ 🐾 <u>WC</u> ⅅ ⟐ ⚲ ⚬

Within the park, *Queen Mary's Rose Garden*, well-laid-out and beautifully manicured, is justly famous. Playing host to more than 60,000 roses – dominated by hybrid teas and floribundas, although also including old-fashioned, shrub and species roses – the sight and scent of the garden in high summer is a magnet for thousands of visitors. It must be said, however, that this style of rose garden is not to everyone's taste. The roses are grown with almost military discipline and are in perfect condition. Swagged and garlanded climbers surround the circular rose garden, but the herbaceous borders are also worth visiting, particularly in late July and August, as is the large ornamental lake with its central island. It attracts many varieties of waterfowl, including herons which nest on the island. The Avenue Garden at the southern end of the Broad Walk (five minutes away, between the Inner and Outer Circle towards Cambridge Gate) is another exquisitely maintained Victorian-style area of planting. Its side walks are lined with urns and fountains following Nesfield's originals. Italian cypresses line the paths. There are 32 ornamental urns and tazzas (shallow bowls) and eight fountains. Nesfield's planting precision has been described as performing the same function as a military band – it provides entertainment for park visitors. Adjacent to this is the charming English Garden added by Nesfield's son Marham. Do not miss the little St John's Lodge garden. Nearby, at 66 Portland Place, W1 (a short walk from Oxford Circus) is the *Royal Institute of British Architects* (RIBA). The delightful roof garden on the first floor adjoining the cafe which features gleaming steel containers with clipped box and other architectural foliage plants, and a William Pye fountain, is open to the public during office hours. Another stylish sculpture garden in the area, which also has a cafe, is to be found at *The Wallace Collection* in Manchester Square.

The Roof Garden [Historic Garden Grade II]
99 Kensington High Street, London W8 5ED. Tel: (020) 7937 7994

Virgin Group • In Derry Street off Kensington High Street by lift • Telephone to check gardens open before attempting to visit • Entrance: free ● ✕ ♀

A fantasy one-and-a-half-acre garden 30 metres above the ground on the sixth floor of what was Derry and Toms 1938 department store. Now a private members' club with restaurant facilities, the gardens which surround the bar and dining room are also used for functions and conferences. Ralph Hancock designed them to give three distinct illusions – a formal Spanish garden with canal, an English woodland garden and a Tudor garden. The soil is nowhere thicker than a metre, so it is remarkable that more than 500 varieties of trees and shrubs, including palms, figs and vines, survive up here. Ducks swim about in their high-rise ponds, watched over by flamingos, and there is a delightful maze of small paths, bridges and walkways, with peepholes in the outer walls giving glimpses across the city skyline.

The Rookery [Historic Garden Grade II]
Streatham Common South, London SW16. Tel: (020) 8671 0994

Lambeth Council • Streatham High Road (A23), then Streatham Common South. No entrance by car from Streatham North Crown Lane • Open all year, daily except 25th Dec, 9am – dusk • Entrance: free • Other information: Dogs on leads on top terrace only ○ ☕ ♨ WC ♿ ♒

This surprising garden space up the hill from Streatham High Road was once part of a private garden. In over a quarter of a mile there is much to enjoy: an abundantly planted English garden with quiet seating areas, a rock garden and stream, a small yew-hedged pond area close by a wisteria-clad pergola. The white garden, at its peak in July, almost rivals Sissinghurst. Further down the hill through shrubbery-lined paths is a quiet orchard picnic ground. On the way back up the hill seek out the well – one of the three original wells of Streatham's spa waters, dating from 1659. A fenced and gated play area with large paddling pool, much used by local families, is next to the parking area.

Roots and Shoots
The Vauxhall Centre, Walnut Tree Walk, London SE11 6DN. Tel: (020) 7587 1131/7582 1800.

Trustees of Roots and Shoots Charity • Off Kennington Road; entrance in Fitzalan Street next to stables or Walnut Tree Walk • Open all year, Mon – Fri, 9am – 4pm, plus Sats, May and June, 10am – 2pm; also open for NGS 10th and 11th June, 11am – 4pm, 12th and 26th July, 6.30 – 8.30pm • Entrance: free (events charge £1) • Other information: Several events and conservation advice service – telephone for details [NEW] ○ WC ♿ ♨ 🚻 ♀ B&B

Lambeth's hidden green lung – a 0.5-acre wildlife garden five minutes' walk from the Imperial War Museum, built on the rubble of a demolition site. As you walk up the entrance traffic sounds seem to fade; waving echiums greet you from the

Mediterranean garden and a banana plant is growing tall at the office door. Local schools come here for pond-dipping and to learn about the abundant wildlife. Robinias, *Mimosa dealbata*, quince and apple trees provide shade and interest, beehives stand in the long grasses; in June the unpruned roses flower among wandering stony paths, and in July the wildflower meadow steals the limelight. The London Beekeepers Association is based here, and their honey is often for sale. Remember also to telephone for details of National Apple Week in October, when single variety apple juice is pressed in the apple barn, then sold to those first in a long queue. A cutting-edge learning centre with solar electricity and water heating, planted roofs, and a rainwater collection opened in 2005.

167 Rosendale Road

West Dulwich, London SE21 8LW. Tel: (020) 8766 7846

Mr and Mrs A. Pizzoferro • Off South Circular Road at junction of Rosendale and Lovelace Roads. Nearest train stations Tulse Hill or West Dulwich • Open for NGS, and by appt • Entrance: £2 ●

The warm colour theme of the front garden gives no hint of the charm to be found in the small woodland area, the natural winter stream and child-safe wildlife pond in the back garden. This is a place to visit for ideas: bamboo canes topped with holed flints; massed perennials and winding bark paths, one of which leads to an old wooden ladder leaning against a fruit tree; grasses massed in pots, houseleeks at home in bricks, hostas planted at eye level for inspection, agapanthus and bulbs in pots are just a few of the visual delights.

Royal Botanic Gardens ★★ [Historic Park Grade I]

Kew, Richmond, Surrey TW9 3AB. Tel: (020) 8332 5655 (24–hour message)

Trustees • Kew Green, S of Kew Bridge • Kew Palace (maintained by Historic Royal Palaces) opens after refurbishment, May 2006 • Gardens open all year, daily except 24th and 25th Dec, 9.30am – 4.15pm/7.30pm depending on season; glasshouses close earlier. Guided tours daily from Victoria Gate visitor centre, 11am and 2pm • Entrance: £10 (late entry charge variable), OAPs, students £7, children under 17, blind, partially sighted and essential carers free, season ticket (for Kew and Wakehurst Place) £35, season ticket for couples £65. Other season tickets and Friends of Kew Membership available (2005 prices) • Other information: Parking on Kew Road (free)/Brentford Gate car park in Ferry Lane (£3.50 per day). Coach parking in Kew Road. Wheelchairs may be reserved in advance free of charge. Guide dogs permitted
○ ● ✕ ▨ wc & ℘ ▦ ♀ ℺

Kew's delightful and varied gardens and grounds of 300 acres have something for everyone: in spring, the flowering cherries, crocuses, daffodils and the fine rock garden; in May and June, the bluebell wood, the lilacs (made famous by the song) and the water-lily house; in summer the Duke's Garden, the rose garden; in autumn bulbs and trees; in winter, the winter-flowering cherries. The 14,000 trees include oaks, conifers and the famous ginkgo and pagoda trees. Year-round pleasures are Decimus Burton's Palm and Temperate Houses and the elegant modern Princess of Wales Conservatory (named after Princess Augusta, founder of the Botanic Gardens in 1759) with its computer-controlled microclimates. The huge glasshouses, some of which are kept at tropical temperatures, have their unique collections of exotic and unusual plants, ranging from banana trees to giant water lilies. There is an Evolution House, and Museum No. 1 (opposite the Palm House) contains the plants and people exhibition. The somewhat formal rose garden, the delightful rock garden and the grass and bamboo gardens should not be missed. The Japanese gateway has been completely restored and the area around landscaped. All these buildings and gardens are elements in 'working' Kew, which is primarily a botanic research institution, collecting, conserving and exchanging plants from all over the world. There is another Kew – historic and royal. The palace (currently undergoing major restoration, reopening in 2006) became in 1729 home to Frederick, Prince of Wales. His wife, Princess Augusta, commissioned the gardens here and, the 3rd Earl of Bute, created them. After Frederick's death, Princess Augusta commissioned Sir William Chambers to design the splendid buildings which today give Kew its historical hinterland – the three temples dedicated to Aeolus, Arethusa and Bellona, the 1761 orangery, the ruined arch and the pagoda. A relic of an earlier age, the seventeenth-century Queen's Garden beside the palace, has been re-created in period style. The disabled will find most parts of Kew accessible; indeed the Secluded Garden, designed by Anthea Gibson, was created with the partially sighted and disabled in mind. Children will enjoy the imaginative mangrove swamps, Mohave desert and carnivorous plants in the Princess of Wales Conservatory, the palm house with its bananas and marine display showing seaweeds and fish from around the world and Climbers and Creepers, the UK's first botanical play zone. In 2003 Kew was awarded World Heritage Site status as an international unique cultural landscape – a great fillip for the world's greatest botanic garden.

Royal Hospital, Chelsea (Ranelagh Gardens) [Historic Park Grade II]

Royal Hospital Road, London SW3 4SR. Tel: (020) 7881 5204

Royal Hospital Chelsea • Through Royal Hospital London Gate in Royal Hospital Road, and through next gate into South Grounds, then through small gate on left • Open all year, daily (except 25th, 26th Dec, 1st Jan, and mid-May to mid-June due to Chelsea Flower Show), 10am – sunset (Sun, 2pm – sunset only) • Entrance: free

○ WC & ⚙

The elegant and attractive gardens are sited to one side of the Royal Hospital, with over a mile of wide walkways through undulating park-like grass and handsome tree and shrub plantings, and a few perennial and shrub borders. Formerly the pleasure grounds of Ranelagh, complete with a large rotunda (now demolished) and laid out in formal style, they were redesigned by Gibson in the nineteenth century, turned into allotments for pensioners between the two world wars, and later reconstructed according to Gibson's plan. The refurbished summerhouse by Sir John Soane stands near the entrance to the garden. The fine trees include many species of poplar, birch, beech, holly, cherry, chestnut, lime, oak and so on, with a couple of more exotic ones – the tree of heaven and the maidenhair tree. To one side of the park is the area used to house the main exhibits of the Chelsea Flower Show. A long avenue of plane trees marks the western boundary of the gardens.

60 South Croxted Road

Dulwich, London SE21 8BD. Tel: 07958 921264

Grainne Farren and Anthony Tuite • Turn right off South Circular Road (A205) after Thurlow Park Road into Rosendale Road, left into Park Hall Road, then right into South Croxted Road. Bus 3 from Brixton underground station; mainline station West Dulwich (10-min. walk) • Open Open 25th June, 2 – 6pm, and for parties of 5 or more by appt • Entrance: £3 NEW ● ▇

The elegant box parterre figure-of-eight set in gravel behind a row of standard photinias in front of the Victorian house hints at artistry, and the garden laid out behind reveals that it is also the abode of a knowledgeable plantsman. Anthony Tuite, a professional gardener, has wrought marvels in a long, narrow plot, secluded on three sides by curtains of foliage. The space is broken up by weathered decking and a central fish-shaped lawn, with the focus directed initially to a strong young 'Snow Queen' birch. At the end of the garden wooden blocks set in gravel lead to a patch of deep shade lightened by a powder-blue shed with a festive tracery of scarlet geraniums. The planting is similarly unfussy and unrestrained, and the intermingling of hundreds of different species and varieties has been choreographed with a sure eye for colour and texture. Seven different roses and nine clematis, plus purple leaves, white flowers, grasses for movement, ferns for levity, gunnera for bulk. Pots have settled in clusters around the garden, planted with such scene-stealers as *Macleaya cordata*, and a dazzle of coloured splinters reveals a giant mosaic salamander hidden in the undergrowth.

Southwood Lodge

33 Kingsley Place, Highgate, London N6 5EA. Tel: (020) 8348 2785

Mr and Mrs Christopher Whittington • Off Southwood Lane, Highgate • Open one day for NGS, 2 – 6pm, and April to July by appt • Entrance: £2, children 50p • Other information: Plants for sale on NGS Sun only ● ▇

An imaginatively designed garden created in 1963 from a much larger, older one, set at the highest part of London with a magnificent view to the east 'as far as the Urals'. In approximately a third of an acre on a fairly steep site, there is much variety of mood and planting. By the house, a densely planted paved area is enclosed on two sides by a high beech hedge, through which steps lead down to a grassy walk edged with shrubs, clematis and herbaceous plants. A wooded area in the lowest part of the garden, planted with many shade-lovers, leads up past three pools to the soothing sound of trickling water. Alpines grow in troughs on a low wall.

7 St George's Road ★

St Margaret's, Twickenham TW1 1QS. Tel: (020) 8892 3713

Mr and Mrs R. Raworth • Off A316 between Twickenham Bridge and St Margaret's roundabout • Open 4th June, 2 – 6pm, and for parties of 10 or more by appt • Entrance: £3.50, children 50p, evening opening £3 including wine • Other information: Home-made teas and plants for sale on open days only ● ▇ ⚘

A most successful result of garden design, inspired by Hidcote and Tintinhull on a miniature scale. This is one of the most interesting and well-maintained private gardens in the west London area and well worth going out of one's way to see. Among its many striking features are impressive hedges of privet, yew, box and hornbeam, which enclose various rooms and a new formal knot garden. Entering through a sunken Mediterranean garden and a sink garden full of interesting small plants, the visitor passes by a rose-covered pergola to an emerald grass carpet, flanked by flower borders backed by old trees in a private park. In one corner is a bog garden surrounded by wooden decking and crossed by a charming bridge. The new parterre gives an air of formality amongst the rare shrubs and containerised plants; plant lovers will also be drawn to the large and elegant conservatory on the north-facing wall, filled with old-fashioned Victorian plants.

St James's Park ★ [Historic Park Grade I]

London SW1A 2BJ. Tel: (020) 7298 2000

Royal Parks • Extends from Buckingham Palace on W to Horse Guards Parade on E, The Mall on N and Birdcage Walk on S • Open all year, daily, 5am – midnight • Entrance: free ○ 🍽 ✕ <u>WC</u> ᴋ ⬧ 🎔 ℺

One of the smaller royal parks but one of the prettiest. It was Henry VIII who turned this swampy field into a pleasure ground and nursery for deer. After the Restoration in 1660, Charles II sought advice from Louis XIV's garden designer André Le Nôtre, who planned the gardens at Versailles, to refashion the park into a garden. He gave advice, via his nephew, Claude Desgots, on a formal canal and included a pitch for the king to play the old French game of *paille maille*, a crude form of croquet, which gave its name to neighbouring Pall Mall. Nash remodelled the lake and gardens between 1827 and 1829, and the islands are still home to a wide variety of birds. Don't miss the picturesque skyline view from the bridge across the lake looking east. Bands play on summer weekend afternoons near Marlborough Gate, and there is a small playground for younger children at the western end of the park.

Syon Park ★ [Historic Park Grade I]

Brentford TW8 8JF. Tel: (020) 8560 0882

The Duke of Northumberland • 2m W of Kew Bridge, marked from A315/310 at Bush Corner • Telephone for house opening dates, times and entrance charges • Garden open all year, daily except 25th, 26th Dec, 10am – 5.30pm (or dusk if earlier) • Entrance: £3.75, concessions/children £2.50, family £9 ○ 🍽 ✕ 🍴 <u>WC</u> ᴋ ♿ 🎔

The Tudor house, with interiors redesigned by Robert Adam c.1760, is the London seat of the Percy family. The park shows British gardening on a grand scale and is one of the oldest landscapes in the country. A few statistics: 3200 trees here, one in four of which are over 100 years old and about one in seven over 200 years old. There are wonderfully mature oaks and swamp cypresses among over 200 different species in this park landscaped by 'Capability' Brown, but the most glorious asset is the great curving conservatory designed by Charles Fowler, which is said to have inspired Paxton when he was working at Chatsworth. One wing is full of scented flowers, leading to a collection of succulent plants, the other is planted with vines, leading to a fern-covered waterfall; the central part with its renovated dome is used for receptions and contains palms in timber planters. The formal garden in front of it has been simplified and now has an austere Italianate feel. The brashly commercial architecture of the garden centre and the crude, unshielded parking area in front of the house have done great damage to the setting, yet the house remains serene and the direct view to the river from it is remarkably untouched. The surrounding park and lakeside walk are of great interest, and a new path was opened in 1999 to allow visitors to walk the complete circuit of the lake. Wildflower areas are being developed, including a spectacular display along the entrance drive in midsummer. The rose garden has been redesigned and replanted with old varieties. One of the glories of Syon has always been the view from the ha-ha across water meadows towards the Thames; here new vistas and the famous axis to the Palm House at Kew are being opened up, and soon it will be possible to see across to the observatory and the pagoda. Much work still needs to be done, but there is a continuing programme for improvement and conservation, including work in the woodland garden and a new gravel garden planted with grasses and perennials. The future is bright indeed. Nearby *Osterley Park* [Historic Park Grade II*] – 650 acres surrounding the neo-classical villa by Robert Adam – has a farm, ornamental lakes and classical buildings, and is a delightful place for a walk, especially in May when the paddocks and chestnut trees are in flower. [Open all year, daily, 9am – 7.30pm or sunset.]

Thames Barrier Park ★

Barrier Point Road, off North Woolwich Road, London E16 2HP.
Tel: (0207) 511 4111

London Borough of Newham • On N bank of River Thames, between North Woolwich Road and Thames Barrier in Silvertown. Nearest underground station: Canning Town. Docklands Light Railway (DLR): Pontoon Dock. Mainline Station: North London Line, Silverlink service between Richmond and North Woolwich Silvertown for Thames Barrier Park. Buses 69, 474 • Open all year, daily, 7am – dusk • Entrance: free • Other information: No direct access between Thames Barrier Park on north bank and Thames Barrier Information and Learning Centre on south bank. No public access to Thames Barrier structure itself from either location ○ 💽 🏠 WC ⚿ 🐕 🍴 ♿

The finest modern park in Britain, and the only new riverside public park to be created since the war, opened in 2000. The distinguished French landscape designers Alain Provost and Alain Cousseran of Groupe Signes teamed up with English architects Patel Taylor and engineers Ove Arup to transform a contaminated brownfield site into a 22-acre park on the north bank adjacent to the river's most significant modern work of engineering, the giant stainless-steel 'cockleshells' of the Thames Flood Prevention Barrier. It is simultaneously a brave act of regeneration and a landscape *tour de force*. The river promenade gives a setting to the Barrier, and a raised walkway opens up views along and over the river. The flatness of the high-level plateau emphasises its spaciousness – think ten or more football pitches of lawns and wildflower meadows framed by bands of shrubs and interspersed with broad mown paths. The greatest surprise and pleasure is, however, the Green

Dock – the largest sunken garden in London by far. Stretching the length of the park, this simulation of a marine dock is a glorious, accessible garden dug deep and crossed by two viewing bridges. Look down and the planting is a tidal flow of wave-cut hedges alternating with beds of perennials stretching into the distance. At the north end are fountains – children dance and splash amid the water jets, and explore the imaginative play area.

64 Thornhill Road

London E10 5LL. Tel: (020) 8558 5895

Paul Minter and Michael Weldon • Off Oliver Road, near Leyton Orient football ground. Buses 69, 58, 158; nearest underground Leyton (10-min. walk) • Open 21st May and 11th June, 2 – 6pm, and by appt 22nd April to 25th June, Sat and Sun only • Entrance: £3 • Other information: Teas on NGS open days only [NEW] ● WC

In the unusually elongated garden stretching behind the 1888 house, the owners have gone for geometry and drama. The space is divided into four distinct areas, linked by a central brick path and focusing on a weeping lime which casts its huge shadow at the far end; a handsome wooden gate into this last enclosure is cleverly positioned to give the impression that infinite woodland stretches beyond. Plants are skilfully combined throughout, with a quincunx of birches, fruit trees, a metasequoia and 'Paul's Himalayan Musk' and 'Rambling Rector' roses adding exuberant height. Near the house a Gorgon fountain is surrounded by succulents, and mature box spirals stand alongside blue-and-gold Korean incense burners. An intriguing and enjoyable piece of theatre.

Victoria and Albert Museum (The John Madejski Garden)

Cromwell Road, London SW7 2RL.

In Cromwell Road, close to South Kensington tube station • Open all year, daily except 24th to 26th Dec, 10am – 5.45pm (closes 10pm Weds) • Entrance: free • Other information: Refreshments during summer only. Music, wine and food lectures, etc. available on Wed evening openings (seasonal) – telephone (020) 7942 2000 for details ○ ● ✕ WC ﹠ ⊞ ♟ ℀

The V&A's new garden has been designed by Kim Wilkie. He has opted for a simple, elegant, flexible design, replacing the current row of trees by just two liquidambars to make the facade of the museum more clearly visible. At the centre is an elliptical sunken stone area rather like a Roman bath, which can be flooded or drained at will. There are stone steps around the edge for people to sit on and water jets at the end. Specially designed planters containing lemon trees (replaced in winter by hollies) stand at the margins of grass; others around the perimeter hold colourful herbaceous perennials. A tranquil daytime garden can be transformed at the blink of an eye into a sparkling evening party space. On the corner of Cromwell Road and Exhibition Road is *The Natural History Museum Wildlife Garden*, a pleasant surprise among the many museums in this area of London. Pursuing a programme of conservation and scientific monitoring, the one-acre garden reveals a range of British lowland habitats, including woodland, meadow, reed-bed and pond. [Open April to October, daily except in bad weather. Tel: (020) 7942 5011; for school workshops telephone (020) 7942 5555.]

82 Wood Vale ★

London SE23 3ED. Tel: 07789 865156

Nigel and Linda Fisher • Near Dulwich Park, off South Circular where it joins Lordship Lane, but before Horniman Museum. House is between Langton Rise and Melford Avenue. Ample off-street parking; nearest station Forest Hill; bus 63 passes house or 176, 185, 312 nearby • Open for NGS, and for parties of 10 or more June and July, Sat and Sun, by appt • Entrance: £2 NEW ◑ &*

The sizeable back garden sloping gently uphill to the disused Crystal Palace railway line is confirmation (if any were needed) that Christopher Bradley-Hole's medal-winning show plots at Chelsea translate triumphantly into a real-garden setting. Hornbeam hedges – now running with the grain of the garden, now at right angles to it – rein in but do not fully enclose a jigsaw of perennial and grass bays. These low barriers almost give the impression that they could be moved around at will to change the flow and articulation of the garden. A canal is set in paving at the base of the slope; halfway up is a decking area, while the lawn at the top, at the foot of the tall trees concealing the railway line, is planted simply with amelanchiers. A clever, intricate design. It is the army of perennials and grasses, however, that pack the real punch. *Calamagrostis* x *acutiflora* 'Karl Foerster', *Achillea* 'Feuerland', *Euphorbia amygdaloides* var. *robbiae* and *Verbena bonariensis* are just some of the stalwarts in the simple, restrained palette of oranges, browns, clarets and purples. A winning combination.

London's Open Spaces

OTHER LONDON PARKS

W10: *Emslie Horniman Pleasance Park* in Kensal Road has bespoke timber benches and sculptures set among colourful perennials and shrubs.

NW3: *Golders Hill Park*, North End Way, a 36-acre park with a vibrant two-acre flower garden, a water garden and a menagerie.

N19: *Waterlow Park*, Dartmouth Park Hill [Historic Park Grade II], has three ponds, tree-lined walkways, mature shrub beds and a terraced garden surrounding historic Lauderdale House, all set on undulating hillside with panoramic views.

E7: *West Ham Park*, Forest Gate, originally a late-eighteenth-century garden rivalling Kew, now a well-maintained 77-acre park with fine trees, Victorian bedding schemes, a rose garden and entertainments for children and adults.

E10: *Lee Valley Regional Park* totals 10,000 acres. Telephone the information centre at Waltham Abbey Gardens (01992) 702200 for details.

SE9: *Avery Hill Park*, Eltham, is notable for its rose gardens, three giant conservatories and aviary.

SE10: *Greenwich Park*, Greenwich [Historic Park Grade I], the oldest enclosed royal park, covering 183 acres, has sensational views, especially from the observatory and historic buildings. Deer park, flower garden, rose and herb gardens, playground and children's entertainments.

SE20: *Crystal Palace Park*, Crystal Palace Park Road [Historic Park Grade II*], 200 acres surrounding Paxton's resited Crystal Palace created for the Great Exhibition of 1851 (alas burnt down in 1936). Terraces and features remain, and there is plenty of family interest.

SE24: *Brockwell Park,* Tulse Hill [Historic Park Grade II], a peaceful refuge with a walled garden, shrubs, trees, formal bedding and three ponds.

Morden: Just over the border in Surrey is *Morden Hall Park* [Historic Park Grade II], a former deer park with ancient haymeadows, waterways and collection of stables, mills and cottages. Nearby is a garden centre, a city farm (closed Mons except Bank Holidays) and craft workshops (closed Tues).

CITY OF LONDON PARKS AND GARDENS

Although there is inevitably a certain similarity in the design and planning of any group of gardens administered by a public body, those within the City of London (numbering around 150), being principally located on bomb sites, churchyards and former churchyards, have more variety than might be expected. For tourists and workers these gardens provide a welcome respite from the City traffic, and almost all are provided with lots of benches. *They are open 8am – 7pm or dusk, 7 days a week unless otherwise stated.*

EC1: *Christchurch – Greyfriars Rose Garden,* Newgate Street. A collection of hybrid teas and climbing roses trained up wooden pillars with linking ropes. *Postman's Park,* Aldersgate Street (close to St Paul's Cathedral). Formal bedding in the centre with mature trees and shrubs, a small pool with fountain and goldfish, together with tombs and headstones – the area is still a churchyard. An arcade protects the Watts Memorial, a tiled wall commemorating the deeds of those who died in their efforts to save others.

EC2: *Finsbury Circus* [Historic Garden Grade II]. [Closed Oct to March at weekends.] The largest public open green space in the City and London's first public park (1606). Apart from the ubiquitous London plane trees, it also boasts the only bowling green in the City, surrounded by low box hedges, bedding plants, shrubs, a drinking fountain and a small bandstand. *St Anne and St Agnes Churchyard,* Gresham Street. [Permanently open.] Here the church still stands, alongside the remains of part of London Wall and those of a Roman fort, surrounded by trees and shrubs. St *Botolph-without-Bishopsgate Churchyard,* Bishopsgate. [Permanently open.] Apart from the usual planting, there is also a tennis court and a netball court and a former school house, restored in 1952 by the Worshipful Company of Fan Makers to serve as a church hall. *St Mary Aldermanbury,* Love Lane. [Permanently open.] Made within the low ruined walls of a Wren church destroyed in the Blitz, the stumps of remaining pillars mark different levels of the garden. A shrubbery encloses a monument to Shakespeare's pals, John Heminge and Henry Condell. There is also a small knot garden. *St Mary Staining,* Oat Lane. [Permanently open.] Another patch of grass surrounded by shrubs, roses and benches. A rare opportunity to see a design by the late David Hicks is available at *Salter's Garden,* Fore Street. Hicks before his death ensured that there were benches for office workers and visitors. Paved areas alternate with grass alleys dividing rectangular box-edged beds. Formally placed obelisks in the beds have been planted with climbing roses and some of the *allées* run below honeysuckle-clad tunnels. Three fountains. *St Alphage Highwalk Garden,* London Wall is nearby. [Permanently open.] This roof garden beside London Wall can be reached via the escalator at Moorgate station and consists of a series of raised beds and extensive trellis work. The planting is a mixture of shrubs, climbers and herbaceous plants with an interesting collection of grasses as a centrepiece.

EC3: *Pepys Garden,* Seething Lane. [Open weekdays only, 9am – 5.30pm.] A splinter of garden on the site of the Navy Office, where Samuel Pepys lived and worked. A surprising number of trees in a tiny area. *St Dunstan-in-the-East Church Garden*, St Dunstans Hill. The most romantic garden in the City, it has been created within the walls of a Victorian Gothick church which was bombed during World War II. Only the Wren tower survived and was restored. The remaining walls, containing arched windows and doorways, are covered with creepers and climbing plants and the spaces between planted with small trees and shrubs. There is a small fountain surrounded by benches and large tubs with standard fuchsias and bedding plants.

EC4: *Bow Churchyard*, just off Cheapside, will interest US visitors as in its small garden is the statue of Captain John Smith, 'citizen and cord-wainer', who was leader of the first settlers in Virginia.

E1: *Portsoken Street Garden*, between Portsoken Street and Goodman's Yard. A tiny oasis with a bubbling fountain, brick walls, small trees and shrubs.

LONDON SQUARES

When this *Guide* first appeared in 1990, the squares of London were mostly municipal in appearance, even though the majority of them were in fact private, and their gates firmly locked to visitors except residents or those with a key. Now the story is different. The gardens in the squares get much more attention from professionals as well as amateurs, and for several years now many are open to the public on the second Sunday in June. Some have events such as Punch and Judy shows as well as the opportunity for visitors to buy plants. London has about 400 squares, of which only about 15 per cent are currently open on one day in the year designated London Garden Squares Day, though a few of the others welcome the public more frequently, some on a daily basis.

The squares were mostly built in the eighteenth and nineteenth centuries to provide an outlook for the fashionable houses which surrounded them and in not-so-fashionable areas like Pimlico so that the lesser classes could imitate the behaviour of their betters. A few squares still remain the joint property of the owners of houses (and today, flats) round them, the grandest being Belgrave Square built by Basevi in 1825, Cadogan Square and Eaton Square. Other private squares, hardly less grand, include Brompton, Carlyle, Edwardes, Lowndes, Montpelier, Onslow, Pembroke and others to the west of Hyde Park Corner.

Many of London's squares are listed on the English Heritage *Register*. Historic Gardens Grade II* are Gray's Inn, Lincoln's Inn and Victoria Embankment, while the Inner and Middle Temple are Grade II. Historic Squares Grade II* are Bedford and Bloomsbury; Grade II are Belgrave, Eaton, Eccleston, Russell, Brunswick, Mecklenburgh, Tavistock, Woburn, Edwardes, Berkeley, Grosvenor, St James's and Cadogan.

One enthusiast, Roger Phillips of Eccleston Square, says that in order to keep the squares going for the benefit of residents and the visual pleasure of passers-by, it is necessary to wage a horrendous battle against potential developers. By contrast, Michael Heseltine once said that 'someone, somewhere, should get a grip' on London squares. There should be tree-planting schemes, seats for the elderly, statues or water features – possibly provided by sponsors.

Amongst gardens which have recently joined the 'open day' scheme are Eaton Square, the Inner and Middle Temple Gardens, Little Venice along the canal, and Portman Square in the West End. For information about the scheme, tickets and descriptive booklets are available from May by writing with a s.a.e. to

London Gardens Squares Day, c/o London Historic Parks and Gardens Trust, Duck Island Cottage, St James Park, London SW1A 2BJ. Of the many other squares and 'gardens' open to the public outside the one-day scheme, the following may be worth a visit.

Northern area: *Russell Square* has been imaginatively restored, thanks to a £1.4m lottery grant, to Repton's original design of 1800, with elegant railings, a new fountain, a hornbeam hedge and an ornamental shrubbery around the perimeter. So too has *Bloomsbury Square,* familiar haunt of the Bloomsberries in the early part of the twentieth century. Then come *Queen Square,* with its statue of Queen Charlotte, after whom it is named; *Brunswick Square,* beyond which is the walled garden, usually a haven of peace; *Coram's Fields* [Historic Garden Grade II], also restored with Lottery money, is a children's play area, open 10am-5pm with *Mecklenburgh Square* adjoining; *Tavistock Square* (quietest in the area); *Woburn Square*; *Gordon Square* (closed weekends); and *Fitzroy Square,* the work of Sir Geoffrey Jellicoe (not open but viewable). Further north is *Edward Square,* Copenhagen Street/Caledonian Road, with a small orchard, nature and picnicking areas. Nearby is *Gibson Square,* with plenty of seats, much grass, fine trees and too many municipal roses.

Central area: *Berkeley Square*; *Cavendish Square*; *Grosvenor Square*. *Phoenix Gardens,* a community-run site with a 20-year lease which shows what can be done by London residents, and which, unlike many others, is open 24 hours a day; and *St James's Square,* the earliest London square, begun 1665, and the quietest. *Mount Street Gardens* is a well-hidden leafy retreat much loved by locals while the throng of the city seems to pass it by. Tasteful planting and lofty trees make it the perfect spot to take your ease after shopping. Versailles tubs planted with palms, beds of sugar-pink and white geraniums or other interesting and varied schemes can be enjoyed from dozens of wooden benches donated by those who have enjoyed this garden's charm. [Open spring and summer, weekdays, 8am – up to 9.30pm; autumn and winter, 8am – 4.30pm; Sun and Bank Holidays, open from 9am.] Also within walking distance are *Covent Garden* and *Soho Square* and *St Paul's Churchyard,* a visual treat and a much-needed restful space under the shadow of St Paul's, with well-designed, densely planted beds, an oval lawn and many seats.

Eastern area: *Embankment Gardens,* if rather municipal, are leafy and tranquil. At *Gray's Inn* Field Court is open to the public during weekday lunchtimes in the summer. *Inner and Middle Temple Gardens* stretch up from the Embankment (no entrance here) to Fleet Street. Their fourteenth-century origins are reflected in the names of some of the individual squares. The Inner Temple's Great Gardens, with majestic trees, were extended in the early eighteenth century and again in the nineteenth. The smaller Middle Temple has fine borders and a small rose garden. At *Lincoln's Inn* one of the 'squares', New Hall, is open Mon – Fri, 12 noon – 1.30pm only. The newest square in London is surrounded by offices, not houses. This is *Arundel Great Court,* which may be viewed from The Strand, south of Aldwych and entered from Arundel and Norfolk Streets. To the south is the luxurious courtyard garden of the *Norfolk Hotel.*

Southern area: *Cadogan Place* (above the car park halfway down Sloane Square (to its E) and *Cadogan Square* (to the W) are sometimes open for two or three days in early June for the Chelsea Festival.

OTHER LONDON 'PUBLIC' SPACES

N1: *New River,* a narrow man-made stream and park off Canonbury Road. *St Mary's Churchyard Gardens,* Upper Street, opposite the King's Head Theatre.

EC1: *Angel/Upper Street.* Three charming courtyard gardens have been built below the new office block, Regent's House, in Upper Street, just a few metres from the Angel tube exit. Nowhere to sit, but a pleasant strolling space. *Bunhill Fields Burial Ground,* between Bunhill Row and City Road. [Open Mon – Fri, 7.30am – 7pm (closes 4pm Oct to March), weekends 9.30am – 4pm.] A burial ground, unused since 1853, containing many fine tombs and memorials, including those of William Blake and John Bunyan. Most of the tombs are behind railings, but part of the grounds which were bomb-damaged has been planted with grass, trees and shrubs. Fine planes and a mulberry. *Fortune Street Garden,* NW of the Barbican between Beech Street and Old Street. *Myddleton Square,* St John Street, which houses St Mark's Church.

EC3: *Trinity Square,* Tower Hill, home to Wyatt's Trinity House.

SE1: The gardens of *Southwark Cathedral* are newly reconfigured, making this the only historic green space remaining under continuous development in Bankside. The new *Globe Theatre* may have an Elizabethan knot garden on its one-acre site. For further details contact Shakespeare Globe Trust (Tel: (020) 7902 1400). At *Tate Modern* Bankside, close block planting of young birch trees and wide grass verges flank the main entrance path, while in the South Garden a green amphitheatre of crab apples and quinces creates a quiet, open space. *The London Eye* has been given a narrow public space between County Hall and Jubilee Gardens with seating areas, yew hedging and an avenue of *Prunus avium* to encourage orderly queues.

SE15: *Centre for Wildlife Gardening,* 28 Marsden Road, near East Dulwich railway station, gives information and sells plants for gardeners who want to attract wildlife. [Open Tues – Thurs and Sun, 11am – 4pm, but telephone first (020) 7252 9186 🐞 ♿ ℘ ⛲ ♀.]

SE23: *Sydenham Hill Woods,* near Forest Hill railway station. Over 180 species of trees and plants.

SW1: *Whitehall Court.* Parallel to N bank of River Thames, between Horseguards Avenue, Whitehall Place and Victoria Embankment. A Grade-II-registered garden, owned by Westminster City Council, re-created in 1994. The excellent planting plan takes into account the proximity of heavy traffic along Victoria Embankment and gives occasional views of the River Thames. Cross over Northumberland Place and visit the rest of *Victoria Embankment Gardens,* especially Bryant's small lily pond and Sullivan's Victorian memorial, which are well supported by planting. Maintenance is to a high standard. *Tate Britain* in Millbank is a pleasant place to stroll after visiting the gallery – an exercise in restraint and a garden for all seasons. Abutting the Thames and the busy traffic of Millbank is the newly created *Riverside Walk* – a shallow granite terrace with curved resin-bound paths set among mown grass. The sculpture 'Locking Piece', on loan from the Tate, gives gravitas.

WC2: *Somerset House,* The Strand. The Great Courtyard and River Terrace open up a walk from Covent Garden to the South Bank.

W9: *Clifton Nurseries* is a commercial establishment for the sale of plants and garden paraphernalia, but for all that it has the charm of a small enclosed London green space, worth visiting at all times of year (nearest tube station: Warwick Avenue) WC ⬧ ⬧ ⬧ . Nearby is *Rembrandt Gardens*, a small municipal triangle by the side of the canal where, if the weather is suitable, the newspaper can be read in pleasant surroundings.

W10: Some London cemeteries have a gardenesque style, or have acquired one over the centuries. *Highgate* [Historic Cemetery Grade II*] in N6 is one of the best known. The longest-surviving cemetery still in private ownership is the 77-acre *Kensal Green* [Historic Cemetery Grade II*] in Harrow Road. (Tube to Kensal Green on Bakerloo line or bus No 18. Parking access via West Gate WC ⬧ ⬧.) It also has more free-standing mausoleums than any other in England – the majority were constructed to the owners' approved designs before being put to use. Several are Grade-II-listed. There are fine trees here as well as grand graves. The company which established Kensal Green in 1832 aimed to create a spacious park that would complement the fine monuments. They succeeded, and their work is now assisted by subscription-paying 'Friends'. [Open April to Sept, 9am – 5.30pm, Oct to March, 9am – 4pm (opens 10am Suns and Bank Holidays). Guided tours 2pm on Suns throughout the year.]

A TOTALLY INDEPENDENT PUBLICATION
The *Guide* makes no charge for entries, which are written by our own inspectors. The factual details are supplied by owners. This is a totally independent publication and its only revenue comes from sales of copies in bookshops.

OPENING DATES AND TIMES
Times of access given are the best available at the moment of going to press, but some may have been changed subsequently. In the entries, the times given are inclusive – that is, an entry such as May to Sept means that the garden is open from 1st May to 30th Sept inclusive, and 2 – 5 pm means that entry will be effective during that period. Please note that many owners will open their gardens to visitors by appointment, and they will often arrange to give a personally conducted tour on these occasions. Unavoidably some owners cannot give their opening details before we go to press, and in such cases we attempt to give the best guidance we can. If in doubt, it is wise to telephone before making a long journey.

SYMBOLS
[NEW] entries new for 2006; ○ open all year; ◐ open most of year; ◑ open during main season; ● open rarely and/or by appt; ⬧ teas/light refreshments; ✕ meals; ⬧ picnics permitted; WC toilet facilities; **WC** toilet facilities, inc. disabled; ⬧ partly wheelchair-accessible; ⬧ dogs on lead; ⬧ plants for sale; ⬧ shop; ⬧ events held; ⬧ children-friendly; B&B bed and breakfast available.

MANCHESTER AREA

We have included some gardens with Manchester postal addresses in Cheshire and Lancashire for convenience, so it is also worthwhile consulting pages 36–50 and pages 208–214.

Bramall Hall

Bramall Park, Bramhall, Stockport, Cheshire SK7 3NX Tel: (0161) 485 3708

Stockport Metropolitan Borough Council • 3m S of Stockport on A5102 between Bramhall and Stockport. Signposted • Hall open Jan to March, Sat and Sun, 1 – 4pm; April to Sept, daily, 1 – 5pm; Oct to Dec, daily except Mon, 1 – 4pm. Closed 25th and 26th Dec • Grounds open all year, daily, dawn – dusk • Entrance: free (hall £3.95, OAPs and children £2.50) (2005 prices) ○ ☕ WC ᴖ ⬧ ⛪

These gardens are a missed opportunity. The black-and-white timber-framed house is such a magnificent building and in such a wonderful position that to have a large expanse of tarmac on one side and terraces of an inappropriate brick on the other seems a sad waste. There is a herbaceous border and some beds of bright annuals a short distance from the hall, otherwise little of interest. The parkland is another matter. In the valley of a small river, broad areas of grassland encircle a number of small lakes. Woods, which contain some very large beech trees, surround the park and hide all sign of the suburbs of Stockport, and the riverside walk has banks covered in wild flowers.

Dunham Massey ★ [Historic Garden Grade II*]

Altrincham, Cheshire WA14 4SJ. Tel: (0161) 941 1025

The National Trust • 3m SW of Altrincham off A56 • House open 26th March to 29th Oct, Sat – Wed, 12 noon – 5pm • Garden open as house, daily, 11am – 5.30pm. Park open all year, daily • Entrance: car park £4, garden £4.50, house and garden £6.50 • Other information: Manual wheelchairs and batricar available. Dogs in park only, on lead ◑ ☕ ✕ 🍴 WC ᴖ ⬧ ⛪ 🍵 ♿

Between the conurbations of Liverpool and Manchester sits the 3000-acre estate of Dunham Massey, where fallow deer still roam freely in their 300-acre park. The house is an eighteenth-century replacement of the Elizabethan mansion, but the broad stretch of water curling around its north and west sides is the original Elizabeth moat, while the semi-circular promontory jutting out into the moat was the site of an Elizabethan mount and possibly even of the Norman motte which preceded it. The other miraculous survivals are the five avenues, which predate the English Landscape School of the eighteenth century. Enough of the formal, seventeenth-century Baroque lay-out of the park to the west and the south remained for the Trust to replant the long avenues radiating out from a *patte d'oie* in front of a triple row of lime trees each side of the southern forecourt. The gardens seem to improve every year, with some excellent new planting. Close to the entrance, bordering a small stream, are huge drifts of moisture-loving perennials, including hostas, rodgersias and a striking clump of *Rheum palmatum rubrum*. Further along, beside a rustic bridge, are *Meconopsis* x *sheldonii*, damp-loving ferns and a collection of acers. Fine specimen trees, including a *Quercus suber*, are to be found on the expansive lawn, which is overlooked by an eighteenth-century orangery containing abutilons and surrounded by banks of shrubs. In the Garden Wood is a large collection of azaleas and hydrangeas. Don't miss the formal courtyard garden at the centre of the house.

Fletcher Moss Botanical and Parsonage Gardens ★

Mill Gate Lane, Didsbury M20 2SW. Tel: (0161) 445 4241

Manchester City Council Leisure Department • 5m S of city centre on Mill Gate Lane, S of A5145, close to centre of Didsbury • Open all year, daily, 9am – dusk • Entrance: free ○ 🅿 🍴 <u>WC</u> ♿ ⬥

Here, close to a busy part of south Manchester, is a tranquil green oasis with a large range of plants, an historic rockery, and a water garden. What's more, it's free. It was in 1889 that Robert and Emily Williamson began to create this garden, focusing on its most important feature, the large rockery (in effect a mountainside in miniature) on which to grow their collection of alpines. It is still impressive. Large stones embedded in the steep south-facing slope form a series of terraces with pockets of soil for the plants and paths for the visitor, and in them are massed alpines, bulbs and small shrubs, plus many conifers and the odd well-placed small tree. Japanese maples cast their light shade in places; there is a large tulip tree, and sheltered at one end of the garden a collection of Chusan palms. A small stream cascades down the rocky terraces to the rich foliage of the water garden. A restful walled terrace gives views across the garden to the meadows and trees of the Mersey Valley. Emily Wiliamson had another interest beside plants: she founded the RSPB here in 1889. Close by are the public *Parsonage Gardens*, entered through an old stone arch in Didsbury's busy High Street. Rhododendrons, camellias, magnolias, hellebores and ferns grow beneath the canopy of trees, and in a brighter area a deep L-shaped herbaceous border is backed by a wisteria-covered wall.

Haigh Hall Gardens

Haigh Country Park, Haigh, Wigan WN2 1PE. Tel: (01942) 832895

Wigan Leisure and Culture Trust • 2m NE of Wigan, N of B5238. Signposted
• Open all year, daily, during daylight hours • Entrance: free, but parking charge
• Other information: Wheelchairs available from information centre. Craft gallery.
Children's rides, model village and railway ○ 🅿 ✕ 🍴 <u>WC</u> ♿ ⬥ 🏛 ☕

The hall is set in the midst of mature parkland, and a short distance to the east are formal gardens, probably of Victorian and Edwardian origin. In an open area of lawn rose beds and specimen shrubs surround an oval pool. Three walled gardens adjoin. The middle one contains a good herbaceous border and a well-stocked shrub border. The second, to the south, has shrubs against the walls and young specimen trees planted in a lawn in the centre, and the low wall to the south gives a view across a wild garden with a pond. The third, at the northern end, is formal, with roses, yew hedges and lawns; on the west side a landscaped area has heathers and conifers. The arboretum, featuring acers set in woodland, is developing well.

Heaton Hall [Historic Park Grade II]

Heaton Park, Prestwich M25 2SW. Tel: (0161) 773 1231/1085 (Hall enquiries); (0161) 773 1085 (Park enquiries)

Manchester City Council • 4m N of Manchester city centre on A576, just S of junction 19 off M60 • House open April to Oct • Park open all year, daily, during daylight hours • Entrance: free, but parking charge on Sun and Bank Holiday Mons • Other information: Some areas in hall possible for wheelchairs but telephone first
○ ◗ ✕ ⬛ wc ♿ ⬥ ⚕ ♨ ♀

The hall, designed in 1772 by James Wyatt, was described by Pevsner as 'the finest house of its period in Lancashire', and the planting in the pleasure ground is appropriate to the period. The 650-acre park, landscaped between 1770 and 1830, contains a number of other neo-classical buildings. The landscape around the hall has been restored with the help of a Heritage Lottery Fund grant and features such as the ha-ha and the western pleasure ground have been reinstated. A path leads through a tunnel to an attractive dell of mature trees and many rhododendrons, then follows a stream through a series of pools and waterfalls to a large boating lake. On the Prestwich side of the park small demonstration gardens are enclosed within the old walled garden.

The ITV Granada Garden

Atherton Street, Manchester, B60 9EA.

Granada Television • From Deansgate in city centre, go down Quay St; turn left at Granada office block (large sign on building) and call at security lodge • Open 13th and 20th May, 10th and 17th June, 10am – 4pm • Entrance: £2, children £1 [NEW] ◗

Originally the set for Granada's gardening programme hosted by Jeff Turner, the garden is virtually the backyard to Coronation Street and stands within the Granada Studios complex. Although it must be said that it's Jeff that's big and not the garden, there is still a lot packed into this disused but still thriving half acre. A good selection of small trees and tall shrubs gives a sense of seclusion from the tall surrounding buildings. At the centre stands an attractive modern building of glass and timber, complemented by an area of decking and planting of a Mediterranean feel, including large clumps of senecio and phlomis. Two Chinese moon gates form the entrance, and close by is a pomegranate over 150 years old. An informal pool crossed by a rustic bridge is planted with water lilies and marginals; another is square and forms the focal point of a more formal paved area with a pergola covered in wisteria, roses and clematis and a distinctive tree fountain based on Chatsworth's famous weeping tree, built by Jeff and the Granada plumbing department. A welcome splash of green in the heart of a major city.

Lyme Park ★ [Historic Garden Grade II*]

Disley, Stockport, Cheshire SK12 2NX. Tel: (01663) 762023/766492

The National Trust • 6m SE of Stockport just W of Disley on A6 • House open as garden, 1 – 5pm • Garden open 27th March to 29th Oct, daily, 11am – 5pm; Nov to 18th Dec, Sat and Sun, 12 noon – 3pm. Guided tours by arrangement • Entrance:

garden £3.50; park: pedestrians free, car and occupants £4.50 (house and garden £6.50) ◐ 🍴 ✕ 🛍 wc ♿ 🏛 🍷

The Palladian-style mansion is set in spectacular parkland in the foothills of the Pennines with panoramic views of the Cheshire Plains. The 17-acre gardens are of great historic importance, retaining many original features from Tudor and Jacobean times. It is regarded as one of the foremost National Trust gardens for its high-Victorian-style bedding in magnificent formal beds, using many rare and old-fashioned plants such as *Penstemon* 'Rubicundus' (bred at Lyme in 1906). Important features include Lewis Wyatt's orangery of 1814, which contains two venerable 150-year-old camellias; a spectacular Dutch garden with a rare example of a *parterre de broderie* using Irish ivy; a fine Gertrude Jekyll-style herbaceous border designed by Graham Stuart Thomas; a wooded ravine garden with a stream and fine collections of rhododendrons, azaleas, ferns and other shade-loving plants; a collection of rare trees and plants associated with that eminent plantsman, the Hon. Vicary Gibbs; a large lake; a 300-year-old lime avenue; extensive lawns and a recently restored Edwardian rose garden. A rare garden designed by Lewis Wyatt in 1817 has been re-created and the Sundial Terrace restored.

17 Poplar Grove ★

Sale M33 3AX. Tel: (0161) 969 9816

Gordon Cooke • SW of city centre off M60 junction 6. From A6144 at Brooklands Station turn into Hope Road; Poplar Grove is 3rd turning on right • Open two days for NGS, and by appt in June • Entrance: £3, children 50p • Other information: Teas on NGS open days only ◐ wc 🌿 🍷

That the owner is a landscape gardener and potter is soon evident, for in a suburban setting and a fairly small area he has created a most distinctive garden. A masterstroke was to set the paths at diagonals to the main axis and this, together with the changes in level and varied use of building materials, creates interest throughout. Many of the plants are chosen for their foliage shape and colour: phormiums, thistles, alliums, euphorbias, cordylines, grasses and ferns all contribute to the variety. A 'living roof' has been added to a porch, and an unusual grotto sunk into the ground with plants growing over the top, overlooking a long rectangular pool surrounded by pieces of modern sculpture. Other water features and fine ceramics are spread around the garden, and within a new exhbition space.

Rivington Terraced Gardens [Historic Garden Grade II]

Rivington Lane, Horwich, Bolton, Lancashire BL6 7SB.
Tel: (01204) 691549 (Great House Information Centre, Rivington)

United Utilities • 1m NW of Horwich. Follow signs to Rivington from A673 in Horwich or Grimeford. Gardens are 10-min. walk from Rivington Hall and Hall Barn • Open all year, daily • Entrance: free • Other information: Parking, refreshments, toilet facilities at Hall Barn; refreshments, toilet facilities and information at Great House Barn ○ 🍴 🛍 wc 🐕

These are not gardens as such but the remains of gardens built by Lord Leverhulme and designed by Thomas Mawson in the early part of the twentieth century. Set mainly in woodland on a steep west-facing hillside, they have fine views across Rivington reservoirs. Particularly impressive is a rocky ravine, the remains of a Japanese garden and the restored pigeon tower. The number and variety of mature trees and rhododendrons indicate that this must once have been a very grand estate. Take care on the steep, sometimes slippery paths.

Wythenshawe Horticultural Centre

Wythenshawe Park, Wythenshawe Road M23 0AB. Tel: (0161) 998 2117

Manchester City Council • 7m S of Manchester city centre, 0.25m S of M63 junction 9, 0.5m SE of M56 junction 3, S of B5167 • Open all year, daily except 25th Dec, 10am – 4pm • Entrance: free ○ 🍴 🥾 wc ♿ 🌿 🏪 💡

Once this nursery within the Grade-II-listed Wythenshawe Park grew bedding stock for the city's parks; now it is a demonstration garden where a large number of different plants can be seen growing. To the right of the entrance a large lawned area runs along a chain of pools planted in large effective clumps with many moisture-lovers, including irises and astilbes. The developing area, backed by mature woodland, already looks attractive. The Safari Walk through a long array of greenhouses leads past a series of plant collections – cacti, tropical plants, carnivorous plants, a fernery – and some unusual displays, including one on rice-growing. Behind the greenhouses is an area of demonstration gardens: a heather garden, a pool and rockery, a collection of shrubs and small trees, a well-labelled herbaceous border and a section of dwarf conifers. Another area is devoted to fruit, with many of the bushes and trees grown as cordons.

13 Yew Tree Cottages

Compstall, Beacomfold, Nr Stockport SK6 5JU. Tel: (0161) 427 7142

Mr M. Murphy • Off B6104 Marple Bridge – Romiley road. Turn into Compstall village signed to Etherow Country Park, and take 2nd left after Andrews Arms pub • Open end-May to Sept by appt • Entrance: £4, children £1 ● 🍴 🌿 ♿

A small garden that is a delight to visit, not just for its horticultural merits but also its superb location high on a hillside overlooking the Etherow Country Park and the historic mill town of Compstall. You can start your visit by drinking tea on the grass terrace, surrounded by beds of small shrubs and perennials, and from here a number of small stone paths lead up through winding routes into the steeply rising garden, which is dotted with pools, streams and water features and has areas devoted to moisture-lovers. Pergolas and trellises giving height and structure accommodate many climbers, and shrubs and small trees are used to create distinct and intimate areas. Shrub roses and geraniums are well represented, but there are many other perennials, including a bed of delphiniums. The other, more formal section of the garden lies across a small track, on a site that is less sloping and more sheltered. Scented and climbing roses and clematis wind up pergolas and other structures in an attractive, mainly gravelled area. There is also a vegetable garden with views across the valley, and a shaded area where hostas and ferns grow beneath small trees.

NEWCASTLE UPON TYNE AREA

Bede's World Herb Garden

Church Bank, Jarrow, South Tyneside NE32 3DY. Tel: (0191) 489 2106

Bede's World • 8m NE of Gateshead off A185, or S entrance to Tyne Tunnel off A19
• Museum open all year except 14th April (telephone for Christmas opening times)
• Garden open all year, daily except 14th April, 10am – 5.30pm (opens 12 noon
Sun, closes 4.30pm Nov to March). Telephone for details of Christmas openings
• Entrance: free ○ 🍽 ✗ <u>WC</u> ♿ ⊞ 🔦 ☕

A small garden of interest to the herbalist, with a wide range of herbs in four sections: culinary, Anglo-Saxon medicinal, aromatic and medicinal. There are also narrow beds in a second part of the garden based on the plans of a medicinal herb garden found at St Gall (*c.* AD 816), and a bricked area at the top of the garden with seating, planted around with rosemary, lavender and with two banks of herbs below it leading down to the St Gall area. An 'Anglo-Saxon' farm has been developed on adjacent land – an 11-acre site with fields, crops, animals and timber buildings. Some herbs and early vegetable strains are grown here, together with pond and stream plants and trees of species available at the time of the Venerable Bede (AD 673–735). The adjacent museum building has a courtyard with four raised beds planted in the style of a late-medieval formal garden. The herb garden is maintained by a team of volunteers.

Gibside [Historic Garden Grade I]

Burnopfield, Gateshead NE16 6BG. Tel: (01207) 541820

The National Trust • 6m SW of Gateshead, 20m NW of Durham from B6314, off
A694 at Rowlands Gill. Signed from A1(M) • Open all year, daily, 10am – 4.30pm,
except 25th Dec and 1st Jan • Entrance: £5, children £3 • Other information:
Chapel open, service first Sun each month ○ 🍽 🍴 <u>WC</u> ♿ ⬦ ⊞ 🔦 ☕

Gibside was once one of the finest designed landscapes in England of the eighteenth century, created by a Whig MP, George Bowes of the Bowes Lyon family, another of whom fashioned St Paul's Walden Bury (see entry in Hertfordshire). In 1729, amongst wooded slopes cut through with radiating avenues, he commissioned and positioned a series of buildings – an early, more formal version of Stowe (see entry in Buckinghamshire). Each building was admirably sited, and all were constituents of a harmonious plan. Employing various architects, he built a Gothick banqueting house, a Palladian chapel and stables. The landscape *pièce de résistance* was a grand terrace with a statue to British Liberty – on a column taller than Nelson's in London – at one end and the architectural masterpiece, James Paine's stately Palladian chapel, at the other. The Trust, assisted by the National Heritage Memorial Fund, has acquired 354 acres to secure the future of this great landscape garden and to protect the chapel's setting. Well-marked walks have been opened up with views to the ruined hall, orangery and other estate buildings in the grounds. Restoration of the ruined buildings and removal of the Forestry Commission's intrusive tree planting is ongoing. Bowes also made a walled garden, part of which is now the car park and part devoted to varieties of heritage vegetables, fruit and flowers that were grown up to 1874.

Jesmond Dene [Historic Park Grade II]

Jesmond NE7 7BQ. Tel: (0191) 281 0973

Newcastle City Council • 1m E of city centre along Jesmond Road • Open all year, daily • Entrance: free • Other information: Parking in Benton Bank. Visitor Centre open at weekends. Cafe open daily ○ 🍽 🍴 WC ♿ ⇪ ♀ ❀

Presented to the city in 1883 by Lord Armstrong, the famous engineer, and only a mile from the city centre, this steep-sided, thickly wooded dene provides extensive walks in an entirely natural setting, complete with a waterfall, a ruined mill and some fine old buildings. There is a well-run pets' corner, and from Freeman Road the upper park has a children's play area and a pond. For a city park, its condition is quite exceptional. Cragside (see entry in Northumberland) was also the creation of Lord Armstrong.

Mowbray Park and Winter Gardens [Historic Park Grade II]

Burdon Road, Sunderland, Tyne and Wear SR1 1PP. Tel: (0191) 553 2323

Sunderland Museum and Winter Gardens • In city centre • Open all year, daily: park, 7am – dusk, winter gardens, 10am – 5pm (opens 2pm Sun) • Entrance: free ○ 🍽 ✗ WC ♿ 🏛 ♀ ❀

Restored to its former Victorian splendour, Mowbray Park is awash with colour – in rose arbours, in colourful shrub borders and in formal bedding displays. Winding paths lead to a quarry garden and a limestone crag at the more naturalistic southern end. Not to be missed within the park are the Winter Gardens, which are attached to the museum. Here is an amazing glass and steel structure housing a variety of exotic plants. Tree ferns, banana plants, citrus trees and scented flowering shrubs create a lush canopy, which can be viewed from a tree-top walk, and a specially commissioned water sculpture by William Pye cascades in torrents, adding to the exotic atmosphere. A newly planted section on the south side of the Winter Gardens aims to re-create the habitat and atmosphere of a Mediterranean hillside of stream, olive and citrus grove and drystone terracing. The cracks in the wall are filled with colourful spring-flowering plants like *Aristolochia sempervirens*, *Clematis cirrhosa balearica*, cyclamen and the sea squill (*Urginea maritima*).

2007 GUIDE
The 2007 *Guide* will be published before Christmas 2006. Reports on gardens for consideration are welcome at all times of the year, but particularly by early summer (May 2006) so that they can be inspected that year.

NORFOLK

Two-starred gardens are marked on the map with a black square.

Besthorpe Hall ★

Besthorpe, Attleborough N17 2LJ. Tel: (01953) 450300

Mr J.A. Alston • 14m SW of Norwich, 1m E of Attleborough on Bunwell Road.
Entrance on right, past church • Open by appt only ● 🍴 WC ♿

A pool and fountain occupy the centre of the entrance forecourt. Beyond the house, more pools and fountains are set within red-brick Tudor enclosures, their walls hung with roses, clematis and honeysuckles, and these provide the backdrop to long herbaceous borders. The largest lawn, believed to have been a tilt yard once, has mature topiary, while on another is an enormous and shapely Wellingtonia. Among the many fine trees are paulownias and a variety of birches, acers and magnolias, including a sumptuous *M. delavayi*. There is also a walled kitchen garden, a nuttery and a herb garden. A small lake is home to wildfowl, and on another pool lives a pair of black swans. Bearded irises are a June feature. *Peter Beales Roses*, London Road, Attleborough is close by [open daily, 9am – 5pm (4pm on Sun)], and has added a bistro to its horticultural attractions.

Blickling Hall ★ [Historic Garden Grade II*]

Aylsham, Norwich NR11 6NF. Tel: (01263) 738030

The National Trust • 15m N of Norwich, 1.5m NW of Aylsham on N side of B1354
• House open end March to early Nov, Wed – Sun, 1 – 4.30pm • Garden open
Jan to March, Sat and Sun, 11am – 4pm; end-March to 2nd Nov, Wed – Sun and
Bank Holiday Mons, plus Tues in Aug, 10.15am – 5.15pm; 3rd Nov to Dec,
Thurs – Sun, 11am – 4pm • Entrance: £4.20, children £2.10 (house and gardens
£6.90) (2005 prices) • Other information: Picnics in walled garden only. Dogs in
park only, on lead ① 🍽 ✕ WC ♿ 🌿 🎁 🍴 ☕

Although the gardens appear to be the perfect setting for the handsome Jacobean house, they are a panorama of garden history from the seventeenth to the twentieth centuries. The massive yew hedges flanking the entrance to the gardens are from the earliest period. To the east is the parterre with a central pool, where four large corner beds planted by Norah Lindsay in the 1930s are surrounded by borders of roses edged with nepeta. Flights of steps mount to the highest terrace, from which a vista cut through blocks of woodland leads to the Doric temple of 1730 raised above parkland beyond. The two blocks are intersected by *allées* in seventeenth-century style but planted in 1861–4 and now replanted using Turkey oak, lime and beech. To the south, the 1782 orangery houses half-hardy plants and a 1640s' statue of Hercules by Nicholas Stone. On the corner of the northern block is the Secret Garden, originally eighteenth-century, which now consists of a lawn with a central sundial surrounded by high beech hedges. The shrub border through which it is approached is by Norah Lindsay, who was also responsible for the dry moat surrounding the house. North of the parterre is a raised grassy area, possibly a remnant of the Jacobean mount; here grows an enormous, sprawling Oriental plane. Landscaped parkland to the north-west descends to the curving lake, formed before 1729 and later extended. West of the house stands a cedar of Lebanon and a collection of magnolias around a nineteenth-century fountain. In the park too is the 1773 Gothic tower and the 1796 mausoleum – a pyramid nearly 14 metres square by Joseph Bonomi. The Trust has now restored the park to its 1840 extent and replanted the Great Wood. Truly a garden which is a palimpsest of gardening history, but also one filled with colour and interest right through from the spring flowering of over 100,000 narcissi to the spectacular display of autumn leaves.

Bradenham Hall ★

Bradenham, Thetford IP25 7QP. Tel: (01362) 687243/687279

*Mr and Mrs Christian Allhusen • 8m E of Swaffham, 5m W of East Dereham S off A47 • Open April to Sept, 2nd and 4th Suns in month, 2 – 5.30pm, and for NGS 23rd April, 23rd July, 24th Sept. Coach parties on open days or at other times by written appt (with meals if requested) • Entrance: £4, children under 12 free • Other information: Plant sale 27th Aug ● ● WC & *

Surrounding the fine early-Georgian brick house (not open), these exceptional gardens are sheltered and divided by many yew hedges, which screen 90 yards of herbaceous borders, backing onto shrubs and the Philosophers' Walk, a paved garden and a large old-fashioned rose garden. The other borders contain a plantsman's collection of shrubs, flowers and trees. The house and garden walls are covered with a wide range of shrubs, climbers and fruit. The walled kitchen garden has vegetables, cut flowers and a mixed border backed by laburnums, and there are two glasshouses, an attractive old barn and a millennium aviary. The arboretum, of about 800 well-labelled varieties, is underplanted for spring with fritillaries and large drifts of naturalised daffodils (some 90 cultivars).

Bressingham Gardens ★

Bressingham, Diss IP22 2AB. Tel: (01379) 686900

Blooms Nurseries Ltd and Mr and Mrs Adrian Bloom • 2.5m W of Diss on A1066 • Open March to Oct, daily: Dell Garden and Foggy Bottom, 10.30am – 5.30pm (closes 4.30pm March, April, Sept and Oct) • Entrance (includes entry to Bessingham Steam Experience): £10, OAPs £8, children £6 • Other information: Special guided tours available outside normal open season ● ● × ● WC & ● ● B&B

Fifteen acres of beautiful gardens still under creation by the Bloom family with over 8000 species and varieties of plants on display in five gardens. Alan Bloom created the six-acre *Dell Garden* with its famous 'island beds' set in park-like meadow between 1955 and 1962. Planted with perennials to give colour and interest from spring to autumn, the wide and varied collection includes many Bressingham-raised varieties. The Summer Garden at the entrance includes a National Collection of miscanthus. *Foggy Bottom*, designed and created by Adrian Bloom over 30 years ago, sparkles with colour, not only from the excellent collection of blue and gold conifers, shrubs and ornamental trees, but from seasonal plantings of perennials, grasses and bulbs. The 'River of Blood', a snaking broad drift of massed planting of the Japanese blood grass *Imperata cylindrica* 'Rubra', is a stunning sight from midsummer onwards. Linking the Dell Garden and Foggy Bottom, a new pathway goes through the Shrub Garden and Adrian's Wood, now being developed and planted with a collection of North American native plants. Then visit the national Dad's Army Collection and the steam museum where engines and trains chug away and whistle – but these nostalgic sounds do not detract from the overall peace of the garden.

Castle Acre Priory

Stocks Green, Castle Acre PE32 2AF. Tel: (01760) 755394

English Heritage • 5m N of Swaffham, 0.5m W of Castle Acre, off A1065 • Open – telephone for details • Entrance: £4.20, OAPs £3.20, children £2.10, family £10.50 (2005 prices) ○ 🐝 WC ♿ ⬆ 🏛 💡 ℞

A walled herb garden divided into four sections containing medicinal, decorative, culinary and strewing herbs. Lavenders line the walls, where there are also three apple trees dating from the sixteenth century; a central circular bed contains a bay tree. Two small beds on the outside of the boundary wall are planted with medieval-period flowers.

Congham Hall Hotel

Lynn Road, Grimston, King's Lynn PE32 1AH. Tel: (01485) 600250

Julie Woodhouse, General Manager • 7m NE of King's Lynn. From A149/A148 interchange, follow A148 signed to Sandringham/Fakenham/Cromer; after 100 metres, turn right for Grimston; hotel is 2.5m on left • Open April to Sept, daily except Sat. Small parties by appt at other times • Entrance: free • Other information: Coaches must pre-book ➊ 🍴 ✕ WC ♿ ⬆ ℘ 🏛 💡 B&B

The hotel, set in 30 acres of parkland with a neat parterre full of bright bedding at the entrance, has a formal herb garden with about 700 varieties of both culinary and medicinal herbs along with herbaceous plantings and rose-covered pergolas. A 'woodery' accommodates the increasing collection of herbs, using timber salvaged from fallen trees instead of rocks.

Corpusty Mill Garden ★

Corpusty, Norwich NR11 6QB Tel: (01263) 587223

Roger Last • 6m S of Holt. Turn off B1149 at Corpusty; mill is in centre of village • Open for parties only by appt • Other information: Teas by arrangement • Entrance: £6 ● ⬆

The four-acre garden is as unexpected as it is intriguing, gradually revealing itself as a complex series of interlinked spaces. The planting is varied and lush with a rich collection of trees, shrubs, herbaceous and water-loving plants. Water is everywhere, in fountains, ponds, a stream, a small lake and a river. Buildings and follies are discovered as the garden unfolds: a long high flint wall inset with heads of Roman emperors, a Gothic arch with knapped flints, and a pitch-dark and mysterious four-chambered grotto, built of moss-covered ginger sandstone. Elsewhere, a Gothick ruin with a spiral staircase, a flint humpback bridge and a classical pavilion in the kitchen garden, with ornamental compost containers. A separate area, rich in trees, has been developed as a landscaped meadow. Here a small lake with a raised bank and walkway on one side is dominated by a gunnera and a tall, slender stainless steel cone and a water-filled cave reveals a figure drowning or rising up from the mud. To the north, the River Bure forms a tranquil natural boundary. By the house a contemporary formal garden, with a stainless steel water column and a central rill and pool, completes a highly eclectic but well-judged sequence of different styles and moods.

Courtyard Farm ★

Ringstead, Kings Lynn PE36 5LQ.

Lord Melchett • 16m NE of King's Lynn, 3.5m E of Hunstanton, 2m E of Ringstead, on road crossing Ringstead Common to Chosely and Burnham Market • Open all year, daily • Entrance: free ○ 🐾 🔼

The primeval gardener was a stone-age farmer who enjoyed the wild flowers that spattered his little fields of ripening grain, and Courtyard Farm harks back to those prehistoric days of marigolds and corncockles. The best time to visit is in July. Take a circular walk through fields of ripening grain and acres of wild flowers – 150 plant species have been identified to date. This is not gardening on a small scale, but it is a most praiseworthy effort to retain our natural heritage of wild and cultivated plants. As the whole 800 acres are managed organically, wildlife abounds and hares and skylarks are spotted regularly. Most heartening.

East Ruston Old Vicarage ★★

East Ruston, Norwich NR12 9HN. Tel: (01692) 650432 (daytime)

Graham Robeson and Alan Gray • 15m NE of Norwich, 4m E of North Walsham. Turn off A149 onto B1159 signed to Walcot and Bacton, then left at T-junction. After 2m, the house is next to the church • Open 26th March to 28th Oct, Sat, Sun, Wed, Fri and Bank Holiday Mons, 2 – 5.30pm, and by appt for coach parties • Entrance: £4.50, children £1, season ticket £14 ◑ 🍴 🐾 wc ᵹ 🌿 🍽

The twin strengths of this much-publicised garden are the architectural framework of walls and hedges and an astonishing profusion of plants. Two Norfolk churches and a lighthouse play a fundamental role as focal points at the end of skilfully crafted vistas. Within the garden the value of theatre is not forgotten. Tall dark hedges with openings beckon the visitor on to yet more discoveries: a box parterre and sunken garden, superb herbaceous borders, a Mediterranean garden and, one of the most striking elements, an exotic garden recently trebled in size. Rare plants are everywhere, set in gravel or in borders; because of the garden's coastal setting, many are semi-hardy and shrubs from the southern hemisphere are well represented. On the perimeter, a cornfield achieves an astonishing density and brilliance of summer colour, and a Desert Wash has mature palms, agaves, dasylirions, colourful lampranthus, delospermas, cacti and self-sown annuals, all left out for winter.

The Exotic Garden

6 Cotman Road, Thorpe, Norwich NR1 4AF. Tel: (01603) 623167

Mr W.R.S. Giles • In E Norwich off A47 Thorpe road, 0.25m from Norwich station. From Yarmouth follow one-way system towards city centre, turn right at traffic lights opposite DEFRA building. New entrance and car park via side entrance of Alan Boswell Insurance, 126 Thorpe Road, next to DEFRA building • Open 18th June to 8th Oct, Sun, 1 – 5.30pm, and for parties of 10 or more by appt • Entrance: £4, children free, parties £5 per person incl. refreshments ● 💷 🏠 WC ✍ ⚲

An exotic garden of half an acre on a south-facing hillside, with tall trees and hedges creating a sheltered microclimate. The unusual collection of plants includes gingers, bananas, aroids and succulents. The garden reaches its peak in high to late summer, when such exotics as cannas and brugmansias are in full bloom. It is renowned for its use of house plants as bedding plants – tillandsias may be spotted in the branches of trees which are underplanted with codiaeums, guzmanias and tradescantias, and philodendrons and *Monstera deliciosa* are also used in this way, flourishing in the summer months. There are many flint walls and two raised pools. A feeling of fantasy pervades the whole place, especially in the evening when the various scents are at their headiest. A new half-acre garden has been added for hardy exotics that need far less maintenance and tolerate winter cold.

Fairhaven Woodland and Water Garden ★

School Road, South Walsham, Norwich NR13 6DZ. Tel: (01603) 270449

The Fairhaven Garden Trust • 9m NE of Norwich. At South Walsham, follow brown tourist-signs on A47 at junction with B1140 • Open all year, daily except 25th Dec, 10am – 5pm; May to Aug, Wed and Thurs, 10am – 9pm. Guided walks for parties • Entrance: £4, OAPs £3.50, children £1.50, under 5 free. Annual membership £15, family membership £35, dog membership £2.50, wildlife sanctuary £1.50. Discounts for parties • Other information: Boat trips available May to Aug ○ 💷 ✕ 🏠 WC 🏠 ⚲ ✍ 🚻 ⚲ ⚲

A garden created in natural woods of oak and alder extending to about 180 acres and surrounding the unspoiled (private) South Walsham Inner Broad. Paths wind among banks of azaleas and large-leaved rhododendrons and lead to the edge of the broad itself. Much of the area is wet and supports a rich variety of primulas, especially candelabras, with lysichitons, hostas, astilbes, ligularias and gunneras of exceptional size merging into the natural vegetation, among which are many royal ferns and some majestic oaks. Although particularly colourful during the spring flowering of the azaleas and rhododendrons, and with the turning of the leaves in autumn, the garden gives pleasure at all times of the year if natural beauty is preferred to man-made sophistication. Three miles of woodland walks with fine views.

Felbrigg Hall ★ [Historic Garden Grade II*]

Felbrigg, Norwich NR11 8PR. Tel: (01263) 837444

The National Trust • 2m SW of Cromer off A148. Entrance on B1436 • Hall open as garden, 1 – 5pm • Garden and walled garden open 25th March to 29th Oct,

Sat – Wed, 11am – 5pm; garden also open 20th July to 1st Sept, Thurs and Fri,
11am – 5pm. Park and woodland walks open all year, daily, dawn – dusk
• Entrance: £3, children £1.50 (house and gardens £7, children £3.50, parties
£6 per person) • Other information: Self-drive scooter available • Garden: ❶ ⬛ ✕
🐌 <u>WC</u> ♿ ♨ ♨ ⛟ ♀ ⚲ *Park:* ○ ⏃ ⚲

The Jacobean house faces south across the park, which is notable for its fine woods
and lakeside walk. A ha-ha separates the park from the lawns of the house, where
there is an orangery planted with camellias. To the north the ground rises and there
are specimen trees and shrubs, including many of North American origin. At some
distance to the east a large walled kitchen garden is now richly planted with a combination of fruit, vegetables and flowers in a formal design behind clipped hedges;
it contains a vine house and a great brick dovecot with a flock of doves. In early
autumn there is a display of many varieties of colchicums: a National Collection is
kept here. The gardens are in immaculate order, and restoration, renewal and
replacement continue at a brisk pace.

Fritton Lake Countryworld

Fritton, Great Yarmouth NR31 9HA. Tel: (01493) 488208

Lord and Lady Somerleyton • 5m SW of Great Yarmouth off A143 • Open April to
Sept, daily, 10am – 5.30pm • Entrance: £6.50, OAPs £5.50, children £4.50.
Discounts for parties • Other information: Falconry, heavy horses, golf, putting, boats,
children's farm, pony rides, fishing, viking fortress, miniature tractors, miniature
railway, cycle trail, self-catering accommodation ❶ ♿ ♨ ⛟ ♀ ⚲

The large lake remains almost unspoilt and separate from the tea rooms and other
commercial attractions of this country park. An unusual feature is a Victorian garden
of about half an acre in the gardenesque style with irregular beds surrounded by
clipped box hedges and filled with shrubs and herbaceous perennials. In addition to
the formal lakeside gardens there are woodland walks and gardens, including the
Lost Gardens of Fritton Hall – the Victorian hall burned down in 1957 and the
gardens were left to go wild – which contain a large collection of rhododendrons
and azaleas intersected by paths.

The Garden in an Orchard

Mill Road, Bergh Apton, Norwich NR15 1BQ. Tel: (01508) 480322

Mr and Mrs R. W. Boardman • 6m SE of Norwich off A146 at Hellington Corner
• Open Bank Holiday weekends and several others May to Sept, 11am – 6pm (but
check before visiting) • Entrance: £2 ❶ ⬛ 🐌 ⏃ ♨

The garden, which started as a commercial orchard, over the years has been planted
up bit by bit with rare and unusual plants and trees, and now extends to 3.5 acres.
Narrow paths meander through dense plantings of species roses, giving
eye-to-eye contact with their flowers, then open up to similar plantings of herbaceous walks. Mr Boardman is a professional plantsman and among his rare trees are
Phellodendron amurense, Prunus padus 'Colorata' and nine species of eucalyptus.
Lonicera ledebourii catches the eye, along with *Malva sylvestris* subsp. *mauritanica* and
many special clematis scrambling through trees. A half-acre wildflower meadow, with
a wide range of British flora, is maturing.

Hales Hall

Hales, Loddon NR14 6QW. Tel: (01508) 548507

Mr and Mrs Terence Read • 12m SE of Norwich, off A146. Signposted • Open all year, Mon – Sat, 10am – 4pm, Sun and Bank Holiday Mons, 11am – 4pm. Closed 14th April. Guided parties by arrangement • Entrance: £2 (Great Barn and gardens) • Other information: Fifteenth-century thatched Great Barn ○ WC ♿

A moat surrounds the remaining wing of a vast house of the late fifteenth century and a central lawn with well-planted borders and topiary of box and yew backed by high brick walls. Work is continuing on the restoration of the garden after centuries of neglect. A fruit garden has been planted and there is a pot-grown orchard. The owners specialise in rare and unusual perennial plants, and look after National Collections of citrus, figs and greenhouse grapes. The associated century-old nurseries offer an extensive range of conservatory plants, vines, figs, mulberries, and many peach, apricot, nectarine and greengage varieties.

Holkham Hall ★ [Historic Garden Grade I]

Wells-next-the-Sea NR23 1AB. Tel: (01328) 710227; (01328) 711636 (nursery gardens)

The Earl of Leicester • 23m W of Cromer, 2m W of Wells on A149 • Hall open 15th, 16th and 17th April; then June to Sept, Thurs – Mon, 1 – 5pm • Nursery gardens open Jan and Feb, daily, 11am – 4pm, March to Oct, daily, 10am – 5pm. Terrace gardens open as hall but Mon (except Bank Holiday Mons), Thurs and Fri only • Entrance: Terrace and nursery gardens free (hall £6.50, children £3.25; Bygones Museum £5, child £2.50). Discount for parties of 20 or more • Terrace gardens: ◑ ✕ WC ♿ *Nursery gardens:* ○

The vast park, famous for its holm oaks, was laid out originally by William Kent but altered by 'Coke of Norfolk' and the 2nd Earl. On the west side of the house, lawns sweep down to the great lake. The terrace which fronts the south façade was added in 1854, but the scale of the house and park is so great that, from a distance at least, this does not seriously disrupt the vision of the two. The formal beds designed by W.A. Nesfield flank a great fountain representing St George and the Dragon, said to be designed by R. Smith. These days, alas, the fountain flows only briefly – from 3 to 3.45pm on Thursdays, Fridays and Mondays (but not on Bank Holidays) during the visitor season. The nursery gardens in the original eighteenth-century walled kitchen garden in the grounds extend to over six acres, subdivided into six areas with perenial borders and the original green-houses. Alpines, shrubs, perennials, herbs, roses, bedding and house plants are for sale.

Houghton Hall ★★ [Historic Garden Grade I]

King's Lynn PE31 6UE. Tel: (01485) 528569

The Marquess of Cholmondeley • 13m NE of King's Lynn off A148 • Hall open as garden but 1.30 – 5pm • Park and gardens open 16th April to 28th Sept, Wed, Thurs, Sun and Bank Holiday Mons, 11am – 5.30pm • Entrance: £4.50, children £2 (hall, park and gardens £7, children £3, family £16) (2005 prices) • Other information: Battery-powered buggies available for disabled visitors ① 💻 ✕ 🏠 <u>WC</u> & ⬗ 🌳 🏛 🏺 ⚲

One of the most magnificent houses in Britain curiously never seems to have had a formal garden in the eighteenth century: it was not until the 1890s that it acquired a garden on the west front. Recent tree-planting on an impressive scale will settle the house into its landscape, but it is the five-acre walled kitchen garden that has undergone the most radical change. The centrepiece is a double herbaceous border; the remainder of the space is divided by yew hedges into 20 different garden rooms, each with an individual character and all immaculately maintained. One is a box-edged rose parterre, and a wide outer border has some of the older rose varieties and a mixture of foxgloves, pinks and delphiniums. In the kitchen garden proper are trained fruit trees, an outsize rustic fruit cage and vegetable beds filled with unusual varieties; elsewhere, pleached limes surround a grassy area planted with 200 plum trees and spring and summer bulbs. The cherry walk is underplanted with irises, and a wisteria pergola runs along the western edge of the garden. Behind, a border is given over to peonies and lilies, while an autumn border of asters, Japanese anemones and sunflowers provides a blaze of colour from August onwards. The rebuilt glasshouses contain an expanding orchid collection and an unusual water feature by Julian Bannerman. A rustic temple, a Kent seat, Italian statues, a sunken pool and a modern obelisk add architectural flourishes.

Hoveton Hall Gardens

Wroxham, Norwich NR12 8RJ. Tel: (01603) 782798

Mr and Mrs Andrew Buxton • 9m NE of Norwich, 1m N of Wroxham on A1151 • Open 16th April to 10th Sept, Wed, Fri, Sun and Bank Holiday Mons, plus Thurs in May and June, all 10.30am – 5pm (opens 11am – 6pm Bank Holidays). Coach parties and tours by arrangement • Entrance: £4, wheelchairs £2, children (5–14) £1.50, season tickets £9.50, family £20 ① 💻 🏠 <u>WC</u> & 🌳 ⚲

Situated as they are in the Norfolk Broads, the gardens are amply supplied with water and streams. For mid-May and early June the rhododendrons and azaleas, many rare varieties, are spectacular, dominating and scenting the woodland walks. The formal walled garden, planted and enclosed in 1936, with herbaceous borders of that period, has in part been redesigned; a delightful gardener's cottage is set picturesquely in one corner, covered in roses. The adjoining walled kitchen garden is a good example of traditional vegetable planting. The entrance to the two walled gardens has an intriguing iron gate in the shape of a spider, hence the formal garden is called the Spider Garden. A water garden, leading to the lake, has good water plants, vast *Gunnera manicata*, peltiphyllums, hostas and fine stands of bamboos. The whole area is laced with streams and interesting bridges, and birds, both migratory and native, abound.

How Hill Farm ★

Ludham, Gt. Yarmouth NR29 5PG. Tel: (01692) 678558

Mr P.D.S. Boardman • 15m NE of Norwich, 1m W of Ludham off A1062. Follow signs to How Hill. Farm Garden S of How Hill • Open probably 21st May, 2 – 5pm, and to parties at other times by appt • Entrance: £3, children free ● 💻 <u>WC</u> & ⬗ 🌳

The garden around the farm is comparatively conventional, with a new garden and pond in the old bullock yard and a large Chusan palm planted in a dog cage from which it threatens to escape. Here, too, is a collection of over 100 varieties of *Ilex aquifolium* as well as many other rare holly species. Over the road in the river valley is a rich combination of exotics mingled with native vegetation, and a wide variety of trees and shrubs. Around a series of pools, banks of azaleas merge into reed beds, rhododendron species rise over thickets of fern, wild grasses skirt groves of the giant *Arundo donax*, with birches, conifers and a collection of 40 different bamboos against a background of a recently created three-acre Broad, thick with water lilies.

Kettle Hill ★

Blakeney NR25 7PN. Tel: (01263) 741147

Richard and Frances Winch • 11m W of Cromer, just outside Blakeney on B1156 Langham road • Open for parties by appt • Entrance: £5 (includes coffee), children free ● ● WC ㄴ

With the help of Mark Rumary, the owners have transformed this garden into a luxurious and elegant delight. A box-edged rectangular parterre with heart-shaped beds, heightened by topiary spirals and mop heads, reflects their interest in the *Romantic Garden Nursery* at Swannington. A cleverly sited brick wall shelters a long mixed border packed with colour and unusual plants and leads to a circular secret garden. A large lawn, featuring a delightful Gothick summerhouse by George Carter, extends from the house to mature woodland, to which many ornamental trees have been added and which is carpeted in spring with bluebells and naturalised lilies. A new rose garden has been planted adjoining the house, and the old one deep in the wood has been rejuvenated.

Lake House Water Gardens

Roman Drive, Postwick Lane, Brundall, Norwich NR13 5LU. Tel: (01603) 712933

Mr and Mrs Garry Muter • 5m E of Norwich. From A47 roundabout take Brundall turn and turn right at T-junction into Postwick Lane • Open for NGS, and for parties of 20 or more by appt • Entrance: £3, children free • Other information: Sale of unusual plants on NGS open days ● ● ● ◁

Two acres of water gardens, once part of a 76-acre private estate and arboretum planted about 1880, are set in a steep cleft in the river escarpment. From the top of the hill the gardens fall away to a lily-covered lake at the bottom. Water features, a fountain and waterfall have recently been added. Plant associations throughout the garden reflect Mrs Muter's talent as a flower arranger. Surrounding the formal areas are drifts of primroses, bluebells and daffodils in season; wild flowers abound. The formal planting has many rare and interesting species: *Zantedeschia aethiopica* 'Green Goddess' and 'Crowborough' in a large clump cool down a flamboyant *Hemerocallis* 'Frans Hals'. A wide variety of hardy geraniums blooms in succession, a good collection of hybrid helianthemums awaits those who visit in June, and it is worth making an appointment with the spectacular late-autumn colour.

Lawn Farm

Cley Road, Holt NR25 7DY. Tel: (01263) 713484

Mr and Mrs G.W. Deterding • From Holt take Cley Road opposite King's Head pub in High Street. After 1m, turning is signposted on right after Holt Hall School gates • Open March to Aug by appt • Entrance: £3, children free ● WC ♿

The six-and-a-half-acre garden was designed and laid out by the owners in 1987. There are five natural ponds with three water gardens, and a damp wooded area with hydrangeas and azaleas. A completely different atmosphere is to be found in the two medieval flint-walled courtyards; here roses and many interesting and unusual shrubs and climbers flourish in the hot and sheltered microclimate. Mrs Deterding has a magpie's eye for the rare and difficult to find, including a good collection of unusual trees.

Lexham Hall [Historic Garden Grade II]

East Lexham, King's Lynn PE32 2QJ. Tel: (01328) 701288/701341

Mr and Mrs Neil Foster • 6m N of Swaffham, 2m W of Litcham off B1145 • Open 5th, 12th, 19th Feb for snowdrops – please telephone for details; 14th and 21st May, and May to July mid-week for parties of 20 or more by appt • Entrance: £3, parties £5 per person ● 🍽 🏠 WC ♿ 🐕 🌿

The seventeenth- and eighteenth-century hall sits well amid beautiful parkland with sheep and interesting trees. The ground falls away to the river forming a lake and canals crossed by elegant bridges; the garden was the inspiration of the present owner's mother who, with the help of the late Dame Sylvia Crowe, laid out its bones. Massive yew hedges reveal intimate views of the park, taking the eye to the distance beyond. Wide terracing to the south of the house is well planted and colourful, and a long grass walk edged with herbaceous plants and shrubs progresses to woodland full of rhododendrons, azaleas, camellias, rare trees and spring bulbs. (In early spring, the parkland and adjoining churchyard are also awash with snowdrops.) There is a colourful rose garden, and the kitchen garden has an early eighteenth-century crinkle-crankle wall covered with fruit, a cutting border, greenhouses with plants for the house and tender vegetables, the whole a picture of health. A wood to the south, known as the American Gardens, is reputedly planted from seeds collected in America.

Mannington Hall ★ [Historic Garden Grade II]

Saxthorpe, Norwich NR11 7BB. Tel: (01263) 584175

Lord and Lady Walpole • 5m SE of Holt off B1149. Signposted • Open May to Sept, Sun, 12 noon – 5pm; also June to Aug, Wed – Fri, 11am – 5pm • Entrance: £4, OAPs and students £3, children free ● 🍽 🏠 WC ♿ 🐕 🏛 ♀ ⚲

A romantic garden of 20 acres with a fifteenth-century house. Lawns run down to the moat, crossed by a drawbridge, to herbaceous borders backed by high walls of brick and flint. The moat also encloses a secret, scented garden in a design derived from one of the ceilings of the house. Outside the moat are borders of flowering shrubs flanking a Doric temple, and woodlands beyond contain the ruins of a Saxon church and nineteenth-century follies. Within the walls of the former kitchen garden, a series of rose gardens has been planted following the design of gardens from medieval to modern times and featuring roses popular at each period. A twentieth-century rose garden incorporates a planthouse, a vegetable plot and a children's garden. There are now more than 1500 varieties of roses here. In 2003 a sensory garden was created on the south lawn with a narrow channel of water and four large beds with plants chosen for scent, touch, sight, taste and hearing. A lake, woods and meadowland with extensive walks are other features.

Norfolk Lavender

Caley Mill, Heacham, King's Lynn PE31 7JE. Tel: (01485) 570384

Norfolk Lavender Ltd • 13m N of King's Lynn on A149 • Open all year, daily except 25th, 26th Dec, 1st Jan, 9.30am – 5pm (closes 4pm Nov to March) • Entrance: free
○ ⬤ ✕ WC ⅋ ⟁ ⅋ ⛪ ⚑ ⚲

Fields of lavender, stretching into the distance like giant stripes of corduroy, are a splendid sight in July and August. There is a more intimate display of named lavender (designated as a National Collection) near the Victorian watermill that serves as the visitor centre for this major commercial enterprise. A small herb garden is well tended and labelled, and the beds in the rose garden are lavender-edged. The four-acre fragrant garden has helped to reduce the pressure of visitors, particularly in July and August.

Oxburgh Hall [Historic Garden Grade II]

Oxborough, King's Lynn PE33 9PS. Tel: (01366) 328258

The National Trust • 7m SW of Swaffham off A134 • House open 25th March to 29th Oct, Sat – Wed, 1 – 5pm (Bank Holiday Mons opens 11am) • Garden open 7th Jan to 19th March, Sat and Sun, 11am – 4pm; 25th March to July, 2nd Sept to 29th Oct, Sat – Wed; Aug, daily; all 11am – 5.30pm; 4th Nov to 17th Dec, 6th Jan to 25th Feb, Sat and Sun, 11am – 4pm • Entrance: £3.25, children £1.65 (hall and garden £6.50, children £3.25, family £17) ○ ⬤ ✕ WC ⅋ ⅋ ⛪ ⚑ ⚲

The gatehouse is the glory of Oxburgh, and the mellow red-brick early-Tudor manor house seems to float in its rectangular moat above a haze of fringed water lilies. Both house and garden are concealed from view until you have walked past the orchard of quince, plum and greengage trees. Then you look down over the formal parterre, a Victorian copy of a Le Nôtre design consisting of a moderately restrained pattern of beds edged with clipped box hedges, punctuated by clipped tumps of yew. Yellow, red, violet and silver are the colours of the annual bedding – a vibrant carpet. Behind a long yew hedge is a narrow border edged with wispy catmint, with repeat-clumps of colourful perennials. There are some fine trees, and circular walks lead into the park and woodland, full of snowdrops and winter aconites in early spring.

Pensthorpe

Pensthorpe, Fakenham NR21 0LN. Tel: (01328) 851465

Mr and Mrs W. Jordan • 1m E of Fakenham on A1067 Norwich – Fakenham road. Signposted • Open all year, daily, 10am – 5pm (closes 4pm Jan to March)

• *Entrance: £7, OAPs £5.50, children £3.50. Special rates for parties of 15 or more*
○ ⬛ ✕ 🍴 <u>WC</u> ♿ 🌱 ♨ 🔫 ⚲

The 200-acre park and nature reserve has two features of considerable interest to gardeners. Piet Oudolf's 1999 Millennium Garden, overlooking one of the lakes, is planted in his trademark perennial style, with large drifts and clumps of herbaceous plants, interspersed with grasses; it is at its peak from July to September, but also looks good in the autumn, when the flowers are slightly duller and the seed heads come through. As a style it is both spectacular and sensitive, blending into the environment of the park where a traditional English garden would have looked out of place; as a garden it is a paradise for huge numbers of butterflies, bumble-bees and insects. Julie Toll's 2005 Wave Garden is by deliberate contrast awash with colour from early spring through to summer. It too blends seamlessly into the surrounding woodland and meadows, thanks to a clever mix of wildflowers and cultivated plants. Drifts of thalictrums, aquilegias and campions stand out against clipped hedges of golden yew that give the garden its structure and form secretive seating areas with views over the lake to the nature reserve beyond. A woodland garden was planted in 2002. There is also an adventure playground for children and walk-through aviaries for all ages.

The Plantation Garden [Historic Garden Grade II]

4 Earlham Road, Norwich NR2 3DB.
Tel: (01603) 621868 (Trust Chairman: Mr B.M. Adam)

Plantation Garden Preservation Trust • Entrance off Earlham Road, next to Beeches Hotel • Open all year, daily, 9am – 6pm, or dusk if earlier, but sometimes closed Sat (check on website listed at back of Guide). Guided parties by arrangement • Entrance: £2 (honesty box) (2005 price), accompanied children free, guided parties by arrangement ● WC ♿ 🌱 🔫 ⚲

This unusual surviving example of a high-Victorian suburban garden, framed by mature trees, was created by Henry Trevor in a disused chalk quarry just outside the medieval walls of Norwich. The first feature in his garden, an idiosyncratic Gothick fountain, was built in 1857. There followed terraces with walls in the medieval style, built using an extraordinary conglomeration of materials: industrial waste, locally made fancy bricks, flint and stone. Flights of steps with Italianate pedestals and balustrades, a rustic-style bridge and summerhouse, flower beds and woodland paths combine to make a garden simultaneously typical of its period and the personal vision of one individual. Conservation and restoration continue. It is also an area of ecological interest with birds and lime-loving wild flowers. The replica summerhouse on the upper terrace gives a view over the whole garden.

Raveningham Hall [Historic Garden Grade II*]

Raveningham, Norwich NR14 6NS. Tel: (01508) 548152

Sir Nicholas Bacon • 14m SE of Norwich off A146. Turn left at Hales on B1136, then first right • Telephone for dates and times of opening • Entrance: £2.50, children free ● ⬛ <u>WC</u> ♿ 🕊 🌱

Set in a fine landscaped park, the garden has a rich variety of trees, shrubs and herbaceous plants, and is notable in spring for a large collection of snowdrop species and cultivars. Its eighteenth-century and Victorian past are still in evidence: the herb garden incorporates physic plantings, and the walled kitchen garden and greenhouses are still in use. An arboretum with some unusual trees is being extended towards the lake. Sculpture is well placed all around this peaceful garden.

Sandringham House ★ [Historic Garden Grade II*]

Sandringham, King's Lynn PE35 6EN. Tel: (01553) 772675

H.M. The Queen • 9m NE of King's Lynn on B1440 near Sandringham Church • House open as garden • Garden and park open Easter to July, early Aug to Oct, daily, 11am – 4.45pm • Entrance: museum and grounds £5.50, OAPs £4.50, children £3.50, family £14.50 (house, museum and grounds £8, OAPs £6.50, children £5, family £21) ◑ 🍽 ✕ <u>WC</u> ♿ ⟡ ♨ ⛪ ♟

The huge Victorian house stands among broad lawns with an outer belt of woodland through which a path runs past plantings of camellias, hydrangeas, cornus, magnolias and rhododendrons, with some fine specimen trees. The path passes the magnificent cast- and wrought-iron Norwich Gates of 1862. In the open lawn are specimen oaks planted by Queen Victoria and other members of the royal family. To the south-west of the house the eastern side of the upper lake is built up into a massive rock garden using blocks of the local carrstone, and now largely planted with dwarf conifers. Below the rock garden, opening onto the lake, a cavernous grotto was intended as a boathouse; above is a small summerhouse built for Queen Alexandra. There are thick plantings of hostas, agapanthus and various moisture-loving plants around the margin of the lake. The path passes between the upper and lower lakes set in wooded surroundings. To the north of the house is a garden designed by the late Sir Geoffrey Jellicoe for King George VI: a long series of box-hedged beds, divided by gravel and grass paths and flanked by avenues of pleached lime, one of which is centred on a gold-plated statue of a Buddhist divinity.

Sheringham Park ★ [Historic Garden Grade II*]

Wood Farm, Upper Sheringham NR26 8TL. Tel: (01263) 820550

The National Trust • 4m NE of Holt off A148 • Open all year, daily, dawn – dusk • Entrance: £3 per car inc. parking and all occupants. Coaches £9 • Other information: Coaches must pre-book during rhododendron season. Refreshments available April to Sept only ○ 🍽 🍴 <u>WC</u> ♿ ⟡ ♨ ⛪

The house and park, both designed by Humphry Repton, are located in a secluded valley at the edge of the Cromer/Holt ridge, close to the sea but protected from its winds by steep wooded hills. The park is remarkable not only for its beauty and spectacular views but also for an extensive collection of rhododendrons which thrive in the acid soil. Crowning an eminence is a modern classical temple based on a Repton design and erected to mark the 70th birthday of Mr Thomas Upcher, the last descendant of the original owner to live at Sheringham. This is the most-admired and best-preserved work of Repton.

Stow Hall ★

Stow Bardolph, King's Lynn PE34 3HU. Tel: (01366) 383194

Lady Rose Hare • 2m N of Downham Market, E of A10 • Open for NGS 23rd April, 2 – 5pm, 23rd June, 5 – 9pm, and for parties by appt • Entrance: £3, children free
● ● ● wc ● ● ● ●

Majestic plane trees, beeches and cedars of Lebanon provide a changing backdrop for a garden that is in effect a long series of imaginative and interesting gardens linked by a straight path of red bricks and gravel. The high, warm walls of the old stableyard and the house are swathed in old roses and wisteria, and shrubs more usually seen in milder gardens also have congenial homes in the shelter of these walls. Off the path from the house to the walled kitchen garden are small elegant formal gardens, a mixed perennial garden including irises, a Dutch garden, cloisters with more roses, and a croquet lawn. The kitchen garden has formal beds of fruit and vegetables, gnarled apple trees and pear trees, a venerable mulberry, and yet more roses; The cottage garden next to a greenhouse is an exuberant mixture of scented plants, herbs and alpines.

Thrigby Hall Wildlife Gardens

Filby, Great Yarmouth NR29 3DR. Tel: (01493) 369477

Mr K.J. Sims • 6m NW of Great Yarmouth on A1064. Signposted • Open all year, daily, 10am – 5pm (or dusk if earlier) • Entrance: £7.50, OAPs £5.50, children (4 – 14) £4.50 (2005 prices) ○ ● ● wc ● ● ●

The chief attraction here is a collection of Chinese plants arranged to form the landscape of the willow-pattern plate, complete with pagodas and bridges across a small lake. Complementing the collection of Asiatic animals, the plants are those particularly associated with temple gardens and include *Ginkgo biloba*, *Pinus parviflora*, *Paeonia suffruticosa*, *Nandina domestica* and *Chimonobambusa quadrangularis*, set against a background of willows of many species.

Wretham Lodge

East Wretham, Thetford IP24 1RL. Tel: (01953) 498997

Mr Gordon Alexander • 6m NE of Thetford off A1075. Turn left by village sign, right at crossroads, then bear left • Open 16th and 17th April, 11am – 5pm, 18th June, 2 – 5pm, and for parties by appt • Entrance: £2.50, children free
● ● wc ● ●

Extensive lawns surround the handsome flint-built former rectory set in its own walled park; there are wide mixed borders around the house and within the walled kitchen garden. Roses are massed in informal beds and cover the high flint walls, and plants worthy of note include espalier and fan-trained fruit trees, a large indoor fig and unusual vegetables in the fully productive kitchen garden. A wide grass walk runs around the park and through mature and recently established trees where daffodils are naturalised; a long walk among narcissi and bluebells leads to a grove of ornamental trees. Spring sees the flowering of many bulbs, and in summer the double herbaceous borders and the wildflower meadows are a haze of colour.

NORTHAMPTONSHIRE

Two-starred gardens are marked on the map with a black square.

Althorp House [Historic Garden Grade II*]

Althorp, Northampton NN7 4HQ. Tel: (01604) 770107 (House and Park Office)

Earl Spencer • 6m NW of Northampton on A428 Northampton – Rugby road • House and grounds open July to Sept, 11am – 5pm (closed 31st Aug) – telephone for exact dates • Entrance: house and gardens £12, OAPs £10, children (5–17) £6

● ◗ ▓ WC ᕷ ⬚ ♞

The Caroline-fronted Elizabethan house was surrounded by formal gardens with a vast walled garden to the east. John Evelyn remarked in 1675 on Althorp's 'stately woods and groves in a Park and with a Canale' and 'Gardens furnished with the choicest fruite in England and exquisitely kept'. They were all swept away during the fashionable eighteenth-century improvements by the architect Henry Holland, helped by Samuel Lapidge, 'Capability' Brown's assistant. The present gardens were laid out in the 1860s by the architect W.M. Teulon and enclosed by stone walls and balustrades. To the side and rear the gardens are also laid to lawn, although the talented designer Dan Pearson has recently planted beds with a subtle blend of bronze fennel, aconitum, potentillas and *Verbena bonariensis* outside the stable block, which now houses a shop, and the same restricted palette is used in other borders, harmonising wonderfully with the honey-coloured stone. This was the home of the late Diana, Princess of Wales, and the Earl, her brother, engaged Pearson to produce an unusual memorial – a two-mile walk in the grounds through the park and house to the island where the Princess is buried, leading through a green meadow of long grasses and wild flowers by the lake colonised by 1000 white water lilies and a variety of water fowl.

Boughton House Park [Historic Park Grade I]

Kettering NN14 1BJ. Tel: (01536) 515731

The Duke and Duchess of Buccleuch and Queensberry • 2m NE of Kettering off A43, entry via Geddington. Signposted • House open as garden • Garden open Aug, daily, 2 – 5pm. Park and plant centre open May to 1st Sept, daily except Fri, 1 – 5pm. Specialist and educational parties welcome at other times by prior arrangement • Entrance: £1.50, OAPs and children £1 (house, gardens and park £6, OAPs and children £5) • Other information: Tea room open August and weekends only. Dogs in park only, on lead ◑ ◗ ▓ WC ᕷ ⬳ ⌔ ⬚ ♞ ⚲

Although only limited formal gardens remain, Boughton will be attractive to garden enthusiasts and the whole family. The large sixteenth- and seventeenth- century house, with monastic origins and a strong French influence, contains an extensive collection of paintings and furniture. The magnificent surrounding park, with its lakes and canalised river, and avenues of trees, was laid out by the 1st Duke of Montagu before 1700 with the help of a Dutch gardener, Van der Meulen, who had experience of reclamation work in the Fens. The 2nd Duke, known as John the Planter, added a lake and a colossal network of avenues of elms and limes in the 1730s to an ambitious plan by Bridgeman, though not even the planter was prepared to carry out the complete network, and indeed he sacked Bridgeman in 1731. Even so the avenues stretched to 23 miles with rides through woods extending another 20 or so. Today, the garden close to the house includes herbaceous borders and some fine planted vases. To the south of the house a small circular rose garden leads to the outstanding rectangular lily pond, beyond which the walled garden houses a long herbaceous border and a well-stocked plant centre. Work is ongoing to restore some of the more important features, such as the Star Pond and its cascade. In the 350-acre park are walks and trails, including one for the disabled, and a woodland adventure play area for children (open subject to weather conditions).

Canons Ashby House [Historic Garden Grade II*]

Canons Ashby, Daventry NN11 3SD. Tel: (01327) 860044

The National Trust • 6m S of Daventry off A361 Daventry – Banbury road • House open • Garden open 25th March to Sept, Sat – Wed, 11am – 5.30pm, or dusk if earlier (closes 4.30pm in Oct); Nov to 17th Dec, Sat, Sun, 12 noon – 4pm • Entrance: £2.20 (house and garden £6.10, children £3.10, family £15.20. Reductions for pre-booked parties) • Other information: Parking 200 metres from house. Disabled telephone in advance and park near house. Wheelchairs available. Tape and braille guide available. Picnics in car park. Dogs in home paddock only, on lead ❶ 🍽 🛍 <u>WC</u> ♿ ⏱ 🌣 🏛 🍴 ⚲

The brooding, romantic house where Spenser wrote part of The Faerie Queene was the first to be rescued by the National Heritage Memorial Fund, and the historical framework of the garden has been painstakingly re-created over the past decade. Formal, with axial arrangements of paths and grass terraces in London and Wise style, high stone walls, lawns and gateways, the design dates almost entirely from the beginning of the eighteenth century; a cedar planted in 1781 survives from the original six. The garden is maturing well, with trees and shrubs beginning to give the required height and scale. Hexagonal beds, part of the later Inigo Trigg's plan of 1901, have been reinstated and feature seasonal bedding. Borders have majestic plants such as acanthus and cardoons, while the green court contains fine topiary. Old varieties of soft fruit bushes and fruit trees include espaliered pears grown from the original stock planted in 1710 by Edward Dryden, whose family owned the house. The wild gardens are in direct contrast to the formal, carefully maintained terraces at the highest level, from where the eye is irresistibly drawn down the principal vista to the Lion Gates and the fine Baroque gate piers. The 2-acre paddock to the east of the garden is being transformed into a wildflower/hay meadow.

Castle Ashby Gardens [Historic Garden Grade I]

Castle Ashby, Northampton NN7 1LQ. Tel: (01604) 696187

Earl Compton • 5m E of Northampton, between A45 Northampton – Wellingborough road and A428 Northampton – Bedford road • Open all year, daily, 10am – 6pm (closes 4pm Oct to March), with occasional closures when house can be hired as corporate venue. Tours for parties by appt • Entrance: (tickets from machine when entrance unattended) £2.80, OAPs/children £1.90, family £8, season ticket £34 (2005 prices) • Other information: Teas available in garden for coach parties or larger groups if pre-booked. Possible for wheelchairs but uneven paths. Farm shop and craft centre in village ○ ⅃ ⬮ ⬮ ⬮

The first impression as you walk past the Elizabethan house is of a vast space. 'Capability' Brown worked on the park, but the gardens open to the public are more intimate, laid out by Matthew Digby Wyatt in the 1860s with sunken lawns and immaculate yew cones surrounded by well planted borders. The fine orangery has a central circular fish pool seven feet deep and is filled with borderline-hardy shrubs. More garden buildings, also glazed to their rear, close this view and, beyond, tall box hedges enclose the Butterfly Garden, the Summerhouse Garden and the Rainbow Border. Ornamental fowl, rabbits and guinea pigs run and hop in the child-friendly farmyard. A spring walk leads to an informal arboretum, where dogs are invited to roam free and paths meander to the terracotta bridge spanning a series of ponds; the wider water of the lake is in view, but inaccessible.

Church Farm

Blakesley, Towcester NN12 8RA. Tel (01327) 860364

Alexander and Gillian Foster • 4m W of Towcester off A43/A5 junction. In Blakesley take first turn right at village green (Church Street); house on right immediately past church • Open April to July by appt only • Entrance: £2.50, children (6-16) £1 • Other information: Teas by arrangement NEW ◐ ◑ WC ⬮

The immaculate gravelled front courtyard with its simple, effective planting of shrubs and roses is a perfect frame for the fifteenth-century ironstone house (still a working farm). Behind the house the eye is drawn immediately to an impressive variety of trees through to the field beyond, grazed by Manx Loghtan sheep and a breeding herd of bright chestnut South Devon cattle. The one-and-a-half-acre garden, which benefits from a neutral clay soil and a natural stream, has been created and developed since 1986 by the present owners (Gillian Foster is also a talented botanical artist). They have engineered a natural flow from one area to the next: a terrace with a stunning display of agapanthus and geraniums; a subtle pink, blue and mauve border set off by a well-maintained lawn; shaded areas lightened by clever use of variegated foliage; a stream-fed pond on two levels surrounded by hostas, astilbes, primulas, blue *Iris sibirica* and densely planted mixed borders. In spring the garden is awash with tulips, fritillaries, hellebores, pulmonarias, while summer brings a spectacular display of roses. 'Cécile Brünner', 'Wedding Day', 'Bobbie James' and *R. mulliganii* clamber enthusiastically over buildings, greenhouse and mature trees in a spectacular way, and many old-fashioned varieties are also grown, including the pink scented 'Fritz Nobis' and *R. mundi*. A traditional garden combining flair and plantsmanship, full of interest, surprise and ideas to take home.

Coton Manor Garden ★★

Guilsborough, Northampton NN6 8RQ. Tel: (01604) 740219

Mr and Mrs Ian Pasley-Tyler • 10m NW of Northampton, 11m SE of Rugby near Ravensthorpe Reservoir, signed from A428 and A5199 • Open April to Sept,

Tues – Sat and Bank Holiday Suns and Mons, plus Suns in April and May, all 12 noon – 5.30pm • Entrance: £4.50, OAPs £4, children £2.50 ◑ 💺 ✕ wc ♿ ⚘ ♨

Dating from the 1920s, when the original seventeenth-century farmhouse was bought and added to by Mr Pasley-Tyler's grandparents, this is a beautifully maintained garden of exceptional charm, with unexpected vistas at every turn. There is something for everyone here: a most attractive assortment of pelargoniums in pots on the terrace by the house leading to the rose garden, a contrastingly shady woodland garden, a water garden, lush lawns sloping down to a large pond complete with black swans and ornamental ducks, and magnificent mixed borders, particularly striking in July with campanulas and philadelphus. There is a surprise around every corner (do not rub your eyes should you think you see a real crane or flamingo beside the neatly clipped yew hedge – no verdigris imitations here) and strategically placed seats from which to enjoy the views and effects of Susie Pasley-Tyler's marvellous eye for colour. The garden has continued to develop since the present generation moved into the house. The Mediterranean bank, rose walk and herb garden are now well established, along with the replanted rose bank and the midsummer and late-summer borders. The bluebell wood is magical in May, the wildflower meadow a mass of colour during June and July, and the autumn foliage shines out in September. A water staircase was recently completed running down between old apple orchards.

Cottesbrooke Hall ★★ [Historic Garden Grade II]

Cottesbrooke, Northampton NN6 8PF. Tel: (01604) 505808

Mr and Mrs A. Macdonald-Buchanan • 10m N of Northampton between A5199 and A508 (A14, junction 1 – A1/M1 link road) • House open as garden • Garden open May to Sept, Thurs and Bank Holiday Mons, plus Wed, May and June; all 2 – 5.30pm; and for individuals and parties by appt • Entrance: £4, children £2 (house and gardens £6, children £3) ◑ 💺 wc ♿ ♨

A beautifully maintained formal garden surrounding a fine Queen Anne house, set in a large park (also open) with lakes and a stream, vistas and avenues. Designs by Edward Schultz, Geoffrey Jellicoe, Dame Sylvia Crowe and the late Hon. Lady Macdonald-Buchanan are being continued by the present family – particularly the planting. The result is a series of delightful enclosed courtyards and gardens around the house with superb borders, urns and statues. Be sure to visit the intriguingly named Dilemma Garden and to wander through the Statue Walk. The spinney garden is at its best in spring with bulbs and azaleas. New trees, borders, yew hedges, gates and vistas have recently been added, and Philip Astley, formerly head gardener at Hardwick, is making his mark here. Beyond the thatched Wendy house, the wild garden surrounds a stream and cascades, with azaleas, rhododendrons, acers, cherries, spring bulbs and wild flowers. The magnolia, cherry and acer collections and the ancient cedars are notable.

Deene Park [Historic Garden Grade II]

Corby NN17 3EW. Tel: (01780) 450278/450223

Mr Edmund Brudenell • 6m N of Corby off A43 Kettering – Stamford road • House open • Gardens open 12th and 19th Feb (snowdrop days), 16th, 17th and 30th

April, 1st, 28th and 29th May; then June to Aug, Sun and Bank Holiday Mon; all 2 – 5pm. Parties by appt • Entrance: £3.50, children (10–14) £1.50, accompanied children under 10 free (house and gardens £6, concessions, £5.50, children (10–14) £2.50, accompanied children under 10 free) (2005 prices) ◐ ◖ ▧ <u>WC</u> ♿ ⚙ ♟

The house, created by generations of the Brudenell family, is an amalgam of architectural styles of all periods which co-exist without a quarrel. The glory of Deene is its trees. Fine mature specimens and groups fringe the formal areas and frame tranquil and enchanting views of the parkland and countryside. The main features of the garden are the long borders, the old-fashioned roses, the parterre and the huge winding lake, crossed by a commanding bridge. The parterre, designed by David Hicks, is a fine feature, running along the whole south side of the house. Gardens, parkland, house and church together provide an interesting and relaxing afternoon for visitors in what was the home of the Earl of Cardigan who led the Charge of the Light Brigade in 1854.

Evenley Wood Garden

Mill Lane, Evenley NN13 5SH. Tel: (01280) 703329

Mr and Mrs R.T. Whiteley • 0.75m S of Brackley on A43. Go through village towards Mixbury, then turn left down unmade road for 0.25m • Open 16th and 17th April, 30th April and 1st May, 28th and 29th May, and for parties by appt • Entrance: £3.50, children £1 [NEW] ◐ ◖ ▧ ♿ ◈

In 1970, the present owner observed that the mature trees in the central 10 acres of the 60 acre wood adjoining his garden sheltered a prosperous colony of *Rhododendron ponticum* in an otherwise alkaline landscape. He was able to buy the wood in 1979 and set about the gargantuan task of clearing the brambles and brush-wood before planting a variety of azaleas, rhododendrons, camellias and magnolias. He then added spring bulbs, particularly snowdrops (80 species and varieties at the last count), and now scillas and other 'small blue bulbs', narcissi and fritillarias are followed in July and August by a wide range of lilies, both species and varieties. New plantings have continued year by year, reaching right through the alkaline woodland. A stream prattles through to a small dam, and the tranquillity of natural woodland pervades the garden. An orchestra of birdsong greets the spring, and the fires of autumn colour lead to the filigree of hoarfrost on the birch trees; truly a place for all seasons.

Holdenby House Gardens and
Falconry Centre [Historic Garden Grade I]

Holdenby, Northampton NN6 8DJ. Tel: (01604) 770074

Mr and Mrs James Lowther • 7m NW of Northampton, signed from A5199 and A428 • House, garden and falconry centre open. Telephone for opening dates and times • Entrance: £4.50, OAPs £4, children £3 (house and gardens £6, OAPs £5, children £4) (2005 prices) • Other information: Meals by appt. Special events Easter, May Day, Whitsun and Aug Bank Hols, 11am – 6pm ◑ ◖ ▧ <u>WC</u> ♿ ◈ ✿ ⚙ ♟ ⚲

Two grassed terraces, a fish pond and the palace forecourt with its original arches remain of the extensive Elizabethan garden which surrounded the vast mansion built by Elizabeth I's chancellor, Sir Christopher Hatton, in the late sixteenth century. The gardens still link the surviving remnant of the house (one-eighth of its former size) to its past, especially the delightful Elizabethan garden, designed in 1980 by the late Rosemary Verey as a miniature replica of Hatton's original centrepiece, using only plants available in the 1580s. Other garden features include the fragrant border (now replanted by Rupert Golby), part of the nineteenth-century garden, a silver border and a kitchen garden, the falconry centre, and an authentically re-constructed seventeenth-century farmstead. A children's garden is currently being planned by garden designer Roddy Llewellyn with bronze statuary, magic planting and hidden surprises.

Kelmarsh Hall ★

Kelmarsh, Northampton NN6 9LT Tel: (01604) 686543

The Kelmarsh Trust • 11m N of Northampton on A508 near A14 junction 2 • House open 16th April to Sept, Sun and Bank Holiday Mons, 1st Sun in every month, plus Thurs, May to Aug; all 2 – 5pm • Garden open as house plus Tues – Thurs, 2 – 5pm • Entrance: £3.50, OAPs £3, children £2 (house and garden £4.50, OAPs £4, children £2.50) ◑ 💷 WC ᕕ ⤳ 🌿 🌷

James Gibbs's 1730s' Palladian house was set in a contemporary landscape with obligatory lake and vistas; in the twentieth century, Nancy Lancaster lived here and created a more intimate garden with advice from Norah Lindsay and Geoffrey Jellicoe. Huge, bulgy box hedges entice you on, to a strategic seat with quintessentially English views across meadows grazed by British White cattle. The old drying-ground is enclosed by ancient yews, like a screens passage in a Tudor house, and planted with rich herbaceous borders. The triangular walled garden, planted anew with vegetables, fruit and cut flowers, includes ornamental elements like a simple turf maze and beautifully restored central glasshouse. Dazzling pots of tulips on steps and by doorways are replaced later in the season by dahlias and glowing annuals. Geoffrey Jellicoe's Philadelphus Garden is being restored, with some replants propagated from the original 1950s' stock. For the sophisticate there is a shaded white garden, for the naturalist a rural lakeside ramble.

Kirby Hall [Historic Garden Grade II*]

Deene, Corby NN17 5EN. Tel: (01536) 203230

English Heritage • 4m NE of Corby off A43 on road W of Deene • Open April to June, daily except Tues and Wed, 10am – 5pm; July and Aug, daily, 10am – 6pm; Sept and Oct, daily except Tues and Wed, 10am – 5pm; Nov to March, daily except Tues and Wed, 10am – 4pm. Closed 24th to 26th Dec, 1st Jan. Please telephone before travelling • Entrance: £4.30, concessions £3.20, children £2.20, family £10.80 (2005 prices) ○ 💷 🏠 WC ᕕ ⤳ 🏛 🌷 ⚲

The gardens date from at least the period when Sir Christopher Hatton owned the hall in Elizabethan times. However, it was in the late seventeenth century that they achieved considerable fame through the work of the 4th Sir Christopher, who devoted his energies to the gardens until his death in 1705. In the 1930s the Great Garden was laid out according to the prevailing idea of how a Baroque formal garden might have looked. Since then, following extensive research of the period, the 1930s' garden has been buried and the parterre re-created using a design based on Longleat (see entry in Wiltshire), which provides a more accurate view of how this garden would have looked in 1686. Over 80 two-metre-high clipped yew cones, holly mopheads and box balls, many placed in oak barrels similar to those used in the Hampton Court restoration, surround the dramatic geometric design of the *gazon coupé* parterre of wide gravel paths and cut-through patterns of lawn. The north border was replanted in 1995 with species following as closely as possible those mentioned by Hatton in his notebooks. These include old varieties of fruit trees – apples, pears and cherries – trained against the walls.

Lamport Hall and Gardens [Historic Garden Grade II]

Lamport, Northampton NN6 9HD. Tel: (01604) 686272

Lamport Hall Trust • 8m N of Northampton on A508 • House open as garden, with tours at 2.30pm and 3.30pm. Telephone for details of fair openings • Garden open 16th April to 1st Oct, Sun and Bank Holiday Mons; plus Aug, daily except Sat, 14th and 15th Oct, 18th and 19th Nov; all 2.15 – 5.15pm. Coach parties at any time by arrangement • Entrance: (Hall and gardens) £5.50, OAPs £5, children £2 • Other information: Dogs in grounds only, on lead. Regular programme of events – telephone for details. Agricultural museum ● ● WC ♿ ⇪ ♥

The principal facade of the hall is one of the only surviving country houses by John Webb, subsequently extended by the Smiths of Warwick. The original grounds were laid out by Gilbert Clarke in 1655; they now contain lawns, mixed borders and fine herbaceous borders backed by mellow brick walls clothed with spreading wisterias. There is also a small Italianate garden with a box parterre and a shell and coral fountain. An impressive row of huge and shapely Irish yews marches across the southern boundary before the mounded ha-ha. Sir Charles Isham's ironstone rockery, fully five metres tall and surprisingly close to the house – more like a quasi-ruin than anything occurring in nature – was home to the first garden gnome.

Lyveden New Bield [Historic Garden Grade II*]

Oundle, Peterborough PE8 5AT. Tel: (01832) 205358

The National Trust • 4m SW of Oundle off A427, 3m E of Brigstock • House, Elizabethan water garden and visitor information room open April to Oct, Wed – Sun; Aug, daily; all 10.30am – 5pm; Nov, Feb and March, Sat, Sun, 10.30am – 4pm • Entrance: £3.50, children free • Other information: Access 0.5m along farm track; parking at property for less able visitors. Teas for groups by prior arrangement ● ● WC ⇪ ♥ B&B

This is not so much a garden, more the remains of an unfinished late-Elizabethan endeavour. Its principal elements were water and sculpted landform, both of which remain largely intact. Part of the canal system survives, as do the remains of a banqueting house or lodge. The latter is a three-storey building in the shape of an equal-armed cross as a celebration of the Passion of Christ. Alas, there is no planting of the period, though the raised grass terrace with its broad walk is still in place, with turf pyramids at each end. The Trust is undertaking a project to reveal the extensive remains of an elaborate water garden, containing a series of truncated pyramids and circular mounds, surrounded by moats and terraces, and has now re-planted the Elizabethan orchard containing over 300 pre-seventeenth-century fruit trees.

The Menagerie [Historic Park Grade II]

Horton, Northampton NN7 2BX.
Tel: (01604) 870957 (Leave message for Administrator)

Mr A. Myers • 6m SE of Northampton, on B526 turn left 1m S of Horton into field. Watch out for tiny notice on gate • Open May to Sept, Mon, Wed and Thurs, 2 – 6pm, also last Sun of these months, 2 – 6pm • Entrance: £5, concessions £4, children £1.50 ● ● WC ఈ ☞

When Horton House was demolished in the 1930s, a few of the landscape follies remained; this fine building was Lord Halifax's private zoo and is one of the most important surviving works of Thomas Wright of Durham. In a ruinous state, it was rescued by Gervase Jackson-Stops and Ian Kirby, who created the garden in the 1980s. They planted the bones and the formal structure of a lime avenue, adding an acaena-covered mount and radiating hornbeam *allées*, each with a dramatic pond and fountain. Following the untimely deaths of its creators, years of neglect left the flesh of their garden sadly puffy and misshapen, but in the last five years much has been done to restore it. Although this is an uphill task on a wetland site and heavy clay, moisture-loving plants are in their element: the camassias stand four feet tall and trilliums burgeon in the rich planting of the Vernal Garden. One of the pair of thatched follies is now a chapel, and there is a newly built walled garden.

The Old Rectory

Mixbury, Brackley NN13 5RR. Tel: (01280) 848336

Mr and Mrs Ben Collins • 5m SE of Brackley, 6m W of Buckingham off A421. Turn left off A421 to Mixbury, house is on right just before church • Open for charity June to mid-Oct, for individuals and parties by appt • Entrance: £3.50 (£4.50 for parties, including refreshments) • Other information: Garden design courses by Angela Collins all year; email: ac.gardendesign@talk21.com for details ●

This is a country garden of traditional bones and refreshingly modern planting – the two in perfect harmony. Step around the side of the attractive, ungrand Victorian house, past the hornbeam avenue, and the first impression is typically rectory – a huge, gently sloping lawn, a terrace flanked by beds, a background of mature trees. Look again, and refocus. On the left-hand side a broad, delicately coloured herbaceous border swirls past characterful garden buildings before giving way on both sides to meadows spangled with alliums and oxeye daisies; to one side a mown path winds to a secluded little garden with a circular bed and a laburnum tunnel. Facing the house at the end of the lawn is a bold contemporary statement – a large oval bed planted with grasses and perennials, plus three rectangular beds defined by box edging and topiary and filled with stronger-coloured flowers and foliage. Angela Collins is a clever and sophisticated plantswoman: her palette is quite small but she combines ravishingly pretty plants with atonal surprises. Even the surrounds to the tennis court, with its tumbledown Hansel and Gretel cottage, and the swimming pool hidden behind a waterfall of roses triumphantly resolve the problems of these twin evils.

The Old Rectory ★

Sudborough, Kettering NN14 3BX. Tel: (01832) 733247

Mr and Mrs Anthony Huntington • 7m SE of Corby off A6116 Corby – Thrapston road, A14 junction 12 • Open for individuals and parties by appt only • Entrance: £4.50 (£6 with tea and biscuits), children under 16 free • Other information: Evening parties by arrangement ● 🏫 WC ♿

A delightful three-acre rectory garden in a beautiful stone and thatch village. Interest is sustained throughout the year, with a fine collection of hellebores in spring, a variety of climbers and many containers, planted especially for a fine summer show. A profusion of planting is evident throughout – surrounding the pond and in the exuberant mixed borders. The *potager*, begun in 1985 by the late Rosemary Verey and completed by Rupert Golby, is charming, with small beds and brick paths leading to a central wrought-iron arbour; standard roses, gooseberries and tents of runner beans and marrows provide vertical features. A small wild garden with interesting trees and a woodland walk along the stream bring a most enjoyable visit to a naturalistic conclusion.

The Prebendal Manor House

Nassington, Peterborough PE8 6QG. Tel: (01780) 782575

Mrs Jane Baile • 6m NE of Oundle off A1, in Nassington opposite church • Open 17th April to Sept, Wed, Sun and Bank Holiday Mons, 1 – 5.30pm • Entrance: £4.50, children £2 ➊ 🏫 🍴 WC ♿ ⟐ 🍴 ☕

From a window sill of the early thirteenth-century tawny stone house two carved heads gaze down, guardians of the secrets of this ancient place. Scattered around the six acres are reconstructions of various types of medieval garden. The herber has grass seats, a fig tree and scented plants, while the trellis garden's compartments overspill with poppies and mallows. Concealed by an ancient wall and protected by a fine withy fence is a vegetable patch with broad beans, herbs and wheat; nearby is a small vineyard, and a nut walk leads to two fishponds. Patches of wild flowers sit in the lawn; old willows, the other guardians of the manor's secrets, billow silvery in the breeze. The tithe barn contains an interpretative museum display, and the wattle-and-daub medieval gardeners' hut some replica garden tools. Rare-breed sheep and pigs are in fine fettle in June and early July.

Rockingham Castle Gardens [Historic Garden Grade II*]

Market Harborough LE16 8TH. Tel: (01536) 770240

James and Elizabeth Saunders Watson • 2m N of Corby on A6003. Signposted • Castle open as garden but from 1pm • Garden open 16th and 17th April; May, Sun and Bank Holiday Mon; June to Sept, Sun and Bank Holiday Mons and Tues; all 12 noon – 5pm • Entrance: £4.50 (castle and gardens £7.50, OAPs £6.50, children £4.50, family £19.50, parties of 20 or more £6.50 per person) • *Other information: Disabled park near entrance* ◑ ⬛ ✕ 🍴 <u>wc</u> ⴺ ⬦ ⬛ 🦮 ⚲

The castle sits on a hilltop fortress site with stunning views of three counties. It has remains from all periods of its 900-year history, with important features ranging from formal seventeenth-century terraces and yew hedges to the romantic wild garden of the nineteenth century. There is a circular rose garden surrounded by a yew hedge and also good herbaceous borders. The wild garden was replanted with advice from Kew Gardens in the late 1960s and includes over 200 species of trees and shrubs. The result is a delightful blend of form, colour, light and shade.

Woodchippings

Juniper Hill, Nr Brackley NN13 5RH. Tel: (01869) 810170

Richard Bashford and Valerie Bexley • *2.5m S of Brackley off A43. 200 yds after junction with B4031 (southbound exit only), turn left signed to Juniper Hill, and continue for 0.3m. Park on grass verge at 30mph sign and walk down unmade road on right; house is last on left* • *Open 22nd Feb to 26th July, Wed, 2.30 – 6pm, and for individuals and parties by appt* • *Entrance: £2.50* [NEW] ◐ ⬛ WC 🌿

Juniper Hill – Lark Rise in Flora Thompson's account of a dying rural tradition, published at the onset of the Second World War – is a hamlet of cottages hidden among hedges. Furthest from the road lies a horticultural gem. The owners have divided the garden between them, and each has a distinctive style and palette of favoured plants. It is virtually a mower-free zone, brimming with the unusual and rare, all grown to perfection despite the difficulties of deep chestnut shade and greedy hedges. If you visit in January/February for the snowdrops and hellebores, your delight will be tempered by the concern that it will be dull in June. If you go for the old roses and alstroemerias in June and the grasses and bright-coloured perennials in July, you worry that it will be bare in autumn. It won't be, it never is! This plantsman's paradise includes a small nursery offering some of the rarities on show, including hybrid hellebores.

THE NATIONAL GARDENS SCHEME

The NGS started in 1927, and now some 3300 gardens, chosen by county organisers and their teams, open their gates each year for charity (more than £15m has been raised over the past decade). The entries in the famous annual Yellow Book are, unlike those in the *Good Gardens Guide*, written by the garden owners themselves; a useful diary section lists all gardens in a county open on any particular day.

ASSOCIATION OF GARDENS TRUSTS

Founded in 1993 in response to growing unease among conservationists and owners of historic gardens about their future security, 36 individual county garden trusts shelter under its umbrella. They are charitable bodies with no legal powers, able to influence planning and other governmental decisions only through vigilance and lobbying. For further details, contact: The Association of Gardens Trusts, 75 Cowcross Street, London EC1M 6EL (Tel: (020) 7251 2610, Tues and Thurs only; www.gardenstrusts.org.uk).

NORTHUMBERLAND

Two-starred gardens are marked on the map with a black square.

The Alnwick Garden ★ [Historic Park and Garden Grade I]

Alnwick NE66 1YU. Tel: (01665) 511350 (Mon – Fri), (01655) 511100 (Infoline)

Duke and Duchess of Northumberland • 35m N of Newcastle upon Tyne. Take A1 and turn W at Alnwick. Signposted • Castle open Easter to Oct (extra charge) • Grounds open, daily, 10am – 5pm (or dusk if earlier) (last admission 4.15pm). Closed 25th Dec. The Alnwick Garden open all year, daily except 25th Dec, 10am – 7pm (or dusk if earlier) • Entrance: £4, OAPs/students £3.75, accompanied children (under 16) free; parties of 14 or more £3.50 per person (2005 prices) ◐ 🍵 WC ♿ ⬇ ☕

Set in a 'Capability' Brown landscape, the castle (remodelled in the 1850s) and its grounds have long been open to the public. The landscape survives almost intact, but in 2001 the first stage of an ambitious and dramatic new garden – The Alnwick Garden – was completed within the sloping 12-acre Victorian walled former kitchen garden. A grand cascade designed by the Wirtz father and sons team from Belgium has become the spine of the garden. Enclosed by an arched hornbeam tunnel with clipped openings along its length, it sends water tumbling down a series of 27 weirs; the pattern of the fountains changes every half hour. The path then leads through trees to a formal ornamental garden, reached through three interlinked stone arches. This walled enclosure contains the largest collection of European plants in Britain (16,500) – a must for any plant lover. Pergolas and arbours are covered in ramblers and vines, and rills lead to secret enclosed gardens with yew hedges. To the right of the entrance is a pretty rose garden. Four equally grandiose projects have also been completed: one of the largest treehouses in the world – the size of two Olympic swimming pools – containing a restaurant, shop and walkways in the sky; a poison garden featuring some of the world's deadliest plants; a bamboo labyrinth by Adrian Fisher; and the Serpent Garden, where masterly William Pye water sculptures rise above a sinuous holly hedge. A new pavilion and visitor centre is due to open in 2006.

Ashfield

Hebron, Morpeth NE61 3LA. Tel: (01670) 515616

Barry and Rona McWilliam • 3m N of Morpeth, 1m E of A1 on C130 S of Hebron • Open all year by impromptu appt • Entrance: £2.50, children free ◐ 🍵 🏠 WC ♿ 🌿

The original half-acre garden surrounding the house overlooks a terrace dense with bulbs in spring and a carpet of alpines, many tumbling over the supporting wall. The lawn slopes gently downwards, sheltered by beech and prunus hedges and punctuated by island beds filled with bulbs, shrubs and small trees, including many varieties of sorbus. Beyond this is a three-acre garden developed from a ploughed field over the past fifteen years. Here again is an expanse of lawn with colourful herbaceous borders, together with a small pinetum, beds of shrubs, a willow 'temple' and a crab-apple walk. In the one-and-a-half-acre wood the mature trees form a canopy for spring bulbs, hellebores, hostas, other shade-loving plants, and small trees – sorbus, betulas, acers. Many plants come from abroad and have been grown from seed, as in the scree bed planted with Sino-Himalayan alpines near the entrance. The owner is a keen plantsman and the five-acre garden reflects his knowledge and enthusiasm. Planting and development continue.

Belsay Hall, Castle and Gardens ★★ [Historic Garden Grade I]

Belsay, Newcastle-upon-Tyne NE20 0DX. Tel: (01661) 881636

English Heritage • 14m NW of Newcastle on A696 • Hall and castle open • Gardens open April to Oct, daily, 10am – 6pm (closes 4pm Oct); Nov to March, Thurs – Mon, 10am – 4pm. Closed 24th to 26th Dec, 1st Jan • Entrance: £5.30, OAPs £4, children £2.70, family £13.30. Reductions for parties of 11 or more • Other information: Advance notice preferred for coaches. Refreshments Easter to Oct only. Wheelchairs available for loan ❶ 🅿 🖺 <u>WC</u> ﴾ 🌳 ℘ ⛲ 🍴 ♿

The 30-acre gardens are the creation of two men who owned Belsay in succession from 1795 to 1933. Sir Charles Monck built the severe neo-classical hall with formal terraces leading through woods to a 'garden' inside the quarry which provided the building with its stone. Sir Arthur, his grandson, took over in 1867, adding Victorian features. Both were discerning plantsmen. The result is an exceptionally well-cared-for collection of rare, mature and exotic specimens in a fascinating sequence; the lily and snowdrop collections are also important. The terrace looks across to massed June rhododendrons. Other areas (flower garden, magnolia terrace, winter garden) lead to woods, a wild meadow and the quarry garden itself. This was carefully contrived and stocked to achieve a wild romantic effect, and the sheltered microclimate has resulted in the luxuriant growth of some remarkable and exotic trees and shrubs, dramatically beautiful in the light and shade of the sandstone gorge. Here, among the massive hewn slabs silvered by lichen are memorable corners: the well of a natural amphitheatre, cascading with ferns; stepped rock ledges carpeted with moss; a host of fritillaries naturalised in grass. The path from the eighteenth-century hall leads through formal gardens to the quarry garden and thence to the fourteenth-century castle, a distance of about half a mile, all on fairly level ground. The winter garden, with its heathers, also has a 28-metre-high Douglas fir planted in 1839 and rhododendrons. An unexpected pleasure is the croquet lawn, which is in regular use. The one-and-a-half-mile Crag Wood walk is a stepped, serpentine path which passes by the lake and through the hanging woods opposite the hall to the south.

Bide-a-Wee Cottage ★

Stanton, Netherwitton, Morpeth NE65 8PR. Tel: (01670) 772238

Mark Robson • 7m NW of Morpeth, 3m SW of Longhorsley, off A697 Morpeth – Coldstream road towards Stanton • Open 22nd April to 26th Aug, Sat and Wed, 1.30 – 5pm. Parties of more than 18 by appt • Entrance: £2.50 ❶ ﴾ ℘

One of the most enchanting and richly planted gardens in the North-East. Combining formal, informal and wild features, it occupies a long-abandoned stone quarry and some of the higher surrounding land. The varied topography, soil and climate allow for a diversity of plants to be grown, from marsh-loving to drought-tolerant species. The beauty of the natural rock faces has been exploited to the-maximum and enriched by truly sympathetic planting. More quarry wall has been exposed with new planting and another seat from which to view the garden. As well as being a highly refined plantsman, the owner is also a splendid mason whose stonework has done much to embellish the garden, and a shady corner has a timber summerhouse with an adjacent planting of arisaemas. A National Collection of centaureas is held here. Many of the plants are well labelled, and there is an excellent plant sales area with unusual species (catalogue available).

Chillingham Castle [Historic Park and Garden Grade II]

Chillingham NE66 5NJ. Tel: (01668) 215359/215390

Sir Humphry Wakefield, Bt • 12m NW of Alnwick between A1 (signposted), A697, B6346 and B6348 • House open • Gardens open May to Sept, Sun – Fri, 12 noon – 5pm, and by appt • Entrance: £6.50, OAPs £5.50, children (5–16) £3, parties of 10 or more £5.30 per person. Guided tours £30 ◑ 💺 ✕ WC ♨ ♿ 🍴 ♿ B&B

Since the 1200s this has been and continues to be the family home of the Earls Grey and their relations. The present owner has restored the ancient castle and garden along with the grounds, landscaped in 1828 by Wyatville (of Windsor Castle and Royal Lodge fame). The Elizabethan-style walled garden has been virtually excavated to rediscover its intricate pattern of clipped box and yew (enlivened by scarlet tropaeolum), with rose beds, fountains, a central avenue and a spectacular herbaceous border running the whole length. Outside are lawns and a rock garden, delightful woodland and lakeside walks through drifts of snowdrops, spring displays of daffodils, bluebells and, later, rhododendrons. The medieval castle provides a spectacular backdrop to the gardens.

Chipchase Castle Garden

Wark NE48 3NT. Tel: (01434) 230203

Mrs P. Torday • 11m NW of Hexham on B6320 to Wark and Kielder. Turn right in centre of Wark following brown tourist-signs and right again on far side of bridge; Chipchase 1m • Castle open 1st to 28th June, daily, 2 – 5pm • Garden open 17th April to July, Thurs – Sun and Bank Holiday Mons, 10am – 5pm • Entrance: £3, concessions £2.50 (house and garden £5, concessions £4) ◐ WC ♿ ♨

The impressive castle was built in 1621 incorporating a fourteenth-century pele tower. The eighteenth-century walled garden with immaculate beds of vegetables and herbaceous borders has been redesigned by the present owners, who are also responsible for the fine herbaceous borders in the formal garden extending on two terraces to the castle walls, with superb views across the North Tyne valley. In the 1860s' pond garden a high canopy of fine old trees, including a Wellingtonia and a Douglas fir, shelters rhododendrons, magnolias and specimen trees planted for spring and autumn colour, and there is more colour beside the lake, where hostas, irises, candelabra primulas, ligularias, deutzias and much else bestow a succession of flowering interest. The one-and-a-half-acre nursery in an adjoining walled garden is under separate management and well worth a visit (Tel: (01434) 230083).

Cragside House [Historic Garden Grade II*]

Rothbury, Morpeth NE65 7PX. Tel: (01669) 620333

The National Trust • 13m SW of Alnwick off A697 between B6341 and B6344 • House closed throughout 2006 for re-wiring • Gardens and estate open 1st April to 29th Oct, Tues – Sun and Bank Holiday Mons, 10.30am – 7pm (last admission 5pm); Nov to 17th Dec, Wed – Sun, 11am – 4pm (last admission 3pm) • Entrance: Gardens and estate £6.50, children (5-17) £3, family £16, parties of 15 or more £5.50 per person • Other information: Main car parks either near to house (with 0.5 m walk to formal garden) or near formal garden, with further car parks along estate drive. Visitor centre (some distance from garden) with toilet facilities, restaurant and shop ○ ▬ ✕ ▤ <u>WC</u> ⟐ ⬦ ⚲ ⬛ ⚲

Lord Armstrong, one of the greatest of Victorian engineers, clothed this hillside above the Coquet Valley with millions of trees and shrubs as the setting for a house designed by R. Norman Shaw (the first ever lit by hydro-electricity) that was then the wonder of the world. From the car park nearest to the house the path (sign-posted 'Garden') affords views of the rock gardens below the house. These are planted with an impressive display of heathers, shrubs, alpines and dwarf rhododen-drons, spectacular in spring. The path descends sharply into the Debdon valley, crosses the river by a rustic bridge (magnificent views of the elegant iron bridge soaring above) and climbs through majestic conifers to the 1864 clock tower which overlooks the formal garden. This area, laid out in high-Victorian style, is set on three terraces and restoration is continuing. The upper terrace was once dominated by a huge glasshouse range, containing ferneries and grottoes. The middle terrace contains the imposing orchard house with rotating fruit pots of sixteen types of fruit, to one side of which is a bed planted with small foliage plants in formal patterns typical of the 1870s. Carpet bedding is taken literally at Cragside: two of the beds mirror the design of floor-coverings and fittings in the house. In the formal beds some 6000 tulips are planted in autumn for spring colour. Between the middle and lower terraces is the Dahlia Walk, planted annually with 650-700 mixed culti-vars and at its best in September and October. On the lower Italian terrace is the loggia made of bold, pierced cast-iron, another unique remnant of the extensive range of glass structures once found on this terrace. The quatrefoil pool has been reinstated as the centrepiece of the whole terrace, giving a focal point to the overall design and an Italian feel to the area. The walk back through the valley impresses on the visitor the contrasting forces of wild romanticism and industrial technology which influenced this estate in equal measure. Two hundred rare North American coniferous species, given to the Trust by the Royal Botanic Gardens in Edinburgh, have been planted on the estate. The climatic conditions and historic landscape of the property make it an ideal site for a collection of specimen conifers. Major engineering work is in progress (a five-year project) to restore and improve deteriorating water systems and to ensure the restoration and long-term preser-vation of the rock garden.

The Garden Cottage
Bolam Hall, Bolam, Morpeth NE61 3UA. Tel: (01661) 881660

Heather and John Russell • 15m NW of Newcastle. Turn off A696 after turn to Belsay Hall, follow sign to Bolam – telephone in advance for directions • Open for NGS and charity, and for individuals and parties by appt • Entrance: £3 • Other information: Possible for wheelchairs but gravel paths. Refreshments for parties by arrangement ● WC ⎣ ℘

Protected by a long south-facing wall, the owners – who have been gardening here for twenty years – have been able to overcome the problems of the cold and wet Northumbrian site and to create a one-acre garden of great artistry and imagination. The centrepiece is a large bed modelled on a dry gravelled river course and surrounded by a terrace with beds built up to suggest river banks, creating the impression of a sunken garden. Everywhere there is an exuberance of colours, both warm and cool, and an inspiring range of planting variations, with new and unusual plants regularly introduced. Structural planting is well conceived – a beech arch, buttressed by a pair of cone-shaped yews, finds an echo in a single beech near the southern boundary – and winter interest is sustained by the coloured stems of cornus and willow. Abstract and animal sculptures enliven the main garden, where there are also secluded areas with seats for relaxation. North of the protective wall a large meadow garden is maturing.

The Garden Station
Langley, Hexham NE47 5LA. Tel: (01434) 684391

Jane Torday • 9m W of Hexham off A69 Newcastle – Carlisle road. Turn onto A686 near Haydon Bridge. Continue past Langley Castle Hotel for 2m, then follow yellow signs • Open May to Aug, Tues – Sun and Bank Holiday Mons, 10am – 5pm, and for small parties Mon – Fri by appt • Entrance: free • Other information: Gardening and art courses early March to Nov – essential to book ● ⬤ WC ⎣ ⎯ ℘ ⎈ ⎤ ℀

One of the most unusual and attractive gardens in Northumberland, surrounding a pretty, restored railway station and itself sheltered by mature woodland. The main garden is on three different levels. On one side is a heavily wooded bank, which drops down to the old platform, now the stage for a small gravel suntrap full of pots; along the foot of the station building are beds of scented plants arranged in the traditional English manner, while a deep row of plants for sale creates the illusion of a herbaceous border. The lowest level is the railway track, now laid to lawn; a richly planted woodland walk extends the garden along the route of the old railway line, passing under the arches of two magnificent Victorian railway bridges, which frame a long vista.

Herterton House ★
Hartington, Cambo, Morpeth NE61 4BN. Tel: (01670) 774278

Frank and Marjorie Lawley • 11m W of Morpeth, 2m N of Cambo off B6342, signed to Hartington • Open May to Sept, Mon, Wed, Fri – Sun, 1.30 – 5.30pm • Entrance: £2.80, children 5–15 £1 ◑ WC ℘

The Lawleys took over this land and near-derelict Elizabethan building, with commanding views over picturesque upland Northumberland, in 1976. With vision and skill they have created four distinct areas. In front is a formal winter garden with views over the Northumbrian countryside; alongside, a cloistered 'monastic' knot garden of mainly medicinal, occult and dye-producing herbs; and to the rear, their most impressive achievement, a flower garden with perceptively mingled hardy flowers chosen with an artist's eye. This part of the garden contains some impressive topiary (spirals, columns and balls), which is altogether appropriate to this formal setting in front of a period house. Many unusual varieties of traditional plants (including many species from the wild) flourish within the newly built sheltering walls. The fourth area, the Fancy Garden, has a parterre and a gazebo raised on a terrace. The views from the gazebo contrast well; to the north over a large field of cattle and to the south over this new garden and beyond to the formal garden with its flowers and topiary.

Howick Hall ★ [Historic Garden Grade II]

Howick, Alnwick NE66 3LB. Tel: (01665) 577285

Lord Howick of Glendale (Howick Trustees Ltd) • 6m NE of Alnwick, 2m N of Longhoughton, off B1339 • Open April to Oct, daily, 12 noon – 6pm • Entrance: £4, concessions £3, children under 16 free ◑ ⬛ ✕ wc ♿

There have been Greys at Howick since 1319, and the church and graveyard within the grounds are filled with their tombs and memorials, including that of the 2nd Earl, the great reforming Prime Minister. Surrounding the imposing Georgian house reconfigured by George Wyatt in 1809 and Sir Herbert Baker in 1928 are 15 acres of gardens. Created largely between 1920 and 2001, the present generation has continued the tradition – essentially that of plantsmanship and dendrology on a grand scale executed with appealing informality. (The excellent guide book is likewise written with scholarship lightly worn.) It is worth visiting at every season. Drifts of snowdrops followed by a spectacular display of old daffodil varieties, with fritillaries to follow and tulips mingling with wild flowers in a 'Botticelli' meadow. The borders around the hall then burst into life, and the woodland garden (Silverwood) flowers with a rich variety of rhododendrons, camellias and magnolias, including two magnificent *M. campbellii*, all underplanted with drifts of shade-lovers. The bog garden surrounding a pond has a most interesting range of late-summer-flowering plants grown from seed collected from the wild by the present owners. Woodland walks to the west take in a new arboretum planted with over 10,500 trees and shrubs.

Lindisfarne Castle

Holy Island, Berwick–upon–Tweed TD15 2SH. Tel: (01289) 389244

National Trust • 14m S of Berwick, 6m E of A1, across causeway to Holy Island (crossing times vary according to tide – telephone for details) • Open all year, daily • Entrance: £1 [NEW] ○ ⬧

In 1911, when Lutyens was restoring the ruined castle in its unique setting on Holy Island for Edward Hudson, owner and founder of *Country Life*, Gertrude Jekyll was asked to provide plans for the small (25.5m x 27m) walled garden lying across a field on the hillside north of the castle. The garden had previously been used to grow vegetables for the garrison. She responded with a selection of her favourite plants, set out in gradations of colour within paving designed by Edwin Lutyens. Jekyll's intention was for a permanent planting of shrubs, herbaceous perennials and annuals, with a single border set aside for vegetables. Following the discovery in California in 1972 of the original plans, the garden was re-created by the National Trust and the University of Durham, using as many of Jekyll's original plants as were still available; it has now been replanted in the same spirit. Creating a garden on such an exposed, windswept and relatively inaccessible site was a challenge; visiting it today in bad weather may appeal only to Jekyll devotees. On a fine calm August day, however, it adds its mite to the unique atmosphere of Lindisfarne.

Loughbrow House

Hexham NE46 1RS. Tel: (01434) 603351

Mrs Kenneth Clark • 20m E of Newcastle, 1m S of Hexham. Take B6306 off Whitley Chapel road, at fork is brick lodge and long drive to house • Open May to July, Wed, 12 noon – 3pm; 6th Aug, 2 – 5pm, and by appt at other times • Entrance: £2, children free ● ⬤ WC & ⬦ ⚘ B&B

The garden here is expansive and a source of inspiration for both plant lovers and those who enjoy original design concepts. The lawns are generous, the planting of shrubs and roses bountiful. On the terrace is an interesting canal. The two deep herbaceous borders show the owner's colour concepts to great advantage, and beyond is a woodland garden, maturing well. There is also a kitchen garden. The small lake from which the house derives its name ('lake on the brow of the hill') has been re-created, the bog garden extended, and an arboretum developed around the lake.

Mindrum

Cornhill-on-Tweed TD12 4QN. Tel: (01890) 850246

The Hon. P.J. Fairfax • 14m SW of Berwick-upon-Tweed. From A697 turn onto B6351 at Akeld, join B6352 towards Kirk Yetholm and continue 3m to Mindrum • Open for NGS, and by appt • Entrance: £2 • Other information: Teas and plants for sale on open days only ●

From the nineteenth-century house built on level ground there are fine views to the valley of the Bowmont Water (you can actually see the Scottish Borders to the south). The creators of the three-acre garden have taken good advantage of any changes of level. From the lawn at the side of the house – over 90 metres above sea level – a path leads down a gentle slope to a walled garden with many flowering shrubs and roses; opposite this is a rose garden with yew hedges on the far sides. The path then descends steeply, winding down a rocky bank beside a small stream which flows into a pool at the foot and then joins a tributary of Bowmont Water. The bank is densely planted with a rich variety of colourful perennials and flowering shrubs at every level – old-fashioned roses, clematis, many varieties of acer, abutilons, irises and candelabra primulas by the water, with spires of white foxgloves adding to the dramatic effect. The tributary is crossed by wooden bridges leading to the riverside walk. The far bank has rhododendrons, azaleas, acers, and planting still continues, including a 'dry pond' in a boggy area with willows, campions and wild moisture-loving plants.

Northumberland College at Kirkley Hall

Ponteland NE20 0AQ. Tel: (01670) 841200

11m NW of Newcastle off A696; turn right at Ponteland on C151 for 2.5m.
Signposted • Open April to Sept, daily, 10am – 3pm. Other information: NCCPG
plant sale mid-June • Entrance: free ◑ <u>WC</u> & ℘ ♟

The 10-acre grounds with a three-acre Victorian walled garden have in the past been
a showcase for all the gardening arts. The long border in front of the hall and the
many colourfully planted containers make a brilliant show. The lawns and hedges are
well maintained, and the succession of beds carefully planted with many mature
trees, shrubs and perennials give variety of profile and continuity of colour. A
National Collection of beeches is held here. The sunken garden is almost completely
restored with cushions of alpines on the raised beds and the herbaceous borders in
the three-acre walled garden are again filled with a great variety of colourful perennials. New projects include a small wildlife garden with a living willow arch. It is
cheering to see progress being made after a period of neglect.

Nunwick ★ [Historic Garden Grade II]

Simonburn, Hexham NE48 3AF.

Mrs L.G. Allgood • 8m NW of Hexham on B6320 • Open 18th June, and for parties
by appt in writing • Entrance: £3 • Other information: Teas on open day only ◑

This is one of the most interesting gardens in a county full of remarkable ones. The
house (not open) was described by Pevsner as perfect for its date (1760). It looks
out over lawns and parkland, with fine trees which the owner has been meticulous
in caring for and replacing when necessary. Walking down to the gardens, it is clear
that the design combines a clever sense of colour and shape with an interest in
unusual plants. The herbaceous borders are cut back from their sheltering wall to
ease maintenance, and there are fine beech hedges and shrub roses to provide shelter on the orchard side. The large Victorian walled kitchen garden is excellently
maintained. Mrs Allgood experiments with varieties of vegetables, and there are
good flowers, too, along the walks. Behind one wall is a small and elegant orangery
containing a camellia over 100 years old. The other fascinating feature is the woodland path to the bog garden (*en route* note the stone wellhead), where the visitor
first becomes aware of a profusion of hostas. The latter become evident again after
crossing the recently built stone bridge over the burn and reaching the eighteenth-
century Gothick kennels. Its four rooms, now open to the sky, house a spectacular
collection of hostas, and the walls are planted with purple erinus, ivies of many kinds,
toadflax and ferns. Trees and plants are well labelled. Back beside the house is a large
collection of stone farm troughs with alpines, and an attractive large fountain. It is
difficult to do justice in words to the charm of this garden.

Seaton Delaval Hall [Historic Garden Grade II*]

Seaton Sluice, Whitley Bay NE26 4QR. Tel: (0191) 237 1493/0786

Lord Hastings • 10m NE of Newcastle, 0.5m inland from Seaton Sluice on A190
• Parts of house open together with coach house, stables and ice-house • Garden open

1st, 29th May; June to Sept, Wed, Sun and Bank Holiday Mon; all 2 – 6pm
• Entrance: £4, OAPs £3.50, children £1 ◑ 💻 <u>WC</u> ♿ ⬦ ⊞ ☕

The original grounds of this architectural masterpiece by Vanbrugh no doubt matched its magnificence, but little is known save for an early painting showing a swan lake. A notable weeping ash survives from that time, and there is a venerable and impressive rose garden, its beds outlined by box hedges 60 cm high and 30 cm wide. Since 1950 an excellent parterre has been laid out by Jim Russell, now embellished by a large Italianate pond and fountain. An attractive shrubbery (rhododendrons, azaleas, etc.), herbaceous borders and a laburnum walk have been established on the south side towards the fine Norman chapel. Replanting continues, including many ornamental trees, and the garden is clearly in good hands.

Wallington ★ [Historic Garden Grade II*]

Cambo, Morpeth NE61 4AR. Tel: (01670) 773600

The National Trust • 20m NW of Newcastle off A696 (signed on B6342) • House open • Walled garden open April to Oct, daily, 10am – 7pm (closes 6pm Oct) or dusk if earlier; Nov to March, daily, 10am – 4pm. Grounds open all year, daily, during daylight hours • Entrance: £6 • Other information: Self-drive scooters and guided tours available ○ 💻 🍴 <u>WC</u> ♿ ⬦ ♻ ⊞ 🍽

The handsome eighteenth-century house is set in a 100-acre landscape of lawns, terraces (fine views) and flower beds – serene and quintessentially English – but it is the walled garden, some distance away across the entry road via an attractive woodland walk, which has the most appeal. A rill runs from the pond to narrow lawns fringed with beds on two levels, and climbers cluster in prodigal numbers on the lovely old walls. (Alas, two of the elegant statues that graced the balustrade were stolen and the rest have been removed for safe-keeping.) The sloping site reveals the layout and invites exploration of the harmonious and generously filled herbaceous border. There is a garden house designed in Tuscan style by Daniel Garrett; the Victorian peach house is now restored, and the spectacular Edwardian conservatory is home to many treasures, with a rich tapestry of colour at every turn. Outside, the walks step down from a classical fountain past beds re-designed by Lady Trevelyan in the 1930s, including notable heathers and many herbaceous perennials. Trees planted by the Duke of Atholl in 1738 include a great larch, the survivor of three, by the China Pond.

OPENING DATES AND TIMES
Times of access given are the best available at the moment of going to press, but some may have been changed subsequently. In the entries, the times given are inclusive — that is, an entry such as May to Sept means that the garden is open from 1st May to 30th Sept inclusive, and 2 — 5 pm means that entry will be effective during that period. Please note that many owners will open their gardens to visitors by appointment, and they will often arrange to give a personally conducted tour on these occasions. Unavoidably some owners cannot give their opening details before we go to press, and in such cases we attempt to give the best guidance we can. If in doubt, it is wise to telephone before making a long journey.

NOTTINGHAMSHIRE

Clumber Park [Historic Park and Garden Grade I]

Clumber Estate Office, Clumber Park, Worksop S80 3AZ. Tel: (01909) 476592

*The National Trust • 4.5m SE of Worksop off A1 and A57, 11m from M1 junction
30 • Open all year, daily during daylight hours, except 16th July, 20th Aug, 25th
and 26th Dec • Walled kitchen garden open April to 1st Oct, daily, 10am – 5.30pm
• Entrance: £1. Vehicle charge for car park (cars and caravans, mini-buses and trailers)
£5.50 • Other information: Wheelchairs available for adults and children. Bicycles
for hire. Chapel open (telephone for details)* ○ **WC** & ◁ ♀

The park of 3800 acres was enclosed from Sherwood Forest in the eighteenth
century, and the garden was largely the creation of the 9th Earl of Lincoln (subsequently the 2nd Duke of Newcastle) in the second half of the eighteenth century.
He landscaped the park, and laid out the pleasure ground, serpentine walks and
shrubberies, and commissioned two temples and a bridge for the lake, which remain
today. The Atlantic cedars and sweet chestnut trees in the cedar avenue are of
breath-taking size. In 1824 William Sawrey Gilpin created the Italianate terrace to
the south of the house, island beds and picturesque walks in the pleasure ground.
The two-mile-long lime avenue of 1838 and the Lincoln Terrace of 1845 were
completed by other hands. From the nineteenth century also are Charles Barry's
stable block and clock tower and G.F. Bodley's ornate Gothic chapel built in the
pleasure garden. Since the demolition of the great house in 1938 (Barry's being the
last in the line), the chapel has become the focus of the garden. The Trust purchased
Clumber in 1946. The vinery and palm house have been restocked and the extensive
glasshouses (138 metres) are the best and longest in the Trust's properties. The
walled kitchen garden contains a 110-metre-long herbaceous border, currently being
replanted to an historic colour gradation, as well as cut-flower, fruit and vegetable and
herb borders, a collection of old varieties of apple trees and a working Victorian apiary. The lower kitchen garden has now been taken in hand by the Trust, and from
March 2006 will be open as a 'work-in-progress'.

Felley Priory ★

Underwood NG16 5FL. Tel: (01773) 810230

*The Hon. Mrs Chaworth Musters • 10m NW of Nottingham, 0.5m from M1
junction 27. Take A608 signed to Heanor and Derby. Garden is on left • Garden
and nursery open all year, Tues, Wed, Fri, 9am – 12.30pm (March to Oct, 2nd and
4th Weds in month, 9am – 4pm, 3rd Sun in month, 11am – 4pm). Snowdrop Sun
13th Feb, 11am – 4pm. Also open for NGS 9th April, 11am – 4pm, and for parties
by appt at other times • Entrance: £3, OAPs £2.50, children free. Other information:
NCCPG plant fairs 4th June, 1st Oct, 12 noon – 4pm* ◑ ⬤ **WC** ⚘ ♀

Despite the M1 being only half a mile away, the first impression is of a garden
surrounded by wooded countryside which can be seen across the grass-edged pond

planted with bamboos, irises, roses, eucomis and primulas. The owner has, with the use of hedging, created several gardens within the one, the original ancient walls unifying the parts as well as providing shelter and support for borders filled with unusual trees, shrubs, perennials, bulbs and climbers. It is a garden for all seasons: an astonishing display of snowdrops is followed by hellebores, daffodils massed under orchard trees, and colourful summer flowers in herbaceous borders. There is also an old-fashioned rose garden, a medieval garden and a small arboretum.

Hodsock Priory ★

Blyth, Worksop S81 0TY. Tel: (01909) 591204

Sir Andrew and Lady Buchanan • 5m NE of Worksop, 2m W of A1 at Blyth off B6045 Blyth-Worksop road • Open 28th Jan to 5th March, Mon – Wed, 2 – 5pm, and for NGS • Entrance: £4, children (6–16) £1) • Other information: Best displays depend on weather (telephone before travelling). Coaches must book. Dogs in park only ◑ ▆ ▓ WC ♿ ✿

Beyond the imposing red-brick Tudor gatehouse which is the entrance to Hodsock Priory (not open) stretches one of the most beautiful winter gardens in England. Snowdrops, magenta cyclamen and golden aconites are everywhere – spreading through the borders of the five-acre garden, in the grass and under the trees, and there is an additional walk in the snowdrop wood from which to enjoy the astonishing display. Coloured stems of cornus and willow, and the brilliant white trunks of *Betula jacquemontii* reflect in the lake. There are two ferneries and banks of hellebores (almost 1000 plants in one), and the hedges of sarcococca and avenues of winter honeysuckle add fragrance to the whole. The working Victorian apiary is a great attraction, and the Victorian Fan Garden was re-created in 2002. Among the many old and interesting trees are *Cornus mas*, *Catalpa bignonioides*, swamp cypress, tulip trees, acers and a paulownia.

Holme Pierrepont Hall [Historic Garden Grade II]

Radcliffe-on-Trent NG12 2LF. Tel: (0115) 933 2371

Mr and Mrs R. Brackenbury • 5m SE of Nottingham off A52/A6011. Continue past National Water Sports Centre for 1.5m • House open as garden • Garden open Feb and March, Mon – Wed, 2pm – dusk, and for NGS. Parties by appt all year, inc. evening visits • Entrance: £2 (house and garden £4.50, children £1.50) ◑ ▆ WC ♿ ✿ ▥

The hall is a medieval brick manor house, but the listed garden and box parterre of 1875 have been restored by the present owners. The parterre is the outstanding feature of the gardens, and the herbaceous borders next to the York-stone path (replacing old rose beds) enhance the courtyard garden further. (The Jacob sheep are friendly lawnmowers.) The owners work hard with improvements and new plantings in this peaceful house and garden and willingly provide information. Their innovations include a winter garden, an outer east garden and the planting of yews, shrubs, roses and fruit trees. Recent years have seen great improvements as these mature and increase.

Mill Hill House

Elston Lane, East Stoke, Newark NG23 5QJ. Tel: (01636) 525460

Mr and Mrs R.J. Gregory • 5m SW of Newark. Take A46, turn left into Elston Lane (signed to Elston); house is first on right • Open April to Sept for parties and individuals by appt; also open for NGS • Entrance: £2, accompanied children free • Other information: Parking 100 metres past house on right ◑ 🐝 WC 🔁 🌿

A half-acre cottage garden generously filled with a wide variety of plants provides year-round interest and tranquillity. The garden is well screened from the road and is a haven for birds, bees and butterflies which have no difficulty in finding it. Trees now stand on the site of the former nursery, with mown paths winding among them, and in the sheltered corner once occupied by the polytunnel a path circles around a cobbled area, with a seat from which to enjoy the collection of herbaceous and climbing plants not usually found in this cold county: euryops, melianthus, berberidopsis, and a stunning *Euphorbia characias* 'Silver Swan'. The garden also holds a National Collection of berberis.

Newstead Abbey ★ [Historic Garden Grade II*]

Newstead Abbey Park, Nottingham NG15 8NA. Tel: (01623) 455900

Nottingham City Council • 11m N of Nottingham on A60 • House with Byron memorabilia open April to Sept, 12 noon – 5pm • Open all year, daily except 24th Nov and 25th Dec, 9am – dusk • Entrance: £3, children £1.50 (house and grounds £6, children £2.50) ○ 🍴 ✕ 🐝 WC ♿ 🔁 ⛲ 🍵 ☕

Water predominates in the estate which the poet Byron inherited, and where he lived from 1808 to 1814. In most of the extensive and immaculate gardens there is much of interest. The Japanese gardens are justly famous and the rock and fern gardens worth visiting. The waterfalls, wildfowl, passageways, grottos and bridges also provide plenty of fun for children, but in addition there is an excellent, imaginatively equipped play area with bark mulch for safety. The tropical garden and the monks' stewpond are visually uninteresting but they are of laudable age. It is a pity that the large walled kitchen garden is now a rose garden – rose gardens, however pretty, are commonplace, but large kitchen gardens to the great houses are now rare. The old rose and carnation garden, until recently the iris garden, has been replanted as a herb garden.

'Pure Land' Japanese Garden

North Clifton, Nr Newark NG23 7AT. Tel: (01777) 228567

Buddha Maitreya • 10m N of Newark on Trent on A1133. Signposted • Open 25th March to 29th Oct, Tues – Fri, 10.30am – 5.30pm, Sat, Sun and Bank Holiday Mons, 10am – 5.30pm • Entrance: £4.50, OAPs £3.50, children £2.50 (under 5 free), season ticket £28, OAPs £23 • Other information: Limited access for wheelchairs ◑ 🍴 ✕ WC ♿

The 1.5 acre garden, created since 1980, is laid out in the Japanese style to provide a calm and contemplative setting for the relaxation and meditation centre based here. Narrow paths, steps and stepping stones lead the visitor up and down to various features, including the pagoda, tea house, Zen gravel garden and koi-filled pond. Ornaments and sculpture combine with carefully pruned and shaped trees and shrubs to create an oriental atmosphere which never descends into cliché. The sound of running water is always present from the small waterfalls and streams that weave their way through the garden. The hardy herbaceous, essentially English planting is informal and relaxed, contrasting successfully with the cloud pruning of many familiar conifers. A new garden has been created using clear crystals, amethyst and semi-precious stones representing hills, mountain, stream and sea. 1.25 tonnes of rose quartz stands in the middle of this glittering 'landscape' as a centerpiece. An inspiration for any visitors thinking of adding a Japanese element to their own gardens.

Rufford Country Park [Historic Park Grade II]

Ollerton, Newark NG22 9DF. Tel: (01623) 822944

Nottinghamshire County Council • 9m NE of Mansfield, 2m S of Ollerton on A614 • Rufford Abbey Cistercian area open • Park open all year, daily, 9am – 5pm • Entrance: free. Parking charge at certain times throughout the year • Other information: Four wheelchairs and two electric vehicles available for pre-booking ○ 🎟 ✕ 🏠 WC ⅃ ⟁ 🅿 ♿ 🚻 ♨ ⚲

This contains almost everything that might be expected of an important country park: lake, lime avenue, mature cedars, etc. A visit to the eight themed gardens within the formal gardens is well worthwhile, and there is a rose garden in front of the abbey ruins. Large areas are managed with wildlife in mind, but ball games are allowed on the lawns beneath cut-leaved beeches and cedars. The Reg Hookway arboretum, established in 1983, has a good collection of oaks and birches, all well labelled.

Wollaton Park [Historic Park and Garden Grade II*]

Nottingham NG8 2AE. Tel: (0115) 915 3900

Nottingham City Council • W of city centre on A609. From M1 junction 25 take A52, turn left onto A614 and left onto A609 • Natural history museum in hall open all year, daily, 11am – 5pm. Closed 24th to 26th Dec, 1st Jan • Garden open all year, daily, 11am – 5pm, (closes 4pm Oct to March) • Entrance: Mon – Fri free, charge at weekends and Bank Holiday Mons ○ 🎟 🏠 WC ⅃ ⟁ 🚻 ♨ ⚲

This large park and garden – the setting for Robert Smythson's masterpiece – is surrounded by the city, but because of its size the visitor feels deep in the country, although near the periphery of the park the roar of traffic dispels that illusion. The polyanthus in spring are spectacular, as are the colourful summer bedding planting schemes. The formal gardens at the top of the hill afford views of huge cedars and holm oaks, lime avenues and the deer in the park.

A TOTALLY INDEPENDENT PUBLICATION
The *Guide* makes no charge for entries, which are written by our own inspectors. The factual details are supplied by owners. This is a totally independent publication and its only revenue comes from sales of copies in bookshops.

OXFORDSHIRE

Two-starred gardens are marked on the map with a black square.

Ashdown House [Historic Park and Garden Grade II*]

Lambourn, Newbury, Berkshire RG16 7RE. Tel: (01488) 72584 (Estate Office)

The National Trust • 9m E of Swindon, 3.5m NW of Lambourn on W side of B4000 • House open • Garden open April to 28th Oct, Wed, Sat, 2 – 5pm. Woodlands open all year, Sat – Thurs, dawn – dusk. Parties must pre-book in writing • Entrance: Woodlands free (house £2.40). No reduction for parties • Other information: Parking 250 metres from house. New visitor reception and information area in South Lodge ● 🏪 & ♀

Set in a hauntingly beautiful valley, the exquisite hunting lodge built by the 1st Lord Craven for Elizabeth of Bohemia appears at first to have a tall central section complete with cupola flanked by two lower wings. It is only when the visitor approaches the front entrance that it becomes obvious that the wings are quite separate from the central block. The remains of a large formal park are present in a western lime avenue, and a complementary lime avenue planted in 1970 to the north of the house is maturing well; the avenue west of the parterre has been replanted. A.H. Brookholding-Jones's appropriately intricate parterre was laid out in the 1950s; the avenue west of the parterre has been replanted. In spring thousands of snowdrops, naturalised in the avenue and woodland, are at their showiest.

Blenheim Palace ★★ [Historic Park and Garden Grade I]

Woodstock, Oxford OX20 1PX. Tel: (01993) 811091

The Duke of Marlborough • 8m NW of Oxford. At Woodstock on A44 • House open as garden • Park open all year, daily except 25th Dec, 9am – dusk (closes 6pm in winter). Garden open 11th Feb to 10th Dec, daily (but closed Mon and Tues in Nov and Dec), 10.30am – 5.30pm (last admission 4.45pm) • Entrance: Park and formal gardens only, £8, concessions £6, children (5–15), £4, family £20 (2005 peak prices) • Park: ○ 🏪 & ⬧ 🏛 ♀ ♀ *Gardens:* ◐ 🖥 ✕ <u>WC</u> & ⌂ 🏛 ♀ ♀

Walking through Hawksmoor's Triumphal Arch into Blenheim Park, the visitor is greeted by one of the greatest contrived landscapes in Britain. The architect Vanbrugh employed Bridgeman and Henry Wise, Queen Anne's master gardener and the last of the British formalists. Wise constructed a bastion-walled 'military' garden, laid out kitchen gardens, planted immense elm avenues and linked Vanbrugh's bridge to the sides of the valley. The gardens were ready when the 1st Duke of Marlborough moved into the palace in 1719. Major alterations were made by the 4th, 5th and 9th Dukes, one of the earliest of which was the removal and grassing-over of Wise's formal gardens by 'Capability' Brown after 1764. Brown also landscaped the park, installing the lake and cascade, and removed Wise's military garden. The gardens today include formal areas designed by Achille Duchêne in the early nineteenth century to replace those destroyed by Brown. He made formal gardens to the east and west, the latter as two water terraces in the Versailles style. To the east of the palace is the elaborate Italian garden of patterned box and golden yew, interspersed with various seasonal plantings. To the south-west from the terraces are the rose garden and arboretum. From the vast south lawn 'one passes through a magnificent grove of cedars ... part shrubberies of laurel and an exedra of box and yew, the whole exemplifying the Victorian pleasure grounds'. In 1991, as a contribution to the celebration of the 300th anniversary of the replanting of the maze at Hampton Court, the present Duke planted in part of the kitchen garden a maze which is maturing well. The former garden centre has been redeveloped as a lavender and herb garden.

Blewbury Manor

Blewbury OX11 9QJ. Tel: (01235) 850246

Alice Coptcoat • 4m SE of Didcot off A417. In Blewbury turn into Westbrook Street, after 0.35m bear right at sign to village hall (park in village hall car park). Continue into Berry Lane; house is 18 metres on left • Open 30th April and 18th June, 2 – 6pm for NGS, plus 4th and 18th May, 1st and 15th June, 2 – 5pm, and for parties of 20 or more by appt • Entrance: £4, children (5-16) £2 • Other information: Teas and plants for sale on NGS open days NEW ● WC &*

Walking up the drive flanked by an avenue of *Crataegus prunifolia* towards the part-seventeenth-century house, visitors come across first the newly created Dial Garden, an innovative sunken space with perennial beds set in gravel and surrounded by avenues of hornbeams. It is a fitting harbinger of the varied and accomplished delights to come. In early May there is a spring walk with 7000 creamy-white pheasant's eye daffodils and snake's head fritillaries, with all the borders and the pergola planted with a large variety of tulips. By the moat 'Wedding Day' and 'Rambling Rector' roses engulf their host trees, and in room after room – curving and relaxed, box-edged and precise – are flower and shrub borders planted in hot or cool colours. A shady stream is fringed with lilies, ferns and candelabra primulas, a little wooden bridge overhung with roses and wisteria. There is even a spiral mound. It comes as no surprise that the owner is a designer, for this is a garden of style, plantsmanship and immense attention to detail. She has 10 acres here in which to hone her skills, so what others can only do in miniature has been realised here on a generous and satisfying scale.

Bridewell Organic Gardens

Wilcote, Nr Witney OX7 3EB. Tel: (01993) 868445

4m N of Witney, 3m S of Charlbury, E of B4022 • Open 25th June, 1 – 6pm, and for gardening and other interested parties evenings by appt • Entrance: free ● ■ WC & ◁▷ ◊ ◊

This most original one-acre walled garden was once the kitchen garden of Wilcote House (see entry). It is run by an award-winning charity that supports people with mental health problems. A box parterre in the shape of a Celtic knot has standard photinias clipped into balls to emphasise its corners; nearby is a sundial with steps up to a viewing platform. A little arbour hung with clematis near the entrance leads into a walled enclosure with a lily pond. A fruit cage protects redcurrants trained as goblets and blueberries in willow baskets, and there are vegetables in raised beds and herbs in a herb wheel surrounded by pleached hornbeams. A *potager* has been laid out as a series of diamond-shaped and semi-circular beds. A tribute to Monet's garden at Giverny includes a slate 'lake' crossed by a wooden bridge and roses clambering over arches; a *trompe-l'œil* painting on one of the garden walls beckons the visitor through the open front door of the painter's house. Beyond the wall is a five-acre vineyard on sloping ground with an adjacent apiary. As if all this were not enough, there is also a gipsy caravan and a traditional smithy making ironwork for the garden. Something here for all ages.

Brook Cottage ★

Well Lane, Alkerton, Banbury OX15 6NL. Tel: (01295) 670303/670590

Mrs D. Hodges • 6m NW of Banbury. From A422 Banbury – Stratford-upon-Avon road, turn W signed to Alkerton. With small war memorial on right, turn left into Well Lane and right at fork • Open 17th April to Oct, Mon – Fri, 9am – 6pm. Weekends, evenings and all group visits by appt only • Entrance: £4, OAPs £3, children free • Other information: Refreshments for parties must be pre-booked. Unusual plants for sale ◑ 🖵 🐾 WC ♿ 🔽 ⌀

A four-acre garden of great originality and variety, created since 1964 in a west-facing valley as a series of interconnecting and intensively planted areas. It is the work of the plantswoman owner and her late husband and shows what can be achieved by those who 'Consult the Genius of the Place in all'. Once past the terrace below the house, slivers of paths force visitors into single file, making their emergence onto open lawn above the stream and lower pond all the more exciting. Here, the planting is bold and confident, grouped tellingly in individual clumps or in beds with skilful combinations of colour. In the bog garden a splendidly broad band of foliage plants contrasts with feathery or piercing flower spikes. The hanging garden of shrub roses is the most famous feature in its season, but for those who wish to see a profusion of plants disposed in a masterly way, Brook Cottage is a living workshop of ideas at any time.

Broughton Castle ★ [Historic Garden Grade II]

Broughton, Banbury OX15 5EB. Tel: (01295) 276070

Lord Saye and Sele • 2.5m SW of Banbury on B4035 • Castle open • Garden open 16th and 17th April; May to 16th Sept, Wed, Sun and Bank Holiday Mons (plus Thurs, July and Aug); all 2 – 5pm. Also by appt for parties all year • Entrance: £2.50 (house and garden £6, OAPs and students £5, children £2.50, family £14). Party rates for private guided tours • Other information: Teas on open days only. Refreshments for parties by arrangement ◑ 🖵 🐾 WC ♿ 🔽 ⌀ ⛪

More of a house than a castle, with gardens that are unexpectedly domestic within the confines of the moat, Broughton sits in a beautiful flat-bottomed valley. In 1900 there were 14 gardeners, now there is one maintaining the overall splendour The most important changes were made after 1969 following a visit from Lanning Roper, who suggested opening up the views across the park. There are now two magnificent borders, where great planting skill is evident in the serpentine flows of colour. The west-facing border, backed by the battlement wall, is based on blues and yellows, greys and whites, the other on reds, mauves and blues. On the south side is the walled 'ladies' garden' with box-edged, fleur-de-lys-shaped beds holding floribunda roses. Another wonderful border rises up to the house wall. Everywhere is a profusion of old-fashioned roses and original planting.

Broughton Grange ★

Wykham Lane, Broughton OX15 5DS. Tel: (07715) 749767

From Banbury take B4035 to Broughton. At Saye and Sele Arms, turn left up Wykham Lane (one-way) and follow road for 0.5m out of village; entrance is on right • *Open several days for NGS and charities* • *Entrance: £5* • *Other information: Teas and plants on open days only* [NEW] ● WC &

Surrounding the house are formal gardens and informal plantings – a yew terrace, a knot garden, a parterre, long borders backed by hedges, an orchard, a wildflower meadow and a young arboretum. Tom Stuart-Smith's six-acre perennial flower garden stands aloof and alone in this traditional English setting, screened by Ptolemy Dean's boldly patterned wall, stepped and buttressed on its eastern side. Descending on its longest axis between a pleached lime *allée* and a beech tunnel, with a viewing terrace at the top of the enclosure and the spire of Bloxham Church as an eye-catcher in the distance among the surrounding hills, it is a garden unlike any other. Colour wells down the slope in crests and troughs. The second terrace is occupied by a water tank and a rill of classical simplicity crossed by stepping stones, and below that is a modern English *parterre de broderie*, enamelled in spring with thousands of tulips. It is a fabulous beast of a garden, groomed and burnished by head gardener Iain Davies, at its peak in high summer but reinventing itself at every season. Quite simply one of the most significant and scintillating gardens to be created in twenty-first-century Britain.

Buscot Park ★ [Historic Park and Garden Grade II*]

Faringdon SN7 8BU. Tel: (01367) 240786

Administered by Lord Faringdon on behalf of The National Trust • *On A417 between Lechlade and Faringdon* • *House open as garden (but closed Mon and Tues)* • *Garden open 3rd April to Sept, daily, except weekends of 22nd and 23rd April, 6th and 7th, 20th and 21st May, 3rd and 4th, 17th and 18th June, 1st and 2nd, 15th and 16th, 29th and 30th July, 5th and 6th, 19th and 20th Aug, 2nd and 3rd, 16th and 17th Sept, 2 – 6pm* • *Entrance: £5, children £2.50 (house and grounds £7, children £3.50)* • *Other information: Teas available when house open* ◑ 💷 📖 WC & ⚘

The huge walled estate is situated in the flatlands of the Thames, with a house built between 1780 and 1783. Its garden, however, was only developed during the twentieth century. The water-garden-within-a-wood was created by Harold Peto in 1904; later, avenues linking lake to house were cut through, branching out from a goose-foot near the house, with fastigiate and weeping varieties of oak, beech and lime. The Egyptian avenue created by Lord Faringdon in 1969 is guarded by sphinxes and embellished with Coade-stone statues copied from an original from Hadrian's Villa. Two new gardens at *allée* intersections – the Swinging Garden and the Citrus Bowl – provide enclosed areas of great charm. The large walled kitchen garden was rearranged in the mid-1980s, and is now intersected by a pleached avenue of ostrya (hop hornbeam) and a Judas tree tunnel. Deep borders under the outside walls have unusual and skilled planting by Tim Rees, mixing old roses and climbing vegetables (gourds, marrows, beans, cucumbers) which lay themselves out over the rose bushes after their flowering is over. Walkways both outside and inside the kitchen garden are between wide borders which use the exterior and interior walls and trellises as screens. In the latter the planting by the late Peter Coats and imaginative development by Lord Faringdon is exceptionally effective. The small garden at the elegant seventeenth-century *Buscot Old Parsonage*, also a Trust property, has different opening times.

Chastleton House [Historic Garden Grade II*]

Chastleton GL56 0SU. Tel: (01608) 674355

The National Trust • 6m NE of Stow-on-the-Wold off A436 • Open 29th March to 30th Sept, 4th to 28th Oct, Wed – Sat, 1 – 5pm (closes 4pm Oct) (last admission 1 hour before closing). Ticket numbers restricted and prospective visitors strongly advised to telephone in advance. Pre-booked guided tours available (charge applies including NT members). Groups of 11 – 25 by prior appt only • Entrance: (house and garden) £6.50, children £3.30, family £16.30 • Other information: No large coaches. Parking 270 metres from house – telephone for details of parking for disabled. Braille guide available ◑ WC ঙ

The beguiling, somewhat gawky early seventeenth-century house was in a state of pleasing decay when it was in private hands, but the Trust has sensitively retained the atmosphere. The garden, which was at its peak in the early twentieth century and survived more or less intact until the 1960s, has been treated in the same spirit. The impressive topiary, probably a Victorian re-creation of a seventeenth-century design, still makes an emphatic statement; the rest provides a pleasant setting for the enchanted house. The rules of modern croquet were first codified at Chastleton and one of the original croquet lawns has been restored. At *Chastleton Glebe* Prue Leith's garden is usually open one day a year for the NGS.

Clock House

Coleshill, Swindon, Wiltshire SN6 7PT.
Tel: (01793) 762476

Denny Wickham and Peter Fox • 3.5m SW of Faringdon on B4019 • Open by appt only • Entrance: £2, children free ◐ 🏵 ঙ

Situated on a hillside with inspiring views over the Vale of the White Horse, this exuberant, delightful garden was created by Michael and Denny Wickham in the last forty years on the site of one of the most beautiful Caroline houses, Coleshill (tragically burned, then wilfully demolished in the 1950s). The ground-plan of the original house is planted out in box and lavender, to show the layout of walls and windows. The gravel 'rooms' are full of self-sown poppies in June and *Verbena bonariensis* in late July. There is a courtyard with a collection of plants in pots, and a sunny walled garden in the old laundry-yard with roses and mixed planting. The lime avenue at the front of the house sweeps down to the views, and a pond and terrace are sheltered by tall shrubs. The mixed herbaceous borders are filled with interesting and unusual plants. This is an original garden, designed by an artist, with a large collection of plants in imaginative settings.

Cotswold Wildlife Park and Gardens ★

Burford OX18 4JW. Tel: (01993) 823006

John and Reggie Heyworth • Open all year, daily; March to Sept, 10am – 6pm (last admission 4.30pm), Oct to Feb, 10am – 4.30pm (last admission 3.30pm). Closed 25th Dec • Entrance: £9, children (3–16) £6.50, OAPs £6.50 (discount for parties of 20 or more) • Other information: Miniature train runs through part of park, April to Oct, usually 11.30pm – 4.30pm (£1 extra, OAPs and children 50p)
○ 🍽 ✗ 🦮 wc ♿ ♨ ⛲ ⚑ ℘

Varied and extensive grounds – 140 acres in all – surround the listed Victorian Gothic manor house. Head gardener Tim Miles and his team have achieved wonders here in the last few years. The tropical house, which has been completely refurbished and replanted, is outstandingly atmospheric with its spectacular plants and birds – the original Eden Project in miniature – and the exotic theme is carried through into the exuberant walled garden. Here are hot colours and the largest collection of tender perennials in the country, together with immaculate traditional bedding in an effective combination of pink and silver shades, fruiting bananas and avocados, and a range of containers and hanging baskets with original and flamboyant displays. The planting schemes throughout complement and enhance the settings of the various animals and birds: don't miss the meerkats in their landscaped desert with its flowering cacti and succulents. The terrace beside the house, which has a formal pond and parterre, is in cool contrast, featuring blues and mauves and masses of white roses. Areas of prairie planting with grasses and bamboos continue to develop, and the parkland, home to many endangered animals, has fine specimen trees: Wellingtonias, giant redwoods, cedars and an immense oak six hundred years old. There are delights here for all ages, whether in prams or wheelchairs.

Greys Court ★ [Historic Garden Grade II]

Rotherfield Greys, Henley-on-Thames RG9 4PG. Tel: (01491) 628529

The National Trust • W of Henley-on-Thames, E of B481. From town centre take A4130 towards Oxford, at Nettlebed mini-roundabout take B481. Signposted to left shortly after Highmoor • House open April to Sept, Wed – Fri and Bank Holiday Mons, plus 1st Sat in month (closed 25th March), 2 – 6pm • Gardens open March and Oct, Wed, 2 – 6pm; April to Sept, Tues – Sat and Bank Holiday Mons, 2 – 6pm • Entrance: £3.70, children £1.70, family £8.70 (house and garden £5.20, children £2.40, family £12) (2005 prices) • Other information: Picnics in car park only
◑ 🍽 wc ♿ ⚑ ℘

The statue symbolising St Fiacre, the protector of gardeners and commemorating Charles Taylor, a former head gardener, stands modestly in this beautiful garden, or several gardens, set against the ruins of a fourteenth-century fortified house. The largest area, an orchard, is divided by hedges of *Rosa mundi*. An ancient wisteria forms a canopy over a walled area, approached on one side through a tunnel of wisterias and *Robinia hispida*. The impeccably kept peony bed and rose garden glow against the ancient walls. Beyond the kitchen garden – now an ornamental garden of unusual vegetables – across the nut avenue, is the grass Archbishop's Maze, interesting for its symbolism. Seek out also the donkey wheel and the restored ice-house. In collaboration with the HDRA, the garden was part of a pilot project aimed at providing the Trust with an organic gardening blueprint for the future.

The Harcourt Arboretum [Historic Arboretum Grade I]

Nuneham Courtenay, Oxford OX44 9PX. Tel: (01865) 343501

Oxford University Botanic Garden • 6m S of Oxford off A4074 • Open Dec to March, Mon – Fri, 10am – 4.30pm (closed 22nd Dec to 3rd Jan); April to Nov, daily, 10am – 5pm (last admission 4.15pm) • Entrance: free, but £2 car parking charge • Other information: No coaches ○ 🍂

The village and church of Nuneham were demolished in the 1670s to make way for a classical landscape to be seen from the Georgian house (not open); Oliver Goldsmith's 1770 poem *The Deserted Village* is said to be based on that upheaval. Horace Walpole, in 1780, described the gardens, designed by 'Capability' Brown and William Mason (the poet-gardener), as the most beautiful in the world. The garden was then full of flowers, not only along the walks, but also in carefully planted beds. The 85-acre site, one and a half miles from the house, is now owned by Oxford University Botanic Garden. It dates from 1835 when Lord Harcourt, who owned the Nuneham estate at the time, planted an eight-acre pinetum with the help of William Sawrey Gilpin. Many of those plantings – of such mighty trees as noble fir, Wellingtonia, Japanese and incense cedars – are now magnificent mature specimens underplanted with camellias, rhododendrons, bamboos, magnolias and a collection of acers. There is also a 10-acre bluebell wood and a 30-acre wildflower meadow. The pleasure of walking among these majestic and ancient trees almost cancels out the traffic noise and gigantic pylons that bedevil the site.

Hill Court

Tackley. (Enquiries to Court Farm, Tackley, Kidlington OX5 3AQ. Tel: (01869) 331218)

Mr and Mrs Andrew C. Peake • 9m N of Oxford, off A4260. From Oxford turn opposite Sturdy's Castle; from S turn off at Tackley sign • Open 10th and 11th June, 2 – 6pm, and for individuals and parties by appt • Entrance: £2.50, children free ● 💺 WC & ℘ ℺

A two-acre, sixteenth-century walled garden formerly attached to the house, which was demolished c. 1960. Remains of the manor house, also demolished, can be seen across the park, which dates from 1787. The garden, the design of which was influenced by Russell Page, is unusual because it is terraced uphill from the entrance. The rose beds were removed over a decade ago and the sensitive and original plantings of silver, pink and blue which replaced them is the work of Rupert Golby. Many rare and unusual plants.

Home Farm

Balscote, Banbury OX15 6JP. Tel: (01295) 738194

Mr and Mrs G.C. Royle • 5m W of Banbury, 0.5m off A422 • Open March to Oct by appt • Entrance: £3 ● ● ● WC & ●

With views over the village roof-tops of grazing sheep and nearby Claydon Wood, this peaceful garden has been cleverly designed to make the most of its half acre. It is a gem, with abundant flowering shrubs, herbaceous plants and bulbs, foliage and grasses achieving a natural effect full of interest and colour all year. In early summer deep purple abutilons beside the paler wisteria against the walls of the seventeenth-century house catch the eye, along with the rock garden and the brilliant cascade of helianthemums next to the terrace, where you can sit and enjoy it all. Potentillas creep between the steps, and pink perennial geraniums frame a stone seat in a shady far corner – a haven of refreshingly uncluttered informality.

Kelmscott Manor [Historic Garden Grade II]

Kelmscott, Lechlade, Gloucestershire GL7 3HJ. Tel: (01367) 252486

The Society of Antiquaries • 4m NW of Faringdon, 2m E of Lechlade in Kelmscott • House open as garden • Garden open April to Sept, Wed, 11am – 5pm; also 1st and 3rd Sat, July and Aug, and 3rd Sat, April to June and Sept, 2 – 5pm. Tours for parties by appt on Thurs and Fri • Entrance: £2, children free (house and garden £8.50, children/students £4.25) ● ● ● WC & ●

'A magical house in a remarkably unchanged village' was *Country Life's* verdict. Its strange atmosphere will be relished by those who are attracted by the Pre-Raphaelite Brotherhood in general, and William Morris in particular. The impression one forms of all his gardens is that they had an unruly beauty where weeds might well have been encouraged as long as they were decorative. Above all the choice of flowers was essentially artistic and romantic because, for him, gardens were places of magic and mystery, fairytale worlds where lovers met under rose-covered arbours. The present garden, designed by Colvin and Moggridge, re-creates some of that romanticism – what Morris himself described as 'a heaven on earth ... and such a garden! Close down on the river, a boat house and all things handy.'

Kingston Bagpuize House

Kingston Bagpuize, Abingdon OX13 5AX. Tel: (01865) 820259

Mrs Virginia Grant • 5.5m W of Abingdon off A415. Follow signs to house along Rectory Lane • Open 5th, 6th, 26th to 28th Feb, 19th to 21st March, 16th to 19th and 30th April, 1st to 3rd and 28th to 31st May, 23rd to 26th July, 27th to 30th Aug, 17th to 19th Sept; all 2 – 5pm. Open to parties by appt all year. Guided tours available • Entrance: £3 (house and garden £5, OAPs £4.50, children (5–15) £2.50) • Other information: Home-made teas. Meals available for groups by arrangement ● ● WC & ● ● ●

The beautiful mellow brick Baroque house, neither too small nor too large, is set in its compact park; it was owned by Miss Marlie Raphael, an enthusiastic and much-travelled plant collector, from 1939 until her death in 1976. With the help of

Sir Harold Hillier and other friends, she created a 15-acre garden with its mind-boggling variety of rare and unusual trees, shrubs and plants. After inheriting the house in 1995, the present owner, together with her late husband Francis, successfully uncovered and restored much of Miss Raphael's original planting, adding to it with their own complementary and innovative ideas. Within the framework of mellow brick walls and hedges of yew, beech and laurel (and even of brachyglottis), there is an air of relaxed informality, the plants thriving in the fertile greensand soil. An enormous mixed border 10 metres deep is packed with tall perennials, many self-sown, covering a broad spectrum of harmonious colours. At every turn in the three-acre woodland garden are rare and interesting trees and shrubs, including several magnolias. Many of them are quite spectacular, and beneath the jungle canopy are carpets of snowdrops and other bulbs, followed by drifts of geraniums, astrantias, campanulas, vincas, hellebores, lilies and other shade-loving perennials. Church Copse has now been cleared and in spring is a mass of naturalised snowdrops; many more native woodland bulbs and perennials are being planted here. Along the edge of the Garden Park with its beech avenue, Wellingtonias and other specimen trees, the shrub border reveals yet more rarities. The terrace walk has a growing cistus collection and provides an excellent vantage point from which to enjoy a view of the house and different aspects of the garden, which is planned to give colour and interest throughout the year.

Lime Close ★

35 Henleys Lane, Drayton OX14 4HU.

M.C. de Laubarede • 2m S of Abingdon off B4017; turn left into Henleys Lane, house 200 yds on left • Open 16th April and 4th June, 2 – 5.30pm, and at other times, Feb to June and Oct, for parties of 10 or more by written appt • Entrance: £3, children under 12 free ● ● & ⬧ ⬧

The owner, a garden designer, has created an unexpected three-acre oasis here, following in the footsteps of her grandfather, Charles Christie-Miller, a tree, shrub and iris specialist, and her aunt, an alpine enthusiast, from whom she inherited the garden. Grassy walks and vistas, and mixed and shade borders distinguished by rare perennials (including *Clematis recta* 'Lime Close') and clever colour combinations, are all surrounded by mature trees and a wide variety of more recently planted rare trees and shrubs. Yew hedges and topiary are beautifully maintained and privet hedges enclose the flower-filled *potager* with its Italian-Renaissance-style pergola and increasing iris collection. Beside the Elizabethan house formal areas include a parterre, a charming little herb garden designed by the late Rosemary Verey, a lawn and herbaceous borders. Peonies, roses, honeysuckles and clematis put in an appearance everywhere. The planting throughout is relaxed and informal, the colour effects enviably subtle and delicate. Masses of bulbs from late February onwards, and good autumn colour and berries. A new cottage garden was planted in 2004 focusing on colour combinations.

The Mill House

Sutton Courtenay, Abingdon OX14 4NH. Tel: (01235) 848219

Mrs Jane Stevens • 1.5m S of Abingdon off B4016. Leaving town over river bridge, entrance gates in main street opposite Fish pub • Open by appt for parties of 10 or

more • Entrance: £5 per person • Other information: Teas by prior arrangement
● WC &

Although the stone house behind high walls suggests promise, the romantic experience of the garden cannot be guessed at as the visitor approaches through the winding main street of the village. Of course, few gardeners have the gift of the Thames in their territory, but the present owner has made remarkable use of it. She had the benefit of a structure laid out by Colonel Peter Laycock, a colleague of Eric Savill, who planted rare and unusual trees and has added imaginative touches of her own – like the circles of comfrey. This eight-and-a-half-acre garden is to be walked in, sat in and savoured. The old mill in the middle of the garden, now a ruin, was used for printing banknotes up until the middle of the eighteenth century. There are formal areas near the early Georgian house, but once past these, the wanderer will be lost in a sylvan idyll amongst the water, trees and groves. There are three islands, planted with a mass of wild flowers, and seasonal interest comes from the fine bulbs in spring, old-fashioned roses in summer and charming autumn colours. For those who like to conjure up dreams of previous owners, Herbert and Margot Asquith lived here before 1916 while he was Prime Minister and entertained all the great figures of the day for Friday-to-Monday weekends.

Old Church House

2 Priory Road, Wantage OX12 9DD. Tel: (01235) 762785

Dr and Mrs Dick Squires • Near Wantage Market Square next to parish church and opposite Vale and Downland Museum • Open April to Oct, Tues – Sat, 10.30am – 4.30pm, Sun, 2 – 5pm, and by appt • Entrance: By donation to charity (tickets available at museum) • Other information: Park in nearby public car park. Refreshments and toilet facilities at museum ● 🏠 & 🌳 ▮ ◦ B&B

An unusual and exciting town garden running down to Letcombe Brook. The present owner and his wife have transformed his childhood garden into a series of rooms leading away from the existing lawns and mature trees. There is a sunken water garden, a Mediterranean garden, a pergola garden and a wild garden, all filled with unusual plants and shrubs, follies and highly imaginative building. Late May and June is the best season to visit, but it is an inspiration at any time to see what can be achieved in less than three years. Some fascinating documentation shows the development of the planning and the work itself in before-and-after style.

The Old Rectory ★

Farnborough, Wantage OX12 8NX. Tel: (01488) 638298

Mr and Mrs Michael Todhunter • 4m SE of Wantage off B4494 • Open for NGS, and by appt • Entrance: £2.50, children free (2005 prices) • Other information: Teas nearby on charity open days and for parties ● WC & 🌿

At nearly 250 metres, and despite being prey to winds from the Downs, this four-acre garden has been created over thirty years, based on a good original structure of large trees and hedges, with magnificent views. Its house is as pretty as any village old rectory could be, and sits at the heart of the garden looking out at the downs. Deep, parallel herbaceous borders are backed by yew hedges. The planting by the front of house is subtle and effective, and smaller areas have been laid out for sun- or shade-loving plants. Woodland contrasts with shrubs and lawns, and the fast-growing arboretum now contains over 150 trees. The swimming pool is surrounded by a large *Hydrangea sargentiana* and potted lilies, with mixed roses and clematis around the outside walls. There is a collection of old roses and small-flowered clematis, and wild flowers line the front lawn by the ha-ha. The tennis court has been turned into a *boule à drôme* – a place in the middle to play boule – with four large beds, pretty wrought-iron gates and a gazebo. Those who like John Betjeman's poetry will be interested to know that he lived here from 1945 to 1950 and can look for the ghost of Miss Joan Hunter Dunn in the shrubberies. A John Piper window in the church is in his memory.

Oxford Botanic Garden
(see UNIVERSITY OF OXFORD BOTANIC GARDEN)

Oxford College Gardens
Most colleges are helpful about access to their gardens, although the more private ones, such as the Master's or Fellows', are rarely open. Specific viewing times are difficult to rely on because some colleges prefer not to have visitors in term time or on days when a function is taking place. The best course is to ask at the porter's lodge or to telephone ahead of visit. However, it is fair to say that some Oxford college gardens will always be open to the visitor, by arrangement with porters, even if others are closed on that particular day. Some colleges have a policy of allowing public entrance on official guided tours only and others now make a charge for entry.

There are eight college gardens that are on the English Heritage *Register*. Each one is identified in the text that follows. As well as these, amongst the college gardens of particular interest are the following: *Christ Church*: the War Memorial Gardens on St. Aldate's, with its attractive herbaceous borders, and, just beyond, the rose garden with its water feature [Open daily except 25th Dec, Mon–Sat, 9am – 5.30pm, Sun, 11.30am – 5.30pm]. So are the splendid Christ Church Meadows [Historic Park Grade I], with the herd of Old English Longhorns resident in summer and autumn months. Most of the other gardens – Master's, Cathedral and Pocock – are open once a year, usually mid-Aug, for the NGS, allowing a sight of the Oriental plane planted in 1636 and of the Cheshire Cat's horse chestnut tree – a reminder of the college's connection with Lewis Carroll wc & ♀. *Corpus Christi* [Historic Garden Grade II]: the smallest college, with an attractive small garden overlooking Christ Church Meadow [Normally open 1.30 – 4pm]. *Exeter*: Fellows' Garden [Open most days, 2 – 5pm] is walled on all sides with part of boundary formed by the old Bodleian Library and Divinity Schools. The mound at the end gives excellent views across Radcliffe Square with the Camera, Church of St Mary the Virgin and All Souls College all clearly visible. Visitors are requested to keep to the paths. Herbaceous borders, shrubs and mature trees. Also the Rector's private garden [Open for NGS in conjunction with New College Warden's Garden one Sun in late June/early July, 2 – 5pm]. *Green College*: alas this institution with its environmental name is only open to the public once a year. *Holywell Manor*, part of Balliol: a restful, well-maintained garden of one acre [Open 10.30am – 6.30pm]. *Kellogg College*: an unusual and pleasant inner courtyard with three separate walled gardens at the back situated in Rewley

House, Wellington Square [Open all year – telephone (01865) 270383 WC &]. *Lady Margaret Hall*: eight formal and informal acres, mainly designed by the Edwardian architect Blomfield, who was also responsible for some of the buildings. Fine specimen trees and good borders [Open 2 – 6pm or dusk if earlier. All visitors are requested to call at the porter's lodge &]. *Magdalen College* [Historic Park Grade I]: 100 acres of meadows including a deer park adjacent to the college buildings and Fellows' Garden (open to the public). The water meadows bounded by the River Cherwell and circled by Addison's Walk, named after the eighteenth-century essayist and garden enthusiast, are famous for the display of fritillaries in April [College and gardens open nearly all year, 2–6pm. Refreshments sometimes available ♥ WC &]. *New College* [Historic Garden Grade I]: admirers of the writings of Robin Lane Fox will be able to see examples of his plantings, outstanding mixed borders against Oxford city wall, rose borders, cloister garden. The mound was completed in 1649. [Open Easter to Oct at New College Lane Gate, 11am – 5pm; winter at Holywell Gate, 2 – 4pm]. *Nuffield*: formal gardens in two quadrangles with water features and sculpture by Peter Randall-Page [Open Mon – Fri, 9am – 5pm, but closed Christmas, Easter and August Bank Holiday. No large parties]. *Queen's*: The gardens are a worthy modern setting to a college with a history stretching back to the fourteenth century. Wrapped around the buildings on several levels, they are planted with elegance, flair and a vital sense of colours that work well together [College, Fellows' and Provost's garden open 26th June for charity, but not to casual visitors during year except those on guided tours arranged through the Information Centre]. *Rhodes House*: not a college and not a pretty building but an unexpectedly pleasant garden behind [9am – 5pm weekdays only]. *St Catherine's* [Historic Garden Grade II]: in the midst of so much ancient charm in garden design it is pleasing to be able to recommend a modern garden created 1960–4 by the distinguished Danish architect Arne Jacobsen (1902–71). Noted for his concern for integrating building and landscape, this is a remarkable example. It has a fine water feature, and John Brookes says that, later in the season, when the water planting is at its best, the canal comes into its own [Open except Easter, Aug and Christmas]. *St Hilda's*: five acres of lawns and beds extending along the banks of the River Cherwell; flood plain meadow with wild flowers including fritillaries. Jacqueline du Pré Music Building accessible for visits and concerts [Open during daylight hours but dogs not permitted]. *St Hugh's*: an interesting 10-acre garden largely created by Annie Rogers, a Fellow. [All visitors are requested to call at the porter's lodge &]. *St John's* [Historic Garden Grade II]: landscaped in the eighteenth century and still immaculately kept. Striking in spring when bulbs in flower. William Pye has designed a new water sculpture. See also the new Garden Quad, opened in 1993, designed by MacCormac Jamieson & Pritchard and described as 'one of the most important buildings of the 'nineties anywhere in Britain' [Open daily, 1 – 5pm or dusk if earlier. Better to go during the week, rather than at weekends, to avoid crowds &]. *Trinity* [Historic Garden Grade II]: broad sweeping lawns, magnificent herbaceous borders and informal woodland carpeted with bulbs in spring; interesting trees including a 1737 catalpa and a splendid fraxinus. Remarkable stone Baroque gateway at the end of Trinity College's garden onto Parks Road, probably by Hawksmoor [Open daily, 10.30am – 12 noon, 2 – 5pm WC &]. Trinity Fellows' and President's Gardens, recently developed with choice plants, statuary and fountain [Open for NGS, one Sun in late March or early

April and Aug, 2 – 5pm ☕ 🌿]. *Wadham* [Historic Garden Grade II]: herbaceous borders, new 'fragrant' garden, rare and fine old trees [Open 1 – 4.30pm WC ♿]. *Wolfson*: nine acres designed around modern college buildings by Powell and Moya. Mature beds of perennials and shrubs, formal lawns and mature trees in a peaceful riverside setting. [Open daily, daylight hours WC ♿ 🌿]. *Worcester* [Historic Garden Grade II*]: the only true landscaped garden in Oxford, including a lake, made from a swampy area in 1817. Brightly coloured beds in front quad [Open term time 2 – 6pm, vacation 9am – 12 noon and 2 – 6pm. Organised parties not admitted except by prior written arrangement]. The Provost's Garden, open on special occasions, has a charming rose garden stretching to wooded lakeside walks and orchards. *The University Parks* (a short walk from Rhodes House past the amazing museum): these were laid out in 1864 and are the perfect place for walking in all weathers and across the bridges to Mesopotamia or the Spalding Nature Reserve. The herbaceous border near South Lodge Gate is laid out in colour themes. The borders along the West and North Walks contain a broad collection of shrubs and groundcover plants chosen especially for their drought tolerance, grouped in strong associations to create a focus in the middle distance. The extended pond provides a habitat for moisture-loving plants, while Cox's Corner has an emphasis on winter colour. The Parks have a fine collection of mature trees mixed with newer plantings [Open daily, except 3rd Sept, 8am – dusk WC ♿].

Pettifers ★

Lower Wardington, Banbury OX17 1RU. Tel: (01295) 750232

Mr J. and The Hon. Mrs Price • 5m NE of Banbury on A361 Daventry Road from M40 junction 11. Opposite church • Open for NGS, and by appt • Entrance: £5 (£6 for private visits) ●

Pettifers has a town-house front garden and a country-house rear garden which pays due homage to its stunning view. It is a garden of levels, with narrow retaining walls packed with plants beneath the terrace of the seventeenth-century house giving way to broad borders facing each other across a central lawn, one of them backed by a 'battered' yew hedge. Pairs of Irish yews and *Rosa californica* 'Plena' announce the descent to a crocus lawn and a cutting/winter parterre garden with mini box buttresses and clipped yew cones creating architectural structure. Beyond, the garden begins to merge into the countryside with an avenue of *Malus transitoria* and a meadow spangled with spring bulbs. A slate circle in the paddock makes a stylish seating area. Gina Price has worked on the garden since 1988, acquiring in the process a passion for plants – many of them rare or unusual – and an instinctive, unconventional ability to combine them. Travels in India have liberated her sense of colour, so that in summer purple alliums, *Rosa* 'Reine des Violettes', scarlet 'Beauty of Livermere' poppies and the wonderful orange *Euphorbia griffithii* 'Fern Cottage' catch the eye in the borders; later in the year come kniphofias, powerful sedums, purple asters. Seats painted lilac and blue can be spotted among the borders. A garden building has diamond-panelled doors painted in pale blue and terracotta, with windows inspired by the Taj Mahal. You sense an interesting and creative mind behind the trowel.

The Priory

Charlbury OX7 3PX. Tel: (01608) 810417

Dr D. El Kabir and others • On B4022 Witney – Enstone road. In Charlbury adjacent to church • Open 25 June, 2 – 6pm, and occasionally for individuals and parties by appt • Entrance : £2, children 50p ● & ⏀ ⌀

In this formal terraced topiary garden with Italianate features, the owners have aimed to create a poetic and contemplative atmosphere through terraces, parterres, foliage colour schemes, statuary and water features. They have also tried to make it low-maintenance and accordingly have ruled out annuals. Over one acre is planted with many unusual specimen trees and shrubs, mainly in various 'rooms' and a young three-acre arboretum has about 200 different trees.

Rousham House ★★ [Historic Park and Garden Grade I]

Nr Steeple Aston, Bicester OX25 4QX. Tel: (01869) 347110

Charles Cottrell-Dormer • 11m N of Oxford, 2m S of Steeple Aston off A4260 and B4030 • House open May to Sept, Sun and Bank Holiday Mons, 2 – 4.30pm • Garden open all year, daily, 10am – 4.30pm • Entrance: £4 • Other information: children under 15 not admitted ○ ▨ **WC** &

Here William Kent's design of 1738 is effectively frozen in time, and historical enlightenment can be combined with the enchantment of the setting and the use he made of it. In fact, before Kent it was already a famous garden, described by Alexander Pope as 'the prettiest place for water-falls, jetts, ponds, inclosed with beautiful scenes of green and hanging wood, that ever I saw'. Kent's design, influenced perhaps by stage scenery, created a series of effects. There are splendid small buildings and follies, fine sculpture, water and many seats and vantage points. The best way to view the garden is to follow these one by one, in the order he intended, and for this a guidebook is necessary. By taking the effects *seriatim*, a feeling for the whole will then gradually emerge. This was also one of the first places where the garden took in the whole estate, 'calling-in' the surrounding countryside, to use Pope's words. Walled gardens next to the house, which pre-date Kent, are a major attraction in their own right, with a parterre, a rose garden, a fully tenanted dovecote and a wonderfully productive vegetable garden; particularly attractive are the exuberant herbaceous borders spilling out over their box edging.

Shotover House [Historic Park and Garden Grade I]

Shotover Estate, Wheatley, Oxford OX33 1QS.

Lt Col Sir John Miller • 6m E of Oxford on A40 (S carriageway) • Open probably April and July for NGS, but check Oxford Times newspaper for dates • Entrance: £1.50, children free • Other information: Possible for wheelchairs but some unsurfaced paths ● ▨ ▨ **WC** & ⏀ ⌀ ▮ ♀

The landscaped park and garden were begun c. 1718, and William Kent was involved in the design in the 1730s, constructing a domed octagonal temple (now ringed by cherry trees) and, on another axis, an obelisk – he was working at nearby Rousham (see entry) from 1738. Rare cattle and sheep, including black varieties, greet visitors as they walk from the car park at the end of the drive round to the colonnaded back of the eighteenth-century house (not open). Much is being done to enliven the planting in the formal garden surrounding it and to revive the statuary. From the rear arcade the view is of a long canal ending in a Gothick folly, which can be reached by walking via the pet cemetery and interestingly decorated wooden chalet. From the west front of the house, visitors will enjoy strolling down the long avenues carved out of what was once part of the royal forest of Wychwood. Allow an hour to explore this pleasant park, but be warned that the noisome A40 is all too present.

Stansfield

49 High Street, Stanford-in-the-Vale, Faringdon SN7 8NQ. Tel: (01367) 710340

Mr and Mrs D. Keeble • 16m SW of Oxford, 3.5m SE of Faringdon. Turn off A417 opposite Vale Garage • Open 4th April, 2nd May, 6th June, 4th July, 1st Aug, 5th Sept, 10am – 4pm, and by appt; parties and evening visits welcome • Entrance: £2
● ❦ & ❧

A one-acre-plus plantsman's garden with many island beds and borders, and a large collection of plants for both damp and dry conditions. All-year round interest is provided by a wide use of foliage and seasonal flowers, starting with species spring bulbs – indeed, attention is focused on the number and variety of plants rather than the design and layout, which includes woodland, a grass border, a scree garden and a model vegetable garden. Alpines in sinks and troughs give interest on a smaller scale. Rabbit-proof fencing encloses perforce the entire property.

Stonor Park [Historic Park Grade II*]

Stonor, Henley-on-Thames RG9 6HF. Tel: (01491) 638587

Lord Camoys • 5m N of Henley-on-Thames on B480 • House open • Open 2nd April to 24th Sept, Suns and Bank Holiday Mons, plus Weds in July and Aug; all 1 – 5.30pm. Parties by arrangement Tues, Wed or Thurs (am and pm) • Entrance: £3.50 (house and gardens £6, children under 14 in family parties free). Party rates on application (2005 prices) • Other information: Lunches for parties by arrangement
◐ 🍽 WC & ♿ ♀

The long southern facade of the house masks a complex E-shaped Tudor building with twelfth-century origins. It is set in a bowl on the south side of a hill facing south to open parkland and large trees. Behind and to the side of the house on higher land, sheltered against the hill, are flower and vegetable gardens. Lawns lead up to a terrace with pools, stone urns and planting along the steps. The orchard, with its cypresses and espaliered fruit trees, and the lavender hedges are attractive features.

University of Oxford Botanic Garden ★★ [Historic Garden Grade I]

Rose Lane, Oxford OX1 4AZ. Tel: (01865) 286690

University of Oxford • In city centre opposite Magdalen College near bridge • Open all year, daily: May to Sept, 9am – 6pm (closes 5pm March, April, Sept and Oct; closes 4.30pm Jan, Feb, Nov and Dec) • Closed 25th Dec and 14th April • Entrance: £2.60, children in full-time education accompanied by a family member, free; Nov to

Feb by donation • Other information: Plants for sale March to Oct. Professional photography by arrangement ○ 🐌 <u>WC</u> ♿ 🌿 🏛 ▮ ☕

This is the oldest botanic garden in Britain, founded in 1621 for physicians' herbal requirements, surrounded by a Grade-I-listed wall and entered through a splendid archway by Nicholas Stone. Nowhere else on earth, it is claimed, are so many different plants clustered in four and a half acres: 8000 species in all, representing over 90 per cent of families of flowering plants. One yew survives from the 1650 plantings, and there is a series of family beds containing herbaceous and annual plants in systematic and labelled groups. The old walls back beds with tender plants, including roses and clematis. To the left is a collection of glasshouses, modern ones replacing those built in 1670. A rock garden has been renovated, as has the water garden and late summer/autumn borders. A National Collection of euphorbias is held here. Recently, Nori and Sandra Pope, from Hadspen in Somerset (see entry), were commissioned to make some new autumn borders, and they have planted dark and silver shrubs with spectacular autumn colour at the back of the border. The site amply justifies its original purpose 'to promote learning and glorify the works of God'. Six miles away at Nuneham Courtenay (south of the A4074) is the Harcourt Arboretum (see entry). Guided tours of both gardens are available – contact the Botanic Garden for details.

Waterperry Gardens

Wheatley, Oxford OX33 1JZ. Tel: (01844) 339226

9m E of Oxford, 2.5m N of Wheatley off M40 junction 8 from London, or 8A from Birmingham. Signposted • Open all year, daily, 9am – 5pm but closed Christmas and New Year holidays. 13th to 16th July open only to visitors to Art in Action (enquiries (020) 7381 3192) • Entrance: £4.25, OAPs £3.75, children £3 (under 10 free), coach parties of 20 or more by appt only, £3.25 per person • Other information: Art and craft gallery. Teashop and museum closed 13th to 16th July ○ 🍽 ✕ <u>WC</u> ♿ 🌿 🏛 ▮

The 20 acres of gardens are difficult to categorise. There is a strong educational atmosphere going back to the 1930s when Miss Beatrix Havergal opened up a small horticultural school, and also a commercial garden centre occupying large areas of the walled garden. The herbaceous nursery stock beds are in the ornamental gardens and form a living catalogue, with the plants grown in rows and labelled. Intermixed with this are major features of the old garden, lawns and a substantial herbaceous border – also beds containing collections of alpines, dwarf conifers and other shrubs, a rose garden and a water-lily canal. The clay bank is planted with shade-lovers. The greenhouses in the nursery are interesting; one in the old walled garden, has an enormous citrus tree which is 100 years old. A few miles east down the M40 is *Le Manoir aux Quat' Saisons*, in Church Road, Great Milton (off A329 Thame–Stadhampton road). The 12-acre garden surrounding Raymond Blanc's renowned hotel includes an impressive *potager*, a water garden, a Japanese garden, an orchard etc. It is open of course to patrons, and once a year for the NGS.

Westwell Manor ★★
Burford OX18 4JT.

Mr and Mrs T.H. Gibson • 10m W of Witney, 2m SW of Burford off A40 • Open 11th June, 2 – 6.30pm, and by written appt for horticultural parties of 20 or more (£10 per person) • Entrance: £4, children 50p • Other information: Teas available in village on open day ◐ ✕ ℘

It is worth braving the inevitable crowds on the one day a year on which this seven-acre garden is open for the sheer variety and ingenuity which Mrs Gibson, a garden designer, has achieved here since 1979. Expecting perhaps a traditional Cotswold manor garden, the visitor will find that there is much more to discover. The Tudor manor hides behind huge walls, and even through the gate, the forecourt gives no hint of what lies beyond. Each of the 20 or so garden rooms behind the house and barn leads to another, some traditional, others – a charming water garden and a black-dyed *pièce d'eau* complete with boat – surprising and original. Notable too are twin rills lined by a pleached lime *allée*, an unusual lavender terrace, a sundial garden, a moonlight garden, an alder basket, a knot garden and splendid deep herbaceous borders in muted pastels contrasting with areas of meadow and long grass. There is also a vegetable garden, a nut walk and a Bunny Walk laid along a ley line. Mown paths lead to a mount constructed from surplus earth moved during the making of a ha-ha. The garden continues to develop with flair and unrestrained enthusiasm: a miniature paddy-field with rice from the Camargue, in all its varying shades of greeny-yellow, a grass amphitheatre in the old orchard. A late-summer border with umbelliferous plants and an orchard with carefully selected old fruit tree varieties are new additions, and a mown grass spiral is the most recent project.

Wilcote House ★
Wilcote, Finstock, Chipping Norton OX7 3DY. Tel: (01993) 868606

The Hon. and Mrs Charles Cecil • 4m N of Witney, 3m S of Charlbury E off B4022 • Open by appt • Entrance: £3, children free, parties negotiable • Other information: Conducted tours for private parties on weekdays by arrangement. Teas available by prior arrangement ◐ WC ♿ ⬥

Surrounding and complementing a fine sixteenth- to nineteenth-century Cotswold stone house, the large garden is itself a period piece, with extensive beds of old-fashioned roses and mixed borders and a 40-metre laburnum walk at its best at the end of May. An unusual feature is the large wild garden intersected by grass paths, planted within the last two decades with nearly 200 varieties of trees chosen for both spring flowering and autumn colour.

Wroxton Abbey [Historic Park and Garden Grade II*]
Wroxton, Banbury OX15 6PX. Tel: (01295) 730551

Wroxton College of Fairleigh Dickinson University of New Jersey, USA • 3m W of Banbury off A422 • House open 29th May and 28th Aug, 2 – 5pm • Grounds open all year, daily, dawn – dusk, but closed for 3 weeks in Aug and late Dec to early Jan

• *Entrance: free (house £2)* • *Other information: Parking in village; vehicles not permitted in grounds* ○ &

The drive that leads up to the Jacobean house is lined with trees. Its gardens and parkland with its extensive lawns, specimen trees and woodlands, natural-looking waters and 'eye-catcher' buildings are of considerable historic interest, a good example of the early Picturesque style of gardening. The formal garden designed by Tilleman Bobart, pupil of Henry Wise, which was laid out between 1727 and 1732, was swept away. The grounds were remodelled and extended less than ten years later by Sanderson Miller for the first Earl of Guilford. Well-kept lawns flow down the valley behind to the Great Pond and Great Cascade, the serpentine river, the Chinese bridge and the Little Cascade, with a viewing mount. Miller's various buildings include a Gothick dovecot, an ice-house and a Doric temple above the formal rose garden and knot garden, with a vista to the obelisk – most of which were restored from their derelict state by the American owners in the late 1970s. There are 56 acres in all, with pleasant lakeside and woodland walks.

RESEARCHING GARDEN HISTORY

The Register of Parks and Gardens of Special Historic Interest is the official record of the nation's historic landscapes produced by English Heritage. It has been substantially revised and upgraded, parks and gardens added, and threatened landscapes 'spot-registered'. At the beginning of August 2005, the total number of entries was 1588. Each site is documented in a description of its historical evolution, accompanied by specially drawn paper maps delineating the historical boundaries of the park or garden and chronicling its development.

The *Register* is available for public consultation at English Heritage's National Monuments Record Centre in Swindon (open Tues — Fri, 9.30am — 5pm). Copies of individual entries or complete county registers can also be purchased and sent by post. For more information contact NMR Enquiry & Research Services (Tel: (01793) 414600; Fax (01793) 414606; Email: nmrinfo@english-heritage.org.uk). Additionally, each local planning authority will have a copy of the relevant descriptions and maps within their jurisdictions. Be sure to telephone in advance of a visit.

SYMBOLS

[NEW] entries new for 2006; ○ open all year; ◑ open most of year; ◐ open during main season; ◕ open rarely and/or by appt; ☕ teas/light refreshments; ✕ meals; 🧺 picnics permitted; WC toilet facilities; <u>WC</u> toilet facilities, inc. disabled; & partly wheelchair-accessible; ⬥ dogs on lead; 🌿 plants for sale; 🏠 shop; ⚑ events held; ⚘ children-friendly; B&B bed and breakfast available.

RUTLAND

For gardens in Leicestershire, see pages 215–219.

Ashwell House

Ashwell, Oakham LE15 7LW. Tel: (01572) 722833

Mr and Mrs S.D. Pettifer • 3m N of Oakham via B668 towards Cottesmore, turn left to Ashwell • Open by appt only • Entrance: £1 ● ● × wc & ☕

Next to the fourteenth-century church of St Mary's Ashwell, the spacious vicarage garden has been designed by the present owners to provide all-year colour in the shrubs and borders. Fine trees on all sides, some distant, give the impression of a park-like setting. Architectural features by George Carter enliven some shaded areas, and a classical summerhouse offers a peaceful retreat. The colour schemes achieve a successful balance of light and dark: in the front garden *Cedrus atlantica* 'Glauca', eucalyptus and white roses act as a cool foil to the copper beech and red-leaved berberis on the other side. A striking group of silver birches fans out in two arcs, surrounded by purple cut-leaf alders and 'Ispahan' and 'Blanche Double de Coubert' roses. The old walled vegetable garden, although well stocked with fruit and vegetables, has in part been taken over by the pool and millennium gardens, with an abundance of roses: an avenue of standard 'Iceberg', a fan of 'Wedding Day', and columns draped with purple 'Raubritter'.

Barnsdale Gardens

The Avenue, Exton, Oakham LE15 8AH. Tel: (01572) 813200

Nick and Sue Hamilton • 3m NE of Oakham off A606 • Open March to Oct, daily, 9am – 5pm (closes 7pm June to Aug), Nov to Feb, daily, 10am – 4pm (last admission 2 hours before closing). Parties by appt • Entrance: £6, OAPs £5, children £2, family £15 • Other information: Pre-booked wheelchairs available on free loan ● ● × wc & ☕ ⛪ ♿ ♨

Here are the show gardens immortalised by the late Geoff Hamilton on *Gardeners' World*, and now run by his son and daughter-in-law. They are impressive in their range and variety. Themes include town and country paradises, modern estate, cottage, allotment and ornamental kitchen gardens, woodland, stream, bog and parterre – all excellent aids to planning or redesigning green spaces. The adjoining nursery sells a wide range of plants propagated from the gardens.

The Court House

Geeston, Ketton, Stamford PE9 3RH. Tel: (01780) 720770

Mr and Mrs Bas Clarke • 5m W of Stamford • Open by appt • Entrance: £1.50 ● ● ⛲ wc & ☕

The attractive stone house, built in 1996 in seventeenth-century style by the present owner (a builder in stone who has now retired to breed ducks), faces south with views down an attractive valley to the river. The terrace garden immediately behind the house, designed by Bunny Guinness to reinforce the Elizabethan impression, has herbs massed around a circular pool shaded by four quince trees, and immaculate squares of lawn defining the space. Below this a wild meadow leads down to the river through a copse well planted with rhododendrons and sheltering cleverly placed follies. The way back leads past a small walled vegetable garden and a green-house which looks genuinely Victorian but of course is no such thing. A charming garden and an enjoyable experience for all ages.

Lyddington Bede House

Blue Coat Lane, Lyddington LE15 9LZ. Tel: (01572) 822438

English Heritage • In Lyddington, 7m S of Oakham, 1m E of A6003 • Open April to Oct, Thurs – Mon, 10am – 5pm • Entrance: £3.30, concessions £2.50, children £1.70, family £8.30 (2005 prices) • Other information: Parking off road 20 metres from entrance via cobbled alley ❶ 🏷 ♿ ⬗ 🏛 ❗ ☕

Originally a medieval palace of the Bishops of Lincoln, the house retains many of its original features; it was later converted into an almshouse. It is set in small gardens among picturesque golden stone cottages and beside the handsome parish church of St Andrew. Situated in a sunny corner at the entrance and backed by walls, the herb garden forms an L-shape and includes culinary and medicinal herbs of the period. Beds are edged with low box hedging.

The Old Hall

Market Overton, Oakham LE15 7PL. Tel: (01572) 767276

Mr and Mrs T. Hart • 6m NE of Oakham, 2m N of Cottesmore off B668 • Open one day for NGS, 2 – 6pm, otherwise by appt only • Entrance: £2.50, children 50p ● WC ♿

Five acres of softly agreeable grounds. Carefully coloured borders lead from a sunken lawn which falls away gently to distant vistas; the formal enclosed swimming pool in the walled kitchen garden has views through ornamental gates and avenues of mature trees. Two large borders, designed by Neil Hewertson, have been planted on the old tennis court lawns against the stone walls. The long borders are divided by yew buttresses and have wide steps in the centre coming down from the cro-quet lawn terrace. There are many interesting focal points, including a raised pond with enchanting tiny frog sculptures that spout from lily leaves into the jaws of a lion mask. The pleached lime screen now coming into its own is elegant and well placed. The whole is at one with its beautiful surroundings of Rutland stone and rolling land-scape. Spring and autumn are the best times to book a visit.

The Old Rectory

Teigh, Oakham LE15 7RT. Tel: (01572) 787681

Mrs D.B. Owen • 5m N of Oakham between Wymondham and Ashwell • Open by appt in April, June and July. Parties welcome • Entrance: £1 • Other information: Teas by arrangement ● 🅿 🏷 WC ♿ B&B

This delightful, partially walled 0.75-acre garden, first laid out in the 1950s, has been evolving and improving for the past thirty years. The swimming-pool garden and some of the beds have been replanted recently in gentle and soothing colour schemes, using traditional favourites like poppies and campanulas, deutzias and philadelphus, hostas in variety, and the small-flowered rambler rose 'Phyllis Bide'. Much successful thought is given to colour and the juxtaposition of plants; roses are used cleverly to connect the shapes and contrasting foliage of surrounding plants. Peonies and geraniums make a fine display, and a whole bed near the house is devoted to *Alstroemeria ligtu* hybrids. Fine trees and climbing plants abound, complementing the mellow stone walls of the eighteenth-century rectory. Although the show of bulbs and blossom makes spring a good time to visit, the garden is at its peak from is mid-June to early July. The beautiful Strawberry Hill Gothick church next door is also well worth a visit.

SYMBOLS

NEW entries new for 2006; ○ open all year; ◑ open most of year; ◑ open during main season; ● open rarely and/or by appt; ⚍ teas/light refreshments; ✕ meals; 🧺 picnics permitted; WC toilet facilities; __WC__ toilet facilities, inc. disabled; ⚐ partly wheelchair-accessible; ⚑ dogs on lead; 🌿 plants for sale; 🏪 shop; ⚐ events held; ⚘ children-friendly; B&B bed and breakfast available.

GARDEN AND FLOWER SHOWS 2006

*   11th to 14th May: Spring Gardening Show, Malvern
    (Three Counties Showground, Malvern, Worcestershire)
    Ticket hotline: (01684) 584924; www.threecounties.co.uk
*   23rd to 27th May: Chelsea Flower Show
    (Royal Hospital, Chelsea, London SW3)
*   6th to 8th June: Wisley Show
    (RHS Garden, Wisley, Woking, Surrey)
*   Mid-June: BBC *Gardeners' World* Live
    (National Exhibition Centre, Birmingham)
    Ticket hotline: (0870) 902 0555; www.necgroup.co.uk
*   16th to 18th June: Three Counties Show, Malvern
    Ticket hotline: (01684) 584924
*   4th to 9th July: Hampton Court Flower Show
    (Hampton Court Palace, East Molesey, Surrey)
*   26th to 30th July: (probable date) RHS Flower Show, Tatton Park
    (Tatton Park, near Knutsford, Cheshire)
*   22nd to 24th Aug: Wisley Show
*   23rd and 24th Sept: Autumn Garden & Country Show, Malvern
    Ticket hotline: (01684) 584924

Unless otherwise given, for details of all these shows telephone the Royal Horticultural Society on (020) 7834 4333 or consult www.rhs.org.uk.

SHROPSHIRE

Two-starred gardens are marked on the map with a black square.

Attingham Park [Historic Park Grade II*]
Attingham, Shrewsbury SY4 4TP. Tel: (01743) 708162

The National Trust • 4m SE of Shrewsbury. Turn off B4380 at Atcham • House open 4th to 19th March, Sat and Sun; 25th March to 30th Oct, Mon, Tues, Fri – Sun; all 1 – 5pm • Deer park and grounds open all year, daily (except 25th Dec), 10am – 8pm (closes 5pm Nov to Feb). Snowdrop weekends 4th and 5th, 11th and 12th, 18th and 19th Feb • Entrance: £3.30, children £1.65, family £8.20 (house and grounds £5,80, children £2.90, family £14). Party and out-of-hours rates available (2005 prices) • Other information. Two self-drive electric scooters available

○ ⬤ 🏠 wc ♿ ⟟ 🌳 🏛 🍴 ♺

This is a landscape mainly of large trees and shrubs, including a magnificent grove of Lebanon cedars, as the setting for a grand neo-classical pile. A mile-long ambulatory walk created by the River Tern in the eighteenth century is enlivened by daffodils in spring followed by azaleas and rhododendrons; autumn colour is provided by dogwoods and American thorns. A longer walk through the deer park affords fine views of the house and the restored Repton landscape. The Trust has bravely and rightly removed the formal 1920 garden in front of the house and returned it to Reptonian grass. The eighteenth-century orangery has also been restored.

Benthall Hall
Broseley TF12 5RX. Tel: (01952) 882159

The National Trust • 4.5m S of Telford, 1m SW of Broseley off B4375 • Part of house open same times as garden • Garden open April to June, Tues, Wed and Bank Holiday Suns and Mons; July to Sept, Sun, Tues, Wed and Bank Holiday Mon; all 1.30 – 5.30pm. Coaches and parties by arrangement only • Entrance: £2.50 (house and gardens £4, children £2) • Other information: Parking 150 metres down road

◑ wc ♿ ♺

A small garden containing interesting plants and features, including topiary. George Maw and Robert Bateman both lived in the house and contributed to the garden design and plant collection. The rose garden has fine plants and a small pool and there is a delightful raised scree bed. A good collection of geraniums and ground-cover plants, together with a peony bed, and clematis and roses growing through trees and shrubs, create a pleasant place for a stroll. The old kitchen garden now contains a collection of crab apples, roses, wall plants, etc. In spring daffodils and the crocus introduced by George Maw provide interest, and the large specimens of Scots pine, beech and chestnut are stunning features. A monument to botanical history.

Brownhill House

Ruyton XI Towns, Shrewsbury SY4 1LR. Tel: (01939) 261121

*Roger and Yoland Brown • 10m NW of Shrewsbury on B4397 • Open May to Aug
by appt, and several times in summer for NGS, 1.30 – 5pm • Entrance: £3, children
free • Other information: Parking at Bridge Inn 100 metres away* ☕ 🍽 WC ⚘ ♨ B&B

Out of an impossible north-facing cliff a most unusual and distinctive garden of great
variety has been created since 1972. The slope has been transformed from a scrap-
covered wilderness into a series of terraces and small gardens connected by over
600 steps that wander up and down the hill through plantings of trees and shrubs,
patches of wild flowers and open flower-filled spaces. At the bottom a riverside garden runs from an open lawn to a bog garden. A series of formal terraces includes a
laburnum walk, and at the top there are paved areas with a pool, gazebo, parterre,
a long walk with herbaceous border, flower beds and a large kitchen garden with
glasshouses. Also incorporated into the design are a folly, a Thai spirit house, a grotto, a summerhouse, a large Arabic arch, a cascade and a unique design of Menorah.
Developments are continuing on the extensive terracing on which grow many of the
collection of over 100 varieties of hedera, and a Japanese 'dry' garden has replaced
the rockery. This is a garden that has to be seen to be believed, and fun for children,
who can tax their brains with a challenging quiz. A few miles away, just west of the
A5 at Kinnerley, is *Hall Farm Nursery*, which has an award-winning selection of herbaceous perennials.

Cruckfield House

Shoot Hill, Ford, Shrewsbury SY5 9NR. Tel: (01743) 850222

*Mr and Mrs G.M. Cobley • 5m W of Shrewsbury off A458. Turn left signed to Shoot
Hill • Open one Fri in June and July, and for parties of 25 or more by appt • Entrance:
£4, children £1* ☕ 🍽 WC ♿ ♨

Sheltered and surrounded by mature trees, the romantic and tranquil four-acre garden, managed organically for many years, is designed in traditionally English formal
style with an abundance of roses and peonies as part of the attraction. There are
exuberant plantings of shrubs and herbaceous plants, many of them rare or unusual. Specimen trees set in wildflower grassland and a pretty bog area surround a large
pond. The ornamental kitchen garden is set off by attractive outbuildings and an
adjoining courtyard garden.

David Austin Roses

Bowling Green Lane, Albrighton, Wolverhampton WV7 3HB. Tel: (01902) 376334

*Mr and Mrs David Austin • 8m W of Wolverhampton between A41 and A464. Take
junction 3 off M54 towards Albrighton. In High Street, take second turning on left
after Shrewsbury Arms pub. Follow brown tourist signs • Open all year, daily, 9am –
5pm. Closed 25th Dec to 1st Jan • Entrance: free* ○ 🍽 ✕ WC ♿ ⟁ ♨ 🏛

David Austin is one of the country's leading rose breeders, so this is an ideal place
for inspecting them *en masse*. There are about 900 varieties, including shrub, climbing, species and old roses. The famous plant centre sells not only one of the largest

collections of container roses in the country, but also an extensive range of herbaceous perennials, trees and shrubs.

Dorothy Clive Garden

(see Staffordshire)

The Dower House

Morville Hall, Morville, Bridgnorth WV16 5NB. Tel: (01746) 714407

The National Trust • 3m NW of Bridgnorth at A458/B4368 junction, within Morville Hall grounds • Open 2nd April to 27th Sept, Wed, Sun and Bank Holiday Mons, 2 – 6pm; 11th June, 2 – 5pm, with other local gardens for NGS; and at other times, inc. evenings, for parties by appt • Entrance: £3, children (under 16) 50p • Other information: Parking in churchyard ❶ 🍽 ⟁ ⬥ ℺

Starting in 1989, the present tenant Katherine Swift, a well-known gardening writer, has transformed a one-and-a-half-acre site within the grounds of Morville Hall, with the aim of relating the history of English gardens in a sequence of separate features: a turf maze, a medieval cloister garden, a knot garden, a seventeenth-century plat and flower beds, a William and Mary canal garden with formal water feature and box-edged *plates-bandes*, an eighteenth-century flower garden, a Victorian rose border, a nineteenth-century wilderness and, finally, an ornamental fruit and vegetable garden. Particular attention is given to the use of authentic plants and construction techniques; old varieties of tulips, irises and roses are a speciality.

Dudmaston [Historic Park and Garden Grade II]

Quatt, Bridgnorth WV15 6QN. Tel: (01746) 780866

The National Trust • 4m SE of Bridgnorth on A442 • House open • Garden open 2nd April to 27th Sept, Sun – Wed, 12 noon – 6pm (last admission 5pm). Special openings for pre-booked parties only, Mons. Estate open free of charge for pedestrian access all year • Entrance: £4, children £2, family £9, parties of 15 ore more £3 per person (house and garden £5, children £2.50, family £12.50, parties £4) • Other information: Batricar available. Dogs in Dingle only, on lead ❶ 🍽 🏠 wc ⟁ 🌿 ⊞ 🍴 ℺

To garden historians, Dudmaston is a shrine. Its valley wilderness is the best surviving exemplar of William Shenstone's gardening philosophy of the Picturesque – 'pleasing the imagination by scenes of grandeur, beauty or variety'. The Dingle is a romantic creation of the late eighteenth century by one of Shenstone's former gardeners, working directly with the owners, the Whitmores of Dudmaston. The William and Mary house sits on the other side of the park, in a landscape of woods, hills and water. The terraces which connect the hall to the Big Pool – actually the largest of a series of lakes – were made in 1816; they anticipated the creation of more formal gardens here. Today eight acres of garden in proximity to the house include a large pool and bog garden, island beds filled with shrubs, azaleas, rhododendrons, viburnums and fine old roses. Large specimen trees, old fruit trees and mature shrubs lend an established feel. The rock garden has been restored and the Big Pool is now framed by attractive plantings. There are two estate walks.

Gate Cottage

English Frankton, Ellesmere SY12 0JU. Tel: (01939) 270606

G.W. Nicholson and Kevin Gunnell • 10m N of Shrewsbury on A528. At Cockshutt take road to English Frankton; garden is 1m on right • Open for NGS 14th May and 18th June, 1 – 5pm, and for parties by appt • Entrance: £2.50, children 50p • Other information: Teas on charity open days only ◐ ⍩ ⌑ ✈

This garden is changing and developing all the time to accommodate a vast range of plants. Roses and clematis scramble through old fruit trees, and there are many other fine roses along the exterior fence and in the herbaceous borders. Aquatic interest comes from pools and a bog garden with primulas. In the extended area shrubs have been planted for colour effect. Large pebbles create attractive features, and there are unusual brown and black foliage plants and some interesting grasses. The rock and gravel plantings now include an area of hardy carnivorous plants.

Hawkstone Park [Historic Park Grade I]

Weston-under-Redcastle, Shrewsbury SY4 5UY. Tel: (01939) 200611

The Redemptionists • 13m NE of Shrewsbury via A49, 6m SW of Market Drayton on A442 Telford – Whitchurch road. Entrance on road from Hodnet to Weston-under-Redcastle. Signed from Hodnet • Open Jan to March, Sat and Sun, 10am – 3pm; April and May, Wed – Sun, 10am – 4pm; June to Sept, daily, 10am – 4pm; Oct, Wed – Sat, 10am – 3.30pm. Closed Nov, but open for Christmas events in Dec by appt • Entrance: £5.75, concessions £4.75, children £3.75, family £17 (2005 peak prices). Reduced rates for pre-booked parties ◐ ⍩ ▧ WC ⌑ ▥ ▯ ⌁ B&B

In its day Hawkstone was as famous as Stowe and Stourhead, and the grounds have now been returned to their eighteenth-century grandeur and sublimity (the latter was supposed to induce awe if not fear). A series of monuments, now reconstructed, is linked by winding paths and tunnels. Ascending towards the White Tower, the visitor passes the thatched buildings, in one of which was a mechanical hermit famous for his artificial cough (now replaced by a hologram), then a grotto and the so-called Swiss bridge (a fallen tree across a gorge). Much remains to be done to the Red Castle, which is genuinely medieval. The whole thing is a triumph for all involved, including English Heritage. A walk through the park is approximately three and a half miles, but visitors should be warned that it involves climbing and descending many steps.

Hodnet Hall ★★ [Historic Park Grade II]

Hodnet, Market Drayton TF9 3NN. Tel: (01630) 685786

Mr A.E.H. and The Hon. Mrs Heber-Percy • 12m NE of Shrewsbury, 5.5m SW of Market Drayton, at A53/A442 junction • Open April to Sept, Tues – Sun and Bank Holiday Mons, 12 noon – 5pm • Entrance: £4, OAPs £3.50, children £2 ◐ ⍩ ▧ WC ⌖ ⌑ ✈ ▥ ⌁

The 60-acre parkland offers a constant succession of interest, although the greatest effect comes in autumn when the acers, sorbus and birches present their display. The grounds are grouped around a series of lakes and water gardens, home to black swans. This is essentially splendid large-scale parkland planting: magnolias, azaleas, rhododendrons in late spring are followed in summer by fuchsias, astilbes and gunneras, matched with water lilies on the lakes. For the herbaceous gardener there are shrub roses, tree peonies and the more traditional border plants. The working walled kitchen garden is well maintained, and there are also displays of flowers and pot plants grown especially for use in the hall, together with many varieties of fruit and vegetables.

Limeburners

Lincoln Hill, Ironbridge, Telford TF8 7NX. Tel: (01952) 433715

Mr and Mrs J.E. Derry • 4m SW of Telford. Turn off B4380 W of Ironbridge at traffic island. Take Church Hill for 0.5m; garden is on left below Beeches Hospital • Open April to Sept by appt • Entrance: £2.50, children free ● WC &

The garden was started in 1970 with the then not-so-fashionable vision of planting for wildlife. Now the mature garden continues to act as a haven for butterflies and birds with its collection of buddleias, nectar-rich flowers and native trees and shrubs of holly, broom, blackthorn, alder and dogwood. Shrub roses abound. The central pool (which looks natural but is man-made) features a waterfall with a stream splashing in.

Lower Hall ★

Worfield, Bridgnorth WV15 5LH. Tel: (01746) 716607

Mr and Mrs C.F. Dumbell • 4m NE of Bridgnorth. Take A454 Wolverhampton/ Bridgnorth road, turn right to Worfield and after village stores and pub turn right • Open 24th and 25th June, 2 – 6pm, and May to July for parties by appt • Entrance: £3.50, children under 12 free • Other information: Access for large coaches nearby. Garden room available for parties of 20 – 40 for pre-booked refreshments ● ⬤ 🏠 WC & ⬠

This modern four-acre plantsman's garden has been developed by the present owners since 1964, helped originally by Lanning Roper. The courtyard and its fountain are featured in many design books. The walled garden has a magnificent display of roses, clematis and irises in season. Everywhere the use of colour combinations and plant associations is good – a red border, another of white and green giving a cool effect. Roses abound. The water garden is separated from the woodland garden by the River Worfe with two bridges and two weirs. A deck built over the pool exploits the view across to the colourful primula island. The woodland garden includes rare magnolias, a collection of birches with bark interest, acers, cornus, azaleas and amelanchiers – all-year variety and colour.

Millichope Park [Historic Park Grade II*]

Munslow, Craven Arms SY7 9HA. Tel: (01584) 841234

Mr and Mrs L. Bury • 8m NE of Craven Arms, 11m N of Ludlow on B4368 • Open for NGS, and by appt • Entrance: £3, children 50p • Other information: Teas on Bank Holidays only. Picnics in woodland only ● WC ⬠

The glory of Millichope is its magnificent landscaping, commissioned in the 1760s by a father seeking a fitting memorial to his four sons, all of whom had predeceased him. The main memorial was an elegant Ionic temple now dramatically sited away from the house across a lake. The present owners have commissioned a fine Chinese-style bridge across one of the gorges, and Mrs Bury has added a set of herbaceous borders disposed in elegant 'rooms' framed by yew hedges. Away from Georgian classicism, romantic wilderness plantings of roses and philadelphus combine to make this a most beautiful park and garden; below the lake the grass has been managed as a flower-rich haymeadow.

Oteley

Ellesmere SY12 0PB. Tel: (01691) 622514

Mr and Mrs R.K. Mainwaring • 8m NE of Oswestry, 1m E of Ellesmere near A528/495 junction. From N past the Mere turn left opposite convent • Open 1st and 29th May, 2 – 6pm, and for parties of 10 or more by appt • Entrance: £3, children 50p • Other information: Possible for wheelchairs if dry ● 💺 WC ⟳ ⚘

The magnificent 10-acre garden, set in park and farmland with glimpses of the Mere beyond surrounding trees, has extensive lawns with architectural features, interesting and old handsome trees set about the lawns, a grey/silver border, decorative island beds, rhododendrons, azaleas, roses and shrubs in a gracious setting, with a collection of peonies flowering simultaneously. Herbaceous borders are backed by high walls covered with roses, clematis and other climbing plants, and a folly and a walled kitchen garden provide the finishing touches. All this plus a superlative plant stall.

The Patch

Acton Pigot, Acton Burnell, Shrewsbury SY5 7PH. Tel: (01743) 362139

Mrs Margaret Owen • 8m SE of Shrewsbury between A49 and A458. From Acton Burnell take Cressage Road. After 0.5m turn left signed to Acton Pigott • Open 26th Feb for snowdrops, 11am – 3pm, 16th April, 2 – 5pm, for camassias in May by appt (coaches welcome), 7th June, 19th July, 2 – 6pm, 24th Sept, 2 – 5pm, and for parties by appt at other times • Entrance: £2.50, children free ● 💺 WC ⟳ ⚘

Do not be deceived by this one-acre garden – allow time. It is filled with beauties, starting in spring with snowdrops, hellebores, erythroniums, dicentras, trilliums and violas. On into summer go *Paeonia mlokosewitschii* and *P. daurica*, roses and epimediums. National Collections of camassias, dictamnus and veratrums are held here, and other specialities include nerines and schizostylis. The garden is bordered by a broad grassy path, and at its centre lies a white garden. It is graced with tree rarities such as *Eucalyptus pauciflora* spp. *debeuzevillei*, *Styrax obassia*, *Toona sinensis*, *Sorbus aria* 'Chrysophylla' and *Malus coronaria* 'Charlottae'.

Preen Manor

Church Preen, Church Stretton SY6 7LQ. Tel: (01694) 771207

Mrs A. Trevor-Jones • 5m W of Much Wenlock on B4371. After 3m turn right for Church Preen and Hughley; after 1.5m turn left for Church Preen, over crossroads.

Drive is 0.5m on right • Open several dates in summer and autumn for NGS, and by arrangement for parties of 15 or more in June and July • Entrance: £3.50, children 50p ● ● ● ● WC ♨

The grounds are blessed with a beautiful south-east aspect facing Wenlock Edge. Despite the attractions of the more formal part of the gardens, it is the wooded landscaped walks beside the pools and natural stream that are the most outstanding feature. Rodgersias, *Primula japonica*, *Rhododendron ponticum* hybrids and magnificent yews and cedars create a noble setting on the banks which fall away from the former manor house. The formal gardens are akin to a pretty cottage garden, with roses, deutzias and violas planted to good effect. Other gardens, including a chess garden, pebble garden and gazebo complete with parrot and cat, demonstrate an esoteric style of gardening which may appeal to some. East of Preen are *Wenlock Abbey* [Historic Park Grade II] and the ruined *Wenlock Priory* with imaginative topiary.

Radnor Cottage

Clunton, Craven Arms SY7 0JA. Tel: (01588) 640451

Mr and Mrs David Pittwood • 12m W of Ludlow, 8m W of Craven Arms. 1m E of Clun on B4368 between Clun and Clunton • Open 21st March, 18th April, 13th June, 2 – 6pm, and for parties by appt • Entrance: £2.50, children 50p ● ● ♨

Overlooking the Clun valley in A.E. Housman's Marcher countryside, the two-acre garden has been continually developing since it was taken on in the 1980s by its present enthusiastic owners. Set on a south-facing slope, it embraces the surrounding countryside by means of drystone walling, a wildflower meadow with snakeshead fritillaries and the old cottage-garden pheasant's eye narcissi. The wide range of garden habitats includes sunny terracing and paving, alpine troughs, and damp shade lightened by golden foliage. There is a pond, a stream, and a small arboretum with native sorbus; roses are of the old-fashioned variety such as *Rosa mundi*.

Ruthall Manor

Ruthall Road, Ditton Priors, Bridgnorth WV16 6TN. Tel: (01746) 712608

Mr and Mrs G.T. Clarke • 7m SW of Bridgnorth. Ruthall Road signed near garage; garden is 0.75m further on • Open by appt and for parties • Entrance: £2.50 ● WC ♿ ♨

Set below the heights of Abdon Burf, the one-acre garden, designed for ease of maintenance, is now coming to maturity. It offers a mixture of settings – from a delightful old pond planted to great natural effect and at its peak in June and July, to more formal plantings near the house, a woodland area and a vegetable garden – and a variety of well-sited trees and shrubs combined with climbers and perennials. A gravelled area beyond the lawn stretching out from the house will be given over to an increasing collection of modern sculpture.

Swallow Hayes ★

Rectory Road, Albrighton, Wolverhampton WV7 3EP. Tel: (01902) 372624

Mrs Michael Edwards • 9m SE of Telford, 7m NW of Wolverhampton. Turn off M54 at junction 3, then off A41 into Rectory Road after garden centre • Open 15th Jan (for National Collection of witch hazels), 11am – 4pm, 30th May, 2 – 5pm, and several days in spring by appt – telephone for details • Entrance: £3 (on open days), parties £3.50 per person (incl. tea and biscuits), children 10p • Other information: Teas on open days only ● 🍽 🏠 WC ♿ ⟁ ℗ ℺

A delightful two-acre modern garden with many design features, colour and foliage contrasts, and a beautiful display of plants, shrubs and trees. Although easy maintenance is an object, it contains nearly 3000 different types of plants (most of them are labelled), and gives year-round interest. The Mediterranean wall has tender plants, and elsewhere small pools, ferns and a woodland area provide contrast. National Collections of witch hazels and lupins are here, plus an interesting area of small gardens to copy at home, vegetables and fruit trees, nursery stock beds and a hardy geranium trial of over 100 labelled hardy varieties.

Walcot Hall [Historic Park Grade II]

Lydbury North SY7 8AZ. Tel: (01588) 680570

Mr C.R.W. Parish • 7m NW of Craven Arms, 3m S of Bishop's Castle, off B4385. Turn left by Powis Arms in Lydbury North • House open for parties by appt • Garden open May to Oct, Fri – Mon, 12 noon – 4.30pm; also house and garden open for charity 28th and 29th May, 1.30 – 5.30pm • Entrance: £3, children free; house on charity days £1 extra ◑ 🍽 🏠 WC ♿ ⟁ 🍴

The handsome red-brick eighteenth-century house was remodelled by Sir William Chambers for the 1st Lord Clive of India. Don't miss the courtyard stabling. Its beautiful landscape setting enhances the arboretum planted by his son. Rhododendrons and azaleas sweep down to pools and are set amid many fine specimen trees and the lake and pools display the fine collection to advantage, enhanced by the lovely vision of Chambers' clock towers among the rolling borderland hills.

Weston Park ★ [Historic Park Grade II*]

Weston–under–Lizard, Shifnal TF11 8LE. Tel: (01952) 852100

Weston Park Enterprises • 6m E of Telford on A5, 7m W of M6 junction 12, 3m N of M54 junction 3 • House open as garden • Garden open April to Sept (enquire for days, times and events list) • Entrance: park and gardens £3.50, OAPs £3, children £2.50, family £11 (house, park and gardens £6.50, OAPs £5.50, children £4.50, family £16) ◑ 🍽 ✗ 🏠 WC ⟁ 🎠 🍴 ℺

A handsome seventeenth-century house with a distinctive 'Capability' Brown park as its setting. There are almost 1000 acres of delightful woodland planted with spring bulbs, bluebells, rhododendrons and azaleas, together with beautiful pools; magnificent trees form a handsome backcloth to the many shrubs. A rose walk leads to the deer park, and the rose garden by the house and the Italian parterre garden have been restored. The architectural features in the park – Temple of Diana, Roman bridge and orangery – were all designed by James Paine. Children will enjoy the adventure playground, the Weston Park Railway and the new maze in the walled garden.

Wollerton Old Hall ★★

Wollerton, Hodnet, Market Drayton TF9 3NA. Tel: (01630) 685760 (Daytime)

John and Lesley Jenkins • 12m NE of Shrewsbury off A53. Brown-signed off A53 between Hodnet and Tern Hill • Open 14th April to Sept, Fri, Sun and Bank Holiday Mons, 12 noon – 5pm • Entrance: £4, children £1 ● 💮 ✕ <u>WC</u> ♿ ⌖ ♥

In design and layout this is a garden in the classic English mode. Within a little over three acres is a series of beautifully planted rooms, each distinct in character yet very much part of the whole. This effect is achieved through the careful positioning of a number of principal and secondary axes upon which the overall plan of the garden depends. The framework, seemingly a constant, has on occasion had to change. A wonderful new planting of yews replaced the former box-edged compartments (struck by the dreaded fungal disease), creating an all-embracing, deeply green atmosphere. Within the different garden rooms, contrasts are much in evidence. Fiery borders in the hot garden, stunning in August, are tempered with cool whites in a scented garden; openness, in the form of a broad expanse of lawn, contrasts with the intimacy of a pergola dripping with roses and clematis. But this garden is not just about plantsmanship and design. It is charged with atmosphere, enhanced by a number of most appealing structures; in recalling the Arts and Crafts Movement of the early years of the last century, it is redolent of many fashionable ones of the present.

THE HERITAGE BULB CLUB

This is both a commercial venture and a conservation-minded horticultural service, based at Tullynally (see entry in Ireland). The club has over 500 members, who receive a year's worth of bulbs, chosen so that a different variety is in flower each month. The choice is between the Heritage Collection and the Plantsman Collection. The stories surrounding the discovery of these bulbs or the uses put to them are written up, as are growing requirements, with the help of renowned bulb expert Martyn Rix. Membership fees range from £45 to £110 p.a., and a sample box is also available for £25. The club aims to kindle interest and spread knowledge, with visits to gardens here and abroad, expeditions to see wild species in flower (Turkey in 2006) and the opportunity to buy normally unobtainable bulbs and exchange seeds. A wholesale list of bulbs for naturalising and a heritage vegetable seed list are also available. Enquiries to Heritage, Tullynally Castle, Castlepollard, Co. Westmeath, Ireland. Tel: 0845 300 4257 (UK), 044 62744 (Ireland); info@heritagebulbs.com; www.heritagebulbs.com.

SOMERSET

Two-starred gardens are marked on the map with a black square.

Ammerdown House [Historic Garden Grade II*]

Radstock, Bath BA3 5SH.

The Hon. Andrew Jolliffe • 10m S of Bath, 0.5m off A362 Radstock – Frome road on B3139 • Open for charity 17th April, 1st and 29th May, 28th Aug, 11am – 5pm, and to parties by appt at other times • Entrance: £3, children free • Other information: Pre-booked catering for parties at Ammerdown Centre. Tel: (01761) 433709 ● ● WC ঠ ⇗ ৩

The Bath-stone house was designed by James Wyatt, with panoramic views on one side and a garden on the other; the garden was a brilliant conception by Lutyens, who wanted to link the house with the orangery. Walking through the Italianate 'rooms' of yew and sculpture and parterre, one is unaware of the tricks of space that are being played. Massive yew planting, now mature and nearly four metres high, creates enclosed formal areas which lead irresistibly one from another – the spaces between being almost entirely filled with hedging. The originality and grandeur remain, as do some clever details such as the clipped Portugal laurels, honeysuckles trained over wire umbrellas, and ancient lemon verbenas in pots in the orangery and on terraces. Daffodils, narcissi and cowslips are spring features; fountains and statues add architectural interest at all seasons.

Barford Park ★

Spaxton, Bridgwater TA5 1AG. Tel: (01278) 671269

Mr and Mrs M. Stancomb • 5m W of Bridgwater. From Bridgwater – Spaxton road, turn to Enmore • Open May to Sept, by appt only • Entrance: £4, children free ● ● WC ঠ ⇗

A garden in the eighteenth-century style developed since the early 1970s, set in parkland and protected by a ha-ha on three sides. After watching the golden orfe darting around the lily pond, stroll down a sweep of lawn to a stand of tall trees. In spring the woodland glade is a carpet of many shades of primulas. The eighteenth-century walled garden unusually is sited in view of the house – a lawn with deep herbaceous borders on each side makes a colourful vista.

Barrington Court Garden [Historic Garden Grade II*]

Barrington, Ilminster TA19 0NQ. Tel: (01460) 241938

The National Trust • 5m NE of Ilminster, on B3168 in Barrington • Open March and Oct, Thurs – Sun, 11am – 4.30pm; April to Sept, Thurs – Tues, 11am – 5.30pm • Entrance: £6, children £3, family £14.50 (2005 prices) • Other information: Self-drive buggy and wheelchairs available, booking essential, telephone (01460) 242614 ① ● ✕ ● WC ঠ ৩ ⌂ ৠ

In 1917, at the end of her career, Gertrude Jekyll planned the planting for the Lyle family, and planting schemes today are based on her original ideas. Set in a park with avenues of mature chestnut trees, the gardens are in the Hidcote style of separate 'rooms'. The lily garden has a central pool with surrounding beds of annuals and perennials planted with a 'hot' theme of oranges, reds and yellows. The white-flowering and silver-leaved plants are seen in the White Garden à la Sissinghurst, though this is a Lyle, not a Jekyll, scheme. This was originally part of a farm, and the early-nineteenth-century cattle sheds and troughs are part of the appeal. Beyond, a pergola supports clematis, wisteria and honeysuckles in profusion. The vast walled kitchen garden produces a wide variety of fruit and vegetables, and further afield a cider orchard provides raw material for liquid refreshment.

Bath City Gardens

The City of Bath has two interesting gardens which are well worth a visit. At the *William Herschel Museum* in New King Street, historical research has resulted in the re-creation of a charming town garden with a curious arbour and plants that might have existed in the great astronomer's time. [Open 1st Feb to 15th Dec, daily except Wed, 1 – 5pm (11am – 5pm at weekends).] On Lansdown Hill the Grade-II burial ground adjacent to *Beckford's Tower* is planted with shrubs as used by the writer, collector and aesthete in his extensive garden. The Greek Revival building of 1827 was designed for him by Goodridge as a retreat. The graveyard offers a splendid panorama. [Open Easter to Oct, Sat, Suns and Bank Holiday Mons, 10.30am – 5pm.]

Cannington College Gardens

Cannington, Bridgwater TA5 2LS. Tel: (01278) 655000

Cannington College • 3m NW of Bridgwater on A39 • Open April to Oct, daily, 9am – 5pm, and for parties by appt • Entrance: £2, OAPs and children (5–16) £1 (2005 prices) • Other information: Teas for parties by arrangement. Guide dogs only ◑ 🍴 <u>WC</u> ♿

The 2.5-acre gardens, enclosed within a medieval priory wall surrounding the fifteenth-century Cannington Court, contain one of the largest collections of rare and unusual plants in the South-West, including National Collections of abutilons, argyranthemums, osteospermums and wisterias. The gardens are planted individually on various botanical themes, among them an Australasian garden and the Bishop's Garden, featuring plants from the eastern Mediterranean.

City of Bath Botanical Gardens

Royal Victoria Park, Upper Bristol Road, Bath BA1 2NQ.

City of Bath • In Royal Victoria Park • Open all year, daily, 8.30am – dusk • Entrance: free • Other information: Toilet facilities in park ○ ♿ 🌀 ⬥ 🍴 ♦

The gardens were formed in 1887 to house a collection of plants assembled over a lifetime by Mr C.E. Broome of Batheaston, an enthusiastic amateur botanist and plant collector. It has become one of the finest collections, certainly in the West Country, of plants on limestone. To mark the centenary in 1987, the gardens were extended to take in the adjacent Great Dell, and the herbaceous border was replanted in 1990. Improvements to the plant collections and educational aspects are ongoing thanks to a grant from the Heritage Lottery Fund, and developments are also afoot in the park.

Claverton Manor [Historic Garden Grade II]

Claverton, Bath BA2 7BD. Tel: (01225) 460503

The American Museum • 2m SE of Bath off A36, signed to American Museum • Garden open late-March to Oct, daily except Mon, 12 – 6pm. Pre-booked private garden tours by arrangement • Entrance: grounds and galleries: £4, children £2.50. House, grounds and galleries: £6.50, OAPs £6, children £4 (2005 prices). Garden tours by arrangement ❶ 💻 ✕ 🍴 <u>WC</u> 🔄 🌶 🏛 🍴 ℗

The house, designed by Jeffry Wyatville, and garden are set on the side of the valley of the Avon in a stunning position with splendid views. The rather stark high walls of the house and the terrace support honeysuckle, clematis and old climbing roses, and fastigiate yews make strong buttress shapes up the south-facing wall. The Colonial Herb Garden is modest in size but the little herbarium is popular for seeds, herbs, tussie-mussies and so on. The Mount Vernon Garden, a colonial interpretation of George Washington's famous garden, with rampant old-fashioned roses, trained pear trees and box and beech hedges, is surrounded by white palings. There is a replica of the octagonal garden house used as a school room for Washington's step-grandchildren. The seven-acre arboretum, which contains a fine collection of exclusively native American trees and shrubs, is believed to be the only one of its kind outside the USA. An orchard contains American apple varieties, and there is also a fernery, a cascade and a waterfall. The Lewis and Clark trail includes a selection of the flora encountered by the explorers as they made their way to the west coast of North America, and a short circular walk through the old parkland and a woodland walk above the manor house have also been opened up.

Cothay Manor ★★

Greenham, Wellington TA21 0JR. Tel: (01823) 672283

Mr and Mrs Alastair Robb • 5m W of Wellington. From W (M5 junction 27) take A38 signed to Wellington, then after 3.5m turn left to Greenham. From N (junction 26) take Wellington exit; at roundabout take A38 signed to Exeter. After 3.5m turn right to Greenham (1.5m) and right again on left-hand corner at bottom of hill. House is 1m further, always keeping left • House open for parties by appt • Garden open May to Sept, Wed, Thurs, Sun and Bank Holiday Mons, 2 – 6pm • Entrance: £4 • Other information: Coaches by appt ● 💻 <u>WC</u> ⑂ 🌶 🍴

Although these outstanding gardens appear integral to the beautiful medieval manor house – each a natural extension of the other – they were in fact laid out only in the 1920s. They have been redesigned and replanted over the last few years, within the original yew-hedged compartments which were created to provide a seventeenth-century promenade complete with 'conversation arbours'. A 70-yard-long avenue of *Robinia pseudoacacia* 'Umbraculifera', underplanted with *Nepeta* 'Six Hills Giant', is a wonderful sight in May when a thousand white tulips in bloom appear through the nepeta. Surrounding meadows, planted with specimen trees, shrubs and spring bulbs, lead on to herbaceous borders, a cottage garden and a magical white garden. There is also a bog garden. Masterly planting is everywhere evident, exuberance balanced by restraint, as the owners are never afraid to repeat a theme within an enclosed space. Particularly unusual is the effective way in which complementary greys and mauves flow into the house walls. The newly created pond beyond the main garden and the bog garden alongside the fast-flowing river are beginning to make an impact.

Crowe Hall ★ [Historic Garden Grade II]

Widcombe Hill, Bath BA2 6AR. Tel: (01225) 310322

Mr John Barratt • Behind Bath Spa station off A36 within walking distance of station • Open for NGS 9th April, 11th June, also 14th May, 2 – 6pm, and for parties by appt • Entrance: £3, children £1 ◐ ▣ WC ⅏ ◈

These gardens, which extend to 11 acres on the hillside above Widcombe, are some of the most mysterious and beautiful in Bath. The owner describes it as an island of classical simplicity surrounded by romantic wilderness. Around the Regency-style house are Italianate terraces, a pond, grottoes, tunnels, woods, glades, kitchen gardens and a long walkway with a stone statue facing a stunning view of Prior Park (see entry). Vistas and views are a feature of this steeply banked garden, where down one walk you suddenly come upon the roof of the fifteenth-century church of St Thomas à Becket. Beyond the restored grotto is a meadow garden and an amusing garden dedicated to Hercules, with a theatrically ferocious hero who appears in a mosaic pool as well as on dry land. Magnificent trees include mulberries, beeches and limes. The charming little enclosed Sauce Garden, with its trelliswork and canal-like pool, was created in 1995, and the 1852 greenhouse has been restored to its former glory. The Teazle Garden (in memory of a much-loved dog) has a cascade, a fountain, a pergola and many climbing plants. For its stunning setting in the meadows above and facing away from Bath and for the romantic ambience, Crowe Hall is an experience not to be missed.

Dunster Castle ★ [Historic Garden Grade I]

Dunster, Minehead TA24 6SL. Tel: (01643) 821314

The National Trust • 3m SE of Minehead on A39 • Castle open 19th March to 6th Nov, 11am – 5pm (closes 4pm 31st Oct to 6th Nov) • Garden and park open all year, daily: 1st Jan to 17th March, 30th Oct to 31st Dec, 11am – 4pm; 1st March to 29th Oct, 10am – 5pm. For Christmas details telephone (01643) 823004 • Entrance: £3.90, children under 16 £1.70, family £9.50 (castle, garden and park £7.20, children £3.60, family £17.80) • Other information: Self-drive batricar and volunteer-driven multi-seater available ○ WC ⅏ ⬚ ♀ ⚲

The Luttrell family, who had lived here since the fourteenth century, gave the castle and gardens to the Trust in 1976. A fine border of rare shrubs surrounds a lawn by the keep, while sub-tropical plants, camellias and azaleas thrive on the formal terraces below and along the river. Thousands of bulbs have been planted, and after the daffodils and snowdrops come fine displays of forsythias, camellias and early rhododendrons. There is a National Collection of arbutus and a huge 18-metre *Magnolia campbellii*. Views stretch across to Exmoor, the Quantocks and the Bristol Channel. The park totals 28 acres in all.

East Lambrook Manor Gardens [Historic Garden Grade I]

South Petherton TA13 5HH. Tel: (01460) 240328

Robert and Marianne Williams • 2m NE of South Petherton off A303. Follow brown flower signs • Open Feb to Oct, daily, 10am – 5pm • Entrance: £3.95, OAPs, students, groups £3.50, children £1 • Other information: Special snowdrop study day 4th Feb (ticket only). Art gallery and café open throughout summer ☾ 💻 ✕ wc ♿ ✿ ⛲ ☕

In essence this is a cottage-style garden with mixed areas of planting, small lawns and narrow paths, but it remains iconic as the creation of the great plantswoman Margery Fish, who established the garden for endangered species famous in its day for its controlled luxuriance of growth, colour and scent. It still houses a remarkable collection of rare plants, many of which she saved from extinction. An extensive collection of geranium (cranesbill) species and cultivars also remains here. The present owners aim to improve all areas of the Grade-I-listed garden, famous not only for its plants but also for its controlled luxuriance of growth, colour and scents. The terrace area and the hellebore woodland garden have been restored, and Margery Fish's nursery has been relocated to its original site.

Gants Mill and Garden

Bruton BA10 0DB. Tel: (01749) 812393

Alison and Brian Shingler • 0.5m SW of Bruton, signed off A359 • Open 15th May to Sept, Sun, Thurs and Bank Holiday Mons, 2 – 5pm, and for parties by appt • Entrance: £3 (mill and garden £5) ☾ 💻 ✕ ♿ 🐟 ⛲ B&B

Approached down the greenest of lanes on the edge of historic Bruton are the old buildings of Gants Mill. The mill itself (still working) dates from 1290, but today's visitor can also revel in the half-acre English summer garden designed by Philip Brown and realised by Alison Shingler since 1995. The emphasis is on the masses of repeat-flowering climbing roses and clematis on pergolas, surrounded by swathes of perennials and summer bulbs in complementary shades. The vibrant scent and colour from successive waves of irises and Oriental poppies, roses and delphiniums, daylilies and dahlias create an unforgettable effect from mid-May until late September, while the strong and intricate design holds all together. The backdrop of river and trees provides a calm setting, and the skilful use of water as a main feature contributes sound and movement overall. An annually changing exhibition of sculptures – some abstract, many figurative, and all for sale – benefits the garden as well as the artists.

Greencombe ★★

Porlock TA24 8NU. Tel: (01643) 862363

Greencombe Garden Trust (Miss Joan Loraine) • 7.5m W of Minehead, 0.5m W of Porlock off B3225 • Open April to July, Sat – Wed, 2 – 6pm • Entrance: £5, children £1 • Other information: Coaches by arrangement ☽ 💻 wc ♿ ✿ ⚲

Created in 1946 by Horace Stroud, this garden has been extended by the present owner over the last three decades. Set on a dark hillside overlooking the Bristol

Channel, it glows with colour. The formal lawns and beds round the house are immaculate. Roses, lilies, hydrangeas, maples and camellias thrive. By contrast the woodland area, traversed by a maze of narrow paths, provides a walk of great interest; here a wide variety of rhododendrons and azaleas flowers in the shelter of mature trees, and ferns and woodland plants flourish. No sprays or chemicals are used in the cultivation of this completely organic garden, which contains National Collections of erythroniums, gaultherias, polystichums and vacciniums. *Woodborough* (see entry) is nearby.

Hadspen Garden and Nursery ★★

Castle Cary BA7 7NG. Tel: (01963) 351856

N. and S. Pope • As we go to press, we learn that the garden will be closed during 2006, but is expected to re-open after major refurbishment in spring 2007.

Set in parkland, this is a classic English walled garden, but curved to raise the temperature within. The basic plan was devised by Margaret Hobhouse in the Victorian gardening 'boom' days, to provide a setting for the eighteenth-century hamstone house. Over the years the garden became overgrown and formless until it was reclaimed in the mid 1980s by Canadians Nori and Sandra Pope, who retained the best of the original plan and have embellished it with a variety of new plantings. Their thing is colour — bold, innovative, thought-provoking colour. Indeed, you could say it is their trademark. The borders therefore have schemes ranging from silver and white through the spectrum to the deepest purple and black; flowers and foliage are combined in the most effective ways. Other features include a lily pond, shrub walks and a wildflower meadow. Hostas are a speciality.

Hapsford House

Great Elm, Nr Frome BA11 3NW. Tel: (01373) 463557

Mrs A. Enthoven • 2m NW of Frome off A362 Frome – Radstock road. 0.5m after Frome turn left to Great Elm, Mells and Hapsford; house is 0.5m further on left • Open 20th and 27th May, 2nd, 9th, 16th, 23rd and 30th June, 11am – 7pm • Entrance: £3, children £2 NEW ●

The 14 neglected acres of garden surrounding the Regency house have been rein-vented since 1989 by the present owner with the help of Pam Lewis, a pioneer of the naturalistic style at Sticky Wicket in Dorset (see entry). Governed by the priceless legacy of gigantic beeches, oaks, chestnuts and sycamores, native plants and grasses have been combined with sympathetic garden plants within the surviving framework of riverside, woodland, orchard, hedgerow and meadow. Buttressed by the past, this is nonetheless very much a garden of today.

Hestercombe Gardens ★ [Historic Garden Grade I]

Cheddon Fitzpaine, Taunton TA2 8LG. Tel: (01823) 413923

HGP Ltd/Somerset County Council • 4m NE of Taunton off A361, just N of Cheddon Fitzpaine. Signposted • Open all year, daily, 10am – 6pm (last admission 5pm). Parties by written appt only • Entrance: £5.75, OAPs £5.25, children free (2005 prices) • Other information: Coaches by arrangement ○ 🍽 ✕ 🧺 <u>WC</u> ♿ ⬦ 🌶 🏛 💡 ♋

This is a superb product of the collaboration between Edwin Lutyens and Gertrude Jekyll, blending the formal art of architecture with the art of planting. The detailed design of steps, pools, walls, paving and seating is Lutyens at his most accomplished, and the rills, pergola and orangery are also fine examples of his work. To the north of the house is the Combe, laid out two centuries earlier than the main gardens and a unique example of eighteenth-century pleasure grounds unchanged until the timber was felled in the 1960s. Visitors are now able to see the eighteenth-century parkland designed between 1750 and 1786 by Coplestone Warre Bampfylde, and his (restored) Great Cascade; he also designed the cascade from the lake at Stourhead (see entry in Wiltshire). He described Hestercombe's as one 'that will rivet you to the spot with admiration'. This ambitious restoration of a Grade-I-listed landscape is likely to continue for a further five years, and will form a 35-acre landscape garden in its own right. The repair of the Victorian terrace is now complete, and a programme is well advanced to re-create the shrubbery in the style of William Robinson, c. 1880. Be sure to see the Doric temple, the mausoleum, the rebuilt witch's hut and the Gothic alcove, which commands views of Taunton Vale. There is still a sense of nature enhanced rather than transformed, with the set pieces so well sited and spaced that they seem to relax into the natural setting. A major reassessment and renewal of Jekyll's planting is underway and the formal garden has been replanted, as close as possible to her original plans. In 2005 a splendid new visitor and interpretation centre was opened in the restored Victorian stables.

Jasmine Cottage

26 Channel Road, Clevedon BS21 7BY. Tel: (01275) 871850

Mr and Mrs Michael Redgrave • 12m W of Bristol. From M5 junction 20, take road to seafront, continue N on B3124 and turn right at St Mary's church • Open May to July, Thurs, 11am – 4pm, and by appt May to Sept • Entrance: £2, children free • Other information: Plants for sale in nursery ☾ WC

Concealed behind a perfectly ordinary house front is a stylish and imaginative garden. Something for everyone in this exuberant garden: old-fashioned roses, climbers, mixed shrubs and a 50-strong collection of salvias. Herbaceous borders, island beds, a pergola walk and a vegetable garden are all crammed into one-third of an acre. An inspiration for suburban enthusiasts, especially as it is only about 100 metres from the sea. The rectangular shape is cleverly disguised, with island beds in one area, and a secret garden enclosed by a hedge over 3.5 metres high and cut annually. Through the hedge is the so-called cottage garden with unusual climbers, including *Rhodochiton atrosanguineus, Dregea sinensis* and *Dicentra macrocapnos.*

Lady Farm ★

Chelwood, Bristol BS39 4NN. Tel: (01761) 490770

Malcolm and Judy Pearce • 9m S of Bristol on A368, 0.5m E of Chelwood round-about (A37/A368) • Open July to Sept, Sun, 2 – 6pm, and for parties by appt • Entrance: £4, children free but under 14s not encouraged ☾ 🍽 WC ⬦

The garden is blessed with a south-west-facing valley setting and with an abundance of natural water, but it is the vision and commitment of Judy Pearce that have since 1992 turned the 12 acres into an outstanding amalgam of contemporary styles. The formal plantings around the farmhouse include a modern interpretation of a cottage garden with a thatched summerhouse and a 'bobble garden' of standard topiary. The style becomes more natural as the garden extends down the valley and blends into the surrounding fields. A spring-fed water course, planted in shades of gold and russet, flows into the top lake, where an impressive rockwork by Anthony Archer-Wills is sited to command the view. A shady hosta walk, with birches and hydrangeas, leads to the bottom lake created from a stream, which is surrounded by natural planting and blends into a wildflower meadow. The stream cascades into a deep ravine before returning to its natural course. The innovative planting schemes elsewhere, initiated by Mary Payne, are the hallmark of the garden – none more so than the widely praised 'steppe' and 'prairie' areas. The first, peaking from May to July, has rhythmical clumps of foliage plants and splashes of colour from strong-hued summer flowers. The other, at its most colourful from July to December, is filled with substantial groups of heleniums, achilleas, rudbeckias, eupatoriums and the like, and many ornamental grasses. A new area of grasses and perennials was planted in 2005.

Lower Severalls

Crewkerne TA18 7NX. Tel: (01460) 73234

Mary Pring • 1.5m NE of Crewkerne off A30 • Open March to Sept, Mon – Wed, Fri and Sat, 10am – 5pm (but please telephone to check) • Entrance: £3 • Other information: Coaches by appt. Teas for pre-arranged parties only. Plants for sale in nursery ◑ 🍽 🏛 WC ⑤ ⇪ ℗ ♀

A typical cottage garden of some two and a half acres with herbaceous borders against the stone-walled house. The garden extends through stone pillars which make a frame for the view of the valley over lawn and varied shrubs and a bog garden. Additional features include arches made from recycled farm machinery, and a 'dogwood basket'. Water gardens, fed from a spring in adjacent farmland, have been created, together with a *wadi* or dry garden built up to form a windbreak for a sheltered valley. A pavilion for contemplation – a green-roofed octagonal building covered in sedums and sempervivums – has replaced the old horse chestnut of 200 years' standing.

Lytes Cary Manor [Historic Garden Grade II]

Charlton Mackrell, Somerton TA11 7HU. Tel: (01458) 224471

The National Trust • 9m N of Yeovil, 2.5m NE of Ilchester, signed from A303 • Open 22nd March to 29th Oct, Wed, Fri, Sat, Sun and Bank Holiday Mons, 11am – 5pm (or dusk if earlier) • Entrance: £5, children £3 • Other information: Building works to house roof may cause some disruption ◑ 🏛 WC ⑤ ℗

Once the house of the Elizabethan herbalist Henry Lyte (although nothing of his botanic garden remains), the main feature is a long, wide border, which has been replanted in line with Graham Stuart Thomas's original design with a mixture of roses, shrubs and herbaceous plants. There are also pleasing lawns with hedges in Elizabethan style and some topiary and a large orchard with naturalised bulbs and mown walks with a central sundial. A little over five miles to the west, at Langport, is the legendary nursery *Kelways*, a leading grower of peonies (Tel: (01458) 250521). [Open all year, daily, 9am – 5pm, but opens 10am at weekends and closes 4pm on Sunday.]

Manor Farm ★

Middle Chinnock, Crewkerne TA18 7PN. Tel: (01935) 881706

Simon and Antonia Johnson • 5m W of Yeovil off A30 • Open one day for NGS, and by appt • Entrance: £3, children free ● 💻 WC ♿ ⬇ ⚲

The two-acre garden surrounding the hamstone farmhouse has an air of timelessness and maturity that blends with the handsome fifteenth- and sixteenth-century buildings. It is however entirely the work of the owners, a garden designer and his wife, who have created it since 1992 to complement the fine setting in a way that is at once innovative and traditional. Both scale and proportion are perfect throughout, and the architectural framework of mellow stone walls and yew and hornbeam hedges allows for areas of great contrast and individuality. In the front garden iris and box alternate *en bloc*, and there are sweeping greys and creams along the drive. A lush and densely planted secret garden surrounds a small pond and there is an attractive orchard with a little slate-roofed house on stilts for the children. Everywhere you look are enviable combinations of plants used formally – for example as a border along the main lawn – or more informally as the garden spreads out towards the pond and the surrounding landscape.

Milton Lodge ★ [Historic Garden Grade II]

Wells BA5 3AQ. Tel: (01749) 672168

Mr D.C. Tudway Quilter • 0.5m N of Wells. From A39 Wells – Bristol road turn N up Old Bristol Road, entrance is first gate on left • Open 14th April to Oct, Tues, Wed, Sun and Bank Holiday Mons, 2 – 5pm • Entrance: £3, children under 14 free • Other information: Parties and coaches by special arrangement. Teas on Sun and Bank Holiday Mons only ◑ 💻 WC ⚲ ♨

The terraced garden, replanted by the present owner in the 1960s, is cultivated down the side of a hill overlooking the Vale of Avalon, affording a magnificent view of Wells Cathedral. A wide variety of plants, all suitable for the alkaline soil, provides a succession of colour and interest from March to October. Many fine trees can be seen in the garden and in the seven-acre arboretum opposite the entrance to the car park.

Montacute House ★ [Historic Garden Grade I]

Montacute TA15 6XP. Tel: (01935) 823289

The National Trust • 4m W of Yeovil. Signposted from A3088 and A303 near Ilchester • House open as garden but closed Nov to Feb • Park open all year, daily, dawn – dusk • Garden open 22nd March to 29th Oct, daily except Tues, 11am – 6pm; 30th Oct to 28th Feb, Wed – Sun, 11am – 4pm (or dusk if earlier) • Entrance: March to Oct, garden and park £3.90, children £1.80; Nov to March,

£2, children £1 (house, garden and park £7.40, children £3.70, family £17) • *Other information: Plants for sale April to Sept* ○ 💷 ✕ 🍴 <u>WC</u> ❤ ⬦ ⛪ 💡 ✎

This Elizabethan garden of grass lawns surrounded by clipped yews set in terraces is a triumph of formality. The surrealism of the topiary, which some claim was inspired by a dramatic snowfall, adds immensely to the effect. A large water feature has replaced the original Elizabethan high circular mount, and there is a charming raised walk, two original pavilions and an arcaded garden house probably devised by Lord Curzon while he was a tenant. Colour is provided by herbaceous borders and from midsummer by twin scented rose borders. An avenue of 72 limes is now established, and the gardens are surrounded by graceful parklands giving vistas and an impression of space.

2 Old Tarnwell

Upper Stanton Drew BS39 4EA. Tel: (01275) 333146

Mr and Mrs K. Payne • *6m S of Bristol, W of Pensford between A368 and B3130* • *Open June and July for small groups by appt* • *Entrance: £2.50* 🌑

A tiny garden full of contrasts and interest. The front garden was remodelled in 2003 to reflect the owners' interest in steppe-style planting, proving that it can be effective on a miniature scale. Based on apricots, coral, yellows and brown, with a hint of purple, this random planting style of contrasting foliage effects is set against flint gravel. Slate monoliths add interest and structure, echoed by columnar box and *Ilex crenata*. The back garden retains its cottage style of cool colours encased by rampant clematis. Features include a misty pool, a wall covering of clipped ivy and auricula theatres, all enhanced by good planting.

Prior Park Landscape Garden ★ [Historic Garden Grade I]

Ralph Allen Drive, Bath BA2 5AH. Tel: (01225) 833422 (General Enquiries)

The National Trust • *No parking at garden or nearby; catch bus from city centre or walk up A3062 from Widcombe* • *Open Feb to Nov, Wed – Mon, 11am – 5.30pm; Dec to Jan, Fri – Sun, 11am – dusk. Closed 25th, 26th Dec and 1st Jan* • *Entrance: £4, children £2* • *Other information: Small area for disabled parking (must be pre-booked), but limited access for disabled* ☽ 💷 🍴 <u>WC</u> 💡 ✎

The Palladian mansion, designed by the architect John Wood from 1735 for Bath's leading entrepreneur and philanthropist Ralph Allen, dominates the steeply sloping landscape and provides stunning views of the city. While the mansion is owned and used by Prior Park College and is not open to the public, the grounds below are well worth the circular walk (allow 1½ hours) from the entrance gate off Ralph Allen Drive. Allen landscaped and planted continuously from 1734 to 1764, helped by several gardeners, notably 'Capability' Brown, who eliminated areas of formality. Alexander Pope inspired the Wilderness, which includes a Rococo sham bridge and the ruins of Mrs Allen's grotto. The walk continues from the mansion viewpoint down the east side of the valley (steep in places) to the lakes and the Palladian bridge of 1755, returning by the west side of the valley via the Rock Gate. Undoubtedly two-star are the views of the Palladian bridge, the mansion from the bridge and the city of Bath; the 'Priory path' leading into the field next to the garden gives a panoramic view over the whole city.

Sherborne Garden

Pear Tree House, Litton BA3 4PP. Tel: (01761) 241220

Mr and Mrs J. Southwell • 15m S of Bristol, 7.5m N of Wells on B3114, 0.25m beyond Litton and The Kings Arms • Open mid-Feb for snowdrops and hellebores; then 28th May to 25th Sept, Mon and occasional Suns, 11am – 6pm. Telephone for details of Feb and Oct opening dates and times • Entrance: £3, children free
● ● ● wc ⑤ ⑤ ⑤ ⑤

A large, rather surreal garden that displays a very personal choice of specimen trees, grasses and water garden features in a six-and-a-half-acre site reclaimed from farmland. It is an excellent example of how natural pasture land may be tamed and surface water channelled into ponds. The owners are compulsive tree people who since 1963 have planted hundreds of native and exotic trees, expanding the original cottage garden and paddock into a mini-arboretum. The garden now boasts a one-acre spinney of native species, a pinetum, nut hedges, a collection of species roses, gravel beds with collections of giant and miniature grasses and about 200 varieties of hemerocallis, a Prickly Wood that offers 100 varieties of holly, and a collection of over 250 ferns. In such experienced and creative hands this garden never stands still, and the twin themes of trees and water – a *wadi* was constructed as a millennium project – are continually being celebrated and extended.

Ston Easton Park ★ [Historic Garden Grade II]

Ston Easton, Bath BA3 4DF. Tel: (01761) 241631

Von Essen Hotels • 11m SW of Bath, 6m NE of Wells on A39 • Open all year, daily, 10am – 5pm (closes 6pm Sat and Sun) • Entrance: free • Other information: Teas and toilet facilities in hotel ● ● ✕ wc ⑤ ⑤ ⑤ B&B

The magnificent Palladian house is set in a park replanned and replanted by Humphry Repton in 1792, reached by a suitably impressive drive winding past the old stables. The glory is the view from inside the great Saloon, or from the terrace immediately outside, over the River Norr with a bridge and an elegant stepped cascade. Repton made a Red Book with his proposals for improvement, and the previous owners worked on the restoration of the park to his plans. Beyond the terrace are wide lawns with fine specimen trees and extensive woodland with many glades and paths. At some distance from the house is a vast sheltered walled garden, partly ornamental and partly productive, divided by Penelope Hobhouse into beech-hedged enclosures. Many new projects and plans are now under way in this area.

Tintinhull House Garden [Historic Garden Grade II]

Farm Street, Tintinhull, Yeovil BA22 9PZ. Tel: (01935) 822545

The National Trust • 5m NW of Yeovil, 0.5m S of A303. Signposted • Open 22nd March to 29th Oct, Wed – Sun and Bank Holiday Mons, 11am – 5pm • Entrance: £4.50, children £2.20 • Other information: Disabled parking by arrangement ◑ ●
wc ⑤ ⑤

Developed from the 1930s by Phyllis Reiss, the two-acre modern garden achieves an impression of greater size by means of walls, hedges and vistas. Like Hidcote, it has a sequence of garden rooms. The Eagle Court near the house passes on to a small white garden; from here, an opening leads to the kitchen garden with an orchard beyond. The pool garden has 'hot' and 'cool' borders, and the Cedar Court some venerable trees, including a yew said to be 400 years old. The standards of planting and maintenance are not, alas, what they were in the garden's heyday.

Wayford Manor ★ [Historic Garden Grade II]

Crewkerne TA18 8QG. Tel: (01460) 73253

Mr and Mrs R.L. Goffe • 3m SW of Crewkerne off B3165 at Clapton • Open 9th and 30th April, 1st and 21st May, 11th June, 2 – 6pm, and for parties of 10 or more at other times by appt • Entrance: £3, children (6-15) £1; garden tours £5 per person ● ● wc ⬦ ⬦

Four acres of gardens surround a fine manor house dating from the thirteenth century with Elizabethan and Victorian additions. This is a good example of the work of Harold Peto, who redesigned the garden in 1902. The formal upper terrace with yew hedges and topiary fronting the house has panoramic views over west Dorset. Steps down to the second terrace lead to a new stone-pillared pergola complementing the loggia designed by Peto, which in turn complemented the Elizabethan porch to the house. Below the rockery and grass tennis court is an area of partly wild woodland gardens with plantings of mature trees and shrubs, including fine maples, cornus, magnolias, rhododendrons and spring bulbs. Colourful displays of candelabra primulas, arum lilies, gunneras and other moisture-lovers fringe the lower ponds. Natural spring water is used throughout this south-facing, multi-layered garden, where widespread planting continues apace.

Woodborough

Porlock Weir TA24 8NZ. Tel: (01643) 862406

Mr and Mrs R.D. Milne • 6m W of Minehead. From A39 at Porlock take B3225 towards Porlock Weir. At Porlock Vale House on right, take tarmac lane uphill immediately opposite; garden is first on right • Open by appt only • Entrance: £2.50, children under 10 free • Other information: No coaches ● ⬦

This interesting garden created on a steep (1 in 4) hillside has magnificent views over Porlock Bay. The wide variety of shrubs includes some of the lesser-known hybrid rhododendrons and a number of Ghent azaleas. The garden is at its most colourful in May but a bog garden and two pools designed by the owners' landscape architect son add interest over a longer season. The owners will happily share with visitors their hard-won experience in garden restoration and their battle with the dreaded honey fungus. Greencombe (see entry) is nearby.

Yarlington House

Yarlington, Wincanton BA9 8DY. Tel: (01963) 440344

Count and Countess Charles de Salis • In village of Yarlington S of Castle Cary, signposted off A371 • Open one day for NGS, and for parties of 10 or more by appt • Entrance: £2.50, children free ● ● ● wc ⬦ ⬦ ● B&B

A large and varied formal garden blessed with an ideal mix of design and planting. The fine pleached lime square surrounding the rose garden and the romantic sunken Italian garden, complete with classical statuary and balustrades and awash with scent and soft colours, complement the scale and style of the distinguished 1780s' house. Created by the present owners over forty years, the garden is at a satisfying stage of maturity within the setting of the fine surrounding parkland. Within some two acres it achieves skilful mood changes, moving gradually from the more formal areas to an unusual circle of crab apples trained in the shape of a bandstand (J.C. Loudon's 'apple house') and down towards a dell replete with ferns and shade-loving specimens. Vegetables and fruit trees are grown within a magnificent walled garden approached through impressive gates. Early in the year the daffodils make their point before the laburnum walk comes into flower over a Gothic-arched pergola. The Emperor Napoleon is commemorated in the Italian garden, surrounded by roses – 'Empress Josephine' and 'Souvenir de la Malmaison' of course. A dovecote is stationed within the small childrens' garden.

SYMBOLS

[NEW] entries new for 2006; ○ open all year; ◑ open most of year; ◐ open during main season; ● open rarely and/or by appt; 💬 teas/light refreshments; ✕ meals; 🧺 picnics permitted; WC toilet facilities; <u>WC</u> toilet facilities, inc. disabled; ♿ partly wheelchair-accessible; 🐕 dogs on lead; 🌿 plants for sale; 🏪 shop; 🎪 events held; 🌞 children-friendly; B&B bed and breakfast available.

BED & BREAKFAST FOR GARDEN LOVERS

The biennial paperback contains some 200 B&Bs (mostly in Britain, with a smattering in the Republic of Ireland, France and Italy) run by keen and knowledgeable owners with fine gardens of all types and sizes – rural and urban, traditional and contemporary. Prices for a double room range from £55 per night. The guide is available from Alastair Sawday Publishing – telephone (01275) 464891 or consult www.specialplacestostay.com.

ASSOCIATION OF GARDENS TRUSTS

Founded in 1993 in response to growing unease among conservationists and owners of historic gardens about their future security, 36 individual county garden trusts shelter under its umbrella. They are charitable bodies with no legal powers, able to influence planning and other governmental decisions only through vigilance and lobbying. For further details, contact: The Association of Gardens Trusts, 75 Cowcross Street, London EC1M 6EL (Tel: (020) 7251 2610, Tues and Thurs only; www.gardenstrusts.org.uk).

STAFFORDSHIRE

Two-starred gardens are marked on the map with a black square.

Alton Towers ★ [Historic Park Grade I]

Alton ST10 4DB. Tel: (08705) 204060

Alton Towers • From N take M6 junction 16 or M1 junction 28, from S take M6 junction 15 or M1 junction 23A. Signposted • Theme park, ruins and grounds open March to Oct daily, 9.30am – 5pm, 6pm or 7pm • Entrance: Charges vary seasonally – maximum for individuals £28, OAPs £14, children £21. Party rates available (2005 prices) ○ 🍽 ✕ 🛍 <u>WC</u> ♿ 🚽 🍴 ⚲ B&B

This fantastic Elysium of ornamental garden buildings was created between 1814 and 1827 by the 15th Earl of Shrewsbury. It contains many beautiful and unusual features, including the three-storey cast-iron Chinese pagoda fountain – a copy of the To Ho pagoda in Canton. W.A. Nesfield was active here (one of his parterres is still *in situ* though in need of restoration). The enormous rock garden is planted with a range of conifers, acers and sedums. The fine domed conservatory houses geraniums etc. according to the season, and the terraces have rose and herbaceous borders. There is a Dutch garden, Her Ladyship's Garden featuring yew and rose beds, an Italian garden, a yew-arch walkway and woodland walks. Water adds further beauty and interest. All this plus the manifold attractions of the theme park.

Biddulph Grange Garden ★★ [Historic Garden Grade I]

Grange Road, Biddulph, Staffordshire Moorlands ST8 7SD. Tel: (01782) 517999 (Garden Office)

The National Trust • 3.5m SE of Congleton, 7m N of Stoke-on-Trent. Access from A527 Biddulph/Congleton road • Open 25th March to 29th Oct, Wed – Sun and Bank Holiday Mons, 11.30am – 5.30pm (or dusk if earlier); 4th Nov to 19th Dec, Sat and Sun, 11am – 3pm. Guided tours by appt only • Entrance: £5, children £2.50, family £12.50, parties of 15 or more £4.20 per person; Nov and Dec £2, children £1, family £5 (2005 prices) ○ 🍽 WC ♿ 🐕 🚽

This is one of the most remarkable and innovative gardens of the nineteenth century. There is an Egyptian garden with a pyramid and obelisks of clipped yew. The Chinese garden has a joss house, a golden water buffalo overlooking a dragon parterre, a watch tower and a temple reflected in a calm pool. In front of the house terraces descend to a lily pond. The stumpery demonstrates an innovative Victorian way of displaying suitable plants. The verbena, araucaria and rose parterres and the Shelter House and dahlia walk (with over 600 dahlias) have now been restored just as they were in the middle of the nineteenth century, and the long Wellingtonia avenue, felled and replanted in 1995, is beginning to make its presence felt again. In all, one of the country's most unusual gardening rediscoveries and restorations – it should not be missed.

12 Darges Lane

Great Wyrley, Walsall WS6 6LE. Tel: (01922) 415064

Mrs A. Hackett • 2m SE of Cannock. From A5 (Churchbridge junction) take A34 towards Walsall. First turning on right over brow of hill. House on right on corner of Cherrington Drive • Open 30th April, 28th May, 2 – 6pm, and by appt • Entrance: £2.50 • Other information: Plants for sale on open days ● ◗ ✿

A quarter-acre garden on two levels, attractively laid out, well stocked and of great interest to plantsmen. Fine trees and large variety of shrubs and foliage plants are the background to a comprehensive collection of flowering plants and small shrubs, among them prunus, spiraea, azara and abutilon Some are unusual, even rare, and there is room too for 93 varieties of clematis and a National Collection of lamiums. There are borders and island beds, and a small water garden with a circular paved area and a water feature. Every inch is used to grow or set off the plants, and there is year-round appeal for flower arrangers. Spring is the owner's favourite time, when hellebores, erythroniums and trilliums ar in flower, along with tulips and *Paeonia* 'Joseph Rock' The overall effect is attractive as well as enticing to the plant lover. Plants for sale include some more unusual ones.

The Dorothy Clive Garden ★

Willoughbridge, Market Drayton, Shropshire TF9 4EU. Tel: (01630) 647237

Willoughbridge Garden Trust • 7m NE of Market Drayton, 1m E of Woore on A51 between Nantwich and Stone • Open 11th March to Oct, daily, 10am – 5.30pm • Entrance: £4.20, OAPs £3.60, children (11–16) £1, under 11 free • Other information: Disabled parking ● ◗ ✕ ▩ WC ♿ ❧ ♀

Created by the late Colonel Clive in memory of his wife, with the help of distinguished gardeners including the late John Codrington, this garden has wide appeal in terms both of design and inspired planting. The guidebook identifies the highlights season by season. These include the rhododendrons and azaleas in the quarry garden and the pool with the scree garden rising on the hillside above it. In spring there are unusual bulbs and primulas, in summer colourful shrubs, unusual perennials and many conifers; other trees provide autumn colour. The scree garden must give gardeners many good ideas. The garden has been extended, and new features include a laburnum arch with roses and other climbers, and a small pool with a bog garden.

The Garth

2 Broc Hill Way, Milford, Stafford ST17 0UB. Tel: (01785) 661182

Mr and Mrs David Wright • 4.5m SE of Stafford. On A513 Stafford – Rugeley road, at Barley Mow pub turn right, then left after 0.5m • Open 4th and 25th June, 2 – 6pm, and by appt for parties • Entrance: £2, children free ● ◗ WC ♿ ✿

This half-acre garden surrounded by countryside is laid out on a steep slope with old caves to discover at the bottom. It contains specialist areas which should give inspiration and ideas to any gardener. The range of plants is astonishing: six unusual beeches, 20 different ferns, 30 varieties of clematis, magnolias, rhododendrons, pulmonarias, hostas, azaleas, penstemons and astilbes, berberis, fothergillas, garryas, amelanchiers and *Holodiscus discolor*, all planted to provide foliage interest and colour combinations. Archways are covered with roses and loniceras, and in the herbaceous borders are heathers, campanulas and osteospermums. There is also a pool and new herbaceous borders containing a wide variety of plants popular with flower arrangers.

Moseley Old Hall

Moseley Old Hall Lane, Fordhouses, Wolverhampton WV10 7HY.
Tel: (01902) 782808

The National Trust • 4m N of Wolverhampton, 5m SW of Cannock. From S take M6 then M54, exiting at junction 1 on A460 to Wolverhampton. From N on M6 exit at junction 11, then take A460. Coaches must use A460 • House open as garden • Garden open 18th March to 29th Oct, Wed, Sat and Sun; also Bank Holiday Mons and Tues following; all 1 – 5pm but opens 11am Bank Holiday Mons; 5th Nov to 17th Dec, Sun, 1 – 4pm • Entrance: £5, children £2.50, family £12.50; parties of 15 or more £4.30 per person (house and garden) ◑ ▆ ✕ ▆ <u>WC</u> & ⬠ ⏁ ⬛ ♀ ◖

Around the Elizabethan house where Charles II hid after the Battle of Worcester is a garden mainly for the specialist interested in old species, as all are seventeenth-century except for a few fruit trees. The knot garden derives from a design of 1640 by the Rev. Walter Stonehouse. A wooden arbour is covered with clematis and *Vitis vinifera* 'Purpurea'. Fruit trees include quince, mulberry, medlar and a morello cherry. The walled garden has topiary and annual borders, and fritillaries grow in the nut walk. There is a small herb garden and boles for bees. It is interesting to see plants grown in times past to provide dyes and for cleansing and medicinal purposes.

Oulton House

Oulton, Stone ST15 8UR. Tel: (01785) 813556

Mr and Mrs W.A. Fairbairn • 8m N of Stafford, 0.5m NE of Stone. From Stone take road signed to Oulton; after Oulton village sign turn left, and after houses turn right up long drive • Open February to July by appt • Entrance: £3, children 75p ◑ ▆ ▆ WC &

This three-acre garden with fine views, surrounded by parkland, has been developed by the present owner over more than 25 years. A range of large trees provides shelter. The conservatory contains vines, camellias and roses. Herbaceous borders are distinguished by interesting colour combinations and a wide range of plants, including geraniums, delphiniums, euphorbias and astrantias. Old shrub roses abound, and a grey-and-silver border by the house has clematis and roses climbing its walls. A new border features yellow, blue and white perennials and the bank behind is covered with ivies, loniceras and roses. There is also a rhododendron walk, a large rockery, a patio area, a golden corner, a white area, and a large vegetable and fruit garden. Although not a weed-free garden, there is plenty to delight the eye, especially in spring with the flowering of a mass of snowdrops, hellebores and spring bulbs.

Rode Hall

(see Cheshire)

Shugborough ★ [Historic Park Grade I]

Milford, Stafford ST17 0XB. Tel: (01889) 881388

Staffordshire County Council/The National Trust • 6m E of Stafford on A513 • House, museum and Park Farm open • Garden open March to Oct, daily, 11am – 5pm. Open for pre-booked parties all year from 10.30am; guided tours available • Entrance: £3 per vehicle to parkland, gardens, picnic area, walks and trails. Extra charge for house, museum and farm • Other information: Guided tours available. Batricars available. Dogs in park only, on lead ◑ 🅿 ✕ 🍴 WC 🚻 ♿ 🛈 🔍

Shugborough is of interest to garden historians because Thomas Wright of Durham worked here. Many of the buildings and monuments are ascribed to James 'Athenian' Stuart and were built for Thomas Anson from the 1740s onwards. These are some of the earliest examples of English neo-classicism, and there is also an early example of Chinoiserie based on a sketch made by one of the officers on Admiral Anson's voyage round the world. It has been suggested that the buildings were randomly scattered, but another view is that they were put in place as 'hidden architectural treasures' to surprise. As for the garden, the Victorian layout with terraces by Nesfield was revitalised for the Trust in the mid-1960s by Graham Stuart Thomas, who also worked on the Edwardian-style rose garden. Due to an outbreak of phytophthora, all the roses except the ramblers have been replaced by herbaceous plantings specifically chosen to attract bees and butterflies, harmoniously grouped in small beds. Seasonal attractions include massed plantings of daffodils along the river bank, azaleas, rhododendrons, a fine long-flowering herbaceous border and good autumn colours. In the park the aim is to restore the landscape to its eighteenth-century appearance; over 1000 trees, predominantly oak and sweet chestnut, have already been planted. Wild flowers and grasses are also being re-established. Parkland walks include the re-created eighteenth- and nineteenth-century woodland walks with fine views to the Derbyshire hills and the impressive Hadrian's Arch monument.

15 St Johns Road

Pleck, Walsall WS2 9TJ. Tel: (01922) 442348

Mr and Mrs Allen • 10m NW of Birmingham. From M6 junction 10, head towards Walsall on A454 Wolverhampton road, and turn right into Pleck Road (A4148). St Johns Road is fourth right • Open one Sun for NGS, and for individuals and parties of up to 30 by appt • Entrance: £2, children free ◑ 🅿 ♿ 🔍

This comparatively small garden is skilfully landscaped so as to appear larger. It contains a wide range of delights, from a tropical area near the house, past a pool and a varied collection of trees, shrubs, climbers (33 different clematis) and flowers, to a Japanese feature at the far end, where a stream runs under a little bridge leading to a tea house. The smaller trees include acers, and there are shrubs, grasses, ferns, hostas, perennials and clematis blooming through the season, with annuals adding splashes of colour. In 2004 a new garden was reclaimed from waste land, trees and shrubs planted in gravel, a wildlife pool dug, and a shaded woodland path made under a large willow tree.

Trentham Gardens [Historic Park Grade II*]

Stone Road, Trentham, Stoke-on-Trent ST4 8AX. Tel: (01782) 657341

Trentham Leisure Ltd • 2m S of Stoke-on-Trent on A34, 2m E of M6 junction 15 • Open all year, daily, 10am – 6pm • Entrance: £3.50, concessions/children £2.50, family £11 (2005 prices) ◑ WC ♿

Over several centuries, the progressive aggrandisement of Trentham Hall and the Leveson-Gower family went hand-in-hand. In 1759 'Capability' Brown was brought in to relandscape the 750-acre park and in 1833 Charles Barry commissioned to lay out the Italian Flower Gardens – the two most important features remaining today. When in 1911 the 2nd Duke of Sutherland sold up, most of the hall was demolished and the grounds degenerated into a public amenity space, although some magnificent trees and decaying garden buildings remained as reminders of the glory days. Now, under the banner of a seemingly enlightened and well-intentioned property company, a posse of knights has galloped to the rescue: Dominic Cole of Land Use Consultants, respected designers Piet Oudolf and Tom Stuart-Smith, and Michael Walker, formerly gardens manager at Waddesdon. The upper part of the Italian Gardens has been restored and the lower part reinterpreted in the modern perennial style. Following this, trees will be planted in perimeter woodlands and in the western pleasure ground to connect the formal gardens to the park, while wildflower and perennials meadows will lead to a grass amphitheatre overlooking the lake. If the project fulfils its ambitions it will be a worthy chapter in a grandiose history.

GARDENING WEBSITES

Many gardens now have their own websites, and we list these at the back of the *Guide*. Others useful for garden visitors are:

- Dept of Environment (Ireland): www.heritageireland.ie
- English Heritage: www.english-heritage.org.uk
- Historic Houses Association: www.hha.org.uk
- Historic Royal Palaces: www.hrp.org.uk
- Historic Scotland: www.historic-scotland.gov.uk
- Landmark Trust: www.landmarkrust.org.uk
- National Gardens Scheme: www.ngs.org.uk
- National Trust: www.nationaltrust.org.uk
- National Trust for Scotland: www.nts.org.uk
- Royal Horticultural Society: www.rhs.org.uk
- Welsh Historic Monuments: www.cadw.wales.gov.uk

SUFFOLK

Two-starred gardens are marked on the map with a black square.

Abbey Gardens [Historic Garden Grade II]

Bury St Edmunds.

*Borough of St Edmundsbury • In town centre • Open all year, daily, 9am – dusk
• Entrance: free • Other information: Refreshments available Easter to Oct only*
○ ● × ▣ WC ⌖ ⬥ ℘ ⛪ ⚑ ⚲

This is a most surprising garden. In 945 the Benedictines founded the Abbey, which
undoubtedly had gardens for herbs and vegetables. The abbey ruins (it was dissolved
in 1539) form the bones of the present-day landscape; if for no other reason, visit
the place to see the great walls, like some extraordinary geological feature, now
dissolving into flinty stumps. Then think forward 900 years and bring to mind that
one Nathaniel Hodson actually formed a botanic garden on this site in 1821. The
present arrangement of formal beds on the site of the Great Court of the abbey
mirrors his garden, of which perhaps only a few trees remain. The planting in the
central area is bright – lots of begonias and busy lizzies in summer and polyanthus
and pansies in the winter and spring. A sensory garden for the visually impaired has
been created and the water garden and wall shrub border have been refurbished.
Excellent free leaflets are available at the Bowling Green office.

Bedfield Hall

Bedfield, Woodbridge, IP13 7JJ. Tel: (01728) 628380

*Mr and Mrs Timothy Easton • 15m N of Ipswich off A140. Turn right onto A1120,
and in Earl Soham turn left after church, signed to Bedfield. With Bedfield primary
school and red phone box on left, take right turn into Church Road; house is just past
church. Parking on green by church • Open June to Oct by appt for parties of 8 or
more • Entrance: £3 for independent viewing or £6 per person inc. tea/coffee and
introductory talk* NEW ●

Timothy Easton is an artist and architectural historian, Christine a conservator. Their
artistic bent is immediately obvious in the two-acre garden surrounding the
Gothicised house dating from 1450 to 1830. One acre – The Platform – is girdled
by a thirteenth-century moat, with a secondary moated area of nuttery and wild
woodland; there is also an island. Central to the plan is a formal herb, vegetable and
picking garden hidden behind high yew hedges and arched wooden gates. It is ringed
by calmer areas of varied greenery: yew and box topiary, grey-olive wooden arches,
and no fewer than five bridges, also painted grey-olive and inspired by the Gothick
finials on the house. The way forward leads over these bridges and high walkways
from one area to another with elevated views over colourful and exuberant
plantings of irises, roses, lavender, clematis, honeysuckles, grasses and much more.
Without ever retracing your steps, you then pass through a new orchard with a
hen-house and along a topiaried yew walk beside the water, lengthened by false
perspectives, with vistas deliberately drawing in the surrounding arable fields.

The whole has been created with strong bones and instinctive, well-informed planting. Church, tower and house make an interesting architectural group with the garden.

Blakenham Woodland Garden

Little Blakenham, Ipswich IP8 4LZ. Tel: (07760) 342131

4m NW of Ipswich, 1m off B1113. Signed from The Beeches in Little Blakenham, 1m off old A1100 (now B1113) • Open March to June, 10am – 5pm. Parties welcome by appt • Entrance: £3 ◑ 🍴 ⓺

The Tory cabinet minister who became Lord Blakenham planted five acres on a hill above the village between 1950 and 1982. It was his rural retreat from urban political life where he could hear the birdsong and relax in its peace. He succeeded admirably, and his passion for planting and the atmosphere he created have been intensified by the present generation. Though the woodland is clearly managed, the birds still sing in the trees above a carpet of native primroses and bluebells in due season. Other planting is more exotic: rhododendrons, azaleas and magnolias now flower blithely alongside bamboos and phormiums, interspersed with sculptures, belvederes and rustic huts from which to enjoy the serenity. At the heart of the wood is a surprise which never fails to enchant visiting children: a tilting, spiralling grass landform with a central chalk 'plughole', ringed by tall sycamores. At Blakenham even the badgers have their own reserved dell. A delight on a spring or early-summer day.

Bucklesham Hall ★

Bucklesham, Ipswich IP10 0AY. Tel: (01473) 659263

Mr and Mrs D.R. Brightwell • 6m SE of Ipswich, 0.5m E of Bucklesham. Entrance opposite and N of primary school • Open for NGS, and by appt • Entrance: £3.50 • Other information: Coaches by appt. Refreshments by arrangement ◐ 🍴 ⓺ ☕

The great interest of Bucklesham is how these seven acres of interlocking gardens, terraces and lakes have been created from scratch since 1973 by the previous owners and added to and further improved by the present owners since 1994. A Monet-type bridge was built in 1999 with a waterfall falling between two lakes. A 16-step water staircase has also been made so that the water flows from an island lake into the streams. Round the house are secret gardens packed with flowers; beds of old-fashioned roses overflow their borders, and a courtyard garden has been created with the use of every kind of container. Descending terraces of lawns, ponds and streams lead to the woodland and beyond; round each corner is a new vista and a fresh delight. Spring is particularly spectacular here, with displays of daffodils and tulips, rhododendrons, camellias and rare Japanese maples.

Columbine Hall ★

Stowupland, Stowmarket IP14 4AT. Tel: (01449) 612219

Hew Stevenson and Leslie Geddes-Brown • 1.5m NE of Stowmarket. Turn N off A1120 opposite Shell garage across village green, then right at T-junction into Gipping Road. Garden drive is on left just beyond de-restriction sign • Open by appt • Entrance: £3, children free ◐ WC ⓺ ⊕

A garden of great subtlety, gentle order and picturesque charm. The lime-washed manor house, a characterful example of medieval craftsmanship, stands proudly in its rhomboidal moat like a ship in dock. In the entrance courtyard, French in feeling, architectural plants – clipped standards and box mounds, cardoons, a fig and a vine – spring out of gravel or hug the house. The architectural embellishments are eye-catching too. What is clever about the garden (much of the work of George Carter) is that it has a series of uncluttered spaces defined by hornbeam hedges. These are not outdoor rooms, for they allow movement through generous openings, glimpses into other parts of the garden and views out to the countryside. Flowers cluster at the base of pleached limes or in strips running parallel to grass paths. Towards the perimeter, rides are mown through meadows beneath native trees. There is one surprise: a hidden, sinuous bog garden planted with great discrimination.

East Bergholt Place

East Bergholt CO7 6UP. Tel: (01206) 299224

Mr and Mrs Rupert Eley • 8m SW of Ipswich, 2m E of A12 on B1070 • Open March to Oct, daily, 10am – 5pm. Closed 16th April • Entrance: £2.50, children free ❶ 🏠 <u>WC</u> �🚻 🅿 🎋 🍴

The bones of this charming, meandering woodland garden were laid out by the current owner's great-grandfather, Charles Eley, between 1900 and 1914; many of the rare mature trees, azaleas and rhododendrons came from George Forrest, the great plant collector. Rupert Eley has built on this sure foundation creating woodland walks, formal and informal ponds and streams while keeping the atmosphere of an English garden loosely inspired by the Himalayas – the whole is a mixture of the romantic and the disciplined. Many of the exotic trees and shrubs are labelled. The walled garden has been turned into an extensive and well-kept nursery.

Euston Hall ★ [Historic Park Grade II*]

Thetford, Norfolk IP24 2QP. Tel: (01842) 766366

The Duke and Duchess of Grafton • 11m NE of Bury St Edmunds, 3m S of Thetford on A1088 • House open as garden • Garden open 15th June to 14th Sept, Thurs, plus 25th June, 16th July and 3rd Sept; all 2.30 – 5pm • Entrance: house and garden £5, OAPs £4, children £2 (under 5 free), parties of 12 or more £4 per person 🍴 🚌 🏠 <u>WC</u> ⚬ 🎋

The epitome of the English landscape park. The pleasure grounds were laid out in the seventeenth century by John Evelyn, have grown into a forest of yew, but straight rides trace out the original formal layout. Also from this period are the stone gate piers which, together with the remnants of a great avenue, mark the original approach to the house. Fronted by terraces, the mellow red-brick hall stands among extensive lawns and parkland along a winding river, the work of William Kent in the 1740s, as is the splendid domed temple isolated on an eminence to the east and the pretty garden house in the formal garden by the house. The small lake was the work of 'Capability' Brown. Today, the planting is admirably restrained, with many fine specimen trees and a wealth of shrub roses, leaving the original designers' genius intact; further evidence of their brilliance is visible from the rooms of the house.

Garden House Farm ★

Rattlesden Road, Drinkstone, Bury St Edmunds IP30 9TN. Tel: (01449) 736434

Mr and Mrs Hans Seiffer • 8m E of Bury St Edmunds, 3m SW of Woolpit off A14. In centre of village turn left and follow signs to Drinkstone, then Drinkstone Green. Pass village hall, and turn first left into Rattlesden Road; after 0.75m turn left down lane • Open 23rd April, 2 – 5.30pm, and by appt • Entrance: £3, children free ● ● ● ● B&B

These intensive, high-maintenance gardens spread over 11 acres were once the display areas of Barcocks Nursery. Elizabeth Seiffer is a fine and dedicated plantswoman constantly planning new effects. The summer garden, planted with many old-fashioned roses and exuberant herbaceous perennials, contrasts with a fiery-coloured foliage and flower garden. In the formal secret garden paths radiate from a central pond. There is also a winter garden and extensive woodland areas filled with rare and unusual plants and many fine trees, complemented by a large, still lake.

Haughley Park ★

Stowmarket IP14 3JY. Tel: (01359) 240701

Mr R.J. Williams • 4m NW of Stowmarket, signed to Haughley Park (not to Haughley) on A14 • House open by appt • Garden open 30th April and 7th May for bluebells, then May to Sept, Tues, 2 – 5.30pm • Entrance: £3, children under 16 free • Other information: Coaches by appt. Teas and plants for sale on bluebell Suns ● WC & ⬧ ♥

A curious mixture of eighteenth-century-style landscaped park and nineteenth-century evergreens, plus rhododendrons and azaleas, gives this huge garden a unique atmosphere. Unexpected secret gardens with clipped hedges or flint and brick walls hide immaculate flower beds, climbers and flowering shrubs; each garden has its own character. The main lawn is surrounded by herbaceous borders, with a splendid lime avenue at the end drawing the eye across open countryside. Rhododendrons, azaleas and camellias grow on soil which is, unexpectedly for Suffolk, lime-free. The trees include a 12-metre-wide magnolia and a flourishing oak reputed to be a thousand years old. Beyond are the walled kitchen garden, greenhouses and shrubbery. In spring the broad rides and walks through the ancient woodland reveal not only the newly planted trees, specimen rhododendrons and other ornamental shrubs, but also 10 acres of bluebells, two acres of lilies-of-the-valley and half a mile of mauve *ponticum* rhododendrons.

Helmingham Hall Gardens ★★ [Historic Garden Grade I]

Helmingham, Stowmarket IP14 6EF. Tel: (01473) 890799 (Contact Sarah Harris)

Lord Tollemache • 9m N of Ipswich on B1077 • Open 7th May to 17th Sept, Sun, 2 – 6pm; also Wed, 2 – 6pm • Entrance: £4.50, OAPs £4, children £2.50, parties of 30 or more £4 per person ● ● ● WC & ⬧ ♥ ♿ ♥

Nineteen generations of Tollemaches have lived here, and though there have been many changes over the past five centuries the property retains a strong Elizabethan atmosphere. The double-moated Tudor mansion house of great splendour and charm, built of warm red brick, stands in a 400-acre deer park. A nineteenth-century parterre, edged with a magnificent spring border, leads to the

Elizabethan kitchen garden which is surrounded by the Saxon moat with banks covered in daffodils. Within the walls the kitchen garden has been transformed into an enchanting *potager* most subtly planted; the meticulously maintained herbaceous borders and old-fashioned roses surround beds of vegetables separated by arched tunnels of sweet peas and dangling gourds. Large beds along the walls have been cleverly split up with iron dividers and planted with geometrically arranged herb and box beds. Outside is a lushly planted south-facing spring border which includes many irises and peonies. There are also wildflower areas, fruit trees, a shady yew walk, knot and herb gardens. Lady Tollemache is a gifted plantswoman and designer, and her own garden increasingly benefits from her skill.

Ickworth Park [Historic Garden Grade II*]

Horringer, Bury St Edmunds IP29 5QE. Tel: (01284) 735270

The National Trust • 3m SW of Bury St Edmunds; signposted • Park open all year, daily (except 25th Dec), dawn to dusk. Garden open all year, daily (except 24th Dec to 1st Jan), 10am – 5pm (closes 4pm Nov to March) • Entrance: £3.10, children 90p (2005 prices) ○ 🍽 ✕ 🧺 wc ♿ ✿ 🏛 🌳

The vast park, girdled by woodland, is in part the work of 'Capability' Brown and provides a formidable setting for the late-eighteenth-century house. At first the building is not obvious, but the huge rotunda soon looms large, and the great domed drum emerges with its vast curving wings, dominating the gardens which surround it A formal garden, in the Italian style, lies to the south of the house. It features many Mediterranean species and provides an intriguing point of contrast to the bucolic English landscape of the grazed parkland beyond its boundary wall. Within the Italian garden, there is box everywhere (the property holds a National Collection). Bands of Jerusalem sage and catmint, and bedded-out scarlet pelargoniums, provide occasional colour. A waiting discovery behind the clipped hedges is a series of hidden gardens – spring, silver and gold – and the extraordinary stumpery complete with bits of the Giant's Causeway. The park and woods at Ickworth contain many other delights, including an ornamental canal and summerhouse which pre-date the house, a recently planted vineyard, miles of way-marked woodland walks, and a deer enclosure complete with hide.

Magnolia House ★

High Street, Yoxford IP17 3EP. Tel: (01728) 668321

Mark Rumary • In main street, next to Griffin Inn • Open by appt • Entrance: £2.50 ●

In this diminutive garden laid out behind a village house and surrounded by high walls, the designer Mark Rumary has managed to create at least four different moods and a coherent plan – paths always lead somewhere. Near the house is a paved area. The largest part of the garden is laid to lawn surrounded by plants chosen for their leaf shapes, colours and textures – phormiums, berberis, cardoons. A beech arch leads to a more formal Italian section with a lily pond, a fountain and a dovecote complete with 'dun nun' doves; the walls are planted with figs and daturas, and colours here are basically white, yellow and blue. A dell at the far end has shady bamboos and ferns beside a water trough.

Melford Hall [Historic Garden Grade II*]

Long Melford, Sudbury CO10 9AA. Tel: (01787) 379228

The National Trust • 14m S of Bury St Edmunds, 3m N of Sudbury, W of A134 in village • Hall open with Beatrix Potter exhibition • Garden open April, Sat, Sun and Bank Holiday Mon; May to Sept, Wed – Sun and Bank Holiday Mons; Oct, Sat and Sun; all 1.30 – 5pm • Entrance: £5, children £2.50, family £12.50 • Other information: Disabled driven to hall. Wheelchairs provided ◑ 🐾 <u>WC</u> ⇪ ♀

The magnificent mellow red brick house is set in a park and formal gardens. The park was originally separated from the hall by a walled enclosure surrounded by a moat; part of this is now the sunken garden. The avenue at the side of the house has been replanted with oaks grown from the original acorns. To the north, overlooking the village green, is a rare and beautiful survival – an octagonal brick banqueting house – surrounded by clipped box hedges, with a bowling-green terrace leading past dense shrubbery. There are many good specimen trees, including the rare *Xanthoceras sorbifolium*. Great domes of box punctuate the lawns, and an interesting detail is the arrangement of yew hedges to the north of the house. All is in perfect harmony: the peaceful gardens merge into the Suffolk landscape and complement the dignified and impressive Elizabethan house.

North Cove Hall ★

North Cove, Beccles NR34 7PH. Tel: (01502) 476631

Mr and Mrs B. Blower • 3.5m E of Beccles, 50 metres off A146 Lowestoft road • Open by appt only • Entrance: £3, children free ◓ 🐾 WC & ⇪ ℺

Climbing roses adorn the sunny Georgian house set in lawns surrounded by mature park trees. The walled garden partly encloses the half-acre pond studded with water lilies and bordered by majestic *Gunnera manicata, Taxodium distichum* var. *imbricatum* 'Nutans', a group of *Betula jacquemontii* and *Alnus glutinosa* 'Imperialis'. A small stream with waterfalls has recently been constructed and planted. Inside the walls are herbaceous and shrub borders, pergolas and a kitchen garden. Outside are woodland walks among mature trees and various younger conifers; the autumn colours make this a good time to visit. It is worth walking across the park to see the church and its restored wall paintings.

The Old Rectory

Orford, Woodbridge IP12 2NN. Tel: (01394) 450063/450266

Mr and Mrs Tim Fargher • 10m E of Woodbridge. Take B1084 Woodbridge – Orford road; house is on left behind church • Open mid-April to mid-July, Tues – Sat, 10am – 4pm – please telephone in advance • Entrance: £3.50, children £2 • Other information: Parking for disabled only. No dogs. Visitors are asked to make themselves known to gardener, or at the house ◓ & ℘

Church of England rectors once did themselves well and the eighteenth-century incumbent surrounded himself with 4.5 acres of garden. Today this includes woodland, wildflower meadows, a vegetable garden and a generous old greenhouse. The main part of the garden, however, designed for the owners' parents by Lanning

Roper, with later additions by Mark Rumary, is a 1960s' classic. Beds are informal with the emphasis on texture and variety, colours preponderantly white, yellow and blue. Tim Fargher, a painter and sculptor, has one work (a centaur) on show and sculptures by others along with a huge steel disc known as 'the wok', which acts as a water feature. Although the garden is surrounded by houses (except alongside the church, where the party wall is made with fragments from the ruined chancel), the atmosphere is still rural and peaceful.

Playford Hall

Playford, Ipswich IP6 9DX. Tel: (01473) 622509

Mr and Mrs Richard Innes • 3m NE of Ipswich, 1m N of A1214 between Ipswich and Woodbridge, on edge of Playford • Open by appt only • Entrance: £5 ● ▆ ▓ WC

The Tudor red-brick house is the central feature of this 10-acre garden. Its surrounding moat runs between high brick walls and a bridge at one side and then, because of the lie of the land, the water is level with the ground at the other. Huge old roses like 'Paul's Himalyan Musk' cover the walls and drip down towards the water. Beyond the moat, the gardens vary from gently sloping lawns planted with splendid trees – a weeping lime, a swamp cypress and the poisonous Persian wing nut – to rose-hedged orchards, a formal vegetable and herb garden and wild woodland walks. The carefully thought-out borders of herbaceous plants and shrubs backed by evergreen hedges draw the eye irresistibly back to the impressive house.

The Priory ★

Stoke by Nayland CO6 4RL. Tel: (01206) 262216

Mr and Mrs Henry Engleheart • 8m SE of Sudbury on B1068 • Open 21st May, 18th June, 2 – 5.30pm, and by appt in writing • Entrance: £3, children free ● ▆ ▓ WC & ⟐ ▨

An exceptional nine-acre garden with fine views over Constable country. Around the house is a splendid selection of plants and roses in terraces and mixed borders. Lawns slope down to six small lakes, planted with a mass of water plants and water lilies; spring-flowering rhododendrons and azaleas ring the water under large trees. A Chinese bridge links to a tea pavilion by one of the lakes. A garden of mixed planting in the walled garden leads into the greenhouse/conservatory, with its colourful collection of tender plants. Beyond is a kitchen garden with raised beds.

Shrubland Park ★ [Historic Park and Garden Grade I]

Coddenham, Ipswich IP6 9QQ. Tel: (01473) 830221

Lord de Saumarez • 4m N of Ipswich. Turn off A140/A14 interchange slip road towards Ipswich, then turn signed to Barham • Open 16th, 17th and 30th April, 1st, 28th and 29th May, 27th and 28th Aug; plus June, Sun; July and Aug, Sun and Wed; all 2 – 5pm. Guided tours for parties of 10 or more at other times by appt • Entrance: £3, OAPs and children £2 (2005 prices) ● WC & ▨

The magnificence of the hall is reflected in the Victorian gardens, laid out by Sir Charles Barry and later modified by William Robinson. They are among the most important of their type remaining in England. From the upper terrace outside the house visitors descend by a stunning cascade of a hundred steps and terraces to a garden of formal beds, fountain and eye-catcher loggia. Beyond is the wild garden, which merges into the woods and is bordered by the park with its many fine trees, some reputed to be 800 years old. The gardens are punctuated by a series of enchanting follies, ranging from a Swiss chalet to an alpine rockery and magnificent conservatory. The box maze is now established and growing well, and the old dell garden undergoes slow restoration. The hot wall has been restored.

Somerleyton Hall and Gardens ★★ [Historic Garden Grade II*]

Somerleyton, Lowestoft NR32 5QQ. Tel: (0871) 222 4244

Hugh Crossley • 5m NW of Lowestoft, 8m SW of Great Yarmouth on B1074. Signposted • House open as garden, but 12 noon – 4pm • Gardens open 9th April to Oct, Thurs, Sun and Bank Holiday Mons; July and Aug, Tues, Wed, Thurs, Sun and Bank Holiday Mon, 10am – 5pm. Private tours of hall and gardens for parties by arrangement with Administrator • Entrance: £4.50, OAPs £3.50, children (5 – 16) £2.50, parties of 20 or more rates on application (2005 prices). Check prices and opening details on website ❶ 🍵 ✕ 🎁 WC ♿ 🐾 ⬛ ♞*

The Jacobean house was extensively rebuilt in the mid-nineteenth century by Sir Morton Peto as an Italianate palace, and the gardens splendidly reflect this magnificence with 12 acres of formal gardens, a beautiful walled garden, an aviary, a loggia and a winter garden surrounding a sunken garden displaying statues from the original nineteenth-century winter garden. Of special note are the 1846 William Nesfield yew hedge maze, and the 90-metre-long iron pergola covered in wisteria, vines and roses, and the extraordinary peach cases and ridge-and-furrow greenhouses designed by Sir Joseph Paxton and now containing peaches, grapes and a rich variety of tender plants. The Victorian kitchen garden has been redeveloped, and there is also a museum of bygone gardening equipment.

The Thumbit

Badwell Road, Walsham-le-Willows IP31 3BT. Tel: (01359) 259414

Mrs Ann James • 10m NE of Bury St Edmunds off A143. From crossroads by church, follow road signed to Badwell Ash to outskirts of village. Parking on roadside • Open 6th July for NGS, 2 – 6pm, and by appt • Entrance: £2, children free 🍵 WC ♿ 🐾

The garden of this tiny thatched cottage is no bigger than a town garden, but the owner has designed the space so skilfully that it includes a fish pond, fed by an ancient iron kettle and an ornamental herb garden with a frame of runner beans. Winding paths of the most immaculate grass edge circular and curvaceous beds, heavily planted with colourful perennials and given height by a pergola, and trellises covered in clipped ivy, with plenty of places to sit out. Even the cornfield beyond has been hijacked to give a long view over the Suffolk countryside.

Woottens of Wenhaston ★

Blackheath, Wenhaston, Halesworth IP19 9HD. Tel: (01502) 478258

Michael Loftus • 14m SW of Lowestoft, 0.5m S of Blythburgh off A12. Turn left in Wenhaston by marked sign • Garden open April to Sept, Tues – Thurs, 9.30am – 5pm.

Iris field open 24th May to 10th June; hemerocallis field open 15th, 16th, 22nd, 23rd, 29th and 30th July, 9.30am – 5pm • Entrance: donation box NEW ●

Excavating a car park for the nursery's new iris field left the owner with enough topsoil to remove the lawn from his private garden and create a series of raised beds. These are now planted, with an excellent eye for a good plant and a good combination, in a glorious herbaceous abandon. Beds range from shaded greens and whites to exuberant mixes of poppies, alliums, columbines and irises. The two-acre iris field and one-acre hemerocallis field have special openings (see above) for their brief but fabulous flowering seasons. Since most of the plants are clearly labelled and many are for sale in the exceptional nursery adjoining, inspired visitors can take his ideas home and re-create the effects in their own gardens. An informative and well-designed handbook is also available.

Wyken Hall ★

Stanton, Bury St Edmunds IP31 2DW. Tel: (01359) 250287

Sir Kenneth and Lady Carlisle • 9m NE of Bury St Edmunds on A143. Leave A143 between Ixworth and Stanton. Signed to Wyken Vineyards • Open April to Oct, daily, except Sat, 2 – 6pm • Entrance: £3, OAPs £2.50, children under 12 free • Other information: Vineyard ○ ☕ ✕ WC ㅎ ⛲ ▨ ♨ ♨

The combination of Sir Kenneth, a RHS committee member, and his enterprising American wife Carla, has created an outstandingly exuberant four-acre garden full of invention and surprise. It is divided into a series of rooms, starting with the wild garden and winter garden, which leads into the south and woodland garden, and so into the dell. Mown paths meander between shrubs and into the newly planted copper beech maze next to the nuttery and gazebo, then on to the rose garden, enclosed on three sides by a hornbeam hedge and on the fourth by a rose-laden pergola. Beyond the wall are the knot and herb gardens, separated by yew hedges and designed by Arabella Lennox-Boyd. An 'edible garden' and a kitchen garden have been planted to the north of the house, and there is a new pond just beyond the garden. The whole place is remarkable for its colours and scents, particularly in high summer. Fields and orchards with wandering hens, peacocks, guinea fowl and llamas enhance the relaxed atmosphere, while the outbuildings painted in American pioneering colours are the personal touches of Lady Carlisle.

NCCPG

The National Council for the Conservation of Plants and Gardens publishes a *National Plant Collections Directory*. Those interested in seeing some of the rarer species and garden varieties of particular families of plants will find this an invaluable publication. The latest edition, which offers information on about 600 collections comprising more than 50,000 plants and contains articles by holders of the collections, is available from NCCPG, The Stable Courtyard, RHS Garden, Wisley, Woking GU23 6QP (Tel: (01483) 221465; Fax: (01483) 212404; Website: www.nccpg.com. The new edition will be published in February or March 2006.

SURREY

We have included some gardens with Surrey postal addresses in the London section for convenience. So before planning a day out in Surrey it is worth consulting pages 235–70.

Two-starred gardens are marked on the map with a black square.

Busbridge Lakes [Historic Park Grade II*]

Hambledon Road, Godalming GU8 4AY. Tel: (01483) 421955

Mr and Mrs Douetil • 1.5m S of Godalming off B2130 Hambledon road • Open 17th April, 30th April, 1st, 28th and 29th May, 20th to 28th Aug; all 10.30am – 5.30pm; pre-booked parties any day April to Sept by appt • Entrance: £5, OAPs and children £3.50, under 5 free • Other information: Refreshments weekends and Bank Holidays only ● ● ● WC & ●

Parkland was created here in the 1650s and the grounds were landscaped in 1750 by Philip Webb MP. Beside the largest of the three lakes stands an early-nineteenth-century Gothick boathouse, recently restored, with delicate blind windows, a room with a fireplace and two verandahs. At the end of the lake, what appears to be a bridge, multi-arched and built of rocks, proves to be an illusion. Huge plane trees dominate the lakeside; the 30-metre chestnuts, probably planted in 1660, may be the tallest in England. Tulip trees (*Liriodendron tulipifera*) and a fine cedar of Lebanon stand near the orchard; a sequoia towers above the house. Across the canal lake is a hermit's cave, excavated in 1756 as a tomb for the then owner's wife and two of their children. Further up, a late-eighteenth-century Doric temple with two porticos has recently been restored; below it a grotto contains the spring which feeds the lakes. There are peacocks on the lawns, and the site abounds with attractive, rare and endangered species of ducks, geese, swans and pheasants, all flourishing – as are the gardens. 2m SW of Godalming on the A3100 is *Secretts Garden Centre*, Portsmouth Road, Milford (Tel: (01483) 426633), where the plants for sale are placed in imaginatively designed settings and a garden with a large pond displays National Collections of cornus and kalmias.

Clandon Park [Historic Park Grade II]

West Clandon, Guildford GU4 7RQ. Tel: (01483) 222482

The National Trust • 3m E of Guildford on A247 at West Clandon; or take A3 to Ripley then join A247 via B2215 • House open as garden • Garden open April to Oct, Tues – Thurs, Sun and Bank Holiday Mons, 11am – 5pm. Pre-booked parties, Tues – Thurs and Sun from 2pm • Entrance: House and garden £6, children £3, family £15, parties of 15 or more £5 per person, combined ticket with Hatchlands (see entry) £9 • Other information: Disabled parking near front of house ○ ● ✕ ● WC & ●

The house was built by the Venetian architect Giacomo Leoni in the early 1730s for the 2nd Lord Onslow, whose family still owns the park although the house and garden are owned by the National Trust. The seven-acre garden is on a hillside and gives a fine view of the lake. An interesting feature is the Maori meeting house, known as 'Hinemihi', brought from New Zealand over a century ago by the then Lord Onslow. Note also the grotto, parterre and herbaceous border, and the bedding and colours in the sunken Dutch garden. Another important historic garden is close by and well worth a visit, although open very infrequently: the 14 acres of pleasure grounds at *Albury Park*, Albury, designed by John Evelyn in the mid-1600s. [Telephone (01483) 202964; open for NGS.]

Claremont Landscape Garden ★ [Historic Park Grade I]

Portsmouth Road, Esher KT10 9JG. Tel: (01372) 467806

The National Trust • E of A307, just S of Esher • House (not NT) and belvedere open – telephone for details • Garden open Jan to March, daily except Mon, 10am – 5pm; April to Oct, Mon – Fri, daily, 10am – 6pm (closes 7pm Sat, Sun and Bank Holiday Mons); Nov to Dec, daily except Mon, 10am – 5pm or sunset if earlier. Closed 25th Dec. Coach parties must book • Entrance: £5, children £2.50, family £12.50, pre-booked parties £4.20 per person • Other information: Dogs, Nov to March only, on lead ○ ⚌ ✕ 🍴 WC ᵹ 🏸 ♿ ♒

One of the most important historic landscapes in England. Practically all the great landscape designers of the eighteenth century adapted it in turn for the new owner, the immensely wealthy man who became Duke of Newcastle. He bought the house from Sir John Vanbrugh and, for him Vanbrugh designed the belvedere (the views from the top are amazing). The Duke then employed Bridgeman in 1716, followed by Kent in the 1730s; the latter adapted the garden to create picturesque settings, evoking various moods, and also enlarged the pond to make the lake, with a pavilion (recently restored). When the Duke died, Clive of India purchased the estate. He brought in 'Capability' Brown, who also designed the house and, in typical form, diverted the London-Portsmouth road to improve the viewpoints, the most striking of which is the grass amphitheatre. In the nineteenth century it was a favourite retreat of Queen Victoria and her younger son. The 50 acres restored by the Trust are only a part of the original estate, which was broken up in 1922 when the house became a school. A useful leaflet describes the various contributions to the park, which will appeal to everyone interested in its sensitive reconstruction of the eighteenth-century English style, even if it has little to please a plant lover, except perhaps the camellia terrace. A few miles east, in Leatherhead Road, Chessington, *Chessington Nursery* (Tel: (01372) 744490) offers a wide range of plants for both house and garden, attractively displayed. [Open all year, daily, 9am – 6pm (10am – 4pm on Suns).]

Coverwood Lakes, Garden and Farm

Peaslake Road, Ewhurst, Cranleigh GU6 7NT. Tel: (01306) 731101

Mrs C.G. Metson and Mr and Mrs N. Metson • 7m SW of Dorking, 6m SE of Guildford, 0.5m S of Peaslake off A25 • Gardens and farm open 16th, 23rd, 30th April, 7th, 14th, 21st May, 2 – 6pm; 22nd Oct, 11am – 4.30pm; and for parties by appt • Entrance: £3.50, children £2 • Other information: Home-made teas available

on April and May open days, hot soup and sandwiches on Oct open day
🍃 **B&B**

Immensely tall rhododendrons, planted in Edwardian times, tower over camellias and azaleas, with little paths bordered by hostas, candelabra primulas, trilliums and lilies-of-the-valley winding among them. In the bog garden, the tiny streams that moisten groups of lysichitum and *Gunnera manicata* flow on to feed the four lakes that lie at the heart of the woodland estate. The first and most formal of these has a pergola with stone pillars and seats running along one side; the furthest and largest lies beside a 3.5-acre arboretum planted in 1990 with specimens from all over the world and already looking well established. A marked farm trail gives wonderful views from the highest field.

Crosswater Farm

Millais Nurseries, Crosswater Lane, Churt, Farnham GU10 2JN.
Tel: (01252) 792698

Mrs R.B. Millais and family • 6m SE of Farnham, 6m NW of Haslemere, 0.5m N of Churt off A287. Signed 'Millais Nurseries' • Open 17th April to 9th June, daily, 10am – 5pm • Entrance: £2.50, children free ● 🅿 🍴 **WC** ♿ 🍃 🎏

These six acres of woodland gardens were begun in 1946 by Ted and Romy Millais, who specialised in azaleas and rhododendrons and assembled an exceptional international collection. Among the mature and some more recent plantings are rare species collected in the Himalayas and hybrids raised by them, including *Rhododendron* 'High Summer'. The plants are labelled and most are available from the adjoining nursery, which grows more than 750 different varieties. There is also an excellent collection of sorbus trees. The surrounding garden features a stream, ponds and attractive companion plantings, including magnolias, Japanese maples and woodland perennials.

Dunsborough Park ★

Ripley, Woking GU23 6AL. Tel: (01483) 225366

Baron and Baroness Sweerts de Landas Wyborgh • 3m NE of Guildford. Take A247 or A3 to Ripley. Entrance across Ripley Green • Open three times a year for charity, and by appt (please telephone for dates) • Entrance: £3, children £1.50 ● 🅿 **WC** ♿ 🍃

The restoration of the 10-acre garden, together with its Victorian glasshouses and palm house, is now virtually complete and makes a fitting showcase for the extensive collection of statuary and ornaments displayed among the plants. Double herbaceous borders have been cleared of bindweed and replanted by Rubert Golby with perennials in a colour scheme of blue and white, and a former colour-themed border has been replaced with vibrant late-summer herbaceous perennials. There are two walled gardens. One has been divided by Penelope Hobhouse into separate rooms, each one different and each filled with unusual and interesting plants; the other shelters shrub roses and, behind a unique ginkgo hedge, a display of garden ornaments. The main part of the water garden, crossed by stepping stones, has been restored and replanted to Mykola Khrystenko's design, and can be viewed from the delightful belvedere on the bridge. The secluded white garden is dominated by an ancient, spreading mulberry.

Feathercombe

Feathercombe Lane, Hambledon, Godalming GU8 4DP. Tel: (01483) 860264

Campbell • 4m SW of Godalming between A283 and B2130. Feathercombe Lane is off Hambledon Road between Hydestile crossroads and Merry Harriers pub • Open by appt during May only • Entrance: £3.50 ● ⟲ ℘

The romantic 12-acre garden was designed and created from 1910 by Surrey author and journalist Eric Parker and his wife Ruth, daughter of Ludwig Messel of Nymans (see entry in West Sussex); now it is maintained by their grandchildren. High banks of rhododendrons, azaleas, tree heathers and shrubs, including a huge exochorda, are sheltered by mature trees – in spring spectacular tall *Embothrium coccineum* (Chilean firebush) blaze out their scarlet flowers. A mature yew topiary garden surrounds a formal goldfish pool, and *Wisteria floribunda* cascades from a pergola. There are amazing views to the Surrey and Sussex hills: Blackdown, Hindhead and the Hog's Back.

Gatton Park [Historic Park Grade II]

Reigate RH2 0TW. Tel: (01737) 649068 or (0794) 157 2434

The Royal Alexandra and Albert School • 3m NE of Reigate. From A23 or Gatton Bottom, turn into Rocky Lane • Open for snowdrops 5th Feb, 1 – 5pm, 12th Feb, 10am – 3pm, 15th Feb, 12 noon – 3pm; then March to Oct, 1st Sun each month, 1 – 5 pm • Entrance: £3, children free. Snowdrop talk and walk 4th Feb, £8 per person ● ☕ <u>WC</u> ⅋ ⟲ ℘ ⓘ ♿

The Domesday Book records a manor and deer park here, and a diminutive town hall still stands as a reminder of Gatton's days as a rotten borough. In the eighteenth century 'Capability' Brown landscaped the grounds and created the 28-acre lake, and in the late-nineteenth and twentieth centuries Jeremiah Colman, the mustard magnate, built a dramatic rock and water garden, together with a Japanese garden with its thatched tea house, bridge and lanterns. An enthusiastic band of volunteers has been restoring the gardens since 1996, most recently the ponds, cascades and the Serpentine feeding the lake, which is home to a heronry on one of the islands. The rock garden has been planted anew with alpines and small shrubs, and the drystone arch restored too; next on the list is the walled garden. Set in a circle near North Downs Way are ten Caithness stones three metres high engraved for the Millennium with texts from the last 1000 years.

Goddards

Abinger Common, Dorking RH5 6JH.
Tel: (01306) 730871 (Ticket bookings during office hours)

The Landmark Trust • 10m SE of Guildford, 4m SW of Dorking off A25. At Wotton take right turn for Abinger Common. House on green opposite Victorian well • Open 29th March to 25th Oct, Wed only, 2.30 – 5pm, strictly by appt • Entrance: £3 • Other information: Limited parking, must be booked ● WC ♿

Sir Edwin Lutyens designed the house originally in 1898 as a home of rest for ladies of small means. He planned it around a courtyard garden, facing slightly west of south and overlooked by all the principal rooms – in effect an outdoor room. Gertrude Jekyll collaborated on the structure of the garden, which remains intact. A dipping well in the centre, providing water for the plants, is surrounded by paved paths, low walls, curved beds and a raised sundial. There are flower borders under the windows and vines and wisterias grow against the house walls. Architectural yew hedges enclose the formal gardens around the house, and yew arches give vistas over lawns, a ha-ha and across a meadow to a curving backdrop of woods. The house, cared for by the Landmark Trust, may be rented for self-catering holidays. Strangely, Goddards is not on the English Heritage Register of Gardens.

Great Fosters ★ [Historic Garden Grade II*]

Stroude Road, Egham TW20 9UR. Tel: (01784) 433822

Great Fosters (1931) Ltd • 1m SW of Staines off M25 junction 13, 1m S of Egham. From railway station follow Manorcroft Road into Stroude Road and continue 1m. Hotel on left • Open all year, daily, during daylight hours • Entrance: free • Other information: Refreshments and toilet facilities in hotel ○ ➍ ✕ <u>WC</u> ♿ B&B

Although the house was built in the late-sixteenth century, the topiary parterres were created in 1918 within an original U-shaped moat and more recently restored. A Japanese bridge, festooned with wisteria, leads to a pergola and a circular, sunken rose garden with an octet of steps leading down to a lily pond and fountain. Nearby are two modern gardens and a vista garden with serpentine hedges. A lake surrounded by marginals and a woodland area are recent additions. But the most dramatic and innovative development is undoubtedly Kim Wilkie's vast amphitheatre at the end of the lime avenue, carved out against a bund made especially to block out the pervasive roar of the M25.

The Green House

69 Station Road, Chertsey KT16 8BN. Tel: (01932) 567725

Steven Leon and Stephanie Grimshaw • Leave M25 junction 11 for A317. Turn left at roundabout, left at Eastworth Road, left at Highfield Road, then right into Station Road • Open by appt only • Entrance: £2 ◗ ♿ ✤

The Japanese-style bridge leads over a pond into an enchanted garden just seven metres wide. Mature trees – hazel, ash and eucalyptus – look down on tall shrubs and arches swathed with climbers, and architectural plants, flowers and bulbs thrive in the shelter and seclusion. Raised beds have been given extra height by lowering the level of the central path to make gardening easier for the disabled owner. Mirrors and holes cut in the fence create a *trompe-l'œil* effect, giving the garden extra width. Covered seating and dining areas are decorated with *objets trouvés*, and at the far end is a fantasy building and a little folly.

Guildford Castle Gardens

Castle Street, Guildford GU1 3TU. Tel: (01483) 505050

Guildford Borough Council • From High Street walk through arches into Tunsgate. Castle opposite at far end • Open all year, daily, dawn – dusk • Entrance: free ○ ▥ ♿ ✤ ☕

This ruined keep built by William the Conqueror (close to the present city centre) once formed part of the garden of a private house bought by Guildford Corporation in 1885. Clever use has been made of the original moat. A path runs around the bottom, and shaped beds, retaining their Victorian designs, are cut into the sloping turfed sides. They are bedded out for spectacular spring and summer displays with much the same plants as the Victorians would have used. There are plenty of seats. A tunnel, its damp, shady approach brightly planted, leads up to a bandstand and a bowling green with attractive borders and clipped hedges. The castle, now restored and reroofed, features a permanent exhibition on its history.

Hannah Peschar Sculpture Garden

Black and White Cottage, Standon Lane, Ockley RH5 5QR. Tel: (01306) 627269

Hannah Peschar • 6m S of Dorking, 1m SW of Ockley off A29. Follow signs for 'Golf and Country Club'. Entrance on right in Standon Lane 400 metres past low bridge over stream • Open May to Oct, Fri and Sat, 11am – 6pm, Sun and Bank Holiday Mons, 2 – 5pm; other days, except Mon, by appt only • Entrance: £9, OAPs £7, children under 16 £6 • Other information: Refreshments and meals for parties by arrangement only. Details of lecture tours, party and school visits on request ❶ 🏵 WC ♿ 🖤 B&B

In Victorian times the heart of the 20-acre valley garden was part of the Leith Vale Estate, and when Hannah Peschar and her husband, the landscape designer Anthony Paul, came here in 1977, the place had been neglected for many years. He kept the old trees, and under their canopy has encouraged some 400 native species to spread among his favourite, more restricted palette of architectural plants – dynamos such as gunneras, *Ligularia* 'The Rocket', a variety of grasses and stands of bamboo. It is an other-worldly experience to wind along the narrow paths looking down on streams, lakes and precarious wooden bridges; and the romantic buildings at the heart of the garden enhance the effect. But the garden is only half the story. It has primarily been designed as a showcase for Hannah Peschar's own business – the sale of contemporary sculpture of the highest quality, placed among vegetation or against water to bring out the character and quality of each piece.

Hatchlands Park

East Clandon, Guildford GU4 7RT. Tel: (01483) 222482

The National Trust • 5m NE of Guildford, E of East Clandon, N of A246 • House and garden open April to Oct, Tues – Thurs, Sun and Bank Holiday Mons, also Fri in Aug, 2 – 5.30pm; park walks and grounds open April to Oct, daily, 11am – 6pm. Parties by appt Tues – Thurs only • Entrance: park walks £3 (house, garden and walks £6, family £15, parties of 15 or more £5 per person, combined ticket with Clandon (see entry) £9) ❶ 💷 🏵 WC ♿ ⛪ 🔍

The Gertrude Jekyll garden has herbaceous planting and roses. Beside the garden is a magnificent 200-year-old London plane tree, a temple and an ice-house. A wildflower meadow is left uncut until July. The 430-acre parkland has four way-marked walks to enjoy, including a bluebell wood.

Knightsmead

Rickman Hill Road, Chipstead CR5 3LB. Tel: (01737) 551694

Mrs C. Jones and Miss C. Collins • 7m E of Epsom, 1m SW of Coulsdon, 3m SE of Banstead, off B2032 • Open 4th May, 11am – 4pm, 7th May, 2 – 5pm, and by appt • Entrance: £2.50, accompanied children 50p ● ● WC ⅋ ⌼

When the present owners came here over a decade ago, the half-acre garden was overshadowed by vast Lawson cypresses. Now there are shrub roses and clematis, with arcs of smaller trees underplanted with spring bulbs and woodland plants such as erythroniums, trilliums and pure-colour-bred hellebores. A graceful 20-metre deodar cedar dominates this well-designed plantsman's garden, and a lily pond, roses climbing over an arch and beds of shrubs and perennials give year-round interest. On heavy clay soil, a bog garden, peat bed and limestone scree provide ideal conditions for choice plants. Walls support climbers and a conservatory extends the range. There is also a pergola and water features.

22 Knoll Road

Dorking RH4 3EP. Tel: (01306) 883280

David and Anne Drummond • From one-way system turn left up Horsham Road (A2003). Knoll Road is on right just after Bush Inn • Open 14th and 17th May, 10.30am – 5.30pm for NGS, and for individuals and parties by appt • Entrance: £2, children free ● ● ● WC ⅋ ⌼ ⌀

Approaching up a short steep drive cut through banks, the visitor is introduced first to the garden lying behind the house. The owners' love of plants is evident everywhere: in the large collection of alpines in troughs and raised beds, and in the interesting mixed borders surrounding the lawn, which has a labyrinth of ancient design cut into it. A catalpa stands in a miniature meadow, and room is also found for a pond, a peat bed, a fern *allée* and a conservatory. Arranged around the garden are intriguing artefacts from many countries; a list with their histories is available. The front garden, with its pebbles and dramatic plants, comes as a complete surprise.

Langshott Manor

Langshott, Horley RH6 9LN. Tel: (01293) 786680

Mr and Mrs Peter Hinchcliffe • 6m S of Redhill, 4m N of Crawley. From Horley on A23 turn right at Chequers Hotel roundabout into Ladbroke Road and continue about 1m. Manor is on right • Open all year, daily • Entrance: free ○ ● ✕ WC ⅋ ⌖ B&B

This beautifully restored Grade-II Elizabethan manor house, draped in roses, clematis and a huge *Magnolia grandiflora*, is tucked away down a country lane; it is now a hotel. The peaceful setting is enhanced by a garden whose design complements the house. A sunken rose garden with borders edged in box contains an interesting star-shaped brick-and-tile feature with roses growing up a central pillar. The terrace of mellow stone and brick is edged with lavender. A pleached lime avenue curves around one side of the croquet lawn, and a hornbeam pergola leads from the entrance drive down towards it. A small orchard of old varieties of fruit contains a turf seat and a colourful mixed bed of herbs and salad plants. There is also a small lake with ducks and a rustic stone bridge separating the birds' domain from the ornamental part, planted with water lilies and moisture-loving plants.

Leith Hill Rhododendron Wood

Tanhurst Lane, Coldharbour. Tel: (01306) 712711

The National Trust • 5m S of Dorking. Take Coldharbour Road and continue to Leith Hill. At next junction keep right, then fork left. Wood immediately on left • Tower open 25th March to 29th Oct, Fri, Sat, Sun, and Bank Holiday Mons (plus Wed in Aug), 10am – 5pm; 4th Nov to March, Sat and Sun, 10am – 3.30pm. Closed 25th Dec • Rhododendron wood open all year, daily, during daylight hours • Entrance: £2 per car for wood • Other information: Light refreshments when tower open ○ 🐾 ⅙ ⊲⅋

The wood was originally part of the estate of Leith Hill Place, once the home of the composer Ralph Vaughan Williams. Beside the car park is an extensive picnic area, and below this the rhododendrons and azaleas are a blaze of colour in April, May and June. There has been some replanting and the paths have been improved. An immense tulip tree, *Liriodendron tulipifera*, can be seen in the field beyond, and there are spectacular views. Further on, the mature trees create a shady area for rhododendrons in soft colours.

Little Lodge

Watts Road, Thames Ditton KT7 0BX. Tel: (020) 8339 0931

Mr and Mrs Peter Hickman • 1m N of Esher. From London take A3. In Thames Ditton village follow High Street down Watts Road. Giggs Hill Green is ahead, house is opposite library • Open 28th May, 11.30am – 5.30pm, 7th June, 2.30 – 8.30pm, and by appt at other times • Entrance: £2.50 (£3.50 after 6pm), children free ● 🔲 WC ⅙ ⅋

The house rests comfortably in its own lush surround, and in the front garden a pond and wild planting with formal topiary beds give little hint of the large cottage garden behind the house. Against the densely covered house walls is a paved suntrap with a wide variety of containers and unusual plants. The main lawned area has herbaceous borders and island beds with secret spots defined by yew hedges. A vegetable garden with raised well-stocked beds edged in box adds to the charm of this much-visited garden.

Loseley Park ★

Compton, Guildford GU3 1HS. Tel: (01483) 304440

Mr and Mrs M.G. More-Molyneux • 3m SW of Guildford, W of A3, off B3000 • House open May to Aug, Tues – Thurs, Sun and Bank Holiday Mons, 1pm – 5pm • Garden open May to Sept, Tues – Sun and Bank Holiday Mons, 11am – 5pm • Entrance: £4, OAPs/disabled £3.50, children £2 (house and garden £7, OAPs/disabled £6.50, children £3.50) ◑ 🔲 ✕ 🐾 WC ⅙ ⅋ 🏛 ♀ ⊶

The Elizabethan house is surrounded by parkland. Hidden away at the side of the house, the vast walled garden has been transformed: six gardens have been created based on a Gertrude Jekyll design, each with their own theme and character. The old mulberry is still there, also a medlar with a group of palms. An enchanting rose garden with low box hedges is filled with old-fashioned roses, carefully labelled; box balls and circles emphasise the design, while pillars of roses and hollies give height. Along one side is an arcade of vines and clematis. A herb garden displays culinary, medicinal and ornamental herbs in triangular beds and others used in cosmetics, lotions and dyes, all well labelled. Quartets of domed acacias stand at the intersections of the main paths, and golden malus (crab apples) form a square avenue in the fruit and flower garden, which is planted in bold fiery colours. In contrast, the fountain garden is laid out with white and silver flowers and foliage to create a romantic atmosphere. A wide range of produce is grown in the attractive organic vegetable garden. Future plans include a wildflower meadow. The moat walk shelters a long border of sun-loving plants, including yuccas (don't step back while admiring them). Near the entrance to the garden is an ancient wisteria and a good herbaceous border.

Munstead Wood [Historic Garden Grade I]

Heath Lane, Busbridge, Godalming GU7 1UN. Tel: (01483) 417867

Sir Robert and Lady Clark • From Godalming take B2130 to Busbridge. Heath Lane is on left opposite church • Open 23rd April, 28th May and 25th June, 2 – 6pm, and by appt • Entrance: £3, OAPs £2, children free ● 💭 WC ♿ 🐕 🌳 🏛

Gertrude Jekyll began to make her own garden here in 1883, when she was forty; the house, designed by Edwin Lutyens, was built thirteen years later. The garden, carefully restored to Jekyll's original plans over the past decade, reveals the extent of her genius for both planting and design. A river of daffodils flows onto the front lawn from a birch copse. A wide grass path through mature rhododendrons creates a vista to and from woodland and the house, and there are walks among scented azaleas in soft and vibrant colours. The wide west lawn leads past a sunken rock garden and shrubbery to the main border, 60 metres long, backed by a high wall of local Bargate stone. Jekyll grew hot red and orange flowers in the centre, shading out through yellows, blues and mauves to white at either end. The spring and summer gardens are reached through an arched doorway. Returning towards the house, past the rose-covered pergola and summerhouse, visitors discover the nut walk and the aster garden, white borders and lavender-fringed paths; a primula garden is hidden away to one side. At the back of the house is a cool courtyard with festoons of *Clematis montana*, paving and a pool. Jekyll had eight gardeners tending 15 acres: now 10 acres are maintained by just two.

Painshill Park ★★ [Historic Garden Grade I]

Portsmouth Road, Cobham KT11 1JE. Tel: (01932) 868113

Painshill Park Trust • 4m SW of Esher, W of Cobham. From M25 junction 10, take A3 and A245. Entrance 200 metres from A245/A307 roundabout • Open all year, daily except 25th and 26th Dec: March to Oct, 10.30am – 6pm (last admission 4.30pm); Nov to Feb, 11am – 4pm or dusk if earlier (last admission 3pm). Parties of 10 or more (incl. school parties) by appt • Entrance: £6, concessions £5.25, children

(5–16) £3.50 • Other information: Children under 16 must be accompanied.
Wheelchairs and electric buggies available by prior booking ⏰ 🍽 ✕ 📷 <u>WC</u> ♿ 🚻 🍴 ♺

The Hon. Charles Hamilton created the 160-acre landscaped park – contemporary with Stowe and Stourhead – between 1738 and 1773, when it was sold after he ran out of funds. The garden was well maintained until World War II, then in 1948 it was sold off in lots and all but lost. Between 1974 and 1980 Elmbridge Council bought up most of the land; the following year the Painshill Park Trust was formed and began the task of restoration. To the north is a crescent of parkland with clumps of trees, and the ornamental pleasure grounds to the south were designed around a serpentine 14-acre lake and spectacular waterwheel fed from the River Mole. The restored Chinese bridge, opened in 1988, leads to an island and a magical grotto, the main chamber of which is 12 metres across, hung with stalactites and lined with shards of glistening felspar. The mausoleum, near the river, was depicted on one of the plates of Catherine the Great's Wedgwood 'Frog Service'; a further reach of the lake reflects an abbey ruin. The focal point of the garden is the elegant Gothick temple on higher ground. It is approached across a grassed 'amphitheatre' encircled by formal eighteenth-century-style shrubberies. A dramatic blue and white Turkish tent with a gold coronet stands on a plateau among informal plantings; in the distance is the Gothick tower. The great cedar of Lebanon, 36.5 metres high and with a girth of 10 metres, is reputedly the largest in Europe. The vineyard has been replanted on a southern slope as it was in Charles Hamilton's day, and the hermitage rebuilt. A major new attraction is the 'American Roots' exhibition within the old walled garden, which celebrates the seventeenth-century influx of exotica from the New World. Plans are afoot to complete the restoration of the grotto and rebuild more of the original features, including the 'missing' Temple of Bacchus.

Polesden Lacey ★ [Historic Garden Grade II*]

Dorking RH5 6BD. Tel: (01372) 452048/458203 (Infoline)

The National Trust • 5m NW of Dorking, 2m S of Great Bookham off A246
Leatherhead – Guildford road • House open • Gardens and grounds open all year,
daily, 11am – 5pm, or dusk if earlier; telephone for details of snowdrop openings
• Entrance: £6, children £3, family £15 (house and grounds £9, children £4.50,
family £22.50) • Other information: Parking 150 metres away. Disabled parking
area. Batricar available on pre-booked basis. Braille guide available. Picnics and
dogs permitted outside formal garden only. Open-air theatre and concerts in June
○ 🍽 ✕ <u>WC</u> ♿ 🌿 🍴 🍷 ♺

Richard Brinsley Sheridan, the dramatist, lived here for twenty years until his death in 1816, and extended the Long Walk with its fabulous views across the valley. A few years later the present house was built by Cubitt in the Greek classical style and over 20,000 trees were planted. The Edwardian society hostess, The Hon. Mrs. Greville, added the Edwardian facade and laid out the formal walled gardens, although the outbreak of the First World War and the death of her husband prevented the plans for an original elaborate Italianate terrace from being carried out. In her day 36 gardeners tended the 30 acres; today a quarter of a million people visit the garden annually. Now pergolas draped with ramblers enclose the paths in the rose garden, peony, lavender and iris gardens lead to the winter garden and the thatched bridge, and there is a long herbaceous border designed by Graham Stuart Thomas sheltered by a wall. A programme of restoration is under way: a new oak bridge has been built and walks have been created, including one suitable for wheelchairs. The rock garden will be restored and the orchard replanted.

Ramster

Chiddingfold, Godalming GU8 4SN. Tel: (01428) 654167

Mr and Mrs P. Gunn • NE of Haslemere, 1.5m S of Chiddingfold on A283 • Open 8th April to 25th June, daily, 10.30am – 5pm, and for parties by appt • Entrance: £4, children under 16 free • Other information: Possible for wheelchairs in dry weather only ❶ 🅿 🍽 <u>WC</u> ⟁ ⚘ 🍷

A local nursery originally laid out the garden in 1890 in the Japanese style fashionable at the time. Bamboos, stone lanterns and a splendid double row of *Acer palmatum* 'Dissectum Atropurpureum' remain from that time. In 1922 the property was bought by Sir Henry and Lady Norman, Mrs Gunn's grandparents. Lady Norman grew up at Bodnant and many of the plants at Ramster came from there. The 20 acres of natural woodland, stream and lakes provide an ideal setting for rhododendrons and azaleas, camellias, magnolias and unusual trees. A collection of over 200 old hardy hybrid azaleas is a more recent addition, and a bog garden was planted in 1998. The millennium garden on the old tennis court, by contrast, is paved, with two ponds connected by a rill, and four raised beds of three tiers each, built of concrete blocks. The planting follows the colour wheel, with an appropriate tree (*Acer palmatum* 'Senkaki' in the 'hot' section), underplanted with bulbs, herbaceous perennials and shrubs.

RHS Garden Wisley ★★ [Historic Garden Grade II*]

Wisley, Woking GU23 6QB. Tel: (01483) 224234

Royal Horticultural Society • 7m NE of Guildford, on A3. Signed from M25 junction 10 south. Trains to West Byfleet or Woking; taxi service usually available at stations • Open all year, daily, 10am – 6pm (opens 9am Sat and Sun, closes 4.30pm Nov to Feb) (last admission 1 hour before closing) • Entrance: £7, children (6–16) £2, under 6 free; companion for wheelchair-bound or blind visitors free (2005 prices) • Other information: Disabled and shaded parking ○ 🅿 ✕ 🍽 <u>WC</u> ♿ ⚘ ⛲ 🍷 ✂

Wisley Garden was presented to the Royal Horticultural Society in 1903 by Sir Thomas Hanbury, who created the famous La Mortola garden in Italy. The Society's first major development was the rock garden, a fashionable feature at the time, sections of which were reconstructed in the 1980s. The broadwalk leads between double mixed borders, each over 120 x 5 metres, to a country garden designed by Penelope Hobhouse, then to rose gardens and onwards to Battleston Hill and East Battleston, with azaleas, rhododendrons, hydrangeas and lilies. Over the crest of the hill, on the southern slope, is the Mediterranean garden, planted since the 1987 storms and, beyond it, the Portsmouth Field. Here the Society, as the leading international trials institution, holds trials of plants, flowers and vegetables, including, every year, delphiniums, sweet peas and dahlias. To the west the 32-acre Jubilee Arboretum encircles the fruit field, where growing trees can be compared. 2006 sees the continuing construction of the new Bicentenary Glasshouse. Considerably larger than the old glasshouses, there will be three climate zones and a large educational area. Completion is due in 2007. The popular model gardens include a collection of bonsai and prize-winning gardens transported from the Chelsea Flower Show; others display fruit and vegetables – 1000 varieties of top, bush and soft fruit are grown. Lucy Huntington's redesigned herb garden is now open. The peaceful pinetum, the riverside walk and the new heather garden in Howard's Field lie beyond the restaurant. The lakes nearby have been enlarged and made more naturalistic, with planting mainly for winter effect. Sir Geoffrey Jellicoe designed the canal and loggia in front of the laboratory. Martin Lane Fox and the garden staff have transformed the walled garden – a sun trap which now shelters Italian cypresses, Chusan palms, tree ferns and a host of tender plants. Beyond the rock garden along the lower path through the trees are new, dramatic meadow-style borders, each 11 metres deep and 146 metres long, designed by the Dutch garden designer and plantsman Piet Oudolf. An avenue of *Cornus kousa* var. *chinensis* and shrubs backs herbaceous perennials and grasses planted in diagonal drifts to give a ribbon effect. At the top is the staff's own millennium project, a fruit mount with a spectacular view of the Surrey countryside; step-over apples grow round the base and the spiral path is bordered by blackberries and vines. Occasional displays of sculpture are among the most recent attractions. The laboratory, built in 1916 in Tudor style, is the hub of the Society's advisory service to members: identifying plants, answering queries on pests and diseases and gardening problems. Talks and demonstrations of gardening techniques are given, informative walks conducted, and a training programme run for students. The combination of learning and pleasure is the essence of Wisley, as well over half a million visitors discover each year as they explore the 240 acres. The Garden Library, open to all visitors, is near the restaurant, and the bookshop should be visited before leaving.

Savill Garden (Windsor Great Park) ★★ [Historic Park Grade I]

Wick Lane, Englefield Green TW20 0UU. Tel: (01753) 847518

Administered by the Crown Estate Commissioners • 4m W of Staines, 5m S of Windsor. From A30, turn into Wick Road and follow signs, or follow signs from Englefield Green • Open all year, daily, 10am – 6pm (closes 4pm Nov to Feb). Closed 25th, 26th Dec • Entrance: £3.55 – £5.50, OAPs/parties £3-£5 (all seasonal), accompanied children under 16 free (2005 prices). Guided tours available ○ 🍽 ✗ WC ♿ 🐾 🏛 ⚑

A particularly fine woodland garden covering some 35 acres, it contains a wide range of rhododendrons, camellias, magnolias, hydrangeas and a great variety of other trees and shrubs producing a wealth of colour throughout the seasons. A wonderful collection of hostas and ferns flourishes in the shadier areas. Meconopsis and primulas are splendid in June, while lilies are the highlight of high summer and the tweedy autumn colours are almost as satisfying in their mellow-ness as the jauntier spring hues. A more formal area is devoted to modern roses, herbaceous borders, a range of alpines and an interesting and attractive dry garden. The Golden Jubilee Garden, planted in cool colours, has a central vista lined by pink and blue lavender; at its heart is a water sculpture designed by Barry Mason. An imposing temperate house was opened in 1995 where tender subjects – tree ferns, mimosas, eucryphias and delicate shrubs – are arranged in tiered beds and underplanted with exotics. Metal obelisks support non-hardy climbers; *Lapageria rosea* is on the main wall. The minimum temperature maintained in the 36 x 18-metre glasshouse is only 2°C (38°F), easily achieved in a conservatory.

41 Shelvers Way

Tadworth KT20 5QJ. Tel: (01737) 210707

Mr and Mrs K.G. Lewis • 6m S of Sutton off A217 Take first turning on right after Burgh Heath traffic lights, heading south; house on left 400yds down Shelvers Way • Open 23rd April and 20th Aug, 1 – 5.30pm, and by appt • Entrance: £2.50, children free • Other information: Plants for sale on April open day NEW ● ▇

In spring over 80 varieties of daffodils bloom in this plantsman's garden alongside an impressive show of tulips and other bulbs, but there is interest here at all seasons. It is divided into two rooms. In one beds of perennials displaying the best varieties are interlaced by paths and backed by unusual shrubs and mature trees; in the other cobbles and shingle support grasses and special plants that prefer dry conditions. The planting is dense and detailed, but the owners have thoughtfully provided plenty of seats from which to contemplate the profusion.

Stuart Cottage

East Clandon, Guildford GU4 7SF. Tel: (01483) 222689

Mr and Mrs J.M. Leader • 4m E of Guildford. From A246, go through village, take road signed to Ripley and follow yellow signs • Open for NGS, and for parties of 15 or more by appt • Entrance: £2.50, children free ● ▇ WC & ⬧ ⍟

Originally this was a cowman's cottage. The present owners arrived in 1975 and, confronted with nothing but grass and two old trees, have made a delightful cottage garden on the alkaline clay soil. It is partially walled, connected and divided by wisteria and rose pergolas. A formal, circular area has colour-themed borders curving round a central fountain, and a hot border of cannas and dahlias thrives in the shelter of a sunny wall. There is also a decorative organic kitchen garden and a small orchard. Secret places and a variety of nooks and crannies make the whole seem much larger than half an acre.

Titsey Place [Historic Garden Grade II]

Titsey Hill, Oxted RH8 0SD. Tel: (01273) 407017/407056 (Information line)

Trustees of the Titsey Foundation • 1m E of Oxted, 9m W of Sevenoaks. Leave M25 at junction 6. From A25 E of Oxted, turn left into Limpsfield (signed to Warlingham). At end of High Street fork left into Blue House Lane and first right into Water Lane • House open • Garden open 17th April, then 10th May to 27th Sept, Wed, Sun and Bank Holiday Mons; all 1 – 5pm • Entrance: £2.50, children £1 (house and garden £5, no concession for children) • Other information: Parking through park near walled garden, or by gate for woodland walks with long walk to garden ● ▇ WC &

The recently restored 18-acre gardens and grounds have been in the same family for 400 years. An unusual knot border stretches across the front of the house, and below it herbaceous borders curve round a fountain. An ancient yew guards old gravestones. Two modern rose gardens are attractively planned, but the colour schemes are unappealing. Magnificent mature trees dominate the lawns, which lead down to two lakes divided by a bridge and a cascade; the larger lake has an island, and a stream has been planted with marginals. The walls of the one-acre Victorian kitchen garden support espaliered fruit behind deep borders of old-fashioned roses and annuals. It is divided classically at crossing points, two ironwork gazebos giving height in the centre. Box-edged beds are filled with vegetables, salad crops, herbs and 100 varieties of tomatoes, raised from seed collected all over the world. There are strawberries too, and flowers for cutting. Against the south wall greenhouses shelter collections of alstroemerias, pelargoniums and tender varieties of tomatoes and peaches. The central glasshouse displays exotic and more familiar plants in pots, and from here the central path leads out into the gardens. Two woodland walks are open, free, all the year.

Vale End

Albury, Guildford GU5 9BE. Tel: (01483) 202296

Mr and Mrs J. Foulsham • 4.5m SE of Guildford. From Albury take A248 W for 0.25m • Open 8th June, 6 – 8.30pm; 11th June, 10am – 5pm; 6th July, 6 – 8.30pm • Entrance: £2.50, evening openings £4 and £3.50 ● ● ● WC ❧ ✿

In an idyllic setting with views of a mill pond backed by woodland, this one-acre walled garden is arranged on different levels. In spring it has a mass of bulbs, especially tulips. The sloping lawn is bordered by old roses and old favourites as well as less familiar perennials. The terrace in front of the house is a sun trap, the border filled with subjects that thrive in hot, dry conditions. Beyond a yew hedge, a cool area is shaded by a spreading magnolia; above, edging a walk, stand clipped yew boxes and a catenary of posts and rope swags, festooned with roses, wisteria and vines. An attractive courtyard is hidden behind the house. Steps by a new pantiled cascade lead up to a fruit, vegetable and herb garden level with the roof.

The Valley Gardens (Windsor Great Park) ★★

Wick Road, Englefield Green TW20 0VU. Tel: (01753) 847518

Administered by the Crown Estate Commissioners • 4m W of Staines, 5m S of Windsor. From A30 turn into Wick Road and look for burgundy-coloured signs to car park entrance adjoining Valley Gardens, avoiding a 2m round walk • Open all year, daily, 8am – 7pm (or dusk if earlier). Possible closure if weather inclement • Entrance: car and occupants £4 (April, May £5.50) (10p, 20p, 50p and £1 coins only) (2005 price) • Other information: Refreshments and plants for sale at Savill Garden (see entry) ○ ❧

One of Britain's most discriminating and experienced garden visitors, the late Arthur Hellyer, suggested that the Valley Gardens are among the best examples of the 'natural' gardening style in England. With hardly any artefacts or attempts to introduce architectural features, they are merely a tract of undulating woodland (on the north side of Virginia Water) divided by several shallow valleys, that has been enriched by the introduction of a fine collection of trees and shrubs. They were started by the royal gardener Sir Eric Savill when he ran out of room in the

Savill Garden. One of the valleys is filled with deciduous azaleas. In another, the Punchbowl, evergreen azaleas rise in tiers below a canopy of maples. Notable too are collections of flowering cherries, a garden of heathers which amply demonstrates their ability to provide colour during all seasons, and one of the world's most extensive collections of hollies. Lovers of formal gardening might be forgiven for suggesting that the Valley Gardens have something of that rather too open, amorphous, scrupulously kept feel found in America. *Virginia Water Lake* [Historic Park Grade I], off the A30, adjacent to the junction with the A329, was a grand eighteenth-century ornamental addition to Windsor Great Park created by the Duke of Cumberland, who became its Ranger in 1746. It had dams, rockwork and a cascade. There was a fake 'Mandarin yacht', a Chinese pavilion and a Gothick belvedere with a mighty single-arch bridge spanning the water. Alas, almost all have disappeared, but the woodland and the lovely one-and-a-half-mile lake, full of fish and wildfowl, survive, and so too a colonnade of pillars from the Roman site of Leptis Magna in Libya.

Vann [Historic Garden Grade II*]

Hambledon, Godalming GU8 4EF. Tel: (01428) 683413

Mrs M.B. Caroe • 11m S of Guildford, 6m S of Godalming. Take A283 to Wormley, turn left at Hambledon crossroads into Vann Lane and continue for 2m • Open for NGS three weeks end-March to June, and by appt. Parties of 15 or more by written appt • Entrance: £3.50, children 50p • Other information: Refreshments for parties by prior arrangement and on some open days only. Limited toilet facilities. Limited access for wheelchairs ◑ ✍

The Grade-II*-listed house (not open), standing in five acres of garden, dates from 1542 – the name is derived from the word 'fen'. The oldest part of the garden is at the front, enclosed by clipped yew hedges, divided by paths and planted in cottage-garden style. Behind the house a stone pergola (W.D. Caröe, 1907), underplanted with shade-lovers, strides out towards an old enlarged field pond. The woodland water garden was designed with Gertrude Jekyll, who supplied the plants in 1911. It has a winding stream, crossed and recrossed by Bargate-stone paths and swathed in lush planting; above the pond a narrow, stone-walled stream is enclosed by a yew walk planted in 1909. A serpentine crinkle-crankle wall supports fruit trees, and there are two mixed herbaceous borders in the vegetable garden and island beds in the orchard.

The Walled Garden

Sunbury Park, Thames Street, Sunbury-on-Thames.
Tel: (01784) 451499 (Community Services)

Spelthorne Borough Council • 3m E of Staines, in Sunbury-on-Thames via B375 Thames Street. Entrance through car park • Open all year, daily except 25th Dec, 8am – dusk • Entrance: free • Other information: Wheelchair available on request ○ 🏠 WC ᷾

The original house was built for a courtier of Elizabeth I, and the hearth return for 1664 shows it, with its 27 hearths, to have been the largest domestic building in

Sunbury. A later house was pulled down in 1946 and the site bought by Surrey County Council; the local borough council began to develop the walled garden in 1985. A pergola leads to beds of roses of the Victorian era. Adding interest are knot gardens of lavender and box, parterres, modern roses and island beds of plants from all over the world. There are climbers against the walls and gates which lead through to Sunbury Park. During the summer, exhibitions of sculpture, paintings, etc. are on view and a band plays at published times.

Winkworth Arboretum

Hascombe Road, Godalming GU8 4AD. Tel: (01483) 208477

The National Trust • 2m SE of Godalming, E of B2130. Signposted • Open all year, daily, dawn – dusk (but may be closed in bad weather, especially high winds) • Entrance: £4.50, children (5–16) £2, family £10, cyclists and public transport users 50% discount, carers with the disabled free (2005 prices). Pre-booked guided tours available • Other information: Coaches must pre-book. Disabled parking. Possible for wheelchairs but some steps and steep paths. Shop and tearoom open daily during bluebell time and autumn; closed Mon and Tues, but open Bank Holiday Mons ○ 🍽 🍴 WC ♿ 🚭 ♨ 🌳 ☕

Dr Wilfrid Fox bought the curving, steeply sloping 110-acre hillside site from the actress Beatrice Lilley in 1937. Helped by his connections with Kew and Hilliers, he set about establishing extensive collections of trees – among them birch, holly, magnolia and a National Collection of sorbus. In 1952 he gave the arboretum to the National Trust. Eucryphias, glorious in August, stand sentinel on either side of his memorial looking down his beloved valley. Carpets of bluebells in spring are followed by cherries, rhododendrons and azaleas in bright splashes, and in autumn acers, liquidambars and nyssas provide rich colour. The hillside setting has glorious views over the lake to the hills beyond. After problems with the dams, the lower lake has been drained to form a wetland area, crossed by a handsome bridge with a viewing platform, built (somewhat improbably) of reconstituted plastic – it is the highpoint of a new woodland walk.

Wotton House

Guildford Road, Dorking RH5 6HS. Tel: (01306) 730000

Hayley Conference Centres Ltd • 3m W of Dorking on A25 Dorking – Guildford road. Entrance signed next to Wotton Hatch pub • Open 2nd, 9th, 16th, 23rd July, 11am – 4pm, and throughout the year for lunches on Sats • Entrance: £2.50, children free NEW 🍽 🍴 ✕ 🍴 WC ♿ 🚭 B&B

John Evelyn, the diarist and gardening writer, was born here in 1620. Greatly influenced by his travels in Europe during the Civil War, he designed the garden originally for his elder brother George, but inherited the estate at the age of 79 on his brother's death. The dominant feature of the garden, set against a backdrop of mature trees, is the spectacular mound rising on three levels with a classical temple at its base; in front is a circular pool with a fountain, surrounded by a parterre of interlocking box triangles filled with a variety of plants. Near the house are two Pulhamite grottoes, one with a pool, and a fernery. Hidden away in a walled enclosure is a tortoise house in the style of an Italian temple, and rectangular pools, intended originally for terrapins. Waterers Landscape have restored the garden, and a drained lake is being transformed into a water meadow.

NCCPG

The National Council for the Conservation of Plants and Gardens publishes a *National Plant Collections Directory*. Those interested in seeing some of the rarer species and garden varieties of particular families of plants will find this an invaluable publication. The latest edition, which offers information on about 600 collections comprising more than 50,000 plants and contains articles by holders of the collections, is available from NCCPG, The Stable Courtyard, RHS Garden, Wisley, Woking GU23 6QP (Tel: (01483) 221465; Fax: (01483) 212404; Website: www.nccpg.com. The new edition will be published in February or March 2006.

POSTCODE PLANTS DATABASE

It is often difficult to find out which plants are local to an area. The Postcode Plants Database locates the names of flowers, trees, butterflies and birds for each of Britain's 26 million home addresses. The website is www.nhm.ac.uk/science/projects/fff; simply by typing in the first four characters of their postcode, householders, schools, garden centres and councils can obtain tailor-made lists of local plants which are both hospitable and garden-worthy. Also included are the names of butterflies and birds most likely to visit gardens in each area. The lists come from innovative software, developed by Royal Mail and *FLORA-for-FAUNA* in conjunction with the Natural History Museum, which searches through hundreds of distribution maps of fauna and flora in the British Isles.

OPENING DATES AND TIMES

Times of access given are the best available at the moment of going to press, but some may have been changed subsequently. In the entries, the times given are inclusive — that is, an entry such as May to Sept means that the garden is open from 1st May to 30th Sept inclusive, and 2 — 5 pm means that entry will be effective during that period. Please note that many owners will open their gardens to visitors by appointment, and they will often arrange to give a personally conducted tour on these occasions. Unavoidably some owners cannot give their opening details before we go to press, and in such cases we attempt to give the best guidance we can. If in doubt, it is wise to telephone before making a long journey.

SUSSEX, EAST

Two-starred gardens are marked on the map with a black square.

Bateman's [Historic Garden Grade II]

Burwash, Etchingham TN19 7DS. Tel: (01435) 882302

The National Trust • 14m E of Uckfield, 10m SE of Tunbridge Wells, 0.5m S of Burwash off A265 • House and mill (which grinds flour most Sats in open season) open 18th March to Oct, Sat – Wed, 11am to 5pm • Garden open 4th to 12th March, Sat and Sun; 18th March to Oct, 11 am – 5pm • Entrance: £6.20, children £3.10, family £15.50, pre-booked parties of 15 or more £4.90 per person (house, mill and garden) • Other information: Picnics in area provided. Dog creche available ◑ ☞ ✕ WC ⅖ ⅏ ♿

Kipling may be more screened than read these days, but his home from 1902 to 1936 is much visited. The house was built in 1634 and the rooms and study remain as they were during the period when he wrote many of his best-known works. Much of the garden was his doing and contains formal lawns with yew hedges, a rose garden and pond, a wild garden, and, on the right as you descend from the car park, an exceptional herb garden. Not far away in Rottingdean is the *Grange Museum* [open weekdays, 10am – 4pm, and Sun, 2 – 4pm], opposite which are two acres of garden, formerly part of the house the Kiplings rented on their return from India. These *Kipling Gardens* are open on weekdays.

Bates Green

Tye Hill Road, Arlington, Polegate BN26 6SH. Tel: (01323) 485152

Mrs Carolyn McCutchan • 7m NW of Eastbourne, 2.5m SW of A22, 2m S of Michelham Priory (see entry) at Upper Dicker. Approach Arlington passing Old Oak Inn on right, continue for 350 metres, turn right along Tye Hill Road. Signposted • Open for NGS, and by appt • Entrance: £3 ☞ WC ⅖ ♿

Successful and original groupings of plants express the owner's flair for using colour and foliage to create atmosphere and effect. Overall this might be described as a 'plantsman's artistic garden'. A splendid mature oak isolated after the 1987 hurricane has been underplanted with foliage plants rejoicing in the dappled shade. Bark paths interweave between the planting and under the young trees. The warm and sheltered area of the former vegetable garden has colour-themed borders of sun-loving plants and foliage contrast. A serpentine path leads from the front of the old farmhouse to the pond where water-loving plants are skilfully grouped. Views from the pond are of the adjoining woodland where there are delightful walks in the bluebell season. A raised-bed vegetable area includes a glasshouse and frames and an adjacent monocot garden.

Brickwall [Historic Garden Grade II]

Northiam, Rye TN31 6NL. Tel: (01797) 253388

The Frewen Educational Trust • 9m N of Hastings on B2088 • Write or telephone for details of opening times • Entrance: £3, children under 10 free (2005 price) • Other information: Coaches by appt ● ⅁ ⏃ ℘

Generations of Frewens have made their contribution to Brickwall: early records show an orchard on the site and two mulberry trees dated to 1670 still exist. The basic framework is the garden laid out between 1680 and 1720 by Jane Frewen, which has been preserved and planted in part with the flowering plants she used. The 110-acre deer park and the bowling green made for the amusement of the Stuart ladies recall more leisurely times when the estate owned most of the land towards Hastings. A dramatic landmark was created in the 1830s by Thomas Frewen Turner, who planted a superb pleached beech walk; at eight metres high it is the tallest hedge in the county. New topiary, a modern box parterre and a unique garden of green and gold yew chess pieces have been added more recently. The house is now a school, but its magnificent seventeenth-century plaster ceilings can be viewed by appointment.

Charleston

Firle, Lewes BN8 6LL. Tel: (01323) 811265

The Charleston Trust • 6m E of Lewes on A27 between Firle and Selmeston • House and garden open April to Oct, Wed – Sun and Bank Holiday Mons, 2 – 6pm (opens 11.30am July and Aug, 2pm Suns and Bank Holiday Mons) • Entrance: £2.50, children £1.50 (house and garden £6.50, children £4.50) ● ⏚ ⏚ WC ⅁ ℘ ⏚ ⏚ ⚲

Created by artists of the Bloomsbury Group, this is a delightful example of a garden fashioned during the 1920s by an idiosyncratic group of highly creative people. The walled garden has been meticulously restored through painstaking research and from the memories of people who visited when Vanessa Bell and Duncan Grant lived at the farmhouse and of those like Angelica Garnett and Quentin Bell who spent their childhood there.

Clinton Lodge ★

Fletching, Uckfield TN22 3ST. Tel: (01825) 722952

Sir Hugh and Lady Collum • 4m W of Uckfield off A272. Turn N at Piltdown and continue 1.5m to Fletching. House is in main street surrounded by yew hedge • Open 7th May, 9th, 16th, 18th, 23rd and 30th June, 7th and 14th July, 4th Aug, 2 – 5.30pm, and for parties by appt • Entrance: £4, parties £6 per person ● ⏚ WC ⅁ ℘

The house was enlarged by the Earl of Sheffield for his daughter, who married Sir Henry Clinton, one of the three generals of Waterloo. The eighteenth-century facade is set in a tree-lined lawn, flanked by a newly created canal and overlooking parkland. The 1987 storm removed the old oaks but these have been replanted in a Repton-style landscape leading to a tall stone pillar on the hill. The garden itself is of about six acres of clay soil divided into areas by period. The Elizabethan herb garden has camomile paths and turf seats, and four knot gardens. The Victorian era is represented by a tall white, yellow and blue herbaceous border; the Pre-Raphaelites by an *allée* of white roses, clematis, purple vines and lilies; the twentieth century by an unusual swimming pool garden encircled by an arcade of apples. A wildflower meadow is reached through an avenue lined with fastigiate hornbeams, and a pleached lime avenue leads to the medieval herb garden and a *potager*. An enclosed garden of old roses is trained at nose height to enjoy the scent. New gardens continue to be made: a small, shady glade, a small knot garden, a canal garden and an orchard planted with crinums.

Great Dixter ★★ [Historic Garden Grade I]

Dixter Road, Northiam, Rye TN31 6PH. Tel: (01797) 252878

Christopher Lloyd and Olivia Eller • 10m N of Hastings, 0.5m N of Northiam. Turn off A28 at Northiam post office • House open • Garden open April to Oct, daily except Mon (but open Bank Holiday Mons), 2 – 5pm • Entrance: £5, children £1.50 (house and garden £6.50, children £2) ◑ 🍵 WC ♿ ✿ 🏛

Enfolded by its glorious gardens, the medieval house at Great Dixter appears historically authentic. Yet the house, bought by Christopher Lloyd's parents in 1910, was reinvented by architect Edwin Lutyens, who enlarged it in the local vernacular, and designed the gardens. Respect for the past and enjoyment of present possibilities prevail side by side today. The enthusiastic forward-thinking team headed by Fergus Garrett make a visit here a stimulating experience. Meadow gardening is a striking feature, with the entrance flanked by long grass filled with *Camassia quamash*, and colonies of bulbs and early purple orchids in the orchard. The famous Long Border is a spectacular mixture of shrubs, climbers, perennials and annuals, reflecting Lloyd's determination to combine colours unconventionally to exuberant effect. The sheltered Exotic Garden is a riot of tropical colours and unfamiliar plant shapes, and throughout the complex linked garden spaces is a myriad of inspired plant associations. In the High Garden, approached through superb topiary, stock plants and vegetables grow together in an intriguing and aesthetic melange. This is gardening with sheer *joie de vivre*.

Hailsham Grange ★

Hailsham BN27 1BL. Tel: (01323) 844248

Mr Noel Thompson • 8m N of Eastbourne off A22. Turn off Hailsham High Street into Vicarage Road and park in public car park • Open 4th June and 2nd July, 2 – 5.30pm, and for parties by appt • Entrance: £2, children free ● 🍵 WC ♿ ✿ ✿ B&B

The present owner has devised a horticultural stage set with the handsome early-eighteenth-century former vicarage centre-stage. Masterly use of stilted hornbeam and box hedging divides the garden into a series of formal rooms where the restraint of clipped foliage, gravel and brick contrasts with romantic, colour-themed planting. A central turf path leading to a rose-swagged gazebo reveals a *coup de théâtre* of hidden double borders filled with cream, yellow and apricot perennials, skilfully planted for texture and form and set against the backdrop of church and sheltering trees. Box parterres, a tiny white garden, a shady wilderness and a bulb-filled spinney combine with topiary and statuary to create a classical estate in miniature.

Herstmonceux Castle [Historic Garden Grade II*]

Hailsham BN27 1RN. Tel: (01323) 833816

Queen's University (Canada) • 14m N of Eastbourne, off A271 Hailsham – Bexhill road • Open 15th April to 29th Oct (closed 25th July), daily, 10am – 6pm (last admission 5pm) • Entrance: £4.95, children (under 15) £3, children (under 5) free, concessions £3.95, family £12.95 ◐ ▆ 🌺 wc ⚥ ⟁ ⚘

The approach to the impressive and beautiful red-brick fifteenth-century castle, set in parkland, is past the science centre housed in the erstwhile observatory buildings. The path continues alongside the moat (filled with water lilies) and under gnarled but stately 300-year-old sweet chestnuts. The gardens are contained within ancient walls and yew hedges, some castellated; they include a herb garden, a Shakespeare garden, rose gardens and herbaceous borders. An orchard has been planted with old varieties of fruit trees. A woodland area has a rhododendron walk and a lake, sculptures and a folly garden. In all, 550 acres of woodland and gardens, including a nature trail.

Ketleys

Rosemary Lane, Flimwell TN5 7PS. Tel: (01580) 879300

Helen Yemm • 12m SE of Tunbridge Wells on A21. At Flimwell traffic lights turn onto B2087 signed to Ticehurst. Rosemary Lane is 0.5mile on right • Open for NGS, and for small parties of 10 – 25 by appt • Entrance: £3, children 50p (2005 price) • Other information: Parking limited ◖ ▆

The two-and-a-half acres surrounding the weather-boarded farmhouse have been transformed in the last seven years by garden writer Helen Yemm into distinctively contrasting areas. The tiny cottage front garden and sheltered gravel garden near the kitchen are filled with a profusion of herbs, low-growing grasses, euphorbias, alliums and annual poppies. Little wooden gates lead to the old orchard, filled with wild flowers, where roses scramble through the apple trees, and to a sophisticated lawned area with distant views of Bewl Water with a formal pool shaded by a huge willow. There is a tiny kitchen garden and beyond this lies the informal area, where a shrubbery, a natural pond and a bog garden lush with gunnera and bamboo have been created. Mown paths lead through a spinney of larch and birch filled with bracken and foxgloves to a circular glade. The skilled planting demonstrates how to use plants for varying situations; to explore the garden in the company of its lively and knowledgeable owner brings the whole place alive.

King John's Lodge

Sheepstreet Lane, Etchingham TN19 7AZ. Tel: (01580) 819232

Mr and Mrs R.A. Cunningham • 10m NW of Hastings, 2m SW of A21/A265 junction. In Etchingham, turn into Church Lane leading to Sheepstreet Lane • Open April to Sept, daily, 11am – 6pm, and by appt • Entrance: £3, children free • Other information: Shop selling statuary ◐ ▆ 🌺 wc ⚥ ⟁ ⚘ ℗ ☕ B&B

The fine Jacobean house with earlier parts and later additions stands hidden down a lane amongst wooded hills; legend has it that King John was held captive here in the fourteenth century. The present owners have increased its romantic appeal by their restoration of the four-acre gardens. Smooth lawns where white doves and cockerels strut are bounded by a formal lily pool with fine views into peaceful parkland. Wisteria and rambling roses cover the mellow stone walls of the house, and sun-loving perennials fill flowing borders around the terrace. In complete contrast, the orchard has paths mown through long meadow grasses filled with wild flowers, where in summer a gazebo and arches are swagged with fragrant old roses. A shady woodland is densely underplanted with hellebores, bulbs, ferns and foxgloves and a natural pool complete with waterfall is surrounded by a bog garden with a dramatic spring colony of drumstick primulas. Further exploration reveals attractive barns, a summerhouse and garden cottage where B&B guests can stay, and the owners' son has established a nursery next door.

Lamb House

West Street, Rye TN31 7ES. Tel: (01797) 229542

The National Trust • In centre of Rye, in West Street, facing W end of church • House open • Garden open 25th March to Oct, Wed, Sat, 2 – 6pm • Entrance: house and garden £2.90, children £1.40, family £7.25, groups £2.50 per person • Other information: No parking near house ◖

Although the author Henry James professed to have no horticultural knowledge, with help from Alfred Parsons he left a town garden of charm and interest. An oasis of calm in this crowded town, there are unusual trees and shrubs, vegetable and herb gardens and herbaceous plantings enclosed within the one-acre walled garden.

Latchetts

Freshfield Lane, Danehill, Haywards Heath RH17 7HQ. Tel: (01825) 790237

Laurence and Rebeka Hardy • 7m S of East Grinstead on A275. In Danehill, turn at war memorial into Freshfield Lane. Latchetts is 1 mile further (not Latchetts Farm) • Open six times for NGS and for individuals and parties by appt • Entrance: £3.50 [NEW] ◖ 🖤 WC ⟐ ⬦ ⚲

A garden remarkable in its diversity, filled by its creative owners with assured planting for every situation. Five acres of flowing spaces surround the house high above a wooded Wealden valley. Velvety lawns surrounded by mature trees and huge shrub borders slope to raised beds massed with sun-loving perennials; a rill trickles from a water garden fringed with giant gunneras into a cool wild wood sheltering tree ferns and bamboo. Bold swathes of prairie planting provide late colour sheltered by a high bank of shrub roses. At every turn there is something new: a mysterious pool with mist rising from the water and sculptures creating sound, a rose-laden tunnel leading to a vegetable garden, an intimate millennium garden filled with Christian symbolism and the soothing sound of water, a desert garden laid out around a giant sundial with a mound for the energetic to climb, looking over a wild flower meadow with a mini-labyrinth cut into it. Everywhere there are benches, summerhouses and vantage points from which to enjoy the varying views.

Marchants Hardy Plants

2 Marchants Cottages, Mill Lane, Laughton BN8 6AJ. Tel: (01323) 811737

Graham Gough and Lucy Goffin • 6m E of Lewes. From Laughton crossroads on B2124 (at Roebuck Inn), travel E for 0.5m. At next crossroads turn S, signed to Ripe, down Mill Lane; entrance is on right • Garden and nursery open mid-March to 22nd Oct, Wed – Sat, 9.30am – 5.30pm • Entrance: £2, children free, season ticket £5 NEW ◑ ♿ ❀

Graham Gough, esteemed as a nurseryman and gardener, bought the derelict cottage sitting on two acres of neglected land on the spur of the moment. What he did not anticipate was the intractable clay that lay beneath. Building up the soil and improving its structure was a long haul and a terrible labour, but he was rewarded with a panoramic view of the South Downs. Now it is filled with grasses, trees and shrubs in harmony with the lush countryside. Personal herbaceous favourites – agapanthus, kniphofias and sedums – are guaranteed a place, together with other enthusiasms like sanguisorba, thalictrum and persicaria, and grasses such as *Miscanthus sinensis* 'Silberspinne', *M.s.* 'Malepartus' and the elegant *Stipa gigantea*. Most of the plants for sale are propagated on site. This is not just a nursery – it is also a fabulous garden with a view.

Merriments Gardens ★

Hawkhurst Road, Hurst Green TN19 7RA. Tel: (01580) 860666

Mr David and Mrs Percy Weeks • 7m N of Battle, on A229 (formerly A265) between Hawkhurst and Hurst Green • Open 14th April to Sept, daily, 10am – 5.30pm (opens 10.30am Sun) • Entrance: £4, children £2 ◑ ☕ ✕ WC ♿ ❀

Pools and pergolas surrounded by boldly curving beds of impressive colour-themed planting create a rich source of inspiration particularly relevant to modern gardens, Well-designed and labelled schemes show plant associations for every situation, from a shady bog garden filled with lush marginals to the sun-baked gravelled garden. Between these extremes are imaginatively stocked borders in every colour combination, filled with herbaceous plants and shrubs underplanted with tulips, alliums and hostas. Fine specimen trees like *Gleditsia triacanthos* 'Sunburst' and *Catalpa bignonioides* 'Aurea' have been chosen for their decorative foliage. Benches, arbours and summerhouses afford good vantage points, and handsome containers and sculpture make effective focal points. The health and vigour of the plants, which include many excellent varieties of clematis, is remarkable. A welcoming tea room and a shady terrace combine with a superbly stocked nursery.

Michelham Priory ★

Upper Dicker, Hailsham BN27 3QS. Tel: (01323) 844224

Sussex Past • 10m N of Eastbourne off A22 and A27. Signposted • House, museum and gardens open March to Oct, Tues – Sun and Bank Holiday Mons, 10.30am – 5pm; Aug, daily, 10.30am – 5.30pm (closes 4pm March and Oct) • Entrance: £5.40, OAPs and students £4.60, children (5–15) £2.80, family £13.80. Rates available for pre-booked parties of 15 or more (2005 prices) • Other information: Working watermill and museum ❶ 💭 ✕ 🍴 WC ♿ 🌿 🏛 ❗ ⚲

Initially, the main horticultural interest of this historic monastic site – more a Tudor manor than a monastery – was the physic garden, but every visit reveals new areas of interest within the moated site of the old priory. The stewponds have been re-excavated and fringed with exotic waterside plants, particularly those with dramatic foliage. The widely sweeping herbaceous border is planted in swathes of bold colour and form and leads into areas of mixed planting alongside the moat and adjoining the buildings. A fine ornamental *potager* with vegetables, flowers and a central pergola lies behind the walls of a yew hedge, and there is also an orchard. Young liquidambars and catalpas are gaining strength and enliven the foreground to the more natural moatside planting. A cloister garden in the well courtyard, inspired by illustrations of medieval Marian gardens, includes an arbour, turf seat and raised beds for medicinal plants. Sculptures are dotted throughout the gaden.

Monk's House ★

Rodmell, Lewes BN7 3HF. Tel: (01892) 890651

The National Trust • 4m S of Lewes off old A275, now C7. In Rodmell follow signs to church and continue 400 metres to house • House and garden open April to 29th Oct, Wed, Sat, 2 – 5.30pm. Pre-booked group tours available on Thurs but must be booked four weeks in advance – telephone (01372) 453401 • Entrance: £3, children £1.50, family £7.50 ◐ 🍴 WC ⚲

This was the cottage home of Virginia and Leonard Woolf from 1919 until his death in 1969. There are three ponds, one in dewpond style. An orchard, underplanted with spring bulbs, contains a comprehensive collection of daffodils, and Leonard's vegetable area is still thriving. Flint stone walls and yew hedges frame the more formal herbaceous areas, leading to a typical Sussex flint church at the bottom of the garden. The one-and-three-quarter-acre garden is a mixture of chalk and clay, nurturing a wide variety of plants. Among the interesting specimen trees are *Salix hastata* 'Wehrhahnii', *Magnolia liliiflora*, walnut and mulberry.

Pashley Manor ★

Ticehurst TN5 7HE. Tel: (01580) 200888

Mr and Mrs James A. Sellick • 16m N of Hastings, 10m SE of Tunbridge Wells on B2099 between Ticehurst and A21. Signposted • Open early April to Sept, Tues – Thurs, Sat and Bank Holiday Mons, 11am – 5pm. Coach parties by appt only • Entrance: £6 (2005 price) ❶ 💭 WC ♿ 🌿 🏛 ❗

The Grade-I-listed Tudor timber-framed ironmaster's house of 1550 with a George I rear elevation dated 1720 stands in some ten acres of formal garden, being completely renovated with advice from Anthony du Gard Pasley. The planting is subtle, with emphasis on colour and form, pale colours blending with carefully chosen foliage. From the terrace and over the magnificent fountain there is a view of the Mad Jack Fuller obelisk at Brightling Beacon several miles away. A series of enclosed gardens is surrounded by beautiful eighteenth-century walls. Grass paths, some concealing the original Victorian gravel beneath, lead through camellia and rhododendron shrubberies. A large fountain, and the natural springs which feed a series of ponds falling away from the house and medieval moat, ensure that the sound of falling water is heard over most of the garden. A golden garden has been created, and other projects include an extensive planting of tulips to complement the tulip festival held in May; an avenue of pleached pear trees underplanted with box so arranged as to give a view through to magnificent hydrangeas; and a garden of old-fashioned roses to complement the rose weekend held in June. In the 1.5-acre garden to the south-east of the old walled garden, ample herbaceous borders are planted with strong colours and sculptural plants for late-summer flowering.

Royal Pavilion Gardens [Historic Garden Grade II]

Brighton BN1 1EE. Tel: (01273) 290900

Brighton & Hove City Council • In central Brighton • Royal Pavilion open April to Sept, daily, 9.30am – 5pm; Oct to March, daily except 25th, 26th Dec, 10am – 4.30pm • Garden open all year, daily • Entrance: gardens free (Royal Pavilion £6.10, concessions £4.30, children under 16 £3.60) (2005 prices) • Other information: New garden entrance to Brighton Museum and Art Gallery (open Tues – Sun) ○ 🏪 WC ᶜ

The seven-acre gardens surrounding the Royal Pavilion have been restored to their original splendour, closely following John Nash's plans of the 1820s. Nash conceived the building and grounds as a unity, and his fascinating vision will be fully realised as the plants and shrubs continue to flourish and mature. The beds are of mixed shrubs and herbaceous plants, a combination first applied at that time, and species and varieties have been selected to conform as closely as possible to the original lists of plants supplied to the Prince Regent (later King George IV). In summer orange tiger lilies with their spotted purple markings, brought from China in 1804, provide an exotic foreground to more familiar and native plants, while a profusion of roses – such as R. 'Petite Lisette', a damask first introduced in 1817 – contribute their colour and scent to the ornamental shrubberies. The gardens and grounds reflect the great revolution in landscape gardening that began in the 1730s, when straight lines and symmetrical shapes were banished, and in their place appeared curving paths and 'natural' groups of trees and shrubs undulating gracefully over the lawn. As visitors pass through the grounds, the magical building is disclosed by a succession of varying views through the shrubs and thickets.

Sarah Raven's Cutting Garden ★

Perch Hill Farm, Willingford Lane, Brightling, Robertsbridge TN32 5HP, Tel: (0845) 050 4849

Sarah Raven and Adam Nicolson • At Burwash Weald on A265, turn down Willingford Lane opposite Wheel Inn; garden is 1m further • Open 29th April, 1st May, possibly 24th June, 26th and 28th Aug, 10th Sept, and for parties by appt • Entrance: £4, children free • Other information: Talks by Sarah Raven on open days (must pre-book). Wide range of courses available ● 💻 WC ᶜ ⚘ 🏛 ⚘

Set high on a windy hill, with stunning views across valleys to the distant Brightling Beacon, the Sussex farmhouse is surrounded by a series of characterful garden spaces – 1.5-acres in all. The Oast Garden, sheltered by a loggia and handsome walls, is planted with bold architectural plants and washes of brilliant colour. The vegetable garden, divided by brick paths and chestnut hurdles, is filled with unusual vegetables on trial, and the herb garden is a decorative delight defined by box topiary. The hot colours of cosmos and cannas add late-season interest in the dahlia garden. A constant supply of favourite flowers for Sarah Raven's courses comes from the large cutting garden, where a hazel tunnel clothed in sweet peas is sensational in summer. Inspirational.

Sheffield Park Garden ★★ [Historic Park Grade I]

Sheffield Park TN22 3QX. Tel: (01825) 790231

The National Trust • 5m NW of Uckfield, midway between East Grinstead and Lewes E of A275 • Open 7th Jan to 12th Feb, Sat and Sun; 14th Feb to 30th April, 6th June to 1st Oct, 1st Nov to 23rd Dec, Tues to Sun; 1st May to 4th June, 2nd to 31st Oct, daily; 27th to 31st Dec, Wed to Sun; all 10.30am – 6pm (closes 4pm in winter) • Entrance: £6.20, children £3.10, family £15.50, pre-booked parties £5.25 per person, children £2.60 • Other information: Wheelchairs and self-drive powered vehicles available – telephone (01825) 790302 ☕ 🍴 🛍 WC & ℘ ♿ 🌳 🎁 ♥

A 120-acre landscape garden and arboretum with two lakes (later extended to four, in an inverted-T formation below the house) created by 'Capability' Brown for the Earl of Sheffield in 1776. Repton worked here in 1789, and a waterfall and cascades were added later. Between 1909 and 1934 a collection of trees and shrubs notable for their autumn colour was planted, including many specimens of *Nyssa sylvatica*. These and other fine specimen trees, particularly North American varieties, provide all-year-round interest. The Trust aims to plant 9000 new trees and shrubs over the next five years to repair storm damage. Features include good water lilies in the lakes, the Queen's Walk and, in autumn, two borders of the Chinese *Gentiana sino-ornata* of amazing colour. Three new beds of brightly coloured azaleas include varieties recently rediscovered, expanding a National Collection of Ghent azaleas.

Stone House

Rushlake Green, Heathfield TN21 9QJ. Tel: (01435) 830553

Peter and Jane Dunn • 5 miles SE of Heathfield off A265. Turn right onto B2096 to Punnetts Town, then follow signs for Rushlake Green; house is on corner of green • Open March to Oct for parties by appt • Entrance: £4.50 • Other information: Spring and autumn day courses on culinary topics (must pre-book) ☕ WC & ℘ 🎁 B&B

At the elegant Stone House hotel, master chef Jane Dunn has created a productive decorative potager in the old walled garden, supplying fresh produce both for her innovative cuisine and her courses on growing and cooking vegetables and herbs. Surrounding a sundial, the beds are filled with unusual varieties grown both for flavour and for aesthetic impact. Trained fruit clothes the walls, rambling roses form arbours, herbaceous plants provide blooms for the house, paths are fringed with fragrant and edible flowers and herbs. Outside the walled garden is a yew-hedged enclosure with an apple and pear walk, massed in spring with *Iris reticulata* of every colour, glasshouses, intensively grown soft fruit, asparagus and artichokes. Old-fashioned roses lead to a grand semi-circular lime walk, glowing with daffodils in spring and encircling falling pools. Beside the croquet lawn, a huge mixed border provides a fitting foreground to the part-Tudor house with its handsome Georgian frontage, and across a tranquil lake lie the wooded valleys of deepest Sussex. A worthwhile visit for gardeners who enjoy growing vegetables for their visual and edible potential.

Warren House

Warren Road, Crowborough TN6 1TX. Tel: (01892) 663502

Mr and Mrs M.J. Hands • 7m NE of Uckfield off A26. From Crowborough Cross turn towards Uckfield, take 4th turning on right; garden is 1m down Warren Road. From south, take 2nd turning on left after Blue Anchor pub • Open for NGS, and by appt • Entrance: £2.50 on NGS open days ● ● WC & ℘

Situated in a commanding position overlooking Ashdown Forest, this is a splendid example of a garden made and tended by the owner alone – all nine acres of it. Extensive plantings of trees, shrubs, grasses and flowers skirt the sweeping lawns, and a series of different vistas display a wealth of rhododendrons and azaleas. There are wisteria and laburnum walks, and the woodland, with its ponds and tree-lined avenues, is a peaceful place in which to stroll. The original infrastructure of walls, paths and terraces has been restored, blending the garden harmoniously into the surrounding forest.

Wellingham Herb Garden

Wellingham Lane, Nr Lewes BN7 5SW. Tel: (01435) 883187

Grant Bricknell • 2m N of Lewes off A26 • Open Easter to Sept, Sat and Sun, 10.30am – 5.30pm • Entrance: free ● WC & ⬧ ℘ ⛪ ♀

Within sight of the South Downs, the present owner, a landscaper and designer, has created a delightful herb garden hidden within the walls of the former kitchen garden of the eigtheenth-century house. A heraldic lion makes a striking centrepiece to a formal pattern of box-edged beds and gravel paths. Within this framework herbs are planted in natural drifts and fruit trees create shade. The walls are clothed in fragrant shrubs, and trained fruit – including peaches, plums and medlars – old roses, yew hedges, statuary and a handsome octagonal summerhouse complete the elegant picture. This is a tranquil place with the atmosphere of a secret garden. A wide range of herbs is available in the nursery area.

SUSSEX, WEST

Two-starred gardens are marked on the map with a black square.

Berri Court

Yapton, Arundel BN18 0ED. Tel: (01243) 551663

Mr and Mrs J.C. Turner • 8m E of Chichester, 5m SW of Arundel on B2233, in Yapton between post office and Black Dog pub • Open for NGS, and by appt • Entrance: £2.50, children free (2005 price) ◐ ◻ WC & ♨ ℺

A series of gardens within a one-and-a-half-acre garden of great interest to plant enthusiasts. Daffodils flowers *en masse* in spring, together with azaleas and rhododen-drons, while the borders have an impressive display of herbaceous plants and many varieties of shrubs and climbing roses. Around the house are magnificent *Magnolia grandiflora*, *Drimys winteri* and *Clematis rehderiana*. Elsewhere, *Clematis* x *jackmanii* clambers through trees, and different varieties of eucalyptus are grown throughout the garden. The vigorous *Rosa glauca* (syn. *Rosa rubrifolia*) provides spectacular foliage colour contrast, and *Tropaeolum speciosum* create splashes of vermilion through the borders.

Borde Hill Garden ★ [Historic Garden Grade II*]

Balcombe Road, Haywards Heath RH16 1XP. Tel: (01444) 450326

Borde Hill Gardens Ltd • 1.5m N of Haywards Heath on Balcombe – Haywards Heath road • House open to groups by appt • Garden open all year, daily, 10am – 6pm (or dusk if earlier); guided tours by arrangement • Entrance: March to Oct £6, children £3.50 (reduced rates Oct to Dec) ○ ◻ ✕ ◈ WC & ⟡ ♨ ⾕ ♀ ℺

One of Sussex's fine plant-hunter gardens. Created from 1893 with trees and shrubs collected from Asia, Tasmania, the Andes and Europe, it has award-winning collections of azaleas, rhododendrons, magnolias and camellias surrounded by 220 acres of parkland and bluebell woods. The classic rose and Italian gardens were designed by Robin Williams, and Heritage Lottery funds used to restore the glasshouse area and refashion the surroundings of the old potting sheds as a series of small rooms filled with rare southern-hemisphere shrubs. In the Long Dell Sino-Himalayan species surround Chusan palms, while the Round Dell is a lush hidden area with more Chusan palms, bamboos and huge gunneras. A white garden was created in 2002. Additional attractions include a pirates' adventure playground, coarse and children's fishing, extensive woodland walks and lakes.

Burpham Place

Burpham, Arundel BN18 9RH. Tel: (01903) 884833

Elizabeth Woodhouse • 0.5m S of Arundel, turn off A27 Arundel – Worthing road and continue for 2m through Wepham to Burpham • Open by appt • Entrance: charge ◐ ◻ B&B

Most of the small garden was redesigned in 2002 by the garden designer/owner. New colour-themed herbaceous borders were introduced around two circles of grass with a succession of unusual and native plants. Special emphasis is on 'sad' colours – black, brown, peach, silver and grey plants and grasses flow through several beds. New varieties of verbascum, foxglove and iris star, and other beds feature mauve/lime and magenta/pink plantings. A Gothic arch leads to a path in the small wild garden full of cow parsley and mullein which meanders through silver birch trees down to a stream and folly. The whole is designed to blend with the Downs beyond.

Cass Sculpture Foundation ★

Goodwood, Chichester PO18 0QP. Tel: (01243) 538449

Kate Simms • 7m N of Chichester, 3m S of East Dean, between A286 and A285 (telephone (01243) 771114 for directions or consult www.sculpture.org.uk) • Open March to Oct, Tues – Sun and Bank Holiday Mons, 10.30am – 4.30pm (last entrance 3:30pm) • Entrance: £10 ◑ WC �& ♿ ⚑ ℺

Twenty-six acres of woodland have been shaped to give a finer setting for twenty-first-century British sculpture than any indoor gallery. The quality of the work is outstanding; the trees act as screens, giving each piece its own stage, and sometimes opening to give a backdrop of the Sussex countryside. Beautiful gates by Wendy Ramshaw herald the entrance to the park, while at the end of one walk the spire of Chichester cathedral is borrowed sculpture of the most majestic kind. Over 72 large, ever-changing outdoor works are on show at any one time, ranging from Gavin Turk's glass maze – 'The Golden Thread' – Lynn Chadwick's mobile 'Ace of Diamonds' and a DNA helix made from shopping trollies by Abigail Fallis. The largest exhibition of Tony Cragg's outdoor work in Britain to date can be seen in a newly landscaped chalk pit within the grounds.

Champs Hill

Coldwaltham, Pulborough RH20 1LY. Tel: (01798) 831868

Mr and Mrs D. Bowerman • 2m SW of Pulborough off A29. At Coldwaltham turn W towards Fittleworth. Garden is 300 metres on right • Open 25th and 26th March, 21st May, 12th and 13th Aug, 2 – 5pm. Private parties welcome – please telephone • Entrance: £4, children free • Other information: Nineteenth-century Dutch art exhibition in music room 12th May, 6 – 9pm, and 13th May, 11am – 4pm (special price for garden and exhibition incl. refreshments) ◑ 🍴 WC �& ℺

This fine and unusual heathland garden, with over 300 varieties of heather grown alongside dwarf conifers and other interesting plants, is complemented by spectacular views of the Arun Valley and South Downs. The heathers are best viewed in March and August, but a walk in May through the 27 acres of natural woodland interplanted with a wealth of rhododendrons and azaleas is a real bonus, and sculptures and a trickling stream add to the appeal.

Chantry Green House

Church Street, Steyning BN44 3YB. Tel: (01903) 814824

Mr R.S. Forrow and Mrs J.B. McNeil • 8m N of Worthing, 10m NW of Brighton off A283. From Steyning High Street, opposite White Horse Inn, turn into Church Street. House is 150 metres on left • Open 10th and 11th June, 2 – 5pm • Entrance: £2, children 50p • Other information: Parking in Fletchers Croft car park opposite church ● ➹

A sheltered and well-maintained one-acre town garden with some interesting features – a water garden, a kitchen garden, an American garden and an arboretum with unusual trees, including *Liriodendron tulipifera* 'Aureomarginatum', *Lagerstroemia indica*, the crape myrtle, and *Eriobotrya japonica*, the Japanese loquat. In a corner, an old wall fountain is the focus of a shady area planted with ferns and hostas. Also of note are the many varieties of cistus.

Chidmere House

Chidham Lane, Chidham, Chichester PO18 8TD. Tel: (01243) 572287

Jackie and David Russell • 6m W of Chichester, 4m E of Emsworth, S of A259. Turn right at S end of Chidham • Open 7th May, 2 – 6pm, 20th Aug, 2 – 7pm, and by appt • Entrance: £2, children free ● **WC** ♿ ➹

The Tudor house (not open) is excitingly situated next to Chidmere Pond, so much so that the well-filled greenhouse which borders the mere feels almost like a house-boat. The garden was laid out in the 1930s, divided into separate compartments by tall hedges of hornbeam and yew. Flowering cherries, sheets of daffodils and bluebells ensure that it is spectacular in the spring. There are other fine flowering trees, while the house supports a Banksia rose and two wisterias. Later, the roses, a well-stocked herbaceous border, a tulip tree and *Taxodium distichum* command attention. The garden has been expanded by 12 acres and now includes a wildflower meadow and additional orchards of fruit trees.

Coates Manor

Fittleworth, Pulborough RH20 1ES. Tel: (01798) 865356

Mrs G.H. Thorp • 3m W of Pulborough, 0.5m S of Fittleworth off B2138 • Open 21st May, 11am – 5pm, and by appt • Entrance: £2.50, children free ● ➹ 🏠 ♿

This one-acre garden has an abundance of trees and shrubs carefully chosen to give long-term pleasure. There are ferns, grasses such as *Stipa gigantea* like frozen waterfalls, *Phlomis italica* and *P. chrysophylla*, blue and white agapanthus, and many specimen trees chosen for their foliage, berries or autumn colour. A small paved walled garden has *Clerodendrum trichotomum*, clematis, phlox and other scented flowers. The owner is particularly interested in colour contrasts and light and shade, and goes to considerable lengths to find the best species available. Look out for a variegated ivy contrasting well with *Cotinus coggygria* 'Notcutt's Variety' on a wall by the house; a mature copper beech tree stands nearby. The delightful Elizabethan house is partly covered in variegated ivy and euonymus, linking it to the surrounding countryside.

Denmans ★

Denmans Lane, Fontwell, Arundel BN18 0SU. Tel: (01243) 542808

John Brookes • 5m E of Chichester. Turn S off A27, W of Fontwell racecourse • Open all year, daily, 9am – 5pm (closed 24th to 26th Dec and 1st Jan) • Entrance: £3.75, OAPs £3.25, children over 4 £1.95, family £10, parties of 15 or more £3 per person if pre-booked (2005 prices) ◑ 💭 ✕ 🥄 **WC** ♿ ⚘ 🏛

John Brookes, one of Britain's most influential designers, moved here in 1980. The whole site relies for its drama on foliage plants – even in spring, visitors come away with minds full of euphorbias, yuccas, phormiums and mounds of clipped box. The centre of the garden is a river of pebbles and gravel against which the leaves of thistles and bamboo show up dramatically. There are some choice tulips and other spring bulbs, interesting primulas and spring-flowering shrubs. In late summer a large border of *Romneya coulteri*, the Californian tree poppy, is at its best, while autumn and winter interest are given by the stems of willow and cornus, and by the leaves of staphylea and *Parrotia persica*. The walled garden contains many old roses as well as a herb garden and perennials. Outside the house is the south garden; very tender species are planted in another gravel area near a circular pond.

Frith Lodge

Northchapel, Petworth GU28 9JE. Tel: (07769) 978520

Mr and Mrs Geoffrey Cridland • 7m N of Petworth on A283. Turn E in centre of Northchapel into Pipers Lane; after 0.75m turn left into bridleway • Open 30th April and 11th June, 3 – 6pm, and by appt • Entrance: £4, children £2 NEW ● 🥄 ⬸ ⚘

If you like roses you will love this place, for the enchanting gamekeeper's cottage is surrounded by them. The owner, a landscape designer, has fashioned a romantic cottage garden around a 100-year-old box hedge, adding miniature rooms enclosed by hornbeams. The one-acre garden starts on either side of the drive with old-fashioned roses, summer perennials and silver pears. In the upper garden the palette is mauve and silver, with large cardoons echoing the silver pears outside. On either side of a pink and white rose walk are two small hidden rooms with a central bed of *Clematis* 'Arabella' and 'Dark Lady' roses, with lollipops of *Lonicera americana* at the corners. Behind these rooms are the arbutus gardens (another matching pair). Follow the lawn round past the hornbeam arbour to where the old piggery is disappearing under a curtain of 'Paul's Himalayan Musk', and continue round to the front of the cottage. Here is a small brick terrace with lavender hedges and box parterres, and more roses of course – 'Pink Bells' and 'Little White Pet', with 'Phyllis Bride' on the fence, one side of which is lined with a yew hedge interspersed with buttresses and infilled with *rugosa* roses and other plants unattractive to rabbits. Then cross the drive to the newly created woodland garden to take in the stunning 180-degree panorama of the South Downs.

Gravetye Manor [Historic Garden Grade II*]

Vowels Lane, East Grinstead RH19 4LJ. Tel: (01342) 810567

Mr Andrew Russell • 4m S of East Grinstead between M23 and A22. By M23, take exit 10 onto A264 towards East Grinstead. After 2m, at roundabout take 3rd exit on

B2028. 1m after Turners Hill fork left and follow signs • Open all year to hotel and restaurant guests, perimeter footpath only for public, Tues and Fri • Entrance: free • Other information: Parking in drive in lay-by before gates ● ● × WC & B&B

This historically important garden has been carefully restored in the style pioneered here by William Robinson. The area around the hotel (which can only be visited by guests or visitors having lunch or dinner) can be viewed from a public footpath which passes through wildflower meadows to the north and south. Several large shrubs and trees – parrotias, rhododendrons and pines – are part of the original planting. The path down the magnolia walk bordered by shrubbery and large camellias leads down through Smugglers Lane to a lake, continues along the lakeside and completes the circumnavigation back to the entrance.

Hammerwood House

Iping, Midhurst GU29 0PF. Tel: (01730) 813635

The Hon. Mrs Lakin • 3m W of Midhurst, 1m N of A272 • Open 7th and 14th May, 2 – 5pm • Entrance: £3, children free ● ● WC & ◈ ☙

This is a peaceful country garden, formerly part of a Regency vicarage, planted with care and a fine eye for good plants. Although the rhododendrons and azaleas give it its most spectacular flowering season, there are some splendid camellias, magnolias, cornus and other specimen trees. Across a meadow from the main garden is the woodland walk by a stream. Wild flowers abound.

High Beeches Gardens ★ [Historic Garden Grade II*]

Handcross RH17 6HQ. Tel: (01444) 400589

High Beeches Gardens Conservation Trust • 5m S of Crawley, 1m E of Handcross, S of B2110 • Open mid-March to Oct, Thurs – Tues, 1 – 5pm • Entrance: £5.50, accompanied children under 14 free. Guided parties of 10 or more by appt any day or time, £8 per person with refreshments by arrangement ◐ ● × ▣ WC ♉

The delightful woodland and water garden of over 25 acres encourages its visitors to explore the different walks that meander, like the streams, through the collection of rare trees and unusual shrubs. Alongside a National Collection of stewartias are glades of rhododendrons, azaleas and magnolias. Originally designed by Colonel Loder in 1906, the garden is always extending its well-labelled collection. There are many benches and a summerhouse from which to enjoy the scents and colours. Starting with bluebells in spring, stunning cornus, a wildflower meadow, a glade of *Gentiana asclepiadea* (the only naturalised site of willow gentian in Britain) and *Eucryphia glutinosa* in late August, and a carpet of *Cyclamen hederifolium* at the base of the oak tree at Centre Pond adding to the wonderful autumn colours, this is a garden of many seasons.

Highdown [Historic Garden Grade II*]

Littlehampton Road, Goring-by-Sea BN12 6PE. Tel: (01903) 501054

Worthing Borough Council • 3m W of Worthing, N of A259 • Open April to Sept, daily, 10am – 6pm; Oct to March, Mon – Fri, 10am – 4.30pm (closes 4pm Dec and Jan)

• Entrance: free – donation box • Other information: Refreshments at peak times only. Toilet facilities available to wheelchair users only with key ○ 🍵 **WC** ♿ ♒

Sir Frederick Stern's selected this site in 1910 in and around a bare chalk pit, and his garden was donated to Worthing Council in 1968. The season starts with a mass of hellebores; narcissi and cowslips follow, and then peonies and irises. Brilliant scarlet anemones are naturalised in the grass; later come agapanthus, eremurus and autumn crocus. And these are just the flowers. There are also fine specimen trees – davidia, arbutus and cornus – and many shrubs, including roses, ceanothus, kolkwitzias and laburnum, with buddleias and paulownias to follow. Dramatic banks of pittosporum are a striking feature. Highdown is a plantsman's garden – it doesn't have a lot of shape – and unfortunately there are few labels.

Leonardslee – Lakes and Gardens ★★ [Historic Garden Grade I]

Lower Beeding, Horsham RH13 6PP. Tel: (01403) 891212

The Loder family • 4m SW of Handcross and M23 on B2110/A281 • Open April to Oct, daily, 9.30am – 6pm • Entrance: April £6; May, Mon – Fri £7, Sat, Sun £8; June to Oct, £6, children £4. Season tickets £16 (2005 prices) • Other information: Victorian motor car collection ◑ 🍴 ✕ 🍵 **WC** ♒ ♿

The gardens were originally started in 1801 and remnants of the original planting can still be found in the dell garden, including some of the oldest and largest specimens of rhododendron and magnolia in the country. In 1889 Sir Edmund Loder, famously remembered for his *Rhododendron loderi* hybrids, moved to Leonardslee. These are a breathtaking sight on the Top Walk in May, as is the rock garden with its brilliantly coloured Kurume azaleas and rare Chusan palms. With 240 acres, seven lakes, sweeps of bluebells and important collections of camellias, acers and magnolias, this is not a place to rush round in a hurry. The immense scale and the mature trees give the garden a special quality and later in the season the autumn colours and their reflections in the water are incredibly beautiful. After the devastation of the 1987 storm new vistas were opened up, the whole area east of the lakes cleared and replanted with oaks and maples, and plans are afoot to plant more cornus to extend the high points of the season. While you are there take time to visit the Ken Norman bonsai collection, the alpine house, the wallabies (assistant lawnmowers), the 'Behind the Dolls' House' exhibition, which now includes a 'local town', and the Loder family collection of Victorian motor cars. Selehurst (see entry) is opposite.

Little Wantley

Fryern Road, Storrington RH20 4BJ. Tel: (01903) 740747

Hilary Barnes • 10m NW of Worthing, 1m N of Storrington on Fryern Road towards West Chiltington; entrance on right • Open for parties of 10 or more by appt • Entrance: £3.50 • Other information: Teas by arrangement ◑ 🍴 **WC** ♿ ♒

Before 1997 the garden was 1.5 acres with a 2.5-acre field adjoining. The owners bought the field, wanted a lake and got one – all 1.5 acres of it! By the top pond *Rosa* 'Grouse' creates an enchanting arch over the waterfall into the main lake, which has lush marginal planting. The surrounding area, including newly landscaped mounds, has been extensively planted. Among the willows, bamboos, birches and conifers is a pretty stand of cut-leaf alders and a trio of swamp cypresses. Once the trees are more mature the autumn colour will be stunning. There is also a nut walk and a rose walk (*R. pimpinellifolia*), terminated by a new stumpery planted with ferns and hellebores. Roses are a passion and abound everywhere. There are walks from which you can look down on the lake and the views back to the house; the run-off from the lake has been planted up as a lush stream with a path beside it. An arch of golden hop leads into a *potager* with four standard *Rosa* 'Helexa' (*R.* 'Super Excelsa') standing sentinel. Beyond the hedge is the front drive and lawn with a beautiful copper beech, a cedar and a dawn redwood. The long front border has magnificent hostas, and tucked away behind the rhododendrons is a fern gully. On the other side of the house an old wooden pergola heralds a small hidden garden, and a new metal pergola smothered in roses, wisteria and clematis invites the visitor round another border and back towards the lake.

Nymans ★★ [Historic Garden Grade II*]

Handcross, Haywards Heath RH17 6EB. Tel: (01444) 400321

The National Trust • 4m S of Crawley. At southern end of Handcross, off A23/M23 and A279. Signposted • House open 15th March to 29th Oct • Garden open 15th Feb to 29th Oct, Wed – Sun and Bank Holiday Mons, 11am – 6pm (or dusk if earlier); 4th Nov to 11th Feb, 11am – 4pm, Sat and Sun • Entrance: house and garden £7, children £3.50, family £17.50, parties of 15 or more £5.95 per person. Joint ticket available with Standen (see entry) Wed – Fri only, £10 • Other information: Coaches must pre-book. Batricar, wheelchairs and braille/audio guide available on free loan. Map of wheelchair route available ○ ⬤ ✕ 🍽 WC ♿ ♨ 🏠 🍴 ⚲

An historic collection of fine trees, shrubs and plants in a beautifully structured setting, full of outstanding and almost theatrical effects: sheets of white narcissi under sorbus trees, a circle of camellias around a lawn with an urn in the centre, a vista down a lime avenue with a 'prospect' at the end and several borders of great splendour. Originally started by Ludwig Messel in 1890, the garden was continued by his son Leonard and daughter-in-law Maud, and then by his granddaughter, Anne, Countess of Rosse; it was given to the Trust in 1954. The library and drawing room are open to the public and lead out to the forecourt and a knot garden. The picturesque ruins of the original building (built *c.* 1928 to resemble a medieval manor house and largely destroyed by fire in 1947) are planted with clipped yew and other topiary. The Messel creations include a pinetum, a sunken garden with a stone loggia, a laurel walk, a croquet lawn, a heather garden, a rose garden, and magnificent herbaceous borders. Some of these areas can be viewed from on high from the mound. Bedding is always beautifully done and the whole is exceptionally well maintained. *Magnolia* x *loebneri* 'Leonard Messel' and *Eucryphia* x *nymansensis* were both raised here. An exhibition of garden history situated within the garden is a recent welcome addition. On the opposite side of the road is the wild garden, and there are also 250 acres of free-access woodlands

Parham House and Gardens ★ [Historic Garden Grade II*]

Nr Pulborough RH20 4HS. Tel: (01903) 742021/744888

4m SE of Pulborough on A283, equidistant from A24 and A29 • House open as garden but 2 – 6pm (last admission 5pm) • Garden open 16th April to Sept, Wed,

Thurs, Sun and Bank Holiday Mons, 12 noon – 6pm (last admission 5pm),
also Tues and Fri in Aug. 8th and 9th July for garden weekend, and 9th and 10th
Sept for flower-arranging weekend. Private parties and guided tours on other days
• *Entrance: £5, OAPs £4.50, children £1, family £10, season ticket £18 single, £30*
double; (house and garden £6.50, OAPs £5.50, children £2.50, family £15.50, sea-
son ticket £28 single, £50 double) (2005 prices) • *Other information: Advance notice*
required for wheelchairs. Telephone for details of garden study and flower arranging
courses ❶ 💻 🐄 wc ♿ ⬆ 𝄢 ⛲

Set in the heart of a medieval deer park on the slopes of the South Downs,
the award-winning gardens of this Elizabethan house are approached through
Fountain Court. A broad gravelled path leads down a gentle slope through a
wrought-iron gate guarded by a pair of Istrian stone lions to a walled garden of
about four acres, which retains the original quadrant layout divided by broad walks
and includes an orchard and teak walk-through greenhouse. The scope and character
of the walled garden have been progressively enhanced with new borders and plantings
of Edwardian opulence, reaching their peak from July onwards. There is also a
potager, a rose garden and a green border, planted along the outer west wall, and a
lavender garden. In one corner is an enchanting miniature house with its own garden,
a delight for both children and adults. The pleasure grounds of about seven acres
provide lawns and walks under stately trees to the lake, with views over the cricket
ground to the South Downs. A brick and turf maze is a feature here. This is a garden
for all seasons, and in spring it is dominated by the splendid 'sacred' grove of 'Mount
Fuji' white-flowering cherry, over fifty years old.

Petworth House ★ [Historic Park Grade I]

Petworth GU28 0AE. Tel: (01798) 342207

The National Trust • *6.5m E of Midhurst on A272 in Petworth* • *House open April*
to Oct, Sat – Wed, 11am – 5pm (but open Good Friday) • *Pleasure ground open 19th*
to 29th March, Sat – Wed, 12 noon – 4pm, then April to Oct, Sat – Wed, 11am – 6pm.
Deer park open all year, daily, 8am – dusk • *Entrance: pleasure ground £2, children*
£1; deer park free (house and pleasure ground £7.50, children £4, family £19.
Pre-booked parties of 15 or more £6.50 per person) • *Other information: Parking*
0.5m N of Petworth on A283. Disabled visitors by arrangement, special parking
available. Refreshments only on days house open • *Pleasure Ground:* ❶ 💻 ✕ 🐄
wc ♿ 𝄢 ⛲ 🍴 ☕ *Deer park:* ○

The stately palace, with one of the finest late-seventeenth-century interiors in
England, sits in a magnificent park developed over centuries from a small enclosure
for fruit and vegetables in the sixteenth century to its present size of 705 acres;
it is enclosed by an impressive five-mile-long stone wall. George London worked
here at the end of the seventeenth century, and from 1751 to 1763 'Capability'
Brown was employed by the 2nd Earl of Egremont to modify the contours of the
ground, plant cedars and many other trees and construct the serpentine lake in
front of the house; it was one of his earliest designs. Turner painted fine views of the
park (as well as the interior of the house) and it is interesting to see these and have
them in one's mind. It is not a place for the botanist, but it is a splendid experience

all year round, with a fine show of daffodils and bluebells and glorious autumn colour. The individual trees and shrubs, including Japanese maples and rhododendrons, deserve close study, and majestic veteran trees now tower over wildflower meadows and ornamental shrubs, providing interest throughout the year. It is worth noting that at the turn of the century Petworth had over two dozen gardeners (they were always counted in dozens). Far fewer staff have, since the storms of 1987 and 1990, planted in the region of 40,000 trees and continued to replant the pleasure grounds in Brownian style.

Rymans

Apuldram, Dell Quay, Chichester PO20 7EG. Tel: (01243) 783147

Mrs Suzanna Gayford • 1m SW of Chichester. Turn off A259 (old A27) at sign to Dell Quay, Apuldram, garden on left • Open for NGS, and by appt • Other information: Teas on open days • Entrance: £3 ● ▣ ◁

Surrounding a fifteenth-century house with a mellow Ventnor-stone exterior, the garden is being developed by the present owner. Two new box parterres flank *Rosa odorata* 'Mutabilis' in front of the house. A walled garden filled with wisterias, flowering shrubs and roses and furnished with a new pergola leads to a modern architectural water feature. The paddock opposite the old stables is now planted with a selection of trees and two wildflower glades. Seen from within the walled garden an avenue of black poplars, *Populus nigra*, stretches beyond a magnificent wrought-iron gate to nearby twelfth-century Apuldram church. Planted with massed daffodils, the avenue is a splendid sight in springtime. A spiral *potager* is maturing, and there is a new dahlia walk which, together with the collection of salvias, steals the show in August and September.

Selehurst

Lower Beeding, Horsham RH13 6PR. Tel: (01403) 891501

Mr and Mrs M. Prideaux • 4.5m SE of Horsham on A281, opposite Leonardslee (see entry) • Open 14th May, 2 – 6pm, and for parties by appt • Entrance: £3 ● ▣ ▣ WC & ✈ ◷

Originally part of the Leonardslee estate (see entry) there are still original 'Loderi' rhododendrons to be found here, and the tallest *Eucalyptus gunnii* in the country, dating from the 1890s. The rest of this romantic landscape garden has been created since 1976 by garden designer and novelist Sue Prideaux. It is a place of glorious views, large-scale planting and a highly individual vision. Near the house the picture is classic and traditional: walled garden, Italian borders, laburnum and rose tunnel, herb knot, herbaceous borders and topiary, with wisteria, roses, iris, lilies as the keynote plants. Crossing the meadow down to bluebell woods and a stand of copper beeches echoing the distant view of Chanctonbury Ring is a different and enchanting world. Here is a crinkle-crankle hornbeam hedge, a 'magnolia axis' underplanted with bluebells, a calm green amphitheatre; nearby is a 5000-year-old petrified Irish yew root set on a mound within a copper beech circle. In the larch wood a new walk is lined with columnar cypresses and *Cornus* 'Eddie's White Wonder'. There are no fewer than six ponds, each different in outline and atmosphere. In one is reflected a Gothick folly tower decorated with shells, and from here the path meanders through magnolias, azaleas, cornus and tree ferns to a hornbeam *allée*. Alternatively you can take the original 1890s' woodland walk back to the topmost pond and Chinese pavilion. On the other side of the house are plantings of eucryphia, stewartia and camellia, and a lime walk leading to a wildflower meadow.

Shulbrede Priory

Linchmere, Haslemere, Surrey GU27 3NQ. Tel: (01428) 653049

Laura Ponsonby and Ian and Kate Russell • 2m SW of Haslemere off B2131 • Open 28th, 29th May, 27th, 28th Aug, 2 – 6pm, and by appt • Entrance: house and garden £3, children £1, parties (maximum 30) £4 per person (guided tour included) ◐ ⬤ ▧ WC ⅁ ⚏

Originally an Augustinian priory, twelfth-century Shulbrede became the home of Lord Ponsonby, a writer and former pacifist MP early in the twentieth century. He and his wife Dorothea created a garden here which delighted Dorothea's father, Sir Hubert Parry, the composer and Director of the Royal College of Music, who often visited Shulbrede and composed the *Shulbrede Tunes* for piano. Their grand-daughter, Laura Ponsonby, continues to improve the garden. Cottage-style borders are seen and smelt from the house, a sunken garden gives an Italianate air, a waterside walk in the wild garden inspires a sense of mystery, and vast yew hedges enclose a series of individual gardens planted to great effect. A gem on the Sussex/Surrey borders.

St Mary's House

Bramber BN44 3WE. Tel: (01903) 816205

Peter Thorogood • 8m NE of Worthing off A283 in Bramber, 1m E of Steyning • Open May to Sept, Thurs, Sun and Bank Holiday Mons, 2 – 6pm (last entry 5pm). Parties by appt daily, 9am – 6pm, except during public open times • Entrance: house and gardens £6, concessions £5, children £2.50 (2005 prices) ◑ ⬤ WC ⅁ ⚏ ⚘

From the small gravel garden with clipped box and yew, the path leads over a pretty stone balustraded bridge and up to the topiary garden (strange animals and birds) in front of the charming fifteenth-century timber-framed house. The yew tunnel beyond the gate leads to the ivy-clad Monk's Walk. The upper lawn is enclosed by herbaceous beds, while the lower lawn has clipped yew hedges and roses; there is an exceptional example of the prehistoric *Ginkgo biloba*. The Victorian Secret Garden includes a rose garden and a border planted in memory of the late Queen Mother. The formerly circular orchard has been re-landscaped and includes a semi-circular pergola. A rural museum has been created in the Boulton and Paul potting shed, while the unusual 40-metre fruit wall has been cleared and replanted, and the pineapple pits with their original stove-house proclaim their purpose once again. Two herbaceous borders and new yew hedges give structure to the planned herb and rose gardens. The woodland walk has been underplanted with bluebells and primroses but is mostly left to the native wildlife, with a huge fallen willow starting into growth again as an amazing living structure.

Standen

East Grinstead RH19 4NE. Tel: (01342) 323029

The National Trust • 2m S of East Grinstead, signed from A22 at Felbridge, and from B2110 • House open as garden, 11am – 5pm • Garden open 25th March to 29th Oct, Wed – Sun and Bank Holiday Mons, 11am – 6pm; 18th Nov to 17th Dec, Sat and Sun, 11am – 3pm • Entrance: £4, children £2; joint ticket available with Nymans Wed – Fri only • Other information: Picnics in picnic area only. Dogs in woodland walks only ☕ 🍽 ✕ <u>WC</u> ❤ ⚘ 🏛 ▼

The Philip Webb House with its Morris and Co interiors may be the main reason for visiting Standen, but the 12-acre hillside garden is also worth seeing as a reflection of the Arts and Crafts Movement. It is divided into small compartments, notably an enchanted hidden jungle known as the Quarry Garden and a rose garden planted with *R. rugosa* edged with nepeta. Across the croquet lawn the Bamboo Garden is being cleared to reveal the site of the old swimming pond with its cascades and steps; this area is being replanted with China roses, deciduous azaleas and herbaceous and bog plants. From the Top Walk stunning views look across to the Weirwood reservoir. Three woodland walks, one crossing a wildflower meadow, can be muddy, but one is mostly path and boardwalk.

Stansted Park Victorian Walled Garden

Rowlands Castle, Hampshire PO9 6DX. Tel: (023) 9241 3090

7m W of Chichester, 2m N of Westbourne, off B2149 • Garden centre open all year, daily, 9am – 1pm (Sun 10.30am – 4.30pm); walled garden open 16th April to Oct, daily, 9am – 5pm; Nov to 7th April, daily, 10am – 4pm (closes 3pm Sun) • Entrance: free ☕ 🍽 WC ⚘ 🏛

Now a garden centre, the Victorian glasshouses, conservatories and complex of walled gardens, and the circular well-head garden in the arboretum, have recently been restored. The upper walled garden holds a collection of sculptures from the 'Sculpture in the South' organisation; all of these are for sale. The site also includes a seven-acre arboretum, a falconry and a resident glass-blower on site. In the lower walled garden, Ivan Hicks' quirky and intriguing *Garden in Mind* has been replaced by a formal yew maze.

Town Place ★

Ketches Lane, Freshfield, Nr Scaynes Hill RH17 7NR. Tel: (01825) 790221

Mr and Mrs Anthony McGrath • 3m E of Haywards Heath. From A275 turn W at Sheffield Green into Ketches Lane (signed to Lindfield); garden is 1.75m on left • Open 11th, 15th, 25th June, 2nd, 9th and 13th July, and for parties of 20 or more by appt • Entrance: £4, children free, parties £6 per person ☕ 🍽 WC ❤ ⚘

A wonderful three-acre garden created since 1990 by an ultra-keen husband-and-wife team – each year it gets a bit bigger. Wrought-iron gates open onto a lawn enclosed by low walls and old brick paths; the one to the left leads up steps to an apple tunnel and herb garden with wide downland views, then down past a big hollow oak to the dell with its attractive free-form raised pond and fountain. From here you look back across the main lawn to the 1650s' house (not open) and a 46-metre-long herbaceous border backed by a magnificent flame tapestry hedge. A rose pergola shields a sunken rose garden, replanted in 2005 with over 140 English roses, and this in turn leads into the orchard and a new area by the pool with gravel paths and beds block-planted with box, screened by a line of *Rosa* 'Excelsa'. Amble through the orchard, carpeted in spring with daffodils, to the shrubbery, where you are surrounded by the astonishing circular, clipped, striped conifer hedge; beyond is the English rose garden, box-edged and planted with over 400 roses of 36 different cultivars. Tucked away in a corner are a spring garden and a hidden garden – follow the sound of water. There is more – copper beech hedges, a hornbeam walk, a *potager* and cutting garden and the New Territories, where a hornbeam *allée* and cloister have recently been planted. From here you can return to the main lawn to soak up a bit more of that sumptuous border.

Trotton Old Rectory

Trotton, Petersfield GU31 5EN. Tel: (01730) 813612

Captain and Mrs John Pilley • 3m W of Midhurst on A272 • Open for NGS and parties by appt • Entrance: £3 ●

Set in the pretty Rother valley, the two-and-a-half-acre garden consists of several different areas of varying shapes and sizes, each with its own character. Many are lavishly planted, and they are separated from each other by hedges of yew, holly and beech as well as a trellis screen and walls. To the north of the house are newly planted pleached limes and box, to the south a terrace leads out into a formal rose garden. This is planted with attractive pink and white roses, contrasting with the old roses in the circular rosarium in the garden beyond, which is surrounded by mixed borders where lavender, delphiniums, campanulas and many other plants provide a riot of colour. A restful enclosure dominated by a venerable oak has gunneras, clipped yew and a lawn speckled with bulbs in spring to give variations of texture and shades of green; against the hedge are the graves of family pets. Another garden surrounds the croquet lawn. To the east of the house at a lower level is a large pond surrounded by clumps of handsome *Iris ensata*. Walks lined with shrubs and hostas, hemerocallis and lilies link the different areas.

Wakehurst Place Garden and
Millennium Seed Bank ★★ [Historic Garden Grade II*]

Ardingly, Haywards Heath RH17 6TN. Tel: (01444) 894066 (Infoline)

The Royal Botanic Gardens, Kew • 5m N of Haywards Heath on B2028. From London take A(M)23, A272, B2028 or A22, B2110 • Part of house open • Garden open all year, daily, except 24th and 25th Dec, 10am – 6pm (closes 4.30pm autumn and winter). Guided walks available 11.30am and 2.30pm on Sat, Sun and Bank Holiday Mons • Entrance: £8, children (under 17) free, season tickets £16 • Other information: Many events throughout the year – telephone for details ○ ● ✕ ●
WC ♿ ♨ ♨ ♀ ♒

Dating from Norman times, the estate was bought by Gerald W.E. Loder (Lord Wakehurst) in 1903. He spent thirty-three years developing the gardens, a work carried on by Sir Henry Price. The gardens have been managed by the Royal Botanic Gardens, Kew, since 1965. They have a fine collection of hardy plants arranged geographically and display four comprehensive National Collections – betulas, hypericums, nothofagus and skimmias. Unique is the glade planted with species growing at over 3000 metres in the Himalayas. A plantation of Japanese irises is part of the extensive and fascinating water gardens. There are two walled gardens, one given over to colourful bedding schemes, the other to herbaceous borders, delightfully planted in subtle shades. Wakehurst is a place for the botanist, plantsman and garden lover, offering features of year-round interest, particularly the winter garden which bursts into colour about late November. The Wellcome Trust Millennium Building, home to an international seed bank and interactive public exhibition, opened in 2000 – futuristic in appearance, the design and presentation are masterly.

Weald and Downland Open Air Museum
Singleton, Chichester PO18 0EU. Tel: (01243) 811348

Weald and Downland Open Air Museum • 5m N of Chichester on A286 • Open March to Oct, daily, 10.30am – 6pm (last admission 5pm); Nov to Feb, Wed, Sat and Sun, 10.30am – 4pm • Entrance: £7.70, children £4.10, under 5 free, family £21, OAPs £6.70 (2005 prices) ○ 🍴 🛍 wc ♿ ⌷ 🐾 🏛 🍽 ✆

Set in the heart of the South Downs, the main exhibits of this museum (founded in 1967) are over 45 traditional buildings, ranging from medieval to Victorian, rescued from certain destruction, restored and rebuilt on the museum's countryside site. Complementing the buildings, seven historic gardens have been researched and planted to demonstrate the changes and continuities in domestic gardens from the early 1400s to 1900. The earliest garden has only a few plants, including wild garlic and edible weeds such as fat hen. A complete medieval farmstead has been re-created around Bayleaf Farmhouse, and the replica fifteenth-century garden is planted to fulfil the gastronomic and medical needs of six adults, their children and servants from beds over four metres long and a metre wide. By the Victorian era, represented by a typical cottage garden of the period, the gardens were not only practical but showed the introduction of flowers for their beauty alone.

West Dean Gardens ★ [Historic Garden Grade II*]
West Dean, Chichester PO18 0QZ. Tel: (01243) 818210

Edward James Foundation • 6m N of Chichester on A286 • Open March to Oct, daily, 10.30am – 5pm (opens 11am March, April, Oct); Nov to Feb, Wed – Sun, 11am – 4.30pm, and for parties by appt • Entrance: £5.50, OAPs £5, children £2.50. Pre-booked parties of 20 or more £5 per person ◑ 🍴 ✕ 🛍 wc ♿ 🐾 🏛 🍽 ✆

There have been gardens here since 1622; in 1836 a number of rare trees were mentioned by J.C. Loudon, and in 1891 William James bought the property and Harold Peto designed the magnificent 100-metre-long pergola. If you want to see fruit and vegetables growing in profusion, this is the garden to visit. The restored Victorian glasshouses are immaculate and the regimented rows of fruit and vegetables excellently labelled. In the orchard, backed by an old crinkle-crankle wall, are fruit trees trained in a variety of shapes and an unusual circular thatched apple store. The potting sheds now house garden-themed exhibitions. Outside the 3.5-acre walled garden you can explore the 35 acres of ornamental grounds – designed around the house (now an Arts and Crafts College). Stroll the length of the pergola with its lush planting designed to flower from spring through to early autumn, then relax in the sunken garden, a mass of tulips in spring, before taking the woodland walk. The west end of the garden has been restored and replanted. The spring garden, with its enchanting summerhouse, laburnum tunnel and flintwork bridges over the River Lavant, is given an exotic jungle atmosphere by a planting of Chusan palms and bamboos; beyond is the wild garden, which has some unusual trees and is planted in more naturalistic style to blend into the surrounding parkland. From here there is an enjoyable walk through the park, with panoramic views of the mansion house, grounds and the surrounding downland landscape, to the 49-acre *St Roche's Arboretum*, carpeted in spring with wild daffodils, where Edward James is buried beneath the trees he loved so much.

HOW TO FIND THE GARDENS
Directions to each garden are included in the entry. This information has been supplied by the owners and garden inspectors. It is aimed to be the best available to those travelling by car, and has been compiled to be used in conjunction with a road atlas. Some gardens may be reached by train or bus, but the unreliability of these makes it unrewarding to include details, particularly as many garden visits are made on Sundays.

GARDENING FOR THE DISABLED
•The Gardening for the Disabled Trust (Charity No. 255066) collects donations to assist people with improvements to their gardens, or to supply equipment which will enable them to continue to garden. Information from Mrs Angela Parish, Frittenden House, Nr Cranbrook TN17 2DG (Fax: (01580) 852120; Email: apparish@hotmail.com.
•Thrive is a national charity promoting the use of gardens and horticulture as a therapy for restricted or disabled gardeners (Tel: (0118) 988 5688; Email: info@thrive.org.uk; Website: www.thrive.org.uk or www.carryongardening.org.uk
•For information on the Disabled and Older Gardeners' Association (including workshops etc.), write to Growing Point, Holme Lacy College, Hereford or telephone Sue Eaton on (01432) 268876.
•Demonstration gardens to assist the disabled are on view at a number of properties open to the public and are also featured in the *Guide*. They include two in Battersea Park (for an appointment with the Horticultural Therapy Unit telephone (020) 7720 2212), Capel Manor and Broadview Garden.

SYMBOLS
[NEW] entries new for 2006; ○ open all year; ◐ open most of year; ◑ open during main season; ● open rarely and/or by appt; ▆ teas/light refreshments; ✕ meals; 🧺 picnics permitted; WC toilet facilities; <u>WC</u> toilet facilities, inc. disabled; ♿ partly wheelchair-accessible; 🐕 dogs on lead; ✿ plants for sale; 🏠 shop; ♟ events held; ◔ children-friendly; B&B bed and breakfast available.

WARWICKSHIRE

Arbury Hall ★ [Historic Garden Grade I]

Arbury, Nuneaton CV10 7PT. Tel: (024) 7638 2804

The Viscount and Viscountess Daventry • 10m N of Coventry, 3.5m SW of Nuneaton off B4102 Fillongley/Nuneaton road • House and garden open 16th, 17th and 30th April, 1st, 28th and 29th May, 27th and 28th Aug, 2 – 6pm (house closes 5pm) • Entrance: £5, children £3.50 (hall and gardens £6.50, children £4, family £18, parties of 25 or more £6 per person) ● ● WC & ⬧ ⛪

A formal rose garden and climbing roses are features of this delightful, peaceful garden, distinguished also by the lakes with their wildfowl, the parkland, the drive and the bluebell woods. Especially memorable are the pollarded limes, the old walled garden and the beautiful old trees. Bulbs at the start of the season are followed by rhododendrons and azaleas, then roses in June and autumn colour from trees and shrubs. A canal system was installed years ago as a method of transport.

Avon Cottage

Ashow, Kenilworth CV8 2LE. Tel: (01926) 512850

Neil Collett • 5m NE of Warwick, 1.5m E of Kenilworth. From A452 Kenilworth – Leamington road turn onto B4115 (signed to Ashow and Stoneleigh), after 0.25m turn right into Ashow and right again. Continue to end of Ashow; cottage is beside church • Open 24th and 25th June, 9am – 6pm, and by appt • Entrance: £2, children 50p • Other information: Refreshments and toilet facilities available in village club on Suns ● ● & ⛲

A peaceful one-and-a-half-acre garden surrounding a picturesque eighteenth-century listed cottage in a lovely riverside setting. The owner, a landscape architect, has worked organically to protect valuable wildlife habitats and there is plenty of interest in the sensitive use of reclaimed materials. Moving through archways covered with clematis, roses and honeysuckles there are surprises at every turn, and seats are strategically placed to enjoy the views, including a new one of camomile on slate. There are riotous mixed herbaceous borders, with vegetables and herbs growing among the flowers, an orchard area with domestic and water fowl, a rhododendron walkway, a collection of old-fashioned shrub roses and masses of daffodils in spring. Don't leave without crossing the footbridge past the twelfth-century church, or you will miss a sensational view of the garden.

Baddesley Clinton [Historic Garden Grade II]

Rising Lane, Baddesley Clinton, Knowle, Solihull B93 0DQ. Tel: (01564) 783294

The National Trust • 7.5m NW of Warwick, 6m S of M42 junction 5, 0.75m W of A4141 Warwick – Birmingham road, at Chadwick End • House open as garden but March to 5th Nov, 1.30 – 5pm • Garden open March to 10th Dec, Wed – Sun,

12 noon – 5pm • Entrance: £3.40, children £1.70, parties £5.80 per person (house and garden £6.80, children £3.40, family £17) • Other information: Combined entrance with Packwood House available NEW ◗ 🥄 ✕ WC ♿ ♨

In spring the driveway and the path to the church are lined with daffodils, while primroses, cowslips and bluebells colour the woodland. The courtyard of the medieval moated manor house is planted with red and golden annuals in the shape of the heraldic shield of the Ferrers family, who lived here until 1633. In the walled garden herbs, herbaceous borders, a circular rose bed and a large bed filled with dahlias give a succession of summer and autumn colour. Nut trees and crab apples intersperse with pampas grass line the Undine Walk, leading to a new kitchen garden filled with fruit and vegetables destined for the tables of the acclaimed restaurant.

Barton House ★

Barton-on-the-Heath, Moreton-in-Marsh, Gloucestershire GL56 0PJ.
Tel: (01608) 674303

Mr and Mrs I.H.B. Cathie • 6m S of Shipston-on-Stour off A3400, 4m E of Moreton-in-Marsh off A44 • Open for NGS 28th May, 2 – 6pm, and by appt for parties of 25 or more • Entrance: £4, children £2, parties £5 • Other information: Refreshments in coach house on open day ◖ 🥄 WC ♿ ⌗ ♒

Borders of rhododendrons greet the visitor to the six-acre garden, set around a manor house by Inigo Jones (not open), and throughout the garden an excellent collection of American, species and hybrid rhododendrons provides a long flowering period, with autumn colour filling many trees. A secret garden has magnolias and maples underplanted with camellias, pieris, embothriums, arbutus, crinodendrons, euphorbias and geraniums. Viewing points have been made to enjoy the surrounding countryside, and there are some fine mature trees, many rare plants plus National Collections of nothofagus, stewartias and arbutus, and masses of spring bulbs. Among the varied features and surprises are a catalpa walk, a collection of moutan tree peonies (*Paeonia suffruticosa*), *Paulownia fargesii* and *P. tomentosum,* a rose garden with beds of individual colours surrounding an oblong lily pool, a Himalayan garden, a Japanese garden, herbaceous and shrub beds, statues, archways and a copy of the portico of St Paul's, Covent Garden. A paved roundel in the centre of the walled kitchen garden is being developed as a Mediterranean garden with palm trees, olives and cypresses. The ornate cast-iron atrium from the Royal Exchange in Threadneedle Street forms the roof of the orangery. The ha-ha has been lined with clay, filled with water and furnished with an ornate iron bridge, a Neptune platform and a garden house. A vineyard planted in 2000 produces red and white wine which can be bought in the Coach House. Also well worth seeing is *Whichford Pottery* off the other side of the A3400 [open all year, daily except Sun]. Although not strictly a garden, it is well worth visiting for its design ideas as well as its stylish pots, and Jim Keeling's own garden, if you can get to see it, is inspirational.

Charlecote Park [Historic Park Grade II*]

Charlecote, Wellesbourne, Warwick CV35 9ER. Tel: (01789) 470277

The National Trust • 5m E of Stratford-upon-Avon, 1m W of Wellesbourne • House open as garden until 29th Oct, but 12 noon – 5pm • Garden and grounds open 4th

*March to 29th Oct, Fri – Tues, 10.30am – 6pm (closes 4pm Oct); 4th Nov to 17th
Dec, Sat and Sun, 11am – 4pm. Parties by appt • Entrance: £3.30, children £1.65
(house and garden £6.60, children £3.30, family £16) • Other information: Braille
guide available* ❶ 👄 ✕ <u>WC</u> ♿ ♨ ♀ ✎

Home of the Lucy family since the thirteenth century, the pink brick gatehouse is
the only remnant of the early Tudor house left untouched. A courtyard garden has
been designed in front of the house and a parterre re-instated. The wild garden is
interesting and the cascade will attract those who like water features – these
include a pond in the small wilderness garden. The Shakespeare border has now
been made smaller and is situated in front of the summerhouse. A new herbaceous
border has been created to give colour from early spring to the first frosts, and
there is also a new sensory garden. The park was laid out by 'Capability' Brown, who
was directed not to destroy the avenues of elms (later eliminated by Dutch elm
disease).

The Coach House

Bitham Hall, Avon Dassett CV47 2AH. Tel: (01295) 690255

*Mr and Mrs G.J. Rice • 12m SE of Warwick, 7m N of Banbury off B4100. Leave
M40 junction 12 at Gaydon, or from Leamington take A462 to join Banbury road.
3m after Gaydon turn left to Avon Dassett; entrance to garden is on hill. Parking on
hill and in village • Open for NGS, and by appt • Entrance: £2, children free* ● **WC**
♿ ⟁

These two acres, set on sloping ground overlooking Edgehill, originally formed part
of a Victorian garden, and are now planted for year-round interest, with many varieties
of trees, shrubs, climbers and perennials. Walls give shelter to tender plants. Two
areas are devoted to bush and cordon fruit trees and vegetables, and there is also a
wet garden. The woodland has well-established trees and some 70 young native
trees, underplanted with new shrubs, including camellias, rhododendrons and
peonies. Flowering bulbs and primroses give spring interest.

Compton Scorpion Farm

Ilmington, Shipston–on–Stour CV36 4PJ. Tel: (01608) 682552

*Mrs T.M. Karlsen • 8m S of Stratford-upon-Avon, 4m NW of Shipston-on-Stour off
A3400. Take left fork uphill at Ilmington village hall. After 1.5m turn left down steep
narrow lane and house is on left • Open 19th to 30th June, daily, 2 – 5pm, and by appt
• Entrance: £2, children free* ● **WC** ♿ ⟁

One of the most stunning views in the county unfolds as you drive along the ridge
from Ilmington towards this farmhouse, which in 1989 was surrounded by a mere
meadow, sloping steeply towards the house. The owner has worked wonders, from
the small walled garden behind the house aiming at Jekyll-inspired single colour
schemes, to the rose-encrusted slope beyond and the rabbit-proof vegetable garden
around the old sheep shed. A spring-fed pond has been added in the orchard, and a
wildflower meadow in the wild garden on the hillside is now well established. In
countryside as beautiful as this you could say that she started with an advantage, but
the stylish planting is all her own.

Coombe Country Park

Brinklow Road, Binley, Coventry CV3 2AB. Tel: (024) 7645 3720 (Ranger Service)

Just E of Coventry on B4027 • Open all year, daily, 7.30am – dusk • Entrance: free but parking charge ○ 👜 ✗ 🍽 WC ♿ ⬥ 🏛 🌢 ☕

Over 400 acres of beautiful parkland including woodland and lakeside walks, all-weather pathways, wildflower meadows and historic gardens by William Andrews Nesfield and William Miller. There are also the remains of a duck decoy and an arboretum: a SSSI includes the vast lake originally designed as part of the 'Capability' Brown landscape, which is home to wildlife, a bird hide and a heronry. Facilities include an information centre, a history video, a wildlife discovery centre and play areas.

Coughton Court ★

Alcester B49 5JA. Tel: (01789) 400777

Mrs C. Throckmorton • 8m NW of Stratford-upon-Avon, 2m N of Alcester on A435 • House and garden open. Dates vary seasonally – telephone or consult website at back of book for details. Also open for parties of 15 or more by appt • Entrance: £5.10, children £2.50 (under 5 free), family £15, parties £4.10 (house and garden £7.45, children £3.95 (under 5 free), family £26.50) (2005 prices) ◑ 👜 ✗ 🍽 WC ♿ ⬥ 🌲 🏛 🌢 ☕

The grounds complement the mid-sixteenth-century house and include a variety of gardens both formal and informal. The main garden, courtyard and walled garden were designed by Christina Williams, Mrs Throckmorton's daughter. The redesigned orchard contains many old local varieties and there is also a chef's herb garden. The large lawn is bordered by cloistered lime walks, while a peaceful stroll beside the River Arrow reveals willows, wild garlic, ferns, hellebores and native trees and shrubs. In spring there is a bluebell wood and many bulbs to enjoy. A second lake has been drained to form a bog garden. One of the finest features is the large walled garden with 'hot' and 'cold' herbaceous borders dedicated to Professor d'Abreu – Mrs Throckmorton's father – containing a superb display of plants to give colour and interest through the seasons. The red and white gardens are surrounded by hornbeam hedges being trained to provide windows. In the rose labyrinth masses of roses and clematis grow over arches and pedestals, with herbaceous underplanting. In the early summer garden wisteria is trained over raised hoops with peonies beneath, and pale colours change to deeper shades of blue and red. The architectural features are also good. A pond and fountain is surrounded by benches and planted in green and white as a peaceful place for contemplation.

Elm Close

Binton Road, Welford-on-Avon CV37 8PT. Tel: (01789) 750793

Mr and Mrs E. W. Dyer • 5m SW of Stratford-upon-Avon on B439. Turn left after 4.5m to Welford • Open for NGS, and for parties by appt • Entrance: £2.50, children free ● WC ♿ 🌲

A relatively small garden filled with fresh ideas and a wide range of plants. Clematis (over 300) are trained over pergolas and climb through trees and shrubs, and there are dwarf conifers, a rock garden, hellebores, a pool, alpine troughs, raised beds and an excellent variety of bulbs. Herbaceous plants and shrubs, including a wealth of peonies, cornus, hostas, daphnes and magnolias, provide interest and colour throughout the year.

Farnborough Hall [Historic Garden Grade I]

Farnborough, Banbury, Oxfordshire OX17 1DU. Tel: (01295) 690002

The National Trust/Mr and Mrs Holbech • 5m N of Banbury, 0.5m W of A423 or 1.5m E off B4100 • House open as garden • Grounds open 5th April to 23rd Sept, Wed and Sat, and 1st May; all 2 – 5.30pm • Entrance: garden and terrace walk £2, (house and grounds £4, children £2) ◗ WC ♿ ⬥

The house has been in the same family since 1684. It was reconstructed in the eighteenth century with fine Rococo plasterwork and the grounds were improved in the 1740s with the aid of Sanderson Miller, the architect, landscape gardener and dilettante who lived at nearby Radway. Climbing gently along the ridge looking towards Edgehill is the fine S-shaped terrace walk built by William Holbech in order to greet his brother on the adjoining property. *The Oxford Companion* describes it as a majestic concept marking the movement towards the great landscaped parks at the end of the eighteenth century. There are two temples and a game larder along the walk and an obelisk at the end. The trees are beech, sycamore and lime. Beyond a giant cedar is part of the site of the former orangery, a rose garden, and a yew walk with steps at the end, where there is a seat with a fine view over the river, the cascade and the countryside towards Edgehill. The cascade fountain suppresses the otherwise-invasive hum of the M40. A uniquely interesting site.

The Hiller Garden

Dunnington Heath Farm, Alcester B49 5PD. Tel: (01789) 772771

Hillers Farm Shop • 9m W of Stratford-upon-Avon, 3m SW of Alcester between A46 and A422, S of Weethley village • Open all year, daily, 10am – 5pm • Entrance: free ○ ⬤ ✗ WC ♿ ⬥ 🌿 🏬 ✎

An established two-acre garden with year-round interest. Large beds of herbaceous perennials with frequent new introductions enable visitors to the garden centre to see mature, well-labelled plants in good colour combinations and so judge their suitability for personal use. The garden also embraces an extensive rose garden, which includes more than 200 varieties and has a Victorian rose area as its centre-piece. The owners' adjacent private garden is also open for pre-booked visits by horticultural societies.

Jephson Gardens [Historic Public Park Grade II]

Leamington Spa CV32 4AD.
Tel: (01926) 450000 (Amenities Department, Warwick District Council)

Warwick District Council • In Leamington Spa, main entrance off Parade • Open all year, daily, 8am – dusk (opens 9am Sun and Bank Holiday Mons) • Entrance: free • Other information: Parking in Newbold Terrace ○ ⬤ WC ♿ ⬥

The spa town has always made a great effort to provide floral displays in its streets, and this vibrancy can also be enjoyed at its peak in the intensive bedding-out of the principal formal public garden. Besides flowers, it contains a remarkable collection of trees. Leamington has a string of parks and gardens running along the River Leam right across the town – an almost unique piece of town planning of a century ago. It is possible to walk their length: Mill Gardens, Jephson Gardens, Pump Room Gardens, York Promenade and Victoria Park. There are some fine listed examples of Victorian iron bridges, as well as earlier stone ones. On the outskirts of nearby Kenilworth is the ruined *Kenilworth Castle*, where the Tudor garden and its parterres has been reconstructed [Historic Garden Grade II*].

The Master's Garden [Historic Garden Grade II]

Lord Leycester Hospital, Warwick CV34 4BH.
Tel: (01926) 491422 (Contact: The Master)

Board of Governors of Lord Leycester Hospital • In High Street • Open 29th March to Sept, daily except Mon (but open Bank Holiday Mons), 10am – 4.30pm • Entrance: £2 ❶ 🍴 WC ♿

The restoration work undertaken here is remarkable. Old cobbles from the summerhouse have been relaid in a new circular house with a thatched roof of Norfolk reeds, and archways dating from the 1850s have been copied to support roses, clematis and other climbers. A brick pathway through the centre of the garden repeats the feathered pattern. The 150-year old pleached lime avenue remains. An eighteenth-century dovecot has been converted into a gazebo, and a pineapple frame has been restored. A circular herb garden has a sundial at its centre, and the vegetable and fruit area is bursting in season with gooseberries and redcurrants. A twelfth-century Norman arch frames a Nileometer – a finial from a stone column installed by the Romans on the Nile to record the rise and fall of the river – and leads into the other half of the garden, which includes a Victorian rock garden, shrubs, roses and perennials. Also in Warwick, at Hill Close, the *Victorian Pleasure Gardens* are an interesting example of nineteenth-century plots grown by local craftsmen, and tradesmen. They are now being restored to their old pattern of high hedges, summerhouses and old fruit trees.

Packwood House ★ [Historic Garden Grade II*]

Lapworth, Solihull, Birmingham B94 6AT. Tel: (01564) 782024

The National Trust • 11m SE of central Birmingham, 2m E of Hockley Heath on A3400 • House open March to 5th Nov, Wed – Sun, Good Fri and Bank Holiday Mons, 12 noon – 4.30pm • Garden open March to 5th Nov, Wed – Sun and Bank Holiday Mons, 11am – 4.30pm (closes 5.30pm May to Sept) • Park open all year, daily • Entrance: £3.10, children £1.55 (house and garden £6.20, children £3.10, family £15.50. Parties of 15 or more by written appt only • Other information: Picnic site opposite main gates. Combined entry ticket with Baddesley Clinton ❶ 🍴 WC ♿ ♿ 🚻 ♟*

Hidden away in a rather suburban part of Warwickshire, this garden is notable for its intact layout, dating from the sixteenth and seventeenth centuries when the original house was built. There are courtyards, terraces and brick gazebos. Even more remarkable is the almost surreal yew garden, unique in design. Tradition claims that it represents the Sermon on the Mount, but in fact the 'Apostles' were planted in the 1850s as a four-square pattern round an orchard. Never mind, the result is now homogeneous. A spiral mount of yew and box is a delightful illusion; note also the clever use of brick. G. Baron Ash, who gave the property to the Trust, made a sunken garden in the 1930s and restored earlier design features. He also introduced colourful border plantings, and now the gardens are worth seeing at all seasons of the year. In spring drifts of daffodils follow the snowdrops and bluebells carpet the copse, while shrubs flower on red-brick walls. The herbaceous border, the sunken garden, the terrace beds and climbing roses and honeysuckles are a riot of colour in summer, and autumn brings changes in foliage. New herbaceous borders flank a pathway lead-ing from the house and framing distant views of the yew garden, while the walled kitchen garden has been greatly improved after many years of neglect; it promises to be splendid. Don't miss the attractive lakeside walk and wildflower meadows.

Ragley Hall [Historic Park and Garden Grade II*]

Alcester B49 5NJ. Tel: (01789) 762090

The Marquess and Marchioness of Hertford • 8m W of Stratford-upon-Avon, 1m S of Alcester off A435 • House open as garden, but 12 noon – 4.30pm (last entry) • Garden and park open April to Sept, Thurs – Sun and Bank Holiday Mons; daily during school holidays, 10am – 6pm • Entrance: £6.50, concessions £5.50, children £4.50 (house, park and garden, £7.50, concessions £6.50, children £4.50) • Other information: Dogs in park only, on lead ◑ 💽 ✕ 🦐 WC ᕦ ⬟ 🏛 🔊 ☕

The 27 acres of formal and informal gardens date from the 1870s and include some vast trees – blue cedar, picea, abies and Wellingtonia. Near the house (the scene of a great range of entertainments) is a border of unusual and tender perennials and, beyond, the rose garden with beds of individual varieties. There are also roses on the pillars of the house. There is a 'fumpery' with ferns, rhododendrons, hydrangeas and foxgloves. The Secret Garden has a central fountain and beds of herbaceous plants. A new bog garden is planted with gunneras, primulas and astilbes to encour-age wild life, and a meadow contains wild flowers, orchids and fritillaries. There are lovely views of the surrounding parkland and pleasant walks through woodland and by the lake. Children will enjoy an adventure area.

Ryton Organic Gardens

Ryton-on-Dunsmore, Coventry CV8 3LG. Tel: (024) 7630 3517

HDRA – the organic organisation • 7m NE of Leamington Spa, 5m SE of Coventry. Turn off A45 onto Wolston road • Open all year, daily except Christmas period, 9am – 5pm • Entrance: £4.50, OAPs £4, children £2. Discount for parties of 14 or more • Other information: Pre-booked guided tours available. Guide dogs only ◯ 💽 ✕ WC ᕦ 🌿 🏛 🔊 ☕

Ryton was set up in 1985 to be a centre of excellence for organic horticulture. Since then the 10 acres have been steadily developed, in a beautifully landscaped setting, to provide a wide range of inspirational and educational displays of herbs, roses, unusual vegetables, fruit, wildlife gardening and plants for bees. At the heart of the garden is a vibrant display of herbaceous perennials in an informal drift of form and colour. The individual gardens include demonstrations of organic methods of looking after soil, and of pest and disease control. There are also gardens for the visually impaired and those with other special needs, a garden for the enthusiastic cook, a Paradise Garden created by Isabelle Van Groeningen, and new displays relating to vegetables and seeds. Events and courses are held throughout the year, and there is plenty to amuse and interest children of all ages.

The Shakespeare Houses and Their Gardens

Stratford–upon–Avon. Tel: (01789) 204016

Shakespeare Birthplace Trust • Located in Stratford-upon-Avon and surrounding area • All properties open all year, daily, except 23rd to 26th Dec. Opening and closing times vary – times and prices on application • Other information: Parking on site at Anne Hathaway's Cottage and Mary Arden's House, otherwise in town car parks. Restaurant/tea shop at Hall's Croft and cafe and picnic area at Mary Arden's House
○ WC 🚶 🐾 ♿ ☕

Some claim that little is known about Shakespeare and less still about his gardens. The Trust has made them interesting adjuncts to the houses. They include: *The Birthplace Garden*, a small informal collection of over 100 trees, herbs, plants and flowers mentioned by the Bard. *Mary Arden's House*, the front a *mélange* of box, roses and flowers, the rear a stretch of lawn with a wild garden beyond. Country museum with tools, etc. *Anne Hathaway's Cottage* [Historic Garden Grade II]: a typical English cottage garden dating from the end of the nineteenth century, including a small garden with varieties of Victorian vegetables, and a nearby tree garden with examples of those mentioned in the *Works*, where a circular yew maze was planted in 2001 based on an Elizabethan model. Garden centre with plants and herbs for sale grown by the Trust's gardeners, and a small display of Victorian and Edwardian garden tools. *Nash's House* belonged to his granddaughter and grandson-in-law, and *New Place* had been bought by Shakespeare for his retirement. The house was demolished in the eighteenth century but the foundations are planted with a garden beyond which, it is suggested, his orchard and kitchen garden lay. Reconstructed Elizabethan knot garden with oak palisade and 'tunnel' or 'pleached bower' of that time. *Hall's Croft*: a walled garden, including a herbal bed, bearing little resemblance to its probable form in the period when it was owned by the Bard's son-in-law. All the above are Trust houses and fee-charged. Beyond the knot garden is the *Great Garden* with free access. Also free, but not part of the Trust, are *Bancroft Gardens* in front of the Theatre and the long stretch owned by the Royal Shakespeare Theatre, along the River Avon between the Swan Theatre and the church where Shakespeare is buried.

Stoneleigh Abbey [Historic Park and Garden Grade II*]

Kenilworth CV8 2LF. Tel: (01926) 858535

Stoneleigh Abbey Ltd (Charitable Trust) • 4m N of Leamington Spa, 5m NE of Warwick, 7m S of Coventry, off M40 junction. Turn off A46 onto B4115, then follow signs to Ashow; entrance on right between two lodges • House open as garden • Garden open 14th April to Oct, Tues – Thurs, Sun, 10am – 5pm • Entrance: £2.50, children (under 12) free (house £6, OAPs £4, one child free, additional child £2.50) ☕ 🍽
♿ WC ⚑

Over the last few years, extensive restoration has included the Baroque west wing of the abbey and its grand state rooms, the fourteenth-century gatehouse, the conservatory overlooking the River Avon, and the early-nineteenth-century stables and riding school. The park and gardens, one of Humphry Repton's most imaginative and picturesque landscape plans, is gradually being reinstated. The estate was the focus in 1809 of one of his finest and largest Red Books. Not all Repton's proposals were executed, but under his aegis the Avon was widened, a stone bridge built, an inspirational reflective pool created to mirror the south facade, and next to it, as counterpoint, a weir built to churn the waters of the river. Work is concentrated on the development of the water features which played such a part in Repton's proposals. This takes in such eclectic features as the eel catchers' hut. Later hands responsible for shaping the landscape included a pupil of Wyatville, C.S. Smith, who in the 1810s and 1820s provided many of the buildings in the park, and Percy Cane who restored and replanted the western terrace. W.S. Nesfield's strident Italianate garden, created overnight for a visit by Queen Victoria in 1858, may be left as a footnote in gardening history, but two herbal parterres have been planted in the manner of Nesfield in front of the west wing.

University of Warwick

Gibbet Hill Road, Coventry CV4 7AL. Tel: (02476) 524189 (Estate Office)

Warwick University • Nearer to Coventry than Warwick, most direct access is off A46 signed 'University of Warwick/Stoneleigh' just S of Coventry • Open all year, daily • Entrance: free ○ 💷 ✕ WC &

The university buildings, developed since the 1960s, have been assimilated within the grounds by clever landscaping, including the creation of new sports fields south of Gibbet Hill Road, the planting of many trees and the use of bedding schemes. Interesting in a smaller space is a wisteria-covered pergola in the Social Studies quadrangle. Formal gardens are being created, and around the Warwick Arts Centre and at sites across the university is a sculpture trail which features work by Richard Deacon, Liliane Ljin, Keir Smith, Bettina Furne, William Pye *et al.* A large formal water feature provides a centrepiece in the new academic square on the central campus. The university now has seven lakes with a wetlands environment and nature reserve. There are several walks through and around the extensive grounds.

Upton House ★ [Historic Garden Grade II*]

Banbury, Oxfordshire OX15 6HT. Tel: (01295) 670266

The National Trust • 12m SE of Stratford-upon-Avon, 7m NW of Banbury on A422 • House open (timed tickets on Bank Holidays) • Garden open March to Nov, Mon – Wed, 12 noon – 5pm, Sat, Sun and Bank Holiday Mons, 11 – 5pm. Telephone for winter opening times. Parties of 15 or more by appt • Entrance: £3.50 (house and garden £6.50, children £3.50). Reduction for parties of 15 or more (2005 prices) • Other information: Coaches by arrangement with Property Office. Possible for wheelchairs in parts but very steep in places. Motorised buggy with driver available on request for access to and from lower garden. Early eighteenth-century banqueting house available as holiday cottage ◑ 💷 ✕ WC & ♨ 🏛 🍷 ☕*

The house, which dates from 1695, stands on ironstone, over 210 metres above sea level on Edgehill, near the site of the famous battle. Below a great lawn, the garden descends in a series of long terraces, along one end of which an impressive flight of stone steps leads down to the large lake. In the centre of the terraced area is a huge sloping kitchen garden, well labelled to indicate varieties, and below this a mirror pool has been restored to its eighteenth-century grandeur. The grand scale of the plan is the main interest, but there are many unusual plants, particularly perennials and bog plants, and a National Collection of asters spp. *amellus*, *cordifolius* and *ericoides* is here. *The National Herb Centre*, with small display gardens, good herb nursery, research glasshouses, exhibition and herb bistro, is nearby on the B4100 at Warmington [open all year, daily, 9am – 5.30pm. Tel: (01295) 690033].

Warwick Castle ★ [Historic Park Grade I]

Warwick CV34 4QU. Tel: (0870) 442 2000

The Tussauds Group • In Warwick • Castle open • Grounds open all year, daily except 25th Dec, 10am – 6pm (closes 7pm weekends in Aug, closes 5pm Oct to March) • Entrance: Charges vary seasonally – maximum for individuals £14.50, OAPs £10.50, students £10.75, children £8.75, family £39 (2005 prices) ○ ● ✕ 🏠 <u>WC</u> ♿ 🚻 ⓘ ☕

The castle stands on the banks of the River Avon, surrounded by 60 acres of beautiful grounds landscaped by 'Capability' Brown. He had previously been employed as gardener to Lord Cobham at Stowe, but after the latter's death in 1749 decided to take on commissions of his own. His work at Warwick Castle for Francis Greville is thought to have been his first independent commission, for which he received much praise, encouragement and publicity. He removed the old formal garden outside the wall and shaped the grounds to frame a view using an array of magnificent trees, notably cedars of Lebanon. In 1753 he began to landscape the courtyard, removing steps, filling in parts of the yard and making a coachway to surround the large level lawn. He then worked on the creation of a park on the other side of the eleventh-century mound. In 1779, when Brown's remodelling was barely twenty years old, George Greville embarked on a grandiose scheme of expansion which involved demolishing several streets in the town. In 1786 he constructed the conservatory at the top of Pageant Field, which today houses a replica of the famous Warwick Vase. From here visitors can view the panorama before them – the Peacock Garden and the tree-lined lawn of Pageant Field which meanders down to the gently sloping banks of the River Avon. On the other side of the castle entrance is the Victorian rose garden re-created in 1986 from Robert Marnock's designs of 1868. Also in the town is The Master's Garden (see entry) at Lord Leycester Hospital. The castle itself is ★★.

Woodpeckers ★

The Bank, Marlcliff, Bidford-on-Avon B50 4NT. Tel: (01789) 773416

Drs Andrew and Lallie Cox • 7m SW of Stratford-upon-Avon off B4085 between Bidford and Cleeve Prior • Open by appt all year • Entrance: £3, children free • Other information: Wheelchair users must be accompanied ● ● 🏠 WC ♿ 🌱 ☕

This two-and-a-half-acre garden, planned for year-round interest, contains a wide range of design and planting ideas, and blends well with the surrounding countryside. A small arboretum with a wide selection of choice trees provide contrast in form and colour. February visitors will enjoy the many varieties of snowdrops here. Moving around the garden, there are many surprises – a wooden figure of St Fiacre carved by Andrew Cox amongst a collection of old roses with clematis climbing through, an attractive small *potager*, colourful and unusual herbs and vegetables. A knot garden has been created from three varieties of box, and room has been found for topiary, an ivy arbour with statue, a fern border, several island beds with splendid ranges of colour and plants, a Mediterranean garden, a cactus and succulent greenhouse and a round greenhouse for tender plants including mimosa, abutilon, callistemon and clematis. The terrace has a range of troughs and alpine plants, and there is a delightful pool and bog garden. A belvedere of framed English oak affords fine views of the garden, including a wildflower area in spring. A two-storey oak building with a balcony overlooks the arboretum and rose garden. It is also worth visiting in winter to see the trees and a border designed to look interesting at this neglected time of year.

NCCPG

The National Council for the Conservation of Plants and Gardens publishes a *National Plant Collections Directory*. Those interested in seeing some of the rarer species and garden varieties of particular families of plants will find this an invaluable publication. The latest edition, which offers information on about 600 collections comprising more than 50,000 plants and contains articles by holders of the collections, is available from NCCPG, The Stable Courtyard, RHS Garden, Wisley, Woking GU23 6QP (Tel: (01483) 221465; Fax: (01483) 212404; Website: www.nccpg.com. The new edition will be published in February or March 2006.

BED & BREAKFAST FOR GARDEN LOVERS

The biennial paperback contains some 200 B&Bs (mostly in Britain, with a smattering in the Republic of Ireland, France and Italy) run by keen and knowledgeable owners with fine gardens of all types and sizes – rural and urban, traditional and contemporary. Prices for a double room range from £55 per night. The guide is available from Alastair Sawday Publishing — telephone (01275) 464891 or consult www.specialplacestostay.com.

THE NATIONAL GARDENS SCHEME

The NGS started in 1927, and now some 3300 gardens, chosen by county organisers and their teams, open their gates each year for charity (more than £15m has been raised over the past decade). The entries in the famous annual Yellow Book are, unlike those in the *Good Gardens Guide*, written by the garden owners themselves; a useful diary section lists all gardens in a county open on any particular day.

WILTSHIRE

Two-starred gardens are marked on the map with a black square.

Abbey House Gardens ★

Malmesbury SN16 9AS. Tel: (01666) 822212

Barbara and Ian Pollard • In town centre next to Abbey • Open 21st March to 21st Oct, daily, 11am – 5.30pm, and for parties by appt • Entrance: £5.50, OAPs/students £4.75, children (5–15) £2, discount for parties of 20 or more • Other information: Car park close to garden ◗ ⬛ 🐾 <u>WC</u> ♿ ✦ 🏆

A remarkable five-acre garden, created since 1996. The owners' passion and enthusiasm are reflected in the exuberant planting schemes. The setting around a late Tudor house beside the abbey is unique, the effect overwhelming, with an enormous arcade-encircled herb garden, a generously proportioned laburnum tunnel, a knot garden in the form of a Celtic cross echoing its historic surroundings, huge herbaceous borders in riotous colours, water features including a waterfall, a river and woodland walk (with kingfishers and water voles if you are lucky), a foliage walk, a maple walk and a scree garden. In all there are over 10,000 different species and varieties of plants here. The season starts with a dazzling display of 70,000 tulips and meconopsis followed by roses (the largest private collection in the country), clematis and rhododendrons, and continues right through to the autumn. There is also a large and interesting collection of cordon fruit trees around an arcade, with sweet peas for added colour.

Avebury Manor

Marlborough SN8 1RF. Tel (01672) 539250

The National Trust • 6m W of Marlborough, 1m N of A4 Bath road on A4361. House on N side of High Street, behind church • House open Mon, Tues, Sun and Bank Holiday Mons, 2 – 4.40pm • Garden open April to Oct, daily except Wed and Thurs, 11am – 5pm • Entrance £3, children £1.50 (house and garden £4, children £2) • Other information: Parking in outer village. Alexander Keiller Museum, galleries, refreshments and shop adjacent ◗ ⬛ ✕ <u>WC</u> ♿ ✦ 🏛

The atmospheric but much-altered house, monastic in origin, with notable Queen Anne alterations, was purchased by the Trust in 1991. The rose garden in the shadow of the church tower is a fragrant delight, herbaceous borders are set neatly behind low box hedging, and there is a splendid lavender walk at the main entrance to the house, which on the south-west is framed by lawns and topiary. The orchard has been replanted with old apple varieties from Wiltshire. In the topiary garden the pond has been restored and the box hedges are in the design of overlapping diamonds, inspired by a plaster ceiling in the house.

Bolehyde Manor ★

Allington, Chippenham SN14 6LW. Tel: (01249) 652105

Earl and Countess Cairns • 1.5m W of Chippenham on A420 Bristol road. Turn N at Allington crossroads; garden is 0.5m on right • Open for NGS, and for parties by appt • Entrance: £3 • Other information: Teas and plant sales on NGS open day only ● &

A four-acre garden at once steeped in tradition and bursting with innovative ideas. The characterful manor house dates from the fifteenth century. Owned by the Abbot of Glastonbury until after the dissolution of the monasteries, Bolehyde was sold in 1635 to the Case family, who lived there for the next 400 years. The house, outbuildings and gatehouses developed into a charming huddle of beautifully weathered Cotswold stone buildings, and this is reflected in the series of linked garden rooms disposed around the house. Within a semi-formal framework are splendid contrasts, gracefully achieved: a pear walk, some lovely wildflower meadow planting, a new and exciting *potager*. Sheltered and sunny formal areas are edged with colourful narrow beds, and satisfyingly chunky topiary abounds. Planted for year-round interest, the garden is nevertheless at its stunning best in midsummer, when masses of roses bloom on the old walls, and the half-hardy planting of the courtyard – much of it in darkly glowing jewel colours – is nearing the peak of a brilliant display.

Bowood House ★ [Historic Park and Garden Grade I]

Bowood House, Derry Hill, Calne SN11 0LZ. Tel: (01249) 812102

The Marquis and Marchioness of Lansdowne • 3m SE of Chippenham, 2.5m W of Calne off A4, 8m S of M4 junction 17. Separate rhododendron walks off A342 Chippenham – Devizes road midway between Derry Hill and Sandy Lane • House open • Garden and pleasure grounds open April to Oct, daily, 11am – 6pm or dusk if earlier. Rhododendron walks open daily end-April to early June (depending on flowering season) • Entrance: House and gardens £6.60, OAPs £5.50, children (5–15) £4.30, (2–4) £3.40, rhododendron walks £3.70 extra, children free (2005 prices) ◑ ➤ ✕ 🐌 WC & 🏛 ♞ ⚲

The house and its pleasure grounds cover over 100 acres and lie in the centre of 'Capability' Brown's enormous park. Other splendours include a tranquil lake, arboretum and pinetum, Doric temple, cascade waterfall and hermit's cave. Thousands of bulbs bloom in spring. The Robert Adam orangery (converted into a gallery) is particularly fine, and in front are formal Italianate terraces with rose beds, standard roses and fastigiate yews. *Fremontodendron californicum* flourishes on the Italianate terrace. The upper terrace was laid out in 1817 and the present fountains were added in 1839. In the twentieth century, when elaborate bedding schemes became too time-consuming, the parterre was planted with hybrid tea roses, thus blurring the edges. Mary Keen advised replacing the grass paths with gravel and compensating for the loss of green by putting box hedges around the beds. New planting has ensured that the flowering season starts almost three months earlier than it used to. In the nineteenth century it was the aim of every garden to be 'as clean as a drawing room', and Bowood is now in this class once again. The rhododendron walks are situated in a separate 60-acre area, which is only open when the rhododendrons are flowering from late April to mid-June. Robert Adam's mausoleum (a little gem well worth a visit) is in this area.

Broadleas Garden

Broadleas, Devizes SN10 5JQ. Tel: (01380) 722035

Lady Anne Cowdray/Broadleas Garden Charitable Trust • 1m S of Devizes on A360. Signed from Devizes town centre • Open April to Oct, Sun, Wed and Thurs, 2 – 6pm • Entrance: £5, children (under 10) £1.50, parties of 10 or more £4.50 • Other information: Coaches must use Devizes town centre approach. Teas for parties by arrangement ❶ WC ♿ ◁ 🌢

This garden was bought just after World War II by Lady Anne Cowdray in a combe below Devizes. Mature and semi-mature magnolias grow on each side of a steep dell. As good as any Cornish garden, it is stuffed with fine things that one would think too tender for these parts – large specimens of everything (much of it now over forty years old), including *Paulownia fargesii, Parrotia persica*, all manner of magnolias, azaleas, hydrangeas, hostas, lilies and trilliums of rare and notable species. There has also been much planting in recent years, including many rhododendrons and camellias. It is a garden of tireless perfectionism, at its most stunning in spring when sheets of bulbs stretch out beneath the flowering trees. Rarely seen in such quantities for instance are the erythroniums or dog-tooth violets. There is also a woodland walk, a sunken rose garden and a silver border. This is serious plantsmanship and dendrology. Some of the more unusual plants, both shrubs and perennials, are grown for sale.

Chisenbury Priory

East Chisenbury, Nr Pewsey SN9 6AQ. Tel: (07810) 483984

Mr and Mrs John Manser • 3m SW of Pewsey. Turn E off A345 at Enford, then N to East Chisenbury; main gates 1m on right • Open one day in June for NGS, and by appt • Entrance: £3 • Other information: Teas on NGS open day NEW ❺

A fine avenue of mature chestnuts and sycamores leads to the handsome eighteenth-century house front, with richly planted herbaceous borders on each side of the lawn. But the priory is much older than that, and 400 years of history have been enriched by skilful and imaginative planting in its surrounding four acres of garden. A great curving pergola by Paul Elliot in galvanised steel, dripping with roses and late-flowering *Clematis viticella*, forms a dramatic and unique feature. Also his work is the fine bridge over the leat in the wild garden, an offspring of the River Avon. Water was an important element in the redesign of the garden in the 1960s, when many of the mature shrubs and trees were planted. Now mown paths wander past iris-fringed pools, down a nut walk and through flowery orchards offering glimpses of striking modern sculptures. Sheltered enclosures nearer the house are ablaze with colour from early spring to the end of July – successive waves of alliums and aquilegias followed by superb delphiniums, lilies, campanulas and masses of roses. This traditional English garden has now been brought to its full glory; a broad vision and close attention to detail have combined to produce an atmosphere of romantic, controlled exuberance within an ancient and peaceful framework.

Conock Manor [Historic Garden Grade II]

Conock, Devizes SN10 3QQ.

Mrs Bonar Sykes • 5m SE of Devizes, off A342 near Chirton • Open 21st May, 2 – 6pm • Entrance: £3, children under 16 free ● ⬤ ⬤ ⬤ ⬤

Set between distant views of Marlborough Downs and Salisbury Plain, the Georgian house looks out over lawns with specimen trees, ha-has and a recently planted arboretum, which includes unusual trees, such as *Aesculus* x *mutabilis* 'Induta' and *Catalpa fargesii* f. *duclouxii*. From a Reptonesque thatched dairy near the house, a long brick wall and a mixed shrub border lead to the stable block, in early Gothic Revival style, with a copper-domed cupola. Between the house and the stable block is an unusual and elaborate water feature. Beyond, yew and beech hedges and brick walls frame unusual trees and shrubs, a small kitchen garden and a 1930s' shrub walk. Beech forms attractive bays and box makes clipped balls. Notable are the pleached limes and a magnolia garden also planted with malus, sorbus, prunus and eucalyptus.

Corsham Court [Historic Garden Grade II*]

Corsham SN13 0BZ. Tel: (01249) 701610

James Methuen-Campbell • 4m W of Chippenham on A4 • House open • Garden open Jan to 18th March, Sat and Sun, 2 – 4.30pm; 21st March to Sept, daily except Mon and Fri (but open Bank Holidays), 2 – 5.30pm; Oct and Nov, Sat and Sun, 2 – 4.30pm. Closed Dec. Also open by appt for parties of 15 or more • Entrance: £2.50, OAPs £2, children £1.50 (2005 prices) • Other information: Teas by prior arrangement for parties ● WC ⬤ ⬤

Approaching from Chippenham, look out for a glimpse of the house on your left, once framed by an avenue of elms now replaced by some lime trees. The house, which has a fine collection of pictures and furniture, is surrounded by a landscape of 'Capability' Brown's devising finished off by Humphry Repton (the lake and boat-house particularly). It is an example of this kind of gardening at its best. Rare and exotic trees look entirely at home: black walnuts, Californian redwoods, cedars, Wellingtonias, and the most astonishing layered Oriental plane tree, shading beeches, oaks, sycamores and Spanish chestnuts. There are 340 tree species. The bath house designed by Brown leads out into a small enclosed garden with flowers and catalpas. Repton's fashion of training roses over metal arches encircling a round pond is a rare surviving illustration of the elegance of early-nineteenth-century flower gardens. Here the borders contain the unusual *Clerodendrum trichotomum* and enormous iron supports for roses and *Clematis* x *jackmanii*. A box-edged garden, a hornbeam *allée*, urns, arbours and seats add further elegant touches.

The Courts Garden ★ [Historic Garden Grade II]

Holt, Trowbridge BA14 6RR. Tel: (01225) 782340/782875

The National Trust • 3m SW of Melksham, 3m N of Trowbridge, 2.5m E of Bradford-on-Avon on B3107 • Open 18th March to 15th Oct, daily except Wed,

11am – 5.30pm, and by appt at other times • Entrance: £4.80, children £2.40, family £12.20 • Other information: Parking at village hall ❶ ♿ ❦ ℀

The distinguished eighteenth-century house, surrounded by a well-defined framework of lawns, topiary and hedging laid out originally in the 1920s, has acquired an overlay of dynamic and creative plantings. Passing through huge stands of cotinus and other red-leaved shrubs, the visitor reaches water gardens which include a rectangular lily pond bordered by hundreds of pale *Iris sibirica* with a luxuriant planted 'dye pond' beyond, dating from its old history as a mill. Borders are brilliantly conceived and maintained – the blue and yellow one is particularly fine – within traditional enclosures of yew, beech and holly. There is also a colourful and productive vegetable garden and orchard, and the arboretum beyond is peaceful and beautiful all year round, with rare and splendid trees and masses of scillas and narcissus in spring. In 2005 the sunken garden on the boundary of the garden was resurrected around a paved courtyard, where Mediterranean and sun-loving plants enjoy the warmth and protection of the drystone walls and the encircling beech hedge; a standard wisteria forms the centrepiece.

Fonthill House

Tisbury, Salisbury SP3 5SA. Tel: (Estate Office) (01747) 820246

Lord and Lady Margadale • 12m W of Salisbury, E of Hindon on B3089. Entrance is S of Fonthill Bishop, on farm road over bridge and through deer park • Open usually three or four times a year during April to July for charity, 2 – 6pm. Telephone for details • Entrance: £2.50, children free (2005 prices) ● ◍ WC ♿ ◈ ♨ ℀

The neo-Georgian 1970s house, built on the site of a demolished Detmar Blow masterpiece on the estate, stands at the head of a combe with fine views and is backed by mature beech and oak trees. Throughout this woodland grow camellias and rhododendrons and, in spring, a carpet of bluebells. The charm and isolation of the place add to its magic, particularly in spring when the woodland is a mass of colour. Five acres in all. For children, there is a heated swimming pool open from mid-May.

The Fovant Hut

Fovant, Salisbury SP3 5LN. Tel: (01722) 714756

Christina and Nigel Oates • Off A30 between Salisbury and Shaftesbury. At W end of Fovant, take road signed to Broadchalke and Bowerchalke. Follow road up steep hill and just before crest turn right into unmade-up road; garden is few hundred yards on right • Open for parties by appt ●

The 'hut' – in fact an old coaching inn – stands on an ancient byway in an area of outstanding natural beauty, and the most impressive feature of the garden is the successful blending of the more intimate areas with the vast and beautiful panorama of the surrounding downland. It is a 'modern' garden in the best sense – conceived and realised since 1992 by garden designer Christina Oates and her husband Nigel. Through design and planting they have succeeded in creating a brilliant one-acre garden on a north-facing sloping site with chalky soil and fierce winds. Skill and dedication have enabled them to achieve areas of shelter, generously planted with specimens that suit the conditions, and distinguished by an original and fresh use of many familiar ideas. Decking is used imaginatively; water leads to a most delightful garden room/conservatory; in the fruit garden masses of alliums flower under a fine lilac. The area around a small wildflower patch has produced further new ideas and experiments – note, for instance, the 3-metre-high clipped *leylandii* drums used as a windbreak.

The Garden Lodge ★

Chittoe, Chippenham SN15 2EW. Tel: (01380) 850314

Mrs Juliet Wilmot • Off A342 Chippenham – Devizes road, signed to Chittoe; garden marked on right after 1m • Open by appt only • Entrance: £3 ● WC & B&B

In 1990 the present owner bought the house and its abandoned 2-acre Victorian walled garden in the peaceful hamlet of Chittoe. Since then, taking advantage of a sheltered, sloping site, she has created within the mellow surrounding walls a formal garden of immaculate design. The upper level consists of a long curving sweep of lawn, backed by a deep raised border which leads to a fine mature oak tree. A large pond on a lower level is lavishly furnished with marginal and water plants, and a stone rill drops to an amphitheatre and a central area planted with 'Sander's White' rambler roses. Clematis and roses abound on walls, pillars and pergolas. Original features include a grass-and-brick maze and a brick sundial let into the grass, and a serpentine yew-edged path leads to an elegant pavilion complete with an ingenious snakes-and-ladders game. The seclusion in this appealing garden is accentuated by the borrowed landscape of mature trees on the encircling skyline.

Goulters Mill

Nettleton, Nr. Castle Combe, Chippenham SN14 7LL. Tel: (01249) 782555

Mr and Mrs Michael Harvey • 6m W of Chippenham on B4039 between Burton and The Gibb • Open 16th and 17th April, 29th May, 2 – 5pm, then April to Sept by appt • Entrance: £3.50 ● ● WC & ❀ B&B

The idyllic 0.75-acre garden lies deep in seclusion and silence. Ancient tracks radiate from the mill, mentioned in the Domesday Book, and the present seventeenth-century house preserves an atmosphere of timelessness and peace. Looking out from the house a sea of colour and movement is achieved with beautifully chosen hardy perennials and self-sown annuals, framed by attractive paths and accented by topiary figures. The dense planting leads to a small lawn surrounded by ancient apple trees entwined with roses and overlooking a lily-fringed stream and pool, then on to a happily planted gravel area. Irises and sisyrinchiums abound here, and poppies and eremurus are also a speciality. The river, tree house and vine planting may be glimpsed beyond a wild area currently under review. The spring invites walks to bluebell woods beyond, and in the summer there is a wash of wild flowers and rare butterflies in the meadow paths.

Great Chalfield Manor [Historic Garden Grade II]

Melksham SN12 8NH. Tel: (01225) 782239

The National Trust • 3m SW of Melksham off A350 and B3107 via Broughton Gifford Common • Open April to Oct, Tues – Thurs, 11.30am – 5pm, Sun, 2 – 5pm, and for parties by appt • Entrance: £4.60, children £2.30, family £12, parties £4.20, children £2.10 (2005 prices) ◐ **WC** ও ✿ B&B

The moated fifteenth-century house and its surroundings were restored by Robert Fuller in the early 1900s, and given to the National Trust forty years later. It remains the home of his grandson's family, and they now manage the property. Fuller employed Sir Harold Brakspear as his architect, and Alfred Parsons designed the gardens to complement the house; Brakspear also contributed a gazebo. The spacious lawns are broken up by vast topiary yew shapes and have substantial borders, recently replanted. Spring flowers are abundant in April, apple blossom in May, roses in June, and asters in October. The borders are at their best in June and September, and there are some splendid old-fashioned and rambling roses. A new rill leads down to the river and good views open up from the moat walk; nearby, a shrubbery is managed as a semi-natural area with woodland plants, and a woodland walk is developing.

Hazelbury Manor [Historic Garden Grade II]

Box, Corsham SN13 8HX. Tel: (01225) 812088

5m SW of Chippenham. From Box take A365 towards Melksham, turn left onto B3109, next left, and right immediately into private drive • Open one weekend for NGS, and by appt • Entrance: £2.80, OAPs £2, children £1, under 6 free ◐ WC ও

Richly architectural in character, the gardens are entirely in keeping with the history and scale of the fifteenth-century fortified manor house they surround. Following an Edwardian renaissance, they were largely rescued in the 1970s by Ian Pollard (currently gardening at Abbey House – see entry), who reconfigured them on a lavish scale with eight acres of formal gardens around the house and 10 more of landscaped grounds. Since 1997 the present owner has restored and improved them, and added a profusion of medicinal herbs and plants – his particular interest – which are grown organically throughout the garden. But the glory of Hazelbury is the main lawn, dramatic in its proportions and framed by magnificent yew hedges and grand colour-themed borders backed by grassy banks leading to mature beech *allées*. The formal structure of the hedging is the determining feature, allowing great freedom of planting and contrasts through the bold sequence of compartments surrounding the great lawn. The unique topiary chess set has reached perfection and the tall laburnum tunnel and broad lime walk add extra dimensions. All are imaginatively and richly underplanted to sparkle through spring and early summer. The front of the house is seen across lawns and borders ablaze with spring bulbs, while behind is an historic archery walk – exactly 40 paces long. To the west of the house the mood becomes more relaxed and intimate, with informal plantings of shrubs and perennials opening onto the surrounding landscape. There is a fine organic vegetable garden and a flowery mead sprinkled with crocuses, fritillaries and martagon lilies. Beyond the garden lies a mound and a circle of seven megaliths placed in a great saucer in homage to the famous prehistoric monuments of this ancient part of Wiltshire.

Heale Garden ★ [Historic Garden Grade II*]

Middle Woodford, Salisbury SP4 6NT. Tel: (01722) 782504

Mr and Mrs Guy Rasch • 4m N of Salisbury between A360 and A345 • Open all year, Tues – Sun and Bank Holiday Mons, 10am – 5pm. Snowdrop Sundays 5th and 12th Feb • Entrance: £4, children (5–15) £2, under 5 free ○ 🍽 WC ✿ ♿ ♟

This is an idyllic garden with mature yew hedges, much of it designed by Harold Peto. A tributary of the Avon meanders through, providing the perfect boundary and obvious site for the sealing-wax red bridge and thatched tea-house straddling the water. This was brought over from Japan and assembled in 1910 with the help of four Japanese gardeners and extends under the shade of *Magnolia* x *soulangeana* along the boggy banks planted with bog arums, *Rodgersia aesculifolia*, candelabra primulas and irises. There are two terraces to the west of the house. The topmost has beds containing two aged wisterias among tall herbaceous plants, backed by clipped yew. A central path of old York stone links both terraces and is rampant with alchemilla. The other has two stone lily ponds and two small borders given height by tall wooden pyramids bearing roses, clematis and honeysuckles. The Long Border contains many dark-leaved plants, including *Sambucus* 'Black Beauty', *Physocarpus* 'Diabolo', and interesting herbaceous perennials; behind is a border of musk roses. The walled kitchen garden achieves a satisfying marriage between practicality and pleasure: the formal nature of rows of vegetables is made into a feature, and plots are divided by espaliered fruit trees forming apple and pear tunnels, and by a pergola and hedges. The wonderful flint-and-brick wall provides protection for many plants, including *Cytisus battandieri* and an ancient fig tree. It is tempting to linger on the seats and in the shaded arbours and enjoy and admire the extraordinary tranquillity of the place. Look out for the ancient mulberry, the very old *Cercidiphyllum japonicum* (the second tallest known in Europe), and the *Magnolia grandiflora*. The plant centre is comprehensive and the shop appeals to the discerning. Unique wrought-iron plant supports can be bought here.

Home Covert Gardens and Arboretum ★

Roundway, Devizes SN10 2JA. Tel: (01380) 723407

Mr and Mrs John Phillips • 1m N of Devizes. Turn off A361 on edge of built-up area NE of town, signed to Roundway. In Roundway turn left towards Rowde. House is 0.75m on left. Signposted • Open by appt. Guided parties (12–40 persons) welcome • Entrance: £4, children free ● ❧ WC & ⬧

This garden, developed in the 1960s, has been created by the present owners out of amenity woodlands of the now-demolished Roundway House. In front of the house is a large lawn on a plateau edged with grasses, herbaceous plants and alpines producing colour throughout the year. Beyond this, grass pathways meander through a collection of trees and rare shrubs. A steep path drops from the plateau to a water garden, lake, waterfall and bog garden, rich with colour from bog primulas and other moisture-loving plants, and shaded by fine specimen trees. Excellent collections of magnolias, camellias, erythroniums and hydrangeas are scattered informally throughout, and roses and clematis scramble over walks and through trees. Described as 'a botanical madhouse', this garden offers wonderful contrasts.

Iford Manor ★★ [Historic Garden Grade I]

Bradford-on-Avon BA15 2BA. Tel: (01225) 863146

Mrs Cartwright-Hignett • 2m S of Bradford-on-Avon off B3109, 7m SE of Bath via A36. Signposted • Open April, Sun; May to Sept, Tues – Thurs, Sat, Sun and Bank Holiday Mons; Oct, Sun; all 2 – 5pm. Other times and parties by appt • Entrance:

£4.50, OAPs, students and children over 10 £4. Children under 10 free, Tues – Thurs
only • Other information: Teas May to Aug, Sat, Sun and Bank Holiday Mons only
❶ 🍽 WC ♿ ❓

Harold Peto found himself a near-ideal house in the steep valley through which the River Frome slides langorously towards Bath. The topography lends itself to the strong architectural framework favoured by Peto and the creation of areas of entirely differing moods. The overriding intention is Italianate with a preponderance of cypresses, junipers, box and yew, punctuated at every turn by sarcophagi, urns, terracotta, marble seats and statues, columns, fountains and loggias. In a different vein is a meadow of naturalised bulbs, most spectacularly martagon lilies. A path leads from here to the cloisters – an Italian-Romanesque building of Harold Peto's confection made with fragments collected from Italy. From here one can admire the whole, and the breathtaking valley and the walled kitchen garden on the other side. Perhaps somewhat incongruously, at the top of the garden, there is a Japanese area, pleasantly done but not apparently completed by Peto himself. Westwood Manor (see entry) is nearby.

Lacock Abbey [Historic Park Grade II]

Lacock, Chippenham SN15 2LG. Tel: (01249) 730227

The National Trust • 3m S of Chippenham off A350 • Abbey open 25th Feb to 29th
Oct, daily, 11am – 5.30pm (closed 14th April). Also open 11th, 12th, 18th and 19th
Feb, 11am – 4pm, for NGS • Grounds, cloisters and museum of photography open
March to Oct, daily, 11am – 5.30pm. Closed 25th March • Entrance: £5, children
£2.50 • Other information: Refreshments and shop in village. Batricar available
❶ WC ♿ ❓

The thirteenth-century abbey, set in meadows beside the River Avon, was turned into a private house by Sir William Sharington after the Dissolution, and was Gothicised by John Ivory Talbot in the eighteenth century. The romantic Victorian woodland garden is best viewed in spring when sheets of crocuses, daffodils and later, fritillaries, replace the large drifts of snowdrops and aconites. Lady Elisabeth's Rose Garden, originally created for the mother of William Henry Fox Talbot, inventor of photography, has been re-created from the original photograph of 1840, which is probably the earliest known photograph of a garden. Fox Talbot was also an eminent botanist, and planted many unusual trees which can still be seen today, including specimens of the American black walnut, the Judas tree and the swamp cypress. His walled 'Botanic Garden', once given over to allotments, has reopened after restoration, and a project to rebuild his glasshouses is underway.

Larmer Tree Gardens [Historic Garden Grade II*]

Rushmore Estate, Tollard Royal, Salisbury SP5 5PT. Tel: (01725) 516228

Mr W. Gronow Davis • 16m SW of Salisbury, 7m SE of Shaftesbury off B3081.
Signposted • Open 16th April to Sept, daily except Fri, 11am – 5pm; Oct to March,
Mon – Fri, 11am – 4.30pm. During summer months gardens may be closed for
private events: telephone or consult website (listed at back of book) • Entrance: £3.75,
concessions and groups £3, children £2.50 (under 5 free), family £12.50. Discount

entry available with Chettle House (see entry in Dorset) • *Other information: Shop and refreshments open 11th April to Sept* ◑ ☕ 🏠 WC ♿ 🚻 B&B

These 12-acre pleasure grounds were laid out in 1880 by General Pitt-Rivers as a place of public enlightenment and entertainment. Today, they remain an exceptionally fine example of Victorian vision and extravagance. The gardens contain a unique collection of buildings, including a Roman temple, an open-air theatre and Nepalese rooms which the General introduced as points of interest for those with limited knowledge of the outside world. The buildings surround the main lawn, off which radiate laurel-hedged rides forming small enclosed wooded arbours originally intended for picnickers. Restoration of the gardens began in the 1990s with the aim that they would continue to be a place of pleasure and entertainment. Regular concerts, theatrical events and festivals are held throughout the summer and local bands play on the stage Sundays in August. The gardens provide stunning views north to the Cranborne Chase and south to the Solent.

Longleat [Historic Park and Garden Grade I]

Warminster BA12 7NW. Tel: (01985) 844400

The Marquess of Bath • *3m SW of Warminster, 4.5m SE of Frome on A362* • *House open* • *Garden open all year, daily: Easter to Sept, 10am – 5.30pm; Oct to March, 11am – 3pm. Closed 25th Dec* • *Entrance: £3, OAPs and children £2, coaches free (house extra) (2005 prices)* • *Other information: Helicopter landing pad available by prior request* ○ ☕ ✕ 🏠 WC ♿ 🐕 🎪 🚻 ♻

This garden has been rearranged and developed by most of the great names in English landscape history. There is nothing left today of the two earliest gardens here – one Elizabethan, the other, spectacularly elaborate, created by London and Wise in the 1680s–90s. Sadly it was barely half a century before 'Capability' Brown ironed out the formality and landscaped a chain of lakes set amongst clumps of trees and hanging woods, best admired today from Heaven's Gate. The park was slightly altered by Repton in 1804 and added to in the 1870s when it became fashionable to collect exotic trees and to make groves of rhododendrons and azaleas. It remains both beautiful and rewarding for all who delight in trees. In the twentieth century the fortunes of the garden came under the guiding hand of Russell Page. The nineteenth-century formal garden in front of the orangery to the north of the house was simplified and improved upon by him to great effect, although, alas, most of his work has since been swept away. The orangery itself is a dream of wisteria. A quarter of a mile to the south there is a pleasure walk in a developing arboretum, with many spring bulbs and wild flowers. To the immediate west of the house the small private garden is not open to the public. Lord Bath says this was designed around the two commas within the yin and yang symbols: bulbs and fruit trees in the first and a lily pond in the second. There is a large dovecot in one corner – inspired by the turrets on the roof of the house. The 6th Marquess planted one of the world's longest hedge maze at Longleat in 1975, and new ones planted by the present Marquess are at various stages of growth, from the Sun Maze and Lunar Labyrinth to the east of the house to the Love Labyrinth in front of the orangery. Future examples of the genre will encompass a variety of styles and materials. Elsewhere, the safari park and other attractions.

Mompesson House

The Close, Salisbury SP1 2EL. Tel: (01722) 335659

The National Trust • In city centre, N of Choristers' Green in Cathedral Close • House open as garden • Garden open 25th March to 29th Oct, Sat – Wed (but open Good Friday), 11am – 5pm • Entrance: 90p (house and garden £4.20, children £2.10, parties £4.20 per person) (2005 prices) • Other information: Parking in city centre. Teas when house open. NT shop nearby ❶ 💭 WC ⅄ ⑨

If visiting Salisbury, the Cathedral and the Close are a must. Take time also to visit this small walled garden, which is in the Old English style. Its tranquil atmosphere is very refreshing. Summer is best, with the old-fashioned roses in bloom, but it is attractive throughout the open season.

The Old Malthouse

Lower Westwood, Bradford-on-Avon BA15 2AG. Tel: (01225) 864905

Simon and Amanda Relph • 1.5m NW of Trowbridge, 1.5m SW of Bradford-on-Avon on B3109 • Open 18th June for NGS, and April to Sept by appt • Entrance: £2.50, children free ● 💭 ⅄ ⬦

In this one-acre garden created by a film producer and his ex-actress wife, it is appropriate that drama and wit should be at the forefront of the design. A work in progress since 1995, its level has been raised to create vistas of Westwood Manor (see entry) and the church of this medieval village. Within the garden the scene changes constantly: from the Arts and Crafts mood at the front of the house, with its drystone walls, water rills and spouts, lavenders and lavateras, via a large rustic barn, to a stretch of lawn overlooking fields and a long herbaceous border in shades of green and white. An old orchard with long grass and daisies elides into a *potager* where fruit and vegetables are presented with panache: the fruit cage is an eight-foot tall metal sculpture, a jewel box for fruit. The main garden has a stream and a view into the cloister garden, where espaliered fruit trees and roses roam over pergolas. On the paved terrace above, silver, white and blue planting makes a soft background for sculpted furniture; the enclosing walls support wisterias and ramblers in drifts, and self-seeding plants are encouraged to rampage. Above all, and everywhere, there is sculpture – carvings, seats, fountains, cages and surreal details – setting and stealing the scene in every part of this original and inspiring garden.

The Old Mill

Ramsbury SN8 2PN. Tel: (01672) 520266

James and Annabel Dallas • 5m NE of Marlborough. Go down High Street, turn right at The Bell pub (signed to Hungerford); garden is 90 metres on right behind yew hedge • Open 10th May, 21st June and 13th Sept, 2 – 5pm, and by appt • Entrance: £3.50, children free ● 💭 ⑨

It would be hard to imagine a more idyllic setting for a garden than the grounds of this ancient rambling mill house. The River Kennet runs through and therefore divides the garden, so that from the formal areas near the house on one side of the river there are lovely views of a wilder and more natural landscape across the flow of water. The pool, mill stream, mill race and numerous channels, all once part of the original working mill, dominate and shape the five acres of cultivated land, giving the garden its special allure and character. The design never intrudes on the natural beauty of the site – this is due to Annabel Dallas's light touch with colour and choice of plants, many of them grown from seed, which veers away from anything that looks too contrived. The whole place is full of experiment and ideas which are constantly being developed. There are many spring bulbs and good autumn colour, but summer is the high point here. Close to the house are ebullient borders of salvias, other colour-themed borders and an attractive area combining an informal arrangement of pots with planting in gravel. Wooden bridges cross streams to extend the garden in different directions: an enclosure of lawn and herbaceous borders leads into a green garden backed by an old brick wall, and thence to the bog garden and wilder parts at the periphery.

The Old Vicarage ★
Edington, Westbury BA13 4QF. Tel: (01380) 830512

J.N. d'Arcy • 4m NE of Westbury on B3098 to West Lavington. Signposted • Open once for charity in mid-June, and by appt • Entrance: £4, children free (includes other neighbouring gardens) • Other information: Parking in church car park ● &

Every year new discoveries mark the travels of a peripatetic gardener who has created a varied, scented garden on a two-and-a-half-acre escarpment set high on the north side of Salisbury Plain. To be shown round by Mr d'Arcy is a treat as he mixes wit with erudition. Swags of clematis, cistus and mahonias enliven the plain facade of the former vicarage; a wide lawn – croquet of course – leads to a meadow artful with wild flowers beneath rare varieties of chestnut, sorbus and maple. A National Collection of evening primroses gives pleasure after dusk. Stunning views towards Edington Church lift the visitor's eyes through well-planted vistas. Dividing the garden is a yew hedge, and the *allée* of fastigiate hornbeams points the view towards Devizes, and brick walls create rooms and shelter exotic plants and trees. Waves of phlomis species mark the hot garden, while a sunken garden to the rear of the house is romantically planted in cool shades round a 15-metre well. Nepetas, a particular passion, run riot. Towards the end of the tour a gravel bed is a sea of agapanthus and eryngiums, and everywhere seedlings push through the gravel.

Old Wardour Castle [Historic Garden Grade II*]
Tisbury, Salisbury SP3 6RR. Tel: (01747) 870487

English Heritage • 2m SW of Tisbury off A30 • Open April to Oct, daily, 10am – 5pm (closes 4pm in Oct); Nov to March, Sat and Sun, 10am – 4pm. Closed 24th to 26th Dec, 1st Jan • Entrance: £3, concessions £2.30, children £1.50 (2005 prices)
○ ● ● WC & ⬦ ⬛ ▮

In a picture-book setting, the ruins of this fourteenth-century castle stand overlooking a lake and surrounded by woodland. The small garden was laid out in the eighteenth century when the nearby New Wardour Castle was built, and remnants of this landscape can still be seen in some fine trees and shrubs. There is a pavilion in Gothic style and a picturesque grotto built of stone, brick and plaster by Josiah Lane, a noted creator of rockwork grottos in Wiltshire in the eighteenth century. Paths and tunnels twist between ancient-looking weathered rocks containing nooks and alcoves. Notable among the trees is a stand of yews around 400 years old, Atlas Mountain cedars of between 150 and 200 years old, and a mighty cedar of Lebanon.

Pound Hill Garden

West Kington, Chippenham SN14 7JG. Tel: (01249) 783880

Mr and Mrs Philip Stockitt • 8m W of Chippenham, 2m NE of Marshfield between A420 and M4 – follow the brown-tourist signs • Open March to Oct, daily, 2 – 5pm, and for parties by appt • Entrance: £3.50 • Other information: Plants for sale in adjacent plant centre open daily except Jan, 10am – 5pm ☾ 💷 ✕ WC ᕕ ♨ 🏧 ♀

The two acres surrounding the sixteenth-century stone house are laid out as a series of garden rooms of very different character. An 'old-fashioned rose garden' (planted and labelled David Austin roses) leads to a Victorian vegetable garden with espaliered fruit trees, then through a wisteria, rose and clematis tunnel to an orchard, a Cotswold garden with topiary, a herbaceous border and drystone walls showing off a parterre of clipped box, *Rosa* 'The Fairy', seasonal pots and rose-covered obelisks. A water garden, filled with shade-loving as well as moisture-loving plants, is surrounded by yew hedging to create another small garden. A corridor lined by *Betula utilis* var. *jacquemontii*, underplanted with *Pulmonaria officinalis* 'Sissinghurst White' and 'Queen of the Night' tulips, leads on to a rose walk lined with clipped sweet chestnuts underplanted with old-fashioned roses and *Hebe rakaiensis*. The nursery sells a wide variety of rarer and commoner plants. A new box garden with a cloud hedge encloses a wide selection of grasses and topiary shapes.

The Priory ★

Kington St Michael, Chippenham SN14 6JG. Tel: (01249) 750360

Mme Anita Pereire • 3m N of Chippenham off A350 between Chippenham and M4 junction 17. Drive through village, then turn left down lane opposite stud farm on right at bottom of hill • Open by appt only • Entrance: £3 ☾ 🍴 WC ᕕ

Since 1994 the owner, a well-known writer and garden designer, has created a magical garden around the buildings of an ancient priory. A firm overall structure and lavish planting have combined to make this a most satisfying and elegant garden. Radiating from a central patchwork stone path lined with an avenue of weeping silver pears (Mme Pereire's signature tree) are well-defined and separate areas. These include a breathtaking 'French' garden of topiary and standard roses (the long-lasting 'The Fairy' and 'Ballerina'), an exquisite water garden, a ha-ha ablaze with rock plants, perennials and flowering shrubs, and a classic rose garden filled with colour and scent from masses of old-fashioned varieties. Beyond the hedge-enclosed part of the garden lies a meadow with mown paths forming a maze among the long grasses. In the wild garden further mown grass paths, edged with wild roses, lead down to a gravel garden which blends seamlessly into the surrounding meadowland. The latest additions are a white and silver sun garden full of artemisias and cistus, and a new rose garden built into a stone walk.

Ridleys Cheer

Mountain Bower, Chippenham SN14 7AJ. Tel: (01225) 891204

Mr and Mrs Antony Young • 8m W of Chippenham off A420. Turn N at The Shoe, take second left, then first right • Open 9th April, 7th May, 4th June, 2 – 6pm, and for parties by appt • Entrance: £3, children under 14 free, parties of 10 or more £4 per person • Other information: Picnics in meadow only, from 1pm ● ▬ 🍴 WC & 🐾 B&B

The garden, created since the early 1980s by a garden designer and his wife, covers some three acres, two of which hold a young and interesting arboretum, and there is also a three-acre wildflower meadow. The garden is on two levels, connected by a broad flight of steps with a wrought-iron rose arbour at the top and a grass walk, and contains many fine examples of rarer shrubs and trees. Spring is ushered in with bulbs and magnolias. The shrub roses, including some 125 species and hybrids seldom encountered, are a major summer feature; notable too are the displays of white martagon lilies and *Meconopsis betonicifolia*. There is a small *potager*, and a gravel garden planted with box and yew outside the conservatory. Autumn colour is given by a growing number of maples, beeches, tulip trees, oaks and zelkovas. In the main, this in an informal garden, full of appeal for plantsmen, who can derive much information from the knowledgeable owners. A small nursery sells trees, shrubs and perennials, many of them unusual. Pound Hill House (see entry) is nearby.

Sharcott Manor

Pewsey SN9 5PA. Tel: (01672) 563485

Captain and Mrs David Armytage • 1m SW of Pewsey off A345 • Open for NGS April to Oct, first Wed in month, 11am – 5pm, plus two Suns, 2 – 6pm. Also open for parties by appt • Entrance: £3 • Other information: Teas on NGS open days and for parties on request ● WC & 🐾 ♀

A fine six-acre garden, mainly informal in character and largely created over the last twenty-five years. More formal areas with lawns and generous borders lead on to water and woodland plantings which include many rare and beautiful trees. The owner is an avowed plant collector and enthusiast, and the whole garden is densely planted with a rich choice of colourful subjects. The family atmosphere of the garden is much appreciated by visitors, and those more expert can revel in the fine effects and groupings that have been achieved. The widely varied plantings ensure interest at all seasons. Thousands of bulbs bloom in the woodlands in spring and climbing roses cascade through the trees in late June, while an avenue of *Pyrus calleryana* 'Chanticleer', leading down the lower lawn towards the stream, gives good autumn colour. The small collection of waterfowl is an unexpected delight.

Special Plants Nursery (Hill Farm Barn)

(see Gloucestershire)

Stourhead ★★ [Historic Garden Grade I]

Stourton, Warminster BA12 6QF. Tel: (01747) 841152

The National Trust • 3m NW of Mere (A303) at Stourton off B3092 • House open 18th March to Oct, Fri – Tues, 11.30am – 4.30pm (or dusk if earlier) • Garden open all year, daily, 9am – 7pm (or dusk if earlier) • Entrance: House or garden £5.80, children (5–16) £3.20, family £14.20 (house and garden £9.90, children £4.80, family £23.50) • Other information: Refreshments in restaurant or at Spread Eagle Inn at garden entrance. Wheelchairs available. Buggy service from car park in peak season. Dogs Nov to Feb only ○ 🍴 WC ⅏ ⚘ 🏛 ♿ 🐾

An outstanding example of an English landscape garden, designed by Henry Hoare II between 1741 and 1780, a paragon in its day and almost the greatest surviving garden of its kind. The sequence of arcadian images is revealed gradually if one follows a route anti-clockwise around the lake, having come from the house along the top route, so seeing the lake from above. Each experience is doubly inspiring: visitors glimpse classical temples across the water, almost unattainable and mirage-like, and when they reach their goal some other vision always attracts the eye – the boat-house, Temple of Flora, turf bridge, Temple of Apollo, rock bridge, cascade (these two are tucked away and very surprising), Pantheon, Gothic rustic cottage and grotto. The view from the Temple of Apollo (1765) was described by Horace Walpole as 'one of the most picturesque scenes in the world', by which he meant that it was as fine as a painting. To gain a better idea of how these buildings would have looked had the surrounding planting remained as it was originally, take a walk by Turner's Paddock Lake below the cascade. Between 1791 and 1838 Hoare's grandson Richard Colt Hoare planted many new species, particularly from America, including tulip trees, swamp cypresses and Indian bean trees. He also introduced *Rhododendron ponticum*. From 1894 the 6th Baronet added to these with the latest kinds of hybrid rhododendrons and scented azaleas, and a large number of copper beeches and conifers, such as the Japanese white pine, Sitka spruce and Californian nutmeg, of which many are record-sized specimens. In the early nineteenth century Stourhead boasted one of the best collections of pelargoniums in the world, over 600 varieties, and the latest effort to emulate Richard Colt Hoare's passion consists of over 100 varieties in a 1910 lean-to greenhouse. Especially wonderful in winter when the garden is quiet, and more views are afforded through the bare trees. Adjacent to Stourhead, and sharing the same car park but with separate entry charges, is *Stourton House Flower Garden*, a colourful five-acre garden of interest at all times of year, where a wide range of wild and cultivated plants grow happily together. Telephone Mrs Bullivant on (01747) 840417 for details. [Open April to Nov, Wed, Thurs, Sun and Bank Holiday Mons, 11am – 6pm.]

West Wind

Manton Drove, Manton, Marlborough SN8 4HL. Tel: (01672) 515380

Mr and Mrs Neil Campbell-Sharp • 1m W of Marlborough off A4. In Manton bear right past Odd Fellows Arms, then after 180 metres left into Manton Drove. House is up hill on right • Open by appt • Entrance: £5 NEW ● 🍴 ⅏

An outstanding and very personal garden created over 20 years by Neil and Jerry Campbell-Sharp in a wonderful downland setting. Their expertise as garden photographers is allied with wide horticultural experience to achieve a visual feast and fine perspectives in this one-acre garden alive with colour, form and scent from May right through to November. Wonderful viewpoints highlight the strong outlines and lush planting radiating from the house. A restful enclosed garden leads to a skilfully planted double border awash with old-fashioned roses, then descends to a woodland

walk planted for spring flowering. The garden fits happily into the surrounding landscape, viewed through slender silver *Betula jacquemontii* and home to a rich assortment of wild life. The superbly grown and placed grasses are an outstanding feature.

Westwood Manor

Bradford–on–Avon BA15 2AF. Tel: (01225) 863374

The National Trust • 1.5m NW of Trowbridge, 1.5m SW of Bradford-on-Avon off
B3109. In Westwood beside church • Open April to Sept, Sun, Tues and Wed,
2 – 5pm, and at other times for parties of up to 20 by written appt with s.a.e.
• Entrance: £4.60 (2005 price) ◑

Turning from the Italianate glories of Iford Manor (see entry) one mile away,
topiarists and others might like to contemplate the dense green geometry of the
garden here. There are no flowers, other than the lilies in the pond set into the lawn
and the swathes of wisteria on the wall leading to the entrance. A small garden links
the ancient barns to the medieval manor house which the yew hedges enfold and
enclose. This simple design looks centuries-old but dates from the early part of the
twentieth century, when Mr Edgar Lister purchased and restored the house and
created and designed the garden, both of which he later left to the Trust. The late
James Lees-Milne wrote that the exquisite manor in its present form 'was his
[Lister's] creation and should be his memorial'. It must be emphasised that the
garden should be visited as an adjunct and a complement to the house, which is lived
in and administered by the Trust's tenant.

Wilton House ★ [Historic Garden Grade I]

Wilton, Salisbury SP2 0BJ. Tel: (01722) 746729

The Earl of Pembroke • 3m W of Salisbury on A30 • House open • For opening times
2006, telephone or consult website (as listed at back of Guide) • Entrance: £4.50,
children £3.50, family £14 (house, grounds and exhibition areas £9.75, OAPs
£7.50, children (5–15) £5.50, family £24, parties £7 per person) (2005 prices)
• Other information: Plants for sale in garden centre ◑ 🍽 🍴 WC ♿ 🚻 ♨ ☕

The first garden the visitor used to see, in the north courtyard, was designed by
David Vickery in 1971. It incorporates formal pleached limes in a rectangular layout,
the geometry being further emphasised by a box parterre infilled with lavender and
a torrential central fountain which provides a cool haven in summer. A wrought-iron
gate adjoining the courtyard leads to the east front with wall-trained shrubs
and extensive herbaceous borders. Looking to the south, the Palladian bridge built
in 1737 spanning the River Nadder is a focal point. Beside this stands a fine golden
oak, *Quercus robur* 'Concordia', raised and grafted in 1843 at a nursery in Ghent.
Going east along the broad gravel walk among many specimen trees set in
eighteenth-century landscaped parkland, the visitor reaches the walled rose garden
containing a large collection of old-fashioned English roses. This adjoins a pergola
clothed with climbing plants and a water garden containing roses, aquatic species
and ornamental fish. Beyond is the Whispering Seat with its unusual acoustic
properties and a loggia facing the statue from the Arundel collection, all enclosed
by a short avenue of *Quercus ilex*, with the river a glistening vista in the distance.
Within the central courtyard of the house, the 17th Earl commissioned Xa

Tollemache to design the fourth new garden (visible but not visitable) where, echoing designs from the central, ninth-century Venetian wellhead, a border of cotton lavender encloses quadrants of clipped box hedge. For children there is fun and excitement in a large adventure playground; for historians, interest in searching out those parts of the garden which show the work of Isaac de Caus (c. 1632), the 8th Earl, the 9th 'Architect Earl', Sir William Chambers and James Wyatt (1801). Tree-trail leaflet available. Nearby is *Philipps House*, Dinton (Tel: (01985) 843600), a National Trust house by Wyatville c. 1816, open all year with 100-acre *Dinton Park*. The house (ground floor only) is open 8th April to 30th Oct, Mon, 1 – 5pm, and Sat, 10am – 1pm. Walks in the park and woodland start from the car park.

THE HERITAGE BULB CLUB

This is both a commercial venture and a conservation-minded horticultural service, based at Tullynally (see entry in Ireland). The club has over 500 members, who receive a year's worth of bulbs, chosen so that a different variety is in flower each month. The choice is between the Heritage Collection and the Plantsman Collection. The stories surrounding the discovery of these bulbs or the uses put to them are written up, as are growing requirements, with the help of renowned bulb expert Martyn Rix. Membership fees range from £45 to £110 p.a., and a sample box is also available for £25. The club aims to kindle interest and spread knowledge, with visits to gardens here and abroad, expeditions to see wild species in flower (Turkey in 2006) and the opportunity to buy normally unobtainable bulbs and exchange seeds. A wholesale list of bulbs for naturalising and a heritage vegetable seed list are also available. Enquiries to Heritage, Tullynally Castle, Castlepollard, Co. Westmeath, Ireland. Tel: 0845 300 4257 (UK), 044 62744 (Ireland); info@heritagebulbs.com; www.heritagebulbs.com.

PARKS AND GARDENS DATA PARTNERSHIP

A major new national database is being set up under the aegis of the Association of Gardens Trusts, the Welsh Historic Gardens Trust and the University of York, funded by a £1-million grant from the Heritage Lottery Fund. This ambitious three-year project, which will complement English Heritage's *Register* of fewer than 1600 properties, aims ultimately to make available to the general public detailed information on some 30,000 historic parks, gardens and landscapes throughout Britain. The initial database will be established in 2006 and some 6000 records provided by 2008.

SYMBOLS

[NEW] entries new for 2006; ○ open all year; ◑ open most of year; ◐ open during main season; ◕ open rarely and/or by appt; 🍵 teas/light refreshments; ✕ meals; 🧺 picnics permitted; WC toilet facilities; <u>WC</u> toilet facilities, inc. disabled; ♿ partly wheelchair-accessible; 🐕 dogs on lead; 🌿 plants for sale; 🏬 shop; 🎪 events held; ✾ children-friendly; B&B bed and breakfast available.

WORCESTERSHIRE

24 Alexander Avenue

Droitwich WR9 8NH. Tel: (01905) 774907

David and Malley Terry • Take M5 exit 5 or 6, then A38. At Copcut roundabout on southern outskirts of Droitwich, take Worcester Road signed to town centre. After 0.75m, just after old-style pedestrian crossing, turn left into Alexander Avenue • Open 2nd April, 11th June, 9th July, 2 – 6pm, for NGS, and by appt • Entrance: £2.50 ● & ℗

This small garden is a lesson in what can be done in a small space and a short time. The present owners moved here in the winter of 1995 and have turned a barren patch of grass into a paradise. High hedges obscure the views of neighbouring houses, and through them climb some of the 100 clematis the garden grows. The borders are stuffed with a dazzling array of interesting plants, many of them rare; most shrubs have climbers growing through them. The early-flowering perennials and bulbs make April a good time to visit. There is a fine collection of ferns, and alpines grow in many old stone troughs or the gravel bed in front of the house. A garden of immaculate artistry.

Arley Arboretum

Upper Arley DY12 1XG. Tel: (01299) 861368/861868

R.D. Turner Charitable Trust • 6m NW of Kidderminster 9m SE of Bridgnorth, between A442 and B4194 • Open April to mid-Nov, Wed – Sun, 11am – 5pm • Entrance: £4, children £1 ❶ ● 🍴 <u>WC</u> & ⬦ ℗

The arboretum at Arley forms part of what remains of an important Picturesque landscape, laid out and planted over the late-eighteenth and nineteenth centuries by two families with distinguished botanical connections. Embellishing the already renowned grounds of Arley House, George Annesley, Earl of Mountnorris, a Fellow of the Royal and Linnean Societies, began planting trees in the 1790s, and through the nineteenth century the Woodward family, related by marriage to Sir Joseph Hooker, Director of Kew, continued his work. Situated above the River Severn, with exquisite views over the surrounding countryside, the remaining walled garden and arboretum retain a romantic atmosphere. The mature trees include Crimean pines and an ancient layered beech, and walks wind beneath them through daffodils in spring, followed by bluebells, magnolias and rhododendrons. The arboretum has recently been extended and planting continues, while the walled garden with its intact castellated gatehouse, is also being restored and replanted.

Barnard's Green House

10 Poolbrook Road, Barnard's Green, Great Malvern WR14 3NQ. Tel: (01684) 574446

Mr and Mrs Philip Nicholls • Just E of Great Malvern at B4211/B4208 junction • Open April to Sept, Thurs, 2 – 6pm; plus 12th Feb, 2nd April, 18th June and at other times by appt • Entrance: £3, children free ● ● 🍴 WC & ℗ ♀

The immaculately kept, quintessentially English garden, set behind a neat seven-teenth-century house, has at its centre a tranquil lawn with a great cedar and a cut-leaved beech. Beyond this, winding paths and gateways lead to areas of differing character, the highlights in spring being the drifts of daffodils and the crocus lawn, in summer the splendid herbaceous borders. Mrs Nicholls is a plantswoman with an eye for colour, and here mauves, blues and pinks are lifted by touches of magenta and by gold and silver foliage. Pink roses cascade over a pergola behind. Entered through an arch cut into a venerable yew hedge, and set beneath mature limes and horse chestnuts, is a shady garden filled with euphorbias, ferns, hostas, geraniums, epimediums and hydrangeas; a small stumpery has been added here. A vegetable, fruit and impressive cutting garden lays out its offerings in a more formal hedged enclosure, intersected by traditional herringbone brick paths and edged with box. Elsewhere are white, red, shrub and rose borders, a rockery and a pond. Now the old tennis court has been turned into an ashphalt garden, laid out as 16 colourful beds edged with Malvern stone; a giant urn surrounded by silver foliage dominates the whole.

Burford House Gardens ★

Tenbury Wells WR15 8HQ. Tel: (01584) 810777

Burford Garden Company • 19m SW of Kidderminster, 1m W of Tenbury Wells on A456; 8m S of Ludlow via A49 and A456 • Open all year, daily, 9am – 6pm (or dusk if earlier). Closed 25th, 26th Dec • Entrance: £3.95, children £1. Parties of 20 or more by prior arrangement £3 per person • Other information: Plants for sale, especially clematis, at Burford Garden Company opposite ○ ⬤ ✕ 🍴 WC ⬥ ❀ ⬛

John Treasure's gardens, planned and planted over a period of forty years from 1954, are now mature and a classic of their time. A huge variety of species is grown here in the broad sinuous mixed borders which cross the smooth lawns, with much of the herbaceous planting devised for late summer colour; elsewhere, streamside gardens are attractive in spring and early summer, while *Erigeron mucronatus* clothes the more formal terraces against the house, which is draped with a magnificent *Wisteria macrobotrys* 'Burford'. The gardens remain a showcase for clematis, in which the garden centre specialises. Across the brook which skirts the main garden is the meadow garden, the work of the designer Charles Chesshire: mown grass paths curve through the meadows into circular enclosures of amelanchier or cherry, or dive into a maze of beech hedging, and a tiny track leads down through the wild flowers to the banks of the River Teme. The whole forms a perfect counterbalance to the more contrived informality of the original gardens.

Conderton Manor

Conderton, Tewkesbury, Gloucestershire GL20 7PR. Tel: (01386) 725389;

Mr and Mrs William Carr • 8m SW of Evesham, 5.5m NE of Tewkesbury between A46 and B4079. Opposite Yew Tree Inn in Conderton • Open by appt • Entrance: £4 • Other information: Refreshments by prior arrangement and at Yew Tree Inn. Toilet facilities by arrangement ◖

The fine seventeenth-century manor house had little garden remaining when the previous owners began the present layout in the 1960s. The present owners have expanded the planting, especially of trees, with the emphasis on preserving and enhancing the magnificent surrounding views. The atmosphere is relaxed and informal. Within the old walled garden rose arches frame views across the garden to the wider landscape, and beds of old roses are underplanted with lavenders and bearded irises alongside cottage-style mixed herbaceous plantings. Through a yew arch a small summerhouse nestles in a sheltered corner, and beyond this a mown grass path leads along a large shrub border carefully planted for foliage effects. Winding walks lead through secret areas enclosed by trees and shrubs, such as a boggy hollow with hostas, ferns, gunneras and drumstick primulas Near to the house a small parterre is kept deliberately low and subtle to merge into the countryside.

Croome Park [Historic Park Grade I]

Builders Yard, High Green, Severn Stoke WR8 9JS. Tel: (01905) 371006

The National Trust • 8m SW of Worcester off A38 and 6m W of Pershore off B4084 • Open March to May, Wed – Sun and Bank Holiday Mons, 10am – 5.30pm; June to Aug, daily, 10am – 5.30pm; Oct, Nov and Dec, Wed – Sun, 10am – 4pm (closes 5.30pm Oct). Advisable to telephone before travelling. Guided tours by appt in writing • Entrance: £3.70, children £1.80, family £9 • Other information: For disabled access, telephone in advance. Car parking £2 ◑ 💷 🥾 <u>WC</u> ♿ ⇭ 🍴 ✿

'Capability' Brown's career as an independent landscape designer and architect was effectively launched at Croome Court, of which today's park was once an integral part. The house (not open) was sold by the family who commissioned it and remains in private hands. Brown created a serpentine lake, complete with grotto, and a mile-long artificial river. Paths wind through shrubberies and past charming and ornate garden buildings, and the wider parkland contains stunning follies by Robert Adam, James Wyatt and others. The Trust's ambitious ten-year restoration, due to be completed in 2006, has involved dredging the lake and river and restoring the bridges across the lake, the classical temples and grotto, and the listed park buildings. More than 2000 trees and 14 acres of shrubberies have been planted to replace those lost from the original planting scheme.

Eastgrove Cottage Garden Nursery ★

Sankyns Green, Shrawley, Little Witley WR6 6LQ. Tel: (01299) 896389

Malcolm and Carol Skinner • 8m NW of Worcester on road between Shrawley (B4196) and Great Witley (A443) • Open 13th April to 29th July, Thurs – Sat and Bank Holiday Mons; 7th Sept to 14th Oct, Thurs – Sat; all 2 – 5pm. Closed Aug • Entrance: £4 (£3.50 April, Sept, Oct), children free ◑ WC ♿ ✿ ✿

An intimate, deceptively simple garden which is both superbly planted and impeccably maintained, with the added value of a nursery full of choice plants. The masterly planting, with a careful but also relaxed and instinctive approach to colour and wonderful use of foliage, divides the small plot into smaller sections of distinct character. A garden of cottage favourites – aquilegias, geraniums, irises and violas – invites quiet sitting, while the Great Wall of China diplays alpines and other small plants deserving of close study in an admirably natural manner. A stroll leads through shady walks and open lawns, with luscious planting on all sides, and even wilder areas further from the cottage are carefully presented. A young two-acre arboretum has an oval concave 'labyrinth' for children to enjoy.

Hanbury Hall ★ [Historic Garden Grade I]

School Road, Hanbury, Droitwich WR9 7EA. Tel: (01527) 821214

The National Trust • 4.5m E of Droitwich, off B4090 or B4091 • House open as garden, but 1 – 5pm • Garden open 4th to 12th March, Sat and Sun, 11am – 5.30pm, 18th March to 1st Nov, Sat – Wed (but open Good Friday), 11am – 5.30pm • Entrance: £3.70, children £1.90, family £8.70 (house and garden £5.70, children £2.80, family £13.50, parties £4.80 per person) (2005 prices) • Other information: Batricar available

The hall, remodelled in 1701 and unaltered since, is a jewel of a house, and the setting provided by the surrounding gardens and parkland is magnificent. The restoration of the early-eighteenth-century gardens on the west side is proving a triumph as they acquire maturity. The sunken parterre, surrounded by yew hedges, and the adjoining fruit garden with its trellis pavilions, have been authentically planted. The pattern of clipped box is filled with individual specimens of choice small plants of the period – auriculas, tulips and marigolds – laid out in colourful regular patterns; citrus and clipped bay trees in pots are displayed on the surrounding gravel walks. Beyond, in the Wilderness and especially the Grove, fastigiate junipers and low box in a calm green space backed by sprightly young trees give a fine and unaccustomed sense of how such formal woodland gardens would have appeared to their creators. Shrubberies rejuvenated with box, laurel, phillyrea and philadelphus stand neatly on vast expanses of smooth lawn, contrasting with fine trees extending into the parkland. The orangery has been brought back into use, with pots of tender plants lining its terrace in the summer, as has the curious mushroom house attached. An orchard of old apple varieties occupies part of the vast walled gardens, and a walk across the park leads past a well-preserved ice-house and a magnificent cedar avenue.

Lakeside

Gaines Road, Whitbourne, Worcester WR6 5RD. Tel: (01886) 821119

Mr D. Gueroult • 9m W of Worcester off A44. Turn left at county boundary sign, signed to Linley Green (ignore sign to Whitbourne) • Open April to June by appt for parties of 10 or more • Entrance: £3, children free

The first glimpse of this six-acre garden is a moment of sheer delight: a dramatic vista of the lake at the bottom of a steep grassy slope. The main part of the garden lies within the walls of what was the fruit garden of Gaines House nearby and consists of mixed beds and borders with many unusual plants, including bulbs and climbers. The main lake is the largest of three medieval stewponds. A small pinetum is maturing well, as is a large bog garden. A woodland path, bordered by ferns and different varieties of holly, leads to the attractive lakeside walk. Don't miss the view from the top of the heather garden.

Little Malvern Court

Little Malvern, Nr Malvern WR14 4JN. Tel: (01684) 892988

Mrs T.M. Berington • 4m S of Great Malvern on A4104 S of junction with A449 • Open 19th April to 20th July, Wed, Thurs, also 26th March and 1st May for NGS, all 2 – 5pm. Private visits and parties (maximum 35 people) welcome weekdays only by appt • Entrance: £4.50, children £1 (house and garden £5.50, children £2) ● WC &

Tucked into the side of the Malvern Hills, and spread out beside an ancient gabled manor house and priory church, this is a garden of great romantic charm. The medieval fish ponds, bulging yew hedges clipped into fantastic shapes and a venerable lime tree remain from earlier gardens, but much dates from 1982 onwards, originally laid out by Arabella Lennox-Boyd and continued by Michael Balston. Close to the house, a classic English combination of clipped hedges and pergolas defining formal areas filled with soft planting creates satisfying contrasts. Moving from area to area, themes develop and vistas are opened up. Pale colours and soft textures are used to great effect, and the garden gains a modern edge by the elegant simplicity of some of the planting, such as a clipped box hedge set against a clipped yew hedge and a billowing choisya in the entrance forecourt, and elsewhere a simple horseshoe of pleached limes around a small lawn. Below the house a series of small lakes connected by weirs is embraced by mown grass paths, flanked by wildflowers and maturing trees. At the top of the first lake is a new rock garden and a watery gravel bed where primulas and irises are naturalising. This evolving, imaginative and immaculately presented garden repays several visits.

Luggers Hall

Springfield Lane, Broadway WR12 7BT. Tel: (01386) 852040

Mr and Mrs R. Haslam • In Broadway turn off High Street by Swan Hotel, bear left into Springfield Lane, garden is 270 metres on left • Open two days for NGS, and May to Sept for parties of 20 or more by appt • Entrance: £2.50, children free ● ● WC ♨ 𝄪 B&B

The Victorian painter of gardens and landscapes Alfred Parsons built the house for himself in 1911 and designed the 2.5-acre garden in the style typical of the Arts and Crafts Movement centred around Broadway at that time. The present owners have been gradually restoring the garden since 1995, retaining its overall character and adding ideas of their own. The main lawn, with hedged compartments opening off it, has a splendid battlemented yew hedge to one side, and the rose garden remains unchanged with criss-cross paths of broken Cotswold stone. The parterre, reconstructed with the aid of an original black-and-white aerial photograph, has been replanted with white roses and blue perennials. Mrs Haslam's colour effects are superb: themed borders in the walled garden and elsewhere range from palest yellows through blues to intense shades of pink, with many unusual plants including a wide variety of salvias. A white garden is tucked away, and there is also a *potager* and a tranquil leafy corner where the former swimming pool has been transformed into a home for the koi carp. Gravel paths with strategically placed seats connect the different areas, and Broadway Tower can be glimpsed between the trees.

Overbury Court ★ [Historic Garden Grade II*]

Overbury, Tewkesbury, Gloucestershire GL20 7NP.
Tel: (01386) 725111 (office hours)

Mr and Mrs Bruce Bossom • 9m SW of Evesham, 5m NE of Tewkesbury, 2.5m N of Teddington (A46/A435) roundabout • Open by appt only • Entrance: minimum charge £20 ● &

The superb garden, largely laid out in the late nineteenth and early twentieth centuries, provides the setting for a fine early-eighteenth-century house; an interesting church adjoins. It is bordered by lush parkland giving unspoiled views in all directions. Everywhere there is water. Behind the house, a brook issues into a tufa grotto. Rough steps wind between cascades and through naturalistic plantings of hostas, filipendulas, wild garlic and ferns, backed by mature box bushes. The brook, emerging along a broad rill bordered on one side by meadow and on the other by lawn, descends through gentle cascades and winds around a series of pools beyond a great lawn. Huge plane and lime trees contrast with the smoothness of grass and water; the simplicity is magical. Massive yew hedges separate this part of the garden from the more formal area to the south, where the centrepiece is an avenue of Irish yews flanked by a sunken bowling lawn and a formal pool. Again, the planting is simple yet stunning – to the east a glorious crinkle-crankle border of gold and silver foliage by Peter Coates, and to the west a sunken double mixed border displaying old-fashioned and species roses, underplanted with geraniums and *Alchemilla mollis*. Near the house is a terrace with silver and white borders, and well-trained shrubs and climbers clothe the house walls.

Pershore College

'Avonbank', Pershore WR10 3JP. Tel: (01386) 552443

7m SE of M5 junction 7, 1m E of Pershore on B4084 • Open Mon – Fri by appt for large parties • Entrance: £1, coaches by appt ●

The grounds are working areas designed with an educational bias, and include 'model gardens' created by students, and a variety of specialist gardens. There is also an arboretum, orchards, automated glasshouses and a hardy plant production nursery and plant centre. The RHS Pershore Centre is on the campus, and the Alpine Garden Society has its national HQ here; the college also holds National Collections of penstemons and philadelphus.

The Picton Garden

Old Court Nurseries, Colwall, Great Malvern WR13 6QE. Tel: (01684) 540416

Mr and Mrs P. Picton • 3m SW of Great Malvern on B4218 • Open 2nd to 31st Aug, Wed – Sun; Sept to 22nd Oct, daily; all 11am – 5pm • Old Court Nurseries open as garden plus May to July, Fri, Sat and Sun • Entrance: £2.50, children under 15 free ◑ ✍

Ernest Ballard began selling asters, many of his own breeding, at Old Court Nurseries in 1906. The present owner's father, Percy Picton, took over in 1952, and the impressive plantsman's garden has developed alongside the continuing breeding programme and National Collection as a setting for a splendid display of asters and other late-summer perennials. It owes much to the naturalistic prairie planting style, with rudbeckias and echinaceas, heleniums and helianthus mingling with the great swathes of Michaelmas daisies, together with seedheads of spent flowers and towering stands of bamboos. Trees and shrubs for autumn interest – cornus, acers, hydrangeas and liquidambars – are being added, and a new shrub bed is planned for 2006. To celebrate the nurseries' centenary, Michaelmas Day (29th September) will mark the beginning of a weekend forum, including a discussion and a conducted tour of the collection.

Riverside Gardens

Wychbold, Droitwich Spa WR9 0DG. Tel: (01527) 860000

Webbs of Wychbold • On A38 between Droitwich Spa and Bromsgrove, just off M5 junction 5. Signposted • Open all year, daily except 16th April and 25th and 26th Dec, 9am – 8pm (closes 6pm Sat and Bank Holiday Mons and during Jan and Feb; 1st Jan and all Suns, 10.30am – 4.30pm) • Entrance: free ○ 💻 ✕ 🍴 <u>WC</u> ♿ ➪ 🌿 ⛓ 🍵 ⚲

A series of imaginative themed gardens planted in just over an acre on the banks of the River Salwarpe. The noise of the motorway and the bustle of a huge garden centre have been reduced by a planting of screening trees, and the gardens themselves are peaceful and full of interest. Great thought has been given to show plants for all situations. An orchard of flowering cherries is underplanted in spring with primroses, fritillaries and cowslips, while a seat in a willow arbour is a good place to view a garden filled with silvery bark and foliage and white flowers. A delightful area based on *A Midsummer Night's Dream* has a willow sculpture of Titania and Bottom with elves and fairies in attendance. There is also a wisteria walk, collections of clematis and potentillas and an attractive potager. Roses hang along ropes, with lavenders and *Elaeagnus ebbingei* for extra fragrance and chocolate cosmos for show. Colour is the key to the Spectrum Garden, with its range of plants from red through pink, orange, yellow, green, blue and purple. The latest addition, Noel Kingsbury's New Wave Gardens, are laid out on a slope on the opposite bank of the river. A limited number of species is chosen and then repeated in waves, creating a strong sense of rhythm.

Shuttifield Cottage

Birchwood, Storridge, Malvern WR13 5HA. Tel: (01886) 884243

Angela and David Judge • 8m SW of Worcester off A4103. Turn right opposite Storridge church to Birchwood. After 1.25m turn left down tarmac drive. Park on road and walk down this drive (limited parking at house for disabled) • Open 23rd April, 6th and 20th May, 10th and 17th June (rose days), 12th Aug, 16th Sept, 1 – 6pm, and at other times by appt • Entrance: £3, children free 🌸 💻 WC 🌿

This unusual garden has lawns leading down to a woodland rose garden through a succession of beds and borders containing shrubs and flowering plants designed to give pleasure and interest throughout the year. The rose garden has space for a large collection of old varieties to spread, sprawl, climb and bloom abundantly. Beyond is a 20-acre wood carpeted with wood anemones and bluebells, azaleas and rhododendrons, traversed by winding paths. In other parts are colour-themed beds, including newly planted stump and primula beds, splendid trees and a vegetable garden. The seven-acre valley to the south is home to a herd of sika deer, and beside one of two ponds set among wild flowers and orchids is a thatched tea house. The planning is skilful, the effect natural and unstudied.

Spetchley Park [Historic Park Grade II*]

Spetchley, Worcester WR5 1RS. Tel: (01453) 810303

Trustees of Spetchley Gardens Charitable Trust • 3m E of Worcester on A44 • Open 21st March to 30th Sept, Wed – Sun and Bank Holiday Mons, 11am – 6pm (last admission 5pm); Oct, Sat and Sun, 11am – 4pm (last admission 3pm) • Entrance: £5, children £2 ❶ 💭 WC ⅄ ♀

The grand Victorian gardens, surrounded by seventeenth-century parkland, were laid out and extended by successive generations of the Berkeley family. Ellen Willmott, a relative, was a frequent visitor and helped to fashion the planting, evidenced by *Eryngium* 'Miss Willmott's Ghost' still self-seeding in the vast herbaceous borders. The current owner, a plant collector, is expanding the area under cultivation, with a view to allowing the plants to do their own thing, even in more formal parts within and around the old walled garden. Everywhere gravel or daisy-strewn grass walks lead you on between yew hedges or old shrubberies to discover further areas punctuated by statue and fountain, and a visit in June is rewarded by spectacular expanses of naturalised martagon lilies, together with *Campanula lactiflora*. In the extensive woodland garden, the varied collection includes many dogwoods and acers, and extensive recent plantings supplement the many fine mature trees. The Park Lake is fringed with water lilies and bulrushes, with views to the deer park beyond.

Stone House Cottage Gardens ★

Stone, Kidderminster DY10 4BG. Tel: (01562) 69902

Mr and Mrs James Arbuthnott • 2m SE of Kidderminster via A448 • Open March to mid-Sept, Wed – Sat, 10am – 5pm, and Oct to March by appt • Entrance: £3, children free ❶ WC ⅄ ✒

The garden has been created since 1974, and looking round it now, it is difficult to believe that the whole area was once flat and bare. The owners have skilfully built towers and follies to create small intimate areas and at the same time provide homes for many unusual climbers and shrubs. Yew hedges break up the area to give a vista with a tower at the end, covered with wisteria, roses and clematis. Hardly anywhere does a shrub grow in isolation – something will be scrambling up it, usually a small late-flowering clematis. Raised beds are full to overflowing, shrubs and unusual herbaceous plants mingle happily. In a grassed area shrubs are making good specimens. In June during two evenings of music the towers have a secondary purpose as platforms for wind ensembles. You are invited to picnic in the garden for a modest fee – the effect is akin to non-pretentious Glyndebourne transplanted to San Gimignano. At other times you may ascend the towers to view the garden as a whole for the price of a donation to the Mother Theresa charity.

Witley Court [Historic Garden Grade II*]

Worcester Road, Great Witley, Worcester WR6 6JT. Tel: (01299) 896636

English Heritage • 10m NW of Worcester on A443 • Open April to Oct, daily, 10am – 6pm (5pm in Oct); Nov to March, Wed – Sun, 10am – 4pm. Closed 25th, 26th Dec, 1st Jan. Evening guided tours available by appt • Entrance: £4.90, OAPs £3.70, children £2.50, family £12.30 (2005 prices) • Other information: Disabled parking available ☾ 🅿 🖪 <u>WC</u> ♿ 🐕 ✿ 🏛 🍴 ☕

The spectacular ruin of Witley Court, once boasting to be master of all it surveyed, looks out now over the ghost of a garden to ploughed farmland where once would have stretched acres of parkland. However, the gardens are being brought to life by the restoration of the truly magnificent Italianate fountains which formed the centrepiece of a vast and elaborate Nesfield parterre. The planting is being only partly replicated, to give an impression of the setting for the fountains and other remaining stonework: twin pavilions flanking the semi-circular bowl of the parterre, with an elaborate and decaying ha-ha dividing this from the land beyond. The imagination provides the rest, and to see the fountains playing again with all the guests departed cannot fail to be a moving experience. Elsewhere in the grounds are the nineteenth-century woodland and wilderness walks, also being restored, a picturesque lake with cascade, and a modern sculpture park, as well as the ruined mansion, which can be visited, and the superb Baroque church adjoining.

GARDEN AND FLOWER SHOWS 2006
- 11th to 14th May: Spring Gardening Show, Malvern
  (Three Counties Showground, Malvern, Worcestershire)
  Ticket hotline: (01684) 584924; www.threecounties.co.uk
- 23rd to 27th May: Chelsea Flower Show
  (Royal Hospital, Chelsea, London SW3)
- 6th to 8th June: Wisley Show
  (RHS Garden, Wisley, Woking, Surrey)
- Mid-June: BBC *Gardeners' World* Live
  (National Exhibition Centre, Birmingham)
  Ticket hotline: (0870) 902 0555; www.necgroup.co.uk
- 16th to 18th June: Three Counties Show, Malvern
  Ticket hotline: (01684) 584924
- 4th to 9th July: Hampton Court Flower Show
  (Hampton Court Palace, East Molesey, Surrey)
- 26th to 30th July (provisional dates): RHS Flower Show, Tatton Park
  (Tatton Park, near Knutsford, Cheshire)
- 22nd to 24th Aug: Wisley Show
- 23rd and 24th Sept: Autumn Garden & Country Show, Malvern
  Ticket hotline: (01684) 584924

Unless otherwise given, for details of all these shows telephone the Royal Horticultural Society on (020) 7834 4333 or consult www.rhs.org.uk.

YORKSHIRE (N. & E. RIDING)

Two-starred gardens are marked on the map with a black square.

Aldby Park ★ [Historic Park and Garden Grade II*]

Buttercrambe, York YO41 1XU. Tel (01759) 371398

Mr and Mrs G.M.V. Winn • 7m NW of York off A166 Bridlington road. Turn left at sign to Buttercrambe and continue 0.5m past Gate Helmsley • Open two Suns for charity, and by appt • Entrance: £3, children £1 • Other information: Teas and other refreshments on open days only. Plants for sale in adjacent nursery ● <u>WC</u> �& ⬨

The fine 1726 house stands on a wooded hillside site which includes the mound and dry moat of King Edwin's seventh-century castle. The original terraced garden was created by Thomas Knowlton in 1746. In 1964 Mr Winn, who had known and loved the pre-war garden as a child, took over the house and began the huge task of restoring the garden. The result is a triumph – a truly romantic garden which lifts the heart as it reveals itself to you. A glimpse through ornamental trees leads to a grassy terrace around a mound, decked on the sunny side with daylilies, yuccas and agapanthus. Pale colours contrast with the dark yews and box and range from white and yellow to silver and pink. In shady areas electric-blue geraniums take over, and a band of hostas flourishes free of slugs, thanks to hungry hedgehogs. Golden elders, *Hypericum* 'Hidcote' and corkscrew hazels add interest. Now a steep drop to the river is revealed, and the path leads down to a grassy walk along the water's edge, where kingcups and primulas glow and dark ferns thrive. On the water are black swans, greylag geese and ducks. Back up towards the house, a 'Kiftsgate' rose has smothered a large yew tree, and fine shrub roses, selected for looks and fragrance, abound.

Arden Hall

Hawnby, York YO62 5LS. Tel: (01439) 798396

The Earl and Countess of Mexborough • 11m NE of Thirsk, 9m NW of Helmsley off B1257 • Open two or three times a year for charities, and possibly by prior appt to suitably interested parties • Entrance: £3 ● ▬ WC ⬨

Formerly the site of a Benedictine convent, the house (not open) was built in the eighteenth century, and the gardens are a series of formal terraces, dominated by a massive yew hedge at least 250 years old. A natural spring supplies four gallons of water a minute, a bonus imaginatively developed under the direction of gardener Stephen Mead. A formal Italianate pond is fed through a series of rills in stone troughs which pass through the terraces. An 27-metre-long laburnum walk and splendid borders have been made by the old croquet lawn. A 1920s' swimming pool (too cold for use) has been converted into a wildlife-oriented pond which flows into a stream and a series of pools before disappearing down the valley, rich in wild plants, especially wood garlic. Starting with a flourish of spring bulbs, the garden is at its fresh best from mid-May to mid-June.

Beningbrough Hall [Historic Garden Grade II]

Shipton–by–Beningbrough, York YO30 1DD. Tel: (01904) 470666

The National Trust • 8m NW of York off A19 York – Thirsk road at Shipton • House open as garden, but 3rd June to 29th Oct only, 12 noon – 5pm • Gardens open April to 29th Oct, Sat – Wed, plus Fris in July and Aug, 11am – 5.30pm (last admission 4.30pm); 4th Nov to March, Sat and Sun, 11am – 3.30pm • Entrance: £4.50, children £2.50, family £10 (house, galleries and gardens £7, children £3.50, family £16) • Entrance: Gardens and exhibitions £5.30, children £2.70, family £13 (house, gardens and exhibitions £6.30, children £3.20, family £14.50 (2005 prices) • Other information: Picnics in walled garden only ❶ 🍽 ✕ <u>WC</u> ♿ 🌿 🏛 🍴 ⚲

The main formal garden, made up of geometrically patterned parterres, was laid out at the time the house, with its superb Baroque interior, was built in 1716, but replaced during the late eighteenth century by sweeping lawns and specimen trees, part of an estate of 365 acres. This is essentially a pleasure garden with an historic framework, amongst which considerable recent planting has been integrated. The wilderness and two privy gardens have been restored to the original standards, and there is a nineteenth-century American garden and a Victorian conservatory. New planting has brought the main border and the walled garden back to life, including more than 5000 lavender plants, flowers for cutting, blocks of vegetables, and soft fruit, with vegetables surplus to the restaurant requirements sold in the shop.

Bolton Percy Churchyard

Bolton Percy, York YO23 7BA.

7.5m SW of York, 5m E of Tadcaster • Open all year, daily • Entrance: donation welcome ○ ♿ 🜄

The enthusiasm of one man has brought a wilderness under control in the splendid one-acre village churchyard, and it is now in all respects a paradise of garden plants growing in the new perennial style of gardening, with limited maintenance required – a lesson for churchwardens the country over. Roger Brook, who still maintains the churchyard, is now converting *Worsborough Village Cemetery* on the same principles [located five minutes from M1 at A61, near St Mary's Church, Birdwell, Worsborough].

Burnby Hall Gardens and Museum ★

The Balk, Pocklington, East Riding YO42 2QF. Tel: (01759) 307125

Stewart's Burnby Hall Gardens and Museum Trust • 13m E of York off A1079 in Pocklington • Open April to Sept, daily, 10am – 6pm • Entrance: £3.25, OAPs £2.60, children (5–15) £1.50, under 5 free. Parties of 20 or more £2.25 per person

❶ 🍽 🏠 <u>WC</u> 🌿 🏛 🍴 ⚲

When the gardens were established on eight acres of open farmland in 1904 by Major Stewart, the original ponds, which covered two acres, were constructed for fishing, but in 1935 they were converted to water-lily cultivation. The large collection of hardy water lilies here forms part of a National Collection. They may be seen from June to mid-September in a normal year, and in July and August the two lakes are covered in blooms from 80 different varieties.

Burton Agnes Hall

Burton Agnes, Driffield, East Riding YO25 4NB. Tel: (01262) 490324

Mrs Susan Cunliffe-Lister/Burton Agnes Preservation Trust Ltd • 5m S of Bridlington, 5m NE of Great Driffield on A166 • House open • Garden open mid-Feb for snowdrops, then April to Oct, daily, 11am – 5pm • Entrance: £2.75 (hall and garden £5.50, OAPs £5) • Other information: Gardeners' Fair 10th and 11th June

❶ ● ✕ 🖾 wc ♿ ⟠ ♨ ⛬ ♀ ⚘

The beautiful Elizabethan hall – designed by Robert Smythson, master mason to Elizabeth I and builder of Longleat and Hardwick – is approached through the gatehouse archway, up a wide gravel drive flanked by rows of fig-shaped yew hedges, with lawns beyond. Little evidence remains of the garden's history, any former flower planting in sight of the hall having succumbed to lawn on all sides. However, the walls of the former enormous kitchen garden conceal a riot of colour (including campanulas, thymes, clematis, hardy geraniums and old roses). The *potager* of vegetables and herbs supplies the needs of the household. There are two herbaceous borders, a scented garden, a jungle of bamboos and giant exotic species, and a maze. A series of large-scale games (including chess, draughts and snakes and ladders) is laid out on paving at the end of the walled garden. Behind the hall is a woodland garden and a one-mile arboretum walk. Adjoining is the English Heritage *Burton Agnes Manor House*, a rare example of a Norman house, open 'any reasonable time'.

Castle Howard ★★ [Historic Park Grade I]

York YO60 7DA. Tel: (01653) 648333

Castle Howard Estates Ltd • 17m NE of York, 5m SW of Malton off A64 • House open • Garden open March to early Nov, daily, 10am – 4.30pm. Special tours of woodland garden and rose gardens available for pre-booked parties • Entrance: £6.50, children (4–16) £4.50, (house, gardens and grounds £9.50, OAPs £8.50, children (4–16) £6.50) (2005 prices). Rates for garden tours on request ❶ ● ✕ 🖾 wc ♿ ⟠ ♨ ⛬ ♀ ⚘

Described as one of the finest examples of the heroic age of English landscape architecture, the house and grounds were first designed by Sir John Vanbrugh, assisted by Nicholas Hawksmoor. This architectural framework still basically exists, although over time features have been added, for example the impressive fountains designed by Nesfield. Although known principally as a fine landscape with remarkable park and buildings, there is also much for the garden lover. It holds one of the largest collections of old-fashioned and species roses in Europe. The Ray Wood and the adjacent area accommodate fine collections of magnolias, rhododendrons, sorbus and vacciniums, an adjunct to the newly extended arboretum, which will soon be one of the largest and most important in the country. An association has been formed between the Royal Botanic Gardens, Kew and Castle Howard to manage the wood. Most plants are well labelled.

Constable Burton Hall [Historic Park Grade II]

Leyburn, North Yorkshire DL8 5LJ. Tel: (01677) 450428

Mr Charles Wyvill • 16m NW of Ripon, 3m E of Leyburn on A684 • Open 21st March to 12th Oct, daily, 9am – 6pm. Tulip Festival 29th April to 1st May • Entrance: £3, OAPs £2.50, children 50p (honesty box) ◑ 🏠 wc & ⬤ 🍽

In a walled and wooded parkland setting is a perfect Palladian mansion designed by John Carr of York in 1768. Built of beautiful honey-coloured sandstone, it rises from the lawns shaded by fine mature cedars. A delightful terraced woodland garden of lilies, ferns, hardy shrubs, roses and wild flowers drops down to a lake enhanced by an eighteenth-century bridge (no access). Near to the entrance drive are a stream and rock garden, and a new lily pond has been added. This substantial garden is a pleasure to visit because, after placing their entry coins in the honesty box, visitors can follow the numbered directional arrows using the concise notes to pass from one area of the garden to another – a technique that many other gardens could use with advantage. Surprises abound, such as the yellow Turk's cap lily in profusion and many mad climbers and shade-loving ground-cover plants. A herbaceous garden and several grand borders (over 6000 tulips planted each year to spectacular effect in May) have replaced the old formal rose garden.

Duncombe Park [Historic Park Grade I]

Helmsley, North Yorkshire YO62 5EB.
Tel: (01439) 770213/771115 (during open hours)

Lord Feversham • 12m E of Thirsk, 1m SW of Helmsley off A170 • House and garden open May to Oct, Sun – Thurs – telephone for details. Parkland Centre and part of National Nature Reserve also open • Entrance: gardens and park £3.50, concessions £3, children (10 – 16) £1.75, parties of 15 or more £2.75 per person; park £2, children £1 (house, garden and park £6.50, concessions £5, children £3, family £13.50, parties of 15 or more £4.75 per person). Discounts for pre-booked parties visiting house and grounds • Other information: Parking at Parkland Centre. Alternative entrance for wheelchair users ◑ 🅿 ✗ 🏠 wc & ⬤ 🍽 🍴

Built in 1713, possibly with advice from Vanbrugh, it is the grass terrace, similar to that at nearby Rievaulx (see entry), for which the garden is justly famous. As Christopher Hussey observed, these two are 'unique, and perhaps the most spectacularly beautiful among English landscape conceptions of the 18th century'. From the Ionic rotunda a broad sweeping grass terrace stretches half a mile in extent, resembling a wonderful green crescent moon. It leads to another, grander temple in the Doric order, where the river in the valley below turns 300 degrees, giving the impression that the temple is set upon a promontory. Further back towards the house, partly hidden in woodland, is a conservatory built by Barry in 1851, of which only the central orangery remains intact. On either side of the house are sunken parterres originally laid out in 1846 and recently restored. The south parterre is planted as a white and grey garden, while its northern neighbour has a red and purple scheme. They contrast well with the huge yews partially encircling the perimeter, which in spring are bedecked with *Clematis montana*. The house dominates the great square lawn with its large figure of Father Time (attributed to

Van Nost and dating from 1715) sitting at the junction of grass and terrace. As a landscape it is a wonderfully simple composition – an essay in tones of green broken only by the extravagant display of a roaming peacock.

Fountains Abbey
(see STUDLEY ROYAL AND FOUNTAINS ABBEY)

Gilling Castle [Historic Park Grade II]
Gilling East, North Yorkshire YO62 4HP. Tel: (01439) 788238

The Ampleforth Abbey Trust • 20m N of York on B1363 York – Helmsley road • Great chamber and entrance hall of castle open by appt during term only • Garden open by appt, daily, 10am – 4pm • Entrance: donation to honesty box ◖

A lovely garden in outstanding scenery. The terraces have been constructed on the south-facing side, four of them tumbling down the slope from an expansive lawn at the top. Many old-fashioned flowers grow in the borders, with a backdrop of majestic trees.

Hackfall Wood [Historic Landscape Park Grade I]
Grewelthorpe, North Yorkshire. Tel: 01476 581135

Woodland Trust • 6m NW of Ripon off A6108, between Grewelthorpe and Masham • Open all year, daily • Entrance: free • Other information: The Ruin is available for holiday bookings – telephone the Landmark Trust on (01628) 825925 ○ 🐾 ⇗

The site is a spectacular gorge cut out by the River Ure. Now being restored after years of neglect, this romantic woodland garden, painted by Turner and praised by Wordsworth, was laid out by William Aislabie between 1750 and 1765 as a counterpoint to the splendour of Studley Royal (see entry) created by his father. In the 117 acres of entirely overgrown semi-natural scenery, paths lead to a pool, a grotto and a number of small Arcadian ruins. The ruin at Mowbray Point, on the western edge of the wood – the traditional climax to the woodland walk with fine views over the Ure valley and beyond – has recently been restored by the Landmark Trust, and a footpath in front of the building runs across the terrace, which is open between 11am and 4pm each day. Restoration of the paths, sometimes soggy, is underway. Spring sees masses of flowering wild garlic and bluebells, and tall ferns flourish in late summer amid beech, oak, ash and alder.

Harlow Carr Botanical Gardens
(see RHS GARDEN HARLOW CARR)

Helmsley Walled Garden
Cleveland Way, Helmsley YO62 5AH. Tel: (01439) 771427

Helmsley Walled Garden, Registered Charity • 12m E of Thirsk on A170, in centre of Helmsley, at rear of castle • Open April to Oct, daily, 10.30am – 5pm • Entrance: £3.50, OAPs £2.50, children free • Other information: Parking at Cleveland Way pay and display. Disabled parking at garden NEW ◖

The five-acre walled garden lying beneath the walls of Helmsley Castle, formerly the kitchen garden for Duncombe Park (see entry), was saved from total dereliction and ruin by the determination and vision of the late Alison Ticehurst. It is part demonstration garden, part show garden and part ornamental garden. The British Clematis Society use it as their National Display Garden and the enclosing walls are richly endowed with clematis as well as fruit trees. The display gardens include a small white garden laid out in memory of Diana, Princess of Wales, plus a wildflower meadow and a peony garden. Lavender and grasses flank part of the central walk, while beyond the dipping well rainbow borders in hues fading gradually from fiery reds and oranges to cool mauves, purples and blues are set between a hedge of purple beech. Some of the ground is used for the cultivation of organic vegetables and fruit. The glasshouses are being restored, and a Victorian vine collection has been established. The garden is dedicated to horticultural therapy and is very much a local community effort, being partly maintained with the help of a dedicated team of volunteers.

Humanby Grange

Wold Newton, Driffield YO25 3HS. Tel: (01723) 891636

Mr and Mrs T. Mellor • Midway between Bridlington and Scarborough, off A165 or B1249, 4m SW of Filey. House is between Wold Newton and Humanby on Burton Fleming-Fordon road. • Open April to Sept, Wed, 1 – 5pm; plus May, June and July, 1st Sun in month, 11am – 5pm • Entrance: £2.50, children free NEW ◑ ☕ WC ♿ 🐾

Situated three miles from the sea high on the chalk wolds, the garden has been carved slowly but steadily since 1984 from pasture land. Now generous shelter belts cut out the winds, and the garden has been further subdivided by hedges to create a series of characterful rooms. The orchard, underplanted with daffodils and camassias, with irises on the sunnier face, greets the visitor. To the north lies a pond and gravel garden complete with two ponds, one for goldfish and one for frogs. Beyond lies the croquet lawn, its eastern edge defined by a laburnum tunnel copied from the famous one at Barnsley House (see entry in Gloucestershire) – the owner once worked for Rosemary Verey. The tone changes yet again with the more intense planting of an enclosure created as an outdoor dining room and filled with plants for scent and autumn colour, a particular feature of the garden as a whole. On the windier east side of the house is a border of shrub roses underplanted with bulbs and hardy geraniums, all in grass, giving onto a bold circular lawn forming a hub, with 'hot' borders making a good contrast to the cool grasses and shrubs which went before. The woodland garden runs down to the tennis court, flanked by a border planted on a spoil mound with bold groups of shrubs; backing onto this a small copse is centred on a fine view of the open countryside. The large elliptical house lawn, with an almost 270-degree view, is even more exposed. Shrubs and some good island-bed planting abounds, revealing the same flare for originality: an old greenhouse base has been turned into an annual and biennial garden with an outdoor chess set. A well-designed and carefully thought-out garden with numerous subtle changes in atmosphere and mood.

Millgate House ★

Richmond, North Yorkshire DL10 4JN. Tel: (01748) 823571

Austin Lynch and Tim Culkin • In Richmond, in corner of Market Square opposite Barclays Bank • Open for special snowdrop days Feb and March (weather permitting) by appt only, then mid-March to mid-Oct, daily, 10am – 5.30pm, and at other times by appt • Entrance: £2 ◖ B&B

From the Market Square a green-painted door opens onto a corridor leading to a narrow stepped lane ('snicket' in the Yorkshire vernacular) set between house and boundary wall. Pots filled with bold foliage line the path, while a golden hop and a *Clematis montana* festoon the walls. The garden opens off to the right, laid out before the charming Regency-fronted house, and is composed of two comparatively small rectangles set on two different levels linked by broad rustic steps. The top area has a small naturalistic shaped lawn, but the space is dominated by a large *Rosa helenae* trained over an iron support in the shape of a medieval tent – an appropriate nod at Richmond's long military history. This is balanced by the house by a fine *Magnolia* x *kewensis* casting its shade over a small tank with a lion mask; the sound of water echoes that of the waterfalls on the River Swale in the valley below. The garden is particularly rich in old roses and there are well over forty different varieties scattered throughout the garden. These are allied with evergreen shrubs to give winter interest, including many specimens of variegated holly, yew and box. The underplanting is particularly skilful, never feeling contrived, just natural and generous. This delightful garden, like York Gate at Adel near Leeds (see entry), is a wonderful education in the art of handling a small restricted space.

Mount Grace Priory

Staddle Bridge, Northallerton, North Yorkshire DL6 3JG. Tel: (01609) 883494

English Heritage • 12m N of Thirsk, 7m NE of Northallerton on A19 • Open April to Sept, daily, 10am – 6pm; Oct, daily, 10am – 4pm; Oct to March, Thurs – Mon, 10am – 4pm. Closed 24th to 26th Dec, 1st Jan • Entrance: £3.60, concessions £2.70, children £1.80, family £9 ◑ 🍴 WC & ⚘ 🏛 ♿ ⚲

The ruins of the priory guest house, incorporated into a seventeenth-century manor, were combined in 1900–1901 with a larger house which is an important example of the Arts and Crafts Movement. The monks' cells in the monastery were occupied from 1398 to its dissolution in 1539, and each cell had its own garden. Some have been replanted, with the latest crop of herbs illustrating varieties used for medicinal purposes. The design of the cell-garden is in the form of paths and raised beds. A low box hedge surrounds the central bed, which is filled with blocks of herbs; every second year these follow a different theme. The one-acre early-twentieth-century garden of stepped terraces falling away from the house is being re-created, with rock plants spilling over the edges. There are shrubberies and narrow borders and a garden with ponds, colourful maples, rhododendrons and azaleas.

Nawton Tower ★

Highfield Lane, Nawton, York YO62 7TU. Tel: (01439) 771218

Mrs Sylvia Ward • 14.5m E of Thirsk, 2.5m NE of Helmsley, off A170 Scarborough road. In Nawton and Beadlam, turn left up Highfield Lane for 2m • Open 29th and 30th April, 1st, 6th, 7th, 13th, 14th, 20th, 21st, 27th, 28th, 29th May, 2 – 6pm; and at other times in spring by appt • Entrance: £1.50, children 75p ● ⇩ ℗

This remarkable, atmospheric 12-acre garden on the edge of the North York Moors was created during the 1930s by the Earl of Feversham. It consists of a series of formal grassy walks between living tapestries woven from a masterly selection of trees, rhododendrons, azaleas and old shrub roses. Every junction from the central walk leads to a fresh surprise: a statue on a pedimented gazebo as the focal point of another pathway; a yew-hedged topiary garden; a quiet contemplative clearing with a silent stone fountain at its centre. A magical experience.

Newby Hall and Gardens ★★ [Historic Garden Grade II*]

Ripon, North Yorkshire HG4 5AE. Tel: (0845) 450 4068

R. Compton • 4m SE of Ripon on B6265, 3m W of A1 • Open April to June and Sept, Tues – Sun and Bank Holiday Mons; July and Aug, daily; all 11am – 5.30pm • Entrance: £6.70, OAPs £5.70, children £5 (house and gardens £8.20, OAPs £7.20, children £5.70) • Other information: Wheelchairs available. Dogs in area adjacent to picnic area only. Events such as craft and plant fairs held in summer, with special admission prices ① ⬤ ✕ ▦ WC ♿ ℗ ⛐ ⛥ ⚲

The much-loved home of the Compton family, who have restored this famous Adam house to its original beauty and have renovated and developed 25 acres of award-winning gardens. Some features remain from the nineteenth century, such as the east-to-west walk marked by Venetian statuary and backed by yew and purple plum. The south front has long wide green slopes down to the River Ure, with herbaceous borders on either side backed by clipped yew hedges and flowering shrubs. Cross-walks lead to smaller gardens full of interest. These include species roses and tropical, autumn, rock and stepped water gardens, as well as a fine woodland area attributed to Ellen Willmott. A National Collection of cornus is here. There is also a garden restaurant, a children's adventure garden, a miniature railway and a woodland discovery walk. A contemporary sculpture park is open from June to September.

Norton Conyers

Wath, Nr Ripon HG4 5PQ. Tel: (01765) 640333

Sir James and Lady Graham • 4m N of Ripon off A61 on Ripon-Wath road. At Baldersby Gate flyover turn onto A61 for Ripon, right again at road signed to Melmerby • Open all year, Thurs, 10am – 4pm. Also 16th and 17th April, 23rd April to 20th Aug, Suns and Bank Holiday Mons; 3rd to 8th July, daily; all 2 – 5pm • Entrance: Free (house £5.50, OAPs £4, children under 16 free) [NEW] ① ▦ WC ♿ ⇩ ℗

Home to the Graham family for over nearly four centuries, Norton Conyers is perhaps best know for its connection with Charlotte Brontë, who visited in 1839 and used the house as a model for Thornfield Hall in *Jane Eyre*. To visit in June, when the drive is lined with milky-white cow parsley, one could believe little had changed. The house with its Dutch-style gables is of great antiquity and sits at the edge of a wide terrace separated from the park by a sweeping ha-ha, said to be the longest in Yorkshire; to the west lies the old bowling green where King Charles I once played. At the western end of the ha-ha, beyond the stables built in the 1780s, lies the old walled garden. Approaching from the rear, the newly restored eighteenth-century orangery commands a splendid vista, looking down flanking borders set between massive walls of yew before passing through a early-eighteenth-century wrought iron gate into the park beyond. The deep borders are filled with a traditional collection of herbaceous plants and shrubs. To the east is a broad peony border planted by the late Lady Graham for her 'peony parties'. Iris borders line the eastern cross-path, and in the north-east quarter a new garden is being developed.

Ormesby Hall

Ormesby, Middlesbrough, North Yorkshire TS7 9AS. Tel: (01642) 324188

The National Trust • 3m SE of Middlesbrough, W of A171 • Open 23rd March to Oct, Fri – Mon, 1.30 – 5pm • Entrance: £2.90, children £1.30 (house, garden, railway and exhibitions £4.10, children £2, family £10.50). Party rates available • Other information: Disabled parking near house. Braille guide available. Dogs on leads, in park only ❶ 🅿 🍽 ♿ 🏛 ♟ ✂

There have been recent developments in the gardens, including the reintroduction of the original ironwork fencing and the planting of many new bulbs and shrubs. The main rose beds have been renewed, and further ground-cover planting is taking place in the Holly Walk. The hall itself is licensed for wedding ceremonies, and the stable block is used by the local mounted police.

Parcevall Hall Gardens ★ [Historic Garden Grade II]

Skyreholme, Skipton, North Yorkshire BD23 6DE. Tel: (01756) 720311

Walsingham College (Yorkshire Properties) Ltd • 10m NE of Skipton, 1m NE of Appletreewick off B6265 Pateley Bridge – Skipton road • Open April to Oct, daily, 10am – 6pm, in winter by appt, and for NGS • Entrance: £3.50, children 50p • Other information: Teas available – for opening times telephone (01756) 720630. Picnics in orchard only ❶ 🅿 🍽 WC ♿ 🐕 🏛

Purchased in 1926 by Sir William Milner Bt., a godson of Queen Mary, the garden is set on a steep hillside with a glorious view to a craggy distant peak known as 'Simon's Seat'. Broad graceful terraces follow the slope, and the whole composition is strongly in the Arts and Crafts tradition, respecting local vernacular style. The planting has been sympathetically renovated and includes a border of hardy fuchsias, a white border and two fine *Prunus* x *yedoensis* 'Shidare-yoshino'. A newly planted orchard containing old late flowering apple varieties flanks the red borders which form the finale. The garden and its environs lie on the South Craven Fault, so above the house a magnificent rock garden was created by stripping away the thin soil to expose the bedrock. The result, set within light woodland and bisected by small streams, is spectacular. Masses of Himalayan poppies enjoy the dappled shade, while in summer the air is rich with the scent of the *Primula florindae* naturalised amongst the rocks and little rills. Below, a rose garden said to be based on a traditional Mogul design (Sir William's sister, Lady Linlithgow, was a Vicereine of India) has been replanted with modern English varieties. A camellia walk leads back down the hill towards the beck, where the acid soil is ideal for rhododendrons, many unique to the garden. Set within the Dales National Park, with only the call of the corncrake to be heard instead of the ubiquitous hum of traffic, such an utterly peaceful place, with so glorious a view, deserves to be much better known.

Plumpton Rocks [Historic Park Grade II*]

Plumpton, Knaresborough HG5 8NA. Tel: (01289) 386360

Edward de Plumpton Hunter • Midway between Harrogate and Wetherby, 1m SE of A661 junction with Harrogate S bypass • Open March to Oct, Sat, Sun and Bank Holiday Mons, 11am – 6pm • Entrance: £2, concessions £1 • Other information: Guided tours by arrangement ◑ 🐾 ⟁

This is not so much a garden as a dramatic natural feature enhanced by man. Owned by the Plumpton family since the 1080s, the present Lord of the Manor of Plumpton represents the 27th generation of the family. The estate was acquired around 1750 by Daniel Lascelles, who set about creating the wonderful pleasure grounds painted by Turner and surviving today. Two thousand mixed trees were set out in 'plumps': 'acorns, beech mastes, chestnuts and fir seeds of all sortes were sown and left to take their chances'. In 1757 he gave instructions for a huge number of flowering shrubs and evergreens to be planted. On Lascelles' death the estate passed to his cousin, the owner of Harewood, and it remained in the ownership of the Harewood family until 1950, when it passed back to the Plumptons. Within the 30 acres is a six-acre lake (originally a string of fishponds), and paths run over the massive reddish-purple rocks, under the rocks, alongside the lake and through woodlands. It is impossible to become tired of this imposing yet restful place.

RHS Garden Harlow Carr ★

Crag Lane, Harrogate, North Yorkshire HG3 1QB. Tel: (01423) 565418

Royal Horticultural Society • 1.5m W of Harrogate on B6162 Otley road • Open all year, daily, 9.30am – 6pm (closes 4pm Nov to March) (last entry 1 hour before closing) • Entrance: £6, accompanied children 6–16 £1.60, under 6 free, parties of 10 or more £4.60 • Other information: Manual wheelchairs for loan. Guide dogs only ○ 🍵 ✕ 🐾 WC ♿ 🌿 🏛 🎁 ✎

Acquired by the RHS in 2001, Harlow Carr had been the home of the Northern Horticultural Society since 1949. The 58 acres are currently subject to an extensive programme of renewal and redevelopment which will take several years to complete. The beautifully planted streamside, criss-crossed by numerous picturesque 'packhorse' bridges, is still an object lesson in such planting and justly famous for its wonderful strain of candelabra primulas. From the lake a magnificent avenue rolls through the woodland and into the arboretum, passing a broad wildflower meadow and bird hide. Elsewhere are display and trial gardens, including a large herb garden, a shrub rose walk, a scented garden and a border of ornamental grasses. A kitchen garden has been created using the raised-bed system, separated from the neighbouring fruit garden by modern herbaceous borders, and during the summer of 2005 the old long walk, leading from the former entrance gates to the streamside, was replanted with perennials in the fashionable prairie style. To celebrate the RHS bicentenary in 2004, the BBC commissioned a landmark gardening series, 'Gardens through Time'. Seven gardens were created exploring fashions and tastes from the Regency period through the Victorian era and to the twentieth century, concluding with a contemporary garden designed by Diarmuid Gavin. Harlow Carr may not be as extensive as Wisley, its southern sister, but in its position and diversity it more than holds its own.

Richmond Castle (The Cockpit Garden)

Richmond DL10 4QW Tel: (01748) 822493

English Heritage • In centre of Richmond, off Market Square • Open April to Sept, daily, 10am – 6pm; Oct to March, Thurs – Mon, 10am – 4pm. Closed 24th to 26th Dec and 1st Jan • Entrance: £3.60, concessions £2.70, children £1.80, family £9
NEW ○

The garden was designed by Neil Swanson in 2002 as part of English Heritage's initiative to create contemporary gardens within historic spaces. The Cockpit lies at the foot of the Gold Hole Tower and may once have been the Privy Garden. The ground slopes towards the river in the valley below and has been laid out as a recreational and performance space on a series of grass terraces. On the upper one, dominated by a large old apple tree, a topiary garden has been made, but to a strikingly modern design. Yew circles of varying size are set in a gravel walk, each representing one of the sixteen 'Absolutists', conscientious objectors who were held in the castle jail during the First World War. Below, a yew hedge skirts around the space and provides a suitable backdrop for a modern interpretation of an herbaceous border, using grasses as a backbone. Oriental poppies, Japanese anemones, euphorbias and rudbeckias, arranged in big bold patches, bring a continuous display of colour and form. Against the outer bailey the wall is covered with shrubs. Both contemporary and complementary to its setting, the garden can only improve over time as the hedges develop and mature.

Rievaulx Terrace ★ [Historic Park Grade I]

Rievaulx, Helmsley, North Yorkshire YO6 5LJ. Tel: (01439) 798340

The National Trust • 10m E of Thirsk, 2.5m NW of Helmsley on B1257 • Open 18th March to 5th Nov, daily, 10am – 6pm (last admission 5pm) (closes 5pm Oct, last admission 4pm). Ionic temple closed 1 – 2pm • Entrance: £3.80, children £3, family £9.60, parties £3.20 per person (2005 prices) • Other information: Coach park. Possible for wheelchairs but steps to temples. Electric runaround available for pre-booking; one manual wheelchair also available. Exhibition of landscape design in basement of Ionic temple ◑ 🐝 <u>WC</u> ⬙ ♿ ♟ ♘

This is a unique example of the eighteenth-century passion for the romantic and the picturesque – that is, making landscape look like a picture. The work was done at the behest of the third Thomas Duncombe around 1754 and consists of a half-mile-long serpentine grass terrace high above Ryedale with fine views of the great ruins of one of the finest of all of Britain's Cistercian abbeys. At one end is a Palladian Ionic temple-cum-banqueting-house with furniture by William Kent and elaborate ceilings, at the other a Tuscan temple with a raised platform, from which are views to the Rye Valley. The concept is wonderfully achieved, its beauty breath-taking. Those who want to see flowers must concentrate their attention on the grass bank below the terrace, which is managed for wildflower content – fine displays of cowslips, primroses, orchids, violets, bird's foot trefoils, ladies' bedstraws, etc. Blossom throughout the spring season comes from cherries, blackthorns, rowans, whitebeams, elders and lilacs.

Ripley Castle [Historic Park Grade II]

Ripley, Harrogate, North Yorkshire HG3 3AY. Tel: (01423) 770152

Sir Thomas Ingilby, Bt • 3.5m N of Harrogate off A61 Harrogate – Ripon road • Castle open June to Sept, daily; Jan to March, Sat and Sun; Oct, April and May, Tues, Thurs, Sat and Sun; all 10.30am – 3pm • Entrance: £4, OAPs £3.50, children £2.50. Parties of 25 or more £3.50 per person • Other information: Guide dogs only ○ 🍽 ✕ 🏪 <u>WC</u> ♿ ⚲ ⚓ 🕯 �’ B&B

The mid-eighteenth-century 'Capability' Brown landscape with formal gardens has been developed by Peter Aram for a family that has lived here since the fourteenth century. The formal areas have been completely restored and the huge herbaceous borders – a total of 110 metres long – are amongst the most spectacular in the north of England. Other features include a lake with an attractive Victorian iron bridge, an eighteenth-century orangery and summerhouses. There are fine displays of snowdrops and bluebells, and magnificent specimen trees. A woodland walk leads to a temple with fine views, and a lakeside walk takes the visitor through the deer park, while some of the ancient oaks and chestnuts are believed to be over 1,000 years old. Extensive plantings of a rich variety of spring-flowering bulbs have been made to complement a National Collection of hyacinths. The tropical plant collection formerly owned by Hull University is now here in the restored listed greenhouses, and the vegetable garden has rare species adopted from the Henry Doubleday Research Association. Nearby, at the arts centre in Knaresborough, is a 'garden of the senses' designed for *Henshaw's College* for children with disabilities. Telephone (01423) 886451 for details.

Scampston Hall

Malton YO17 8NG. Tel: (01944) 759111

Sir Charles and Lady Legard • 5m E of Malton off A64 York – Scarborough road • House open 22nd June to 23rd July, daily except Mon, 1.30 – 5pm (last entry 4pm) • Walled garden open 15th April to 15th Oct, daily except Mon (but open Bank Holiday Mons), 10am – 5pm. Also open for parties of 20 or more, and for special garden tours, by appt • Entrance: £5, concessions £4.50, children (12–16) £3 • Other information: Cookery courses and demonstrations for adults and children – for further information telephone (01944) 759000 ◑ 🍽 ✕ <u>WC</u> ♿ ⚲

The handsome bow-fronted house, externally of the early 1800s, sits at the heart of the 70-acre park laid out by 'Capability' Brown; traces also remain of Bridgeman's earlier landscape and of a garden he probably also designed. In 1998 the present generation of Legards commissioned Piet Oudolf to create a remarkable modern garden within the derelict four-and-a-half acre walled kitchen garden. His design divides the space into a series of beech-hedged compartments, each with a distinctive character. Along the long wall, backing onto the house, a 500-metre-long border walk runs under an avenue of limes. The border is densely planted with spring-flowering shrubs and underplanted with *Paeonia rockii, Tetrapanax papyrifer, Comptonia peregrina* and *Edgeworthia chrysantha*. Stretching almost the length of the parallel wall is a huge glasshouse divided into three compartments with a high-roofed and projecting conservatory as the centrepiece. The heart of the garden is taken up by a perennial meadow displaying a rich palette of reds, yellows, purples and oranges. Other areas feature giant clipped cubes of box and double banked yew hedges clipped in contrapuntal waves, surrounded by herbaceous borders; a flat-topped grass pyramid some three metres high complete with stone steps provides a spectacular viewing point over the entire garden. This is Oudolf at his inventive and confident best fulfilling his largest private commission to date – an historic garden of the future.

Shandy Hall

Coxwold, York YO61 4AD. Tel: (01347) 868465

The Laurence Sterne Trust • 18m N of York, 7m SE of Thirsk. From York, take A19 towards Thirsk, turn off to Easingwold and follow signs to Coxwold. From crossroads go 150 metres past church • House open May to Sept, Wed and Sun, 2 – 4.30pm • Garden open May to Sept, daily except Sat, 11am – 4.30pm • Entrance: £2.50 (house and garden £4.50, children £1.50) • Other information: Refreshments in village nearby. Permanent Sterne exhibition ❶ 🏠 WC ♿ 🐕 🌿 🏛 🍽

A delightful small-scale, three-part garden, full of year-round interest, surrounds the pretty fifteenth-century cottage in which Laurence Sterne wrote *Tristram Shandy* during the 1760s. In the Barn Garden, borders of herbaceous plants and shrub roses enfold on three sides, with a view out to Byland Abbey and the North York Moors beyond. The Old Garden is approached through a small orchard where some of the gnarled trees are covered with climbing roses. A wide selection of old-fashioned roses in raised beds against drystone walls is interspersed with herbaceous planting in which careful thought is given to plant associations for colour and form. The foliage of a silver poplar provides a perfect backdrop for shrub roses such as 'Kassel', 'Fantin-Latour' and 'La Reine Victoria'. The third section is a surprise – a garden created within a long-abandoned adjacent quarry and devoted mainly to a wonderful display of wild flowers underplanted with bulbs. Starting in the spring with narcissi and then bluebells, the tree-fringed quarry garden changes colour through the year, from yellow to blue to pink, then purple (in July) and on to a deep bosky green, punctuated by clematis and climbing roses, before moving into autumn colours. Four magnificent ash trees form a centrepiece, and grassy paths wind through its undulations, past rustic seats and bowers.

Sledmere House [Historic Park Grade I]

Sledmere, Great Driffield, East Riding YO25 3XG. Tel: (01377) 236637

Sir Tatton Sykes, Bt • 9m NW of Great Driffield off A166. Signposted • House open
• Garden open April to Sept, Wed – Fri, Sun; plus 14th to 17th April and Bank
Holiday Sats, Suns and Mons; all 11am – 4.30pm • Entrance: £4, children £1
(house, park and garden £6, OAPs £5.50, children £2) ◑ ⬛ ✕ 🍴 <u>wc</u> ♿ ⌖ ✿ 🏛 ❢
✆ B&B

Sledmere is among the best-preserved of 'Capability' Brown's landscape schemes.
Dating from the 1770s, it clearly reveals his characteristic belting and clumping of
trees and carefully controlled diagonal vistas to distant 'eye-catchers'. His use of a
ha-ha allows the park to flow up to the windows of the house (whence it is best
seen) across extensive tree-planted lawns. To the rear of the house is a well-stocked
herbaceous border and parterre. The eighteenth-century walled gardens are planted
mainly with roses, herbaceous plants and fruit trees, and there is an attractive iron
pergola running the length of this area.

Sleightholme Dale Lodge

Fadmoor, Kirbymoorside, North Yorkshire YO62 7JG. Tel: (01751) 431942

Dr and Mrs O. James • 20m NE of Thirsk, 3m N of Kirbymoorside, 1m from
Fadmoor off A170 Thirsk – Scarborough road • Open for NGS and NHS, and by
appt in writing • Entrance: £2.50, children 50p • Other information: self-catering
cottages available ◑ 🍴 wc ⌖

The garden occupies a unique position on the side of a wooded valley opening onto
the moors. In the spring it is a blaze of blossom, wild daffodils and azaleas, and
through the summer the walled garden, which runs steeply up the hill to the north,
is breathtaking in the colour and exuberance of its parallel borders. It has been
described as 'a gardeners' garden' and there are many rare plants to be seen, notably
meconopsis. Descending terraces, built at the beginning of the century to the south
of the house, have deep shrubberies, and a grass platform at the bottom separated
from the meadow beyond by a ha-ha. A fine series of steps runs down through the
terraces.

Stillingfleet Lodge ★

Stillingfleet, York YO19 6HP. Tel: (01904) 728506

Mr and Mrs J. Cook • 6m S of York. From A19 York – Selby road take B1222 signed
to Sherburn in Elmet. In Stillingfleet turn opposite church; garden is at end of lane
• Open May to July, Wed, Fri and Sat; Aug and Sept, Wed and Fri; all 1 – 4pm.
Plus 7th May and 18th June, 1.30 – 5pm, for NGS • Entrance: £2.50, children 50p
• Other information: Parking and plants for sale at nursery ◑ ⬛ 🍴 wc ♿ ✿ ✆

An eclectic and most attractive garden has been unfolding here since the owners
started developing their windswept plot sloping down to the River Fleet in 1974.
Vanessa Cook is a notable plantswoman with an instinctive feeling for both naturalistic and formal planting styles. The wilder areas which include a meadow, a grassy
walk dominated by beehives and wild flowers, a nature trail and a large pool

generously fringed with exotic and native species have no quarrel with the magnificently ordered double herbaceous borders, furnished with trees, shrubs and many bulbs for year-long colour interest. Many climbing roses and clematis, and a good use of foliage plants in soft colours, give the garden a romantic feel. Rare breeds of poultry make their own contribution to the atmosphere. A National Collection of pulmonarias is here. The nursery, well stocked with unusual plants, is also well worth a visit. [Open April to mid-Oct, Wed, Fri and Sat, 10am – 4pm. (Closed Sat in Aug.)]

Studley Royal and Fountains Abbey ★★ [Historic Park Grade I]

Ripon, North Yorkshire HG4 3DY. Tel: (01765) 608888

The National Trust • 4m SW of Ripon, 9m N of Harrogate. Follow Fountains Abbey sign off B6265 Ripon – Pateley Bridge road • Deer park open all year during daylight hours. Abbey and garden open all year, daily except 24th, 25th Dec and Fridays from Nov to Jan, 10am – 5pm (closes 4pm Oct to March, or dusk if earlier). Free guided tours April to Oct, daily • Entrance: Studley park free. Abbey, mill and garden £6.50, children £3.50, family £17.50. Special rates for pre-booked coach parties – telephone (01765) 643197 • Other information: Parking free at main visitor centre car park but £3 at Studley park (pay-and-display, NT members free). Self-drive powered runarounds available by prior booking ○ 💷 🖥 WC & 🕸 🅿 🏛 ⓘ ℀

The gardens of Studley Royal were created by John Aislabie, who had been Chancellor of the Exchequer but whose career was ended by his involvement with the South Sea Bubble in 1720; he retreated to his estate in 1722 and worked until his death in 1742 to make the finest water garden in the country. The lakes, formal canals and water features, with buildings such as the Temple of Piety, turned what is essentially a landscape with large trees and sweeping lawns into one of the most beautiful green gardens in the world. The views from Colen Campbell's Banqueting House are remarkable. Then there is its intimate and dramatic relationship with Fountains Abbey – probably the noblest monastic ruin in Christendom – visible at first only distantly from the Surprise View, a door in a small building. Studley Royal Park is deservedly a World Heritage Site. Restoration of Anne Boleyn's seat, a timber gazebo with a fine view, is now complete, and a further £10 million is being sought to continue a major programme of restoration.

Sutton Park ★

Sutton-in-the-Forest, York YO61 1DP. Tel: (01347) 810249/811239

Sir Reginald and Lady Sheffield • 8m N of York on B1363 • House open April to Sept, Sun, Wed, and Bank Holiday Mons, plus 14th April, 1.30 – 5pm. Private parties by appt at other times • Gardens open April to Sept, daily, 11am – 5pm • Entrance: £3.50, concessions £2.50, children £1 (house and gardens £6, concessions £5, children £3.50, parties of 15 or more £5.50 per person) • Other information: Coaches by appt (£3 per person). Specialist plant fair 4th June ◑ 💷 ✕ 🖥 WC & 🕸 🏛 ⓘ ℀

Moving reluctantly from Normanby Hall (see entry in Lincolnshire) in 1962, Nancie Sheffield, herself a keen and knowledgeable gardener, engaged Percy Cane to help redesign the garden. They set about enclosing part of the park laid out originally in the 1750s by Adam Meikle, a follower of 'Capability' Brown, and planted three terraces, each with a distinct and different character. Large panels of lawn and crisp paving characterise the topmost one, flanked by borders filled with shrubs, old roses and herbaceous perennials, with a wisteria tumbling out of a large old conifer. Broad steps lead on down past a fine Judas tree to a narrower terrace with a double parterre punctuated by eight weeping pears clipped to resemble silvery green umbrellas. On the lowest terrace a beech hedge marks the boundary while a magnificent cedar of Lebanon gave an instant air of maturity. This terrace became a water garden with a stone-edged canal pool characteristic of Cane's work; a pair of white painted wirework gazebos festooned with roses act as full stops at either end. To the west the garden becomes more natural. An old Edwardian rock garden is being developed as a fernery, and beyond some fine old trees stretches a long low laburnum walk. Since 1997 the garden has been developed further by the present generation, and the old walled kitchen garden is now a wildflower maze, with a smaller organic kitchen garden created in its stead.

Thorp Perrow Arboretum and Woodland Garden ★ [Historic Arboretum Grade II]

Bedale, North Yorkshire DL8 2PR. Tel: (01677) 425323

Sir John Ropner, Bt • 10m N of Ripon, 2m S of Bedale, signed off B6268 Masham road • Open all year, daily, dawn – dusk • Entrance: £5.75, OAPs and concessions £4.40, children (4–16) £2.95 • Other information: Electric wheelchair available. Tea room open mid-Feb to mid-Nov, thereafter weekends only ○ 🍴 🍽 <u>WC</u> & ⚐ ⚒ 🏛 ❢ ⚲

The arboretum was established many years ago and has one of the finest collections of trees in England, containing over 2000 species. Within the 85 acres is a Victorian pinetum, sixteenth-century woodland and National Collections of ash, limes, laburnums and walnuts. You can follow the tree trail, the nature trail or simply amble at your own leisure. Thousands of naturalised daffodils and bluebells in spring, glorious wild flowers in summer and stunning autumn colour. There are new plantings, a new one-acre bog garden with raised walkway, and continual improvements in the arboretum. Falconry demonstrations and children's play area.

Valley Gardens ★ [Historic Public Park Grade II]

Valley Drive, Harrogate, North Yorkshire. Tel: (01423) 500600

Harrogate Borough Council • In centre of Harrogate; main entrance near Pump Room Museum and Mercer Art Gallery • Open all year, daily during daylight hours • Entrance: free • Other information: Art exhibition 29th May, 25th to 27th July, 28th Aug in Sun Pavilion (also available for events – telephone (01423) 522588 for details) ○ 🍴 🍽 <u>WC</u> & ⚐ ❢ ⚲

One of the best-known public gardens in the north of England, laid out earlier this century at the time Harrogate was fashionable as a spa. The Sun Pavilion has been restored. The standard of formal bedding remains high, and the dahlia border gives a fine display in late summer. Children will enjoy the range of activities on offer – paddling and boating pools, a play area, tennis courts, a pitch-and-putt course and crazy golf.

Wytherstone Gardens

Pockley, York YO62 7TE. Tel: (01439) 770012

Lady Clarissa Collin • 15m E of Thirsk, 2.5m NE of Helmsley off A170. In Pockley, past church • Open June to Aug, Wed, 1 – 5pm, and by appt • Entrance: £2.50 (2005 price) ● WC ♨

A large, expanding and enchanting plantsman's garden created from a greenfield site over thirty-five years, with a wide range of rare shrubs, trees and perennials not normally considered hardy in the north of England, such as *Melianthus major*, thriving and flowering year after year. It consists of a series of garden rooms, inter-linked so that the whole is revealed little by little. The spring garden is a riot of colour with azaleas, rhododendrons, meconopsis, trilliums and other ericaceous plants. This leads into a Mediterranean garden and a small rock garden, home to some rather rare alpines. The front of the house is covered in pineapple brooms and carpenterias. Behind the 3-metre-high beech hedges are smaller spaces, each with its own individual feel. A pathway meanders along a large terrace made of railway sleepers up to a secret doorway; beyond lie a young arboretum and a wildlife pond, and steps flanked by peony borders lead to the colour-themed and highly scented conservatory garden where roses threaten to smother the trees.

PARKS AND GARDENS DATA PARTNERSHIP

A major new national database is being set up under the aegis of the Association of Gardens Trusts, the Welsh Historic Gardens Trust and the University of York, funded by a £1-million grant from the Heritage Lottery Fund. This ambitious three-year project, which will complement English Heritage's *Register* of fewer than 1600 properties, aims ultimately to make available to the general public detailed information on some 30,000 historic parks, gardens and landscapes throughout Britain. The initial database will be established in 2006 and some 6000 records provided by 2008.

POSTCODE PLANTS DATABASE

It is often difficult to find out which plants are local to an area. The Postcode Plants Database locates the names of flowers, trees, butterflies and birds for each of Britain's 26 million home addresses. The website is www.nhm.ac.uk/science/projects/fff; simply by typing in the first four characters of their postcode, householders, schools, garden centres and councils can obtain tailor-made lists of local plants which are both hospitable and garden-worthy. Also included are the names of butterflies and birds most likely to visit gardens in each area. The lists come from innovative software, developed by Royal Mail and *FLORA-for-FAUNA* in conjunction with the Natural History Museum, which searches through hundreds of distribution maps of fauna and flora in the British Isles.

YORKSHIRE (S. & W. AREA)

Bramham Park ★ [Historic Park Grade I]

Wetherby LS23 6ND. Tel: (01937) 846000

Mr G. Lane Fox • 10m NE of Leeds, 15m SW of York, 5m S of Wetherby just off northbound A1 • House open to parties of 10 or more by written appt only • Garden open April to Sept, daily, 11.30am – 4.30pm (closed for horse trials and Leeds Festival: please telephone for dates) • Entrance: £4, OAPs/children £2, under 5s free. Reduced rates for parties of 20 or more ◐ 🍽 🏠 <u>WC</u> ♿ ⟐ 🏮

Created by Robert Benson after the style of Le Nôtre nearly 300 years ago, this is one of the most important formal landscape gardens in the French style to survive in this country. Although a great storm early in 1962 caused extensive damage to trees and avenues, the original concept has been maintained and the layout restored. Apart from their unique design, the gardens also have a fine spring flowering, a substantial rose garden providing summer-long colour, and an interesting herbaceous border replanted in typical English style by Mary Keen and John Sales. However, it is the splendid architectural features (such as the Gothic pavilion) combined with trees and water that are outstanding. Mary Keen has termed it 'forest gardening' – a genre practised by generations of the owner's family. In 1991 the remains of a massive eighteenth-century cascade were found.

Brodsworth Hall [Historic Garden Grade II*]

Brodsworth, Doncaster DN5 7XJ. Tel: (01302) 722598

English Heritage • 5m NW of Doncaster. Access from A1(M) junction 37 off A635 • House open as garden, but from 1pm • Garden open April to Sept, Tues – Sun and Bank Holiday Mons, 12 noon – 5.30pm, Oct to March, Sat and Sun, 11am – 4pm • Entrance: £4.50, concessions £3.50, children £2.50 (hall and gardens £6.50, concessions £5, children £3.50) ◐ 🍽 ✕ 🏠 <u>WC</u> ♿ 🌿 🏛 🏮 ✎

The 15 acres were designed and planted when the Italianate house was being built in the mid-1860s on a site with many fine established trees. It also featured a long, deep quarry dating from the eighteenth century. Main features in the garden are tamed evergreen shrubberies and a border where trimmed shrubs are underplanted with Japanese anemones, daylilies, aconites, ferns and fuchsias. Beyond, around a marble fountain, an intricate bedding scheme uses the original shapes cut in the lawn and filled with such delights as tulips and nineteenth-century pelargonium varieties. Trees overhanging the old quarry shade a maze of walkways and bridges in fine rockwork offering vistas into the recently restored fern dell. Cooled by an elegant cascade, it is planted with an historic collection of period ferns together with shrubs, bulbs, herbaceous perennials and dwarf conifers. This part of the garden and the rose garden have been restored and planted. The lawns are rich in natural flora. A collection of the Portland group of roses has been planted here, along with other historic varieties, and a large herbaceous border provides a fine backdrop. The woodland garden near the house has been restored, with new paths and planting.

East Riddlesden Hall

Bradford Road, Riddlesden, Bradford BD20 5EL. Tel: (01535) 607075

The National Trust • 1m NE of Keighley off B6265, 3m NW of Bingley • House open • Garden open April to 5th Nov, Sat, Sun, Tues and Wed, 12 noon – 5pm. Also open Good Friday, Bank Holiday Mons and Mons in July and Aug. Parties must pre-book • Entrance: £4, accompanied children £2, family £ ◐ 💷 🏰 <u>WC</u> ♿ ⬧ ♿ 🏘 💡 ⚲

Set on a promontory overlooking the River Aire, there has been a dwelling on the site since at least AD680. The oldest parts of the present house date from the thirteenth century, although it was 'modernised' in 1640 and a later eighteenth-century west wing was partially demolished in 1905. Seen across the small lake, the house with its large rose window presents a particularly romantic prospect. The garden on the south face was laid out in the 1970s by the late Graham Stuart Thomas, with a simple holly hedge partly enclosing the site and pyramidal fruit trees lining a central path. A sunken rose garden wraps around the surviving west facade, and the ghostly outline of the whole wing has been traced by a chequered pattern of standard acacias planted on a strip of lawn. Further west still an old orchard containing a number of old varieties of apple traditional to Yorkshire gardens is being developed as a wild garden in homage to William Robinson and Gertrude Jekyll. A fragrant medicinal herb border based on Culpeper's *Herbal* lies at the foot of the east front of the house, overlooking a grass maze and picnic area in the meadow beside the riverbank.

Golden Acre Park ★

Otley Road, Leeds. Tel: (0113) 246 3504

Leeds City Council • NW of Leeds off A660 Leeds – Otley road at approach to Bramhope • Open all year, daily, during daylight hours • Entrance: free ○ 💷 WC & ⬧ 🏘 ⚲

Until 1945, when it was purchased by Leeds Corporation for £18,500, this was a privately owned pleasure park. Since then it has been developed as an important public park and minor botanic garden. It stands on a pleasant undulating site leading down to a lake, and has an extensive tree collection. Rhododendrons are a feature, together with alpine plants both in the rock garden and the alpine house. The park is noted for its fine collection of sempervivums and heathers. Demonstration plots are maintained where instruction is provided for home gardeners; the quality of planting and vegetables improves annually.

Harewood House ★ [Historic Park and Garden Grade I]

Harewood, Leeds LS17 9LQ. Tel: (0113) 218 1010

The Earl and Countess of Harewood • 7m N of Leeds on A61 • House open, 11am – 4.30pm • Grounds open 4th Feb to Oct, daily, Nov to mid-Dec, Sat and Sun, all 10am – 4pm • Entrance: Grounds and bird garden £8.25, OAPs £7.50, children £5.50, freedom ticket £11, OAPs £9.50, children £6.50 • Other information: Regular garden tours and talks programme ◕ 💷 ✕ 🏰 <u>WC</u> & ⬧ ⬧ 💡 ⚲

In 1772 'Capability' Brown was commissioned to 'improve' the park surrounding a new mansion built by Carr of York. The natural terrain was much in his favour, and his refashioned landscape, described as 'most delectable' by Dorothy Stroud, was painted by Turner. He would still recognise the park, but the house was 'Italianised' in 1843 by Sir Charles Barry, who also laid out a broad terrace. His elaborate box parterre with its mile of hedging has been restored and planted with blue hyacinths in spring and heliotropes in summer – the effect against the yellow-tinged stone of the house and walls is quite stunning. A broad herbaceous border, mixing perennial and tender plants as in Victorian days, continues the soft pastel colour scheme. On the upper west terrace a simple and sophisticated modern garden was laid out by David Hicks in 1993, with hornbeam hedging reflecting the massive bulk of the house centred around a terracotta dolphin fountain. Beneath the bastion wall, as a contrast to the cool subtle colours directly round the house, lies another border planted with 'hot' colours, using many tender subjects not readily associated with Yorkshire gardens. Behind Carr's stable block lies the famous Bird Garden, where the geographical zones are defined by plants; this leads on to a woodland garden densely planted in the nineteenth century with a fine collection of rhododendrons. At the head of the lake lies the Himalayan garden, a sunken glade originally laid out in the 1770s and now graced by a stupa, a Buddhist memorial shrine built of local stone under the supervision of a Bhutanese lama. In the old walled garden a spiral labyrinth was installed in 1999 – the family's interest in developing house and grounds continues unabated.

Hillsborough Walled Garden

Middlewood Road, Sheffield S6 4HD. Tel: (0114) 281 2167

Hillsborough Community Development Trust • Adjacent to Hillsborough Library • Open all year, Mon – Fri, 9am – 5pm (closes 4.30pm Fri), Sat and Sun (during summer months only), 2 – 5pm, and Bank Holidays (check before travelling) • Entrance: free but donations welcome • Other information: Parking for disabled only ○ 🖢 🕮 🕭 🕭 🕮 🕭 ℚ

The peaceful site embraces four different gardens: a wildlife area, a lawn with herbaceous borders, a woodland glade and a formal garden with raised beds for easy use by disabled gardeners. There are many architectural features, and varied gardens including herb, a vegetable and nursery gardens, a Georgian heated wall and a garden for the visually impaired. Planned, created and run by the community, this is not just an area to look at and enjoy, but everyone is encouraged to help with its upkeep – tools are available on site and plants always welcomed.

The Hollies Park ★

Weetwood Lane, Leeds LS16 5NZ. Tel: (0113) 247 8361 (Parks and Countryside)

Leeds City Council • In NW Leeds, off A660 Leeds – Otley road • Open all year, daily, during daylight hours • Entrance: free ○ 🕮 **WC** ♿

The original layout is Victorian, and the gardens were given to Leeds Corporation in 1921 by the Brown family in memory of a son killed during World War I. The fine informal, largely woodland garden features woody plants, especially rhododendrons. Ferns flourish throughout the gardens and a varied collection of hydrangeas provides late summer colour. Many slightly tender subjects thrive in the pleasant microclimate. Several National Collections are held here, including those of hemerocallis, hostas and deutzias, and probably the most comprehensive philadelphus collection in Europe.

Land Farm ★

Colden, Hebden Bridge, Calderdale HA7 7PJ. Tel: (01422) 842260

Mr and Mrs J. Williams • 3.5m NE of Todmorden, off A646 between Sowerby Bridge and Todmorden. Call at visitor centre in Hebden Bridge for map • Open May to Aug, Sat, Sun and Bank Holiday Mons, 10am – 5pm. Parties welcome • Entrance: £3, Parties £5 per person incl. refreshments ◑ 🏠 WC ♿ ⬥ ℘ ⛪ ᵠ

The four-acre garden created by the owners on a north-facing site high in the Pennines combines good design, excellent planting and interesting sculpture. The impact of sculpture in a garden depends so much on its positioning – here it is done to perfection and at times achieves a real drama. Planted for ease of maintenance, the emphasis is on shrubs, herbaceous perennials and alpines. In the woodland garden, acers, cornus and rhododendrons have an understorey of herbaceous plants. Large banks are massed with *Cardiocrinum giganteum*, making a fantastic display in July and August with their tall and scented spires, and *Tropaeolum speciosum* runs in glorious riot through other parts of the garden. The former barn is now an art gallery.

Lister Park [Historic Public Park Grade II]

Keighley Road, Bradford. Tel: (01274) 437673

City of Bradford Metropolitan District Council • 1.5m N of Bradford centre (Forster Square) on A650 Bradford – Keighley road • Open all year, daily, during daylight hours • Entrance: free • Other information: Cartwright Hall, City Art Gallery and Museum open all year, daily except Mon (but open Bank Holiday Mons) ○ 🅿 WC ♿ ⬥ ⛾ ᵠ

The 55-acre park was given to the city by a local mill owner, Sir Samuel Cunliffe-Lister, in 1870, and has been restored through a Heritage Lottery Fund grant. Six of its features are listed. There is an attractive formal bedding display in front of the Cartwright Hall and gallery and an interesting floral clock – a rare example of Victorian ingenuity. The tranquil Mughal garden adjoining illustrates the simplicity and symmetry of the fusion of Islamic and Hindu styles. The old botanical garden behind the hall includes a geological trail and boating, games and summer entertainments are on offer for both children and adults.

Nostell Priory [Historic Park Grade II*]

Doncaster Road, Nostell, Wakefield WF4 1QE. Tel: (01924) 863892

The National Trust • 6m SE of Wakefield on A638 • House open as garden, 1 – 5pm • Garden open 13th to 19th Feb, daily, 11am – 4.30pm; 4th March to 5th Nov, Wed – Sun and Bank Holiday Mons, 11am – 6pm • Entrance: £4, children £1.75 (house and garden £6.50, children £3.25, family £16) • Other information: Dogs in park only. Batricar available. Special events and fairs ◑ 🅿 🏠 WC ♿ ⛪ ᵠ

The dark, brooding eighteenth-century mansion by Robert Adam sits in open parkland with an attractive lake and a variety of well-established trees. A fine rose garden is the main gardening feature, together with extensive lakeside gardens planted with magnolias and rhododendrons, a summerhouse, a Gothick archway and a cock-fighting pit. One of the most attractive Gothick buildings, with later additions by Robert Adam, has been restored.

The People's Park [Historic Public Park Grade II*]

Hopwood Lane, Halifax HX1 5ER. Tel: (01422) 323824

Metropolitan Borough of Calderdale • Open all year, daily, 8am – dusk • Entrance: free ○ 🍴 <u>WC</u> & ⬦ 🍷 ♿

A gift by Francis Crossley to the town, this is a good example of a Victorian park. Designed by Joseph Paxton, it was opened in 1857, and in 1874 a bandstand was added. Queen Victoria presented two swans to the park in 1861. The pavilion was designed by Stokes and has a statue of Crossley by Joseph Durham; the statues on the terrace are by Francesco Bienaime. Restoration of the park, including the water features and the pavilion, and new landscaping, is now complete, and the atmosphere is being rejuvenated with a varied events programme and community involvement. Brass bands play every Sunday afternoon, from 2 – 4.30pm, from the second week of May to the second week of August.

Sheffield Botanical Gardens [Historic Public Park Grade II]

Sheffield S10 2LN. Tel: (0114) 267 6496

Sheffield Council • 0.5m from A625, 1.5m SW of city centre • Open all year, daily except 25th Dec, 10am – dusk • Entrance: free ○ 🍴 ✗ 🍴 <u>WC</u> & ⬦ 🏛 🍷 ♿

These historic gardens, designed by Robert Marnock in the Gardenesque style with several interesting garden buildings, opened in 1836. Today they provide residents and visitors to Sheffield with an invaluable 19-acre green lung; more importantly, they are the only botanical gardens in the UK to have undergone a major (£6.69m) facelift. The jewels in the crown – the three impressive glass pavilions with their linking glass corridors (one of the earliest curvilinear glass house complexes in the country) – have been beautifully restored and display plant collections from around the warm temperate world. An evolutionary garden shows the development of plants, the rosarium the history of the rose. National Collections of weigelas and diervillas are displayed on the main lawn, and an archive of botanical illustrations depicting plants growing in the gardens is being built up.

Temple Newsam Park [Historic Garden Grade II]

Leeds LS15 0AD. Tel: (0113) 264 5535

Leeds City Council • 3m E of Leeds, signed off A63/A6120 ring road junction and junction 46 on M1 • House open all year, Tues – Sun, 10.30am – 5pm (closes 4pm in winter) • Park open all year, daily, dawn – dusk; National Collections open daily, 11am – 3pm (closes 2pm Sat and Sun) • Entrance: free ○ 🍴 🍴 <u>WC</u> & ⬦ 🏛 🍷 ♿

Most people visit the house to see its remarkable collection of furniture, but set in the remnants of a 'Capability' Brown landscape of the 1760s is a wide diversity of gardens. A rhododendron and azalea walk leads to small ponds with a bog garden and arboretum, beyond which is a large walled rose garden and greenhouses containing bougainvilleas and a collection of South African plants that formed part of the Nelson Mandela garden at Chelsea 2004. Several National Collections, including delphiniums, phlox, asters, charm and cascade chrysanthemums, are held here. Also within the large walled garden are traditional borders considered to be amongst the best in England.

Tropical World ★ [within Roundhay Park – Historic Park Grade II]

Roundhay Park, Roundhay, Leeds LS8 2ER. Tel: (0113) 266 1850

Leeds City Council • S of A6120 northern ring, off A58 Roundhay Road from city centre • Open all year, daily, except 25th and 26th Dec, 10am – 6pm • Entrance: £3, children (8–15) £2, under-8s and Leeds card holders free • Other information: Dogs in park only, on lead ○ 💁 ✕ 🍴 WC ♿ ♨ 🚻 ♒

The 700-acre parkland with its fine trees and wildflower meadows is a wonderful setting for the pure horticultural extravaganza of the canal gardens with their formal bedding and generous collections. Nearby are the Monet and the Alhambra gardens. These were once the kitchen and ornamental gardens of the estate purchased by Thomas Nicholson in 1803, who developed a ravine, landscape gardens, woodland, a lake, waterfalls and a sham castle – all the trappings of the time – before selling up to the Leeds Corporation in 1871. The exotic houses have the largest collection outside Kew, with exotic butterflies and birds. Waterfalls and pools are surrounded by tropical plants, and the arid house holds a large collection of cacti and succulents. There is an underwater world of plants and fish, a recreated rainforest environment and a nocturnal house where bush babies, monkeys and other animals can be seen.

Wentworth Castle Gardens ★ [Historic Park Grade I]

Lowe Lane, Stainborough, Barnsley S75 3ET. Tel: (01226) 776040

Wentworth Castle and Stainborough Park Heritage Trust • 3m SW of Barnsley off M1 junction 37, 2m along minor roads between Stainborough and Hood Green. Follow signs for Northern College • Open March to Oct, Sat and Sun, 2 – 5pm (last admission 4pm); also for parties of 15 or more Mon to Fri, by appt 💁 🍴 WC ♿

Less than an hour from Leeds and Sheffield is one of the most exciting gardens in Yorkshire – 600 acres of parkland, 50 acres of pleasure gardens, a walled garden and a three-quarter-mile-long serpentine lake, laid out mainly under the direction of Thomas Wentworth and his son William between 1708 and 1791. A £15m project, which includes a £10.3m Heritage Lottery Fund grant, is underway to revitalise the estate, and visitors are encouraged to tour the gardens to see this ambitious work in progress. The first phase includes the restoration of the gardens, including the Union Jack Garden, the Victorian secret garden, Stainborough Castle, and the park and woodland. The derelict home farm will be transformed into a visitor centre and cafe.

York Gate ★

Back Church Lane, Adel, Leeds LS16 8DW. Tel: (0113) 267 8240

Perennial (formerly The Gardeners' Royal Benevolent Society) • 2.25m SE of Bramhope, off A660 • Open April to Sept, Thurs, Sun and Bank Holiday Mons, 2 – 5pm, plus 22nd and 29th June, 6th July, 6.30 – 9pm, and for parties by appt • Entrance: £3.50, children free • Other information: Café closed in April and May ◐ ☕ WC ✿

A garden created by the Spencer family and bequeathed by the late Sybil Spencer to the Gardeners' Royal Benevolent Society. Bought by the Spencers in 1951, this was a bleak farmhouse and unpromising area of land. When her husband died, her son took over the design and in a tragically short life achieved a garden of rare delight, using local stone, cobblestones and gravel to create a structure of impeccable taste and style and great horticultural interest. The late Arthur Hellyer remarked on its debt to Hidcote and commented on the clever use of architectural features and topiary. It is also a plantsman's garden, with rare and unusual plants to be discovered in a sequence of individual settings. These include an extraordinary miniature pinetum, a dell with a stream, a canal garden, fern and peony borders, a herb garden with a summerhouse, a kitchen garden and white borders. Sybil's Garden has recently been redesigned by Alistair Baldwin in a more contemporary style but using materials sympathetic to the rest of the garden.

Yorkshire Sculpture Park [within Bretton Park Historic Park Grade II]

West Bretton, Wakefield WF4 4LG. Tel: (01924) 832631

Yorkshire Sculpture Park, Independent Charitable Trust • 6m NW of Barnsley, 6m SW of Wakefield at West Bretton. Leave M1 at junction 38 • Open all year, daily, 10am – 6pm (closes 5pm in winter). Telephone for Christmas openings • Entrance: free but donation welcomed. Parking £3 per car • Other information: Coaches by prior arrangement. Access Sculpture Trail suitable for wheelchairs. Visitor centre and indoor galleries ○ ☕ ✕ WC ♿

This, Britain's first permanent sculpture park was established in 1977, and is now considered to be one of Europe's leading open-air galleries. The 500 acres of formal gardens, woods, lakes and parkland provide a fine setting for temporary and permanent exhibitions. The layout makes it possible to view sculpture in garden as well as 'public' settings that demand a more monumental approach by the sculptor. The park hosts temporary exhibitions by international sculptors, as well as rotating its own permanent collection.

FEEDBACK

Readers are invited to advise the *Guide* of any gardens which in their opinion should be listed in future editions, and where possible arrangements will be made to review such suggestions. Readers who would like to add information about gardens listed are warmly invited to write to the *Guide* with their comments, which may be used in future editions without attribution. Please send letters to the publishers, Frances Lincoln Ltd, 4 Torriano Mews, Torriano Avenue, London NW5 2RZ. All letters are acknowledged by the editors.

THE REPUBLIC OF IRELAND & NORTHERN IRELAND

Two-starred gardens are marked on the map with a black square.

NORTHERN IRELAND

The National Trust Ulster Gardens Scheme runs private garden openings on special days and by appointment. For a list of gardens opening in 2006 telephone (028) 9751 0721.

Annesley Garden and National Arboretum ★★ [Historic Demesne]

Castlewellan, Co. Down BT31 9BU. Tel: (028) 4377 8664

Forest Service, Dept of Agriculture (Northern Ireland) • 25m S of Belfast, 4m NW of Newcastle, in Castlewellan • Open all year, daily • Entrance: cars £4, minibuses £10, coaches £25 (2005 prices) • Other information: Disabled parking. Refreshments in summer only. Caravan and camping ground in park ○ 🅿 🍴 WC ♨

The walled garden contains an outstanding collection of mature trees and shrubs, planted since 1849 by the Earl Annesley. Original specimens of some of Castlewellan's cultivars thrive here, in fine condition. In the spring and summer there are many rhododendrons in bloom and scarlet Chilean fire bushes (*Embothrium coccineum*). In midsummer, a snow-carpet consists of the fallen petals of an unequalled collection of eucryphias. In all, there are 34 champion specimen trees in one area of just nine acres, including 15 southern-hemisphere broad-leaved champions; half of these specimens are also thought to be the oldest examples in cultivation. Apart from the trees there are bulbs, herbaceous borders, two restored fountain pools, topiary of Irish yew and, in summer, an impressive show of tropaeolum. Beyond the walls the arboretum extends for a further 85 acres in the Forest Park, where signposted walks lead round a magnificent lake, the Cypress Pond, where the dramatic view to the Mourne Mountains has been restored. A major new piece of landscaping, the largest and longest yew-hedge maze in the world, represents the path to peace in Northern Ireland.

Antrim Castle Gardens [Historic Garden]

Randalstown Road, Antrim, Co. Antrim BT41 4LH. Tel: (028) 9448 1338

Antrim Borough Council Arts and Heritage Service • Access from A6 Randalstown Road • Open all year, daily, 9.30am – dusk. Guided tours for parties at any time by arrangement • Entrance: Individuals free; small parties £2, concessions £1; parties of 40 or more £1 per person; school parties 50p per child • Other information: Refreshments by arrangement for groups. Interpretative display in Clotworthy Arts Centre ○ 🅿 🍴 WC & ♨ 🛈

A rare example of a demesne where the main elements survive as laid out for a late-seventeenth-century castle (now demolished). The canals, connected by a cascade, are lined with clipped lime and hornbeam hedges. Paths criss-cross through the wooded wilderness, the main avenue of which leads to an airy clearing with a round pond reflecting sky and trees. Following a restoration project, a large parterre has been planted with varieties known in the seventeenth century and is set off by a quincunx grove of standard hornbeam (new) and an immense yew hedge (old). The adjacent Anglo-Norman motte retains its spiral path; access can be gained by collecting a key from the arts centre (£5 refundable deposit), and it is worth a climb to the top to see the lower course of the Sixmilewater river, the centre of the town of Antrim, and the 37-acre ornamental site below – a fraction of a once-vast estate stretching as far as the eye could see.

The Argory [Historic Demesne]

Moy, Dungannon, Co. Tyrone BT71 6NA. Tel: (028) 8778 4753

The National Trust • 4m NE of Moy, 3m from M1 junction 14 • House open • Grounds and garden open all year, daily, 10am – 7pm (closes 4pm Oct to April) • Entrance: £4.50, children £2.40. Parking charge £2.50 • Other information: Coaches must use M1 junction 13 because of weight restrictions. Parking 100 metres from house ◑ 🅿 🅱 <u>WC</u> ♿ ⬦ ⚓ ☕

The lawns of the pleasure ground slope down past yew arbours to two pavilions, one a pump house, the other a garden house. Beyond, the visitor can walk under pollarded limes along the banks of the Blackwater River, and there are other woodland walks in this tranquil landscape. A splash of summer colour near the house attracts the eye to an enclosed early-nineteenth-century sundial garden of box-edged rose beds. The riverside walk runs for 1.5 miles.

Ballywalter Park [Historic Garden]

Ballywalter, Nr Newtownards, Co. Down BT22 2PP. Tel: (028) 4275 8264

Dunleath Estates • 20m E of Belfast, 10m SE of Newtownards off B5 between Greyabbey and Ballywalter. Turn right at T-junction facing gates and follow wall to entrance on left opposite farm • Open by appt only (please telephone Mon – Fri, 9am – 1pm) • Entrance: house or garden £6 (house and garden £10) • Other information: Self-catering accommodation. PYO in season ◑ 🅿 WC ♿ 🌿 ☕

The fine mid-nineteenth-century Italianate house by the architect Lanyon, with an elegant conservatory wing, was praised by Sir John Betjeman. The surrounding grounds are an amalgam of two earlier 'landscaped' demesnes, embellished for the present house by a rock garden around a stream with bridges, also by Lanyon. The notable rhododendron collection is sheltered by mature trees throughout the park. A rose pergola and seven restored glasshouses decorate the walled garden.

Belfast Botanic Gardens Park [Historic Park]

Stranmillis Road, Belfast City BT7 ILP. Tel: (028) 9032 4902

Belfast City Council Parks Department • Between Queen's University and Ulster Museum, Stranmillis. Buses 69, 84 and 85 • Open all year, daily, 7.30am – dusk.

Palm House and Tropical Ravine, summer, weekdays, 10am – 5pm, weekends and public holidays, 2 – 5pm (closes 4pm in winter). Guided tours and parties at any time by arrangement • Entrance: free. Guided tours £10 • Other information: Refreshments in Ulster Museum ○ 🐌 <u>WC</u> �& ⊕ 🎈

Established in 1828, this became a public park in 1895. As well as two magnificent double herbaceous borders and a rose garden with 8000 roses, there is another reason to visit this park – the curvilinear iron and glass palm house (1839–52), one of the finest Victorian glasshouses. Richard Turner built only the wings; the dome is by Young of Edinburgh, restored in the 1970s. It contains a finely displayed collection of tropical plants, while massed pot plants are changed throughout the seasons in a cooler wing. The Tropical Ravine House is the greater delight, a perfect piece of 'High Victoriana' with ferns, bananas, lush tropical vines and tree ferns, goldfish in the Amazon lily pond, and a waterfall worked with a chain-pull. Marvellous, evocative of crinoline days.

Benvarden House [Historic Garden]

Ballybogey, Ballymoney, Co. Antrim BT53 6NN. Tel: (028) 2074 1331

Mr and Mrs Hugh Montgomery • 4m E of Coleraine off B67. Signposted • Open June to Aug, Tues – Sun and Bank Holiday Mons, 12 noon – 5.30pm, and at other times by appt • Entrance: £3 ◑ 🍴 <u>WC</u> ⅋ ⊕ 🌱

The eighteenth-century house is set in lawns where the visitor can wander along the banks of the Bush River, which is spanned at this point by an elegant Victorian iron bridge, 36 metres long. A large pond is surrounded by Irish yews and many rhododendrons, camellias and azaleas. The walled garden has a curved and brick-faced three-metre high wall, lined with old espalier-trained apple and pear trees and focused on a round goldfish pond and fountain. Climbers scramble over the former glasshouse frames, beneath which seats are provided. The adjoining one-acre traditional kitchen garden is in full production and contains fruit trees and box hedges, melon and tomato houses, potting sheds and a gardener's bothy.

Castle Ward [Historic Demesne]

Strangford, Downpatrick, Co. Down BT30 7LS. Tel: (028) 4488 1204

The National Trust • 7m NE of Downpatrick, 1.5m W of Strangford on A25, on S shore of Strangford Lough. Entrance by Ballyculter Lodge • House open – telephone for details • Estate, gardens and grounds open Oct to April, daily, 11am – 4pm, May to Sept, 10am – 8pm • Entrance: Estate and grounds £3 (estate, grounds and house £4.70). Parking charge £1 when house and other facilities closed ○ 🍴 ✕ <u>WC</u> ⅋ ⊕ ⚓ 🎈 ⚲

Beautifully situated on a peninsula near the mouth of Strangford Lough, the landscape park enhances the 1760s' house with its classical west front and Gothick east front. Both house and decorative Lady Anne's Temple command the heights; below lie an impressive canal and yew walks, features retained from the gardens of a previous early-eighteenth-century house. The sunken Windsor Garden has lost much of its intricate bedding but there are colourful borders containing an interesting range of plants, some quite rare, which lead to the rockery and a sentinel row of cordylines and Florence Court yews.

Castlewellan National Arboretum
(see ANNESLEY GARDEN AND NATIONAL ARBORETUM)

Florence Court [Historic Demesne]
Florencecourt, Enniskillen, Co. Fermanagh BT92 1DB. Tel: (028) 6634 8249

The National Trust • 8m SW of Enniskillen, via A4 Sligo road and A32 Swanlinbar road, 4m from Marble Arch Caves • House open 17th to 19th March, April, May and Sept, Sat, Sun and Bank Holiday Mons; June, daily except Tues; July and Aug, daily; all 1 – 6pm, but opens 12 noon in Aug • Estate open all year, daily, 10am – 7pm (closes 4pm Nov to March) • Entrance: Forest park and Pleasure Gardens £3 per car (house £4.25, children £2, family £10.50, parties of 15 or more £5 per person) • Other information: Tearoom and shop open as house, but closes 5.30pm. Batricar available ○ 💬 ✕ 🐌 <u>WC</u> ♿ ⏛ 🏛 ⚱ ⚲

The original, the mother of all Irish yews (*Taxus baccata* 'Fastigiata'), still grows in its original garden site – accessible by well-marked woodland paths and about a quarter of a mile from the splendid mansion. Well worth the walk, the gravel path allows glimpses of the mountains and the handsome 'Brownian' park in front of the house. Some fine weeping beeches, Japanese maples and old rhododendrons grow in the pleasure grounds, and the garden buildings include an ice-house, a water-driven saw mill, a restored summerhouse, an eel bridge, a hydraulic ram, and the listed Rose Cottage in the three-acre walled garden. The nearby caves are worth visiting too.

28 Killyfaddy Road
Magherafelt, Co. Londonderry BT45 6EX. Tel: (028) 7963 2180

Ann Buchanan • 10m NE of Cookstown off A31. From Magherafelt, take Moneymore road. After 0.25m Killyfaddy Road is 2nd on left opposite filling station. Gardens 1m further along, both sides of road • Open April to Sept, Wed – Sat, 1 – 5pm, and by appt • Entrance: donation to charity ◔ 🐌 WC ♿ ⚱ ⚲

An acre of informal country garden created over three decades, densely planted with an extensive range of herbaceous perennials plus trees, shrubs, alpines, fruit, vegetables and a small orchard. The 'wild' garden in a separate site across the road has woodland and shade areas and a wildlife pond with associated bog plants. There is also a small wildflower meadow with marsh orchids flowering in June – coinciding with the candelabra primulas.

Mount Stewart ★★ [Historic Garden]
Greyabbey, Newtownards, Co. Down BT22 2AD. Tel: (028) 4278 8387

The National Trust • 15m E of Belfast, 5m SE of Newtownards on A20 Portaferry road • House open different times – telephone for details • Lakeside gardens and walk open March to Nov from 10am, closing times vary depending on season. Formal garden open March, Sat, Sun and 17th March, 10am – 4pm; April to Oct, daily, 10am – 8pm (closes 6pm April and Oct) • Entrance: £4.20, children £2.20, family £9.30, parties £3.95 per person (2005 prices) • Other information: Parking 300 metres away. Two pre-bookable battery wheelchairs available ◑ ▣ ✕ 🐚 <u>wc</u> ♿ ⬧ ▨ 🏛 🍴 ⚲

Of all Ireland's gardens this is the one not to miss. Any adjective that evokes beauty can be applied to it, and it's fun too. In the gardens fronting the eighteenth- and nineteenth-century house is a collection of statues depicting British political and public figures as animals. The planting here is formal, with rectangular beds of hot and cool colours. Beyond in the informal gardens are mature trees and shrubs – a botanical collection with few equals, planted with great panache and maintained with outstanding attention to detail. Spires of cardiocrinums, aspiring eucalyptus, banks of rhododendrons, ferns and blue poppies, rivers of candelabra primulas, and much more. Walk along the lakeside path to the hill that affords a view over the lake to the house. Rare tender shrubs such as *Metrosideros umbellata* from Australasia flourish here outside the walled family cemetery; leading from it is the Jubilee Avenue with its statue of a white stag. The Temple of the Winds, James 'Athenian' Stuart's banqueting hall of 1782–5, is also memorable. The garden should be seen several times during the year truly to savour its rich tapestry of plants and water, buildings and trees.

Rowallane Garden ★★ [Historic Garden]

Saintfield, Ballynahinch, Co. Down BT24 7LH. Tel: (028) 9751 0131

The National Trust • 0.5m S of Saintfield on A7 Belfast – Downpatrick road • Open all year, daily, 10am – 4pm (closes 8pm 15th April to 15th Oct). Closed 25th and 26th Dec, 1st Jan • Entrance: £3.70, children £1.70, family £9.10, parties £2.80 per person (2005 prices) ○ ▣ 🐚 <u>wc</u> ♿ ⬧ ▨ 🍴

While famous as a 52-acre rhododendron garden and certainly excellent in this regard, Rowallane has much more to interest keen gardeners. In summer, the walled garden blossoms in lemon and blue, while hoherias scatter their white petals in the wind and in secluded places a pocket-handkerchief tree blows. There is a restored Victorian bandstand (music-filled on some summer weekends) and a rock garden with primulas, meconopsis, heathers, etc. Any season will be interesting, and for the real enthusiast there are rhododendron species and cultivars in bloom from October to August. A National Collection of large-flowered penstemons is here. A feature is made of *Hypericum* 'Rowallane' at the entrance to the walled garden; within are the original plant of *Viburnum plicatum* 'Rowallane' and the original *Chaenomeles* x *superba* 'Rowallane'. The wildflower meadows are famed for such comparative rarities as wild orchids, and as the garden is cultivated organically, wildlife abounds.

Seaforde House [Historic Garden]

Downpatrick, Co. Down BT30 8PG. Tel: (028) 4481 1225

Mr Patrick and Lady Anthea Forde • 22m S of Belfast on A24 Belfast – Newcastle road • Open March to Oct, Mon – Sat, 10am – 5pm, Sun 1 – 6pm; Nov to Feb,

Mon – Fri, 10am – 5pm. Closed 25th Dec to 1st Jan • Entrance: £3, children £2
○ 🍽 ✕ 🗺 ♿ ♨ ⛪ ⚲

The fine landscaped park can be glimpsed on the way to the vast walled garden. Half of this is a commercial nursery with the attraction of a butterfly house which also displays a collection of tropical plants, the other half is an ornamental garden bedecked in late summer with blooms of eucryphia that make up a National Collection. The hornbeam maze has a rose-clad arbour at the centre, the vantage point for which is a 1992 Mogul tower. Beyond the walled garden is the Pheasantry, a verdant valley enclosed by mature trees, full of noteworthy plants collected over many years and still expanding.

Sir Thomas and Lady Dixon Park [Historic Park]

Upper Malone Road, Belfast. Tel: (028) 906 03359/903 20202

Belfast City Council • S of Belfast city centre, on Upper Malone Road • Open all year, daily, 8am – sunset • Entrance: free ○ 🍽 WC ♿ ♨ ⚲

This 128-acre park, presented to the City of Belfast in 1959, is part of a demesne established in the eighteenth century. The main feature today is the International Rose Trial area, where some 40,000 rose bushes can been seen in carefully labelled beds following the contours of the park. One display has old varieties demonstrating the history of the rose. Elsewhere there are riverside meadows by the River Lagan, a walled garden, international camellia trials and a Japanese garden. A secluded children's playground and band performances during the summer make it enjoyable for all the family.

THE REPUBLIC OF IRELAND

No register of Historic Gardens has been published for the Republic of Ireland. The GGIRP refers to The Great Gardens of Ireland Restoration Programme, initiated in 1994, which has seen the renaissance of 26 historic parks and gardens.

Altamont

Tullow, Co. Carlow. Tel: (59) 91 59444

Office of Public Works • 19km SE of Carlow, 8km S of Tullow, off Tullow-Bunclody road (N80/81) near Ballon • Telephone for opening times and details • Entrance: Pre-booked guided tours €2.75, OAPs €2, students/children € 1.25, family € 7, groups €2 per person ◑ 🗺 WC ♿ ♨ ♨

The lily-filled lake, surrounded by fine, mature trees, forms a backdrop for a gently sloping lawn. A central walkway formally planted with Irish yews and roses leads from the house to the lake. There is a beautiful fern-leaved beech, and other ancient beeches form the Nun's Walk. The passion of the late owner, Mrs North, for trees, old-fashioned roses and unusual plants is evident, and the garden will be kept in the spirit she intended; a flower border in her memory was planted in 2000. A long walk through the demesne leads to the River Slaney with diversions to a bog garden, through an Ice-Age glen of ancient oaks undercarpeted with bluebells.

Amergen
Walshestown, Ovens, Co. Cork. Tel: (21) 733 1326

Mrs Christine Fehily • Take N22 Cork – Killarney road, 9km W of Cork, turn right at Dan Sheahan's pub, follow road to crossroads, turn right into cul-de-sac for about 1.5km. Garden on right • Open for parties by appt • Entrance: € 4.50 ● WC & ⬧

A plantsman's garden in a beautiful setting overlooking the valley of the River Lee. Behind the house is a modest arboretum that merges into mixed borders interspersed with informal lawns. The driveway divides the main garden from a slope thickly planted with shrubs and trees. Paths meander through this area, where lush *Geranium maderense* and handsome dogwoods vividly demonstrate the mildness of the Cork climate. Many tender plants can be grown outdoors, including *Melianthus major*, *Acacia melanoxylon* and correa, so interesting and unusual shrubs and perennials abound.

Annes Grove
Castletownroche, Near Mallow, Co. Cork. Tel: (22) 26145

Mr and Mrs F.P. Grove Annesley • 2.5km N of Castletownroche, between Fermoy and Mallow • Open 17th March to Sept, Mon – Sat, 10am – 5pm, Sun, 1 – 6pm, and at other times by appt • Entrance: € 6, OAPs and students € 4, children € 2. Reductions for pre-booked parties • Other information: Self-catering accommodation available ❶ 🍴 WC & ⬧ ⬧

This is a wild garden of an archetypically Robinsonian kind. Rhododendron species and cultivars arch over and spill towards the pathways, carpeting them with fallen blossoms. Steep, sometimes slippery paths descend at various places into the valley of the Awbeg river (which inspired Edmund Spenser). Seek out the eighteenth-century pen pond at the bottom of the valley – a star-shaped artificial pond used for attracting and snaring wild duck, rare in Ireland. The statuesque conifers planted in the valley make a colourful tapestry behind the river garden, with mimulus, daylilies and candelabra primulas in profusion. The glory of the garden is, however, the collection of rhododendron species, many of them introduced through subscription to Kingdon Ward expeditions. Visitors may spot hidden surprises – a superb *Juniperus recurva* 'Castlewellan', a mature pocket-handkerchief tree (*Davidia involucrata*) and other exotic flowering trees. A fernery is being constructed at the back of limestone rocks at the top end of the garden.

Ardcarraig ★
Oranswell, Bushypark, Co. Galway. Tel: (91) 524336

Mrs Lorna MacMahon • 4km W of Galway city centre off N59. Oranswell turn is approx 2km past Glenlo Abbey Hotel; house is approx 230 metres up hill on left • Open 17th May, 10am – 9pm, and by appt • Entrance: €5, parties of 15 or more €5 per person • Other information: Refreshments and plants for sale on open day only ● WC

In front of the house is a collage of heathers and conifers, with spring and autumn-flowering bulbs; ordinary but attractive. Beside it is a formal, sunken garden, with a clematis-draped pergola and a terracotta *pithoi* as the focal point; handsome, but not unusual. The path then enters a wild hazel wood carpeted with bluebells, ramsons and ferns; nature's garden. A clearing ablaze with scented azaleas in spring and roses and geraniums in summer is the first surprise. The path winds on to a pool surrounded by blue Himalayan poppies, hostas and candelabra primulas. And on ... to a bubbling peat-stained stream that chatters over granite rocks to a bog garden with heathers and skunk cabbages, to a stunning tranquil Japanese hill and pool garden, while the boulder beyond suggests Mount Fuji. And on ... to Harry's Garden, full of plants given to Lorna in memory of her late husband, and planted (with a pick!) among the natural granite boulders. The latest venture is a moss garden in the Japanese style.

Ardgillan Castle and Garden

Balbriggan, Co. Dublin. Tel: (1) 849 2212 (Castle), (1) 849 2324 (Garden)

Fingal County Council Parks • 24km N of Dublin, between Balbriggan and Skerries. Signposted off M1 and N1 • Castle open all year, daily except Mon (but open Bank Holiday Mons and Mons in July and Aug). Closed 23rd Dec to 1st Jan • Garden open all year, daily, 10am – 6pm (closes winter 4.30pm). Park open all year, daily, 10am – 6pm (closes up to 9pm depending on season). Conducted tours June to Aug, Thurs, 3.30pm • Entrance: free but groups € 3.50 guided tours € 6 (castle tours € 6, concessions € 3.50, family € 12) ○ 🍴 🏠 WC ⅃ ⬦ ⚲

The approach to the castle is one of the most spectacular in Ireland, with views northwards along the coast to Carlingford and the Mourne mountains, and the castle itself nestled in a hollow. Built in 1738 by the Revd Robert Taylor, it now houses an eclectic assortment of eighteenth- and nineteenth-century furniture, and an important collection of seventeenth-century 'Down Survey' maps of Ireland. The demesne today covers about 194 acres, and within it are various gardens. A fine Victorian conservatory rescued from another house has been re-erected and is now the centrepiece of the formal rose garden. The walled garden is divided into sections which include box-edged herb and vegetable gardens, a fruit garden and ornamental gardens displaying a good mix of shrubs, perennials and rock plants. Many of the beds were created recently and are not part of the original layout, but they contain some choice plants. A unique, free-standing brick wall with 20 alcoves is now planted with fruit. The garden has been grant-aided under the GGIRP for remedial work on its woodland paths, the rose garden (which now includes Edwardian and Victorian cultivars) and a small garden museum, and to provide some new plant stock to extend its collections. A National Collection of potentillas is held here. Don't miss the ice-house, a short way along the woodland walk.

Ballindoolin House and Garden

Carbury, via Edenderry, Co. Kildare. Tel: (46) 973 1430

The Molony family • 5km N of Edenderry on R401 • House open; guided tours only (extra charge) • Garden open May to July, Wed – Sun, 12 noon – 6pm, and by appt at other times • Entrance: € 6, children over 5 € 4 ○ 🍴 🏠 WC ⅃ 🌼 🏛 ⚱ ⚲

A medium-sized demesne surrounding an 1821 Georgian house which still retains its original interior and furnishings. Some of the farmyard buildings and outhouses await repair, but the two-acre walled garden has been restored under the GGIRP. It has aged espaliered apple trees in various stages of decrepitude, which have been carefully kept and are charming, setting the atmosphere for the garden. A melon-pit ruin has also been conserved. The soil is rich and fertile, and the old borders have been beautifully replanted with a wide range of herbaceous perennials, roses and herbs. Every year the new plantings get better and better, and a good variety of vegetables and fruit thrive once again in the warm microclimate, providing much of the produce for the restaurant. The wonderfully preserved walls include a high, brick-lined south-facing fruit wall, which has also been replanted. Outside the walled garden a path leads past a quirky little rockery towards the trefoil-shaped dovecote, on to the lime kiln, the 'Iron Age' mound and the woodland walk, where a long beech avenue leads into the woods and back towards the house.

Ballinlough Castle Gardens

Clonmellon, Co. Westmeath. Tel: (46) 9433234

Alice Nugent • On N52 between Kells and Mullingar, 3km from Clonmellon • Open May to Sept, Sun and Bank Holiday Mons, 12 noon – 6pm, and at other times by appt. Check opening times before travelling • Entrance: € 6, concessions € 5, party rates on application ● ● WC &

The gardens, woods and lakes were restored in 1998 under the GGIRP. The present castle dates from the seventeenth century, with eighteenth- and nineteenth-century additions, but the history of the site goes way back to 1400. The long avenue through the demesne hints at good things to come, and as the house comes into view on its mound above the two lakes it is truly delightful. The arched gateway into the first of four walled enclosures leads to a formal pool, mature trees and flowering shrubs, and on to double herbaceous borders. Lady Nugent has filled the gardens with choice plants, fruit, herbs and vegetables, some old, many newly planted and all well cared for. Most of the work is done by the family, and a real team spirit is evident. The formality of the walled gardens gives way to free-style wild plantings along the woodland paths, leading down to two rock bridges, a summerhouse, and a planted rockery and glade. A walk around the lake is rewarded by the view from the far side, where the castle seems to float above the water's edge. Swans have recolonised the lakes, and other creatures are settling in again.

Ballymaloe Cookery School Gardens

Kinoith, Shanagarry, Co. Cork. Tel: (21) 464 6785

Tim and Darina Allen • 36km E of Cork, between Cloyne and Ballycotton • Open April to Sept, daily, 10am – 6pm. Guided tours for parties by arrangement • Entrance: € 5 • Other information: Booking for groups essential ● & ᵍ ▥ ᵓ

Take the bones of an old Quaker garden and begin afresh – that is what Darina Allen has done at Kinoith (and she hasn't finished yet). The antique beech hedges are being clipped again, and within their shelter are compartments, each one different and refreshing. The first is the flower garden with short herbaceous borders, and beside a small pool is a summerhouse, the floor of which is patterned with shards of Delft. Beyond is the herb garden, where dwarf box hedges delineate a formal pattern of beds planted mainly with culinary herbs. These compartments can be enjoyed from ground level and also from a viewing platform. The pool garden lies outside the old hedges, and has an incomplete folly. A double herbaceous border, planted in 1996, leads to a plain garden house with Gothic windows. 'Please do not touch my insides' is a friendly piece of advice, for the interior of this unassuming building is decorated with myriad shells. The organic vegetable garden appeals directly to the eye with its tapestry of vegetables and edible flowers. The prime flowering months are June and July.

Bantry House and Gardens ★

Bantry, Co. Cork. Tel: (27) 50047

Mr and Mrs E. Shelswell-White • On outskirts of Bantry on Cork road • House open as garden, but closes 5.30pm • Gardens open March to Oct, daily, 9am – 6pm • Entrance: € 5, children under 14 free, (house and garden € 10, concessions and students € 8, children under 14 free) • Other information: Annual music festival, 24th June to 2nd July (house closed) – telephone (27) 50047 for details ◑ ● ✕ ▦ WC ♿ ⟁ 🍴 B&B

Bantry House is worth a visit to see the house in its setting, quite apart from its magnificent garden. The gardens were created from 1844 to 1867 while in the ownership of the 2nd Earl of Bantry, Richard White, who also built up an impressive art collection as a result of his Grand Tour travels. His artistic ambitions drove him to develop the house and its setting, so formal parterres, terraces and beds were laid out around the house; behind is his amazing staircase of a hundred steps stretching up the steep hillside. Those who reach the top are rewarded with the most stunning view of the house and gardens below and Bantry Bay sweeping out to the broad Atlantic beyond. Statues, urns and balustrading encircle and embellish the gardens; copies of original terracotta urns which punctuate the great flight of steps are filled with *Osmanthus delavayi*. There is a definite Italian air about the place, and its warm humid climate has inevitably influenced the plants that will grow there towards Japanese and Chinese wisterias, magnolias, myrtles, *Trachelospermum asiaticum* – the lakeside gardens of Como and Maggiore spring to mind here. The results achieved under the GGIRP are impressive: the extensive drainage system has been recovered, the parterre surrounding the nineteenth-century wisteria circle and fountain completed, the round bed at the entrance to the house replanted, and the 14 round beds to the north overlooking the bay re-created. The rose garden is currently under review.

Belvedere

Mullingar, Co. Westmeath. Tel: (44) 49060

Westmeath County Council • 5km S of Mullingar on N52 Tullamore road • House and garden open all year, daily: May to Aug, 9.30am – 9pm; March, April and Sept, 10.30am – 6pm; Oct to Feb, 10.30am – 4.30pm (last admission 1 hour before closing) • Entrance: € 8, children € 4.50, family € 22 (2005 prices) ○ ● ✕ ▦ WC ♿ ⟁ 🅿 ⛪ 🍴 ♿

The eighteenth-century hunting lodge, Victorian walled garden and landscaped park, extending over 160 acres on the shores of Lough Ennell, have been restored thanks to a € 4.4 million grant. There are fine views of the lough and islands from the terraces. The Jealous Wall is one of those typically Gothick-Irish follies, built in 1760 to separate squabbling brothers. It looks antique and is impressive. There are also 3km of trails and three children's play areas. An exhibition in the restored stables relates the story of the Wicked Earl and the Mary Molesworth scandal, the history of the estate and its restoration. Its real glory is the eighteenth-century parkland, follies – including Thomas Wright's Gothick arch – and woods.

Birr Castle Demesne ★

Birr, Co. Offaly. Tel: (509) 20336

The Earl and Countess of Rosse • 130km SW of Dublin, 38km S of Athlone, on N52 in Birr • Open all year, daily, March to Oct, 9am – 6pm; Nov to Feb, 10am – 4pm. Guided tours by arrangement • Entrance: € 8.50, OAPs and students € 6.50, children €4.50, family € 25 (2005 prices) • Other information: Parking outside castle gates ○ 🅿 🅱 <u>WC</u> ♿ ⚓ ⌖ 🏮 🍴

The Gothick front of the castle (not open) dominates vistas which strike through the park and at whose centre is the restored 'Leviathan' (the Great Telescope which made Birr the world's astronomical Mecca in the middle of the nineteenth century and of which demonstrations are given regularly). All around, in profusion, are rare trees and shrubs, many raised from seed received from central China from the 1930s. Over one of the rivers is a fine suspension bridge, while a hidden glen boasts a Victorian fernery with its own waterfall and fountain. Evergreen conifers, golden willows, carpets of daffodils, and world-record box hedges, magnolias galore, a cherry avenue and the original plant of *Paeonia* 'Anne Rosse' are mere selections of the many attractions. Recent improvements include the transformation of the old formal terraces with millennium gardens; new water features and wooden statuary complement the hornbeam cloisters. A secret winter garden with a romantic thatched winter bower dominating a glade of snowdrops has been restored. The demesne contains over 50 of the champion trees of the British Isles, as well as geographic collections from Mexico, Pakistan and Yunnan, the last in a corner of Tipperary to which it extends across a further bridge.

Bunratty Castle and Knappogue Castle

Bunratty, Co. Clare. Tel: (61) 360788

Shannon Heritage • Both castles located between Ennis and Limerick off N18. Signposted • Open: Bunratty, all year, daily, 9.30am – 5.30pm (last admission 4.15pm). Closed Good Friday and 24th to 26th Dec. Knappogue, mid-April to early Oct, daily, 9.30am – 5pm (last admission 4.15pm) • Entrance: charge 🅿 ✕ <u>WC</u> 🏮 🍴 ♿

The two fifteenth-century castles, under the same ownership, have a variety of gardens offering an enjoyable family day out. The grounds of Bunratty Castle are now occupied by the vernacular buildings of the Folk Park, each complemented by an appropriate garden. At the far end of the park is the early-nineteenth-century *Bunratty House*, next to a pretty Regency-style walled flower garden with a traditional gardener's bothy. Knappogue Castle has a large walled garden in a tranquil setting close by.

Planted today as a flower and herb garden, the wall borders are filled with an attractive mixture of shrubs and herbaceous plants. Spacious lawns are divided by the old path systems and amply supplied with seats.

Coolcarrigan House and Gardens

Naas, Co. Kildare. Tel: (45) 863527/863524

Mr and Mrs Wilson-Wright • 17.5km N of Naas, 14.5km W of Clane on minor road. Signposted • Open April to Sept, Mon – Fri, by appt only • Entrance: €8 ● ♨ WC &

The 15-acre gardens are mainly planted with shrubs and trees. The large and much-admired collection of rare and unusual trees and shrubs was formed with the advice of Sir Harold Hillier many years ago; they are dotted about the lawns in informal style as specimens. A large and well-maintained Victorian greenhouse dominates the main garden, and a fine herbaceous border fronted by an immaculate lawn completes the picture.

Derreen ★

Lauragh, Killarney, Co. Kerry. Tel: (64) 83588

Charles Bigham • 24km SW of Kenmare on R571 road along S of Kenmare Bay, towards Healy Pass • Open April to July, Sept and Oct, daily; Aug, Thurs – Sun; all 11am – 6pm • Entrance: €6, children €2 • Other information: Picnic area near car park only ● ♨ 🏠 WC ⇎ ℺

The broad sweep of plush lawn and the bald outcroppings of rock by the house do not prepare visitors for the lushness of the walks which weave through native woodlands and palisades of jade-stemmed bamboo. The evocatively named King's Oozy – a path that has a hankering to be a river – leads to a grove of tall, archaic tree ferns (*Dicksonia antarctica*) with socks of filmy ferns. Wellies are the plantsman's only requirement to enjoy the large collection of rhododendrons that shelter among clipped entanglements of *Gaultheria shallon*. This is probably one of the wettest places in these islands, a fact you're reminded of by the lushness of planting throughout.

The Dillon Garden ★★

45 Sandford Road, Ranelagh, Dublin 6

Helen and Val Dillon • 10-min. drive or 30-min walk from city centre in cul-de-sac off Sandford Road just after Merton Road and church • Open March, July and Aug, daily; April to June and Sept, Sun only; all 2 – 6pm. Parties of 15 or more at any time by written appt • Entrance: €5 • Other information: Refreshments for pre-booked parties. Possible for wheelchairs but limited access ● WC & ℺

The renowned plantswoman Helen Dillon does not let the grass grow under her feet – literally, these days. The front garden is now a plain square of pink granite surrounded by *Betula* 'Fascination', and the rectangular walled garden at the rear, typical of Dublin's Georgian town houses, lost its lawn to a canal a while back. This is one of the best town gardens in Britain. The mixed borders of shrubs and herbaceous perennials against the walls are changeful, each season revealing unusual plants and exciting colour combinations. Exploration reveals a necklace of secret rooms with raised beds for rarities, such as lady's slipper orchids or double-flowered *Trillium grandiflorum*. On the sunken terrace, terracotta pots sprout more rare plants. Clumps of *Dierama pulcherrimum* arch over the sphinxes, and a small alpine house and conservatory shelter the choicest species – *Lapageria rosea*, prize-winning ferns, alpines and bulbs. A new area of dramatic foliage plants is being developed. On the way out, take a peek into the shell-encrusted 'grotto' that is the visitors' toilet – the classiest, surely, on the garden-visiting circuit.

Dunloe Castle Gardens

Hotel Dunloe Castle, Beaufort, Killarney, Co. Kerry. Tel: (64) 44111

Killarney Hotels Ltd • 6km W of Killarney, off Killorglin Road. Signposted • Open early May to Sept, but opening date varies – check with hotel. Parties by appt only • Entrance: individuals free, parties €10 per person (incl. guided tour) • Other information: Toilet facilities in hotel ❶ 🍷 ✕ <u>WC</u> ♿ ⬙ ℺ B&B

On a superb site facing the Gap of Dunloe lie the imposing buildings of the castle (now a hotel), opened in 1965, surrounded by acres of parkland and gardens with magnificent and unusual trees and shrubs. Visitors and hotel guests may wander freely and appreciate the well-kept lawns and colourful planting, the walled garden and the ruined fort of Dunloe Castle. The more serious garden visitor will spot such tender specimens as *Eriobotrya deflexa*, *Glyptostrobus pensilis*, *Banksia marginata* and *Telopea oreades* with the aid of the plan and catalogue compiled by Roy Lancaster. Plantings of 1920 have been continually added to and the whole is impeccably maintained. Plants, however, are becoming crowded and tough decisions will have to be made in the near future to allow the choicest to achieve their full potential.

Enniscoe Gardens

Castlehill, Ballina, Co. Mayo. Tel: (96) 31112

Mrs Susan Kellett • After Ballina, turn sharp left in Crossmolina at statue, and drive for 4km on R315 (Pontoon and Castlebar road). Gates and signs on left • Open April to Sept, daily, 10am – 6pm (opens 2pm Sat and Sun) • Entrance: €6, children €2 ❶ 🍷 <u>WC</u> ♿ ⬙ ⛪ B&B

Set near the shores of Lough Conn, the estate dates from the seventeenth century, the picturesque house (now a country house hotel with good fishing and cuisine) from the eighteenth. The surrounding landscape is beautiful and unspoilt. The pleasure grounds were developed in the 1870s, but the woods may be a remnant of original woodland taken into ownership in the 1600s and managed ever since. The walled gardens were derelict from the 1950s until the present owner received grant aid from the GGIRP. The ornamental garden within the old walls has been faithfully restored to its Edwardian origins, and is vibrant with annual bedding and borders filled with perennials and shrubs – at their brightest and best from early June through August. The paths are smartly gravelled, the box hedging trim and the lawns settling down. The fruit and vegetable garden linked to it by a fern-draped rustic arch has been taken over by a small local co-operative, and sells produce to visitors.

An Féar Gorta (Tea and Garden Rooms)

Ballyvaghan, Co. Clare. Tel: (65) 707 7157

Catherine and Brendan O'Donoghue • In Ballyvaghan, on sea-front • Open June to mid-Sept, Mon – Sat, 11am – 5.30pm • Entrance: free ◑ 🛒 wc ⅙ ⬙

The Burren, John Betjeman's 'Stony seaboard, far and foreign' ... is this simple garden's dramatic backdrop. Catmint spills over the native limestone, shrubby cinquefoils sparkle in the sun, butterfly bushes burst with blossom and are a-flutter with insects. There are several compartments, in front of and behind the traditional cottages, all different but each one filled with shrubs and perennials that thrive by the edge of the sea. A conservatory contains other joys, including the red banana passion flower (*Passiflora antioquiensis*) and, appropriately, the cup-and-saucer vine (*Cobaea scandens*). You can sit under their shade, sipping tea and eating scrumptious cakes, enjoying the view.

Fernhill Gardens

Sandyford, Dublin 18. Tel: (1) 295 4257

Mrs Ann Burnett • 13km S of city centre on R117 Dublin – Enniskerry road • Open all year, Tues – Sat and Bank Holiday Mons, 11am – 5pm, Sun, 2 – 6pm • Entrance: €5, concessions/students € 4, children € 4 (under 5 free) ◑ 🏠 wc ⅙ ⬙

The garden is situated on the eastern slope of the Dublin Mountains and has a laurel lawn, some fine nineteenth-century plantings and an excellent flowering specimen of *Michelia doltsopa*. The plantings of rhododendron species and cultivars provide spectacles of colour from early spring into midsummer; many of the more tender rhododendrons flourish here. The walkways through the wooded areas wind steeply past many other shrubs – pieris and camellias are also outstanding. Nearer the house are water and rock gardens. Daffodils appear in sheets in spring, and summer sees the flowering of roses and a good collection of herbaceous plants, many used as underplanting through the woodland.

Fota Arboretum and Gardens ★

Fota Estate, Carrigtwohill, Co. Cork. Tel: (21) 481 2728

Office of Public Works • 15.5km E of Cork, on Cobh road • Arboretum open all year, daily, 9am – 6pm (opens 11am Sun, closes 5pm Nov to March). Closed 25th Dec. Walled garden open April, May, Sept, Oct, Mon – Fri, 9am – 3.30pm; June to Aug, daily except Sat and Sun, 2 – 5pm • Entrance: free. Automatic pay barrier to car park • Other information: Refreshments and shop in Fota House ◑ 🏠 wc ⅙ ⬙ ⚑

Perhaps the wonders of Fota are best appreciated in summer when the obvious distractions like camellias, embothriums, drimys, pieris and most of the rhododendrons have finished flowering. There is no lack of colour: the walls sparkle with abutilons and cestrums, and the myrtles take on a pinkish hue. *Davidia involucrata* may be bereft of handkerchiefs, but admire instead the elaborate flowers of *Magnolia* x *wieseneri*, or the frothy white blooms of *Eucalyptus delegatensis*. Now is the time to appreciate the complicated growth of the Chilean hazel, the immense canopy of the fern-leaved beech, a perfect *Pinus montezumae* and the marvellous bark of the stone pine. Note the wickedly spiny species of colletia and the elegance of *Restio subverticillatus*, then spend a few minutes in the cool fernery and the Victorian orangery, which contains a fine collection of contemporary plants. This, and a section of the Pleasure Gardens known as the Italian Garden, have both been restored.

Garinish Island

(see ILNACULLIN)

Gash Gardens

Castletown, Portlaoise, Co. Laois. Tel: (502) 32247

The Keenan family • S of Mountrath, 1km off N7 Dublin – Limerick road. Signposted
• Open May to Sept, daily except Sun, 10am – 5pm. Parties welcome by appt
• Entrance: € 4 • Other information: Children under 10 not admitted ◑ **WC** ♨

Developed by the late Noel Keenan and now lovingly looked after by his daughter Mary, this plantsman's garden full of treasures deserves to be better known. Water features include a circular pond, a stream garden, a cascade and a bog garden. There is also an extensive rock garden, fine and varied herbaceous borders, a riverside walk, a beech walk and a laburnum arch.

Georgian House and Garden

2 Pery Square, Limerick, Co. Limerick. Tel: (61) 314130

Limerick Civic Trust • In Limerick • House and garden open all year, Mon – Fri, 9am – 4.30pm, Sat and Sun for parties by appt . Closed Christmas period and Bank Holidays • Entrance: € 6, OAPs/students € 4, family € 14 ○ **WC** ♿

The handsome early-nineteenth-century town house in a terrace overlooking the public gardens of Pery Square has recently been conserved and renovated, and the garden at the rear, enclosed by high brick walls and backed by its coach house, restored. The central lawn is surrounded by neatly maintained wall borders planted with favourites of the era to sustain interest throughout the year.

Glenveagh Castle Gardens ★

Glenveagh National Park, Churchill, Co. Donegal. Tel: (74) 37088/37090/37262

Department of Environment • 24km NW of Letterkenny • Castle open • Garden open 15th March to 2nd Nov, 10am – 5pm, and at other times by appt • Entrance: € 2.50, OAPs and parties per person € 2, students and children € 1.50 • Other information: Parking at visitor centre. Access to garden and castle by shuttle bus (€2) ◑ 💷 ✕ 🍴 **WC** ♿ ☕

The centrepiece of the Glenveagh National Park is the castle and surrounding gardens, set above Lough Veagh and encircled by high peat-blanketed mountains in the middle of the Donegal highlands – there can be few places where the contrast between the wild and rugged landscape and the carefully tended gardens is so marked. In the garden the surprises are countless, with each outdoor room given a different treatment. The two-acre lawn in the pleasure grounds is fringed by rhododendron shrubberies, tree ferns, eucryphias and mass plantings of hostas, rodgersias and astilbes. Beyond, pathways wind through oak woods in which grow scented rhododendrons and numerous other tender trees and shrubs. Here classical elements are added: visitors happen upon terraced enclosures furnished with Italian statuary and massive terracotta pots. The *jardin potager* next to the castle is bounded by herbaceous borders, each plot planted with heritage vegetable varieties, Irish apple cultivars, the unique single red *Dahlia* 'Matt Armour' and rank upon rank of flowering herbs. This is a paradise for plantsmen and gardeners keen on seeing fine and unusual specimens. Linger, tour the castle, and walk the mountain sides, then take the last bus back to the remarkable heather-roofed visitor centre with its imaginative landscaping.

Glin Castle Gardens

Glin, Co. Limerick. Tel: (68) 34173/34112

Madam Fitzgerald and the Knight of Glin • 48km W of Limerick on N69 • Open by appt only • Entrance: € 5 ◑ 🏛 B&B

The stylish and romantic castle looks over a formal setting to the north and a well-wooded demesne to the south. The formal garden could not be simpler, with its lawns and two domed bays flanking a path to a sundial flanked by cone-shaped yews and an elegant *Parrotia persica*, beyond which is a meadow with daffodils and a woodland with fine old trees. Magnolias and bluebells bring their spring flowering, and in early summer rhododendrons are still providing a splash of colour, in contrast to the two earlier-flowering huge *Drimys winteri* and the ancient Chilean lantern bush (*Crinodendron hookerianum*), while the grey walls of the castle are relieved by climbing plants. Shell-pink, white, yellow, scarlet – spotlights of colour switch on and off all around the garden. A shady walk with broad-leafed rhododendrons is being developed in a wood east of the main garden. An outstanding feature is the walled garden on a steep slope, with its mathematically neat rows of organic vegetables and herbs, figs and fruit, walls and arches dappled with roses and clematis, castellated henhouse, rustic temple with marble incumbent, and lovely view across the Shannon over the walls and undulating slate roofs of the old battlemented, cobblestoned stableyard. If you like kitchen gardens, Glin's will please you. Behind, a path ascends gently to a circle of twentieth-century standing stones and, beyond, to a Gothic hermitage surrounded by ferns and a winding woodland walk.

Graigueconna ★

Old Connaught, Bray, Co. Wicklow. Tel: (1) 282 2273

Mr and Mrs John Brown • 19km SE of Dublin city centre. Take N11, then slip road to Bray and turn right at traffic lights. From S take N11 towards Dublin, then slip road signed to Bray/Enniskerry/Rathmichael. Turn left for Graigueconna • Open May to July, 9am – 6pm, by appt only for parties of four or more • Entrance: € 5 • Other information: Coffee provided for small groups by arrangement ● WC ♿

The three-acre garden was created early last century by Lewis Meredith, who wrote *Rock gardens – how to make and maintain them* (1906), one of the earliest 'text books' on this topic. His rock garden lies hidden at the end of a specially laid railway track along which rocks were trundled. Today, this track is a grassy path, punctuated by Irish yews and lined with excellent mixed borders of shrubs and herbaceous perennials many of them uncommon. The rock garden, while intact, is planted for easier maintenance with ground-cover species, bulbs and ferns, along with many interesting southern-hemisphere shrubs. There are numerous 'old' roses on the walls and in shrubberies. Tender and unusual plants are to be found near the house, while the conservatory houses tender southern-hemisphere species and a collection of arisaemas. The whole place is painstakingly cared for.

Heywood Garden

Ballinakill, Co. Laois. Tel: (502) 33563

Department of Environment • 5km SE of Abbeyleix. Turn E in Abbeyleix signed to Ballinakill. Outside Ballinakill • Open all year, daily, during daylight hours • Entrance: free ○ &

Edwin Lutyens' walled garden with pergola and lawns is acknowledged as his finest small-scale work in Ireland. This gem has now been recognised as a heritage garden of historic and architectural importance and restored close to its original state as far as the walls and ornaments are concerned. On the driveway leading towards the school buildings is an eighteenth-century folly.

Ilnacullin (Garinish Island)

Glengarriff, Co. Cork. Tel: (027) 63040

Department of Environment • On island in Bantry Bay • Open March and Oct, Mon – Sat, 10am – 4.30pm, Sun, 1 – 5pm; May to Sept, daily, 10am – 6.30pm (opens 9.30am July and Aug; opens 11am Suns) (last landing 1 hour before closing). Closed Nov to Feb • Entrance: €3.50, OAPs €2.50, students and children €1.25, family €8.25, parties of 20 or more €2.50 per person (2005 prices) ◗ ⬛ WC & ⬥ ⚲

The boat trip across the sheltered inlets of Bantry Bay past sun-bathing seals, with views of the Caha Mountains, is doubly rewarding; landing at the slipway you gain entrance to one of Ireland's gardening jewels, begun in the early 1900s. Most visitors cluster around the Casita – an Italianate garden – and reflecting pool, designed by Harold Peto, to enjoy (on clear days) spectacular scenery and some quite indifferent annual bedding. But walk beyond, to the Temple of the Winds, through shrubberies filled with plants usually confined indoors, tree ferns, southern-hemisphere conifers, rhododendron species and cultivars. A flight of stone steps leads to the Martello tower, and thence the path returns to the walled garden with its double-sided herbaceous border.

Iveagh Gardens

Clonmel Street, Dublin 2. Tel: (1) 475 7816

Department of Environment • Access via Clonmel Street, Hatch Street or National Concert Hall, Earlsfort Terrace • Open all year, daily, 8.30am – 6pm (opens 10am Sun and Bank Holiday Mons, closes earlier Oct to March). Closed 5th Dec, 17th

*March • Entrance: free • Other information: Wheelchairs via Clonmel Street and
Hatch Street entrances* ○ &

Ranked among the finest and least known of Dublin's parks and gardens, they were
designed by Ninian Niven in 1863 and include a rustic grotto, a cascade, fountains, a
maze, a rosarium, archery grounds, a wilderness and woodlands. An ongoing
programme of restoration is underway, and many of the highlights of the gardens –
the fountains, the cascade and the rosarium – have already been tackled, but a lot
remains to be done and good plantings are needed.

The Japanese Garden

Irish National Stud, Tully, Kildare, Co. Kildare. Tel: (45) 521617/522963

*Irish National Stud • 40km SW of Dublin, 1.5km off M7 and R415 outside Kildare
• Open mid-Feb to mid-Nov, daily, 9.30am – 5pm. Guided tours available • Entrance:
by combined ticket for Japanese Garden, St Fiachra's Garden, Irish National Stud and
Horse Museum €9, OAPs and students €7, children €4.50, family €20 • Other
information: Picnics in car park only* ○ ☕ × WC & ⬧ ⬧ ⌁

Devised by Colonel William Hall-Walker (later Lord Wavertree), a wealthy
Scotsman of a famous brewery family, and laid out 1906–10 by the Japanese Eida and
his son Minoru, the garden symbolises the 'Life of Man'. This is not a plantsman's
garden, and few of the plants are Japanese; to be sure there are some excellent old
maples, but many of the trees and shrubs are clipped and shaped beyond reason.
The overshadowing Scots pines are exquisite. A pathway meanders through artificial
caves into a watery stream, past the tranquil ponds and on to the weeping trees
of the grave. In all, there are four acres of woodland and lakeside walks. Beautiful
stone lanterns grace the site, which is in the style of a Japanese tea garden. New in
1999 was the creation of *St Fiachra's Garden*, 'a garden in commemoration of the
Patron Saint of Gardeners in his home country of Ireland', as the National Stud
puts it.

John F. Kennedy Arboretum

New Ross, Co. Wexford. Tel: (51) 388171

*Office of Public Works • 12km S of New Ross • Open all year, daily except 14th April
and 25th Dec, from 10am (closes 6.30pm April and Sept, 8pm May to Aug, 5pm Oct
to March) • Entrance: €2.75, OAPs €2, students and children €1.25, family
€7 (2005 prices) • Other information: Refreshments and shop available mid-March to
Oct, sometimes Suns only. Visitor centre with Kennedy memorial* ○ ☕ WC & ⬧ ⬧ ⌁

A spacious modern arboretum laid out in botanical sequence with rides. From the
summit of a nearby hill a superb panorama stretches out, not only of the arboretum
but also of parts of six counties, and it is best to begin at the viewpoint – turn left
just beyond the main entrance and drive to the summit car park to see the layout.
At the arboretum be prepared for a long walk; fortunately those not keen on
gardening tend to linger near the cafe so that the distant reaches are quiet and
empty. Planting began in the 1960s, and now 4500 different trees and shrubs are
growing, ranging from conifers to flowering shrubs. In autumn, the colour of the 170
different kinds of maple can be quite spectacular. Most species are represented by

several specimens, and keen plantsmen can take their time examining the groups. A colourful planting of dwarf conifers is on the western side, a small lake on the east. While primarily a scientific collection, the arboretum is now achieving an established reputation. A special feature in spring and early summer is the 12-acre ericaceous garden, which contains 500 different rhododendrons and many varieties of azaleas and heathers.

Kilfane Glen and Waterfall

Thomastown, Co. Kilkenny. Tel: (56) 7724558

Mrs Susan Mosse • 19km SE of Kilkenny, 6.5km N of Thomastown, signed off N9 • Open July, Aug, daily, 11am – 6pm, and for parties of 20 or more at other times by appt • Entrance: €5.50, OAPs €5, children €4.50, family €15 ◑ 🏠 WC ♨

This romantic woodland garden dates from 1790, when the glen was designed to display nature in all her terrifying beauty, *à la* Wordsworth. It has the requisite romantic traits including a hermit's grotto, a *cottage orné* and a waterfall, so that present-day visitors can enjoy the beauties just as their predecessors did under the tuition of the gentry of Kilfane House. A good leaflet with a suggested walk tells the reader when to feel the *frisson*.

Killruddery House and Gardens ★

Bray, Co. Wicklow. Tel: (0) 404 46024

The Earl and Countess of Meath • 23km S of Dublin, just beyond Bray. Follow signs off roundabout on Bray/Greystones road. From N11 (1st exit for Bray travelling N; 3rd exit for Bray/Greystones travelling S) follow signs off roundabout • House open May, June and Sept, daily, 1 – 5pm, with conducted tours, and at other dates and times for pre-arranged parties • Garden open April, Sat and Sun, 1 – 5pm; May to Sept, daily, 1 – 5pm • Entrance: €6.50, OAPs/students €4, children €2 (house and garden €8, OAPs/students €6.50, children €3). All children must be accompanied • Other information: Teas and meals for groups by arrangement ◑ WC ♿ ♀

Killruddery is unique in having the most extensive early formal gardens surviving in Ireland in their original style. They date largely from the seventeenth century with nineteenth-century embellishments. The joy of the gardens is the formal hedging, known as 'The Angles', set beside the formal canals which lead to a ride into the distant hills. There is a collection of nineteenth-century French cast statuary, a sylvan theatre created in bay, and a fountain pool enclosed in a beech hedge. The fine nineteenth-century conservatory has been completely re-roofed, its original Turner dome put back and its unique collection of statues conserved and restored. The garden deserves to be better known. Nearby is the *National Gardens Exhibition Centre* at Kilquade, a one-stop shop for gardeners with individual gardens created by different designers.

Kilmacurragh

Kilbride, Rathdrum, Co. Wicklow. Tel: (1) 647 3000

Department of Environment • 48km S of Dublin, 8km S of Wicklow off N11. Turn right at Old Tap pub. After 1m turn left at T-junction. Entrance through gate-

way with curved granite wall and sequoiadendrons • Opening dates and prices: for information ring National Botanic Gardens on (1) 837 4388 ◕

This garden is rated highly because of its atmosphere and magnificent ancient plants. It was created by Thomas Acton in the mid- to late-nineteenth century. Behind the derelict eyesore of a house there was an incomparable avenue composed of alternating Irish yews and crimson rhododendrons, although in recent years there has been much storm damage. Beyond, paths wind through the arboretum under mighty rhododendrons. The trees include many unequalled specimens – rare conifers abound. If you can, visit it when crocus blossom is in the meadow, when the rhododendron flowers are tumbling down, at any time for elegant decrepitude. The garden is now managed, as Thomas Acton always wished, as an adjunct to the National Botanic Gardens, Glasnevin (see entry).

Kilmokea

Great Island, Campile, Co. Wexford. Tel: (51) 388109

Mark and Emma Hewlett • 13km S of New Ross, 0.5km off R733 New Ross – Great Island road towards River Barrow • Open March to Oct, daily, 10am – 6pm • Entrance: €6, OAPs €5, accompanied children under 16 €3 ◑ ✕ WC ♿ B&B

The gardens of the rectory, developed since 1940, have matured splendidly in the gentle microclimate of Waterford Harbour. The contrast between the formal and the informal is marvellously displayed here. It is impossible to decide which is the more inspired – a series of enclosed gardens featuring an herbaceous border, topiary and an Italian garden, etc., or the woodland garden, which was started on the site of an old mill and where the smaller and rarer rhododendrons, candelabra primulas and tender shrubs excel beneath a canopy of conifers and exotic trees, alongside a stream and its falls. The influence of Peto is discernible, the imaginative hand of the previous owners, the Prices, is paramount. Admire also the pergolas, gazebos and boardwalks. A yin and yang garden has been planted by the present owners, with white and yellows representing the cool element and reds and oranges the hot, and a large organic *potager* was added in 2003.

Knockabbey Castle

Louth, Co. Louth. Tel: (16) 778816

Cyril O'Brien • 13m SW of Dundalk, 8M NW of Ardee. Take M1 to Ardee, at second roundabout take Tallanstown exit – castle signposted from there • Open May to September, Tues – Sun and Bank Holiday Mons, 10.30am – 5.30pm • Entrance: €6, children €4, family €16 (tower house and gardens €10, children €8, family €28) ◑ WC

The grounds have evolved over many generations and have been skilfully revived in recent years by the present owner, with grant aid from the GGIRP. Terraces from the attractively castellated house lead, via an expertly maintained double herbaceous border, to mown paths in the parkland that meander between fine mature specimen trees. Beyond, well-constructed paths are linked by metal bridges and run through woodland beside a series of ornamental ponds, once formal fish ponds. The culmination of this walk is a restored eighteenth-century stone garden building, known as the tea house, which is encircled by majestic lime trees. There are many carefully placed seats and a wooden summerhouse from which to enjoy the view back towards the replica Victorian glasshouse and its colourful surrounding bedding.

Kylemore Abbey

Kylemore, Connemara, Co. Galway. Tel: (95) 41146

Order of Benedictine Nuns • On N59 9km NE of Letterfrack • Abbey, church and mausoleum open all year, daily except Christmas week and Good Friday, 9.30am – 5.30pm; Nov to March, 10.30am – 4pm • Garden open 16th April to Oct, daily, 10.30am – 4.30pm • Entrance: Abbey buildings and garden €11, concessions €7, parties of 10 or more €7 per person ◐ ◙ ✕ <u>WC</u> & ℘ ⊞ ◕

Set in spectacular Connemara landscape, the 1860s' Scottish Baronial house is reflected in a lake and backed by tree-covered mountains. The trees are some of the hundreds of thousands planted by the original owner, Mitchell Henry, who also established an elaborate six-acre walled garden in a clement spot a mile away from the castle. Kylemore Castle became Kylemore Abbey when it was bought by Benedictine nuns in the 1920s. A portion of the walled garden was maintained for many years, but it had become overgrown and the buildings dilapidated until the nuns, aided by a GGIRP grant, decided in 1995 to restore the walled garden to its late-nineteenth-century splendour and to conserve the buildings. Half the garden has become again an ornamental flower garden, containing typical annual beds in lawns, the other half was a fruit and vegetable garden, now fully replanted. The two areas are separated by a tree-lined stream. Restoration of the 21 glasshouses in a handsome range has begun. The head gardener's house (sadly not lived in), bothy, toolshed and lime kiln (from which the heat for the glasshouses was piped) are on view, and traditional Victorian favourites and exotic plants can be enjoyed once more.

Lakemount ★

Barnavara Hill, Glanmire, Co. Cork. Tel: (86) 811 0241

Brian Cross • 8km E of Cork off R639, at top of Barnavara Hill above Glanmire • Open all year, by appt • Entrance: €5.50 ◐ ◙ WC & ℘

A skilfully designed and immaculately maintained two-acre hillside garden, with rhododendrons, azaleas and camellias in spring and a wealth of summer interest and colour, especially from hydrangeas. There are paved areas on different levels, a poolhouse and planthouse with exotics such as iochromas, cassias and tibouchinas, while to the rear of the house a lawn slopes gently from a rock garden to beds with a mixed planting of trees, shrubs and herbaceous plants. This is an evolving garden with many unusual plantings, most recently in the old orchard and in meadows now filled with wild flowers fringed with rare trees and shrubs. A large pond has also been added.

Larchill Arcadian Gardens
Kilcock, Co. Kildare. Tel: (1) 628 7354

Michael and Louisa de las Casas • 5km from Kilcock on Dunslaughlin Road • Open May, Sept, Sat, Sun and Bank Holiday Mons; June to Aug, daily except Mon; all 12 noon – 6pm • Entrance: €7.50, children €5.50, family €27.50, parties by arrangement ● ◪ ▦ <u>WC</u> ♿ ⬠ ℘ ⛪ ⛲ ᕫ

The modest mid-eighteenth century house overlooks a tree-lined parkland landscape. A circulatory walk through the trees leads to several unique rustic follies, including the Fox's Earth and a sham fort on an island in the lake (no longer used for mock sea battles but by nesting wild fowl). The follies have been conserved, the lake flooded and the entire site restored with the aid of a grant from the GGIRP. Larchill is a very unusual survival: an intact *ferme ornée*, with the largest collection of rare breeds of cattle and other domestic animals in Ireland, living in fields and in the attractive farmyard. Near the house, contemporary design and colourful planting in the walled garden contrast with the restful greens of the parkland.

Lismore Castle Gardens
Lismore, Co. Waterford. Tel: (58) 54424

The Duke and Duchess of Devonshire • 57.5km SW of Waterford in Lismore • Open April to Sept, daily, 1.45 – 4.45pm (opens 11am June to Aug) • Entrance: €6, children under 16 €3. Parties of 20 or more during working hours €5.50 per person, children €2.50 • Other information: Toilet facilities, inc. disabled, nearby ◑ ▦ ♿ ⬠ ᕫ

The situation of the castle overlooking the River Blackwater is stunning; Edmund Spenser is said to have written *The Fairie Queene* here. There are two gardens linked by the gatehouse entrance: the upper, reached by a stairway in the gatehouse, leads to a terrace with vegetables and flowers, a reduced glasshouse by Joseph Paxton (with an interesting ridge-and-furrow roof) and a fine view from the main axis to the church spire emphasised by a new herbaceous border. In the lower garden, several steps down from the gatehouse, are a few meritricious plants, but the principal feature, an ancient yew walk, is wonderful. Remarkable too are the contemporary sculptures so skilfully inserted into the landscape. The west wing of the castle is being converted into a contemporary art space to host exhibitions from all over the world.

Lisnavagh
Rathvilly, Co. Carlow. Tel: (59 91) 61104

Lord and Lady Rathdonnell • 2.5km SE of Rathvilly off N81. Signposted • Open by appt only • Entrance: €5, children €2 ● <u>WC</u> ♿

Originally designed by Daniel Robertson in the 1850s with panoramic views of the Wicklow hills and Mount Leinster, the 10-acre gardens have a wonderful array of majestic trees and shrubs, including magnificent rhododendrons, azaleas, camellias, embothriums and many unusual plants, as well as some spectacular Irish yews. They also boast a large walled garden with peacocks strutting amongst the old fruit trees, mixed borders and a small rock garden. There are endless woodland walks with all sorts of wildlife.

Lodge Park Walled Garden
Straffan, Co. Kildare. Tel: (1) 628 8412

Mr and Mrs Robert Guinness • 20km W of Dublin. Take N4 to Maynooth or Lucan or N7 to Kill. At traffic lights in Kill on N7 follow signs for Steam Museum (adjoins garden) • Open June to Aug, Wed – Sun and Bank Holiday Mons, 2 – 6pm, May and Sept by prior appt • Entrance: €7, concessions €5, family €20 ● ● × ● WC ● ● ● ● ●

The two-acre walled garden dates from the late eighteenth century and provided produce and flowers for the house. The present owners have been restoring it over a number of years, adding their own personal touches to the layout. It is filled with a great assortment of rare flowering plants, herbs, salad crops and fruit and is beautifully kept – the potting shed must be the most perfect example of its kind for cleanliness and order. The lack of commerciality is refreshing, and despite being relatively unknown its high standards mark it out as a gardener's garden.

Loughcrew Historic Gardens
Oldcastle, Co. Meath. Tel: (49) 854 1922

Mr and Mrs Charles Naper • 85km NW of Dublin off N3, 5km from Oldcastle off Mullingar road • Open 19th March to Oct, daily, 12.30 – 5pm; Nov to 18th March, Sun, 1 – 4pm. Closed 25th Dec • Entrance: €5, OAPs €4.50, children €3, family €15, parties €4.50 per person ○ ● ● WC ● ● ● ● ● ●

An extraordinary survival of a seventeenth-century demesne, retaining many of its features through the waxing and waning of the family fortunes. The remarkable yew walk dates from the mid-1660s and has few rivals for the beauty and girth of its individual trees. The lime avenue runs down in a straight and elegant sweep to an ancient burial ground. The tower house alone is worth a visit. A massive centre motte is the focal point of the garden; behind it a huge cedar spews a water cascade from its base into a dark pool. This 'devil's cauldron' has been planted in fiery colours and terminates the main herbaceous border. A yew parterre fronts the site of the ruined seventeenth-century longhouse, where a carved wooden doorframe echoes the original. A slender and elegant canal flows parallel to the replanted herbaceous border, which itself skirts the outside of the old walled garden. Many of the original features of the garden and pleasure ground have been repaired, restored or unashamedly reinvented. The atmosphere of the whole place is one of considerable antiquity blended with an artistic approach.

Marlay Park
Grange Road, Rathfarnham, Dublin 18. Tel: (1) 493 4059

Dun Laoghaire-Rathdown County Council • In Rathfarnham, signposted on Brehon Road/Grange Road • House open by appt • Park open, all year, dawn – dusk. Walled garden open May to Sept, Tues – Sun, 12 noon – 5pm • Entrance: park free, walled garden €3, children €2 ○ ● ● WC ● ● ● ● ● ●

The extensive 200-acre public park under the Dublin mountains, with the Little Dargle River running through, contains a lake, lawns and fine old trees. Once the demesne of the La Touche banking family, the late-eighteenth-century house has recently been sensitively restored for public use; the adjacent large walled garden has also been restored with the aid of a grant from the GGIRP. The garden was traditionally divided into three parts, two of which are on view. On entering through the head gardener's house, the central position is taken by an attractive Regency-style ornamental flower garden, containing colourful flowerbeds of mixed bedding fashionable in that era. Features of interest, such as a shrubbery, an orangery, a rustic summerhouse and a fountain embellish the site. Another section of the walled garden houses a large kitchen garden, set out in a traditional early-nineteenth-century manner and containing vegetables and fruit known to have been grown at that time, many now rare.

Mount Congreve ★★

Kilmeaden, Co. Waterford. Tel: (51) 384115 (Office)

Mr Ambrose Congreve • Open April to Oct, Thurs, 9am – 5pm, strictly by appt for conducted tours and coach parties • Entrance: individuals free, coaches €300 – €400 per coach • Other information: No children under 12 ◐ WC

In emulation of Exbury, the owner has amassed an unequalled collection of rhododendron, camellia and magnolia species and cultivars, with many other trees as icing on the cake. It is a staggering collection which cannot be described adequately in a single entry: 70 acres of shrubs, mass upon mass, since every cultivar is planted in groups. In addition to the flowering shrubs, which include Mount Congreve hybrids, there are many other splendours, including a whole series of surprises, one of the most spectacular being a pagoda at the base of 25-metre cliffs. Highlights are memorable. In early March a forest of *Magnolia campbellii* offers pink to white goblets to the rooks. A languid walled garden has a fine eighteenth-century vinery and range of glasshouses. In the borders is an extensive collection of herbaceous plants arranged in order of monthly flowering – May to July, a large arrangement for August, plus a border for September and October – an unusual idea. There is far too much here to appreciate on a single visit and it is satisfying to know the garden has been left to the nation.

Mount Usher ★★

Ashford, Co. Wicklow. Tel: (404) 40116/40205

Mrs Madelaine Jay • 50km S of Dublin, 6.5km NW of Wicklow, off the N11 at Ashford • Open 17th March to Oct, daily, 10.30am – 6pm • Entrance: €6.50, OAPs, students and children €5. Special rates for parties of 20 or more. Guided tours (€40) must be pre-booked ◑ ⬤ ✕ WC ⅊ ♨ ♀

The Vartry River flows through this exquisite garden over weirs and under bridges which allow visitors to meander through the collections. It is a plant-lovers' paradise. *Pinus montezumae* is always first port of call, a shimmering tree, magnificent when the bluebells are in flower. Throughout are drifts of rhododendrons, fine trees and shrubs, including many that are difficult to cultivate outdoors in other parts of

Britain and Ireland. The grove of eucalyptus at the lower end of the valley is memorable; a kiwi-fruit vine (*Actinidia chinensis*) cloaks the piers of a bridge, and beside the tennis court is the gigantic original *Eucryphia* x *nymansensis* 'Mount Usher'. In spring, bulbs, magnolias, a procession of rhododendrons and camellias, in summer eucryphias and leptospermums, in autumn russet and crimson leaves falling from maples – a garden for all seasons.

Muckross House and Gardens ★

Killarney National Park, Killarney, Co. Kerry. Tel: (64) 31947/31440

National Parks and Wildlife Service • 6.5km S of Killarney on N71 Kenmare road • House open (admission charge) • Gardens open all year, daily • Entrance: free
○ ▆ ✕ 🦽 wc ♿ ⚓ ♨ ♋

The garden around the house is almost incidental to the spectacle of the lakes and mountains of Killarney; indeed, it is principally renowned as a viewing area for the wild grandeur of the mountains. The lawns sweep to clumps of old rhododendrons and Scots pines, and there is a huge natural rock garden. Quiet corners abound along the lough-shore walks, and anyone interested in trees and shrubs is strongly recommended to head for the recently developed arboretum area (it can be reached by car easily – follow the signpost) and is a short walk from the house). There, good specimen trees surround a wooden pergola of imaginative design, and there are plantings of tender shrubs in the wild, shaded woods beyond, which, with their unique flora and ancient yews and the almost immortal strawberry trees (*Arbutus unedo*), are enticing.

National Botanic Gardens, Glasnevin ★

Glasnevin, Dublin 9. Tel: (1) 804 0300 (Visitor centre (1) 857 0909)

Office of Public Works • 1.5km N of city centre on Botanic Road close to cemetery • Open all year, daily except 25th Dec: summer, 9am – 6pm, winter, 10am – 4.30pm (opens 11am Sun). Opening times for glasshouses posted at entrance • Entrance: free, parking €2 • Other information: Pre-booked guided tours €2; free tour every Sunday at 2.30pm ○ ▆ ✕ wc ♿ ♨ ♋

This historic garden is changing yearly but retains much of its Victorian atmosphere. The plant collections and glasshouses are undergoing restoration and renewal, there are interesting new planting schemes near the entrance and around the Curvilinear Range, and the Great Palm House of 1884 reopened in 2004. The Turner Conservatory (1843–69), the finest in Ireland, has been restored and planted with cycads and related plants, south-east Asian rhododendrons (sect. Vireya) and plants from the South African fynbos and dry temperate areas of Australia and South America. Recent developments include a sensory garden and a greatly expanded display of Chinese plants. Glasnevin is undoubtedly worth visiting and highlights are hard to enumerate, but a few outstanding plants should be mentioned: *Zelkova carpinifolia* (especially in winter a marvellously architectural tree); the ancient wisteria on the Chain Tent (*c.* 1836); the weeping Atlas cedar (*Cedrus atlantica* 'Pendula'); Chusan palms planted in 1870; *Parrotia persica* (near entrance, wonderful in February and October); and of course 'The Last Rose of Summer'.

The Phoenix Park

Dublin 8. Tel: (1) 821 3021

Office of Public Works • N of River Liffey. From city centre follow signs to 'The West', or take No. 10 bus to Phoenix Park • Open all year, daily • Entrance: free • Other information: Visitor centre near Phoenix Monument. Guided tours of àras an Uachtarin (residence of President of Ireland) and Farmleigh Estate from visitor centre, Sat from 9.45am ○ 🍵 ✕ 🥬 <u>wc</u> ♿ ⏃ 🔦 ✑

This is one of the largest enclosed parks in any European city, replete with a herd of fallow deer, some splendid monuments and great houses, most of which are accessible to the public by request. The Phoenix Monument has been relocated to its original position on the main avenue. The planting is large-scale – the avenues of horse chestnuts, limes and beeches are spectacular in blossom and in autumn, and gas lights twinkle at night the whole way along the ceremonial avenue. The People's Garden, near the main city entrance, is the only part where there is intensive gardening, but the park is a place to be lost in among the hawthorns and the wild flowers.

Powerscourt ★

Enniskerry, Co. Wicklow. Tel: (1) 204 6000

Slazenger family • 19km S of Dublin, just outside Enniskerry • House open, with exhibition on history of estate and gardens • Gardens open all year, daily except 25th and 26th Dec, 9.30am – 5.30pm (closes dusk Nov to Feb) • Entrance: charge • Other information: Apartment available ○ 🍵 ✕ <u>wc</u> ♿ ⏃ 🌿 ♨ 🔦 ✑

This is a 'grand garden', a massive statement of the triumph of art over the natural landscape. In its present form, with an amphitheatre of terraces and great central axis (mid-nineteenth century), it is largely the design of the inimitable Daniel Robertson. In some ways it is beyond compare – the axis formed by the ceremonial stairway leading down to the Triton Pond and jet, and stretching beyond to the Great Sugarloaf Mountain, is justly famous. We recommend that you walk along the terrace towards the Pepperpot, and on through the mature conifers collected by Lord Powerscourt. The Pepperpot tower has been restored and visitors can climb it to view 'the killing hollow' and the North American specimen trees in the tower valley. Wander on to the edge of the pond and look up along the stairway past the monumental terraces to the facade of the house. That's the view of Powerscourt that is breathtaking – a man-made amphitheatre guarded by winged horses. Statuary and the famous perspective gate, an avenue of monkey puzzles and a beech wood along the avenue add to the glory.

Primrose Hill ★

Lucan, Co. Dublin. Tel: (1) 628 0373

Mr Robin Hall • 13km W of city centre off N4. Turn right signed to Lucan, drive through village and, after Garda (police) station, take steep, narrow Primrose Lane on left. Continue to top and through black gateway • House open • Garden open Feb,

daily, 2pm – dusk, June to July, daily, 2 – 6pm, and at other times by appt
• Entrance: € 5 ◑ 🦽 ℘

The garden is approached up a beech avenue, flanked by a developing three-acre arboretum. The garden itself is not much bigger than one acre, yet it succeeds in housing a fine collection of snowdrops, including some of their own 'Primrose Hill' seedlings, glorious in flower. It is unusual for a garden to boast that February is its best month – but undoubtedly it is here, starting the visiting season; to return in late spring and summer when the borders are in full colour is an added joy. The herbaceous plants are lovingly cared for and planted in humus-rich compost in large clumps, giving a generous effect to the borders. Irises are high on the priority list, and so are lobelias (two named ones originated here), lilies, kniphofias and, of course, *Primula auricula* 'Old Irish Blue', plus many others.

45 Sandford Road

(see THE DILLON GARDEN)

St Anne's Park

Raheny, Dublin 3. Tel: (1) 833 8898/1859

Dublin City Council, Mount Prospect Avenue • Open all year, daily, during daylight
hours • Entrance: free ○ 🦽 WC ♿ ⟁ 🍴 ⚲

The park was once the grounds to a grand Victorian mansion, long since demolished but retaining many features of the gardens and fine mature trees. The establishment of the rose garden was inspired by the memory of the vigorous pinky-white Bourbon rose, 'Souvenir de St Anne's', which was discovered in the gardens. The main reason for visiting the large public park today is to see the outstanding display of roses in the 14-acre rose garden where thousands of blooms flourish. The height of the season, June and July, peaks with the Rose Festival held each July. It is one of the few rose gardens which holds trials for the newest unnamed varieties of roses judged by a jury of local and world experts each year. There is also a garden dedicated to patio and miniature roses.

Strokestown Park ★

Strokestown, Co. Roscommon. Tel: (071 96) 33013

The Westward Group • 23km W of Longford on N5 • House open • Park open mid-
March to Oct, daily, 10am – 5.30pm. Parties by arrangement • Entrance: park free;
house, museum and garden € 12.50, concessions € 11, children € 5.70, family € 28
• Other information: Restaurant, garden shop and toilet facilities at Famine Museum
🍽 ✕ 🦽 WC ♿ ⟁ ℘ ⛪ 🍴

The neo-Palladian house, entered from one of the broadest streets in Ireland, was purchased in 1979 by a local company, who put in motion a restoration plan involving the refurbishment of the house, the replanting of the remaining parkland and the creation of new gardens within the old walls. In the five-acre garden is one of the largest double herbaceous borders in these islands, resplendent from the top – silver, blue and white – to the bottom – purple, red and yellow – and repeated for much of its 146 metres. Handsome gates (moved here from Rockingham near Boyle) have been restored and re-erected, the pool and the pergola completed, a yew and beech hedge planted. The old summerhouse is close by the new maze and croquet lawn. A rose garden, a wildflower meadow and a fern walk are the latest achievements. The two-acre Georgian walled fruit and vegetable garden, the 1780 vinery, the 1740 banqueting folly and the Regency gazebo tower have all been restored.

Talbot Botanic Gardens ★

Malahide Castle, Malahide, Co. Dublin.
Tel: (1) 846 2456; (1) 890 5629 (Parks Department, Dublin)

Fingal County Council • 16km N of Dublin in Malahide • Castle open • Gardens open May to Sept, daily, 2 – 5pm, and to parties by appt. Conducted tour of walled garden and glasshouses, May to Sept, Wed, 2pm, and by appt • Entrance: €4, parties €3.50 per person (2005 prices) ◗ ⬤ ✕ 🍴 WC ♿ ⬦ 🛍 ⚲

A 22-acre botanic garden within the 290-acre estate of Malahide with the castle centre stage. The castle was home to the Talbot family for 800 years until the death of Lord Milo Talbot in 1973; in 1976 the estate was acquired by the local authority. The garden is in two sections – the 18-acre West Lawn area of non-ericaceous plants, and a four-acre walled garden of more tender species. The seven well-filled glasshouses range from a large Victorian conservatory to a small pit house. A National Collection of olearias has been established here, and pittosporums, nothofagus, azaleas and hoherias are also well represented. Non-horticultural entertainments include a model railway, a doll's museum and a children's playground.

Turlough Park

Castlebar, Co. Mayo. Tel: (9490) 24444

Mayo County Council • 5m E of Castlebar on N5 • Open all year, daily except Bank Holiday Mons (museum closed on Mons), 10am – 5pm (opens 2pm Suns) • Entrance: free • Other information: Garden tours by prior arrangement ○ ⬤ WC ♿ ⬦ 🏛 ⚲

The house is now part of the National Museum of Ireland's Museum of Country Life, and a visit to the extensive grounds can be combined with one to the museum. The core of the landscape park surrounding the now-ruinous eighteenth-century house survives with gardens superimposed upon it as a setting for the replacement Victorian mansion. The Castlebar River flows near the lake, recently reflooded as part of a restoration scheme; supposedly a turlough, it was dammed up in the late nineteenth century and made into an ornamental lake, containing three tree-planted 'picnic islands'. Above these are grass terraces, formal bedding, restored lean-to vinery and a fully planted free-standing replica glasshouse built onto an original base. An award-winning museum building, contemporary sculpture and the vista to a nearby round tower and ruined monastery add to the uniqueness of the site today.

Tullynally Castle

Castlepollard, Co. Westmeath. Tel: (44) 61159/62746

Thomas Pakenham • 1.5km NW of Castlepollard on R395 Granard road • Castle open to pre-booked parties only • Gardens open May, Sat and Sun, then June to Aug, daily, all 2 – 6pm, and at other times by appt • Entrance: €6, children €3 ◐ 🅿 ♿ ⬥ ⛩ 🚻 ♨

An elaborate early-eighteenth-century formal garden of canals and basins was succeeded by romantic parkland and pleasure grounds in the best Reptonian manner. They encompass two artificial lakes and a recently restored grotto, made of eroded limestone from nearby Lough Derravaragh and decorated within by carved wooden gargoyles. The present owners have added new features: two Gothick summerhouses, a Chinese garden complete with pagoda and a Tibetan garden of waterfalls and streams. The walled gardens have extensive flower borders and an avenue of memorable 200-year-old Irish yews. The energetic can undertake a mile-long walk around the lower lake, which offers splendid views of the castle.

Vandeleur Walled Garden

Vandeleur Demesne, Killimer Rd, Kilrush, Co. Clare. Tel: (6590) 51760

42km SW of Ennis on N67 in Kilrush; also 9km NW of Shannon ferry (Killimer – Tarbert) • Open all year, daily, 10am – 6pm (closes 5pm Oct to April) • Entrance: €5, OAPs €3, children €2, family €10, party rates available • Other information: Garden tours available by appt ○ 🅿 WC ♿ ⬥ ♨ 🚻 ♨

Hidden by forest, criss-crossed by paths, the ancient stone walls are a major feature of the two-acre garden that once contained humdrum produce for the Vandeleur family. Cleared after years as a nursery for the Forest Service, the original path system and the lay-out were restored but a completely new design has been introduced in each area, complemented by vibrant contemporary planting. The abundant wall borders and bedding displays include unusual, tender and scented plants. A horizontal maze (don't cheat – keep to the path!) and a more traditional beech maze, a red fountain surrounded by a collection of hebes and plenty of lawn space add to the attractions.

Woodstock Gardens and Arboretum

Inistioge, Co. Kilkenny. Tel: (87) 8580502/8549785

Kilkenny County Council • Just outside Inistioge midway between Kilkenny and New Ross off R700 • Open all year, daily, dawn – dusk • Entrance: €3.50 car parking charge. Bus charges on request ○ 🅿 🍴 WC ♿ ⬥ 🚻 ♨

The 50-acre gardens surrounding the mid-eighteenth-century house (now ruinous) were redesigned in the latter half of the Victorian era by Colonel William Tighe and his wife Lady Louisa (Lennox) in fashionable style and became renowned for the arboretum and intricately planted terraced gardens. Much has recently been conserved and restored with the aid of a GGIRP grant after seventy years of neglect.

Beautifully situated on a sloping site, high above the attractive village of Inistioge and the River Nore, many fine mature exotic trees are well spaced in grass and paths lead through the towering Monkey Puzzle and Noble Fir Walks. The walled garden now contains a double herbaceous border. The rose garden beyond has been replanted and the rustic summerhouse rebuilt, and a newly installed fountain is enclosed by rhododendrons. A dovecot and a garden building (later tiled as an ornamental dairy) pre-date the Victorian lay-out. A vast granite and white quartz rockery, assembled in 1862, awaits sympathetic planting in the next phase of improvement.

HOW TO FIND THE GARDENS

Directions to each garden are included in the entry. This information has been supplied by the owners and garden inspectors. It is aimed to be the best available to those travelling by car, and has been compiled to be used in conjunction with a road atlas. Some gardens may be reached by train or bus, but the unreliability of these makes it unrewarding to include details, particularly as many garden visits are made on Sundays.

OPENING DATES AND TIMES

Times of access given are the best available at the moment of going to press, but some may have been changed subsequently. In the entries, the times given are inclusive — that is, an entry such as May to Sept means that the garden is open from 1st May to 30th Sept inclusive, and 2 — 5 pm means that entry will be effective during that period. Please note that many owners will open their gardens to visitors by appointment, and they will often arrange to give a personally conducted tour on these occasions. Unavoidably some owners cannot give their opening details before we go to press, and in such cases we attempt to give the best guidance we can. If in doubt, it is wise to telephone before making a long journey.

GUIDANCE ON SYMBOLS

Wheelchair users: the symbol &, denoting suitability for wheelchairs, refers to the garden only — if there is a house open, it may or may not be suitable. Additionally, some areas of the garden may not be accessible by wheelchair, or may require assistance.

Dogs: ⌒ indicates that there is somewhere on the premises where dogs may be walked, preferably on a lead. The garden itself is often taboo — parkland, or even the car park, are frequently indicated for the purpose.

Picnics: ▦ means that picnics are allowed, but usually in certain restricted areas only. It does not give visitors the all-clear to feast where they please!

Children-friendly: the bat-and-ball symbol ⚲ suggests that there are activities specifically designed for children, such as an adventure playground or a discovery trail, or that the garden itself is likely to appeal to them.

SCOTLAND

Two-starred gardens are marked on the maps with a black square.

Abbotsford [Historic Scotland Inventory]

Melrose, Scottish Borders TD6 9BQ. Tel: (01896) 752043

1m S of Galashiels, just S at A72. 3m W of Melrose on A6091, turn SW onto B6360 • House open as garden • Garden open 20th March to Oct, daily, 9.30am – 5pm (Sun opening times vary seasonally) • Entrance: £5, children £2.50, parties £3.90 per person, children £1.95 ◐ 🅿 🐾 <u>WC</u> ♿ ⏏ ⛪

Sir Walter Scott's magnificent house astride a river valley was built between 1817 and 1821 to satisfy his yearning to become a laird, and its garden is rich in Scottish allusions. A yew hedge to the south of the house has medallions inset from an old cross, which was also used to make a fountain in the same formal garden. The River Tweed flows past the house, and there are fine views across a stretch of garden. Herbaceous beds lead to a Gothic-type fern house filled with plants other than ferns. However, dedicated Scott scholars will find most interest in the house, among historical relics collected by the laird himself.

Abriachan Garden and Nursery

Loch Ness Side, Inverness, Highland IV3 8LA. Tel: (01463) 861232

Mr and Mrs Davidson • On A82 Inverness – Fort William road. Ignore side roads signed to Abriachan (centre of village is in hills 2 miles above garden and nursery) • Open Feb to Nov, daily, 9am – 7pm • Entrance: £2 (collecting box) ○ 🅿 ⏏ ⚘

Although this is officially a retail nursery, it is also a fascinating hillside garden of over four acres – a plantsman's joy with paved viewing areas and secluded seats from which to contemplate the ever-mysterious Loch Ness. The clever terracing of the beds ensures that plants are seen from every angle and level, and visitors will not be able to resist climbing onwards and upwards along the network of paths meandering into the woodland. The owners have obviously worked hard, and the planting content is comprehensive and professional, ranging from bog plants to gravel lovers and alpines, especially *Primula auricula*, meconopsis, gentians and campanulas. Several new beds have been planted with unusual woodland plants. Enticingly, most of the plants on view are also for sale.

Achamore Gardens ★ [Historic Scotland Inventory]

Isle of Gigha, Argyll and Bute PA41 7AD. Tel: (01583) 505390

Isle of Gigha Heritage Trust • Take A83 to Tayinloan then ferry to Gigha • Open all year, daily, dawn – dusk • Entrance: £3.50, children £1, collecting box • Other information: Refreshments at hotel ○ ◑ WC ♿ ⏏ ⚘

An amazing idea to create such a superb garden on the Isle of Gigha. The journey there is via most beautiful countryside finishing up with the ferry trip, surrounded by squawking sea birds. In 1944 Sir James Horlick purchased the whole island with the sole purpose of creating a garden in which to grow the rare and the unusual. This was accomplished with the advice of James Russell, and the overall effect is tropical. A delightful woodland landscape was planted with a vast collection from around the world. Few gardens outside the national botanic collections can claim such diversity and rarity. The rhododendrons are unsurpassed in variety, quality and sheer visual magnitude, with fine specimens of tender species such as *R. lindleyi, R. fragrantissimum*, and *R. macabeanum*, and there are many varieties of camellias, cordylines, primulas and Asiatic exotica. Many genera are represented by very good specimens, thriving in the mild climate. There is a fine *Pinus montezumae* in the walled garden; drifts of Asiatic primulas feature around the especially pretty woodland pond. A visit to Gigha is a must for the keen plantsman and avid gardener; now that it has been put in trust for the local community, its future seems secure.

Achnacloich [Historic Scotland Inventory]

Connel, Oban, Argyll and Bute PA37 1PR. Tel: (01631) 710796

Mrs T.E. Nelson • 3m E of Connel off A85 • Open 18th March to Oct, daily, 10am – 6pm • Entrance: £2, OAPs £1, children free • Other information: Dogs on lead please ◑ &

A small castellated Scottish baronial house beautifully situated above the loch on a rocky cliff, with fine views to Loch Etive and the surrounding countryside. A curved drive sweeps past massed bulbs in spring, and later there are azaleas and fine Japanese maples; autumn colour is good throughout the garden. The natural woodland with its interlinked glades is beautiful in spring with bluebells, primroses and wood anemones, while other gaps are planted with primulas, magnolias, rare shrubs and rhododendrons. There are two water gardens, and the garden walks have been extended, taking in an oak wood underplanted with large-leaved rhododendrons.

Allangrange

Munlochy, Black Isle, Ross and Cromarty, Highland IV8 8NZ. Tel: (01463) 811249

Major and Mrs A. Cameron • 5m N of Inverness, signed from A9 • Open for parties by appt • Entrance: £2, children 20p ● wc & ⬥ ⬥

A most attractive garden which spills down the hillside in a series of descending terraces merging naturally with the rolling agricultural landscape of the Black Isle. The formal part incorporates white and mauve gardens, many old and shrub roses, tree peonies and a small corner for plants of variegated foliage. In July, climbing Himalayan roses, including *Rosa filipes* 'Kiftsgate', make a spectacular display. There is also a small pool garden, and to the rear of the house a woodland garden with unusual rhododendrons, primulas, meconopsis and *Cardiocrinum giganteum*. The hand of an accomplished flower painter, Elizabeth Cameron, shows itself everywhere.

An Cala [Historic Scotland Inventory]

Easdale, Isle of Seil, Argyll PA34 4RF. Tel: (01852) 300237

Mrs Sheila Downie • 16m SW of Oban. Signed to Easdale on B844 off A816 Oban – Campbelltown road • Open April to Oct, daily, 10am – 6pm • Entrance: £2 ◑ 🐾 wc & ⬥

A jewel of under five acres designed in the 1930s in front of a row of old distillery cottages, nestling into the surrounding cliffs. The stream, with its ponds and little waterfall, is an essential element in a series of different spaces filled with sophisticated colour. A small wooden temple lined with a mosaic of fir cones stands at the far end of one of the ponds. This is how azaleas and rhododendrons should be planted on the small scale – enhancing rather than dominating the picture. Local slate paths invite the visitor into each well-planned corner. Just over the gate, in a different world, are ocean and islands.

Arbuthnott House [Historic Scotland Inventory]

Laurencekirk, Kincardineshire AB30 1PA. Tel: (01561) 361226

The Viscount of Arbuthnott • 22m S of Aberdeen, 3m W of Inverbervie on B967 between A90 (A94) and A92 • Open all year, daily, 9am – 5pm • Entrance: £2, children £1 • Other information: Refreshments available at Grassic Gibbon Centre in village ○ **WC**

The enclosed garden dates from the late seventeenth century and with the policies is contained within the valley of the Bervie Water. The entrance drive is flanked by rhododendrons, and in spring the verges are full of primroses and celandines. The drive crosses a fine bridge topped by imposing urns before reaching the house set high on a promontory, with most of the garden sloping steeply to the river. The design is unusual in that it has always been treated as an extension of the house, rather than being laid out at some distance. The sloping part has four grassed terraces and this pattern is dissected by diagonal grassed walks radiating out in a manner reminiscent of the Union Jack. This fixed structure creates long garden rooms and vistas as the garden is explored. Although the garden plan is very old, much of today's mature planting was done by Lady Arbuthnott in the 1920s, and this is continued by the present Lady Arbuthnott. Herbaceous borders, old roses, shrub roses and ramblers, shrubs underplanted with hostas, primulas, meconopsis and lilies, lilacs and viburnums provide colour throughout the summer. A metal stag for target practice stands at the bottom of the slope by the lade (millstream).

Ardanaiseig Garden and Hotel [Historic Scotland Inventory]

Kilchrenan, Argyll and Bute PA35 1HE. Tel: (01866) 833333

4m E of Kilchrenan on B845 • Open April to Oct, 9am – 8pm • Entrance: by collection box at car park, £2, OAPs and children free (2005 price) • Other information: No children under 8. Refreshments at hotel ◑ **⬤** ✕ **WC** ⬥ **B&B**

A picturesque 10-mile drive from Taynuilt down the peninsular makes a fitting introduction to this traditional Argyll garden. Attractive slate paths guide the visitor round 20 acres of well-planted woodland set behind an 1834 baronial house, now a comfortable hotel, with lovely views across Loch Awe. The species and hybrid rhododendrons are particularly fine. Note the unusual curved walls of the walled garden.

Ardchattan Priory [Historic Scotland Inventory]

Oban, Argyll PA37 1RQ. Tel: (01796) 481355

10m NE of Oban. Cross Connel Bridge on A828 N and turn first right to Ardchattan • Open April to Oct, daily, 9am – 6pm • Entrance: £2.50 ◑ **WC** ♿ ⬥

A charming garden with spectacular views over Loch Etive. The extensive lawn to the front of the house is encircled by herbaceous, rose and shrub borders and a rockery. Either side of the drive, the wild garden is full of roses, shrubs and ornamental trees. The garden surrounds a priory (now a private house) founded by the Valescaullian Order in 1230, and the ruined chapel and its early graveyard are open with the garden.

Ardkinglas Woodland Garden [Historic Scotland Inventory]

Cairndow, Argyll and Bute PA26 8BH. Tel: (01499) 600261

Mr David Sumsion • On A83 Loch Lomond – Inveraray road. Signposted • Open all year, daily, during daylight hours • Entrance: £3, children under 16 free

○ ➍ ✕ ➍ wc ᕦ ℘

Following a large-scale, long-term programme aimed at conserving and rejuvenating the historic plant collection, a sense of balance and atmosphere is being restored to this dramatic landscape setting above the shores of Loch Fyne. The garden contains eight champion trees, including the 'mightiest conifer in Europe', a silver fir (*Abies alba*) with a girth in excess of 10 metres, and one of the tallest trees in Britain, a grand fir (*Abies grandis*) at just over 62 metres. The next generation of plants is well and truly established amongst bluebells and ferns. There are panoramic views from the gazebo (linger to read the literary quotations inscribed within). A further area has new footpaths and a bridge over the River Kinglas giving access to a seventeenth-century mill.

Ardmaddy Castle

By Oban, Argyll PA34 4QY. Tel: (01852) 300353

Mr and Mrs Charles Struthers • 13m SW of Oban. Signed from B844 to Easdale along narrow road • Open all year, daily, 9am – dusk • Entrance: £2.50 ○ ➍ wc
ᕦ ⬠ ℘ ℺

The handsome but modest fifteenth-century castle, with steps up to its *piano nobile*, faces both ways – outwards with wide views to the islands and the sea, inwards on the garden side towards steep surrounding woods and a formal walled garden. In the eighteenth century Ardmaddy marked the western extent of the Earl of Breadalbane's estate, enabling him to ride from one side of Scotland to the other on his own land – until all was gambled away in the early twentieth century. The walled garden set below the castle has traditional box hedge compartments, large numbers of species and hybrid rhododendrons and an increasing collection of herbaceous plants and flowering shrubs and trees as well as immaculate vegetables. A water garden with two ponds, and a woodland garden with walks, add further interest. There is always a good selection of home-grown plants and vegetables (in season) on sale.

Ardtornish [Historic Scotland Inventory]

Lochaline, Morvern, Highland PA34 5UZ. Tel: (01967) 421288 (Estate Office)

Ardtornish Estate Company • 30m SW of Corran. From Corran ferry, 9m SW of Fort William, cross to Morvern and take route left on A861 towards Lochaline, then left on A884. Gardens are 2m before Lochaline on left • Open April to Oct, daily,

9am – 6pm • Entrance: £3, children free (collecting box) • Other information: 12 self-catering units available, 5 in house ◑ WC ♿ ⬦

A plantsman's garden with a particularly fine and extensive collection of unusual shrubs, deciduous trees and rhododendrons set against a background of conifers, a loch and outstanding Highland scenery. The first house on the site was built by a London distiller in the 1860s, and the gardens have developed over the past hundred years or more. They are on a steep slope and rainfall is heavy. Mrs Raven's late husband wrote a book, *The Botanist's Garden* (now republished), about their other garden, Docwra's Manor (see entry in Cambridgeshire), and here too he assisted his wife to follow in her parents' footsteps in trying to establish a plantsman's paradise. Apart from the area around the house, there is a pleasing air of informality about the gardens, which include Bob's Glen with *Rhododendron thomsonii* and *R. prattii*, a larger glen with still more species and hybrid rhododendrons, and a kitchen garden under separate management nearby, where good-quality plants are for sale.

Arduaine Garden ★★ [Historic Scotland Inventory]

Oban, Argyll and Bute PA34 4XQ. Tel: (01852) 200366

The National Trust for Scotland • On A816, 20m S of Oban, 18m N of Lochgilphead. Joint entrance with Loch Melfort Hotel • Open all year, daily, 9.30am – sunset • Entrance: £5, concessions and children £4, family £14 • Other information: Refreshments at hotel adjacent – coach parties must pre-book, telephone (01852) 200233 ○ 🍴 WC ♿

Arduaine was conceived and begun in 1898 by James Arthur Campbell, possibly with advice from Osgood Mackenzie, creator of Inverewe Garden (see entry). The Essex nurserymen Edmund and Harry Wright restored the garden after they acquired it in 1971 and gave it to the Trust in 1992. This plantsmen's garden consists of an outstanding 20 acres on a promontory bounded by Loch Melfort and the Sound of Jura, climatically favoured by the North Atlantic Drift. Make the effort to climb to the high viewing point to enjoy the panorama of ocean, coasts and islands. Although its fame rests largely on its outstanding rhododendrons, azaleas, magnolias and other rare and tender trees and shrubs (the rhododendron collection, with around 400 species, ranks high in importance in Scotland), the garden has far more than botanical interest to offer. Trees and shrubs, some over a hundred years old and thickly underplanted, tower overhead as they, and visitors, climb the glen, while at the lower level hostas, ferns, candelabra primulas, meconopsis and numerous other flower and foliage perennials cluster around lawns and along the sides of the watercourses.

Armadale Castle Gardens [Historic Scotland Inventory]

Armadale, Sleat, Isle of Skye IV45 8RS. Tel: (01471) 844305

Clan Donald Lands Trust • 14m S of Broadford at S end of Skye, close to Mallaig ferry • Open April to Oct, daily, 9.30am – 5.30pm • Entrance: £4.80, concessions £3.50, family £14, parties of 8 or more £3.20 per person • Other information: Guided tours available. Two electric wheelchairs available ◑ 🖵 ✕ WC ♿ ⬦ 🌿 ⛪
🔦 ⚲

This fine garden is so well groomed that it has almost the atmosphere of a city park. The cultivated areas have been sympathetically developed to include pond gardens with scree planting, a long herbaceous border with a raised walk behind the ruined castle, lawns with ornamental trees and a romantic garden planted within one of the ruined sections of the castle. Surrounding the cultivated area are four miles of nature trails set in 50 acres of woodland and wildflower meadows. Although Armadale is further north than Moscow, the climate is warm and everywhere there are inspiring views up Loch Nevis to Mallaig and Knoydart. Allow plenty of time to get here: the 14-mile approach road is single-track in places and every oncoming driver must be acknowledged and thanked. The new *Museum of the Isles*, located within the garden, is included in the admission charge and worth visiting.

Attadale

Strathcarron, Wester Ross, Ross-shire IV54 8YX. Tel: (01520) 722217

Mr and Mrs Ewen Macpherson • 15m NE of Kyle of Lochalsh, on A890 between Strathcarron and Strome • Open April to Oct, daily except Sun, 10am – 5.30pm • Entrance: £3, children £1, disabled free • Other information: Honesty box, maps and leaflets inside gate. Car park 50 yards from garden; disabled parking by Attadale House. Meals available at Carron Restaurant 1.5m away. Cottages available ◐ 🖳 🍴 wc ♿ ⬦ ☂ ℘

Inside the gate a stream and ponds all along one side of the drive are beautifully planted with candelabra primulas, irises, giant gunneras and bamboos. A bridge over a waterfall links the water garden with the upper rhododendron walk, commanding views of the sea and hills. Sculpture from Zimbabwe and bronzes by Bridget McCrum and Elizabeth Macdonald Buchanan are reflected in the ponds, and a bronze crested eagle perches on a cliff. The formal kitchen garden has a slate urn by Joe Smith; beyond, a recently built geodesic dome houses a collection of exotic ferns and is surrounded by hardy ferns, including tree ferns, backed by dripping cliffs. A path leads down to a dell of rhododendrons planted by the Schroder family nearly a century ago, then on along a woodland path to the new Japanese garden, where lichened rocks and gravel imitate the River of Life and the Mystic Isles of the West. The symmetrical sunken garden in front of the 1755 house (not open) provides a complete contrast. Visitors are advised to wear waterproof shoes.

Baitlaws

Lamington, Biggar, Lanarkshire ML12 6HR. Tel: (01899) 850240

Mr and Mrs M. Maxwell Stuart • 10m SE of Lanark, 5m SW of Biggar, 5m NE of Abington, off A702 above Lamington village • Open one day for SGS, and June to Aug by appt • Entrance: £3, children (over 12) 25p ◐ wc ♿ ⬦ ℘

Approached up a long, stony and winding road, in a glorious setting of encircling hills, this delightful garden lies 300 metres above sea level. Everything has to be very hardy, therefore, but this has not cramped Kirsty Maxwell Stuart's style, and colour co-ordination and plantsmanship are important features of the garden. Generous crescent-shaped herbaceous borders blaze out on either side of the main lawn, one side planted mainly in shades of yellow, bronze, gold and red, the other with cool blues, mauves and white. Beyond, shrubs and small trees act as a screen to the outhouses. Stone steps lead down to a sunken garden: a large-scale parterre of mixed shrubs and small trees grouped in clever shapes and colour effects. The partially walled nursery area, furnished with cold frames and a new greenhouse with every modern facility, contains a variety of vegetables and two more long borders. Behind the house a pretty little area for shade-loving plants is being expanded into a woodland glade; another recent addition is a small pond surrounded by waterside planting. Then make your way to the 'bubble conservatory' attached to the house – really an observatory on stilts – the better to view most of the garden and the wider landscape.

Ballindalloch Castle

Grantown-on-Spey, Banffshire, Moray AB37 9AX. Tel: (01807) 500205

Mrs Oliver MacPherson-Grant Russell • Halfway between Grantown-on-Spey and Keith on A95. Signposted • Castle open • Garden open 14th April to Sept, daily except Sat, 10.30am – 5pm, and at other times by appt • Entrance: grounds £2 (castle and gardens £6) (2005 prices) • Other information: Dog-walking area ◑ 🍽 🍴 WC ♿ ⏻ 🏛 🐕

What a pleasure to find a garden of this scale and calibre set in the magnificent Spey valley. One of the most attractive feature is the 1937 rock garden, which comes tumbling down the hillside onto the most impressive lawn in the land. It takes three men two days to mow and edge it. The owners have completely renovated all the borders over the years and transformed the old walled garden into a rose and fountain parterre garden which has matured most attractively. The daffodil season and the river/woodland walks are particularly lovely. A small parterre at the side of the house shows how stunning humble nepeta and *Alchemilla mollis* can be when all else is eaten by the deer, and an intriguing new feature is the grass labyrinth.

Balmoral Castle [Historic Scotland Inventory]

Ballater, Aberdeenshire AB35 5TB. Tel: (013397) 42534 (Estates Office)

H.M. The Queen • 6m W of Ballater on A93 at Crathie • Castle ballroom and carriage exhibitions open • Gardens and grounds open April to July, daily, 10am – 5pm • Entrance: £6, OAPs £5, children (5–16) £1, under 5 free ◑ 🍽 ✕ 🍴 WC ♿ ⏻ 🎨 🏛

Balmoral, the personal home in Scotland of Her Majesty the Queen, is Gaelic for 'majestic dwelling'. There had been earlier castles on the same site before the estate was purchased in 1852 by Prince Albert, consort to Queen Victoria. She called Balmoral 'this dear paradise', and she and the Prince immediately began making a three-acre garden about the castle and planting the grounds with rare coniferous and broad-leaved forest trees. Queen Mary added the sunken rose garden in 1932, and since 1953 there have been improvements and extensions, including a water garden created in 1979 close to Queen Victoria's garden cottage. There are herbaceous borders, but generally the gardens are natural in style. Throughout the grounds statues and cairns have been erected in memory of Queen Victoria's family and their descendants, and specimen trees labelled with the names of the visiting dignitaries who planted them.

The Bank House

Glenfarg, Perth PH2 9NZ. Tel: (01577) 830275

Mr and Mrs C.B. Lascelles • 10m SW of Perth off B996 between M90 junctions 8 and 9. In Glenfarg, 50 metres along Ladeside, by Glenfarg Hotel • Open by appt • Entrance: £5, children free ● 🐌 **WC** ⑃ ❀

The main garden is approached through a paved area with additional planting above low retaining walls. An apple and clematis tunnel leads the visitor onwards to large curved beds set into lawns on a gently sloping site. A horseshoe-shaped yew hedge underplanted with yellow archangel and star of Bethlehem is a fine spring feature; bulbs and early-flowering herbaceous plants carry the display through to summer. The owners have built up an eclectic collection of rare and unusual plants of much merit, and these are grown to perfection using organic gardening techniques. The careful planting, with great regard to colour and form, makes for an instructive visit. A smaller garden across the street, with a 'flowform cascade' water feature and a yin and yang circular bed, may be visited at any time. Ornamental trees have been planted in a field, where a pond has been created and a wildflower meadow sown.

Bargany [Historic Scotland Inventory]

Girvan, South Ayrshire KA26 9QL. Tel: (01465) 871249

John Dalrymple-Hamilton • 18m SW of Ayr off B734 Girvan – Dailly road • Open May, daily, 12 noon – 5pm • Entrance: £2, children under 12 free ◐ 🐌 ⑃ ❀ ♨

This is a woodland garden with a lovely relaxed family atmosphere, densely planted with splendid ancient rhododendrons, azaleas, fine trees and conifers. Wonderfully diverse paths encourage visitors to stroll round the charming lily pond, rock garden and walled garden with its magnolias, azaleas and rhododendrons.

Barguillean's 'Angus Garden'

Taynuilt, Argyll and Bute PA35 1HY. Tel: (01866) 822335/822333

Sean Honeyman • 5m SE of Oban, 3m SW of Taynuilt. Take minor road to Kilmore, signed to Glen Lonan, off A85 at Taynuilt Hotel • Open all year, daily, dawn – dusk. Parties welcome by prior appt in writing • Entrance: £2, children free ◐ 🐌 ❀

Set on a Highland hillside overlooking a lochan with views to Ben Cruachan, this is a nine-acre woodland garden with no formal paths or borders, but with areas of established rhododendrons, azaleas and conifers and some rare trees and shrubs. It is interesting to compare the new planting, combining modern rhododendron hybrids from the north-west of the United States within native birch and oak woodland, with established rhododendron gardens of the west coast. Described by its owner as a place of tranquillity and love, it was created by Betty Macdonald in memory of her writer/journalist son, killed in Cyprus during the 1956 troubles.

Beatrix Potter Garden

Birnam, Perth and Kinross PH8 0DS. Tel: (01350) 727674 (Birnam Institute)

Perthshire and Kinross Council • 13m NW of Perth in Birnam, at centre of short loop diversion from A9 • Open all year, daily except 25th and 26th Dec, 1st and 2nd Jan • Entrance: free • Other information: Refreshments and shop at new B.I. Arts Community and Conference Centre nearby, plus Beatrix Potter exhibition ○ ☕ ✕ 🖐 <u>WC</u> ♿ ◁ 🏛 🍴 ﹢ B&B

The garden displays bronze sculptures of animals in their natural surroundings, as they were first observed by Beatrix Potter before she anthropomorphised them as her enduringly famous characters. Only on an ornamental roadside gate donated by Frederick Warne do we find Peter Rabbit in the blue jacket so familiar to his fans. In her diaries Potter reveals that some of her characters were based upon people she met in the Birnam area during her many visits.

Bell's Cherrybank Gardens and Scottish National Heather Collection

Bell's Cherrybank Centre, Cherrybank, Perth PH2 0PF. Tel: (01738) 627330

Off A93 in southern outskirts of Perth, approx 1m from Broxden roundabout • Open under Scotland's Garden Trust – telephone (01738) 627330 for details • Entrance: charge • Other information: Guide dogs only ◐ ☕ <u>WC</u> ♿ 🌿 🏛 🍴 ﹢

This modern garden surrounding commercial offices is in fact two gardens. The first, laid out in the early 1970s, was augmented from 1983 by the Scottish National Collection of heathers; there are now over 900 varieties, all in superb condition. Other plant collections are well maintained and beautifully designed, and interest is sustained by water features, modern sculptures, pleasant vistas, a tiny putting green, tubular bells and an aviary. The play area includes a roundabout for wheelchair-bound children. The second garden consists of the Bell's Pride of Perth Exhibition. Ownership having passed to Scotland's Garden Trust, these seven acres are being subsumed into Scotland's first national garden – 62 acres in extent, described as a 'garden for the 21st century', with a variety of features including a rocky gorge, an arboretum, water gardens, grass terraces and a wildflower meadow. It is due to be completed in 2007.

Benmore Botanic Garden ★★ [Historic Scotland Inventory]

Dunoon, Argyll, Argyll and Bute PA23 8QU. Tel: (01369) 706261

Royal Botanic Garden Edinburgh • 7m N of Dunoon, W of A815 at Benmore. Signposted • Open March to Oct, daily, 10am – 6pm (closes 5pm March and Oct), and at other times by appt • Entrance: £3.50, concessions £3, children £1, family £8. Membership inc. Dawyck and Logan Botanic Gardens (see entries) available ◑ ☕ ✕ <u>WC</u> ♿ 🌿 🏛 🍴 ﹢

This regional garden of the Royal Botanic Garden Edinburgh is a magnificent mountainside garden set in the dramatic location of the Cowal Peninsula. It is world-famous for its collections of flowering trees and shrubs. From Britain's finest avenue of giant redwoods (*Sequoiadendron giganteum*) planted in 1863, a variety of trails spreads out. More than 400 species of rhododendron and an extensive magnolia collection provide a positive array of colour on the hillside beside the River Eachaig. Other features include a formal garden with stately conifers, an informal pond, the Glen Massan arboretum with some of the tallest trees in Scotland, a Chilean rainforest and a Bhutanese glade. A short climb leads to a stunning viewpoint looking out across the garden, Strath Eck and the Holy Loch to the Firth of Clyde and beyond.

Biggar Park ★

Biggar, South Lanarkshire ML12 6JS. Tel: (01899) 220185

Capt. and Mrs David Barnes • 30m SW of Edinburgh at S end of Biggar on A702 • Open May to July to individuals and especially to parties by appt • Entrance: £3 • Other information: Teas by arrangement ● 🐝 ও ⬧

A Japanese garden of tranquillity welcomes the visitor to this well-planned 10-acre plantsman's garden. The efficient labelling adds greatly to the enjoyment when walking through the woodland and the small arboretum and well-planted ornamental pond. The planting is carefully designed to give year-round interest, starting with a stunning display of daffodils, with a little field of snake's head fritillaries blooming at the end of April, then followed by masses of meconopsis, rhododendrons and azaleas in early summer before the huge herbaceous borders burst into colour. The centrepiece, however, must be the outstanding walled garden, reached through a fine rockery bank beside the eighteenth-century mansion house. The view through the wrought-iron gate stretches the length of a 45-metre double herbaceous border, attractively backed by swags of thick ornamental rope hanging from rose 'pillars', whilst either side is divided into intensively planted sections intersected by pleasing grass paths and plots of fruit and vegetables.

Blackhills House

Lhanbryde, Elgin, Moray IV30 8QU. Tel: (01343) 842223

Mr and Mrs John Christie • 4m E of Elgin off A96. Take B9103 southwards, then minor road • Open 14th and 21st May, and by appt at other times • Entrance: £2, children free • Other information: Teas on open days only. Self-catering accommodation ● 🍺 🐝 WC ও ⬧

The east coast of Scotland is not, with a few exceptions, noted for its rhododendron gardens, but this garden in the Laich of Moray should be visited for its collection of species rhododendrons in early May and hybrids in late May. Both sorts are spread under tree cover in a steep-sided valley with many fine specimen trees. These include a davidia, a Japanese red cedar (*Cryptomeria japonica*), Brewer's weeping spruce and a golden chestnut (*Chrysolepis chrysophylla*) – a rare chestnut relative from North America. The finest rhododendrons are those in the subsections Falconera, Grandia and Taliensia, but the genus is well represented as a whole. The wooded valley opens to reveal two lakes with plantings of maples and other Asiatic plants. Thomas North Christie, who was responsible for the early planting in the 1920s, corresponded at length and exchanged the latest introductions with his neighbour the Brodie of Brodie.

Blair Castle ★ [Historic Scotland Inventory]

Blair Atholl, Pitlochry, Perthshire PH18 5TL. Tel: (01796) 481207

The Manager, The Blair Charitable Trust • 35m N of Perth on A9 at Blair Atholl. Signposted • House open as garden • Garden open April to 27th Oct, daily, 9.30am – 5.30pm (last entry 4.30pm), Nov to March by appt • Entrance: £2.30, children £1.20, family £5.40 (house and grounds £7.20, OAPs £6.20, students £5.90, children £4.50, family £17.50) ○ 🍽 ✕ 🏪 wc ᏉᏙᎵ ◁● 🏛 🍵 ℃

The blazing white castle remains one of Scotland's most important, most visited and best presented historic houses in private hands. The 2500-acre managed park and landscape were begun in 1730 by the 2nd Duke of Atholl in the French manner, with geometrically patterned avenues and walks radiating out from the castle. His most important legacy was the nine-acre walled Hercules Garden of 1758, named after the life-size lead statue by John Cheere which overlooks it. It is unique, not only for its scale, but also for the fact that it contains extensive water features. A series of delightful ponds, planted islands and peninsulars form a central axis from which fruit tree orchards – faithfully reproduced, but without the original underplanting of fruit and vegetables – slope gently upwards to herbaceous borders, yew buttresses and elegant gravel walks backed by the original eighteenth-century walls. A charming apple-store museum, a nineteenth-century folly, statuary, an ogee-roofed pavilion and a Chinoiserie bridge all add to the beauty of this unusual garden in its splendid Highland setting.

Bolfracks [Historic Scotland Inventory]

Aberfeldy, Perth and Kinross PH15 2EX. Tel: (01887) 820344

Mr R.A. Price • 2m W of Aberfeldy on A827 towards Loch Tay • Open April to Oct, daily, 10am – 6pm • Entrance: £3, children free (honesty box at gate) ◑ wc ℘ ℃

There has been a garden on this site for over two centuries, but the present garden was started by the owner's grandparents in the 1920s and reshaped by his uncle over the last thirty years. Three acres of plantsman's garden are well laid out within a walled enclosure and demonstrate the potential of an exposed hillside site with a northerly aspect. Astounding views over the Tay Valley are matched by the garden's own interesting features, including peat walls and a stream garden. There are masses of fine bulbs in spring and good autumn colour. An excellent collection of mainly dwarf rhododendrons has been established over the years and gives a wonderful display in May and June. Gentians, meconopsis, ericaceous plants and celmisias do well on this soil. The walled garden contains a collection of old and modern shrub roses and rambling roses and a great variety of herbaceous perennials.

Branklyn Garden ★ [Historic Scotland Inventory]

116 Dundee Road, Perth, Perth and Kinross PH2 7BB. Tel: (01738) 625535

The National Trust for Scotland • 0.5m from Friarton Bridge on A90, then A859 to Perth • Open April to Oct, daily, 10am – 5pm • Entrance: £5, Concessions £4, family £14. Pre-booked parties of 20 or more £4.50 per person • Other information: Steep lane to garden. Parking for disabled and coaches at entrance. Possible for wheelchairs but some paths too narrow ◑ 🍽 wc ℘ 🏛 🍵

John and Dorothy Renton created this garden nearly within sight and certainly within sound of the centre of Perth. Work commenced in 1922, and in 1955 Dorothy was awarded the Veitch Memorial Medal by the Royal Horticultural Society. The National Trust for Scotland took over the garden in 1968, after the death of Dorothy in 1966 and of her husband the following year. It extends to nearly two acres, the main interest being its Sino-Himalayan alpine and ericaceous plants and magnificent scree/rock gardens. There is also a splendid collection of dwarf rhododendrons and a National Collection of the Mylnefield lilies bred by Dr Chris North. Essential work continues to maintain Branklyn's rightful reputation as an outstanding plantsman's garden. It is impossible to describe all the fascinating things to be found here, from the fine trees to the comprehensive collection of dwarf and smaller rhododendrons, the meconopsis to the notholirions. This is a garden that repays many visits.

Brodick Castle ★ [Historic Scotland Inventory]

Isle of Arran, North Ayrshire KA27 8HY. Tel: (01770) 302202

The National Trust for Scotland • On Isle of Arran, 2m N of Brodick. Ferry from Ardrossan or Kintyre • Gardens and country park open all year, daily, 9.30am – dusk. Walled garden open April to Oct, daily, 9.30am — 5pm • Entrance: £5, concessions £4, parties of 20 or more £3 per person (castle and gardens £8, concessions £6, pre-booked parties of 20 or more £6 per person) • Other information: Wheelchair available ○ ☕ ✕ 🍴 WC ♿ 🐾 🌳 🏧 ♨ ℞

High above the shores of the Firth of Clyde and guarding the approaches to Western Scotland is a castle of locally quarried sandstone. The garden was an overgrown jungle of rhododendrons until it was restored by the Duchess of Montrose after World War I. She was much helped after 1930 when her daughter married John Boscawen of Tresco Abbey (see entry in Cornwall). Many trees and plants arrived at that time by boat from Tresco in the Scillies; others came from subscriptions to the second generation of great plant-hunters like Kingdon Ward and, in particular, George Forrest, one of the greatest of all collectors. Plants from the Himalayas, Burma, China and South America, normally considered tender, flourish in the mild climate. There is a good display of primulas in the bog garden. The walled formal garden to the east of the castle is over 250 years old and has recently been restored as an Edwardian garden with herbaceous plants, annuals and roses. It is impossible to list all the treasures of the woodland garden, but perhaps the most surprising is the huge size of the specimens in the lower rhododendron walk, where *R. sinogrande* are found with enormously long leaves. Opposite Brodick on the W side of the island, 5 miles north of Blackwaterfoot, is *Dougarie Lodge*, an impressive castellated terrace garden created in 1905 to celebrate the marriage of Mary Louise, daughter of the 12th Duke of Hamilton, to the 6th Duke of Montrose. A fine plantsman's garden with a good range of semi-hardy trees and plants, and lovely views towards the Mull of Kintyre. [Open one day in summer for SGS and by appt; telephone Mr and Mrs Gibbs on (01475) 337355 for details.]

Broughton House ★ [Historic Scotland Inventory]

12 High Street, Kirkcudbright, Dumfries and Galloway DG6 4JX.
Tel: (01557) 330437

The National Trust for Scotland • 28m SW of Dumfries. Take A75 from Dumfries past Castle Douglas, then 1m past Bridge of Dee take A711 to Kirkcudbright. Signposted • House open 14th April to Oct, daily, 12 noon – 5pm (opens 10am July and Aug) • Garden open as house plus Feb to 13th April, 11am – 4pm • Entrance: House and garden £8, OAPs £5; garden Feb to 13th April, donation box ❶ WC ♿ ♨

Created by an artist, E.A. Hornel, who lived here from 1901 to 1933, this fascinating garden reflects an interest in Oriental art following his visit to Japan, and incorporates both Japanese and Scottish features. After his death the house became a museum and its surroundings were gradually restored. The garden starts with a sunken courtyard, beyond which is a pleasant hybrid, a cross between 'fantasy Japan' and fantasy old-world cottage garden'. Japanese cherries blossom over skilful low-level planting in the sunken courtyard, and further down are all the elements of a much larger garden: rose parterre, pergola, glasshouse, box hedges and herbaceous borders, all looking remarkably uncrowded. Charming lily pools have flat stepping stones and dramatic boulders. At the end of the long central walk, beyond a hedge, is the River Dee with its mudflats and saltings.

Bughtrig

Leitholm, Coldstream, Berwickshire, Scottish Borders TD12 4JP.
Tel: (01890) 840678

Major General and The Hon. Mrs Charles Ramsay • 5m N of Coldstream, 0.25m E of Leitholm on B6461 • Open 15th June to 15th Sept, daily, 11am – 5pm • Entrance: £2, children under 18 £1, inc. donation to SGS • Other information: Special arrangements for bona fide parties to garden, and occasionally to house. Sometimes possible for parties of up to 8 persons to stay in house ❶ 🍴 ♿ ♨

Bughtrig has been owned by just three families since the fourteenth century. The traditional Scottish family garden was designed for amenity; unusually it is hedged rather than walled, and sited close to the house. Its two-and-a-half acres contain an interesting combination of herbaceous perennials, shrubs, annuals and fruit, surrounded by fine specimen trees which provide remarkable shelter.

Cally Gardens and Nursery [Historic Scotland Inventory]

Gatehouse of Fleet, Castle Douglas, Dumfries and Galloway DG7 2DJ.
Tel: (01557) 815029 (Infoline)

Mr Michael Wickenden • 30m SW of Dumfries via A75. Take Gatehouse turning and turn left through Cally Palace Hotel gateway. Signposted • Open 15th April to 24th Sept, Tues – Fri, 2 – 5.30pm, Sat and Sun, 10am – 5.30pm • Entrance: £2.50, children under 13 free ❶ WC ♿ ♨ ♨

Three hundred Glasgow children 'dug for Victory' here in World War II and the gardens have flourished since the present owner arrived. A specialist nursery in the two-and-three-quarter-acre, eighteenth-century walled garden has large beds of herbaceous plants and many unusual varieties, well worth a visit by plant lovers. There is a impressive collection of perennial geraniums, kniphofias, crocosmias and others – 3500 varieties in all. Almost all the plants in the sales area are propagated on the premises, some from seed collected abroad or sent in botanic garden exchanges, and a changing selection of several hundred is available pot-grown. A favourite with visitors is the spread of meconopsis (Himalayan blue poppies) when in season in early June. The Cally Oak Woods which surround the nursery have nature trails. Catalogue available (3 x 1st-class stamps).

Cambo Gardens

Kingsbarns, St Andrews, Fife KY16 8QD. Tel: (01333) 450313

Mr and Mrs P. Erskine • 6m SE of St Andrews on A917 between Kingsbarns and Crail • Open all year, daily, 10am – dusk • Entrance: £3, children free • Other information: Self-catering accommodation available ○ 🏠 WC & ⚓ ℘ 🍴 ♒ B&B

This romantic Victorian walled garden is designed around the Cambo burn with weeping willows, a waterfall and rose-clad wrought-iron bridges. Naturalistic plantings of rare and interesting herbaceous perennials add to the informal atmosphere of the garden. There are masses of spring bulbs, a lilac walk with 26 cultivars, over 250 old-fashioned and rambling roses, and glowing September borders. Beyond the walled garden a woodland garden includes a September meadow of colchicums, and 70 acres of woodland walks leading to the sea are carpeted in early spring with snowflakes, aconites and a spectacular display of snowdrops (over 200 specialist varieties).

Carnell [Historic Scotland Inventory]

Hurlford, Kilmarnock, South Ayrshire KA1 5JS. Tel: (01563) 884236

Mr and Mrs J.R. Findlay and Mr and Mrs Michael Findlay • 4m SE of Kilmarnock, NW of Mauchline on A76, 1.5m off A719 • Open probably 30th July, 2 – 5.30pm, and to private parties by appt • Entrance: charge ● 💽 WC & ⚓ ℘ ♒

Eighty years ago this was a limestone quarry – now it is an exquisite example of 90 metres of linear herbaceous borders facing a rectangular pool, with informal planting as a contrast on the opposite bank. There is a phlox and shrub border, an interesting rock garden and a walled garden. Oriental features include a Chinese gazebo and Burmese dragons, all mementos of Commander Findlay's travels. Climbing the slope behind the pavilion in the south-east corner is the rock garden. The garden adjacent to the house, which has a sixteenth-century pele tower, has long herbaceous borders and a shrub and lily collection. The entrance is through an archway bedecked with a 'Kiftsgate' rose.

Castle Fraser [Historic Scotland Inventory]

Sauchen, Inverurie, Aberdeenshire AB51 7LD. Tel: (01330) 833463

The National Trust for Scotland • 15m NW of Aberdeen, off B993 near Kemnay • Castle open Easter, then May to Sept, daily, Oct, weekends • Garden open all year, daily, 9am – 6pm • Entrance: free. Castle and garden £7, concessions £5.25, family

£19, parties £5.60 per person, school parties £1 per child (2005 prices) • *Other information: Dogs on dog trail only* ○ 🅿 🍴 <u>wc</u> ♿ ◁▷ ♨ ♨ 🍴 ♨

The grounds – the setting for one of the most spectacular of the castles of Mar – consist of a designed landscape of the last seventeenth and early eighteenth centuries with eighteenth-century agricultural developments; the work of Thomas White (1794) was followed by 'natural-style' improvements of c. 1800. The deep, south-facing herbaceous border, designed in 1959 by James Russell, has been reworked to accommodate a greater selection of plants tolerant of the brisk climate. The historic walled garden has been completely replanted and the original cross- and perimeter paths have been reinstated. A woodland garden is being developed around the walled garden, together with a woodland play area with an amphitheatre. Extensive walks in the grounds include superb views of the castle in its parkland setting and outwards to nearby hills, notably Bennachie.

Castle Kennedy ★★ [Historic Scotland Inventory]

Stranraer, Wigtownshire, Dumfries and Galloway DG9 8BX.
Tel: (01776) 702024/(01581) 400225

The Earl of Stair • *5m E of Stranraer on A75* • *Open April to Sept, daily, 10am – 5pm* • *Entrance: £4, OAPs £3, children £1. Discount for parties of 20 or more (2005 prices)* ◐ 🅿 🍴 <u>wc</u> ♿ ◁▷ ♨ 🍴

One of Scotland's most famous gardens, set on a peninsula between two lochs and well worth a visit for its sheer 75-acre magnificence and spectacular spring colour. The gardens, originally laid out in the late seventeenth century, were later remodeled by Field Marshal the 2nd Earl of Stair. He used his unoccupied dragoons to effect a major remoulding of the landscape around the ruined castle, which had burnt down in 1716, combining large formal swathes of mown grassland with massive formal gardens, criss-crossed by avenues and *allées* of large specimen trees. The garden is internationally famous for its pinetum, for its good variety of tender trees and for its species rhododendrons, including many of Sir Joseph Hooker's original introductions from his Himalayan expeditions. The monkey-puzzle avenue, now sadly a little tattered, was once the finest in the world; there is also an avenue of noble firs underplanted with embothriums and eucryphias. An impressive two-acre circular lily pond puts everyone else's in their proper place, and a good walk from this brings the visitor back to the ruined castle and its walled garden, well planted with themed borders.

Castle of Mey [Historic Scotland Inventory]

Thurso, Caithness, Highland KW14 8XH. Tel: 01847 851473

The Queen Elizabeth Castle of Mey Trust • *1.5m from Mey on A836* • *Open mid-May to Sept, daily except Fri, 10.30am – 4pm, but closed first two weeks in Aug. Important to telephone for exact opening dates* • *Entrance: £3, concessions £2.50, children free (castle and gardens £7, concessions £6, children free) (2005 prices)* ◐ <u>wc</u> ♿ ◁▷ ♨ 🍴

The castle dates from the late sixteenth century and was renovated by H.M. The Queen Mother between 1952 and 1955. Gardening would not be possible in such an exposed position without the protection of the 'Great Wall of Mey'. Within the walled garden, she collected her favourite flowers; many were gifts and have special meaning. The personal private feeling pervades the whole garden, which is well planted and well maintained. The colour schemes are very good, blending the garden with the vast natural panorama within which it is situated.

Cawdor Castle ★ [Historic Scotland Inventory]

Cawdor, Nairn, Highland IV12 5RD. Tel: (01667) 404401

The Dowager Countess Cawdor • Between Inverness and Nairn on B9090 off A96 • Castle open • Garden open May to 8th Oct, daily, 10am – 5.30pm • Entrance: £3.70 (castle and garden £7, OAPs £6, children £4.30, family £22, parties of 20 or more £6.10 per person) ◐ 💺 ✕ 🍴 wc & ⇪ 🍴 ⛪

Frequently referred to as one of the Highland's most romantic castles and steeped in history, Cawdor Castle is a fourteenth-century keep with seventeenth- and nineteenth-century additions. The surrounding parkland is handsome and well kept, though not in the grand tradition of classic landscapes. To the side of the castle is the formal garden, where recently added wrought-iron arches frame extensive herbaceous borders, a peony border, a very old hedge of mixed varieties of *Rosa pimpinellifolia* (the Scots or Burnet rose), a rose tunnel, old apple trees with climbing roses, interesting shrubs and lilies. An abundance of lavender and pinks completes a rather Edwardian atmosphere. The castle wall shelters exochordas, *Abutilon vitifolium*, *Carpenteria californica* and *Rosa banksiae*. Pillar-box red seats create an unusual note in this splendidly flowery place, but the owner likes them. The walled garden below the castle has been restored with a holly maze, a thistle garden, a laburnum walk and a white garden. The latter is a 'Paradise garden', preceded by Earth represented as a knot garden, and between the two lies Purgatory. There are fine views everywhere of the castle, the park and the surrounding countryside, which one can enjoy more actively by walking one of the five nature trails, varying in length from half a mile to five miles. Further developments include the Auchindoune gardens, where Arabella Lennox-Boyd helped with the planting.

Clan Donald Visitor Centre

(see ARMADALE CASTLE GARDENS)

Cluny House ★ [Historic Scotland Inventory]

Aberfeldy, Perth and Kinross PH15 2JT. Tel: (01887) 820795

Mr J. and Mrs W. Mattingley • 32m NW of Perth. N of Aberfeldy, over Wade's Bridge, take A827 Weem – Strathtay road. House signed after 3m • Open March to Oct, daily, 10am – 6pm • Entrance: £3, children free ◐ 🍴 ⇪ 🌳 ♿

Unlike most other gardens, this is as truly wild as one can find – friendly weeds grow unchecked for fear of disturbing an extensive collection of Asiatic primulas. Sheltered slopes create a moist microclimate where all the plants flourish abundantly, including a Wellingtonia with the British near-record girth of over 11 metres. In the superb woodland garden many of the plants were propagated from seed acquired by Mrs Mattingley's father on the Ludlow/Sherriff expedition to Bhutan in 1948. Special treats are the carpets of bulbs, trilliums and meconopsis, a fine selection of Japanese acers, *Prunus serrula*, hundreds of different rhododendrons, *Cardiocrinum giganteum*, massive lysichitons and many fine specimen trees. The garden is managed on strictly organic principles, and it is delightful to see native wild flowers and garden plants growing together in harmony and profusion, and red squirrels putting in a welcome appearance.

Colzium Lennox Estate

Kilsyth, Glasgow G65 0PY. Tel: (01236) 828150

North Lanarkshire Council • 14m NE of Glasgow, 0.5m E of Kilsyth on A803 • House and museum open by appt • Estate open all year, daily. Walled garden open April to Sept, daily, 12 noon – 7pm; Oct to March, Sat and Sun only, 12 noon – 4pm • Entrance: free ○ WC & ⇦ 🎈

An outstanding collection of conifers, including dwarf cultivars, and rare trees in a beautifully designed large walled garden. Everything is well labelled and immaculately maintained; even gravel paths are raked. There are also 100 varieties each of snowdrops and crocuses. Other attractions include a seventeenth-century ice-house, a glen walk, a fifteenth-century tower house, an arboretum, a curling pond and a clock theatre.

Corsock House

Corsock, Castle Douglas, Dumfries and Galloway DG7 3DJ. Tel: (01644) 440250

Mr and Mrs M.L. Ingall • 10m N of Castle Douglas on A712. Signed from A75 onto B794 • Open one Sun in May for SGS, and by appt • Entrance: £3, children free (2005 prices) • Other information: Refreshments on open day ● 🍽 ⇦

A most attractive 20-acre woodland garden with exceptionally fine plantings both of trees (beech, Wellingtonia, oak, Douglas fir, cercidiphyllum, acer) and of rhododendrons (*R. thomsonii, lacteum, loderi, prattii, sutchuenense*). The knowledgeable owner has contributed most imaginatively to the layout of the gardens over the last forty years, creating glades, planting vistas of azaleas and personally building temples and a *trompe-l'oeil* bridge which give the gardens a classical atmosphere. An impressive highlight is the large water garden, again cleverly laid out and with water-edge plantings set off by a background of mature trees with good autumn colour.

Crarae Garden ★★ [Historic Scotland Inventory]

Minard, Inveraray, Argyll and Bute PA32 8YA. Tel: (01546) 886614

National Trust for Scotland • 11m SW of Inveraray on A83 • Open all year, daily, 9.30am – sunset • Entrance: £3.50, concessions and children £2.60, family £9.50 (2005 prices) • Other information: Visitor centre open April to Sept, daily, 10am – 5pm ○ 🍽 🍴 WC & ⇦ ⌂

Crarae, previously owned by the Crarae Charitable Trust, and one of the most important of Scottish woodland gardens, was forced to close in June 2001 due to lack of resources. A successful £1.5 million fund-raising campaign by the National Trust for

Scotland raised an endowment sufficient to take on the property and to guarantee the continuity of the garden. It reopened in April 2002, and a phased programme of restoration is underway. The gardens were originally planned by Grace, Lady Campbell in the early part of last century, possibly inspired by her nephew Reginald Farrer, the famous traveller and plant collector. Subsequently her son, Sir George Campbell (1894–1967), spent many years creating this superb Himalayan ravine set in a Highland glen, the whole enlivened by splendid torrents and waterfalls. Using surplus seed from the great plant expeditions, numerous gifts from knowledgeable friends and the shared expertise of a network of famous horticulturists, he planted a variety of rare trees (his first love), together with exotic shrubs and species rhododendrons, which now form great canopies above the winding paths. This must be a unique opportunity to see 440 different varieties of rhododendron, some exclusive to the garden, which, together with many other plants from the temperate world, make a magnificent spectacle of colour and differing perspectives. The autumn colouring of sorbus, acers, prunus, cotoneasters and berberis is one of the great features of the garden, which contains a National Collection of nothofagus.

Crathes Castle Garden ★★ [Historic Scotland Inventory]

Crathes Castle, Banchory, Aberdeenshire AB31 5QJ. Tel: (01330) 844525

The National Trust for Scotland • 3m E of Banchory, 15m SW of Aberdeen on A93 • Castle open April to Sept, daily, 10.30am – 5.30pm (timed entry system; last admission 4.45pm), Oct, daily, 10.30am – 4.30pm (last admission 3.45pm), Nov to March, Thurs – Sun, 10.30am – 4pm, and at other times by appt • Garden and grounds open all year, daily, 9am – dusk • Entrance: £8, concessions and children £5 (castle, garden and grounds £10, concessions and children £7, family £25, single adult family £20. Pre-booked parties of 20 or more £7.50 per person, concessions £5.25) • Other information: Parking 400 metres from gardens (charge for non-Trust members). Dogs on nature trail in grounds only ○ 💭 ✕ 🍴 WC & 🌸 🌿 ⛪ 🍵 Q

The romantic castle, set in flowing lawns, dates from 1596, and looks much as it did in the mid-eighteenth century. There is no record of how the garden looked then, although the splendid yew topiary of 1702 survives. Sir James Burnett, who inherited the estate in the 1920s, was a keen collector, his wife an inspired herbaceous garden designer, and the garden today reflects their achievements. In all there are eight gardens, each with a different character and varied planting schemes, often compared to Hidcote but with evident inspiration from Jekyll. The terraces and sloping terrain increase the dramatic effect. Rare shrubs reflect Burnett's interest in the Far East, while the splendid wide herbaceous borders with clever plant associations were Lady Burnett's creation, the most famous being the white border. There are many specialist areas, such as the trough garden; the large greenhouses contain a National Collection of Malmaison carnations. The extensive wild gardens and grounds are furnished with picnic areas and marked trails.

Cruickshank Botanic Garden

St Machar Drive, Aberdeen AB24 3UU. Tel: (01224) 272704

The Cruickshank Trust and University of Aberdeen • 1.5m N of city centre in Old Aberdeen. Entrance in Chanonry. Signposted • Open all year, Mon – Fri, 9am – 4.30pm;

May to Sept, Sat, Sun, 2 – 5pm • Entrance: free • Other information: Children must be accompanied by adult ○ 🐌 ♿

The garden was endowed in 1898 by Miss Anne H. Cruickshank, who stipulated that it should be used to advance the study of science at the university and also be enjoyed by the people of Aberdeen. Both hold good today. The original six acres were designed by George Nicholson of Kew, but that layout disappeared with World War I. The long wall, herbaceous border and sunken garden date from 1920 but much reverted to vegetable cultivation during World War II. In 1970 the garden was extended and a new rock garden made. Today it is planted with a series of connecting pools, interestering alpines, bulbs and dwarf shrubs. A terrace garden was added by the long wall in 1980, a new rose garden completed in 1986 and the peat walls restored in 1988. There is also a sunken garden and beech, birch and azalea lawns. A small woodland area is rich in meconopsis, primulas, rhododendrons and hellebores. Proximity to the North Sea does not permit good growth of large conifers, with the exception of dawn redwood and *Pinus radiata*, but there are fine species lilacs, witch hazels, and the long wall shelters more tender exotics. The total area of the present garden is 11 acres, of which four are planted as an arboretum – this is reached by a path from the summit of the rock gardens.

Culross Palace [Historic Scotland Inventory]

Culross, Dunfermline, Fife KY12 8JH. Tel: (01383) 880359

The National Trust for Scotland • 12m W of Forth Bridge off A985 • House open 14th April to Sept, daily, 12 noon – 5pm • Garden open all year, daily, 10am – 6pm (or sunset if earlier) • Other information: Refreshments and toilet facilities when house open; shop open during main season • Entrance: Garden free when palace closed. Palace and garden £8, OAPs £5, family £20 (2005 prices) ◑ 💻 🐌 WC 🌶 🏭 ♀

A small area packed full of fascinating plants and features, including the old poultry breed, the Scots Dumpy. The atmosphere of the seventeenth-century garden is evoked by the crushed-shell paths, and great attention paid to detail – clay watering cans, plants in baskets and hurdles, bee skeps in wall niches. On the walled terrace a kitchen and ornamental garden of the period is planted with an abundance of fruit, vegetables and herbs. Head gardener Mark Jeffery describes this as an historical showpiece which runs on organic principles; the walled area contains truly old-fashioned vegetables flourishing in a relatively frost-free environment.

Culzean Castle ★ ★ [Historic Scotland Inventory]

Maybole, South Ayrshire KA19 8LE. Tel: (01655) 884400

The National Trust for Scotland • 12m S of Ayr on A719 coast road • Castle open • Gardens and country park open April to Oct, daily, 10am – 5pm • Entrance: £8, concessions and children £5, parties £8 per person (castle, grounds and country park £12, concessions £8, family £30, parties £10 per person) (2005 prices) ◑ 💻 ✕ 🐌 WC ♿ ♿ 🌶 🏭 ♀ ⚲

Culzean is regarded by many as the Trust's flagship. The castle was originally a medieval fortified house atop the Ayrshire cliffs, but was extensively restructured by

Robert Adam from 1777 in what has become known as his 'Culzean style'. His patron was the 10th Earl of Cassilis – he and Adam were both to die in 1792, the year of the castle's completion. This is reflected in the many fine architectural features scattered throughout the grounds, and in particular the handsome home farm courtyard, now a visitor centre. Restoration work continues. A major undertaking was the consolidation and partial rebuilding of Robert Adam's unique viaduct. The camellia house, a picturesque 1818 glasshouse, has been beautifully restored to its original use as an orangery, the fountain in the garden below the castle repaired and replumbed, the southern walled garden completely redesigned and the vinery rebuilt on the original site based on its Victorian plan. The Swan Pond buildings have been conserved and repaired along with the beautiful bridge to the north. The restored pagoda is now spectacular, and the Dolphin House has been turned into an environmental education centre for school visits. The country-park landscape covers 600 acres with a network of woodland and cliff-top paths; the gardens themselves occupy a spacious 30 acres and include all the traditional elements of a grand garden at the turn of the century.

Dawyck Botanic Garden ★ [Historic Scotland Inventory]

Stobo, Peeblesshire, Scottish Borders EH45 9JU. Tel: (01721) 760254

Royal Botanic Garden Edinburgh • 20m SW of Edinburgh, 8m SW of Peebles on B712 • Open Feb to Nov, daily, 10am (closing times vary), and at other times by appt • Entrance: £3.50, concessions £3, children £1, family £8. Season tickets inc. Logan and Younger Botanic Gardens (see entries) available • Other information: Guide dogs only ◑ 🅿 🏠 <u>WC</u> ♿ ⚘ ♨

This is a specialist garden of the Royal Botanic Garden Edinburgh (see entry). With over 300 years of tree planting, it is one of the world's finest arboretums; its collections include rare Chinese conifers and the unique Dawyck beech. At the entrance is the formal azalea terrace which leads the visitor into Scrape Glen, and from here paths cross the slopes of Scrape Hill, with the burn tumbling down under the Swiss bridge in the middle of the glen. The mature specimen trees tower majestically above a variety of flowering trees and shrubs. From further up the hill there are magnificent views of the garden, including the beech walk with its tree-top outlook. In the Heron Wood is the first cryptogamic sanctuary and reserve for non-flowering plants; illustrated panels provide details of the essential role played by these plants. The fine stonework and terracing on bridges, balustrades and urns were produced by Italian craftsmen in the 1820s.

Druimavuic House Gardens

Appin, Argyll and Bute PA38 4BQ. Tel: (01631) 730242

Mr and Mrs Newman Burberry • 4m S of Appin on A828 Oban – Fort William road, turn left at new road bridge. Signposted • Open April to June, daily, 10am – 6pm • Entrance: £2, children free ◑ 🏠 ⚐ ⚘

A romantic site which was begun after World War I but has now been replanted and cultivated by its dedicated owners. The humorous and descriptive guide states that 'the real architect of Druimavuic Gardens is Nature', but they have certainly embellished her work most successfully. The stream garden makes an immediate impact with colourful clumps of many varieties of primulas (*P. pulverulenta*, 'Inverewe' and *helodoxa*) and meconopsis mixed in with other varied spring plantings. The well-planted woodland garden has lovely open oil-painting views of cattle watering in the loch below. In the an excellent working kitchen garden strawberries are grown at eye level.

Drum Castle [Historic Scotland Inventory]

Drumoak, by Banchory, Aberdeenshire AB31 5EY. Tel: (01330) 811204

The National Trust for Scotland • 10m W of Aberdeen, 3m W of Peterculter, off A93 • Garden open April to Sept, daily, 10am – 6pm. Grounds open all year, daily, 9.30am – sunset • Entrance: Grounds free, garden only £2.50, concessions £1.90 (castle, garden and grounds £8, children and concessions £5; parties of 20 or more £6.50 per person) (2005 prices) • Garden: ◐ 🍽 🏠 <u>WC</u> & ℘ ⛲ ♿ *Grounds:* ○ ⟳ ९

Within the old walled garden of the castle, the Trust has established a 'garden of historic roses' which was officially opened in June 1991 as part of its Diamond Jubilee celebrations. The four quadrants of the garden are designed and planted with roses and herbaceous or other plants appropriate to the seventeenth, eighteenth, nineteenth and twentieth centuries. The central feature is a copy of the gazebo at Tyninghame, East Lothian (see entry), and a small garden house in one corner, now restored, acts as an interpretative centre. The grounds around the castle also contain a pond garden, interesting conifers, spacious lawns and walks in the Old Wood of Drum, designated a SSSI.

Drumlanrig Castle [Historic Scotland Inventory]

Thornhill, Dumfries and Galloway DG3 4AQ. Tel: (01848) 331555

The Duke of Buccleuch • 16m SW of M74 Junction 14, 18m NW of Dumfries, 3m N of Thornhill on A76, between A77 and A75. Signposted • Castle, garden and country park open – telephone for details • Entrance: £3 (extra charge for house) (2005 price) ◐ 🍽 🏠 <u>WC</u> & ⟳ ℘ ⛲ ♿ ९

Built in the late seventeenth century by William Douglas, 1st Duke of Queensberry, Drumlanrig is one of Scotland's finest and most palatial residences. The formal terraces and parterres around and below the house reflect this contemporary 'grand manner', in a magnificent setting. The parterres were first restored to their former glory in the Victorian era by two of the foremost designers of their day, Charles M'Intosh and David Thomson, who, interestingly, used heathers instead of bedding plants as infill. They also introduced a variety of foreign plants and shrubs as well as many of the exotic conifers still thriving in the woodland walk today. These include one of the oldest Douglas firs in the UK, the tallest weeping beech (*Fagus sylvatica* 'Pendula') and an early fan-trained *Ginkgo biloba*. A charming heather-root pavilion in the woodland walk overlooks the tumbling Marr burn. The gardens were simplified during the two world wars and are now being restored again to a very high standard. The four parterres, all with different plants and colour themes, are a stunning sight from the 200-metre-long terrace above; the Shawl Parterre in particular has a pretty design using circles, ovals and hearts. Annuals are used on an impressive scale.

Drummond Castle Gardens ★★ [Historic Scotland Inventory]

Muthill, Crieff, Perth and Kinross PH5 2AA. Tel: (01764) 681433

Grimsthorpe and Drummond Castle Trust Ltd • 2m S of Crieff on A822 • Open 14th to 17th April, then May to Oct, daily, all 1 – 6pm (last admission 5pm) • Entrance: £4, OAPs £3, children £1.50 ◑ **wc** ᕳ ⬧ ℘

These magnificent parterre gardens were first laid out in 1630 by the 2nd Earl of Perth; at their centre was a multi-faced obelisk sundial which still indicates the time all over the world. The gardens were greatly enhanced during the seventeenth century and reached their zenith during the 1830s when a descendant created one of the most significant revival gardens of the period, much admired by Queen Victoria. Parterres were traditionally designed as architectural extensions of the mansion or castle. The one here takes the form of a long St Andrew's Cross and is one of the finest in Scotland, particularly when viewed from the 120-metre-long terrace 20 metres above. The whole garden is ornamented by 36 statues and numerous fountains and urns, all strategically placed as focal points or at the end of long vistas. Numerous box-edged compartments of intricate design are infilled, mostly with roses, antirrhinums, dahlias and lavenders, in the Drummond heraldic colours. The visual impact of the 207 clipped evergreens, intricate box compartments and stonemasonry is unforgettable.

Dun Ard ★

Main Street, Fintry, Stirlingshire G63 0XE. Tel: (01360) 860369.

Mr Alastair Morton and Mr Niall Manning • 17m SW of Stirling, 17m N of Glasgow on B822 • Open by appt only • Entrance: free ◑

An exceptionally well-planned organic garden incorporating many of the most stimulating elements of contemporary horticultural design, all carved out of a sloping three-acre field. Areas of exuberant planting are interspersed with minimalist, restful or wild areas, so that visitors are always ready for the next surprise as they climb ever onwards and upwards, culminating with a sandstone pyramid with a bird's-eye view over the whole garden, the valley and the mountains beyond. All the features sought after by today's gardeners are here – a *potager*, an early garden, a rose parterre, a bulb meadow, a still pool enclosed by a beech hedge, a bog garden, a formal pleached hornbeam avenue and, best of all, a late garden planted in hot colours in the increasingly popular continental matrix style, combining wild and herbaceous patchwork planting, viewed in all its deliciousness from a smart decking platform.

Dunbeath Castle ★

Dunbeath, Caithness KW6 6EY. Tel: (01593) 731308

Mr and Mrs S.W. Murray Threipland • 6m NE of Berriedale off A9. Turn right to Dunbeath village post office, then right again • Open for parties by appt • Entrance: £4, OAPs and children £2 ◑ ⬛ ◈ **wc** ᕳ ⬧

The immaculately harled clifftop castle, dating from the fourteenth century, is dramatically outlined against the sea as one approaches down a tunnel of trees giving way to steep, deep-cut grass banks crowned on each side by two large walled gardens. The right-hand one has now been beautifully re-created with the help of the designer Xa Tollemache with a turret viewpoint over the garden as a whole and behind to the castle and the glinting sea. Although the layout is traditional, with three mown grass axes and a central path creating eight compartments, these are broad and generously scaled, with the outer paths unusually wide and the whole threaded together with decorative metalwork. A water feature with cupola, a laburnum pergola across the width of the garden, a gazebo, plant supports and border backdrops are all designed using the same metalwork, giving the garden structure, height and unity. Two well-clipped fuschia hedges run the length of the garden, providing the outer shelter walls of the compartments and small parterres. These are paired so as to make a colourful and attractive pattern of vegetables, fruit and flowers. The outer walls themselves have herbaceous planting at their feet and are clad alternatively with *Cytisus battandieri*, *Hydrangea petiolaris*, actinidia, lonicera, escallonia, *Humulus lupulus* 'Aureus' and a variety of roses. Dunbeath's outstanding position and the quality and design of its garden makes this an exceptional visit, combined perhaps with Langwell, Dunrobin and West Drummie (see entries).

Dunrobin Castle Gardens ★ [Historic Scotland Inventory]

Golspie, Sutherland, Highland KW10 6SF. Tel: (01408) 633177/633268

The Sutherland Trust • 1m NE of Golspie on A9 • Castle open • Garden open April to 15th Oct, daily, 10.30am – 4.30pm (opens 12 noon Sun, April, May and Oct; closes 5.30pm June to Sept) • Entrance: £6.80, concessions £5.80, children £4.70, family £18, parties of 10 or more £5.60 per person, OAPs, £5 • Other information: Falconry displays ● ➡ ▨ WC ♿

These Victorian formal gardens were designed in the grand French style to echo the architecture of the castle, which rises high above and looks out over the Moray Firth. They were created by the architect Sir Charles Barry in 1850. Descending the stone terraces, one can see the round garden (evocative of the Scottish shield, perhaps), grove, parterre and herbaceous borders laid out beneath. The round ponds, all furnished with fountains, are a particular feature, together with the wrought-iron Westminster gates. Roses have been replaced with hardy geraniums, antirrhinums and *Potentilla fruticosa* 'Abbotswood'; the interest continues from tulips in spring through to hardy fuchsias, including *F.* 'Dunrobin Bedder' (raised c. 1860) and the autumn-flowering dahlias. An eighteenth-century summerhouse, converted into a museum in the nineteenth century, is now also open to the public and well worth seeing. Other developments include the removal of the shrubbery and its replacement by 20 wooden pyramids covered in roses, clematis and sweet peas and interplanted with small ornamental trees to continue the French style visible elsewhere. In the policies there are many woodland walks.

Dunvegan Castle [Historic Scotland Inventory]

Isle of Skye IV55 8WF. Tel: (01470) 521206

MacLeod Estate • 14m NW of Portree, beyond A850/A863 junction • Castle open • Garden open all year, daily, mid-March to Oct, 10am – 5.30pm, Nov to mid-March,

11am – 4pm • Entrance: £4.50, OAPs £2.50, children £2.50 (castle and gardens £6.50, OAPs £5.50, children £3.50) (2005 prices) ○ 🍽 ✕ 🧺 <u>WC</u> ♿ ⟳ 🐾 ♨ B&B

A superb backcloth for the castle which stands on the shores of Loch Dunvegan, the gardens have three areas of interest. First, a round garden with a boxwood parterre of 16 triangular beds, three mixed borders for summer show and a fern house. Second, an expanding woodland waterfall dell, which carries the season on past rhododendron time. The meconopsis and giant cardiocrinums are breathtaking in this setting, but note also tiny maidenhair ferns, native woodsage and other treasures. Third, an exciting two-acre walled garden, created by head gardener Thomas Shephard on a long-derelict site and open to the public since 1998. Laid out on a formal plan, the four quarters each have a focus of interest: a lawn with a sorbus avenue; a raised pool with gravel surround pierced by plants; a triangle with an internal yew triangle; and an unusual stepped 'temple' evocative of Mayan architecture. The surrounding paths spill over with helianthemums, cistus and other Mediterranean plants. Non-gardeners can take an exciting boat trip to the nearby seal colony – on a calm day.

Edzell Castle [Historic Scotland Inventory]

Edzell, Brechin, Angus DD9 7UE. Tel: (01356) 648631

Historic Scotland • 6m N of Brechin. Take A90 (A94) and after 2m fork left on B966 • Castle ruins open (closed Thurs and Fri in winter) • Garden open April to Sept, daily, 9.30am – 6pm (closes 4pm Oct to March) • Entrance: £3.30, OAPs £2.50, children (5–16) £1.30, under 5 free ○ 🧺 <u>WC</u> ♿ ⟳ ♨ 🚻 ♀

In 1604 Sir David Lindsay made a remarkable small walled garden at his fortress at Edzell; as reconstructed, it gives us a clear idea of how his garden might have looked in its heyday. By the time they came under the care of H.M. Office of Works in 1932, the garden and castle had lain in ruins for over 150 years. Although the plantings date from the 1930s, they are elaborate examples in the manner of the period of the early seventeenth century. Meticulously kept parterres of box, lawn, and bedding are contained within the original walls of unique and curious design. There are 23 panels of alternating chequered niches and 21 sculptured symbolic figures with large recesses below for flowers. The whole is laid out to be viewed from a corner summerhouse and the windows of the castle. Edzell itself is a good example of an ordered Victorian Scottish Highland village, with shops, tea rooms and two hotels.

Falkland Palace Garden [Historic Scotland Inventory]

Falkland, Fife KY15 7BU. Tel: (01337) 857397

The National Trust for Scotland • 11m N of Kirkcaldy via A92 and A912. M90 junction 8 from Forth Road Bridge • Palace open as garden (last tour of palace 5pm) • Garden open March to Oct, Mon – Sat, 10am – 6pm, Sun, 1 – 4.30pm • Entrance: £5, concessions and children £3.50 (palace and garden £10, concessions and children £7, family £25) • Other information: Parking 100 metres from palace. Toilet facilities in town car park and next to NTS shop ◑ 🧺 ♿ ♨ 🚻 ♀

This was originally the garden at the sixteenth-century palace, which was the hunting lodge for the Stuart monarchs. Kings and queens from James II to Charles II enjoyed the Fife landscape and the grounds of the Renaissance palace. During World War II the garden was a 'Dig for Victory' effort and was thereafter remodelled by the landscape designer Percy Cane. The palace itself lends a gracious and dignified atmosphere to this three-acre garden. The shrub island borders are now fully mature and provide a good illustration of how to break up large areas of lawn. The main herbaceous border, recently replanted, runs the full depth of the garden and is maturing well. In addition, visitors can see the royal tennis court (i.e. real tennis) where occasional competitions of this old game are still staged, and an outdoor chequers game near the herb garden. There is also an orchard. Note the interesting village houses nearby.

Finlaystone [Historic Scotland Inventory]

Langbank, Renfrewshire PA14 6TJ. Tel: (01475) 540505

Mr George Gordon MacMillan of MacMillan • 8m W of Glasgow Airport, on A8 W of Langbank • Open all year, daily, 10.30am – 5pm • Entrance: £3.50, OAPs and children £2.50 • Other information: Doll museum and Celtic exhibition in visitor centre. Play area ○ 🍽 🐕 WC ♿ ⬆ 🏛 🚻 ♿

Designed in 1900 and enhanced and tended over the last fifty years by the late Lady MacMillan, much respected *doyenne* of Scottish gardens, and her family, this spacious garden is imaginatively laid out over 10 acres, with a further 70 acres of mature woodland walks. There are large, elegant lawns framed by long herbaceous borders, interesting shrubberies and mature copper beeches looking down over the River Clyde. John Knox's tree, a Celtic paving 'maze', a paved fragrant garden and a bog garden are added attractions, and for children there are unusual woodland play areas. A walled garden is planted in the shape of a Celtic ring cross.

Floors Castle [Historic Scotland Inventory]

Roxburghe Estates Office, Kelso, Roxburghshire TD5 7SF. Tel: (01573) 223333

The Duke of Roxburghe • Well-signposted on outskirts of Kelso • Open April to Oct, 11am – 4.30pm • Entrance: Grounds and gardens £3, OAPs £1.50 (house, grounds and garden £6, OAPs/students £5, children £3.25, family £16) ○ 🍽 ✕ 🐕 WC ♿ ⬆ 🅿 🏛 🚻 ♿

Floors is, architecturally, one of Scotland's grandest country houses – a real swagger castle – magnificently situated with glorious views across a huge sweep of open parkland. The 1857 walled kitchen garden is of equally stately proportions and contains the classic mix of glasshouses, herbaceous borders, fruit, vegetables and annuals. The borders – long, broad and packed with colour – have a backing of chain swags covered with the bright pink rose 'American Pillar'. Groups of apple trees using the three historic Scottish cultivars – 'Bloody Ploughman' (thereby hangs a tale), 'Galloway Pippin' and 'Scottish Dumpling' – have been trained in the traditional French style as goblets and dwarf and full pyramids. The large children's playground is conveniently, but not aesthetically, sited within the walled garden. Recent additions are a woodland garden and a two-acre parterre, designed in the French style and featuring the intertwined initials of the present Duke and Duchess. Much use has been made of traditional box, with contrast and highlighting provided by *Euonymus fortunei* 'Emerald 'n' Gold'.

Glamis Castle [Historic Scotland Inventory]

Glamis, Forfar, Angus DD8 1RJ. Tel: (01307) 840393

The Earl of Strathmore and Kinghorne • 5m W of Forfar on A94 • Castle open, guided tours • Garden open March to Dec, daily, 10am – 6pm (last admission 4.30pm) • Entrance: £3.50, OAPs, students and children (5–16) £2.50, disabled persons free (castle and grounds £7, OAPs and students £5.70, children (5–16) £3.80, family £20). Reductions for parties of 20 or more ◑ 💽 ✕ 🍴 <u>WC</u> ♿ 🌳 ☕

At the end of a long, tree-lined avenue and against the backdrop of mountain and moorland, the turrets and spires of Glamis Castle beckon the visitor. Although much older, the park was landscaped in the 1790s by a garden designer working under the influence of 'Capability' Brown, and the avenue was replanted about 1820. On the lawn near the castle is an intriguing Baroque sundial, six and a half metres tall and with a face for every week of the year. On the east side of the castle a two-acre Italian garden consists of high yew hedges, herbaceous borders, a fountain and seventeenth-century-style gazebos. The pinetum, planted c.1870, is now open to visitors. Glamis was the childhood home of the late Queen Mother.

Glasgow Botanic Gardens [Historic Scotland Inventory]

730 Great Western Road, Glasgow G12 0UE. Tel: (0141) 334 2422

Glasgow City Council • Near city centre on corner of Great Western Road and Queen Margaret Drive • Open all year, daily, 7am – dusk. Glasshouses open 10am – 4.45pm (closes 4.15pm in winter) • Entrance: free ○ 💽 🍴 <u>WC</u> ♿ 🌳 ☕

A pleasant afternoon's walk among well-maintained herbaceous, shrub and annual borders. A greatly extended herb garden has recently been completed and includes a unique garden containing plants native to Scotland with explanatory labels on how they have been utilised over centuries. In the nearby tropical glasshouses are displays of orchids and a National Collection of species begonias, also cacti and economic plants – all meticulously maintained. The Arid Adaptations house has on display some of the most bizarre plants in the world; the unique development of island plants is also demonstrated here. Although the Victorian Kibble Palace – the chief attraction here – will not reopen until July 2006, there is a new rose garden of mainly scented shrub roses to enjoy.

14 Glebe Crescent

Tillicoultry, Clackmannanshire FK13 6PB. Tel: (01259) 750484

Mrs Joy McCorgray • 8m W of Stirling on A91 at east end of village; signed by yellow arrow at Glebe Crescent • Open for SGS, and by appt • Entrance: £2, children free

This delightful half-acre plantsman's garden is designed to fill every corner with a different plant setting and thus a different 'feel'. Clever terracing of the natural slope ensures that the garden does not seem unduly overcrowded and yet, believe it or not, there is a Japanese koi carp pool, a collection of bonsai, a perfumed garden, a formal courtyard area, a conifer lawn, over 40 ornamental grasses and a woodland area with a large collection of rare ferns, arisaemas, hellebores and trilliums. Notable are the unusual *Cercidiphyllum japonicum* 'Ruby', and the variegated angelica tree (*Aralia elata* 'Aureovariegata') and many people covet the beautiful Japanese umbrella pine (*Sciadopitys verticillata*). The owner says: 'There's a lot squashed into this garden.' Indeed there is.

Glen Grant Garden

Rothes, Aberlour, Moray AB38 7BS. Tel: (01340) 832118

Glen Grant Distillery • 10m SE of Elgin on A941, on main roundabout in Rothes • Open April to Oct, daily, 10am – 4pm (opens 12.30pm on Sun) • Entrance: free • Other information: Distillery tours ❶ WC & ♿

The garden was originally developed in 1866 up the sides of the distillery's glen by 'The Major' James Grant, son of the founder, and a legendary innovator, socialiser and traveller. Using exotic plants collected on his travels, he enhanced the natural setting with paths that meandered through orchards, lawns and wooded glades up to the gorge and a rustic bridge over the tumbling burn which flows through on its way to the River Spey. Thanks to the firm of Chivas Brothers, the garden is currently being restored with exact replicas, including the heather-thatched dram hut.

Glenarn [Historic Scotland Inventory]

Rhu, Helensburgh, Dunbartonshire G84 8LL. Tel: (01436) 820493

Michael and Sue Thornley • On A814 between Helensburgh and Garelochhead. Go up Pier Road to Glenarn Road • Open 21st March to 21st Sept, daily, dawn – dusk • Entrance: £3, OAPs/children £1.50 • Other information: Refreshments on certain open days only and by arrangement. Plant sales March to June ❶ 🐶 WC ♿

Established in the 1920s by the Gibson family, the 10 acres of woodland owe an incalculable debt to the earlier Victorian garden fed by the famous plant expeditions. Well-kept paths meander round a sheltered bowl, sometimes tunnelling under superb giant species rhododendrons (including a *R. falconeri* grown from seed supplied by Hooker in 1849), sometimes allowing a glorious vista across the garden to the Clyde estuary, and sometimes stopping the visitor short to gaze with unstinted admiration at 12-metre magnolias, pieris, olearias, eucryphias and hoherias. The owners, both professional architects, acquired Glenarn some years ago and with almost no help are successfully replanting and restoring where necessary, whilst retaining the special atmosphere created by such magnificent growth. The rock garden falls steeply down past the daffodil lawn to the house with its tall, twisting chimney pots; work has been completed to expose the quarry face and is continuing on the restoration of the scree bed.

Glenbervie House [Historic Scotland Inventory]

Drumlithie, Stonehaven, Kincardineshire AB39 3YA. Tel: (01569) 740226

Mrs C.S. MacPhie • 8m NE of Laurencekirk, 6m from Stonehaven off A90 Laurencekirk – Stonehaven road. On minor road 3m W of Drumlithie • Open one day for charity, and by appt • Entrance: £3, children 80p ● ● WC ℗

Two very different gardens may be enjoyed here – a traditional Scottish walled garden on a slope, and a woodland garden by a stream. Occupying one wall of an enclosed garden is a fine example of a Victorian conservatory, with a great diversity of pot plants and climbers on the walls. Elsewhere in the walled area is a typical mix of herbaceous plants, fruit, vegetables and summer bedding. There are many shrub and old roses, and on walls and pillars a variety of climbing and rambler roses. Spring brings good displays of bulbs, and the woodland garden with its drifts of primulas, ferns and interesting shrubs is beautiful in early summer. There are fine trees near the house.

Glendoick Gardens [Historic Scotland Inventory]

Glendoick, Glencarse, Perth and Kinross PH2 7NS. Tel: (01738) 860205 (Nursery); (01738) 860260 (Garden Centre)

Mr and Mrs Peter Cox and Kenneth Cox • 8m E of Perth, 14m SW of Dundee on A90 • Open mid-April to mid-June, Mon – Fri, 10am – 4pm, 7th and 21st May for SGS • Entrance: £3, children free ● ● ✕ WC ⅋ ℗ ⊞

One of the most comprehensive collections of rhododendrons in the world, started by Euan H.M. Cox in the 1920s and considerably augmented since then by his son, daughter-in-law and grandson; many specimens were collected by them in the Himalayas and China. The rhododendrons are enhanced by an understorey of perennials, including meconopsis, primulas, trilliums, lilies and nomocharis, swelled by naturalised and native plants. Near the fine Georgian mansion are dwarf rhododendrons and azaleas, a small arboretum and a collection of conifers complement the many mature trees. Trial beds of new hybrid rhododendrons have been planted in the walled garden.

Glenwhan Garden

Dunragit, Stranraer, Wigtownshire, Dumfries and Galloway DG9 8PH. Tel: (01581) 400222

Mr and Mrs Knott • 7m E of Stranraer, 1m off A75 at Dunragit. Signposted • Open April to Sept, daily, 10am – 5pm, and by appt. Evening visits by arrangement • Entrance: £4, OAPs £3, children £1, toddlers free, family £8.50, season ticket £10, conducted tours for parties of 20 or more £15 • Other information: Picnics permitted on request. Dogs strictly on leads (dog-walking area). Plants for sale in nursery ◑ ● ✕ ❀ WC ⅋ ⊞ ⊞ ♨ ⚲

This magical 12-acre garden has spectacular views over Luce Bay and the Mull of Galloway, and is set in an area of natural beauty with many rocky outcrops. Because of the Gulf Stream and consequent mild climate, exotic plants thrive amongst the huge collections of trees, shrubs and plants from all over the world. Seats and walkways abound in the maze of hilly plantings, mostly overlooking the central lakes and bog gardens, and sculptures are placed in carefully selected locations. Collections, whether of genera, reminders of friends or particular themes of interest, are to be seen everywhere. The garden, started in 1981, is maturing well. There are enchanting woodland walks where species rhododendrons flourish amongst many different kinds of primulas, and a new 17-acre moorland walk sprinkled with native wild flowers.

Greenbank Garden ★ [Historic Scotland Inventory]

Flenders Road, Clarkston, Glasgow G76 8RB. Tel: (0141) 616 5125/5126

The National Trust for Scotland • From Clarkston Toll in S Glasgow take Mearns Road for 1m. Signposted • Open all year, daily except 25th, 26th Dec and 1st, 2nd Jan, 9.30am – sunset • Entrance: £5, concessions and children £4 (2005 prices) • Other information: Conducted tours and demonstrations on second Sat of each month. Refreshments in summer only. Catering for parties and guided tours by arrangement. Dogs in woodland only, on lead ○ 🐾 <u>WC</u> ♿ ⌖ ⚙ ♀

The large old walled garden of an eighteenth-century house has been divided into many sections, offering imaginative practical demonstrations to illustrate the design and planting of small gardens. The colour combinations are especially good. All the plants are in good condition and admirably labelled. An old hard tennis court in the corner has been converted into a spacious and pleasant area full of ideas for disabled and infirm gardeners, with raised beds and a waist-high running-water pond. Wheelchair access to the glasshouse and potting shed allows disabled people to attend classes and work here. Woodland walks are filled with spring bulbs and shrubs and there are usually Highland cattle in the paddock. A National Collection of bergenias is held here.

Greywalls

Gullane, East Lothian EH31 2EG. Tel: (01620) 842144

Mr and Mrs Giles Weaver • 17m SE of Edinburgh on A198, 3m W of North Berwick. At east end of Gullane, signed to Greywalls Hotel; house is on right • Open May to Oct, daily, during daylight hours • Entrance: £2.50 NEW ◑ <u>WC</u> ⌖ B&B

Greywalls was designed in 1901 by Sir Edwin Lutyens as a golfing holiday house and enjoys eye-refreshing views over Muirfield golf course and the Firth of Forth to distant hills known as the Paps of Fife. The whole property is surrounded by local honey-coloured stone walls topped with grey Dutch tiles – their relationship with the house is one of the most interesting features. The 5-acre formal garden is possibly the only one in Scotland attributed to Gertrude Jekyll. The main garden lying to the south, where a Yorkstone terrace opens onto the old rose garden, has recently been redesigned by Laura Mackenzie retaining the original design of 20 beds and using Jekyll's favourite plants such as iris, heuchera, anemone, campanula, achillea, *Crambe cordifolia*, romneya and yucca. Honeysuckles, clematis and roses climb up ornamental metal pyramids surrounded by *Thalictrum flavum*, *Verbascum phlomoides* and *Kniphofia* 'Yellowhammer'. An *oeil-de-boeuf* in the stone wall provides a fine vista through to the Lammermuir Hills. Beyond this garden, box compartments contain whitebeams underplanted with vincas and white foxgloves, backed by holly-hedged chambers containing cherry trees and sculptures. Beyond this again are double herbaceous borders, a lavender border, and a charming parterre of box and santolina with green bean pyramids – all Jekyllian in design and content. The garden combines the 'prettiness' of that particular era of English gardening with wonderful Scottish views and the tang of the sea, while the house is an exceptionally comfortable hotel and open to visitors for dinner. Time your arrival carefully.

Harmony Garden

St Mary's Road, Melrose, Ettrick and Lauderdale, Scottish Borders TD6 9LT.
Tel: (01721) 722502

The National Trust for Scotland • On A6091 in Melrose • Open April to Sept, daily, 10am – 5pm (opens 1pm Sun) • Entrance: honesty box ☽ ⅃ ⌗

The two-and-a-half acre garden, like Priorwood (see entry) falls within the Melrose Abbey precinct complex. The house was built *c.* 1807 by a plantation owner who named it after his Jamaican estate. The garden is well named, for it exudes an aura of peace and tranquillity in the middle of a bustling town, with fine view of the abbey and the Eildon Hills. Just inside the entrance gate is the Golden Border, planted to celebrate the last owners' golden wedding anniversary with such things as *Rhododendron* 'Sun Chariot' and *R.* 'Persil', 'Grandpa Dickson', 'Allgold' and 'Golden Showers' roses, *Trollius* x *cultorum* 'Golden Cup' and *Iris* 'Ola Kala'. The kitchen garden has all the usual vegetables and a good variety of wall-trained fruit trees: a fig, an apricot, a peach, plums and a greengage. In front of the house generous herbaceous borders surround a beautifully balanced natural lawn with a mass of spring-flowering bulbs and wild and exotic flowers, including fritillaries, colchicums, erythroniums, crocus and alliums. Several narcissus species are unique to the garden.

Hill of Tarvit [Historic Scotland Inventory]

Cupar, Fife KY15 5PB. Tel: (01334) 653127

The National Trust for Scotland • 2.5m S of Cupar off A916 • House open April to 1st Oct, daily, plus 7th and 8th Oct, all 1 – 5pm • Grounds open all year, daily, 9.30am – sunset • Entrance: House and grounds £8, children and concessions £5, family £20, parties of 20 or more £4 per person. Car parking charge extra • Other information: Shop and tea room open from 12 noon daily ○ ☕ 🍴 WC ⅃ ⌗ ⌗ ⌗ ⌗ ⌗

The garden surrounds the charming Edwardian mansion designed in 1906 for a Dundee financier by Sir Robert Lorimer, who also laid out the grounds to the south of the house: the views over Fife are particularly fine. Good-size borders are filled with an attractive variety of perennials, annuals and heaths, and the grounds as a whole contain many unusual ornamental trees and shrubs now reaching maturity. The plantings are regularly upgraded to include newer and more unusual specimens. The rose garden is charming. A massive two-day plant sale for SGS is held the first weekend in October – there is no entry charge, and the public queue at the gate well before the opening.

The Hirsel [Historic Scotland Inventory]

Coldstream, Berwickshire TD12 4LP. Tel: (01573) 224144

The Earl of Home • 9m NE of Kelso, 15m SW of Berwick-on-Tweed, W of Coldstream on A697 • Open all year, daily during daylight hours • Entrance: parking charge £2 per car • Other information: Craft workshops ○ 💬 ✕ 🏠 wc & ⬧ ⚲

The house is not open, but at all seasons of the year the grounds have much of interest and enjoyment for the visitor who values the peace and ever-changing beauty of the countryside. There is something here for the ornithologist, botanist, geologist, forester, zoologist, historian and archaeologist. In spring, snowdrops and aconites and then acres of daffodils herald the coming summer as the birds, resident and migrant, of which 169 have been definitely identified within the estate boundaries, start busying themselves around their nesting sites. In May and June the rhododendron wood, Dundock, is justly famous for its kaleidoscopic colouring and breathtaking scents. Rose beds, herbaceous and shrub borders follow through the summer. In October and November the leaves turning on trees and shrubs provide attractive autumn colouring, and hundreds of duck, geese and gulls make the lake their nightly home. In winter the same trees are stark but magnificent in their skeletal forms against storm clouds and sunsets.

House of Pitmuies ★★ [Historic Scotland Inventory]

Guthrie, By Forfar, Angus DD8 2SN. Tel: (01241) 828245

Mrs Farquhar Ogilvie • 1.5m W of Friockheim, on A932 • House open for parties by appt • Garden open 25th March to Oct, daily, 10am – 5pm, and at other times by appt • Entrance: £2.50 by collection box • Other information: Teas by arrangement for parties visiting house ◑ 🏠 wc & ⬧ 🌿

In the grounds of an attractive eighteenth-century house and courtyard, these beautiful walled gardens lead down towards a small river with an informal riverside walk and two unusual buildings – a turreted dovecot and a Gothick wash-house. There are rhododendron glades with unusual trees and shrubs, but pride of place must go to the spectacular semi-formal gardens behind the house, where exquisite old-fashioned roses and a series of long borders containing a dramatic and superbly composed palette of massed delphiniums and other herbaceous perennials in June and July constitute one of the most memorable displays of its type to be found in Scotland. Latterly the gardens have evolved with new plantings, vistas and focal points, and the conversion of a former tennis court has allowed for new habitats and a greater diversity of plants. The supremely knowledgeable owner has lived in the house since 1966 and known the place for half a century.

House of Tongue [Historic Scotland Inventory]

Tongue, Lairg, Sutherland, Highland IV27 4XH. Tel: (01847) 611209

The Countess of Sutherland • 1m N of Tongue off A838 • Open 29th July, 2 – 6pm for charity, and at other times by appt • Entrance: £2.50, OAPs £2 children (under 12) 50p ◑ 💬 & ⬧

Sheltered from wind and salt by tall trees, this walled garden is a haven in an otherwise-exposed environment. Adjoining the seventeenth-century house, it is laid out after the traditional Scottish acre, with gravel and grass walks between herbaceous beds, hedged vegetable plots and orchard, and three beds filled with old-fashioned and new rose varieties. The glasshouse has been restored, and a wildflower meadow is in progress. A stepped beech-hedged walk leads up to a high terrace which commands a fine view over the Kyle of Tongue. The centrepiece of the garden is Lord Reay's 1714 sundial, a sculpted obelisk of unusual design.

Innes House Garden [Historic Scotland Inventory]

Elgin, Moray IV30 8NG. Tel: (01343) 842410

Mr and Mrs Mark Tennant • 5m E of Elgin, off A96 and then B9103 Lossiemouth road • Open to parties of 20 or more by appt only • Entrance: £3.50 • Other information: Meals for parties by arrangement only ● ● WC & B&B

The extensive ornamental garden is divided into compartments and the whole framed by a wide variety of mature and interesting trees. It was replanned and reorientated by the present owner's great-grandmother in 1912, when yew hedges were planted, providing a central walk. The large trees in the park are a major feature of the property – 47 varieties are represented, many estimated to be over 200 years old, including rare oaks, unusual maples, beeches and specimen trees such as *Arbutus menziesii*, *Davidia involucrata* and *Cercidiphyllum japonicum*. There are beautiful mature rhododendrons, different varieties flowering over a long period, and an azalea walk.

Inveresk Lodge Gardens [Historic Scotland Inventory]

Musselburgh, East Lothian EH21 6BQ. Tel: (0131) 665 1855

The National Trust for Scotland • 6m E of Edinburgh, S of Musselburgh via A6124 • Open all year, daily, 10am – 6pm (closes 4.30pm Nov to March) • Entrance: £3 (honesty box) ○ ● WC & ● ●

The large garden of the seventeenth-century house (not open) is surrounded by high and ancient stone walls; the south-facing aspect provides a warm microclimate for tender plants and a wide range of climbers. A small courtyard opens out unexpectedly onto a croquet lawn dominated at one end by an old yew. The large Edwardian glasshouse contains a National Collection of tropaeolums, plus exotic climbers, tree ferns, a grapevine and an aviary. Semi-formal in character, the three acres of garden were redesigned in the 1960s, with a shrub rose border originally planted by Graham Stuart Thomas, an azalea border, a white border flanked by a *Prunus nigra* hedge, a spring border with a circular lawn, and a newly laid juniper terrace. The garden slopes gently downwards, giving fine views of the Pentland Hills. The village itself, a unique, unspoilt example of eighteenth-century villa development, open under the Scotland's Gardens Scheme on alternate years – 2006 is the next occasion. A new pond has been created in the meadow, with paths winding through the grass, and a woodland walk.

Inverewe Garden ★★ [Historic Scotland Inventory]

Poolewe, Ross-shire, Highland IV22 2LG. Tel: (01445) 781200

The National Trust for Scotland • 6m NE of Gairloch on A832 • Open all year, daily, 9.30am – dusk (closes 4pm Nov to March) • Entrance: £8, concessions £5.25, family £20, parties £5.25 per person • Other information: Restaurant and shop open April to Oct only ○ 🍽 ✕ 🛍 WC ♿ 🐕 ♨

This spectacular garden on the shores of a sea loch, Loch Ewe, covers the Am Ploc Ard peninsula and has a long period of colour and interest. Planned as a wild garden around two dwarf willows on peat and sandstone, it has been developed since 1865 as a series of walks through herbaceous and rock gardens, a wet valley, pond gardens and woodland walks. A sloping traditional walled garden with glorious sea views and colourful terraces is filled with a mixture of herbaceous plants, roses and vegetables. It is a plantsman's garden (labelling is discreet), containing nearly 6,000 different plants including many tender species from Australia, New Zealand, China and the Americas, sheltered by mature beech and pine trees. National Collections of olearias and rhododendrons are held here. The garden is well tended and way-marked. Note: midge-repellent is advisable on still and muggy summer days and is on sale at the main desk.

Inwood

Carberry, Musselburgh EH21 8PZ. Tel: (0131) 665 4550

Irvine and Lindsay Morrison • 6m E of Edinburgh. From A1 Edinburgh – Berwick Road take A6094 signed to Dalkeith. Turn left at roundabout and follow signs for Carberry; garden is signed on left • Open April to Sept, Tues, Thurs, Sat and Bank Holiday Mons, 2 – 5pm, and by appt • Entrance: £2, children free ◑ 🍽 WC ♿ 🐕
B&B

A delightful plantsman's garden of just over an acre created since 1984. Full use is made of a small front garden designed for late summer colour containing an exciting variety of tender and lush-foliage plants. Through the garden gate boundary fences blaze with prolific rambling roses ('Blush Rambler', 'Paul's Himalayan Musk' and 'Sander's White Rambler'), and carefully chosen plants – tulips, streptocarpus, begonias, fuchsias and geraniums – complement each other in colour-themed island beds, where roses and unpruned clematis scramble over shrubs to reach up into the central heights of *Viburnum plicatum* 'Pink Beauty', *Pyrus salicifolia* 'Pendula', and a beautiful *Cornus controversa* 'Variegata'. Neat mown lawn extends into the woodland area with appropriate shrubs and ornamental trees; rare plants are constantly being added to the shade beds and pond. The owner has also cleverly created a large polythene-lined 'bog-bed' – an excellent idea that really works and adds glamorous foliage to a dry shady area.

Johnston Gardens

Viewfield Road, Aberdeen. Tel: (01224) 522734

Aberdeen City Council • In Aberdeen, 0.5m S of Queens Road (A944 to Alford), 0.25m W of junction with ring road • Open all year, daily, 8am – 1 hour before dusk • Entrance: free ○ WC ♿ 🐕 🐾

When Johnston House was demolished and the grounds sold for redevelopment, it was impossible to utilise the deepest area of the ravine. This was converted into a water and rock garden by the City of Aberdeen Parks and Recreation Department. The result is a congenial oasis of trees, shrubs and mature rhododendrons surrounding a small lake complete with an island, bridges and resident waterfowl. The rock and scree gardens contain some interesting alpine plants.

Jura House Gardens

Ardfin, Isle of Jura, Argyll and Bute PA60 7XX. Tel: (01496) 820315 (Peter Cool)

Riley-Smith family • On Jura, 5m SE of ferry terminal off A846. Vehicle ferries from Kennacraig by Tarbert to Port Askaig, Islay, and from Islay to Feolin, Jura • Open all year, daily, 9am – 5pm • Entrance: £2.50, children (5-16) £1 (collecting box) • Other information: Teas available June to Aug, Mon – Fri only. Possible for wheelchairs but sloping gravel paths ○ 💻 WC ⅋ ⬧ ⌇ ⚬

A circular walk around the Jura House estate illustrates the rich natural history and geology of the island. Starting from the car park, the visitor walks through native woodland and follows the fuchsia-clad banks of the burn to where it plunges into a ravine, filled with ferns and lichens, over the raised beach to the sea. Spectacular views of the Islay coast accompany the steep path down to the shore. Dykes and rock formations are home to wild scree plants and scrubby trees, and here is an example of machair – dune grassland. After the climb back up the cliff, signs guide the visitor to the garden proper. This organic walled garden is a sheltered haven with many unusual plants, including a collection of Australasian origin. Linger awhile before continuing on the woodland path back to the lodge.

Kailzie Gardens ★ [Historic Scotland Inventory]

Peebles, Peeblesshire, Scottish Borders EH45 9HT. Tel: (01721) 720007

Lady Angela Buchan-Hepburn • 2.5m SE of Peebles on B7062 • Garden and trout pond open all year, daily, 11am – 5.30pm (in winter, during daylight hours) • Entrance: mid-March to May, £3, children (5–12) 75p; June to Oct, £3.50, children (5–12) £1; Nov to mid-March, £2, children 50p (honesty box); snowdrop days, as advertised. Telephone for party rates • Other information: Holiday cottage available ○ 💻 ✕ WC ⬧ ⅋ ⌇ ⛃ ⚲ ⚬

'A Pleasure Garden' is the description in one of the advertisements for Kailzie (pronounced Kailie), and very apt it is too. The gardens of 17 acres are situated in a particularly attractive area of the beautiful Tweed Valley and are surrounded by breathtaking views. The old mansion was pulled down in 1962 and the vast walled garden, which still houses the magnificent greenhouse, has been transformed by the present owner from vegetables to a garden of meandering lawns and island beds full of interesting shrubs and plants, notably fuchsias and geraniums. There are many surprises, including snowdrops in drifts in February and March, a choice flower area, secret gardens, loving seats invitingly placed under garlanded arbours and several thoughtfully sited pieces of statuary. A magnificent fountain at the end of the herbaceous borders leads on to woods and stately trees, and from here you may stroll down the Major's Walk, lined with laburnum and underplanted with rhododendrons, azaleas, blue poppies and primulas. An 18-hole putting green and an osprey-watch viewing centre opened in 2003.

Kellie Castle [Historic Scotland Inventory]

Pittenweem, Fife KY10 2RF. Tel: (01333) 720271

The National Trust for Scotland • 3m NW of Pittenweem on B9171 towards Arncroach • Castle open May to Sept, 1 – 5pm • Garden and grounds open all year, daily, 9.30am – 5.30pm • Entrance: £3, children £2 (castle and garden extra charge) • Other information: Parking 100 metres, closer for disabled. Refreshments and shop only when castle open, 12 noon – 5pm ○ 🍽 🦽 <u>WC</u> ♿ 🐕 🄿 🚼 ♨ ℀

The garden appears to be seventeenth-century in plan, embellished by Professor James Lorimer and his family in late Victorian times. Entered by a door in a high wall, the one-and-a-half acres inspire dreams within every gardener's reach. Simple borders, such as one of nepeta, capture the imagination as hundreds of bees and butterflies work the flowers. Areas of lawn are contained within box hedges, and roses on arches and trellises abound. In one corner, behind a trellis, is a small romantic garden-within-a-garden. A large, green-painted commemorative seat designed by the sculptor Hew Lorimer provides a focus at the end of one of the main walks. There is an orchard, wall-trained fruit, and a collection of old and unusual varieties of vegetables produced by organic gardening methods. Outside the walled garden, mown walks wind through the meadow and woodland, which is a haze of wild garlic in late spring.

Kerrachar Gardens

Kylesku, Sutherland IV27 4HW.
Tel: (01571) 833288 (Garden); (01971) 502345 (Boat)

Peter and Trisha Kohn • 30m N of Ullapool, accessible by boat from Kylesku • Open mid-May to mid-Sept, Tues, Thurs, Sun. Additional visits are arranged for parties of up to 40. Boat departs from Old Ferry Pier 1pm or by arrangement • Entrance: £2.50, children (12 – 16) £1.25, under 12s free (boat fare £10, children (12 – 16) £5, under 12 free) ◑ 🍽 🦽 🐕 🄿

Horticulturally as far north-west as you can go, Kerrachar is one of the few inhabited homes in the UK accessible only by water. The half-hour boat trip down the loch is a scenic pleasure in itself, but this waterside garden would be well worth a visit wherever it was. The areas either side of the house are not particularly large – under an acre each – but this is anyway a garden you want to wander around, so varied and abundant is the planting, with plants and shrubs seemingly continuously in flower. Particular favourites are *Gladiolus cardinalis*, *Morina longifolia*, *Achillea grandiflora*. thalictrums, deep red Martagon lilies, verbascums, liatris, the little red 'thistle' *Cirsium rivulare* and the unfailingly hardy *Hebe eliptica*. As well as a host of roses and herbaceous plants, they also have a fine show of more tender shrubs – crinodendrons, pittosporums, callistemons, olearias and the attractive *Ozothamnus rosmarinifolius* with its woolly white shoots. Finally, what a treat to be able to buy truly home-grown plants from the well-stocked nursery area, most of them grown from seed and well labelled and reasonably priced.

Kilbryde Castle

Dunblane, Perthshire FK15 9NF. Tel: (01786) 824897

Sir James Campbell • 9m NW of Stirling, off A820 Dunblane – Doune road • Open 14th May and 18th June, 2 – 5pm, and by appt • Entrance: £2.50, OAPs and children £2; non-open day charge £3 ● &

The 20-acre garden was created by the present owner's parents, whose passions were rhododendrons, azaleas, clematis and bulbs. The garden is in two parts – a partly walled upper garden with island beds full of colour on a south-facing slope, and a lovely woodland garden on either bank of a stream well planted with rhododendrons and azaleas under a canopy of mature trees. The best time to visit is spring, particularly the end of May.

Kildrummy Castle Gardens ★ [Historic Scotland Inventory]

Alford, Aberdeenshire AB33 8RA. Tel: (01975) 571203/571277

Kildrummy Castle Garden Trust • 2m SW of Mossat, 10m W of Alford, 17m SW of Huntly. Take A944 from Alford, following signs to Kildrummy, and turn left onto A97. From Huntly turn right onto A97 • Open April to Oct, daily, 10am – 5pm • Entrance: £3.50, OAPs £3, children (5–16) free • Other information: Cars park inside hotel main entrance, coaches in delivery entrance. Woodland walks and children's play area ❶ 💷 🍴 <u>WC</u> & ⬧ ⚘ 🏛 ⚲

The gardens are set in a deep ravine between the ruins of a thirteenth-century castle and a Tudor-style house, now a hotel. The rock garden, by Backhouse of York (1904), occupies the site of the quarry which provided the stone for the castle. The narrowest part of the ravine is crossed by a copy of the towering fourteenth-century Auld Brig O'Balgownie (Old Aberdeen Bridge) built by Colonel Ogston in 1900. This affords a spectacular bird's-eye view of both sides of the water garden commissioned from a firm of Japanese landscape gardeners in the same period; Backhouse continued the planting. In April the reflections in the still water of pools increase the impact of the luxuriant *Lysichiton americanus*, and later come primulas, Nepalese poppies and a notable *Schizophragma hydrangeoides*. There are also fine maples, rhododendron species and hybrids, oaks and conifers. Although a severe frost pocket, the garden can grow embothriums, dieramas and other choice plants. The garden is especially beautiful in autumn with colchicums in flower and acers in brilliant leaf.

Kinross House Gardens [Historic Scotland Inventory]

Kinross, Kinross–shire KY13 8ET. Tel: (01577) 862900

Mr James Montgomery • Junction 6 of M90, into Kinross and follow signs • Open 14th April to Sept, daily, 10am – 7pm • Entrance: £2.50, OAPs and students £2, children free ❶ &

Ten acres of walled garden, all beautifully maintained, surround the seventeenth-century mansion. The gardens were designed in the 1680s and reconstructed early last century. The walls, surmounted by fine statuary, have decorative gates. Within, the scene is formal: a spacious lawn, clipped hedging, herbaceous borders, some with colour themes, and rose borders surrounding a fountain. There are yew hedges in interesting shapes, with well-placed seating for those in a contemplative mood or wishing to view *Loch Leven Castle* on the nearby island. It was here that Mary Queen of Scots was imprisoned in 1567, and visitors can make the short boat trip to its sombre walls from the adjoining Kirkgate Park.

Kittoch Mill

Busby Road, Carmunnock, Glasgow G76 9BJ. Tel: (0141) 6444712

Margaret and Les Watson • 4m NW of East Kilbride, on B759 Busby – Carmunnock road • Open for parties by appt • Entrance: £50 per group (max. 20 people) ●

A small organic country garden on the site of an ancient water mill. It includes a 25-foot waterfall and a small Japanese-style garden adjacent to a SSSI and home to 300 hostas.

Landform Ueda at the Gallery of Modern Art

75 Belford Road, Edinburgh EH4 3DR. Tel: (0131) 624 6200

National Galleries of Scotland • Between Scottish National Gallery of Modern Art and Dean Gallery • Open all year, daily, 10am – 5pm (closes 7pm Thurs) • Entrance: free ● ✕ ● wc & ● ● ●

Designed in 2002 by American architectural historian Charles Jencks for the Scottish National Gallery of Modern Art, the Landform Ueda (named for a Japanese scientist) is a serpentine stepped mound of mown grass with three crescent-shaped pools from which rise gentle spiral paths. The design, which is both innovative and strangely pleasing to the eye, is based on the rhythmic patterns that occur in nature, such as weather systems. These create a series of curves which overlap but never repeat and are attracted to a point or basin. Jencks 'looked at the inherent principles of natural movement and designed the Ueda to reflect and heighten these natural forces'. Once you actually see it, the above description becomes quite understandable. The Landform is seven metres high and occupies 300 square metres; from the paths there is also a good elevated view over the two galleries' grounds and their fine collection of sculptures, and towards the handsome Edinburgh skyline. Jencks' own sensational garden, *Portrack* in Dumfriesshire, is open on one day for SGS.

Langwell [Historic Scotland Inventory]

Berriedale, Caithness, Highland KW7 6HE. Tel: (01593) 751237 or (01593) 751278 (Head Gardener)

The Lady Anne Bentinck • 2m W of Berriedale off A9 • Open 6th and 13th Aug for SGS, and by appt • Entrance: £2 ● ● wc & ● ●

A lovely traditional two-acre walled garden. It has a sadly short season, due to the fact that it is almost as far to the north-east as it is possible to go, but inspires commensurate interest and admiration as a result. The cruciform layout lends itself to dramatic 64-metre-long herbaceous borders specialising in plants that are not only colourful but also manage to thrive in these conditions. They are framed by yew hedges, behind which lie vegetable and fruit sections – all immaculately maintained.

Lawhead Croft

Tarbrax, West Calder, West Lothian EH55 8LW.

Sue and Hector Riddell • 12m SW of Balerno, 6m NE of Carnwath on A70 towards Tarbrax • Open for charity June to Sept, daily, at any reasonable time, and for parties by written appt only • Entrance: £2, children 20p • Other information: No coaches down farm road (no turning room) ◐ ⬛

Nearly 300 metres up in the midst of the bleak Lanarkshire moors, the present owners have planted hedges and laboriously carved out a luxuriant garden, set out as an enchanting series of garden rooms, all with a different theme. Grass walks lead from one interesting border to another, full of unusual plants, with colour associations and leaf contrasts are carefully thought out. Great ideas include an excellent bonsai collection. Recently most of the vegetable garden has been swept away and replanted in a great sweep of curved, tiered and circular beds of spectacular and original design.

Leckmelm Shrubbery and Arboretum [Historic Scotland Inventory]

Little Leckmelm House, Lochbroom, Ullapool, Ross-shire IV23 2RH.

Mr and Mrs Peter Troughton • 4m S of Ullapool on A835 • Open April to Oct, daily, 10am – 6pm • Entrance: £2.50 ◐ ♿ ✎

Situated on the shore of Loch Broom and warmed by the Gulf Stream, the 10-acre arboretum is full of fine species rhododendrons and important trees, various shrubs and bamboos. Originally planted in 1870, it was abandoned for fifty years in the 1930s until reclamation started in 1984, and is now restored to its former Victorian glory. Note particularly the venerable old weeping beech whose spread covers at least a third of an acre, and the largest *Chamaecyparis lawsoniana* 'Wisselii' in Europe. A map and planting plan are available in the car park.

Leith Hall and Gardens ★ [Historic Scotland Inventory]

Huntly, Aberdeenshire AB54 4NQ. Tel: (01464) 831216

The National Trust for Scotland • 34m NW of Aberdeen, 1m W of Kennethmont on B9002 • House open (inc. exhibition) 14th to 17th April, then May to Sept, Fri – Tues, 12 noon – 5pm (last admission 4.15pm) • Garden and grounds open all year, daily, 9.30am – dusk • Entrance: £2.50, OAPs and children £1.90, pre-booked parties of 20 or more £2 per person (house and gardens £8, OAPs and children £5, pre-booked parties of 20 or more £5.60 per person) • Other information: Dogs outside walled garden only ○ 🅿 ⬛ WC ♿ ▮

The gardens are being restored and it is the old garden, remote from the house, that offers the greatest pleasure to the enthusiast. This comprises a series of small spaces, sheltered by walls and hedges, rising on a gentle slope from the west drive. It includes long borders and a large, well-stocked rock garden with a stream and gravel paths. The simple, romantic design allows a tremendous display of flowers during the whole of summer and early autumn; especially fine are magenta *Geranium psilostemon* and an entire border of solid catmint. There are no courtyards and no dominating architecture, just massive plantings of perennials and the odd rarity amongst the rocks. The circular moon gate at the top of the garden leads to the old turnpike road. Woodland walks throughout the designed landscape take in ponds and views down the garden.

Linn Botanic Gardens

Cove, Helensburgh, Dunbartonshire G84 0NR. Tel: (01436) 842242

Mr J.H.K. Taggart • 6m S of Garelochhead, 0.75m N of Cove on shore of Loch Long • Open all year, daily, dawn – dusk • Entrance: £3.50, students and teenagers £2.50, children £1 (under 5 free) • Other information: Entirely unsuitable for wheelchairs and prams. Light refreshments for organised tours. Plants for sale in adjacent nursery, open daily, 11am – 5pm ○ 🐾 WC ⬦ 🌳

The garden has been developed to its present form since 1971 by the current owners with thousands of unusual and exotic plants, including large collections of bamboos and temperate ferns. Colour is present at every season, from spring-flowering bulbs through rhododendrons to autumn leaves, set off by the dark foliage of conifers and evergreen trees. Water is a pervasive presence: in the extensive water garden, in formal ponds and fountains, in the glen with its tumbling waterfalls. There are also herbaceous borders, a rockery and a cliff garden; in 2004 a large oval lawn was dug up and replaced by a 'New Zealand heath'. A 1-kilometre signed route takes visitors through all parts of the garden. Fine views look down to the Firth of Clyde and from the terrace across Loch Long to the hills of Argyll.

Little Sparta ★ ★ [Historic Scotland Inventory]

Dunsyre, Lanark, South Lanarkshire ML11 8NG. Tel: (01899) 810252

Dr Ian Hamilton Finlay • Turn off A721 at Newbiggin for Dunsyre. 1m W of Dunsyre turn up unmarked farm track signed to Stonypath and Little Sparta. Alternatively take A702 from Edinburgh, turning off at Dolphinton; road signed to Dunsyre • Open June to Sept, Fri and Sun, 2 – 5pm • Entrance: free, but donation to Little Sparta Trust welcome ◐

Described by Sir Roy Strong as the most original contemporary garden in the country, the garden is now mercifully open to the public once more. On arrival at the gate to the property a beautifully carved wooden sign greets the visitor, giving a hint of the fine craft that combines with the art of this admired sculptor. Hamilton Finlay believes that a garden should appeal to all the senses and provoke thought, both serious and trivial, and he has therefore revived the art of emblematic gardening which died out in Britain in the seventeenth century, although his personal philosophy is inspired more closely by the eighteenth-century poet-gardeners Alexander Pope and William Shenstone. He has achieved an international reputation in the process. It is impossible to describe Little Sparta briefly, except to say that he has transformed a sizeable hill farmstead 350 metres above sea level in the Pentland Hills (starting in 1996 with the idea of establishing a testing-ground for his sculptures) into a garden full of classical inscriptions and images, allusions and symbols. Not all are easily understood or interpreted – *n'importe*, as this is a garden, not a crossword puzzle.

Lochalsh Woodland Garden (Balmacara Estate)

Lochalsh House, Balmacara, Kyle, Ross-shire, Highland IV40 8DN.
Tel: (01599) 566325

The National Trust for Scotland • 3m E of Kyle of Lochalsh off A87 • Open all year, daily, 9am – dusk • Entrance: £2, children £1 (2005 prices) • Other information: Parking off A87 with 0.5m walk to garden, closer parking by prior arrangement ○ 🐾 **WC** 🕊 🌿

Woodland planting on this steep-sided, 11-acre site began in 1887 around the house, and the canopy of beeches, larches, oaks and pines is now outstanding. Ornamental plantings began in the late 1950s with large-leaved rhododendrons, followed from the 1980s to the present day by shrubs from China, Japan, the Himalayas and Australasia. Paths created through the woods give a choice of walks. Alongside these and in glades, logs have been used to build curved, raised beds for plantings which include hydrangeas, fuchsias, bamboos and ferns. There are wonderful views out from the woodland and across the water to the mountains of Skye and Knoydart.

Logan Botanic Garden ★★ [Historic Scotland Inventory]

Port Logan, Stranraer, Wigtownshire, Dumfries and Galloway DG9 9ND.
Tel: (01776) 860231

Royal Botanic Garden Edinburgh • 14m S of Stranraer, off B7065. Signposted • Open March to Oct, daily, 10am – 6pm (closes 5pm March and Oct) and by appt at other times • Entrance: £3.50, concessions £3, children £1, family ticket £8. Local membership scheme, inc. Dawyck and Benmore Botanic Gardens (see entries), available • Other information: Discovery Centre and Sound Alive guided tours. Guide dogs only ◑ 🍽 ✕ **WC** ♿ 🌿 🏛 🛈

This garden deserves far more acclaim and repays you tenfold for the extra effort required to journey to the furthest south-west corner of the UK. Rightly described as the most exotic garden in Scotland, the balmy Gulf Stream climate is ideal not only for the tender sweet-scented rhododendrons which are a speciality, but also allows a remarkable collection of exotic half-hardy plants to flourish outside. Logan specialises in plants from the southern hemisphere (including 40 different species of eucalyptus) and over half of its holdings are fully documented wild-origin plants. In the walled garden paths flow between island beds always full of colour and interest. Scale and structure are well supplied by majestic fern trees, *Cordyline australis*, *Pinus montezumae*. Everywhere there are tender shrubs such as leptospermum, embothrium, olearia, pittosporum, eucryphia – an endless list. The woodland area has a similarly large collection of trees, including a collection of magnolias, shrubs such as carpodetus, metrosideros (related to callistemon), elegant bamboos and tree ferns like the lovely silver fern *Cyathea dealbata* and *Osmunda regalis* . Wander through Tasmania Creek, gasp at the gunnera stand and admire the Chilean collection. Then, since the rainfall here is 40-inches a year, take shelter in the licensed salad bar which looks onto a good display of Scottish native plants.

Logan House Gardens

Port Logan, by Stranraer DG9 9ND. Tel: (01776) 860239

Mr and Mrs Andrew Roberts • 14m S of Stranraer on A716. 2.5m from Ardwell. Signposted • Open Feb to Aug, daily, 9am – 6pm (Feb and March, 10am –5pm) • Entrance: £3, children (under 16) free [NEW] ◗ 🐚 WC ⅋ 🍵 ⚲

The elegant Queen Anne house was built in 1701, but the lands were documented as held by the McDouall family 'Ultra memoriam hominum' ('Before the memory of man').The gardens were planted by them in the 1870s with new shrubs from China, the Himalayas, Australasia and South America. In 1969 the main part of the garden became the Logan Botanic Garden (see entry), and the remaining mainly woodland section round the house was left relatively untended until 1995, when the present owners began an ongoing planting programme.Wide lawns and woodland glades set against the natural rock now enhance the mature trees and giant rhododendrons such as *R. macabeanum, sinogrande* and *russelianum*. Two champion trees, *Eucryphia cordifolia* and *Leptospermum lanigerum*, are both the biggest of their kind in the UK, and there are also exceptional embothriums, nothofagus, auracarias, clethras and Chilean hazels.

Malleny Garden [Historic Scotland Inventory]

Balerno, Edinburgh EH14 7AF. Tel: (0131) 449 2283

The National Trust for Scotland • In Balerno, off A70 Edinburgh – Lanark road • Open all year, daily, 10am – 6pm (or dusk if earlier) • Entrance: £3, OAPs/children £2 ○ 🐚 WC ⅋

Aptly described as the Trust's secret garden, Malleny seems an old and valued friend soon after meeting and reflects the thoughtful planning by the head gardener and his talented wife. An impressive deodar cedar reigns over this three-acre walled garden, assisted by a square of early-seventeenth-century clipped yews and by yew hedges.As well as holding a National Collection of nineteenth-century shrub roses, Malleny's four-metre-wide herbaceous borders are superb, as is the large glasshouse containing a summer display of flowering plants. Don't forget to admire the attractive herb and ornamental vegetable garden, laid out in traditional manner.

Manderston ★ ★ [Historic Scotland Inventory]

Duns, Scottish Borders TD11 3PP. Tel: (01361) 883450

Lord Palmer • 2m E of Duns on A6105 • House open • Gardens open mid-May to Sept, Sun, Thurs and Bank Holiday Mons, 11.30 – dusk, and for parties at any time of year by appt • Entrance: £3.50, children £7, children (12 – 18) £3.50, under 12 free. Reduced rate for parties of 15 or more on open days only ● 🍽 ✕ 🐚 WC ⬦ ♨

One of the last great classic houses to be built in Britain, designed by John Kinross and modelled on Robert Adam's Kedleston Hall. It was described in 1905 as a 'charming mansion inexhaustible in its attractions', and this might equally well apply to the gardens, which remain an impressive example of gardening on the grand scale.

Four magnificent formal terraces planted in Edwardian style overlook a narrow serpentine lake, and a Chinoiserie bridging dam tempts visitors over to the woodland garden on the far side, elegantly effecting the transition from formal to informal. The woodland garden has an outstanding collection of azaleas and rhododendrons, and is at its best in May. The formal walled gardens to the north of the house are a lasting tribute to the very best of the Edwardian era, when 24 gardeners were employed to do what two now accomplish to the same immaculately high standard. Gilded gates open on to a panorama of colourful planting on different levels, with fountains, statuary and a charming rose pergola all complementing one other. Even the greenhouses were given lavish treatment, with the walls created from lumps of limestone to resemble an exotic planted grotto. Fifty-six acres of formal and informal beauty.

Megginch Castle [Historic Scotland Inventory]

Errol, Perthshire PH2 7SW. Tel: (01821) 642222

The Hon. Mrs. Herdman • 8m E of Perth off A85 Perth – Dundee road • Open April to Oct by appt • Entrance: £3, children (over 5) £1 ◑ ⅃ ⬦

Megginch means Beautiful Island, and the castle (not open) was originally built as a tower house in the fifteenth century. Altered in the sixteenth century and again in the early eighteenth century, it was restructured by Robert Adam in 1790 and substantially by subsequent generations. The gardens span the centuries in the same way. The courtyard dates from 1720 – the first known example of brickwork in Scotland. A fountain parterre to the west of the house is of particular interest for its yew and variegated holly topiary, including an unusual yew crown planted to commemorate Queen Victoria's Golden Jubilee. There are four clumps of thousand-year-old yews, at 22 metres the highest in Scotland. The glorious 110-metre double border running the length of the eighteenth-century walled garden will be revived and replanted during 2006. An adjacent sixteenth-century walled area contains an interesting astrological garden with plants relevant to each sign. Peacocks abound.

Mellerstain [Historic Scotland Inventory]

Gordon, Berwickshire TD3 6LG. Tel: (01573) 410225

The Earl of Haddington • 6m NW of Kelso off A6089 • House open as garden, 12.30 – 5pm • Garden open 14th to 17th April; May to Sept, daily except Tues and Sat; Oct, Sun; all 11.30 – 6pm (last admission 5pm), and to parties of 20 or more at other times by appt • Entrance: £3.50, children free (house and garden £5.50, parties of 20 or more £5 per person) • Other information: Craft gallery ◑ 💻 WC ⅃ ⬦ ✒ ♿ ⚲

The house is a rare example of the work of the Adam family; both William and his son Robert worked on the building. The formal garden created by Reginald Blomfield after 1909 to replace William Adam's original design is composed of a trio of dignified balustraded terraces with lawns, clipped yews and rose-filled parterres. The glory of the garden is the landscape, complete with lake and woodlands in the style of Brown and Repton, but redesigned by Blomfield – the view of the Cheviot

Hills from the terraces is one of the finest to be found in this attractive stretch of the Scottish Borders.

Mertoun [Historic Scotland Inventory]

St Boswells, Melrose, Roxburghshire TD6 0EA. Tel: (01835) 823236

The Duke of Sutherland • 8m SE of Galashiels, 2m NE of St Boswells on B6404 • Open April to Sept, Sat, Sun and Bank Holiday Mons, 2 – 6pm • Entrance: £2, OAPs £1.50, children (under 14) 50p ● WC &

Overlooking the Tweed and with the house in the background, this is a lovely garden in which to wander and admire the mature specimen trees, azaleas and daffodils, and the most attractive ornamental pond flanked by a good herbaceous border. The focal point is the immaculate three-acre walled garden, which is everything a proper kitchen garden should be. Walking up from a 1567 dovecot, thought to be the oldest in the county, through a healthy orchard, the visitor reaches the box hedges, raised beds and glasshouses of the main area. Vegetables, herbs and bright flowers for the house vie for attention with figs and peaches in the well-stocked glasshouses.

Monteviot [Historic Scotland Inventory]

Jedburgh, Scottish Borders TD8 6TJ. Tel: (01835) 830380 (mornings)

5m NE of Jedburgh. Turn off A68 onto B6400 to Nisbet. Entrance second turn on right • Open April to Oct, daily, 12 noon – 5pm. Parties must book with Administrator • Entrance: charge, children under 16 free • Other information: Refreshments at Harestanes Countryside Visitor Centre, 0.5m ◑ WC & ♨

The river garden running down to the River Teviot has been extensively replanted with herbaceous perennials and shrubs to a more informal design. Beside it, the semi-enclosed terraced rose gardens overlooking the river have a large collection of hybrid teas, floribundas and shrub roses. The pinetum is full of unusual trees, and nearby a water garden has been created, planted with hybrid rhododendrons and azaleas. A new feature will incorporate cascading water flowing through bridges into a pool. A circular route has been laid out around the gardens, and there are fine views.

Mount Stuart ★★ [Historic Scotland Inventory]

Rothesay, Isle of Bute. Argyll and Bute PA20 9LR. Tel: (01700) 503877

Mount Stuart Trust • Take ferry from Wemyss Bay. Garden is 5.5m S of Rothesay ferry terminal on A844 • House open as garden but 11am – 5pm (opens 10am – 2.30pm, Sat) • Garden open 14th to 17th April, then May to Sept, daily, 10am – 6pm • Entrance: £3.50, OAPs £3, children £2 (house and garden £7, OAPs £5.50, children £3) ◑ ➡ ✕ 🖼 WC & ♨ ♨ 🏺 🍴 ◕

Incorporated in the 300 acres of designed landscape and waymarked woodland walks, there is a wealth of horticultural interest here, and one of the most elegant drives in the country. The gardens contain a considerable mature pinetum of 1860 and a magnificent old lime tree avenue leading to the shore, but they have been restored and augmented over the last decade by the 6th Marquess and his wife.

In conjunction with the Royal Botanic Garden Edinburgh, 100 acres have also been set aside to grow endangered conifer species from all over the world. Rock gardens provide decorative features near the house, but the two most important elements are the kitchen garden and the 'Wee' garden. The latter is actually eight acres of mixed and exotic plantings with emphasis on species from the southern hemisphere. It is set in the mildest part of the grounds and grows some of the most tender plants to be found outside the glasshouse, some flourishing to unusual size. The kitchen garden, originally designed as an ornamental *potager* by the late Rosemary Verey, has been partially redesigned for the 7th Marquess by James Alexander-Sinclair in the form of six large beds, planted with bold imagination in a scheme based on the colour wheel. Set in the middle is the Pavilion Glasshouse planted with rare flora from SE Asia. One of Scotland's finest gardens. Then make time to visit the magnificent Victorian fern house and attractive garden at *Ascog Hall*, just south of Rothesay. [Open Easter to October, Wed – Sun, 10am – 5pm.]

Netherbyres [Historic Scotland Inventory]

Eyemouth, Berwickshire, Scottish Borders TD14 5SE. Tel: (01890) 750337

Colonel S.J. Furness • 8m NW of Berwick-upon-Tweed, 0.25m from Eyemouth on A1107 • Open twice yearly in April and July for charity, and April to Sept for small parties by appt • Entrance: £3, children £1.50 ● &⚘ 🌶

Netherbyres is worth seeing for the unique elliptical walled garden, built before 1740 and thought to be the only one of its kind. The present layout dates from the 1860s, although the Victorian conservatory and vineries were demolished to make way for a modern house and conservatory. It is filled with a traditional mix of fruit, flowers and vegetables still fully cultivated on traditional lines. A central gazebo and a shrub border have been added. Summer is the best time to visit.

Novar

Evanton, Ross-shire IV16 9XL. Tel: (01349) 830126

Mr and Mrs Ronald Munro Ferguson • 7m NE of Dingwall off A9 and B817 between Evanton and junction with A836 • Open for SGS, and for parties of 8 or more by appt. Other information: Refreshments on request • Entrance: £5 ● WC &

A charming series of mature planted natural ponds forms part of the mansion house gardens, fed by streams gushing over stone steps and monumental waterfalls. A formal semi-circular parterre was built to celebrate the millennium, the back edge of which drops down as a 2.75-metre wall to form a handsome ha-ha overlooking the park. There is also a five-acre traditional walled garden with charming arched entrances. Peaceful lawns and mature trees offset a large eighteenth-century oval pond embellished with a contemporary bronze figure.

Pitmedden Garden [Historic Scotland Inventory]

Pitmedden Village, Ellon, Aberdeenshire AB41 7PD. Tel: (01651) 842352

The National Trust for Scotland • 14m N of Aberdeen, 1m W of Pitmedden, 1m N of Udny on A920 • Open May to Sept, daily, 10am – 5.30pm • Entrance: £5, concessions £4, family £14, parties £4 per person • Other information: Coaches please book if tea is required. Wheelchairs supplied. Museum of farming life ◑ 💻 🐾 <u>WC</u> ♿ ⇗ 🐾 🏛 🍴 ☕

The Great Garden at Pitmedden exhibits the taste of seventeenth-century garden-makers and their love of patterns made to be viewed from above. This rectangular parterre garden is enclosed by high terraces on three sides and by a wall on the fourth. Simple topiary and box hedging abound. The south- and west-facing walls, lined by fine herbaceous borders, are covered by a great variety of old apple trees in both fan and espalier styles, producing almost two tons of fruit at the end of the season. Ornamental patterns are cut in box on a grand scale, infilled with 40,000 annuals. The overall impact is striking when viewed from the original ogivally roofed stone pavilion at the north of the garden or when walking along the terraces. When the Trust acquired Pitmedden in 1952 all that survived was the masonry, and since nothing remained of the original design, contemporary seventeenth-century plans for the garden at the Palace of Holyrood in Edinburgh were used in re-creating what is seen today.

Pollok House [Historic Scotland Inventory]

Pollokshaws Road, Glasgow G43 1AT. Tel: (0141) 616 6410

The National Trust for Scotland • 3.5m S of city centre. In Pollokshaws take A736. Signposted • House open • Garden open all year, daily except 25th and 26th Dec, 1st and 2nd Jan, 10am – 5pm • Entrance: free (house £8) ○ 💻 ✕ 🐾 <u>WC</u> ♿ ⇗ 🏛 🍴

A full day's entertainment here. Next to the house is a lovely formal terrace of box parterres, and there are borders near the water and a nineteenth-century woodland garden, famous for its rhododendrons in late spring, on the ridge nearby. The stone gazebos have ogee roofs. The house holds the Stirling Maxwell collection of European paintings, and in the grounds, famous for their bluebells in spring, is the Burrell Collection, one of the world's finest modern galleries, housing decorative and fine arts. The building was designed to complement the woodland, and the parkland around is beautifully planted and maintained.

Portmore ★

Eddleston, Peebleshire, Scottish Borders EH45 8QU. Tel: (01721) 730383

Mr and Mrs D.L. Reid • 0.5m N of Eddleston, on A703 Peebles – Edinburgh road • Open for SGS in mid-July, and for parties by appt • Entrance: £2.50 ◐ WC ⇗

It is a joy to see an old neglected estate brought lovingly back to life. The long drive winds up through woods, fields and little lochs to the Edwardian mansion proudly surveying the rolling acres. Parterres have recently been planted at the far side of the house, and shrub-filled woodland walks are being planned. The wonder of the place is the large walled garden designed and replanted by Chrissie Reid with great taste and flair – she cares particularly about colours and the effect at the entrance is magical. The soft mixture of pale greens, blues, mauves and white delights the eye in the herbaceous borders and leads the gaze to the greenhouses stuffed full of geraniums, pelargoniums, streptocarpus, fuchsias, etc. Leading off these there is an enchanting cool, dripping Victorian Italianate grotto, fern-filled. The remainder of the garden is divided into squares of *potagers*, herb gardens, hawthorn walks, rose gardens, all surmounted by wonderful wrought-iron arches. Even the luxurious-looking fruit is protected by wire held up by three elegant cages. A new water and woodland garden has been planted.

Priorwood Garden [Historic Scotland Inventory]

Melrose, Ettrick and Lauderdale, Scottish Borders TD6 9PX.
Tel: (01896) 822493

The National Trust for Scotland • On A6091 in Melrose • Open 14th April to 24th Dec, daily, 10am – 5pm (opens 1pm Sun) • Entrance: £3, OAPs £2, children £2, family £8 ○ 🐌 ♿ ⬅ 🌿 ⛪

Purchased by the Trust in 1974, this was originally the walled garden belonging to Priorwood House, now Melrose Youth Hostel. The garden has been developed for the production of dried flowers, and by drying them in dessicants – as the ancient Egyptians did – the range of plants has been greatly increased to include some 700 varieties of annual and herbaceous plants. There is also an orchard, which has been designed to show the development of the apple tree in Britain, and a woodland area. The eighteenth-century garden walls are complemented by ornamental ironwork thought to have been designed by Lutyens.

Royal Botanic Garden Edinburgh ★★ [Historic Scotland Inventory]

Inverleith Row, Edinburgh EH3 5LR. Tel: (0131) 552 7171

1m N of city centre at Inverleith. Signposted • Open all year, daily except 25th Dec and 1st Jan, from 10am (closes 4pm – 7pm depending on season). Garden tours operate April to Sept, daily, 11am and 2pm from West Gate • Entrance: free. Glasshouses £3.50, OAPs £3, children £1, family £8 • Other information: Exhibition hall and Inverleith House gallery open. Guide dogs only ○ 🍽 ✕ <u>WC</u> ♿ 🌿 ⛪ 🍴

Set on a hillside with magnificent panoramic views of the city, this is one of the finest botanic gardens in the world; arguably the finest garden of its type in Britain. Established in the seventeenth century on an area the size of a tennis court, it now extends to 75 acres. Rhododendrons and azaleas abound, and in spring their stunning flowers provide a blaze of colour and intriguing scents. The world-renowned rock garden is spanned by a long bridge over the stream. In summer, marsh orchids, lilies, saxifrages and bell-shaped campanulas give brilliant colour. There are also peat and woodland gardens and a stunning herbaceous border. The arboretum sweeps along the garden's southern boundary. A relatively recent addition is the Chinese hillside on a south-facing slope, which includes a spectacular wild-water ravine crossed by bridges, tumbling down into a tranquil pond at the bottom of the hillside. A *T'ing* (pavilion) provides an ideal place to relax. The glasshouses, featuring Britain's tallest palm house, leads the visitor on a trail of discovery through the temperate and tropical regions of the world, featuring passion flowers, cycads (some over 200 years old) and species that provide everyday necessities such as food, clothes and medicine. 7m W of Edinburgh city centre off A90 is *Mons Hill*, within the Dalmeny Estate. It is open for charity one Sunday in late February or early March, when the acres of wild snowdrops, naturalised in woodland, must be seen to be believed. Outstanding also for the views towards the Pentland Hills. Telephone (0131) 331 1888 for details.

Scone Palace Gardens [Historic Scotland Inventory]

Perth, Perth and Kinross PH2 6BD. Tel: (01738) 552300

The Earl and Countess of Mansfield • Just outside Perth on A93 Perth – Braemar road • Palace and grounds open April to Oct, daily, 9.30am – 5.30pm • Entrance: £3.25, OAPs/students £2.65, children £1.80 (palace and gardens £6.95, OAPs/students £5.95, children £4, family £22) ◑ ⬛ ✕ 🍂 WC ♿ ⬗ ⊞ ⬤ ℃

The 100 acres of gardens, surrounding the site of Macbeth's ancient city of Scone, include the famous nineteenth-century pinetum with magnificent towering trees including *Sequoia giganteum* over 48 metres tall; a second pinetum with over 60 specimens was planted in 1977. There is also an acer collection, a 30-metre-long laburnum pergola and a beech maze. Designed by Adrian Fisher and opened in 1998, this comprises 2000 beech trees in the shape of the Murray Star. Taking their turn in season are spectacularly massed daffodils, a primrose drive, many honeysuckles, clematis and roses, and fine rhododendrons and azaleas. Butterflies abound in their designated garden, and red squirrels delight visitors for whom they are a rarity. The renowned explorer/plant collector, David Douglas, born at Scone, supplied the garden with many of his discoveries, and one of his firs survives. His life is marked by an exhibition in the palace. The owners have the largest orchid collection in the country and orchids are always in flower in the State Rooms. It is also worth travelling 7m further north to marvel at the *Meikleour Beech Hedge*, now 30 metres high and a quarter of a mile long, beside the A93. Legend has it that men who planted it in 1745 were called away to fight and not one returned alive from the battle of Culloden.

Shepherd House ★

Inveresk, East Lothian EH21 7TH. Tel: (0131) 665 2570

Sir Charles and Lady Fraser • 7m E of Edinburgh. From A1 take A6094 exit, signed to Wallyford and Dalkeith, and follow brown tourist-signs to Inveresk Lodge Gardens. Shepherd House is opposite lodge at junction of main road and Crookston Road (garden entrance in Crookston Road) • Open April to June, Tues and Thurs, plus 3 times a year for SGS, and for parties by appt • Entrance: £2.50 • Other information: Exhibition of watercolours by Ann Fraser on garden open days. Teas and plant stall on SGS open days only ◐ ♿ ⬗

The most arresting feature of this one-acre plantsman's garden is a timelessly elegant stone water rill, which flows for 37 metres from a raised pond with a four-jet fountain at the end of the garden to a central bronze fountain with a girl washing her hair, set just above the alpine wall of a prettily planted terrace and parterre in front of the seventeenth-century house. Over and beside the rill are alternate arches and blue trellises, pillars clothed with *Vitis coignetiae* and 'Bobbie James', 'Wedding Day', 'Seagull' and bronze 'Ghislaine de Féligonde' roses, underplanted with allium and nepeta. A decorative arbour sets off more old-fashioned and Scottish roses in a special bed protected by the old stone walls of the garden, and the lawn path meanders on past 'cool' and 'hot' borders through shady trees, a meadow garden (which can be admired from a drystone spiral seat), a shrub border, finally curving round to two immaculate *potager* areas with twin arbours of trained pear trees. The garden is also full of sculptural surprises. Some – bird baths, sundials and tulip-filled urns – are elegant, while others – lead pigeons in the undergrowth, a large copper rose stuck in a bush and eye-stopping giant topiary creatures – are delightfully quirky. Lady Fraser, an accomplished botanical artist, has created with her husband one of the best smaller gardens in Scotland.

St Andrew's Botanic Garden

Canongate, St Andrews KY16 8RT. Tel: (01334) 476452/477178

Fife Council • 0.5m from town centre, signed in Canongate • Open all year, daily, 10am – 7pm (closes 4pm Oct to April). Glasshouse open daily, 10am – 4pm • Entrance: £2, concessions and children (5–16) £1 (2005 prices) • Other information: Private tours by prior arrangement ○ 🍽 🏠 WC & ℘ ♿

On its present site the garden dates from 1960, covering 18 acres along the Kinness Burn; in 1987 it was leased by the university to the local council. Although the botanical collections are now increasingly adapted for low maintenance, the areas of specialised planting remain excellent. Visitors will find something of interest all year; even in winter a pleasant afternoon may be spent in the greenhouses among the arid, alpine, tropical and temperate-zone plants. The pond and rock garden are particularly attractive, and the order beds are a valuable educational aid, rarely seen elsewhere. There are good collections of cotoneasters, sorbus and berberis, and stunning clumps of *Lathraea clandestina*.

Stobo Castle Water Gardens [Historic Scotland Inventory]

Peebles, Scottish Borders EH45 8NX. Tel: (01721) 760245

Hugh and Charles Seymour • 6m SW of Peebles on B712, 12m E of Biggar • Open for SGS, and by appt, but advisable to confirm in writing as well as telephoning • Entrance: £2.50, children free ● 🍽 & ♿ ℘ **B&B**

The enduring appeal of water is exemplified here; the planting, although most attractive, takes second place to the visual impact of clear water flowing down a series of cascades and waterfalls. Japanese bridges and stepping stones invite frequent crossings from side to side, and peaceful rills stray from the main torrent to create one huge water garden. In fine landscape-garden tradition, man has contrived to manipulate nature – in this case a large earth dam across a steep valley – into something of classical delight. The dam was faced with stone to create a magnificent waterfall and the resulting flow is impressive even in dry summers. Many fine mature trees, including Japanese maples.

Teviot Water Garden

Kirkbank House, Eckford, Kelso, Scottish Borders TD5 8LE. Tel: (01835) 850253

Mrs Susan Wilson • Between Kelso and Jedburgh on A698 • Open all year, daily, 10am – 5pm • Entrance: free ◑ 🍽 ✕ WC ℘ 🏛 ♿

Created over the years from a stony riverside field, these gardens occupy a spectacular position on a steep north-west-facing bank of the River Teviot. A series of terraces linked by waterfalls displays a wide range of plants, giving a varied show throughout the summer months. Aquatic plants are a speciality, but this intimate and tranquil garden also contains a selection of choice perennials, grasses, ferns and bamboos. The shop stocks plants and other items needed by the water garden enthusiast, from fish to pumps and liners.

Threave Garden and Estate [Historic Scotland Inventory]

Stewartry, Castle Douglas, Dumfries and Galloway DG7 1RX. Tel: (01556) 502575

The National Trust for Scotland • 1m W of Castle Douglas off A75 • House open April to Oct, Wed, Thurs, Fri, Sun, 11am – 4pm • Garden open all year, daily, 9.30am – dusk (walled garden and glasshouses close 5pm) • Entrance: £6, OAPs and children £5, family £15, parties £4 per person, school parties £1 per child (house and garden £10, OAPs £7, parties £7 per person, family £25) • Other information: Exhibition in visitor and countryside centre, Feb to Dec, daily ○ ● ✕ 🥄 wc 🔛 🕸 🦯 🏛 🚻 🐾

The Threave estate, which extends to 1500 acres, includes the famous 65-acre garden which has been used as a school of horticulture since 1960 and caters for trainee gardeners. For the visitor the principal interest is the working walled garden with its range of glasshouses, vegetables, orchard and wall-trained fruit. This may be contrasted with the less formal woodland and rock gardens, heath garden and arboretum. The garden is noted for its collection of daffodils, complemented in spring by rhododendrons, herbaceous perennials in summer, and a good collection of flowering trees and shrubs.

Tillypronie [Historic Scotland Inventory]

Tarland, Aboyne, Aberdeenshire AB34 4XX. Tel: (013398) 81238

The Hon. Philip Astor • 4.5m W of Tarland via A97 Dinnet – Huntly road • Open 4th June and 27th Aug for charity, 2 – 5pm • Entrance: £3, children £1.50 ● ● wc 🦯 🕸 🏛 🐾

Set on the south-facing slope of a hill at over 300 metres above sea level, this is a cold garden, but shelter belts dating from the mid-1800s ensure that a wide range of plants can be grown; more shelter planting was added from 1925 to 1951. The overall layout was completed in the 1920s, the work of George Dillistone of Tunbridge Wells. The terraces below the house date from the same period and support narrow herbaceous borders. The house walls provide shelter for less hardy climbers, and trained *Buddleia davidii* cultivars make a good display in August. Curved stone steps lead between extensive heather gardens to lawns sweeping down to the ponds with their colourful plantings of astilbes, filipendulas, lysichitons, primulas and ferns. Azaleas and rhododendrons feature strongly in June, and there are fine specimens of *Picea breweriana* and many other conifers and an area devoted to dwarf varieties. A rock garden and a Golden Jubilee garden are recent arrivals. Spectacular views end with the Grampians on the horizon.

Torosay Castle and Gardens [Historic Scotland Inventory]

Craignure, Isle of Mull PA65 6AY. Tel: (01680) 812421

*Mr Christopher James • 1.5m S from Craignure. Steamer 6 times daily April to Oct
(2 to 4 times daily Nov to March) from Oban to Craignure. Narrow-gauge railway
from Craignure ferry. Or take Lochaline to Fishnish ferry, then travel 7m S on A849
• Castle open Easter to Oct, 10.30am – 5pm • Garden open all year, daily, 9am – 7pm
(or dusk in winter) • Entrance: £5, OAPs and students £4, children £1.75 (castle
and gardens) (2005 prices)* ○ ➑ 🐚 WC ᕝ ⇗ ℘ ⛪ ℃

The house in baronial castle style by Bryce (1858) is complemented by a formal
Italianate main garden based on a series of descending terraces with an unusual
statue walk. This features one of the richest collections of Italian Rococo statuary
in Britain and alone justifies the crossing from Oban to Mull. Vaguely reminiscent
of Powis Castle (see entry in Wales), it makes a dramatic contrast with the
rugged island scenery. The peripheral gardens around the formal terraces are
also a contrast – a newly restored informal water garden and an Oriental garden
looking out over Duart Bay, and a small rock garden. Rhododendrons and
azaleas are a feature but less important than in other west-coast gardens, and
there is a collection of Australian and New Zealand trees and shrubs. A major
restoration is under way, and 2000 species and cultivars have been planted over
the past five years. Outside the main garden, the owners, in conjunction with the
Royal Botanic Garden Edinburgh, have created a five-acre Chilean wood and
underplanted another two-acre wood with plants from the collection of the late Jim
Russell.

Tyninghame House [Historic Scotland Inventory]

Tyninghame, East Linton, East Lothian EH42 1XW.

*Tyninghame Gardens Ltd • 25m E of Edinburgh between Haddington and Dunbar.
N of A1, 2m E of A198 • Open one day in May and June for charity, 1 – 5pm
• Entrance: £2* ◕ ➑ 🐚 WC ᕝ ⇗ ℘

Tyninghame is renowned for the gardens created by the late Countess of
Haddington. When her husband died in 1986 the house was sold and converted into
separate dwellings with great sensitivity by Kit Martin. The owners have their own
private area of garden, but Lady Haddington's Secret Garden, the stunning
herbaceous border and the woodland area are shared. The parterre on the upper
terrace is laid out in a design of triangular beds, filled with roses that are either
white or yellow, chiefly 'King's Ransom' and 'Iceberg'. The romantic and exuberant
Secret Garden is an eighteenth-century French re-creation, planted with old-
fashioned roses in subdued colours, clematis, philadelphus, white lilacs, peonies and
geraniums, and an apple walk. Through the gateway a path leads to woodland where
many mature trees shelter azaleas, rhododendrons, shrub roses, embothriums and
shrubs selected for their autumn colour. In spring the woods abound with wild
primroses and bulbs. The ruin of the Romanesque St Baldred's Church stands within
the grounds, and there are stunning views across parkland to the Tyne estuary and
the Lammermuir hills.

Tyninghame Walled Garden ★ [Historic Scotland Inventory]

Dunbar, East Lothian EH42 1XW. Tel: (01620) 860559

Mrs Charles Gwyn • 25m E of Edinburgh N of A1. Take turning to North Berwick and Tyninghame on A198; after 1m turn right through archway • Open two day for SGS, and by appt, 1 – 5pm • Entrance: £2, children free (2005 price) ● WC ✕ &
⬙ ⌖

The high brick walls, which were originally heated, and the gateways here date from 1760, making this one of the oldest walled gardens in Scotland. Within are four acres of formal gardens redesigned in 1960 by Jim Russell. The wide grass walk with its high yew hedges forms the backbone of the garden. Classical statues are set in alcoves cut in the yew, while pedestal urns and a very fine Florentine fountain stand at the intersections of two transverse paths that dissect the vista. One path, edged with nepeta, has arched supports for ornamental vines and climbing roses; the second is a beautifully planted rose walk. Extensive borders of mixed plantings, a long border of peonies and an iris border are all impeccably maintained and plant associations are often excellent. There is also a knot garden, an apple orchard, a *potager* and a large woodland area with mature and unusual trees underplanted with huge swathes of perennials. The famous 90-metre-long apple walk outside the walls was planted in 1891 and formed the approach to the walled garden from Tyninghame House (see entry above).

University of Dundee Botanic Garden

Riverside Drive, Dundee DD2 1QH. Tel: (01382) 647190

University of Dundee • 2.5m from city centre on A90 Perth road. Signposted • Open all year, daily, 10am – 4.30pm (closes 3.30pm Nov to Feb). Closed 25th and 26th Dec, 1st and 2nd Jan • Entrance: £2, OAPs £1, children £1, family £5 ● ⬛ ⬛ WC
& ⌖ ⛪ ♔ ℀

Founded in 1971 as a source of plant material for teaching and research purposes, the garden has always been open to the public for their pleasure. The attractive planting around the glasshouse and large pond near the entrance is reminiscent of a private rather than a botanic garden. The large area beyond has plants grouped according to region or habitat, including many Scottish natives; though mainly composed of trees and shrubs, the artistic layout ensures plenty to see of interest as well as beauty. The glasshouse is brimful of fine specimens, from tropical to temperate zones, from rainforest to desert – a pleasure whatever the weather is like outside. In all, a very varied 21 acres.

Wemyss Castle

East Wemyss, Fife KY1 4TE. Tel: (01592) 651327

Michael and Charlotte Wemyss (Wemyss Estate Trustees) • 2m NE of Kirkcaldy on A955 Dysart-Leven tourist route. Entrance in village of Coaltown of Wemyss • Open 9th April, 2pm – dusk, for erythroniums; then May to 10th Aug, Thurs, 12 noon – dusk • Entrance: £4 NEW ◑ WC & ⌖

The traditional six-acre walled garden dates from 1690, but gradually reverted to rough field after the 1890s. The current owners began its re-creation from scratch in

1994, retaining the original three sections and the magnificent Georgian orangery. The romantically informal garden now features long herbaceous borders planted with a large collection of roses and clematis, secret watery nooks, arches and pergolas. There is a magnificent display of erythroniums on the one-day spring opening in April.

West Drummuie Garden

West Drummuie, Golspie, Sutherland, Highland KW10 6TA. Tel: (01408) 633493

Mrs Elizabeth Woollcombe • 1m S of Golspie off A9. At white milestone, turn up hill and bear right at fork to last house • Open mid-April to early Oct by appt only • Entrance: donations welcome • Other information: No coaches please ● ⚘

A small private garden imbued with the spirit of the owner (a gardener of forty years' experience), set on a steep slope at the foot of Ben Bhraggie overlooking the Dornoch Firth. Protected from the salty east winds by hedges of *Griselinia littoralis*, escallonia and *Berberis darwinii*, it is a garden of woodland and water. Pieris, *Crinodendron hookerianum*, *Azara serrata*, hoheria and *Corokia cotoneaster* flower well, and *Myosotidium hortensia* now has its Chatham Island cousins, olearia and astelias, which appreciate their covering of fresh seaweed. *Meconopsis* 'Slieve Donard' and monocarpics (plants that flower and fruit once and then die) also like the conditions. A Jack Russell patrols the garden, and bantams act as slug controllers. Visitors to this northerly spot are made to feel very welcome, and the owner's favourite treasures are propagated and for sale. A recently acquired patch of ground has been planted with the aim of introducing children to the joys of nature and history.

GARDENING WEBSITES
Many gardens now have their own websites, and we list these at the back of the *Guide*. Others useful for garden visitors are:
Dept of Environment (Ireland): www.heritageireland.ie
English Heritage: www.english-heritage.org.uk
Historic Houses Association: www.hha.org.uk
Historic Royal Palaces: www.hrp.org.uk
Historic Scotland: www.historic-scotland.gov.uk
Landmark Trust: www.landmarkrust.org.uk
National Gardens Scheme: www.ngs.org.uk
National Trust: www.nationaltrust.org.uk
National Trust for Scotland: www.nts.org.uk
Royal Horticultural Society: www.rhs.org.uk
Welsh Historic Monuments: www.cadw.wales.gov.uk

SYMBOLS
[NEW] entries new for 2006; ○ open all year; ☾ open most of year; ◐ open during main season; ● open rarely and/or by appt; ☕ teas/light refreshments; ✗ meals; 🧺 picnics permitted; WC toilet facilities; <u>WC</u> toilet facilities, inc. disabled; & partly wheelchair-accessible; 🐕 dogs on lead; ⚘ plants for sale; 🏠 shop; ♛ events held; ℗ children-friendly; B&B bed and breakfast available.

WALES

Two-starred gardens are marked on the map with a black square.

Aberglasney Gardens ★ [Welsh Historic Garden Grade II*]

Llangathen, Llandeilo, Carmarthenshire SA32 8QH. Tel: (01558) 668998

Aberglasney Restoration Trust • 3m W of Llandeilo on A40. Turn S at Broak Oak junction • Open all year, daily, 10am – 6pm (last entry 5pm), (winter 10.30am – 4pm). Closed 25th Dec • Entrance: £6, OAPs £5, disabled £3, children £3, family ticket £15 • Other information: Holiday cottages available ◑ 💻 ✕ 🏵 <u>WC</u> ♿ ⚘ 🏛 🍴

Here are gardens lost in time. Records for Aberglasney go back to the mid-fifteenth century, when mention was made of nine gardens, orchards and vineyards. Around 1600 the Bishop of St David's bought the estate to turn it into a private palace, and it was probably he who built the gatehouse and the marvellous cloister garden. To the side of the house is a rare example of a yew tunnel. After many years of neglect the gardens are being restored with great care and attention to detail. The large upper walled garden was designed by Penelope Hobhouse to complement the historic site, and the lower walled garden is home to vegetables, herbs and plants grown for cutting. The wooded area known as Bishop Rudd's Walk has fine collections of rare and unusual woodland plants. Pigeon House Wood is a natural, unspoilt area where you may sit in the shade of splendid beech trees and other woodland planting. The restoration of the formal cloister garden, devoted to plants typically grown in an early-seventeenth-century garden, was completed in 2001.

Bodnant Garden ★★ [Welsh Historic Garden Grade I]

Tal–y–Cafn, Colwyn Bay, Conwy LL28 5RE. Tel: (01492) 650460

The National Trust • 8m S of Llandudno, just off A470 • Garden open 11th March to 5th Nov, daily, 10am – 5pm • Entrance: £6, children £3, parties over 20, £5 per person • Other information: Parking 50 metres from garden. Plant centre (not NT) adjacent ◑ 💻 ✕ <u>WC</u> ♿ 🏛 🍴

One of the finest gardens in the country, not only for its magnificent collections of rhododendrons, camellias and magnolias but also for its beautiful setting above the River Conwy, with extensive views of the Snowdon range. The 80-acre garden ranks among the best-loved in Britain. The famous laburnum tunnel, an overwhelming mass of bloom, is matched for interest by others including the lily terrace, the curved and stepped pergola, the canal terrace and Pin Mill. In the dell is the tallest redwood in the country, the 45-metre *Sequoia sempervirens*. All these, together with the outstanding autumn colours, make it a garden well worth visiting at any season. The whole effect was created by four generations of the Aberconway family (who bought Bodnant in 1874), aided by three generations of the Puddle family as head gardeners.

Bodrhyddan [Welsh Historic Garden Grade II*]

Rhuddlan, Denbighshire LL18 5SB. Tel: (01745) 590414

Lord Langford • 4m SE of Rhyl. Take A5151 Rhuddlan – Dyserth road and turn left. Signposted • House open • Garden open June to Sept, Tues, Thurs, 2 – 5.30pm • Entrance: £2 (house and garden £4, children under 16 £2) ◑ 💷 🏠 WC ⅙ ⬩ ⌂ ♀

The box-edged parterre was laid out by William Andrews Nesfield – the father of the equally renowned William Eden Nesfield – who designed the 1875 alterations to the house. The paths are bordered by clipped yews and, to the north-west, the two-acre Pleasance, part of a larger area known on very old maps as the Grove. This is probably because it embraces St Mary's Well, revered since pagan times and covered now by a 1612 Inigo Jones pavilion, said to have been used for clandestine marriages. The Pleasance itself, originally a Victorian shrubbery, has been restored; it has four ponds, fine mature trees and many new plantings, and an additional area has been developed as a wild garden, picnic spot and new woodland walk. There is also a millennium summerhouse based architecturally on the Treasury at Petra on which the present Lord Langford's great-great-grandparents inscribed their names when on honeymoon in 1835.

Bodysgallen Hall ★ [Welsh Historic Garden Grade I]

Llandudno, Gwynedd LL30 1RS. Tel: (01492) 584466

Historic House Hotels • 2m S of Llandudno. At A55/A470 junction turn onto A470 towards Llandudno. Hall is 1m on right • Open all year, daily • Entrance: free to guests using hotel facilities • Other information: Refreshments in hotel ○ 💷 ✕ WC ⅙ B&B

The Garden has written that 'there can be few better living examples of early seventeenth-century gardens anywhere in England and Wales'. Both house and gardens have been restored to a high standard. The limestone outcrops provide an interesting array of rockeries and terraces; major features include a parterre sympathetically planted with herbs and a formal walled rose garden. The fine trees and shrubs include a medlar and a mulberry, and woodland walks add a further dimension to a splendid historic garden.

Cae Hir ★

Cribyn, Lampeter, Ceredigion SA48 7NG. Tel: (01570) 470839

Mr Wil Akkermans • 5m NW of Lampeter off A482. Turn left onto B4337 at Temple Bar; garden is 2m on left • Open June, daily except Sun, 2 – 5pm • Entrance: £4.50, OAPs £4, children 50p ◑ 💷 🏠 WC ⅙ ⬩ ⌂ ⌕

Begun twenty years ago, the garden was made and is still managed by just one man. Its six acres – four on one side of the road where the house is situated and two on the other – slope, very gently at first, then more steeply from a natural stream and a series of informal wildlife pools at the bottom to a summerhouse at the top with fine views of the surrounding countryside. Near the top, an 18-metre-long laburnum crescent is underplanted with *Rosa rugosa* and edged with *Geranium macrorrhizum*; immediately below, a neatly clipped yew hedge echoes the crescent shape. This formality of design occurs throughout the garden, and yet there is no formal feel to it – indeed an element of wildness is encouraged, to settle the garden into the landscape. The discreet rooms, several themed by colour, are separated by large swathes of grass punctuated by standard trees. The owner's necessary choice of tough plants that don't need a lot of looking after has been turned to good effect: he uses them dramatically and often in masses. Trees are his passion, and he clearly enjoys trimming some of them into unusual shapes – he has a separate bonsai area. Nearby on the B4342, near Talsarn, is the *Winllan Wildlife Garden*, where several acres bordering the River Aeron are devoted to encouraging wildflowers and wildlife. [Open for NGS, June, daily, 2 – 5pm and in July and Aug by appt only – telephone (01570) 470612.]

Centre for Alternative Technology
Machynlleth, Powys SY20 9AZ. Tel: (01654) 705950

C.A.T. • 3m N of Machynlleth on A487. Also access by water-balanced cliff railway, Easter to Oct • Open all year, daily except 25th Dec and mid-Jan, 10am – 5pm (4pm in winter) • Entrance: £8, concessions £7.20, children under 16 £5.50, family from £24 (2005 prices). Discounts for arrival by public transport or bicycle • Other information: Parking inc. coaches at base of site, but for elderly and disabled at top of steep drive. Guide dogs only ○ 🐾 ✗ 🐾 WC & ℗ 🏛 💡 ℀

High in a former slate quarry, and at the heart of the environmentally friendly community here, is the most exciting garden. Compactly laid out, using natural and recycled materials to form harmoniously shaped raised beds, ponds and walks, the garden is vibrant (in June) with colour and insect life drawn to the organically grown flowers and companion-planted vegetables. There are suggestions, too, for urban gardeners and displays of land reclamation, wildlife gardening, composting, weed and pest control. Wind turbines and solar fountains in different sizes and designs could be considered unusual, if highly functional, garden sculptures. Whether you want to experience the world of the worm in the underground mole hole, or wander gently by one of the lakes, be sure not to miss the view from the balcony of the water-balanced railway. A new information centre has been built from rammed earth and insulated with sheep's wool.

Chirk Castle ★ [Welsh Historic Garden Grade I]
Chirk, Wrexham, Clwyd LL14 5AF. Tel: (01691) 777701

The National Trust • 10m SW of Wrexham, 2m W of Chirk off A5, 1.5m up private drive • Castle open as gardens but 12 noon – 5pm (closes 4pm Oct) • Gardens open for snowdrops 3 weekends in Feb (telephone to check dates), 12 noon – 4pm; then 25th March to Oct, Wed – Sun and Bank Holiday Mons, 11am – 6pm (last admission 5pm). Closes 5pm Oct • Entrance: £6, children £3, family £15 (castle and garden £7, children £3.50, family £17.50) • Other information: Parking 350 metres from garden; courtesy coach offers transport ○ 🐾 ✗ 🐾 WC & ⬧ ℗ 🏛 💡 ℀

The castle, its walls now covered with climbing plants, dates from 1300 and is set in an eighteenth-century landscaped park. Six acres of trees and flowering shrubs, including rhododendrons and azaleas, were mostly planted by Lady Margaret Myddleton; they contrast with the yews in the formal garden, which were planted in the 1870s by Richard Biddulph. The long border has been replanted in four sections, each flowering at a different time of the year: winter, spring, summer and autumn. The addition of many herbaceous plants gives a more open feel to the border and links it to the herbaceous border planted in the 1920s. The rose garden contains mainly old cluster-flowered (floribunda) roses. From the terrace, with its fine views over Shropshire and Cheshire, the visitor passes to the classical pavilion, then along a lime tree avenue to a statue of Hercules. There is interesting nineteenth-century topiary, a rockery and an old hawk house, and a pleasure-ground wood to stroll in. Alas, the Myddleton family no longer live at Chirk.

Clyne Gardens ★ [Welsh Historic Garden Grade I]

Blackpill, Swansea, West Glamorgan SA3 5AR. Tel: (01792) 401737

Swansea City Council • From Swansea take A4067 Mumbles road and turn right into car park of Woodmans Inn • Open all year, daily, 8am – dusk. Telephone for details of garden tours • Entrance: free • Other information: 'Clyne in Bloom' and rare plants sale in May ○ 🏠 WC ఉ 🐦 ♀ ९

Fifty acres of well-kept nineteenth-century woodland garden and open parkland with considerable botanical interest. Three National Collections are held here – pieris, enkianthus and rhododendrons (Trifolia and Falconera subsections) – although they are not easy to find. Tree lovers will be well rewarded: there are many fine specimens, including the tallest recorded magnolia in Britain, M. *campbellii* Alba group. The most interesting time to visit is undoubtedly the spring, when the eno- mous collection of rhododendrons (over 800 varieties, some of them are very rare) are at their best. These are mostly found on the banks of the stream that runs through the garden and make for a glorious walk ending up at the Japanese bridge. The bog garden is also situated in this area with extensive plantings of *Gunnera manicata*, candelabra primulas and other moisture-lovers. Pick your time right and there will also be swathes of bluebells and wood garlic.

Colby Woodland Garden [Welsh Historic Garden Grade II]

Stepaside, Amroth, Narberth, Pembrokeshire SA67 8PP. Tel: (01834) 811885

The National Trust • 10m SW of St Clear, near Amroth on Carmarthen Bay off A477 • Open April to Oct, daily, 10am – 5pm; walled garden 11am – 5pm. Guided walks available with head gardener • Entrance: £3.60, children £1.80, family £9, pre-booked parties of 15 or more £3 per person, children £1.50 • Other information: Parking 50 metres from garden. Coaches welcome. Gallery and annual plant fair – telephone for details ○ 💻 ✕ 🏠 WC ఉ 🐦 ఞ ⛪ ♀ ९

This early-nineteenth-century estate garden round a Nash-style house is now mainly woodland with some formal gardens. The walled garden is planted informally for ornamental effect. The woodland garden has many rhododendrons and some inter-esting trees and the autumn colour is delightful.

Dewstow Grottoes

Dewstow House, Caerwent, Monmouthshire NP26 5AH.
Tel: (01291) 430444

John Harris • 5m SW of Chepstow off A48 • Open April to Oct, Wed and Sun, 10am – 3.30pm, and for parties by appt, Mon – Fri (advisable to telephone or check www.dewstow.com for updated details) • Entrance: £7, concessions £5, children £3.50, under 5 free [NEW] ○ ● ♿ WC ⏪ ♀

The gardens and grottoes of Dewstow were regarded in the lifetime of its Victorian creator, Henry ('Squire') Oakley, as a unique and wondrous local landmark. Above ground were rock gardens, ponds, water features, ornamental areas, tropical glasshouses and a vast variety of plants from around the world. Below ground sprawled one of the most extensive and best-preserved examples of Pulhamite rockwork in the country. A labyrinth of man-made tunnels, fern-filled caverns and artificial tufa grottoes winds its way under the house and past small pools and fountains; parts are illuminated by natural light; in others artificial light is required to negotiate them. Hardy and not-so-hardy ferns, spider plants and *Ficus pumila* thrive in the moist, frost free conditions. This subterranean fantasy world is entered through a shady stumpery and emerges into a brightly planted bog garden ravine with a string of interconnecting lakes and small waterfalls. Dewstow is a family home and next to the house a lively herbaceous border filled with cosmos, crocosmia, stachys, rudbeckia, gladioli and other strong performers has been created below a high wall as a colourful backdrop to the lawn where the children can play.

The Dingle Nurseries and Garden ★

Welshpool, Powys SY21 9JD. Tel: (01938) 555145

Mrs Kerry Hamer • 3m NW of Welshpool. Take A490 for 1m to Llanfyllin then turn left signed to Dingle Nursery or Frochas. After 1.5m fork left • Open all year, daily, except Tues, 9am – 5pm. Closed 25th Dec to 2nd Jan • Entrance: £2.50, children and wheelchair users free • Other information: Possible for wheelchairs but steep in places ○ ● ♿ WC ♿ ⏪ ♫ ♀

Set on the steep slopes of a verdant Welsh valley, this garden is partly a woodland creation of over 4000 carefully chosen trees and shrubs, and colour-co-ordinated beds planned to look good all year. The owners began by damming the stream (the dingle) that flows through the site, and have created a large pool which now sets off the garden superbly. There is a grove of acers, with many other interesting specimens such as *Davidia involucrata*. The real treat has to remain the 120-acre nursery, which is worth driving many, many miles to reach.

Dolwen ★

Cefn Coch, Llanrhaeadr–ym–Mochnant, Powys SY10 0BU. Tel: (01691) 780411

J. Marriott and B. Yarwood • 14m W of Oswestry, on B4580 Oswestry – Llanrhaeadr road. Turn sharp right in Llanrhaeadr opposite The Plough Inn • Open May to Aug, Fri and last Sun in month, 2 – 4.30pm. Parties welcome by appt • Entrance: £2.50 ○ ● ♿ WC ⏪ ♫

Two and a half acres of garden with three large ponds, a stream and a number of different plant habitats used to great advantage. Shade-lovers thriving in the small woodland garden include gunneras, ranunculus, meconopsis, ligularias, hostas and many types of fern. Around the ponds, planting is aimed at good foliage shape, with gunneras, rodgersias, irises and large hostas predominating. The more open areas and those around the cottage provide ideal growing conditions for climbing roses, wisterias and peonies. The main attraction of the garden is its setting in the foothills of the Berwyn Mountains and the way in which it blends into this setting rather than imposing on it. The glacial boulders placed imaginatively around the garden, the slate bridges across the stream and the prospect mount fit perfectly into the garden land-scape.

Donadea Lodge

Babell, Flintshire CH8 8QD. Tel: (01352) 720204

Mr and Mrs Patrick Beaumont • 8m E of St Asaph. Turn off A541 Mold – Denbigh road at Afonwen, signed to Babell, and at T-junction turn left; or take A55 then B5122 to Caerwys and third turn on left • Open May to July by appt • Entrance: £2.50, children free ● WC & ◁ ℗

The garden demonstrates what creative design can achieve on a very long site. On one side an avenue of mature lime trees is a fine feature in its own right. The other side is a mixed border of bays and small islands, each with its own restrained and carefully thought-out colour scheme, often achieved using unusual plants in unexpected but entirely effective combinations. A particular feature is the use of roses and clematis.

Dyffryn Gardens ★ [Welsh Historic Garden Grade I]

St Nicholas, Cardiff, Vale of Glamorgan CF5 6SU. Tel: (029) 2059 3328

Vale of Glamorgan Council • 4m SW of Cardiff on A4232 turn S on A4050 and W to A48 • Open all year, daily, 10am – 6pm (closes 5pm Oct, 4pm Nov to March) • Entrance: £3.50, OAPs and children £2.50, family £7. Free of charge during winter (2005 prices) • Other information: no facilities in winter ○ ● 🐄 WC & ◁ ℗ 🏛 🍴 ☕

What is happening at Dyffryn, one of Wales's largest landscape gardens and also one of its best-kept secrets, is one of the Heritage Lottery Fund's most intelligent acts of garden funding. With the help of a huge grant – some £6.15 million – Thomas Mawson's 1904 plans for the distinguished horticulturist Reginald Cory are being used as the basis for a full-scale restoration. Major projects include the restoration of the walled kitchen garden and its magnificent glasshouse and the reinstatement of the statue collection. Arguably one of the most important gardens of the Edwardian era, here are herbaceous borders on an heroic scale, croquet and archery lawns, flower beds laid out in a traditional pattern, rose gardens, a heather bank, a Victorian fernery, a stumpery, a rockery, an arboretum and a series of themed garden rooms, including the Pompeian Garden with a Grade-II-listed garden building.

Dyffryn Fernant Gardens

Dyffryn Fernant, Llanychaer, Fishguard SA65 9SP. Tel: (01348) 811282

Christina Shand • 2m E of Fishguard off A487 Cardigan road. After long straight hill take small turning to right signed to Llanychaer (at 'Unsuitable for long vehicles' sign). Entrance after 0.5m on left • Open 16th April to Sept, alternate Suns and Bank Holiday Mons, plus 27th Aug; all 10am – 5pm, and by appt • Entrance: £2.50, chil-dren under 16 free • Other information: self-catering cottage available [NEW] ● WC ℗

Since 1995 the owner has created an adventurous five-acre garden on an inauspicious site of boggy and stony ground surrounding her pretty house, making the most of the raw materials and applying a touch of magic to them. She is an enthusiastic plantswoman, and the courtyard garden and the borders immediately surrounding the house display a dizzy profusion of choice plants and shrubs. There is also evidence throughout of a strong grasp of design. The bog garden, formally laid out with slate paving, is dominated by a stainless steel obelisk – an inspired touch. The Rickyard (really a nursery area) has a Mediterranean feel with a ceramic pot in the middle of a cruciform path. At the edges of the garden things quieten down. Nicky's Tree sits in the middle of open rough grass mown to create a labyrinth, and in the furthest corner a large pond, created by damming a stream, sits comfortably in the landscape. New walks are being opened up and wildflower meadows developed. This is a garden of many parts, interesting at all seasons; it all adds up to something really quite special.

Erddig ★ [Welsh Historic Garden Grade I]

Wrexham, Clwyd LL13 0YT. Tel: (01978) 355314

The National Trust • 2m S of Wrexham off A525 or A483 • House open as garden but 12 noon – 5pm (closes 4pm from Oct) (last admission 1 hour before closing) • Garden open 25th March to 29th Oct, Sat – Wed (open Good Friday and Thurs in July and Aug), 11am – 6pm (opens 10am July and Aug, closes 5pm Oct). Conducted tours for parties by prior arrangement • Entrance: £3.80, children £1.90, family £9.20, pre-booked parties of 15 or more £3 per person, (house and garden £7.40, children £3.70, family £18.40, pre-booked parties £6 per person) • Other information: Parking 100 metres from garden. Wheelchairs provided. Dogs in parkland only, on lead ◗ 💺 ✕ WC ♿ ⚲ ⬛

The gardens, a rare example of early-eighteenth-century formal design, were almost lost along with the house, but have now been carefully restored. The large walled garden contains varieties of fruit trees known to have been grown there during that period, and there is a canal garden and fish pool. South of the canal walk is a Victorian flower garden, and other Victorian additions include the parterre and yew walk. A National Collection of ivies is here, also a narcissus collection. Apple Day is celebrated in October.

Foxbrush

Aber Pwll, Port Dinorwic, Gwynedd LL56 4JZ. Tel: (01248) 670463

Mr and Mrs B.S. Osborne • 3m SW of Bangor on B4507 (old Caernarfon road) N of A487. Avoiding new bypass, enter village. House on left after high estate wall, opposite layby. Signed to Felinheli • Open by appt only • Entrance: £2, children free ◐ 🏵 WC ⬱

A private three-acre plantswoman's garden, created single-handedly from a wilderness on the site of a sixteenth-century mill and retaining its wild atmosphere. Narrow paths meander through romantic plantings of rare treasures and sudden surprises, over bridges and under tunnels of laburnum and a 14-metre rose and clematis pergola, past herbaceous borders, a croquet lawn, a river and ponds. Although essentially a spring garden (despite ferocious flooding), it is much admired throughout the summer, too.

Glansevern Hall Gardens [Welsh Historic Garden Grade II*]

Berriew, Welshpool, Powys SY21 8AH. Tel: (01686) 640200

G.E and M.B Thomas • From Welshpool take A483 S. After 5m entrance signposted on left • Open May to Sept, Thurs to Sat and Bank Holiday Mons, 12 noon – 6pm. Parties by appt at other times • Entrance: £3.50, OAPs £3, children free ◑ 💺 ✕ <u>WC</u> ♿ ⬦ 🌡 🏛 B&B

The mature 20-acre garden is set in a wider parkland on the banks of the River Severn, and is noted for its range of unusual trees. A four-acre lake has islands where swans, ducks and other waterfowl breed. The streams, which form a water garden and feed the lake, are planted along the banks with moisture-loving plants and shrubs. A large area of lawn contains mature trees and herbaceous borders. Notable too are the fountain with its surround and walk festooned with wisteria, the restored rockery and grotto, the walled garden (completely replanted in 2002), and the rose gardens.

Llanllyr [Welsh Historic Garden Grade II]

Talsarn, Lampeter, Ceredigion SA48 8QB. Tel: (01570) 470900

Mr and Mrs Robert Gee • 6m NW of Lampeter, on B4337 Temple Bar – Llanrhystud road • Open 18th June for NGS, and April to Oct by appt • Entrance: £3, children 50p ◑ 💺 WC ♿

Llanllyr is an ancient site with a long and interesting history. The basic structure of the garden was laid out around 1830 and has undergone considerable restoration and development by the present owners since 1985. Wide borders surround the house on the north and east sides. Immediately next to the house on its south side is a pretty box parterre; the densely planted shrubbery behind leads to a 127 metre-long colour-themed rose border and a unique inscribed stone (a scheduled ancient monument) to an attractive summerhouse. Running parallel to the rose border is a striking formal pool crossed by a little stone bridge; a large fish pond and bog garden add to the water interest. A recent addition is the labyrinth, loosely based on the dreamer's journey in William Langland's poem *Piers the Plowman*, and a newly planted gravel garden includes a carved oak column measuring the shadow cast by the sun throughout the year. Given considerable prominence in the garden's interesting booklet, its heavy symbolism and quirky ornamentation will not be to everybody's taste.

Maenan Hall

Llanrwst, Conwy LL26 0UL. Tel: (01492) 640441

The Hon. Mr and Mrs Christopher McLaren • 2m N of Llanrwst on E side of A470, 0.25m S of Maenan Abbey Hotel • Open 23rd April, 21st May for charity, and 23rd July, 10.30am – 5.30pm (last admission 4.30pm) • Entrance: £3, children £2 ◑ 💺 WC ♿ ⬦ 🌡

Created in 1956 by the late Christabel, Lady Aberconway are formal gardens surrounding the Elizabethan and Queen Anne house, with less formal gardens in the mature woodland beyond. Her son and daughter-in-law, the present owners, have extended the planting of ornamental trees and shrubs in both settings. Azaleas, rhododendrons and camellias, the latter situated in a dell at the base of a cliff, make a spring visit rewarding, while roses flower in profusion in June and a large number of eucryphias are spectacular in late summer.

Museum of Welsh Life and
St Fagans Castle ★ [Welsh Historic Garden Grade I]

St Fagans, Cardiff, South Glamorgan CF5 6XB. Tel: (029) 2057 3500

National Museum of Wales • Near M4 junction 33. Signposted • Open all year, daily, 10am – 5pm or 6pm. Closed 24th to 26th Dec • Entrance: free ○ ● ✕ ▨ <u>WC</u> ໕ ⬠ ⛫ ⛾ ℺

An historic garden with terraces, herb and knot gardens, a hornbeam tunnel, an old grove of mulberry trees and a vinery. The Rosery of 1900 has been replanted with the original varieties, and the vinery and flower house have been restored. Mature trees, both coniferous and broad-leaved, are an impresssive feature, as are the broad high terraces with massive stone walls hosting many climbing plants; beneath are large fish ponds containing carp, bream and tench, traditionally farmed over the years to feed the household. In the grounds rhododendrons are underplanted with spring bulbs. The restoration and replanting of the formal gardens, including an Arts and Crafts Italian garden, continue to reflect the Edwardian spirit of the place. Gardens attached to re-erected buildings from all over Wales are also being developed to re-create the differences in social status and period, using traditional horticultural techniques, tools and vegetable varieties.

National Botanic Garden of Wales ★ [Welsh Historic Garden Grade II]

Middleton Hall, Llanarthne, Carmarthenshire SA32 8HG.
Tel: (01558) 667132/667134

Trustees, NBGW • 8m E of Carmarthen, 7m W of Llandeilo off A48(M) • Open all year, daily, 10am – 6pm (last admission 1 hour before closing) • Entrance: £7, concessions £5, children £2, family £16 (2005 prices) • Other information: Free buggy hire for disabled. Coaches recommended to pre-book ● ● ✕ ▨ <u>WC</u> ໕ ℘ ⛫ ⛾ ℺

The first national botanic garden of the new millennium, supported by £22 million from the Millennium Commission, is located in the Regency estate of Middleton Hall, deep in the beautiful Towy valley. Its scale and purpose is summed up in its centrepiece, the Great Glasshouse, a stunning 91-metre-long 'teardrop' structure designed by architects Foster and Partners. Within the world's largest single-span glasshouse, visitors can walk through and wonder at plants, landscapes and waterfalls normally found in threatened Mediterranean environments. A 300-metre-long broadwalk of herbaceous plants and flowers leads through the middle of the garden, passing the unique restored double-walled garden, the award-winning Japanese garden and towards the Wallace garden, which demonstrates the history of plant genetics, the apothecaries' garden, the boulder garden and several others. Visitors can also explore a necklace of lakes, features of the late-eighteenth-century water park, where plants cultivated in slate beds adjoin the natural setting of gentle Welsh countryside, parkland and grassland; Paxton's View, site of the former mansion, offers a panorama down the valley.

The Nurtons

Tintern, Gwent NP16 7NX. Tel: (01291) 689253

Adrian and Elsa Wood • 7m N of Chepstow on A466. In Tintern opposite Old Station • Open 14th April to Sept, Wed – Sun, 11am – 5pm • Entrance: £3 NEW ◗ 🍴 ♿ 🌿 🍽 B&B

The sloping 2.5-acre garden with a nursery attached is gardened organically by two botanists. A plantsman's garden, then, with shady walks, hidden corners and a formal, if slightly wild, herb garden. As a result of the owners' love of salvias and other late flowers, it is especially good in late summer. The garden has been lifted out of the ordinary by the recent addition of a large circular lawn, surrounded by a magnificent border and offering wonderful views across the Wye Valley. .

Pant-yr-Holiad ★

Rhydlewis, Llandysul, Ceredigion SA44 5ST. Tel: (01239) 851493

Mr and Mrs G. Taylor • 12m NE of Cardigan. Take A487 coast road to Brynhoffnant, then B4334 towards Rhydlewis for 1m, turn left and garden is second left • Open for pre-booked parties by appt • Entrance: £2.50, children £1 (2005 prices) ◗ 💺 WC 🌿

This five-acre woodland garden, created by the owners since 1971, was started in an area of natural woodland backing onto the farmhouse. Since then hundreds of rhododendrons (species and hybrids) have been planted along the banks, and acers, eucalyptus, eucryphias and many other rare and unusual trees have now reached maturity. Paths wander in and around, and a stream runs through the middle of the garden. Much dredging and replanting will take place during 2006. There is also a summer walk, along which slate-edged beds are filled with herbaceous plants, including a collection of penstemons. A small pergola has a rose-embowered seat with a fine view over the valley, and the remainder of the walk is beneath arches of climbing roses. Nearer the house is a walled garden, alpine beds, a series of pools for ornamental waterfowl and a *potager*-style kitchen garden. Nearby in Pontgarreg is *Gwynfor Growers* nursery with a wide range of intriguing perennials and scented shrubs [open all year, Wed, Thurs and Sun, 10am – 5pm, and by appt – telephone (01239) 654151].

Pencarreg ★

Glyn Garth, Menai Bridge, Gwynedd LL59 5NS. Tel: (01248) 713545

Miss G. Jones • 1.5m NE of A545 Menai Bridge towards Beaumaris. Glan y Menai drive is turning on right, Pencarreg 100 metres on right • Open all year by appt • Entrance: charity box • Other information: Parking in lay-by on main road, limited parking in courtyard for small cars and disabled ◗ WC 🐕

This beautiful garden, with a wealth of species planted for all-year interest, has colour achieved by the use of common and unusual shrubs. A small stream creates another sympathetically exploited feature. The garden ends at the cliff edge and this, too, has been skilfully planted. The views are remarkable.

Penpergwm Lodge

Abergavenny, Monmouthshire NP7 9AS. Tel: (01873) 840208

Mrs C. Boyle • 2.5m SE of Abergavenny off B4598 Usk road. Turn left opposite King of Prussia Inn. Entrance 300 metres on left • Open April to Sept, Thurs – Sun, 2 – 6pm • Entrance: £3 ❶ WC ⅄ ⬥ ⅋ ⛴ B&B

This spacious three-acre garden forms the centrepiece for an established and successful school of gardening, which offers day-long workshops. Broad south-facing terraces command views over wide expanses of lawn well screened by mature trees and shrubs. A vine pergola makes a bold statement and provides a visual link with the house, while a formal garden of yew and box creates a delightful and effective enclosure and a folly tower adds a new dimension to the garden. Old-fashioned roses, herbaceous perennials and an imaginative vegetable garden with a new water canal contribute interest throughout the season. The nursery sells unusual plants.

Penrhyn Castle ★ [Welsh Historic Garden Grade II*]

Bangor, Gwynedd LL57 4HN. Tel: (01248) 353084

The National Trust • 1m E of Bangor on A5122 • Castle open 12 noon – 5pm (opens 11am July and Aug) • Garden open 4th, 5th, 11th and 12th Feb, for snowdrops, 12 noon – 4pm; then 29th March to Oct, daily except Tues, 11am – 5pm (opens 10am July, Aug) • Entrance: £5, children £2.50 (snowdrop weekends, £1) (castle and garden £7, children £3.50, family £17.50, parties £5.50 per person) • Other information: Golf buggy available if pre-booked ❶ ⬤ ✕ ⬥ WC ⅄ ⬥ ⛪ ⛴ ✍

The large garden covers 48 acres with some fine specimen trees, shrubs and a Victorian walled garden in terraces with pools, lawns and a wild garden. Although the original house dated from the eighteenth century, the gardens are very much early-Victorian, contemporary with the present castle designed by Thomas Hopper. A giant tree fern, which will dwarf any children who visit, has been sent from Tasmania to take its place in a specialist collection that also includes another giant, gunnera and the Australian bottle brush plant. These can be found in the spectacular bog garden beyond the walled garden.

Picton Castle ★ [Welsh Historic Garden Grade II*]

Haverfordwest, Pembrokeshire SA62 4AS. Tel: (01437) 751326

Picton Castle Trust • 4m SE of Haverfordwest off A40. Signposted • Castle open for conducted tours April to Sept – telephone for details • Garden open April to Oct, daily except Mon (but open Bank Holiday Mons), 10.30am – 5pm • Entrance: Gardens and gallery £4.95, OAPs £4.75, children £2.50 (castle, gardens and gallery £5.95, OAPs £5.75, children £2.50) ❶ ⬤ ✕ ⬥ WC ⅄ ⬥ ⅋ ⛪ ⛴ ✍

The grounds extend over nearly 40 acres, with woodland walks among massive oaks and giant redwoods. Rarities include the biggest *Rhododendron* 'Old Port' in existence and a metasequoia, a deciduous conifer presumed extinct but rediscovered in China in 1941. In May and June all these exotic shrubs reach their full splendour. In the walled garden are herb borders and summer-flowering plants, with a pond and fountain creating a cool and calming atmosphere.

Plas Brondanw ★ [Welsh Historic Garden Grade I]

Llanfrothen, Penrhyndeudraeth, Gwynedd LL48 6SW. Tel: (07880) 766741

5m NE of Porthmadog between Llanfrothen and Croesor • Open all year, daily, 9am – 5pm • Entrance: £3, children free ○ **WC** ♿ ⚘

This garden, in the grounds of the house given to Sir Clough Williams-Ellis by his father, is quite separate from the village of Portmeirion (see entry), and was created by the architect over a period of seventy years. His main objective was to provide a series of dramatic and romantic prospects inspired by the great gardens of Italy; it includes several architectural features, including an orangery. Visitors should walk up the avenue that leads past a dramatic chasm to the folly, from which there is a fine view of Snowdon – indeed mountains are visible from the end of every vista. Williams-Ellis made a prodigious investment in hedging and topiary (mostly yew) and the former head gardener has calculated that the hedging, if laid flat, would cover four acres. Hydrangeas and ferns flourish in the damp climate.

Plas Newydd ★ [Welsh Historic Garden Grade I]

Llanfairpwll, Anglesey LL61 6DQ. Tel: (01248) 714795

The National Trust • 4m SW of Menai Bridge, 2m S of Llanfairpwll via A5 • House with military museum open as gardens, 12 noon – 5pm • Garden open 18th March to 1st Nov, Sat – Wed, Good Friday and Bank Holiday Mons, 11am – 5.30pm (last admission 4.30pm). Rhododendron garden open 18th March to early June only. Guided tours by arrangement • Entrance: £3, children £1.50 (house and gardens £5, children £2.50, family £12, pre-booked parties of 15 or more £4.50 per person) (2005 prices) • Other information: Parking 0.25m from house. Complimentary minibus service between car park and house, and shuttle service available in garden ◑ 💷 ✕ **WC** ♿ 🚻 ⓘ ☕

The eighteenth-century house by James Wyatt is worth visiting, mainly to see Rex Whistler's largest painting. Humphry Repton's suggestion of 'plantations ... to soften a bleak country and shelter the ground from violent winds' has resulted in an informal open-plan garden, with shrub plantings in the lawns and parkland, which slopes down to the Menai Strait and frames the view of the Snowdonia peaks. There is a formal Italian-style garden to the front of the house. A new arbour has replaced a conservatory on the top terrace with a tufa mound, from which water falls to a pool on the bottom terrace. The pool has a new Italianate fountain to add to the overall Mediterranean effect of this formal area within the parkland. The influence of the Gulf Stream enables the successful cultivation of many frost-tender shrubs, and a special rhododendron garden is open in the spring when the gardens are at their best, although they are expertly tended throughout the year. Major restoration of the Italianate terrace garden continues and includes the building of a deep grotto and the replanting of the mixed borders. The waterside and woodland paths along the Menai Straits have also been restored. Summer brings displays of hydrangeas, while autumn colour appears in the ever-changing arboretum of southern-hemisphere trees and shrubs, and wild flowers appear in their seasons. There is an adventure trail for children.

Plas-yn-Rhiw [Welsh Historic Garden Grade II]

Pwllheli, Gwynedd LL53 8AB. Tel: (01758) 780219

The National Trust • Near tip of Lleyn Peninsular. 16m SW of Pwllheli, take A499 and B4413. Signposted at Botwnnog • House open (numbers limited) • Garden and snowdrop wood open some weekends Jan and Feb (telephone to check); also open 18th March to 30th May, daily except Tues and Wed; June to Sept, daily except Tues; all 12 noon – 5pm; 1st to 23rd Oct, Sat and Sun only; 24th to 30th Oct, Mon – Fri; both 12 noon – 4pm • Entrance: £2.20, children £1.10, family £5.50 (house and garden £3.40, children £1.70, family £8.50. Pre-booked evening parties £1.40 extra per person) • Other information: Parking 80 metres from garden. No coaches
❶ 🦐 wc ⚒ 🏛 ♟

This is essentially a cottage garden, laid out around a partly medieval manor house on the west shore of Hell's Mouth Bay. Flowering trees and shrubs, rhododendrons, camellias and magnolias are divided by formal box hedges and grass paths extending to three quarters of an acre. A snowdrop wood stands on high ground above the garden.

Portmeirion ★ [Welsh Historic Garden Grade II*]

Penrhyndeudraeth, Gwynedd LL48 6ET. Tel: (01766) 770228 (Hotel Reception)

2m SE of Porthmadog near A487 • Open all year, daily except 25th Dec, 9.30am – 5.30pm • Entrance: £6, OAPs £5, children £3, under 5 free, family £14.40, season ticket £35 (2005 prices) • Other information: Parking at top of village. Difficult for wheelchairs as steep in places ○ 💷 ✕ 🦐 wc ⚒ 🏛 ♟ B&B

Architect Sir Clough Williams-Ellis's wild essay into the picturesque is a triumph of eclecticism, with Gothick, Renaissance and Victorian buildings arranged as an Italianate village around a harbour and set in 70 acres of sub-tropical woodland criss-crossed by paths. This light opera is played out against the backdrop of the Cambrian mountains and the vast empty sweep of estuary sands. The gentle humour of the architecture extends to the plantings in both horizontal and vertical planes – in the formal gardens and in the wild luxuriance which clings to the rocky crags. Portmeirion provides one of Britain's most stimulating objects for an excursion, and during the period of the June festival in nearby Criccieth there are other good gardens open in the district. Write for details (with s.a.e.) to Criccieth Festival Office, PO Box 3, 52 High Street, Criccieth LL52 OBW).

Powis Castle and Garden ★★ [Welsh Historic Garden Grade I]

Welshpool, Powys SY21 8RF. Tel: (01938) 551929

The National Trust • 0.75m S of Welshpool on A483. Signposted • Castle open, 1 – 5pm • Garden open 21st March to 30th Oct, Thurs – Mon, 1 – 5pm (closes 4pm 7th to 28th April, 5th Sept to 30th Oct) • Entrance: £6.20, children (5–16) £3.10, under 5 free, family £15.20, parties £5.20 per person (castle, garden and museum £8.80, children (5–16) £4.40, under 5 free, family £22, parties £7.80 per person) • Other information: Events programme and guided tours of garden – telephone for details. Picnics in park outside garden only. Problematic for wheelchairs and pushchairs as very steep with steps ❶ 💷 ✕ wc ⚒ 🏛 ♟ ♟

The garden was originally laid out in the 1680s, based on formal designs by William Winde, who had just finished at Cliveden (see entry in Buckinghamshire) – another cliff-hanger. The most notable features are the broad hanging terraces, interestingly planted and with huge clipped yews. The terraces are inspired by those of the Palace of St Germain-en-Laye near Paris, where the 1st Marquis of Powis joined James II in exile in 1689. On the second terrace, above the orangery, are fine urns. Statuary by van Nost's workshop stands in front of the deeply recessed brick alcoves of the aviary. The late-eighteenth-century changes to the garden as a result of the English landscape style are attributed to William Emes. Advantage was taken of the many microclimates to develop the ornamental plantings during the nineteenth century, and the kitchen garden of the lower garden was transformed into a formal flower garden in 1911 by Lady Violet, wife of the 4th Earl. Unusual and tender plants and climbers now prosper in the shelter of the walls and hedges. The planting schemes are superb. The box-edged terraces have notable clematis and pittosporums; in season *Abutilon vitifolium* 'Tennant's White' matched with *Rosa banksiae* 'Lutea' and *R.* 'Gloire de Dijon' are inspiring, the collection of ceanothus cloaking the terraces magnificent; in late summer the eucryphias repeat the performance. The basket-weave terracotta pots continue to be planted with a masterly touch. The more recent gardens below, lying towards the Severn valley, are planted with old-fashioned roses and cottage-garden plants, with arches of vines continuing the formality in enclosed hedged rooms. This garden is not for the faint-hearted because it is very steep, but it is well worth the effort to enjoy the views which are as fine as any, anywhere.

Ridler's Garden ★

7 St Peter's Terrace, Swansea SA2 0FW. Tel: (01792) 588217

Mr and Mrs Tony Ridler • At M4 Junction 47 turn S on A483. After 3m turn right at traffic lights opposite carpet warehouse; at next traffic lights turn left. Entrance to garden is off footpath for Cockett Pond play area • Open 30th April, 1st, 28th and 29th May , 2 – 5pm, and by appt (children not permitted) • Entrance: £2 ● ⬤ WC

Behind his modest terraced house in the suburbs of Swansea, graphic designer Tony Ridler has created within half an acre one of the most exciting gardens you are likely to see. The drama of the place engages you from the moment you enter, when you are faced with a formal avenue of yew containing a sea of box balls and standard Portuguese laurels clipped neatly into lollipops. In an enclosed compartment off this avenue are exquisitely crafted topiary spirals mulched with white cockleshells. Further paths create new vistas, mostly with focal points of sculpture. Plants, although chosen with care and forethought, play a supporting role – they are there to emphasise and complement the atmosphere, mostly used in blocks and with repetition. The black-painted walls used to define some of the spaces and boundaries make a strikingly successful backdrop to the planting. Beyond a quiet courtyard of grass squares and topiary, the formal kitchen garden is the most intensively planted area. Box pyramids and standard figs add height, and the alternating purple and green foliage of the vegetables reinforces the overall impression of symmetry and order.

Singleton Botanic Gardens ★

Singleton Park, Swansea, West Glamorgan SA2 9DU. Tel: (01792) 298637

Swansea City Council • In Swansea. Entrance in Gower Road • Open all year, daily, 9am – 6pm (4.30pm in winter) • Entrance: free • Other information: Refreshments during Aug only ○ 🅿 🍴 <u>WC</u> ♿ 🌿 ♟

A four-and-a-half-acre garden with herbaceous borders, rockeries, rose beds and an interesting collection of trees and shrubs, including tapestry hedges using a variety of different shrubs. Newly erected temperate and tropical glasshouses contain an extensive range of rare and unusual plants, including orchids, bromeliads and epiphytes. While in Swansea, visit the 1600-square-metre hothouse *Plantasia*. Divided into arid, tropical and humid zones, it contains over 5000 plants and much wildlife. [Signed from city centre and open all year, daily except Mondays.]

Tredegar House [Welsh Historic Park Grade II*]

Newport, Gwent NP10 8YW. Tel: (01633) 815880

Newport City Council • 3m S of Newport. Signed from A48 and M4 junction 28 • House open as garden, 11.30am – 4pm • Garden open April to Sept, Wed – Sun, 9am –5pm • Park open all year, daily, dawn – dusk • Entrance: free (house £5.40, OAPs £3.95, children free) (2005 prices) • Other information: Dogs in park only, on lead ◑ 🅿 🍴 <u>WC</u> ♿ 🌿 🏛 ♟ ☕

Behind the handsome Restoration house and its adjacent orangery and stables are three large walled enclosures. This is the main gardened area. The middle one is dominated by an ancient cedar of Lebanon and several mature magnolias; at the base of the walls a herbaceous border is designed to have colour throughout the summer and autumn months. On one side of this enclosure is the orchard and the head gardener's cottage. But the most interesting area is the Orangery Garden on the other side. Here, recent archaeological excavations revealed the remnant of a massive late seventeenth-century mineral parterre. This unique find has been reconstructed using coal, sand, gravels and sea shells and is punctuated by carefully clipped standards of box. Two large *Magnolia grandiflora* stand at the entrance to the orangery.

Veddw House ★

Devauden, Monmouthshire NP16 6PH. Tel: (01291) 650836

Anne Wareham and Charles Hawes • 5m NW of Chepstow off B4293. In Devauden, signed from pub on green • Open June to Aug, Sun and Bank Holiday Mons, 2 – 5pm, and for parties of 10 or more afternoons or evenings by appt • Entrance: £4, children £1 (2005 prices) ☻ <u>WC</u> ♿ ♟

Situated on a sheltered slope near the Wye Valley, framed by old beech woods and with views in all directions, this garden is the product of enthusiastic labour by the owners since 1987. There are two acres of flower garden and meadow and two acres of woodland where the trees are embellished by decorative plaques and quotations. The generously planted borders include repeat plantings of many unusual varieties, and around every corner is something of interest – a magnolia walk, a cotoneaster walk with rampant rambler roses growing through it, a philadelphus border. In front of the house four rectangular beds are punctuated by balls of clipped evergreens; nearby is a grey border. The formal vegetable garden is enclosed by borders of old scented roses and 40 varieties of clematis on trellis and arches. From here an arch leads into the orchard and meadow, full of bulbs in spring and grasses and wild flowers in summer. Behind the house the ground slopes steeply upwards, with paths and steps leading to viewpoints. Yew hedges enclose a formal garden planted with cornfield annuals, and a new garden has been created with a black reflecting pool and a seat with an arching back that echoes curves found elsewhere in the garden – in long low paths and a sinuous beech hedge. Overlooking these gardens is another fascinating parterre, where box hedges form compartments replicating the 1824 tithe map of the area. The spaces between are filled with a variety of grasses. Further up still is a hazel coppice and the wood with its superb old beeches,sorbus and hornbeams.

Whimble Garden and Nursery

Kinnerton, Presteigne, Powys LD8 2PD. Tel: (01547) 560413

Liz Taylor and Rod Lancett • 6m W of Presteigne; signposted from A44 at Walton (going from Kington towards Rhayader) • Open April to mid-October, Thurs – Mon, 10.30am – 5.30pm • Entrance: £1.50 ◑ 🏵 WC & 🌿

Tucked away on a south-facing slope of the Radnor Valley, this small but richly planted garden is not only a most effective shop window for the adjoining nursery, but a joy in its own right. Specialising in unusual herbaceous plants and climbers, everything is carefully chosen for beauty of colour and form; it is at its peak in August and September. In the main garden a yew walk leads into a box-edged parterre planted with bulbs, perennials and some unusual annuals – a subtle tapestry of colour throughout the season. Beyond, an airy wire-mesh 'church' creates an eccentric and attractive framework for roses and rare clematis. A small garden is scented by a hedge of 'Hidcote' lavender, and a gate cut through a beech hedge leads into a meadow with a nuttery and a 'prehistoric' earthwork. Even finer views of the surrounding hills can be seen from the balustraded 'toposcope' at the far end of the garden. This is an inspiring and satisfying place to visit – you will not go home empty-handed.

Wyndcliffe Court [Welsh Historic Garden Grade II*]

St Arvans, Chepstow, Monmouthshire NP16 6EY.
Tel: (01291) 622352/627597 (Valerie James)

Mr and Mrs H.A.P. Clay • Off Wye Valley road from Chepstow • Open 4th June, and by appt for private parties • Entrance: £2.50 • Other information: Garden only accessible for wheelchairs on terrace ◑ 🏵 🏠 WC & 🔽 🐾

An Arts and Crafts house designed by Eric Francis, with a landscape garden to match created by Avray Tipping. The house and its garden date from 1922, and although maintenance is not up to the high standards of that time it is worth visiting as a period piece that has remained largely unchanged. From a broad paved terrace, two flights of steps descend to the topiary terrace with its semi-circular pool; the topiary yew drums are matched by ten rectangular beds of annuals. The next level is a bowling green, and beyond the charming summerhouse is a sunken garden with a long rectangular pool. Long herbaceous borders lead to the large walled vegetable garden, much of it devoted to flowers and shrubs. Fine views.

CHANNEL ISLANDS

GUERNSEY AND SARK

Candie Gardens

Candie Road, St Peter Port GY1 1UG. Tel: (01481) 717000

States of Guernsey • In St Peter Port, off Candie Road • Open all year, daily, 8am – sunset (5pm in winter) • Entrance: free • Other information: Teas, toilet facilities, (inc. disabled), shop and events in Guernsey Museum and Art Gallery ○ 🍽 🐌 **WC** ♿ ⬦ 🏛 ⚐

Situated on a slope overlooking the harbour at St Peter Port, there are wonderful views over the islands of Herm and Sark from the gardens. Created over a century ago, they contain statues of Queen Victoria and of Victor Hugo, who lived on Guernsey in exile from 1855 to 1871. The Lower Gardens used to be the walled fruit and vegetable garden of Candie House (now the Priaulx Library) but were remodelled as a public garden in 1887. A rare surviving example of a Victorian public flower garden, they have been sympathetically restored. Guernsey's mild climate and the shelter afforded by the garden walls has enabled many varieties of exotic plants from all over the world to be grown, including a magnificent Canary palm considered to be the largest in the British Isles, a huge *Ginkgo biloba*, camellias, rhododendrons, ferns, aquatics and a South African bulb collection which originated in the late nineteenth century. The gardens also contain herbaceous borders and two 1792 show glasshouses in an excellent state of preservation. The Guernsey Museum and Art Gallery, built around an original Victorian bandstand, and the Priaulx Reference and Genealogical Library are here.

The Hermitage

Les Maindonnaux, St Martin GY4 6AJ.
Tel: (01481) 237035 or Guernsey Tourist Information (01481) 723552

Anne and Tony Curr • 1.5m S of St Peter Port • Open one or two days a year, and for private parties by appt • Entrance: £3 ● **WC** ♿

Dating from the 1750s, the house is surrounded by about three acres of landscaped gardens, dominated by a very tall Monterey cypress some 200 years old. From this vantage point visitors can view a small lake surrounded by giant gunneras, ligularias and other moisture-loving plants, fed by freshwater springs to the obvious enjoyment of the resident ducks and moorhens. Nearby azaleas, rhododendrons, camellias and fuchsias grow in abundance in a woodland setting. A walled garden offers shelter to fine specimens of *Cestrum elegans, Clethra arborea, Clianthus puniceus, Crinodendron hookerianum*, giant echiums and many other unusual shrubs and perennials.

Le Manoir ★

La Villette, St Martin GY4 6QQ. Tel: (01481) 235256

John Webb • 3m S of St Peter Port • Open for charities and by appt – telephone for details • Entrance: £3.50 ● &

This remarkable two-and-a-half-acre garden, created by the present owners in just two years, is an object lesson in what can be achieved with skill, knowledge, good taste and hard work – and all without the aid of a gardener. First they planned, then they put in an irrigation system, then they planted, then they mulched with bark. The result is a splendid collection of rare, unusual and more commonplace plants and shrubs assembled in entrancing style in drifts and borders, and including formal, spring and Mediterranean gardens; it is possible to see at a glance which plants enjoy full sun, partial shade or deep shade. This is the second notable garden the Webbs have created on the island – they were also responsible for the Hermitage (see entry). This is even better: already mature and flourishing.

Mille Fleurs

Rue du Bordage, St Pierre du Bois GY7 9DW. Tel: (01481) 263911

Mr and Mrs D. Russell • 6m SW of St Peter Port. 100 metres down lane from Rue de Quanteraine/Rue du Bordage junction • Open one or two days a year, and for parties by appt • Entrance: £3.50 • Other information: Self-catering cottages available ●

Natural country gardens of some three acres set in a peaceful, wooded conservation valley, with much of the planting chosen with wildlife in mind. The areas around the house and holiday cottages are a profusion of roses, clematis, penstemons and other herbaceous perennials, with sweetly scented honeysuckle and jasmine framing arches and doorways. Paths flanked by lilies, lavender and other fragrant plants meander down to the bottom of the valley, where more tender, sub-tropical plants flourish in the sheltered microclimate. A natural spring feeds into two ponds surrounded by mature tree ferns and giant gunneras amid huge stands of arum lilies. A large mature fig tree and a host of terracotta pots brimming with red pelargoniums and cordylines, together with banks of crocosmias, phormiums and euphorbias, lend a Mediterranean feel to the swimming-pool area.

La Petite Vallée ★

Rue de Putron, St Peter Port GY1 2TE. Tel: (01481) 238866

Mrs Jennifer Monachan • 2m S of central St Peter Port • Open occasionally for charity – check with local paper or tourist information office (Tel: (01481) 726611) ● wc &

This is a garden full of surprises and excitement, since it reflects the enthusiasm and passions that the owner has lavished on this three-acre valley going down towards the sea. Wildflower meadows, shrubberies, rose gardens, a folly, a stream, along with herb, water and terrace gardens all flow into each other with effortless ease. One of the best in the Channel Islands.

Les Prés de Jerbourg

St Martin GY4 6BN. Tel: (01481) 236158

Paul Chilcott • Drive to Jerbourg Point car park; garden is at end of little cliff road • Open April to Sept, daily, 2 – 5pm, and by appt • Entrance: £2, children free (all donations to local charities) ❶ WC க் ⬦

A series of gardens has remarkably been created since 1988 from a couple of clifftop fields on one of the most exposed positions in the islands, using sycamore, Scots pine (which figures in a painting by Renoir) and escallonia as windbreaks. It is well worth the 400-metre walk just for the views over virtually all the other islands and France. The garden has now expanded to include a Mediterranean garden, a meadow area, rock, gravel and rose gardens. There are also shrubberies and a conservatory, and the owner continues to take in more land as further windbreaks come into effect. The plants and shrubs native to warmer parts of the world, new to many British gardeners, are particularly interesting, not only from a colour combination and aesthetic point of view, but because of their resistance to high winds off the sea.

Sausmarez Manor Exotic Woodland Garden

St Martins, Guernsey GY4 6SG. Tel: (01481) 235571

Peter de Sausmarez • 1.5m S of St Peter Port, off Fort Road • Manor open mid-week in summer • Garden open all year, daily, 10.30am – 5.30pm (or dusk if earlier). Guided tours for parties by appt • Entrance: £4.50, OAPs/children £3.50, disabled persons and babies free • Other information: Rare plant sale 29th May. Doll's house collection. Pitch and putt course. Sculpture park, ride-on trains. Holiday let available ○ ● ⬛ WC க் ৶ ⬛ ⬤ B&B ✂

Set around two small lakes in an ancient wood is a garden which has been crammed with the unusual and rare to give an exotic feel. It is strewn with plants from many parts of the world, particularly the sub-tropics and the Mediterranean, which survive in Guernsey's mellow maritime climate. Collections of yuccas, ferns, camellias (over 300), bamboos, hebes, bananas, echiums, lilies, palm trees, fuchsias, as well as hydrangeas, hostas, azaleas, pittosporums, clematis, rhododendrons, cyclamens, impatiens, giant grasses etc., all jostle with indigenous wild flowers. No pesticides are used so wildlife flourishes. A new poetry trail winds through the wood. Also here is the Art Park, showing around 200 pieces of sculpture by about 90 British, European, African, American and local artists, all for sale.

La Seigneurie

Sark GY9 0SF. Tel: (01481) 832345 (Sark Tourism)

Seigneur Mr J.M. Beaumont • 0.5m NW of Creux Harbour, Sark • Open 10th April to 24th Oct, Mon – Fri, 10am – 5pm, and Sat, July to Sept for charity • Entrance: £1.80, children 90p ❶ ⬛ <u>WC</u> க் ✂

The grounds and walled garden of La Seigneurie, the residence of the Seigneurs of Sark, are beautifully maintained. Visit in spring and early summer for the camellias, azaleas and rhododendrons, later for roses, old-fashioned annuals, and in autumn for the glowing colours of dahlias and fuchsias. The walled garden contains clematis, geraniums, lapagerias, abutilons, osteospermums and many sub-tropical and tender plants. There is a *potager*, a wild pond area, a restored Victorian greenhouse with vines and bougainvilleas, a hedge maze for children, and a small outdoor museum with antique cannons. The Gothick *colombier* may still be seen behind the house.

Les Videclins Farm

Candie Road, Castel GY5 7BX. Tel: (01481) 254788

Mr and Mrs T.M. Le Pelley • 46 metres from junction with Route des Talbots, near King's Mills • Open 14th April to Sept, Fri, 2 – 5pm, but check before travelling; also occasionally for charity and by appt – telephone (01481) 726611/254788 for details • Entrance: £2, children free ● & ♨

The garden reveals itself as a surprising combination of artistry and plantsmanship, with its plethora of roses rambling over barns, small pottery studio and old walls sheltering a relaxed and spontaneous cottage garden with a selection of interesting plants. The charming organic vegetable garden has young box hedging dividers, and there is interest from spring through to autumn in the main, wild and vegetable gardens. Also surprising are the views across rolling fields to wooded hills, with scarcely a house in sight and access to the meadow in the Fauxquet Valley.

JERSEY

Creux Baillot Cottage

Le Chemin des Garennes, St Ouen JE3 2FE. Tel: (01534) 482191

Judith Quérée • 0.25m N of St Ouen. Location map provided or directions given when booking made • Open May to Sept, Tues, Wed, Thurs, 11am and 2pm (or by arrangement), by appt only for conducted tours • Entrance £5 ● 🍴 ♨

This garden, largely laid out as a cottage garden, belongs to a dedicated plantsperson. With 1700 different species and cultivars, it is a living encyclopaedia of the rare and unusual packed into 0.25 acres in a secluded valley. There are 250 different clematis and 80 types of iris, to name but a few. An unusual feature with a charming sculpture, a curtain of chains for climbers, a raised walkway through a bog garden with a small wooden boat and a collection of anchors lend nautical and humorous touches to a serious garden.

Domaine Des Vaux

La Rue de Bas, St Lawrence JE3 1JG.

Mr and Mrs Marcus Binney • 2m N of St Helier • Open one Sun, 2 – 5pm, for charity (check with Jersey Tourist Board (01534) 500700). Private parties by prior arrangement with owners in writing • Entrance: £3 ● 🍴 🍴 WC ⬧ ▮

Marcus Binney, architectural correspondent of *The Times*, has a passion for the preservation of architecture and landscape, and these tastes are very much reflected in his and his wife Anne's delightful garden. It is in two completely contrasting parts. The top is a formal Italianate garden, set around and above a sunken rectangular lawn, and the borders here are a riot of unusual and familiar perennials and shrubs. This perfect formal garden was created by the previous generation, Sir George and Lady Binney, and designed by Walter Ison. Lady Binney planted with an eye for colour in foliage as much as in flowers, as is evidenced by the grey and silver borders facing the yellow, gold and bronze ones. The present generation have planted a small formal herb garden on a triangular theme and have created a *jardinière* and a pair of long flower borders. The lower garden is a semi-wild and quite steep valley with a string of ponds connected by a stream. In spring the valley and wood are at their best, with a carpet of wild Jersey narcissi under camellias, azaleas and rhododendrons. A magnificent *Magnolia campbellii* has reached maturity and flowers abundantly in March. Of particular note are the camellias in both gardens and an interesting collection of conifers, and other trees planted to give year-round foliage colour in a small arboretum. A newly created Mediterranean garden stands at the top of the valley with a collection of planted pots which reflect the colours of the south of France and Italy.

Eric Young Orchid Foundation

Victoria Village, Trinity JE3 5HH. Tel: (01534) 861963

The Eric Young Charitable Trust • 1.5m N of St Helier • Open all year except 25th, 26th Dec and 1st Jan, Wed – Sat, 10am – 4pm • Entrance: £3, OAPs/students £2, children £1 • Other information: Plants for sale when available ○ 🍽 🥃 wc ♿ ⟁ ☞

This exquisite collection, described as 'the finest private collection of orchids in Europe, possibly the world', was built up by the late Eric Young, who came to Jersey after World War II. In 1958 he merged his own collection with that of a Sanders nursery which was closing down, and continued to acquire new plants. The purpose-built centre, which has won many awards, consists of eight growing houses and a landscaped display area where visitors may view these exotic flowers in close detail. From November to April there are cymbidiums, paphiopedilums, odontoglossums and calanthes, from May to June cattleyas, miltonias and odontoglossums and from June to October, phalaenopsis, miltonias and odontoglossums. (The beauty of these flowers is inversely proportional to the difficulty of their names.)

Howard Davis Park

St Saviour.

In St Helier, between St Clement's Road and Don Road • Open all year, daily: April and May, 8am – 8pm; June to Sept, 8am – 10pm; Oct to March, 8.30am – 4.30pm • Entrance: free (charge for bandstand seats) ○ 🍽 ✕ 🥃 wc ♿ ☕ ⚲

Given by T.B. Davis, a great benefactor of the island, in memory of his son who was killed in World War I, this is the most famous of Jersey's public gardens. Colourful sub-tropical trees and plants flourish here, and the bandstand is the venue for an excellent variety of live entertainment from May to September. Other public parks in St Helier are Parade Gardens, off Parade Place, and Victoria Park, off St Aubins Road/Cheapside. Both contain interesting statues.

Jersey Lavender

Rue du Pont Marquet, St Brelade JE3 8DS. Tel: (01534) 742933

Alastair and Eleanor Christie • 3m W of St Helier near Pont Marquet Country Park • Open 10th May to 18th Sept, Tues – Sun, 10am – 5pm • Entrance: £3.25, children free (2005 prices) ◑ 🖢 ✕ wc ⅙ ⬡ ℘ ⛁

This lavender farm was started in 1983 and now covers nine acres. Visitors are invited to walk around the main fields, planted with six varieties of lavender, to enjoy their different colours and scents. Harvesting starts in late June, and the distillation and perfume-bottling processes may be seen. There is an extensive garden of herbs, including a National Collection of lavenders and a collection of 75 different species of bamboos.

Jersey Zoological Park

Les Augres Manor, Trinity JE3 5BP. Tel: (01534) 860000

Durrell Wildlife Conservation Trust • 2.5m NW of St Helier on B361 • Open daily except 25th Dec, 9.30am – 6pm or dusk if earlier • Entrance: £11.50, OAPs £8.50, children £7.405. Parties of 10 or more £3 less per person, OAPs, students and children £2 less ○ 🖢 ✕ 🐚 wc ⅙ ⛁ ♀ ⚘

Over 100 rare and endangered species of animals reside within the 40 acres of parkland and water gardens. The late author and naturalist Gerald Durrell founded the Zoo as a sanctuary forty years ago. Today Sumatran orang-utans, Andean bears and Montserrat orioles, rescued from beneath the smouldering volcano, live in lush, spacious environments which closely replicate their native habitats. Madagascar lemurs and tiny lion tamarins from Brazil live free in the Zoo's woodland, leaping through the trees. New exhibits include a walk-through aviary and a cloud forest inside the enclosure housing Andean bears, otters and coartis.

Samares Manor

St Clement JE2 6QW. Tel: (01534) 870551

Vincent Obbard • 2m E of St Helier • Manor (guided tours daily except Sun, £2.50 extra) open • Garden open 8th April to 14th Oct, daily, 10am – 5pm • Entrance: £5.60, OAPs £5.20, children £1.95, under 5 free • Other information: Craft centre ◑ 🖢 ✕ 🐚 wc ⅙ ℘ ⛁ ♀

The name Samares is derived from the French for salt marsh, and indeed sea salt was once extracted from marshy land nearby. It is not known who built the existing manor house, which has passed through many owners, but the grounds have developed gradually. By 1680 they were famed for their trees. The present garden was the work of Sir James Knott, who bought the property in 1924 and had it developed, employing 40 gardeners, at a cost of £100,000. Two quite different gardens here: a collection of herbs for every possible use, laid out in a partially walled garden leading to a lake; and a Japanese garden. Of particular note are the camellias, the *Taxodium distichum* in the lake and the rocks imported from Cumberland.

Les Vaux

Rozel Valley, St Martins JE3 6AJ. Tel: (01534) 861102

Rhona, Lady Guthrie • 6m NE of St Helier • Open March to Sept for parties by appt • Entrance: £3 • Other information: Garden steep in parts, so not ideal for unfit or disabled visitors ● 🐌 **WC**

Sheltered within a steep-sided valley, the garden encompasses a variety of styles and an eclectic range of trees, shrubs, herbaceous plants and sculptures. The owner's artistry and love of unusual plants is lavished around lawns and bare rocks, on serene slopes and in richly filled shrubberies and borders. The old potato ground to the north now flowers with 30,000 bulbs, and a field at the head of the valley has been planted with 800 native trees to form a small nature reserve, with two ponds linked by a stream. Red squirrels and hedgehogs are already regular visitors, and peacocks roam the garden.

GARDENING WEBSITES
Many gardens now have their own websites, and we list these at the back of the *Guide*. Others useful for garden visitors are:
Dept of Environment (Ireland): www.heritageireland.ie
English Heritage: www.english-heritage.org.uk
Historic Houses Association: www.hha.org.uk
Historic Royal Palaces: www.hrp.org.uk
Historic Scotland: www.historic-scotland.gov.uk
Landmark Trust: www.landmarkrust.org.uk
National Gardens Scheme: www.ngs.org.uk
National Trust: www.nationaltrust.org.uk
National Trust for Scotland: www.nts.org.uk
Royal Horticultural Society: www.rhs.org.uk
Welsh Historic Monuments: www.cadw.wales.gov.uk

BED & BREAKFAST FOR GARDEN LOVERS
The biennial paperback contains some 200 B&Bs (mostly in Britain, with a smattering in the Republic of Ireland, France and Italy) run by keen and knowledgeable owners with fine gardens of all types and sizes – rural and urban, traditional and contemporary. Prices for a double room range from £55 per night. The guide is available from Alastair Sawday Publishing – telephone (01275) 464891 or consult www.specialplacestostay.com.

SYMBOLS
[NEW] entries new for 2006; ○ open all year; ◐ open most of year; ◑ open during main season; ● open rarely and/or by appt; 🍵 teas/light refreshments; ✕ meals; 🐌 picnics permitted; **WC** toilet facilities; **WC** toilet facilities, inc. disabled; ♿ partly wheelchair-accessible; 🐕 dogs on lead; 🌱 plants for sale; 🏛 shop; ▮ events held; ☺ children-friendly; B&B bed and breakfast available.

EUROPE

Throughout the *Guide* two-starred gardens are marked on the maps with a bold square.

For some years the *Guide* has included a selection of gardens in Europe, concentrating on those which are a reasonable distance from the Channel ports or some other points of entry such as a Eurostar station.

FRANCE

Paris Gardens

Central Paris: *The Tuileries Garden* near the Louvre (being restored, including *Le Jardin du Carrousel*. Christopher Bradley-Hole in his description has written that the Wirtz family 'have used yew hedges, planted in an extensive *patte d'oie* converging on the Arc de Triomphe, to make sense of some of the disparate geometry of the site'); *Parc Monceau on* boulevard de Courcelles (nineteenth-century nannyland); *The Luxembourg Gardens* on the Left Bank (*grandeur ancienne*); The *Fondation Cartier* has a gallery and garden for '*l'art contemporain*' at 261 boulevard Raspail (Tel: 42.18.56.51). Here Patrick Blanc has created a spectacular jungle-like hanging garden above the entrance which links the boulevard trees to the Fondation's rear garden; *Jardin des Plantes* also on the Left Bank, Pont d'Austerlitz; *Place des Vosges*, which landscape architect Gordon Haynes calls 'a masterpiece' of design and an excellent venue for picnics purchased in rue St Antoine and rue Birague to the south. An exhibition was held in 2000 at *Bagatelle* near the Trianon and this may be a regular event; there is also an elegant rose garden there.

Inner suburbs: *Parc André Citroën* (the most exciting modern park in Paris); *Jardin Albert Kahn* at Boulogne Billancourt (several gardens including an authentic Japanese garden); *Fondation Cartier Sculpture Garden* in Jovy-en-Jonas (20 minutes by train or RER line B. Good café). In the Marais is a new garden, simple and elegant, dedicated to the late Diana, Princess of Wales.

Outer suburbs: *Parc Caillebotte*, Yerres, near Orly (garden of the painter who launched Monet); *Roseraie de L'Hay les Roses* (famous rose garden in the corner of a large municipal park near Orly); *La Bagatelle* on the edge of the Bois de Boulogne in Neuilly (perhaps the most elegant display of roses in the world).

Ile de France: *Château de St Jean de Beauregard*, 28km S of Paris at Les Ulis (one of the best *potagers*), which hosts an annual plant fair (telephone 1.60.12.00.01 for details).

Shows

Two other major garden events are held every year within reasonable distance of Paris. Les Journées de Plantes de Courson is held every May and October in the seventeenth-century *Château de Courson*, 35km south of Paris. Dubbed the 'French Chelsea', this is an international plant sale with exhibitors and nurserymen from all over Europe, organised by the château owners, Patrice and Hélène Fustier, who were awarded the RHS Gold Veitch medal in 1993. To reach Courson from Paris, take the train (RER line C) from Alma, Les Invalides or Austerlitz stations to Breuillet or Bruyères-Le-Châtel on Dourden route (first four carriages of train only), then shuttle bus or taxi from Breuillet to Courson (6km). For 2006 dates and prices, telephone 1.64.58.90.12 or consult www.courson.com. Further south, 185km from Paris, the Festival des Jardins, takes place every year at the *Château de Chaumont.* Dozens of miniature gardens are on show, created by designers from all over the world. The festival runs from mid-June to mid-October. There is a regular train service from Austerliz to Chaumont-sur-Loire, sometimes having to change at Blois. For further information and prices, telephone 1.48.04.84.59.

Arboretum d'Harcourt

27800 Harcourt, Normandie. Tel: 2.32.46.29.70

Open March to 12th June, 13th Sept to 13th Nov, daily except Tues, 2pm – 6pm, 16th June to 11th Sept, daily, 10.30am – 6.30pm, 2pm – 6pm

A nine-hectare arboretum set in a 94-hectare forest, started in 1802 and including many fine trees from North America.

Botanica

79 rue de Fruges, 62130 Hernicourt–Sauricourt. Tel: 3.21.04.04.03

Open March to Oct, Thurs – Sun, 10am – 5pm

A beautifully landscaped garden with fine trees and good collections of herbaceous perennials. Landscaped lake with rustic bridge.

Chantilly ★

60500 Chantilly. Tel: 3.44.62.62.62

Open all year, daily, 10am – 6pm. 45-minute train around the park available, with commentary in French and English

Acknowledged as one of André Le Nôtre's greatest creations, notable for its magnificent scale and water features.

Château d'Ambleville

95710 Bray-et-Lû. Tel: 1.34.67.71.34

Open April to June, Sept and Oct, Sat, Sun and public holidays; July and Aug, daily; all 10.30am – 5.30pm

Italian gardens created between the two world wars, with dramatic terraces, topiary and water.

Château de Bagatelle

133 route de Paris, 80100 Abbeville. Tel: 3.22.24.02/69

Open July and Aug, daily except Tues, 2 – 6pm, and for parties by appt

Complementing the picturesque eighteenth-century castle, a box-edged parterre, sculptures and pleached limes. Fine trees in the park.

Château de la Ballue

35560 Bazouges-la-Pérouse, Brittany. Tel: 2.99.97.47.86

Open May to mid-July, Fri – Sun; mid-July to late-Aug, daily; Sept, Fri – Sun; all 1 – 5.30pm, and in winter by appt

A series of theatrical gardens created in 1973 in the Baroque or Mannerist style of the sixteenth and seventeenth centuries, including a fernery, a water trap, an open-air theatre and a maze.

Château de Beaumesnil ★

27410 Beaumesnil. Tel: 2.32.44.40.09

Open April to June, Sept, Fri – Mon; July and Aug, daily, except Tues; all 10am – 12 noon, 2 – 6pm

Designed by La Quintinye in 1640 and extensively remodelled in the eighteenth century. Features include a formal garden, an unusual labyrinth and lakeside walks.

Château de Bizy

27200 Vernon. Tel: 2.32.51.00.82

Open April to Oct, daily, except Mon, 10am – 12 noon, 2 – 6pm

Surrounding the eighteenth and nineteenth-century château, a series of elaborate cascades, fountains and statuary, lime and yew walks and an attractive park.

Château de Bosmelet

76720 Auffay. Tel: 2.35.32.81.07

Open June and Sept, Fri – Sun and public holidays; July and Aug, daily; all 1 – 7pm

A re-creation of the classical French design laid out in 1715 by Le Colinet, first gardener to André Le Nôtre at Versailles, and including an ancient lime avenue and a fine ornamental kitchen garden.

Château de Brécy ★★

14480 St Gabriel-Brécy. Tel: 2.31.80.11.48

Open Easter to 1st Nov, Tues, Thurs and Sun (plus Sat in June), 2.30 – 6.30pm, and for groups at other times by appt

A seventeenth-century garden laid out on five terraces in the Italian style in the 1650s – sophisticated, architectural and compact.

Château de Canon ★★

14270 Mézidon. Tel: 2.31.20.05.07/2.31.20.71.50

Open June to Oct, daily, 2 – 7pm

Unchanged since the mid-eighteenth century, a combination of French and English picturesque styles, including an Anglo-Chinese garden.

Château de Caradeuc ★★

35190 Bécherel, Brittany. Tel: 2.99.66.77.76

Open April to June, Sept and Oct, Sat and Sun; July to Aug, daily, 2 – 6pm

A garden restored in the traditional French manner in the late nineteenth century, distinguished by *allées*, vistas, statues and monuments.

Château de Compiègne ★

60200 Compiègne. Tel: 3.44.38.47.00

Open all year, daily except Tues and public holidays, 8am – 7pm (closes 6pm March to mid-April, Sept to Oct, 5pm Nov to Feb)

An important restoration project, noted especially for the magnificent vista and trellis-covered walk commissioned by Napoleon to complement a garden dating originally from the reign of Louis XV. 1820 rose garden.

Château de Galleville ★

76560 Doudeville, Normandie. Tel: 2.35.96.52.40

Open May to Oct for groups by appt. Guided visits mid-July to Aug

An elegant contemporary design uniting the seventeenth-century château with its garden and magnificent park.

Château d'Harcourt

14220 Thury-Harcourt. Tel: 2.31.79.65.41 or 2.31.79.72.05

Open April and Oct, Sun and public holidays, May to Sept, daily, all 2.30 – 6.30pm

A dazzling spring and summer garden with a profusion of flowers laid out with consummate artistry on a sloping site: a world away from the dramatic ruins of the château destroyed in World War II and its 70 hectares of park and gardens along the banks of the River Orne.

Château de Martinvast

50690 Martinvast. Tel: 2.33.87.20.80

Open early-March to late-Nov, daily, 10am – 12 noon, 2 – 6pm (open afternoons only Sat, Sun and public holidays); late-Nov to early-March, Mon – Fri, 10am – 12 noon, 2 – 6pm

A wooded park created in the English manner in 1820, with extensive water features, complementing the Gothick château.

Château de Miromesnil

Tourville sur Arques, 76550 Offranville. Tel: 2.35.85.02.80

Open April to Oct, daily, 2 – 6pm

A garden notable for its connection with Guy de Maupassant, magnificent beech wood and charming traditional *potager*.

Château de Nacqueville

50460 Urville-Nacqueville, Nr Cherbourg, Manche. Tel: 2.33.03.21.12

Open Easter to Sept, daily except Tues and Fri (unless public holidays). Guided visits only, hourly from 2pm to 5pm

A park in the English style, created in the 1830s, damaged in World War II and now restored, set in a green valley sheltered by wooded escarpments.

Château de Vauville

50440 Vauville, E. Cherbourg. Tel: 2.33.10.00.00

Open for guided tours May, June and Sept, Tues, Fri – Sun and public holidays; July and Aug, daily; all 2 – 6pm

A post-war garden of 4 hectares, informal in its style and Mediterranean in its planting, specialising in exotic and succulent plants arranged in a series of green rooms.

Château de Vendeuvre

14170 Saint-Pierre-sur-Dives.

Open May to Sept, daily; April and Oct, Suns and public holidays; all 11am – 6pm

A classical château and lake and many contemporary ideas, including new plantings and intriguing architectural and water features.

Clos du Coudray

76850 Etaimpuis, Normandie. Tel: 2.35.34.96.85

Open April to Oct, daily, 10am – 7pm

Thousands of different plant species grouped into 22 distinctive areas within clipped hedges or meandering paths – a succession of delightful surprises.

Ermenonville (Parc Jean-Jacques Rousseau)

1 rue Ren de Girardin, 60950 Ermenonville. Tel: 3.44.54.01.58

Open April to Sept, daily, 12 noon – 6.15pm (2 – 7pm on Sat); Oct to March, daily, 1 – 5pm

A natural landscape of grass, trees and water embellished with statues and follies in the Stowe/Painshill tradition and indelibly associated with the great philosopher.

Herbarium des Remparts ★

80230 St Valéry-sur-Somme. Tel: 3.22.26.90.72

Open May to Oct, daily, 10am – 12 noon, 3 – 6pm

A well-laid-out collection of medicinal, aromatic and culinary herbs and other plants useful to man, within the walls of an old convent garden.

Les Hortillonages

54 Boulevard Beauville, 80000 Amiens. Tel: 3.22.92.12.18

Open April to Oct, daily, 2 – 5pm (times vary depending on season)

Unique. Small electric boats take visitors around these former vegetable gardens (filled now with flowers), intersected by numerous small canals. Striking views of Amiens Cathedral.

Jardin d'Angélique

Hameau du Pigrard, Route de Lyons, 76520 Montmain, Normandie. Tel: 2.35.79.08.12

Open mid-April to June, daily; July to Oct, daily except Tues; all 10am – 7pm

A small garden dedicated to the beauty of life in memory of a lost daughter, filled with roses and perennials in a subtle combination of scents and colours, plus a newer, more formal garden.

Jardin de Castillon–Plantbessin

14490 Castillon, Calvados, Nr Bayeux. Tel: 2.31.92.56.03

Open 15th May to 1st June, Mon – Sat; June and July, daily; Aug to Sept, Mon – Sat, all 2.30 – 5.30pm

A delightful setting for a fine nursery, laid out in garden rooms, including herbaceous borders and water, Japanese and herb gardens, terraces accentuated by yew topiary opening onto a border of grasses, an arboretum and maze. A plantsman's delight.

Le Jardin de Claire

4, route d'Inchville, 80770 Beauchamps. Tel: 3.22.26.11.61 or 6.84.90.61.14

Open May to Oct by appt • 10km SE of Le Tréport/EU, just off D1015. In village of Beauchamps take Inchville road; garden is second on right

A plantsman's garden of 1,700 square metres, created in 1995, with many varieties of iris, rhododendrons and peonies. The knowledgeable owner is always delighted to share his love of perennials and shrubs.

Jardins de Maizicourt

80370 Maizicourt. Tel: 3.22.32.69.64

Open May to Oct, Mon – Fri, June and Sept, daily, 2 – 6pm

Clipped box hedges, herbaceous borders and old roses, all planted with impeccable taste. The small church over the garden wall is worth visiting, (key with garden owner) for parties only.

Les Jardins du Pays d'Auge

Route de Trois Bois, 14340 Cambremer. Tel: 2.31.63.01.81

20km E of Caen, 12km W of Liseux. Take exit 29b off A13 autoroute. Signposted in Cambremer • Open May to 15th Nov, Mon – Sat (plus Suns in July and Aug), 9am – 12 noon, 1.30 – 5.30pm. Closed mid-Sept to 1st Oct

A series of themed garden rooms including the Moon Garden, predominantly in silver shades, the Sun Garden, mostly in gold and yellow, the Angel's Garden, featuring plants with a biblical theme, and the Devil's Garden, with toxic plants.

Jardin des Plantes, Caen

5 place Blot, rue Desmoneux, 14000 Caen. Tel: 2.31.30.48.40

Open all year, daily, 8am – between 5.30 and 7.30pm (Suns and public holidays open 2pm). Tropical greenhouses, 2 – 5pm • Entrance: free

A pleasant public garden founded in 1736, with a park added in 1805 – fine trees, rare shrubs, a wide range of native plants, plant order beds and medicinal and rock gardens.

Jardin des Plantes, Rouen

114 ter avenue des Martyrs de la Résistance, 76100 Rouen. Tel: 2.32.18.21.30

Open all year, daily, 8am – between 5.15 and 7.45pm. Greenhouses 8.30 – 11am, 1.30 – 4.30pm • Entrance: free

A well-maintained eight-hectare park with interesting plants, attractive greenhouses and order beds.

Jardins de Valloires

80120 Argoules. Tel: 3.22.23.53.55

Open mid-March to Nov, daily, 10am – 5pm (closes 6.30pm, May to Sept)

Designed by one of France's foremost garden designers, Gilles Clément. Evoking the peace and contemplation of its monastic past, spacious lawns, subdued flower combinations, a rosery and a cloister furnished with yew columns and a parterre, a water garden, a garden of the five senses, and an evolution garden.

Jardin de Yves Gosse de Gorre

2 rue du bois, 62270 Séricourt. Tel: 3.21.03.64.42

Open April to Oct, Tues – Sat, 9am – 12 noon, 2 – 6pm (June to Oct also open Sun and Mon, 3 – 6pm)

Good collection of species roses, chosen especially for their colourful heps, together with amusing topiary, and colour-themed rooms.

Jardin Exotique

Roscoff, 29680 Brittany. Tel: 2.98.61.29.19 (summer)

Open March and Nov, daily, 2 – 5pm; April, May and Oct, daily, 10.30am – 12.30pm, 2 – 6pm; June to Sept, daily, 10am – 7pm

Over 3000 species of exotic plants grown in an informal seaside setting, fringing paths, pools, waterfalls and rocky outcrops. Small but spectacular.

Jardin Georges Delaselle

29253 Ile de Batz, Finistère, Brittany. Tel: 2.98.61.75.65

Open April to June, Sept, daily except Tues, 2 – 6pm; July and Aug, daily, 1 – 6pm; Oct, Sat and Sun, 2 – 6pm

A late-nineteenth-century plantsman's garden with over 1700 species sheltered, nurtured and now restored, with many palms and exotics from the southern hemisphere complementing the Bronze Age tombs and excellent modern sculptures.

Jardins et Pépinières de Cotelle

76370 Derchigny–Graincourt. Tel: 2.35.83.61.38

Open late April to mid-Nov, Mon – Sat, 10am – 12 noon and 2 – 5pm; occasionally open Suns, May, June, Oct

A garden created by a nurseryman and his painter wife around their nursery of unusual plants.

Manoir du Fay

Rue du Grand Fay, 76190 Yvetot, Normandie. Tel: 2.35.56.24.73

Open May to Oct, one Sun per month, 2 – 6pm, and by appt

Behind a seventeenth-century manor house, a *potager* re-created in the traditional manner using entirely organic principles.

Parc Floral de Haute-Bretagne

35133 Le Châtellier. Tel: 33.2.99.95.48.32

Open March to mid-Nov, daily, 2 – 6pm

A nineteenth-century garden in the English style with a series of sixteen gardens on an international theme: Persian, Greek, Himalayan etc.

Parc Floral des Moutiers ★★

76119 Varengeville–sur-Mer. Tel: 2.35.85.10.02

Open 15th March to 15th Nov, daily, 10am – 6pm, and for groups by appt

A Lutyens garden with Jekyll undertones surrounding a Lutyens house, combining formality, exuberant planting and archetypal architectural features in a satisfying Anglo-French alliance.

Shamrock

Route du Manoir d'Ango, 76119 Varengeville-sur-Mer. Tel: 2.35.04.02.33;

Open mid-June to mid-September, daily except Tues, 10am – 12 noon, 2.30 – 6pm; 16th to 30th September, daily except Tues, 2.30pm – 6pm

Possibly the largest collection of hydrangeas in the world, with over 1000 different species and varieties brought together by Corinne Mallet.

Le Vasterival ★★

76119 Ste-Marguerite-sur-Mer. Tel: 2.35.85.12.05

Open all year, by appt only

A garden created since 1957 by an outstanding plantswoman, the Princess Sturdza, informal in layout, immaculately cultivated, fascinating at any season.

BELGIUM

Brussels Gardens

Brussels itself has a number of gardens open at all times, including Abbaye de la Cambre, Bois de la Cambre, the Jean Massart Experimental Garden, Parc Léopold on rue Belliard and the park in the City Centre. Other gardens include Parc Tenbosch (with outstanding trees) on chaussée de Vleurgat, and Maison d'Erasme, 31 rue du Chapitre Anderlecht. Parc Solvay on chaussée de la Hulpe and Jardins du Museé van Buuren, 41 rue Leo Errera are in the south of the city. Ten kilometres north of Brussels is the National Botanic Garden, open daily 9am – sunset. Once a year, usually in April/May, the King of Belgium opens the conservatories in the Laeken Royal Palace on the northern outskirts of the city.

Annevoie ★★

5537 Annevoie-Rouillon, Anhee.

Open April to Oct, daily, 9.30am – 6.30pm

An historically important garden, created in the mid-eighteenth century with elements borrowed from the Italian, French and English styles, linked by a network of water features, including some spectacular fountains, fine urns and statues and superb trees.

Arboretum Kalmthout

Heuvel 2, B-2920 Kalmthout. Tel: 3.666.67.41

Open 15th March to 15th Nov, daily, 10am – 5pm. Hamamelis festival 17th Jan to 13th Feb; hellebores show 10th to 13th Feb; plant fair 17th April and 2nd Oct

The largest dendrological collection in Belgium, a 12-hectare arboretum of outstanding quality with many collections of rare and unusual trees and shrubs.

Château d'Attre

Avenue du Château, 7941 Attre, Brugelette. Tel: 32.68.45.44.60

Open by appt only: April to June, Sept and Oct, Sun and public holidays; July and Aug, Sat, Sun and public holidays; 1 – 6pm

A picturesque 28-hectare park with magnificent old trees and interesting follies and garden building.

Château de Belœil ★

Rue du Château 11, B–7970 Belœil, pres Mons. Tel: 32.69.68.94.26

Open April, Sat, Sun and bank hols; 15th May to 20th Nov, daily; all 1 – 6pm

An exceptional garden with a great six-hectare lake flanked by characterful garden rooms, plus 10km of spectacular hedges and other foliage features.

Château s'Gravenwezel

2970 s'Gravenwezel, Schilde. Tel: 36.58.14.70

Open probably 3rd to 5th June, 2 – 7pm – telephone to check

A 40-hectare formal park surrounding an ancient castle, reinvigorated by leading designer Jacques Wirtz with wide walks, extensive tree planting and the restoration of the eighteenth-century garden plan in the English landscape style, plus an attractive botanical garden and a redesigned walled garden.

Château de Leeuwergem ★

B–9620 Zottegem. Tel: 93.60.08.73

Open May to Sept by appt only

A park with a rare eighteenth-century *théâtre de verdure* (still in regular use), and formal gardens laid out in 1764 in the French classical style splendid counter-point to the spare simplicity of the château.

Hof ter Weyden

Greefstraat 1, 2910 Essen. Tel: 36.77.22.74

Open 2 days in June, 10am – 6pm, and by appt

Three distinctive planting areas surrounding an old farmhouse and its historic barn: a formal rose garden, an architectural garden divided by hedges, and an orchard, with a double row of poplars and a lake linking the garden with the countryside.

Kasteel Hex

B–3870 Heers. Tel: 12.74.73.41

Open 9th to 11th June and 9th and 10th Sept, all 10am – 5pm, and for parties by appt

Eighteenth-century formal gardens and one of the oldest English-style parks on the Continent, inspired by Capability Brown, in a beautiful natural setting. A huge collection of old and wild roses, and a traditional *potager*. Plant sales by holders of National Collections.

Park van Beervelde

Beervelde-Dorp 75, B-9080 Lochristi. Tel: 9.355.55.40

Open 12th to 14th May, 6th to 8th Oct (garden festivals), and by appt at other times

A 20-hectare arboretum and garden in the English landscape style, with stylish buildings and a spectacular flowering of Ghent azaleas in May, Ghent being the host city of important biennial horticultural shows.

Rekem Garden ★

Achter St Pieter 24, 3621 Rekem-Lanaken. Tel: 89.71.46.92

Open by appt

A small, immaculately maintained garden sheltered by fine hedges, with an unusual central pavilion of *Cornus mas* and distinctive areas planted with an artist's eye for design and colour.

De Tuinen van Hoegaarden (The Gardens of Hoegaarden)

1 Houtmarkt, Hoegaarden 3320. Tel: 16.76.78.43/16.76.56.39;

Within an ancient walled park, a permanent exhibition of 24 different types of gardens, all designed by landscape architects and professional gardeners, plus nature trails, a sculpture exhibition and horticultural displays.

NETHERLANDS

Amsterdam Canal Gardens

During the 'Amsterdam Canal Garden in Bloom' weekend of 16th – 18th June some 25 individual, institutional and museum gardens (both classical and contemporary) will open to the public. The entry through the fine seventeenth- and eighteen-century houses is worth the visit by itself. Several houses offer sandwiches and drinks. Opening hours are 10am – 5pm, and a day ticket costs €12. Telephone 0206.24.52.55, email info@canalmuseums.nl or visit the website on www.canalmuseums.nl.

Broekstraat 17 ★

6999 De Hummelo. Tel: 314.38.1120

Nursery open April to 1st Nov, Tues – Sat, 10am – 4pm (closed in July). Garden open June and Aug, Tues – Sat, and grass days 2nd and 3rd Sept, 7th and 8th Oct.

The highly original creation of one of the gurus of the contemporary Dutch style of naturalistic gardening, Piet Oudolf, and his wife Anja, displaying the masterly orchestration of nature that won him the top prize at Chelsea 2000.

Huys de Dohm

De Doom 48–50, 6419 CX Heerlen. Tel: 45.571.0470

Open 3rd, 4th, 10th, 11th, 17th, 18th June for parties of 15 or more by appt.
Check website, www.inekefreue.nl, for opening times

Restored since 1980 as a series of outdoor rooms, including double herbaceous borders, a delightful *potager* and topiary, white, water and wild gardens, reflecting the character of the small, ancient castle and its hunting lodge.

De Kempenhof

Zuiverseweg 4, 4357 NM Domburg. Tel: 118.58.16.47

Open 1st and 2nd July, 10am – 5pm, and by appt

A two-hectare garden focused on a splendid all-season double herbaceous border, with island beds, roses, hellebores and an avenue planted with ornamental grasses for additional seasonal interest.

Leiden Botanic Garden ★

Hortus Botanicus, Rapenburg 73, Leiden. Tel: 71.527.7249

Open all year, daily, 10am – 6pm (closes 4pm and Sats Oct to March). Closed 24th Dec to 2nd Jan

Clusius's late-sixteenth-century garden reconstructed with 60 beds and ancient trees, a Japanese garden, and a more conventional garden with other features of interest.

Paleis Het Loo, National Museum ★★

Koninklijk Park 1, 7315 JA Apeldoorn. Tel: 55.577.2400

Open all year, daily except Mon (but open Bank Holiday Mons), 10am – 5pm

William Prince of Orange's magnificent formal garden of 1684, transformed into a landscape park, then destroyed and now triumphantly restored to its original design, including a sunken garden, parterres, elaborate water conceits, an upper garden with a curved colonnade, and delightful gardens near the palace.

Priona Gardens

Schuineslootweg 13, 7777 RE Schuinesloot. Tel: 523.68.17.34

Open May to Sept, Thurs to Sat, 10am – 5pm, Sun, 2 – 6pm

The naturalistic garden of Henk Gerritsen, combining artistry and a profound knowledge of wild flowers and their habitats.

Rotstuin Bèr Slangen

Ambyerstraet Noord 73, 6225 EB Maastricht.
Tel: 640.12.69.83 or 433.622.918 contact Nico Tillie

Open 14th, 21st, 25th, 28th May, 4th, 5th, 11th June, 10am – 12 noon, 2pm – 5pm, and all year by appt

A unique rock garden constructed after 1950 by Bèr Slangen, 'the grandfather of Dutch rock gardening'. A landscape of giant boulders 5 metres tall is scattered with a profusion of bulbs, herbaceous perennials, alpines, shrubs and conifers, refreshed by streams and a magical pool.

J.P. Thijsse–Park

Prins Bernhardlaan 8, Amstelveen, Amsterdam. Tel: 205.40.42.65

A public 'new-wave' park created post-war and devoted to plants that grow in the wild, with large and varied groups of plants creating an entirely natural feeling, all connected by a long and narrow meandering pond.

De Tintelhof

Golsteinseweg 24, 4351 SC Veere. Tel: 118.61.45.20

Open by appt

A garden of well-balanced herbaceous borders, many old and modern roses in a frame of trimmed hedges and clipped evergreens, and a contrasting area of woodland, all sensitively integrated into its surroundings.

In de Tuinen van Ruinen

Achterma 20, 7963 PM Ruinen. Tel: 522.47.26.55

Open 30th April to Oct, Wed – Sun, 10am – 5pm

A magical meadow-like garden in the new Dutch style contrived by former owner Ton ter Linden, one of the acknowledged masters of the art.

FEEDBACK

Readers are invited to advise the *Guide* of any gardens which in their opinion should be listed in future editions, and where possible arrangements will be made to review such suggestions. Readers who would like to add information about gardens listed are warmly invited to write to the *Guide* with their comments, which may be used in future editions without attribution. Please send letters to the publishers, Frances Lincoln Ltd, 4 Torriano Mews, Torriano Avenue, London NW5 2RZ. All letters are acknowledged by the editors.

GUIDANCE ON SYMBOLS

Wheelchair users: the symbol &, denoting suitability for wheelchairs, refers to the garden only — if there is a house open, it may or may not be suitable. Additionally, some areas of the garden may not be accessible by wheelchair, or may require assistance.

Dogs: ⏏ indicates that there is somewhere on the premises where dogs may be walked, preferably on a lead. The garden itself is often taboo — parkland, or even the car park, are frequently indicated for the purpose.

Picnics: ☙ means that picnics are allowed, but usually in certain restricted areas only. It does not give visitors the all-clear to feast where they please!

Children-friendly: the bat-and-ball symbol ⚇ suggests that there are activities specifically designed for children, such as an adventure playground or a discovery trail, or that the garden itself is likely to appeal to them.

Websites for Gardens in the *Guide*

Many private and publicly owned gardens now have their own websites, and these are listed below. We have not listed individually the websites for gardens owned by the National Trust. The easiest way to access a National Trust garden is to type in their website followed by the house name in full, e.g. nationaltrust.org.uk/mottisfontabbey. For the National Trust for Scotland (nts.org.uk), English Heritage (english-heritage.org.uk) and the Department of Environment in the Republic of Ireland (heritageireland.ie or environ.ie) you should access the main website and follow the instructions. **Note: All website addresses must have www. as a prefix**.

Other useful websites for garden visitors are: CADW (Welsh Historic Monuments) (www.cadw.wales.gov.uk); Historic Houses Association (www.hha.org.uk); Historic Royal Palaces (www.hrp.org.uk); Historic Scotland (www.historic-scotland.gov.uk); Landmark Trust (www.landmarktrust.co.uk); The National Gardens Scheme (www.ngs.org.uk). The website for all the Royal Horticultural Society's gardens is rhs.org.uk.

Bedfordshire
kathybrownsgarden.homestead.com
(The Manor House, Stevington)
shuttleworth.org (The Swiss Garden)
toddingtonmanor.co.uk
woburnabbey.co.uk

Berkshire
englefield.co.uk
royal.gov.uk (Frogmore Gardens)
livingrainforest.org
walthamplace.com
whiteknightsgarden.co.uk

Birmingham Area
birminghambotanicalgardens.org.uk
cbhgt.swinternet.co.uk
(Castle Bromwich Hall Gardens)
birmingham.gov.uk (City Centre Gardens)
botanic.bham.ac.uk
(University Botanic Garden)

Bristol Area
bristol-city.gov.uk (Ashton Court Estate)
bristol-city.gov.uk (Blaise Castle)
bristolzoo.org.uk
emmaushouse.org.uk
goldneyhall.com
bristol-city.gov.uk (The Red Lodge)

Buckinghamshire
ascottestate.co.uk
waddesdon.org.uk

Cambridgeshire
christs.cam.ac.uk
clare.cam.ac.uk
elgoods-brewery.co.uk
eltonhall.com

cont-ed.cam.ac.uk (Madingley Hall)
greenknowe.co.uk
(The Manor, Hemingford Grey)
south-farm.co.uk
botanic.cam.ac.uk
wimpole.org

Cheshire
adlingtonhall.com
arleyestate.com
bluebellcottagegardens.co.uk
bridgemere.co.uk
capesthorne.com
dungevalley.co.uk
eeo.co.uk (Eaton Hall)
gawsworthhall.com
jb.man.ac.uk/scicen (Jodrell Bank Arboretum)
nessgardens.org.uk
nortonpriory.org
crewe-nantwich.gov.uk (Queen's Park)
tattongardensociety.co.uk (The Quinta)
reaseheath.ac.uk
rodehall.co.uk
stapeleywg.com
tattonpark.org.uk (Tatton Park)
warrington.gov.uk (Walton Hall Gardens)
bents.co.uk (Weeping Ash)

Cornwall
tate.org.uk/stives (Barbara Hepworth Museum)
boconnocenterprises.co.uk
bonythonmanor.co.uk
bosvigo.com
burncoose.co.uk
caerhays.co.uk
carwinion.com
edenproject.com
godolphinhouse.com
headlandgarden.co.uk

heligan.com
marshvillagardens.com
penwith.gov.uk (Morrab Subtropical)
mountedgcumbe.gov.uk
oldmillherbary.co.uk
pencarrow.co.uk
penjerrickgarden.co.uk
pine-lodge.co.uk
trebah-garden.co.uk
tresco.co.uk
trevarno.co.uk
trewithengardens.co.uk

Cumbria
brantwood.org.uk
dalemain.com
cragview.demon.co.uk
highcleabarrow.com
holehirdgardens.org.uk
holker-hall.co.uk
hutton-in-the-forest.co.uk
levenshall.co.uk
muncaster.co.uk
rydalmount.co.uk
yewbarrowhouse.co.uk

Derbyshire
chatsworth.org
derbyshire.gov.uk (Elvaston Hall)
fgh.org.uk (Fanshawe Gate Hall)
alpineplantcentre.co.uk (Fir Croft)
gamesleyfold.co.uk
haddonhall.co.uk
leagarden.co.uk
melbournehall.com
paviliongardens.co.uk
sitwell.co.uk (Renishaw Hall)

Devon
bicton.ac.uk (Bicton College)
bictongardens.co.uk
blackpoolsands.co.uk
burrowfarmgardens.co.uk
castlehilldevon.co.uk
hostas-uk.com (Cleave House)
clovelly.co.uk
dartingtonhall.com
doctonmill.co.uk
thegardenhouse.org.uk
gidleigh.com
hartlandabbey.com
heddonhallgardens.co.uk
hillhousenursery.co.uk
marwoodhillgarden.co.uk
paigntonzoo.org.uk
ex.ac.uk (University of Exeter)

Dorset
abbotsbury-tourism.co.uk
mdmusic.com/arnmore (Arnmore House)
athelhampton.co.uk

cranborne.co.uk
domineys.com
fordeabbey.co.uk
kmc.ac.uk (Kingston Maurward Gardens)
knollgardens.co.uk
mapperton.com
moretondorset.com.uk
priest-house.co.uk
sherbornecastle.com
snapestakes.com
springheadtrust.co.uk
stickywicket.co.uk

Durham
auckland-castle.co.uk
bowesmuseum.org.uk
crookhallgardens.co.uk
egglestonhallgardens.co.uk
rabycastle.com
durham.ac.uk (University Botanic Garden)

Essex
bethchatto.co.uk
bridgeendgarden.gov.uk
eastonlodge.co.uk
thegibberdgarden.co.uk
glenchantry.demon.co.uk
langthorns.com
themagnolias.co.uk
randrsaggers.co.uk
woodsidegarden.net

Gloucestershire
batsarb.co.uk (Batsford Arboretum)
bourtonhouse.com
cerneygardens.com
colesbournegardens.org.uk
eastleachhouse.com
framptoncourtestate.uk.com
kiftsgate.co.uk
milldenegarden.co.uk
forestry.gov.uk/westonbirt (The National
    Arboretum, Westonbirt)
freshairart.org
    (The Old Rectory, Quenington)
owlpen.com
rococogarden.co.uk
    (Painswick Rococo Garden)
rodmarton-manor.co.uk
specialplants.net
stanwayfountain.co.uk
sudeleycastle.co.uk
trullhouse.co.uk
lesleyrossergardens.co.uk (Urn Cottage)
westonbirt.gloucs.sch.uk
    (Westonbirt School)

Hampshire & Isle of Wight
applecourt.com
brandymount.co.uk
exbury.co.uk

furzey-gardens.org
gardengallery.uk.com
gilbertwhiteshouse.org.uk
highclerecastle.co.uk
houghtonlodge.co.uk
longstockpark.co.uk
gertrudejekyllgarden.co.uk
    (The Manor House, Upton Grey)
hilliergardens.org.uk
spinnersgarden.com
hants.gov.uk/Staunton
    (Staunton Country Park)
tylneyhall.com
westgreenhousegarden.com.uk
northcourt.info
botanic.co.uk (Ventnor Botanic Garden)

Herefordshire
abbeydorecourt.co.uk
hamptoncourt.org.uk
hergest.co.uk
rogeroates.com (The Long Barn)
monnington-morgans.co.uk

Hertfordshire
ashridge.com
bealeshotels.co.uk (The Beale Arboretum)
beningtonlordship.co.uk
hanbury-manor.com
hatfield-house.co.uk
hopleys.co.uk
knebworthhouse.com

Kent
abbotsmerry.co.uk
bedgeburypinetum.org.uk
belmont-house.org
hadlow.ac.uk (Broadview Gardens)
cottagefarmturkeys.co.uk
doddington-place-gardens.co.uk
godinton-house-gardens.co.uk
goodnestoneparkgardens.co.uk
greatcomp.co.uk
groombridge.co.uk
hevercastle.co.uk
holepark.com
leeds-castle.co.uk
lullingstonecastle.co.uk
marleplace.co.uk
merriments.co.uk
mountephraimgardens.co.uk
nettlesteadplace.co.uk
owlhouse.com
penshurstplace.com
baytrust.org.uk (The Pines Garden)
totallywild.net (Port Lympne)
rockfarmhousebandb.co.uk
squerryes.co.uk
hdra.org.uk (Yalding Organic Gardens)

Lancashire
williamsonpark.com (Ashton Memorial)
arabellalennoxboyd.com (Gresgarth Hall)
hawthornes-nursery.co.uk
hoghtontower.co.uk
leightonhall.co.uk
htnw.co.uk (Pendle Heritage Centre)
bedbreakfast-gardenvisits.com (The Ridges)
towneleyhall.org.uk
woodsidegarden.net
southribble.gov.uk (Worden Park)

Leicestershire
belvoircastle.com
longclose.org.uk
wartnabygardenlabels.co.uk

Lincolnshire
sholland.gov.uk (Ayscoughfee Hall)
burghley.co.uk
doddingtonhall.com
eastonwalledgardens.co.uk
grimsthorpe.co.uk
hall-farm.co.uk
holmdalehouse.co.uk
kexbyhousegardens.co.uk
northlincs.gov.uk
    (Normanby Hall)
hostas.co.uk (The Old Rectory, Somerby)

Liverpool & Wirral
wirral.gov.uk (Birkenhead Park)
croxteth.co.uk
liverpool.gov.uk (Liverpool Botanic)

London
barbican.org.uk
wandsworth.gov.uk (Battersea Park)
royal.gov.uk (Buckingham Palace)
royalparks.gov.uk (Bushy Park)
wildlondon.org.uk
    (Camley Street Nature Park)
merton.gov.uk (Cannizaro Park)
capel.ac.uk
chelseaphysicgarden.co.uk
CIP.com (Chiswick House)
westminster-abbey.org
    (College Garden and Little Cloister)
elthampalace.org.uk
geffrye-museum.org.uk
hallplace.com
hamptoncourtpalace.org.uk
gardenphotolibrary.com (239A Hook Road)
horniman.ac.uk
royalparks.gov.uk (Hyde Park)
royalparks.gov.uk (Isabella Plantation)
royalparks.gov.uk (Kensington Gardens)
wwt.org.uk (London Wetland Centre)
zsl.org (London Zoo)
museumgardenhistory.org.uk

museumoflondon.org.uk
leevalleypark.com (Myddelton House)
bromley.gov.uk (Priory Gardens)
royalparks.gov.uk (Regent's Park)
roots-and-shoots.org.uk
kew.org (Royal Botanic Gardens)
chelsea-pensioners.org.uk
    (Royal Hospital, Chelsea)
royalparks.gov.uk (St James's Park)
syonpark.co.uk
thamesbarrierpark.org.uk
vam.ac.uk (Victoria and Albert Museum)

Manchester
manchester.gov.uk (Heaton Hall)
unitedutilities.com
    (Rivington Terraced Gardens)

Newcastle upon Tyne
bedesworld.co.uk
newcastle.gov.uk (Jesmond Dene)
twmuseums.org.uk (Mowbray Park)

Norfolk
bradenhamhall.co.uk
bressinghamgardens.com
conghamhallhotel.co.uk
e-ruston-oldvicaragegardens.co.uk
exoticgarden.com
norfolkbroads.com/Fairhaven
    (Fairhaven Woodland and Water Garden)
somerleyton.co.uk
    (Fritton Lake Countryworld)
haleshall.com
holkham.co.uk
hovetonhallgardens.co.uk
houghtonhall.com
manningtongardens.co.uk
norfolk-lavender.co.uk
pensthorpe.com
plantationgarden.co.uk
raveningham.com
sandringhamestate.co.uk
thrigbyhall.co.uk

Northamptonshire
althorp.com
boughtonhouse.org.uk
cotonmanor.co.uk
cottesbrookehall.co.uk
deenepark.com
evenleywoodgarden.co.uk
holdenby.com
kelmarsh.com
lamporthall.co.uk
menageriehorton.co.uk
oldrectorygardens.co.uk (The Old Rectory,
    Sudborough)
prebendal-manor.co.uk
rockinghamcastle.com

Northumberland
alnwickgarden.com
bide-a-wee.co.uk
chillingham-castle.com
thegardenstation.co.uk
howickgarden.org.uk
northland.ac.uk
    (Northumberland College at Kirkley Hall)

Nottinghamshire
snowdrops.co.uk
    (Felley Priory/Hodstock Priory)
holmepierreponthall.com
newsteadabbey.org.uk
ruffordcraftcentre.org.uk
wollatonhall.org.uk

Oxfordshire
blenheimpalace.com
bridewellorganicgardens.co.uk
broughtoncastle.demon.co.uk
buscot-park.com
cotswoldwildlifepark.co.uk
botanic-garden.ox.ac.uk
    (The Harcourt Arboretum)
kelmscottmanor.co.uk
kingstonbagpuizehouse.org.uk
botanic-garden.ox.ac.uk (Oxford Botanic)
rousham.org
stonor.com
waterperrygardens.co.uk
wroxtonabbey.org

Rutland
barnsdalegardens.co.uk

Shropshire
eleventowns.co.uk (Brownhill House)
davidaustinroses.com
stmem.com/dower-house-garden
    (The Dower House)
hawkstone.co.uk
walcothall.com
weston-park.com
wollertonoldhallgarden.com

Somerset
bath-preservation-trust.org.uk
    (William Herschel Museum)
cannington.ac.uk
americanmuseum.org (Claverton Manor)
eastlambrook.com
gantsmill.co.uk
hadspengarden.co.uk
hestercombegardens.com
bologrew.pwp.blueyonder.co.uk
    (Jasmine Cottage)
Ladyfarm.co.uk
lowerseveralls.co.uk
stoneaston.co.uk

Staffordshire
altontowers.com
dorothyclivegardens.co.uk
anitawright.co.uk (The Garth)
shugborough.org.uk
trenthamgardens.co.uk

Suffolk
stedmundsbury.gov.uk (Abbey Gardens)
columbinehall.com
eustonhall.co.uk
haughleyparkbarn.co.uk
helmingham.com
shrublandpark.co.uk
somerleyton.co.uk
woottensplants.co.uk
wykenvineyards.co.uk

Surrey
busbridgelakes.co.uk
coverwoodlakes.co.uk
rhododendrons.co.uk (Crosswater Farm)
sweertsdelandas.com (Dunsborough Park)
gattonpark.com
landmarktrust.co.uk (Goddards)
greatfosters.co.uk
guildfordborough.co.uk
    (Guildford Castle Gardens)
hannahpescharsculpture.com
langshottmanor.com
loseley-park.com
painshill.co.uk
ramsterweddings.co.uk
savillgarden.co.uk
titsey.org
cornusweb.co.uk (Winkworth Arboretum)

Sussex, East
batesgreen.co.uk
frewcoll.demon.co.uk (Brickwall)
charleston.org.uk
greatdixter.com
herstmonceux-castle.com
merriments.co.uk
sussexpast.co.uk (Michelham Priory)
pashleymanorgardens.com
thecuttinggarden.com
    (Sarah Raven's Cutting Garden)
royalpavilion.brighton.co.uk
stonehousesussex.co.uk

Sussex, West
bordehill.co.uk
sculpture.org.uk (Cass Sculpture Foundation)
chidmere.com
denmans-garden.co.uk
gravetyemanor.co.uk
highbeeches.com
leonardslee.com
hellyers.co.uk
parhaminsussex.co.uk

stmarysbramber.co.uk
townplacegarden.org.uk
kew.org (Wakehurst Place)
wealddown.co.uk
westdean.org.uk

Warwickshire
coughtoncourt.co.uk
lordleycester.com (The Master's Garden)
ragleyhall.com
hdra.org.uk (Ryton Organic Gardens)
shakespeare.org.uk
stoneleighabbey.org
warwick-castle.co.uk

Wiltshire
abbeyhousegardens.co.uk
bowood.org
corsham-court.com
fonthill.co.uk
secretgardendesigns.co.uk
    (The Fovant Hut)
ifordmanor.co.uk
larmer-tree-gardens.co.uk
longleat.co.uk
poundhillplants.co.uk
wiltonhouse.com

Worcestershire
arley-arboretum.org.uk
burford.co.uk
eastgrove.co.uk
eastnorcastle.com
luggershall.com
overbury.org.uk
pershore.ac.uk
autumnasters.co.uk (The Picton Garden)
webbsofwychbold.co.uk (Riverside Gardens)
spetchleygardens.co.uk
shcn.co.uk (Stone House Cottage Gardens)

Yorkshire (N. & E. Riding)
burnbyhallgardens.co.uk
burton-agnes.co.uk
castlehoward.co.uk
constableburtongardens.co.uk
duncombepark.com
ampleforth.org.uk (Gilling Castle)
humanbygrange.co.uk
millgatehouse.com
newbyhall.com
parcevallhallgardens.co.uk
plumptonrocks.co.uk
ripleycastle.co.uk
scampston.co.uk
asterisk.org.uk (Shandy Hall)
shdcottages.co.uk
    (Sleightholme Dale Lodge)
stillingfleetlodgenurseries.co.uk
fountainsabbey.org.uk
statelyhome.co.uk (Sutton Park)

thorpperrow.com
harrogate.gov.uk (Valley Gardens)
wytherstonegardens.co.uk

Yorkshire (S. & W. Area)
bramhampark.co.uk
harewood.org
hcdt.4t.com (Hillsborough Walled Garden)
bradforddistrictparks.co.uk (Lister Park)
calderdale.gov.uk (People's Park)
sbg.org.uk (Sheffield Botanical Garden)
leeds.gov.uk (Temple Newsam Park)
leeds.gov.uk (Tropical World)
wentworthcastle.org
perennial.org.uk (York Gate)
ysp.co.uk(Yorkshire Sculpture Park)

Ireland
forestserviceni.gov.uk (Annesley Garden)
antrim.gov.uk (Antrim Castle Gardens)
ballywaterpark.com
parks.belfastcity.gov.uk
   (Belfast Botanic Gardens)
benvarden.com
forestserviceni.gov.uk/arboretum.htm
   (Annesley Garden)
seafordegardens.com
parks.belfastcity.gov.uk
   (Sir Thomas and Lady Dixon Park)
annesgrovegardens.com
ardnamona.com
ballindoolin.com
cookingisfun.ie
   (Ballymaloe Cookery School Gardens)
bantryhouse.com
belvedere-house.ie
birrcastle.com
coolcarrigan.ie
dillongarden.com
killarneyhotels.ie (Dunloe Castle)
enniscoe.com
gardensireland.com (Fernhill Gardens)
zenith.ie/fota (Fota Arboretum)
limerickcivictrust.ie (Georgian House)
glincastle.com
irish-national-stud.ie (The Japanese Garden)
NicholasMosse.com (Kilfane Glen)
killruddery.com
kilmokea.com
knockabbeycastle.com
kylemoreabbey.com
lakemountgarden.com
larchill.ie
lismorecastle.com
lisnavagh.com
steam-museum.ie (Lodge Park Walled Garden)
loughcrew.com
irishtabletop.com (Marlay Park)
mount-usher-gardens.com
killarneynationalpark.ie (Muckross House)

botanicgardens.ie
powerscourt.ie
dublincorp.ie (St Anne's Park)
strokestownpark.ie
fingalcoco.ie (Talbot Botanic Gardens)
tullynallycastle.com
kilrush.ie (Vandeleur Walled Garden)
woodstock.ie

Scotland
melrose.bordernet.co.uk/abbotsford
   (Abbotsford)
lochnessgardens.com (Abriachan Garden)
gigha.org.uk (Achamore Gardens)
allangrange.co.uk
gardens-of-argyll.co.uk (An Cala)
ardanaiseig-hotel.com
gardens-of-argyll.co.uk (Ardchattan Priory)
ardkinglas.com
gardens-of-argyll.co.uk (Ardmaddy Castle)
ardtornishgardens.co.uk
clandonald.com (Armadale Castle)
attadale.com
gardensofscotland.org.uk (Atttadale)
ballindallochcastle.co.uk
balmoralcastle.com
gardens-of-argyll.co.uk
   (Barguillean's 'Angus Garden' and
   Ardchattan Priory)
birnaminstitute.com (Beatrix Potter Garden)
rbge.org.uk (Benmore Botanic Garden)
blackhills.org.uk
blair-castle.co.uk
bolfracks.com
branklyngarden.org.uk
callygardens.co.uk
camboestate.com
castlekennedygardens.co.uk
castleofmey.org.uk
carnellestates.com
cawdorcastle.com
northian.gov.uk (Colzium Lennox Estate)
abdn.ac.uk (Cruickshank Botanic Garden)
culzeancastle.net
rbge.org.uk (Dawyck Botanic Garden)
drum-castle.org.uk
buccleuch.com (Drumlanrig Castle)
drummondcastlegardens.co.uk
dunbeath.co.uk
great.houses-scotland.co.uk
   (Dunrobin Castle Gardens)
dunvegancastle.com
finlaystone.co.uk
floorscastle.com
glamis-castle.co.uk
gbg@land.glasgow.gov.uk
   (Glasgow Botanic Garden)
gardens-of-argyll.co.uk (Glenarn)
glendoick.com
maltwhiskydistilleries.com (Glen Grant Garden)

glenwhangardens.co.uk
greywalls.co.uk
hirselcountrypark.co.uk
pitmuies.com
inneshouse.co.uk
inwoodgarden.com
aberdeen.gov.uk (Johnston Gardens)
jurahouseandgardens.co.uk
kerrachar.co.uk
kildrummy-castle-gardens.co.uk
kinrosshouse.com
nationalgalleries.org (Landform Ueda)
rbge.org.uk (Logan Botanic Garden)
manderston.co.uk
mellerstain.com
mountstuart.com
rbge.org.uk
   (Royal Botanic Garden Edinburgh)
scone-palace.co.uk
shepherdhousegarden.co.uk
st-andrews-botanic.org
teviotwatergardens.co.uk
torosay.co.uk
dundeebotanicgardens.co.uk
   (University of Dundee Botanic Garden)

Wales
aberglasney.org.uk
bodnantgarden.co.uk
bodysgallen.com
caehirgardens.ws

cat.org.uk
   (Centre for Alternative Technology)
dewstow.com
dinglenurseries.co.uk (The Dingle)
genuslocus.net (Dyffryn Fernant Gardens)
dyffryngardens.gov.uk
glansevern.co.uk
nmgw.ac.uk (Museum of Welsh Life)
gardenofwales.org.uk (National Botanic)
the nurtons.co.uk
penplants.com (Penpergwym Lodge)
pictoncastle.co.uk
portmeirion-village.com
swansea.gov.uk (Singleton Botanic)
newport.gov.uk (Tredegar House)
pembrokeshirecoast.org.uk (Upton Castle)
veddw.co.uk

Channel Islands
3.gov.gg (Candie Gardens)
millefleurs.co.uk
artparks.co.uk (Sausmarez Manor)
sark-tourism.com (Le Seigneurie)
JudithQueree.com (Creux Baillot Cottage)
ericyoungorchidfoundation.co.uk
jerseylavender.co.uk
durrellwildlife.org (Jersey Zoo)
samaresmanor.com

KEY TO MAPS

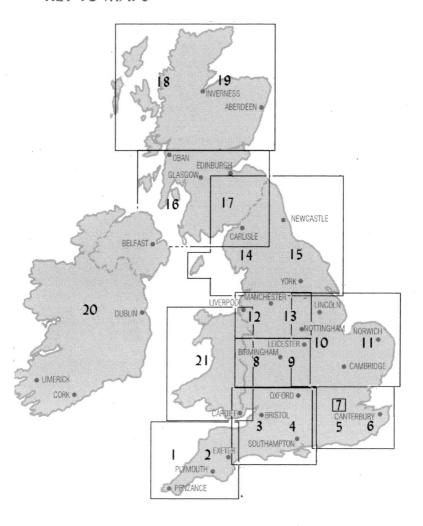

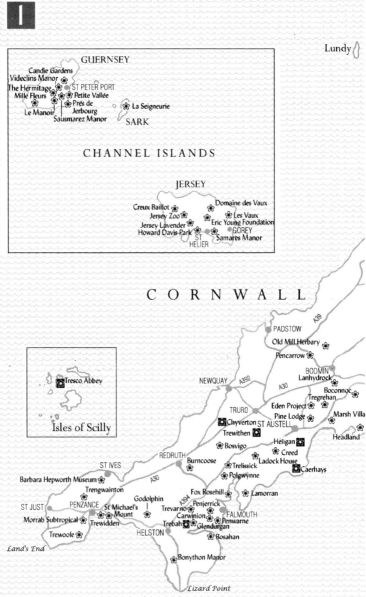

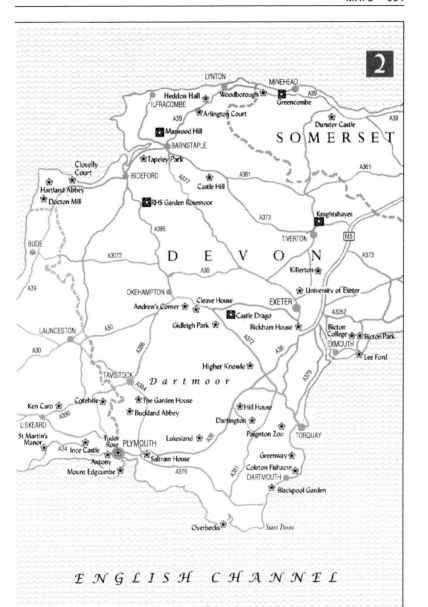

2

LYNTON

MINEHEAD

Heddon Hall
ILFRACOMBE
Woodborough
Greencombe
A39

Arlington Court

A39

Dunster Castle
A39

Marwood Hill

SOMERSET

BARNSTAPLE

A361

Tapeley Park

Clovelly
Court
BIDEFORD
A377
Castle Hill
A361

A361

Hartland Abbey
Docton Mill

RHS Garden Rosemoor

A373

Knightshayes

A386

TIVERTON
M5

BUDE

A3072

D E V O N
A30

A373

Killerton

A39

OKEHAMPTON
Cleave House
University of Exeter
EXETER
A3052

Andrew's Corner
Castle Drago
Bickham House
Bicton
College
Bicton Park
EXMOUTH

LAUNCESTON
A30
Gidleigh Park

A386
A372
A38

Lee Ford

A30

Higher Knowle

A384
Dartmoor
A379

Ken Caro
Cotehele
The Garden House
Buckland Abbey
Hill House
Dartington

LISKEARD
St Martin's
Manor
A390
Lukesland
A38
Paignton Zoo
TORQUAY

Tudor
Rose
PLYMOUTH
A34 Ince Castle
Saltram House
Greenway

Antony
Mount Edgcumbe
A379
Coleton Fishacre
DARTMOUTH

Blackpool Garden

Overbecks
Start Point

ENGLISH CHANNEL

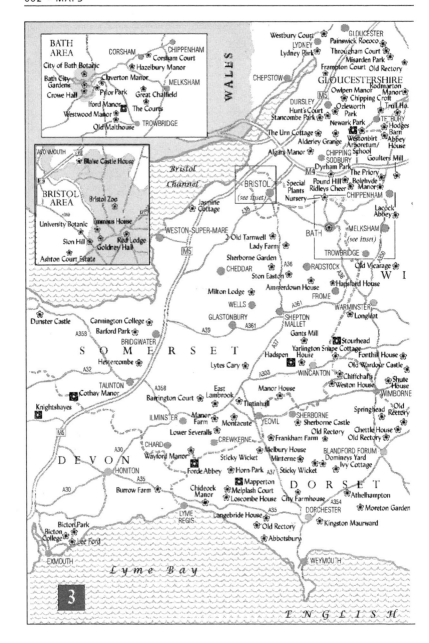

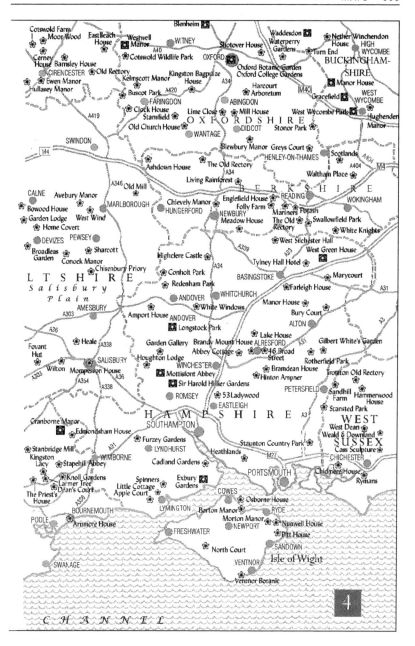

Cotswold Farm
Moor Wood
Eastleach House
Westwell Manor
WITNEY
Blenheim
Waddesdon
Waterperry Gardens
Shotover House
Nether Winchendon House
HIGH WYCOMBE
Turn End
BUCKINGHAM-
SHIRE
Cerney House
Barnsley House
CIRENCESTER
Old Rectory
Cotswold Wildlife Park
OXFORD
A40
Oxford Botanic Garden
Oxford College Gardens
Manor House
WEST WYCOMBE
Ewen Manor
Hullasey Manor
Kelmscott Manor
Kingston Bagpuize House
Buscot Park
A420
Harcourt Arboretum
Gracefield
West Wycombe Park
Hughenden Manor
FARINGDON
ABINGDON
A419
Clock House
Stansfield
Lime Close
Mill House
West Wycombe Park
OXFORDSHIRE
Old Church House
WANTAGE
DIDCOT
Stonor Park
SWINDON
M4
Blewbury Manor
Greys Court
Scotlands
A404
M4
Ashdown House
The Old Rectory
HENLEY-ON-THAMES
A34
Living Rainforest
Waltham Place
BERKSHIRE
CALNE
Avebury Manor
A346
Old Mill
Chievely Manor
Englefield House
READING
WOKINGHAM
Bowood House
MARLBOROUGH
HUNGERFORD
Folly Farm
Mariners Potash
Swallowfield Park
Garden Lodge
West Wind
NEWBURY
Meadow House
The Old Rectory
White Knights
Home Covert
DEVIZES
PEWSEY
West Silchester Hall
Broadleas Garden
Sharcott
A339
West Green House
Conock Manor
Chisenbury Priory
Highclere Castle
Tylney Hall Hotel
WILTSHIRE
Conholt Park
A34
BASINGSTOKE
Marycourt
Salisbury Plain
Redenham Park
Farleigh House
A31
AMESBURY
ANDOVER
WHITCHURCH
Manor House
A303
Amport House
ANDOVER
White Windows
Bury Court
A36
Longstock Park
ALTON
Heale
A338
Garden Gallery
Brandy Mount House
ALRESFORD
Lake House
Gilbert White's Garden
Fovant Hut
Houghton Lodge
Abbey Cottage
46 Broad Street
Rotherfield Park
SALISBURY
A303
Wilton
Mompesson House
A354
A36
A338
Mottisfont Abbey
WINCHESTER
Bramdean House
Hinton Ampner
Trotton Old Rectory
Sir Harold Hillier Gardens
PETERSFIELD
Sandhill Farm
Hammerwood House
ROMSEY
53 Ladywood
EASTLEIGH
Stansted Park
HAMPSHIRE
A3
WEST
Cranborne Manor
SOUTHAMPTON
West Dean
SUSSEX
Edmondsham House
Furzey Gardens
Staunton Country Park
Weald & Downland
Cass Sculpture
Stanbridge Mill
A31
WIMBORNE
LYNDHURST
Heathlands
M27
CHICHESTER
Kingston Lacy
Stapehill Abbey
Cadland Gardens
PORTSMOUTH
Chidmere House
Knoll Gardens
Larmer Tree
Dean's Court
Spinners
Little Cottage
Apple Court
Exbury Gardens
COWES
Rymans
The Priest's House
BOURNEMOUTH
LYMINGTON
Barton Manor
Osborne House
RYDE
POOLE
Arnmore House
Morton Manor
NEWPORT
Nunwell House
FRESHWATER
Pitt House
North Court
SANDOWN
SWANAGE
VENTNOR
Isle of Wight
Ventnor Botanic
CHANNEL
4

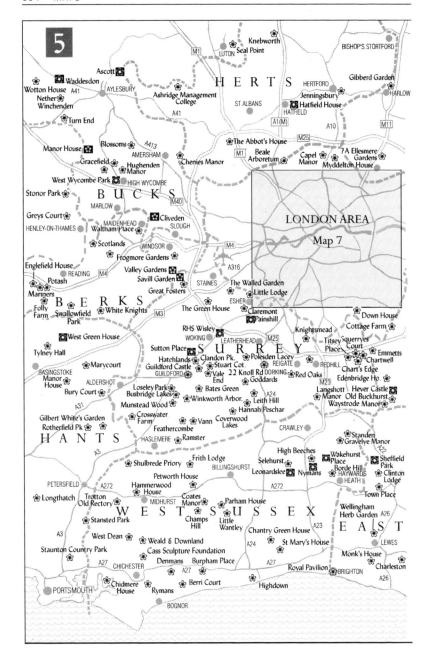

5

Knebworth
LUTON Seal Point
BISHOP'S STORTFORD
M1
Ascott
Waddesdon
Wotton House A41
AYLESBURY
Nether
Winchenden
HERTS
HERTFORD
Jenningsbury
Hatfield House
HATFIELD
Gibberd Garden
HARLOW
Ashridge Management
College
ST ALBANS
A41
A1(M)
A10
M11
Turn End

Manor House
Blossoms
A413
AMERSHAM
Gracefield
Hughenden
Manor
West Wycombe Park
HIGH WYCOMBE
Chenies Manor
The Abbot's House
M1
Beale
Arboretum
M25
Capel
Manor
Myddelton House
7A Ellesmere
Gardens

Stonor Park
BUCKS
M40
MARLOW
Cliveden
SLOUGH

Greys Court
HENLEY-ON-THAMES
MAIDENHEAD
Waltham Place
Scotlands
WINDSOR
Frogmore Gardens
M4

Englefield House
READING
M4
Potash
Mariners
BERKS
Valley Gardens
Savill Garden
Great Fosters
STAINES
A316
The Walled Garden
Little Lodge

Folly
Farm
Swallowfield
Park
White Knights
M3
The Green House
ESHER
Claremont
Painshill
Down House

West Green House
Tylney Hall
RHS Wisley
WOKING
LEATHERHEAD
M25
Knightsmead
Cottage Farm
Titsey
Place
Squerryes
Court
Emmetts

Marycourt
BASINGSTOKE
Manor
House
ALDERSHOT
Sutton Place
Hatchlands
Guildford Castle
GUILDFORD
Clandon Pk.
Stuart Cot.
Vale 22 Knoll Rd
End
Polesden Lacey
REIGATE
DORKING
Goddards
Red Oaks
REDHILL
Chartwell
Chart's Edge
Edenbridge Ho.
M23

Bury Court
A31
Loseley Park
Busbridge Lakes
Munstead Wood
Bates Green
Winkworth Arbor.
A24
Leith Hill
Langshott Hever Castle
Manor Old Buckhurst
Waystrode Manor

Gilbert White's Garden
Rotherfield Pk
HANTS
Crosswater
Farm
Feathercombe
HASLEMERE
Ramster
Vann
Coverwood
Lakes
Hannah Peschar
CRAWLEY
Standen
Gravelye Manor

High Beeches
Shulbrede Priory
Frith Lodge
BILLINGSHURST
Selehurst
Leonardslee Nymans
Wakehurst
Place
Borde Hill
HAYWARDS
HEATH
Sheffield
Park
Clinton
Lodge

PETERSFIELD
A272
Petworth House
Hammerwood
House
MIDHURST
Coates
Manor
Parham House
A272
Town Place

Longthatch
Trotton
Old Rectory
Champs
Hill
Little
Wantley
Chantry Green House
A23
Wellingham
Herb Garden
A26
EAST

A3
Stansted Park
West Dean
Weald & Downland
A24
St Mary's House
LEWES
Monk's House
Charleston

Staunton Country Park
A27
CHICHESTER
Cass Sculpture Foundation
Denmans
Burpham Place
A27
Royal Pavilion
BRIGHTON
A26

Chidmere
House
Rymans
Berri Court
Highdown
A27

PORTSMOUTH
BOGNOR

HERTS
HARLOW
SURREY
WEST SUSSEX
LONDON AREA
Map 7

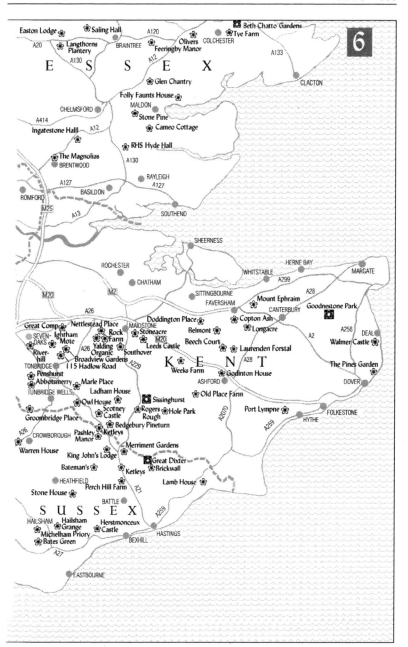

6

ESSEX

Easton Lodge · Saling Hall · A120 · Olivers · COLCHESTER · Beth Chatto Gardens · Tye Farm · A133

A20 · Langthorns Plantery · BRAINTREE · Feeringby Manor · A130 · A12

CLACTON

Glen Chantry

Folly Faunts House

CHELMSFORD · MALDON · Stone Pine

A414 · Cameo Cottage

Ingatestone Hall · A12

RHS Hyde Hall

The Magnolias · A130
BRENTWOOD

A127 · RAYLEIGH · A127

ROMFORD · BASILDON
M25 · A13

SOUTHEND

SHEERNESS

HERNE BAY
ROCHESTER · WHITSTABLE · A299 · MARGATE
CHATHAM · A28

M20 · M2 · SITTINGBOURNE · Mount Ephraim · Goodnestone Park
FAVERSHAM · CANTERBURY

A26 · Doddington Place · Copton Ash · Longacre
Great Comp · Nettlestead Place · MAIDSTONE · Belmont · A256 · DEAL
SEVEN-OAKS · Ightham · Rock · Stoneacre · M20 · Beech Court · Walmer Castle
Mote · Farm · A2
River- · Yalding · Leeds Castle · Laurenden Forstal
hill · Organic · Southover · The Pines Garden
Broadview Gardens · A229 · **KENT**
TONBRIDGE · 115 Hadlow Road · Weeks Farm · A28
Penshurst · Godinton House · DOVER
Abbotsmerry · Marle Place · ASHFORD
TUNBRIDGE WELLS · Ladham House · Old Place Farm
Owl House · Sissinghurst
Scotney · Rogers · Hole Park · Port Lympne · FOLKESTONE
Groombridge Place · Castle · Rough · A2070 · HYTHE
Bedgebury Pineturn · A259
A26 · CROWBOROUGH · Pashley · Ketleys
Warren House · Manor · Merriment Gardens
King John's Lodge · Great Dixter
Bateman's · Ketleys · Brickwall
HEATHFIELD · Perch Hill Farm · Lamb House
Stone House
BATTLE · A21
SUSSEX · A259
HAILSHAM · Hailsham · Herstmonceux
Grange · Castle · HASTINGS
Michelham Priory · BEXHILL
Bates Green
A27

EASTBOURNE

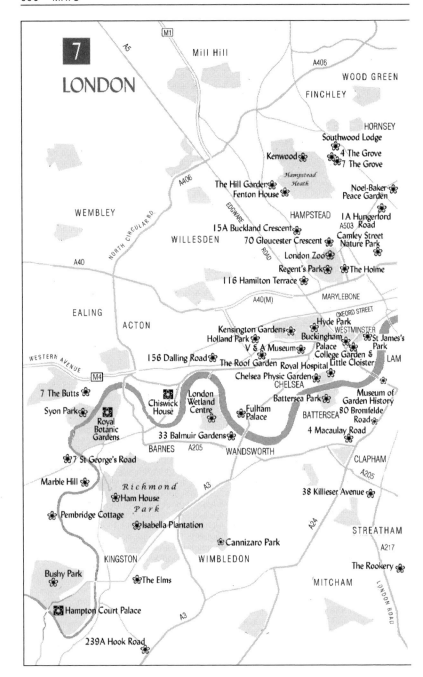

7

LONDON

M1

A5

Mill Hill

A406

WOOD GREEN

FINCHLEY

HORNSEY

Southwood Lodge

4 The Grove

7 The Grove

Kenwood

A406

Hampstead Heath

The Hill Gardens

Fenton House

Noel-Baker
Peace Garden

WEMBLEY

EDGWARE

HAMPSTEAD

1A Hungerford
Road

NORTH CIRCULAR RD.

A503

15A Buckland Crescent

Camley Street
Nature Park

WILLESDEN

70 Gloucester Crescent

ROAD

A40

London Zoo

Regent's Park

The Holme

116 Hamilton Terrace

A40(M)

MARYLEBONE

EALING

ACTON

OXFORD STREET

Kensington Gardens

Hyde Park

WESTMINSTER

St James's
Park

Holland Park

Buckingham
Palace

156 Dalling Road

V & A Museum

College Garden &
Little Cloister

LAM

The Roof Garden

Royal Hospital

Chelsea Physic Garden

CHELSEA

WESTERN AVENUE

M4

7 The Butts

Chiswick
House

London
Wetland
Centre

Battersea Park

Museum of
Garden History

Syon Park

Royal
Botanic
Gardens

Fulham
Palace

BATTERSEA

80 Bromfelde
Road

4 Macaulay Road

33 Balmuir Gardens

BARNES

A205

WANDSWORTH

CLAPHAM

7 St George's Road

A205

Marble Hill

Richmond

A3

38 Killieser Avenue

Ham House

Park

A24

Pembridge Cottage

Isabella Plantation

STREATHAM

Cannizaro Park

A217

KINGSTON

WIMBLEDON

The Rookery

Bushy Park

The Elms

MITCHAM

LONDON ROAD

Hampton Court Palace

A3

239A Hook Road

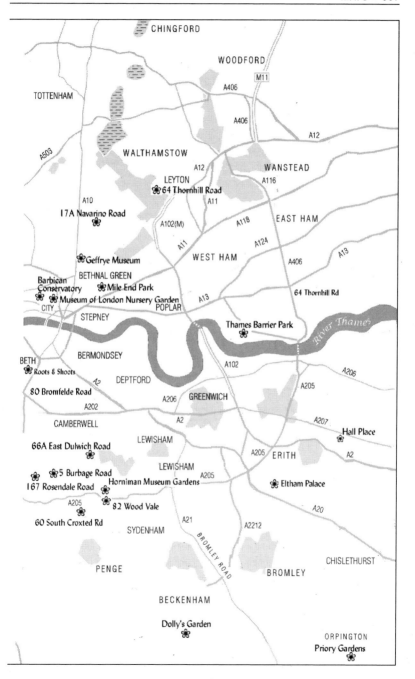

CHINGFORD

WOODFORD

M11

A406

TOTTENHAM

A406

A12

A503

WALTHAMSTOW

A12

LEYTON

WANSTEAD

64 Thornhill Road

A116

A11

A10

17A Navarino Road

A102(M)

A118

EAST HAM

A11

WEST HAM

A124

A13

Geffrye Museum

BETHNAL GREEN

A406

Barbican
Conservatory

Mile End Park

64 Thornhill Rd

Museum of London Nursery Garden

A13

CITY

POPLAR

STEPNEY

Thames Barrier Park

River Thames

BETH

BERMONDSEY

Roots & Shoots

A102

A206

DEPTFORD

A205

80 Bromfelde Road

A202

A206

GREENWICH

CAMBERWELL

A2

A207

Hall Place

LEWISHAM

66A East Dulwich Road

A205

ERITH

A2

LEWISHAM

5 Burbage Road

A205

167 Rosendale Road

Horniman Museum Gardens

Eltham Palace

A205

82 Wood Vale

A20

60 South Croxted Rd

SYDENHAM

A21

A2212

BROMLEY ROAD

CHISLEHURST

PENGE

BROMLEY

BECKENHAM

Dolly's Garden

ORPINGTON

Priory Gardens

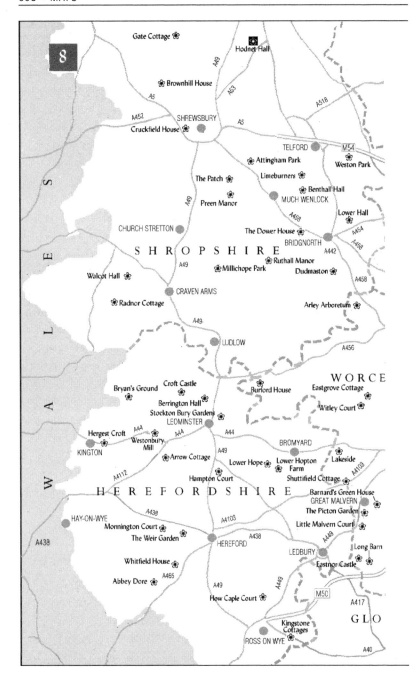

8

Gate Cottage

Hodnet Hall

A49

A53

Brownhill House

A5

A518

A452

SHREWSBURY

A5

Cruckfield House

TELFORD

M54

Weston Park

Attingham Park

Limeburners

The Patch

Benthall Hall

A49

Preen Manor

MUCH WENLOCK

Lower Hall

A458

CHURCH STRETTON

The Dower House

A464

BRIDGNORTH

A442

A458

S H R O P S H I R E

A49

Ruthall Manor

Millichope Park

Dudmaston

A458

Walcot Hall

CRAVEN ARMS

Radnor Cottage

Arley Arboretum

A49

LUDLOW

A456

W O R C E

Bryan's Ground

Croft Castle

Burford House

Eastgrove Cottage

Berrington Hall

Witley Court

Stockton Bury Gardens

Hergest Croft

A44

LEOMINSTER

A44

Westonbury Mill

A49

BROMYARD

KINGTON

Arrow Cottage

Lower Hope

Lower Hopton Farm

Lakeside

A4112

Hampton Court

Shuttield Cottage

A4103

H E R E F O R D S H I R E

Barnard's Green House

GREAT MALVERN

The Picton Garden

A438

A4103

Little Malvern Court

HAY-ON-WYE

Monnington Court

A449

Long Barn

The Weir Garden

A438

A438

HEREFORD

LEDBURY

Whitfield House

Eastnor Castle

Abbey Dore

A465

A49

A449

M50

How Caple Court

A417

G L O

Kingstone Cottages

ROSS ON WYE

A40

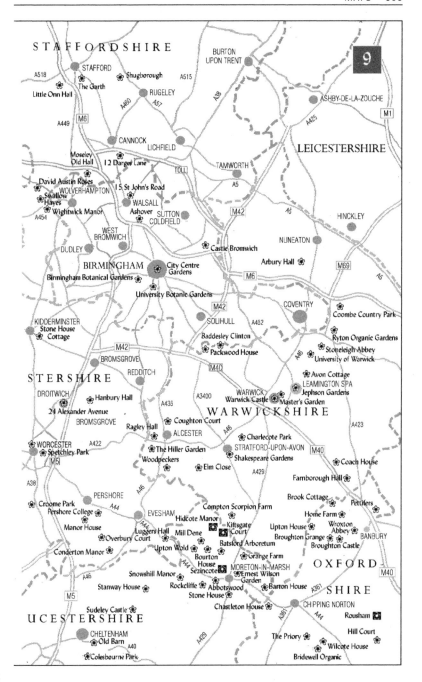

STAFFORDSHIRE

A518
STAFFORD
Shugborough A515
The Garth
Little Onn Hall RUGELEY
A460 A57
A449 M6
BURTON UPON TRENT

9

A38
ASHBY-DE-LA-ZOUCHE
A425
M1

CANNOCK LICHFIELD
Moseley
Old Hall 12 Darges Lane
David Austin Roses
Swallow WOLVERHAMPTON 15 St John's Road
Hayes
Wightwick Manor WALSALL
A454 Ashover SUTTON
WEST COLDFIELD
BROMWICH
DUDLEY

TOLL
TAMWORTH
A5
M42 A5
LEICESTERSHIRE
HINCKLEY

BIRMINGHAM City Centre
Birmingham Botanical Gardens Gardens
University Botanic Gardens

Castle Bromwich
Arbury Hall
NUNEATON
M6 M69 A5

KIDDERMINSTER
Stone House
Cottage
M42
BROMSGROVE
STERSHIRE REDDITCH
DROITWICH Hanbury Hall
24 Alexander Avenue
BROMSGROVE
Ragley Hall
WORCESTER A422
Spetchley Park
M5
A38
PERSHORE
Croome Park A44
Pershore College
Manor House EVESHAM
Overbury Court Luggers Hall Mill Dene
Conderton Manor Upton Wold
Snowshill Manor
Stanway House
M5
Sudeley Castle
UCESTERSHIRE
CHELTENHAM
Old Barn A40
Colesbourne Park

M42
SOLIHULL A452
Baddesley Clinton
Packwood House
M40
WARWICK
Warwick Castle Master's Garden
WARWICKSHIRE
A3400
A435
Coughton Court
ALCESTER
Charlecote Park
The Hiller Garden STRATFORD-UPON-AVON M40
Woodpeckers Shakespeare Gardens
Elm Close A429

COVENTRY
Coombe Country Park
Ryton Organic Gardens
Stoneleigh Abbey
University of Warwick
Avon Cottage
LEAMINGTON SPA
Jephson Gardens

A423

Coach House
Farnborough Hall
Brook Cottage Pettifers
Compton Scorpion Farm Home Farm
Hidcote Manor Kiftsgate Upton House Wroxton
Court Abbey BANBURY
Batsford Arboretum Broughton Grange
Bourton Grange Farm Broughton Castle
House MORETON-IN-MARSH OXFORD
Sezincote Ernest Wilson
Rockcliffe Abbotswood Garden Barton House SHIRE
Stone House A361 M40
Chastleton House CHIPPING NORTON
Rousham A44
Hill Court
The Priory Wilcote House
Bridewell Organic

A46
A46
A429

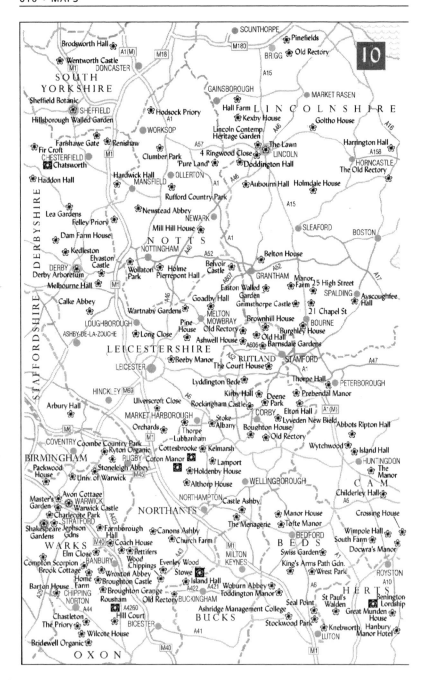

10

SCUNTHORPE
Pinefields
M180
BRIGG
Old Rectory
Brodsworth Hall
A1(M)
M18
Wentworth Castle
M1 DONCASTER
A15
SOUTH
YORKSHIRE
GAINSBOROUGH
MARKET RASEN
Sheffield Botanic
Hall Farm L I N C O L N S H I R E
SHEFFIELD
Hodsock Priory
Kexby House
Hillsborough Walled Garden
A1
Goltho House
A16
WORKSOP
Lincoln Contemp
Heritage Garden
Farnshawe Gate Renishaw
A57
The Lawn
Harrington Hall
Fir Croft
4 Ringwood Close
LINCOLN
A158
CHESTERFIELD
M1
Clumber Park
'Pure Land'
Doddington Hall
HORNCASTLE
Chatsworth
The Old Rectory
Hardwick Hall
OLLERTON
A1 A46
Haddon Hall
MANSFIELD
Aubourn Hall Holmdale House
Rufford Country Park
A15
Lea Gardens
Newstead Abbey
Felley Priory
NEWARK
SLEAFORD
BOSTON
Dam Farm House
Mill Hill House
Kedleston
N O T T S
A1
Elvaston
NOTTINGHAM
A52
Belton House
DERBY
Castle
Wollaton Holme
Belvoir
A52
Derby Arboretum
Park
Pierrepont Hall
Castle
GRANTHAM
Manor
25 High Street
Melbourne Hall
M1
A607
Easton Walled
Farm
SPALDING
A47
Garden
Ayscoughfee
Calke Abbey
Goadby Hall
Grimsthorpe Castle
Hall
Wartnaby Gardens
A46
MELTON
21 Chapel St
LOUGHBOROUGH
Pine
MOWBRAY
Brownhill House
BOURNE
ASHBY-DE-LA-ZOUCHE
Long Close
House Old Rectory
Burghley House
Old Hall
LEICESTERSHIRE
Ashwell House
A606
Barnsdale Gardens
Beeby Manor
RUTLAND
STAMFORD
LEICESTER
The Court House
A1
Lyddington Bede
Thorpe Hall
PETERBOROUGH
A47
HINCKLEY M69
Kirby Hall
Deene
Prebendal Manor
Arbury Hall
Ulverscroft Close
A6
Rockingham Castle
Park
MARKET HARBOROUGH
CORBY
Elton Hall
A1(M)
M6
Orchards
Stoke
Lyveden New Bield
Abbots Ripton Hall
Thorpe
Albany
Boughton House
COVENTRY Coombe Country Park
M1
Lubbenham
Old Rectory
Wytchwood
Island Hall
Ryton Organic
Cottesbrooke Kelmarsh
HUNTINGDON
BIRMINGHAM
RUGBY Coton Manor
Lamport
The
Packwood
Stoneleigh Abbey
Holdenby House
C A M
House
Univ. of Warwick
M45
Manor
Althorp House
WELLINGBOROUGH
Avon Cottage
Childerley Hall
Master's
WARWICK
NORTHAMPTON
Castle Ashby
A6
Garden
Warwick Castle
NORTHANTS
Manor House
Crossing House
Charlecote Park
The Menagerie
Tofte Manor
STRATFORD
Wimpole Hall
Shakespeare Jephson
Farnborough
Canons Ashby
BEDFORD
South Farm
Gardens
Gdns
M40 Coach House
Church Farm
M1
B E D S
Docwra's Manor
WARKS
Elm Close
Pettifers
MILTON
Swiss Garden
ROYSTON
Compton Scorpion BANBURY
Wood
Evenley Wood
KEYNES
King's Arms Path Gdn.
A10
Brook Cottage
Chippings
Stowe
Wrest Park
H E R T S
Home
Wroxton Abbey
Island Hall
A6
Barton House Farm
Broughton Castle
Woburn Abbey
St Paul's
Benington
CHIPPING
Broughton Grange
A422 A421 Toddington Manor
Walden
Lordship
NORTON
Rousham
Old Rectory BUCKINGHAM
Seal Point
Great Munden
A44
A4260
Ashridge Management College
House
Chastleton
Hill Court
B U C K S
Stockwood Park
Hanbury
The Priory
BICESTER
Knebworth
Manor Hotel
Wilcote House
A41
LUTON
Bridewell Organic
M40
M1
O X O N

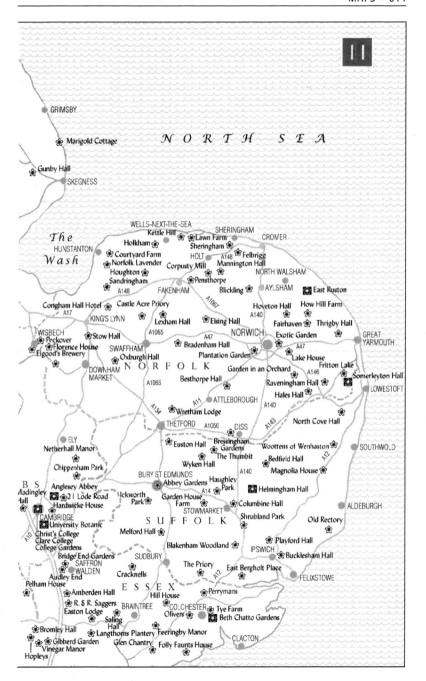

11

GRIMSBY

Marigold Cottage

Gunby Hall

SKEGNESS

NORTH SEA

The
HUNSTANTON
Wash

WELLS-NEXT-THE-SEA
Kettle Hill
Holkham
Courtyard Farm
Norfolk Lavender
Houghton
Sandringham
A148
FAKENHAM

SHERINGHAM
Lawn Farm
Sheringham
HOLT
A148
Corpusty Mill
Pensthorpe
Blickling

CROMER
Felbrigg
Mannington Hall
NORTH WALSHAM
AYLSHAM
East Ruston

Congham Hall Hotel
A17
KING'S LYNN
WISBECH
Peckover
Florence House
Elgood's Brewery
DOWNHAM
MARKET
A1065

Castle Acre Priory
Stow Hall
SWAFFHAM
Oxburgh Hall

A1067
Lexham Hall
A1065
A47
Bradenham Hall

Elsing Hall
NORWICH

Hoveton Hall
A140
Fairhaven
Exotic Garden

How Hill Farm
Thrigby Hall

GREAT
YARMOUTH

N O R F O L K
Besthorpe Hall

Plantation Garden
Garden in an Orchard
A146
Ravelingham Hall
Hales Hall

A47
Lake House
Fritton Lake
Somerleyton Hall
LOWESTOFT

A11
ATTLEBOROUGH
A140
North Cove Hall

A134
Wretham Lodge
THETFORD
A1066
DISS
A143

ELY
Netherhall Manor

Chippenham Park

Euston Hall
Bressingham
Gardens
The Thumbit
Wyken Hall
BURY ST EDMUNDS

Wootens of Wenhaston
Bedfield Hall
A140
Magnolia House

SOUTHWOLD
A12

B S
Madingley
Hall
Anglesey Abbey
21 Lode Road
Hardwicke House
CAMBRIDGE
University Botanic
Christ's College
Clare College
College Gardens
Bridge End Gardens
SAFFRON
WALDEN
Audley End
Pelham House

Ickworth
Park
Garden House
Farm
STOWMARKET

Haughley
A14 Park
Columbine Hall

S U F F O L K
Melford Hall
Blakenham Woodland

Helmingham Hall
Shrubland Park
Old Rectory

Playford Hall
IPSWICH
Bucklesham Hall

ALDEBURGH

Cracknells
The Priory

E S S E X
Hill House

Amberden Hall
R & R Saggers
Easton Lodge
Saling
Hall
BRAINTREE
Langthorns Plantery
Glen Chantry

SUDBURY
East Bergholt Place
A12

Perrymans
COLCHESTER
Olivers
Tye Farm
Beth Chatto Gardens
Feeringby Manor
Folly Faunts House
CLACTON

FELIXSTOWE

Bromley Hall
Gibberd Garden
Vinegar Manor
Hopleys

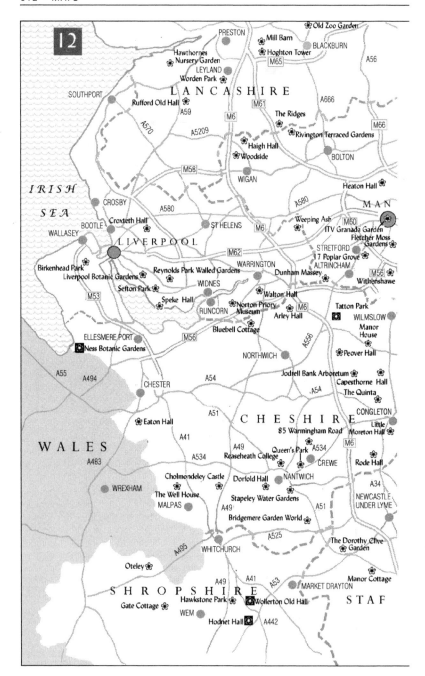

13

Lister Park
BRADFORD
Towneley Park
HALIFAX
Land Farm
People's Park
WAKEFIELD
M62
CASTLEFORD
DEWSBURY

WEST YORKSHIRE

ROCHDALE
M62
HUDDERSFIELD
Nostell Priory
Yorkshire Sculpture Park

OLDHAM
A627
CHESTER
A628
Wentworth Castle Gardens
BARNSLEY
Brodsworth Hall
M1

M67
SOUTH YORKSHIRE
M60
GLOSSOP
ROTHERHAM
A629
STOCKPORT
Gamesley Fold Cottage
13 Yew Tree Cottages
Bramall Hall
High
M18
CHEADLE
Lyme Park
Peak
Hillsborough Walld Garden
SHEFFIELD
A57
17 Hill Top Avenue
Dunge Valley
Gardens
CHAPEL-EN-LE-FRITH
Sheffield Botanical Gardens
Adlington Hall
Hare Hill Gardens
Fanshawe Gate Hall
A61
The Mount
Mellors Gardens
Pavilion Gardens
A623
Renishaw Hall
Henbury Hall
MACCLESFIELD
BUXTON
Fir Croft
A6
Gawsworth Hall
A515
CHESTERFIELD
M1
A536
BAKEWELL
Chatsworth
A619
A617
Haddon Hall
DERBYSHIRE
A61
Hardwick Hall
A53
A6

Biddulph Grange
MATLOCK
MANSFIELD
BIDDULPH
LEEK
Lea Gardens
A38
A523
ALFRETON
A53
A515
A610
A520
Felley Priory
A52
STOKE ON TRENT
ASHBOURNE
A6
A38
Alton Towers
Dam Farm House
Trentham Gardens
Dove Cottage Gardens
A52
Kedleston Hall
A50
A515
Wollaton Park
Oulton House
UTTOXETER
DERBY
A52
STONE
Derby Arboretum
Elvaston Castle
Country Park
FORDSHIRE
A50
A50
M1
M6

STAFFORD
Melbourne Hall Gardens
The Garth
Little Onn Hall
Shagborough

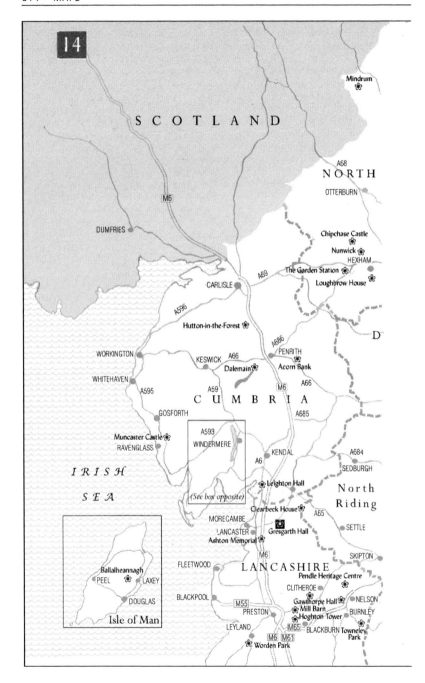

14

S C O T L A N D

Mindrum

N O R T H

A68

OTTERBURN

M6

Chipchase Castle

Nunwick

DUMFRIES

HEXHAM

The Garden Station

A69

Loughbrow House

CARLISLE

A596

D

Hutton-in-the-Forest

A686

WORKINGTON

A66

PENRITH

KESWICK

Dalemain

Acorn Bank

WHITEHAVEN

A595

A59

M6

A66

C U M B R I A

A685

GOSFORTH

A593

Muncaster Castle

WINDERMERE

RAVENGLASS

A6

A684

KENDAL

I R I S H

SEDBURGH

S E A

North

Leighton Hall

Riding

(See box opposite)

Clearbeck House

A65

MORECAMBE

SETTLE

LANCASTER

Gresgarth Hall

Ashton Memorial

Ballaheannagh

SKIPTON

PEEL

LAXEY

M6

FLEETWOOD

L A N C A S H I R E

DOUGLAS

Pendle Heritage Centre

CLITHEROE

NELSON

BLACKPOOL

Gawthorpe Hall

Isle of Man

M55

Mill Barn

BURNLEY

PRESTON

Hoghton Tower

LEYLAND

M65

BLACKBURN Towneley

M6 M61

Park

Worden Park

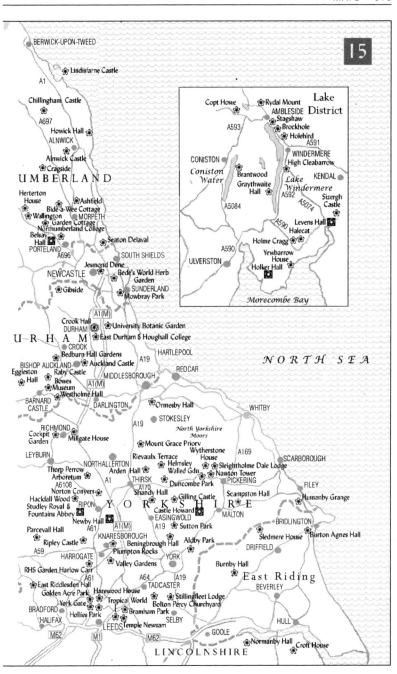

15

BERWICK-UPON-TWEED

Lindisfarne Castle

A1

Chillingham Castle

A697

Howick Hall
ALNWICK

Alnwick Castle
Cragside

UMBERLAND

Herterton
House   Ashfield
      Bide-a-Wee Cottage
   Wallington   MORPETH
   Garden Cottage
   Northumberland College
Belsay
Hall
PORTELAND   Seaton Delaval
        A696

Jesmond Dene
NEWCASTLE   Bede's World Herb
                    Garden
   Gibside   SUNDERLAND
                    Mowbray Park

SOUTH SHIELDS

Lake District

Copt Howe   Rydal Mount   Lake
              AMBLESIDE   District
                 Stagshaw
A593   Brockhole
                 Holehird
                        A591
CONISTON   WINDERMERE
              High Cleabarrow
Coniston   Brantwood
Water   Graythwaite   KENDAL
           Hall   Lake
                  A592   Windermere
A5084   Sizergh
                    A5074 Castle
                   A590
                   Levens Hall
                   Halecat
           Holme Cragg
A590   Yewbarrow
ULVERSTON   House
           Holker Hall

Morecombe Bay

A1(M)
Crook Hall
DURHAM   University Botanic Garden
U R H A M   East Durham & Houghall College
   CROOK
      Bedburn Hall Gardens   HARTLEPOOL
BISHOP AUCKLAND   Auckland Castle   A19
Eggleston   Raby Castle
   Hall   Bowes MIDDLESBOROUGH   REDCAR
           Museum
           Westholme Hall A1(M)
BARNARD
CASTLE   DARLINGTON   Ormesby Hall

NORTH SEA

A19
            STOKESLEY
RICHMOND   *North Yorkshire*
Cockpit   *Moors*
Garden   Millgate House   Mount Grace Priory   WHITBY

LEYBURN   Rievaulx Terrace Wytherstone
          NORTHALLERTON   Helmsley House
Thorp Perrow   Arden Hall   Walled Gdn Sleightholme Dale Lodge
Arboretum   A1   THIRSK   Nawton Tower
A6108   A170 Duncombe Park PICKERING
Norton Conyers   Shandy Hall   Scampston Hall
Hackfall Wood   RIPON   Gilling Castle
Studley Royal &   Y O R K S H I R E
Fountains Abbey   Newby Hall   Castle Howard
              A1(M) EASINGWOLD   MALTON
Parcevall Hall   A19   Sutton Park
        A61 KNARESBOROUGH
   Ripley Castle   Beningbrough Hall Aldby Park
A59   Plumpton Rocks
        HARROGATE   YORK
RHS Garden Harlow Carr   Valley Gardens
        A61
East Riddlesden Hall   A64   A19
Golden Acre Park Harewood House TADCASTER
   York Gate   Tropical World   Stillingfleet Lodge
BRADFORD   Bramham Park Bolton Percy Churchyard
   Hollies Park   SELBY
HALIFAX   LEEDS Temple Newsam

SCARBOROUGH

FILEY
                    Humanby Grange

BRIDLINGTON
Sledmere House   Burton Agnes Hall
DRIFFIELD

Burnby Hall   *East Riding*

BEVERLEY

HULL

M62   M1   M62   GOOLE
                    Normanby Hall Croft House
              L I N C O L N S H I R E

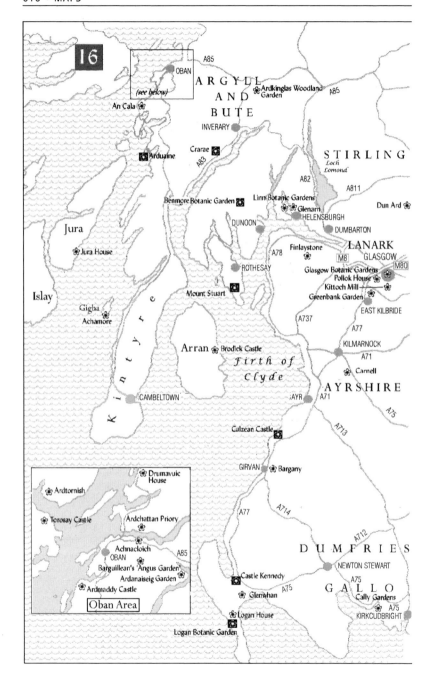

16

OBAN
A85
A R G Y L L
Ardkinglas Woodland Garden
A85
An Cala 🏵
A N D
(see below)
B U T E
INVERARY
Crarae 🏰
S T I R L I N G
Loch Lomond
Arduaine
A83
A82
A811
Benmore Botanic Garden
Linn Botanic Gardens
Glenarn
Dun Ard 🏵
Jura
DUNOON
HELENSBURGH
DUMBARTON
Jura House 🏵
A78
Finlaystone 🏵
LANARK
M8
GLASGOW
ROTHESAY
Glasgow Botanic Gardens
Pollok House
M80
Islay
r
Mount Stuart
Kittoch Mill
Greenbank Garden
Gigha
Achamore
EAST KILBRIDE
A737
A77
Arran 🏵 Brodick Castle
KILMARNOCK
F i r t h   o f
A71
C l y d e
🏵 Carnell
CAMBELTOWN
A Y R S H I R E
AYR
A71
A75
Culzean Castle
A713
GIRVAN 🏵 Bargany
Drumavuic House
🏵 Ardtornish
A77
A714
A712
🏵 Torosay Castle
Ardchattan Priory
D U M F R I E S
Achnacloich
OBAN
A85
NEWTON STEWART
Barguillean's 'Angus Garden'
Ardanaiseig Garden
Castle Kennedy
A75
G A L L O
🏵 Ardmaddy Castle
🏵 Glenwhan
A75
Cally Gardens
A75
Oban Area
Logan House
KIRKCUDBRIGHT
Logan Botanic Garden

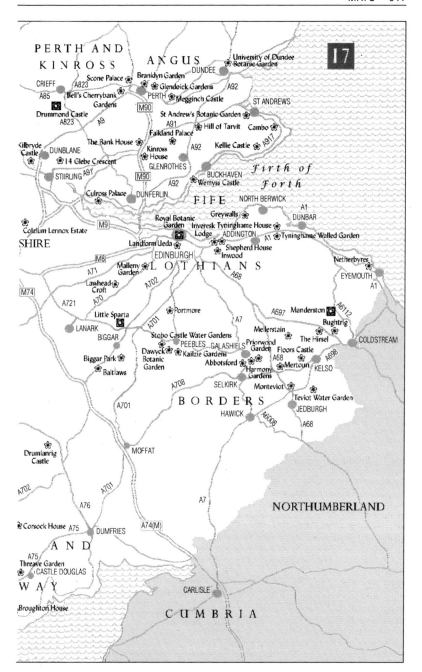

PERTH AND
KINROSS

ANGUS

University of Dundee
Botanic Garden

DUNDEE

CRIEFF   Scone Palace
A823   Branklyn Garden
A85   Bell's Cherrybank   Glendoick Gardens   A92
    Gardens   PERTH   Megginch Castle   ST ANDREWS
Drummond Castle   M90
A823   St Andrew's Botanic Garden
A9   A91   Hill of Tarvit   Cambo
    Falkland Palace
Kilbryde   The Bank House   Kinross   A92   Kellie Castle   A917
Castle   DUNBLANE   House
    14 Glebe Crescent   GLENROTHES   Firth of
STIIRLING   A91   Forth
    BUCKHAVEN
    Culross Palace   A92   NORTH BERWICK
SHIRE   DUNFERLIN   Wemyss Castle
    M9   FIFE   A1
Colzium Lennox Estate   Greywalls   DUNBAR
    Royal Botanic   Inveresk   Tyninghame House
    Garden   Lodge   ADDINGTON   A1   Tyninghame Walled Garden
    Landform Ueda   Shepherd House   Netherbyres
    EDINBURGH   Inwood
    M8   Malleny   L O T H I A N S   EYEMOUTH
A71   Garden   A702   A68   A1
    Lawhead   Manderston   A6112
M74   Croft   A697   Bughtrig
A721   A70   Little Sparta   Portmore   A7   Mellerstain   The Hirsel   COLDSTREAM
LANARK   A701   Stobo Castle Water Gardens   Priorwood   Floors Castle
    BIGGAR   PEEBLES   GALASHIELS   Garden   A68   A698
    Dawyck   Kailzie Gardens   Abbotsford   Mertoun   KELSO
Biggar Park   Botanic   Harmony   KELSO
    Baitlaws   Garden   Gardens
    A708   SELKIRK   Monteviot
A701   B O R D E R S   Teviot Water Garden
    HAWICK   JEDBURGH
    A6008   A68
Drumlanrig
Castle   MOFFAT
A702   A701
A76   A7
    NORTHUMBERLAND
Corsock House   A75   DUMFRIES   A74(M)
A75   A N D
Threave Garden
    CASTLE DOUGLAS
W A Y
Broughton House   CARLISLE
    C U M B R I A

17

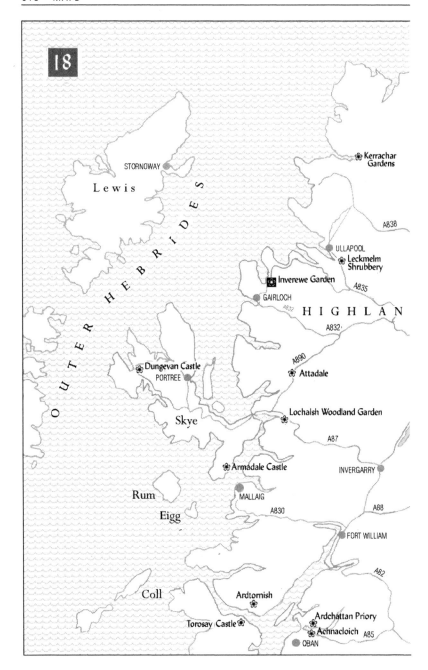

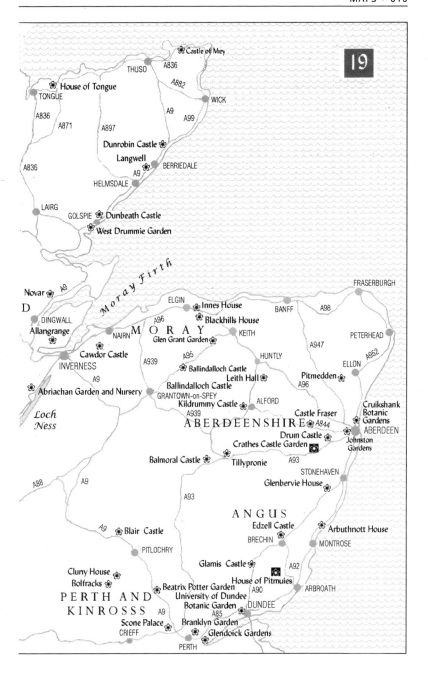

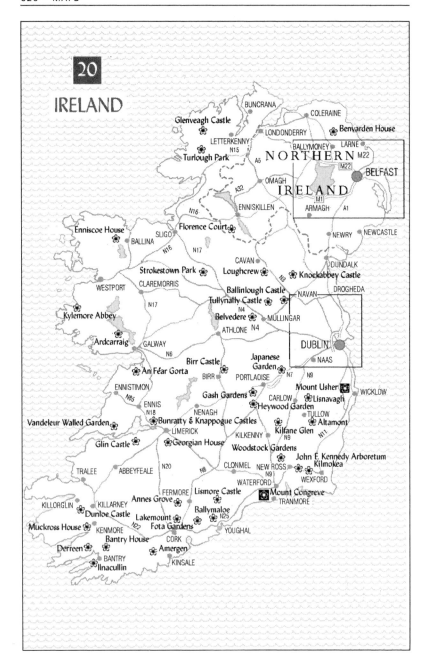

20

IRELAND

BUNCRANA

COLERAINE

Glenveagh Castle

Benvarden House

LETTERKENNY
LONDONDERRY
N15

Turlough Park

BALLYMONEY   LARNE

NORTHERN   M22

A5

M22

BELFAST

OMAGH

A32

IRELAND

M1

ENNISKILLEN

ARMAGH   A1

N16

Florence Court

Enniscoe House

NEWRY   NEWCASTLE

SLIGO

BALLINA

N15

N17

CAVAN

DUNDALK

Strokestown Park

Loughcrew

Knockabbey Castle

N3

WESTPORT

CLAREMORRIS

Ballinlough Castle

DROGHEDA

NAVAN

N17

Tullynally Castle

N4

Belvedere

MULLINGAR

Kylemore Abbey

ATHLONE   N4

Ardcarraig

GALWAY

DUBLIN

N6

Birr Castle

Japanese
Garden

NAAS

An Féar Gorta

BIRR

PORTLAOISE

N7   N9

ENNISTIMON

Mount Usher

WICKLOW

Gash Gardens

Lisnavagh

N85

CARLOW

ENNIS

Heywood Garden

N18

NENAGH

TULLOW

Vandeleur Walled Garden

Bunratty & Knappogue Castles

Altamont

LIMERICK

Kilfane Glen

Glin Castle

Georgian House

KILKENNY

N9   N11

Woodstock Gardens

John F. Kennedy Arboretum

Kilmokea

TRALEE   ABBEYFEALE

N20

N8

CLONMEL   NEW ROSS

WATERFORD

WEXFORD

N9

FERMORE   Lismore Castle

KILLORGLIN   KILLARNEY

Annes Grove

Mount Congreve

Dunloe Castle

Ballymaloe

TRANMORE

Lakemount   N25

Muckross House   KENMORE

Fota Gardens

N22

Bantry House

CORK   YOUGHAL

Derreen

Amergen

BANTRY

KINSALE

Ilnacullin

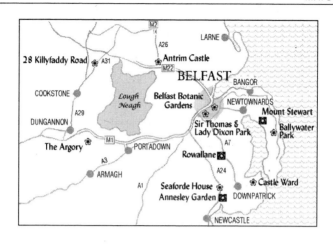

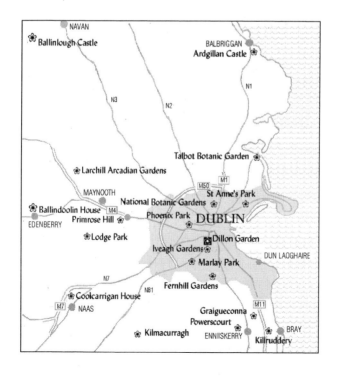

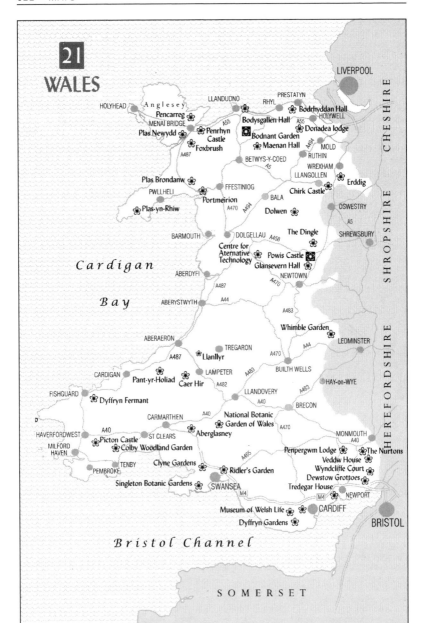

21
WALES

LIVERPOOL

HOLYHEAD
Anglesey
Pencarreg
MENAI BRIDGE
Plas Newydd
Penrhyn Castle
Foxbrush
A487
A5

LLANDUDNO
PRESTATYN
RHYL
Bodrhyddan Hall
HOLYWELL
Bodysgallen Hall
A55
Donadea lodge
Bodnant Garden
Maenan Hall
A494
MOLD
BETWYS-Y-COED
A5
RUTHIN
WREXHAM
LLANGOLLEN
Erddig

CHESHIRE

Plas Brondanw
PWLLHELI
FFESTINIOG
Portmeirion
A470
Plas-yn-Rhiw
BALA
A494
Dolwen
Chirk Castle
OSWESTRY
A5

BARMOUTH
DOLGELLAU
A458
The Dingle
SHREWSBURY

Cardigan
Bay
ABERDYFI
A487
Centre for Alternative Technology
Powis Castle
Glansevern Hall
NEWTOWN
A470

SHROPSHIRE

ABERYSTWYTH
A44
A483
Whimble Garden
LEOMINSTER

ABERAERON
A487
TREGARON
Llanllyr
A470
A44

CARDIGAN
Pant-yr-Holiad
Caer Hir
LAMPETER
A482
A483
BUILTH WELLS
HAY-on-WYE

FISHGUARD
Dyffryn Fermant
LLANDOVERY
A40
A483
BRECON

HEREFORDSHIRE

HAVERFORDWEST
A40
MILFORD HAVEN
Picton Castle
Colby Woodland Garden
ST CLEARS
CARMARTHEN
A40
National Botanic Garden of Wales
Aberglasney
A470
MONMOUTH
A40

TENBY
PEMBROKE
Clyne Gardens
Ridler's Garden
A465
Penpergwm Lodge
The Nurtons
Veddw House
Wyndcliffe Court
Dewstow Grottoes
Singleton Botanic Gardens
SWANSEA
M4
Tredegar House
M4
NEWPORT

Museum of Welsh Life
Dyffryn Gardens
CARDIFF
BRISTOL

Bristol Channel

SOMERSET

EUROPE

On the map which follows we include a selection of fine gardens in France, Belgium and Holland, concentrating on those which are a reasonable distance from the Channel ports or some other points of entry such as a Eurostar station. Regional leaflets are available at many tourist offices and other outlets in those countries. French speakers should pay a visit to the French bookshop (Librairie La Page) at 7 Harrington Road, London SW7 (Tel: (020) 7589 2849), where they may buy or order such useful guides as Michel Racine's *Jardins en France* (published by Acres Sud and revised in 2003) or the Guide Charme *Parcs et Jardins en France*. Alas, Mitchell Beazley's *Gardens of France* by Patrick Taylor and *Gardens of The Netherlands and Belgium* by Barbara Abbs are out of print.

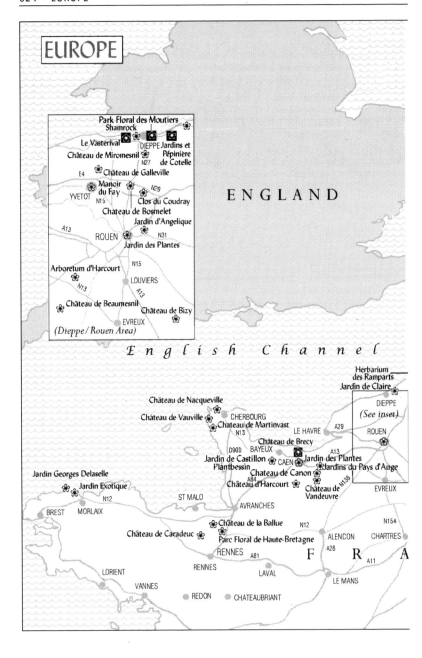

North Sea

GRONINGEN

A7

In der Tuinen
van Ruinen
A28

Priona Gardens

HOLLAND

A7

Palais Het Loo
AMSTERDAM   A28   A50
Broekstraat
LEIDEN   APELDOORN
THE HAGUE   J.P. Thijsse-Park A1
Leiden Botanic Garden   A12   A1   ARNHEM
UTRECHT   A12

BELGIUM   ROTTERDAM
A50
A16   A27
De Kempenhof   De Tintelhof   BREDA

Hof ter Weyden
Arboretum Kalmthout   Château s'Gravenwezel
OSTENDE   ANTWERP
A10   GENT   Château de   Huys de Dom
DUNKIRK   Leeuwergem   Rekem Garden
CALAIS   Park van Beervelde   MAASTRICHT   Rotstuin Bèr Slangen
A16   BRUSSELS   Kasteel de Hex   AACHEN
A14   A3   LIÈGE
BOULOGNE   A25   Vlaamse Toontuinen
Botanica   Château de Beloeil
N1   LILLE   Château d'Attre   A15
Jardin des   A1   MONS
Valloires   Jardin de Yves Gosse de Gorre
Jardins de   ARRAS   Annevoie
ABBEVILLE Maizicourt   CAMBRAI
Château de Bagatelle   N2
AMIENS   A1
N29

Les Hortillonages

A26   N51
BEAUVAIS   Château de Compiègne
COMPIÈGNE
N1   REIMS   VERDUN
N14   Chantilly   A4
Château   Ermenonville
d'Ambleville
N13   CHÂLONS-sur-MARNE
N12
PARIS   NANCY

N   C   E
TROYES

ORLEANS

AUXERRE

GERMANY

Index

An * indicates that the garden or nursery is mentioned in the text of another garden entry. # means that only garden names, addresses and contact details, with perhaps a very brief description, are given.

Notes

Report Form

We welcome readers' comments on gardens they have visited. Use the report form below, or send your comments on a sheet of paper to:

The Daily Telegraph *The Good Gardens Guide,*
Frances Lincoln Ltd, 4 Torriano Mews, Torriano Avenue, London NW5 7RZ

The Daily Telegraph GOOD GARDENS GUIDE REPORT FORM

To the Editors of **The Daily Telegraph** *The Good Gardens Guide:*

From my own experience the following garden should/should not be included in the *Guide:*

GARDEN NAME ....

Address: ....

....

....

Postcode ....

Telephone: ....

Name of owner(s): ....

....

DESCRIPTION ....

1. Location: ....

2. Garden open/times: ....

3. Entrance charge: ....

4. House open/times: ....

5. Brief details of main characteristics: ....

....

....

....

....

....

6. Other notes: ....

....

....

....

....

....

Sent in by (name and address) ....